Cities of the United States

SIXTH EDITION

ISSN 0899-6075

Cities of the United States

SIXTH EDITION

VOLUME 2

THE WEST

GALE
CENGAGE Learning

Detroit • New York • San Francisco • New Haven, Conn • Waterville, Maine • London

Cities of the United States, 6th edition

Product Management: Leigh Ann Cusack

Project Editor: Kristy A. Harper

Imaging and Multimedia: Lezlie Light

Rights and Acquisitions: Jermaine Bobbitt, Dean Dauphinais

Product Design: Pamela A. E. Galbreath

Composition and Electronic Prepress: Evi Seoud

Manufacturing: Rita Wimberley

For product information and technology assistance, contact us at **Gale Customer Support, 1-800-877-4253.**
For permission to use material from this text or product, submit all requests online at **www.cengage.com/permissions.**
Further permissions questions can be emailed to **permissionrequest@cengage.com**

Cover photographs reproduced by permission of kcphotos/Dreamstime (picture of downtown New Orleans) and Shutterstock.com (all other cover photographs). Banner art within text reproduced by permission of photos.com/Jupiterimages.

While every effort has been made to ensure the reliability of the information presented in this publication, Gale, a part of Cengage Learning, does not guarantee the accuracy of the data contained herein. Gale accepts no payment for listing; and inclusion in the publication of any organization, agency, institution, publication, service, or individual does not imply endorsement of the editors or publisher. Errors brought to the attention of the publisher and verified to the satisfaction of the publisher will be corrected in future editions.

Gale
27500 Drake Rd.
Farmington Hills, MI 48331-3535

ISBN-13: 978-0-7876-9629-0 (4-vol. set)   ISBN-10: 0-7876-9629-3 (4-vol. set)
ISBN-13: 978-0-7876-9630-6 (vol. 1)   ISBN-10: 0-7876-9630-7 (vol. 1)
ISBN-13: 978-0-7876-9631-3 (vol. 2)   ISBN-10: 0-7876-9631-5 (vol. 2)
ISBN-13: 978-0-7876-9632-0 (vol. 3)   ISBN-10: 0-7876-9632-3 (vol. 3)
ISBN-13: 978-0-7876-9633-7 (vol. 4)   ISBN-10: 0-7876-9633-1 (vol. 4)

ISSN 0899-6075

This title is also available as an e-book.
ISBN-13: 978-1-4144-3759-0   ISBN-10: 1-4144-3759-5
Contact your Gale sales representative for ordering information.

Printed in the United States of America
1 2 3 4 5 6 7 12 11 10 09 08

Contents

VOLUME 2—THE WEST

VOLUME 3—THE MIDWEST

VOLUME 4—THE NORTHEAST

Introduction

Cities of the United States (CUS) provides a one-stop source for all the vital information you need on 199 of America's top cities—those fastest-growing, as well as those with a particular historical, political, industrial, and/or commercial significance. Spanning the entire country, from Anaheim to Virginia Beach, each geographically-arranged volume of *CUS* brings together a wide range of comprehensive data. The volumes include: *The South; The West; The Midwest;* and *The Northeast.*

Within each volume, the city-specific profiles organize pertinent facts, data, and figures related to demographic, economic, cultural, geographic, social, and recreational conditions. Assembling a myriad of sources, *CUS* offers researchers, travelers, students, and media professionals a convenient resource for discovering each city's past, present, and future.

For this completely updated sixth edition, ten new cities have been added, providing even greater access to the country's growing urban centers. The new city profiles include:

- Aberdeen, SD
- Aurora, CO
- Cambridge, MA
- Chesapeake, VA
- Huntsville, AL
- Missoula, MT
- Shreveport, LA
- Sioux City, IA
- Vancouver, WA
- Winston-Salem, NC

Key Features Unlock Vital Information

Cities of the United States offers a range of key features, allowing easy access to targeted information. Features include:

- Section headings—Comprehensive categories, which include **History, Geography and Climate, Population Profile, Municipal Government, Economy, Education, Research, Health Care, Recreation, Convention Facilities, Transportation,** and **Communications** (including city web sites), make it easy for you to locate answers to your specific questions.

- Combined facts and analysis—Fact-packed charts and detailed descriptions bring you the statistics and the rest of the story.

- "In Brief" fact sheets—One-page "at a glance" overviews provide the essential facts for each state and each city profiled.

- Economic information—Detailed updates about such topics as incentive programs, development projects, and largest employers help you rate the business climate using criteria that matter to you.

- Directory information—Contact information at the end of many entry sections provides addresses, phone numbers, and email addresses for organizations, agencies, and institutions you may need to contact.

- Selected bibliography listings—Historical accounts, biographical works, and other print resources suggest titles to read if you wish to learn more about a particular city.

- Web sites for vital city resources—Access points to URLs for information-rich sources, such as city government, visitors and convention bureaus, economic development agencies, libraries, schools, and newspapers provide researchers an opportunity to explore cities in more detail.

- Enlightening illustrations—Numerous photographs highlight points of interest to you.

- Handy indexing—A referencing guide not only to main city entries, but also to the hundreds of people and place names that fall within those main entries, leading you directly to the information you seek.

Designed for a Variety of Users

Whether you are a researcher, traveler, or executive on the move, *CUS* serves your needs. This is the reference long sought by a variety of users:

- Business people, market researchers, and other decision-makers will find the current data that helps them stay informed.

- People vacationing, conventioneering, or relocating will consult this source for questions they have about what's new, unique, or significant about where they are going.

- Students, media professionals, and researchers will discover their background work already completed.

Definitions of Key Statistical Resources

Following are explanations of key resources used for statistical data:

ACCRA (The Council for Community Economic Research; formerly the American Chamber of Commerce Researchers Association): The Cost of Living Index, produced quarterly, provides a useful and reasonably accurate measure of living cost differences among urban areas. Items on which the Index is based have been carefully chosen to reflect the different categories of consumer expenditures, such as groceries, housing, utilities, transportation, health care, and miscellaneous goods and services; taxes are excluded. Weights assigned to relative costs are based on government survey data on expenditure patterns for mid-management households (typically the average professional worker's home, new construction with 2,400 square feet of living space). All items are priced in each place at a specified time and according to standardized specifications. Information regarding ACCRA and the Cost of Living Index can be found at www.accra.org. Please note that the ACCRA Cost of Living Index and ACCRA housing price information are reprinted by permission of ACCRA.

Metropolitan Statistical Area (MSA): The U.S. Office of Management and Budget (OMB) provides that each Metropolitan Statistical Area must include (a) at least one city with 50,000 or more inhabitants, or (b) a U.S. Census Bureau-defined urbanized area (of at least 50,000 inhabitants) and a total metropolitan population of at least 100,000 (75,000 in New England). The term was adopted in 1983. The term "metropolitan area" (MA) became effective in 1990. During the 2000 Census, the MSA standards were revised, establishing Core Based Statistical Areas (CBSAs). CBSAs may be either Metropolitan Statistical Areas or Micropolitan Statistical Areas. It is important to note that standards, and therefore content of 1990 Census MSAs, are not identical to 2000 Census MSA standards. Additional information regarding MSAs can be found at http://census.state.nc.us/glossary/msa.html.

FBI Crime Index Total: The total number of index offenses reported to the FBI during the year through its Uniform Crime Reporting Program. The FBI receives monthly and annual reports from law enforcement agencies throughout the country. City police, sheriffs, and state police file reports on the number of index offenses that become known to them. The FBI Crime Index offenses are: murder and non-negligent manslaughter; forcible rape; robbery; aggravated assault; burglary; larceny; motor vehicle theft; and arson.

Estimates of population: Between decennial censuses, the U.S. Bureau of the Census publishes estimates of the population using the decennial census data as benchmarks and data available from various agencies, both state and federal, including births and deaths, and school statistics, among other data.

Method of Compilation

The editors of *Cities of the United States* consulted numerous sources to secure the kinds of data most valuable to you. Each entry gathers together economic information culled in part from the U.S. Department of Labor/Bureau of Labor Statistics and state departments of labor and commerce, population figures derived from the U.S. Department of Commerce/Bureau of the Census and from city and state agencies, educational and municipal government data supplied by local authorities, historical narrative based on a variety of accounts, and geographical and climatic profiles from the National Oceanic and Atmospheric Administration. Along with material supplied by chambers of commerce, convention and visitors bureaus, and other local sources, background information was drawn from periodicals and books chosen for their timeliness and accuracy. Through print resources, web sites, email contact, and/or phone calls with agency representatives, the information contained reflects current conditions.

Acknowledgments

The editors are grateful for the assistance provided by dozens of helpful chambers of commerce and convention and visitors bureau professionals, as well as municipal, library, and school employees for their invaluable generosity and expertise.

Comments and Suggestions Welcome

If you have questions, concerns, or comments about *Cities of the United States*, please contact the Project Editors:

Cities of the United States
Gale
27500 Drake Road
Farmington Hills, MI 48331
Phone: (248)699-4253
Toll-free: (800)347-GALE
Fax: (248)699-8075
URL: gale.cengage.com

Cities of the United States

SIXTH EDITION

Alaska

The State in Brief

Nickname: Land of the Midnight Sun; The Last Frontier

Motto: North to the future

Flower: Forget-me-not

Bird: Willow ptarmigan

Area: 663,267 square miles (2000; U.S. rank 1st)

Elevation: Ranges from sea level to 20,320 feet above sea level

Climate: Summers are short and hot, winters long and intensely cold

Admitted to Union: January 3, 1959

Capital: Juneau

Head Official: Governor Sarah Palin (R) (until 2010)

Population

    1980: 402,000
    1990: 570,000
    2000: 626,932
    2006 estimate: 670,053
    Percent change, 1990–2000: 14.0%
    U.S. rank in 2006: 47th
    Percent of residents born in state: 38.85% (2006)
    Density: 1.2 people per square mile (2006)
    2006 FBI Crime Index Total: 28,765

Racial and Ethnic Characteristics (2006)

    White: 460,170
    Black or African American: 21,476
    American Indian and Alaska Native: 88,026
    Asian: 30,151
    Native Hawaiian and Pacific Islander: 3,753
    Hispanic or Latino (may be of any race): 37,498
    Other: 11,968

Age Characteristics (2006)

    Population under 5 years old: 47,481
    Population 5 to 19 years old: 156,469
    Percent of population 65 years and over: 6.6%
    Median age: 33.5

Vital Statistics

    Total number of births (2006): 10,238
    Total number of deaths (2006): 3,316
    AIDS cases reported through 2005: 621

Economy

    Major industries: Oil, government, commercial fishing, food processing, lumber, mining
    Unemployment rate (2006): 9.4%
    Per capita income (2006): $26,919
    Median household income (2006): $59,393
    Percentage of persons below poverty level (2006): 10.9%
    Income tax rate: None
    Sales tax rate: None

Anchorage

■ The City in Brief

Founded: 1915 (incorporated 1920)

Head Official: Mayor Mark Begich (since July 2003)

City Population

> 1980: 174,431
> 1990: 226,338
> 2000: 260,283
> 2006 estimate: 278,700
> Percent change, 1990–2000: 15.0%
> U.S. rank in 1980: 78th
> U.S. rank in 1990: 69th (State rank: 1st)
> U.S. rank in 2000: 75th (State rank: 1st)

Metropolitan Area Population

> 1980: 174,431
> 1990: 226,338
> 2000: 260,283
> 2006 estimate: 359,180
> Percent change, 1990–2000: 15.0%
> U.S. rank in 1980: 78th
> U.S. rank in 1990: 69th
> U.S. rank in 2000: 75th

Area: 1,955 square miles (2000)

Elevation: 132 feet above sea level

Average Annual Temperature: 35.8° F

Average Annual Precipitation: 15.71 inches of rain; 70.6 inches of snow

Major Economic Sectors: services, wholesale and retail trade, government

Unemployment Rate: 5.5% (June 2007)

Per Capita Income: $29,581 (2005)

2005 FBI Crime Index Property: 11,365

2005 FBI Crime Index Violent: 2,031

Major Colleges and Universities: University of Alaska Anchorage, Alaska Pacific University

Daily Newspaper: *Anchorage Daily News*

■ Introduction

Anchorage is the largest city in the state and serves as the center of the state's communication, transportation, commercial, and finance industries. About 42 percent of the state's residents are at home in Anchorage. When its brief modern history is considered—the town of Anchorage was founded in 1915 as a railroad construction headquarters—the fact that Anchorage stands as a sophisticated metropolis in the midst of rugged wilderness can be appreciated as a phenomenon. In 2002, Anchorage was named an All-American City. A visit to the city will dispel myths about its long, dark winters. Anchorage's climate is relatively mild with distinct seasons, winters similar to Denver's, and short daylight periods confined to late December. A relatively high per capita income, low taxes, and a low crime rate are among the positive qualities that have earned Anchorage a place among the country's most livable cities.

■ Geography and Climate

Anchorage is located in south-central Alaska in a wide valley surrounded by several mountain ranges, including the Chugach, Kenai, Talkeetna, Tordillo, Aleutian, and Alaska ranges. This port city is bordered on the west, north, and south by the Knik Arm and Turnagain Arm of Cook Inlet on the Gulf of Alaska. The city is conterminous with the borough of Anchorage. The Chugach Mountains to the east have a general elevation of 4,000 to 5,000 feet, with peaks from 8,000 to 10,000 feet. These mountains block warm air from the Gulf of Mexico, keeping precipitation relatively low. The Alaska

Range to the north protects the city from cold air from the state's interior; thus temperatures in Anchorage are usually 25 to 30 degrees warmer than temperatures in the rest of the state. While the area has four seasons, their length and characteristics differ from those of the middle latitudes; snows generally arrive in October and leave in mid-April, while annual average snowfall is over 70 inches. The average number of daylight hours in the summer is 19.3 hours; the winter average is 5.8 hours.

Area: 1,955 square miles (2000)

Elevation: 132 feet above sea level

Average Temperature: 35.8° F

Average Annual Precipitation: 15.71 inches of rain; 70.6 inches of snow

■ History

Native American Trade Center Transformed by Discovery of Gold

The Anchorage area was settled more than 6,000 years ago as a summer fishing camp for the Tanaina tribe. Until the seventeenth century it was under the dominance of the Pacific Eskimos. In 1650 the Eskimos were defeated in battle by the Tanaina where Point Woronzof is now located on the shore of Knik Arm. By 1700 the area had become a major trade center for Native Americans, Eskimos, and Aleuts.

The first Russian sailors, led by Vitus Bering, may have arrived in about 1743 to establish trading posts. The first European to explore the territory around the inlet was the British explorer Captain James Cook, who claimed the land for England in 1778 and after whom Cook Inlet was named. Russian settlers moved onto Upper Cook Inlet in the late 1890s, establishing settlements inhabited by traders and missionaries. With the sale of Alaska to the United States in 1867, Russia turned over its holdings on Cook Inlet to the Alaska Commercial Company of San Francisco. In 1882 gold was discovered in streams along Turnagain Arm, causing a population explosion as steamships from Seattle brought prospectors who settled in the Matanuska and Sustina Valleys to pan for gold. Alaska became an official U.S. territory in 1912.

City Becomes Major Railroad, Aviation, Military Center

Another growth spurt occurred in 1915 when the area known as Ship Creek valley was chosen as the mid-point construction headquarters for the government-owned Alaska Railroad that was to be built from Seward to Fairbanks. The town site of Anchorage was soon established at Ship Creek. By 1920, the year of its incorporation, Anchorage had developed into a major city. The

Alaska Railroad was completed in 1923; that same year Anchorage's first airfield was built, initiating the aviation industry that within a decade became a vital part of the city's economy. Anchorage established its own airline in 1926 and in 1935 Merrill Field was opened. In 1935 the city also experienced another population boom with the migration of dust bowl farmers from the Midwest into the Matanuska Valley.

The foundation of another important element of Anchorage's economy, the military defense complex, was formed with the military buildup in Alaska during the late 1930s and early 1940s. Fort Richardson and Elmendorf Field Air Force Base were established near the city. The Alaska Highway, the American military supply line to northern defense headquarters and a link between Anchorage and other parts of the country, was completed in 1942. Through World War II and into the early 1950s the city expanded. The population increased to 43,314 in 1950 at a rate of more than 600 percent in a decade. The first terminal of the Anchorage International Airport opened in 1953, making Anchorage a primary connection for transpolar air traffic between Europe and Asia.

City Devastated by Earthquake; Oil Discovered

Anchorage suffered a severe setback in 1964 when it was struck by a devastating earthquake, one of the most serious ever recorded in North America. Damage was extensive, but within the next few years the city had recovered and was moving into another phase of prosperity resulting from the discovery of oil on Cook Inlet. The city and borough governments merged in 1975 to form the municipality of Anchorage and, in 1978, Project 80s was initiated. A development plan of major proportions, Project 80s involved the construction of the George M. Sullivan Arena, the William A. Egan Convention and Civic Center, and the Anchorage Center for the Performing Arts; the final stage of the project, the Center for the Performing Arts, was completed in 1988. A collapse in world crude oil prices brought statewide recession in 1986, causing high unemployment rates and a population decrease in Anchorage.

Oil Spilled in Prince William Sound

Anchorage made international headlines on Good Friday, March 24, 1989, when the grounded oil tanker *Exxon Valdez* spilled nearly 11 million gallons of crude oil into nearby Prince William Sound, forming a slick that eventually reached into the Gulf of Alaska and beyond. Anchorage served as the command post for cleanup efforts costing more than $2.5 billion. Only a small amount of oil remained by the mid-1990s and seals, whales, and bald eagles had returned to the region. U.S. government biologists and scientists for the Exxon Corporation continued to disagree over the issue of damage to animals, with Exxon contending that the damage was less than what government scientists claimed. In 1994 an Anchorage jury ordered Exxon Corp. to pay more than $5 billion to fishermen and others who could show that they had been financially hurt by the oil spill.

A Time of Growth

In the 1990s Anchorage began to experience record economic growth that continued through the early 2000s. In 2002 Anchorage was one of ten cities to receive the 2002 All-American City Award, an award designated by the National Civic League. The Anchorage Economic Development Corporation predicted the creation of 2,500 new jobs in 2007, marking the cities 19th straight year of growth with an increase of 1.7 percent from the previous year. The same year, the city assembly and Mayor Mark Begich announced an idea to cut property taxes by one-third and issue a gross-receipts tax on businesses to fund costs of services such as schools and the police force. The gross-receipts tax would likely result in higher retail costs for the goods and services sold by local businesses. Since a large portion of goods and services offered by Anchorage businesses are sold to tourists and in other cities, the tax would be paid in part by non-residents. The assembly has the right to adopt the tax without voter approval. As of July 2007, a task force had been appointed to consider the impact of such a tax shift.

Historical Information: Anchorage Museum of History and Art Archives, 121 West Seventh Avenue, Anchorage, AK 99501; telephone (907)343-6189; www.anchoragemuseum.org; Municipality of Anchorage, 632 West Sixth Avenue, Anchorage, AK 99501; telephone (907) 343-7100 (public information); www.muni.org

■ Population Profile

Metropolitan Area Residents

   1980: 174,431
   1990: 226,338
   2000: 260,283
   2006 estimate: 359,180
   Percent change, 1990–2000: 15.0%
   U.S. rank in 1980: 78th
   U.S. rank in 1990: 69th
   U.S. rank in 2000: 75th

City Residents

   1980: 174,431
   1990: 226,338
   2000: 260,283
   2006 estimate: 278,700
   Percent change, 1990–2000: 15.0%
   U.S. rank in 1980: 78th
   U.S. rank in 1990: 69th (State rank: 1st)
   U.S. rank in 2000: 75th (State rank: 1st)

Density: 153.4 people per square mile (2000)

Racial and ethnic characteristics (2005)

   White: 185,780
   Black: 16,547
   American Indian and Alaska Native: 15,903
   Asian: 18,514
   Native Hawaiian and Pacific Islander: 2,297
   Hispanic or Latino (may be of any race): 18,584
   Other: 5,377

Percent of residents born in state: 32.1% (2000)

Age characteristics (2005)

   Population under 5 years old: 21,228
   Population 5 to 9 years old: 22,028
   Population 10 to 14 years old: 20,884
   Population 15 to 19 years old: 21,383
   Population 20 to 24 years old: 19,204
   Population 25 to 34 years old: 33,111
   Population 35 to 44 years old: 42,004
   Population 45 to 54 years old: 43,080
   Population 55 to 59 years old: 15,925
   Population 60 to 64 years old: 10,532
   Population 65 to 74 years old: 10,524
   Population 75 to 84 years old: 4,644
   Population 85 years and older: 1,734
   Median age: 33.8 years

Births (2006, County)

   Total number: 4,320

Deaths (2006, County)

   Total number: 1,267

Money income (2005)

   Per capita income: $29,581
   Median household income: $61,217
   Total households: 102,277

Number of households with income of . . .

   less than $10,000: 5,515
   $10,000 to $14,999: 4,100
   $15,000 to $24,999: 9,224
   $25,000 to $34,999: 7,778
   $35,000 to $49,999: 14,356
   $50,000 to $74,999: 20,780
   $75,000 to $99,999: 14,627
   $100,000 to $149,999: 16,799
   $150,000 to $199,999: 5,622
   $200,000 or more: 3,476

Percent of families below poverty level: 10% (2005)

2005 FBI Crime Index Property: 11,365

2005 FBI Crime Index Violent: 2,031

©Jon Arnold Images Ltd/Alamy

■ Municipal Government

The municipality of Anchorage is administered by a mayor-assembly form of government, with the mayor and 11 assembly members elected to three-year terms.

Head Official: Mayor Mark Begich (since July 2003; current term expires June 30, 2009)

Total Number of City Employees: 4,300 (2003)

City Information: Municipality of Anchorage, 632 West Sixth Avenue, Anchorage, AK 99501; telephone (907)343-7100 (public information); www.muni.org

■ Economy

Major Industries and Commercial Activity

The United States government and the oil industry have been integral to the Anchorage economy. The federally funded Alaska Railroad gave Anchorage its start; later the military defense system supported an essentially undiversified economic base. This base expanded in the 1970s when the Trans-Alaska Pipeline, one of the largest construction projects in history, brought thousands of workers and increased service industries.

While the U.S. economy has shown decline in recent years, Alaska's economy has shown a relatively stable growth of about 2 percent annually. Anchorage is the state's primary transportation, communications, trade, service, and finance center. The major growth sectors in the local economy are oil, health care, professional and business services, and leisure and hospitality. In 2007, *Foreign Direct Investment* magazine named Anchorage as fourth in the nation for Best Small Cities of the Future.

Anchorage is not a major center of oil production, but the city acts as the administrative center for the industry. BP and ConcocoPhillips were planning new development activities in 2007 that would result in the addition of over 300 jobs. While the number of jobs in the sector is relative low, the importance to Anchorage's economy is great, accounting for a significant percentage of local salaries and wages each year.

Since Anchorage is a primary center for health care services for most Alaskans, health care has become a major economic driver in the city. The growth is attributed in part to increased federal spending and the increased need for health care in Alaska's growing population. Job growth in the professional and business services sector is seen primarily in engineering, architectural, and related services that meet the growing demand of construction, mining, and oil developments.

The leisure and hospitality industry, along with the service businesses that sprout up around the industry, are a major driving force in Anchorage economy. Mainly due to its central location, Anchorage acts as the gateway to the state of Alaska, thereby funneling tourists, conventioneers and other visitors through the area. Alaska's tourism industry had an estimated economic impact of nearly $151 million in Anchorage in 2006. The market for trade shows and conventions in the city is growing as well. In 2006, conventions held had an economic impact of about $97.7 million dollars.

The military in Anchorage is a constant presence. Elmendorf Air Force Base, Fort Richardson Army Post, and Kulis Air National Guard base are all located at the Ted Stevens Anchorage International Airport. The three military posts employ over 10,000 military personnel. The family members of military personnel contribute to the local economy through employment and consumer spending. Because of the large number of military personnel based in the city, many businesses have experienced temporary slowdowns due to military deployments. In 2006, 2,500 troops were deployed from Fort Richardson.

The transportation industry in Anchorage is the busiest in the state. The Ted Stevens Anchorage International Airport (TSAIA) was the third busiest cargo airport in the world in 2007 (after Memphis and Hong Kong). TSAIA officials estimated that air transportation accounted for one in nine city jobs. The TSAIA flies more than 650 transcontinental cargo flights each week; the airport's economic impact is felt as far away as the North Pole, where jet fuel is refined and loaded onto the more than 100 rail cars that then travel by Alaska Railroad to service TSAIA daily. The Alaska Railroad transports freight and passengers; in summer months the Railroad transports passengers to popular destinations throughout the state. The Port of Anchorage accounts for delivery of more than 90 percent of the consumer goods arriving in Alaska.

Items and goods produced: fisheries' products, wood and wood products, petroleum products, coal, minerals

Incentive Programs—New and Existing Companies

The most widely used local incentives include customized job training programs, low interest loans, municipal revenue bonds, and property tax abatement. Anchorage Economic Development Corporation, a public-private partnership, assists new and existing businesses with information on taxes and utilities and on available sites and buildings, which are said to be plentiful.

Local programs: The Municipality of Anchorage offers a program that exempts some types of economic development properties from taxation. Inventory that is held for shipment outside of Alaska may also be exempt from local inventory taxes.

State programs: The Governor's Office of International Trade provides assistance and information to firms interested in foreign trade and investment, organizes trade missions and promotions, and sponsors trade shows and seminars. Several areas in the city are located in Anchorage's Foreign Trade Zone, the two most notable being the Ted Stevens Anchorage International Airport and the Port of Anchorage. The World Trade Center assists businesses seeking to enter or expand their role in international trade. The Alaska Export Assistance Center helps local businesses expand into foreign markets.

Job training programs: The University of Alaska Anchorage offers classes and degree programs to businesses and individuals on logistics and on doing business in Pacific Asia and the former Soviet Union. The university also partners with the Alaska Economic Development Corporation to provide a Mentor Program that connects students with business leaders. Lunchtime forums highlight a different business industry each time.

Development Projects

In transportation, a $250 million expansion was underway at the Port of Anchorage as of 2007. The expanded facility is expected to generate more than 2,300 jobs once completed and will accommodate the area's cruise and military business. The project is scheduled for completion in 2012. Merrill Field has constructed two new taxiways and an apron expansion in 2005 added more space and accommodations for ski-equipped aircraft in winter and aircraft with tundra tires in summer. A project is currently underway to build an interchange that would link the Glenn and Seward highways. Construction is expected to be completed in 2008. The 2004 summer road construction season completed 41 road and safety projects with a total cost of about $45 million.

To add an additional boost to the growing convention and tourism industry, the city began construction of a new $103 million, 215,000 square-foot convention facility in 2006. The Dena'ina Center will be located about one block away from the existing Egan Civic and Convention Center and the Alaska Center for the Performing Arts. All three buildings will be linked by covered walkways. The project is scheduled for completion in 2008.

Anchorage has a strong commitment to preserving land for recreation. Part of this commitment involves the Foster-A-Flower program; in 2004 downtown businesses bought more than 200 hanging flower baskets, each at $75, to beautify the area. Five new dog parks were created in Anchorage in 2004.

Economic Development Information: Anchorage Economic Development Corporation, 900 West Fifth Avenue, Suite 300, Anchorage, AK 99501; telephone (907)258-3700; toll-free (800)462-7275; fax (907)258-6646; email aedc@aedcweb.com. Municipality of Anchorage, 632 West Sixth Avenue, Anchorage, AK 99501; telephone (907)343-7100 (public information); www .muni.org

Commercial Shipping

Anchorage's seaports and airports combine with its railroad to make the area the primary cargo distributor in the state. The Port of Anchorage, the largest seaport in Alaska, is a year-round shipping point with five terminals served by three major carriers, which bring four to five ships from the Pacific Northwest and Asia each week. More than 4 million tons of iron and steel products, containerized freight, bulk petroleum, cement, wood products, and various other commodities crossed the Port's docks in 2007. The Ted Stevens Anchorage International Airport (TSAIA) was the third busiest cargo airport in the world in 2007 (after Memphis and Hong Kong). More than 50 air carriers and 9 freight forwarders connect Anchorage to the rest of the country and the world beyond. Municipal Merrill Field airport serves the intrastate needs of business, banking, and commerce. The Alaska Railroad provides rail freight service; in 2003 the railroad moved more than 8 million tons of freight across 525 miles of track. More than 30 motor freight carriers link Anchorage with major market areas.

Labor Force and Employment Outlook

Anchorage boasts an abundant and well-educated labor pool with a relatively low median age. As of 2007 about 91.7 percent of residents were high school graduates and approximately 32 percent of Anchorage's adult residents had earned a bachelors degree or higher. Wage rates in Anchorage tend to be higher than wages in other areas of the country due to an abundance of higher-level positions. In 2007 the average monthly earnings across all industries was about $3,550. Anchorage employment levels rose 28 percent between 1995 and 2003, due mainly to a 40 percent increase in the private support sector. In that same period, the services industry increased 114 percent, reflecting the area's attractiveness as a tourist destination.

Expansion and diversification have given Anchorage's economy the ability to absorb fluctuations in the business cycle or unexpected economic events. Anchorage now has a steady year-round employment base, with a summer boost from tourism and construction activities. The international cargo business in Anchorage continues to grow; Anchorage is equidistant to both Asia and Europe, and is nine hours flying time to nearly the entire industrialized world, making it a good location for warehousing and distribution.

According to the Anchorage Economic Development Corporation, job growth in Anchorage is expected to be in the service sector, which would include jobs in health and social services, hospitality, trade, and finance and real estate.

The following is a summary of data regarding the Anchorage metropolitan area labor force, 2006 annual averages.

Size of nonagricultural labor force: 166,800

Number of workers employed in . . .

   construction and mining: 13,800
   manufacturing: 2,100
   trade, transportation and utilities: 37,700
   information: 5,000
   financial activities: 10,000
   professional and business services: 18,000
   educational and health services: 22,400
   leisure and hospitality: 17,500
   other services: 6,300
   government: 34,000

Average hourly earnings of production workers employed in manufacturing: Not available

Unemployment rate: 5.5% (June 2007)

Largest employers (2003)	*Number of employees*
Providence Health System Alaska	3,566
Safeway Stores, Inc.	3,135
Wal-Mart/Sam's Club	2,443
Fred Meyer	2,341
Alaska Airlines	1,726
BP Exploration, Inc.	1,417
Banner Health System	1,243
NANA Management Services	1,227
Yukon-Kuskokwim Health Corporation	1,217
ASRC Energy Services	1,171
Federal Express	1,094
VECO Inc.	1,018

Cost of Living

The personal tax burden in Alaska is extremely low, while the cost of living is significantly higher than much of the rest of the nation. Residents benefit from distributions from the Permanent Fund, a savings account established in 1976 by voters allowing residents to receive 25 percent of the state's royalty oil revenue. Senior citizens enjoy a $150,000 property tax exemption or a renter's rebate.

The following is a summary of data regarding several key cost of living factors for the Anchorage area.

2007 (1st quarter) ACCRA Average House Price: $449,658

2007 (1st quarter) ACCRA Cost of Living Index: 121.0

State income tax rate: None

State sales tax rate: None

Local income tax rate: None

Local sales tax rate: 8.0% on rental cars, fuel, alcohol, tobacco

Property tax rate: Graduated from 7.91 mills to 18.15 mills levied on full assessed value

Economic Information: Alaska Department of Labor and Workforce Development, Research and Analysis Section, PO Box 111149, Juneau, AK 99811-1149; telephone (907) 465-4500. Anchorage Economic Development Corporation, 900 West Fifth Avenue, Suite 300, Anchorage, AK 99501; telephone (907)258-3700; toll-free (800)462-7275; fax (907)258-6646; email aedc@aedcweb.com.

■ Education and Research

Elementary and Secondary Schools

The Anchorage School District has schools in Anchorage, Eagle River, Chugiak, and Girdwood. The district prides itself on test scores that are better than state and national averages, and a diverse student body. In the 1990s Anchorage voters approved more than $500 million in school construction. Two middle schools and nine elementary schools were built and the new South Anchorage High School, serving 1,600 students, opened for the 2004-2005 school year. The new Eagle River High School opened in fall 2005 with 740 students, relieving crowding at Chugiak High School. The Alaska Native Cultural Charter School is scheduled to open in August 2008. Many other Anchorage schools have undergone expansions or upgrades since 1990.

The school system is administered by a nonpartisan, eight-member school board that appoints a superintendent on the recommendation of a selection task force. The system faced budget hardships, making cuts to supplies and services in the 2004/05 school year. A 2005/06 budget was announced with hopes for increased funds, pending approval from state legislature.

The following is a summary of data regarding the Anchorage School District as of the 2005–2006 school year.

Total enrollment: 50,000

Number of facilities

elementary schools: 60
junior high/middle schools: 9
senior high schools: 9
other: 20

Student/teacher ratio: 17.7:1

Teacher salaries (2005–06)

elementary median: $37,432–$51,788 (all levels)
junior high/middle median: Not available
secondary median: Not available

Funding per pupil: $8,282

A small percentage of students attend private and parochial schools in the Anchorage area.

Public Schools Information: Anchorage School District, 5530 E. Northern Lights Blvd., Anchorage, AK 99504-3136; telephone (907)742-4000; www.asd.k12.ak.us

Colleges and Universities

Two fully accredited universities are located in Anchorage: the University of Alaska Anchorage (UAA), which enrolls more than 17,000 students, and Alaska Pacific University, a private institution affiliated with the United Methodist church with about 700 enrolled students. Both institutions offer undergraduate degrees in a wide range of disciplines and master's degrees in such fields as biological sciences, business and management, logistics, and engineering. Charter College, an independent college, offers bachelor's degrees in information technology and associate degrees in business management, medical office administration, computerized accounting, computer technical graphics and computer networking technology. Also located in the Anchorage area are several vocational, specialty, and technical schools.

Libraries and Research Centers

In addition to its main branch downtown, the Anchorage Municipal Libraries system operates five branches throughout the city. Holdings consist of more than 515,255 books, nearly 1,780 periodical subscriptions, and films, records, tapes, art reproductions, and sheet music. Special collections at the system's main Z. J. Loussac Library include the Alaska Collection, featuring more than 25,000 books and documents on Alaska and the North, and the Loussac Children's Collection, with materials for parents and people who work with children. Nearly 50 special libraries and research centers are located in Anchorage, most of them affiliated with the University of Alaska Anchorage and specializing in the fields of environment, natural resources, art, history, law, and education. ARLIS, or Alaska Resources Library and Information Services, features a collection of more than 200,000 books, 700 journals, and a variety of other sources of information about Alaska. Housed on the University of Alaska campus, ARLIS contains the collection of The Oil Spill Public Information Center, featuring scientific data from the *Exxon Valdez* oil spill damage. The National Center for Infectious Diseases Arctic Investigations Program seeks to improve the quality of life of arctic and subarctic people.

Public Library Information: Anchorage Municipal Libraries, 3600 Denali St., Anchorage, AK 99503 (main branch); telephone (907)343-2975; www.anchoragelibrary.org

■ Health Care

Anchorage is a primary medical treatment center for the state of Alaska and is home to the two largest hospitals in the state—Providence Alaska Medical Center and Alaska Regional Hospital. The $157 million 100-bed hospital on Elmendorf Air Force Base opened in 2001. The new Elmendorf Hospital replaced the existing 50-bed hospital, which suffered structural damage during the 1964 earthquake, and serves the state's military population.

Providence Alaska Medical Center, with 341 beds and more than 600 staff physicians, is the main medical referral center in the state, offering such specialized treatment as open heart surgery and neonatal care. In 2001 the hospital added a new state-of-the-art emergency department as part of a 100,000-square-foot expansion. Alaska Regional Hospital provides neurosurgery and spinal and orthopedic surgery; a maternity center, critical care units, and emergency services, including an air ambulance, are maintained. A $7 million renovation at Alaska Regional Hospital included a new trauma and open-heart surgery room.

Alaska Native Medical Center provides service to Alaskan and American Natives throughout the state free of charge. With 150 beds and a staff of about 250 physicians and 700 nurses, it is one of the largest facilities of its kind in the United States. Anchorage Neighborhood Health Center offers three family practice clinics featuring medical, dental, pharmaceutical, and mental health services. The North Star Behavioral Health System provides mental health and substance abuse treatment programs through several facilities.

In 2007 the average cost of an office visit was about $87 and the average daily rate for a hospital room was $800.

■ Recreation

Sightseeing

An ideal way to see the points of interest in downtown Anchorage is to take a walking tour. A circular route—beginning at Old City Hall, original seat of the municipal government, and ending two blocks away at the Pioneer Schoolhouse, the first school in Anchorage—provides a leisurely stroll through the city's history. Principal attractions along the way include the Ship Creek

Viewpoint with a view of the site of Tanaina summer fish camps. Nearby are the David Leopold House, built in 1917 for the city's first mayor and Boney Memorial Courthouse, housing fine examples of nineteenth-century art motifs of Alaskan natives and animals. The Oscar Anderson House Museum in Elderberry Park is Anchorage's only historic house museum, offering visitors a glimpse into the life of the family that occupied the home as well as Anchorage history. The Anchorage Light Speed Planet Walk, beginning at 5th and G streets in downtown Anchorage, is designed to offer an interactive tour of the solar system. The walk through town, in which one step is equal to the distance that light travels in one second, includes information kiosks at each planet location.

Resolution Park, featuring the Captain Cook Monument, commemorates the 200th anniversary of Cook's exploration of the area. Adjacent to the park are historic Anchorage homes, including the first permanent frame residence in the city. Located on the southern edge of downtown is Delaney Park, known as "The Park Strip," once a firebreak for the original town site and later the city's first airfield.

The Alaska Zoo features hundreds of animals; special attractions are the natural land habitat for brown bears and an aquarium for seals and otters. Points of interest in north Anchorage include St. Nicholas Russian Church. The oldest building in the municipality, the church is located at Eklutna Historical Park, the site of the first Tanaina settlement east of Knik Arm; the cemetery's "spirit" houses are reminders of the blend of native tradition and missionary influence.

In south Anchorage are the Potter Section House and Crow Creek Mine, the first non-native settlement. An example of a nineteenth-century placer mine, Crow Creek is still in operation, and rental equipment is available for those wishing to pan for any gold that remains. Local fur factories provide regularly scheduled tours of their facilities. Sightseeing and "flightseeing" tours of the Anchorage area and day trips to attractions such as Mt. McKinley and Portage Glacier can be arranged through bus and air services.

Arts and Culture

Dating back to territory days when opera was staged regularly and when the city had an orchestra before it had paved streets, the performing arts have been an integral part of life in Anchorage. The city's arts community, with more than 75 organizations offering cultural experiences ranging from classical music to native dance, provides a striking contrast to the surrounding wilderness. The Anchorage Concert Association, founded in 1950 to bring international performers to local audiences, is still active, sponsoring about 22 music, dance, and theatre productions each year. The Alaska State Council on the Arts is based in Anchorage.

Many of these performances are presented in the downtown Alaska Center for the Performing Arts, a modern complex housing four theaters, including the Elvera Voth Hall, an 1,800-square-foot performance and rehearsal space opened in 2003. A significant contribution to the Anchorage arts community, the center offers a year-round schedule of more than 600 events and furnishes a showcase for local performers. The center's resident companies include Alaska Dance Theatre, Alaska Junior Theater, Alaska Theatre of Youth, Anchorage Concert Association, Anchorage Concert Chorus, the Anchorage Symphony Orchestra, Anchorage Opera, and Whistling Swan Productions.

The Anchorage Symphony Orchestra, formed in 1946 and today featuring about 80 musicians, hosts a September-to-May season with performances of classics and young people's concerts. Randall Craig Fleischer has been the symphony's music director since 1999. The Anchorage Opera offers three full-scale opera productions per season. The Alaska Chamber Singers, a chorale ensemble of 40 voices, offer performances at various venues throughout the city.

Interest and participation in the visual arts has been encouraged in Anchorage by "1% for Art in Public Places," a 1978 law setting aside for the purchase of commissioned artwork at least one percent of construction costs of all public buildings.

Museums and galleries in Anchorage specialize in science, history, and arts and crafts. The Alaska Aviation Heritage Museum traces the history of state aviation and prominent aviators, with a theater, observation deck, and historic planes. The Alaska Museum of Natural History is located in Anchorage.

The Anchorage Museum of History and Art features a permanent collection of 17,500 objects and 2,000 artifacts; the museum is also responsible for a $5.8 million collection of 276 works of art viewable in public buildings around the city. Groundbreaking for a museum expansion project took place in 2006. The addition of 70,000 feet will include galleries for the first regional office of the Smithsonian Institution's National Museum of Natural History Arctic Studies Center. The Arctic Studies Center will house over 1,000 Alaska Native artifacts relocated from the Smithsonian. The museum will also include a new home for the city's Imaginarium, a science discovery center with a variety of hands-on experience exhibits, a 10-foot tall Tyrannosaurus Rex, a planetarium, and a preschool learning area. The expansion project is scheduled for completion in 2009. The 15,000-square-foot Alaska Gallery in the museum displays a collection of more than 1,000 objects of traditional and modern native art with demonstration exhibits.

At the Alaska Native Heritage Center (opened in 1999) the visitor can explore five distinct Alaska Native cultures through interpretive displays, films, and daily performances by traditional storytellers. A trail from the Welcome House leads to Native Tradition Bearers—artists and performers at five traditional village exhibits surrounding a lake on the 26-acre grounds.

Festivals and Holidays

The year kicks off in Anchorage with the Annual Anchorage Folk Festival, offering more than 120 musical performances by local and guest acts, and the Great Alaska Beer and Barleywine Festival. February offers the Fur Rendezvous, known as the "Fur Rondy" (dating back to 1936 and one of the 10 largest festivals in the nation), a popular 10-day celebration of the annual fur-auctioning and social gathering of trappers and miners. The world-famous cross country Iditarod Trail Sled Dog Race starts in downtown Anchorage the first Saturday in March. Also in March and coinciding with the Iditarod is the Tour of Anchorage, a cross-country ski event with varying race lengths.

April follows up with the Alyeska Spring Carnival and Slush Cup and May brings the Alaska Native Youth Olympics. June events include the Three Barons Renaissance Faire and the Mayor's Midnight Sun Marathon.

Live music can be heard all summer long on Wednesday and Friday afternoons from the park at Fourth Avenue and E Street. Other summer fare includes the annual July 4th Celebration and the Bear Paw Festival at Eagle River in July; August offerings include the Alyeska Blueberry & Mountain Arts Festival and the Arctic Thunder Elmendorf Air Force Base Open House and Air Show.

Among the fall highlights are the Alaska State Fair in late August and early September, followed in October by the Nye Frontier Hockey Classic. Thanksgiving weekend events include an annual production of *The Nutcracker* by the Cincinnati Ballet and the Town Square Tree Lighting Ceremony. The Anchorage International Film Festival takes place in December.

Sports for the Spectator

The Wells Fargo Sports Complex at the University of Alaska Anchorage hosts Seawolves National Collegiate Athletic Association (NCAA) hockey, basketball, and volleyball competition. The Alaska Aces of the East Coast Hockey League are based in Anchorage and play at Sullivan Arena. The Carrs Great Alaska Shootout collegiate basketball tournament is a major event that draws fans from throughout the state and nation. The Anchorage Bucs are part of the Alaska Baseball League (summer collegiate league).

Sled dog racing is the official state sport and Anchorage hosts several main sledding events. The world famous Iditarod Trial Sled Dog Race originates in Anchorage and runs more than 1,000 miles to Nome, the course taking from 10 days to a month to complete. The World Championship Sled Dog Race, the most famous sprint race, is held during the Fur Rendezvous and draws racers from all over the world. The Native Youth

Olympics, sponsored in part by the University of Alaska Anchorage, attracts students from across the state. Competition focuses on games and contests that were once played by Alaska Natives to hone their hunting and survival skills.

Sports for the Participant

With more than 162 parks covering 14,000 acres, residents have a multitude of choices for year-round and seasonal outdoor activities. Park facilities include shelters, pools, camping, more than 40 ball fields, 59 tennis courts, winter ice skating, and programming for recreational events. Mountain climbing can be pursued at the 500,000-acre Chugach State Park, situated within the city limits; hiking and horseback riding trails are located in several other municipal parks. Salmon and trout fishing facilities are maintained on rivers, creeks, and lakes, and licensed hunting is regulated by the Alaska Department of Fish and Game.

During summer the midnight sun provides additional time for recreation. Popular activities include boating, kayaking, and river rafting on the flowing waters within the municipality limits. Free loaner bicycles are available for use on downtown bike trails; among other public facilities are 4 golf courses, 5 indoor pools, several lakes, and 49 tennis courts. With 120 miles of paved trails and 300 miles of unpaved and wilderness trail, Anchorage's extensive trail system attracts both residents and visitors. One of the most popular routes is the Tony Knowles Coastal Trail, an 11-mile asphalt trail that runs from downtown to Kincaid Park (which has its own system of 43 miles of wooded trail). Flattop Mountain is a popular hike; both beginner and expert hikers can summit the 3,510 foot mountain (3 miles roundtrip) as a day hike. Cyclists and runners enjoy the multitude of trails in and around Anchorage. Runners have been traveling to Anchorage to participate in the Mayor's Midnight Sun Marathon since its inception in 1974. *Bicycling* magazine called Anchorage's trail system one of the best in the United States.

Winter sports enthusiasts can find a wide range of choices, including dogsledding, ice skating, skiing, sledding, snowshoeing, snowmobiling, and skating on several rinks, including two Olympic-sized hockey rinks. Dogsled rides and tours are available through local vendors. The municipality maintains more than 200 miles of cross-country ski trails, including 40 kilometers lit for night skiing, plus sledding hills and snowmobile trails. Alaska's largest ski resort is 40 minutes from downtown Anchorage. Alyeska Resort boasts an annual average of 742 inches of snowfall and a lift capacity of more than 10,000 skiers per hour on its nine lifts.

Shopping and Dining

More than a dozen shopping centers, including five major malls, are located in Anchorage. Downtown's Fifth Avenue Mall houses major national retail chains such as Nordstrom, The Gap, and J. C. Penney, but products native to Alaska are the major shopping attractions, with foods, ivory, jewelry, gold, furs, seal oil candles, and Eskimo and Aleut basketry among the most popular items. Shoppers can visit workshops to see fur styling, jewelry crafting, and wool making demonstrations. Dimond Center has over 200 stores, a cinema, and an athletic club. The Anchorage Saturday Market operates both Saturday and Sunday throughout the summer at Third Avenue and E Street. Shoppers will find fresh baked goods and vegetables, handmade jewelry and crafts, and unique Native art.

More than 350 restaurants in Anchorage offer a variety of ethnic cuisines. The local specialty is fresh seafood, particularly salmon, served at most restaurants in settings that offer views of mountain ranges and ocean-going vessels departing the Port of Anchorage.

Visitor Information: Anchorage Convention and Visitors Bureau, 524 West Fourth Avenue, Anchorage, AK 99501-2212; telephone (907)276-4118; www.anchorage.net

■ Convention Facilities

Anchorage is rapidly gaining distinction as a convention and meeting site. The city's downtown convention center is within walking distance of fine restaurants, unique shops, and world-class cultural events. The extraordinary experience of enjoying first-class amenities in close proximity to untouched wilderness attracts an increasing number of groups to Anchorage yearly.

The principal meeting place in Anchorage is the William A. Egan Civic and Convention Center. The complex contains 45,000 square feet of meeting and exhibit space accommodating groups of 20 to 2,776 people; other features include 189 custom exhibit areas, simultaneous interpreting facilities, and complete catering service. Across the street from Egan Center and adjoined by a skybridge is the Alaska Center for the Performing Arts, which provides theater-style meeting halls seating 350 to 2,100 people. In 2006 construction began on the new $103 million, 215,000-square-foot Dena'ina Center. The new convention center will be located about one block away from the Alaska Center for the Performing Arts; however, the project includes the construction of covered walkways to connect all three convention locations. The project is scheduled for completion in 2008.

Located two miles from downtown is the George M. Sullivan Arena, which accommodates trade shows with 32,000 square feet of usable space and parking for 1,800 vehicles. The Anchorage Museum of History and Art is available to host special events in its atrium. Other meeting facilities are available at the University of Alaska Anchorage, Alaska Pacific University, and major hotels in the metropolitan area. Anchorage features more than

8,000 hotel and motel rooms and more than 850 beds in bed and breakfast and hostel accommodations.

Convention Information: Anchorage Convention and Visitors Bureau, 524 West Fourth Avenue, Anchorage, AK 99501-2212; telephone (907)276-4118; www .anchorage.net

■ Transportation

Approaching the City

The majority of travelers come to Anchorage by plane, arriving at Anchorage International Airport located ten minutes west of downtown. A major stop for transpolar flights, the airport is one of the busiest in the country and is served by more than 50 freight and passenger air carriers.

For those heading to Anchorage by car, the major route into the city is Alaska 1, which is Glenn Highway as it enters from the northeast and Seward Highway (scenic S.R. 1/9) as it enters from the south. The Alaska Railroad, headquartered in Anchorage, provides passenger rail service within Alaska.

Traveling in the City

Downtown Anchorage is laid out in a series of square blocks, a pattern typical of early western railroad towns. All lettered streets run north-south and numbered streets run east-west, with Northern Lights Boulevard dividing north from south and A Street dividing east from west.

Anchorage's bus-based public transit system is the People Mover, which provides a convenient way to see the city, as buses stop at major points of interest and extend to all suburbs. The Share-A-Ride service connects people living in the same area for car or vanpooling, and in some cases municipally-owned vans are provided. AnchorRides offers paratransit services to residents with disabilities. Taxi companies and several private shuttle companies offer transportations services throughout Anchorage.

■ Communications

Newspapers and Magazines

The major daily newspaper in Anchorage is the morning *Anchorage Daily News*. *The Anchorage Press* is an alternative weekly. Several other newspapers are published in Anchorage, including *Petroleum News,* a paper covering the petroleum industry in Alaska and Canada; and the *Sourdough Sentinel,* a weekly covering happenings at Elmendorf Air Force Base. Also published in Anchorage

are *Northern Pilot Magazine, Alaska Business Monthly,* which focuses on state business developments, and *Senior Voice.*

Television and Radio

Anchorage has four commercial television stations and one public broadcasting station. The city is also served by cable television and by twelve AM and FM radio stations broadcasting a variety of formats such as adult contemporary, country, and broadcasts from National Public Radio and American Public Radio. The Anchorage Media Group operates six of the radio stations. Telecommunication service companies include Alaska Communication Systems, General Communication, Inc., and AT&T Alascom.

Media Information: *Anchorage Daily News,* P.O. Box 149001, Anchorage, AK 99514-9001 (mailing address); telephone (907)257-4200; www.adn.com

Anchorage Online

Alaska Department of Education and Early Development. Available www.eed.state.ak.us

Anchorage Convention and Visitors Bureau. Available www.anchorage.net

Anchorage Daily News. Available www.adn.com

Anchorage Economic Development Corporation. Available www.aedcweb.com

Anchorage Municipal Libraries. Available www .anchoragelibrary.org

Anchorage School District. Available www.asd.k12 .ak.us

Municipality of Anchorage Home Page. Available www.muni.org

State of Alaska. Available www.state.ak.us

BIBLIOGRAPHY

Fanning, Kay, *Kay Fanning's Alaska Story: Memoir of a Pulitzer Prize-Winning Newspaper Publisher on America's Northern Frontier* (Kenmore, WA: Epicenter Press, 2006)

Muir, John, *Travels in Alaska* (Boston, New York: Houghton Mifflin, 1915)

Rich, Kim, *Johnny's Girl: A Daughter's Memoir of Growing Up in Alaska's Underworld* (New York: Morrow, 1993)

Woodward, Kesler E., *Painting in the North: Alaskan Art in the Anchorage Museum of History and Art* (Seattle, WA: University of Washington Press, 1993)

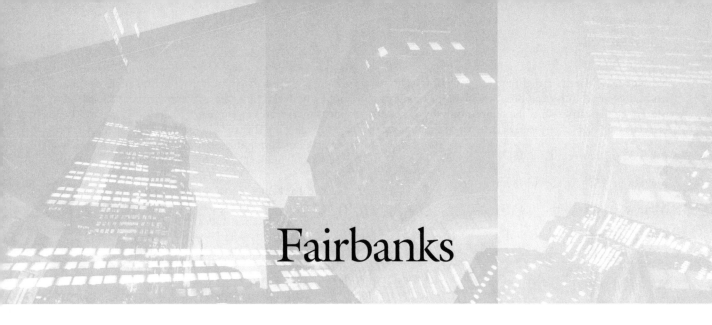

Fairbanks

■ The City in Brief

Founded: 1901 (incorporated 1903)

Head Official: Mayor Terry Strle (since 2007)

City Population

> 1980: 22,645
> 1990: 30,843
> 2000: 30,224
> 2006 estimate: 31,142
> Percent change, 1990–2000: − 2.4%
> U.S. rank in 1980: Not reported
> U.S. rank in 1990: 878th
> U.S. rank in 2000: Not reported (State rank: 3rd)

Metropolitan Area Population

> 1980: 53,983
> 1990: 77,720
> 2000: 82,840
> 2006 estimate: 86,754
> Percent change, 1990–2000: 6.6%
> U.S. rank in 1980: Not reported
> U.S. rank in 1990: Not reported
> U.S. rank in 2000: Not reported

Area: 32.67 square miles (2000)

Elevation: 432 feet above sea level

Average Annual Temperature: 30.4° F

Average Annual Precipitation: 67.8 inches of snow

Major Economic Sectors: services, wholesale and retail trade, government

Unemployment Rate: 5.4% (June 2007)

Per Capita Income: $19,814 (1999)

2005 FBI Crime Index Property: 1,587

2005 FBI Crime Index Violent: 306

Major Colleges and Universities: University of Alaska Fairbanks

Daily Newspaper: *Fairbanks Daily News-Miner*

■ Introduction

Fairbanks, located in east-central Alaska, is sometimes referred to as the "Golden Heart of Alaska." Despite being the trade, transportation, and cultural center of the Alaskan Interior, Fairbanks has maintained much of its frontier character. Mining camps, swinging-door saloons, and unpaved roads mingle with modern hotels and restaurants, a symphony orchestra, and an internationally known research university. The most distinctive feature of the city, however, is its weather. During the months of June and July, Fairbanks has about 20 hours of sunlight, while December and January offer only about four hours of sun each day. With long winter nights and snow covering the ground about nine months of the year, Fairbanks is quintessentially Alaska.

■ Geography and Climate

Fairbanks is located in the Tanana Valley in east-central Alaska, about 358 miles north of Anchorage and 125 miles south of the Arctic Circle. The Alaska Range, including Mt. McKinley, lies to the south and the White Mountains are off to the north. The city is located near the confluence of the Chena and Tanana rivers. It is the largest city in the interior and the second-largest in the state (after Anchorage). It is part of Fairbanks North Star Borough. Significant changes in solar heat during the year produce a wide variation of temperatures from winter to summer. During the summer months (June and July) the sun is above the horizon an average of 20 hours per day and temperatures are often in the high 80s. From

November to March, daylight ranges from 10 to 4 hours daily and temperatures can drop to −50° F. During the winter, ice fog can occur if the temperature drops below −20° F. Fairbanks rarely experiences windy conditions.

Area: 32.67 square miles (2000)

Elevation: 432 feet above sea level

Average Temperature: 30.4° F

Average Annual Precipitation: 67.8 inches of snow

■ History

Discovery of Gold Brings Prospectors, Settlers

Fairbanks was founded accidentally in 1901 by Captain E. T. Barnette. On his way to set up a trading post on the Tanana River, Barnette was instead stranded on the Chena River when the riverboat in which he was traveling was forced to turn back. As he was making plans to move his supplies to a more profitable location, gold was discovered about 12 miles away, near Fox. An Italian prospector, Felix Pedro, is credited with having made the discovery on July 22, 1902. Every year on that date, Fairbanks commemorates the gold strike with the Golden Days celebration.

During the ensuing gold rush, Barnette's trading post became the center of activity for prospectors who swarmed into the area. A settlement grew up and was named for Senator Charles Fairbanks of Indiana who served as vice president under Theodore Roosevelt from 1905-1909; the town was incorporated in 1903. Barnette was elected the first mayor of Fairbanks. He is credited with establishing telephone service, fire protection, sanitation ordinances, electricity and steam heat, but he soon fell into disfavor as a result of his involvement in a bank failure that caused many citizens to lose their savings.

Oil and Military Buildup Replace Gold as Economic Pillars

By 1910 the population of Fairbanks grew to 3,541 people, although more than 6,000 miners lived and worked their claims north of town. During World War I, however, gold activity declined and the population of the town decreased. The start of the construction of the Alaska Railroad brought another boom period, so that by 1930 the population was restored to about half of its previous level.

In 1922 the Alaska Territorial legislature accepted lands granted by the United States Congress, creating the Alaska Agricultural College and School of Mines, which grew into the University of Alaska Fairbanks. During World War II the Alaska Highway was constructed as part of the military buildup and Fairbanks experienced yet another boom period when thousands of military

personnel were located at nearby Eielson Air Force Base and Ladd Field (now Fort Wainwright). Military personnel in the area grew from 10 in 1940 to 5,419 in 1950. Following the war, the Fairbanks population again declined, but during the following decade the community experienced gradual growth. Alaska became a state in 1959.

The Fairbanks North Star Borough was established on January 1, 1964, by an act of the Alaska State Legislature. The borough includes the cities of Fairbanks and North Pole and several unincorporated communities. The borough encompasses about 7,361 square miles (4.7 million acres).

In August 1967, just weeks before the expected winter freeze-up, the city was swept by a flood that inundated 95 percent of its residences and left the city under eight feet of water. Fairbanks recovered from the extensive damage, and with the discovery in 1968 of oil on the north slope of the Brooks Mountain Range, the city entered a new era of expansion.

Construction of the Trans-Alaska oil pipeline triggered one of the city's largest booms, and the population is estimated to have reached 70,000 persons in 1977. With the completion of the pipeline construction, the community's economy went into a serious decline, but it soon recovered with the injection of state revenues in the early 1980s. By the mid-1980s, however, crude oil prices had dropped and Alaska slipped into a severe recession, with Fairbanks experiencing the most abrupt decline in the state. The local economy recovered somewhat, but high unemployment rates continued into the new millennium.

Historical Information: City of Fairbanks, 800 Cushman Street, Fairbanks, AK 99701; telephone (907) 459-6774 (city clerk's office); www.ci.fairbanks.ak.us

■ Population Profile

Metropolitan Area Residents

1980: 53,983
1990: 77,720
2000: 82,840
2006 estimate: 86,754
Percent change, 1990–2000: 6.6%
U.S. rank in 1980: Not reported
U.S. rank in 1990: Not reported
U.S. rank in 2000: Not reported

City Residents

1980: 22,645
1990: 30,843
2000: 30,224
2006 estimate: 31,142
Percent change, 1990–2000: − 2.4%

Walter Bibikow/The Image Bank/Getty Images

U.S. rank in 1980: Not reported
U.S. rank in 1990: 878th
U.S. rank in 2000: Not reported (State rank: 3rd)

Density: 948.7 people per square mile (2000)

Racial and ethnic characteristics (2000)

White: 20,150
Black: 3,370
American Indian and Alaska Native: 2,994
Asian: 821
Native Hawaiian and Pacific Islander: 164
Hispanic or Latino (may be of any race): 1,854
Other: 740

Percent of residents born in state: 30.4% (2000)

Age characteristics (2000)

Population under 5 years old: 2,908
Population 5 to 9 years old: 2,503
Population 10 to 14 years old: 2,233
Population 15 to 19 years old: 2,283
Population 20 to 24 years old: 3,423
Population 25 to 34 years old: 5,588
Population 35 to 44 years old: 4,340

Population 45 to 54 years old: 3,262
Population 55 to 59 years old: 989
Population 60 to 64 years old: 709
Population 65 to 74 years old: 1,086
Population 75 to 84 years old: 700
Population 85 years and older: 200
Median age: 27.6 years

Births (2006, MSA)

Total number: 1,556

Deaths (2006, MSA)

Total number: 439

Money income (1999)

Per capita income: $19,814
Median household income: $40,577
Total households: 11,075

Number of households with income of . . .

less than $10,000: 822
$10,000 to $14,999: 820
$15,000 to $24,999: 1,468
$25,000 to $34,999: 1,615

$35,000 to $49,999: 2,052
$50,000 to $74,999: 2,167
$75,000 to $99,999: 1,086
$100,000 to $149,999: 802
$150,000 to $199,999: 206
$200,000 or more: 94

Percent of families below poverty level: 9.5% (1999)

2005 FBI Crime Index Property: 1,587

2005 FBI Crime Index Violent: 306

■ Municipal Government

The city mayor is elected to a three-year term as the executive and administrative officer of the city; six elected council members serve for staggered three-year terms. The Fairbanks North Star Borough (similar to a county) is governed by a mayor who serves a term of three years and an assembly of nine members, who are elected to three-year terms on a staggered schedule. Administration for the public school system is the responsibility of Fairbanks North Star Borough.

Head Official: Mayor Terry Strle (since 2007; term expires 2010)

Total Number of City Employees: 468 (2005)

City Information: City of Fairbanks, 800 Cushman Street, Fairbanks, AK 99701; telephone (907)459-6774 (city clerk's office); www.ci.fairbanks.ak.us

■ Economy

Major Industries and Commercial Activity

The city economy is closely related to that of the borough as well, and is primarily based on tourism, government services, and the military. The government services sector, including the military, employs more than one-third of the region's workers. The city's international airport serves villages in the region, is a supply point for North Slope oil fields and is a center for the transport of cargo by international carriers. The Williams North Pole Refinery, southeast of Fairbanks, employs about 150 people from Fairbanks and contributes over $2.8 million in property taxes to the borough.

The military presence at nearby Eielson Air Force Base and Fort Wainwright has a significant impact on the city and borough economy. According to the Fairbanks Economic Development Corporation, the total economic impact of the two military bases to the Greater Fairbanks community is over $800 million annually. Active-duty military personnel and their families account for about 20 percent of the total borough population.

Tourism comprises a large percentage of the commercial activity in the region. Each summer, approximately 325,000 visitors travel to Fairbanks. Mining is an important industry as well. To the north of Fairbanks, the Fort Knox gold mine is the largest producing gold mine in the state. It produces about 1,200 ounces of gold daily and employs about 360 permanent year-round workers. More than $200 million in gold has been extracted from the mining district. The mine was expected to remain in operation through 2010.

Incentive Programs—New and Existing Companies

Local programs: The Small Business Development Center (SBDC) offers seminars, counseling, and workshops for new and established businesses to support their existence and help them grow. The Procurement Technical Assistance Center (PTAC) assists businesses who contract with local, state, or federal government.

State programs: The Governor's Office of International Trade provides assistance and information to firms interested in foreign trade and investment, organizes trade missions and promotions, and sponsors trade shows and seminars. The World Trade Center assists businesses seeking to enter or expand their role in international trade. The Alaska Export Assistance Center helps local businesses expand into foreign markets.

Job training programs: A variety of training programs exist to help meet the business needs of Fairbanks employers; many are organized through the local educational institutions. Tanana Chiefs' Conference offers a wide array of programs for tribal populations through its Employment and Training Department. The Chamber of Commerce offers the School Business Partnership, which allows businesses and schools to work together.

Development Projects

In 2005, the Alaska Gasline Port Authority (AGPA) reached a development agreement with Sempra LNG to assist in the development of the All-Alaska Gas Pipeline Project and market the related liquefied natural gas (LNG). The 800-mile natural gas pipeline was designed to run from Prudhoe Bay to Valdez, parallel to the existing Trans-Alaska Oil Pipeline. An LNG plant was planned for construction at Valdez to allow for export to the rest of North America. The first LNG tanker was projected to leave the terminal at Valdez sometime in 2011. A 40 percent portion of project revenues will be shared among the Alaskan municipalities. As of 2007, the cost of the pipeline was projected to approach $9 billion.

In 2007, construction was underway for a multi-million dollar fish hatchery, funded in part by the state. The primary developmental goal was to boost tourism. The hatchery will increase the number of stocked catchable fish available for anglers. The hatchery itself will also be a tourist destination and the source of research dollars for the University of Alaska Fairbanks' fish biology program.

Extreme climate has become a real asset for the area. In 2006, the Research Test Facility (RTF) for the Cold Climate Housing Research Center (CCHRC) was built on land adjacent to the University of Alaska Fairbanks campus. Development in cold weather research and testing, particularly for automotive, aviation, and materials industries, was expected to have an economic impact of about $1.4 million in 2009.

In 2006, the Comprehensive Economic Development Strategies for both the city and county included restructuring projects at Fairbanks International Airport, promotional support for research activities at the University of Alaska Fairbanks, and continued maintenance and development of public transportation systems to support the tourism industry.

Commercial Shipping

Fairbanks is a major transportation hub both for the state and the world. Fairbanks International Airport functions as the air freight distribution and supply center for the region. With low fuel costs and a location that is within 9.5 hours away from major commercial centers in the northern hemisphere, the airport is also used as a major global flight refueling site. The airport handles about 200 million tons of air transit freight each year. Several motor freight carriers transport goods through facilities in the city. Goods are shipped via truck, air, and the Alaska Railroad.

Labor Force and Employment Outlook

Continued slow population growth is projected in the city of Fairbanks, especially among the working-age population. However, the Fairbanks North Star Borough has seen its population steadily increase over the past four decades. The senior population was projected to nearly triple by 2020, while the school-age population was predicted to remain steady. Fairbanks-area businesses that cater to the needs of seniors were expected to prosper, but there will be more competition by employers to find workers. As of 2007 the construction industry was predicted to be the primary source of new jobs. The construction of the All-Alaska Pipeline was expected to bring new jobs to the area.

The following is a summary of data regarding the Fairbanks metropolitan area labor force, 2006 annual averages.

Size of nonagricultural labor force: 38,000

Number of workers employed in . . .

   construction and mining: 2,800
   manufacturing: 600
   trade, transportation and utilities: 7,700
   information: 600
   financial activities: 1,600
   professional and business services: 2,200

   educational and health services: 4,300
   leisure and hospitality: 4,100
   other services: 1,400
   government: 11,800

Average hourly earnings of production workers employed in manufacturing: Not available

Unemployment rate: 5.4% (June 2007)

Largest private employers	Number of employees
Banner Health System	1,204
Alyeska Pipeline Service Co.	1,007
Tanana Chiefs Conference	669
Fairbanks Gold Mining Co.	376
Petro Star	308

Cost of Living

Despite Alaska's reputation for its high cost of living, prices in Fairbanks compare favorably with those in many other North American cities. In 2007, Fairbanks's cost of living index was lower than New York, Boston, and Baltimore, for example. In addition, the personal tax burden for Fairbanks residents is extremely low. Residents benefit from distributions from the Permanent Fund, a savings account established in 1976 by voters allowing residents to receive 25 percent of the state's royalty oil revenue. Senior citizens enjoy a $150,000 property tax exemption or a renter's rebate. The availability of vast natural resources insures utility costs somewhat lower than the national average.

The following is a summary of data regarding key cost of living factors for the Fairbanks area.

2007 (1st quarter) ACCRA Average House Price: $472,800

2007 (1st quarter) ACCRA Cost of Living Index: 125.9

State income tax rate: None

State sales tax rate: None

Local income tax rate: None

Local sales tax rate: None

Property tax rate: 20.777 mills for city of Fairbanks; 7.171 City and 13.606 Borough areawide

Economic Information: Fairbanks Economic Development Corporation, 301 Cushman St., Ste 301, Fairbanks, AK 99701; telephone (888)476-FEDC; www.investfairbanks.com. Fairbanks North Star Borough, Economic Development Division, PO Box 71267,

Fairbanks, AK 99707; telephone (907)459-1300; www
.cometofairbanks.com

■ Education and Research

Elementary and Secondary Schools

Public elementary and secondary schools in Fairbanks are
part of the Fairbanks North Star Borough School District
(FNSBSD). The district is administered by a nonpartisan,
seven-member school board with three non-voting advisory members, which appoints a superintendent. Students in the district come from about 50 different
language backgrounds. In 2007 there were 33 schools in
the district, including 3 charter schools. The high school
graduation rate in the district was about 82 percent. The
district opened a Fairbanks Magnet School for grades K-8
at Barnette Elementary School in fall 2005.

The Yukon-Koyukuk School District, headquartered
in Fairbanks, covers the western interior of Alaska. Serving an area of 65,000 square miles, the district is larger
than the state of Washington. The district sponsors nine
village schools and two correspondence school programs.
More than 90 percent of the students are Tanana or
Koyukon Athabaskan Indians.

The following is a summary of data regarding the
Fairbanks North Star Borough Schools as of the 2005–
2006 school year.

Total enrollment: 14,446

Number of facilities

    elementary schools: 19
    junior high/middle schools: 4
    senior high schools: 5
    other: 5

Student/teacher ratio: 19:1

Teacher salaries (2005–06)

    elementary median: $35,605–$69,073 (all levels)
    junior high/middle median: Not available
    secondary median: Not available

Funding per pupil: $9,597

Private schools, including six religious schools, provide alternative forms of education in the Fairbanks area.

Public Schools Information: Fairbanks North Star
Borough School District, 520 Fifth Avenue, Fairbanks,
AK 99701-4756; telephone (907)452-2000; www
.northstar.k12.ak.us

Colleges and Universities

Fairbanks is home to the University of Alaska Fairbanks
(UAF), which offers 162 degrees in more than 112 disciplines. Programs of study include developmental

programs and certificate, associate, baccalaureate, and
graduate/professional programs in the arts, sciences, career fields, and professions. It is Alaska's only doctoral-
granting institution. UAF possesses unique strengths in
both the physical and natural sciences and offers a broad
array of engineering programs with particular emphasis
on the northern environment. UAF is the state's center
for the study of Alaska native cultures and languages, and
also offers a northern studies program.

Libraries and Research Centers

The Noel Wien Public Library in Fairbanks is the central
branch of the Fairbanks North Star Public Libraries.
There is one branch located in the city of North Pole, 11
miles from Fairbanks. Mail library service is available. The
library houses about 284,400 volumes, 985 periodicals,
14,000 videos, and 12,900 audio materials. The Elmer E.
Rasmuson Library at the University of Alaska Fairbanks
houses more than 1.75 million items, making it the
largest library in the state. Its holdings include books,
periodicals, photography, manuscripts, films, oral histories, rare books, maps, microfiches, tapes, records, and
prints. Its Alaska and Polar Regions collection is one of
the world's finest.

The University of Alaska Fairbanks (UAF) ranks
among the top 100 universities in the nation for its research and development activities. Among UAF's many
outstanding research schools and institutes are the School
of Fisheries and Ocean Science, the Geophysical Institute,
the Institute of Arctic Biology, the Polar Ice Coring
Office, the Institute of Northern Engineering, and the
Agriculture and Forestry Experiment Station. The Arctic
Region Supercomputing Center, a collaboration between
the UAF and the Department of Defense, supports
computational research in science and engineering with
emphasis on high latitudes and the arctic. A $32 million,
100,000-square-foot International Arctic Research Center provides office and research space for scientists from
around the world. Research at the Center focuses on four
major spheres: Arctic Ocean circulation, arctic atmosphere, permafrost/frozen soil, and arctic vegetation.
The Office of Electronics Miniaturization (OEM) boasts
a Class 10,000 Clean Room, equipped with Chip-Scale
Packaging and related technologies. UAF is engaged in
prototyping design development and production through
a cooperative agreement with the Department of
Defense's Defense MicroElectronics Activity (DMEA).
The Poker Flats Research Range, located 33 miles north
of Fairbanks, is a scientific rocket launching facility owned
by the University of Alaska under contract to NASA.
Poker Flat houses many scientific instruments for the
study of the arctic atmosphere and ionosphere. The Cold
Climate Housing Research Center in Fairbanks resear-
ches and develops the latest building technologies and
products for cold climate regions. Alaska's full range of
climatic conditions and a cold season which lasts for six

months or longer provides researchers ample time to conduct experiments and evaluations of housing performance. The Agricultural Research Service projects in the area focus on aquaculture, crop protection, plant diseases, and plant, microbial and insect genetics.

Public Library Information: Fairbanks North Star Borough Public Library and Regional Center, 1215 Cowles Street, Fairbanks, AK 99701; telephone (907) 459-1020; www.library.fnsb.lib.ak.us. University of Alaska Fairbanks, P.O. Box 757500, Fairbanks, AK 99775; telephone (907)474-7211; www.uaf.edu

■ Health Care

Fairbanks Memorial Hospital is the local community-owned hospital, serving an area covering about 250,000 square miles. It is the only major civilian hospital in the area. Operated by the Banner Health System, Fairbanks Memorial is a modern 152-bed facility that has been expanded and remodeled several times since its opening in 1972. The hospital occupies a five-building campus including a cancer treatment center, an imaging center, the Fairbanks Clinic (primary care) and a 24-room emergency department. The hospital's Denali Center, located on the same campus as the hospital, is a 92-bed short- and long-term care facility that is also managed by Banner Health System. The Tanana Valley Clinic and a branch of the Interior Community Health Center also provide basic care in Fairbanks. Other facilities include the Fairbanks Regional Public Health Clinic and Fairbanks Community Behavioral Health Center. Bassett Army Hospital at Fort Wainwright serves military personnel and retirees.

■ Recreation

Sightseeing

Fairbanks is rich in frontier history. One of the main attractions is Pioneer Park, a 44-acre historic theme park on the banks of the Chena River. The Park features a Gold Rush Town with authentic historic buildings, a Native Village with Indian and Eskimo architecture and artifacts, the Pioneer Air Museum, and the riverboat Nenana in drydock. The Kitty Hensley House, home of one of Fairbanks's early citizens, has been restored and is open to the public in Gold Rush Town. A narrow gauge railroad train meanders through the park, and a mini golf course, a mining operation, three museums, and an art gallery are also part of the fun. The Alaska Centennial Center for the Arts is located at Pioneer Park.

There are several National Historic Register buildings within the Fairbanks area, including Creamer's Dairy Wildlife Refuge; these sites are a living testament to the area's rich cultural history. Several churches and buildings in the city are of architectural interest. Muskoxen, caribou and reindeer can be seen at the Large Animal Research Station at the University of Alaska Fairbanks which offers tours of its facility from June through September.

Hot springs, gold dredges, gold camps, and engineering projects such as the first water system in permafrost ground and the Trans-Alaska Oil Pipeline are attractions in the outlying areas. The art of extracting gold from the frozen Alaskan ground is on display at Gold Dredge No. 8, which also has a dining hall and offers an opportunity to pan for gold. The Ester Gold Camp, a popular family attraction, features a 1900s gold camp site and town, a dining hall buffet dinner, a Saloon Show and a view of the Northern Lights set to music. The El Dorado Gold Mine offers two-hour guided tours through a permafrost tunnel, a walking tour of a mining camp, and a chance to pan for gold.

A recommended day trip is a visit to Denali National Park, 120 miles south of Fairbanks. Within its boundaries is North America's tallest mountain, Mt. McKinley (also known locally as Denali). Wildlife such as moose, grizzly bear, mountain sheep, and caribou can be seen in their natural habitat. During the summer months colorful carpets of wildflowers add to the beauty of the park.

The Georgeson Botanical Garden, on the University of Alaska Fairbanks campus, offers tours in the summer months. The sternwheeler Discovery paddles the Chena River for a three-and-a-half hour cruise and makes stops to visit Iditarod kennels, a traditional Athabascan fish camp and an Old Chena Indian Village.

Fairbanks visitors can take advantage of one or more tour packages to explore the area's beauty, wildlife, and opportunities for outdoor fun. Choices for guided tours are plentiful and varied and can include tours by horseback, canoe, raft, boat, car, snowmobile, dogsled, or jet boat. Flightseeing in the form of balloon or helicopter rides is a unique way to enjoy the landscape. Day-long and multi-day trips are available to a number of destinations for individuals and groups.

The Aurora Borealis is one natural wonder that visitors shouldn't miss when visiting the area. Recommended viewing is from September to April, with February, March, September, and October as the very best months (the midnight sun makes viewing difficult in the summer months). There are a variety of options for viewing the Northern Lights, with special guided tours of the Aurora Circle and lodges catering to Aurora viewers.

Arts and Culture

Fairbanks serves as a cultural center for the interior. The Fairbanks Arts Association was incorporated in 1966 and is the oldest community arts council in the state. The Davis Concert Hall of the University of Alaska Fairbanks Fine Arts Complex is home to the Fairbanks Symphony Orchestra and the Arctic Chamber Orchestra. There is also a city youth orchestra. Fairbanks is home to the

Fairbanks Shakespeare Theatre and the Fairbanks Children's Theatre. Musical comedy revues and light opera productions are staged by the Fairbanks Light Opera Theater, the Center Stage, and the Palace Saloon. The Fairbanks Choral Society features an annual "Sing-it-Your-Self-Messiah."

The city has several museums relating to the natural and cultural history of the area. The University of Alaska Museum of the North is one of the most frequently visited tourist attractions in the state and is the only natural and cultural museum in Alaska. Blue Babe, the Ice Age's only restored steppe bison mummy; Alaska's largest public display of gold; and Alaskan native artifacts are on exhibit. Fairbanks Community Museum chronicles the history of Fairbanks from its founding in 1901 to the present with a focus on the Gold Rush era and mining. In the same building is the Dog Mushing Museum which exhibits sleds, clothing, harnesses, trophies, and cold weather expedition gear. Life-size ice sculptures are on view at the Fairbanks Ice Museum which preserves year-round some of the sculptures carved during the World Ice Art Championships held annually in March. The Pioneer Museum and Big Stampede Show is located in Pioneer Park.

The Alaska Public Lands Information Center provides both exhibits and recreation information on state and federal land in Alaska for those planning a trip to the "back country." Information on camping grounds, hiking trails, scenic drives, and fishing spots is available. Several art galleries are also located in Fairbanks, including the Alaska House Art Gallery and Tundra Walker Studio.

Festivals and Holidays

The North American Championship Preliminary Sled Dog Races are held in December and January. In February the Yukon Quest International Dog Sled Race is a 1,000-mile run on gold rush trails. The Tesoro Iron Dog Gold Rush Classic, also in February, is the world's longest snowmobile race. In February or early March the Ice Alaska/Winter Carnival showcases the World Ice Art Championships, an 11-day international ice carving competition. Folk, Celtic, bluegrass, orchestral, and gospel music are all on stage at the Fairbanks Folk Festivals held in February and June. March is the month for the Open North American Sled Dog Championships, which attracts top sprint mushers from the U.S., Canada, Europe, and Japan, as well as the Junior North American Sled Dog Championships. Native people from all over the state gather to share their dancing, singing, storytelling, and traditional arts and crafts at the Annual Festival of Native Arts.

June is a busy month with a variety of events surrounding the summer solstice, such as the Midnight Sun Festival and Midnight Sun Dances. The Yukon 800 Marathon Riverboat Race also takes place in June. Music, theater, story telling, creative writing, visual arts, dance,

and ice skating are on display at the Fairbanks Summer Arts Festival on the campus of the University of Alaska Fairbanks during the last two weeks in July. Also in July, Golden Days celebrates the rich gold-mining history of Fairbanks; a hairy chest, legs, and beard contest is one highlight of the five-day festival. In the World Eskimo-Indian Olympics, another July event, Native people from all over the Arctic compete in games of strength and endurance; among other highlights are storytelling and Native dances. The Midnight Sun Intertribal Powow is a weekend-long dance and drum event open to visitors hoping to learn more about native culture.

The Tanana Valley State Fair is held in August, followed by Oktoberfest. The Athabascan Old-Time Fiddling Festival in November celebrates a musical format that is a composite of French Canadian and Scottish-Arcadian styles fused with Native tunes. Fairbanks celebrates the Winter Solstice each weekend in December with Santa, live music, and family activities downtown.

Sports for the Spectator

Fairbanks is home to the Alaska Goldpanners of the Alaska Baseball League (a summer collegiate league). The University of Alaska Fairbanks Nanooks basketball and ice hockey teams host games on the University of Alaska campus and in the Carlson Center in town.

Dogsledding (mushing) is the official sport of the state of Alaska, and Fairbanks is the site of mushing competitions throughout the winter. Mushing demonstrations can be seen in summer, but serious racing requires cool temperatures and snow. Yukon Quest (in February) is a 1000-mile international sled dog race between Whitehorse, Yukon Territory, Canada, and Fairbanks, Alaska. The Fairbanks Curling Club hosts competitions with teams from throughout Alaska, Canada, and the United States. The Greater Fairbanks Racing Association sponsors summer stock and sprint car racing nearly every weekend starting Memorial Day weekend through Labor Day at the Mitchell Raceway. The Sundawgs Rugby Football Club plays rugby during the Golden Days festival in July. Fairbank's junior ice hockey team is the Ice Dogs, a North American Hockey League team.

Sports for the Participant

Running is a popular activity in Fairbanks. The Equinox Marathon, said to be the second most challenging marathon in the U.S., is a 26-mile race to the top of Ester Dome. The Midnight Sun Run is held in conjunction with the celebration of the summer solstice, and the Chena River 5K Run is held in May.

Many city and area parks offer facilities for a variety of year-round indoor and outdoor recreational activities. Among the most popular pursuits are downhill and cross-country skiing, fishing, canoeing, goldpanning, hiking, hockey, hunting, ice skating, jogging, nature walks, tennis, swimming, volleyball, and racquetball. Smooth paved trails along the Chena River are ideal for biking and rollerblading. Fairbanks boasts three golf courses including one at Fort Wainwright. Winter is a favorite time for swimming in nearby hot springs. A skate board park and volleyball courts are located at Growden Park. Birch Hill Park, a few minutes north of Fairbanks, is a 460-acre park with hiking and running trails, mountain biking, and bird watching in the summer.

Shopping and Dining

Fairbanks has a number of shopping malls and neighborhood stores. Specialty shops feature Alaska native arts and crafts and jewelry fashioned from ivory, jade, and hematite, as well as handmade fur garments. Visitors can watch the manufacture of Alaskan birch bowls at the Great Alaskan Bowl Company where they are also for sale. Santa Claus House, located 13 miles from Fairbanks in the city of North Pole, has become a landmark, drawing visitors from throughout the world to shop for Alaskan gifts, jewelry, and clothing. Local farmers and craft makers display their wares at the Farmers' Market, open Wednesdays and Saturdays from May through the end of summer next to the Tanana Valley Fair Grounds. The city's main commercial district extends along Airport Way, between University Ave. and Cushman St. where most of the fast-food chains and malls can be found. Many bars, restaurants and businesses that cater to the university crowd are located along University Ave. and College Rd.

Dozens of restaurants in Fairbanks provide a wide range of cuisine in casual and elegant settings. Area restaurants specialize in fish from inland waters to more casual fare including miners's stew served in the dining halls of the local gold mines. Visitors can also enjoy Japanese, Korean, Mongolian, and Mexican specialties. Salmon, halibut and cod are the specialties at the Alaska Salmon Bake, one of the more popular venues with its Palace Theater and Saloon in Gold Rush Town. Located in Pioneer Park, it features evening entertainment in the summer with its "Golden Heart Revue."

Visitor Information: Fairbanks Convention and Visitors Bureau, 550 First Avenue, Fairbanks, AK 99701-4790; telephone (907)456-5774; toll-free (800)327-5774; www.explorefairbanks.com

■ Convention Facilities

Fairbanks offers a wide variety of meeting space. The largest meeting and exhibition facility is the Carlson Center, which features a 35,000-square-foot arena and several meeting rooms, for a combined total of 44,220 square feet of space that can accommodate more than 1,200 meeting participants, 200 trade show exhibits, or 4,000 people for a concert or sports event. The Alaska Centennial Center for the Arts at Pioneer Park houses a 384-seat theater, art gallery, exhibit areas, meeting rooms

and all-purpose hall. Also at Pioneer Park is the Birch Hill Cross Country Ski Center which has a 2,400 square foot assembly room. The Chief Peter John Tribal Hall (capacity 750 people) and Mushers Hall are downtown banquet and meeting facilities. The University of Alaska Museum of the North and the Tanana Valley State Fair also provide many options for meeting spaces for any type of function.

Hotel properties with meeting and conference facilities include the Fairbanks Princess Riverside Lodge, Westmark Fairbanks Hotel and Conference Center, River's Edge Resort, Pike's Waterfront Lodge, Regency Fairbanks Hotel, and Fountainhead Hotels. Chena Hot Springs Resort, located 56 miles outside of Fairbanks, offers meeting space that can accommodate more than 100 people.

Convention Information: Fairbanks Convention and Visitors Bureau, 550 First Avenue, Fairbanks, AK 99701-4790; telephone (907)456-5774; toll-free (800)327-5774; www.explorefairbanks.com

■ Transportation

Approaching the City

The Fairbanks International Airport is served by Alaska Airlines, Alaska Central Express, Cargolux Airlines International and Lufthansa. Alaska Airlines has regularly scheduled daily flights to Anchorage and Seattle. Direct connections to major cities and international connections are made through Anchorage International Airport. Airport shuttle service into Fairbanks is available.

Principal routes into Fairbanks are the Alaska Highway, running southeast to northwest, which connects the city with the lower 48 states through Canada, and the George Parks Highway, leading south to Anchorage. Fairbanks is also connected with Anchorage via the Richardson Highway. The Dalton Highway connects Fairbanks to Prudhoe Bay near the Arctic Ocean.

The Alaska Railroad, which links Fairbanks to Anchorage, Denali Park, and Seward on the Kenai Peninsula, has Fairbanks for its northern terminus.

Traveling in the City

Chartered bus tours operate throughout the tourist season in Fairbanks. The Metropolitan Area Commuter System (MACS) operates six bus routes. There are about 10 taxi services in Fairbanks.

■ Communications

Newspapers and Magazines

The major daily newspaper in Fairbanks is the *Fairbanks Daily News-Miner*, published in the morning. The *Northstar Weekly* is distributed in Fairbanks, North Pole and surrounding communities. The University of Alaska Fairbanks publishes the *Sun Star Newspaper*.

Television and Radio

Four television stations broadcast in Fairbanks; cable is available. Eleven AM and FM radio stations broadcast in the Fairbanks, providing a variety of music, news, and information programming. Two of these stations are broadcast from the University of Alaska Fairbanks.

Media Information: *Fairbanks Daily News-Miner*, P.O. Box 70710, Fairbanks, AK 99707-0710; telephone (907)456-6661; www.newsminer.com

Fairbanks Online

City of Fairbanks website. Available www.ci .fairbanks.ak.us

Fairbanks Convention and Visitors Bureau. Available www.explorefairbanks.com

*Fairbanks Daily News-Miner.*Available www .newsminer.com

Fairbanks Economic Development Corporation. Available www.investfairbanks.com

Fairbanks North Star Borough Home Page. Available www.co.fairbanks.ak.us

Fairbanks North Star Borough Public Library and Regional Center. Available www.library.fnsb.lib .ak.us

Fairbanks North Star Borough School District. Available www.northstar.k12.ak.us

Greater Fairbanks Chamber of Commerce. Available www.fairbankschamber.org

State of Alaska. Available www.state.ak.us

University of Alaska Fairbanks. Available www.uaf .edu

BIBLIOGRAPHY

Anders, Joyce J., *Anders of Two Rivers* (Fairbanks, AK: Jenny M. Publishers, 1997)

Blunk, R. Glendon, *Yearning Wild: Exploring the Last Frontier and the Landscape of the Heart* (Montpelier, VT: Invisible Cities Press, 2002)

Cole, Dermot, *Amazing Pipeline Stories* (Fairbanks, AK: Epicenter Press, 1997)

Cole, Dermot, *Fairbanks: A Gold Rush Town that Beat the Odds* (Fairbanks, AK: Epicenter Press, 1999)

Fejes, Claire, *Cold Starry Night: An Alaskan Memoir* (Fairbanks, AK: Epicenter Press, 1996)

Juneau

■ The City in Brief

Founded: 1880 (incorporated 1970)

Head Official: Mayor Bruce Botelho (NP) (since 2003)

City Population

    1980: 19,528
    1990: 26,751
    2000: 30,711
    2006 estimate: 30,737
    Percent change, 1990–2000: 14.8%
    U.S. rank in 1980: Not reported
    U.S. rank in 1990: 1,013th
    U.S. rank in 2000: 989th (State rank: 2nd)

Metropolitan Area Population

    1980: 19,528
    1990: 26,751
    2000: 30,711
    2006 estimate: 30,737
    Percent change, 1990–2000: 14.8%
    U.S. rank in 1980: Not reported
    U.S. rank in 1990: Not reported
    U.S. rank in 2000: Not reported

Area: 3,255 square miles (Borough, 2000)

Elevation: Ranges from sea level to 3,800 feet above sea level

Average Annual Temperature: 41.9° F

Average Annual Precipitation: 91.32 inches

Major Economic Sectors: services, wholesale and retail trade, government

Unemployment Rate: 7.2% (January 2005)

Per Capita Income: $26,719 (1999)

2005 FBI Crime Index Property: 60

2005 FBI Crime Index Violent: 0

Major Colleges and Universities: University of Alaska Southeast

Daily Newspaper: *Juneau Empire*

■ Introduction

The city and borough of Juneau is one of Alaska's most popular tourist destinations and one of the state's most important ports. Juneau is unique in that it is accessible only by air and sea. Annually, more than 800,000 cruise-ship passengers visit the city between May and September. Many are surprised to find a vibrant community with professional theater, museums, art galleries, and historical sites in a small-town atmosphere. The area has a temperate climate with weather on par with that of Seattle. Juneau had been one of the world's major gold mining areas until the 1940s when costs outstripped the value of the gold; however, the industry has had a resurgence with a significant project having gained approval in 2005. The city's economy relies heavily on the government workers who make up the majority of the work force, along with fishermen, loggers, and miners. Nearby Glacier Bay, Admiralty Island, and the Juneau Icefield offer spectacular scenery, and sightseeing flights are available year-round.

■ Geography and Climate

The city of Juneau is located on the mainland of southeastern Alaska's Panhandle on the narrow southeastern strip bordering the Canadian province of British Columbia, approximately 1,000 miles northwest of Seattle, Washington. Most of the city lies on the mainland of Alaska, although Douglas Island, which is connected by a bridge, is also part of Juneau. The Gastineau Channel separates the island from the main part of the city, which is surrounded by the Tongass National Forest. The city climbs the tree-lined slopes of Mount Roberts and Mount Juneau, which rise from the water's edge to more than 3,500 feet.

The city has a mild, rainy climate with a year-round ice-free harbor. The Pacific Ocean currents temper the weather, and average summer temperatures are in the 60s with many days reaching into the high 70s or low 80s. Juneau's winters are comparable to those of Minneapolis or Chicago.

Area: 3,255 square miles (Borough, 2000)

Elevation: Ranges from sea level to 3,800 feet above sea level

Average Temperature: 41.9° F

Average Annual Precipitation: 91.32 inches

■ History

In the late 1800s when gold prospecting began in the Gastineau Channel region, the area was a fishing ground for local Tlingit Native Americans. A mining engineer from Sitka, George Pilz, offered a reward to any local native chief who could show him the site of gold-bearing ore. After Chief Kowee of the Auk Tlingit arrived in Sitka with ore samples from the Gastineau Channel, Pilz outfitted Joseph Juneau and Richard Harris for a trip to investigate the lode.

The prospectors reached the area in 1880, and although they found gold samples, they did not follow the gold to its source. After their return to Sitka, Pilz sent them out again. On the second trip Harris and Juneau climbed Snow Slide Gulch at the head of Gold Creek and observed the mother lode of Quartz Gulch, and Silver Bow Basin. They staked a 160-acre town site on the beach. By the next year more than 100 prospectors had arrived in the settlement, which was later named in honor of Joseph Juneau.

Within a few years, Juneau grew to a center for large-scale hard-rock mining, and tunnels and shafts wound through the surrounding hills. Two great mills were developed, the Alaska-Juneau at the south end of the city and the Alaska-Gastineau at Thane.

In May 1882 John Treadwell established the Alaska Mill & Mining Company with the construction of a five-stamp mill. The Treadwell Gold Mining Company produced more than $70 million of gold before it closed. Treadwell's production peaked in 1915, but a 1917 flooding of three of its mines after a cave-in spelled its demise. The Alaska-Gastineau closed in 1921 when operations became too expensive. The final big mill,

Alaska-Juneau, folded in 1944 as a result of high prices and labor shortages due to World War II.

By the beginning of the twentieth century, Juneau had become a transportation and regional trading center. It assumed the title of Alaska's capital in 1906 following its transfer from Sitka. In 1931 the Federal and Territorial Building, now the State Capitol Building, was constructed. Juneau has remained the state capital despite attempts to move the capital elsewhere. In 2005 the city announced its desire to build a modern, $100 million facility to replace the aging Capitol Building. Today, government—local, state or federal—employs one out of every two workers and tourism is the largest private-sector employer in Juneau. A federally recognized Native American tribe lives within the Juneau community.

With its vast natural wonders, temperate climate, and position as the capital city, Juneau has the foundation for a long-term prosperous community as can be seen in its population growth since 1980. The Juneau Economic Development Council has programs in place to create positive business conditions for new and existing companies.

Historical Information: Juneau-Douglas City Museum, 155 S. Seward St., Juneau, AK 99801; telephone (907)586-3572; email mary_pat_wyatt@ci.juneau.ak.us

■ Population Profile

Metropolitan Area Residents

1980: 19,528
1990: 26,751
2000: 30,711
2006 estimate: 30,737
Percent change, 1990–2000: 14.8%
U.S. rank in 1980: Not reported
U.S. rank in 1990: Not reported
U.S. rank in 2000: Not reported

City Residents

1980: 19,528
1990: 26,751
2000: 30,711
2006 estimate: 30,737
Percent change, 1990–2000: 14.8%
U.S. rank in 1980: Not reported
U.S. rank in 1990: 1,013th
U.S. rank in 2000: 989th (State rank: 2nd)

Density: 11.3 people per square mile (2000)

Racial and ethnic characteristics (2000)

White: 22,969
Black: 248
American Indian and Alaska Native: 3,496

David Job/Stone/Getty Images

Asian: 1,438
Native Hawaiian and Pacific Islander: 116
Hispanic or Latino (may be of any race): 1,040
Other: 323

Percent of residents born in state: 38.0% (2000)

Age characteristics (2000)

Population under 5 years old: 2,003
Population 5 to 9 years old: 2,339
Population 10 to 14 years old: 2,541
Population 15 to 19 years old: 2,321
Population 20 to 24 years old: 1,686
Population 25 to 34 years old: 4,286
Population 35 to 44 years old: 5,781
Population 45 to 54 years old: 5,514
Population 55 to 59 years old: 1,456
Population 60 to 64 years old: 916
Population 65 to 74 years old: 1,084
Population 75 to 84 years old: 615
Population 85 years and older: 169
Median age: 35.3 years

Births (2006, Micropolitan Statistical Area)

Total number: 395

Deaths (2006, Micropolitan Statistical Area)

Total number: 133

Money income (1999)

Per capita income: $26,719
Median household income: $62,034
Total households: 11,534

Number of households with income of...

less than $10,000: 404
$10,000 to $14,999: 407
$15,000 to $24,999: 974
$25,000 to $34,999: 1,111
$35,000 to $49,999: 1,653
$50,000 to $74,999: 2,525
$75,000 to $99,999: 2,183
$100,000 to $149,999: 1,625
$150,000 to $199,999: 390
$200,000 or more: 262

Percent of families below poverty level: 3.7% (1999)

2005 FBI Crime Index Property: 60

2005 FBI Crime Index Violent: 0

■ Municipal Government

Juneau, a home-rule municipality, has a council-manager type of government formed via elections held every three years. In 1970 the city merged with the city of Douglas and other areas of the Juneau Borough to become the city and borough of Juneau. The Borough Assembly is comprised of the mayor and eight assembly members.

Head Official: Mayor Bruce Botelho (NP) (since 2003)

Total Number of City Employees: 1,536 (2004)

City Information: City and Borough of Juneau, 155 S. Seward St., Juneau, AK 99801; telephone (907)586-3300

■ Economy

Major Industries and Commercial Activity

Nearly half of Juneau's working population is employed by the federal, state, or local government. All state departments have offices in Juneau, including the Superior and District Courts. A large federal building houses the regional headquarters of several federal agencies. Those with the largest number of workers are the U.S. Forest Service, National Park Service, National Marine Fisheries Service, Bureau of Indian Affairs, U.S. Fish and Wildlife Service, U.S. Postal Service, and the U.S. Coast Guard. It is estimated that for each government worker, one private sector job is needed to supply the services required by the government workers.

Tourism is the largest private-sector employer. The number of non-Alaskan visitors to Juneau tops 800,000 each year, accounting for about half of the total Alaska visitor market. The majority of visitors travel between May 1 and October 1, though year-round travel is growing. During that time, the harbor is filled with cruise ships bringing tourists from the "Lower 48" and around the world.

Commercial fishing and fish processing are another important sector of the local economy. Salmon hatcheries and a cold storage facility operate in town, the latter processing two million pounds of salmon, halibut, black cod, and crab annually.

Transportation and trading are the other important sectors of the economy. Manufacturing jobs had been almost nonexistent but that area has become a focal point for government programs resulting in a growth spurt.

Kenneccott Greens Creek Mine, on Admiralty Island near the city, produces gold, silver, lead, and zinc, and is one of the largest silver mines in North America. In December 2004 an environmental impact study was completed allowing for the Kensington Gold Mine project to proceed. It is expected to create about 200 construction jobs for two years, then roughly 250 positions for its 10 to 15 years of operation.

The $900 million Regional Corporation Alaska Native Land Claims Settlement Act (ANCSA) was enacted in 1971 to help compensate the native Alaskans for the lands taken from them when the United States purchased the Alaskan Territory from Russia in 1867. Two of Alaska's 13 regional native Alaskan corporations are located near Juneau. Sealaska, the ANCSA regional corporation for Southeast Alaska that serves 17,500 Tlingit and Haida shareholders, has its headquarters in Juneau. Goldbelt Inc., the urban native village corporation, is also located near Juneau and handles about 3,500 shareholders of primarily Alaska Native heritage. The two corporations are in the business of money management, producing timber, and studying diversification into the area of mineral rights. Juneau is also the home of Klukwan Forest Products, Inc., which holds 23,000 acres of forested land within the area's rainforest.

Items and goods produced: processed fish, ore, forest products

Incentive Programs—New and Existing Companies

Local programs: The Southeast Alaska Revolving Loan Fund (RLF), since its formation in 1997, has developed a capital pool of about $5 billion to assist area businesses in retaining and creating jobs. Entrepreneurs can go to the Business Assistance Center (BAC) for information, workshops, and a variety of other services.

State programs: The Governor's Office of International Trade provides assistance and information to firms interested in foreign trade and investment, organizes trade missions and promotions, and sponsors trade shows and seminars. The Office of Economic Development provides business assistance to new and existing Alaskan businesses and industry. Programs include business counseling, Made in Alaska, RAPIDS: Rural Alaska Project Identification and Delivery System, and the Alaska Economic Information System.

Job training programs: Business start up services are offered by the state of Alaska on a case-by-case basis.

Development Projects

A two-phase renovation project to Bartlett Memorial Hospital was approved in 2001, entailing $43 million in improvements. Phase I construction began in 2004 and finished with the addition of a new wing—nearly 55,000 square feet—in early 2007. Phase II is set for completion by spring 2008. The most recent renovations will include a reworked entrance and lobby space, as well as new chemotherapy and medical surgical facilities.

Economic Development Information: Alaska Department of Community and Economic Development, Research & Analysis Section; telephone (907)465-4508; fax (907)465-4506; email raweb@labor.state.ak.us. Juneau Economic Development Council, 612 W. Willoughby Ave., Ste. A, Juneau, AK 99801-1732; telephone (907)463-3662; fax (907)463-3929; email administrator@jedc.org

Commercial Shipping

The Juneau airport includes a paved 8,456-foot runway and a seaplane landing area. Marine facilities include a seaplane landing area at Juneau Harbor, two deep draft docks, five small boat harbors, and a state ferry terminal. The Alaska Marine Highway System and cargo barges provide year-round services. Juneau's docks are used primarily for the cruise ships bringing tourists to Juneau.

Labor Force and Employment Outlook

Because so many are employed in government, Juneau's workforce is better educated than is the statewide workforce and per capita income is higher. However, dependence on one industry leaves Juneau vulnerable to severe economic distress when government falters. Ongoing efforts are being made to diversify Juneau's economy. The overall labor force demonstrated significant increases in all major categories. Manufacturing and financial industries have shown great successes, and construction and mining continue to grow with the Kensington Gold Mine starting production. Employment in the service sector should remain strong. Tourism is vibrant, and there has been a change in the characteristics of the typical visitor to Alaska. Many of the new travelers are younger, more independent, and interested in family, adventure, and environment-related activities.

The following is a summary of data regarding the Southeast Region metropolitan area labor force, 2003 annual averages.

Size of nonagricultural labor force: 36,250

Number of workers employed in...

construction and mining: 2,050
manufacturing: 1,850
trade, transportation and utilities: 7,050
information: 500
financial activities: 1,250
professional and business services: 1,400
educational and health services: 3,450
leisure and hospitality: 3,550

other services: 1,150
government: 13,650

Average hourly earnings of production workers employed in manufacturing: Not available

Unemployment rate: 7.2% (January 2005)

Largest employment sectors and employers (2003)	*Number of employees*
Federal, state, and local government	17,105
Southeast Alaska Regional Health Corp.	705

Cost of Living

The personal tax burden in Alaska is extremely low. Senior citizens enjoy a $150,000 property tax exemption or a renter's rebate. The availability of vast natural resources ensures utility costs somewhat lower than the national average. However, in Juneau, the overall costs are significantly higher than the U.S. average (about 30 percent).

The following is a summary of data regarding key cost of living factors for the Juneau area.

2007 (1st quarter) ACCRA Average House Price: $470,400

2007 (1st quarter) ACCRA Cost of Living Index: 131.5

State income tax rate: None

State sales tax rate: None

Local income tax rate: None

Local sales tax rate: 4.0%

Property tax rate: Varies

Economic Information: Alaska Department of Labor & Workforce Development, Research & Analysis Section, PO Box 25501, Juneau, AK 99802-5501; telephone (907)465-4500; fax (907)465-2101; email raweb@labor.state.ak.us

■ Education and Research

Elementary and Secondary Schools

Juneau's schools offer special programs for secondary school students, including the Project of Assisted Learning, an alternative approach; the Entrepreneurship Program, with an emphasis on vocational education; and special education programs for children with special needs. Due to Juneau's geographic location, the schools also offer programs focusing on the sea.

The following is a summary of data regarding the Juneau School District as of the 2005–2006 school year.

Total enrollment: 5,273

Number of facilities

elementary schools: 7
junior high/middle schools: 2
senior high schools: 2
other: 1

Student/teacher ratio: 17:1

Teacher salaries (2005–06)

elementary median: $34,606–67,305 (all levels)
junior high/middle median: Not available
secondary median: Not available

Funding per pupil: $8,902

Public Schools Information: Juneau School District, 10014 Crazy Horse Dr., Juneau, AK 99801; telephone (907)463-1700

Colleges and Universities

Enrolling 700 full-time and 2,000 part-time students, the University of Alaska Southeast's (UAS) Juneau location on the shores of the Inside Passage serves as the main campus, with two other administrative units of the University of Alaska statewide system (in Ketchikan and Sitka), and focuses on general liberal arts education. The university proper offers certificate, associate of arts, associate of applied science, baccalaureate, professional, and master's degree programs in the applied areas of business, fisheries, liberal arts, science, public administration, and teacher education. The university's two-year and certificate program in vocational and technical education supplies employees for local business and industry.

Libraries and Research Centers

The 18,000 square foot Juneau Public Library has a unique design built upon a parking garage in a beautiful waterfront location, with holdings of about 70,000 volumes. In March 2005 it began offering the Alaska Library Network Catalog (ALNCAT) which provides access to all state libraries' collections. The Juneau Public Library and its two branches are part of the Capital City Libraries consortium, a cooperative catalog and circulation system shared with the Alaska State Library since 1989, the University of Alaska Southeast Egan Library, the Juneau-Douglas High School Library, and the Alyeska Central School Library. Holders of library cards at one of these libraries may borrow from any of the others and have access to library resources from home.

Other libraries in the city include the Alaska State Libraries, Archives & Museums, which encompass legislative information, policy issues and Alaskan history; the U.S. Bureau of Mines Library (with a collection of more than 20,000 publications); the U.S. Forest Service Library; the Alaska Historical Library; and other state level governmental libraries.

Public Library Information: Juneau Public Libraries, 292 Marine Way, Juneau, AK 99801; telephone (907)586-5249

■ Health Care

Juneau is served by Bartlett Memorial Hospital, a city-owned facility that began an extensive $40 million expansion project in 2005. Bartlett Memorial also operates the Juneau Recovery Hospital, a medical model facility for the detoxification and rehabilitation of persons with alcohol or other drug dependencies. Other Juneau health facilities are the Juneau Alliance for Mental Health, Inc. (JAMHI), and the Teen Health Clinic.

■ Recreation

Sightseeing

A good place for visitors to start exploring Juneau is at the Davis Log Cabin Visitor Center, which offers guides and maps. The Downtown Historic District of the city contains many buildings dating back to 1880 and has wider sidewalks reminiscent of the old boardwalks. The Governor's Mansion, built in 1912, is not open to the public on a regular basis but tours can be arranged by contacting the governor's office. Alaska's State Capitol Building, with columns fashioned from a quarry on Prince of Wales Island, houses both the governor's office and state legislative offices and is open for tours. From January through May visitors may watch floor sessions from the galleries. The House of Wickersham, built in 1898 and the former home of famous local judge, James Wickersham (1837–1939), contains historic memorabilia as well as a genuine Chickering grand piano circa late 1800s, and is listed on the National Register of Historic Places.

The Juneau-Douglas City Museum includes various exhibits related to the areas's rich history and provides educational and public programs while concentrating on the city's mining history. Tours are available of the St. Nicholas Orthodox Church, the oldest original Russian Orthodox church in the state, which was founded in 1893. The Shrine of St. Therese, a chapel located on an island north of Juneau that is connected to the city by a narrow path, has stations of the cross on a trail circumnavigating the chapel in the surrounding woods and can be visited year-round.

The Last Chance Basin Historic District, usually referred to as the Jualpa Mining Camp, features many old mine buildings and attractions for visitors such as gold panning and, in summer, an outdoor salmon bake. A

5,000-gallon aquarium full of local sea life is the highlight of the Macaulay Salmon Hatchery, which is located three miles from downtown. Green Angel Gardens is a botanical facility featuring a variety of local plants and a salmon stream located near a low, active volcano.

Nature is the star at Juneau, and the walk-up Mendenhall Glacier, located 13 miles from downtown, is a must-see experience. It features a visitor center, built in 1962, which describes the progression of the glacier and the icecap from which it descends; the visitor center also features a movie and self-guided walking tour map. The 1,500-square-mile Juneau Icefield, the birthplace of the Mendenhall Glacier and 37 others, is located just over the mountains behind the city and is the fifth largest in North America. Light plane charters and helicopters offer an up-close tour.

Many visitors enjoy taking walking tours of Juneau's four local harbors, where fishing boat captains are usually amenable to discussing the day's catch. Whalewatching and wildlife viewing charter boat tours are a popular visitor attraction; a variety of companies offer tours from in or around Juneau, and many guarantee sightings.

Arts and Culture

The Alaska State Museum, established in 1900 when the state was a territory, offers more than 27,000 fine historical, cultural, and artistic collections under one roof. Juneau's gold rush history is captured at the Juneau-Douglas City Museum, which also contains a "Back to the Past" hands-on room for children, and a large relief map of Juneau's topography. Juneau has a very active artists' community, and there are many works of art located in public areas throughout downtown, including sculptures and totem poles.

Alaska's only professional theater company, Perseverance Theatre of Juneau, presents a variety of classic, comedic, and dramatic plays during its fall-winter-spring season that typically draws 20,000 annually. The Naa Kahidi Theater, supported by the Sealaska Heritage Foundation, performs ancient Tlingit legends via storytelling for special events. The Gold Nugget Revue presents comedic historical adventures of Juneau's history, along with cancan dancers and other entertainment.

Festivals and Holidays

April is the time for the annual Alaska Folk Festival, which has been running since the mid-1970s. Music lovers assemble for the 10-day Juneau Jazz & Classics Festival in May. August's Golden North Salmon Derby, a tradition since 1947, offers big prizes, including scholarships, for catching big fish.

Sports for the Spectator

Douglas High School sports receive plenty of media coverage from the daily newspaper, *The Juneau Empire*. Spectators have the chance to cheer on the 2005 State Champion football team, the Crimson Bears, as well as a variety of other athletics programs, such as those centered around baseball, basketball, soccer, track and field, hockey, and volleyball. Spectators should also try to catch one of the men's, women's or co-ed softball games organized by the Juneau Sports Association.

Sports for the Participant

Juneau has five mountain peaks within reasonable day-trip distances, affording many hiking and climbing opportunities. Hiking trails lead from downtown to overlooks on 3,576-foot Mt. Juneau, 3,819-foot Mt. Roberts, and 3,337-foot Mt. Bradley (also known as Mt. Jumbo). The Mt. Roberts tramway travels from Juneau's waterfront to an elevation of nearly 2,000 feet. Guided tours, a restaurant, and theater are available at the upper terminal. The Juneau visitor's center offers free guides to more than two dozen trails to glaciers and historic gold mining ruins.

Fishing, sailing, kayaking, and river rafting are available on the protected waters of the Inside Passage. In summers, operators offer gentle river rafting, salmon watching, and gold panning. Picnics, camping, fishing, and beachcombing are popular on the area's beaches.

Mendenhall is the only golf course in Southeast Alaska, a par-three, nine-hole course built on private land behind the airport and only 10 miles from downtown. Winter downhill skiing and snowboarding are offered at Eaglecrest, 12 miles from the city's downtown, with alpine runs, Nordic trails, and a vertical drop of 1,400 feet. Helicopter ski packages are available from late November through early April.

Juneau also has a racquet club, indoor rock-climbing, several aerobic studios, yoga classes, and local Parks and Recreation Department seasonal sports programs that welcome visitors.

Shopping and Dining

Visitors will find galleries, shops, and restaurants throughout the downtown Juneau area. Specialty shops and gift shops offer hand-crafted work by local artists. Nugget Mall, the largest shopping destination, is within walking distance of the airport; its more than 35 stores feature Alaskan gifts and clothing and the mall has a visitor information center. Senate Shopping Mall houses eight eclectic shops from Native art to flyfishing supplies. Merchant's Wharf, an office and shop complex, is located at harborside. Gift shops and taverns line South Franklin Street. The Emporium Mall contains specialty shops and stores, as well as the Heritage Coffee Co., a sandwich and coffee shop on the main floor. Fantastic mountain views and a traditional steak and seafood menu are signatures of the historic Hangar on the Wharf restaurant.

The state's most famous bar, the lively Red Dog Saloon, provides local pictorial history, music, and excitement, especially when cruise ships are in port.

Visitor Information: Juneau Convention and Visitors Bureau, One Sealaska Plz., Ste. 305, Juneau, AK 99801; telephone (907)586-1737; toll-free (800)587-2201; fax (907)586-1449; email info@traveljuneau.com

■ Convention Facilities

Centennial Hall Convention Center, just across the street from the waterfront, is three blocks away from the heart of Juneau's downtown with its shops and restaurants. Built in 1983, Centennial Hall has 7 meeting rooms ranging from 300 square feet to an 11,275-square-foot, column-free ballroom. The ballroom can be divided into three separate rooms, each with state-of-the-art light and sound systems. Centennial Hall also has two lobbies that provide an additional 4,200 square feet for receptions, displays, and relaxation. Juneau also offers meeting spaces in majestic settings atop Mt. Roberts, on the banks of the Gastineau Channel, or overlooking Auke Lake.

Convention Information: Juneau Convention and Visitors Bureau, One Sealaska Plz., Ste. 305, Juneau, AK 99801; telephone (907)586-1737; toll-free (800)587-2201; fax (907)586-1449; email info@traveljuneau.com

■ Transportation

Approaching the City

Juneau International Airport covers 80,000 square feet of land and is serviced daily by Alaska Airlines. The city is about a two-hour flight north from Seattle, or approximately a 90-minute flight southeast from Anchorage. In 2005 a study was in process to determine the specific renovations needed to modernize the aging facility. Juneau has no direct road and rail links. The Alaska Marine Highway ferry system provides car and passenger connections into Juneau from other southeast communities, as well as Bellingham, Washington (a two and one-half day trip) and Prince Rupert, British Columbia (a 24-hour trip). The ferries have staterooms, observation decks, cocktail lounges, and heated solariums. A variety of regional air taxi services and chartered flights are available to nearby attractions and smaller towns. Barge lines serve Juneau from Seattle several times per week. Power boats, sailboats, and kayaks are also available to rent for trips to the Inside Passage.

Traveling in the City

Egan Drive is one of the major streets in Juneau, running from one end of town to the other and following the shoreline of the Gastineau Channel. The downtown area is divided into a grid with Main Street crossing the numbered streets and passing the Capitol building and other major sites. Bus service is provided by the Capitol Transit line with 16 buses in its fleet. Buses and vans meet every ferry from mid-April to the end of September, providing inexpensive service to downtown and the airport. Local air taxi operators fly both wheel and float planes.

■ Communications

Newspapers and Magazines

Juneau Empire is the city's daily newspaper and *Inside Passage,* the official newspaper of the Catholic Diocese of Juneau, is produced biweekly from September through May and monthly from June to August.

Television and Radio

ABC and PBS television stations are based in Juneau. Cable television is available, and there are five AM and FM radio stations broadcasting news, adult contemporary music, public radio, and album-oriented rock.

Media Information: Juneau Empire, Morris Communications Corp., 3100 Channel Dr., Juneau, AK 99801; telephone (907)586-3740; (907)586-9097

Juneau Online

Alaska Communications Systems. Available www.acsalaska.com

Alaska Department of Labor & Workforce Development, Research & Analysis Section. Available almis.labor.state.ak.us

Alaska State Library. Available www.library.state.ak.us

Alaska State Museum. Available www.museums.state.ak.us/asmhome.html

City of Juneau Home Page. Available www.juneau.org

Juneau Borough Schools. Available www.jsd.k12.ak.us

Juneau Chamber of Commerce. Available www.juneauchamber.com

Juneau Convention and Visitors Bureau. Available www.traveljuneau.comwww.juneau.com

Juneau Economic Development Council. Available www.jedc.org

Juneau Empire. Available www.juneauempire.com

Juneau Public Library. Available www.juneau.org/library/index.php

State of Alaska. Available www.state.ak.us

BIBLIOGRAPHY

Raban, Jonathan, *Passage to Juneau: A Sea and Its Meanings*(New York: Pantheon Books, 1999)

Arizona

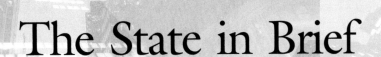

The State in Brief

Nickname: Grand Canyon State

Motto: Ditat Deus (God enriches)

Flower: Blossom of the saguaro cactus

Bird: Cactus wren

Area: 113,635 square miles (2000; U.S. rank 6th)

Elevation: Ranges from 100 feet to 12,670 feet above sea level

Climate: Dry and sunny, but heavy snows in the high central area

Admitted to Union: February 14, 1912

Capital: Phoenix

Head Official: Governor Janet Napolitano (D) (until 2010)

Population

1980: 2,718,000
1990: 3,750,000
2000: 5,130,632
2006 estimate: 6,166,318
Percent change, 1990–2000: 40.0%
U.S. rank in 2006: 16th
Percent of residents born in state: 35.68% (2006)
Density: 52.3 people per square mile (2006)
2006 FBI Crime Index Total: 316,286

Racial and Ethnic Characteristics (2006)

White: 4,741,310
Black or African American: 207,837
American Indian and Alaska Native: 277,732
Asian: 144,858
Native Hawaiian and Pacific Islander: 10,960
Hispanic or Latino (may be of any race): 1,803,377
Other: 633,350

Age Characteristics (2006)

Population under 5 years old: 479,145
Population 5 to 19 years old: 1,313,680
Percent of population 65 years and over: 12.8%
Median age: 34.6

Vital Statistics

Total number of births (2006): 97,176
Total number of deaths (2006): 44,272
AIDS cases reported through 2005: 9,952

Economy

Major industries: Services, trade, manufacturing, agriculture
Unemployment rate (2006): 4.9%
Per capita income (2006): $24,110
Median household income (2006): $47,265
Percentage of persons below poverty level (2006): 14.2%
Income tax rate: 2.59% to 4.57%
Sales tax rate: 5.6%

Flagstaff

■ The City in Brief

Founded: 1881

Head Official: Mayor Joseph Donaldson (R) (since 2000)

City Population
- 1980: 34,743
- 1990: 45,857
- 2000: 52,894
- 2006 estimate: 58,213
- Percent change, 1990–2000: 13.3
- U.S. rank in 1980: 676th
- U.S. rank in 1990: 543rd (State rank: 10th)
- U.S. rank in 2000: 673rd (State rank: 13th)

Metropolitan Area Population
- 1980: Not available
- 1990: 101,760
- 2000: 122,366
- 2006 estimate: 124,953
- Percent change, 1990–2000: 20.2%
- U.S. rank in 1980: Not reported
- U.S. rank in 1990: Not reported
- U.S. rank in 2000: 237th

Area: 63.58 square miles (2000)

Elevation: 6,899 feet above sea level

Average Annual Temperature: 45.8° F

Average Annual Precipitation: 21.3 inches of rain

Major Economic Sectors: services, wholesale and retail trade, government

Unemployment Rate: 3.6% (June 2007)

Per Capita Income: $18,637 (1999)

2005 FBI Crime Index Property: 4,277

2005 FBI Crime Index Violent: 529

Major Colleges and Universities: Northern Arizona University, Coconino County Community College

Daily Newspaper: *Arizona Daily Sun*

■ Introduction

Located along the fabled American highway, Route 66, Flagstaff is the largest city and regional center in northern Arizona. Known as "the Gateway to the Grand Canyon," it is the county seat for Coconino County, the second largest in the nation, with 18,608 square miles. At nearly 7,000 feet, Flagstaff is one of the highest cities in the United States. This attractive community sits at the base of the San Francisco Peaks, Arizona's highest point at 12,633 feet. There are many tales surrounding how the city got its name. A popular one holds that a group from Boston stripped a pine tree on the Fourth of July and placed a flag atop it. Flagstaff boasts a refurbished downtown and a top-rate museum, and its colony of college students make for a lively atmosphere.

■ Geography and Climate

Flagstaff is located 145 miles due north of Phoenix, 323 miles west of Albuquerque, and 467 miles east of Los Angeles.

Flagstaff enjoys a four-season climate. Because of its high elevation, the city has cool summers in which air conditioners are mostly unnecessary, not the desert conditions one might expect. The altitude and low humidity result in clean air and relatively mild weather year round. Occasional late-afternoon thundershowers are common from July through September, and snow usually occurs first in mid-October, and is heaviest December through March. The snow, which averages just under 100 inches per year, generally melts off rather quickly. The city experiences about 300 days of sunshine annually.

Area: 63.58 square miles (2000)

Elevation: 6,899 feet above sea level

Average Temperature: 45.8° F

Average Annual Precipitation: 21.3 inches of rain

■ History

Local Springs and Railroad Draw Settlers

It is said that it is the springs that first drew people to the Flagstaff area of otherwise dry northern Arizona. The Sinagua, Anasazi, and Cohonino tribes were the first to settle there. Ruins of the pueblos and cliff dwellings belonging to the Navaho nation and Hopi tribes can still be found in the forests and lands surrounding present-day Flagstaff. A mountain man named Antoine Leroux knew the location of a source of water at the base of the San Francisco Peaks, and in 1876 a group of New Englanders left from Boston in search of the excellent farm land that they had heard about in highly exaggerated stories. They started a settlement in present-day Leroux Springs later in the year. According to legend, it was this group who placed a flag on top of a denuded pine tree, celebrating the Centennial of the Declaration of Independence, and thus gave the city the name by which it has been known ever since.

In 1882, the arrival in Flagstaff of the Atlantic and Pacific Railroad started a building boom. The site of what is today downtown Flagstaff was selected because the railroad wanted to build its new depot on flat land. Shortly after the arrival of the railroad, a sawmill began operations to accommodate the railroad's need for wooden ties. The new sawmill provided jobs for more than 250 people. Wood was easily attainable, as the city is near the world's largest forest of ponderosa pines.

For more than half a century, beginning in the 1880s, miles of spur rail line extended in all directions from the city. The men who engaged in the sawmill industry developed their own culture. Author Rose Houk describes "logger lingo" in which "coffee was referred to by its brand name, Arbuckle; pancakes were 'blankets;' [and] biscuits were 'doorknobs.'"

Sheep ranching got started in the mid-1880s and became big business in Flagstaff. Many of the sheep ranchers were of Basque or Spanish heritage. At the same time, cattle raising was begun by a group of Mormons at Leroux Spring.

City Becomes Observatory Site

In 1894, Andrew E. Douglass of Boston chose Flagstaff as the site for an astronomical observatory. Douglass placed the Lowell Observatory there in part because of the clear skies that good telescope viewing requires. During that same year a reform school was built, which was later to serve as the first building of what is now Northern Arizona University. In 1930 astronomer V.M. Slipher discovered the planet Pluto at the observatory. Lowell Observatory has stayed in the forefront of science, notably with its research in the area of bodies within the solar system, such as satellites (moons), near-Earth asteroids, and comets.

Wildland-Urban Interface

In June and July 2002 the catastrophic Rodeo-Chediski fire grabbed national attention as the worst fire in Arizona history. Affecting Coconino County and its contiguous neighbors Navajo, Apache, and Gila counties, the fire burned approximately 468,000 acres, the bulk of which was Ft. Apache Indian Reservation and national forest land; destroyed almost 500 homes; and cost $43 million to quell. More than $34 million in federal disaster aid was directed to the area. Flagstaff itself was not directly affected because of city leaders' and civic groups' proactive work in land use planning and response training.

In the past decade, some of Flagstaff's citizens became concerned about increasing development, mostly due to tourism, and preserving the very environment that makes the area special. Plans were developed to ensure a balance between economic opportunity and growth limits. Today, the city seems to have met and exceeded this goal. Mayor Joe Donaldson sums it up: "Flagstaff is a community raved about in many magazines as the place to invest, develop, vacation and just plain enjoy. Flagstaff prides itself in the miles of internal majestic scenic trails, multi modal transportation opportunities...The community boasts of its efforts in achieving sustainable economic strength while preserving its pristine environment through community activism, emulated quality of life ordinances and resolutions driven through extensive community driven processes. Flagstaff is not just a place. It is a way of life where people become one with their environment."

Historical Information: The Historical Society, Northern Arizona University, Cline Library, PO Box 6022, Flagstaff, AZ 86011-6022; telephone (928) 523-5551

■ Population Profile

Metropolitan Area Residents
    1980: Not available
    1990: 101,760

2000: 122,366
2006 estimate: 124,953
Percent change, 1990–2000: 20.2%
U.S. rank in 1980: Not reported
U.S. rank in 1990: Not reported
U.S. rank in 2000: 237th

City Residents

1980: 34,743
1990: 45,857
2000: 52,894
2006 estimate: 58,213
Percent change, 1990–2000: 13.3
U.S. rank in 1980: 676th
U.S. rank in 1990: 543rd (State rank: 10th)
U.S. rank in 2000: 673rd (State rank: 13th)

Density: 831.9 people per square mile (2000)

Racial and ethnic characteristics (2000)

White: 41,214
Black: 927
American Indian and Alaska Native: 4,210
Asian: 660
Native Hawaiian and Pacific Islander: 65
Hispanic or Latino (may be of any race): 8,500
Other: 3,201

Percent of residents born in state: 41.6% (2000)

Age characteristics (2000)

Population under 5 years old: 3,546
Population 5 to 9 years old: 3,410
Population 10 to 14 years old: 3,599
Population 15 to 19 years old: 4,762
Population 20 to 24 years old: 9,004
Population 25 to 34 years old: 8,654
Population 35 to 44 years old: 7,457
Population 45 to 54 years old: 6,433
Population 55 to 59 years old: 1,876
Population 60 to 64 years old: 1,327
Population 65 to 74 years old: 1,658
Population 75 to 84 years old: 909
Population 85 years and older: 259
Median age: 26.8 years

Births (2006, MSA)

Total number: 2,110

Deaths (2006, MSA)

Total number: 619

Money income (1999)

Per capita income: $18,637
Median household income: $37,146
Total households: 19,355

Number of households with income of . . .

less than $10,000: 2,035
$10,000 to $14,999: 1,335
$15,000 to $24,999: 2,866
$25,000 to $34,999: 2,789
$35,000 to $49,999: 3,258
$50,000 to $74,999: 3,360
$75,000 to $99,999: 1,793
$100,000 to $149,999: 1,279
$150,000 to $199,999: 343
$200,000 or more: 297

Percent of families below poverty level: 17.9% (1999)

2005 FBI Crime Index Property: 4,277

2005 FBI Crime Index Violent: 529

■ Municipal Government

Flagstaff has a council/manager form of government with a mayor and six council members elected at large. Mayoral elections are held every two years; council members serve four years, and elections are staggered every two years.

Head Official: Mayor Joseph Donaldson (R) (since 2000; current term expires 2008)

Total Number of City Employees: 689 permanent, 169 temporary or seasonal (2006)

City Information: City of Flagstaff, 211 W. Aspen, Flagstaff, AZ 86001; telephone (928) 774-5281

■ Economy

Major Industries and Commercial Activity

New scientific and high-tech research and development industries have located to Flagstaff, broadening the economic base of tourism, government, education, and transportation, which replaced the lumber, railroad, and ranching eras.

Research activities are important to the city's economy. The most well-known facility, Lowell Observatory, was responsible for the discovery of Pluto and has done pioneering work in observations of near-Earth phenomena such as asteroids, comets, and belt systems; and in the field of interferometric studies, in which a distributed network of small telescopes together create images of celestial bodies with much higher resolutions than any other single telescope can produce.

Airphoto - Jim Wark

Items and goods produced: dog and cat food; surgical/medical instruments and apparatus; wind generators; circuit boards; packaging products; recycled paper products for commercial use

Incentive Programs—New and Existing Companies

Most programs in Arizona are offered at the state level. The Greater Flagstaff Economic Council is a public/private agency that serves the city, county, Chamber of Commerce, and local businesses.

Local programs: The city offers an Infrastructure Assistance Fund with up to $100,000 available per economic development project.

State programs: Flagstaff businesses in Enterprise Zone areas may receive direct state income tax credits based on the number of net new employees hired. Any qualified position is eligible if the position is a full-time permanent job, if the employer pays an hourly wage above the "wage offer by county" (between $7.14 and $13.41 an hour, depending on location), and if the employer provides health insurance and pays at least 50 percent of the insurance cost. If at least 35 percent of new employees live in any Enterprise Zone areas, then all new net employees qualify for eligibility. Any unused state

income tax credits may be carried forward for up to five taxable years, providing the business remains in the Enterprise Zone. Other Enterprise Zone incentives include tax breaks for women-owned, minority-owned, or small businesses, and for businesses that make investments in fixed assets in the zone in the amount of $1 million. Other programs give tax credits on the cost of installing recycling equipment; exemptions for contractors and vendors of solar energy devices, for pollution control, and for the purchase of construction materials; and research and development investment. State lottery proceeds provide fixed-asset loans to companies for expansion, relocation, and consolidation.

Job training programs: The Flagstaff Job Service Center gives aid to employers in advertising openings, evaluating applicants, and immigration certification. The state of Arizona offers matching funds of up to 75 percent to businesses for the training of workers for new jobs in the state. Through the federal Workforce Investment Act (WIA), formerly the Job Training Partnership Act, employers may receive up to 50 percent of their wages back during initial training periods. Customized training programs are also available.

The Small Business Development Center is jointly funded by the U.S. Small Business Administration and Coconino County Community College. This one-stop center offers free one-on-one counseling, training, and technical assistance in all aspects of small business management.

Development Projects

Downtown Flagstaff completed a major $7 million project upgrading its commercial area surrounding the Visitors Center in the 1990s. Flagstaff 2020 Vision Project also began then, when some citizens questioned whether increasing development was compatible with preservation of what made the area special. The plan laid out a five year plan to balance economic opportunity with growth limits, and was replaced in 2002 with the Regional Growth and Transportation Plan, which governs land use, transportation, open space, and trail systems. Heritage Square—at one time a vacant plot of land due to become a parking lot—became a vibrant area in the heart of downtown with shops, galleries, and restaurants. Another development project was the runway expansion at Flagstaff Pulliam Airport. Extension of the airport runway, which will allow jumbo jet travel to the city, had an expected December 2007 completion.

Flagstaff also has planned the development of a non-motorized urban trail network (FUTS), which will interconnect virtually all areas of the city when completed and promises to be important for both transportation and recreation. Flagstaff had completed approximately 32.8 miles of FUTS as of early 2007.

In 2003, the Lowell Observatory and Discovery Communications announced a cooperative effort on a $30 million telescope that will bring unprecedented wide range views and deep imaging surveys of the night skies. The Discovery Channel telescope's unique design will allow it to switch from extremely wide-field focus to much more detailed spectroscopy, infrared imaging and other applications. In addition to significantly advancing capacity for research, the telescope will also be used for real-time worldwide broadcasting and for science education programs for the public. The expected completion date for the telescope is 2009.

Flagstaff is investing in bioscience. The city is constructing a technology incubator that could provide space for up to two dozen companies and many researchers. Construction of the incubator, funded by a $2.5 million federal economic development grant and $1 million from Flagstaff, began in fall 2007. The construction of the technology incubator will be followed by the construction of a 200,000 square foot Science and Technology Park.

Commercial Shipping

Air cargo carriers flying direct from Flagstaff Pulliam Airport are Federal Express and United Parcel Service. The city has a number of motor freight carriers. The one-day truck radius extends to Salt Lake City, San Francisco, Albuquerque, El Paso, Los Angeles, and parts of Mexico.

Flagstaff is served by Burlington Northern Santa Fe Railway.

Labor Force and Employment Outlook

Northern Arizona, which includes Flagstaff, Sedona, and Payson, has experienced a massive influx of tourists and retirees in recent years. After concerns were voiced by residents about the continued development and its impact on the environment, developers and environmentalists started working together to achieve a balance between economy and landscape preservation. Government is one of the largest employment sectors in Flagstaff. Tourism, and the service and construction industries in concert, create employment opportunities as well.

The following is a summary of data regarding the Flagstaff metropolitan area labor force, 2006 annual averages.

Size of nonagricultural labor force: 64,300

Number of workers employed in . . .

construction and mining: 3,600
manufacturing: 3,600
trade, transportation and utilities: 9,800
information: 500
financial activities: 1,800
professional and business services: 3,400
educational and health services: 7,200
leisure and hospitality: 13,000
other services: 1,900
government: 19,600

Average hourly earnings of production workers employed in manufacturing: Not available

Unemployment rate: 3.6% (June 2007)

Largest employers	*Number of employees*
Northern Arizona University	3,393
Flagstaff Medical Center	1,999
Flagstaff Unified School District	1,700
W.L. Gore & Associates	1,300
Coconino County	1,075
City of Flagstaff	948
Grand Canyon Railway	400
Walgreens Distribution Center	400
Coconino Community College	400
SCA Tissue	279
Pepsi Cola Bottling Plant	250

Cost of Living

Housing costs in Flagstaff run somewhat higher than the national average. Food and health care also run a bit higher than the nation as a whole.

The following is a summary of data regarding several key cost of living factors in the Flagstaff area.

2007 (1st quarter) ACCRA Average House Price: $490,350

2007 (1st quarter) ACCRA Cost of Living Index: 115.6

State income tax rate: 2.87% to 5.04%

State sales tax rate: 5.6%

Local income tax rate: None

Local sales tax rate: 1.51% city; .80% county

Property tax rate: $9.89 per $100 of assessed value (2003)

Economic Information: Flagstaff Chamber of Commerce, 101 W. Route 66, Flagstaff, AZ 86001-5598; telephone (520)774-4505; fax (928) 779-1209. Greater Flagstaff Economic Council, 1300 S. Milton Road, Flagstaff, AZ 86001; telephone (928) 779-7658; toll-free (800) 595-7658; fax (928) 556-0940

■ Education and Research

Elementary and Secondary Schools

The Flagstaff Unified School District is widely recognized as one of the finest in the Southwest. It offers a wide range of programs to meet the needs of students with diverse backgrounds, interests, and abilities. Through use of non-traditional approaches, Project New Start helps students on the verge of dropping out, and the Teenage Parent Program assists young mothers in continuing their education while pregnant and during the months following childbirth. Flagstaff was the first school system in the United States to implement drug-and-alcohol prevention programs in both its elementary and secondary schools. Other programs include artists-in-residence, after-school classes for high school credit, the Suzuki violin program, parenting programs, bilingual education, and magnet and alternative programs, among others.

The following is a summary of data regarding the Flagstaff Unified School District as of the 2005–2006 school year.

Total enrollment: 11,500

Number of facilities

elementary schools: 12

junior high/middle schools: 4

senior high schools: 3

other: 1

Student/teacher ratio: 22.8:1

Teacher salaries (2005–06)

elementary median: $35,930

junior high/middle median: $35,260

secondary median: $36,100

Funding per pupil: $6,193

Colleges and Universities

Northern Arizona University (NAU) has more than 14,500 undergraduate and almost 6,000 graduate students. It offers small classes, respected and accessible faculty and advisers, comprehensive libraries, computer labs, research opportunities, career placement, cultural programs and events, recreational facilities, and intramural and NCAA athletics. NAU students can choose from 91 baccalaureate degrees and 55 graduate studies programs, including 47 master's degree programs and eight doctoral programs. Unique programs range from Colorado Plateau-based forestry to global-ranging bioterrorism. Fields such as physical therapy and hotel/restaurant management are also available. The university's Center for Excellence in Education promotes a competency-based approach to teacher education.

Coconino County Community College, a two-year college educating approximately 5,000 students, offers programs for students to continue their higher education or to enter the business world.

Libraries and Research Centers

The Flagstaff City-Coconino County Public Library consists of a main library, the East Flagstaff Community Library, a bookmobile, and nine county affiliate libraries. The main library, built in an attractive ski-lodge style, features four fireplaces and local Native American art. The library contains more than 170,000 volumes and an extensive collection of Arizona and Southwest publications. Other special collections include a U.S. genealogy collection, the Economic Development Information Center, a large print collection, and the City of Flagstaff Archives.

Considering its small population, the city is home to a large number of research collections and special libraries, including Lowell Observatory, the Museum of Northern Arizona, the U.S. Geological Survey, the Arboretum (Transition Zone Horticultural Institute), the Cross Cultural Dance Resources Institution, and Northern Arizona University's Cline Library Special Collections and Archives Division.

The many research centers and institutes at Northern Arizona University include the Colorado Plateau Research Station, the Quaternary Sciences Program, and the

Institute for Native Americans. The university's Distance Learning Network provides a number of classes per day to off-campus students across the state and is used by many private corporations for special research needs. The U.S. Geological Survey Flagstaff Field Center supports such research as space mission support, water locating, earth geology, and image processing.

Public Library Information: Flagstaff City/Coconino County Public Library, 300 West Aspen Avenue, Flagstaff, AZ 86001; telephone (928) 779-7670

■ Health Care

Flagstaff Medical Center (FMC) is Northern Arizona's regional referral medical facility and has the only Level II trauma center in the area. Prominent departments of Flagstaff Medical Center are The Heart Center, The Cancer Center, Imaging/Radiology, Joint Surgery Center, Women and Infants Center, and a Bariatric Surgery Center. FMC has more than 270 inpatient beds and 190 physicians active on staff. The center's parent corporation, Northern Arizona Healthcare, also has facilities in nearby Sedona and Verde Valley.

■ Recreation

Sightseeing

Flagstaff, originally a railroad town, now houses its visitors center in the Tudor revival-style Santa Fe Station, where one can pick up maps for walking tours of the city. The Lowell Observatory, possibly the city's most famous structure, presents visitors with hands-on exhibits, historic displays, and a scenic campus located near downtown. Tours, sky shows, demonstrations, and lectures are offered throughout the year. The observatory's oldest telescope is housed in an historic wooden dome, and night sky viewing is offered in evening hours during most of the year.

The Arboretum at Flagstaff, with the highest elevation of a botanical research garden in the nation, displays a fascinating variety of plant life native to the region, and features a Threatened and Endangered Plant Conservation Program. The Arboretum is home to 2,500 species of plants. Its gardens include an herb garden of 250 specimens, a constructed wetland wherein native plants purify water, a butterfly garden, organic vegetable garden, and other gardens spread over 200 acres with scenic trails. Visitors to Coconino National Forest may spot American bald eagles and black bear in the world's largest ponderosa pine forest, which ranges in elevation from 2,600 to 12,633 feet. The Eldon Pueblo Archaeological Project at the National Forest informs visitors about archaeological concepts, values, laws, and practices through

personal experience. Programs for children are also available.

Guides escort tourists through the Riordan Mansion State Historic Park, a mansion with forty rooms and more than 13,000 square feet of living area. This 1904 duplex contains original artifacts, handcrafted furniture, and personal mementos of the Riordan family, who lived there early in the twentieth century. The park also offers a visitor center, a self-guided tour of the grounds, and picnic tables. Reservations are recommended for tours.

Three national monuments in the area draw visitors for their history and breathtaking beauty. The pristine, stream-cut gorge at Walnut Canyon National Monument offers walking trails that reveal the ancient cliff dwellings built into the steep canyon walls where the Sinagua people lived nearly a thousand years ago. The on-site museum displays artifacts that paint a picture of what life was like for these early inhabitants of the area. Located in the shadow of the San Francisco peaks, the Wupatki National Monument was once home to the farmers and traders of the Anasazi and Sinagua tribes. Four pueblos offering a glimpse into the past can be seen at this monument. (Wupatki is Hopi for "big house.")

Fifty thousand years ago an enormous iron-nickel meteorite, falling through space at about 30,000 to 40,000 miles per hour, struck a rocky plain of northern Arizona with an explosive force greater than 20 million tons of TNT. It left behind a crater, called the Meteor Crater, which today is 550 feet deep and 2.4 miles in circumference. The adjacent Museum of Astrogeology offers exhibits, movies and lectures that vividly describe the impact and the awesome results.

The Grand Canyon is about 80 miles northwest of Flagstaff. There one can view one of the most spectacular examples of arid land erosion in the world. The park covers 1,904 square miles, including 277 miles of the Colorado River. South Rim facilities are open year-round, and North Rim facilities are open mid-May through mid-October. The Grand Canyon Railway lets one travel in grand style on a vintage train from Williams, Arizona to the South Rim, across 65 miles of beautiful Arizona countryside.

Arts and Culture

The Coconino Center for the Arts, a modern glass-front building, is the site of many cultural activities in Flagstaff, including symphonic, orchestral, and choral performances. It is also home to the 10-day Festival of Native American Arts in August. Visual arts and literary and educational programs edify both locals and visitors. The center's 4,000-square-foot gallery presents the work of a variety of artists throughout the year. Annual exhibits of note held at the center include the Youth Art Exhibit held in March or April, which features the works of students throughout Coconino County; and the

Trappings of the American West exhibit in May and June, which highlights contemporary cowboy arts and crafts by artists throughout the Southwest and Canada and also offers cowboy poetry readings and musical performances.

The Flagstaff Symphony Orchestra (FSO) has been bringing enjoyment to local audiences since its founding in 1950. The FSO performs in the 1,500-seat Ardery Auditorium, giving seven concerts during its September through April season, as well as youth concerts, a Lollipop concert in December for very young children, and pops series in nearby ShowLow and Sedona. The Museum of Northern Arizona also plays host to many entertainment events throughout the year. Theatrikos, a popular local theatre group, performs five mainstage productions per year; is involved in project P.E.A.C.E (Prevention, Education, and Creative Expression), which helps to prevent teen violence through theatre and peer interaction; and offers classes on acting, scene building, lighting design, voice, and the like. Theatrikos's home, the Flagstaff Playhouse, was renamed the Doris Harper-White Community Playhouse after one of its founders. It is an intimate black box theatre with 99 seats.

Flagstaff's premier museum is the Museum of Northern Arizona, which introduces museum-goers to the native peoples and natural sciences of the Colorado Plateau region. Permanent galleries and changing exhibits explore anthropology, biology, geology, and fine art. Native American art is for sale at the museum shop and there is a nature trail on the grounds.

The history of Flagstaff from the time of cowboys and lumberjacks to the railroaders and astronomers is presented at the Arizona Historical Society Pioneer Museum. Exhibits include early medical equipment, saddles, household and livestock items, and a 1929 Baldwin locomotive.

Festivals and Holidays

Summer events in Flagstaff center around the rodeo and ethnic cuisine. Fans of the rodeo enjoy the Arizona High School Rodeo finals, which take place the first weekend of every June at the Coconino County Fairgrounds. High school students compete in such events as barrel racing, bareback riding, saddle bronco riding, bull riding, team roping, calf roping, and goat tying. The annual Chili Cook-off held during that same weekend features live music and contests for both adults and children. On the second Saturday in June, the Great Fiesta Del Barrio & Fajita Cook-off celebrates the customs and culture of the local Hispanic community. The third weekend in June brings the Pine Country Pro Rodeo, which draws contenders to the Coconino County Fairgrounds. The Arizona Highland Celtic Festival offers music, Irish dancing, and whiskey tastings. The Festival of Native American Arts, held during July and August, includes an exhibit,

outdoor market, dances, workshops and demonstrations celebrating the arts, crafts, culture, and traditions of Native Americans throughout the Southwest. August's Flagstaff Summerfest Festival in the Pines tops off the summer season with the finest in arts and crafts, food, and entertainment.

Every Labor Day Weekend the Coconino County Fair takes place at the fairgrounds in Fort Tuthill Park. Highlights of the fair include exhibits, livestock, entertainment, a demolition derby, and a carnival. The Flagstaff Festival of Science, a 10-day event held annually at the end of September, promotes science awareness through hands-on exhibits, interactive displays, field trips, and world-class scientist participants.

Flagstaff kicks off the winter season as children young and old delight in the Playthings of the Past exhibit, which runs from November through January and features dolls, trains, cars, and castles from the 1880s through the 1960s. During December, Riordan Mansion offers holiday tours of its festively decorated turn-of-the-century rooms. February's Flagstaff Winterfest features nearly 100 events: sled dog races, skiing competitions, and other snow events; llama play days; sleigh rides; concerts; cultural events; and historic walking tours are all on schedule. The Arizona Special Olympics is a competition for mentally and physically challenged athletes that is held during the last weekend in February.

Sports for the Spectator

The Arizona Cardinals of the National Football League and the Phoenix Suns, affiliates of the National Basketball Association, hold preseason training camps in Flagstaff. A variety of NCAA-sanctioned sports are hosted at Northern Arizona University, including football, men's and women's basketball, volleyball, track and swimming. NAU's Skydome, where many athletic events are held, is one of the largest wood-domed structures in the world; the university's Wall Aquatic Center is a high-altitude training site for U.S. and international Olympic swimmers and divers.

The Coconino County Horse Races—a tradition for more than 50 years—features thoroughbreds and quarter horses and is held annually over the Fourth of July weekend at Fort Tuthill Downs.

Sports for the Participant

Flagstaff has 31 parks with 2 swimming pools, 1 public 18-hole golf course and 4 private ones, an ice-skating rink, 17 tennis courts, 1 bowling alley, a skeet-and-trap facility, and a ski resort. FUTS, the Flagstaff Urban Trails System, runs through the city and provides several multi-use trails varying in length from one to five miles. Northern Arizona University's Wall Aquatic Center has an Olympic size pool that is open to the public. The city's transportation network of interstate highways makes it easy to explore the national forests surrounding the city. Popular forest-based activities include hiking, mountain biking, and horseback riding. Coconino National Forest offers more than 320 miles of hiking trails. In town, trailheads access Mount Elden from the east and west. The Arizona Snowbowl atop the San Francisco Peaks, with a base elevation of 9,000 feet, is higher in elevation than most resorts in Utah, Colorado, and California. It offers skiers a vertical drop of 2,300 feet, 4 chairlifts and more than 30 slopes, the longest of which stretches more than a mile. Its chairlift becomes a 6,450-foot-long "Scenic Skyride" during the summer. Flagstaff Nordic Center, 16 miles north of the city, offers 25 miles of groomed trails for every level of skier.

Shopping and Dining

Flagstaff is the primary commercial center in northern Arizona. The city boasts many fine art galleries, antique shops and specialty shops, as well as a number of major shopping centers. Flagstaff's proximity to a number of Indian reservations provides shoppers with a variety of Native American arts and crafts. The historic downtown shopping area has some 200 gift shops, boutiques, and clothing stores. Import stores downtown specialize in South American and Mexican goods. The Flagstaff Mall is an enclosed shopping center with more than 70 stores. The Gallery Shop at Coconino Center for the Arts specializes in hand-made arts and crafts by area artists.

Flagstaff's more than 200 restaurants range from casual southwestern to European-style, with food served in the historic atmosphere of turn-of-the-century buildings. Ethnic cuisine ranges from Italian, Mexican, and Asian to Middle Eastern and Bohemian. Music fans enjoy visiting the Museum Club, a Depression-era Route 66 road house and the Southwest's largest log cabin, which continues to present popular country musicians.

Visitor Information: The Flagstaff Visitor Center, (928) 774-9541

■ Convention Facilities

Flagstaff's largest conference hotel, with 247 guest rooms, is the Little America hotel. With 10,000 square feet of conference space, the facility can accommodate 360 people classroom-style, 675 people theater-style, and 460 people for banquets. The Radisson Woodlands Hotel, with more than 180 guest rooms, has 6,400 square feet of conference space and can accommodate 168 classroom-style, 375 theater-style, and can handle banquets for up to 350 people. Nearly 70 area hotels offer more than 4,900 rooms.

■ Transportation

Approaching the City

I-40, providing east-west coast access, runs through the center of Flagstaff. Access to the south is via I-17. U.S. routes 89 and 180 run between Flagstaff and the Grand Canyon. At Pulliam Airport, located just four miles south of downtown Flagstaff, America West Express provides hourly flights to Phoenix, where national and international connections can be made. Amtrak offers two daily trains from Flagstaff that connect with trains to Chicago and Los Angeles, and Greyhound-Trailways has interstate and intrastate bus service.

Traveling in the City

Flagstaff has developed many of the traffic congestion problems that come with rapid growth. Some estimates say that traffic has more than tripled since 1974. Two major traffic improvements are underway—one on I-40 and the other a new bridge over the railway at 4th Street and at Route 66. Shuttle and tour bus service is provided by Grayline/Nava-Hopi Tours and Mountain Line.

■ Communications

Newspapers and Magazines

The city's daily newspaper, the *Arizona Daily Sun*, is published weekdays in the evenings and on Saturday and Sunday mornings. The *Canyon Shopper* is published weekly, and the *Navajo-Hopi Observer* serves the Native American peoples of northern Arizona. The monthly *Mountain Living Magazine* features topics of community interest, and the *Arizona Guide* describes things to do and see in the area.

Television and Radio

Flagstaff has three television stations, and cable is available throughout most of the city. Thirteen AM and FM radio stations broadcast out of the city, offering a wide range of formats.
Media Information: The *Arizona Daily Sun*, 1751 S Thompson St., Flagstaff, AZ 86001; telephone (928) 774-4545

Flagstaff Online

Arizona Daily Sun Available www.azdailysun.com
Arizona School Report Cards. Available www.ade
   .state.az.us/srcs/main.asp
City of Flagstaff home page. Available www.flagstaff
   .az.gov
Flagstaff Chamber of Commerce. Available www
   .flagstaffchamber.com
Flagstaff Online. Available www.flagstaff.az.us

Flagstaff Unified School District. Available www
.flagstaff.k12.az.us

BIBLIOGRAPHY

Aitchison, Stewart, *Red Rocks, Sacred Mountains: The Canyons and Peaks from Sedona to Flagstaff* (Stillwater, MN: Voyager Press, 1992)

Ashworth, Donna, *Against This Ground: Biography of a Small Mountain* (Flagstaff, AZ: Small Mountain Books, 1994)

Cline, Platt, *Mountain Town: Flagstaff's First Century* (Flagstaff, AZ: Northland Press, 1994)

Houk, Rose, *The Peaks* (Phoenix, AZ: Arizona Highways, 1994)

Kupel, Douglas E., *Fuel for Growth: Water and Arizona's Urban Environment* (Tucson, AZ: University of Arizona Press, 2003)

Mangum, Richard K., *Flagstaff: Past and Present* (Flagstaff, AZ: Northland Pub., 2003)

Mesa

■ The City in Brief

Founded: 1878 (incorporated 1883)

Head Official: Mayor Keno Hawker (since 2000)

City Population

    1980: 152,404
    1990: 288,091
    2000: 396,375
    2006 estimate: 447,541
    Percent change, 1990–2000: 37.6%
    U.S. rank in 1980: Not available
    U.S. rank in 1990: 53rd (3rd in state)
    U.S. rank in 2000: 51st (3rd in state)

Metropolitan Area Population

    1980: 1,508,030
    1990: 2,122,101
    2000: 3,251,876
    2006 estimate: Not available
    Percent change, 1990–2000: 53.2%
    U.S. rank in 1980: Not available
    U.S. rank in 1990: Not available
    U.S. rank in 2000: 14th

Area: 125.18 square miles (2000)

Elevation: 1,241 feet above sea level

Average Annual Temperature: 84.5° F

Average Annual Precipitation: 8.5 inches

Major Economic Sectors: services, wholesale and retail trade, government

Unemployment Rate: 3.0% (June 2007)

Per Capita Income: $22,325 (2005)

2005 FBI Crime Index Property: 24,071

2005 FBI Crime Index Violent: 2,280

Major Colleges and Universities: Arizona State University East, Mesa Community College, East Valley Institute of Technology

Daily Newspaper: *The East Valley Tribune*

■ Introduction

Founded by Mormon agricultural pioneers, Mesa today is growing like a weed. Far enough from Phoenix to retain its small town feel yet near enough to the big city to encourage the growth of technological and manufacturing industries, Mesa has become more than a retirement community and has evolved into a tourist mecca in its own right. Layers of native, frontier, and Mexican history have combined to form a city of eclectic tastes and offerings, from the prehistoric farming canals deep in the ground to the aviation businesses that take to the skies.

■ Geography and Climate

Desert, mountains, water—somehow Mesa got it all. Located along a spit of the Sonoran Desert, Mesa is warm and arid every month of the year and enjoys the flora and fauna of the desert clime. Saguaro and prickly pear cacti are abundant, along with varieties of cholla, and the dry soil outside the city is wandered by rattlesnakes, jack rabbits, bobcats, hawks, and owls. While Mesa gets 320 days of sunshine annually and temperatures in the 100s during the summer, the city also has easy access to six local lakes and two nearby rivers. The Superstition Mountain range just to the east of the city provides some altitude to the mesas and valleys of the area.

Area: 125.18 square miles (2000)

Elevation: 1,241 feet above sea level

Average Temperature: 84.5° F

Average Annual Precipitation: 8.5 inches

■ History

The First Farmers

More than 2,000 years ago, Mesa's agricultural destiny was carved out by the Hohokam Indians who settled the area. The Hohokam were peaceful farmers who developed a sophisticated and effective network of irrigation canals that turned the arid land around Mesa into arable soil. Eventually, the Hohokam people seemed to disappear from the area; it is theorized that the tribe may have morphed into the Tohono O'dham tribe or that the Hohokam were driven out of the future Mesa area by Apache Indians. Regardless, the tribe left an indelible mark on the desert that served farmers of all nationalities well for centuries.

Spanish explorers and conquistadores followed—both Francisco Vasquez de Coronado and Father Eusebio Kino passed near Mesa as they searched for treasure and sought to convert Native Americans. The Mesa-Phoenix area also lay along the route to the legendary seven cities of Cibola sought by Estevanico (or Esteban), a former Muslim slave who became an explorer after hurricanes and battles with Native Americans decimated his former crew in Florida. As quickly as the Spanish attempted to put down roots in southwestern Arizona, the Apache tribe drove them out again in a tradition that lasted through the 1700s.

The Mexican War and the U.S. Civil War largely occupied the time and resources of the United States military during the early and mid-1800s, and its forces were operating at less than full power when the government decided to intervene in the clashes between native peoples and European settlers in the Southwest after a portion of Arizona was ceded to the U.S. The Western Indian Wars in the later 1800s were spotted with massacres and relocations; in the Mesa area, the U.S. Army did battle with the Apaches until the tribe agreed to re-settlement. Unfortunately, several competing Apache tribes were co-located, resulting in a resumption of hostilities until the military was able to negotiate a surrender by Apache Chief Geronimo in 1886. It was in relative peace that a group of Mormon farmers, dealing with relocation and persecution themselves, established the settlement of Fort Utah in Lehi, just north of Mesa.

Mesa Takes Root

A decade before Chief Geronimo's surrender, the 85 intrepid members of the First Mesa Company left Utah and Idaho. The group was composed of Latter-Day Saints, some of whom practiced polygamy and who had been intrigued by the descriptions of Arizona brought back to church elders by the Mormon Battalion that fought during the Mexican War and traveled through Arizona on its way back to Utah. Stopping briefly in Lehi, the First Mesa Company moved on to the mesa, where they discovered and began clearing the irrigation canals left by the Hohokam people. The Second Mesa Company set out from Idaho about a year later; with the best land in Mesa already claimed, these pioneers established a nearby community called Stringtown, which was eventually absorbed into modern Mesa.

In the late 1800s, a flood in Lehi washed away Fort Utah; it had become evident over time that the lower desert lands were prone to sudden and unexpected flooding, allowing table-top Mesa to flourish. It began to look like a city, complete with an adobe pesthouse to control smallpox outbreaks, a city hall, saloons, and *The Mesa Free Press*, which has existed continuously under a variety of names since 1892 and is currently known as *The East Valley Tribune*.

Dr. A.J. Chandler played a significant role in the foundation of Mesa. Using heavy machinery, he enlarged the Hohokam canals and made them more effective in agricultural enterprises. Dr. Chandler was the force behind the construction of the first office complex in Mesa, and he started the first electric power plant. When the municipal government purchased the utility in 1917, it became one of a handful of Arizona cities to own such a service. Earnings from utilities solely funded capital expenditures until the 1960s and also provided the financial underpinning for Works Progress Administration (WPA) projects during the Great Depression. WPA projects included the first dedicated hospital facility, a new city hall and library, sidewalks, paved streets, parks, and a recreation department for the city.

Layers of Culture

By 1940, Mesa had achieved its standing as the third largest city in Arizona, boasting 7,000 inhabitants. Joining the Tohono O'dham Indians, the Hispanics, and the Mormons living in Mesa in the early 1900s were African American families (including a veterinarian) and families of Chinese and Japanese heritage who farmed and owned a variety of local businesses. This eclectic populace provided an interesting backdrop for events during the second World War, particularly considering the proximity of the internment camp at the Gila River Indian Reservation nearby.

World War II had another lasting cultural and industrial impact with the development of Falcon Field Airport and Williams Air Force Base as training sites for pilots. British pilots trained at Falcon Field, while U.S. pilots trained at Williams; many of those military families stayed in the Mesa area after the war ended. The aeronautical training and supply facilities at Falcon Field and Williams Air Force Base attracted aviation and aerospace companies to Mesa, propelling a switch from citrus and

Brian Stablyk/Stone/Getty Images

cotton farming to high-tech employment in the mid-1960s.

Twenty-First Century Mesa

Williams Air Force Base was closed in September of 1993 and was quickly reborn as Williams Gateway Airport. The aviation industry gives Mesa its wings today, with weather conditions that are near-perfect for training and testing every month of the year. Mesa accounts for close to 20 percent of aerospace related jobs within the Phoenix-Mesa metropolitan area. Both Williams Gateway and Falcon Field are home to national and international aeronautical companies that develop aircraft and aviation systems both for the commercial aviation industry as well as for the military. The climate and geography have also made Mesa a golf destination, to the extent that local universities have developed golf-related degree programs that have been accredited by the Professional Golf Association.

Mesa offers a low cost of doing business, reasonable tax structure, well-educated workforce, low crime rate, high performing schools, affordable housing, and a good regional transportation system. These benefits are some of the reasons why Mesa is one of the fastest-growing cities in the country.

Historical Information: Mesa Historical Museum, 2345 N. Horne Street, Mesa, AZ 85211; telephone (480)835-7358; email mesamuseum@netzero.net

■ Population Profile

Metropolitan Area Residents

> 1980: 1,508,030
> 1990: 2,122,101
> 2000: 3,251,876
> 2006 estimate: Not available
> Percent change, 1990–2000: 53.2%
> U.S. rank in 1980: Not available
> U.S. rank in 1990: Not available
> U.S. rank in 2000: 14th

City Residents

> 1980: 152,404

1990: 288,091
2000: 396,375
2006 estimate: 447,541
Percent change, 1990–2000: 37.6%
U.S. rank in 1980: Not available
U.S. rank in 1990: 53rd (3rd in state)
U.S. rank in 2000: 51st (3rd in state)

Density: 3,171.3 people per square mile (2000)

Racial and ethnic characteristics (2005)

White: 361,116
Black: 10,830
American Indian and Alaska Native: 9,817
Asian: 8,845
Native Hawaiian and Pacific Islander: 371
Hispanic or Latino (may be of any race): 106,325
Other: 41,250

Percent of residents born in state: 33% (2006)

Age characteristics (2005)

Population under 5 years old: 37,267
Population 5 to 9 years old: 31,509
Population 10 to 14 years old: 31,718
Population 15 to 19 years old: 31,425
Population 20 to 24 years old: 32,777
Population 25 to 34 years old: 63,547
Population 35 to 44 years old: 61,601
Population 45 to 54 years old: 51,092
Population 55 to 59 years old: 20,551
Population 60 to 64 years old: 17,748
Population 65 to 74 years old: 35,271
Population 75 to 84 years old: 22,346
Population 85 years and older: 5,593
Median age: 34.1 years

Births (2006, MSA)

Total number: 66,478

Deaths (2006, MSA)

Total number: 26,082

Money income (2005)

Per capita income: $22,325
Median household income: $44,861
Total households: 165,509

Number of households with income of . . .

less than $10,000: 10,016
$10,000 to $14,999: 9,748
$15,000 to $24,999: 21,930
$25,000 to $34,999: 21,145
$35,000 to $49,999: 28,995
$50,000 to $74,999: 31,339

$75,000 to $99,999: 21,751
$100,000 to $149,999: 14,638
$150,000 to $199,999: 3,261
$200,000 or more: 2,686

Percent of families below poverty level: 12.7% (2005)

2005 FBI Crime Index Property: 24,071

2005 FBI Crime Index Violent: 2,280

■ Municipal Government

The city of Mesa has established a charter under which it operates, with citizens of the municipality electing a mayor and six district council members. Council members serve four-year terms; every two years, there is an election for three seats on the council. The mayor serves a four-year term in office. A vice mayor, chosen by the council, assists the mayor and council in administration of the city government.

Head Official: Mayor Keno Hawker (since 2000; current term expires 2008)

Total Number of City Employees: approximately 4,000 (2007)

City Information: City of Mesa, PO Box 1466, Mesa, AZ 85211; telephone (480)644-2011

■ Economy

Major Industries and Commercial Activity

The arid, warm climate of Mesa has made it a top-flight locale for aeronautical industries that range from manufacturing to educational. Boeing maintains a facility at Falcon Field Airport where flight control panels are created, tested, and installed in freighters. The Mesa plant was the site of the development of the Apache Longbow helicopter during the 1990s and continues to research and develop military aeronautical equipment. Boeing Training Services and Systems not only equips pilots with the latest knowledge in flight but puts together training packages that can be administered to prospective pilots in other locations.

The local airports host a number of aviation training businesses, including Arizona Aviation, Learn to Fly Arizona, and SunCountry Flight Services. Airplane and helicopter medical transport, maintenance, and tour operations range from Air Evac Services to LifeNet.

TRW Vehicle Safety Systems, Inc., is the subsidiary of a *Fortune* 500 company and stands at the head of Mesa manufacturers. The plant produces vehicle restraint systems and other safety equipment, which are sold to automakers from around the world. TRW has been on the leading edge of safety system integration of restraint belts, air bags, crash sensors, and steering wheel technologies. Some of those restraint and safety systems might find their way into the heavy machinery and large vehicles produced by Empire Southwest Machinery in Mesa, where buses and caterpillars are researched and refined. The Empire Regional Training Center offers classes in machinery management, maintenance and repair as well.

The technology of golf has evolved into a thriving industry in Mesa. A sophisticated golf driving range and PING Swing Analysis Lab at Arizona State University East supports not only the golf-related majors at the college but also serves the community in perfecting its game.

Items and goods produced: aeronautical equipment, military equipment, vehicles, vehicle safety systems

Incentive Programs—New and Existing Companies

Local programs: Local business development assistance is available through the Neighborhood Economic Development Corporation (NEDCO), a partnership between the public and private sectors in support of community development and community reinvestment. NEDCO oversees the Business Development Loan Program, along with Individual Development Accounts that stimulate the creation of small businesses. Funding support comes from joint ventures between NEDCO and its partner financial institutions, as well as New Markets Tax Credit and private social investment dollars. NEDCO's Mesa Grande Commercial Revitalization Program works hand in hand with low income neighborhood groups to further develop cooperative housing and micro-enterprises.

State programs: The State of Arizona encourages businesses to invest in areas with higher poverty and/or unemployment rates through its Enterprise Zone Program, which provides income or premium tax credits along with property tax benefits. Construction of industrial and manufacturing facilities is supported via the state Private Activity Bond program. New businesses at the Williams Gateway Airport in Mesa can take advantage of the state Military Reuse Zone program, established in 1992 to lessen the economic impact of military base closures. Businesses sited at the former Williams Air Force Base can benefit from property reclassification, tax credits and transaction privilege tax exemptions.

Williams Gateway Airport also lies within a Foreign Trade Zone, an area that is essentially treated as if it were outside of U.S. Custom Territory. This allows for imported goods to be stored in the zone duty-free and without full customs formalities. Foreign Trade Zones

additionally allow businesses to realize significant real and personal property tax reductions.

Other State of Arizona business incentive programs include: tax credits for research and development, pollution control, information technology training, the cost of installing recycling equipment, exemptions for contractors and vendors of solar energy devices, and the purchase of construction materials. The state also offers a Waste Reduction Assistance Program to new and existing businesses. State lottery proceeds provide fixed-asset loans to companies for expansion, relocation, and consolidation.

Job training programs: The Neighborhood Economic Development Corporation (NEDCO) offers technical assistance and workforce training as part of its services locally. Maricopa Workforce Connections is a county branch of the state workforce development office, serving Maricopa County businesses and job seekers. Employers can access recruitment, screening, job matching, corporate restructuring, and job training services, while county residents in search of employment can tap into education and job training opportunities, career planning services, vocational counseling, specialized support services, job placement, and a national job database. The State of Arizona also operates the Arizona Job Training Program to tailor training plans to the evolving industry landscape. The Arizona Apprenticeship System maintains more than 100 registered apprenticeship opportunities that pair education with on-the-job training. The state's job workforce development programs are underscored by job training and hiring tax credits for companies providing specialized training or hiring employees in a targeted group.

Development Projects

The state of Arizona is experiencing exponential growth, as exemplified by Mesa's population and industry leaps since the 1980s; this has spurred the state to institute "Growing Smarter" legislation in reference to municipal planning efforts. The city of Mesa's priority work plans demonstrate this careful approach as it lays out development strategies for the Williams Gateway AREA (WGA). Mesa's long-term plan for the AREA is to set up a vibrant center for business, employment, aviation, education, and technology—providing employment for 100,000 people by 2035.

The "Mesa 2025" strategic plan has identified areas of focus for economic development, including the 4,560 acres that comprise the Falcon Field Airport corridor (business park and industrial usage), the Town Center/Main Street corridor (light rail, other rapid transit, business development, historical, and cultural development), and the Santan Freeway corridor (a combination of residential, commercial, industrial and mixed use).

The city is participating in an ongoing redevelopment and historical preservation effort, with particular emphasis on the town center. Four sites in downtown are on the National Register of Historic Places: the Evergreen area, West 6th Street, Glenwood Wilbur, and Temple. Robson was under consideration for the National Register in 2007. More work is being done on Fraser Fields, Escobedo, Lehi, and Clark Historic Districts to prepare them for consideration on the local and national level. In an effort to support older neighborhoods that are reporting decline, the City of Mesa has instituted a Neighborhood Opportunity Zone plan that coordinates residents, government, businesses, and nonprofits in planning and implementing neighborhood improvements.

Largely funded by the 1998 "Quality of Life" sales tax, the Mesa Arts Center opened its doors in 2005 as a 212,775-square-foot performing arts, visual arts and art education hub for the entire state of Arizona. The Arts Center was designed to reflect the aesthetic sensibilities of the Sonoran Desert on its exterior; inside is a complex of four theaters, exhibit space, art education classrooms, and Mesa Contemporary Arts' Galleries. The Mesa Arts Center is the largest facility of its kind in the state and is expected to drive economic development in the downtown area while it anchors the art scene locally and regionally.

In 2004 the City of Mesa developed a cutting-edge Transportation Management Center as part of its Intelligent Transportation System (ITS), using the latest technology to improve the flow of traffic through the city. Large-scale improvements on freeways, arterial streets and mass transit programs keep Mesa an accessible destination for businesses.

Educational institutions in Mesa in 2006 and 2007 received funding in the field of bioscience that impacts Mesa's economic development. In 2007 Mesa Public Schools received a Science Foundation Arizona grant worth $300,000 annually for three years to train up to 24 teachers assigned to bioscience courses and to provide support for students researching the genome of a bacterium, *Sphingomonas elodea*. In 2006, the school district, along with Mesa Community College and Arizona State University Polytechnic, received a National Science Foundation grant worth $900,000 over three years to create a biotech research project that stretches across all three education levels.

Commercial Shipping

Mesa is served by two local airports, a major international airport 12 miles to the west, and a network of freeways, highways, and rail. The Williams Gateway Airport can accommodate corporate, cargo, military, and general aviation craft. A 21,500-square-foot storage hangar and a 25,000-square-foot air cargo facility are available for shipping concerns, and the airport resides in Foreign

Trade Zone #221, allowing for landing and storing import merchandise without full customs formalities.

Falcon Field Airport doubles as an industrial park, offering a variety of charter, general aviation, and cargo flights daily. Sky Harbor International Airport, located between Mesa and Phoenix, is a major aeronautical enterprise that handled nearly 290,000 tons of cargo and more than 41,400,000 passengers in 2006. Sky Harbor joins Williams Gateway Airport in Foreign Trade Zone #221, easing customs requirements for imported goods and providing some tax relief for those businesses.

Several freeways, U.S. highways, and state highways pass through Mesa, including U.S. 60 (known as Superstition Freeway) and state highways 87 and 89. The Santan Freeway 202 creates a bypass around the more congested downtown area, and Interstates 10 and 17 are quickly accessible from the city. Mesa is the headquarters for several trucking companies of national scope and is located conveniently near many more in Phoenix. Driving conditions are good year-round, and Mesa is within an 8-hour drive of Albuquerque, El Paso, Las Vegas, Los Angeles, San Diego, Tucson, and several major cities in Mexico. Mesa is also served by Union Pacific Railroad.

Labor Force and Employment Outlook

Census data from the 1970s through the 2000s indicates that Mesa will continue to grow, and it's expected that the economy will grow apace. Despite its agrarian past, it seems likely that farming, fishing, and forestry occupations will decline into the 2010s, while healthcare, education, construction, and sales will all likely increase their niche in the local job market.

Certain occupational areas such as architecture, transportation, and industry are expected to experience steady growth or remain stable.

The following is a summary of data regarding the Phoenix-Mesa-Scottsdale metropolitan area labor force, 2006 annual averages.

Size of nonagricultural labor force: 1,894,600

Number of workers employed in ...

   construction and mining: 187,400
   manufacturing: 140,300
   trade, transportation and utilities: 379,500
   information: 32,900
   financial activities: 154,200
   professional and business services: 320,600
   educational and health services: 195,300
   leisure and hospitality: 180,700
   other services: 73,000
   government: 230,700

Average hourly earnings of production workers employed in manufacturing: $15.37

Unemployment rate: 3.0% (June 2007)

Largest employers	*Number of employees*
Mesa Public Schools	10,132
Banner Health System	6,100
Boeing	4,300
City of Mesa	4,105
AT&T	2,800
Wal-Mart	1,775
TRW Safety Systems	1,450
Empire Southwest Machinery	1,000

Cost of Living

The following is a summary of data regarding key cost of living factors for the Mesa area.

2007 (1st quarter) ACCRA Average House Price: $325,251

2007 (1st quarter) ACCRA Cost of Living Index: 101.9

State income tax rate: 2.87% to 5.04%

State sales tax rate: 5.6%

Local income tax rate: None

Local sales tax rate: 0.15%

Property tax rate: None

Economic information: City of Mesa, Office of Economic Development, Mesa City Plaza, 20 E. Main Street, Suite 200, PO Box 1466, Mesa, AZ 85211-1466; telephone (480)644-2390

■ Education and Research

Elementary and Secondary Schools

The Mesa Public Schools System has come a long way from its pioneer farmer roots, when classes were taught in a shack made of cottonwood. These days, the emphasis is on preparing students to function in the new technology of the information age. Classes are geared toward the development of students who can use the latest technology and can think critically in the course of their learning experiences. The school district plans for every student to graduate with a skill or trade that will lead to future employment; to that end, the district has created and implemented a Career and Technical Education (CTE) curriculum. The program is comprised of five areas of concentration, including agricultural education, business education, family and consumer sciences, industrial technology, and informational technology. Hands-on learning is stressed, with some high school

students enrolled in a Cooperative Office Education program that allows them to attend classes in the morning and work at local businesses in the afternoon.

With job preparedness as a district-wide concern, it makes sense that Mesa School District would also contain a well-developed and well-supported service learning program, with community-based education suggested in art, business, computer technology, and foreign language classes.

Mesa Public Schools offers 12 alternative education programs spanning kindergarten to 12th grade and running the gamut from early education centers, to support for home-schooled students, to institutions created for drop-out prevention and retrieval.

Mesa Public Schools works closely with business and community partners to create classes that help develop the skills students require for entering the working world. The district also coordinates with technical schools, Maricopa Community Colleges, and Arizona's three state universities so that students can continue their studies at the post-secondary level. Dual credit is available through Mesa Community College in several areas.

The following is a summary of data regarding the Mesa Public Schools as of the 2005–2006 school year.

Total enrollment: 73,808

Number of facilities

elementary schools: 58
junior high/middle schools: 13
senior high schools: 7
other: 9

Student/teacher ratio: 22:1

Teacher salaries (2005–06)

elementary median: $32,680
junior high/middle median: $37,430
secondary median: $37,020

Funding per pupil: $5,719

Public Schools Information: Mesa Public Schools, 63 E. Main Street, #101, Mesa, AZ 85201-7422; telephone (480)472-0000

Colleges and Universities

Arizona State University (East Campus) in Mesa functions as a polytechnic institute, or vocational college, offering its more than 6,500 students degrees in some 30 educational concentrations including business, agribusiness, engineering technology, professional pilot training, health and wellness, and education. Baccalaureate, masters and doctoral degrees are all available through the Mesa campus. In June 1999, the university received accreditation by the Professional Golfers Association and is one of the first state universities west of the Mississippi to offer both a Professional Golf Management program and a Golf and Facilities Management major.

Masters and doctoral degrees are available through the Arizona School of Health Sciences, which offers programs such as medical informatics, advanced physician assistant studies, sports medicine, occupational therapy, and audiology. Fieldwork experiences occur in a variety of urban and rural placements, allowing for practical application of academic concepts.

The largest of the 10 Maricopa Community Colleges, Mesa Community College (MCC) offers its student body of more than 27,000 the only biotechnology studies program in the state of Arizona. Well-respected Fire Science and Nursing academic programs are underscored by a service learning program that has become a blueprint for community colleges across the country. Courses within a variety of disciplines send their students out into the local community to do meaningful volunteer work that employs the theoretical concepts learned in class. Additionally, MCC provides AmeriCorps service scholarships to students who are performing volunteer work or completing unpaid internships.

East Valley Institute of Technology (EVIT) is billed as Arizona's first regional technological education district, serving high school students from 10 East Valley school districts (including Mesa Public Schools). The programs at EVIT are the result of partnerships with local industry and business in an effort to prepare students with the skills needed for future employment. High school students can attend half-days at EVIT and the rest of the school day at their own school. EVIT additionally offers adult education classes under the banner of Evenings at EVIT.

Highly specialized training is available to would-be pilots and transitioning former members of the military at Williams Gateway Airport Educational Campus, which includes tenants such as Advanced Training Systems International, Inc. and Airline Transport Professionals. Keller Graduate School of Management also maintains a Mesa branch with a range of business-related masters degrees. Adult learners can also enroll at the Mesa campus of Ottawa University and the University of Phoenix.

Libraries and Research Centers

The City of Mesa Library system is comprised of one centrally located main library facility, with two branch libraries covering the southwest and northeast portions of the city. The main library is home to the Mesa Room, an archive of local history items and special collections regarding Mesa. Besides offering general library services, the City of Mesa Library coordinates reading programs for children, book discussion groups, special exhibits and lectures.

The Research Library at the Mesa Southwest Museum contains non-circulating materials dedicated to the natural and cultural history of the Southwest. There are approximately 58,000 objects in the collections of the Mesa Southwest Museum.

The East Library at Mesa's branch of Arizona State University offers access to hundreds of databases and thousands of online journals and periodicals, which can be searched remotely. The library provides a call center for help, along with live tech support. The library features the Naxos Music Library, an online compendium of classical music with a sprinkling of other musical genres.

Arizona State University (ASU) East also houses several high-tech facilities for specialized research, including the Golf Driving Range and PING Swing Analysis Lab, which refine the work of students in Professional Golf and Golf Facilities Management programs. ASU's Agribusiness Center incorporates a Consumer Behavior Research Lab with a Market/Trading Room, along with a testing theater for students in the pre-veterinary medicine program. An altitude chamber and a simulator lab provide the latest facilities for pilot training, while the College of Technology and Applied Sciences benefits from the Microelectronics Teaching Factory, a 15,000-square-foot manufacturing facility available to both students and local industry partners. ASU East constructed a 34,600-square-foot research facility to house Applied Biological Research labs, the Applied Cognitive Sciences Center, the Health Lifestyles Center, and the Plant Made Pharmaceutical Research and Manufacturing Facility.

Public Library Information: City of Mesa Main Library, 64 East First Street, Mesa, AZ 85201; telephone (480) 644-2207

■ Health Care

Mesa is home to four medical centers, three of which are part of the Phoenix-based Banner Health company. The Banner Mesa Medical Center (formerly Mesa Lutheran Hospital) has 258 acute care beds and 62 behavioral health and rehabilitation beds; this full-service community hospital offers acute care for adults, intensive and emergency care, pediatrics, labor and delivery, medical imaging, and surgery. In the fall of 2007 Banner Mesa Medical Center was scheduled to close and reopen as a new, state-of-the-art medical center in the town of Gilbert, to be called Banner Gateway Medical Center. Banner Desert Medical Center offers the community 549 licensed beds for adult acute care, emergency services, intensive care, oncology and cardiology specialties, orthopedics, and neurology. Banner Desert also operates a Children's Hospital staffed by medical specialists in pediatric emergency, and surgical, intensive, and rehabilitative care. The third Banner facility is Banner Baywood Medical Center. A new seven-story patient tower opened in October 2006 after more than two years of planning and construction, adding more than 120 beds to the existing 242. Banner Baywood's Orthopedic Institute has been ranked in the top 100 orthopedic programs nationally, according to the Health Network. Other specialty programs and services include an ambulatory treatment unit, intensive care and emergency services, pain management programs, endoscopy and wound/ostomy care. The Banner Baywood Heart Hospital provides specialized cardiology services to the East Valley community, offering advanced cardiac diagnostics and treatment.

Mesa General Hospital has served the community since 1965, offering 126 licensed beds for care ranging from cardiac services, intensive and critical care, imaging, rehabilitation, and wound treatment. Mesa General is also home to the Arizona Diagnostic and Surgical Center and is a designated Diabetes Care Center of Arizona.

Mesa's proximity to Phoenix allows access to hundreds of medical professionals in family practice, specialty practices, outpatient psychiatric services and alternative medicine practices.

■ Recreation

Sightseeing

A tour of Mesa might best be started at the very beginning, at the Park of the Canals near the intersection of McKellips Road and Horne Street north of the downtown area. Visitors can see the innovative irrigation systems established by the original Hohokam Indian residents of Mesa, with the effectiveness of the canals demonstrated by the Brinton Desert Botanical Garden at the same location. The Botanical Garden hosts special events in season, along with desert gardening workshops and concerts in what can be a surreal setting. The Salt River is just northwest from the Park of the Canals, making for a water-themed day in the desert.

On the way back to Mesa's town center, it's an easy stop at the former Lehi School, circa 1913, which now houses the Mesa Historical Museum and provides snapshots into the lives of early settlers of the communities that have blended to form modern Mesa. The historic downtown section of Mesa features attractions ranging from the Wild West era to modern arcades. The Ellis-Johnson home, the Alhambra Hotel, the Vance Auditorium and the former Southside Hospital all echo back to the beginnings of Mesa. The Sirrine House, built in 1895, is an attractive brick structure restored by the Mesa Historical Society and the City of Mesa. The Mesa Southwest Museum provides scholarly, scientific, and fun background for sites visited in the city and beyond.

Immediately east of the original Mesa town site is the Temple Historic District, encompassing two residential divisions. Homes from the early 1920s line streets that were named for the Mormon pioneers who helped shape present-day Mesa and who laid the foundations for the

Arizona Temple of the Church of Jesus Christ of Latter-Day Saints built in 1927. The temple is open for tours.

From Mesa, visitors and history buffs can embark on sightseeing adventures such as the Apache Trail Jeep Tour, which follows the stagecoach and freight wagon route from Mesa to Globe through the Superstition Mountains. Somewhere in those mountains, the Lost Dutchman Mine waits to be found again. The Goldfield Ghost Town resurrects its history as a thriving mining community that bit the dust when the mine petered out. At its height, there were three saloons, a boarding house, a general store, blacksmith shop, brewery, schoolhouse, and bordello. Along the finger of the Sonoran Desert that points across the East Valley, a smorgasbord of desert succulents can be encountered: saguaro, prickly pear, varieties of cholla, hedgehog cactus, and ocotillos. When the mountains and desert become too dry, visitors can head northeast to Saguaro Lake for a paddleboat excursion on the *Desert Belle* past canyon walls and Arizona wildlife.

Arts and Culture

The Mesa Arts Center, which opened in 2005, is the largest arts center in Arizona at 212,775 square feet of space for performing arts facilities, visual arts galleries and studios, and art education classrooms. The outside of the complex is as inviting as the inside, with a design reflective of the surrounding Sonoran Desert in hue, shape and landscaping. A 700-foot Shadow Walk serves as a cool outdoor plaza for events or relaxing during a tour. Located in the heart of downtown Mesa, the Arts Center campus contains three buildings, including a four-theater complex. The theater spaces are: the 1,588-seat Tom and Janet Ikeda Theater; the 550-seat Virginia G. Piper Repertory Theater; the 200-seat Nesbitt/Elliott Playhouse; and the 99-seat Anita Cox Farnsworth Studio Theater. The other facilities on the Arts Center campus are the Mesa Contemporary Arts Building and the Art Studios' classrooms and work areas.

The Mesa Arts Center is home to Ballet Etudes, offering serious ballet performers an experience akin to a professional dance company. Ballet Etudes stages *The Nutcracker* annually, along with a Spring Repertory performance. The dancers have performed with the Mesa Symphony Orchestra, also located under the Arts Center roof. Besides its five scheduled orchestral performances each season, the Mesa Symphony Orchestra does outreach in the public schools and provides vouchers that allow students and their families to attend future performances at a reduced rate. The Metropolitan Youth Symphony involves 280 excellent young musicians in a minimum of three concerts each season, providing a professional-level experience for aspiring performers. The Sonoran Desert Chorale's 60 vocalists present four major concerts each season, with selections ranging from classical to the Broadway stage.

Billed as "theatre for children by children," the East Valley Children's Theatre encourages creativity, self-confidence, and expression through community theatrical performances. The company puts on three productions each season, along with a host of workshops and classes for youth between the ages of 8 and 18. Also offering three plays per season is the Southwest Shakespeare Company, which strives to bring classical theater to the masses through dynamic live performances. The actors are able to share their appreciation for the Bard via student matinees, post-show seminars, and play introductions. For theater along with edible fare, the Broadway Palm West Dinner Theatre is recommended.

At the Arizona Museum for Youth, exhibits are tailored for young children to 12-year-olds, although adults will also enjoy the explanatory and interactive displays. Tours, opportunities to contribute to masterpieces, art classes, and workshops all happen at this fun and stimulating site located at Robson and Pepper streets.

Housed in the original 1913 Lehi Schoolhouse, the Mesa Historical Museum contains a wealth of artifacts donated by Mesa's pioneer families and linked to the city's colorful past. Also on the grounds is the Settler's Adobe House, reconstructed in the scale and manner of the first permanent homes as the new residents attempted to deal with life in the desert heat.

The natural and cultural histories of Mesa and its environs are the focus of the Mesa Southwest Museum. A $4.5 million expansion completed in 2000 brought the museum to its current size of 80,000 square feet, and another $4.5 million funded new exhibits for the expanded area. Collections include Spanish Colonial relics, artifacts of mining, reflections of Arizona's role in World War II (including Japanese relocation camps), Hohokam ceramics and jewelry, and evidence of Arizona's former function as ocean floor. The museum's Archaeology Team has several active excavations that are open to the public.

Arts and Culture Information: Mesa Arts Center, 1 East Main Street, PO Box 1466, Mesa, AZ 85211-1466; telephone (480)644-6500

Festivals and Holidays

The desert heat in summer dictates that festivals and outdoor events in Mesa are concentrated in winter, spring and fall months with a bit of a summer siesta in between. The year kicks off in January with the Martin Luther King, Jr., Festival, where the civil rights pioneer is feted with music, food, and carnival rides. In February, Mesa joins forces with Phoenix and other East Valley communities to put on the Blues Blast at the Mesa Amphitheatre. National and local blues artists perform a day-long concert that gets central Arizona in the groove. From March through April, Free Community Concerts are performed, including a family series with puppetry

and theater as well as the Courtyard Series on Thursday nights.

Cinco de Mayo festivities start May off, with a two-day cultural fiesta in Pioneer Park. For 45 years, Mesa has held a Fourth of July party; the Mesa Symphony Orchestra typically provides a rousing rendition of "The Star Spangled Banner." Ushering in cooler weather, in September Mesa honors its history during the Annual Constitution Celebration, featuring a parade, picnics and music.

Native American art, culture, music, dancing, and food are the focus of the Mesa Pow Wow in late October. Elaborate native dress and dance competitions attract visitors from many tribes and states. Also in late October is the Mesa Storytelling Festival, which presents the art of the spoken word. National, regional, and youth talent gather to share a wide range of stories: folk tales, tall tales, myths, humor, American legends, and tales from all over the world. From November through April, art takes to the streets with Mesa's Sculptures in the Streets program, during which the public can stroll through temporary sculpture displays along downtown Main Street. In December, Main Street is again the destination for holiday celebrations in the downtown area. Mesa's Merry Main Street decks the halls with lights, gingerbread houses, tempting wrapped packages and a visit by Santa.

Sports for the Spectator

The Chicago Cubs get ready for baseball season at Mesa's own Hohokam Field. In 2004, baseball fans at Hohokam Field broke attendance records for Major League Baseball Spring Training. The Cactus League gets started in early March and wraps the Spring Training season up in approximately a month. Locals and visitors get the opportunity to preview not just the Cubs but also their impressive roster of opponents, including the Colorado Rockies, San Diego Padres, and the Oakland A's.

Baseball doesn't end in March, though—Mesa and Hohokam Field are also host to Fall League baseball. In October and November, Fall League baseball features the Mesa Solar Sox providing a preview of the next generation of Major League Baseball players.

Mesa Community College's Thunderbirds compete in a variety of sports at the National Junior College Athletic Association level, with teams in baseball, basketball, football, soccer, and track. Phoenix offers more professional and collegiate sports options, from the Cardinals football team to the Suns basketball program to the Diamondbacks baseball organization.

Sports for the Participant

The name of the game in Mesa is golf—local courses abound and a short drive provides access to even more holes stunningly situated in desert and mountain terrain. Local courses in Mesa include Fiesta Lakes Golf Club, Royal Palms Golf Course, Augusta Ranch Golf Club, Las

Sendas Golf Club, and Superstition Springs Golf Club, just to name a few. Toka Sticks Golf Course on the grounds of the Williams Gateway Airport offers the unique opportunity to fly in, play 18 holes, and fly out again. Mountain Brook Golf Club is located outside of Mesa but is set in the desert just below the Superstition Mountains, making it a dramatic experience for the golfer.

The Gene Autry Sports Complex contains tennis courts, indoor volleyball courts and beach volleyball pits. Lessons are offered, and players can join leagues or drop in on specified days.

Mesa may be in the desert, but watersports are still available. Rafting and tubing on the Salt River are popular summertime thrills, while local lakes like Saguaro are typically good spots for anglers to try for walleye, large-mouth and brown trout, bluegills, channel catfish, and crappie.

The Superstition Mountains east of Mesa offer hikes of all levels of difficulty and duration, including the 1.5 mile Massacre Grounds trail, the Peralta Trail to the Fremont Saddle, and the steep Siphon Draw trail. The Tonto National Forest to the north of Phoenix and Mesa is the fifth largest forest in the United States, providing opportunities for a range of outdoor activities such as hiking, rock climbing, and camping. For a classic hiking adventure, trekkers can head north to the Grand Canyon.

Shopping and Dining

The Mesa Market Place Swap Meet covers 55 acres with more than 1,600 booths under a canopy to give an outdoor shopping experience with shade and water misters to keep customers cool. The Swap Meet is open year-round with great bargains and unusual merchandise. Antiques and collectibles are often found among the shops in the historic downtown area of Mesa, while more recognizable stores can be encountered at the Fiesta Mall, Superstition Springs Center, the Village at Las Sendas, and The Village Square at Dana Park. Mesa holds a Community Farmers Market downtown all year, with vendors providing fresh produce and other goods in a street fair atmosphere.

As might be expected, Mesa's culinary specialty is Mexican-Southwestern food, with burgers and pizza coming in second and third. There's something for every taste, though, in Mesa's menu of Chinese, Japanese, Italian, Greek, and homestyle eateries. Local and chain coffee shops abound, as well.

■ Convention Facilities

The Mesa Convention Center features 19,000 square feet of exhibit space, along with an additional 19,000 square feet of flexible meeting space that can be used for trade show exhibits, banquets, dances, concerts and other events. The Conference Center features a 100-seat conference theatre that possesses multi-media capabilities for presentations and teleconferences. Breakout rooms and an executive conference room are also available.

The Mesa Amphitheatre hosts more than 70 events per year; festival-style seating can accommodate 4,200 for commercial shows and outdoor festivals.

The Arizona Golf Resort and Conference Center has a 12,000-square-foot space for meetings and exhibitions, bolstered by an additional 5,000 square feet of general session rooms, training rooms, board rooms, outdoor courtyards, and even onsite Championship Golf. The Marriott Phoenix Mesa Hotel and Convention Center offers 52,000 square feet of meeting and function space. The 18,000-square-foot Exhibit Hall is accompanied by the 9,000-square-foot Arizona Ballroom and an outdoor amphitheatre that can accommodate up to 5,200 people.

■ Transportation

Approaching the City

Phoenix Sky Harbor Airport is located approximately 12 miles to the west of Mesa and is served by 23 airlines that connect the East Valley area to more than 100 cities in the United States and around the world. Sky Harbor is a major hub for Southwest and America West airlines but also has services through airlines such as United, Delta Frontier, and Sun Country. Non-stop international flights are available via Aeromexico, Air Jamaica, British Airways, Lufthansa, Air Canada, and America West Airlines. The local airfields, Williams Gateway and Falcon Field, offer charter flights in the southwest. In 2007, Falcon Field airport planned to conduct an airport master plan update. The project was planned to last 12–15 months. The last update was in 1992.

Several freeways, U.S. highways and state highways pass through or near Mesa, including U.S. 60 (known as Superstition Freeway) and state highways 87 and 89. The Santan Freeway 202 creates a bypass around the more congested downtown area, and Interstates 10 and 17 are quickly accessible from the city. Greyhound Bus service maintains a branch in Mesa, with daily departures and arrivals.

Traveling in the City

Mesa is laid out on a straightforward north-south, east-west grid pattern as regards its major streets. Center Street and Main Street are perpendicular to each other and, as suits their names, intersect in the city center in a manner that provides a handy reference point and makes city navigation relatively easy.

Bus service within Mesa is provided by Valley Metro, which runs buses 6 days a week for about 16 hours per day. There are 9 local routes and 4 express routes to Phoenix. Mesa operates a Dial-A-Ride program for people with mobility or vehicle operation issues, plus the city offers RideChoice options to elderly and disabled patrons who either use the bus, cabs, or are driven to their destinations by friends or family members.

Mesa has styled itself as a bicycle-friendly city, with 70 miles of bicycle routes and 40 miles of bicycle lanes. The city plans for more bicycle route and lane construction in the future, along with facilities at bike destinations.

■ Communications

Newspapers and Magazines

The Mesa area is served by *The East Valley Tribune,* which is delivered daily and is available online by subscription. *Get Out,* an affiliate of the daily paper, supplies dining and entertainment information for Mesa residents and tourists alike. Another online news alternative for the East Valley is offered by *Newszap.com.* Mesa Community College publishes its campus paper, *The Mesa Legend.* Spanish language speakers can check out *La Voz* and *Prensa Hispana,* while other local publications write to the interests of the Catholic, Jewish, and senior populations in Mesa.

Television and Radio

Phoenix is Mesa's source for network television broadcast stations, being home to affiliates of CBS, ABC, NBC, and Fox. Mesa Channel 11 provides local coverage of council meetings and announcements of local events.

Mesa is within hearing distance of a wide variety of AM and FM radio stations with signals originating in Phoenix; formats run the gamut from talk radio to National Public Radio to classical music to rock and roll. KDKB 93.3 FM is based in Mesa and plays a hard rock rotation.

Mesa Online

City of Mesa home page. Available www.cityofmesa .org/Home

City of Mesa Library. Available www.mesalibrary.org

Downtown Mesa Association. Available www .downtownmesa.com/

Mesa Chamber of Commerce. Available www .mesachamber.org

Mesa Convention and Visitors Bureau. Available www.mesacvb.com

Mesa Historical Museum. Available www.mesaaz .org/index.htm

BIBLIOGRAPHY

Our Town: The Story of Mesa, Arizona, 1878-1991 (Mesa, AZ: Mesa Public Schools, 1991)

Phoenix

■ The City in Brief

Founded: 1864 (incorporated 1881)

Head Official: Mayor Phil Gordon (since 2003)

City Population
> 1980: 789,704
> 1990: 983,015
> 2000: 1,321,045
> 2006 estimate: 1,512,986
> Percent change, 1990–2000: 34.4%
> U.S. rank in 1980: 9th
> U.S. rank in 1990: 9th
> U.S. rank in 2000: 10th (State rank: 1st)

Metropolitan Area Population
> 1980: 1,509,000
> 1990: 2,238,498
> 2000: 3,251,876
> 2006 estimate: 4,039,182
> Percent change, 1990–2000: 45.3%
> U.S. rank in 1980: 24th
> U.S. rank in 1990: 20th
> U.S. rank in 2000: 14th

Area: 475.09 square miles (2000)

Elevation: 1,058 feet above sea level

Average Annual Temperature: 72.6° F

Average Annual Precipitation: 8.3 inches

Major Economic Sectors: services, wholesale and retail trade, government

Unemployment Rate: 3.0% (June 2007)

Per Capita Income: $22,471 (2005)

2005 FBI Crime Index Property: 93,328

2005 FBI Crime Index Violent: 10,691

Major Colleges and Universities: University of Phoenix, Arizona State University, Maricopa Community Colleges

Daily Newspaper: *The Arizona Republic, The Phoenix Gazette*

■ Introduction

Phoenix, the capital of Arizona, is a study in contrasts. As the center of "the Valley of the Sun," the city has traditionally been associated with Old West myths, tourist resorts, and Sun Belt retirement communities. While it retains strong links with this image—frontier history permeates the city's culture and architecture, tourism continues to thrive, and people still spend their golden years here—Phoenix has also emerged as one of the "newest" cities in the nation. It is among the country's fastest expanding metropolitan areas, and with children under the age of 14 comprising a significant percentage of its inhabitants, Phoenix is adding a youthful contrast to its traditions as a frontier desert town and a place "where the old-timers go to retire." With a growing labor force and population, friendly business environment, affordable housing, and low cost of living, the area is ideal for businesses and residents alike.

■ Geography and Climate

Located in the Salt River Valley in the south central part of the state, Phoenix is situated on flat desert terrain, bordered by lakes and the Superstition Mountains to the east and surrounded by the Phoenix Mountain Preserve. The climate is warm, with low humidity. The most remarkable weather feature is sunshine approximately 325 days per year, making Phoenix one of the sunniest cities in the country.

Area: 475.09 square miles (2000)

Elevation: 1,058 feet above sea level

Average Temperature: 72.6° F

Average Annual Precipitation: 8.3 inches

■ History

Native Americans Removed to Make Way for White Settlers

The city of Phoenix stands on the site of a prehistoric settlement built by Native Americans, the Hohokam tribe, who had established a thriving culture but who vanished without a trace around 1450 A.D. Thought to be the ancestors of the Pima—"Hohokam" means "those who have gone" in Pima—the Hohokam had constructed a sophisticated system of irrigation canals, many of which are still in use today, that remain as evidence of their existence.

Permanent resettlement of the Hohokam site did not come until the late 1860s; in the interim the area shared the history of the rest of the state. Hispanic conquistadors invaded Arizona in the 1500s in search of the Seven Cities of Cibola, bringing with them cattle, horses, and new agricultural methods. They were followed by miners, traders, and farmers whose presence was tolerated by the Native Americans until the 1850s, when it became apparent that the white settlers were encroaching on their land. Battles between the settlers and the tribes brought intervention by the U.S. military and the tribes were eventually confined to reservations.

City Thrives as Trade Center; Irrigation Aids Farms, Industry

In 1864 a U.S. Army post, a supply camp for nearby Camp McDowell, was set up on the ruins of the Hohokam settlement. Then in 1867 the Hohokam's irrigation canals were rebuilt by two settlers, one of whom called the place "Phoenix." He predicted that, like the mythical phoenix bird rising from its own ashes, a great city would emerge from the ruins. Incorporated in 1881, Phoenix rapidly developed into a major trading center with the building of the railroad in 1887 and became the capital of the Arizona territory in 1889; it was named the capital of the state of Arizona in 1912.

Phoenix gained a reputation as a rowdy frontier town because of its saloons, gambling places, and general outlaw atmosphere. Law and order were restored by the turn of the century, however, and Phoenix entered a new phase. The railroad, bringing settlers from throughout the country, established an immigration pattern that has continued steadily without interruption; during the three decades following World War II, for instance, the

population of Phoenix increased from roughly 107,000 to nearly 790,000 people.

Major technological advances during the first half of the twentieth century—the Roosevelt Dam on the Salt River, the Southern Pacific Railroad, the advent of air conditioning, and the Central Arizona Project aqueduct system—brought about agricultural and industrial development that also fueled tremendous growth. In the 1990s Phoenix went through its third major growth boom in four decades, partly a result of a large influx of people from California. The city is experiencing the effects of urban sprawl, including serious air pollution. Entering the twenty-first century, Phoenix's landscape consists of Hispanic colonial and Indian pueblo architecture interspersed with gleaming high-rise office buildings. The economic success of the area has spurred a continuing population growth and nearly all business indicators present positive gains. The City Council has allotted $1 billion in public and private projects to enhance and maintain the community. This foresight, in conjunction with the natural appeal of the environment, prepares the city for boundless prosperity.

Historical Information: Phoenix Museum of History, 105 N. 5th St., Phoenix, AZ 85004-4404; telephone (602)253-2734; email exhibits@pmoh.org

■ Population Profile

Metropolitan Area Residents
    1980: 1,509,000
    1990: 2,238,498
    2000: 3,251,876
    2006 estimate: 4,039,182
    Percent change, 1990–2000: 45.3%
    U.S. rank in 1980: 24th
    U.S. rank in 1990: 20th
    U.S. rank in 2000: 14th

City Residents
    1980: 789,704
    1990: 983,015
    2000: 1,321,045
    2006 estimate: 1,512,986
    Percent change, 1990–2000: 34.4%
    U.S. rank in 1980: 9th
    U.S. rank in 1990: 9th
    U.S. rank in 2000: 10th (State rank: 1st)

Density: 2,781.9 people per square mile (2000)

Racial and ethnic characteristics (2005)
    White: 1,015,038
    Black: 69,687
    American Indian and Alaska Native: 29,049

Image copyright EuToch, 2007. Used under license from Shutterstock.com.

Asian: 27,724
Native Hawaiian and Pacific Islander: 872
Hispanic or Latino (may be of any race): 575,436
Other: 206,728

Percent of residents born in state: 34.6% (2000)

Age characteristics (2005)

Population under 5 years old: 121,471
Population 5 to 9 years old: 110,483
Population 10 to 14 years old: 105,047
Population 15 to 19 years old: 95,316
Population 20 to 24 years old: 107,313
Population 25 to 34 years old: 239,444
Population 35 to 44 years old: 201,219
Population 45 to 54 years old: 182,780
Population 55 to 59 years old: 65,323
Population 60 to 64 years old: 45,908
Population 65 to 74 years old: 59,230
Population 75 to 84 years old: 35,235
Population 85 years and older: 9,211
Median age: 30.9 years

Births (2006, MSA)

Total number: 66,478

Deaths (2006, MSA)

Total number: 26,082

Money income (2005)

Per capita income: $22,471
Median household income: $42,353
Total households: 503,753

Number of households with income of...

less than $10,000: 37,300
$10,000 to $14,999: 29,440
$15,000 to $24,999: 69,007
$25,000 to $34,999: 67,702
$35,000 to $49,999: 85,415
$50,000 to $74,999: 93,360
$75,000 to $99,999: 50,590
$100,000 to $149,999: 44,003
$150,000 to $199,999: 14,681
$200,000 or more: 12,255

Percent of families below poverty level: 12.7% (2005)

2005 FBI Crime Index Property: 93,328

2005 FBI Crime Index Violent: 10,691

■ Municipal Government

The capital of Arizona and the Maricopa County seat, Phoenix has a council-manager form of government. The eight council members serve staggered four-year terms, representing districts of the city, while the mayor is elected at large to a four-year term and also serves as a member of the council. Phoenix has won international recognition and many awards for the quality of management of the city.

Head Official: Mayor Phil Gordon (since 2003; current term expires 2011)

Total Number of City Employees: full time, 14,144; part time, 865 (2006)

City Information: City of Phoenix, 200 W. Washington St., Phoenix, AZ 85003; telephone (602)262-6011

■ Economy

Major Industries and Commercial Activity

Manufacturing and tourism, traditionally the base of the city's economy, continue to be important to Phoenix. Major industrial products manufactured by companies located in the metropolitan area include aircraft parts, electronic equipment, agricultural chemicals, radios, air-conditioning equipment, leather goods, and Native American crafts.

Tourism is an especially vital part of the economy. With more than 10 million visitors from throughout the United States and Canada annually visiting for the warm weather and sunshine in the Valley of the Sun, Phoenix continues to be an important resort center. Flights from Phoenix travel to more than 100 locations within the United States and 18 cities internationally including direct flights to destinations in Mexico, Canada, the United Kingdom, and Costa Rica. The airport is constantly seeking to improve its facilities.

As the result of the population boom, the economy of Phoenix has taken on new dimensions in recent decades by moving into technology and service industries. Tourism and business services in particular account for a large percentage of the area's total employment. Another sector of growth has been financial services and banking as several significant processing and/or regional headquarters operations call Phoenix home: American Express, Chase Bank, Bank of America, Discover Card Services, and Wells Fargo Bank. High technology and aerospace firms hold a considerable share of the manufacturing jobs throughout the state.

Population and economic growth have made Phoenix the center of the state's economy. More than a third of the state's entire labor force works in the Phoenix metropolitan area. Further, many *Fortune* 500 companies

operate within the area such as Boeing, Honeywell, AT&T, and Intel.

Items and goods produced: aircraft and aircraft parts, electronic equipment, steel castings and fabrications, flour, boxes, agricultural chemicals, aluminum products, radios, mobile homes, air conditioning machinery, creamery products, beer, liquor, saddles and leather goods, apparel, Native American and Mexican novelties

Incentive Programs—New and Existing Companies

Funding and assistance for business development in Phoenix are available through the Business Development Finance Corporation, Southwestern Business Financing Corp., the Phoenix Industrial Development Authority (PIDA), the Small Business Innovation Research Program (SBIR), and the Arizona Commerce and Economic Development Commission.

Local programs: Employers locating facilities in the 200-square-mile City of Phoenix Enterprise Zone (COPEZ), as designated by the Arizona Department of Commerce, can earn state corporate income tax credit for each net new job created in the zone. Tax credits can total up to $3,000 per hire (with a maximum of 200 annually) over a three-year period. The city of Phoenix is the administrator of Foreign Trade Zone #75, which allows companies to reduce or defer payment of customs duties on imported products; companies operating in the zone can benefit from an 80 percent reduction in real and personal property tax. EXPAND (Expansion Assistance and Development Program) was formed to facilitate a growing company's need for funds to acquire capital. EXPAND reserve deposits are pledged in amounts from 25 percent to 50 percent of a loan with a ceiling of $150,000. Phoenix Industrial Development Authority (PIDA) bonds provide tax-exempt financing utilizing industrial revenue bonds up to $10 million for the acquisition, construction, equipping, or improvement of manufacturing projects located within Phoenix.

State programs: Arizona has a favorable tax structure for businesses, collecting no corporate franchise tax; in addition, business inventories are exempt from property taxes. The State of Arizona has adopted a four-year accelerated depreciation schedule for certain personal property devoted to any commercial or industrial use. There are weight-distance tax exemptions and transaction privilege tax refunds for the motion picture industry, and exemptions from taxation for secured and unsecured personal property relating to construction work in progress. Qualified employers that provide technical training for their employees are eligible for the Technology Training Tax Credit. A research and development income tax credit is a state tax credit for qualified R&D activities performed in Arizona; the credit includes publicly funded research conducted at a university. The maximum credit is $100,000 in the first year, $250,000 in the second year, $400,000 in the third year, and $500,000 in the fourth and subsequent years.

Job training programs: The Arizona Job Training Program is targeted at new and existing businesses. Funds are available on a grant basis and range from $2,000 to $5,000 per job. In addition, Arizona State University and the Maricopa Community College district work with area employers to maintain continuing education programs for local workers.

Development Projects

A rapidly growing young city, Phoenix has required more recent construction activities than more mature cities. A $600-million construction project for the Phoenix Civic Plaza and Convention Center will, once complete in 2009, triple its size. One research institute, Translational Genomics Research Institute (TGen), was built in the downtown area for $46 million in 2002 while another large facility opened in 2004 on the campus of Arizona State University.

Economic Development Information: City of Phoenix Community and Economic Development Office, 200 W. Washington St., 20th Fl., Phoenix, AZ 85003; telephone (602)262-5040; fax (602)495-5097

Commercial Shipping

Phoenix is located at the center of market areas stretching along interstate highways from southern California to western Texas, Colorado, Utah, and Mexico. More than 50 companies provide motor freight service. Rail service is available from two transcontinental rail lines. The Phoenix metropolitan area economy benefits from air cargo service through Phoenix Sky Harbor International Airport, where American Airlines and American West provide wide-body freight service.

Labor Force and Employment Outlook

The local labor force is described as young, plentiful, and well-educated. Arizona consistently ranks in the top five growth states, and workers are attracted by the quality of life to be enjoyed. A right-to-work state, Arizona has union membership of less than 5 percent in the private sector.

The labor force in Phoenix was expected to top 550,000 jobs by 2012 with significant gains in the professional, service, and technical fields. Maricopa County, with Phoenix as its county seat, registered the second largest gain in the level of employment in the U.S. from December 2005 to December 2006 (with 68,500 new jobs), following Harris County, Texas (76,300).

The following is a summary of data regarding the Phoenix-Mesa-Scottsdale metropolitan area labor force, 2006 annual averages.

Size of nonagricultural labor force: 1,894,600

Number of workers employed in . . .

    construction and mining: 187,400
    manufacturing: 140,300
    trade, transportation and utilities: 379,500
    information: 32,900
    financial activities: 154,200
    professional and business services: 320,600
    educational and health services: 195,300
    leisure and hospitality: 180,700
    other services: 73,000
    government: 230,700

Average hourly earnings of production workers employed in manufacturing: $15.37

Unemployment rate: 3.0% (June 2007)

Largest employers (2006)	*Number of employees*
Wal-Mart Stores Inc.	25,969
Banner Health	19,662
Honeywell International Inc.	12,500
Wells Fargo & Co.	11,800
Intel Corp.	10,900
Raytheon Co.	10,641
Bashas' Supermarkets	9,966
Home Depot Inc.	9,600
Kroger Co.	9,340
JP Morgan Chase & Co.	9,263

Cost of Living

The following is a summary of data regarding several key cost of living factors for the Phoenix area.

2007 (1st quarter) ACCRA Average House Price: $325,251

2007 (1st quarter) ACCRA Cost of Living Index: 101.9

State income tax rate: 2.87% to 5.04%

State sales tax rate: 5.6%

Local income tax rate: None

Local sales tax rate: 1.8% plus 0.7% county rate

Property tax rate: Varies by school district. The 2004 average was $16.95 per $100 of assessed valuation

Economic Information: Greater Phoenix Economic Council, Two North Central Ave., Ste. 2500, Phoenix, AZ 85004; telephone (602)256-7700 or (800)421-4732; email info@gpec.org

■ Education and Research

Elementary and Secondary Schools

A total of 58 separate school districts serve the entire Maricopa County. The city of Phoenix is home to 325 public schools in 30 school districts along with more than 200 charter and private schools. The Greater Phoenix area has an extensive magnet school program with an emphasis on specialized course work in career fields such as aeronautics and aerospace, agri-business, and computer studies, among others.

The following is a summary of data regarding the 30 separate school districts within the city; aggregate data below is from the 2005–2006 school year.

Total enrollment: 731,577

Number of facilities

elementary schools: 95
junior high/middle schools: 32
senior high schools: 67
other: 0

Student/teacher ratio: 22:1

Teacher salaries (2005–06)

elementary median: $32,680
junior high/middle median: $37,430
secondary median: $37,020

Funding per pupil: $8,175

More than 80 private elementary and high schools are also located in Phoenix, providing alternative educational services.

Public Schools Information: Maricopa County Superintendent of Schools, 4041 N. Central Avenue, Suite 1100, Phoenix, AZ 85012; telephone (602)506-3866; fax (602)506-3753

Colleges and Universities

Phoenix has some 80 private technical and business colleges, including the University of Phoenix and Maricopa Community Colleges, the latter being one of the largest higher education systems in the world. The University of Phoenix has garnered the spot as the nation's top private university via its innovative online degree program and more than 190 campuses throughout North America. Both offer undergraduate degrees in a wide range of disciplines and graduate degrees in such fields as business and management and education. Other colleges in Phoenix include Grand Canyon University and two campuses of Arizona State University (ASU), the largest university in the Rocky Mountain area with an enrollment of more than 63,000 students and more than 2,000 full-time faculty, based in nearby Tempe. ASU boasts a strong science orientation; the Phoenix West Campus focuses on upper division and graduate courses.

Libraries and Research Centers

The Phoenix Public Library system consists of the main branch downtown and 16 branches located throughout the city. Located in 280,000 square feet, the central library's collection numbers nearly one million volumes as well as magazines, newspapers, tapes, films, slides, and art reproductions. Special collections include the Arizona Room, which features a variety of resources related to Arizona's rich history. The Arizona State Library, Archives, and Public Records also focuses on the state's history and includes law, government, and genealogy holdings. More than 50 special libraries and research centers are located in Phoenix; most are affiliated with colleges, medical centers, and government agencies and specialize in such fields as medicine, business, and technology. Arizona State University's Engineering Center focuses on microelectronics, CAD/CAM, telecommunications, and computer science.

The Translational Genomics Research Institute (TGen) held its grand opening in March 2005 with a 170,000-square-foot facility. The Arizona Biodesign Institute on the campus of Arizona State University is contributing to Phoenix's growth by luring scientists and biotechnological companies to the area. Four modules are set for completion by 2007; the first opened with 250,000 square feet in the fall of 2004.

Public Library Information: Phoenix Public Library, 1221 N. Central Ave., Phoenix, AZ 85004; telephone (602)262-4636

■ Health Care

Along with population growth in Phoenix has come an increased demand for health care services; meeting this need, the Phoenix medical community has become a major industry in the metropolitan area. More than 33,000 medical personnel are employed in the region. Forty-two licensed hospitals, providing in excess of 8,000 beds, serve the Phoenix metropolitan area; more than 2,000 physicians, dentists, psychiatrists, chiropractors, osteopaths, and ophthalmologists attend to health care needs.

The largest health care facilities in Phoenix are the Maricopa Integrated Health System with more than 600 beds; St. Joseph's Hospital and Medical Center, housing some 520 beds; the 549-bed Banner Desert Medical Center; the Barrow Neurological Institute, known internationally for the treatment of neurological disorders; and Good Samaritan Regional Medical Center, with more than 650 beds. In 2000 a bone marrow transplant program for children was launched after Phoenix Children's Hospital Foundation supplied a grant to underwrite the salary costs for a physician who specializes in pediatric bone marrow transplants.

■ Recreation

Sightseeing

A visitor to the Phoenix metropolitan area will find many sights and attractions, some of them related to frontier history and the natural beauty of Salt River Valley. A principal attraction in Phoenix since 1939 is the Desert Botanical Garden on 50 acres of Papago Park, containing 10,000 desert plants that represent half of the 1,800 existing species of cactus. Also located in Papago Park is the Phoenix Zoo, a privately funded, non-profit zoo, where 1,400 animals are exhibited.

Historic Heritage Square near downtown is a city block of restored Victorian houses preserved as replicas of homes in the late 1800s and converted into museums, shops, and restaurants; a highlight is the elegant Rosson House. In neighboring Scottsdale is Taliesin West, a national historic landmark built as the desert home of architect Frank Lloyd Wright.

Scottsdale is also the site of Rawhide, a replica of a 1880s western town that offers a variety of activities, including stagecoach and burro rides, a petting zoo, and stunt shows. Located in nearby Tempe is Big Surf Water Park, "Arizona's ocean."

Old West-style entertainment, such as stagecoach rides, covered wagon campfire circles, and simulated gunfighter shoot-outs, is available to groups by reservation through various commercial enterprises in the area. Scenic day trips to the Grand Canyon and other sights near metropolitan Phoenix are provided by several bus and airplane charter services. Encanto Park is the home of the Enchanted Island Amusement Park with a variety of rides geared for the younger set.

Arts and Culture

Phoenix has a vital performing arts community, which was enriched with the 1989 opening of the Herberger Theater Center. Located downtown next to the Phoenix Civic Plaza Convention Center and Symphony Hall, the complex is designed to augment existing cultural facilities. The Herberger Theater is used primarily for music, dance, and dramatic performances and includes an art gallery.

The Phoenix Center Youth Theatre, CityJazz, Dance Phoenix, and the Phoenix Children's Chorus call the Phoenix Center for the Arts their home. A variety of theater and drama, including amateur, professional, children/family-oriented, and experimental productions, is offered by companies in the Phoenix area. Founded in 1920, the Phoenix Theatre Little Theatre is one of the oldest continuously running companies in the country. The Arizona Theatre Company, based in Phoenix, is in residence at the Herberger Theater Center and offers about 25 weeks of performances. Other local troupes include Childsplay, Actors Theatre of Phoenix, and Centre Dance Ensemble.

Housed in Symphony Hall, the Phoenix Symphony Orchestra performs an extensive classical repertoire and presents pops concerts with well-known guest artists. Phoenix hosts the state's professional ballet company and other international dance companies. The Arizona Opera also gives regular performances for Phoenix area audiences. Touring artists perform at the America West Arena, Celebrity Theatre, Gammage Auditorium, and the Cricket Pavilion.

More than 40 museums and 150 art galleries in the Phoenix area offer a range of educational and cultural experiences. The Arizona Hall of Fame Museum, opened in 1902, honors people who have contributed to Arizona heritage. Featuring the history of central Arizona, the Arizona Historical Society Museum includes replications of old-time shops and stores. The family-oriented Shemer Art Center and Museum presents primarily local and state artists. The Arizona Science Center provides interactive exhibits for children and adults in such areas as energy, life science, and health. The Hall of Flame Fire Fighting Museum houses the world's most extensive collection of fire-fighting apparatus, equipment, and memorabilia. Anthropological exhibits, fine arts, and historic arts of Native American cultures of the Southwest are specialties at the Heard Museum, which boasts 18,000 works of art and artifacts. The Phoenix Art Museum contains a permanent collection of 17,000 objects focusing on European, American, Western American, Latin American, and Asian arts and costume design.

Festivals and Holidays

Until 2006, the Tostitos Fiesta Bowl Football Classic opened the year with a game between two of the country's best collegiate teams on New Year's Day at Sun Devil Stadium. The Fiesta Bowl, since 2006, has been held at the University of Phoenix Stadium in Glendale, Arizona. Also held in January are the Arizona National Livestock Show (since 1948) and the Parada del Sol Parade and Rodeo.

The Heard Museum Guild Annual Indian Fair and Market takes place in March, featuring Native American culture. Also in March is the St. Patrick's Day Parade and Irish Family Fare. The Desert Botanical Garden's Annual Cactus and Succulent Show and Sale is offered in April. In May the Cinco de Mayo festival celebrates the 1862 Mexican victory over the French with various activities throughout the Phoenix area. The Arizona State Fair, billed as one of the most successful in the nation, takes place in October and November. The fall also brings the Way Out West Oktoberfest. The year ends with the APS Fiesta of Light Parade and Victorian Holiday

Celebration, two December celebrations of the holiday season in downtown Phoenix.

Sports for the Spectator

Phoenix fields teams in all major league sports. The city is home to two professional basketball teams—the Phoenix Suns of the National Basketball Association and the Phoenix Mercury of the Women's National Basketball Association, both of which play their games at the America West Arena. Professional football is represented by the National Football League's Arizona Cardinals and the Arena Football League's Rattlers, while professional hockey is represented by the National Hockey League's Phoenix Coyotes and the East Coast Hockey League's Phoenix RoadRunners. In 1998 the major league baseball team, the Arizona Diamondbacks, were formed and began play at Bank One Ball Park (later renamed Chase Field), built especially for them. In 2001 the expansion team defeated the powerhouse New York Yankees to capture their first World Series crown.

From March through early April, exhibition baseball games are held nearly every day by the 12 major league baseball teams that hold spring training in Phoenix at the Cactus League games. Other popular sporting events are polo matches and greyhound, horse, and auto racing. The Phoenix Greyhound Park features greyhound races year round, and Turf Paradise schedules thoroughbred racing from September through May. The Phoenix International Raceway, built in 1964, boasts one of the world's fastest one-mile oval paved tracks for auto racing, and the Manzanita Speedway holds sprint, midget, and stockcar races.

Annual sporting events in the Phoenix area include professional golf tournaments, such as the FBR Open, with about 500,000 attendees, and the LPGA Safeway International at the Superstition Mountain Golf and Country Club; the Formula One Grand Prix auto race in April; and World Championship Tennis.

Sports for the Participant

Phoenix's consistently warm climate permits such year-round outdoor activities as camping, backpacking, hiking, horseback riding, mountain climbing, swimming, boating, fishing, water skiing, skating, tennis, and golf. In metropolitan Phoenix and the surrounding valley area, there are more than 1,100 tennis and racquetball courts, more than 190 championship golf courses (many designed by golfing legends Arnold Palmer and Jack Nicklaus), and many natural and man-made lakes and waterways with facilities for a variety of water sports. Contained within the city limits is South Mountain Park, said to be one of the largest municipal parks in the world, which offers horseback riding, hiking trails, and a view of the city. Three snow skiing resorts are within traveling distance of the city.

Shopping and Dining

Retail establishments in Phoenix range from large malls and shopping centers—including several downtown—that feature nationally known department stores to small specialty shops offering products made by local artists and craftsmen. Located downtown, the Arizona Center is a uniquely landscaped mall on three acres of land. Close to the center city is Biltmore Fashion Park, a collection of exclusive stores anchored by Macy's and Saks Fifth Avenue. Nearby is Town & Country Shopping Center, considered Arizona's original open-air mall. A variety of shops in metropolitan Phoenix specialize in such items as native American arts and crafts, products made from Arizona copper, leather crafts, and Western apparel.

Restaurants in Phoenix have become more sophisticated with the city's growth and prosperity. They offer a variety of cuisines, including traditional American, Italian, Continental, Oriental, and French fare. Specialties are Southwestern and Mexican dishes with an emphasis on regional foods such as chilies, jicama, local game, and citrus. A popular attraction is Rustler's Roost, a landmark and one of the busiest dining establishments west of the Mississippi. With a scenic mountaintop view of the surrounding area, the restaurant features a mineshaft entrance and walls decorated with the brands of local cattle ranches. Selected by *Food and Wine* magazine as "Distinguished Restaurants of North America" were Different Pointe of View, Wright's, and Vincent Guerithault on Camelback.

Visitor Information: Greater Phoenix Convention & Visitors Bureau, 400 E. Van Buren St., Ste. 600, Phoenix, AZ 85004; telephone (602)254-6500; fax (602)253-4415; email visitors@visitphoenix.com

■ Convention Facilities

Phoenix is a popular gathering place for large and small groups that wish to conduct business in a pleasurable environment. Known for its resorts, Phoenix offers plentiful hotel space (about 10,000 rooms in the central city alone), a year-round warm climate, and a variety of leisure activities. These factors have contributed to an increase in group business in metropolitan Phoenix since 1980. Nearly 40 percent of visitors to the Valley come to attend a convention.

The Phoenix Civic Plaza and Convention Center, with 300,000 square feet of meeting and exhibit space in 43 breakout meeting rooms providing a total seating capacity for more than 29,000 people, has been the city's primary convention facility since 1972. A $600-million expansion was underway in 2007 that will increase the space to 900,000 square feet; phase one was ready for groups in July 2006, while phase two was scheduled to open in late 2008 and be ready for business in early 2009.

Meeting space is also available at Veterans Memorial Coliseum, at Arizona State University, and at area hotels.

Convention Information: Phoenix Civic Plaza and Convention Center, 111 North Third St., Phoenix, AZ 85004; telephone (800)AT-CIVIC

■ Transportation

Approaching the City

Located near downtown, the Phoenix Sky Harbor International Airport is serviced by 23 airlines with direct flights from most cities in the United States and several locations abroad. More than 108,000 passengers are served on a daily basis, which is comparable to the Miami and San Francisco airports. Its importance to the area is highlighted by an estimated $72 million daily economic impact.

Interstate routes into the city are Interstate 10 (the Papago Freeway), entering from the west, and Interstate 17 (the Black Canyon Freeway), entering from the north. These highways join at Van Buren Street and 27th Avenue, becoming the Maricopa Freeway and then forming the Pima Freeway southeast of the city. State Route 89 (Grand Avenue Expressway) enters diagonally from the northwest, joins State Route 60 at Van Buren Street downtown, then intersects the city laterally to the east, becoming the Superstition Freeway. A 20-year "Regional Transportation Plan" was passed by voters in November 2004 to alleviate excessive traffic congestion by building new or renovating existing freeways; 2007 was the earliest projected start date.

Traveling in the City

Travel in the city is facilitated by the simple grid layout. The Valley Metro Transit System provides daily bus service in the metropolitan area.

■ Communications

Newspapers and Magazines

Phoenix's major daily newspaper is the morning daily *The Arizona Republic*. The smaller-circulation *The Phoenix Gazette* is published in the evenings on Monday through Saturday. Among the many other daily and weekly periodicals published in Phoenix are the *Arizona Business Gazette, Arizona Informant, Jewish News of Greater Phoenix,* and *New Times* (which features arts, entertainment, and restaurants). Magazines published in Phoenix include *Phoenix Magazine, Phoenix Home & Garden, Desert Living, Arizona Foothills Magazine, Arizona Highways,* and *Latino Future*.

Television and Radio

Phoenix is served by seven television stations and by two cable television companies. Twenty-six AM and FM radio stations, including Hispanic-language radio, also broadcast in Phoenix.

Media Information: *The Arizona Republic,* 200 E. Van Buren St., Phoenix, AZ 85004; telephone (602)444-8000; toll-free (800)331-9303

Phoenix Online

The Arizona Republic. Available www.azcentral .com/arizonarepublic

Arizona School Report Cards. Available www.ade .state.az.us/srcs

City of Phoenix Home Page. Available www.ci .phoenix.az.us

Greater Phoenix Convention & Visitors Bureau . Available www.phoenixcvb.com

Greater Phoenix Economic Council. Available www .gpec.org

Phoenix Museum of History. Available www.pmoh .org

Phoenix Public Library. Available www .phoenixpubliclibrary.org

BIBLIOGRAPHY

Bartlett, Michael H., and Thomas M. Kolaz, *Archaeology in the City: A Hohokam Village in Phoenix, Arizona* (Tucson, AZ: University of Arizona Press, 1986)

Booth-Clibborn, Edward, ed., *PHX: Phoenix 21st Century City* (London: Booth Clibborn Editions, 2006)

Hait, Pam, *Shifra Stein's Day Trips from Greater Phoenix, Tucson, and Flagstaff* (Charlotte, NC: East Woods Press, 1986)

Scottsdale

■ The City in Brief

Founded: 1888 (incorporated 1951)

Head Official: Mayor Mary Manross (NP) (since 2000)

City Population
> 1980: 88,622
> 1990: 130,099
> 2000: 202,705
> 2006 estimate: 231,127
> Percent change, 1990–2000: 55.8%
> U.S. rank in 1980: 141st
> U.S. rank in 1990: 139th
> U.S. rank in 2000: 99th (State rank: 5th)

Metropolitan Area Population
> 1980: 1,509,175
> 1990: 2,238,480
> 2000: 3,251,876
> 2006 estimate: Not reported
> Percent change, 1990–2000: 45.3%
> U.S. rank in 1980: 26th
> U.S. rank in 1990: 20th
> U.S. rank in 2000: 14th

Area: 184.5 square miles (2000)

Elevation: 1,250 feet above sea level

Average Annual Temperature: 70.3° F

Average Annual Precipitation: 7.05 inches

Major Economic Sectors: services, wholesale and retail trade, government

Unemployment Rate: 3.0% (June 2007)

Per Capita Income: $41,737 (2005)

2005 FBI Crime Index Property: 7,733

2005 FBI Crime Index Violent: 465

Major Colleges and Universities: Scottsdale Community College

Daily Newspaper: *Scottsdale Tribune*

■ Introduction

Scottsdale is a popular winter vacation mecca in the area of Arizona known as the "Valley of the Sun." A tiny farming community of 2,000 people covering only one square mile in 1951, Scottsdale has become a vibrant city of more than 200,000 residents encompassing nearly 200 square miles. Its many golf courses and resorts attract visitors from around the world. Art galleries abound amid the towering palm trees, purple shadowed mountains, and pastel landscapes. The city boasts more than 300 sunny days per year. The lively restaurants, nightclubs, and cultural and sporting events add a metropolitan touch, yet cowboy ranches and Indian reservations are a brief ride away. In addition to its booming tourism industry, Scottsdale has become a diverse high technology center and is becoming recognized as a leader in health care and medical research. It offers a vast array of recreational activities including biking, hiking, white water rafting, horseback riding, and ballooning. The arts are flourishing in the city, which has its own symphony orchestra and more art showcases per capita than almost any other world city.

■ Geography and Climate

Scottsdale is located in central Arizona, just northeast of Phoenix. With an area of more than 184 square miles, the distance between the most extreme northern and southern points in Scottsdale is about 30 miles; the distance between the farthest east and west points is over 10 miles. Scottsdale enjoys more sunshine than any other area in the United States. Low humidity year-round makes even high temperatures comfortable. Most of the yearly rainfall occurs July through September and December through March.

Area: 184.5 square miles (2000)

Elevation: 1,250 feet above sea level

Average Temperature: 70.3° F

Average Annual Precipitation: 7.05 inches

■ History

Irrigation Leads to Thriving Agriculture Industry

Prior to its founding, the Scottsdale area was made up of barren desert lands, distinguished only by the intricate canals of the Hohokam Indians.

Scottsdale was founded in 1888 by U.S. Army Chaplain Winfield Scott, a Baptist minister from New York. That same year the construction of the Arizona Canal, which provided irrigation to a wide geographic area, was completed by Frank Murphy. Winfield Scott and his brother, George Washington Scott, who shared a dream of developing a thriving town in the desert, first grew citrus and other fruits, peanuts, and sweet potatoes on their land.

Air Quality Attracts Settlers, Manufacturers, Artists

Early settlers included people searching for better health and others who were attracted by the fresh desert air. History shows that many of these people were culturally-minded and nurtured the arts from the beginning. The city was first called Orangedale because of the orange orchards along Camelback Mountain, but the name was changed to Scottsdale in 1894 in honor of its founder.

From 1894 through the 1940s Paradise Valley ranchers drove their cattle through the city each spring and fall on their way to the stockyards or the train depot at Tempe, where the cattle were shipped to market.

Modern development began after World War II when Motorola opened a plant in Scottsdale, the first of many electronics manufacturing plants to locate in the area. Artists and crafts persons also became attracted to the city, and the population grew from 2,000 people in 1950 to 10,000 people by 1960. By 1965 the city had grown to 55,000 residents. The city was incorporated in 1951 and received its city charter in 1961.

Through the 1960s the city preserved an Old West look of wood buildings and quaintly lettered signs, calling itself "the West's most Western town." As the "Old West" theme became less prominent, the city began billing itself as the "Arts Capital of the Southwest."

Galleries shared the avenues with western wear stores, and the magnificent Scottsdale Center for the Arts was built, permitting year-round exhibits and concerts for residents and visitors.

Scottsdale's area was greatly increased by the annexation of territory north of the city in the 1980s. A great part of this area is made up of uninhabited desert and hilly land, much of which is maintained in its natural state. Although manufacturing remains the state's largest employer, tourism is now the city's major industry.

In recent years Scottsdale has spent almost $4 million on the renovation of the downtown area with new landscaping, entrances, signage and public art, making it a most appealing desert oasis.

Historical Information: Scottsdale Historical Society, 333 Scottsdale Mall, Scottsdale, AZ 85251; telephone (480)945-4499

■ Population Profile

Metropolitan Area Residents

    1980: 1,509,175
    1990: 2,238,480
    2000: 3,251,876
    2006 estimate: Not reported
    Percent change, 1990–2000: 45.3%
    U.S. rank in 1980: 26th
    U.S. rank in 1990: 20th
    U.S. rank in 2000: 14th

City Residents

    1980: 88,622
    1990: 130,099
    2000: 202,705
    2006 estimate: 231,127
    Percent change, 1990–2000: 55.8%
    U.S. rank in 1980: 141st
    U.S. rank in 1990: 139th
    U.S. rank in 2000: 99th (State rank: 5th)

Density: 1,096 people per square mile (2000)

Racial and ethnic characteristics (2005)

    White: 197,519
    Black: 3,397
    American Indian and Alaska Native: 1,481
    Asian: 6,176
    Native Hawaiian and Pacific Islander: 0
    Hispanic or Latino (may be of any race): 17,079
    Other: 3,417

Percent of residents born in state: 18.3% (2000)

Photo courtesy of City of Scottsdale Downtown Group.

Age characteristics (2005)

Population under 5 years old: 15,216
Population 5 to 9 years old: 13,191
Population 10 to 14 years old: 10,594
Population 15 to 19 years old: 9,715
Population 20 to 24 years old: 9,849
Population 25 to 34 years old: 28,386
Population 35 to 44 years old: 32,305
Population 45 to 54 years old: 33,915
Population 55 to 59 years old: 14,556
Population 60 to 64 years old: 13,249
Population 65 to 74 years old: 18,896
Population 75 to 84 years old: 11,613
Population 85 years and older: 4,448
Median age: 41.2 years

Births (2006, MSA)

Total number: 66,478

Deaths (2006, MSA)

Total number: 26,082

Money income (2005)

Per capita income: $41,737
Median household income: $60,057
Total households: 95,150

Number of households with income of...

less than $10,000: 4,159
$10,000 to $14,999: 3,941
$15,000 to $24,999: 10,209
$25,000 to $34,999: 8,858
$35,000 to $49,999: 13,605
$50,000 to $74,999: 16,118
$75,000 to $99,999: 10,624
$100,000 to $149,999: 13,151
$150,000 to $199,999: 6,256
$200,000 or more: 8,229

Percent of families below poverty level: 12.7% (2005)

2005 FBI Crime Index Property: 7,733

2005 FBI Crime Index Violent: 465

Municipal Government

Scottsdale's government consists of a mayor and six city council members elected at large who serve staggered four-year terms. The council appoints a city manager, city clerk, city treasurer, city attorney, and city judge.

Head Official: Mayor Mary Manross (NP) (since 2000; current term expires June 2008)

Total Number of City Employees: 2,699 (both full and part-time, 2006)

City Information: City of Scottsdale, 3939 N. Drinkwater Blvd., Scottsdale, AZ 85251-4468; telephone (480)312-6500

Economy

Major Industries and Commercial Activity

Tourism is Scottsdale's major industry and largest employer, providing jobs to some 40 percent of the city's workers. Today, Scottsdale is home to more than 60 hotels and resorts with a combined total of more than 12,000 rooms. The city is also home to numerous high-technology firms such as a division of Motorola and JDA Software Group. In addition, it is the location for a number of regional and national corporate headquarters.

Aviation is one of the fastest growing sectors of the Arizona economy. The Scottsdale Airport/Airpark was begun in the 1960s as a fully planned facility specifically designed to meet the needs of employers with air transportation requirements. By the mid-2000s, the Airport/Airpark had become one of Scottsdale's top employment centers, with nearly 50,000 people employed in retail, service, technological, and manufacturing industries. The Airpark houses some 2,500 businesses in all with a combined economic impact of nearly $3 billion annually. In 2007, the Scottsdale Chamber of Commerce sought as a long-term objective to develop a position on and strategy for the direction of the Scottsdale Airport/Airpark.

Items and goods produced: electronics, apparel, aerial maps

Incentive Programs—New and Existing Companies

Local programs: To encourage commercial development and facilitate the paperwork involved, the city offers developers a "One-Stop Shop" where all the necessary permits can be obtained from one office. The Scottsdale Chamber of Commerce administers The Scottsdale Partnership, which is actively involved in attracting and retaining businesses, offering incentives such as entrepreneurial start-up assistance and free, confidential business counseling. To encourage economic development,

Scottsdale recently began a building permit fee waiver program which has spurred investment by hundreds of businesses. In 2007, Scottsdale was looking to establish stronger relationships and partnerships with the Salt-River Pima-Maricopa Indian community. Also that year, the Chamber of Commerce was outlining a strategy for attracting and retaining a workforce to drive "the new economy," determined by knowledge-based, innovative changes wrought by the information revolution.

State programs: Arizona is a pro-business state. It levies no unitary tax, no inventory tax, no franchise tax, no municipal income tax, and no sales tax on direct sales to the state or federal government. It has developed targeted incentives to encourage the recruitment of desirable new businesses and to encourage the growth of existing businesses.

Job training programs: A workforce recruitment and job training program is administered by the state and provides training and retraining for specific employment opportunities with new and expanding businesses and businesses undergoing economic conversion. Scottsdale Community College offers training classes for local businesses ranging from nursing to the hospitality industry, to computer operations and other skills.

Development Projects

Groundbreaking began in 2000 on the $250 million Scottsdale Waterfront project, a retail, dining, entertainment, office, and residential complex planned on 12 acres southwest of Scottsdale and Camelback roads on the north side of the Arizona Canal. The development was scheduled to be home to the Fiesta Bowl headquarters and museum; five acres was to consist of public open space that will feature an outdoor amphitheater, recreation paths along the canal, and public art. Phase One of the project (retail, office, and restaurants) was completed and opened in 2005; Phase Two (residential towers) was due to be completed in 2007; and Phase Three (hotel, residential, and office) was under design/review as of 2006.

Another public development project would reroute the waterfront sanitary sewer line. The city selected an engineering firm to analyze the situation and propose solutions, but as of July 2007, no timeline for construction had been set. However, the city designated $2 million for the project.

In 2004, the City of Scottsdale, Arizona State University, and the ASU Foundation entered into a partnership to develop the ASU Scottsdale Center for New Technology and Innovation on 42 acres of land that was the former site of the Los Arcos Mall. The city agreed to purchase the site, called "SkySong," from the ASU Foundation for $41.5 million with the provision that the site would be available to the ASU Foundation to develop the ASU Scottsdale Center. The Center is designed to focus on technology commercialization, entrepreneurship, and business development. When completed in 2009, the

Center is expected to provide approximately 4,000 jobs and a return of approximately $150 million in direct revenues to the city.

Economic Development Information: Scottsdale Chamber of Commerce, 4725 N. Scottsdale Rd. #210, Scottsdale, AZ 85251-4498; telephone (480)355-2700; fax (480)355-2710

Commercial Shipping

Air freight is handled at Phoenix Sky Harbor International Airport, a 20-minute drive from downtown Scottsdale. Arizona is crisscrossed by five U.S. interstate highways and by a growing system of state roadways. The interstates permit rapid motor freight delivery because of their by-pass features, no slowdown in the metro areas, and no toll roads or toll bridges. Numerous general interstate and transcontinental truck lines serve the city and state. Although there are no railroads in Scottsdale's city limits, the Southern Pacific and the Santa Fe lines connect in adjacent Tempe.

Labor Force and Employment Outlook

Scottsdale's labor force offers a complex blend of skills, abilities, and experience levels, and more than 100,000 highly educated and skilled workers. Scottsdale's economic base is primarily supported by the hospitality and tourism industries; other supports are business, professional and financial services, healthcare, retail, electronics, and corporate headquarters.

The following is a summary of data regarding the Phoenix-Mesa-Scottsdale metropolitan area labor force, 2006 annual averages.

Size of nonagricultural labor force: 1,894,600

Number of workers employed in . . .

    construction and mining: 187,400
    manufacturing: 140,300
    trade, transportation and utilities: 379,500
    information: 32,900
    financial activities: 154,200
    professional and business services: 320,600
    educational and health services: 195,300
    leisure and hospitality: 180,700
    other services: 73,000
    government: 230,700

Average hourly earnings of production workers employed in manufacturing: $15.37

Unemployment rate: 3.0% (June 2007)

Largest employers (2006)	*Number of employees*
Scottsdale Healthcare	4,473
Mayo Clinic Scottsdale	4,000
General Dynamics- Decision Systems	3,600
Scottsdale Unified School District	2,700
Caremark/CVS	2,700
City of Scottsdale	1,700
The Phoenician	1,700
DMS Direct Marketing	1,500
Scottsdale Community College	1,327
Rural/Metro Corporation	1,200
The Vanguard Group	1,118
Scottsdale Fairmont Princess	1,080

Cost of Living

The cost of living in the Phoenix metropolitan area, of which Scottsdale is a part, is slightly above the national average.

2007 (1st quarter) ACCRA Average House Price: $325,251

2007 (1st quarter) ACCRA Cost of Living Index: 101.9

State income tax rate: 2.87% to 5.04%

State sales tax rate: 5.6%

Local income tax rate: None

Local sales tax rate: 1.65%

Property tax rate: $9.30 per $100 of assessed value for a Scottsdale resident living within the Scottsdale Unified School District (2004)

Economic Information: Scottsdale Chamber of Commerce, 4725 N. Scottsdale Rd. #210, Scottsdale, AZ 85251-4498; telephone (480)355-2700; fax (480)355-2710

■ Education and Research

Elementary and Secondary Schools

The Scottsdale Unified School District (SUSD) consistently receives outstanding support from city voters. Its high school students rate high on the SAT and ACT tests. The district offers special education services for all handicapped children, including programs for those that are moderately and severely handicapped, which are strategically located throughout the district. An English-as-a-Second Language program is available to help children who are limited in their ability to speak English. All of the district's elementary schools offer some type of on-campus after-school program. Elementary and middle school students with high academic ability are tested for participation in the district's gifted program. Desert Mountain High School offers the International Baccalaureate (IB) program to qualified students. The accelerated courses across all content areas allow students to complete pre-university work for college credit. Sierra Vista Academy, opened in 2003, is a transitional school for grades 4 through 12 that offers a non-traditional curriculum to students who have not experienced academic success in the traditional learning environment. As of 2007, the SUSD had more excelling schools than any other Arizona school district.

The following is a summary of data regarding the Scottsdale Unified School District as of the 2005–2006 school year.

Total enrollment: 26,000

Number of facilities

elementary schools: 20
junior high/middle schools: 7
senior high schools: 5
other: 1

Student/teacher ratio: 22:1

Teacher salaries (2005–06)

elementary median: $32,680
junior high/middle median: $37,430
secondary median: $37,020

Funding per pupil: $6,110

The Scottsdale/Paradise Valley area has a number of private academies, college prep, charter day, and child-care schools, including the nationally known Judson School and P.A.L.S. Play and Learn Schools.

Public Schools Information: Scottsdale Public Schools, 3811 North 44th Street, Phoenix, AZ 85018; telephone (480)484-6100

Colleges and Universities

Scottsdale Community College is part of the Maricopa Community College system, one of the largest such systems in the country. It offers an extensive selection of educational programs including associate's degrees and technical degrees. The college provides training classes for local businesses, continuing education courses, and community service programs. Ottawa University, based in Kansas, has one of several satellite campuses in Scottsdale; it is designed to meet the higher educational needs of adults with jobs and/or family responsibilities. Also located in Scottsdale are Phoenix Seminary, the

Scottsdale Culinary Institute, Scottsdale Artists School, and the Frank Lloyd Wright School of Architecture/Taliesin West.

Students in Scottsdale also have access to nearby institutions: Arizona State University, located in adjacent Tempe; Southwest College of Naturopathic Medicine & Health Sciences; and the University of Phoenix.

Libraries and Research Centers

The Scottsdale Public Library System, established in 1960, includes one main library and three branch libraries, two of which are shared-use facilities located on the campuses of Desert Mountain Schools and Desert Mountain High School. The library has more than 800,000 items and 700 periodical subscriptions. The library system has a computer network of more than 200 terminals, almost all of which provide direct access to the Internet. The libraries within the system are the Civic Center Library, Mustang Library, Palomino Library (at Desert Mountain High School), and Arabian Library (on the campus of Desert Canyon Schools). The new Arabian Library, an $8.7 million stand-alone facility in McDowell Mountain Ranch Park, was scheduled to be completed in August 2007.

At the Samuel C. Johnson Medical Research Building on the grounds of Mayo Clinic Scottsdale, scientists study molecular genetics, molecular immunology and chemistry, and molecular and cell biology. The Mayo Clinic Collaborative Research Building, a 110,000-square-foot biomedical research facility, was completed in 2005.

Public Library Information: Civic Center Library (Main Library), 3839 N. Drinkwater Blvd., Scottsdale, AZ 85251-4467; telephone (480)312-7323

■ Health Care

Scottsdale offers the services of more than 1,000 doctors and has a full range of medical services available. The largest health care providers are Scottsdale Healthcare and Mayo Clinic Scottsdale. Since its inception in 1962 as the City Hospital of Scottsdale, Scottsdale Healthcare has grown to include three campuses, two hospitals, and outpatient centers. Scottsdale Healthcare offers one of the busiest Level 1 trauma centers in the state, as well as outpatient surgery, cardiology and oncology services, a diabetes center, and weight reduction surgery.

Mayo Clinic Scottsdale, with more than 330 physicians, provides health care in 65 medical and surgical specialties and programs. The Mayo Clinic Hospital provides inpatient care as well as emergency rooms and urgent care services.

■ Recreation

Sightseeing

Scottsdale celebrates the life of the West through a variety of attractions. Old Scottsdale hearkens back to pioneer days with its wooden sidewalks, blacksmith shop, mission, church, and the 1909 Little Red School House, now home to the Scottsdale Historical Society Museum. Rawhide Wild West Town is the state's largest western theme attraction, with a replica of a frontier town, stagecoach and burro rides, gunfights, petting ranch, museum, gold panning, and country music and food. Rawhide closed at the Scottsdale location in 2005 and reopened 35 miles from North Scottsdale. West-World of Scottsdale is a 120-acre equestrian center and special events facility. Many local companies offer trips via jeep, covered wagon, helicopter, and air balloon to the mountains, desert, and canyons surrounding Scottsdale. Day trips can be arranged to Kinishba and Tuzigoot or Canyon de Chelly, which are prehistoric pueblo villages. In Verde Valley, the five-story Montezuma Castle National Monument is a twelfth-century cliff dwelling carved into solid rock by the Sinagua Indians.

Arts and Culture

Scottsdale is a nationally recognized art mecca with more than 125 art galleries, the Scottsdale Center for the Arts, the Scottsdale Artists School, and a variety of public artworks, primarily downtown. Scottsdale has an "ArtWalk" every Thursday night that begins at the Scottsdale Center for the Arts; it offers an opportunity to meet artists and observe their work. Cosanti, an Arizona Historic Site, is a unique complex of concrete structures designed and constructed by Paolo Soleri. Tours of where Soleri Windbells are made and sold are offered. Taliesin West/Frank Lloyd Wright Foundation is an architectural masterpiece and Wright's former home and studio. The Scottsdale Celebration of Fine Art features more than 100 fine artists and crafts persons from across the country. The Scottsdale Museum of Contemporary Art, located in the city's Old Town district, houses modern and contemporary works from around the world. The House of Broadcasting, Inc. celebrates Arizona's radio and television history.

Other museums of interest in Scottsdale include the Buffalo Museum of America, with collections relating to the buffalo, and the Heard Museum North, focusing on Native American artists.

Scottsdale's showcase for the performing arts is the Scottsdale Center for the Arts, where symphonies and Broadway plays are performed. Scottsdale Desert Stages Theatre presents children's, main stage, and professional productions. The newly renovated Theatre 4301 presents live theatre in an intimate setting.

Festivals and Holidays

Scottsdale's annual Barrett-Jackson Classic Car Auction in January is one of the largest in the world. Indian Artists of America showcases 125 of the country's premier talents in January. In February, the Parada del Sol includes a rodeo and ends with the world's largest "horse-drawn parade." Also in February, the Scottsdale Arabian Horse Show—one of the world's largest all-Arabian horse shows—attracts Arabian horse breeders and buyers from around the world.

The Festival of the West, a three-day celebration of cowboy life at Rawhide each March, features western film and television stars, western antiques, western art and music, cowboy poetry, and other events. Also in March, the Scottsdale Arts Festival showcases the work of nearly 200 nationally acclaimed artists.

The Culinary Arts Festival in April showcases local and nationally-known chefs. Scottsdale celebrates the holiday season with the Tree Lighting and Concert at the Scottsdale Mall in December, and with displays featuring more than 100,000 holiday lights at McCormick-Stillman Railroad Park.

Sports for the Spectator

Although Scottsdale fields no major league sports teams, sports fans have easy access to events in Phoenix. Scottsdale is the spring training home of the San Francisco Giants Major League Baseball team. Scottsdale Stadium is also one of the playing sites for the Arizona Fall League, where the stars of the future, including those on the team of the Scottsdale Scorpions, vie for a shot at Major League Baseball in the Arizona Fall League competition.

Professional golf has an enthusiastic following in Scottsdale. January's FBR Open Golf tournament is held at Scottsdale's Tournament Players Club; it attracts the Professional Golfers' Association (PGA) Tour's finest players to one of the most respected national tournaments. One of Scottsdale's more unique golfing events is the Scottsdale Celebrity Chef Golf & Spa Invitational in October.

Sports for the Participant

Scottsdale has more than 500 acres of developed park land, more than 35 acres of lakes, some 40 miles of bike trails, and about 200 miles of non-paved multiuse recreational trails. Many of Scottsdale's nearly 40 parks are located within the Indian Bend Wash Greenbelt, a 7.5-mile-long flood control project that uses a system of parks, lakes, and golf courses as an alternative to a conventional concrete channel. Pools and recreation centers also meet the needs of Scottsdale residents year-round. Residents may participate in youth and adult sports and recreation programs.

There are nearly 200 golf courses in the Scottsdale area, including more than 25 public golf courses. The course for P.F. Chang's Rock 'n' Roll Marathon runs through Scottsdale and nearby cities, beginning at the Arizona State Capitol in Phoenix and ending in Tempe. Held in January, the marathon attracts thousands of distance runners due to its flat, fast course and live musical entertainment. Tennis, horseback riding, swimming, rollerblading, and fishing are among the other year-round recreational opportunities available in Scottsdale.

Shopping and Dining

Scottsdale has more than 2,500 retail shops with everything from hand-stitched leather boots to designer fashions. Upscale shopping centers such as Scottsdale Fashion Square, Biltmore Fashion Park, and Borgata of Scottsdale feature retailers such as Burberry, Gucci, Louis Vuitton and Tiffany & Company. Old Town Merchants Association, with more than 150 shops and restaurants, captures the flair of the Old West with traditional and southwestern merchandise. Scottsdale Pavilions is a shopping center that offers mass retailers such as Target, Home Depot, and Best Buy. El Pedregal Festival and Marketplace has courtyard amphitheater facilities surrounded by boutiques, galleries and restaurants. Native American arts and crafts are available at Chief Dodge Indian Jewelry & Fine Arts, Gilbert Ortega Gallery of Indian Art, and Iverson's Indian Arts.

Scottsdale has an excellent selection of first-class dining establishments among its more than 500 restaurants. Notable among them is Mary Elaine's in The Phoenician resort, which has earned the prestigious AAA Five Diamonds award. Ethnic offerings include Southwestern specialties, Italian, French, Japanese, Chinese, Polynesian, Greek, Thai, Indian, and Continental cuisine. Mesquite grills abound, and Western fare served in cookout or ranch settings is popular.

Visitor Information: Scottsdale Chamber of Commerce, 4725 N. Scottsdale Rd. #210, Scottsdale, AZ 85251-4498; telephone (480)355-2700; fax (480)355-2710

■ Convention Facilities

El Zaribah Shrine Auditorium is a multiuse facility with a 12,000-square-foot ballroom, eight break-out rooms, and a stage that can be used for banquets, seminars, and trade shows. Many hotels and resorts provide meeting space within the city. Among them are the Phoenician Resort, offering 60,000 square feet; the Hyatt Regency Scottsdale at Gainey Ranch, offering 43,000 square feet; Marriott's Camelback Inn Resort; and the Marriott at McDowell Mountains. Rawhide Western Town & Desert Cookouts stages banquets. The Hilton Scottsdale Resort & Villas offers versatile meeting and conference space.

WestWorld is one of the most sought-after equestrian show facilities in the country.

Convention Information: Scottsdale Chamber of Commerce, 4725 N. Scottsdale Rd. #210, Scottsdale, AZ 85251-4498; telephone (480)355-2700; fax (480)355-2710

■ Transportation

Approaching the City

Phoenix Sky Harbor International Airport, located about 15 miles west of downtown Scottsdale, is served by 23 airlines with direct flights from most cities in the United States and several locations abroad. Scottsdale is served by Greyhound Bus Lines and Valley Metro (officially, the Regional Public Transportation Authority, responsible for public transit in Phoenix and Maricopa County). Interstate-10, and I-17, U.S. 60 and 89, and AZ 87 are near the city.

Traveling in the City

Scottsdale Road is the major north-south thoroughfare through the city. Scottsdale Trolley is a free downtown shuttle for tourists and shoppers in operation from November through May. Valley Metro operates public transit bus routes throughout Paradise Valley and links to Scottsdale business and residential districts via the wheelchair-accessible "Scottsdale Connection."

■ Communications

Newspapers and Magazines

The *Scottsdale Tribune* is the city's daily newspaper, published in the morning. Another newspaper published in Scottsdale is *Scottsdale Airpark News*. *Scottsdale Times* is a free human interest community newspaper with a humorous slant. Magazines published locally are *American Indian Art Magazine, Document Management,* and *Frank Lloyd Wright Quarterly*.

Television and Radio

Although Scottsdale does not have any television or radio stations within its borders, television and radio stations do broadcast in Paradise Valley, and cable is available.

Media Information: Scottsdale Tribune, 6991 E. Camelback Road, Suite A110, Scottsdale, AZ 85251; telephone (480)970-2330

Scottsdale Online

Arizona School Report Cards. Available www.ade .state.az.us/srcs/statereportcards

City of Scottsdale Economic Vitality Department.
Available www.scottsdaleaz.gov/departments/
Economics.asp

City of Scottsdale Home Page. Available www
.scottsdaleaz.gov

Scottsdale Chamber of Commerce. Available www
.scottsdalechamber.com

Scottsdale Convention and Visitors Bureau.
Available www.scottsdalecvb.com

Scottsdale Public Library. Available www.library.ci
.scottsdale.az.us

BIBLIOGRAPHY

Frondorf, Shirley, *Death of a "Jewish American Princess:"
The True Story of a Victim on Trial* (New York:
Villard Books, 1988)

Tucson

■ The City in Brief

Founded: 1775 (incorporated 1853)

Head Official: Mayor Bob Walkup (R) (since 1999)

City Population

    1980: 330,537
    1990: 415,444
    2000: 486,699
    2006 estimate: 518,956
    Percent change, 1990–2000: 16.7%
    U.S. rank in 1980: Not reported
    U.S. rank in 1990: 34th
    U.S. rank in 2000: 37th (State rank: 2nd)

Metropolitan Area Population

    1980: 531,000
    1990: 667,000
    2000: 843,746
    2006 estimate: 946,362
    Percent change, 1990–2000: 26.5%
    U.S. rank in 1980: Not reported
    U.S. rank in 1990: 62nd
    U.S. rank in 2000: 57th

Area: 194.7 square miles (2000)

Elevation: 2,390 feet above sea level

Average Annual Temperature: 68° F

Average Annual Precipitation: 11 inches

Major Economic Sectors: services, wholesale and retail trade, government

Unemployment Rate: 3.5% (June 2007)

Per Capita Income: $18,813 (2005)

2005 FBI Crime Index Property: 31,299

2005 FBI Crime Index Violent: 5,048

Major Colleges and Universities: University of Arizona, Pima Community College, University of Phoenix

Daily Newspaper: *The Arizona Daily Star, Tucson Citizen, Daily Territorial*

■ Introduction

Traditionally known for its dry and sunny climate, Tucson is gaining a new reputation for high culture and high technology. With record increases in population, the city has become a Southwest center for opera, theater, ballet, symphony, and visual arts as well as the economic and industrial focal point of an area known as the "Silicon Desert." Consistently pleasant weather and a beautiful desert setting continue to make Tucson a popular tourist attraction. Proud of a multicultural heritage composed of Native American, Spanish, Mexican, and Anglo influences, residents call their hometown "Old Pueblo," a name hearkening back to rough and exciting pioneer days.

■ Geography and Climate

Tucson is located in southeastern Arizona, 60 miles north of the Mexican border. Established in the valley of the Sonoran Desert, the city is surrounded by the Sierrita and Santa Rita mountain ranges to the south and the Rincon Mountains rising to 7,000 feet above sea level to the east. With more than 300 days of sunshine a year, Tucson's climate lends itself to a variety of outdoor activities and enjoyment.

Area: 194.7 square miles (2000)

Elevation: 2,390 feet above sea level

Average Temperature: 68° F

Average Annual Precipitation: 11 inches

■ History

Four Governments Claim Tucson Territory

Tucson is an extremely old settlement with a rich layering of history and pre-history. Archaeological excavations have revealed adobe huts, pit houses, and irrigation systems built by the Hohokam tribe who inhabited and farmed the area nearly 2,000 years ago. The Hohokam have since vanished; in fact, their name, meaning "those who have vanished," was given to them by the Pimas, the Native Americans who occupied the site of present-day Tucson when the first white settlers arrived, and after whom Pima County is named. "Tucson" is also derived from a Pima word, "Stjukshon" or "Chuk-son," meaning "spring at the foot of a black mountain."

Since its founding Tucson has operated under four governments: Spain, Mexico, the United States, and the Confederacy. One of the first Spanish visitors was Father Eusebio Francisco Kino, a Jesuit missionary who arrived in 1687. Tucson was officially founded as a Spanish colony less than one hundred years later, in 1775, and the Spanish settlers built the Presidio of San Augistin del Tucson as protection from the Apache. Part of this walled presidio still exists today, and its nickname, "Old Pueblo," is now extended to the city as a whole.

When Mexico won independence from Spain in 1821, Tucson became a Mexican town. In 1853 the United States acquired from Mexico the Gadsden Purchase, a strip of land that included Tucson. Before 1863, when Arizona gained territorial status, Tucson briefly belonged to the Confederacy, then became the capital of the Arizona Territory in 1867.

Tucson played an integral role in the romance of the Old West. The city was the scene of gunfights, brawls, and attacks by Native Americans; neighboring Tombstone was the site of the legendary gunfight at the O.K. Corral. Tucson also participated in the great gold rush when prospectors moved east from California into Arizona. The effects of this migration were lasting, since Tucson became the center of a mining industry that continued unabated into the 1970s.

Healthy Climate Attracts Settlers, Tourists

By the time it became the 48th state in 1912, Arizona was famous for the sunny climate and dry air that made it ideal as a healthful spot where people could visit and settle. In 1920 Tucson became the first city in the nation to have a municipal airport. At the same time, major highways were being built. Tourism became one of Tucson's strongest industries and remains so today. During World War II the city contributed to the war effort when the government established the Davis-Monthan Air Force Base nearby. Tucson has since emerged as a major cultural center and one of the most sophisticated cities in the Southwest.

Tucson in 2007 was the second largest city in Arizona with more than 900,000 people living in its metropolitan area. Public and private sectors continue to join forces to improve Tucson's standard of living and business environment. With an expanding economy based on high-technology industries, modern Tucson aggressively preserves its multicultural heritage and pioneer spirit.

Historical Information: Arizona Historical Society, Tucson Museum, 949 East Second Street, Tucson, AZ 85719; telephone (520)628-5774

■ Population Profile

Metropolitan Area Residents

1980: 531,000
1990: 667,000
2000: 843,746
2006 estimate: 946,362
Percent change, 1990–2000: 26.5%
U.S. rank in 1980: Not reported
U.S. rank in 1990: 62nd
U.S. rank in 2000: 57th

City Residents

1980: 330,537
1990: 415,444
2000: 486,699
2006 estimate: 518,956
Percent change, 1990–2000: 16.7%
U.S. rank in 1980: Not reported
U.S. rank in 1990: 34th
U.S. rank in 2000: 37th (State rank: 2nd)

Density: 2,500.1 people per square mile (2000)

Racial and ethnic characteristics (2005)

White: 331,181
Black: 19,129
American Indian and Alaska Native: 14,848
Asian: 12,782
Native Hawaiian and Pacific Islander: 759
Hispanic or Latino (may be of any race): 206,958
Other: 113,147

Percent of residents born in state: 38.2% (2000)

Age characteristics (2005)

Population under 5 years old: 42,651
Population 5 to 9 years old: 33,599
Population 10 to 14 years old: 34,935
Population 15 to 19 years old: 32,274
Population 20 to 24 years old: 49,848
Population 25 to 34 years old: 81,313
Population 35 to 44 years old: 69,077

David Bean Photography

Population 45 to 54 years old: 59,335
Population 55 to 59 years old: 24,169
Population 60 to 64 years old: 18,418
Population 65 to 74 years old: 31,266
Population 75 to 84 years old: 23,109
Population 85 years and older: 7,368
Median age: 32.4 years

Births (2006, MSA)

Total number: 13,257

Deaths (2006, MSA)

Total number: 7,738

Money income (2005)

Per capita income: $18,813
Median household income: $34,241
Total households: 208,342

Number of households with income of...

less than $10,000: 23,719
$10,000 to $14,999: 17,785
$15,000 to $24,999: 32,698
$25,000 to $34,999: 32,174
$35,000 to $49,999: 37,277
$50,000 to $74,999: 34,250
$75,000 to $99,999: 14,907
$100,000 to $149,999: 11,164
$150,000 to $199,999: 2,337
$200,000 or more: 2,031

Percent of families below poverty level: 14.7% (2005)

2005 FBI Crime Index Property: 31,299

2005 FBI Crime Index Violent: 5,048

■ Municipal Government

Tucson, the seat of Pima County, has a council-manager form of government, with a seven-member council that includes the mayor. All are elected to four-year terms.

Head Official: Mayor Bob Walkup (R) (since 1999; current term expires December 2011)

Total Number of City Employees: 5,933 (2002)

City Information: City of Tucson, 103 E Alameda St., Tucson, AZ 85701; telephone (520)882-7661

■ Economy

Major Industries and Commercial Activity

Copper mining has traditionally been a vital part of the city's economy; in 1976, for instance, one of every 20 Tucson residents was a copper miner. Seven years later, a combination of foreign competition and depressed copper prices forced a dramatic downturn in mining industries nationwide, with the result that only four-tenths of a percent of the working population was employed in mining by the mid 1980s. The early 1990s saw an upturn in the mining industry again. In Arizona the mining industry continues to contribute to the economy, although locally and globally the industry has experienced a slowdown.

At the time of the mining crisis, Tucson and southern Arizona looked to economic diversity. In the 1980s the area experienced economic growth from Davis-Monthan Air Force Base, with more than 9,200 employees, and the University of Arizona, with more than 11,000 employees, as well as growth in the high-tech and service industries, particularly in banking.

Today the Tucson economy is based on the arts, tourism, manufacturing and high-tech industries. Unique because of Tucson's relatively small size is the fact that a ballet, symphony, live theater, and opera call Tucson home. Tucson's dependably dry and sunny climate assures continuing growth in tourism, an industry that employs about 1 in 10 workers in the metropolitan area labor force and brings in well over $1.5 billion annually. Manufacturing activity doubled from the 1990s to the 2000s, and includes such companies as AlliedSignal, Weiser Lock, 3M, Environmental Air Products, Inc., Krueger Industries, Inc., and Raytheon Missile Systems Company. Marked changes have come about elsewhere in Tucson's economic base, however, with copper mining being most deeply affected.

Tucson has actively promoted expansion in the high-technology industry. More than 300 local companies are directly involved in information technology. Other growing high-technology areas are bioindustry, aerospace, environmental technology, plastics and advanced composite materials, and teleservices. It is hoped that these industries will continue to be a catalyst, drawing companies to Tucson.

Another factor in the renewed strength of Tucson's economic base is the building or relocation of major corporations in the area. Industry leaders include Raytheon Missile Systems, IBM, Texas Instruments, Intuit, America Online, and Bombardier Aerospace.

Tucson has become more involved in international trade and has developed close partnerships with Mexico. One development asset in Tucson is the city's proximity to the Mexican border. The city actively encourages the growth of twin-plant or "maquiladora" industries locating part of their operations in Tucson. Increased expansion is predicted in the manufacture of electronics, aerospace, and computer component products.

Items and goods produced: aircraft and aircraft parts, electronic equipment, steel castings and fabrications, flour, boxes, agricultural chemicals, aluminum products, radios, mobile homes, air conditioning machinery, creamery products, beer, liquor, saddles and leather goods, apparel, native American and Mexican novelties

Incentive Programs—New and Existing Companies

Local programs: The Tucson Regional Economic Opportunities (TREO) serves as the lead economic development agency for the greater Tucson area. TREO focuses on promoting and developing the region's industry strengths. They are: aerospace; biotechnology; environmental technology; information technology; manufacturing; mining; optics; plastics and advanced composite materials; and tourism. The Tucson Metropolitan Chamber of Commerce works to promote a favorable business atmosphere conducive to attracting, sustaining, and expanding industrial and service sector employers. Its Business Development Division provides information, counseling, training, and other services. The University of Arizona, one of the top research universities in the country, plays an active role in attracting businesses and encouraging the entrepreneurial spirit in Tucson.

State programs: Arizona is a pro-business state. It levies no unitary tax, no inventory tax, no franchise tax, no municipal income tax, and no sales tax on direct sales to the state or federal government. It has developed targeted incentives to encourage the recruitment of desirable new businesses and to encourage the growth of existing businesses. Innovative programs designed to encourage job growth include the Workforce Development and Job Training Progam, Enterprise Zones, Foreign Trade Zones, and Research and Development tax credits.

Job training programs: A work force recruitment and job training program is administered by the state and provides training and retraining for specific employment opportunities with new and expanding businesses and businesses undergoing economic conversion.

Development Projects

More than $900 million of investment and tax dollars is funding The Downtown Rio Nuevo project, which will add new attractions, shopping, restaurants, infrastructure, office space and residential housing in downtown Tucson. More than 1,100 housing projects are planned or under construction. Other new developments will include parking garages, streetscapes, and enhancements to arts districts and museums.

Economic Development Information: Tucson Metropolitan Chamber of Commerce, 465 West St. Mary's Road, PO Box 991, Tucson, AZ 85701; telephone (520) 792-1212; fax (520)882-5704. Tucson Regional Economic Opportunities (TREO), 120 N. Stone Ave. #200, Tucson, AZ 85701; telephone (520)243-1900, toll-free (866)600-0331; fax (520)243-1910

Commercial Shipping

Tucson is linked to national and worldwide markets via Tucson International Airport, which receives service from major air cargo carriers. The Union Pacific railroad provides freight service; some 40 motor freight carriers ship goods through facilities in Tucson.

Labor Force and Employment Outlook

Tucson attracts 18,000 to 20,000 new residents each year and offers a work force from which employers can draw relatively young and productive workers. Tucson has committed itself, through its educational institutions, to train and retrain potential employees.

The following is a summary of data regarding the Tucson metropolitan area labor force, 2006 annual averages.

Size of nonagricultural labor force: 379,700

Number of workers employed in . . .

    construction and mining: 29,700
    manufacturing: 28,800
    trade, transportation and utilities: 61,800
    information: 7,000
    financial activities: 17,300
    professional and business services: 49,100
    educational and health services: 52,800
    leisure and hospitality: 40,700
    other services: 15,900
    government: 76,800

Average hourly earnings of production workers employed in manufacturing: $13.22

Unemployment rate: 3.5% (June 2007)

Largest employers (2007)	*Number of employees*
Raytheon Missile Systems	11,184
University of Arizona	10,254
State of Arizona	9,927
U.S. Army Intelligence Center and Fort Huachuca	9,119
Davis-Monthan Air Force Base	8,233
Tucson Unified School District No.1	7,419
Pima County	7,290
City of Tucson	5,848
Wal-Mart Stores Inc.	5,625
Phelps Dodge	4,900

Cost of Living

The following is a summary of data regarding several key cost of living factors for the Tucson area.

2007 (1st quarter) ACCRA Average House Price: $284,165

2007 (1st quarter) ACCRA Cost of Living Index: 99.3

State income tax rate: 2.87% to 5.04%

State sales tax rate: 5.6%

Local income tax rate: None

Local sales tax rate: 2.0% (real estate, groceries, and prescriptions are exempt)

Property tax rate: Average $17.00 per $100 of assessed valuation (2003); rate is assessed at 25% of fair market value of a home

Economic Information: Tucson Metropolitan Chamber of Commerce, 465 West St. Mary's Road, PO Box 991, Tucson, AZ 85701; telephone (520)792-1212; fax (520)882-5704. Pima County Treasurer, 115 N. Church Avenue, Tucson, AZ 85701; telephone (520) 740-8344

■ Education and Research

Elementary and Secondary Schools

Pima County has 17 school districts, of which Tucson Unified School District is the largest, with an enrollment approaching 60,000 students. All districts focus on building basic skills. Gifted, honors, advanced placement, English-as-a-Second-Language, computer literacy, special education, extended school year, sports, music, theater, arts, and homebound programs are among the special offerings. Vocational and business programs prepare students for entry into jobs or further occupational education.

The following is a summary of data regarding the Tucson Unified School District as of the 2005–2006 school year.

Total enrollment: 60,000

Number of facilities

elementary schools: 74
junior high/middle schools: 21
senior high schools: 11
other: 0

Student/teacher ratio: 19.9:1

Teacher salaries (2005–06)

elementary median: $36,080
junior high/middle median: $36,230
secondary median: $33,320

Funding per pupil: $6,683

About 35 self-regulating and parochial schools operate in Pima County. These range from boarding schools offering a college preparatory curriculum to schools that provide basic education with religious instruction. Tucson is also home to the Arizona School for the Deaf and Blind.

Public Schools Information: Arizona Department of Education, 1535 W. Jefferson Street, Phoenix, AZ 85007; telephone (602)542-5393; hotline (800)352-4558

Colleges and Universities

Institutions of higher learning located in Tucson include the University of Arizona, Pima Community College, Tucson College of Business, and the University of Phoenix (Tucson). The University of Arizona has 130 undergraduate and 200 master's, doctoral, and specialist programs in 18 colleges and 12 schools. Pima Community College consists of six campuses in southern Arizona offering on campus, alternative-style and online courses.

Libraries and Research Centers

The Pima County Public Library has 24 locations; the Main Library is located in Tucson. The system's collection consists of more than 1.3 million volumes, some 200,000 book titles, and more than 4,000 periodical subscriptions, plus records, films, and videotapes. A special collection focuses on Southwestern literature for children.

The University of Arizona Library holds about 5 million volumes and more than 25,000 serials and collections that include photography, science-engineering, Japanese and Chinese studies and Southwestern Americana. Also located in the city are a number of specialized scientific libraries associated with high-technology industries.

Biosphere 2, located 30 miles northeast of Tucson, was formerly the site of research into global climate change by Columbia University's Lamont-Doherty Earth Observatory. Tours of the inside and outside of the glass-and-steel geodesic structure are available. Research activities in such fields as architecture, engineering, astronomy, geology, geochemistry, minerals and mining, agriculture, fish and wildlife, arid lands and water, biotechnology, immunology, gerontology, sleep disorders, anthropology, Southwestern culture, and international studies are conducted at centers in the Tucson area.

Public Library Information: Tucson-Pima Public Library, 101 North Stone Avenue, Tucson, AZ 85701; telephone (520)791-4391

■ Health Care

Tucson has long had a reputation for its healthful climate. For the past century its warm, dry air has attracted people suffering from such respiratory illnesses as asthma and tuberculosis. The city continues to attract wealthy residents from across Mexico's border who travel to Tucson for health care.

The 365-bed University Medical Center, the teaching hospital of the University of Arizona (with the state's only medical school), specializes in the research of respiratory illness, cancer, and heart disease. Providing health care to residents throughout southern Arizona, Tucson Medical Center (609 adult and skilled nursing beds, 62 psychiatric beds, and 90 bassinets) houses Southern Arizona's Level One Trauma Center. The 60-bed Tucson Heart Hospital offers inpatient and outpatient cardiovascular and cardiology services. Tucson also offers internationally known health and spa retreats and alternative health care centers. There are more than 10 other hospitals serving the Tucson area.

Health Care Information: Pima County Medical Society, 5199 Farness Drive, Tucson, AZ 85712; telephone (520)795-7985

■ Recreation

Sightseeing

The variety of things to do and see in Tucson extends from the heart of the city to the surrounding area. Three historic districts—El Presidio, Armory Park, and Barrio Historico—provide convenient focal points for a walking tour of downtown Tucson. Around El Presidio, the old adobe wall that was part of the original town, are clustered other historic structures, among them restored homes of the city's early settlers and political leaders, as well as an artisans' marketplace housed in an adobe.

Located in the Barrio Historico district, El Tiradito—the "Wishing Shrine"—is one of the nation's genuine folk shrines. A few blocks away, at the edge of the Armory Park district, is the site of the printing office of a Spanish-language newspaper founded in 1878. Other popular attractions in the city include Tucson's world famous zoo, situated in Gene C. Reid Park, and the Tucson Botanic Gardens.

The ideal way to view the landscape surrounding Tucson is to take a leisurely driving tour that winds through miles of scenic Sonora desert, the only place where Saguaro cactus grows, ending at Mt. Lemmon. Covered with stands of aspen, Ponderosa pine, and Douglas fir, Mt. Lemmon offers vistas of the desert.

Other interesting excursions include Colossal Cave, one of the largest caves in the world, and Sabino Canyon, in nearby Coronado National Forest. Kartchner Caverns State Park, home of the world's largest living cave, offers guided cave tours, hikes, and group use areas. Popular visitor attractions are Old Tucson, a western theme park and the site of a television and movie set, and Mission San Xavier del Bac, called the "White Dove of the Desert" because of its striking appearance from a distance.

Arts and Culture

Tucson is the "arts mecca" of the American Southwest, offering a wealth of cultural activities: theater, opera, ballet, and symphony, as well as galleries and museums. The Tucson Arts District Partnership lies in the heart of downtown Tucson and includes the Tucson Music Hall, the Tucson Community Center, and the Temple of Music and Art. Tucson's Arizona Theater Company, the leading professional theater company in the state, has received national recognition, including grants and citations from the Ford Foundation, the National Endowment of the Arts, and the White House Committee on the Arts. Its productions range from the classics to recent Broadway hits during a September-to-April season at the Temple of Music and Art. Off-Broadway shows and musicals are the forte of the Invisible Theatre.

The award-winning Tucson Symphony offers a nine-month season of classical music at the Tucson Music Hall. The Arizona Opera makes Tucson its home, performing a standard repertoire along with less-frequently performed works. Dance lovers can see performances of Ballet Arizona, which is based in Tucson. The Gaslight Theatre presents old-fashioned melodrama. The "UApresents" series at the University of Arizona Centennial Hall brings performances and groups like the Martha Graham Dance Company, the St. Petersburg Ballet Theatre, I Musici,

Herbie Hancock, Forever Tango, David Sedaris, and Itzhak Perlman to delight audiences.

Tucson is home to several museums and galleries. The Arizona State Museum, specializing in the archaeology and ethnology of Arizona, is noted for having one of the most comprehensive southwestern archaeology collections in existence. The Arizona Historical Society houses a museum, research library, and Arizona mining exhibit; the society also administers Fort Lowell Museum and Sosa-Carrillo-Frèmont House. Featuring military equipment, the Fort Lowell Museum is an 1865 reconstruction of the home of the fort's commanding officer. The Sosa-Carillo-Frèmont House, built around 1858, is one of the oldest adobe houses in Tucson and is furnished in original period pieces. Exhibits such as dinosaur canyon, an ocean discovery center and unique arts for kids can be found at the Tucson Children's Museum. The Pima Air and Space Museum features more than 75 acres of different kinds of military and civilian aircraft.

Arizona-Sonora Desert Museum, 14 miles west of downtown, is one of southern Arizona's most popular attractions. It exhibits hundreds of native plants and animals in their natural habitats. The Flandrau Science Center and Planetarium, on the campus of the University of Arizona, presents exhibits pertaining to optical science, astronomy, and space exploration, many of them encouraging visitor experimentation. For those interested in astronomy, the 56-mile trip to Kitt Peak National Observatory to gaze through one of the telescopes in the world's largest collection of optical solar telescopes is well worth the drive. The Tucson Museum of Art specializes in crafts, textiles, furnishings, and fine arts, including pre-Columbian and western American pieces. The University of Arizona Center for Creative Photography offers permanent and changing exhibitions of photographs and is home to 60,000 works by 2,000 photographers such as Ansel Adams, Richard Avedon, and Edward Weston. Tucson boasts an active community of artists and artisans. Local commercial galleries show their work, which includes paintings, jewelry, and pottery.

Arts and Culture Information: Tucson Museum of Art and Historic Block, 140 North Main Avenue, Tucson, AZ 85701; telephone (520)624-2333. Tucson-Pima Arts Council, 10 E. Broadway Rd. #106, Tucson, AZ 85701; telephone (520)624-0595; email info@ tucsonpimaartscouncil.org

Festivals and Holidays

Tucson celebrates its history and multicultural heritage with a variety of activities throughout the year. Midwinter's La Fiesta de los Vaqueros features riding and roping events. The Tucson Winter Chamber Music Festival takes place in March, as does the Annual Wa:k Pow Wow Conference, which brings together southwestern tribes who present inter-tribal pow wow songs and dances. The month of April offers the Tucson International Mariachi Conference featuring a full week of culture, music and dancing. In May Tucson's Mexican-American community commemorates Mexico's victory against France with the four-day Cinco de Mayo Festival. Tucson's patron saint is honored in the Fiesta de San Augustin in August, and in September the Latin community celebrates Mexico's independence from Spain. El Nacimiento, on the grounds of the Tucson Museum of Art, ushers in the Christmas holiday season with displays of folk art. It is followed by Fiesta Navidad, a Mexican mariachi Christmas celebration.

Tucson is the site of other events of interest to both residents and visitors. For several weeks in the winter colored stones, gems and beads are on show at various locations in the city. The Fourth Avenue Street Fair is held twice each year, usually in March and December.

Sports for the Spectator

Although Tucson does not field any teams in the major leagues, there is plenty of action for sports fans. Tucson is home to the University of Arizona Wildcats teams, which compete in Pacific Athletic Conference (PAC-10) basketball and football. The University of Arizona Icecats play hockey at Tucson Convention Center.

Fans of amateur and professional baseball can enjoy a full schedule. Hi Corbett Field is the spring training site for the Colorado Rockies of the National League. The Tucson Sidewinders, a AAA affiliate of the Arizona Diamondbacks, play a full schedule of summer baseball at Tucson Electric Park. Tucson Electric Park is also the site where the Arizona Diamondbacks and the Chicago White Sox have spring training. Greyhound races are held year-round at Tucson Greyhound Park. Stock car races are on view at Tucson Raceway Park, the only asphalt short track in Arizona.

Golf is very popular in Tucson, and major annual events include the Chrysler Classic of Tucson golf championship in February. Ranked by *Bicycling* magazine as one of the nation's top three cities for cycling, Tucson hosts the prestigious El Tour de Tucson cycling event each fall, as well as many tennis tournaments.

Sports for the Participant

Tucson's warm, sunny climate offers the outdoor sports enthusiast weather that rarely disrupts planned activities. The city of Tucson maintains some 125 parks with jogging tracks, bike paths, riding trails, more than 25 swimming pools, 5 municipal golf courses and a few tennis centers. Swimming, boating, and fishing can be enjoyed in public and private pools and lakes. More than 4,500 participants run or walk in the Tucson marathon, half marathon or 5k each December. Surrounding mountain ranges offer a variety of recreational opportunities. Mount Lemmon ski area receives an average of 175 inches of snow and offers 3 months of skiing each

year. In keeping with Tucson's western traditions, local ranches offer horseback riding; and for those who want to step back into the past, there are even opportunities to pan for gold or participate in a cattle drive.

Shopping and Dining

Shopping for necessities or for pleasure can be equally rewarding in Tucson at neighborhood retail centers, regional malls, shopping plazas, and numerous shops and boutiques conveniently located throughout the area. Downtown's Fourth Avenue historic shopping and arts district is a popular destination, with its more than 100 galleries and unusual shops. Many shops specialize in indigenous goods and crafts such as Mexican handicrafts and decorative items, Indian kachina dolls, baskets, pottery, and moccasins. Traditional western clothing, boots, and other leather goods are also available in Tucson.

The city's restaurants are famous for Southwestern cuisine. Local specialties include carne seca, beef that has been marinated in lime and cilantro and then sun-dried; cinnamon chicken; black bean hummus; and prickly pear cactus. Diners can find a wide diversity of other ethnic fare, ranging from Greek to Thai, as well as traditional American food.

Visitor Information: Metropolitan Tucson Convention and Visitors Bureau, 100 S. Church Ave., Tucson, AZ 85701; telephone (520)624-1817; fax (520)884-7804; email info@visittucson.org

■ Convention Facilities

With an expanded convention center and with additional meeting facilities available in many of the more than 200 hotels and resorts, Tucson is emerging as a primary convention and meeting destination in the Southwest. Besides a consistently warm climate and a wealth of leisure activities, Tucson offers more than 16,000 hotel rooms in the metropolitan area.

To keep pace with hotel and resort developments that have gained for Tucson a reputation as an ideal setting for large and small group functions, the Tucson Convention Center offers flexible facilities for all types of meeting and convention needs. The center offers 205,000 square feet of meeting space and 3 exhibition halls as well as a music hall, arena, small auditorium and 8 meeting rooms for groups of 50 to 1,000 people. A spacious foyer and galleria are designed to accommodate pre-function activities.

Convention Information: Metropolitan Tucson Convention and Visitors Bureau, 100 South Church Ave., Tucson, AZ 85701; telephone (520)624-1817; fax (520) 884-7804; email greatmeetings@visittucson.org

■ Transportation

Approaching the City

Visitors arriving in Tucson by plane are greeted by the recently expanded Tucson International Airport, located a few miles south of the city. In January 2005 the airport completed a terminal expansion project allowing TIA to handle seven million passengers in ticketing and baggage claim. A comprehensive master plan provides for even more development over 20 years to accommodate the area's rapidly growing needs and will include a runway relocation, additional runway, expanded passenger areas and terminal complex, as well as additional cargo, corporate and support facilities. Served by 12 major airlines, Tucson International provides daily flights to cities in the United States, Mexico, and abroad.

Principal highway routes into the city are Interstate 10, which runs between Los Angeles and El Paso and passes through downtown on a northwest-southeast axis, and Interstate 19, which originates at the Mexican border and merges with Interstate 10 in Tucson. Amtrak provides train service and Greyhound provides bus service.

Traveling in the City

Tucson, located in a narrow, elliptical valley, is laid out in a grid pattern. The city is essentially serviced by surface roads, which can be congested during rush hours. Some major cross-town roads may suddenly dead end, necessitating a switch to a roundabout route. Numbered streets south of Speedway Boulevard run east-west, and numbered avenues west of Euclid Avenue run north-south. Residential and commercial pockets are scattered throughout the city, which can cause confusion. Drivers should be aware that during rush hours, the center or left-turn lane on major east-west thoroughfares becomes a one-way traffic lane.

Tucson's public mass transit system, operated by Sun Tran Transit, provides service for 60,000 riders each day to major points within the city and the surrounding area, including the airport. Arizona has deregulated the ground transportation industry so that cab fare in Tucson is negotiable. The Old Pueblo Historic Trolley runs between the Fourth Ave Business District and the University of Arizona campus. Future expansion of the trolley will bring the line downtown to the Tucson Convention Center and the Rio Nuevo Development Area.

■ Communications

Newspapers and Magazines

Tucson readers choose from among three daily newspapers: *The Arizona Daily Star* (every morning), the *Tucson Citizen* (Monday through Saturday evenings),

and the business paper, the *Daily Territorial*. *Desert Airman* is a weekly newspaper for military personnel at Davis-Monthan U.S. Air Force Base. Magazines published in Tucson include *Tucson Weekly*, which contains information about the arts and area news, *Tucson Guide*, which publishes *Tucson Official Visitors Guide* and *Tucson Lifestyle*. Several scholarly journals are also published in Tucson.

Television and Radio

Tucson's eight television stations include five network affiliates, two public stations, and one independent; a cable system is also available. Some 20 AM and FM radio stations broadcast from Tucson, which also receives programming from neighboring communities.

Media Information: The *Arizona Daily Star* and *Tucson Citizen*, TNI Partners, PO Box 26767, Tucson, AZ 85726-6767; telephone (520)573-4400.

Tucson Online

The Arizona Daily Star home page. Available www .azstarnet.com

Arizona School Report Cards home page. Available www.ade.az.gov/srcs/main.asp

City of Tucson home page. Available www.ci.tucson .az.us

Metropolitan Tucson Convention & Visitors Bureau home page. Available atwww.visittucson.org

Tucson Citizen home page. Available www .tucsoncitizen.com

Tucson Metropolitan Chamber of Commerce home page. Available atwww.tucsonchamber.org

Tucson-Pima Library home page. Available www.lib .ci.tucson.az.us

BIBLIOGRAPHY

Griffith, James S., *Hecho a Mano: The Traditional Arts of Tucson's Mexican American Community* (Tucson, AZ: University of Arizona Press, 2000)

Hait, Pam, *Shifra Stein's Day Trips from Greater Phoenix, Tucson, and Flagstaff* (Charlotte, NC: East Woods Press, 1986)

California

The State in Brief

Nickname: Golden State

Motto: Eureka (I have found it)

Flower: Golden poppy

Bird: California valley quail

Area: 163,695 square miles (2000; U.S. rank 3rd)

Elevation: Ranges from 282 feet below sea level to 14,494 feet above sea level

Climate: Extremely varied, with zones ranging from subtropical to subarctic; in the main two seasons— wet from October to April, dry from May to September

Admitted to Union: September 9, 1850

Capital: Sacramento

Head Official: Governor Arnold Schwarzenegger (R) (until 2010)

Population

1980: 23,668,000
1990: 30,380,000
2000: 33,871,653
2006 estimate: 36,457,549
Percent change, 1990–2000: 13.8%
U.S. rank in 2006: 1st
Percent of residents born in state: 52.36% (2006)
Density: 231.7 people per square mile (2006)
2006 FBI Crime Index Total: 1,350,137

Racial and Ethnic Characteristics (2006)

White: 21,810,156
Black or African American: 2,260,648
American Indian and Alaska Native: 265,963
Asian: 4,483,252
Native Hawaiian and Pacific Islander: 129,483
Hispanic or Latino (may be of any race): 13,074,155
Other: 6,296,602

Age Characteristics (2006)

Population under 5 years old: 2,672,666
Population 5 to 19 years old: 7,953,831
Percent of population 65 years and over: 10.8%
Median age: 34.4

Vital Statistics

Total number of births (2006): 561,364
Total number of deaths (2006): 236,031
AIDS cases reported through 2005: 139,019

Economy

Major industries: Agriculture, manufacturing (transportation equipment, electronics, machinery), biotechnology, aerospace, tourism
Unemployment rate (2006): 6.6%
Per capita income (2006): $26,974
Median household income (2006): $56,645
Percentage of persons below poverty level (2006): 13.1%
Income tax rate: 1.0% to 9.3%
Sales tax rate: 7.25%

Anaheim

■ The City in Brief

Founded: 1857 (incorporated 1876)

Head Official: Mayor Curt Pringle (since 2002)

City Population
> 1980: 219,494
> 1990: 266,406
> 2000: 328,014
> 2006 estimate: 334,425
> Percent change, 1990–2000: 23.1%
> U.S. rank in 1980: 62nd
> U.S. rank in 1990: 59th (State rank: 10th)
> U.S. rank in 2000: 64th (State rank: 10th)

Metropolitan Area Population
> 1980: 1,933,000
> 1990: 2,410,668
> 2000: 2,846,289
> 2006 estimate: 3,002,048
> Percent change, 1990–2000: 18.1%
> U.S. rank in 1980: 2nd (CMSA)
> U.S. rank in 1990: 2nd (CMSA)
> U.S. rank in 2000: 2nd (CMSA)

Area: 48.9 square miles (2000)

Elevation: 137 feet above sea level

Average Annual Temperature: 70.0° F

Average Annual Precipitation: 11.0 inches

Major Economic Sectors: services, wholesale and retail trade, government

Unemployment Rate: 4.1% (January 2005)

Per Capita Income: $20,794 (2005)

2005 FBI Crime Index Property: 9,512

2005 FBI Crime Index Violent: 1,616

Major Colleges and Universities: None

Daily Newspaper: *The Orange County Register, Daily Pilot, Los Angeles Times–Orange County*

■ Introduction

Anaheim is the largest and wealthiest (with more than $1 billion in assets) of the 34 cities that comprise Orange County. As the home of the world famous theme park, Disneyland, Anaheim is the center of the Orange County tourism industry and one of the top vacation destinations in the United States. Other major attractions in or near Anaheim range from Knott's Berry Farm and the Movieland Wax Museum to Medieval Times, San Juan Capistrano Mission, and the Anaheim Resort, the centerpiece of the city. In 2001, Anaheim completed a transformation of epic proportions, with a $5 billion renovation of its resort areas. As of 2007 it was estimated that nearly 45 million people visit Anaheim and the surrounding area each year. But theme parks are not the only attraction. The city has been working to develop new housing areas and new businesses in hopes that Anaheim will attract not only tourists, but new residents as well.

■ Geography and Climate

Anaheim is located approximately 21 miles south of downtown Los Angeles and 13 miles from the Pacific coast. Anaheim is the second-largest city in Orange County, which consists of 34 cities. The Santa Ana Mountains lie to Anaheim's east. The Santa Ana River, which rises in the San Bernardino Mountains, flows past the southeast of Anaheim to the Pacific. Industrial and commercial areas along with a majority of the residential sections are relatively flat. The newer residential areas are in rolling terrain in the foothills of the Santa Ana

Mountains. Summers are moderate to hot with cool evenings and winters are mild with very little rain. There are only about 38 days each year with even a one one-hundredth inch sprinkle. The region of Southern California, with several fault lines, is susceptible to earthquakes, though most are of a relatively low magnitude. The Santana Winds (or Santa Ana Winds) that typically occur from late summer to spring, bring warm and dry air down from the high deserts to the San Bernardino Mountains and through the Los Angeles–Orange County Basin. These winds are sometimes accompanied by brush and wildfires.

Area: 48.9 square miles (2000)

Elevation: 137 feet above sea level

Average Temperature: 70.0° F

Average Annual Precipitation: 11.0 inches

■ History

City Settled By German Winemakers

Anaheim was founded in 1857 by a group of German settlers who gave it the German name meaning "home by the river." The settlers were part of a group who first came to the United States during the German Revolution of 1848 and settled in San Francisco. Fifty members of that German community decided to move south when they learned about an abundance of cheap land that was once part of a Spanish land grant. The German colonists purchased the 1,165 acres of coastal plains for $2 an acre. Two of the Germans had a wine-making business. Attracted by the area's moderate climate, the settlers decided to make wine production the region's economic foundation. A civil engineer named George Hansen was hired to plan a carefully thought-out community with fences to protect the planned vineyards from roaming cattle. To allow future growth, specific parcels were set aside for construction of a school and other public buildings.

With the introduction of irrigation, Anaheim remained a prosperous wine producing region until the 1880s. During the period of 1860 to 1885, Anaheim wineries produced more than 1.25 million gallons of wine annually. In the 1880s, a blight completely wiped out the vineyards, destroying a thriving business. The orange and citrus industry was then developed and prospered, as did the city of Anaheim. The Southern California Fruit Growers Exchange, which was later renamed Sunkist, was organized in 1893.

The railroad had a positive effect on the city's development. Railroad service was provided by the Southern Pacific Railway, which established itself in the city in 1875. The Santa Fe Railroad followed soon after. The coming of the railroads permitted the city to expand to include other markets. Businesses prospered and the population grew.

Despite earlier failed attempts to become independent of the city of Los Angeles, Orange County was formed in 1889. Beginning in the late 1920s the city underwent rapid industrial development. A huge flood in 1938 caused the creation of a program to control the Santa Ana River, and the Prado Dam was built upstream to regulate the flow of the sometimes violent waterway.

Disneyland Displaces Agriculture as Major Industry

Agriculture remained the principal industry of the city until the mid 1950s, when the legendary Walt Disney chose Anaheim as the site for construction of his world-famous Disneyland amusement park. Millions of people each year are drawn to the area to enjoy this wonderful fantasy world.

The growth of Anaheim as a recreational attraction increased in the 1960s with the opening of Anaheim Stadium—current home of the Los Angeles Angels of Anaheim baseball team and now called Angel Stadium of Anaheim. In 1967 the Anaheim Convention Center was opened. In December 2000, the center was expanded by 40 percent; by adding 815,000 square feet of exhibit space it became the largest exhibit facility on the West Coast. Disney's California Adventure, an additional 55-acre themed park, opened in February 2001. An adjacent Downtown Disney District was created at the same time, offering restaurants, shopping, and entertainment. Continued expansion of this area into the early 2000s has more firmly established Anaheim as the center of the Orange County tourism industry.

During the early 2000s, the city also made progress in attracting new residents and businesses. In the spring of 2004, the city offered a Home Improvement Holiday, through which all residential home improvement permit fees were waived. The result was an estimated $28 million in individual reinvestment in the local economy. In spring of 2005, a similar Business Tax Holiday was established offering free business licenses to new companies locating in Anaheim. About 540 new businesses took advantage of the offer. In 2004 the city approved plans for a development project known as the Platinum Triangle. This project includes construction of a high density, mixed-use, urban environment that could include up to 9,500 residential units, 5 million square feet of office space, and over 2 million square feet of commercial uses. Another mixed-use development, the Anaheim GardenWalk, opened its first phase in 2007. This project included a set of restaurants along Katella Avenue. A set of retail spaces were scheduled to open as a second phase in 2008 and an 866-room hotel was planned for 2009.

■ Population Profile

Metropolitan Area Residents

1980: 1,933,000
1990: 2,410,668
2000: 2,846,289
2006 estimate: 3,002,048
Percent change, 1990–2000: 18.1%
U.S. rank in 1980: 2nd (CMSA)
U.S. rank in 1990: 2nd (CMSA)
U.S. rank in 2000: 2nd (CMSA)

City Residents

1980: 219,494
1990: 266,406
2000: 328,014
2006 estimate: 334,425
Percent change, 1990–2000: 23.1%
U.S. rank in 1980: 62nd
U.S. rank in 1990: 59th (State rank: 10th)
U.S. rank in 2000: 64th (State rank: 10th)

Density: 6,702.0 people per square mile (2000)

Racial and ethnic characteristics (2005)

White: 199,851
Black: 8,542
American Indian and Alaska Native: 1,787
Asian: 41,438
Native Hawaiian and Pacific Islander: 829
Hispanic or Latino (may be of any race): 175,418
Other: 70,983

Percent of residents born in state: 44.4% (2000)

Age characteristics (2005)

Population under 5 years old: 32,016
Population 5 to 9 years old: 25,716
Population 10 to 14 years old: 27,211
Population 15 to 19 years old: 26,977
Population 20 to 24 years old: 27,866
Population 25 to 34 years old: 47,942
Population 35 to 44 years old: 51,000
Population 45 to 54 years old: 40,047
Population 55 to 59 years old: 13,652
Population 60 to 64 years old: 10,731
Population 65 to 74 years old: 13,987
Population 75 to 84 years old: 9,727
Population 85 years and older: 2,611
Median age: 30 years

Births (2006, Metropolitan Division)

Total number: 46,345

Deaths (2006, Metropolitan Division)

Total number: 16,689

Money income (2005)

Per capita income: $20,794
Median household income: $52,158
Total households: 95,617

Number of households with income of...

less than $10,000: 5,335
$10,000 to $14,999: 5,141
$15,000 to $24,999: 9,569
$25,000 to $34,999: 12,105
$35,000 to $49,999: 13,143
$50,000 to $74,999: 20,813
$75,000 to $99,999: 12,422
$100,000 to $149,999: 11,398
$150,000 to $199,999: 3,137
$200,000 or more: 2,554

Percent of families below poverty level: 8.8% (2005)

2005 FBI Crime Index Property: 9,512

2005 FBI Crime Index Violent: 1,616

■ Municipal Government

Anaheim has a council-manager form of government. The four members of the city council are elected to four-year, staggered terms. Council elections are held every two years. A mayoral election is held every four years. The city council appoints a manager who serves as the head of the government.

Head Official: Mayor Curt Pringle (since 2002, term expires 2010)

Total Number of City Employees: 3,707 (2007)

City Information: Anaheim City Hall, 200 S. Anaheim Blvd., Anaheim, CA 92805; telephone (714)765-5100; www.anaheim.net

■ Economy

Major Industries and Commercial Activity

Tourism is the major industry in Anaheim. An ever-growing number of visitors has caused hotels, motels, restaurants, and retail centers to be built to meet their demands. At the time of Disneyland's opening in 1955, Anaheim had only 87 hotel/motel rooms; presently, those numbers have grown to some 20,000. The rise in tourism has encouraged the city to update and add to its facilities. Since being dedicated in 1967, the Anaheim Convention Center has undergone five major expansions, the most recent of which, completed in December 2000, enlarged the center by 40 percent to 1.6 million square feet. Tremendous infrastructure changes in the Anaheim Resort

Courtesy of the Anaheim/Orange County Convention and Visitors Bureau.

district (surrounding Disneyland and Anaheim Convention Center area) during the past few years have included 15,000 new trees, shrubs, and flowers, as well as improved signage. The Anaheim Convention Center was the largest convention center on the West Coast as of 2007.

In 2006, nearly 45 million visitors spent $8 billion in Orange County. Tourism supports approximately 160,000 jobs either directly or indirectly in Orange County. Anaheim/Orange County also hosted more than 1.2 million convention-goers in 2006, who spent $891 million.

Tourism and business have built a healthy interdependence over the years. The city has become more economically diverse with the development of business and manufacturing firms; Anaheim is currently home to more than 15,000 businesses. It is a center of enterprise for multinational firms, as well as regional and local companies. Located within Anaheim are more than 100 manufacturing plants. The city of Anaheim has been successful in retaining some businesses that had considered leaving by offering loans, tax and utility rebates, subsidies, and job-training incentives.

In addition to the Walt Disney Resort, by far the largest employer in Anaheim, top employers in 2006 included the Kaiser Foundation Hospital, Boeing North America, Alstyle Apparel, Anaheim Memorial Medical Center, Northgate Gonzales Supermarkets, Honda Center, Hilton Anaheim, and Long Beach Mortgage Company, Inc.

Items and goods produced: electronic components, electrical machinery, chemicals, guidance and navigation systems, locks, plastics, processed food, aircraft parts, fabricated metal products, communications equipment

Incentive Programs—New and Existing Companies

Local programs: Anaheim offers qualifying firms economic development rates, new construction incentives, and energy efficiency incentives. Anaheim's "Powerful Partnership for Business," comprised of the city's Community Development and Public Utilities departments, creates customized business programs for economic development support. These include Redevelopment Agency loans and assistance, utility loans and assistance, job training, energy efficiency strategies, environmental assistance, fast-track permitting, and financial assistance and subsidies. The Orange County Small

Business Development Center also offers assistance to new and expanding businesses.

State programs: A variety of programs administered by state and federal sources are available to area businesses. A Research & Development Tax Credit is available of up to 15% against bank and corporate tax liability for certain in-house research. An additional 24 percent credit is available for basic research payments to outside organizations. This is one of the highest research and development tax credits in the nation. A Child Care Tax Credit is available for companies establishing on-site child care facilities. A Net Operating Loss Carryover and New Market Tax Credits are also available. A Work Opportunity Tax Credit is offered for employers who hire individuals from certain target groups.

Job training programs: Anaheim's Job Training Program (JTP) offers subsidies of up to 50 percent of an employee's wages for up to six months in order to assist with customized on-the-job training programs that can help new and expanding businesses. The California Employment Training Panel assists businesses through performance-based customized training contracts for new or existing employees. Reimbursement of costs for developing, implementing, and completing training programs may range from $1,500 to $2,000 per employee. The Anaheim Workforce Center offers industry specific customized training, retraining and new hire training assistance, occupational skills training, on-the-job training programs, and employability skills training.

Development Projects

In 2001 a massive $5 billion renovation of the Anaheim Resort District (the greater Anaheim Convention Center/Disneyland area, comprised of 1,100 acres) was completed. The project began in 1994 when the city of Anaheim approved a $174 million Anaheim Resort Capital Improvement Program designed to transform the district into a more attractive, pedestrian-friendly destination. Among the results are a 55-acre themed park called Disney's California Adventure, brought about by a $1.4 billion investment in all Disney properties. California Adventure, which opened in February 2001 and is adjacent to Disneyland, pays tribute to the Golden State. The Anaheim Convention Center underwent a $177 million expansion, completed in December 2000. The expansion increased the size of the center by 40 percent; it now houses 815,000 square feet of exhibit space, making it the largest exhibit facility on the West Coast. Also completed is a $396 million "freshening" of the entire Resort District with landscaping and infrastructure improvements, including the addition of 15,000 new trees, shrubs, and flowers, and improved signage. The Anaheim Resort Transit (ART), which began operating in 2001, in 2007 featured 32 buses and trolleys providing access to all area resorts, attractions, hotels, restaurants, and shops. In the summer of 2005, Disneyland began an 18-month celebration of its 50th anniversary with several new attractions to draw more visitors to the park than ever before.

In 2004 the city approved plans for a development project known as the Platinum Triangle. This high density, mixed-use, urban environment may contain up to 9,500 residential units, 5 million square feet of office space, and over 2 million square feet of commercial uses. The site is strategically located near Angel Stadium, the Honda Center, and other major city attractions sites. Stadium Lofts, including 390 condominium units, a restaurant, and 2,280 square feet of retail space, was completed at the Platinum Triangle site in 2007. Stadium Towers, a 14,185 square-foot retail center has also been completed. At least two more projects, Stadium Park Apartments and Gateway Centre Condominiums, were under construction in 2007. Several others were pending approval or permits.

Another mixed-use development, the Anaheim GardenWalk, opened its first phase in 2007. This project included a set of restaurants along Katella Avenue. A set of retail spaces were scheduled to open as a second phase in 2008 and an 866-room hotel was planned for 2009.

The Muzeo, a new cultural center, was scheduled to open in fall 2007. The Muzeo includes an exhibit hall, museum space, and a history center. It is located in one of the six mixed-use developments of the CIM Group's downtown revitalization project.

In 2007 John Wayne Airport was undertaking an Airport Improvement Program to meet the needs of its passengers. Among other changes, the program includes an update to existing facilities, the addition of a third terminal (Terminal C), additional parking, and the addition of WiFi in all terminals. The first phase of construction to allow room for the new terminal began in late 2006 and was scheduled to take approximately two years to complete.

Economic Development Information: City of Anaheim Economic Development, City Hall East, 200 South Anaheim Boulevard, First Floor, Anaheim, CA 92805; telephone (714)765-4323

Commercial Shipping

The city's transportation access is excellent and is in proximity to several airports, two major ports of call, interstate access, and an extensive public transit system. The Port of Los Angeles, about 28 miles from the city, has 27 cargo terminals and is the busiest container port in the United States. It is designated as a Foreign Trade Zone. The Port of Long Beach, about 25 miles from the city, was the twelfth busiest container port in the world in 2006.

The Los Angeles International Airport (LAX) has 1,000 cargo flights each day. Handling facilities include the 98-acre Century Cargo Complex, the 57.4-acre Imperial Complex, the Imperial Cargo Center, and several terminals on the south side of the airport. The John Wayne Airport has two all-cargo airlines. Freight service is provided by Southern Pacific, Santa Fe, and Union Pacific railroads, which maintain about 30 miles of railroad track in the city. Many major interstate trucking companies are located within the area.

Labor Force and Employment Outlook

Economic development in Anaheim has created thousands of new jobs. As of 2006, 29.5 percent of people employed in Anaheim worked in wholesale or retail trade; 19.5 percent in services; 10.6 percent in manufacturing; 9 percent in construction, agriculture, mining, and fishing; 8.4 percent in finance, real estate, and insurance; 7.9 percent in medical and other health related fields; 5.7 percent in education and social services; 4 percent in engineering, accounting, and research and development; and 5.4 percent in other fields.

The following is a summary of data regarding the Santa Ana-Anaheim-Irvine Metropolitan Division metropolitan area labor force, 2006 annual averages.

Size of nonagricultural labor force: 1,520,100

Number of workers employed in . . .

> construction and mining: 107,600
> manufacturing: 183,400
> trade, transportation and utilities: 270,700
> information: 31,700
> financial activities: 139,000
> professional and business services: 274,800
> educational and health services: 138,900
> leisure and hospitality: 169,500
> other services: 47,900
> government: 156,500

Average hourly earnings of production workers employed in manufacturing: $14.59

Unemployment rate: 4.1% (January 2005)

Largest private employers (2006)	*Number of employees*
Walt Disney Resort	23,105
Kaiser Foundation Hospital	3,660
Boeing North America	3,500
Alstyle Apparel	1,600
Anaheim Memorial Medical Center	1,185
Northgate Gonzalez Supermarkets	1,000
Honda Center	1,000
Anaheim Memorial Hospital-ER	979
Hilton Anaheim	900
Long Beach Mortgage Company, Inc.	800

Cost of Living

The following is a summary of data regarding key cost of living factors for the Anaheim area.

2007 (1st quarter) ACCRA Average House Price: $855,232

2007 (1st quarter) ACCRA Cost of Living Index: 154.7

State income tax rate: 1.0% to 9.3%

State sales tax rate: 7.25%

Local income tax rate: None

Local sales tax rate: 1.75%

Property tax rate: 1.0% of assessed valuation

Economic Information: Anaheim Chamber of Commerce, 201 East Center Street, Anaheim CA, 92805; telephone (714)758-0222; fax (714)758-0468

■ Education and Research

Elementary and Secondary Schools

Anaheim is served by the Anaheim City School District (ACSD), which operates the elementary schools, and the Anaheim Union High School District, which oversees the junior high and high schools. The city is noted for excellent schools offering a full array of learning programs from basic curriculum instruction to college preparation, athletics, and special education. A Spanish-English Dual Language program is available in some schools. The Gifted and Talented Education Program (GATE) is available to students in grades three to six.

All of the schools in the ACSD are on a year-round schedule. Most of them are on a single-track calendar, but a few schools have a four-track schedule. Loara High School and Kennedy High School offer the International Baccalaureate (IB) program. Walker Junior High School has the Middle Years Program, the junior high component of IB. Career Technical Education Programs are offered at several high school campuses. Specialized accelerated academy programs are also available. Alternative education programs include three Continuation High Schools, offering self-pacing schedules, and an Independent Study Program (Polaris High School) through which students meet all of the requirements for graduation but are only required to meet with a supervising teacher for one hour a week.

The following is a summary of data regarding the Anaheim City and Anaheim Union High School Districts as of the 2005–2006 school year.

Total enrollment: 60,000

Number of facilities

> elementary schools: 23
> junior high/middle schools: 8
> senior high schools: 10
> other: 8

Student/teacher ratio: 23:1

Teacher salaries (2005–06)

> elementary median: $61,360
> junior high/middle median: $62,040
> secondary median: $63,410

Funding per pupil: $7,084

Public Schools Information: Anaheim City School District, 1001 South East Street, Anaheim, CA 92805-5749; telephone (714)517-7500; www.acsd.k12.ca.us. Anaheim Union High School District, 501 Crescent Way, Anaheim, CA, 92803; telephone (714)999-3511; www.auhsd.k12.ca.us

Colleges and Universities

Although there are no major universities in the city of Anaheim proper, there are several smaller institutions offering post-secondary education.

The American College of Law in Anaheim offers classes leading to a Juris Doctor degree. The Southern California Institute of Technology offers four bachelor's degree programs through its School of Business and a College of Engineering and Computer Science. The North Orange County Community College District Anaheim Campus houses one of the district's Schools of Continuing Education. The school offers a variety of basic adult education and vocational programs. Associate degrees are offered through Cypress College and Fullerton College, both of which are operated by the Orange County district. Everest College (formerly known as Bryman College) offers career training programs in dental assisting, medical assisting, massage therapy, nursing, and medical billing and coding. The national ITT Technical Institute maintains a campus in Anaheim.

South Baylo University offers master's and doctoral degree in acupuncture and oriental medicine. It is considered to be one of the best schools of its kind in the nation and offers instruction in Chinese and Korean as well as English. The school operates a clinic in Anaheim.

In the greater Orange County area, California State University–Fullerton offers both undergraduate and graduate programs through eight colleges. Chapman University in Orange offers programs in eight colleges, with one of the most popular being studies in film and television through the Lawrence and Kristina Dodge College of Film and Media Arts. The University of California–Irvine is a research university with 14 colleges and schools.

Libraries and Research Centers

The Anaheim Public Library holds over 512,900 volumes, and over 40,000 audio and video materials. The library's special collections include the Anaheim History Collection. The library is comprised of a central library, four branches—Haskett, Euclid, Sunkist, and Canyon Hills—and two bookmobiles. The Central Branch holds foreign language books in Chinese, Spanish, and Vietnamese. Card holders of the Anaheim Public Library system may also borrow books through the Fullerton Public Library, Placentia Public Library, and Yorba Public Library.

Other Anaheim libraries consist of those of local hospitals and companies, including Anaheim Memorial Medical Center, Western Medical Center Hospital, and Boeing Co. The Richard Nixon Presidential Library & Museum is in Yorba Linda, a 15-minute drive from Anaheim.

The Anaheim Research Center, founded in 2002, conducts psychiatric and medical research. The South Baylo University Research Center was established 2000. It conducts research in acupuncture treatments for high risk populations, such as those with cancer or AIDS, in part by providing free services to patients seeking such care. Research training takes place at the Well Healthcare One Clinic, part of the South Baylo University Integrative Medical Center.

Public Library Information: Anaheim Public Library, 500 West Broadway, Anaheim CA 92805; telephone (714)765-1880; www.anaheim.net/library

■ Health Care

Area hospitals boast state-of-the-art facilities and top quality care. Several hospitals are located within the city. Anaheim Memorial Medical Center offers general medical, critical care, and surgical services, as well as centers for specialized care including: The Advanced Endovascular Institute; The HeartCare Center; The Birth Place, Women's HeartMatters, the Imaging Services Center, the Women's Health and Wellness Center, a Pain Management Center, and the MemorialCare Breast Centers. The Safe Place at Anaheim Memorial is the only hospital-based acute sexual assault response center in the county.

The 70-bed Anaheim General Hospital's main hospital campus includes emergency room services, intensive care, an obstetrical unit, radiology, in-patient and out-patient surgery department, telemetry, and a wide range of additional services. The 219-bed West Anaheim Medical Center is another general medical and surgical hospital. The 167-bed Kaiser Foundation Hospital's key services include: general medical, surgical and intensive care; cardiac intensive care; cardiology, neurology, and orthopedics departments; pediatric medical and surgical care; and obstetrics. Western Medical Center/Anaheim has about 181 beds and offers general medical and surgical service in the following areas: acute medicine and critical care; ambulatory care; behavioral medicine; cardiac rehabilitation; emergency care; radiology services; women's and children's health services; and sleep disorder care.

Well Healthcare One Clinic, part of the South Baylo University Integrative Medical Center, offers Western medicine practice as well as treatments including acupuncture, herbal medicine, and massage in taking a more holistic approach to health care.

The Karlton Residential Care Center in Anaheim is a 70-bed faculty for those with Alzheimer's or other related disorders.

■ Recreation

Sightseeing

Anaheim's crown jewel attraction is Disneyland, America's most popular theme park. Visitors can stroll through the park's eight "lands," which together offer more than 60 major rides, shops, and restaurants: futuristic Tomorrowland provides an out-of-this-world atmosphere; Adventureland reproduces the exotic surroundings of Asia, the Middle East, and the South Seas; Frontierland is based on the Wild West; Fantasyland, with Sleeping Beauty's Castle and the It's a Small World ride, is the heart of Disneyland; Critter Country is home to cute woodland creatures; Main Street U.S.A. is based on small-town America of a century ago; New Orleans Square reproduces the atmosphere of turn-of-the-century New Orleans; and Mickey's Toontown is a cartoon playland. Special entertainment, shopping, and dining are featured at Disneyland year-round. Special attractions include Indiana Jones Adventure; Space Mountain and Star Tours, exciting flight-simulation journeys; Splash Mountain, an 87-foot-high log flume ride based on Disney's "Song of the South" characters; Big Thunder Mountain Railroad; and the Haunted Mansion.

In the summer of 2005 the park celebrated its golden anniversary with several new attractions: Buzz Lightyear Astro Blasters, in Tomorrowland, is an interactive game in which visitors join Buzz Lightyear to battle the evil Emperor Zurg; Space Mountain, also in Tomorrowland, was re-launched with new special effects; at Disneyland's Parade of Dreams, a new Main Street U.S.A. parade, spectators can meet Disney characters and watch floats transform into shows; a new nighttime celebration will feature spectacular pyrotechnics; and Disneyland: The First 50 Years provides an exclusive look at the park's 50 years, through artwork, models and design, and film. In 2007 the park opened the Finding Nemo Submarine Voyage, an underwater adventure inspired by the film *Finding Nemo*. This attraction replaces the original Submarine Voyage of 1954, which was based on the theme of *20,000 Leagues Under the Sea*.

One of Disneyland's newest areas is California Adventure. Requiring a separate admission ticket, it is based on the fun adventures offered by California, and is divided into four themed districts: Paradise Pier has classic "Golden Age" amusement park attractions along the beach; Hollywood Pictures Backlot celebrates the movie business; The Golden State is a tribute to California's natural beauty; and "a bug's land," inspired by the film *A Bug's Life* is designed from a bug's perspective.

Knott's Berry Farm in nearby Buena Park, once a small berry farm business, has grown into one of the most popular theme parks in the country. The park, a 150-acre complex with more than 100 rides and dozens of shops and restaurants, is especially known for its thrill rides. Distinct theme areas are Ghost Town, an Old West mining town reproduction; Camp Snoopy, which features special rides and activities for small children; The Boardwalk, a colorful tribute to the Southern California beach culture that features ocean-related rides and attractions; Indian trails, which showcases the traditions and cultures of Native Americans; Fiesta Village, a celebration of Spanish California; and Wild Water Wilderness water park. Special attractions include Montezooma's Revenge, a roller coaster that goes from 0 to 60 miles per hour in just three seconds; Jaguar!, a roller coaster that twists, spirals, speeds up, and slows down, mimicking a jaguar stalking its prey; Supreme Scream ascends 214 feet and then plunges straight down at about 50 mph; and Bigfoot Rapids is a whitewater river raft ride.

In 2007, as part of the city's 150th anniversary celebrations, a new Anaheim OC Walk of Stars was set on Harbor Boulevard by Disneyland's main entrance. Walt Disney was one of the first stars to be honored.

Other nearby attractions include Buena Park's Movieland Wax Museum, where more than 300 lifelike figures of famous movie stars are on view in realistic costumes and posed in scenes from classic movies; and Medieval Times, an elaborate dinner tournament where eleventh-century knights in armor joust and a feast is presented.

The Discovery Science Center, in Santa Ana, houses hands-on exhibits in themed areas: Discovery Stadium, Quake Zone, Dynamic Earth, Air and Space Exploration, and Kidstation. Hobby City is a 10-acre collection of miniature buildings; it includes a doll and toy museum inside a miniature replica of the White House. Nearby Adventure City is a two-acre theme park for children aged 2 to 12. The Mission San Juan Capistrano, 30 miles south of Anaheim, was founded in 1776 and is the birthplace of Orange County. Beautiful and romantic, it is considered the "jewel of the missions." Its Serra Chapel is believed to be California's oldest standing building.

Arts and Culture

The 3,000-seat Segerstrom Hall at the Orange County Performing Arts Center in nearby Costa Mesa hosts world-class performances of symphony, ballet, and opera, as well as Broadway shows; the 250-seat Founders Hall in the Center offers innovative jazz and cabaret programming as well as the best in chamber music. The Center also includes a 2,000-seat Renée and Henry Segerstrom Concert Hall and the 500-seat multi-functional Samueli Theater. The Center is home to the Philharmonic Society of Orange County, Pacific Symphony Orchestra, Opera Pacific, and Pacific Chorale.

Numerous other theaters dot Orange County. Fullerton Civic Light Opera Company, based in nearby Fullerton, is one of the largest musical theater companies in Southern California; their productions are presented four times annually at Plummer Auditorium. The auditorium, built in 1930, seats more than 1,300 and hosts a variety of theatrical productions and community-oriented cultural programs. South Coast Repertory Theatre, in Costa Mesa, is a Tony award-winning theater that presents professional productions of contemporary and classical plays on its three stages. The Grove Theater Center, in Garden Grove, is home to the 178-seat Gem Theater and 550-seat Festival Amphitheater; the complex offers year-round plays as well as participatory events.

The Honda Center is a 650,000-square-foot arena that hosts concerts and family shows as well as being home to the NHL Anaheim Ducks. Pearson Park Amphitheater is an open-air facility that features family entertainment all summer long and the Grove of Anaheim presents comedy and music artists in an intimate setting.

The Anaheim Museum highlights the history of the city's original German settlers, its establishment as a wine and citrus colony, and the early Disneyland days depicted in changing exhibits. Mother Colony House, one of the city's first buildings, showcases antiques and other historical items of Anaheim's earliest periods. Bowers Museum of Cultural Art, in nearby Santa Ana, occupies a landmark mission-style building; its exhibits reflect cultural arts from California and around the world. Bowers features a hands-on children's section known as the Kidseum.

The Muzeo, opened in 2007 as part of the city's downtown revitalization projects, offers an exhibit hall, a cultural and art museum, and a history center.

Festivals and Holidays

The St. Patrick's Day Festival at the Anaheim Farmer's Market features Irish dancers, music, and food. St. Boniface Parish Fiesta in April features international foods, rides, and games. The first weekend in May brings the Cinco de Mayo Fiesta, featuring a soccer tournament, the crowning of a fiesta queen, and a Sunday bilingual Mass, as well as rides, food, and entertainment; the fiesta draws approximately 100,000 people throughout the weekend.

The Greek Festival, also in May, features Greek foods, pastries, music, and folkdancers, and a marketplace with vendors selling a variety of items. The Anaheim Children's Art Festival in late May draws 7,000 visitors annually to its art-and-craft projects in staffed booths. June's Taste of Anaheim offers ethnic food, fun, and displays. Anaheim Hills 4th of July Festival & Parade includes a pancake breakfast, dog show, 5K and 10K run/walk, parade, food and game booths, and fireworks. At nearby Laguna Beach's Pageant of the Masters, famous paintings and statuary come to life through the use of live models and an orchestra each night during the months of July and August. The Anaheim Fall Festival & Halloween Parade in late October features a parade, pancake breakfast, rides, games, and live entertainment. Knott's Berry Farm transforms into Knott's Camp Spooky and then Knott's Merry Farm to celebrate Halloween and Christmas. The Christmas Parade at Disneyland features many popular Disney characters as well as Santa Claus. Nutcracker Holiday, held the first Saturday in December, features musicians, carolers, and a tree-lighting ceremony.

Sports for the Spectator

The Major League Los Angeles Angels of Anaheim baseball team, World Series Champion in 2002 and American League West Champions in 2007, plays its home games at Angel Stadium of Anaheim, a baseball-only facility with seating for 45,050. The Anaheim Ducks, a National Hockey League team owned by the Walt Disney Company, won the 2003 Western Conference championship and the Stanley Cup in 2007. They play at the four-level, 17,174-seat Honda Center. The Honda Center is also home of National Lacrosse League's Anaheim Storm, which suspended play in 2006, and the J. R. Wooden Classic, which features some of the nation's top basketball teams. The National Basketball Association Development League set up an expansion team for Anaheim in the 2006/07 season. The Anaheim Arsenal is affiliated with the Los Angeles Clippers and play at the Arena of the Anaheim Convention Center.

Los Alamitos Race Course, 15 minutes west of Disneyland, features the world's fastest horses in quarter horse, Arabian, thoroughbred, paint, and Appaloosa racing. Costa Mesa Speedway at Orange County Fairgrounds holds speedway races on Saturday nights, April through October.

Sports for the Participant

Anaheim has 44 parks totaling approximately 650 acres. Among them is Oak Canyon Nature Center, a 58-acre natural park in the Anaheim Hills providing excellent opportunities for short hikes. A year-round stream meanders through the park, which consists of three adjoining canyons with four miles of hiking trails. Tennis is available at several Anaheim hotels and the city maintains more than 50 public courts. Anaheim Hills, a public country club, offers a challenging 18-hole golf course in the natural terrain of the Santa Ana Canyons. H. G. "Dad" Miller is a well kept course surrounded by lovely old trees and a natural lake; it was Tiger Woods' home course during high school. Anaheim ICE, the official training facility of the Anaheim Ducks, offers public skating and pick up hockey.

Orange County has a 42-mile coastline filled with public and state beaches. Sailing cruises, whale watching, surfing, and swimming are available at sites along the coastline. The county has a regional trail system consisting of 220 miles of built trails. The 30-mile Santa Ana River Trail is a running/bike path that follows the Santa Ana River in the San Bernardino Mountains. Snow skiing is available at nearby Bear Mountain ski resort. Orange County is home to 39 public golf courses.

Shopping and Dining

Downtown Disney, a 120-acre shopping, restaurant, and entertainment complex adjacent to Disneyland, features one-of-a-kind Disney-themed shops and trend-setting restaurants. It is open to the public, with no admission charge. Anaheim Indoor Marketplace is an outlet mall with more than 200 variety stores. Timeless Quilts offers fabrics and quilting supplies in a 1920s Craftsman house, while Hobby City offers a collection of antique dolls and toys from around the world. South Coast Plaza Village in Costa Mesa offers an immense collection of international stores clustered around a Village Green in an open-air environment. Fashion Island Newport Center, in Newport Beach, is an upscale shopping area with open-air courtyards and covered patios overlooking the ocean; it features more than 200 shops, 40 restaurants, and two movie theaters. Westfield Shoppingtown MainPlace in Santa Ana is another large upscale center, with more than 200 specialty shops and restaurants. The Anaheim Hills Festival Shopping Center offers a variety of stores similar to those found in typical shopping malls.

Dining experiences in Anaheim run the gamut from ethnic specialties such as Armenian, Cajun, Chinese, Cuban, German, Indian, Italian, Japanese, Mexican, Middle Eastern, Peruvian, and Thai to places with unique ambiance such as canneries, gold mines, and Victorian houses. There are more than 60 restaurants and cocktail lounges in the immediate area of the Anaheim Convention Center. In nearby Orange, Watson Drugs and Soda Fountain, established in 1899, has been the set for several movies; it offers burgers and sweets. In 2007 Ruth's Chris Steak House opened, featuring a New Orleans-inspired menu. Also in 2007, the first phase of the Anaheim GardenWalk opened, offering a unique outdoor dining experience for visitors along Katella Avenue. The GardenWalk is home to the Bubba Gump Shrimp Co., a seafood restaurant themed after the movie *Forrest Gump*; the California Pizza Kitchen; the Cheesecake Factory; McCormick & Schmick Grill; and Roy's of Hawaii.

Visitor Information: Anaheim/Orange County Visitor and Convention Bureau, 800 West Katella Avenue, Anaheim, CA 92802; telephone (714)999-8999; fax (714)991-8963

■ Convention Facilities

The Anaheim Convention Center, a sparkling, glass-walled facility, completed a $177 million expansion and redesign in December 2000. The expansion enlarged the center by 40 percent to 1.6 million square feet. The center houses 815,000 square feet of exhibit space, making it the largest exhibit facility on the West Coast. Pre-function lobby space totals 200,000 square feet. There is also 130,000 square feet of meeting space and a 38,000 square-foot main ballroom. The center hosts an average of more than 1,300 events annually, including national conventions, conferences, corporate meetings, trade shows, and a variety of public events such as concerts and home and garden shows. Situated on 53 acres in the Anaheim Resort district, the center is within walking distance of more than 12,000 hotel rooms.

The Disneyland Hotel at Disneyland Resort offers dozens of meeting spaces, the largest one being the 50,000-square-foot Disneyland Exhibit Hall in Magic Tower. There is a banquet hall to accommodate up to 2,000 people and three restaurants. The Marriott Anaheim offers 35,000 square feet of exhibit space, three flexible ballrooms and eleven meeting rooms. Several other area hotels and restaurants offer meeting and banquet spaces.

Convention Information: Anaheim/Orange County Visitor and Convention Bureau, 800 West Katella Avenue, Anaheim, CA 92802; telephone (714)765-8888; fax (714)991-8963; www.anaheimoc.org

■ Transportation

Approaching the City

The main artery running through Anaheim is Interstate 5 (the Santa Ana Freeway), which also connects Los Angeles and San Diego. I-5 links Anaheim with the Riverside Freeway, the Garden Grove Freeway, the Orange Freeway, and the Costa Mesa Freeway.

There are four airports serving the area. Los Angeles International Airport (LAX), located about 31 miles northwest of Anaheim, is one of the top ten largest airports in the world in terms of passengers handled. The airport is served by over 50 airlines with thousands of flights each year. Long Beach Airport to the west is served by four airlines and LA/Ontario International Airport to the northeast supports 12 airlines. The John Wayne Airport in Santa Ana, owned operated by Orange

County, is about 16 miles southwest of Anaheim. It is served by 11 commercial airlines and 3 commuter lines.

Metrolink, a regional commuter rail system, links travelers to activity centers in Orange and surrounding counties; it has two stations located in Anaheim: Anaheim station and Anaheim Canyon station. Amtrak provides railway transportation with a station located at Angel Stadium. Greyhound offers daily bus service into the city.

Traveling in the City

The Santa Ana Freeway traverses Anaheim's downtown running northwest to southeast. The Garden Grove Freeway runs east and west through the city, and the Orange Freeway runs north and south through the city. The Orange County Transportation Authority operates buses daily with about 80 routes throughout Orange County. Anaheim Resort Transit (ART) buses, trams, and trolleys provide connections between hotels, Anaheim attractions, the convention center, shopping, dining, and evening entertainment locations, along nine interchangeable routes. Beginning October 2007 the ART has offered connecting service to the Anaheim Amtrak Station.

■ Communications

Newspapers and Magazines

The primary daily newspapers serving Anaheim and surrounding Orange County are the *Daily Pilot* (circulation 26,725) and the *Los Angeles Times–Orange County* (circulation 983,727), both published in Costa Mesa; and *The Orange County Register* published in Santa Ana. The *Press-Telegram* is published in Long Beach.

The *Anaheim Bulletin, Orange City News, Placentia News-Times,* and *Fullerton News Tribune* are weekly newspapers published in Anaheim. Other weeklies published in Orange County include *OC Weekly,* an alternative press, and *Excélsior,* a Spanish-language newspaper, both published in Santa Ana.

Television and Radio

There are no television stations broadcasting directly from Anaheim. Most local programming and news is provided through Los Angeles stations. Cable television is also available. There are 30 AM and 44 FM radio stations serving the Orange County/Los Angeles area.

Media Information: *Orange County Register,* Freedom Communications Inc., 625 N. Grand Ave., Santa Ana, CA 92701; telephone (877)469-7344; www. ocregister.com

Anaheim Online

Anaheim City School District. Available www.acsd .k12.ca.us

Anaheim Orange County Visitor & Convention Bureau. Available www.anaheimoc.org

Anaheim Public Library. Available www.anaheim .net/comm_svc/apl/index.html

City of Anaheim home page. Available www .anaheim.net

Greater Anaheim Chamber of Commerce. Available www.anaheimchamber.org

Orange County Department of Education. Available www.ocde.k12.ca.us

Orange County Register. Available www.ocregister .com

BIBLIOGRAPHY

Faessel, Stephen J., *Early Anaheim* (Mount Pleasant, SC: Arcadia Publishing, 2006)

Newhan, Ross, *The Anaheim Angels: A Complete History* (New York: Hyperion, 2000)

Fresno

■ The City in Brief

Founded: 1872 (incorporated 1885)

Head Official: Mayor Alan Autry (since 2001)

City Population

    1980: 217,491
    1990: 354,091
    2000: 427,652
    2006 estimate: 466,714
    Percent change, 1990–2000: 20.7%
    U.S. rank in 1980: 65th
    U.S. rank in 1990: 47th
    U.S. rank in 2000: 40th

Metropolitan Area Population

    1980: 515,000
    1990: 667,000
    2000: 922,516
    2006 estimate: 891,756
    Percent change, 1990–2000: 38.3%
    U.S. rank in 1980: 67th
    U.S. rank in 1990: 59th
    U.S. rank in 2000: 53rd

Area: 99.1 square miles (2000)

Elevation: 328 feet above sea level

Average Annual Temperatures: January, 46.0° F; July, 81.4° F; annual average, 63.2° F

Average Annual Precipitation: 11.23 inches of rain

Major Economic Sectors: services, wholesale and retail trade, government

Unemployment Rate: 8.1% (June 2007)

Per Capita Income: $17,586 (2005)

2005 FBI Crime Index Property: 25,546

2005 FBI Crime Index Violent: 3,897

Major Colleges and Universities: California State University, Fresno; Fresno City College; Fresno Pacific University

Daily Newspaper: *The Fresno Bee*

■ Introduction

The seat of Fresno County, Fresno is the commercial, financial, and cultural center of the San Joaquin Valley and the central California region. The city is the business and transportation hub for four separate agricultural regions in what has been called the agribusiness center of the world. Fresno is also known as the gateway to Yosemite, Kings Canyon, and Sequoia national parks. The city is given an international flavor by a diverse citizenry representing more than 70 nationalities and the largest refugee population in the United States. Over the last two decades, Fresno has been one of the fastest growing cities in the United States, which has offered a challenge for city officials in providing adequate housing, services, and employment for the population. Development projects targeted at building a diverse economy and boosting the city's economic growth have been underway since the early 2000s and may prove to be just what the city needs to ensure successful growth.

■ Geography and Climate

Fresno is located in the fertile San Joaquin Valley in the central part of California, about halfway between San Francisco and Los Angeles. It is the sixth largest city in the state and is the seat of Fresno County. The terrain in Fresno is relatively flat, with a sharp rise to the foothills of the Sierra Nevada Mountains about 15 miles eastward. A network of irrigation canals runs through and round the city. The weather is usually sunny, with over 200 clear days each year. Summers are typically hot and dry, while winters are mild and rainy. Spring and fall are the most pleasant seasons. The area is occasionally subject to severe droughts or winter storms that can cause damage to croplands and homes.

Area: 99.1 square miles (2000)

Elevation: 328 feet above sea level

Average Temperatures: January, 46.0° F; July, 81.4° F; annual average, 63.2° F

Average Annual Precipitation: 11.23 inches of rain

■ History

Settlement of Fresno Delayed Until Arrival of Railroad

Fresno means "ash tree" in Spanish and was the name given by early Spanish explorers to a stretch of white ash trees along the banks of the San Joaquin River. These explorers did not settle the region where Fresno is now located, however, because they considered it uninhabitable. The site was in fact to remain undeveloped until the late nineteenth century. In the early part of the century, potential settlers were discouraged from staying permanently by the presence of the native population. Unlike other California cities Fresno did not get its start during the gold rush. Prospectors simply passed through the area on the way to the Sierras. After the gold rush the land was used for cattle grazing.

The first permanent settlement is said to have been established in the 1860s by an immigrant from Holland who was joined by a few other people; but the cluster of dwellings was not actually considered a town. In 1872 the Central Pacific Railroad was constructed through the San Joaquin Valley; the railroad builders laid out a town, calling it Fresno Station for the name of the county. A station was built on the present site of downtown Fresno.

The county seat at that time was Millerton, a town 25 miles to the south. In order to gain access to rail transportation, Millerton residents voted to transfer the seat to Fresno Station and the entire population moved. The town was rough and desolate and the countryside barren. The introduction of irrigation and grape-growing in the valley brought prosperity and Fresno was incorporated as a city in 1885. Soon vineyards were being planted by local inhabitants as well as Italian, French, and Swiss immigrants who had bought 20-acre parcels of land.

Development of Raisin and Fig Industries

When the dry white wine produced from the area's vineyards proved less than satisfactory, the grapes were cultivated for raisins, which were naturally produced by

the continuous sunlight in the valley. Following an unusually large yield of more than one million pounds of raisins that drove the price down to two cents a pound in 1894, the Raisin Growers Association was organized (in 1898) to protect the raisin industry. In 1886 Frank Roeding and his son began growing figs in the area; having experimented with caprification, the cross-fertilization of the Smyrna fig by the fig wasp, they started another successful industry.

By 1900 the population of Fresno had reached 12,470 people and the city drafted its first charter. During the following decade agriculture continued to flourish, with cotton growing and sweet wine production emerging as new industries. Fresno became the residential and commercial center of an increasingly prosperous region. With the expansion of manufacturing along with agriculture, Fresno was a major metropolitan area by the end of World War II.

Rapid population growth began to strain the city's boundaries. In the late 1970s the city had about 190,000 people. In 1990 the population was 354,000. From 1990 to 2000 the population grew by 20.3 percent. Newcomers included a large number of immigrants, particularly those from Southeast Asia. To keep up with the surge of residents, farmlands were rezoned to allow for new housing developments and the city began to diversify its economy, particularly in retail, strip-mall type developments.

Scandal rocked the town in the early 1990s as the FBI discovered a web of political corruption known as Operation Rezone. It came to light that a number of city council members from Fresno and nearby Clovis were accepting bribes from developers in return for favorable votes on rezoning issues. Several officials were later convicted. At about the same time downtown retail centers began to decline as suburban shopping centers became more popular.

In the early 2000s city officials took measures to strengthen the city through redevelopment. The city became a federal Empowerment Zone in 2002. The city also created its own Municipal Restoration Zone to encourage new businesses. New developments included the 2003 opening of the Save Mart Center, for concerts and sports events, and construction of several office towers in the downtown area.

While Fresno County continues to be one of the nation's leading agricultural counties, producing more than three billion dollars' worth of crops each year, the city of Fresno has become the center of trade, commerce, finance, and transportation for the San Joaquin Valley and city officials have been intent on using these strengths to spawn new growth.

Historical Information: California History & Genealogy Room, Fresno County Library, 2420 Mariposa, Fresno, CA 93721; telephone (559)488-3195

Aerial photo provided by Digital Sky Aerial Imaging

■ Population Profile

Metropolitan Area Residents

1980: 515,000
1990: 667,000
2000: 922,516
2006 estimate: 891,756
Percent change, 1990–2000: 38.3%
U.S. rank in 1980: 67th
U.S. rank in 1990: 59th
U.S. rank in 2000: 53rd

City Residents

1980: 217,491
1990: 354,091
2000: 427,652
2006 estimate: 466,714
Percent change, 1990–2000: 20.7%
U.S. rank in 1980: 65th
U.S. rank in 1990: 47th
U.S. rank in 2000: 40th

Density: 4,315 people per square mile (2000)

Racial and ethnic characteristics (2005)

White: 255,981
Black: 39,396
American Indian and Alaska Native: 4,858
Asian: 58,771
Native Hawaiian and Pacific Islander: 961
Hispanic or Latino (may be of any race): 209,487
Other: 105,448

Percent of residents born in state: 61.7 (2000)

Age characteristics (2005)

Population under 5 years old: 44,238
Population 5 to 9 years old: 43,357
Population 10 to 14 years old: 43,211
Population 15 to 19 years old: 41,012
Population 20 to 24 years old: 38,546
Population 25 to 34 years old: 75,637
Population 35 to 44 years old: 63,240
Population 45 to 54 years old: 54,778
Population 55 to 59 years old: 21,018
Population 60 to 64 years old: 15,061
Population 65 to 74 years old: 18,166

Population 75 to 84 years old: 14,924
Population 85 years and older: 4,063
Median age: 28.1 years

Births (2006, MSA)

Total number: 16,496

Deaths (2006, MSA)

Total number: 5,922

Money income (2005)

Per capita income: $17,586
Median household income: $37,800
Total households: 154,147

Number of households with income of...

less than $10,000: 16,808
$10,000 to $14,999: 12,664
$15,000 to $24,999: 22,754
$25,000 to $34,999: 20,705
$35,000 to $49,999: 23,147
$50,000 to $74,999: 23,853
$75,000 to $99,999: 17,258
$100,000 to $149,999: 11,383
$150,000 to $199,999: 2,862
$200,000 or more: 2,713

Percent of families below poverty level: 20.7% (2005)

2005 FBI Crime Index Property: 25,546

2005 FBI Crime Index Violent: 3,897

■ Municipal Government

Fresno has a strong-mayor form of government. There are seven council members elected by district to four-year, staggered terms. The mayor is elected at large for a four-year term, with a two term limit. A city manager is appointed by the mayor. Fresno is also the Fresno County seat.

Head Official: Mayor Alan Autry (since 2001; term expires 2009)

Total Number of City Employees: 3,787 (2007)

City Information: City of Fresno, 2600 Fresno Street, Fresno, CA 93721; telephone (559)621-2489

■ Economy

Major Industries and Commercial Activity

Agriculture is the backbone of the Fresno area, employing nearly 20 percent of the workforce and providing more than $3.5 billion for the local economy. More jobs

are tied into the agricultural industry than any other industry in the Fresno area; estimates are that one in three jobs are related to agriculture. A majority of America's produce is grown in California's Central Valley, and Fresno County is the number one agricultural county in the United States. By 2007 more than 7,500 farmers were growing 250 types of crops on 1 million acres of some of the world's most productive farmland. Major crops are grapes, cotton, cattle, tomatoes, milk, plums, turkeys, oranges, peaches, and nectarines. A large food processing industry has developed around the agricultural activity; a number of canning, curing, drying, and freezing plants are located in the area.

An Ernst and Young study also tapped Fresno as an ideal location for manufacturing and distribution, due to its proximity within one day's drive of 35 million people. Manufacturing concerns in this Port of Entry region produce farm machinery, metal products, transportation equipment, stone, clay, and glass products, lumber and wood products, furniture and fixtures, and electrical equipment. Government, services, and trade are also important economic sectors.

Some of the largest employers in Fresno in 2007 were: Community Medical Centers, Saint Agnes Medical Center, Beverly Health Care, Kaiser Permanente, Pelco, Quinn Group, Inc., Gottschalks, AT&T, Zacky Farms LLC, and Sun-Maid Growers.

Incentive Programs—New and Existing Companies

Local programs: The City of Fresno is specifically interested in attracting new businesses involved with flexible food manufacturing, irrigation and agricultural technology, agile industrial manufacturing, advanced logistics, smart commerce and customer services. The city offers programs such as Fresno Startup and the Fresno Redevelopment Agency (RDA) and its finance authority that can be useful when considering Industrial Development Bonds. The City has also developed relationships with other agencies such as the Fresno County Workforce Development Corporation and the Fresno Chamber of Commerce and Economic Development Corporation, which offer assistance to the developer and other companies considering a move to the City of Fresno.

State programs: In 2002 the City of Fresno was awarded a lucrative Federal Empowerment Zone designation. The U.S. Department of Housing and Urban Development will fund this program until December 31, 2009. Businesses that are located in the Empowerment Zone are eligible for significant incentives that will encourage expansion, including up to $3,000 per employee per year, tax deductions on property investment and capital gains, tax-free rollover of certain gains, and tax-exempt financing through state or local government bonds. The city of Fresno has one of the largest

Enterprise Zones in California. Benefits of operating in the Enterprise Zone include sales and use tax credits; hiring tax credits; net operating loss carryover and net interest deduction for lenders programs. Fresno businesses may also receive tax incentives as part of a Foreign Trade Zone.

A Research & Development Tax Credit is available of up to 15 percent against bank and corporate tax liability for certain in-house research. An additional 24 percent credit is available for basic research payments to outside organizations. This is one of the highest research and development tax credits in the nation. A Child Care Tax Credit is available for companies establishing on-site child care facilities. A Net Operating Loss Carryover and New Market Tax Credits are also available. A Work Opportunity Tax Credit is offered for employers who hire individuals from certain target groups.

The State Loan Guarantee Program provides working capital loans, and Small Business Administration loans are available to assist in financing fixed-capital and operational expenditures. All programs are administered through the State of California Commerce and Economic Development Program.

Job training programs: The California Employment Training Panel assists businesses through performance-based customized training contracts for new or existing employees. Reimbursement of costs for developing, implementing, and completing training programs may range from $1,500 to $2,000 per employee. The Fresno County Workforce Investment Board offers assistance in on-the-job skills training and training subsidies. The Fresno Neighborhood Job Network also offers job training services. Additional services are available through the Fresno Regional Occupational Program and the Fresno City College Vocational Training Center.

Development Projects

The Save Mart Center on the campus of Fresno State University opened in late 2003 as a venue for national touring concert acts, as well as Fresno State home basketball games. Several downtown developments have revitalized the area, including the Tower at Convention Center Court, an 11-story complex completed in 2003, as well as several other office towers. A new federal courthouse will be the tallest building in Fresno. These and other planned developments are part of the city's Vision 2010 that aims to bring residents back to the area.

In June 2007, Univision—the leading Spanish-language media company in the U.S.—broke ground on a new state-of-the-art 40,000-square-foot facility, estimated at a cost of over $20 million. The facility will house three Spanish-language television stations and three Spanish-language radio stations. In 2007, construction of Phase I of the 230-acre North Pointe Business Park was underway. North Pointe caters to industrial users.

Fancher Creek Business Park will feature a 95-acre town center, retail mixed with residential, and a 29-acre village center that includes housing for seniors. Another 107 acres will be reserved for a business park with mix uses including distribution and possibly manufacturing. Scheduled to open at the end of 2007 was the Woodward Mountain Bike Skills Progression Park, a 10-acre progression-based mountain bike park in the city. Further development of the downtown area is in the planning stages. Projects being considered are a public ice rink, 73,000 square feet of retail shops and restaurants, and 160 apartments in the Selland Arena parking lot. The multi-story development would feature solar panels on the roof to help offset the cost of operating the indoor ice rink.

Economic Development Information: City of Fresno, Economic Development Department, 2600 Fresno Street, Room 3076, Fresno, CA 93721; telephone (559)621-8350; fax (559)488-1078

Commercial Shipping

International freight shipments to and from the entire region flow through the Fresno Yosemite International Airport, a direct port of entry and part of a Federal Foreign Trade Zone. The nation's largest parcel carriers, FedEx, UPS, and Airborne Express, operate from there. Rail freight services are provided by both the Burlington Northern-Santa Fe and Southern Pacific railroads. Nearly 200 truck firms are based within the Fresno County borders.

Labor Force and Employment Outlook

Fresno continues to diversify its economy toward non-agricultural industries. In 2002, two major manufacturers, Sinclair Systems and Rayovac Corporation, moved their headquarters to the Fresno area. Fresno's labor force is productive, motivated, flexible, and relatively young. Steady population growth has occurred faster than local business expansion or new business development. Unemployment rates fluctuate seasonally, due mainly to the high demand for agricultural labor at certain times of the year. A large number of immigrants, both regional and international, provide a continuous supply of employable people with diverse skills. Job availability is aided by a cooperative effort between business and government to attract new industry. In September 2007, the unemployment rate in Fresno County was 7.5 percent, up from 6.3 percent the year prior. In September 2007, the California unemployment rate was 5.4 percent, and the national unemployment rate was 4.5 percent. By September 2007, job growth was occurring the fastest in agriculture; trade, transportation, and utilities; and educational and health services.

The following is a summary of data regarding the Fresno metropolitan area labor force, 2006 annual averages.

Size of nonagricultural labor force: 301,800

Number of workers employed in . . .

  construction and mining: 23,300
  manufacturing: 27,400
  trade, transportation and utilities: 58,200
  information: 4,200
  financial activities: 15,300
  professional and business services: 29,700
  educational and health services: 37,100
  leisure and hospitality: 28,200
  other services: 10,900
  government: 67,600

Average hourly earnings of production workers employed in manufacturing: Not available

Unemployment rate: 8.1% (June 2007)

Largest private employers (2007)	*Number of employees*
Community Medical Centers	4,592
Saint Agnes Medical Center	2,075
Beverly Health Care	2,000
Kaiser Permanente	2,000
Pelco	1,965
Quinn Group, Inc.	1,178
Gottschalks	1,095
AT&T	1,000
Zacky Farms LLC	915
Sun-Maid Growers	600

Cost of Living

The following is a summary of data regarding several key cost of living factors for the Fresno area.

2007 (1st quarter) ACCRA Average House Price: $499,166

2007 (1st quarter) ACCRA Cost of Living Index: 121.5

State income tax rate: 1.0% to 9.3%

State sales tax rate: 7.25%

Local income tax rate: None

Local sales tax rate: Local sales and use tax rate: 1.975%

Property tax rate: Limited to 1% of assessed value by state law. In some cases the local taxing body can add up to 0.15%

Economic Information: Greater Fresno Chamber of Commerce, 2331 Fresno Street, Fresno, CA 93721; telephone (559)495-4800; fax (559)495-4811

■ Education and Research

Elementary and Secondary Schools

The Fresno Unified School District is the fourth largest district in the state. A five-member, nonpartisan board of education hires a superintendent. Overall the district has underperformed due to a wide variety of problems including financial woes, mismanagement, and a highly diverse student population with large numbers of immigrant and non-English-speaking students, many of whom are impoverished. However, in 2007 over half of the district schools made their Academic Growth Index growth targets and five schools were removed from Program Improvement status. The student body is rather diverse, with over 76 languages represented. In 2006, there were 17 magnet and specialty program schools in the district and 10 alternative education schools. The system has seven charter schools.

The Central Unified School District (CUSD) also serves students in the city. In 2007 the CUSD had 18 school sites, but a rapidly expanding population has inspired plans to build several new schools and expand others within the next decade. CUSD offers a full array of programs for all ages.

The following is a summary of data regarding the Fresno Unified School District as of the 2005–2006 school year.

Total enrollment: 79,383

Number of facilities

  elementary schools: 61
  junior high/middle schools: 19
  senior high schools: 8
  other: 0

Student/teacher ratio: 20.8:1

Teacher salaries (2005–06)

  elementary median: $59,190
  junior high/middle median: $59,510
  secondary median: $60,340

Funding per pupil: $6,082

Additionally there are several private schools serving K-12 students in Fresno, including Catholic elementary and high schools, other Christian and religious schools, and secular private institutions.

Public Schools Information: Fresno Unified School District, 2309 Tulare Street, Fresno, CA 93721; telephone (559)457-3733; www.fresno.k12.ca.us. Central Unified School District, 4605 Polk, Fresno, CA 93722; telephone (559)274-4700; www.centralusd.k12.ca.us

Colleges and Universities

California State University, Fresno (commonly known as Fresno State) is part of the 23 campus California State University system. It is a four-year accredited university offering doctoral, graduate, and undergraduate degrees in about 100 fields to its more than 22,000 students. With 26 nationally accredited departmental programs, Fresno State is the largest post-secondary institution in the city and sits on a 388-acre campus and adjacent to a 1,011-acre University Farm in the northeast section of Fresno.

Fresno City College is a two-year community college with more than 21,000 students. California's oldest community college, Fresno City College offers associate's degrees in more than 100 disciplines. Many are designed to transfer to four-year institutions. The University of California San Francisco School of Medicine operates a campus in Fresno that hosts a medical education program, providing medical internship and residency training.

Fresno Pacific University is a Christian liberal arts school affiliated with the Mennonite Brethren. It offers associate's, bachelor's, and master's degrees through four schools: the School of Business; the School of Education; the School of Humanities, Religion, and Social Sciences; and the School of Natural Sciences. Enrollment is over 1,453 students. The Mennonite Brethren Biblical Seminary has a campus in Fresno with about 200 students. The school offers master's degrees and certificate programs in religious and church studies.

The Fresno campus of Alliant International University is one of six locations in the state. Programs at Alliant focus on careers in human relations, applied behavioral, cognitive and economic sciences, and the humanities. The Fresno campus offers graduate and undergraduate degrees through its Marshall Goldsmith School of Management, the California School of Professional Psychology, the Graduate School of Education, and the Center for Forensic Studies.

Libraries and Research Centers

The Fresno County Public Library has a Central Resource Library and 34 branches throughout the Fresno area. The system further links to the San Joaquin Valley Library system, a cooperative network of nine public library systems with shared information databases across six counties in the Central Valley. In addition to more than 1.1 million volumes, the Fresno County Library also offers nearly 2,000 periodical subscriptions, over 1 million government publications, 55,900 video materials, and 96,260 audio materials. There are special services for the handicapped and visually impaired, as well as special collections on the Japanese and Hmong languages, Pulitzer Prize-winning author and Fresno native William Saroyan, oral history, and holdings of the Fresno Genealogical Society. The library is a complete depository for California state documents and a partial depository for the U.S. Government.

The Henry Madden Library at Fresno State has a collection of over 927,860 books and scores and over 151,000 bound periodicals. The library also has over 1.2 million microforms. Special collections include the Arne Nixon Center for the Study of Children's Literature, the Central Valley Political Archive, the Enology and Viticulture Collection, the Map Library, and the Music and Media Library. The Larson Collection on International Expositions and Fairs contains information on world fairs from 1851 to 1940. The Woodward Memorial Library of Californiana, containing information on local history, is also part of the Madden Library's special collections.

Fresno State sponsors several research centers and institutes, including the California Water Institute, the Central Valley Cultural Heritage Institute, the Center for Food Science and Nutrition research, the Viticulture and Enology Research Center, the Center for the Study of Crime and Victimization, and the Engineering Research Institute. The Fresno campus of the University of California San Francisco School of Medicine is home to the Center for Medical Education and Research.

The Center for Mennonite Brethren Studies in Fresno, California is part of the Heibert Library at the Mennonite Brethren Biblical Seminary. The center holds over 18,000 volumes as part of its historical collection and also maintains records and personal papers relating to the Mennonite Brethren Church in North America.

Public Library Information: Fresno County Public Library, 2420 Mariposa Street, Fresno, CA 93721-2285; telephone (559)488-3195; www.fresnolibrary.org

■ Health Care

Community Medical Centers operates the largest health system in the city. The 457-bed Community Regional Medical Center in Fresno is home to the only stroke unit in the area with 24-hour vascular neurology and neurosurgery coverage. It is also the only hospital in the region with a Level I Trauma Center and specialized burn center. It serves as a teaching hospital for the University of California San Francisco School of Medicine. The Fresno Heart and Surgical Hospital is a 57-bed facility primarily dedicated to the full range of cardiac care services. This hospital also offers bariatric and general surgery services. The Community Living Center Fresno is a 109-bed rehabilitation and skilled nursing facility. The DeWitt Subacute and Skilled Nursing Center has 33 beds. Outpatient care is offered through the California Cancer Center, the Community Health Center, and the Community SPORT (sports, orthopedics, rehabilitation, and training) Center.

The St. Agnes Medical Center, a full-service regional hospital, is affiliated with Trinity Health. The Medical Center campus includes the California Eye Institute at Saint Agnes, a comprehensive outpatient facility offering services from routine eye exams to complex eye surgeries, and the Cancer Center at Saint Agnes, offering a holistic approach to cancer care.

Nearby Children's Hospital Central California has more than 255 beds on a 50-acre campus in Madera.

■ Recreation

Sightseeing

The 62-mile self-guided motor tour of Blossom Trail offers arguably the best look at what makes the Fresno area unique, with a plunge into some of the most productive agricultural land in the world. The annual Blossom Trail kickoff comes each February and motorists and hikers through the farm country can come upon stunning displays of blossoming peach, nectarine, plum, orange, and almond trees in full bloom. The family-run Simonian Farms at the end of the trail cultivate more than one hundred varieties of fruits and vegetables and can be toured via a hay wagon.

The Forestiere Underground Gardens offers a unique experience of underground rooms, passageways, and gardens covering 10-acres. The complex was excavated (by hand!) and designed by Baldasare Forestiere in the early 1900s. It includes his five-room underground home, a multilevel aquarium, and an auto tunnel. The gardens include a variety of fruit trees, such as date palm and olive. Guided tours are available at this state landmark.

Fresno is less than an hour away from the Sierra Nevada Mountains and three of the nation's most popular national parks. Yosemite, King's Canyon, and Sequoia National Parks offer spectacular canyons, waterfalls, and forests of 4,000-year-old bristlecone pine trees and giant sequoias, the largest trees in the world.

Downtown Fresno offers the Fulton Mall, a beautiful area of stores, restaurants, landscaped grounds, fountains, and sculpture that covers a ten-block area. It contains one of the finest collections of public art in the nation, arranged throughout the central business district. Roeding Park, two miles northwest of the downtown area, contains the Fresno Chaffee Zoo, the third largest in California; Rotary Storyland and Playland, an amusement park for children; Chaffee Zoological Gardens; and Storyland, offering display and walk-through depictions of children's stories.

Arts and Culture

The William Saroyan Theater is the cultural center of Fresno. Luxurious seating for 2,300 people and near-perfect acoustics highlight the theater, home to the Fresno Philharmonic Orchestra and the Fresno Ballet and

site of many cultural events throughout the year. The Fresno Grand Opera offers two major productions each year at the Saroyan. Other venues for the performing arts are the Good Company Players Second Space Theatre, presenting comedy and drama; Roger Rocka's Dinner Theatre; historic Tower Theatre, presenting touring performers; Theatre Three, presenting eight varied performances annually in a 107-seat facility; and Warnors Center for the Performing Arts. Children's Musical Theaterworks offers young actors a chance to perform at the Veterans Memorial Auditorium. Save Mart Center at Fresno State and the Selland Arena at the Fresno Convention and Entertainment Center offer a wide variety of programs and concerts.

The Fresno City and County Historical Society operates the Kearney Mansion and Fort Miller Blockhouse, two historical museums, extensive archives on the history of Fresno, and tours of the city's historic buildings. Meux Home, a restored historical structure in downtown Fresno, features a number of exhibits relating to the region's history, displayed on a rotating basis. Architecture buffs might wish to contemplate the futuristic design of the City Hall, located near the historic district containing Meux Home and St. John's Cathedral.

The Discovery Museum is a hands-on science museum and outdoor education center; it features Native American exhibits, a cactus garden, worm farms, ponds, and a greenhouse. Downing Planetarium at the California State University, Fresno offers public programs on weekends.

The Fresno Art Museum is the only modern art museum between San Francisco and Los Angeles and has three main galleries, an exhibition concourse, and a unique "Childspace;" it offers art classes for adults and children. The Fresno Metropolitan Museum of Art and Science contains collections of European still lifes, tromp l'oeil oil paintings, and exhibits focusing on the cultural heritage of Central California, including exhibits dedicated to author and Fresno native William Saroyan.

The African American Cultural and Historical Museum offers exhibits on African American contributions in the San Joaquin Valley. The Veteran's Memorial Museum in Veteran's Memorial Auditorium is the only museum in the country dedicated to the recipients of the Medal of Honor, Distinguished Service Cross, Navy Cross, and Air Force Cross.

Arts and Culture Information: Fresno Coalition for Art, Science, and History; 1544 Van Ness Ave., Fresno, CA 93721; telephone (559)650-1880; www.fcash.org

Festivals and Holidays

Fresno schedules a number of special cultural and ethnic events throughout the year. A variety of activities are planned by communities along the Blossom Trail to coincide with the peak growing season, beginning in late February or early March. A Grand Mardi Gras Parade and festival takes place in the Tower District, usually in February. A Renaissance Festival is held annually in March on the campus of Fresno City College. An annual Mariachi Festival also takes place in March at the Selland Arena. The Rouge Performance Festival (March) is a nonjuried art festival for theater, dance, music, film, puppetry, storytelling, visual arts, and more. The Bob Matthias Fresno Relays take place every spring, as they have for more than 75 years. Beginning each June there are bi-weekly free concerts in Woodward Park. July brings the Obon Odori Festival, a Japanese carnival of crafts, games, food, music, and dance. The High Sierra Regatta at Huntington Lake is a prestigious yachting event held on two consecutive weekends in July. The Big Fresno Fair happens at the Fairgrounds in October. Several special treelighting and musical events occur throughout the month of December.

Sports for the Spectator

The Fresno Grizzlies, a Triple-A affiliate of the San Francisco Giants, play baseball at the downtown ballpark, Chukchansi Park. The Central Valley Coyotes play professional Arena Football at 11,000-seat Selland Arena. Minor League ECHL hockey can be seen with the Fresno Falcons at the new Save Mart Center. The Fresno State University Bulldogs play basketball at Selland Arena and football at Bulldog Stadium. Men's baseball and women's softball teams compete at Beiden Field.

Sports for the Participant

A number of area lakes and reservoirs provide a full range of water recreation in the immediate Fresno area. With three of America's great national parks within a 90-minute drive, Fresno offers arguably the greatest range of recreational options of any large metropolitan area in the U.S. Nearby Yosemite, Sequoia/Kings Canyon, and Death Valley National Parks offer flat, scorching desert vistas to high mountain streams and skiing, and everything in between. The numerous streams and rivers in the area offer some of California's finest trout and largemouth bass fishing, as well as rafting and canoeing. The hills and nearby mountains contain many campsites and hiking trails; snow skiing is less than 90 minutes away at Sierra Summit, while Lake Tahoe is just a bit further in the Sierra Nevada range.

More than 2,000 children ages 3 to 12 play on 175 teams in the sports of baseball, basketball, and football, and participate in karate lessons. The city of Fresno operates 3 major regional parks, including the highly popular Chaffee Zoo, as well as 27 playgrounds and community centers, 14 swimming pools, 3 eighteen-hole golf courses, and tennis courts. There are six additional public golf courses in the immediate Fresno area, including the Running Horse Golf and Country Club featuring the first private golf course codesigned by Jack Nicklaus and Jack Nicklaus II.

Shopping and Dining

Fulton Mall, a popular sightseeing spot along the six-block stretch of historic Fulton Street, is the major shopping complex in Fresno's downtown area. Other important shopping centers are the Fashion Fair Mall and Manchester Mall. Fig Garden Village and River Park offer both offer national chains as well as unique boutiques. The Tower District offers a variety of shops, restaurants, and nightclubs. The Sierra Vista Mall in Clovis contains several large retail outlets and a number of smaller specialty shops. Numerous smaller centers and antique shops are spread throughout the city. Of unique interest is the international gift shop in the Mennonite Quilting Center in downtown Reedley.

More than 500 restaurants in Fresno, many housed in historic buildings, offer a wide selection of dining experiences for every taste and price range, including hearty regional and western dishes, Mexican specialties, and European and international cuisines. Visitors might want to stop in at one of the areas local wineries, including Engelmann Cellars, Milla Vineyards, Nonini Winery, and Los Californios Winery.

Visitor Information: Fresno Convention and Visitors Bureau, 808 M Street, Fresno, CA 93721; telephone (559)233-0836; toll-free (800)788-0836; www.fresnocvb.org

■ Convention Facilities

The Fresno Convention and Conference Center is an award-winning complex covering five city blocks in the downtown district. It contains a 168,172-square-foot exhibit hall, a theater that seats 2,300 people, an 11,000-seat arena, and a 13,120 square-foot multi-use ballroom. The William Saroyan Theatre in the convention center complex is home to the Fresno Philharmonic Orchestra and the Fresno Ballet, and is also available for meetings. California State University, Fresno offers several large facilities, and the major hotels in the area feature extensive meeting, banquet, and ballroom accommodations. More than 7,000 hotel/motel rooms are available in Fresno.

Convention Information: Fresno Convention and Visitors Bureau, 808 M Street, Fresno, CA 93721; telephone (559)233-0836; toll-free (800)788-0836; www .fresnocvb.org

■ Transportation

Approaching the City

The Fresno Yosemite International Airport is served by 14 local and national air carriers and offers scheduled service to more than 25 of the nation's major cities.

Fresno Chandler Executive Airport is a secondary general aviation airport serving the area.

State Routes 99, 41, and 180 are the primary entryways into the city. Interstate 5, which runs generally north-south to the west of the city, connects directly with S.R. 99 at points north and south of the city. S.R.180 runs east and west to connect the city with the Sierra Nevada Mountains and western California.

Amtrak provides daily service to the downtown Fresno Amtrak Station through Fresno County with connections to northern and southern California. Fresno County is poised to maintain its dominant rail position in California as the state continues with plans for high speed rail service, which will connect the Central San Joaquin Valley with San Francisco and the Los Angeles basin. The proposed rail service would transport passengers at more than 200 miles per hour and move 68 million passengers annually by 2020. Greyhound also makes a daily stop to a downtown Fresno station.

Traveling in the City

Most of Fresno is laid out in a grid of streets running east-west and north-south. West Avenue is the dividing line for east and west designations and Whites Bridge Avenue and Kings Canyon Road divide the city north and south. State Routes 99, 180, and 41 circle the downtown area.

Fresno Area Express (FAX) has 18 fixed-route bus service lines and Handy Ride Para transit service, all with a fleet of more than 100 buses. A free downtown trolley service is available through FAX. There are over a dozen cab companies serving the city.

■ Communications

Newspapers and Magazines

The Fresno Bee is the only daily paper published in the city. With a daily circulation of about 157,546 in 2007, it was ranked as one of the top 100 newspapers in the country. *Fresno Business Journal* is published weekly. *Vide en el Valle* is a Spanish-language weekly. *Fresno Magazine* comes out monthly. *His Magazine* is a bimonthly publication for men.

Television and Radio

Only four television stations broadcast from the city itself. Cable television is available throughout Fresno. As expected of any mid-sized American city, a wide variety of radio programming is available from 23 FM and AM stations, including foreign language broadcasts.

Media Information: *The Fresno Bee*, 1626 E. Street, Fresno, CA 93786; telephone(559)441-6111; www.fresnobee.com

Fresno Online

California Mission Studies Association. Available www.ca-missions.org

City of Fresno Home Page. Available www.ci.fresno.ca.us

The Fresno Bee. Available www.fresnobee.com

Fresno Chamber of Commerce. Available www.fresnochamber.com

Fresno Convention & Visitors Bureau. Available www.fresnocvb.org

Fresno County Economic Development Corporation. Available www.fresnoedc.com

Fresno County Library. Available www.fresnolibrary.org

Fresno Unified Public Schools. Available www.fresno.k12.ca.us

BIBLIOGRAPHY

Burnett, Brenda Preston, *Andrew Davidson Firebaugh and Susan Burgess Firebaugh: California Pioneers* (Rio Del Mar, CA: Rio Del Mar Press, 1995)

Hunter, Pat, *Fresno's Architectural Past* (Fresno, CA: Craven Street Books, 2006)

Los Angeles

■ The City in Brief

Founded: 1781 (incorporated 1850)

Head Official: Mayor Antonio R. Villaraigosa (D) (since 2005)

City Population

1980: 2,966,850
1990: 3,485,557
2000: 3,694,820
2006 estimate: 3,849,378
Percent change, 1990–2000: 5.9%
U.S. rank in 1980: 3rd
U.S. rank in 1990: 2nd (State rank: 1st)
U.S. rank in 2000: 2nd (State rank: 1st)

Metropolitan Area Population

1980: 7,478,000
1990: 8,863,052
2000: 9,519,338
2006 estimate: 9,948,081
Percent change, 1990–2000: 9.4%
U.S. rank in 1980: 2nd (CMSA)
U.S. rank in 1990: 2nd (CMSA)
U.S. rank in 2000: 2nd (CMSA)

Area: 469.1 square miles (2000)

Elevation: 340 feet above sea level

Average Annual Temperatures: January, 58.3° F; July, 74.2° F; annual average, 66.2° F

Average Annual Precipitation: 15.14 inches of rain

Major Economic Sectors: services, wholesale and retail trade, government

Unemployment Rate: 4.7% (June 2007)

Per Capita Income: $24,587 (2005)

2005 FBI Crime Index Property: 117,285

2005 FBI Crime Index Violent: 31,767

Major Colleges and Universities: University of California, Los Angeles (UCLA); University of Southern California (USC); California Institute of Technology

Daily Newspaper: *Los Angeles Times*

■ Introduction

Los Angeles is the second largest city in the United States in terms of population and one of the largest in terms of area. It is the center of a five-county metropolitan area and is considered the prototype of the future metropolis—a city on the cutting edge of all of the advantages and the problems of large urban areas. The glamour of Hollywood, Beverly Hills, the Sunset Strip, and the famous beaches have added to Los Angeles's reputation as a California paradise and have contributed to the area's phenomenal growth. Los Angeles is a city of fascinating diversity, incorporating one of the largest Hispanic populations in the United States, a major Asian community, and sizable populations of nearly every ethnic background in the world. Los Angeles is also a center of international trade and banking, manufacturing, and tourism. The city offers something for everyone in its large conglomeration of separate and very different districts: a sleek, ultra-modern downtown, miles of beautiful beaches, mansions and stunning canyon homes built with opulent luxury, and some of the world's most glamorous shopping and dining. Beneath the glitter, though, is a troubled, racially divided city, with extremely high unemployment rates for young African Americans and Latinos.

■ Geography and Climate

Los Angeles lies on a hilly coastal plain with the Pacific Ocean as its southern and western boundaries. It is the seat of Los Angeles County. The greater Los Angeles Metropolitan Area is considered to be a major economic region in Southern California. It covers the five counties of Los Angeles, Orange, Riverside, San Bernardino, and Ventura. The harbor at San Pedro Bay offers a port of entry. The communities of Hollywood, San Pedro, Bel Aire, Central City, Sylmar, Watts, Westwood, and Boyle Heights are all part of the city of Los Angeles. The city of Los Angeles stretches north to the foothills of the Santa Monica Mountains and is bounded by the San Gabriel Mountains to the east. Numerous canyons and valleys also characterize the region, making it an area of diverse climatic conditions.

The predominant weather influence is the warm, moist Pacific air, keeping temperatures mild throughout the year. Summers are dry and sunny—the city averages 329 days of sun per year—with most of the precipitation occurring during the winter months. Smog and air pollution are common problems, gathering in the coastal basin during periods of little air movement. Other unusual weather phenomena include the Santa Ana winds, which bring hot, dusty winds of up to 50 miles per hour from the surrounding mountains, and the occasional flash floods in the canyon areas, causing mudslides and rockslides. Wildfires during the driest season can be very destructive. The San Andreas Fault runs to the north of the Los Angeles area, making the area susceptible to earthquakes, though most are of a low magnitude.

Area: 469.1 square miles (2000)

Elevation: 340 feet above sea level

Average Temperatures: January, 58.3° F; July, 74.2° F; annual average, 66.2° F

Average Annual Precipitation: 15.14 inches of rain

■ History

Spanish and Anglos Settle, Trade Industry Thrives

The area around present-day Los Angeles was first explored by Europeans in 1769 when Gaspar de Portola and a group of missionaries camped on what is now called the Los Angeles River. Franciscans built Mission San Gabriel about 9 miles to the north in 1771. In 1781 Felipe de Neve, governor of Alte California, founded a settlement called El Pueblo de Nuestra Senora la Reina de los Angeles, which means "the pueblo of our lady the queen of angels." In its early years, the town was a small, isolated cluster of adobe-brick houses and random streets carved out of the desert, and its main product was grain.

Although the Spanish government placed a ban on trading with foreign ships, American vessels began arriving in the early 1800s, and the first English-speaking inhabitant settled in the area in 1818. He was a carpenter named Joseph Chapman, who helped build the church facing the town's central plaza, a structure that still stands. After Mexico, including California, gained its independence from Spain in 1821, trade with the United States became more frequent. The ocean waters off the coast of California were important for whaling and seal hunting, and a number of trading ships docked at nearby San Pedro to buy cattle hides and tallow. By the 1840s, Los Angeles was the largest town in southern California.

City Becomes American Possession; Gold Discovered

During the war between the United States and Mexico in 1846, Los Angeles was occupied by an American garrison, but the citizens drove the fifty-man brigade out of town. The Treaty of Cahuenga, signed in 1847, ended the war in California, adding Los Angeles and the rest of California to American territory. The Sierra Nevada gold strike in 1848 in the mountains to the north of Los Angeles provided the town with a booming market for its beef, and many prospectors settled in the area after the gold rush. Los Angeles was incorporated in 1850 with a reputation as one of the toughest towns in the West. "A murder a day" only slightly exaggerated the town's crime problems, and suspected criminals were often hanged by vigilante groups. Lawlessness reached a peak in 1871, when, after a Chinese immigrant accidentally killed a white man, an angry mob stormed into the Chinatown district, murdering sixteen people. After that, civic leaders and concerned citizens began a successful campaign to bring law and order to the town.

The Southern Pacific Railroad reached Los Angeles in 1876, followed by the Santa Fe Railroad nine years later. The two rival companies conducted a rate war that eventually drove the price of a ticket from the eastern United States down to five dollars. This price slashing brought thousands of settlers to the area, sending real estate prices to unrealistically high levels. By 1887, lots around the central plaza sold for up to one thousand dollars a foot, but the market collapsed in that same year, making millionaires destitute overnight. People in vast numbers abandoned Los Angeles, sometimes as many as three thousand a day. This flight prompted the creation of the Chamber of Commerce, which began a worldwide advertising campaign to attract new citizens. By 1890, the population had climbed back up to fifty thousand residents.

Oil, Agriculture, Moving Pictures, Manufacturing Build City

In the 1890s, oil was discovered in the city, and soon another boom took hold. By the turn of the century almost fifteen hundred oil wells operated throughout Los Angeles. In the early 1900s, agriculture became an important part of the economy, and a massive aqueduct project was completed. The city's growth necessitated the annexation of the large San Fernando Valley, and the port at San Pedro was also added to give Los Angeles a position in the international trade market.

The motion picture industry thrived on the Los Angeles area's advantages after the first decade of the twentieth century, and by 1930 it had earned the city the nickname of "Tinseltown." Large manufacturing concerns also began opening factories during that time, and the need for housing created vast areas of suburban neighborhoods and the beginnings of the city's massive freeway system. The Depression and the Midwestern drought of the 1930s brought thousands of people to California looking for jobs.

To accommodate its growing population, the city instituted a number of large engineering projects, including the construction of the Hoover Dam, which channeled water to the city from the Colorado River and provided electricity from hydroelectric power. The area's excellent weather made it an ideal location for aircraft testing and construction, and World War II brought hundreds of new industries to the area, boosting the local economy. By the 1950s, Los Angeles was a sprawling metropolis. It was considered the epitome of everything new and modern in American culture—a combination of super highways, affordable housing, and opportunity for everyone.

City Grapples with Pollution, Racial Unrest

The Los Angeles dream began to fade in the 1960s. Despite the continued construction of new freeways, traffic congestion became a major problem; industry and auto emissions created smog and pollution. Frustration over living conditions came to a head in August 1965, when riots erupted in the African American ghetto of Watts, and more unrest developed in the Hispanic communities of East Los Angeles.

Reacting to these new problems, the city adopted strict air pollution guidelines and took steps to bring minorities into the political process, culminating in the 1973 election of Mayor Tom Bradley, the city's first African American mayor. Over the next two decades, public transportation was improved, and a subway system was funded and began limited operations. The downtown area became a thriving district of impressive glass skyscrapers.

The city's reputation was severely tarnished by a rebellion that broke out in April 1992 following the acquittal of four white police officers accused of beating an African American motorist—a beating that was captured on videotape by a bystander and broadcast worldwide. The ensuing melee left more than 50 people dead and resulted in an estimated $1 billion in damage.

Los Angeles Enters Twenty-First Century

Los Angeles began to emerge from the recession of the mid-1990s, but like much of the country, the city was dealt another blow after the terrorist attacks of September 11, 2001. In response to the ensuing economic downturn, the mayor created the Los Angeles Economic Impact Task Force, which brought together business leaders from across the city to develop recommendations for strengthening the local economy. The result was an increase in tourism, retail sales, and other continuing signs of recovery. In the early 2000s the city also made progress toward improvement of the environment. City officials set a goal of recycling 70 percent of all waste by the year 2015 and a Million Trees LA program was launched to add 35 new parks to the city. The city also began investing in renewable energy resources and established water conservation programs. In 2007 the mayor announced plans to develop a comprehensive climate change plan for the city directed, in part, toward reducing the overall reliance on fossil fuels.

The problem of gang violence in the city has been another major challenge. In his 2007 state of the city address, the mayor reported that over 400 different gangs, with more than 39,000 youth and adult members, were active in the area. Plans were made to add 780 new police offers to the city and to appoint a new Director for Gang Reduction and Youth Development as part of the Mayor's Office staff. Approximately $168 million was budgeted for spending in youth and anti-gang programs.

Historical Information: The Historical Society of Southern California, Charles F. Lummis Home and Garden, 200 East Avenue 43, Los Angeles, CA 90031; telephone (323)222-0546; www.socalhistory.org. Los Angeles City Historical Society, P.O. Box 41046, Los Angeles, CA 90041; telephone (213)891-4600; www.lacityhistory.org

■ Population Profile

Metropolitan Area Residents

1980: 7,478,000
1990: 8,863,052
2000: 9,519,338
2006 estimate: 9,948,081
Percent change, 1990–2000: 9.4%
U.S. rank in 1980: 2nd (CMSA)
U.S. rank in 1990: 2nd (CMSA)
U.S. rank in 2000: 2nd (CMSA)

City Residents

1980: 2,966,850
1990: 3,485,557
2000: 3,694,820
2006 estimate: 3,849,378
Percent change, 1990–2000: 5.9%
U.S. rank in 1980: 3rd
U.S. rank in 1990: 2nd (State rank: 1st)
U.S. rank in 2000: 2nd (State rank: 1st)

Density: 7,876.8 people per square mile (2000)

Racial and ethnic characteristics (2005)

White: 1,831,467
Black: 368,711
American Indian and Alaska Native: 15,082
Asian: 415,652
Native Hawaiian and Pacific Islander: 9,732
Hispanic or Latino (may be of any race): 1,824,373
Other: 1,002,868

Percent of residents born in state: 50.2% (2000)

Age characteristics (2005)

Population under 5 years old: 287,230
Population 5 to 9 years old: 265,343
Population 10 to 14 years old: 288,309
Population 15 to 19 years old: 257,284
Population 20 to 24 years old: 280,287
Population 25 to 34 years old: 594,344
Population 35 to 44 years old: 596,361
Population 45 to 54 years old: 482,100
Population 55 to 59 years old: 194,593
Population 60 to 64 years old: 139,599
Population 65 to 74 years old: 179,082
Population 75 to 84 years old: 129,504
Population 85 years and older: 37,401
Median age: 33.3 years

Births (2006, Metropolitan Division)

Total number: 156,687

Deaths (2006, Metropolitan Division)

Total number: 59,775

Money income (2005)

Per capita income: $24,587
Median household income: $42,667
Total households: 1,284,124

Number of households with income of . . .

less than $10,000: 140,031
$10,000 to $14,999: 88,374
$15,000 to $24,999: 172,757
$25,000 to $34,999: 141,434

$35,000 to $49,999: 174,033
$50,000 to $74,999: 221,100
$75,000 to $99,999: 127,501
$100,000 to $149,999: 116,348
$150,000 to $199,999: 42,757
$200,000 or more: 59,789

Percent of families below poverty level: 16.3% (2005)

2005 FBI Crime Index Property: 117,285

2005 FBI Crime Index Violent: 31,767

■ Municipal Government

The city has a mayor-council form of government. The fifteen-member city council and the mayor are elected to four-year terms, as are the city attorney and the controller. The council members are elected to single-member districts with staggered terms and a limit of terms. There are 41 departments, bureaus, commissions, and offices operating as part of city government. The Board of Harbor Commissioners assists in governance of the Port of Los Angeles. The county of Los Angeles is governed by a five-member board of supervisors, although many districts are separate and self-governing. Neighborhood Councils serve to promote public participation in city government.

Head Official: Mayor Antonio R. Villaraigosa (since 2005; term expires 2009)

Total Number of City Employees: 47,700 (2006)

City Information: City Hall, 200 North Spring Street, Los Angeles, CA 90012; telephone (213)485-2121; www.lacity.org

■ Economy

Major Industries and Commercial Activity

California has always been known as an "incubator" of new ideas, new products and entrepreneurial spirit. Southern California has led the way in celebrating and nurturing that spirit. The people, institutions of knowledge, great climate and infrastructure have enabled the Los Angeles region to emerge as a leading business, trade and cultural center—a creative capital for the twenty-first century. The city is part of the largest manufacturing center in the West, one of the world's busiest ports, a major financial and banking center, and one of the largest retail markets in the United States.

The economy of Los Angeles County is diverse. The leading industries are direct international trade, tourism, motion picture and television production, technology, and business and professional services.

Image copyright Byron W. Moore, 2007. Used under license from Shutterstock.com.

The Port of Los Angeles is part of the nation's largest Customs District in terms of value of two-way trade. It is also the busiest container port in the United States. The top five trading partners in 2006 were China, Japan, Taiwan, South Korea, and Thailand. The top containerized exports that year were paper products, cotton, pet and animal feed, metal scrap, and resins, plastics, and rubber. The port itself had 847 employees in 2007. Port related employment, however, included 16,000 local jobs and 259,100 regional jobs. About $1.4 billion of state and local tax revenue is generated by the port for Southern California. The city's prominence in international trade is also evidenced by the nearly 50 U.S. headquarters of foreign companies located in the area.

Tourism accounted for over 267,400 jobs in the area in 2006. In 2006 the county hosted about 25.4 million overnight visitors who spent about $13.5 billion dollars. Entertainment, in the form of film, television, and music production, is the best known industry in Los Angeles, focusing worldwide attention on the city and making Los Angeles a major tourist destination. The motion picture and television production industries sponsored over 254,300 jobs in 2006. In the first quarter of 2007 there were 10,414 location filming days in the county.

Technology is considered to lead the "new economy" of the area. This sector includes computer and electronics manufacturing, aerospace products manufacturing, software publishing, Internet services, computer system design, scientific and technical consulting, and wholesale electronic markets, agents, and brokers. In 2006 this sector sponsored over 225,500 jobs. Business and professional services (excluding the insurance industry) employed about 178,100 workers. The banking and finance industry in Los Angeles is one of the largest in the country. More than 100 foreign and countless domestic banks operate branches in Los Angeles, along with many financial law firms and investment banks.

Los Angeles is the largest major manufacturing center in the United States. In 2005 there were about 470,400 workers in manufacturing. The largest components are apparel (61,500 jobs), computer and electronic products (60,500 jobs), transportation products (51,900 jobs), fabricated metal products (48,200 jobs), food products (43,400 jobs), and furniture (25,500 jobs).

In the United States, only Detroit produces more automobiles than the Los Angeles area, a fitting statistic for the city with more cars per capita than any other in the world. The "big three" U.S. auto manufacturers, along with Honda, Mazda, Nissan, Toyota, Volkswagen, and

Volvo, have all located design centers in Los Angeles. The manufacture of heavy machinery for the agricultural, construction, mining, and oil industries contributes significantly to the local economy. Los Angeles is also a major producer of furniture and fixtures, as well as petroleum products and chemicals, print material, rubber goods, electronic equipment, and glass, pottery, ceramics, and cement products.

In 2007 there were six *Fortune* 1000 companies headquartered in Los Angeles: Northrop Grumman, Occidental Petroleum, KB Home, Reliance Steel and Aluminum, Mercury General, and Univision Communications. Other prominent industries in the Los Angeles area include health services, education, high-technology research and development, toy manufacturing, and a large construction business, both commercial and residential.

Items and goods produced: agricultural and seafood products, aircraft and aircraft parts, furniture, ordnance missiles, electrical and electronic equipment, jewelry, apparel, textiles, toys, fabricated metals, rubber, plastic, motion pictures, petroleum

Incentive Programs—New and Existing Companies

Local programs: LA's Business Team, part of the Mayor's Office of Economic Development, is a one-stop shop for business developers. Through strategic industry and government alliances, the Business Team links businesses to a network of opportunities including financing, tax incentives, real estate, low-interest loans, job training programs, permits, and more. It is also working to develop emerging industries in Los Angeles, such as the environmental technology and biomedical industries. The Team will even cross jurisdictional lines to open doors for businesses at the federal, state, and country levels. Financial incentives are available in one Empowerment Zone, five Enterprise Zones, and one Renewal Community. The city is part of Foreign Trade Zone 202. Businesses wishing to expand or locate in Greater Los Angeles will find assistance through the Los Angeles County Economic Development Corporation.

Effective January 2006 the city approved new business tax reform measures to retain and attract new businesses. For 2007 these include a Small Business Exemption for businesses with total gross receipts under $100,000; a restructured tax ranges for motion picture, television, and radio producers; and business tax rate reductions of up to 50 percent.

Small- or medium-sized businesses may be eligible for technical assistance at one of the six Los Angeles Business Assistance Centers (BACs). The centers are operated by community based organizations and/or local colleges and universities and are funded by the City of Los Angeles Industrial and Commercial Development

Division (ICD). Assistance is provided through a combination of in-house counselors, school faculty and private business professionals.

State programs: A variety of programs administered by state and federal sources are available to Los Angeles businesses. These include special incentives in Enterprise Zones, Foreign Trade Zones, Federal Empowerment Zones, and Redevelopment Areas. Enterprise Zone Credits include a sales and use tax credit and hiring tax credits. A Research & Development Tax Credit is available of up to 15 percent against bank and corporate tax liability for certain in-house research. An additional 24 percent credit is available for basic research payments to outside organizations. This is one of the highest research and development tax credits in the nation. A Child Care Tax Credit is available for companies establishing on-site child care facilities. A Net Operating Loss Carryover and New Market Tax Credits are also available. A Work Opportunity Tax Credit is offered for employers who hire individuals from certain target groups.

Job training programs: The California Employment Training Panel assists businesses through performance-based customized training contracts for new or existing employees. Reimbursement of costs for developing, implementing, and completing training programs may range from $1,500 to $2,000 per employee. The Los Angeles Workforce Investment Board (WIB) helps to provide educational facilities and mentoring programs for both youth and adult students. The WIB sponsors eight WorkSource Centers to assist both businesses and individuals.

Development Projects

Greater Los Angeles was bustling with construction activity at the turn of the twenty-first century. The Los Angeles downtown area has undergone a renaissance, with new museums, entertainment centers, sports venues, and more. Among the many projects were the Walt Disney Concert Hall, the home of the Los Angeles Philharmonic since the 2002-2003 concert season, and the New Catholic Cathedral, a $189 million Mother Church for the Archdiocese of Los Angeles that was completed in 2002. Los Angeles Center Studios, a $105 million project described as the largest full-service independent film studio to be developed since the 1920s, began an expansion at the end of 2002 that added 900,000 square feet, including a full-service commissary, additional offices and meeting rooms, and eight additional stages.

Hollywood is being refurbished as well, with the famous Mann's Chinese Theatre having undergone a major renovation. A new shopping, dining, and entertainment center located in the heart of Hollywood is designed to mirror a 1916 classic movie set. The five-story, open-air complex, called Hollywood and Highland, includes the Renaissance Hollywood Hotel, more than 60 specialty shops, public art exhibitions, six movie screens, restaurants, nightclubs, and the Kodak Theatre.

In September 2005, ground was broken on LA Live, a $2.5 billion development with more than 4 million square feet of residences, hotels, and entertainment venues. Also called Times Square West, the development is located south of downtown. The centerpiece of the project will be a 54-story tower with a Marriott hotel and Ritz-Carlton condominium development. In addition, the development will include: a 7,100-seat theatre to host concerts, musicals, and special events; a 14-screen movie theatre; West Coast broadcast facilities for ESPN; and eight restaurants, including concepts by Los Angeles chef Wolfgang Puck. LA Live is expected to have a $10 billion economic impact, create more than 25,000 jobs, and bring in more than $18 million in annual tax revenue.

Another development project in the works is Grand Avenue. The $2 billion Grand Avenue project, adjacent to the Walt Disney Concert Hall, is being designed by the architect Frank Gehry. Grand Avenue will be developed in three phases over the next decade. The first phase will include: two residential towers with 20% of the 1,000 units reserved for affordable housing; a Mandarin Oriental hotel; a 16-acre park; and a sports club, retail stores, and restaurants. The project will create 29,000 union construction jobs and generate $109.5 million in annual tax receipts. The first phase will be completed in 2011.

In December 2006, NBC/Universal unveiled a $3 billion, 25-year plan to expand Universal City from a movie studio and theme park into a major residential and office center. The proposal represents the single largest investment in the San Fernando Valley and is expected to create 17,000 construction jobs and double the number of jobs at the studio.

Economic Development Information: Los Angeles County Economic Development Corporation, 444 South Flower Street, 34th Floor, Los Angeles, CA 90071; telephone (213)622-4300 or (888)4-LAEDC-1; fax (213)622-7100; www.laedc.org

Commercial Shipping

International trade is a major component of the Los Angeles area economy. The Los Angeles Customs District (including the ports of Long Beach and Los Angeles, Port Hueneme, and Los Angeles International Airport) is the nation's largest based on value of two-way trade, which was valued at $329.4 billion in 2006. The Port of Los Angeles has 27 cargo terminals and is the busiest container port in the United States. It is designated as a Foreign Trade Zone. The Los Angeles International Airport (LAX) has 1,000 cargo flights each day. Handling facilities include the 98-acre Century Cargo Complex, the 57.4-acre Imperial Complex, the Imperial Cargo Center, and several of terminals on the south side of the airport.

The Alameda Corridor, a 20-mile high-speed cargo rail system, connects the Port of Long Beach and the Port of Los Angeles to the transcontinental rail network links near the city of Los Angeles. In 2007 an average of 50 trains per day made the trip. Several transcontinental rail lines serve the area. All of the major interstate truck companies maintain large facilities in the metropolitan area.

Labor Force and Employment Outlook

Los Angeles offers a diverse employment pool, with a wide range of schooling and skills. A large number of immigrants—international, national, and regional—provide a steady source of labor with strong links to important trading partners like Mexico and Asia. With Los Angeles International Airport serving as the so-called new Ellis Island for foreign immigration to this country, the metropolitan region has achieved a new ethnic and cultural diversity in its workforce.

Services, wholesale and retail trade, manufacturing, government, financial service industries, transportation, utilities, and construction contribute significantly to local employment. The County of Los Angeles is the top ranked county in manufacturing in the United States.

By the end of the 1990s biotechnology emerged as one of California's largest employers at 210,000 jobs, surpassing such traditional strongholds as aerospace and the entertainment industry. Greater Los Angeles already is home to significant biotech manufacturing. More than 2,500 companies in Southern California make pharmaceuticals and other medical products. Other major industries showing growth at the start of the twenty-first century are international trade and tourism.

From 1996 through May 2007, the Los Angeles Economic Development Corporation had helped retain, attract, or expand more than 133,700 jobs, providing $5.5 billion in direct economic impact and $95 million in local tax revenue contributions. The industry leaders for 2007 and 2008 were forecast to be professional, scientific, and technical services; leisure and hospitality services; and government. Industry laggards were construction; durable goods manufacturing; and management of companies. The Riverside-San Bernadino area was a leader in employment growth in the Los Angeles metropolitan region, and Orange County was a laggard when it came to employment growth in the metropolitan region.

The following is a summary of data regarding the Los Angeles-Long Beach-Santa Ana metropolitan area labor force, 2006 annual averages.

Size of nonagricultural labor force: 5,612,600

Number of workers employed in ...

  construction and mining: 268,300
  manufacturing: 645,700

trade, transportation and utilities: 1,084,800
information: 241,400
financial activities: 387,000
professional and business services: 869,400
educational and health services: 620,200
leisure and hospitality: 557,100
other services: 193,700
government: 745,100

Average hourly earnings of production workers employed in manufacturing: $14.55

Unemployment rate: 4.7% (June 2007)

Largest employers (Los Angeles County, 2002)	*Number of employees*
County of Los Angeles	93,354
Los Angeles Unified School District	78,085
Federal Government	56,100
University of California, Los Angeles	36,354
City of Los Angeles	35,895
State of California (non-education)	32,300
Kaiser Permanente	27,635
Boeing Co.	23,468
Ralph's Grocery Co.	17,211
Long Beach Unified School District	14,000

Cost of Living

Living costs in the metropolitan area are significantly higher than the national average.

The following is a summary of data regarding key cost of living factors for the Los Angeles area.

2007 (1st quarter) ACCRA Average House Price: $823,101

2007 (1st quarter) ACCRA Cost of Living Index: 153.3

State income tax rate: 1.0% to 9.3%

State sales tax rate: 6.25%

Local income tax rate: None

Local sales tax rate: 2.0% (county)

Property tax rate: Varies according to location

Economic Information: Los Angeles Area Chamber of Commerce, 350 South Bixel Street, Los Angeles, CA 90017; telephone (213)580-7500; fax (213)580-7511; www.lachamber.org

■ Education and Research

Elementary and Secondary Schools

The Los Angeles Unified School District (LAUSD) is the country's second largest district. Geographically, it encompasses 710 square miles, an area that includes the City of Los Angeles and eight surrounding cities, as well as parts of 24 other cities and some unincorporated areas of Los Angeles County. For administrative purposes, the district is broken down into eight smaller local districts. Over 70 percent of all students are Hispanic. Dual Language Programs, in which instruction is given in English and a second language, are sponsored district-wide for students who speak Spanish or Korean. Several classes are available for those learning English as a second language.

Most district schools are on a single-track schedule with a school year running September through June. About 200 schools in the district operate on one of two-different year-round schedules. Under the four-track "90-30" system, students are divided into four groups or tracks. With staggered starting dates, each track of students attend school for 90 days, then take 30 days off. Under a three-track (Concept 6), the school year is broken up into separate blocks with two two-month vacation blocks. At any given time, two tracks are in session while the third is on vacation. The year-round calendars were designed to serve a student body that is too large to be accommodated by the district's limited facilities. New school building projects are under way through a $19.3 billion construction program designed to add over 100 schools to the district by 2012. Thirteen new schools opened in 2006.

In 2007, the district had 96 independent charter schools and centers, over 150 magnet schools and centers, and 19 special education schools. There were also 43 state-sponsored preschools and 26 schools for basic and skills-based adult education.

The following is a summary of data regarding the Los Angeles Unified School District as of the 2005–2006 school year.

Total enrollment: 704,417

Number of facilities

elementary schools: 435
junior high/middle schools: 74
senior high schools: 61
other: 489

Student/teacher ratio: 22.3:1

Teacher salaries (2005–06)

elementary median: $51,310
junior high/middle median: $56,900
secondary median: $56,700

Funding per pupil: $8,571

There are over 75 private schools in the city of Los Angeles and well over 100 including those in the LAUSD area. These include religious affiliated schools, independent schools, Montessori's, and special education facilities.

Public Schools Information: Los Angeles Unified School District, Office of the Superintendent, 333 South Beaudry Avenue, 24th floor, Los Angeles, CA 90017; telephone (213)241-7000; www.lausd.k12.ca.us.

Colleges and Universities

The two largest schools in Los Angeles are the University of California–Los Angeles (UCLA) and the University of Southern California (USC). UCLA was ranked as twenty-fifth among the best universities in the nation by *U.S News and World Report* for 2008. The university consists of the College of Letters and Science and 11 professional schools, offering 118 undergraduate degrees and 200 graduate degrees. Enrollment at UCLA was about 25,432 in 2006/07. USC was ranked as twenty-seventh in the nation by *U.S News and World Report.* The University consists of the College of Letters, Arts and Sciences; a Graduate School; and 17 professional schools. Enrollment in 2006/07 was about 33,000. There are over 77 majors offered.

California Institute of Technology (CALTECH) was ranked as fifth in the nation for best universities by *U.S News and World Report* for 2008. As of 2007 there were 31 CALTECH faculty and alumni on the list of Nobel laureates and 49 National Medal of Science recipients. Enrollment in 2006/07 was about 2,086. Undergraduate and graduate degrees are available in biology; chemistry and chemical engineering; engineering and applied science; geological and planetary sciences; humanities and social sciences; physics, mathematics and astronomy; and nine interdisciplinary programs.

Loyola Marymount University, a private Jesuit-affiliated institution, has a total enrollment of about 8,972 students. They offer 80 undergraduate degree programs and 30 graduate programs through seven schools and colleges. Pepperdine University, an independent university affiliated with the Churches of Christ, ranks as one of the top 100 best universities by *U.S News and World Report.* There are about 8,300 students enrolled in five colleges and schools. The Graduate School of Education and Psychology has a campus location in Los Angeles. The main campus, however, is in Malibu. Mount St. Mary's College is an independent Catholic liberal arts college for women. The school offers associate's degrees in five fields, bachelor's degrees in 22 fields, 6 master's degrees, and a doctorate in physical therapy. Certificate programs are available in gerontology, advanced religious studies, Hispanic pastoral ministry, and youth and young adult ministry. Enrollment is about 2,480 women. The Claremont Colleges, a consortium of five undergraduate

and two graduate institutions, are located to the east of the city.

The Los Angeles Community College District has nine campuses in the Los Angeles area, three of which are in the city limits (Los Angeles City College, Los Angeles Southwest College, and Los Angeles Trade-Technical College). A wide variety of programs are offered throughout the system. The colleges have a combined total enrollment of about 114,777.

The American Film Institute's Conservatory offers graduate programs for those entering the film industry. A Master of Fine Arts degree is available in six discipline specific programs: cinematography, directing, editing, producing, production design, and screen writing. The campus includes the Warner Communications/Warner Brothers Building, which contains a state-of-the-art sound stage, and the Sony Digital Arts Center, a post-production facility.

There are many other specialized schools in the city that offer both general higher educational opportunities and career specific programs. These include such schools as the American Barber College, the National Bartenders School, the Otis College of Art and Design, Samara University of Oriental Medicine, and the American Jewish University.

Libraries and Research Centers

The Los Angeles Public Library System operates a central library and 71 branches throughout the metropolitan area with a total of more than 6.3 million volumes. Forty-four branches and the central library are located in Los Angeles. The Mexicana Collection, with information on Mexico and the impact of Mexican culture on California, is considered to be a core collection with items located at several branches in the system. Other core collections cover special topics such as bullfighting, pacific voyages, food and wine, costumes, the history of the book and printing, California history, and ornithology. Special collections include the George Smith Biblioteca Taurina (Bullfight Collection), photographs by Ansel Adams and Edward Weston, the Tom Owen Collection of Bookplate Art, and the Paul Fritzche Collection of Culinary Literature. The system also maintains holdings of maps, audio tapes, films and videos, art reproductions, mobile libraries, and special services for the visually impaired.

The County of Los Angeles Public Library, headquartered in Downey, operates 84 regional and community library branches and 4 bookmobiles. With over 7.7 million titles, the system was ranked as one of the largest public library systems in the nation by a report from the American Library Association. There are 10 library branches within the city of Los Angeles. The Anthony Quinn Library branch contains over 3,000 items of memorabilia related to the actor. Special homework centers are located at several branches.

The UCLA library collection ranks among the top 10 academic libraries in the nation with over 8 million volumes. The Clark Library holds special collections on Oscar Wilde and Western Americana. The East Asian Library includes numerous Chinese, Japanese, and Korean language materials. The USC libraries contain over 3.9 million volumes. Special collections include American Literature, the Boeckmann Center for Iberian and Latin American Studies, the California Social Welfare Archives, the Natural History Collection, and the Shoah Foundation Visual History Archive. There are several regional history collections as well.

The Los Angeles County Law Library consists of nine branches with a collection totaling more than 700,000 volumes in all areas of law and legal issues. More than 150 other specialized and private libraries serve the Los Angeles area.

The Louis B. Mayer Library of the American Film Institute holds over 14,000 books and 100 journal titles on industry related topics such as film, television, video, photography, theater, and costume design. The library also holds over 5,000 unpublished American film scripts. Special collections include the Martin Scorsese Collection, the Charles K. Feldman Collection, the Robert Aldrich Collection, and the Fritz Lang Collection. Most items are non-circulating, but are available for in-house use by visitors as well as students and film professionals.

Some of the most advanced research in the world is conducted at Los Angeles's three major institutions of higher learning: UCLA, USC, and the California Institute of Technology. There are dozens of research centers and institutes at UCLA with topics ranging from scientific to social and religious. Scientific and technological research facilities include the Basic Plasma Science Facility, the Center for High Frequency Electronics, the Center for Planetary Chemistry and Physics, Earth and Space Sciences–Geodynamics Research Group, the Electronic Thin Film Lab, and the Fusion Science and Technology Center. Health research centers include the Alzheimer's Disease Center, the Cardiovascular Research Lab, the Center for Collaborative Research on Drug Abuse, the Center for Human Nutrition, the Center for Molecular Medicine, and the Gonda Neuroscience and Genetics Research Center. Cultural studies are supported by the Center for Buddhist Studies, Center for Chinese Studies, the Center for East Asian Studies, the Center for Jewish Studies, and the Institute for America Cultures. Other research topics include business, communications, labor and industry, and environmental studies.

Research at USC is just as extensive. Centers for scientific research include Center for Excellence in Genomic Science, the Center for Robotics and Embedded Systems, the Loker Hydrocarbon Research Institute, and the Space Sciences Center. Cultural and social research is covered through Center for Feminist Research, the Center for Religion and Civic Culture, the East Asian

Studies Center, the Institute of Modern Russian Culture, and the Center for Research on Children, Youth and Families. Health research institutes include the Andrus Gerontology Center, the Center for Alcoholic Liver and Pancreatic Diseases and Cirrhosis, the Hepatitis Research Center, and the Research Center for Liver Disease. The Southern California Earthquake Center is also located at USC. The USC Stevens Institute for Innovation helps students and faculty turn new inventions and discoveries into practical applications.

Research institutes at CALTECH are known worldwide. They include the Beckman Institute, a multi-disciplinary center for research in the chemical and biological sciences; the Infrared Processing and Analysis Center; the NASA Jet Propulsion Laboratory; the Laser Interferomoeter Gravitational Wave Observatory; and the Space Infrared Telescope Facility. There are nine observatories sponsored in part by CALTECH. The Keck Observatory at Mauna Kea, Hawaii, is a joint program of CALTECH and the University of California.

Public Library and Research Information: Los Angeles Public Library System, Central Branch, 630 West Fifth Street, Los Angeles, CA 90071-2097; telephone (213)228-7000; www.lapl.org. USC Office of the Vice Provost for Research Advancement, Bovard Administration Building, Suite 300; Los Angeles, CA 90089-4019; telephone (213)740-6709; www.usc.edu/research/centers. UCLA Office of the Vice Chancellor of Research, UCLA, 2147 Murphy Hall, Los Angeles, CA 90095; telephone (310)825-7943; www.ucla.edu/research

■ Health Care

Los Angeles is the primary health care and treatment center for the southern California region. It is one of the largest health care markets in the country and is at the forefront of major changes taking place in the health care industry. In the vast metro Los Angeles area, there are over 800 hospitals and clinics.

With more than 600 beds, UCLA Medical Center is known worldwide as a health care innovator. Its highly experienced staff consists of more than 1,000 physicians and 3,500 nurses, therapists, technologists, and support personnel. Offering comprehensive care from the routine to the highly specialized, its physicians are some of the best in the country. Other factors contributing to the Center's top rankings include specialized intensive care units, state-of-the-art inpatient and outpatient operating suites, a Level-1 trauma center, and the latest diagnostic technology. UCLA Medical Center includes The Mattell Children's Hospital; the Jules Stein Eye Institute; the Doris Stein Eye Research Center; UCLA's Jonsson Cancer Center, officially designated by the National Cancer Institute as one of the most comprehensive cancer centers in the country; and a network of health care facilities that brings UCLA-quality care to a growing number of California communities. In 2007 the UCLA Medical Center received several high marks from the annual *U.S News and World Report* for best hospitals in the nation. These include a first place ranking in geriatrics; fourth place in urology; fifth place in rheumatology, digestive disorders, psychiatry, and ophthalmology; seventh in kidney disease; and eighth in neurology/ neurosurgery and cancer care. Other top 20 rankings were given for orthopedics, heart, and pediatric care.

The private, non-profit Children's Hospital Los Angeles is affiliated with the Keck School of Medicine of the University of Southern California. The 314-bed hospital features Level I Pediatric Trauma Center, a Newborn and Infant Critical Care Unit, a Pediatric Intensive Care Unit, and a Cardiothoracic Intensive Care Unit. The hospital made headlines in 2006 when a team of doctors successfully separated conjoined twins who were joined at the mid-abdomen and pelvis. The hospital was ranked among the top 20 best pediatric hospitals in the nation in 2007 by *U.S News and World Report.*

The LAC–USC Medical Center is among the largest teaching hospitals in the country. Specialized facilities and services include a state-of-the-art burn center, Level III neonatal intensive care unit, Level I trauma service, an NIH-funded clinical research center and a HIV/AIDS outpatient center. USC University Hospital is a private, 293-bed referral, teaching, and research hospital. Advanced services include neurointerventional radiology, cardiac catheterization, and interventional cardiology. The hospital is also known for its surgical care in organ transplantation, neurosurgery, and plastic and reconstructive surgeries. The Doheny Eye Institute, also affiliated with USC, was ranked eighth in the nation for ophthalmology in *U.S News and World Report.* The 408-bed Good Samaritan Hospital is also affiliated with USC.

Cedars-Sinai Medical Center (CSMC), with 877 beds, is one of the largest nonprofit hospitals in the west. The CSMC Campus is located near the borders of Los Angeles, Beverly Hills, and West Hollywood. The 2007 *U.S. News & World Report* ranked Cedars-Sinai as part of its "Best of the Best" Honor Roll. The hospital ranked as one of the top twenty hospitals nationwide for digestive disorders, heart care, endocrinology, and neurology and neurosurgery. It ranked in the top forty for kidney diseases, geriatrics, respiratory disorders, gynecology, orthopedics, and urology. The CSMC Samuel Sochin Comprehensive Cancer Institute is one of the largest of its kind in Southern California. Other Specialty centers include the Cedars-Sinai Institute for Spinal Disorders, the Heart Center, and the Center for Chest Diseases. The hospital has a comprehensive transplant center.

The Los Angeles County Department of Health Services operates several community clinics in the area.

■ Recreation

Sightseeing

The immense size of Los Angeles and the innumerable activities offered by the city make its attractions seem limitless. Different sections of the city offer a wide range of sights and diversions, from the more than 40 miles of city-operated Pacific beaches in the west to the mountains in the east and the vast urban areas in between. The downtown district not only forms one of the nation's most modern skylines, but also preserves many historic buildings. Some of the original structures in the city can be found in El Pueblo de Los Angeles State Historic Park. To the east is Olvera Street, a Hispanic district that recreates the atmosphere of old Mexico's open-air markets. Chinatown is just north of the downtown area, and to the south Little Tokyo is the social, cultural, religious, and economic center for southern California's more than 200,000 Japanese American residents, the largest concentration of Japanese people outside of Asia.

Hollywood and other districts devoted to the film and television industry are among the most popular attractions in Los Angeles. Universal Studios Hollywood features guided tours of some of the world's most famous imaginary places, and live tapings of television shows can be viewed at several studios. The world's first psychological thrill ride—the Revenge of the Mummy—opened there in June 2005. Nearby Beverly Hills, an independent community completely surrounded by the city, is home to many film stars, where opulent mansions enjoy proximity to some of the world's most exclusive stores and restaurants. A trip to Los Angeles is not complete without a visit to the newly refurbished Mann's Chinese Theatre and the "Walk of Fame" sidewalk featuring the handprints and footprints of movie legends.

Griffith Park, the city's largest, the Los Angeles Zoo, with more than 2,000 animals; Griffith Observatory, which contains two refracting telescopes; and the Greek Theater, a natural outdoor amphitheater. Train rides are also available in the park. Hancock Park contains the Rancho La Brea Tar Pits, where prehistoric fossil remains are displayed alongside life-size renditions of the species common to the area in prehistory.

Three of the nation's most popular theme parks are located in the Los Angeles area. Six Flags Magic Mountain is 25 minutes north of Hollywood in Valencia and features 260 acres of rides and family-oriented fun. Knott's Berry Farm in Buena Park offers rides, attractions, live entertainment, shops, and restaurants. World-famous Disneyland, located in Anaheim, is home to eight imaginary lands, rides, adventures, and the famous Disney characters.

The Pacific oceanfront provides a variety of attractions, including carnival-like Venice Beach and Muscle Beach, home to hundreds of bodybuilders. Marina Del Ray, known as "L.A.'s Riviera," is the world's largest man-made marina. Catalina Island features island tours and a casino.

Arts and Culture

The performing arts thrive in the city of Los Angeles. Many consider it the entertainment capital of the world, where major television and film projects develop daily. One of America's premier symphony orchestras, the Los Angeles Philharmonic, performs during the winter at the Walt Disney Concert Hall; the orchestra gives summer concerts at Hollywood Bowl, an open-air amphitheater designed by Frank Lloyd Wright. The Los Angeles Opera and Master Chorale performs at the 3,197-seat Dorothy Chandler Pavilion.

Theater in Los Angeles benefits from the motion picture and television industry. Famous personalities can often be seen in area theaters, including the Henry Fonda Theatre, the Ahmanson Theatre, and the Center Theatre Group at the Mark Taper Forum. The internationally acclaimed Joffrey Ballet performs and maintains offices in Los Angeles.

The Los Angeles area is filled with museums for every taste. The Natural History Museum of Los Angeles County features displays of paleontology and history, minerals, animal habitats, and pre-Columbian culture. The Page Museum located at the Rancho La Brea Tar Pits is one of the world's most famous fossil localities, recognized for having the largest and most diverse collection of extinct Ice Age plants and animals in the world. The Hollywood Wax Museum houses more than 350 wax figures depicting famous people. The California Museum of Science and Industry, one of the most visited museums in the West, includes the Mitsubishi IMAX Theatre, the Gehry-designed Aerospace Hall, Technology Hall, the Kinsey Hall of Health, and the California Science Center. The Los Angeles Children's Museum is a hands-on museum, designed to help children learn as they experiment with a number of exhibits. The history of California comes alive at the Gene Autry Western Heritage Museum in Griffith Park, the Southwest Museum, the Hollywood History Museum, and the Wells Fargo Museum. The early Spanish colonial history of the region can be experienced by visiting one of nine mission churches located in and around the city. The Museum of Tolerance is a high-tech, hands-on experiential museum that focuses on racism and prejudice in America and the history of the Holocaust through unique interactive exhibits.

The Museum of Contemporary Art houses a large permanent collection of approximately 5,000 objects in all visual media, ranging from masterpieces of abstract expressionism and pop art to recent works by young and emerging artists. Paintings, drawings, sculpture, illuminated manuscripts, decorative arts, and European and American photographs are on display at the J. Paul Getty Museum, which completed major construction projects in 2006. The Los Angeles County Museum of Art features permanent installations of pre-Columbian, Far Eastern, European, and American artwork, as well as a number of traveling exhibits. Other museums in the region include the California African American Museum, the Chinese American Museum, the Armand Hammer Museum of Art at UCLA, and the many museums to be found on "Museum Row" on the city's west side.

Festivals and Holidays

Los Angeles' events calendar begins with the Tournament of Roses Parade in Pasadena on New Year's Day, an event featuring floral floats decorated by hand. Chinese New Year is celebrated each February in Chinatown with the Golden Dragon Parade and other celebrations. In March or April Olvera Street is host to a Blessing of the Animals festival on the Saturday before Easter. April features the spectacular Easter Sunrise services at the Hollywood Bowl and the annual Academy Awards event sponsored by the Academy of Motion Picture Arts and Sciences.

Cinco de Mayo, a Mexican festival in May, is celebrated in a number of places throughout the Southern California area. May also brings the Calico Spring Festival at Calico Ghost Town in Yermo and the elegant Affaire in the Garden, a fine arts and crafts show in Beverly Hills. June features the Ojai Wine Festival in Ojai and the Playboy Jazz Festival at the Hollywood Bowl. The Fourth of July is celebrated in a variety of ways throughout the city, including fireworks on the oceanfront. July also features the Orange County Fair in Costa Mesa and the International Surf Festival on the South Bay. One of the oldest Japanese American festivals, the Nisei Week Japanese Festival occurs each August in Little Tokyo.

Los Angeles celebrates its birthday each September in the downtown Plaza and Catalina Island hosts the Annual Art Festival, a September tradition since 1958. September also brings the L.A. County Fair in Pomona, a two-week celebration of agriculture and livestock featuring horse races and prize pies. Mexican Independence Day is also celebrated with a fiesta for three days in mid-September in El Pueblo de los Angeles State Historic Park. The annual Music Center Family Festival in September at Music Center Plaza offers international music and dance performances along with free arts and crafts workshops. The October Eagle Rock Music festival is a street fair that is family-friendly, offering food from local restaurants and live entertainment. The Screamfest Horror Film Festival also takes place in October at the Mann Chinese Theatre. November features the Dia de Los Muertes, the "Day of the Dead," a traditional Mexican festival on the first of November. The AFI Film Fest, a 10-day event in November, is the longest running film festival in Los Angeles (established 1987) and is considered to be one of the most influential in North America.

One of the newest festivals for November is the Los Angeles International Tamale Festival, initiated in 2005 at MacArthur Park as a weekend event with activities for kids of all ages. The holiday season begins in December with the Christmas Afloat Boat Parade and the L.A. Art Fair, offering for sale museum-quality artworks from around the world. Los Posadas, a traditional Mexican festival recreating the New Testament story of Mary and Joseph's journey to Bethlehem, takes place each year during the week before Christmas.

Sports for the Spectator

The 21,000-seat Staples Center is home to the National Basketball Association's Clippers and Lakers, and the National Hockey League's Kings. Baseball's National League Dodgers play an April- October season at a refurbished Dodger Stadium. Los Angeles is also home to the Women's National Basketball Association team, the Sparks, and Major League Soccer team, the Galaxy. The Los Angeles Angels of Anaheim professional baseball team and the Anaheim Ducks professional hockey team play in nearby Anaheim.

Collegiate sports are represented by UCLA and USC, both Division I National Collegiate Athletic Association (NCAA) institutions. Both schools field championship caliber teams in every major sport. The annual Rose Bowl, one of the major traditional postseason college football games, is played on New Year's Day in Pasadena. Hollywood Park and Santa Anita Park are both nationally known thoroughbred racing facilities.

Sports for the Participant

The Los Angeles area offers a broad range of activities for the athletically inclined. The miles of city-operated beaches along the Pacific are popular for swimming, surfing, and all forms of boating. Winter skiing areas are less than an hour's drive away from the city. The Los Angeles Parks and Recreation Department operates several hundred parks and recreation centers. These include 54 public swimming pools, 9 dog parks, and 7 skate parks. There are three special Therapeutic Recreation Centers for children and adults with disabilities. The city also has three universally accessible playgrounds, designed to accommodate children of all ability levels. The city maintains seven bike trails.

Shopping and Dining

Los Angeles is a shoppers' paradise, with more than 1,500 department stores as well as countless smaller specialty shops, a number of fashionable shopping plazas, and many large urban malls. An exclusive group of stores along Rodeo Drive is the most famous shopping district in the area, but there are a number of others, including Melrose Avenue, offering the latest and wildest trends in fashion. Westwood Village is a collection of interesting boutiques and restaurants that offers a thriving night life. The Beverly Center in West Los Angeles is one of the nation's busiest malls. Celebrity sightings there are not uncommon, and Japanese tourists come by the thousands to shop as part of planned sightseeing tours. The Hollywood and Highland Center in Hollywood offers dining, shopping, and entertainment at one stop.

Ethnic specialty shops can be found in Little Tokyo, Koreatown, Chinatown, East Los Angeles, and on Olvera Street. The Farmer's Market and Shopping Village in downtown Los Angeles offers fresh produce, import shops, and elegant cafes. Westwood Village and the neighboring UCLA campus are a cultural and entertainment hub filled with shops, bistros, and architectural landmarks.

The Los Angeles area, home to some of America's finest restaurants, enjoys some 20,000 dining establishments, from fast food chains to exclusive gourmet restaurants frequented by Hollywood stars. Ethnic specialties from nearly every country in the world can be found in Los Angeles. Fresh seafood and beef, as well as produce from the nearby agricultural regions, are served in most of the city's restaurants. While in the city, visitors might want to stop at a few of the Los Angeles "original" restaurants. Philippe the Original restaurant, for instance, is the home of the first French dip sandwich, created by accident by the then-chef and owner Philippe Mathieu in 1918. Chansen's Restaurant in Beverley Hills is the birthplace of the Shirley Temple cocktail, invented for the actress of the same name when she first entered the acting scene. Wood-fired pizzas were introduced by Wolfgang Puck, the famous chef and owner of Spago.

Visitor Information: Los Angeles Convention & Visitors Bureau, Visitor Center, 685 S. Figueroa St., Los Angeles, CA 90017; telephone (213)689-8822; www .greaterlosangeles.com

■ Convention Facilities

The major convention and meeting facility in Los Angeles is the Los Angeles Convention Center. Situated on 63 landscaped acres, the complex is centrally located within easy access of hotels, restaurants, nightlife, shops, recreational activities, and sightseeing attractions. With 720,000 square feet of exhibition and 147,000 square feet of meeting room space, the center has become the largest convention facility on the West Coast. There are more than 14,000 hotel rooms and two major airports near the convention center. The California Market Center downtown offers 168,000 square feet of exhibit and banquet space. The Kodak Theatre and the Pantages Theatre are sometimes available for private events. Meeting spaces may also be available at the local universities.

Convention Information: Los Angeles Convention & Visitors Bureau, Visitor Center, 685 S. Figueroa St., Los Angeles, CA 90017; telephone (213)689-8822; www.greaterlosangeles.com

■ Transportation

Approaching the City

Los Angeles International Airport (LAX), just west of the downtown area, is one of the top ten largest airports in the world in terms of passengers handled. The airport is served by over 50 airlines with thousands of flights each year. Special FlyAway buses take visitors from LAX to downtown or to the Van Nuys Airport (a noncommercial regional airport). Nearby Burbank-Glendale-Pasadena Airport, now referred to as the Bob Hope Airport, is served by eight major airlines. Travelers may also choose to enter the area through Long Beach Airport to the south, which is served by four airlines, or LA/Ontario International Airport to the east, which supports 12 airlines.

Greyhound carries passengers to a terminal in downtown Los Angeles. Amtrak has invested $100 million in new passenger trains in recent years. Its *Pacific Surfliner* carries passengers from San Diego through Los Angeles to San Luis Obispo. Three other Amtrak routes pass through the city with about 17 trains passing through LA's Union Station.

Three interstate highways converge in the Los Angeles area: I-5 approaching from Canada in the north, I-15 from Las Vegas to the west, and I-10 connecting Los Angeles with Arizona and the Southwest. State Highway 1, the Pacific Coastal Highway, skirts the city along the ocean.

Traveling in the City

Los Angeles is perhaps best navigated by automobile, however the city's massive, complex web of limited-access freeways, one of the most extensive in the nation, still struggles to accommodate heavy commuter traffic. The Los Angeles Department of Transportation has implemented a state-of-the-art computer system to manage the city's street traffic, but Los Angeles is still among the places with the worst traffic in the nation, according to a study by Cambridge Systematics for the American Highway Users Alliance.

The Los Angeles County Metropolitan Transit operates frequent local and express bus service with 200 metro buslines throughout the city and to major area attractions. Light rail service is also available. The Metro Blue Line runs north and south between Long Beach and Los Angeles. The Metro Green Line runs between Norwalk and Redondo Beach. The Metro Red Line subway provides service through Downtown to North Hollywood, then connects to the Orange Line, which

travels west into the San Fernando Valley. The Metro Purple Line subway runs through Downtown and continues to the Mid-Wilshire area. The Metro Gold Line connects with the Red Line at Union Station and runs northeast to Pasadena.

The City of Los Angeles Department of Transportation operates the DASH shuttle system. Six downtown DASH lines link major business, government, retail and entertainment centers within downtown. The Convention Center, the Garment and Jewelry districts, Olvera Street, the Metro Blue Line, and Union Station are easily accessible via DASH lines.

■ Communications

Newspapers and Magazines

Los Angeles has two main daily papers. The *Los Angeles Times* is based in the city. In 2006 it ranked as the fourth largest newspaper in the nation with a circulation of about 851,832. The *Daily News*, published out of Oxnard, has a circulation of about 432,000. The *Los Angeles Daily Journal* and *Investors Business Journal* serve the business community with daily papers. The *Los Angeles Business Journal* is a weekly publication. *La Opinion* is the largest Spanish-language newspaper in the United States, with a daily circulation of about 100,880. Other Spanish-language papers published in LA include *La Prensa de Los Angeles* and *LA Voz Libre*.

More than 100 foreign-language, special-interest, business, alternative, and neighborhood papers are published weekly in Los Angeles area. Those published within the city include the *Los Angeles Independent*, *Westsider*, and *Hollywood/West Hollywood Independent*, all distributed on Wednesday. The *Los Angeles Downtown News* is distributed on Monday. *LA Weekly* is an alternative press publication distributed on Thursday. Weekly newspapers serving the African American community include *Fireston Park News*, the *Herald Dispatch*, and the *Los Angeles Sentinel*. Numerous English and foreign language papers serve the ethnic communities, including the *Beirut Times* (in Arabic), *Pacific Times* (Chinese and Taiwanese), and *California-Staats Zeitung* (German). The *Rafu Shimpo* (Japanese) and *Korea Times* (Korean) are daily papers. The *Jewish Journal of Greater Los Angeles* is published weekly and *Jewish News* is published monthly.

Los Angeles magazine, a monthly covering events and topics of importance to the metropolitan area, and a number of nationally distributed magazines, such as *Guns and Ammo*, and *Bon Appetit* are also published in the city.

Television and Radio

Eleven television stations broadcast in the Los Angeles area. The 12 AM and 20 FM radio stations broadcasting there feature a wide assortment of music, news, and information programming; stations broadcasting in surrounding communities are also received in Los Angeles.

Media Information: *Los Angeles Times,* 202 W. First Street, Los Angeles, CA 90012; telephone (213)237-5000; www.latimes.com

Los Angeles Online

City of Los Angeles Home Page. Available www.lacity.org

La Opinion. Available www.laopinion.com

Los Angeles Area Chamber of Commerce. Available www.lachamber.org

Los Angeles Convention and Visitors Bureau. Available www.greaterlosangeles.com

Los Angeles Economic Development Corporation. Available www.laedc.org

Los Angeles Public Library. Available www.lapl.org

Los Angeles Times. Available www.latimes.com

BIBLIOGRAPHY

Allende, Isabel, *The Infinite Plan* (New York: HarperCollins, 1993)

Cameron, Robert W., *Above Los Angeles* (San Francisco, CA: Cameron and Co., 1990)

Cole, Carolyn Kozo, and Kathy Kobayashi, *Shades of Los Angeles: Pictures from Ethnic Family Albums* (New York: Norton, 1996)

Gebhard, David, and Robert Winter, *Architecture in Los Angeles* (Salt Lake City, UT: Gibbs M. Smith Inc., Peregrine Smith Books, 1985)

Hacker, Andrew, *Two Nations: Black and White, Separate, Hostile, Unequal* (New York: Scribner, 1992)

Mosley, Walter, *White Butterfly* (New York: W.W. Norton, 1992)

Monterey

■ The City in Brief

Founded: 1770 (incorporated 1850)

Head Official: Mayor Chuck Della Sala (since 2006)

City Population

    1980: 27,558
    1990: 31,954
    2000: 29,674
    2006 estimate: 28,803
    Percent change, 1990–2000: −8.9%
    U.S. rank in 1980: Not reported
    U.S. rank in 1990: Not reported
    U.S. rank in 2000: Not reported (State rank: 237th)

Metropolitan Area Population

    1980: 290,000
    1990: 355,660
    2000: 410,762
    2006 estimate: Not reported
    Percent change, 1990–2000: 13%
    U.S. rank in 1980: Not reported
    U.S. rank in 1990: 102nd (PMSA)
    U.S. rank in 2000: 103rd (MSA)

Area: 8.44 square miles (2000)

Elevation: 10 feet above sea level

Average Annual Temperature: 57° F

Average Annual Precipitation: 19.29 inches

Major Economic Sectors: services, wholesale and retail trade, government

Unemployment Rate: 5.4% (September 2007)

Per Capita Income: $27,133 (1999)

2005 FBI Crime Index Property: 1,295

2005 FBI Crime Index Violent: 172

Major Colleges and Universities: Monterey Peninsula College, Monterey Institute of International Studies, Naval Postgraduate School

Daily Newspaper: *The Monterey County Herald*

■ Introduction

Monterey, the largest city on the Monterey Peninsula, is a beautiful seaside community with a vast array of recreational and cultural activities. Cannery Row, the district made famous by novelist John Steinbeck that once marked Monterey as the "Sardine Capital of the World," has become a bustling retail site with fashionable restaurants, shops, and nightspots. Monterey has preserved more of its history than any other California city. Once the capital of the Spanish territory of California, Monterey has restored its historic buildings and Spanish adobes, and displays these treasures on the magnificent crescent of blue water that is Monterey Bay.

■ Geography and Climate

Monterey is located on the Monterey Peninsula, which is 120 miles south of San Francisco, 60 miles south of San Jose, and 345 miles north of Los Angeles. The peninsula is bordered by Monterey Bay to the north, the Pacific Ocean to the west, and Carmel Bay to the south.

Although characterized by cool, dry summers and wet winters, the regions of Monterey County exhibit considerable climatic diversity. The warmest months are July through October, and the rainiest are November and April. Summer months often can be foggy, especially early and late in the day, due to the chilly and unchanging water temperatures of the Pacific Ocean. The city lies in an area surrounding by six active fault lines putting the city at risk for earthquakes.

Area: 8.44 square miles (2000)

Elevation: 10 feet above sea level

Average Temperature: 57° F

Average Annual Precipitation: 19.29 inches

■ History

Early Settlements

Native Americans known as the Esalen lived in the area of present-day Monterey from 500 B.C. to 500 A.D. and probably much longer. The Esalen were displaced in 500 B.C. by the Ohlone Indians, who were drawn to the area by the abundance of fish and wildlife and other natural resources. The Indians hunted quail, geese, rabbit, bear, and other wildlife, gathered plants, and caught fish, mussels, abalone, and shellfish. Several of their village sites have been identified and preserved.

Monterey was first seen by Europeans when Portuguese explorer Juan Rodriquez Cabrillo spotted La Bahia de los Pinos (Bay of Pines) in 1542 on a journey in search of riches in the New World. But high winds prevented him and his crew from landing. In 1602 Spanish explorer Don Sebastian Viscaino officially named the port in honor of Spain's Count of Monte Rey under whose order he was sailing. Viscaino's 200 men gave thanks for their safe journey in a ceremony held under a large oak tree overlooking the bay.

In 1770 an expedition by land and sea brought Gaspar de Portol and Franciscan Father Junipero Serra to Monterey. There they established the Mission and Presidio (military post) of San Carlos de Borromeo de Monterey and the City of Monterey. Under the same oak tree where Viscaino's crew members had prayed, Father Serra said mass for his brave group. A year later Father Serra moved the mission to nearby Carmel, which offered a better agricultural and political environment; the Presidio Church in Monterey, however, continued in use.

Becomes Capital of Spanish California

In 1776 Spain named Monterey the capital of Baja (lower) and Alta (upper) California. This same year Captain Juan Bautista de Anza arrived with the first settlers for Spanish California, most of them bound for San Francisco. For decades Monterey's soldiers and their wives lived at the Presidio. In 1818 Argentinean revolutionary Hippolyte Bouchard sacked the town in an effort to destroy Spain's presence in California. Soon the residents began to expand outside the Presidio, creating homesteads throughout Monterey.

In April 1822, when Mexico gained its independence from Spain, Monterey became the Mexican capital. California soon pledged its loyalty to the Mexican government.

Spain had not allowed foreigners to trade with California, but Mexico opened up the area to international trade, and Monterey was made California's sole port of entry. Traffic with English and American vessels for the hide and tallow trade became an important part of the economy. A dried steer hide valued at about a dollar was termed a "California bank note." The hides were shipped to New England, where they were used to make saddles, harnesses, and shoes. Tallow was melted down in large rendering pots and poured into bags of hides or bladders to be delivered to the trading ships; in the end, most of the tallow was made into candles.

By 1827 foreign trade had become very important and a custom house was built in Monterey. The booming trade, especially with New England, attracted a number of Americans—called "Yanquis"—to Monterey. Many of them married into Mexican families and became Mexican citizens. In the mid-1830s, Mexican rulers redistributed much of the local land formerly run by the Catholic Church and huge cattle ranches were formed. An elite class of landed "Californios" grew up in the area. In 1842 the U.S. government sent Thomas Larkin to Monterey to head the first American consulate in California.

Statehood Attained

In July 1846 Commodore John Drake Sloat's flagship arrived in Monterey Bay and his troops raised the American flag, claiming the region for the United States, and gaining the territory without a fight from the Mexicans. American occupation continued until the Treaty of Guadalupe Hidalgo was signed in 1848, making all of Alta California part of the United States. This included the land now known as California, Utah, Nevada, and parts of Arizona, Colorado, New Mexico, and Wyoming.

In Monterey, U.S. Naval Chaplain Walter Colton was appointed to serve as Monterey's first American Alcalde, a position defined as mayor and judge. Colton, a well-educated and just man, was considered well qualified to hold this important position. In 1846 he and Robert Semple established California's first newspaper, *The Californian*. Colton also designed and supervised the construction of the first public structure built under the American flag, Colton Hall, which served as a public school and town meeting hall.

In 1849 delegates from throughout Alta California met in Colton Hall in Monterey to create a constitution for the people of the new U.S. territory. The new constitution was signed on October 13, 1849. In 1850 the U.S. Congress voted to adopt California as the thirty-first state of the Union. San Jose was chosen as the seat for the first legislature. (The official definition of a state capital is where the legislature sits; therefore Monterey never was the state capital.)

During the next decade Monterey lost much of its political influence. But at the same time it was becoming an important center for the whaling industry. Asian and

European fishermen began arriving there, drawn by the developing fishing industry. Influences from these Japanese, Chinese, Portuguese, and Italian immigrants formed a basis for the city's culture that lives on to today.

Serves as County Seat; Sardine Trade Develops

After California gained its statehood, the legislature formed counties. Monterey served as the Monterey County seat of government until 1873, when Salinas was named to that role. Further transformation of Monterey took place in the 1870s when the first railroad was built, connecting the quiet fishing town with cosmopolitan San Francisco and cities beyond. In the 1880s the local whaling industry disappeared and civic leaders turned to tourism to revive the local economy. By the mid-1880s tourism flourished in the area, with thousands flocking to the seaside resort annually.

By the 1920s the sardine market had grown greatly and the section of Monterey known as Cannery Row was established. During the next two decades, a score of canneries and reduction plants grew up in the area. Workers processed an estimated 250,000 tons of sardines each year. Monterey became known as the "Sardine Capital of the World." The rough and rollicking vicinity of Cannery Row was made famous in the John Steinbeck novels *Cannery Row* and *Sweet Thursday*.

Abandoned Warehouses Revitalized; Tourism Grows

In the 1940s, for reasons still in dispute, the sardine population began a rapid decline. Theories explaining the sardines' disappearance range from water pollution to a change in currents to warmer climates or just being "fished out." The once-thriving Cannery Row soon became a ghost town of empty warehouses.

That changed in the second half of the twentieth century, as the old abandoned warehouses were converted into shops, restaurants, and galleries and tourism began to take root. In the early 2000s tourism was a major industry in Monterey, growing out of the city's efforts to preserve its historic and natural resources.

In March 2007 the city council met to develop a new vision, mission, and strategic plan for the city. It was the first time in about 20 years that such a comprehensive plan was established. In hopes of building Monterey into a model city for residents, businesses, and visitors alike, the strategic initiatives within the plan listed a diverse set of actions including the improvement and expansion of basic city services and utilities, housing, and library and cultural resources, as well as ideas on ways to balance the budget and inspire economic growth.

Historical Information: Monterey County Historical Society, PO Box 3576, Salinas, CA 93912; telephone (831)757-8085; www.mchsmuseum.com

■ Population Profile

Metropolitan Area Residents

1980: 290,000
1990: 355,660
2000: 410,762
2006 estimate: Not reported
Percent change, 1990–2000: 13%
U.S. rank in 1980: Not reported
U.S. rank in 1990: 102nd (PMSA)
U.S. rank in 2000: 103rd (MSA)

City Residents

1980: 27,558
1990: 31,954
2000: 29,674
2006 estimate: 28,803
Percent change, 1990–2000: −8.9%
U.S. rank in 1980: Not reported
U.S. rank in 1990: Not reported
U.S. rank in 2000: Not reported (State rank: 237th)

Density: 3,516.9 people per square mile (2000)

Racial and ethnic characteristics (2000)

White: 23,985
Black: 749
American Indian and Alaska Native: 170
Asian: 2,205
Native Hawaiian and Pacific Islander: 86
Hispanic or Latino (may be of any race): 3,222
Other: 1,603

Percent of residents born in state: 41.6% (2000)

Age characteristics (2000)

Population under 5 years old: 1,477
Population 5 to 9 years old: 1,421
Population 10 to 14 years old: 1,263
Population 15 to 19 years old: 1,961
Population 20 to 24 years old: 2,695
Population 25 to 34 years old: 5,382
Population 35 to 44 years old: 4,638
Population 45 to 54 years old: 4,031
Population 55 to 59 years old: 1,279
Population 60 to 64 years old: 1,117
Population 65 to 74 years old: 1,974
Population 75 to 84 years old: 1,699
Population 85 years and older: 737
Median age: 36.1 years

Births (2001, Monterey County)

Total number: 7,176

Airphoto-Jim Wark

Deaths (2001, Monterey County)

Total number: 2,470

Money income (1999)

Per capita income: $27,133
Median household income: $49,109
Total households: 12,656

Number of households with income of . . .

less than $10,000: 887
$10,000 to $14,999: 621
$15,000 to $24,999: 1,262
$25,000 to $34,999: 1,431
$35,000 to $49,999: 2,261
$50,000 to $74,999: 2,865
$75,000 to $99,999: 1,403
$100,000 to $149,999: 1,307
$150,000 to $199,999: 304
$200,000 or more: 315

Percent of families below poverty level: 4.4%(1999)

2005 FBI Crime Index Property: 1,295

2005 FBI Crime Index Violent: 172

■ Municipal Government

Monterey operates with a council-city manager form of government. The city council is the policymaking branch of the city government and consists of five members. The mayor is elected to a two-year term and four council members are elected to four-year terms. The city manager, appointed by the council, serves as the city's professional administrator.

Head Official: Mayor Chuck Della Sala (since 2006; term expires November 2008)

Total Number of City Employees: over 800 (2007)

City Information: City of Monterey, 580 Pacific Street, Monterey, CA 93940; telephone (831)646-3799; www.monterey.org

■ Economy

Major Industries and Commercial Activity

Once a leading fishing and whaling port, Monterey County's economic mainstays now are tourism and the military. While tourism has always been a major component in the city's economy, it has become the dominant industry in the last 30 years, supporting more than one third of Monterey jobs. Today, hotel taxes provide some 30 percent of the city budget and the main source of funding for municipal services is derived from the visitor industry. The prime tourist season runs April through Thanksgiving. While the city's economy suffered greatly from the lack of travel due to the events of September 11, 2001, Monterey tourism is on the rebound. The Monterey Bay Aquarium is the prime attraction, and numerous restaurants, art galleries, gift shops, and an Antiques Mall have created a wide variety of shopping opportunities. Tourists also come to observe the special events tied to the historic Cannery Row Area, made famous by novelist John Steinbeck, local son of the nearby city of Salinas. Its reputation as a world class golfing destination brings golfers to the championship golf courses at Pebble Beach and other area courses. Independent travelers (those not with a tour group) make up the largest class of overnight visitors to the Monterey Bay Area and are primarily from elsewhere in California. It is estimated that 4 million people visit Monterey each year. The city's population increases to nearly 70,000 during tourist seasons.

Due to its strategic location, Monterey has historically been a key military outpost. Today, the city's military installations continue to provide tremendous support to the economy, particularly through its educational institutions. The Army's Defense Language Institute provides language instruction for agents of the FBI, Drug Enforcement Administration, and Border Patrol. The Naval Postgraduate School offers advance classroom training for Naval officers. The Fleet Numerical Meteorology and Oceanography Center, operated by the Navy, is one of the world's leading numerical weather prediction centers. According to *The Monterey County Herald,* these institutions contribute $1 billion to the local economy. The economic impact of spending by the School and employees of the Naval Postgraduate School alone amounts to more than $140 million channeled into the local economies of Monterey County. However, the changing needs of the military, coupled with its efforts to streamline operations, threaten the closure of many of the country's military bases and those in California are not exempt.

Agriculture is the largest industry in Monterey County, accounting for more than 21 percent of all employment. The government employs approximately 18 percent of the county's workforce. Other significant sectors of Monterey's economy include trade, transportation and utilities, which account for 16 percent of all employment in the county. Workers in the leisure and hospitality sector, including arts, recreation, entertainment, accommodations and food service, make up 12 percent of the workforce.

As Monterey looks to the future, the challenge will be to balance the cyclical nature of the tourist economy while finding ways to provide higher paying jobs. Monterey will increasingly see its economy based on educational and research activities. Marine biology and the environmental sciences are expected to make a very large impact on the economy of the region. The information technology sector is also becoming more important; Monterey County has a need for computer software engineers and network systems and data communications analysts. Air transportation workers and pharmacy aides were also in demand in 2007.

Some of the largest employers in Salinas Valley in 2007 were: Dole Fresh Vegetables; Tanimura and Antle, Inc.; Escamilla and Sons, Inc.; Spreckels; Salinas Valley Memorial Healthcare System; D'Arrigo Brothers Company of California; Fresh Express, Fresh Food; and the CDC Correctional Training Facility, Soledad.

Items and goods produced: vegetables, fish and seafood, light manufactured products

Incentive Programs—New and Existing Companies

Local programs: The California Coastal Rural Development Corporation operates a variety of small business loan programs, as well as Monterey's Microloan Program. The Central Coast Small Business Development Center (SBDC) provides no-cost, hands-on technical assistance and support to small businesses on California's Central Coast. Confidential counseling, classes, workshops, seminars, and loan programs are available through the SBDC.

State programs: With the Manufacturers' Investment Credit, companies that purchase manufacturing or R&D equipment for use anywhere in California are allowed a tax credit equal to six percent of the costs paid or incurred for acquiring the property. Other incentives include the California research and development tax credit, which allows companies to receive a credit of 15 percent against bank and corporate tax liability for certain research done in-house. An additional 24 percent credit is available for basic research payments to outside organizations. This is one of the highest research and development tax credits in the nation. A Child Care Tax Credit is available for companies establishing on-site child-care facilities. A Net Operating Loss Carryover and New Market Tax Credits are also available. A Work Opportunity Tax Credit is offered for employers who hire individuals from certain target groups.

Job training programs: The Private Industry Council (PIC) offers specialized services designed for laid off workers who have been displaced from their jobs due to plant closures or relocation. Programs for older workers,

limited English speakers, offenders, physically handicapped youth, teen parents, and other at-risk youth are
also available. The city of Monterey can also provide information about agencies that assist international businesses with training employees. JobLINK of Monterey
County provides employment and training opportunities
and services to laid off workers, long-term unemployed,
displaced homemakers, and persons over 55. The California Employment Training Panel assists businesses
through performance-based customized training contracts for new or existing employees. Reimbursement of
costs for developing, implementing, and completing
training programs may range from $1,500 to $2,000 per
employee. Monterey Peninsula College, a two-year
school, provides job training.

Development Projects

When a change in military needs led to the downsizing of
Fort Ord in 1993, the 13,000 soldiers and family members
who lived there were relocated. The city is making efforts
to replace the lost revenue by redeveloping the area into an
educational, residential, commercial and light industrial
center. A Base Reuse Plan has been developed to guide the
planning and implementation process through 2014.
Plans include removing toxins from military use from the
site and constructing housing at all income levels, making
recreational improvements, and conserving a portion of
the land for endangered species. Once the process is
started, it is estimated that it will take five to seven years to
complete the relocation, rehabilitation, hazard abatement,
and demolition removal activities at the Fort. In 2005, the
U. S. Army had finished a substantial amount of the clean-
up, but more funds were needed to complete the project.
The Defense Language Institute, the Naval Postgraduate
School and the Coast Guard station now occupy 750 acres
of the property, which has been annexed to the Presidio of
Monterey. California State University at Monterey Bay
and the Monterey Institute of International Studies have
opened campuses there, as well as the University of California at Santa Cruz, with a new research center on the
property. The remaining half of the property is being
turned over to the U.S. Bureau of Land Management to
manage as open spaces.

Monterey City Council approved a building permit
for the construction of an IMAX theater in Cannery Row;
design plans were approved in 2006, and the city was
expecting to receive building plans in 2007. Also on
Cannery Row, a Monterey Peninsula Hotel was under
construction in 2007 and is expected to open in May
2008. A Trader Joe's was being remodeled in 2007.

Economic Development Information: California
Coastal Rural Development Corp., 2121 M120 Main St.,
Suite 301, Salinas, CA 93901; telephone (831)424-1099.
Central Coast Small Business Development Center at
Cabrillo College, 6500 Soquel Drive, Aptos, CA 95003;
telephone (831)479-6136

Commercial Shipping

Monterey is not a major commercial transportation hub;
however, there are a number of motor freight carriers that
serve the surrounding area.

Labor Force and Employment Outlook

Monterey County's civilian labor force in September
2007 totaled approximately 206,800 workers; 11,200 of
them were unemployed (5.4 percent of the labor force).
The area employs both seasonal and year-round workers
since the visitor industry accounts for such a large part of
the economy. According to the Monterey Peninsula
Chamber of Commerce, the ratio of people in the labor
force and employment roles have remained constant since
1998. One challenge to attracting new employees to the
city of Monterey has been its lack of affordable housing.
Since the jobs fueled by the tourist industry in Monterey
tend to be lower paying jobs, affordable housing is especially needed. In 2007, the occupations with the fastest
job growth over the 2004–2014 period were projected to
be computer software engineers, network systems and
data communications analysts, air transportation workers,
and pharmacy aides.

The following is a summary of data regarding the
Monterey area metropolitan area labor force, 2003 annual averages.

Size of nonagricultural labor force: 130,000

Number of workers employed in . . .

    construction and mining: 6,700
    manufacturing: 7,700
    trade, transportation and utilities: 25,200
    information: 2,400
    financial activities: 6,600
    professional and business services: 14,400
    educational and health services: 12,100
    leisure and hospitality: 19,400
    other services: 4,400
    government: 31,000

**Average hourly earnings of production workers
employed in manufacturing:** $15.50

Unemployment rate: 12.9% (December 2004)

Largest employers employees *(Salinas Valley)*	*Number of employees*
Dole Fresh Vegetables	4,700
County of Monterey	4,435
Tanimura and Antle Inc.	3,000
Naval Postgraduate School	2,600
Escamilla and Sons Inc., Spreckels	2,060

Salinas Valley Memorial Healthcare System	1,900
D'Arrigo Bros. Co. of CA	1,700
Fresh Express, Fresh Food	1,650
CDC Correctional Training Facility, Soledad	1,531
Household	1,526

Cost of Living

The following is a summary of data regarding several key cost of living factors for the Monterey area.

2007 (1st quarter) ACCRA Average House Price: $827,270 (San Jose area)

2007 (1st quarter) ACCRA Cost of Living Index: 155.1 (San Jose area)

State income tax rate: 1.0% to 9.3%

State sales tax rate: 7.25%

Local income tax rate: None

Local sales tax rate: 1.25% (county)

Property tax rate: 1% of assessed value

Economic Information: Monterey Peninsula Chamber of Commerce, 380 Alvarado St., Monterey, CA 93940; telephone (861)648-5360; fax (831)649-3502; email info&mpcc.com.

■ Education and Research

Elementary and Secondary Schools

The Monterey Peninsula Unified School District encompasses Monterey City schools as well as those of Marina, Fort Ord, Sand City, Seaside, and Del Rey Oaks. In addition to a well-rounded curriculum, the schools offer a gifted and talented program (GATE) for fourth and fifth grade students and an independent study program for motivated students who wish to study on their own. Special academies for high school students include the Art Careers Academy, Monterey Academy of Oceanographic Science, and Sports Professions and Recreation Careers, all at Monterey High School, and Health Professions Pathway at Seaside High School. The Monterey Adult School offers a regional occupational program as well as other courses for students age 16 and above.

The following is a summary of data regarding the Monterey Peninsula Unified School District as of the 2005–2006 school year.

Total enrollment: 10,252

Number of facilities

elementary schools: 12
junior high/middle schools: 4
senior high schools: 4
other: 2

Student/teacher ratio: Not available

Teacher salaries (2005–06)

elementary median: $34,186–$68,022 (all levels)
junior high/middle median: Not available
secondary median: Not available

Funding per pupil: $7,186

Monterey is also home to several religious schools and to the York School associated with the Episcopal Faith, Santa Catalina School (Catholic school for girls), and Possibility House, a Montessori pre-school.

Public Schools Information: Monterey Peninsula Unified School District, 700 Pacific St., Monterey CA 93940-5730; telephone (831)645-1200; www.mpusd.k12.ca.us

Colleges and Universities

Monterey's major institution of higher learning is Monterey Peninsula College. It is one of 109 schools in the California Community College System. Enrollment is over 16,900 students.

The college offers associate's degrees and certificate programs in a wide variety of fields, including business administration, accounting, law enforcement, art history, computer technology, visual arts, drama, music, hospitality, medical assisting, nursing, and many others.

The Monterey Institute of International Studies, an affiliate of Middlebury College (Vermont) offers graduate programs in international policy studies, language translation and interpretation, language and educational linguistics, and international business. The school also offers tailored courses for individuals requiring intensive language and cultural training for work outside their native country or with foreign nationals in the United States.

The Naval Postgraduate School is an academic institution whose emphasis is on study and research programs relevant to the U.S. Navy's interests, as well as to the interests of other arms of the Department of Defense. Its campus houses state-of-the-art laboratories, academic buildings, a library, government housing, and recreational facilities to serve its nearly 1,500 students. The student body consists of officers from the five U.S. uniformed services, officers from approximately 30 other countries, and a small number of civilian employees. The school offers master of arts degrees in national security affairs, master of science degrees in a wide variety of fields, and bachelor's and doctoral degrees in various engineering fields. Another educational institution associated with the military is the Defense Language Institute operated by the Army. Its Foreign Language Center, located on the Presidio of Monterey, is the world's largest language institute.

Golden Gate University's Monterey Bay Campus offers undergraduate and graduate degree programs in business, public administration, health care, and technology. The Orange County-based Chapman University maintains a Monterey campus which offers baccalaureate degrees in a variety of subjects. California State University's Monterey Bay campus on the grounds of Fort Ord offers 12 undergraduate programs to approximately 3,500 students.

Libraries and Research Centers

Monterey Public Library is the largest public library on the Monterey Peninsula. The library houses more than 120,000 volumes, video and audio cassettes, and CDs, subscribes to 375 magazines and newspapers, and operates one bookmobile. The California History Room contains a unique collection of books, selected magazine and newspaper articles, maps, government documents, photographs, and archival material about the city of Monterey and the Monterey Peninsula. Additional library programs and collections include the Local History Partners, which provides access to local history materials through a partnership with the Colton Hall Museum, the Monterey History and Art Association, and the Teen Zone and Youth Services collections.

Other local libraries include the Colton Hall Museum Library, the CTB McGraw-Hill Library, the Maritime Museum of Monterey Library, the Monterey Bay Aquarium Library, the Community Hospital of the Monterey Peninsula Medical Library, The Monterey County Herald Library, and the U.S. Navy Library. College libraries are housed at the Monterey Institute of International Studies, the Naval Postgraduate School, and Monterey Bay Peninsula College.

The Monterey Institute of International Studies is home to the Center for East Asian Studies, the James Martin Center for Nonproliferation Studies, the Center for Globalization and Localization of Business Exports (GLOBE), and the Center for Russian and Eurasian Studies. Naval Postgraduate School is home to dozens of research institutes and centers that support the Navy and Department of Defense, including the Turbo Propulsion Laboratory, the Ocean Acoustic Observatory, the Spacecraft Research and Design Center, and the Center for Autonomous Underwater Vehicle Research. The Monterey Bay Aquarium Research Institute's research program focuses on deep-sea exploration in Monterey Bay, one of the most biologically diverse bodies of water in the world. The Institute's two research vessels and remotely-operated vehicles provide access to the

Monterey Canyon, an underwater canyon two miles deep. The Naval Research Laboratory is the Navy and Marine Corps' corporate research lab. The lab conducts research on the atmosphere, develops weather interpretation systems for the Department of Defense, and studies the effects of the atmosphere on Naval weapons systems.

Public Library and Research Information: Monterey Public Library, 625 Pacific St., Monterey, CA 93940; telephone (831)646-3932; fax (831)646-5618. Naval Postgraduate School, Office of the Dean of research, Halligan Hall, Monterey, CA 93943; www.nps.edu/research

■ Health Care

Community Hospital of the Monterey Peninsula is a nonprofit system serving the Monterey Peninsula and surrounding communities with 15 locations that include outpatient facilities, satellite laboratories, mental health clinics, and two hospice facilities. The main hospital houses a comprehensive cancer care center, an emergency department, a family birth center, and a health resource library. The system also includes the Breast Care Center, the Carmel Hill Professional Center, the Diabetes and Nutrition Therapy Center, the Hartnell Professional Center, and Ryan Ranch Outpatient Campus. The 172-bed Natividad Medical Center, an acute care hospital in nearby Salinas, is owned and operated by Monterey county and is affiliated with the University of California at San Francisco School of Medicine.

■ Recreation

Sightseeing

Monterey's Cannery Row, popularized by the books of Nobel and Pulitzer award winner John Steinbeck, is one of America's most famous streets. Cannery Row features over 200 shops, restaurants, galleries, and attractions, including American Tin Cannery Premium Outlets and A Taste of Monterey Wine Tasting Room. The Blue Fin Cafe & Billiards overlooks Steinbeck Plaza and offers a panoramic view of Monterey Bay and Cannery Row. Steinbeck's Spirit of Monterey Wax Museum recreates the history of Cannery Row through life-sized characters and narration. The Edgewater Family Fun Center, across from the Cannery, has the area's largest video arcade, a snack bar, old-time photos, a magic shop, and bike and surrey rentals. Other amusements in Cannery Row include a shop which rents reproductions of old roadster convertibles, an old-fashioned portrait studio, and a ceramic painting studio.

Fisherman's Wharf and Wharf No. 2 stretch side-by-side into the Monterey Harbor. Fisherman's Wharf is lined with seafood restaurants, fish markets, art galleries, shops, candy stores, a theater, and fish and diving companies. Municipal Wharf No. 2 is a working fish pier where commercial fishing boats can be seen unloading their daily catch. On holidays, the fisherman often decorate their craft with colorful strings of lights.

Cannery Row's Monterey Bay Aquarium features marine life ranging from playful sea otters to drifting jellyfish, octopuses, giant ocean sunfish, green sea turtles, swirling yellow-fin tuna, and hundreds of other creatures. A recent addition is a white shark, the only one on exhibit in the world. The Ocean's Edge: Coastal Habitats of Monterey Bay exhibit has been popular since its opening in 2005. The aquarium showcases the largest ocean sanctuary in the United States in a three-story-tall living kelp forest, the million-gallon Outer Bay exhibit, a jellyfish gallery, expanded touch pools, and dozens more recently renovated galleries and exhibits.

Monterey State Historic Park downtown marks the spot where the U.S. flag was first officially raised on July 7, 1846, heralding California's statehood. Ten buildings, including the Custom House, California's first theater, and several former 1830s residences, now museums, preserve the area's heritage.

Tours are available of Colton Hall, a local landmark from the time when Monterey was the capital of Alta California. The hall was built to serve as a public school and town meeting hall and now is a museum. California's first constitution was drafted there 150 years ago.

Visitors to the area enjoy whale watching (best in winter) and fishing trips. Other popular tours departing from Monterey can be guided or self-guided. Wine tasting, sightseeing, and agricultural education tours are available, as well as movie tours of scenes from popular movies filmed in the area. Point Pios Lighthouse at the northernmost tip of the Monterey Peninsula is open for guided tours. The 17-mile drive along the coast through Pebble Beach affords spectacular views of rugged coastline and animals in their natural habitats.

Arts and Culture

The Monterey Museum of Art has a fine collection of early Christian, Asian, American folk, ethnic, and tribal art. It also offers photographic exhibits and rotating exhibits of major American artists. The museum is housed in two facilities, Pacific Street and La Mirada. Pacific Street, located across from Colton Hall in the historic center of Monterey, includes eight galleries as well as the Buck Education Center and Library. The Monterey Museum of Art at La Mirada is situated in one of Monterey's oldest neighborhoods and is surrounded by magnificent gardens and picturesque stone walls. It began as a two-room adobe structure and later became an elegant home where international and regional celebrities were entertained. Visitors today experience the same exquisitely furnished home and spectacular rose and rhododendron gardens. Visitors view the museum's permanent collection and changing exhibitions in four contemporary galleries, including the Dart Wing designed by renowned architect Charles Moore, that complement the original estate.

The Monterey Conference Center features impressive permanent and rotating collections. Sculptures, paintings, and tapestries from contemporary local artists adorn its walls and public spaces. Visitors are greeted by *Two Dolphins*, a nine-foot-tall sculpture composed of thousands of pieces of inlaid wood. The work, created by Big Sur artist Emile Norman, depicts two dolphins in flight as they dance across the sea. On the center's second floor, the Alvarado Gallery presents an ever-changing array of art from Peninsula artists.

The Golden State Theatre features live shows and concerts by musical guests and comedians and also serves as a film theater for old movies. It is the site for the Monterey International Film Week. The Bruce Arris Wharf Theater at Fisherman's Wharf offers live shows as well.

Festivals and Holidays

Colorful events fill Monterey's calendar throughout the year. In January the annual migration of the gray whales is saluted through a variety of events such as art projects, story telling, whale watching, and exhibits. The sounds of Dixieland and Swing fill the March air during the three days of Dixieland Monterey, held in various venues with dance floors and special events.

The spotlight is on young, up-and-coming musicians during the three-day Next Generation Jazz Festival held annually in April. The Annual Sea Otter Classic, the largest bicycle festival in the country, features road cycling, mountain biking, downhill, and BMX events. Original hand-made arts and crafts are for sale at the Spring Arts & Crafts Fair. The Old Monterey Plein Air Painting and Art Promenade showcases artists of all ages busy at work on the streets of Monterey. The Monterey Wine Festival, held at the end of April, featuring California wines exclusively, consists of tastings, educational seminars, and cooking demonstrations.

On May 15, Cannery Row celebrates the life and times of Ed "Doc" Ricketts, a revolutionary marine biologist and mentor of John Steinbeck. Mountain bikers can race solo or team up to ride as many laps as possible in the 24 Hours of Adrenalin Cycle Race. The Back to the Boatyard Beer Festival is a lively celebration of great beers in May. Three days of blues music on three stages is the focus of the Monterey Bay Blues Festival at the Monterey Fairgrounds in June.

July's big events include the Community Fourth of July Parade, picnic and fireworks, the commemoration of John Drake Sloat's landing in Monterey on July 8, and the Obon Festival at the Buddhist Temple. August is enlivened by the Annual Winemaster's Celebration, the Turkish Festival, the Monterey County Fair, and the Historic Automobile Races. Crowds dine and dance at September's Annual Bay ReggaeFest, Rock and Art Festival, Annual Greek Festival, Festa Italia-Santa Rosalia Festival, the Cherry's Jubilee classic car show, the Fishermen's Fiesta and the Monterey Beer Festival. The world-famous Monterey Jazz Festival offers non-stop jazz by top performers as well as food, art, and jazz clinics. Fresh seafood, music, and crafts are the focus of October's Old Monterey Seafood & Music Festival. A reenactment of California's first Constitutional Convention takes place each October on California Constitution Day. International Day in October celebrates cultural diversity in entertainment, food and cultural demonstrations from 35 countries. A week-long focus on the history of Monterey is History Fest Monterey. The Monterey Sports Car Championships features Le Mans style racing as the main event at the Mazda Raceway Laguna Seca.

November's annual Great Wine Escape Weekend showcases the products of local vintners. Runners of all ages participate in the Big Sur Half Marathon and 5K Run and the Cannery Row Christmas Tree Lighting welcomes the arrival of Santa Claus to the city. Christmas in the Adobes showcases Monterey's historic buildings illuminated and decorated for the holidays. December also brings the Annual Monterey Cowboy Poetry and Music Festival. First Night Monterey draws crowds throughout the city to music, dance, and poetry events to welcome in the New Year.

Sports for the Spectator

World-class automobile racing events are held at the Laguna Seca Raceway, east of downtown Monterey. The raceway also hosts five major racing events annually including Indy car, motorcycle, and historic automobile events. The World Superbike Championships and the Honda Grand Prix are also held at the Raceway.

Sports for the Participant

The City of Monterey Sports Center is the largest family fitness facility on the Monterey Peninsula, offering a full range of fitness activities, as well as two pools and a water slide. The city has several neighborhood parks. The El Estero Park complex, a 45-acre city-wide multi-use recreation area in the center of the city, offers paddleboats, swimming, picnicking, and an exercise course. Located in the park complex are a number of recreational facilities including the Dennis The Menace Park, designed by the popular cartoon character's creator Hal Ketcham. It features a steam engine, sway bridge, a sandy hills slide, a rollers-slide, sun bridge, garden maze, and a handicap play area. The Monterey Youth Center is a multi-use recreation facility for youth and adult activities. The Monterey Youth Center Dance Studio is a professional

dance studio with a wooden floor, wall mirrors, ballet bars, and a public address system. Located next to Lake El Estero is the Monterey Skate Park designed for skateboarders and inline skaters. The Monterey Tennis Center has six courts. The city has five ball fields.

Monterey Bay Waterfront Park/Window on the Bay offers 4.1 acres of turf and landscaped areas adjacent to the beach that feature five sand volleyball courts and picnic and grill facilities. The Monterey Tennis Club has six lighted tennis courts and a pro shop.

Private sea kayak outfitters help visitors discover Monterey by sea, by paddling through the kelp forest along Cannery Row and observing sea otters and the abundant marine life. Diving, skydiving, and sailing are all available to sports enthusiasts on Monterey Bay.

Shopping and Dining

Del Monte Center, Monterey's traditional regional shopping center, anchored by Macy's and Mervyn's, has approximately 90 businesses offering a wide variety of goods and services. Recent additions to the center include California Pizza Kitchen, Ann Taylor Loft, and a Century 13 Theatre. Monterey has a busy downtown shopping area. The Old Monterey Market Place is one of the largest in the United States, attracting thousands of tourists and residents downtown every Tuesday afternoon. New Monterey, an emerging commercial area with an eclectic mix of new businesses, includes Lighthouse Avenue, and is located three blocks up the hill from Cannery Row. The former sardine canning factories of Cannery Row have become the center of more than 50 factory outlets. North Fremont, adjacent to the Monterey Fairgrounds, is a high traffic area and serves the many tourists who attend activities at the Monterey Fairgrounds.

The Salinas Valley has been called the "Salad Bowl of the Nation" for the wide variety of fruits and vegetables produced there. These, plus Monterey's extensive marine life and the Native American, Spanish, Mediterranean Rim, and Asian heritages of its citizens from various eras, have influenced the local cuisine. Restaurant choices run the gamut from American Regional to Asian, British, California, Continental, French, Indian, Island Grill, Italian, Mexican, Swiss, and seafood cuisines. Monterey restaurant chefs are inspired by the abundance of robustly flavored signature area crops such as lettuce, artichokes, garlic, strawberries, and a variety of mushrooms. Visitors may want to explore the local wineries, including the Baywood Cellars Tasting room, A Taste of Monterey, Silver Mountain Vineyards, Terranova Fine Wines, Ventana Vineyards, and Wine from the Heart.

Visitor Information: Monterey County Convention & Visitors Bureau, 150 Olivier St., PO Box 1770, Monterey, CA 93942; telephone (831)649-1770; toll-free (888)221-1010; www.montereyinfo.org

■ Convention Facilities

Convention activity in Monterey is heaviest from early April through Thanksgiving. The Monterey Conference Center, with 58,000 square feet of meeting space, a 19,600-square-foot exhibit hall, a 1200-seat ballroom, and a 494-seat theater, hosts more than 220 events annually. The Monterey County Fairgrounds has eight buildings for exhibits or meeting spaces and two outdoor music arenas seating 5,850 and 2,000 people.

The Monterey Meeting Connection, located in the heart of the city's historic district and adjoining Fisherman's Wharf, is an alliance of the Monterey Conference Center and its adjoining hotels—the Portola Plaza, the Monterey Marriott, and the Hotel Pacific. The Connection features 800 guest rooms and suites, an amphitheater, and 61,000 square feet of flexible function space. Other hotels that offer a variety of spaces for meetings are the Hyatt Regency Monterey, Hilton Monterey, Monterey Plaza Hotel and Spa, Casa Munras Garden Hotel, and the Monterey Beach Resort. A variety of other facilities also feature spaces for large functions including Adventures by the Sea, Alexander Julien Wine Estate, Culinary Center of Monterey, and the Monterey Bay Aquarium.

Convention Information: Monterey Conference Center, One Portola Plaza, Monterey, CA 93940; telephone (831)646-3370; fax (831)646-3777. Monterey County Convention & Visitors Bureau, 150 Olivier St., PO Box 1770, Monterey, CA 93942-1770; telephone (831)649-1770; toll-free (888)221-1010; www.montereyinfo.org. Monterey Convention Authority, 380 Alvarado St., Suite 201, Monterey, CA 93940; telephone (831)646-3388; toll-free (888)742-8091

■ Transportation

Approaching the City

Direct access to Monterey is provided from San Jose and San Francisco via Highway 156 off State Route 101. Access from Los Angeles is achieved via State Route 101 and Highway 68. Monterey Peninsula Airport, 3.5 miles from downtown Monterey, provides passenger service on five airlines from Monterey with non-stop flights to Los Angeles, San Francisco and Phoenix and connections to 200 domestic and foreign locations. Airlines serving Monterey include American Eagle, Delta Airlines, Express Jet, United/United Express, and U.S. Airways. Five major car rental companies operate from the airport. Monterey Salinas Transit buses (Route 21) also service the airport.

The Monterey-Salinas Airbus provides 11 trips daily to the San Jose and San Francisco international airports from downtown Monterey. Pick up service is available from hotels and private homes. Greyhound Lines offers regular bus service in Salinas with connections to Monterey. Amtrak's Coast Starlight train also stops at Salinas, with free bus service into downtown Monterey.

Traveling in the City

Five taxi companies operate in Monterey County. The Monterey-Salinas Transit (MST) operates 84 buses on 33 routes, and covers the Monterey Peninsula and Salinas Valley. MST provides rural transit service to Carmel Valley and seasonal service to Big Sur. Its Waterfront Area Visitors Express (WAVE) Shuttle Service provides free trolley transportation to the Monterey Bay Aquarium and other waterfront areas during the summer months.

■ Communications

Newspapers and Magazines

Monterey's local daily newspaper is *The Monterey County Herald,* which also publishes a Salinas edition. *Monterey County Weekly* is an alternative press publication covering news, art and entertainment.

Television and Radio

Monterey is home to one commercial television station and four AM and FM radio stations. Commercial television stations are picked up from nearby cities and cable service is available.

Media Information: *The Monterey County Herald,* 8 Upper Ragsdale Drive, Monterey, CA 93940-5730; telephone (831)372-3311; www.montereyherald.com

Monterey Online

California Coastal Rural Development Corporation. Available www.calcoastal.org

City of Monterey home page. Available www.monterey.org

Community Hospital of the Monterey Peninsula. Available www.chomp.org

Monterey Conference Center. Available www.montereyconferencecenter.com

Monterey Convention Authority. Available www.montereyconventionauthority.com

Monterey County Convention & Visitors Bureau. Available www.montereyinfo.org

The Monterey County Herald. Available www.montereyherald.com

Monterey County Historical Society. Available www.mchsmuseum.com

Monterey Jazz Festival. Available www.montereyjazzfestival.org

Monterey Peninsula Chamber of Commerce. Available www.mpcc.com

Monterey Peninsula Unified School District.
Available www.mpusd.k12.ca.us
Monterey Public Library. Available www.monterey
.org/library

BIBLIOGRAPHY

Benson, Jackson J., *True Adventures of John Steinbeck, Writer: A Biography* (New York: Penguin Books, 1990)

Fink, Augusta, *Monterey: The Presence of the Past* (San Francisco, CA: Chronicle Books, 1972)

Fisher, Anne B., *No More a Stranger* (Stanford, CA: Stanford University Press, 1946)

Ford, Tirey Lafayette, *Dawn and the Dons: The Romance of Monterey, with Vignettes and Sketches by Jo Mora* (San Francisco, CA: A.M. Robertson, 1926)

Hobbs, Fredric, *The Spirit of the Monterey Coast* (Palo Alto, CA: Tioga Pub., 1995)

Jeffers, Robinson, *Selected Poems* (New York: Vintage, 1965)

Reinstedt, Randall A., *Ghosts, Bandits, and Legends of Old Monterey* (Carmel, CA: Ghost Town Publications, 1974)

Steinbeck, John, *Cannery Row* (New York: Viking, 1945)

Steinbeck, John, *Tortilla Flat* (New York: Grosset and Dunlap, 1935)

Oakland

■ The City in Brief

Founded: 1820 (incorporated 1854)

Head Official: Mayor Ron Dellums (since 2006)

City Population
1980: 339,337
1990: 372,242
2000: 399,484
2006 estimate: 397,067
Percent change, 1990–2000: 7.3%
U.S. rank in 1980: 43rd
U.S. rank in 1990: 39th
U.S. rank in 2000: 50th (State rank: 8th)

Metropolitan Area Population
1980: 1,762,000
1990: 2,108,078
2000: 2,392,557
2006 estimate: Not reported
Percent change, 1990–2000: 12.6%
U.S. rank in 1980: 5th (CMSA)
U.S. rank in 1990: 4th (CMSA)
U.S. rank in 2000: 5th (CMSA)

Area: 56 square miles (2000)

Elevation: 42 feet above sea level

Average Annual Temperature: 56.7° F

Average Annual Precipitation: 23 inches

Major Economic Sectors: services, wholesale and retail trade, government

Unemployment Rate: 4.4% (June 2007)

Per Capita Income: $25,739 (2005)

2005 FBI Crime Index Property: 23,027

2005 FBI Crime Index Violent: 5,692

Major Colleges and Universities: Holy Names University, Mills College, Patten University, Merritt College, California College of the Arts, Laney College

Daily Newspaper: *The Oakland Tribune*

■ Introduction

The city of Oakland is known as the heart of the East Bay section of the San Francisco Bay Area. It is a heavily populated and industrialized belt that is home to one of the most ethnically and culturally diverse populations in the state. An important seaport, Oakland has been a major business and manufacturing center. Oakland was among the first ports globally to specialize in the intermodal container operations whose advantages have revolutionized international trade. With its strategic Pacific Rim location, a majority of Oakland's foreign trade is with Asia. In the new millennium, the city has built a reputation for green business. In 2007 Oakland was ranked as first in the nation for renewable energy by SustainLane Government and received a City Solar Award from the NorCal Solar Energy Association. City officials have hopes to make Oakland a Model City for residents and businesses. With community projects and development initiatives that focus on health, education, safety, and the environment, that goal may not be too far away.

■ Geography and Climate

Oakland lies near the center of the Pacific Coast between Canada and Mexico. It is located on the east side of the San Francisco Bay and is connected to the city of San Francisco by the San Francisco-Oakland Bay Bridge. Oakland boasts 19 miles of coastline to the west and magnificent rolling hills to the east. The flat plain of San Francisco Bay comprises about two-thirds of the city and the remainder of the city's terrain lies in the foothills and hills of the East Bay range. Residents and area visitors can take advantage of one of the most beautiful views in the world—the San Francisco Bay, the Golden Gate and Oakland Bay Bridges, and the sparkling Pacific Ocean. Cities adjacent to Oakland include Berkeley to the north; San Leandro to the south; Alameda across the estuary; Piedmont, a small city completely surrounded by Oakland; and Emeryville, a city that lies on the bay between Oakland and Berkeley. Oakland is the seat of Alameda County. Oakland is the only city in the United States with a natural saltwater lake wholly contained within its borders—the 115-acre Lake Merritt.

Oakland has earned the nickname "bright side of the Bay" because of its sunny skies and moderate year-round climate. Humidity remains high while precipitation is low. Almost all the city's rainfall occurs between October and January. The temperature usually reads about five degrees warmer than San Francisco, and the warmest months are September and October. The entire San Francisco Bay area lies between the Pacific and North American Tectonic Plates. The city of Oakland itself rests on the Hayward Fault, which is one of seven fault lines (also including the San Andreas Fault) affecting the area. This zone of continual seismic activity marks the city as highly susceptible to damaging earthquakes and landslides.

Area: 56 square miles (2000)

Elevation: 42 feet above sea level

Average Temperature: 56.7° F

Average Annual Precipitation: 23 inches

■ History

Spaniards Settle Area, Followed by Hunters, Loggers

The first inhabitants of present-day Oakland were the Ohlone (also known as Costanoans), peaceful tribes known for their basket making and the success of their hunting and gathering way of life.

In 1772 the first Europeans arrived through an expedition from Spain led by Lieutenant Pedro Fages and Father Crespi, who camped along Lake Merritt. The area that is now Oakland came more directly under European control in 1820, when Don Luis Maria Peralta received the land as a grant from the Spanish crown in recognition of his soldiering career. Don Luis never lived on his ranch, but divided the land among four of his sons who settled and operated ranches in the area. At that time the territory was governed by the Republic of Mexico, which had become independent of Spain in 1821.

In the 1840s hunters and loggers came to the area, followed by adventurers traveling to the gold fields. Some stayed and built squatter shacks on the Peralta land, creating several small settlements which later became part of Oakland.

In 1848, the Treaty of Guadalupe-Hidalgo officially ceded California to the U.S. and, two years later, California became the thirty-first state in the Union. Regulation of land deeds became the responsibility of the new state government. The Peraltas presented their claim to the Federal Land Commission in 1852.

Railroad Spurs Growth

In 1850 Edson Adams, Horace Carpentier, and Andrew Moon had settled on land near the present foot of Broadway. They planned a town, sold lots, and secretly rushed "An Act to Incorporate the Town of Oakland" to the State Legislature. The city, which was named for the groves of lovely oaks that grew along the hills, was granted a charter on May 4, 1852, about the same time that ferry service to San Francisco was initiated. It became an incorporated city with an elected mayor and council two years later. During this period the Peralta land case continued through the American legal system. By the time the land claim was finally confirmed in 1877, the Peraltas had sold most of their property to pay legal fees and taxes.

The completion of the Southern Pacific railroad line in 1869 transformed Oakland, which had been chosen as the terminus of the transcontinental railroad, into an important part of the Metropolitan Bay Area, second only to San Francisco. For the next several decades the railroad controlled the city's political and economic life. The railroad also stimulated economic development and the creation of an electric street car system which spurred rapid population and territorial growth.

Originally, the area of the city was quite small, but annexations in 1872, 1891, 1897, and finally in 1910 brought the city to its present size. Along with the 1906 earthquake in San Francisco, which resulted in a sizable number of new residents in-migrating, Oakland experienced a rapid rise in population that reached over 150,000 people by 1910 and continued its growth through World War II. By the 1920s Oakland had become the core city of the East Bay, the Alameda County seat, and a rival to San Francisco for leadership in the Bay Area as a whole.

Oakland experienced great losses from the 1989 Loma Prieta earthquake, which caused the upper deck of the Nimitz freeway in West Oakland to collapse, killing 41 people. The earthquake also caused part of the San Francisco Bay Bridge to fall down on the Oakland side and a number of buildings in the business district and residential areas suffered severe damage. In 1991

Oakland was struck by a firestorm, which burned more than 3,000 homes to the ground, killed 25 people, and accrued $1.5 billion in damage. The fire remains one of the most damaging firestorms in the history of the state.

By the end of the 1980s, Oakland was the sixth largest city in the state with a highly diverse and integrated population of more than 350,000 residents. Population growth continued into the 1990s, when Oakland began to experience an increasing vitality. In 1998 former California governor and presidential candidate Jerry Brown was overwhelmingly elected mayor of Oakland. Brown brought sweeping change to the city, ranging from fixing potholes to increasing the size of the police force to forcing the resignations of entrenched managers and department heads, and encouraging business development in the city. In March 2004, Oakland voters approved a measure which affirmed the "strong mayor" system by altering the city charter to give the mayor chief executive power rather than the city manager, as had been the case.

As the city entered the new millennium, it was still faced with the mounting challenges of a high crime rate, a troubled school system, and a lack of affordable housing. In 2003 the state of California took over control of the financially strapped Oakland Unified School District and appointed a state administrator to oversee the district's operations. While property values soared in Oakland and surrounding areas in the early part of the new millennium, there was a lack of affordable housing necessary to attract new residents to the city. A new 10K Downtown Housing Initiative was developed to attract 10,000 new residents to downtown Oakland by encouraging the development of subsidized housing units. By 2005 more than 5,100 units towards the goal of 6,000 had been built.

A new mayor, Ron Dellums, took office in 2007 and soon began work with other city officials on continued development to make Oakland a "model city" in health, education, economy, environmental issues, and social and cultural strength and diversity. The city partnered with schools and the county hospital to offer new health prevention and education projects for both children and adults. The local school board was able to regain control over some aspects of school governance, such as community relations, but the state continued to maintain primary control over decisions relating to financial management, facilities, student achievement, and personnel. The police force was increased. The Oakland Partnership was established as a public-private collaboration to shape a workplan that would bring more jobs to the city. The Green Initiative partnership began between Pacific Gas and Electric Company and the city for environmental and economic development. This Green Initiative was a continuation of programs that had already been in place to encourage green business and sustainability in the city. In 2007 Oakland was ranked as first in the nation for renewable energy by SustainLane Government and

received a City Solar Award from the NorCal Solar Energy Association.

Historical Information: Oakland History Room, Oakland Public Library, 125 14th Street, Oakland, CA 94612; telephone (510)238-3222; www.oaklandhistory.com

■ Population Profile

Metropolitan Area Residents
1980: 1,762,000
1990: 2,108,078
2000: 2,392,557
2006 estimate: Not reported
Percent change, 1990–2000: 12.6%
U.S. rank in 1980: 5th (CMSA)
U.S. rank in 1990: 4th (CMSA)
U.S. rank in 2000: 5th (CMSA)

City Residents
1980: 339,337
1990: 372,242
2000: 399,484
2006 estimate: 397,067
Percent change, 1990–2000: 7.3%
U.S. rank in 1980: 43rd
U.S. rank in 1990: 39th
U.S. rank in 2000: 50th (State rank: 8th)

Density: 7,126.6 people per square mile (2000)

Racial and ethnic characteristics (2005)
White: 121,075
Black: 115,952
American Indian and Alaska Native: 2,072
Asian: 61,358
Native Hawaiian and Pacific Islander: 3,426
Hispanic or Latino (may be of any race): 93,582
Other: 52,243

Percent of residents born in state: 47.1% (2000)

Age characteristics (2005)
Population under 5 years old: 27,039
Population 5 to 9 years old: 27,187
Population 10 to 14 years old: 23,636
Population 15 to 19 years old: 21,636
Population 20 to 24 years old: 23,471
Population 25 to 34 years old: 62,548
Population 35 to 44 years old: 58,431
Population 45 to 54 years old: 50,655
Population 55 to 59 years old: 22,259
Population 60 to 64 years old: 15,687
Population 65 to 74 years old: 21,632

©Ambient Images/drr.net

Population 75 to 84 years old: 14,545
Population 85 years and older: 5,184
Median age: 35.2 years

Births (2006, Metropolitan Division)

Total number: 34,604

Deaths (2006, Metropolitan Division)

Total number: 16,601

Money income (2005)

Per capita income: $25,739
Median household income: $44,124
Total households: 146,282

Number of households with income of . . .

less than $10,000: 17,357
$10,000 to $14,999: 9,890
$15,000 to $24,999: 18,765

$25,000 to $34,999: 13,388
$35,000 to $49,999: 21,995
$50,000 to $74,999: 22,578
$75,000 to $99,999: 15,509
$100,000 to $149,999: 16,108
$150,000 to $199,999: 5,701
$200,000 or more: 4,991

Percent of families below poverty level: 10.3% (2005)

2005 FBI Crime Index Property: 23,027

2005 FBI Crime Index Violent: 5,692

■ Municipal Government

In 2004 voters approved Measure P which altered the city charter to create a strong-mayor form of government in place of the previous city-manager form. The city manager position was redefined as a city administrator, appointed by and reporting to the mayor. The mayor and eight council members are elected to four-year terms. Seven council members are elected as district representatives and one member serves at large.

Head Official: Mayor Ron Dellums (elected 2006; term expires 2010)

Total Number of City Employees: 5,044 (2002)

City Information: City of Oakland, One Frank Ogawa Plaza, Oakland, CA 94612; telephone (510)444-CITY; www.oaklandnet.com

■ Economy

Major Industries and Commercial Activity

Oakland's leading industries are business and health care services, transportation, food processing, light manufacturing, government, arts, culture, and entertainment. The Port of Oakland is one of the busiest ports in the world for container ships. Nearly 200,000 jobs are related to the movement of cargo through Oakland marine terminals. Chief exports at the port include fruits and vegetables, waste paper, red meat and poultry, resins, chemicals, animal feed, raw cotton, wood and lumber, crude fertilizers/minerals, industrial machinery, and cereal. Oakland's principal imports include auto parts, computer equipment, apparel, toys, games and items made of plastic, processed fruits and vegetables, fasteners and household metal products, red meat, pottery, glassware and ceramics, iron and steel, beverages, and lumber products.

Oakland's business community faced some major problems in the 1980s and 1990s. The Loma Prieta Earthquake in 1989 not only caused physical damage but caused many companies to consider relocation. Although Alameda County had economic growth in the 1980s, Oakland did not participate in that growth and the economy actually declined. Major plant closures in the late 1980s and 1990s included Gerber Products, General Electric, National Lead, American Can, and Oakland's largest manufacturing facility, Transamerican Delaval, which had employed 1,600 workers. The ripple effect of these closures led to the closing of many small businesses that had been suppliers to these firms. The city received a designated Urban Enterprise Zone to help alleviate the employment situation, particularly for inner city residents. By the late 1990s Oakland's economy was showing some vitality. In 2002, Oakland was ranked the 8th best city in the nation for business in the *Forbes* annual survey of the Best Places in America for Business and Careers. By 2007, Oakland was benefiting from a strong and diverse business environment. Among its major corporations are Clorox, Kaiser Permanente, Cost Plus, Dreyer's Grand

Ice Cream, APL Limited, and Rainin Instruments. According to the Landauer Realty Group, out of the 60 largest office markets in the United States, Oakland was expected to have the strongest market for the next several years.

Rated the fifth most sustainable city in the U.S., Oakland has done much to expand its work with "green" businesses in an effort to grow the economy and create jobs while improving environmental conditions. As of 2007, Oakland was planning on creating a citywide wireless broadband infrastructure. Indeed, Oakland's infrastructure is a major attraction in the global information industry. In 2006, there were 19,720 businesses operating in Oakland, 3,184 of them new businesses.

Items and goods produced: processed foods, transportation equipment, fabricated metal products, non-electrical machinery, electrical equipment, clay and glass products

Incentive Programs—New and Existing Companies

Local programs: Oakland takes full advantage of existing state and federal programs to provide a full set of incentives and has a municipal lending unit to assist businesses looking for capital, technical assistance, and training. Oakland has been designated as an Enhanced Enterprise Community (EEC), a designation that allows businesses that hire from the EEC zone to be eligible for federal tax incentives including the Work Opportunity Tax Credit and the Welfare to Work Tax Credit. Improvement grants of $10 per square foot are offered to downtown tenants through the retail and Entertainment Catalyst Tenant Improvement Program. Façade improvement grants are also available. The city of Oakland's Business Development Corporation (OBDC) assists businesses in getting established, finding suitable locations, and in expansion and growth. Business loans are available through the OBDC and through the city's Industrial Development Bond Program. The Operation Hope Center offers financial services, including loans, to businesses that bring economic self-sufficiency to low-income communities. The Mills Act Program allows for property tax abatement contracts between the city and private owners for businesses that need assistance in rehabilitating or maintaining qualified historic structures. Oakland's Development Action Team works directly under the mayor and city manager to streamline all economic development, redevelopment, planning, zoning, building services, and housing development processes in support of key development projects. Incentives range from an industry-specific business tax abatement program to assistance with locating space and identifying its workforce. A Business Improvement District Assistance program supports six improvement districts in the city.

State programs: Business incentives and tax credits are provided to those businesses that operate or invest within the state-designated Oakland Enterprise Zone, which includes the airport, Downtown, and several industrial areas in the city, and within the Oakland Foreign Trade Zone. Enterprise Zone credits include a Sales and Use Tax Credit and Hiring Tax Credits. Oakland is also part of a state-designated Recycling Market Development Zone, enabling businesses involved in recycling to utilize low-interest loans, technical assistance, siting and permitting assistance, and reduced permit application fees. The Research & Development Tax Credit is available of up to 15% against bank and corporate tax liability for certain in-house research. An additional 24 percent credit is available for basic research payments to outside organizations. This is one of the highest research and development tax credits in the nation. A Child Care Tax Credit is available for companies establishing on-site child care facilities. A Net Operating Loss Carryover and New Market Tax Credits are also available. A Work Opportunity Tax Credit is offered for employers who hire individuals from certain target groups. The credit can result in a reduction in federal tax liability by as much as $2,400 per new hire.

Job training programs: The city of Oakland serves as the liaison between new and existing companies and all of the educational and training organizations in the East Bay, including Oakland Higher Education Center, Eastbay Works One-Stop Career Center, the Department of Adult Education, Alameda County Workforce and Investment Board, and the Oakland Private Industry Council. The Oakland Workforce Investment Board offers a multitude of assistance and training opportunities to assist small businesses in recruiting a qualified workforce. The California Employment Training Panel assists businesses through performance-based customized training contracts for new or existing employees. Reimbursement of costs for developing, implementing, and completing training programs may range from $1,500 to $2,000 per employee.

Development Projects

As of 2007, public and private investment had driven more than 75 major development projects, including market-rate residential housing to attract 10,000 new downtown residents. Oakland was rated at the top of 55 U.S. commercial real estate markets measured by rental growth over two years ending 2007. More than $50 million has been invested to turn the Old Oakland historic district into a sophisticated turn-of-the-century retail and commercial area, while preserving each building's ornate Victorian facade. Jack London Square, a popular waterfront retail and entertainment district, was completed in 2002. The Wood Street Development Project is a redevelopment of the former Central Station, warehouses, and signal tower into 1,570 housing units, retail

shops, and non-retail commercial space. The "Oak to Ninth" project is a 10-year redevelopment of 62 acres of waterfront property owned by the Port of Oakland. Plans call for the construction of 3,100 residences, commercial space, structured parking, approximately 27 acres of public open space, 2 renovated marinas, and a wetlands restoration area. As of 2007, there were plans to build a high-rise mall in Oakland combined with commercial office space.

The Port of Oakland's $500-$600 million Vision 2000 program will expand and improve marine terminals and develop transportation infrastructures. Two new maritime terminals will be developed, as well as a new intermodal rail facility. The Port of Oakland and the U.S. Army Corps of Engineers are working together on a harbor deepening project to accommodate the new generation of container vessels arriving in Oakland. Other slated projects include widening and deepening the harbor entrance, the outer and inner harbor channels, and two turning basins to 50 feet, as well as relocating utility lines. The Port is also deepening its berths and strengthening its wharves as part of the project. All dredged material is being reused to restore Bay Area wetlands.

Economic Development Information: City of Oakland Business Development Office; telephone (510)238-3627; toll-free (877)2OAKLAND. Oakland Metropolitan Chamber of Commerce, 475 Fourteenth Street, Oakland, CA 94612-1903; telephone (510)874-4800; fax (510)839-8817

Commercial Shipping

The Port of Oakland is one of the largest container ports in the United States and the world. The Port of Oakland occupies 19 miles on the mainland shore of San Francisco Bay, one of the finest natural harbors in the world. There are 10 container terminals, 20 deepwater berths, and 37 container Gantry cranes. On-dock storage space exceeds 600,000 square feet. The port's facilities are backed by a network of local roads and interstate freeways, warehouses, and intermodal railyards. Rail service is provided through Burlington Northern Santa Fe and Union Pacific. All major motor freight carriers serve the port and many maintain terminals in the harbor area. The port is part of the Oakland Foreign Trade Zone No. 56. Cargo service is also provided at Oakland International Airport through 16 airlines. On-site U.S. Customs personnel are available at the airport on a scheduled basis.

Cargo service at San Francisco International Airport is available from 57 airlines, including 17 cargo-only airlines. The airport supports 11 cargo facilities with a total of about 989,000 square feet of warehouse and office space. The Port of San Francisco has five berths, on-dock rail, and over 550,000 square feet of covered storage for weather-sensitive cargo. There are six shipping service companies serving the port. The port is part of Foreign Trade Zone No. 3.

Port Information: Port of Oakland, 530 Water St., Oakland, CA 94607; telephone (510)627-1100; www .portofoakland.com

Labor Force and Employment Outlook

The Oakland labor force is described as skilled, educated, and available to employers who need managerial/executive, professional, sales, technical, and clerical staff. Oakland has been rated one of the nation's top ten technology cities. Nearly one-third of area residents have a college degree, and about 100,000 students attend local institutions of higher learning. Employment growth rates through 2015 were projected to be highest in the area of manufacturing. Oakland has a civilian workforce of nearly 200,000. Oakland rates high in the percentage of women-owned businesses.

The following is a summary of data regarding the San Francisco-Oakland-Fremont metropolitan area labor force, 2006 annual averages.

Size of nonagricultural labor force: 2,007,300

Number of workers employed in . . .

construction and mining: 117,700
manufacturing: 140,400
trade, transportation and utilities: 358,500
information: 68,600
financial activities: 158,000
professional and business services: 346,500
educational and health services: 225,600
leisure and hospitality: 205,800
other services: 73,300
government: 313,000

Average hourly earnings of production workers employed in manufacturing: $17.98

Unemployment rate: 4.4% (June 2007)

Largest private employers (East Bay)	*Number of employees*
Kaiser Foundation Health Plan Inc.	22,500
SBC Communications Inc. (Pacific Bell)	10,132
Alameda County	9,638
University of California at Berkeley	9,168
Contra Costa County	8,467
U.S. Postal Service, Oakland District	8,283
Lawrence Livermore National Lab	7,837
Safeway Inc.	7,680
State of California	7,600

Cost of Living

The following is a summary of data regarding key cost of living factors for the Oakland area.

2007 (1st quarter) ACCRA Average House Price: $674,704

2007 (1st quarter) ACCRA Cost of Living Index: 146.2

State income tax rate: 1.0% to 9.3%

State sales tax rate: 7.25%

Local income tax rate: None

Local sales tax rate: 1.25%

Property tax rate: ranges from 1.22% to 1.3773% of assessed values (2005)

Economic Information: Oakland Metropolitan Chamber of Commerce, 475 Fourteenth Street, Oakland, CA 94612-1903; telephone (510)874-4800; fax (510)839-8817

■ Education and Research

Elementary and Secondary Schools

The Oakland Unified School District (OUSD) is one of the largest school districts in the state. The district has a rich ethnic diversity with a little more than one-half African American students and the rest a mixture of Hispanic, white, combined Asian, and other students, including Native Americans. Gifted and Talented Education (GATE)/High Potential programs are available for students of all ages, as are special education programs. The district supports three adult education centers. There are several charter schools.

In 2003 the district's financial crisis led to a takeover by the State of California and the appointment of a state administrator. In 2007 the local school board regained control over all aspects of community relations, but the state continued to maintain primary control over decisions relating to financial management, facilities, student achievement, and personnel. Oakland Unified is the only district in the state to allocate funds directly to each school based on enrollment and student demographics.

The following is a summary of data regarding the Oakland Unified School District as of the 2005–2006 school year.

Total enrollment: 40,080

Number of facilities

elementary schools: 70
junior high/middle schools: 21

senior high schools: 26
other: 41

Student/teacher ratio: 20.2:1

Teacher salaries (2005–06)
elementary median: $53,000
junior high/middle median: $57,230
secondary median: $57,690

Funding per pupil: $8,129

Oakland has over 50 private schools, including both independent and faith-based schools. Of particular note is the Mills College Children's School, a laboratory school that is operated through the Mills College School of Education.

Public Schools Information: Oakland Unified School District, 1025 Second Avenue, Oakland, CA 94606; telephone (510)879-8200; webportal.ousd.k12.ca.us

Colleges and Universities

Mills College is a private liberal arts school with an enrollment of more than 1,100 students that serves female undergraduates, but admits men to its graduate school. The college grants bachelor's and master's degrees and offers courses leading to California teaching credentials. Undergraduate enrollment in 2007 was 948; graduate enrollment was 506.

Two of the four Peralta Community College District campuses are located in Oakland; they are Merritt College, a publicly supported coeducational junior college with an enrollment of nearly 6,000 students and Laney College, which offers associate's degrees in arts and science, pre-apprenticeship programs, and job retraining to its more than 11,000 students. The school offers liberal arts, technical-vocational, and general education programs in both day and evening schools. Holy Names University is a Catholic, liberal arts college that enrolls more than 1,100 students. The college provides both bachelor's and master's programs, including a Master of Science in Nursing and a Master of Music.

More than 700 students are enrolled at Patten University, a private co-educational school affiliated with the Christian Evangelical Churches of America, Inc. Patten awards associate's and bachelor's degrees in 15 majors. The school also offers a master's degree in education. Certificate and training programs are offered through the School of Extended and Continuing Education.

California College of the Arts is a four-year independent college of art and design. Its Oakland campus houses undergraduate art students and hosts the Center for Art and Public Life. The San Francisco campus of the California College of the Arts houses the schools graduate program and hosts the CAA Watts Institute for Contemporary Arts. The Oakland campus of Samuel

Merritt College offers degrees at the undergraduate and graduate level in five disciplines: nursing, occupational therapy, physician assistant, physical therapy and podiatric medicine.

The San Francisco State University College of Extended Learning in Oakland offers a number of certificate and professional development programs, as well as degree credit courses through its Open University.

Naropa University of Boulder, Colorado, maintains a branch campus in Oakland; it offers an accredited Master of Liberal Arts in Creation Spirituality.

Libraries and Research Centers

The Oakland Public Library consists of a main library, 15 branches, and 1 bookmobile. The library has over 1.2 million books and other materials system wide. The main library houses a special Business Collection and the Oakland History Room. The main library is also a government documents repository. The system has a few unique collections. The Asian Library contains over 74,000 print and audio materials, with both reference and general subject titles, in eight Asian languages: Chinese, Japanese, Korean, Vietnamese, Thai, Cambodian, Tagalog and Laotian. The branch also features an in-depth English-language Asian Studies collection.

Also unique to the system is the Temescal Tool Lending Library, which offers over 2,700 tools available for loan, as well as books and how-to videos for home repairs. The Temescal branch offers workshops on tool safety and home repair topics.

The African American Museum and Library at Oakland is a non-circulating reference library system. The collection contains 12,000 volumes by or about African Americans, including materials about the military, Martin Luther King, Jr., Malcolm X, the Black Panther Party, Africa, genealogy, and California history. The museum houses exhibits on African American art, history, and culture.

Oakland has two research centers associated with the University of California: the California Agricultural Experiment Station and the Tobacco-Related Disease Research Program. Another major research center in the city is the Children's Hospital Oakland Research Institute (CHORI). It is one of the top 10 federally funded pediatric research facilities in the nation. CHORI contains six specialized centers: the Center for Cancer Research; the Center for Genetics; the Center for Immunobiology and Vaccine Development; the Center for Nutrition and Metabolism; the Center for Prevention of Obesity, Cardiovascular Disease and Diabetes; and the Center for Sickle Cell Disease and Thalassemia. The Earthquake Engineering Research Institute, a non-profit technical professionals society, is based in Oakland as well.

Public Library Information: Oakland Public Library, 125 Fourteenth Street, Oakland, CA 94612; telephone (510)238-3134; www.oaklandlibrary.org

■ Health Care

Oakland's largest private, not-for-profit medical center is the Alta Bates Summit Medical Center with three campuses and two acute care hospitals in the Oakland region. The Medical Center was formed from the January 2000 merger of Summit Medical Center, Alta Bates Medical Center, and Sutter Health. Its Summit campus specializes in cardiovascular care, orthopedics, women and infants, wellness and prevention, and seniors. The Alta Bates campus, based in Berkeley, is recognized for its care of women and infants, In Vitro Fertilization Program, and its high risk obstetrics program. Alta Bates includes the Herrick Campus, once known as Herrick Hospital and Health Center. The 205-bed Children's Hospital Oakland has the region's only pediatric trauma center, largest pediatric intensive care unit, and one of largest sickle cell treatment and research centers in the world.

The 236-bed Highland Hospital is part of the Alameda County Medical Center (ACMC) system. Highland is home to a Level II Emergency/Trauma Center and the Bright Beginnings Family Birthing Center. The hospital also serves as a teaching and training facility with accredited programs in emergency medicine, internal medicine, general surgery, and oral and maxillofacial surgery. The ACMC Eastmont Wellness Center is home to over 40 primary and medical specialty services, including an immigration clinic and refugee health screening clinic.

The Kaiser Permanente Oakland Medical Center, with 346-beds, is considered to be Kaiser's flagship hospital for Northern California. It offers a full range of acute care services. Urgent care and primary care services are located on the campus as well. The hospital supports a drop-in HIV testing clinic and a domestic violence support services program. As an extension of the center's Medical Weight Management Program, the hospital sponsors the Oakland Food Mill Farm'acy. The Farm'acy, located directly across the street from the main hospital, is managed through Food Mill, a natural and organics food market, and stocks only those foods that products that are compatible with the weight-control plans encouraged by the center. Educational materials on healthy lifestyles are also available at the store and a health educator is often on-site to answer questions of diet and nutrition.

■ Recreation

Sightseeing

Historic buildings in Oakland include the Camron-Stanford House, a beautifully restored Victorian house on Lake Merritt. The Pardee Home Museum is an historical treasure in the heart of the Preservation Park Historical District. Dunsmuir House and Gardens features 40 acres of hills and gardens that are the site of public events. The Greek Orthodox Church of the Ascension is a modern Byzantine architectural gem, with icons painted on the dome; the church is nestled in the Oakland Hills. The Oakland Temple and Visitor's Center, of the Church of Jesus Christ of Latter-day Saints (Mormons), is another notable architectural site. The visitor's center offers exhibits on the Mormon faith. The Morcom Amphitheater of Roses provides a stunning horticultural display of more than 8,000 rose bushes surrounded by Mediterranean architecture. The landmark Paramount Theatre is a restored 1930s movie palace that still hosts a variety of arts events.

Popular entertainment and amusement sites include Children's Fairyland, a three-dimensional theme park with more than 60 sets recreating nursery rhymes, fairy tales, and legends; and the Western Aerospace Museum, displaying aeronautical artifacts and housing an aircraft library and gift shop. The Oakland Zoo in Knowland Park is home to 440 native and exotic animals and an African Lion Exhibit. The Valley Children's Zoo is a three-acre sight within the larger zoo that includes a Reptile and Amphibian Discovery Room, the Bug House, and a Goat and Sheep Barn, as well as a playground area. Curious persons of all ages are welcome at the Chabot Space and Science Center which completed its new facility in January 2000 and features a planetarium, observatory and exhibits.

Another popular spot is the Jack London Square and Village, which was once the stomping grounds of the city's most colorful literary figures. It houses many quaint shops, restaurants, and a Farmer's Market along its scenic Boardwalk. The Presidential Yacht Potomac, Franklin Delano Roosevelt's "floating white house," hosts dockside tours and history cruises from its port at Jack London Square. Several museums are part of the Jack London Square complex including the African American Museum and Library, Lightship Relief floating lighthouse, the Museum of Children's Art, and the Oakland Museum of California. The Oakland Museum of California is lauded for its displays of California art, history and natural science. The Ebony Museum of Art at Jack London Village displays and sells African American art. The Museum of African American Technology Science Village, opened in 2004, sponsors exhibits on the technical achievements of African Americans.

Arts and Culture

The Oakland East Bay Symphony presents symphonic music during its November through May subscription concert series, which is presented at the Paramount Theatre. The Malonga Casquelourd Center for the Arts (the former Alice Arts Center) is home to Axis Dance Caomany, Citicentre Dance Theater, Dimensions Dance Theater, Oakland Youth Orchestra, and Bay Area Blues Society. Oakland Ensemble Theatre, the city's only professional resident theater, produces contemporary, insightful works from an African American perspective. Blues, jazz, and gospel concerts are promoted by the Bay Area Blues Society. Woodminster Summer Musicals are performed July through September in the open-air Woodminster Amphitheater in the scenic Joaquin Miller Park in the Oakland hills.

New to the Oakland civic center area are the Craft & Cultural Arts Gallery and the Oakland Art Gallery which opened in 2001. Samuel's Gallery features a large collection of cards, prints, posters, and original graphics by African American artists.

Festivals and Holidays

The African Cultural Festival, popularly known as "The Africans are Coming," features dance in its many African forms performed by five sub-Saharan repertory companies. Oakland celebrates its birthday on May 4th with its annual Celebration in the Plaza, featuring live music with guest performers, famous Oakland celebrities, living history exhibits, walking tours, food booths, and art exhibits. Oakland's rich Spanish heritage is saluted at the annual Cinco de Mayo celebration which includes a parade and many festival activities. June's Festival at the Lake is a multi-cultural festival that features entertainment, arts, children's activities, an international food fair, and community programs. The Annual Scottish Highland Games take place in July. August's Chinatown Streetfest with its arts, food and crafts of the cultures of China, Vietnam, Japan, Korea, the Philippines, and others, celebrates the city's Asian community. The Laurel World Music Festival, also in August, celebrates the diverse culture of the city.

The first week in September is the date for the Art & Soul Festival with more than 150 artisans displaying their music and crafts at multiple stages around the city. The Montclair Jazz and Wine Festival also takes place in September. Another annual fall occurrence is the Black Cowboy Parade downtown, always held the first Saturday in October. The holiday season is greeted by a Christmas Tree Lighting Celebration, a parade of lighted yachts at Jack London Square's waterfront and a holiday parade sponsored by *The Oakland Tribune*.

Sports for the Spectator

The National Football League's Oakland Raiders play at McAfee Coliseum, also home to the Oakland Athletics of major league baseball's American League. The National Basketball Association's Golden State Warriors play at the ORACLE Arena. Both the arena and coliseum are part of the Oakland-Alameda County Coliseum Complex. The Oakland Banshees play women's tackle football, with home games at Chabot College in Hayward. Infineon Raceway in nearby Sonoma offers a wide variety of motorsports events year round. The excitement of thoroughbred racing is offered at Golden Gate Fields in Albany, only minutes from Oakland.

Sports for the Participant

Joaquin Miller Park offers 10 trails featuring spectacular views of the entire Bay Area. Joggers enjoy the 3.18-mile jogging path that encircles the shoreline of Lake Merritt. Surrounded on three sides by Lake Merritt, 122-acre Lakeside Park offers picnic areas, putting greens, lawn bowling, boat rentals, and Japanese and herb gardens. The Redwood Regional Park and Roberts Regional Recreation Area covers more than 2,000 acres in the city of Oakland and Contra Costa County. They include an amphitheater fire circle, horse and hiking trails, picnic and play areas, volleyball court, exercise course, and heated outdoor swimming pool. The Temescal Regional Recreation Area's 48 acres, which include a 13-acre lake, provide swimming, fishing, picnicking, and a children's play area. Willows Skate and Surf in nearby Alameda offers roller skating, skate boards, and surf boards. Ice skating is available seven days a week at the Oakland Ice Center. Oakland's three municipal golf courses, Metropolitan Golf Links, Lake Chabot Golf Course, and Montclair Golf Course, accommodate avid and beginning golfers alike. Oakland also maintains 53 athletic fields, over 40 outdoor tennis courts and 7 public outdoor pools located throughout the city.

Shopping and Dining

Boutiques and specialty shops offering men's and women's apparel, household goods, toys and ethnic gift items are featured at Jack London Village. Other shopping areas include the City Center downtown, Rockridge, Piedmont Avenue, Lakeshore, and Grand Avenues. City Center is a popular pedestrian plaza with a mix of shops and restaurants. The Oakland Artisan Marketplace is open Fridays in Oakland's Frank Ogawa Plaza and Saturdays and Sundays in Jack London Square. One of the oldest and most culturally diverse markets in the city is the Old Oakland Farmer's Market, open year-round on Fridays downtown where shoppers find Asian produce, fresh flowers, potted plants, herbs, bakery items, fresh fish and seafood, and wild game and poultry. Visitors might want to enjoy the Asian restaurants, specialty shops, and bakeries of Chinatown, located along Broadway, Alice, 13th, and 7th Streets.

From upscale to modest, Oakland has offerings for traditionalists as well as adventurous gourmets. The Jack London Square is home to a variety of restaurants in a wonderful waterfront setting. Unusual fare and cuisine from around the world is offered at 12 eateries on the Square. Restaurants include specialties such as Mexican, Indonesian, Cajun, Northern Italian, Greek, Japanese, sushi, seafood, and classic American cuisine. Some favorite stops for both locals and visitor's include T. J.'s Gingerbread House, a highly-decorated establishment offering Louisiana-style cuisine; Yoshi's Japanese Restaurant; and Ratto's Italian deli.

Local wineries are well worth a stop for visiting wine connoisseurs. JC Cellers, founded by winemaker Jeff Cohn, offers winemaking demonstrations and a selection of Rhone varietals. Enat Winery specializes in Ethiopian-style honey wines, made from honey, water, and yeast. Dashe Cellers feature wines made from grapes from Dry Creek, Alexander Valley, and Mendocino counties.

■ Convention Facilities

The Oakland Convention Center/Marriott Oakland City Center complex is one of the first structures in California to house both a convention center and hotel. An atrium lobby joins the two-story convention center with the 483-room hotel. Convention center meeting facilities can accommodate 6,000 people and banquet facilities seat 3,900 diners. There is a 48,000-square-foot exhibition hall that can be divided into smaller halls, 12 additional meeting rooms, and a parking garage. Approximately 7,500 square feet of additional meeting space is available on the center's second level, with 8,000 square feet inside the hotel. The Marriott offers an additional 25,000 square feet of flexible function space.

The Henry J. Kaiser Convention Center is a multifunction facility consisting of the Kaiser Arena, Calvin Simmons Theatre and two banquet/ballrooms. Kaiser Arena can accommodate up to 8,000 patrons for a variety of events and has a banquet capacity of 1,500 people. The arena's 23,000-square-foot hardwood floor accommodates up to 150 eight-foot by ten-foot trade show booths. The 1,900-seat Calvin Simmons Theatre has been restored to European splendor with a gilt-trimmed proscenium stage. The center's ballroom and goldroom host many functions of all types.

Other large facilities include the Oakland-Alameda County Coliseum Complex, featuring the indoor ORACLE Arena; and the outdoor McAfee Coliseum, the state-of-the-art County of Alameda Conference Center; and the California Ballroom. Several local museums and theaters offer meeting and event space for smaller groups.

Visitor Information: Oakland Convention and Visitors Bureau, 463 11th Street, Oakland, CA; telephone (510)839-9000; www.oaklandcvb.com

■ Transportation

Approaching the City

Oakland International Airport, located only 12 minutes from downtown, has 13 domestic and international airlines serving 14.4 million passengers each year. Bay Area Rapid Transit (BART) offers a dedicated connection to and from the airport and high-speed rail service between East Bay cities and San Francisco with eight stations in Oakland. Four shuttles also serve the airport. The

Alameda-Contra Costa Transit District (AC Transit) provides bus service to and from the airport via the 50 and 805 lines. Amtrak schedules frequent arrivals through its terminal at Jack London Square. Greyhound bus service is also available.

Interstate 980 is the main north-south artery to the city. I-880 and I-580 connect to I-980, as does State Route 24.

Some travelers may wish to fly in through the San Francisco International Airport. Oakland can be reached from San Francisco by traveling east across the Bay Bridge via Interstate 80 and continuing south to Oakland on I-580 or I-980.

Traveling in the City

The Alameda-Contra Costa Transit District (AC Transit) is the third-largest public bus system in the state, serving 13 cities in Alameda and Contra Costa counties. There are dozens of routes through the city, with some routes connecting to the Bay Area Transit System (BART), which provides wide-ranging subway service on four East Bay lines into San Francisco. The Alameda/Oakland Ferry cruises into Jack London Square from San Francisco's Ferry terminal and Pier 41. Three taxi companies service the city. The city has 87 miles of bicycle lanes and routes.

■ Communications

Newspapers and Magazines

The Oakland Tribune is the city's daily newspaper. The *Berkeley Voice*, *The Montclarion*, and *Piedmonter* are popular weeklies. The *Oakland Post* is a weekly serving the African American community while *El Mundo* serves the Hispanic population.

Among the magazines and journals published in Oakland are *Oakland Magazine*, *The Black Scholar*, and *California Agriculture*.

Television and Radio

Oakland has one commercial network television station (KTVU-Fox), a government cable access channel, and 3 AM radio stations offering talk radio and children's programming. Several television and radio stations are picked up from the surrounding area and cable programming is available.

Media Information: *The Oakland Tribune*, 401 13th Street, Oakland, CA 94612; telephone (510)208-6300; www.insidebayarea.com/oaklandtribune

Oakland Online

City of Oakland Home Page. Available www .oaklandnet.com

Community and Economic Development Agency. Available www.business2oakland.com/main

East Bay Economic Development Alliance for Business. Available www.edab.org

Oakland Convention and Visitors Bureau. Available www.oaklandcvb.com

Oakland Metropolitan Chamber of Commerce. Available www.oaklandchamber.com

Oakland Public Library. Available www.oaklandlibrary.org

Oakland Tribune. Available www.insidebayarea.com/oaklandtribune

BIBLIOGRAPHY

Bradford, Amory, *Oakland's Not for Burning* (New York: McKay, 1968)

Irvin, Dona L., *The Unsung Heart of Black America: A Middle-Class Church at Midcentury* (Columbia, MO: University of Missouri Press, 1992)

Levy, Frank, *Urban Outcomes: Schools, Streets, and Libraries* (Berkeley, CA: University of California Press, 1974)

Rhomberg, Chris, *No There There: Race, Class, and Political Community in Oakland* (Berkeley, CA: University of Press, 2004)

Self, Robert O., *American Babylon: Race and the Struggle for Post-War Oakland* (Princeton, NJ: Princeton University Press, 2003)

Riverside

■ The City in Brief

Founded: 1870 (incorporated 1883)

Head Official: Mayor Ronald O. Loveridge (since 1994)

City Population

    1980: 170,591
    1990: 226,546
    2000: 255,166
    2006 estimate: 293,761
    Percent change, 1990–2000: 12.6%
    U.S. rank in 1980: 83rd
    U.S. rank in 1990: 68th
    U.S. rank in 2000: 78th

Metropolitan Area Population

    1980: 1,558,000
    1990: 2,588,793
    2000: 3,254,821
    2006 estimate: 4,026,135
    Percent change, 1990–2000: 25.7%
    U.S. rank in 1980: 2nd (CMSA)
    U.S. rank in 1990: 2nd (CMSA)
    U.S. rank in 2000: 2nd (CMSA)

Area: 85.6 square miles

Elevation: 847 feet above sea level

Average Annual Temperature: 66.0° F

Average Annual Precipitation: 10.2 inches

Major Economic Sectors: services, wholesale and retail trade, government

Unemployment Rate: 5.6% (June 2007)

Per Capita Income: $20,924 (2005)

2005 FBI Crime Index Property: 13,425

2005 FBI Crime Index Violent: 1,954

Major Colleges and Universities: University of California, Riverside; California Baptist University; La Sierra University; Riverside Community College

Daily Newspaper: *The Press-Enterprise*

■ Introduction

The city of Riverside, located within one hour of the city of Los Angeles, began as the center for the navel orange-growing industry in the United States. The city has since developed a diverse economy that includes a growing number of high-tech and research and development firms.

Recreational opportunities such as beaches, ski slopes, and desert resorts are within an hour's drive. Cultural activities run the gamut from community theater to symphonic concerts to ballet. The Mission Revival style hotel built in the city's early days has become the world-famous Mission Inn favored by presidents, royalty, and movie stars. Riverside is blessed with an abundance of space. Through coordinated city planning, Riverside has combined the best of the past with the promise of unlimited future possibilities.

■ Geography and Climate

Riverside is located in Southern California at the center of the metropolitan area that encompasses Riverside County and San Bernardino County. This area is typically known as the Inland Empire. Riverside is 10 miles southwest of San Bernardino and 53 miles east of Los Angeles. The city is located on the Santa Ana River, near the San Bernardino Mountains.

The climate is characterized as mild and semi-arid. Summer highs frequently reach over 90 degrees, but evening temperatures can drop as much as 30 to 49 degrees accompanied by cool breezes. Low humidity generally keeps even hot summer days from being oppressive. The Santana Winds (or Santa Ana Winds) that typically occur from late summer to spring bring warm and dry air down from the high deserts to the San Bernardino Mountains and through the counties of Los Angeles, Orange, San Bernardino, and Riverside. These often strong winds are sometimes accompanied by brush and wildfires. The San Andreas Fault line lies just to the northeast of Riverside. This area in Southern California is highly susceptible to earthquakes, some of which can be very severe.

Area: 85.6 square miles

Elevation: 847 feet above sea level

Average Temperature: 66.0° F

Average Annual Precipitation: 10.2 inches

■ History

The Rancho Era

The first European visitors to the area of present-day Riverside were Captain Juan Bautista de Anza and his 34 seasoned soldiers, who arrived in the area from Arizona in 1774 in search of a land route to California. At that time the Valley of Paradise was inhabited by Native Americans who lived in the niches in the rocky hills and foraged for food. The natives lived in the area relatively undisturbed until 1821, when the lands of California became the property of Mexico.

Shortly thereafter Juan Bandini, a prominent political figure in California, was given a piece of land called El Rancho Jurupa, which he later presented to his son-in-law, Abel Stearns. The Stearns sold the land to Louis Rubidoux, who along with other ranchers, ruled the land. After Rubidoux's death part of the land was purchased by John North. He decided to build a community of ethical people devoted to establishing good schools, churches, and libraries. The new town was called Riverside and its original square, called "Mile Square," remains the heart of the city. Within a few years of its founding, railroad tracks were built connecting the city to far-off places.

In 1873 James Roe, a druggist and teacher, moved to the city and by the late 1870s had launched the *Riverside Press* weekly newspaper that later became the current daily publication, *The Press-Enterprise*.

Oranges and Irrigation

Around 1875 a mutant Brazilian orange tree that produced fruit with no seeds was brought to the city. In the rich soil by the Santa Ana River the fruit flourished under the abundant sunshine. By 1887 the navel orange had become the dominant crop in Riverside and other California cities.

About the same time, with the financial aid of people from England, Matthew Gage, an immigrant from Canada, began work on a canal to bring water to all of Riverside, parts of which had no water available. With the irrigation made possible by Gage's canal, Riverside's greatest growth period began. Three new subdivisions—White's Addition, Hall's Addition, and Arlington Heights—were developed.

Economic strides were made in the 1880s when a number of local fruit growers joined together to pick and sell fruit under one brand name and to grade their oranges for quality. The plan expanded and by 1893 a group of all California growers was formed under the name of the Southern California Fruit Exchange, now known as Sunkist. The development of refrigerated railroad cars and innovative irrigation systems established Riverside as the state's wealthiest city per capita by 1895.

World Wars Establish Military Presence

During World War I, March Field, now the March Air Reserve Base, was established for the training of aviators. In 1920, Ernest Louis Yeager began the E. L. Yeager Construction Company, Inc., which, with the assistance of his three sons, completed over a half century of master construction projects. In the latter half of this century the Food Machinery Corporation was formed to produce machinery for packing citrus fruits efficiently and rapidly. During World War II March Field was expanded and another base, Camp Haan, was begun across from March Field. The site is now occupied by the new National Veteran's Cemetery. A third base was built, called Camp Anza, which later became a subdivision called Arlanza.

In 1997 a joint use agreement with the U.S. Air Force allowed for over 300-acres of March Field to be used as a civilian airport, which is now known as the March Inland Port.

A Promising Future

In the late 1990s and into the early 2000s, Riverside began to focus much attention on diversifying its economy and creating a sustainable community. One major development was an agreement between the city, county, and the University of California, Riverside for the creation of University Research Park (URP), a 39-acre site designed to house high-tech research facilities as well as office spaces for technology-based companies. The first lot opened in 2000. By 2007 the tech companies calling URP their home included the Pacific Fuel Cell Corporation, Viresco Energy, Centrum Analytical Laboratories, and Ambryx Biotechnology. Other tenants included Farmer's Insurance Group, Nationwide Health Plans, Qmotions, and Protection One. An innovative Riverside Renaissance Initiative was set in place in the early 2000s

Photograph by Michael J. Elderman. Courtesy of Riverside. Reproduced by permission of the photographer.

to begin the process of redeveloping and expanding the general infrastructure of the city as well as allowing for capital improvements. Through the initiative, over $780 million will be invested in projects to include parks, libraries, museums, public safety facilities, office and retail developments, utilities upgrades, and general transportation improvements. In a move toward sustainable community, the city began to promote the use of alternative fuel vehicles for public and private use and opened a compressed natural gas fast-fill fueling station for the public.

In 2004 Partners for Livable Communities recognized Riverside as one of America's "Most Livable Communities" in the mid-sized city category. The award—which is given out every decade—recognizes Riverside's strides in preparing itself for a global economy through strategic business plans. However, it also acknowledges Riverside's constant nurturing of its community—something the city has done since it blossomed in 1883.

Historical Information: Riverside Metropolitan Museum, 3580 Mission Inn Avenue, Riverside, CA 92501; telephone (951)826-5273; www.riversideca .gov/museum

■ Population Profile

Metropolitan Area Residents

1980: 1,558,000
1990: 2,588,793
2000: 3,254,821
2006 estimate: 4,026,135
Percent change, 1990–2000: 25.7%
U.S. rank in 1980: 2nd (CMSA)
U.S. rank in 1990: 2nd (CMSA)
U.S. rank in 2000: 2nd (CMSA)

City Residents

1980: 170,591
1990: 226,546
2000: 255,166
2006 estimate: 293,761
Percent change, 1990–2000: 12.6%
U.S. rank in 1980: 83rd
U.S. rank in 1990: 68th
U.S. rank in 2000: 78th

Density: 3,104 people per square mile (2000)

Racial and ethnic characteristics (2005)

> White: 160,725
> Black: 21,346
> American Indian and Alaska Native: 2,981
> Asian: 16,853
> Native Hawaiian and Pacific Islander: 2,614
> Hispanic or Latino (may be of any race): 131,849
> Other: 76,529

Percent of residents born in state: 56.5% (2000)

Age characteristics (2005)

> Population under 5 years old: 24,116
> Population 5 to 9 years old: 23,200
> Population 10 to 14 years old: 23,185
> Population 15 to 19 years old: 21,112
> Population 20 to 24 years old: 30,137
> Population 25 to 34 years old: 53,498
> Population 35 to 44 years old: 40,341
> Population 45 to 54 years old: 32,855
> Population 55 to 59 years old: 13,974
> Population 60 to 64 years old: 7,498
> Population 65 to 74 years old: 12,311
> Population 75 to 84 years old: 8,877
> Population 85 years and older: 2,955
> Median age: 28.9 years

Births (2006, MSA)

> Total number: 64,217

Deaths (2006, MSA)

> Total number: 26,484

Money income (2005)

> Per capita income: $20,924
> Median household income: $50,416
> Total households: 93,405

Number of households with income of...

> less than $10,000: 7,365
> $10,000 to $14,999: 4,704
> $15,000 to $24,999: 10,731
> $25,000 to $34,999: 9,995
> $35,000 to $49,999: 13,372
> $50,000 to $74,999: 20,301
> $75,000 to $99,999: 11,484
> $100,000 to $149,999: 10,593
> $150,000 to $199,999: 2,855
> $200,000 or more: 2,005

Percent of families below poverty level: 13.2% (2005)

2005 FBI Crime Index Property: 13,425

2005 FBI Crime Index Violent: 1,954

■ Municipal Government

Riverside has a council-manager form of government. The seven-member council is comprised of persons elected for four-year terms from geographically designated wards. A mayor is elected from the city at large for a four-year term and acts as the presiding officer of the council.

Head Official: Mayor Ronald O. Loveridge (since 1994; term expires 2009)

Total Number of City Employees: 2,623 (2005)

City Information: City of Riverside, 3900 Main Street, Riverside, CA 92522; telephone (951)826-5311; www.riversideca.gov

■ Economy

Major Industries and Commercial Activity

Although Riverside's beginnings are steeped in agriculture, today the economy has become more diversified, while still relying heavily on government, education, professional/business services, and retailing.

The largest city employers are the University of California, Riverside and the Riverside Unified School District. The city is also home to many state and county government offices as well as county, state, and federal courts. In addition, the city has become an important center for financial and professional services. There are numerous legal and accounting firms, software firms, architectural and engineering offices, and banking institutions that call the city home.

In recent years Riverside has placed a major emphasis on expanding its technology areas by developing high-tech industrial business parks. For example, the city, county, and University of California at Riverside have partnered together to create University Research Park within the 856-acre Riverside Regional Technology Park. The complex offers a high-speed fiber optic telecommunications system that supports voice, video, and data information. Bourns Inc., Centrum Analytical Labs, and Luminex Software, Inc. have all chosen Riverside for new headquarters operations. Other high-tech firms in Riverside include Adelphia Communications, Goodrich (aerospace), Pacific Fuel Cell Corporation, and Biovent Medical.

Riverside also has taken strides in developing its industrial and manufacturing sectors. Riverside has attracted more than 125 industrial employers in the last decade, according to the city's Development Department. Riverside's diverse manufacturing base now includes such sectors as electrical instruments; plastics; wood, glass, and metal fabrication; food processing; recreational vehicles; and imaging equipment.

Riverside enjoys substantial economic growth with the addition of shipping company DHL to its fold. The $18.6 billion company chose the March Air Reserve Base as its West Coast hub over two other Inland Empire locations in 2004. In 2007 DHL established a new International Gateway operation, investing nearly $3 million at the Riverside facility. The newly expanded operation came online with the arrival on March 27, 2007 of a flight from DHL's Central Asia SuperHub in Hong Kong into the facility.

In addition Riverside's retail industry continues to grow as population continues to rise.

Items and goods produced: electrical instruments; plastics; wood, glass, and metal fabrication; recreational vehicles; food processing; aircraft parts; motorcycle parts; citrus-packing; precision plastic injection molders; home furniture; and medical imaging equipment

Incentive Programs—New and Existing Companies

Local programs: The City of Riverside Development Department offers many programs and services to help businesses grow and succeed in the Southern California marketplace. These programs and services include: industrial development bond financing, local and state designated Enterprise Zones, redevelopment incentives, accelerated processes for plan checks and building permit fees, employment hiring and training programs, mapping services, high-speed Internet bandwidth within the city limits, and very competitive electric and water utility rates. The Inland Empire Small Business Development Center and Inland Empire Economic Partnership, both located in the research park, offer additional assistance to small, emerging and technology-based businesses. The TriTech Small Business Development Center promotes high-tech/high-growth business sectors including particularly bioscience, computer hardware/software, and communications.

State programs: The Agua Mansa Enterprise Zone, which is partially located in the northeast corner of Riverside, is one of the state's designated Enterprise Zones. Business incentives and tax credits are provided to those businesses that operate or invest within a designated enterprise zone. Riverside also is home to a state Recycling Market Development Zone that offers financial incentives to companies interested in promoting recycling as part of their manufacturing process. Enterprise Zone Credits include a Sales and Use Tax Credit and Hiring Tax Credits. The Research & Development Tax Credit is available of up to 15% against bank and corporate tax liability for certain in-house research. An additional 24 percent credit is available for basic research payments to outside organizations. This is one of the highest research

and development tax credits in the nation. A Child Care Tax Credit is available for companies establishing on-site child care facilities. A Net Operating Loss Carryover and New Market Tax Credits are also available. A Work Opportunity Tax Credit is offered for employers who hire individuals from certain target groups.

Job training programs: The federal Workforce Investment Act (WIA) provides a cooperative effort between employers and the Riverside County Workforce Development Board. An employer can receive assistance with employer-specific training and financial incentives, such as reimbursements, tax credits, and direct payments for the training of new employees. Employers can also receive reimbursement for a portion of the employee's wages during an on-the-job training period. The California Employment Training Panel assists businesses through performance-based customized training contracts for new or existing employees. Reimbursement of costs for developing, implementing, and completing training programs may range from $1,500 to $2,000 per employee.

Development Projects

Riverside has seen its industrial sector grow with the addition of the 56-acre University Research Park (URP), a project with the University of California, Riverside. URP is housed within Hunter Park and is the core of the recently designated 856-acre Riverside Regional Technology Park. Future plans for the Park include a 40,000 square foot technology business incubator.

Downtown Riverside also has been the focus of a rash of new developments. In 2002 Riverside Community Hospital opened a $20 million Emergency Room and Trauma Center. The Market Street Gateway, which is the entrance to Riverside off State Highway 60, has undergone vast aesthetic changes to attract more residential and retail developments. Market Street is the home of a new 126,000-square foot Corporate Center, located across from Fairmount Park.

The historic Fox Theater located downtown is currently undergoing restoration to become another multi-use venue in Riverside. The 1,600-seat venue is slated to become Riverside's premier performing arts center, hosting Broadway shows, concert performances, and ballets. The Fox Theater is expected to complement the Fox Plaza, a proposed project of 900 condominiums, 200 lofts, a hotel, and 800,000 square feet of commercial space nearby. The Fox Theater restoration was one of the largest projects included in the Riverside Renaissance Initiative, the city's plan for $785 million worth of projects in the five years from 2007 to 2012.

The Riverside Planning and Building Department has presented its General Plan for 2025. This plan outlines objectives for the future of Riverside in regards to housing, circulation, land use, economic outlook, arts and culture, and education. Some of the projects proposed in the General Plan for 2025 include improvements to the Riverside Municipal Airport, city parks, March Air Reserve Base/March Inland Port Airport, and more. The General Plan also proposes continuing support of the development of a contemporary state-of-the-art campus for the Riverside School of the Arts near White Park in downtown Riverside. The addition of shipping company DHL to the area in 2004 and its expansion of its international operations in Riverside in 2007 greatly benefited the economy.

Commercial Shipping

Riverside is adjacent to one of the major rail-freight centers in the state. Burlington Northern Santa Fe links and United Pacific Southern Pacific both link to the Ports of Los Angeles and Long Beach. The Port of Los Angeles has 27 cargo terminals and is the busiest container port in the United States. It is designated as a Foreign Trade Zone. The LA/Ontario International Airport has six airlines providing cargo service. The John Wayne Airport, about 44 miles away in Santa Ana, has two all-cargo airlines. About 70 miles away, Los Angeles International Airport has 1,000 cargo flights each day. The March Inland Port/March Airfield, just outside of the city limits, is a joint use facility serving both military and commercial interests. It has been designated as a Foreign Trade Zone. The Riverside Municipal Airport, an excellent general aviation facility, accommodates private aircraft, charter services, and air-related businesses. More than sixty-five trucking companies are based in or have facilities in Riverside and provide a broad range of interstate, regional, and local freight services. The one-day area served from Riverside has a population of more than 30 million people, which is more than one-tenth of the U.S. population.

Labor Force and Employment Outlook

The Inland Empire used to be the bedroom community for the larger metropolitan area. A relatively high percentage of the labor force commuted to jobs outside the two counties. But from 1980 to 2000 about 1.3 million people migrated to the area because it offered large tracts of affordable residential land, more than in coastal areas. The California Employment Development Department notes that Inland Empire's affordable housing and advantageous location have helped it create more new jobs than any other area. And the future forecast is just as bright. The influx of skilled professionals has helped the Inland Empire's economy become more focused on high tech, professional, and corporate jobs. The Southern California Association of Governments forecasted that the Inland Empire's employment base would expand by 408,946 jobs from 2000–2010. Job growth in the Inland Empire from 2000–2010 in the high tech/professional/corporate office sector was projected to reach 3.9 percent. By 2007, the Inland Empire had realized job growth of

25.6 percent in the past ten years, one of the fastest job growth rates of any metropolitan area of the country.

The following is a summary of data regarding the Riverside-San Bernardino-Ontario metropolitan area labor force, 2006 annual averages.

Size of nonagricultural labor force: 1,271,200

Number of workers employed in . . .

construction and mining: 130,900
manufacturing: 124,000
trade, transportation and utilities: 289,000
information: 15,200
financial activities: 51,800
professional and business services: 142,200
educational and health services: 122,700
leisure and hospitality: 128,700
other services: 42,600
government: 224,200

Average hourly earnings of production workers employed in manufacturing: $13.85

Unemployment rate: 5.6% (June 2007)

Largest city employers	*Number of employees*
University of California, Riverside	5,336
Riverside Unified School District	3,553
City of Riverside	2,642
Pacific Bell	1,800
Kaiser Permanente	1,700
The Press Enterprise Co.	1,300
Alvord Unified School District	1,200
Riverside Community Hospital	1,053

Cost of Living

Residential housing costs within Riverside are among the lowest in Southern California, a fact that has caused numerous companies and individuals to relocate to the area in recent years.

The following is a summary of data regarding several key cost of living factors for the Riverside area.

2007 (1st quarter) ACCRA Average House Price: $488,334

2007 (1st quarter) ACCRA Cost of Living Index: 116.0

State income tax rate: 1.0% to 9.3%

State sales tax rate: 7.25%

Local income tax rate: None

Local sales tax rate: Local sales and use tax rate: 1.75%

Property tax rate: Approximately 1.25% of assessed valuation; assessment ratio = 100% for residential

Economic Information: City of Riverside Development Department, 3900 Main Street, Riverside, CA 92522; toll-free (877)RIV-SIDE (877-748-7433); email devdept@riversideca.gov. Greater Riverside Chamber of Commerce, 3985 University Avenue, Riverside, CA 92501; telephone (951)683-7100; fax (951)683-2670

■ Education and Research

Elementary and Secondary Schools

There are two school districts serving the city. The Riverside Unified School District (RUSD), the 14th largest in the state, serves an area that includes most of Riverside as well as the Highgrove and Woodcrest areas just outside of the city. The district reports that most students match or exceed national and statewide performance on achievement tests and over 75 percent of high school graduates enroll in post-secondary training. The RUSD GATE Program offers special cluster classes or day classes for elementary students beginning in second grade. Advanced programs are offered for middle school and high school GATE students, including Advanced Placement classes, an International Baccalaureate, and college credit classes. The Alvord Unified School District accommodates the southwestern part of the city and adjacent unincorporated areas. Alvord also offers a GATE program for students in elementary school through high school. Both districts offer magnet schools for science and the performing arts, regional occupational programs, a wide variety of special education programs (generally serving students through age 21), and adult education classes.

The At Home in Riverside program serves area homeschoolers. There are several independent and church-oriented private schools in and around the city.

The California School for the Deaf, Riverside is part of the state Department of Education. The school has an enrollment of about 500 students from Southern California with day and residential programs. Students range in age from about 18 months to 22 years. Educational programs are also available for parents and community members.

The following is a summary of data regarding the Riverside Unified School District as of the 2005–2006 school year.

Total enrollment: 42,000

Number of facilities

    elementary schools: 29

    junior high/middle schools: 6

    senior high schools: 5

    other: 5

Student/teacher ratio: 22.3:1

Teacher salaries (2005–06)

    elementary median: $57,010

    junior high/middle median: $55,840

    secondary median: $54,950

Funding per pupil: $6,275

Public Schools Information: Alvord Unified School District, 10365 Keller Avenue, Riverside, CA 92505; telephone (951)509-5000; www.alvord.k12.ca.us. Riverside Unified School District, 3380 14th Street, Riverside, CA 92501; telephone (951)788-7134; www.rusd .k12.ca.us

Colleges and Universities

The University of California, Riverside (UCR) is considered to be a major research university and national center for the humanities. UCR offers bachelor's degrees in more than 78 majors, 38 doctoral programs, and 50 master's degree programs. The School of Education offers master's and doctoral programs in addition to teaching credentials in several other programs; UCR also offers a College of Engineering. The UCR California Center for Native Nations, established in 2003, encourages research and educational programs for Native populations. The UCR/UCLA Thomas Haider Program in Biomedical Sciences is the only medical program in the county. UCR was ranked as one of the top 100 national universities for 2008 by *U.S. News & World Report.*

La Sierra University (LSA), with more than 1,900 students, is a Seventh-Day Adventist institution that offers course work in undergraduate and graduate programs. LSA has four schools: the College of Arts and Sciences, the School of Business, the School of Education, and the School of Religion.

California Baptist University, affiliated with the Southern Baptist Convention, is a liberal arts institution with more than 3,700 students that offers 90 undergraduate and 25 graduate majors in such areas as behavioral sciences, business administration, liberal arts, and Christian studies. The school was ranked as one of the top 50 master's universities in the West for 2008 by *U.S. News & World Report.*

California Southern Law School, which operates part-time evening classes, offers programs in the practice and theory of law as students prepare for the state bar exam. Riverside City College, part of the Riverside Community College District, is a two-year school serving over 19,000 students each semester. Its main campus in downtown offers a number of associate degree programs in a variety of fields, including a School of Nursing.

Moreno Valley and Norco also have campuses that are part of the Riverside Community College District.

Other institutions of higher learning within the greater Riverside area include California State University–San Bernardino, California State University–Fullerton, Chapman University, University of Redlands, and Cal Poly Ponoma.

Libraries and Research Centers

The Riverside Public Library, with over 600,000 books, has one of the largest public library collections in the Southwest. The general collection includes print items representing 29 different languages. Casa Blanca Library and Family Center features a collection of over 7,000 volumes in Spanish. The main library facility is located in historic downtown and five other branches operate within the city. The Riverside Local History Research Center is a partnership between Riverside Municipal Museum and Riverside Public Library. Special collections at the Riverside Public Library include genealogy, local history, historical photographs, and U.S. documents.

The Riverside County Library System has 32 libraries and 2 bookmobiles serving the county. The Riverside County Library, San Bernardino County Library, Moreno Valley Public Library, Murrieta Public Library, and College of the Desert libraries are part of the Inland Library Network, an automated network that deploys approximately 350 computer/terminal workstations in library branches throughout the region.

The Riverside County Law Library is a state government document depository library. The University of California, Riverside (UCR) libraries contain over 2.3 million volumes and over 22,000 serial subscriptions. There are four facilities. The Tómas Rivera Library is home to the famed Eaton Collection, the world's largest cataloged collection of science fiction and fantasy. There is also the Science Library, the Music Library, and the Media Library.

The University of California, Riverside sponsors many research projects and facilities. The Citrus Experiment Station has developed over 40 new citrus varieties and provides research to help growers fight pests and diseases. The Institute for Integrative Genome Biology and the Center for Nanoscale Science and Engineering are leading research facilities. The Insectary and Quarantine Facility is an advanced laboratory for research in the study of non-native insects.

University Research Park is a cooperative development between the city, the county, and UCR. The development covers 39 acres in the Hunter Park Area and includes such companies as Centrum Analytical Labs, Encore Pharma, the Pacific Fuel Cell Corporation, Center for Environmental Microbiology, and Digital Angel. As of 2007 plans for continued development included an incubator facility containing chemical, biological, and electronics laboratories, as well as office space for emerging technology-based companies.

Public Library Information: Riverside Public Library, 3581 Mission Inn Avenue, Riverside, CA 92501; telephone (951)826-5201; www.riversideca.gov/library.

■ Health Care

Riverside Community Hospital, with 373 beds, is one of the largest acute care community hospitals in the county. The facility includes a Level II Trauma Center, the HeartCare Institute, the Cancer Center at Riverside, Family BIRTHplace, and a transplant services department for kidney and pancreas transplants. A full array of other medical services are provided. Kaiser Permanente Riverside Medical Center offers a wide variety of hospital and primary care services. The hospital has 215 beds. Specialty centers include the HEARx West Hearing Care Center and the Optix Vision Center. Other Kaiser facilities in Riverside include the Magnolia Village geriatric and long-term care facility, Canyon Crest Mental Health Offices, Van Buren Medical Offices, and Polk Street Medical Offices. Parkview Community Hospital Medical Center, with 193 beds, is a not-for-profit acute care hospital.

The addition of the 362-bed Riverside County Regional Medical Center in Moreno Valley adds to the quality health care, specialty clinics, and research facilities that are easily accessible to area residents.

■ Recreation

Sightseeing

One of Riverside's most attractive sites, Victoria Avenue, was constructed in 1891-92. The 8.3 miles of divided street are planted with hedgerow roses, eucalyptus, palm, and crepe myrtle trees with a multipurpose trail. Thirty-nine acres of hilly tree-lined paths with more than 3,000 blooming plant species from around the world are on view at the Botanical Gardens of the University of California, Riverside. The Gardens are also a wildlife sanctuary with almost two hundred bird species officially observed. The Mission Inn, a completely renovated National Historic Landmark hotel, is a unique blend of architectural styles and houses priceless pieces of art. The Teen Challenge Program is headquartered in the Spanish-style Benedict Castle, which was built in 1931. Overlooking the city of Riverside is the 1,337-foot Mt. Rubidoux, which is the site of the World Peace Tower and a large cross dedicated to Father Junipero Serra.

Heritage House, a restored two-story Victorian home completed in 1892 in the Queen Anne style, is open for tours. Visitors are also welcome at the Jensen-Alvarado Ranch, a historic ranch completely restored to portray rural life. The ranch features a variety of live animals, a duck pond, and citrus groves and fruit orchards.

Castle Park, a 25-acre family recreation park, features miniature golf, arcades, amusement rides, and a restored 1909 carousel. A model railroad at Hunter Park offers train rides when operating. Cuttings from the Parent Navel Orange Tree, planted in 1875, started the entire billion-dollar citrus industry in the United States. The tree, which can be seen at the Magnolia and Arlington area, still bears fruit.

Arts and Culture

Riverside is home to a variety of performing arts, theater, dance, and music organizations. The Performing Arts Program of the University of California, Riverside offers quality plays, musicals, and other acts through its University Theatre and other campus venues. The historic Riverside Municipal Auditorium—located in downtown Riverside—showcases live performances that range from popular music acts to comedy to dance throughout the year. The Riverside County Philharmonic performs four subscription concerts each year October through May at the Riverside Municipal Auditorium.

The Riverside Community Players, founded in 1926, is one of the oldest continuously active community theater groups in the United States and holds workshops in acting and staging techniques in addition to performing six productions annually. The Riverside Youth Theatre provides training for much younger thespians and showcases their talents with a few reasonably priced performances per year.

The free public concerts of the Riverside Concert Band, Inc. provide an opportunity for young musicians to perform with more experienced players at official functions in the city. Riverside Community College's Civic Light Opera offers its Performance Riverside season at the college's Landis Auditorium.

Dance enthusiasts will enjoy traditional Mexican dances performed by The Ballet Folklorico de Riverside, whose members range in age from 5 to 23 years old. Annual professional productions of the *Nutcracker* plus a spring performance are offered by the California Riverside Ballet, founded in 1969. The Riverside Ballet calls the historic Aurea Vista Hotel its home. It is only one of the many art groups found in the building. Another historic structure that serves as an art center in Riverside is the Life Arts Building. Built as a YMCA in 1909, the Life Arts Building is home to more than 30 artists' studios and includes art galleries for the Riverside Community Arts Association and Media Sound Productions, a high-tech recording studio.

The Riverside Community Arts Association, a non-profit organization staffed by volunteers, presents classes, demonstrations, shows, and sales of artworks. Members promote the cultural life of Riverside through leadership in educational, financial, and technical assistance to artists, art organizations, and community groups.

Riverside has an interesting variety of museums to be enjoyed by residents and visitors alike. The March Air Force Museum displays more than 60 aircraft and missiles, both inside and outside, on a 35-acre site adjacent to March Field. The Riverside Municipal Museum tells the story of the city's history, depicts the development of the citrus and other local manufacturing industries, and features touring exhibits. One of the largest collections of cameras and photos in the world is on display at the University of California, Riverside/California Museum of Photography. Rare Indian artifacts, basketry, pottery, and handicrafts are on view at the Sherman Indian Museum. The Mission Inn Museum, located at the historic Mission Inn, presents an eclectic display of historic artifacts, paintings of the California Missions painted in the 1800s, oriental *objects d'art,* arts and crafts furniture, marble sculptures, and many photographs. The Riverside Arts Museum, which offers 20 major exhibits a year, also is located downtown near the Mission Inn Museum.

Festivals and Holidays

February brings the annual Dickens Festival, a literary festival honoring the writer Charles Dickens that encourages reading and enjoyment of the dramatic and cultural arts by the general public. Riverside also hosts the Black History Parade and Expo on the third Saturday in February. And the Riverside Ballet Theatre hosts its Sweetheart Dance in February, which is open to the public. The Riverside County Fair and National Date Festival is also a February highlight.

In March the Riverside Arts Council presents Evening for the Arts to benefit the local arts community. April brings the annual Riverside Airshow at the Riverside Municipal Airport and the annual Orange Blossom Festival. The Orange Blossom Festival is two days of entertainment, vendors, a parade, turn-of-the-century costumes and events that celebrate Riverside's citrus heritage. Apple Festival Weekend is also typically in April. May's Cinco de Mayo is a celebration with music, entertainment, and food. The Vintage Home Tour and Restoration Faire featuring historically significant homes takes place in June. June also marks the beginning of Riverside Wednesday Night in downtown Riverside; the program lasts until September and offers a certified Farmer's Market, arts and crafts, food, live entertainment, petting zoo, pony rides, and kiddie rides.

In the summer months Fairmount Park offers a wide range of family programs and a peaceful setting. Independence Day features fireworks atop Mt. Rubidoux and two other city sites, which can be viewed from Riverside's Wheelock Field.

Fall ushers in a new lineup of programming in Riverside. September is the month of the Annual Mayor's Ball for the Arts, with an evening of banquets, costumes, prizes, and awards. Riverside Jazz Fest goes on for a weekend in September at Fairmount Park. October features Fiesta de la Familia in celebration of Hispanic Heritage month and Festa Italiana, an Italian food festival. Halloween weekend brings spooky tales of ghouls with Ghostwalk Riverside.

November brings the Mission Inn 5K/10K Run through notable areas of downtown. But it also kicks off the holiday season with the Christmas Tree Lighting and Mission Inn Festival of Lights. December's Christmas Open House brightens spirits with music and entertainment at the Riverside Municipal Museum, and the Riverside Ballet Theatre Company performs the annual *Nutcracker* ballet.

Sports for the Spectator

The University of California, Riverside is part of the NCAA Division I and participates in the Big West Conference. Men's and women's competitions include soccer, basketball, tennis, golf, cross country, and track and field. Men's baseball is played at the Riverside Sports Complex, which is jointly owned by the city and the university. Women's softball is played at the Amy S. Harrison Field.

Sports for the Participant

Riverside has over 21 city parks and 2 state parks available to sports enthusiasts. Six neighborhood parks have tennis courts and swimming pools. The city parks also have a combined total of 15 soccer fields and more than 40 ballfields, which includes the lighted baseball stadium at Riverside Sports Complex that seats 3,500.

County parks offer natural environments for hiking, horseback riding, cycling, fishing, and camping. The 180-plus acre Fairmount Park offers fishing and sailing on Lake Evans, paddleboats, wildlife and bird watching, lawn bowling, golfing, playgrounds, and evening concerts. An outdoor recreational facility on 350 acres, Rancho Jurupa Park (a county park) has 10 miles of hiking and horseback riding trails, stocked lakes, campsites with utility hookups, and the Louis Rubidoux Nature Center.

The California Citrus State Historic Park is currently being expanded for visitors. Lake Perris State Recreation Area has 8,800 lakeside acres waiting for water-skiing, boating, sailing, and windsurfing. Skiing in the nearby Big Bear area and hot air ballooning near the Temecula wineries are two popular winter activities.

Golfers can choose from six public and three private courses. Miniature golf enthusiasts can find four different 18-hole miniature courses at the Castle Amusement Park. Bicyclists can find out about a wealth of trails and events through the Riverside Bicycle Club. Riverside bike trails connect to Crest the Coast trails along the Santa Ana River. Even bowlers and skaters have numerous options within Riverside's city limits.

Shopping and Dining

The Inland Empire's shopping outlet is Ontario Mills, home to more than 200 specialty stores and 24 anchor stores. Riverside itself has two other major shopping malls: the 1.1-million square foot Galleria at Tyler and Riverside Plaza. The Riverside Plaza, housed within Riverside's Magnolia Center and historic craftsman-era "Wood Street" neighborhood, now sports a "Main Street" look and feel to its stores and shops. Downtown Riverside also offers a wide arrange of specialty stores. The Canyon Springs shopping center located on the eastern edge of Riverside has national retail stores, while Canyon Crest Towne Center has specialty shops in a residential area five minutes from downtown. Mission Village offers a more upscale shopping experience.

From coffeehouse fare to Cantonese favorites, Riverside has restaurants for every taste. Sandwich shops and casual eateries abound along with purveyors of ethnic delights including Mexican, French, Italian, Greek, Japanese, Thai, and British fish 'n' chips. The Mission Inn restaurant, Citrus City Grille, Creola's Fine Dining, Gerard's French Restaurant, and Café Sevilla are just a few of the local restaurants listed as the best in the city.

Visitor Information: Riverside Convention and Visitors Bureau, 3750 University Ave., Suite 175, Riverside, CA 92501; telephone (951)222-4700; www.riversidecb.com

■ Convention Facilities

Riverside Convention Center is located near downtown and has 45,000 square feet of multiuse space that can accommodate up to 2,000 people for special events. The Convention Center also has an outdoor, well-lit plaza available for open-air exhibits. Numerous hotels are within walking and easy driving distance from the Convention Center. Meeting spaces are available at Riverside Marriot and Mission Inn Hotel, as well as at several other hotels. The Riverside Municipal Auditorium, built in the Spanish Revival style with Moorish accents, is the home of the local symphony orchestra, opera, and ballet and is available for special events.

Convention Information: Riverside Convention and Visitors Bureau, 3750 University Ave., Suite 175, Riverside, CA 92501; telephone (951)222-4700; www.riversidecb.com

■ Transportation

Approaching the City

Most travelers take advantage of services at the LA/Ontario International Airport, which is located about 17 miles northwest of Riverside and is served by 12 commercial airlines. Riverside Municipal Executive Airport serves small corporate and business travelers. The John Wayne Airport is about 44 miles away in Santa Ana and is served by 11 commercial airlines and 3 commuter lines.

Several interstate highways passing through or near the city of Riverside include I-215 and I-15, which run north-south, and I-10, which runs east-west just north of the city. Other major freeways in the area are State Route 60 and State Route 91. These routes provide direct access to metropolitan areas of Los Angeles and Orange County. Nearly 3,000 miles of county-maintained roads and nearly 700 miles of roads maintained by the state provide service to business, industry, and motorists in the region. A toll lane for commuters traveling between Riverside and Orange County on Highway 91 is the newest freeway addition.

Metrolink is a regional rail system that includes commuter and other passenger services and links Riverside to employment and activity centers in Los Angeles, Orange, Ventura, San Bernardino, and San Diego counties.

Greyhound Bus Lines offers both intrastate and interstate service. The Riverside Transit Agency provides service to Riverside County within a 2,500-square-mile area; it also maintains two commuter routes to Orange County, San Bernardino, and Los Angeles. Amtrak serves the city through its Southwest Chief route, with two daily trips to Chicago through Albuquerque and Kansas City.

Traveling in the City

Within the city of Riverside, State Route 91 runs northwest and southeast through the city, and State Highway 60 runs northwest to southeast through the northern part of the city. Major thoroughfares include Magnolia Avenue, Allesandro Boulevard, University Avenue, and Arlington Avenue. The Riverside Transit Agency (RTA) has 40 routes in and around the city, with two trolley service routes near downtown. Bike racks are available on all fixed-route busses. RTA is a Dial-A-Ride service for those with disabilities, with 62 vans available.

■ Communications

Newspapers and Magazines

The city's daily newspaper is *The Press-Enterprise,* which has an average circulation of about 182,000. Other newspapers are UC-Riverside's *Highlander,* California

Baptist University's *The Banner, Black Voice News* (weekly), *Riverside Green Sheet* (a shopper), and *La Prensa* (a Spanish weekly). Magazines, newsletters, and journals published in Riverside include *Riverside Business Journal, Riverside Review, Hispanic Lifestyle, Inland Empire Magazine,* and *Inland Empire Family Magazine.*

Television and Radio

No television stations are based in Riverside, but cable is available. Riverside has four AM and six FM radio stations featuring contemporary hits, adult contemporary, and religious programming. One station is hosted by the University of California, Riverside.

Media Information: The Press Enterprise, PO Box 792, Riverside, CA 92502-0792; telephone (951)684-1200; www.pe.com

Riverside Online

Alvord Unified School District. Available www .alvord.k12.ca.us

City of Riverside home page. Available www .riversideca.gov

Greater Riverside Chamber of Commerce. Available www.riverside-chamber.com

Press Enterprise. Available www.pe.com

Riverside Community Online. Available www .smartriverside.com

Riverside Convention and Visitors Bureau. Available www.riversidecb.com

Riverside County. Available www.countyofriverside. us

Riverside County Library System. Available www .riverside.lib.ca.us

Riverside Unified School District. Available www .rusd.k12.ca.us

BIBLIOGRAPHY

Patterson, Tom, *A Colony for California: Riverside's First Hundred Years* (Riverside, CA: The Museum Press of the Riverside Museum Associates, 1996)

Traf, Clifford, *Native Americans of Riverside County* (San Francisco, CA: Arcadia Publishing, 2006)

Sacramento

■ The City in Brief

Founded: 1839 (incorporated 1850)

Head Official: Mayor Heather Fargo (since 2000)

City Population

> 1980: 275,741
> 1990: 369,365
> 2000: 407,018
> 2006 estimate: 453,781
> Percent change, 1990–2000: 3.0%
> U.S. rank in 1980: 52nd
> U.S. rank in 1990: 41st
> U.S. rank in 2000: 49th

Metropolitan Area Population

> 1980: 1,100,000
> 1990: 1,481,102
> 2000: 1,796,857
> 2006 estimate: 2,067,117
> Percent change, 1990–2000: 21.3%
> U.S. rank in 1980: 32nd
> U.S. rank in 1990: 26th
> U.S. rank in 2000: 24th (Sacramento/Yolo CMSA)

Area: 97.2 square miles (2000)

Elevation: 30 feet above sea level

Average Annual Temperatures: January, 46.3° F; July, 75.4° F; annual average, 61.1° F

Average Annual Precipitation: 17.93 inches of rain

Major Economic Sectors: services, wholesale and retail trade, government

Unemployment Rate: 5.2% (June 2007)

Per Capita Income: $22,841 (2005)

2005 FBI Crime Index Property: 26,083

2005 FBI Crime Index Violent: 5,265

Major Colleges and Universities: California State University, Sacramento; University of California at Davis, School of Medicine; American River College; Sacramento City College; Cosumnes River College

Daily Newspaper: *The Sacramento Bee*

■ Introduction

Sacramento, the capital of the state of California, began its life as a Gold Rush city when thousands of prospectors descended upon Captain John Sutter's settlement, New Helvetia, in hopes of striking the mother lode. Today Sacramento is a city of gracious tree-lined streets, famous for flowers that bloom all year—the "Camellia Capital of the World." A significant percentage of the food that America consumes is produced in Sacramento, which is at the center of the fruitful Sacramento Valley. Since the nineteenth century the city has been a major transportation hub for the West Coast.

■ Geography and Climate

Sacramento lies in the center of California's broad and fruitful Sacramento Valley at the confluence of the Sacramento and American Rivers, 72 miles northeast of San Francisco. Shielded by the Sierra Nevada Mountains to the east, the California Coast ranges to the west, and the Siskiyou Mountains to the north, the city enjoys a mild climate for most of the year. In the summer, however, "northers" blow from the Siskiyou Mountains, bearing pollen and heat. This is mitigated by Sacramento's extremely low humidity and the cool ocean breezes. The winters are rainy. The city lies to the northeast of several major fault lines, making the area susceptible to earthquakes. However, most quakes experienced in the city are of lower, less damaging magnitudes than those that may occur in the coastal San Francisco Bay Area.

Area: 97.2 square miles (2000)

Elevation: 30 feet above sea level

Average Temperatures: January, 46.3° F; July, 75.4° F; annual average, 61.1° F

Average Annual Precipitation: 17.93 inches of rain

■ History

Gold Rush Begins in Sacramento

The Sacramento area was originally inhabited by the Nisenan, a branch of the Maidu, who lived in the valley for 10,000 years before white settlers arrived. Spanish soldiers from Mission San Jose under the command of Lieutenant Gabriel Morago discovered the Sacramento and American rivers in 1808. The area was not settled until 1839. That year, with the permission of Mexico, Captain John Sutter, a Swiss immigrant who had fled his homeland to escape debtor's prison, built a settlement on 76 acres and called it New Helvetia after his homeland. He built a fort called Sutter's Fort (which has been restored and can still be seen today). Sutter also constructed a landing on the Sacramento River that he called the Embarcadero and contacted a millwright, James Marshall, to help build the settlement. It was Marshall who in 1848 discovered a gold nugget, thus precipitating the great California Gold Rush of 1849. Sutter's Embarcadero became the gateway to the mines, but Sutter was financially ruined by the influx of newcomers from all over the world who trampled his settlement; even his employees left him to make their fortune.

Sacramento, Spanish for "Holy Sacrament," was originally the name of a nearby river that is now called the Feather River; in 1849 the name was taken for the town, which was incorporated in 1850. Sacramento was a rowdy place, full of successful miners who spent their money on gambling and dance halls. In its early days the town encountered difficulties, with floods in 1849 and 1853 and a fire in 1852. But Sacramento survived to become the capital of California in 1854, paying the state $1 million for the honor.

Railroad Arrives; Agriculture Surpasses Gold Mining

In 1855 construction began on the Sacramento Valley Railroad with the financial backing of shopkeepers known as the Big Four: Collis P. Huntington, Mark Hopkins, Charles Crocker, and Leland Stanford (after whom Stanford University is named). In 1856 Sacramento became the terminus of California's first railroad. Then

came the Pony Express and, in 1861, the transcontinental telegraph. The Central Pacific Railroad joined the east and west coasts in 1869, permitting Sacramento farmers to ship their produce to the east. The railroad also transformed what had been a six-month trip between the coasts to six days; in time it also superseded the river as a means of transportation. In another important change, agriculture eventually replaced the gold mines as the primary industry.

Mather Field was established to prepare planes to fly to Europe during World War I; McClellan Air Force Base was established in 1937 and was an important base of operations during World War II. These military installations drew a large influx of people into the area, many of whom stayed after World War II and spurred the development of the private sector. The first suburban shopping mall in the United States was established in North Sacramento in 1945. However, like many cities in the United States, downtown Sacramento had fallen into decay by the end of the 1950s, since most of the moneyed population had moved to the suburbs. The city eventually experienced a resurgence marked by the redevelopment of the downtown area, with the city's historical sections being preserved and restored. Sutter's Embarcadero, for instance, was redeveloped to house shops and restaurants.

The 1990s brought a decrease in the once major military presence. Mather Air Force Base officially ceased military operation in 1993. The Air Force transferred the base to the County of Sacramento, which opened the Mather Airport for civilian use in 1995. McClellan Air Force Base officially ceased operations in 2001, but the site continued to house federal employees from the Department of Defense and is the site of the Veteran's Administrations medical and dental clinics.

Into the early 2000s, federal, state, and local government services continued to be a major source of employment in the city; however, city officials also continued to work on development projects that encouraged the reemergence of retail, entertainment, culture, and arts as primary forces in the downtown economy. Population within the six-county Sacramento Region increased by 20 percent between 1990 and 2000. Into the 2000s, the city also continued to work on projects to provide affordable housing and quality service for the continually growing population.

Historical Information: Sacramento Room, Sacramento Public Library, 828 I Street, Sacramento, CA 95814-3576; telephone (916)264-2700; www.saclib.org/sac_room/index.htm

■ Population Profile

Metropolitan Area Residents

1980: 1,100,000
1990: 1,481,102

2000: 1,796,857

2006 estimate: 2,067,117

Percent change, 1990–2000: 21.3%

U.S. rank in 1980: 32nd

U.S. rank in 1990: 26th

U.S. rank in 2000: 24th (Sacramento/Yolo CMSA)

City Residents

1980: 275,741

1990: 369,365

2000: 407,018

2006 estimate: 453,781

Percent change, 1990–2000: 3.0%

U.S. rank in 1980: 52nd

U.S. rank in 1990: 41st

U.S. rank in 2000: 49th

Density: 4,189.2 people per square mile (in 2000)

Racial and ethnic characteristics (2005)

White: 203,456

Black: 72,501

American Indian and Alaska Native: 5,739

Asian: 81,944

Native Hawaiian and Pacific Islander: 3,867

Hispanic or Latino (may be of any race): 111,559

Other: 59,073

Percent of residents born in state: 56.5% (2000)

Age characteristics (2005)

Population under 5 years old: 32,112

Population 5 to 9 years old: 28,857

Population 10 to 14 years old: 36,449

Population 15 to 19 years old: 32,595

Population 20 to 24 years old: 32,098

Population 25 to 34 years old: 75,497

Population 35 to 44 years old: 62,346

Population 45 to 54 years old: 58,488

Population 55 to 59 years old: 22,445

Population 60 to 64 years old: 16,338

Population 65 to 74 years old: 23,341

Population 75 to 84 years old: 19,070

Population 85 years and older: 5,651

Median age: 33 years

Births (2006, County)

Total number: 21,396

Deaths (2006, County)

Total number: 9,883

Money income (2005)

Per capita income: $22,841

Median household income: $44,867

Total households: 168,782

Number of households with income of . . .

less than $10,000: 14,564

$10,000 to $14,999: 11,518

$15,000 to $24,999: 21,190

$25,000 to $34,999: 18,898

$35,000 to $49,999: 24,295

$50,000 to $74,999: 30,972

$75,000 to $99,999: 21,736

$100,000 to $149,999: 17,627

$150,000 to $199,999: 5,074

$200,000 or more: 2,908

Percent of families below poverty level: 12% (2005)

2005 FBI Crime Index Property: 26,083

2005 FBI Crime Index Violent: 5,265

■ Municipal Government

Sacramento has a council-manager form of government. The council is comprised a mayor elected at large and eight council members elected by district; all serve staggered four-year terms. A city manager is hired by the council.

Some urbanized areas within the county of Sacramento are not part of any incorporated city, therefore, they are still governed by a system designed for rural counties.

Head Official: Mayor Heather Fargo (since 2000, term expires 2008)

Total Number of City Employees: 4,695 (2004)

City Information: City Hall, 915 I Street, Suite 205, Sacramento, CA 95814; telephone (916)264-5011; www.cityofsacramento.org

■ Economy

Major Industries and Commercial Activity

Sacramento began as a city rich from gold and railroad money. Productive mines still operate in the area, and the city remains an important transportation center. Sacramento's deep-water port, connected to the San Francisco Bay via a 43-mile channel, is an important West Coast hub for the handling of cargo from ocean-going ships. As the junction of the state's major railroad, the Union Pacific, Sacramento maintains its position at the top of the rail transportation industry. As state capitol of California, Sacramento's largest employment sector has historically been federal, state, and local government. As is true of California in general, the Sacramento area is rich in agriculture; products of the fertile Sacramento Valley

Image copyright lixxim, 2007. Used under license from Shutterstock.com.

region include fruits and vegetables, rice and other grains, meat, beet sugar, and almonds.

Today the city's economy is broadly based. Government and transportation are the largest sectors of employment in the area, and agriculture and mining—while still important in the region—have been surpassed by information, technology services, leisure and hospitality, education and health services, and construction. Technology-related companies such as Intel, Apple, and Hewlett-Packard are among the Sacramento area's largest employers; proximity to research centers, and a well-educated labor pool, have drawn such companies to the area. Sacramento's fastest-growing employment areas in the 2000s include financial activities, professional and business services, and education and health services.

Some of the other large employers in Sacramento in 2007 were Johnson Brothers Corporation, Azteria LLC, Sutter Health, Hospital Jobs Online, and Think Energy, Inc.

Items and goods produced: high-technology items, medical equipment and other health-related products, dairy products, feeds, meat, brick and clay products, mining equipment, lumber boxes

Incentive Programs—New and Existing Companies

Local programs: A number of organizations work to attract and assist businesses in the Sacramento area. Among them are the Sacramento Metro Chamber of Commerce, the Downtown Development Group, and the Sacramento Area Commerce and Trade Organization (SACTO). Sacramento's Economic Development Department and its partners offer loan programs to assist the development of small businesses. The city of Sacramento's facade rebate programs help businesses pay for building improvements. The Sacramento Municipal Utility District, California's largest customer-owned utility, offers discounts for new and expanding businesses. The Grow Sacramento Fund is a local, community-based lender that offers loans to eligible small businesses. The EnterFund Micro Loan program is also available to some small businesses that are not able to access capital through conventional lenders.

State programs: A variety of programs administered by state and federal sources are available to Sacramento businesses. The city has three state-designated Enterprise Zones: Northgate/Norwood, Oak Park/Florin Perkins, and the Sacramento Army Depot zone. Benefits of operating in the Enterprise Zone include sales and use tax credits; hiring tax credits; net operating loss carryover and net interest deduction for lenders programs. Sacramento also has two LAMBRA (Local Agency Military Base Recovery Area) areas: Mather Field and McClellan Park. LAMBRA incentives are similar to those for Enterprise Zones. Sacramento is part of a state-designated Recycling Market Development Zone, enabling businesses involved in recycling to utilize low-interest loans, technical assistance, siting and permitting assistance, and reduced permit application fees. A Research & Development Tax Credit is available of up to 15 percent against bank and corporate tax liability for certain in-house research. An additional 24 percent credit is available for basic research payments to outside organizations. This is one of the highest research and development tax credits in the nation. A Child Care Tax Credit is available for companies establishing on-site child care facilities. A Net Operating Loss Carryover and New Market Tax Credits are also available. A Work Opportunity Tax Credit is offered for employers who hire individuals from certain target groups.

Job training programs: The Sacramento Training and Response Team (START), a partnership of 20 job assistance and training programs, helps companies recruit, train, and hire employees. The California Employment Training Panel assists businesses through performance-based customized training contracts for new or existing employees. Reimbursement of costs for developing, implementing, and completing training programs may range from $1,500 to $2,000 per employee.

Development Projects

Sacramento's healthy economy is reflected in the city's numerous recent development projects. Developments in Sacramento's downtown area include: a five-story, 200,000-square-foot expansion of City Hall, which opened in 2005; new hotels including a 32-story hotel that opened in 2001 and an 8-story hotel that opened the following year; and construction of the Wells Fargo Pavilion, a 2,500-seat theater that replaces the Music Circus tent. Two of Sacramento's medical centers—University of California at Davis Medical Center and Kaiser Permanente's South Sacramento Hospital—were undergoing massive expansions in 2007.

Economic Development Information: Sacramento Metro Chamber of Commerce, One Capitol Mall, Suite 300, Sacramento, CA 95814; telephone (916)552-6800; fax (916)443-2672

Commercial Shipping

With an international airport, rail hub, seaport, and junction of three freeways within ten miles of downtown, Sacramento is ideally situated for commercial shipping.

Inland 79 miles from San Francisco, the Port of Sacramento admits international ocean-going vessels through a deep-water channel connecting it with San Francisco Bay. The port's specialty is handling dry-bulk cargos and it utilizes the most modern equipment on the West Coast for that purpose. About 1.3 million tons of cargo is handled each year. The port is served by over 50 major trucking companies and three major rail lines: BNSF Railway, Union Pacific Railroad, and Sierra Northern. The Sacramento International Airport is served by 10 cargo airline carriers.

Labor Force and Employment Outlook

Employers have access to a large and well-educated labor pool. The Sacramento region's economy is among the strongest in California, and job growth has remained positive in the 2000s. Government employment is the largest employment sector in the area. Among California's approximately 470,000 government employees, some 25 percent are employed in the Sacramento area. As of 2007, as much as 80 percent of new employment in the Sacramento region was due to the expansion of existing companies. *Time* magazine has rated Sacramento as the nation's most integrated city. Among the most popular occupations in Sacramento are management, professional, and related occupations, 34 percent; sales and office occupations, 24 percent; and service occupations, 16 percent. Approximately 62 percent of workers in Sacramento work for companies, some 23 percent work for the government and 6 percent are self-employed. Regarding the educational level of the workforce, in 2007, 24 percent of workers had some college, but no degree; 8 percent held an associate's degree; 19 percent held a bachelor's degree; and 9 percent held a graduate or professional degree. As of September 2007, the number of Sacramento jobs had decreased by 11 percent since March 2006. In August 2007, Sacramento had an unemployment rate of 5.4 percent, compared the national average of 4.6 percent.

The following is a summary of data regarding the Sacramento–Arden-Arcade–Roseville metropolitan area labor force, 2006 annual averages.

Size of nonagricultural labor force: 900,300

Number of workers employed in ...

   construction and mining: 71,800
   manufacturing: 49,200
   trade, transportation and utilities: 153,200
   information: 19,900
   financial activities: 65,300
   professional and business services: 106,300
   educational and health services: 92,000
   leisure and hospitality: 85,700
   other services: 28,700
   government: 228,400

Average hourly earnings of production workers employed in manufacturing: $16.43

Unemployment rate: 5.2% (June 2007)

Largest employers (non-government)	*Number of employees*
UC Davis Medical Center	8,500
Intel	6,500
Sacramento City Unified School District	6,000
Hewlett-Packard Co.	4,500

Cost of Living

Sacramento's housing prices relative to San Francisco and southern California have been kept low by an abundance of cheap land.

The following is a summary of data regarding several key cost of living factors for the Sacramento area.

2007 (1st quarter) ACCRA Average House Price: Not reported

2007 (1st quarter) ACCRA Cost of Living Index: 122.8

State income tax rate: 1.0% to 9.3%

State sales tax rate: 6.25%

Local income tax rate: None

Local sales tax rate: 1.5% (county)

Property tax rate: 1.0% of total assessed value

Economic Information: Sacramento Metro Chamber of Commerce, One Capitol Mall, Suite 300, Sacramento, CA 95814; telephone (916)552-6800; fax (916)443-2672

■ Education and Research

Elementary and Secondary Schools

The Sacramento City Unified School District, among the largest in the state, is Sacramento's main school district. Students of all ages are served throughout the district, which offers a full range of programs that include charter schools, alternative schools, independent study, preschool, and adult education. There were 88 schools in the district in 2007. Other districts with schools in Sacramento include the Elk Grove Unified School District, Folsom-Cordova Unified School District, the San Juan Unified School District, the Grant Joint Union High School District, Natomas Unified School District, North Sacramento Elementary School District, Robla Elementary School District, and Del Paso Heights School

District. The California Education Authority, which specifically serves students who are convicted juvenile offenders, maintains one school in Sacramento.

The following is a summary of data regarding the Sacramento City Unified School District as of the 2007–2008 school year.

Total enrollment: 50,000

Number of facilities

elementary schools: 60
junior high/middle schools: 8
senior high schools: 6
other: 14

Student/teacher ratio: 20.9:1

Teacher salaries (2005–06)

elementary median: $36,408–67,918 (all levels)
junior high/middle median: Not available
secondary median: Not available

Funding per pupil: $8,294

Sacramento also has about 80 private and parochial schools.

Public Schools Information: Sacramento City Unified School District, 5735 47th Avenue, Sacramento, CA 95824; telephone (916)643-7400; www.scusd.edu

Colleges and Universities

Sacramento is home to a number of colleges and universities. Four-year institutions include California State University, Sacramento (CSUS), typically known as Sacramento State, with an enrollment of approximately 28,000 students. CSUS has the following academic divisions: Arts and Letters; Business Administration; Education; Engineering and Computer Science; Health and Human Services; Natural Sciences and Mathematics; Social Sciences and Interdisciplinary Studies; and Continuing Education. CSUS offers 60 undergraduate degree programs and 40 graduate programs.

Golden Gate University, which offers undergraduate and graduate programs in business and management, information technology, taxation, and law, has a Sacramento campus (its main campus is in San Francisco). Nearby is the University of California at Davis, which boasts a highly regarded medical center—the primary teaching facility of the University's School of Medicine—located in Sacramento. In 2007 UC Davis School of Medicine was ranked among the top 25 schools for primary care methodology and in the top 50 for research methodology by *U.S. News & World Report*. The University of Southern California's School of Policy, Planning, and Development is located in Sacramento. There is a regional campus of the University of San Francisco in Sacramento as well, offering both bachelor's and master's degree programs for a student body of about 250. The University of the Pacific's McGeorge School of Law at Sacramento offers full-time and part-time study programs. Joint degrees are available with UC Davis and CSUS.

Two-year colleges in Sacramento are American River, Cosumnes River, and Sacramento City colleges.

Libraries and Research Centers

The Sacramento Public Library operates a 160,000-square-foot Central Library, and 27 branches and 2 bookmobiles. Holdings include over 1.8 million volumes and 3,952 periodical subscriptions, plus audio and video tapes, recordings, maps, and art reproductions. Among the special collections are Californiana, the history of printing, and city planning and urban development. The Arden-Dimick Community Library branch houses a special collection for the deaf with about 500 books and magazines and 400 sign language videos. The Schwab-Rosenhouse College Resource Center and the Sacramento Room (for local history) are located at the Central Library. A College and Career Center is based at the Colonial Heights branch.

The California State University, Sacramento, Library holds over 1.2 million volumes, 4,444 e-books, nearly 5,000 periodical subscriptions, 12,847 audio/visual materials, plus maps and government documents.

Sacramento is also the headquarters of the California State Library with special collections of federal and state government documents; its holdings include over 777,509 volumes. The Braille and Talking Book Library is one of the special collections at the State Library. It has over 55,000 titles and 15 periodical subscriptions, including a limited number of materials in foreign languages. The Witkin State Law Library of California is also part of the State Library.

The Western Ecological Research Center (WERC), which has 14 field stations in California and one in Nevada, is headquartered in Sacramento. WERC offers its clients and partners the research and technology needed to support the management of Pacific Southwestern ecosystems. WERC's scientists are experts in such fields as herpetology, conservation biology, wetlands ecology, and ecological restoration. The research centers and institutes of the nearby University of California at Davis (UC) perform research in a wide variety of areas such as food safety and cleaner fuel technologies. UC Davis Health System, which is based in Sacramento, conducts hundreds of research studies through its specialized clinics. The UC Davis Health System research centers include the AIDS Clinical Trials Unit, the Alzheimer's Disease Center, the Center for Healthy Aging, the Mouse Biology Program, the Genomics Program, and the Center for Nursing Research. The M.I.N.D. Institute has performed cutting edge research in such areas as autism and cancer. The California National Primate Research Center is a federally funded biomedical research facility affiliated with UC Davis. The center is part of a network of eight national primate research centers sponsored by the National Institutes of Health for studies of human and animal health.

California State University, Sacramento sponsors several research institutes and centers, including the Institute for Social Research, the Center for Pacific Asian Studies, the Applied Research Design Center, the High Power Electronics Center, the Archaeological research Center, and the Polymer Research Center.

Public Library Information: Sacramento Public Library, Central Library, 828 I Street, Sacramento, CA 95814-3576; telephone (916)264-2770;www.saclib.org

■ Health Care

Sacramento is well served by medical care facilities. The acclaimed University of California at Davis Medical Center is located in Sacramento. Its 141-acre campus includes a 528-bed hospital. Originally founded in 1852 as Sacramento County Hospital, it was acquired by the university and renamed The University of California, Davis Medical Center in 1973. The campus's Shriner's Hospital for Children, providing pediatric care in three specialty programs—orthopaedics, spinal cord injury treatment and rehabilitation, and acute burn treatment and rehabilitation—was built in 1997. The medical center is the region's only Level I comprehensive adult and pediatric trauma center. Specialty services include a trauma service that utilizes Life Flight; a Burn Center; a Transplant Center for kidney, pancreas, and liver transplants; a regional poison control center; a corneal transplant service; a regional mental health program; an extensive family practice program; a neonatal intensive care unit; a comprehensive rehabilitation center; and seven specialized intensive care units including a neurological surgery intensive care unit. The UC Davis Cancer Center is the only National Cancer Institute-designated cancer center in Northern California. The Clinical Trials Program at the Cancer Center is one of the largest in the country.

Sutter Medical Center, Sacramento, includes Sutter General Hospital, Sutter Memorial Hospital, Sutter Oaks Midtown Nursing Center, and Sutter Center for Psychiatry. In 2003, Sutter Memorial Hospital and Sutter General Hospital became the first hospitals on the West Coast to begin utilizing electronic ICU with advanced video and electronic monitoring as a remote high-tech surveillance system of their most critically ill patients. The 306-bed Sutter General offers general acute medical and surgical care. Among the specialties of the hospital are critical care, neuroscience, renal dialysis, respiratory rehabilitation, spinal care, and urology. The 346-bed Sutter Memorial is a specialty medical center with particular focus on cardiovascular services, transplants, and women's and children's specialty care. Sutter Center for Psychiatry provides psychiatric and mental health services to adults, adolescents and children age five and older. Sutter Oaks provides short-term rehabilitation services.

Mercy General Hospital, operated by Catholic Healthcare West, offers specialty services that include a birth center, eye and heart institutes, a stroke center, and orthopedic, neuroscience, spine, and rehabilitation services. Mercy has 304 acute care beds and 38 skilled nursing beds. Mercy also sponsors the MercyClinic Norwood primary healthcare facility and MercyClinic Loaves and Fishes, a medical clinic for homeless residents in Sacramento. Methodist Hospital of Sacramento, also operated by Catholic Healthcare West, has 162 acute care beds. The emergency department at Methodist is expected to expand to include a trauma center by the end of 2008. Special programs and centers include the Family Birth Center, featuring a level II neonatal ICU; the Orthopedic and Sports Medicine Center; the Hand Therapy Program; and the Occupational and Physical Therapy Center. Bruceville Terrance is a 171-bed long-term skilled nursing facility licensed to Methodist Hospital.

Kaiser Permanente's South Sacramento Medical Center is a 179-bed full service facility. It has one of the largest labor and delivery services in the area. Along with standard services such as 24-hour emergency care, surgery, nuclear medicine, and cardiology, the hospital provides HIV/AIDS programs, home health, hospice, a nutrition service, pain management, and a sleep lab. South Sacramento Medical Center is a teaching hospital for UC Davis School of Medicine.

The Veteran's Administrations maintains a 45-bed inpatient medical center in Sacramento.

■ Recreation

Sightseeing

Sacramento is a river town, virtually created by the California Gold Rush. Along the bank of the Sacramento River is the Old Sacramento Historic Area, a 28-acre National Historic Landmark that attracts more than 5 million visitors annually. This atmospheric area, with wooden-slat sidewalks and horse-drawn carriages on its cobblestone streets, gives the visitor a sense of the vitality and bustle generated by the thousands of hopeful prospectors who streamed through Sacramento in the mid-nineteenth century. Old Sacramento's museums, shops, and restaurants preserve its historical character. The Old Sacramento Waterfront offers a variety of activities, including touring and riding on nineteenth-century boats, visiting the depots of the Central Pacific railroad, and exploring the bustling Public Market. In midtown Sacramento, Sutter's Fort, the first Euro-American settlement in Sacramento, has been restored and preserved.

The 1839 adobe fort contains relics of pioneer and goldrush days. Exhibits include living quarters, a blacksmith shop, a bakery, a prison, and livestock areas. The State Capitol building within 40-acre Capitol Park was built in 1869; it is similar in style to the U.S. Capitol building. Underneath its 120-foot high rotunda are ornate chandeliers, imposing staircases, and marble floors. Visitors can tour the offices of the governor, attorney general, secretary of state, and treasurer, and view exhibits about the history of California's state government. In Sacramento's south side, the Sacramento City Cemetery, established in 1849, contains the graves of more than 25,000 pioneers, immigrants, their families, and descendants; among its first interments were more than 600 victims of the 1850 cholera epidemic.

The Sacramento Zoo displays more than 400 exotic animals in their natural settings, including red pandas, snow leopards, lemurs, zebras, chimpanzees, jaguars, and many others. The zoo emphasizes protection of endangered animals, and faithful recreation of natural habitats. Adjacent to the zoo is Fairytale Town for children, a park based on themes from fairy tales and nursery rhymes. Waterworld California, the only wave pool in Northern California, has the highest water slides in the West, including the Honolulu Halfpipe and the Cliffhanger.

Sacramento is within easy driving distance of other atmospheric Gold Country towns: Coloma has Marshall Gold Discovery State Historic Park, where James Marshall's discovery of gold in 1848 started the Gold Rush; Placerville features Hangtown's Gold Bug Mine, a fully-lighted mine shaft; Sutter Creek has a charming array of Victorian homes and balconied buildings; Jackson retains a European character from its early Italian- and Serbian-American miners; Columbia has Columbia State Historic Park, where visitors can ride a stagecoach and pan for gold. Sacramento is conveniently located for day trips to Northern California's outdoor attractions. The city is only a few hours away from Yosemite National Park; from the Napa-Sonoma Valley, where most of California's finest wines are produced; and from Lake Tahoe.

Arts and Culture

Sacramento is rich in theater. California's largest nonprofit musical theatre—The California Musical Theatre, formerly known as Sacramento Light Opera Association or SLOA—is based here. It provides Music Circus productions during the summer and Broadway Series productions during the rest of the year. Since its first performance in 1951, Music Circus has staged numerous productions of some 150 musicals; classics such as *The King and I, Oklahoma!,* and *Show Boat* are well represented. Music Circus presented its music theatre under a circus-style open-air tent until its move in 2003 to the 2,200-seat Wells Fargo Pavilion. Performances are in the round, with 360-degree seating. California Musical

Theatre's Broadway Series, begun in 1989, offers Broadway hits with national stars. Productions are at the 2,452-seat Sacramento Community Center Theater, across from the Capitol building.

The Sacramento Community Center Theater is also home to The Sacramento Ballet, Sacramento Opera, Sacramento Philharmonic, Sacramento Choral Society and Orchestra, Sacramento Community Concerts, and the Sacramento Speakers Series. The Sacramento Opera has performed more than 40 operas; the opera season runs from September to March and includes about three performances. The 73-member Sacramento Philharmonic generally presents five concerts annually from November through May. Special chamber orchestra concerts are also offered throughout the season. The Sacramento Ballet performs both classical and contemporary ballet. They present about five performance series annually. Also for music lovers, the all-volunteer (by audition) Camellia Symphony season runs from October through mid-May and includes about six concerts (one of which, at the Sunrise Mall on Mother's Day, is free) and several special fundraising concerts.

The 24th Street Theatre, a 296-seat auditorium at the Sierra 2 Center for the Arts and Community, is home to the Light Opera Theatre of Sacramento (LOTS), which brings light opera, such as the works of Gilbert and Sullivan, to the Sacramento area. The Sacramento Theater Company maintains its own resident company offering classical and modern plays at its 300-seat Mainstage and 85-seat Stage Two. The B Street Theatre, Sacramento's Professional New Works Theatre Company, produces contemporary theatrical works. Garbeau's Dinner Theatre, in nearby Rancho Cordova, is housed in a restored winery. In all, more than 80 groups present live theatrical performances throughout the region.

Sacramento is home to the oldest art museum in the West. Established in 1873, the Crocker Art Museum's permanent collection features European paintings by such masters as Rembrandt and Bruegel; a renowned collection of drawings; Indian and Persian miniature paintings; American (especially Californian) paintings; decorative arts and ceramics; photography; and contemporary art. The California State Railroad Museum displays the history of the railroads and makes special note of the fact that Sacramento was once the terminus of the transcontinental railroad. The 100,000 square-foot-museum displays 21 locomotives and railroad cars, half of which may be walked through, as well as 46 exhibits. On weekends between April and September, visitors can ride the Museum's Sacramento Southern Railroad on a six-mile route along the Sacramento River. The Discovery Museum features interactive history, science, and technology exhibits examining the evolution of everyday life in Sacramento, on such topics as the gold rush and other periods of local California history, the history of the

Sacramento Valley's topomorphology, and food processing technology. The Towe Auto Museum explores car culture and automotive history, and has more than 150 vintage automobiles on display. The State Indian Museum on the grounds of Sutter's Fort displays the jewelry, art, clothing, baskets, and other artifacts of the native Americans who lived in the area.

Festivals and Holidays

Sacramento Jazz Jubilee, the world's largest congregation of jazz bands, takes place during Memorial Day weekend; it features more than 100 bands and attracts more than 100,000 listeners. The Bridge to Bridge Waterfront Festival in July is a two-day event featuring boat races, boating exhibitors, and Coast Guard and wakeboard demonstrations. From mid-August through early September Sacramento hosts the California State Fair, one of the largest agricultural fairs in the country, at the California Exposition; the fair's features include a concert series, rides, horse racing, numerous competitions, extreme sports demonstrations, indoor and outdoor exhibits and shows, and a kids park. During the four-day Gold Rush Days festival over Labor Day weekend, the Gold Rush era is recreated in Old Sacramento, with historic characters, covered wagons and horse-drawn carriages, street dramas, musicians, dancers, arts and crafts, and exhibits; the streets of Old Sacramento are covered with dirt and only horse-drawn vehicles are permitted.

Sports for the Spectator

The NBA Sacramento Kings and WNBA Sacramento Monarchs bring professional basketball to Sacramento; they play at Arco Arena, a 442,000-square-foot venue that seats 17,317. The Kings won Pacific Division titles in 2001-02 and 2002-03, and advanced to the 2002 Western Conference Finals. In 2000, professional minor league baseball returned to Sacramento after a 27-year absence when the Sacramento River Cats, formerly the Vancouver Canadians, moved to 11,092-seat Raley Field. The River Cats have won five Pacific Coast League South Division titles (in 2000, 2001, 2003, 2004, and 2007) and PCL Championships in 2003, 2004, and 2007. Professional tennis is represented by the Capitals of the World TeamTennis League. As of 2007, the 20-year-old team has been five-time champion of the World Team-Tennis (WTT) League Championship and King Trophy. The Sacramento Knights play at Cosumnes River College as part of the National Premier Soccer League. The Sacramento State Hornets are among the Sacramento area's college sports teams.

Sports for the Participant

Sacramento, the "River City," provides many forms of water recreation. The American River offers boating, swimming, and calm- and white-water rafting. Nearby

Folsom Lake and Lake Natoma offer sailing and windsurfing. All the waters in the Sacramento area are stocked with fish; king salmon run in the American and Sacramento Rivers. The American River Bike Trail, stretching from Sacramento's Discovery Park to Folsom Lake, provides nearly 35 miles of scenic trail used by cyclists, walkers, joggers, and bird watchers. Over 210 city parks and recreation areas dot Sacramento encompassing over 2,000 acres, including sites for skate parks, dog parks, a rifle and pistol range, bocce ball, disc golf, playgrounds, and community gardens. There are four municipal golf courses and four county courses.

Sacramento is roughly two hours from five national forests. The Sacramento area's municipal golf courses comprise 540 acres. Sacramento has several equestrian centers and many horseback riding trails. More than two dozen ski resorts, most within 120 miles, are located in the nearby Sierra-Nevada Mountains. The California International Marathon in December starts in Folsom and ends at the Sacramento State Capitol building.

Shopping and Dining

Sacramento is home to several shopping malls and hundreds of boutiques and specialty shops. Old Sacramento is a popular and atmospheric shopping area; its Public Market is a European-style, open-air market featuring bakeries, fish, poultry, meat, produce, flowers, and assorted ethnic shops. Other major shopping areas in Sacramento include: Westfield Downtown Plaza, with more than 100 shops, many restaurants, and a cinema; Town and Country Village, with 55 shops, was built in 1946, making it Sacramento's oldest shopping center; Arden Fair has more than 165 shops, restaurants, a cinema, and foodcourt; Pavilions offers cosmopolitan shopping and fine dining; Sunrise Mall and Florin Mall each have approximately 100 shops and restaurants and a cinema; and Folsom Premium Outlets has more than 80 stores.

Restaurants are plentiful in Sacramento, featuring cuisine ranging from traditional American, to inventive Californian, to a wide variety of ethnic fare. Many eateries are concentrated in Old Sacramento, as well as along J Street and Capitol Avenue between 19th and 29th streets and Fair Oaks Boulevard between Howe and Fulton streets. A few local favorites include Fran's Café (Mediterranean), Aioli Bodega Espanola (Spanish), Addis Ababa (Ethiopian), Ambrosia Café (Californian), Bangkok Garden (Thai), and La Bonne Soupe Café (French).

Visitor Information: Sacramento Convention and Visitors Bureau, 1608 I Street, Sacramento, CA 95814; telephone (916)808-7777; www.sacramentocvb.org

■ Convention Facilities

The principal meeting place is the Sacramento Convention Center Complex, located downtown. The complex contains three buildings: the 134,000-square-foot Exhibit Hall can be divided into 5 areas and is equipped with risers to create arena seating for 6,500 people; the elegant 25,000-square-foot Ballroom, which can be divided into 10 meeting rooms, accommodates 1,500 people banquet-style or 2,500 theater-style; and the 11,200-square-foot Activity Building features 12 meeting rooms. Nearby Memorial Auditorium, built in 1926 and registered as a historic landmark, provides seating for a maximum of 3,800 people; the building contains Memorial Hall, the Little Theater, and meeting rooms. The 2,452-seat Sacramento Community Center Theater is located near Capitol Park.

Located five miles from downtown is the California Exposition (Cal Expo), a large facility with more than 200,000 square feet of exhibit space on a 780-acre site. Designed for events such as agricultural shows and trade conventions, the center provides outdoor exhibit areas and unlimited parking. Arco Arena also hosts trade shows and business events in its 442,000-square-foot main floor.

Hotels and motels in the metropolitan area, providing more than 10,000 rooms, offer meeting facilities for large and small groups.

Convention Information: Sacramento Convention and Visitors Bureau, 1608 I Street, Sacramento, CA 95814; telephone (916)808-7777; www.sacramentocvb.org

■ Transportation

Approaching the City

The Sacramento International Airport, 12 miles northwest of downtown, receives service from 14 major carriers and 1 commuter airline. The airport served 10.4 million passengers in 2006. There are non-stop and direct flights from 52 cities. Also in Sacramento, the Executive Airport serves private and business planes.

The primary north-south routes to Sacramento are I-5 (the Pan American Highway) and U.S. 99; the major east-west routes are I-80 and U.S. 50, connecting Sacramento to San Francisco to the southwest, and Lake Tahoe to the northeast.

Passenger train service is available through Amtrak on three lines. Greyhound also has a route to the city, and boat/bus excursions are offered between Sacramento and San Francisco.

Traveling in the City

Most of Sacramento's downtown streets are one-way, with a synchronized traffic light system. The major thoroughfares are the freeways: Interstate 80 and Business 80, which run from the west to the northeast, and Interstate 5, which runs north and south. Other important roads are the Garden Highway, running east and west, and State Highway 99, coming from the southern part of the city to join Business 80. In downtown Sacramento, the streets running east and west are named by letter; streets running north and south are designated by number.

Sacramento Regional Transit District (RT) operates 254 buses on 97 area bus routes. The RT also owns the electrically powered light rail system, which consists of 76 light rail vehicles traversing 36.87 miles of light rail, connecting the suburbs with downtown. The bus and rail systems are accessible to the disabled community. The system had more than 30 million passengers in 2005.

■ Communications

Newspapers and Magazines

Sacramento offers one major daily newspaper, the morning *The Sacramento Bee*. The "Sacbee," as it is sometimes called by locals, is one of the top five newspapers in the state and was one of the top 25 papers in the nation by circulation in 2007 (279,032 daily). The *Sacramento News and Review*, a weekly alternative paper is distributed for free throughout the city. The *Sacramento Gazette* is a small weekly paper that began publication in 1996. *The Sacramento Observer* is considered one of the finest African American newspapers in the country. *El Hispanio* is a weekly Spanish and English publication for the Hispanic community.

The *Sacramento Business Journal* reports on happenings in business and industry. *Sacramento Magazine* highlights local entertainment and lifestyles. Nearly 30 magazines and journals are published in Sacramento. *Parent's Monthly* is a free family-oriented magazine. *MGW Newsmagazine* is a monthly publication featuring local and national news for the gay and lesbian community. *Catholic Herald*, for the Diocese of Sacramento, is published twice a month.

Television and Radio

There are five television stations that broadcast in Sacramento, where cable is also available. In the Sacramento listening range, there are 50 AM and FM radio stations broadcast music, news, talk, Spanish, and Christian programming; only about 20 broadcast directly from Sacramento.

Media Information: *The Sacramento Bee*, 2100 Q Street, Sacramento, CA 95852; telephone (916)321-1000; www.sacbee.com

Sacramento Online

City of Sacramento Home Page. Available www .cityofsacramento.org

The Sacramento Bee. Available www.sacbee.com

Sacramento City Unified School District. Available www.scusd.edu

Sacramento Convention & Visitors Bureau. Available www.sacramentocvb.org

Sacramento Metro Chamber. Available www .metrochamber.org

Sacramento Public Library. Available www .saclibrary.org

BIBLIOGRAPHY

Kelley, Robert Lloyd, *Battling the Inland Sea: American Political Culture, Public Policy, and the Sacramento Valley, 1850–1986* (Berkeley, CA: University of California Press, 1989)

San Diego

■ The City in Brief

Founded: 1769 (incorporated 1850)

Head Official: Mayor Jerry Sanders (R) (since 2005)

City Population

    1980: 875,538
    1990: 1,110,623
    2000: 1,223,400
    2006 estimate: 1,256,951
    Percent change, 1990–2000: 10.1%
    U.S. rank in 1980: 8th
    U.S. rank in 1990: 6th
    U.S. rank in 2000: 11th

Metropolitan Area Population

    1980: 1,862,000
    1990: 2,498,016
    2000: 2,813,833
    2006 estimate: 2,941,454
    Percent change, 1990–2000: 12.6%
    U.S. rank in 1980: 19th
    U.S. rank in 1990: 15th
    U.S. rank in 2000: 17th

Area: 324.3 square miles (2000)

Elevation: Ranges from sea level to 1,591 feet above sea level

Average Annual Temperatures: January, 57.8° F; July, 70.9° F; annual average, 64.4° F

Average Annual Precipitation: 10.77 inches of rain

Major Economic Sectors: services, wholesale and retail trade, government

Unemployment Rate: 4.6% (January 2005)

Per Capita Income: $29,497 (2005)

2005 FBI Crime Index Property: 46,213

2005 FBI Crime Index Violent: 6,603

Major Colleges and Universities: University of California, San Diego; University of San Diego; San Diego State University; Scripps Institution of Oceanography

Daily Newspaper: *The San Diego Union-Tribune*

■ Introduction

San Diego, "the Birthplace of California," is a city of many guises. It is not only a major naval base and an important natural harbor, but it is also a top tourist attraction and resort area, a prominent high-technology, aerospace, and aviation production community, and a fertile agricultural area. San Diego's port and its proximity to Mexico give the city an international flavor, and a revitalized downtown area adds to the exciting atmosphere. The mild climate attracts many new residents and industries each year. A nondescript town until the 1940s, San Diego now has more than 1.2 million residents and is California's second largest city. San Diego's phenomenal growth has brought it well-deserved national attention. The city keeps this growth balanced by careful preservation of history and a strong emphasis on art, culture, and recreation.

■ Geography and Climate

San Diego is just 20 miles north of Mexico, situated in the rolling hills and mesas that rise from the Pacific shore to join with the Laguna Mountains to the east. Its bay is one of the country's finest natural harbors. The city covers a large area of vastly different terrain: miles of ocean and bay shoreline, densely forested hills, fertile valleys, and mountains, canyons, and desert. The climate varies in a similar manner. On the coast, the temperatures are mild and constant, while in the desert areas, the temperature can fluctuate as much as 30 degrees in one day. San Diego is about 120 miles south of Los Angeles.

The climate in San Diego is tempered by the Pacific Ocean air, keeping the summers cool and the winters warm. Severe weather is rare in the area; snow is almost unknown, and the city averages only three thunderstorms a year. September and October often bring hot eastern winds from the desert, producing what are usually the hottest days of the year.

Area: 324.3 square miles (2000)

Elevation: Ranges from sea level to 1,591 feet above sea level

Average Temperatures: January, 57.8° F; July, 70.9° F; annual average, 64.4° F

Average Annual Precipitation: 10.77 inches of rain

■ History

Spanish, Mexicans, Americans Lay Claim to San Diego Region

Portuguese explorer Juan Rodriguez Cabrillo, the discoverer of California, sailed into what is now San Diego Bay and claimed the surrounding region for the King of Spain in 1542. The bay was named in 1602 by another Spanish explorer, Don Sebastian Viscaino. The first European settlement there was established in 1769, when the Franciscan fathers established a mission on a hill overlooking the bay, close to a large Native American village. The mission was the first in a chain of twenty-one that the sect built throughout California. The mission was burned down by the local tribes and later almost completely destroyed by an earthquake, but the determined Franciscans rebuilt each time. Today, the restored mission still conducts Mass every Sunday.

By the 1830s, a small but thriving trading village had developed on the bay, in the district now called "Old Town." The town was an important shipping point for cattle hide and quarried stone. The famous cobblestone streets of Boston are said to have been paved with San Diego stone. San Diego became the capital of Mexican California after Mexico achieved independence from Spain in 1822. It was a much fought-over prize during the Mexican War, changing hands numerous times before the U.S. Army established permanent American rule in late 1846. The town was incorporated as a city in 1850.

City Thrives, Declines, Thrives Again

Throughout the next twenty years the town was an important whaling port. Then in 1867, San Francisco land-developer Alonzo E. Horton bought a 1,000-acre plot of what was to become downtown San Diego. Horton laid out streets, built a wharf and a hotel, and donated land for churches. A gold strike in 1870 and numerous land booms in the area increased the population rapidly. In 1885, when the Santa Fe Railroad and a number of eastern investors arrived, 40,000 people lived in the city.

By the turn of the century, however, San Diego was plunged into a slump. Failed businesses and unwise real estate speculations caused the population to dwindle to 17,000 people. The city began a period of slow, steady growth, helped by the Panama-California Exposition in celebration of the completion of the Panama Canal in 1915. The fledgling aircraft industry, which found the desert climate and terrain an ideal testing environment, also aided San Diego's recovery. An aggressive policy of attracting new people and industry contributed to growth, but the city remained relatively obscure, overshadowed by Los Angeles and San Francisco to the north.

City Becomes Naval Base; Rise of Agriculture and Industry

Japan's bombing of Honolulu's Pearl Harbor at the beginning of World War II forced the U.S. Navy to seek another suitable Pacific base. They chose San Diego, and almost overnight the city became a busy military center, home base for a large number of naval trainees, many of whom relocated to the city as civilians after the war. In the post-war era the city emerged as the headquarters of the Eleventh Naval District and the Naval Air Command; installations included major U.S. Navy and Marine training centers, the West Coast's main supply depot, a naval hospital and laboratories, and a large fleet stationed in the bay. Along with the military came related support industries and a large number of naval and aviation defense contractors.

Growth begun during World War II has continued unabated. San Diego spread to extend almost 20 miles in each direction, developing small, distinct communities in the nearby canyons and valleys; these areas retain a separate identity while being incorporated into San Diego. With this growth came diversity. To the south, San Diego connects with a rich agricultural area that produces much of California's famous fruit and vegetable produce, shipped worldwide from the easily accessible port. To the north the wealthy leisure class developed a resort community of hotels, spectacular cliff homes, and recreational amenities. Throughout the city commercial and industrial corridors began growing, and many corporations moved their headquarters to the region.

Downtown Declines, Revives

During the 1960s and early 1970s the San Diego downtown area declined when businesses and residents moved to the suburbs in large numbers. The city's growth continued despite these problems, and by the mid-1970s San Diego had surpassed San Francisco as

California's second largest city. An efficient freeway system and a coordinated effort by the Centre City Development Corporation—a comprehensive group of developers, financial experts, and civic leaders—kept the downtown area alive.

Today downtown San Diego is revitalized with new energy and is experiencing a renaissance as growth continues though areas like the Gaslamp District. Thoughtful planning has produced an impressive skyline of mirrored office towers blended with innovative shopping and residential developments, parks, and historic districts, all designed to serve the people who use them. Atria, attractive public gathering spaces, and overhead walkways encourage visitors and residents alike to enjoy the downtown area.

Historical Information: San Diego Historical Society, Museum of San Diego History, 1649 El Prado, Balboa Park, San Diego, CA 92101; telephone (619) 232-6203

■ Population Profile

Metropolitan Area Residents

1980: 1,862,000
1990: 2,498,016
2000: 2,813,833
2006 estimate: 2,941,454
Percent change, 1990–2000: 12.6%
U.S. rank in 1980: 19th
U.S. rank in 1990: 15th
U.S. rank in 2000: 17th

City Residents

1980: 875,538
1990: 1,110,623
2000: 1,223,400
2006 estimate: 1,256,951
Percent change, 1990–2000: 10.1%
U.S. rank in 1980: 8th
U.S. rank in 1990: 6th
U.S. rank in 2000: 11th

Density: 3,771.9 people per square mile (in 2000)

Racial and ethnic characteristics (2005)

White: 763,661
Black: 81,630
American Indian and Alaska Native: 6,046
Asian: 190,893
Native Hawaiian and Pacific Islander: 6,281
Hispanic or Latino (may be of any race): 312,767
Other: 117,263

Percent of residents born in state: 40.3% (2000)

Age characteristics (2005)

Population under 5 years old: 93,399
Population 5 to 9 years old: 78,333
Population 10 to 14 years old: 82,378
Population 15 to 19 years old: 77,575
Population 20 to 24 years old: 96,545
Population 25 to 34 years old: 211,166
Population 35 to 44 years old: 183,516
Population 45 to 54 years old: 158,608
Population 55 to 59 years old: 60,170
Population 60 to 64 years old: 42,963
Population 65 to 74 years old: 62,781
Population 75 to 84 years old: 47,144
Population 85 years and older: 13,753
Median age: 33.5 years

Births (2006, MSA)

Total number: 47,359

Deaths (2006, MSA)

Total number: 19,685

Money income (2005)

Per capita income: $29,497
Median household income: $55,637
Total households: 466,579

Number of households with income of...

less than $10,000: 29,598
$10,000 to $14,999: 21,765
$15,000 to $24,999: 47,694
$25,000 to $34,999: 44,038
$35,000 to $49,999: 67,775
$50,000 to $74,999: 85,266
$75,000 to $99,999: 59,376
$100,000 to $149,999: 64,683
$150,000 to $199,999: 22,776
$200,000 or more: 23,608

Percent of families below poverty level: 11% (2005)

2005 FBI Crime Index Property: 46,213

2005 FBI Crime Index Violent: 6,603

■ Municipal Government

San Diego uses a council-manager form of government, which it adopted in 1931. The mayor and eight council members are elected every four years, and they appoint the city manager.

Head Official: Mayor Jerry Sanders (R) (since 2005, current term expires 2009)

Total Number of City Employees: 20,700 (2007)

Image copyright iofoto, 2007. Used under license from Shutterstock.com.

City Information: City Hall, 202 C Street, San Diego, CA 92101; telephone (619)236-5555

■ Economy

Major Industries and Commercial Activity

San Diego's economy, once dominated by military and defense endeavors (now the city's second largest economic sector) is led by manufacturing, particularly in the areas of shipbuilding and repair, industrial machinery and computers, metals production, and the manufacture of toys and sporting goods. Computer and electronic manufacturing bring annual revenues of more than $9.2 billion to the San Diego region. International trade is an important part of San Diego's economy, accounting for 37 percent of its manufacturing dollars. The border between the San Diego area and Tijuana is the busiest in the world. Defense and transportation manufacturing have become important as well, and and the city is home to the Space and Naval Warfare Systems Center (SPAWAR),

which brings in more than $1.2 billion annually in contracts and salaries to the region.

Since the founding of San Diego, the city's economy has been tied to San Diego Bay, a natural harbor which today is one of California's five major ports. It is an important link in the nation's international shipping trade; the port's two marine cargo facilities are the National City Marine Terminal, which is a primary port of entry for Honda, Acura, Volkswagen, Isuzu, Mitsubishi Fuso, and Hino Motors vehicles; and Tenth Avenue Marine Terminal, which handles a wide variety of commodities. The port also has a growing cruise ship operation, with more than 190 cruise ships docking annually.

San Diego's harbor has had the most significant impact on the local economy, however, through the Eleventh Naval District Headquarters, the base for the U.S. Navy Pacific fleet, which is located on the bay. San Diego is the Navy's principal location for West Coast and Pacific Ocean operations. Increases in military and homeland defense spending during the early 2000s has contributed to economic growth in San Diego. The military/defense industry is the city's second largest economic sector, bringing more than $13.4 billion into the local economy annually. The San Diego region has the largest military concentration in the nation. The Marine Corps Base Camp Joseph H. Pendleton, the Marine Corps Recruit Depot, Marine Corps Air Station at Miramar, Naval Air Station North Island, Naval Station San Diego, and Naval Submarine Base Point Loma, San Diego, are among San Diego's military installations.

With the San Diego Zoo and Sea World, a variety of historical and cultural attractions, and year-round good weather, San Diego is a top destination for tourists. In 2004, *Travel and Leisure* magazine ranked it America's second favorite city (behind Honolulu). San Diego's tourism industry is the third largest segment of its economy, with more than 26 million visitors to the county bringing more than $5.6 billion in annual revenues. Service industries have seen continued growth in recent years, specifically in areas such as dining, lodging, shopping and recreation services. San Diego regularly ranks as a top-10 U.S. vacation destination for international travelers.

San Diego is a center for high technology and biotechnology. In 2005 the software industry contributed $3.4 billion to the local economy. High technology growth areas include the biomedical, software, telecommunications and security sectors. Biotechnology firms have an estimated $8.5 billion annual economic impact on the local economy. Quick growth in the wireless and telecommunications sectors have earned San Diego the nickname "Telecom Valley." The city is home to more than 850 communications firms, which received $160.1 million worth of venture capital investment in 2004 and 2005. San Diego has the highest concentration of wireless employment in the United States, and the industry has an annual impact of over $11.5 billion dollars a year.

San Diego County is also a top producer of nursery products, flowers, foliage plants, and avocados.

Items and goods produced: acoustical materials, adhesives, airplane parts, bamboo, dairy products, electronics transmission and distribution equipment, plastic, rubber products, awnings, beverages, paper, clothing, dental products, detergents, computers, televisions

Incentive Programs—New and Existing Companies

Local programs: The city of San Diego offers permit and regulatory assistance, problem solving, regulatory reform, and project troubleshooting for large companies interested in expanding in the San Diego area. Most of these companies must be creating or retaining 200 or more jobs, generating $500,000 in annual revenue to the city, or be located in the San Diego Regional Enterprise Zone. Other incentives include water-sewer capacity

fee reductions, fee waivers, and sales/use tax rebates. The city's Business Cooperation Program offers incentives that can lower operating and facility costs for a variety of businesses. San Diego has 19 business improvement districts, 15 redevelopment project areas, 1 enterprise zone, a foreign trade zone, recycling market development zones, and a renewal community.

State programs: A variety of programs administered by state and federal sources are available to San Diego businesses. These include special incentives in Enterprise Zones, Foreign Trade Zones, Federal Empowerment Zones, and Redevelopment Areas. Enterprise Zone Credits include a sales and use tax credit and hiring tax credits. A Research & Development Tax Credit is available of up to 15 percent against bank and corporate tax liability for certain in-house research. An additional 24 percent credit is available for basic research payments to outside organizations. This is one of the highest research and development tax credits in the nation. A Child Care Tax Credit is available for companies establishing on-site child care facilities. A Net Operating Loss Carryover and New Market Tax Credits are also available. A Work Opportunity Tax Credit is offered for employers who hire individuals from certain target groups.

Job training programs: The city of San Diego works closely with the San Diego Workforce Partnership, a nonprofit community corporation that supports the region's workforce and employers through education, training, and employment services. The California Employment Training Panel assists businesses through performance-based customized training contracts for new or existing employees. Reimbursement of costs for developing, implementing, and completing training programs may range from $1,500 to $2,000 per employee.

Development Projects

In 2002, a $312.3 million program to build or improve 24 San Diego libraries was approved. Since then several new branches have been built, including the College-Rolando, North University Community, Point Loma/Hervey, and Serra Mesa-Kearny Mesa branches. A new main library, slated to be completed by 2011, was estimated to cost $185 million and comprise 297,581 square feet. In 2006 work began on the former Campbell shipyard to transform it into the Hilton San Diego Convention Center Hotel, intended to be a 32-story, 1.65 million-square-foot structure. That same year, work began on the Old Police Headquarters & Park Project, intended to revitalize the Downtown Historic Harbor with retail shops, restaurants and public space at the water's edge and expected to be complete by 2008. Also in 2006 work began on the Setai San Diego hotel, a 21-story condo hotel, consisting of 185 condo-hotel units, the House of Blues, the Foundation Room, Whiskey Bar lounge, Ivan Kane's Forty Deuce, a sky bar, private wine cellar, health spa, fitness center, and pool. The project was expected to be completed by 2008.

Since 1975 the Centre City Development Corporation has been supporting the redevelopment of downtown San Diego. In 2007 the organization supported nearly fifty projects, mainly commercial and residential undertakings in the core of the downtown area. Several major infrastructure projects were in the planning stages, including a new County Courthouse, the North Embarcadero Visionary Plan, and the C Street Revitalization Master Plan. No completion dates had yet been finalized.

Economic Development Information: City of San Diego Economic Development Division, 600 B Street, Suite 400, San Diego, CA 92101; telephone (619)533-4233; fax (619)533-5250; email sdbusiness@sandiego.gov

Commercial Shipping

The Port of San Diego handles hundreds of merchant ships each year and saw revenues of $117 million in fiscal year 2005; nearby Tijuana, Mexico, is also a duty-free port. The Burlington Northern Santa Fe (BNSF) railroad connects San Diego to major market areas. More than 80 trucking companies are established in metropolitan San Diego, providing freight, hauling, or equipment services. Air cargo services are maintained at San Diego International Airport, which handled 156,410 tons of cargo in 2005, representing nearly a 25 percent increase over the previous year.

Labor Force and Employment Outlook

A large portion of the San Diego work force is derived from in-migration, creating a diverse population. The workforce is also young, since the median age of San Diego's population is 33.5, with two-thirds younger than age 35 and only 10 percent older than 65. One third of the population over 25 has at least a bachelor's degree. Among the three occupations expected to see the most growth in San Diego in the early twenty-first century, all were in the information technology field. A 2005 report by the San Diego Workforce Partnership indicated that the occupations with the highest growth rate between 2001-2008 were expected to be computer support specialists (57.9 percent growth), network and computer systems administrators (51.9 percent), and network systems and data communications analysts (50.0 percent). According to the same report, occupations forecasted to have the most opportunities for job seekers—the most job openings between 2001 and 2008—included janitors and cleaners, security guards, laborers, stock clerks, computer support specialists, bookkeepers, and elementary school teachers.

In August 2007 the unemployment rate for the San Diego-Carlsbad-San Marcos MSA was at 4.8 percent, a jump of nearly a percentage point from January of that year. The ten-year unemployment low occurred in 1999, with 2.8 percent unemployment.

The following is a summary of data regarding the San Diego-Carlsbad-San Marcos metropolitan area labor force, 2006 annual averages.

Size of nonagricultural labor force: 1,299,900

Number of workers employed in . . .

construction and mining: 93,100
manufacturing: 103,600
trade, transportation and utilities: 221,000
information: 37,200
financial activities: 83,700
professional and business services: 213,800
educational and health services: 124,700
leisure and hospitality: 156,200
other services: 48,900
government: 217,700

Average hourly earnings of production workers employed in manufacturing: $14.96

Unemployment rate: 4.6% (January 2005)

Largest employers (2007)	*Number of employees*
Federal Government	39,100
State of California	37,100
University of California, San Diego	24,790
City of San Diego	20,700
County of San Diego	18,900
Sharp HealthCare	13,872
United States Postal Service	11,611
Scripps Health	10,313
Kaiser Permanente	7,386
Qualcomm Inc.	6,000

Cost of Living

The following is a summary of data regarding key cost of living factors for the San Diego area.

2007 (1st quarter) ACCRA Average House Price: Not reported

2007 (1st quarter) ACCRA Cost of Living Index: 147.7

State income tax rate: 1.0% to 9.3%

State sales tax rate: 6.25%

Local income tax rate: None

Local sales tax rate: 2.5% (county)

Property tax rate: 1.00% of assessed valuation in city proper

Economic Information: San Diego Regional Chamber of Commerce, 402 West Broadway, Suite 1000, San Diego, CA 92101; telephone (619)544-1300

■ Education and Research

Elementary and Secondary Schools

The San Diego Unified School District is the second largest school district in the state and eighth largest urban school district in the country. There are around 133,000 students enrolled in the district, which was one of only three large urban school districts in the state of California to meet the national performance standards of the "No Child Left Behind" program in 2006. Its nonpartisan five-member board is elected every four years, and the superintendent is hired by the board. The district operates 24 magnet schools offering in-depth studies in areas ranging from science and research to journalism and telecommunications. In 2007 fifteen of the high schools in the school district were named to the *Newsweek* list of "America's Best High Schools." Additionally, in 2007 Balboa Elementary School was selected by Intel to be its 2007 "School of Distinction" for its marked improvement in mathematics performance. The growing school district expected to open five new schools by the fall of 2008.

The following is a summary of data regarding the San Diego Unified School District as of the 2005–2006 school year.

Total enrollment: 133,000

Number of facilities

    elementary schools: 114
    junior high/middle schools: 23
    senior high schools: 27
    other: 52

Student/teacher ratio: 20.7:1

Teacher salaries (2005–06)

    elementary median: $60,350
    junior high/middle median: $66,990
    secondary median: $58,090

Funding per pupil: $8,007

Public Schools Information: San Diego City Schools, Eugene Brucker Education Center, 4100 Normal Street, San Diego, CA 92103; telephone (619)725-8000

    The San Diego area is also served by a number of parochial and private schools.

Colleges and Universities

Major universities in San Diego include the University of California at San Diego (UCSD), San Diego State University (SDSU), and the University of San Diego (USD), which is a Catholic university. UCSD, one of the University of California's 10 campuses, is regarded as a top institution for higher education and was rated eighth best public university in the nation for 2008 by *U.S. News and World Report.* In 2006 the school was named the "hottest" institution in the nation for students to study science by *Newsweek* and the *Kaplan/Newsweek College Guide,* and 4th best university in the nation by *Washington Monthly's 2007 College Guide,* based on the positive impact the university has had on the country. Campus enrollment is approximately 26,000. UCSD has six undergraduate colleges all on one campus, each maintaining its own set of requirements while sharing departmental majors: Thurgood Marshall College, John Muir College, Revelle College, Roosevelt College, Sixth College, and Warren College. UCSD's graduate and professional schools include: the acclaimed Scripps Institution of Oceanography (one of the oldest and largest centers for marine science research and graduate training in the world), School of Medicine, School of International Relations and Pacific Studies, School of Pharmacy and Pharmaceutical Sciences, Jacobs School of Engineering (graduate and undergraduate), and Rady School of Management. SDSU, the oldest and largest university in San Diego and fifth largest in the state, has an enrollment of nearly 34,000 and in 2006 awarded 6,476 bachelor's degrees. One in seven adults in San Diego who holds a college degree attended SDSU. A readers' poll in the *San Diego Union-Tribune* in 2004 ranked SDSU "Best Local College/University." SDSU offers bachelor's degrees in 81 areas of study, 59 master's degrees, and 13 joint-doctoral degrees. In 1970 the university founded the first women's studies program in the country. USD, a private, Roman Catholic university, has an enrollment of more than 7,000; the university offers more than 60 bachelor's, master's and doctoral degrees, and is particularly noted for its law and nursing schools.

Libraries and Research Centers

San Diego is served by two major library systems, the city and county. The San Diego Public Library operates 33 branches in addition to the main library, maintaining more than 2.8 million volumes, nearly 5,000 periodical subscriptions, audio/visual materials, and collections such as local and state history, rare books and the history of printing, and U.S. Department of Patents documents. In 2002 the mayor and city council approved a $312.3 million program to build or improve 24 libraries. Since then several new branches have been built, including the College-Rolando, North University Community, Point Loma/Hervey, and Serra Mesa-Kearny Mesa branches. A new main library, slated to be completed by 2011, was estimated to cost $185 million and comprise 297,581 square feet.

The San Diego County Library system consists of a main branch and 31 branches, two bookmobiles, and an adult literacy site with an annual circulation of over four million items. In 2005-2006 library use increased 24 percent. Special collections include audio and videotapes, films, art reproductions, extensive Filipino, Spanish, and Vietnamese collections, and special services for the deaf, including closed-captioned video tapes and talking books. More than 30 other public, private, and research libraries serve the metropolitan area.

A large number of specialized research centers functioning in such subject areas as oceanography, nuclear energy, astronomy, and biological sciences are scattered throughout San Diego. Among the most prominent research centers are the Salk Institute for Biological Studies, which focuses on molecular biology, genetics, neuroscience, and plant biology; and the Palomar Observatory, a center for astronomy research, located atop San Diego county's Mount Palomar.

Public Library Information: San Diego Public Library, 820 E Street, San Diego, CA 92101; telephone (619)236-5800.

■ Health Care

The San Diego county medical community includes 26 accredited hospitals, with a total of more than 6,600 beds. The largest networks are ScrippsHealth and Sharp Healthcare, which maintain hospitals and walk-in clinics throughout the county. Scripps Mercy Hospital, the city's longest-running and largest hospital, was established in 1890 and has 700 licensed beds, more than 3,000 employees and 1,300 physicians. Scripps is one of the ten-largest hospitals in California, and was voted "Best Hospital" by readers of the *San Diego Union-Tribune* and *Sign-On San Diego* each year between 2000 and 2006. Additionally, in 2006 Scripps Memorial Hospital La Jolla was named one of America's Best Hospitals for cardiac care by *U.S. News and World Report*. Sharp Healthcare consists of seven hospitals, three affiliated medical groups and nearly 14,000 employees. Its largest hospital is Sharp Memorial, the designated trauma center for San Diego. Sharp Memorial's best-known programs include cardiac and vascular care, cancer treatment, pulmonary care services, rehabilitation, and multi-organ transplantation. In 2007 Sharp HealthCare was named San Diego's "Best Health Care Provider" and "Best Hospital" in the *San Diego Union-Tribune's* "Best of San Diego" Readers' Poll. San Diego's research and specialty institutions include the Salk Institute of Biology—established by Jonas Salk, developer of the polio vaccine—which conducts research in such areas as genetics and neuroscience; Children's Hospital and Health Center, the county's designated Pediatric Trauma Center; the Naval Medical Center, which provides care to officers, personnel, and their dependents and is among the largest and most technologically advanced military health care centers in the world; and the Scripps Research Institute, internationally recognized for its research in immunology, molecular, and cell biology.

Health Care Information: San Diego County Medical Society, 3702 Ruffin Road, Suite 206, San Diego, CA 92123; telephone (858)565-8888

■ Recreation

Sightseeing

San Diego and its surrounding communities offer a wide range of tourist attractions for every taste, from amusement parks to historic buildings and scenic wilderness.

Animals play a major role in San Diego's tourist trade. The world-famous San Diego Zoo, 100 acres of lush, tropical landscape filled with more than 4,000 animals representing some 800 species, contains some of the rarest species in captivity. Moving sidewalks, an aerial tramway, and open-air buses run through the exhibits. Highlights include giant pandas, Australian koalas, rare Chinese golden monkeys, a large reptile collection, a 1-acre children's zoo, and a beautiful free-flight walk-through aviary. Habitats have been crafted to replicate desert, tropical rain forest, savanna, scrubland, island, tundra, ocean and coastline, prairie and steppe, temperate forest and taiga, river, lake, and wetland ecosystems as closely as possible. Among the habitats are Ituri Forest, which simulates a four-acre African rainforest; Tiger River, an Asian rainforest; and Polar Bear Plunge, representing Arctic tundra. Absolutely Apes features orangutans and siamangs living together as they would in the wild. Absolutely Apes is the first phase of the under-construction New Heart of the Zoo, which will be a three-acre Asian and African rainforest containing many rare and endangered animals in the center of the zoo.

The San Diego Wild Animal Park, a 2,200-acre preserve operated by the San Diego Zoo, is located 30 miles north of downtown. Designed to protect endangered species, the park features more than 3,500 animals living in natural habitats modeled after African, Asian, and Australian terrain. The park is known for its successful breeding of such species as the southern white rhino and Arabian oryx. Visitors can walk the park or use the monorail system that traverses through the heart of the park. During summer months, the rail system also operates after dark, and lamps light the active animal areas. Nairobi Village provides special exhibits, refreshments, and other services.

Sea World San Diego, home of Shamu the killer whale and Baby Shamu (the original Shamu died long ago, but his successors bear his name), is a 150-acre marine park, located along Mission Bay, that offers a number of marine exhibits, live shows, aquariums, the world's largest shark exhibit, playgrounds and rides, and the $25 million Places of Learning educational complex. Sea World's Wild Arctic area is a massive, multimillion dollar project combining motion simulation theater technology, live marine mammal viewing, and interactive educational exhibits. At Shark Encounter, visitors come face to face with sharks by walking through a 57-foot tube that passes through a 280,000-gallon habitat. Shipwreck Rapids transforms visitors into island castaways who journey on raftlike inner tubes trying to find their way back to civilization.

LEGOLAND California, located in Carlsbad, stimulates creativity and imagination through hands-on recreation. Six play areas feature attractions, rides, building opportunities, and more than 1,000 LEGO models. AQUAZONE Wave Racers, one of the park's rides, are "Wave Activated Vehicles Equipped with Radar Antennas Capable of Evading Random Sprays" as they hydroplane across wakes created by dual carousels. New in 2005 was Knights' Tournament, a unique robotic coaster ride that allows participants to choose their own destiny.

The center of San Diego preserves two separate historic districts representing two different periods. Old Town evokes San Diego's Spanish and Mexican heritage. Many of its nineteenth-century adobe buildings have been restored and filled with museums, shops, and restaurants. Old Town was preceded, in 1769, by the Spanish establishment of California's first mission and military fortress, on nearby Presidio Hill. Gaslamp Quarter is a 16-block restored Victorian district downtown, featuring antiques, arts and crafts, offices, shops, and restaurants. Two-hour walking tours of the district depart from William Heath Davis House, one of the area's first residences, on Saturdays.

Several of the original missions in the area, including California's first—Mission Basilica San Diego de Alcalá, which moved from Presidio Hill to its present site in 1774—still hold Mass and are open to the public for tours. San Diego Bay harbors the *Star of India*, a 100-year-old sailing vessel, and several U.S. Navy ships that are open to the public. At Point Loma the Cabrillo National Monument commemorates the spot where California was discovered and includes a restored lighthouse, a whale overlook, and a visitor's center.

The nearby 600,000-acre Anza-Borrego Desert State Park, east of San Diego, is a unique collection of geological formations, plants, and animals that has been described by *Flower and Garden* magazine as "a perfect first desert encounter." The Cleveland National Forest north of the city, and other local cliffs, mesas, and canyons offer an abundance of natural scenic pleasures on 460,000 acres, as do the many flower plantations in the hills outside of San Diego. Tijuana, Mexico, the most visited border town in the world, is an exciting and exotic adventure for shoppers, sightseers, and sports enthusiasts.

The Mexican border is a 20 minute ride away, accessed by restored trackless trolleys that depart from the renovated Santa Fe Railway Depot in downtown San Diego.

Arts and Culture

San Diego's citizens and business community are very supportive of the arts. Drama, music, and the visual arts are important elements of the city's personality. Theater, in all its varieties, is available year round. Musical offerings range from formal affairs, symphonies, and operas, to oceanside picnic concerts under the stars and arena-sized rock concerts. Over 90 area museums as well as a number of small art galleries cater to the historic- and artistic-minded.

A large theater community is rising to national prominence in San Diego, and the area's proximity to Hollywood attracts many stars to the more than 40 innovative local theater companies. The centerpiece of San Diego culture is the Simon Edison Centre for the Performing Arts, called "one of the best theater complexes in the U.S." by *Time* magazine. It consists of the Lowell Davies Festival Theater, a large outdoor arena; the Cassius Carter Centre Stage, a 225-seat theater-in-the-round; and the Tony Award-winning 581-seat Old Globe Theater, a reproduction of Shakespeare's Globe Theater. The theatre complex stages classic and contemporary works throughout the year, with an emphasis on Shakespeare during the summer. Numerous other theater groups are located in the area, including the La Jolla Playhouse at University of San Diego at La Jolla, which stages plays and musicals from April through December at the university's 492-seat Mandell Weiss Theatre and 384-seat Mandell Weiss Forum; the San Diego Repertory Theatre, which produces progressive, culturally diverse plays at the Lyceum Theatre's 545-seat Stage Theatre and 270-seat Space Theatre; and the Lamb's Players Theater, which stages musicals, dramas, comedies, and adventurous world premieres, primarily at the company's 350-seat resident theatre in Coronado and the Joan B. Kroc Theatre for the Performing Arts at the Salvation Army Ray and Joan Kroc Corps Community Center. San Diego has a thriving dinner-theater population as well.

Music and dance are also well-represented in San Diego. The San Diego Symphony performs classical masterworks, interactive performances, outdoor summer pops, family festivals, and community concerts. The La Jolla Music Society presents visiting orchestras, soloists, and ensembles. The San Diego Chamber Orchestra presents its classical repertoire and Carnival Concerts Series (designed for families) at venues across San Diego County. The acclaimed San Diego Opera attracts star international performers; its grand productions at the San Diego Civic Theatre run from January through May. The California Ballet Company provides year-round contemporary and classical professional ballet, while historical and cultural dance exhibitions are offered by organizations such as the Traditional Chicano-Azteca Dance Circle, the Samahan Philippine Dance Company, the Pasacat Philippine Performing Arts Company, and Teye Sa Thiosanne, an African drum and dance company.

Balboa Park is the nation's largest urban cultural park. Covering 1,200 acres, it is home to the San Diego Zoo, most of San Diego's museums, performing arts venues, and restaurants, as well as cultivated and wild gardens and a number of historic buildings and exhibits. In all, more than 85 cultural and recreational organizations are located here. The park was originally the site of the Panama-California International Exhibition in 1915 and 1916 (which celebrated the opening of the Panama Canal), and most of the buildings are restored exhibit halls from that period, serving as examples of Spanish Revival architecture.

There are 15 museums located in Balboa Park. Among them is the San Diego Museum of Art, established in 1922; it is the oldest and largest art museum in the region. Highlights of the museum's permanent collections include its Spanish baroque, Renaissance, and contemporary California paintings; Indian miniatures; South Asian art; and numerous works by Toulouse-Lautrec. Traditional and modern sculpture is exhibited in an outdoor garden. The Mingei International Museum emphasizes traditional and modern folkart, craft, and design from outside the United States and Europe. The Museum of Photographic Arts, devoted to collecting, conserving and exhibiting still photography and film, has a permanent collection of more than 7,000 works, as well as a state-of-the-art 226-seat movie theater and a 20,000-volume library. The San Diego Natural History Museum features exhibits on local plants, animals, and geological specimens; in 2001, the opening of a new 90,000-square-foot wing more than doubled the museum's size. The San Diego Air & Space Museum features aeronautical exhibits, from the dawn of flight through the space age. The Reuben H. Fleet Science Center houses more than 100 scientific hands-on exhibits, the nation's first Omnimax theater, a virtual reality attraction, and a motion simulation ride. The San Diego Museum of Man, devoted to anthropology, is comprised of a group of buildings documenting the history of mankind, Indians of the three Americas, and human birth, plus various temporary exhibits. The San Diego Model Railroad Museum is the world's largest operating model railroad museum, at 28,000 square feet; highlights include four massive scale model layouts and a toy train gallery. The San Diego Hall of Champions Sports Museum is the largest multi-sport museum in the country at 70,000 square feet.

Other attractions in the park include the House of Pacific Relations, a cluster of 15 cottages representing 30 nationalities, and the Spreckels Organ Pavilion, containing the largest outdoor organ in the nation, played on Sundays by a civic organist. The Spanish Village Art Center presents artists and craftspeople at work in buildings resembling a charming town square in Spain, and the San Diego Art Institute features prominent local artists.

The Junipero Serra Museum is located on the site where Father Junipero Serra and Captain Gaspar de Portola established California's first mission and military fortress, in Presidio Park overlooking Old Town. It displays exhibits covering the history of the San Diego area from 1562 to the present. The San Diego Maritime Museum, located on the waterfront, is comprised of three historic ships—the 1863 tall ship *Star of India*, the 1898 ferry *Berkeley*, and the 1904 steam yacht *Medea* —as well as numerous nautical exhibits. The Museum of Contemporary Art San Diego (MCASD), with San Diego and La Jolla locations, presents more than 3,000 artworks, created after 1950, in its permanent collection; across the street from the San Diego location, the historic 1915 Santa Fe Depot baggage building was remodeled to become part of MCASD and opened in 2006.

Arts and Culture Information: City of San Diego Commission for Arts and Culture 1010 Second Avenue, Suite 555, San Diego, CA 92101; telephone (619)533-3050

Festivals and Holidays

San Diego's events calendar begins with the New Year's Day Race, a yacht regatta in San Diego Bay. In March, the San Diego Latino Film Festival, spanning 10 days, is the largest Latino film festival in the country. ArtWalk is a two-day April event showcasing visual and performing fine arts exhibits in San Diego's Little Italy neighborhood. May events include the Cinco de Mayo Celebration, which brings historical reenactments, folkloric music and dance, and Mexican food and fun to Old Town; Gator by the Bay two-day Cajun zydeco music and food festival; and the Ethnic Food Fair, featuring food from more than 25 nations.

A gala celebration on the Fourth of July features special events throughout the region, including several parades, outdoor concerts, a hot-air balloon race, and fireworks. The Harlem of the West Fest, also in July, is a premier African American festival held in the Gaslamp Quarter. Another July event, held at Imperial Beach, is Sand Castle Days, the world's longest-running and largest sand castle competition. America's Finest City Week is celebrated city-wide in August and features a large variety of events including concerts, sports events, carnivals, and more. The San Diego Film Festival in September celebrates American and international cinematic arts.

In late September, the city celebrates the Cabrillo Festival to commemorate the discovery of California by Spanish explorer Juan Rodríguez Cabrillo. The San Diego Bay Wine & Food Festival in November is a culinary celebration featuring more than 150 wineries and cuisine from many fine area restaurants. The San Diego Thanksgiving Dixieland Jazz Festival is a five-day classic jazz event held during Thanksgiving weekend, showcasing traditional, swing, and dixieland jazz. The Christmas season inspires some of the major celebrations of the year, sparking festivals, parades, and light displays in many locations. Other Christmas events include the Parade of Lights, a display of decorated boats in San Diego Bay; the festive rituals of Las Posadas; and the Pacific Life Holiday Bowl, a college football game. December also marks the beginning of the whale migration season off Point Loma.

Sports for the Spectator

Sports are varied in San Diego. Major League Baseball's San Diego Padres play April through September at PETCO Park, which opened in 2004; PETCO, located downtown, has 42,000 seats, and its seating bowl sections are named after neighborhoods. The National Football League's San Diego Chargers 2004 AFC West Division champions play at 71,500-seat Quallcomm Stadium. Quallcomm is also home to San Diego State University's Aztecs. San Diego also hosts a major bicycle Grand Prix race each year. Nearby Del Mar Thoroughbred Club, founded by entertainer Bing Crosby in 1937, offers horseracing from July through September, and Tijuana, Mexico features the excitement of jai alai, bullfighting, and greyhound racing.

Sports for the Participant

Sports Illustrated magazine calls San Diego "the sports and fitness capital of the U.S." The Pacific Ocean and numerous bays in the area provide a wide range of activities: swimming, sailing, water skiing, snorkeling, and deep sea sport fishing, among others. Mission Bay Park is the largest aquatic park in the nation; it consists of 4,235 acres. The park offers 44 miles of beachfront recreation area, as well as inland trails and jogging tracks. San Diego-La Jolla Underwater Park and Ecological Reserve at La Jolla Cove provides excellent snorkeling and scuba diving opportunities. San Diego's public park system maintains extensive recreation facilities, public pools, jogging paths, and playing fields. There are more than 1,300 public and private tennis courts in the county, as well as more than 90 golf courses. The most popular bike and running route in the area is Route S21, which extends 15 miles along the beach between La Jolla and Oceanside. Winter sports such as skiing are available in the nearby mountains.

Shopping and Dining

San Diego offers a wide variety of shopping experiences, from small shops in renovated historical districts such as Old Town, which resembles a Mexican marketplace, and the Gaslamp Quarter, where Victorian buildings house antique stores, art galleries, and boutiques, to the large suburban shopping malls, many located in the Mission Valley region. Downtown San Diego's massive Westfield Horton Plaza, adjacent to the Gaslamp district, is a five-

level, open-air plaza filled with department stores and nearly 200 upscale specialty shops. Seaport Village is a 14-acre shopping, dining, and entertainment complex featuring over 50 shops and restaurants in a harborside setting. Nearby Tijuana provides a colorful variety of bazaars, open-air markets, and handcrafted goods.

Seafood and authentic Mexican cuisine are dining specialties in the San Diego area. Many distinctive restaurants, ranging from formal luxury dining to sidewalk cafes, can be found in the historical districts, the modern plazas, and along the waterfront. A large number of international and ethnic restaurants add variety to the dining fare.

Visitor Information: San Diego Convention & Visitors Bureau, 2215 India Street, San Diego, CA 92101; telephone (619)232-3101; email sdinfo@sandiego.org

■ Convention Facilities

The San Diego Convention Center, which doubled in size upon an expansion in 2001, is located downtown along San Diego Bay. The 1.7 million-square-foot facility features 615,701 square feet of exhibit space; 204,114 square feet of meeting space, including two 40,000-square-foot ballrooms; and 284,494 square feet of pre-function, lobby, and registration space. The center is within a mile of 7,500 first-class hotel rooms, and is only 10 minutes from the airport. Meeting space is also available at the 2,975-seat Civic Theatre, a multipurpose convention and performing arts center adjacent to City Hall.

A number of downtown hotels are designed to accommodate major conventions, providing extensive meeting and banquet facilities, as well as exhibit space. Over 50,000 rooms are available in the San Diego area.

Convention Information: San Diego Convention & Visitors Bureau, 2215 India Street, San Diego, CA 92101; telephone (619)232-3101; email sdinfo@-sandiego.org

■ Transportation

Approaching the City

San Diego International Airport Lindbergh Field is located 3 miles from downtown and provides major domestic and foreign air service from 18 passenger carriers and 6 cargo carriers. There are close to 300 departures daily, and San Diego is the 30th busiest passenger aiport in the U.S. and the busiest single-runway commercial service airport in the nation. Amtrak's *Pacific Surfliner* route carries passengers from San Diego through Los Angeles, Oxnard, and Santa Barbara, to San Luis Obispo. Amtrak's San Diego station is in the historic Santa Fe

Depot, north of Seaport Village. A commuter rail service, The Coaster, runs between San Diego, Solana Beach, Encinitas, Carlsbad, and Oceanside.

San Diego is located at the junction of two major north-south routes that originate in Canada. Interstate 5 from Los Angeles and I-15 from Las Vegas meet in San Diego and continue to the Mexican border. I-8 enters San Diego from the east.

Traveling in the City

The San Diego Metropolitan Transit System serves over 86 million riders annually and operates 82 bus routes covering San Diego, El Cajon, La Mesa, National City, as well as portions of San Diego County's unincorporated area. The San Diego Trolley travels in the downtown area, through Mission Valley and east county communities, and to the Mexican border. Carriage rides through the downtown area are available from Embarcadero Marina Park.

■ Communications

Newspapers and Magazines

San Diego is served by *The San Diego Union-Tribune,* the result of the 1992 merger of the city's two dailies. Readers can choose from among a number of weekly, ethnic, and community papers as well, such as *La Prensa San Diego,* a weekly English/Spanish newspaper. *San Diego Magazine* publishes articles of regional interest; several other technical and special interest magazines, such as *San Diego Home/Garden Lifestyles, Computer Edge,* and *San Diego Metropolitan* (focusing on business news), are also published in the area.

Television and Radio

Ten television stations broadcast in the San Diego area, representing ABC, CBS, NBC, FOX, WB, Univision (two stations), PBS, a local independent station focusing on news, and an Oceanside-based station focusing on local government and media. The region is also serviced by cable television. More than 30 radio stations serve the San Diego area, providing a wide variety of musical and information programming, some broadcasting in Spanish.

Media Information: *The San Diego Union-Tribune,* PO Box 120191, San Diego, CA 92112; telephone (619) 299-3131. *San Diego Magazine,* 1450 Front Street, San Diego, CA 92101; telephone (619)230-9292

San Diego Online

City of San Diego Home Page. Available www.ci .san-diego.ca.us

San Diego Convention & Visitors Bureau. Available www.sandiego.org

San Diego County Library. Available www.sdcl.org

San Diego Daily Transcript. Available www.sddt .com

San Diego Public Library. Available www.sannet .gov/public-library

San Diego Regional Chamber of Commerce. Available www.sdchamber.org

San Diego Unified School District. Available www .sandi.net

The San Diego Union-Tribune. Available www .uniontrib.com

BIBLIOGRAPHY

Cameron, Robert, *Above San Diego: A New Collection of Historical and Original Aerial Photographs of San Diego* (San Francisco, CA: Cameron and Co., 1990)

Ford, Larry, *Metropolitan San Diego: How Geography and Lifestyle Shape a New Urban Environment* (Philadelphia, PA: University of Pennsylvania Press, 2005)

Schad, Jerry, *Afoot and Afield in San Diego* (Berkeley, CA: Wilderness Press, 1998)

Urrea, Luis Alberto, *Across the Wire: Life and Hard Times on the Mexican Border* (New York: Anchor Books/ Doubleday, 1993)

San Francisco

■ The City in Brief

Founded: 1776 (incorporated 1850)

Head Official: Mayor Gavin Newsom (D) (since 2004)

City Population
1980: 678,974
1990: 723,959
2000: 776,733
2006 estimate: 744,041
Percent change, 1990–2000: 3.0%
U.S. rank in 1980: 13th
U.S. rank in 1990: 14th
U.S. rank in 2000: 18th

Metropolitan Area Population
1980: 1,489,000
1990: 1,603,678
2000: 1,731,183
2006 estimate: 4,180,027
Percent change, 1990–2000: 7.8%
U.S. rank in 1980: 5th (CMSA)
U.S. rank in 1990: 4th (CMSA)
U.S. rank in 2000: 5th (CMSA)

Area: 47 square miles (2000)

Elevation: 155 feet above sea level

Average Annual Temperatures: January, 52.3° F; July, 61.3° F; annual average, 58.3° F

Average Annual Precipitation: 22.28 inches of rain

Major Economic Sectors: services, wholesale and retail trade, government

Unemployment Rate: 4.4% (June 2007)

Per Capita Income: $39,554 (2005)

2005 FBI Crime Index Property: 34,269

2005 FBI Crime Index Violent: 5,985

Major Colleges and Universities: San Francisco State University; University of California, San Francisco; University of San Francisco; Golden Gate University

Daily Newspaper: *San Francisco Chronicle; The Examiner*

■ Introduction

The term "melting pot" is used to describe many American cities and towns. This is indeed true for San Francisco, one of the few truly international cities in the United States. The neighborhoods are varied, yet each features a cohesiveness as unique as its inhabitants. Rows of elegant houses, the famous cable cars, clusters of ethnic neighborhoods, and the colorful waterfront all add to the distinctive international flavor of the city. The city's well-known hills offer stunning views of the Pacific Ocean and San Francisco Bay and feature a wide array of shops, restaurants, and cosmopolitan nightlife. In addition to its diversity and charm, San Francisco is a major financial and insurance center, an international port, and the gateway to Silicon Valley, America's premier high-technology center. The consistently spring-like weather and unique atmosphere attract corporations as well as visitors, and the solid economic base keeps them there.

■ Geography and Climate

San Francisco occupies the tip of a peninsula halfway up the coast of northern California, surrounded by the Pacific Ocean to the west, the Golden Gate strait to the north, and the San Francisco Bay to the east. The city is laid out in a grid over some 40 hills, reaching heights of nearly 1,000 feet; this sometimes causes wide variations in temperature and sky conditions in different areas of town. The Pacific air keeps the temperatures generally moderate, rarely ranging above 75 degrees or below 45 degrees, leading San Francisco to be called "the air-conditioned city." The climate is very similar to coastal areas on the Mediterranean.

Although temperatures remain relatively constant, there are two definite seasons—wet and dry—with more than 80 percent of annual precipitation taking place between November and March. Perhaps the most distinctive feature of the local climate is the banks of fog that can roll in off the ocean, quickly covering various areas of the city, and then disappear just as quickly. The fog is most common on summer mornings, coming off the cooler ocean and backing up against the hills, but it also comes from the colder inland areas during the winter. The fog affects different elevations in varying amounts, covering the city in complex patterns of fog and sunshine.

The San Francisco Bay area lies between the Pacific and North American Tectonic Plates. The city of San Francisco itself rests in the San Andreas Fault, which is one of seven fault lines affecting the area. This zone of continual seismic activity marks the city as highly susceptible to damaging earthquakes and at high-risk for tsunamis. Landslides are another natural hazard.

Area: 47 square miles (2000)

Elevation: 155 feet above sea level

Average Temperatures: January, 52.3° F; July, 61.3° F; annual average, 58.3° F

Average Annual Precipitation: 22.28 inches of rain

■ History

Spanish Discover City; Franciscan Friars Build Missions

Because thick fog banks usually obscure the narrow entrance to the bay, the area where San Francisco now stands and the adjacent natural harbor remained undiscovered by seafaring adventurers for more than 200 years after the original Spanish explorers found California. It was left to an overland expedition of Spanish soldiers from Mexico to stumble upon the bay by accident in 1769 while trying to reach Monterey. In 1776 Colonel Juan Bautista de Anza founded the first European settlement in the Bay Area by establishing a military garrison, or Presidio, on the southern shore of the Golden Gate. That same year the Franciscan Order built Mission Dolores, the sixth Roman Catholic mission in what eventually became a chain of 21 missions along the coast of California.

Until the 1830s almost all of the inhabitants were missionaries, trying—without much success—to convert the local Costanoan tribe to Christianity, but eventually a small village was built up around the Presidio and the mission. The village, called Yerba Buena, was mapped out in 1839 by Jean Jaques Vioget, a Swiss surveyor, but it continued to be small and remote throughout most of the 1840s. The quiet town of a few hundred inhabitants was visited infrequently by whaling ships, traders from the East Coast, and frontier hunters and trappers. Farming and a small but steady market in trading cattle hides and tallow were the main sources of commerce.

America Wins California; Gold Discovered

The American flag was raised in the town's central square in 1846, marking the annexation of California by the United States after the war with Mexico; one year later the name of the town was changed to San Francisco. Soon after the annexation, the town's population was nearly doubled by the arrival of a group of 238 Mormon settlers, led by Sam Brannan. It was Brannan who ran through the muddy streets of San Francisco less than two years later shouting "Gold!," thus altering the city's fate. Within a year, more than 40,000 people had journeyed through the area on their way to the gold fields around Sutter's Mill in the Sierra foothills, about 140 miles away. Some 35,000 of those people stayed on to live in San Francisco. The city was incorporated in 1850.

The gold prospectors came from all corners of the globe and tended to settle in areas according to their nationalities, one reason for the distinctive international flavor of modern San Francisco. Demand for food and shelter outstripped the supply, and many people lived in tents, cooking over campfires. Whole crews abandoned their ships in the harbor, leaving hundreds of empty hulls that were brought ashore and used as temporary warehouses, stores, and as the foundations of the town's new buildings. Gambling halls, saloons, hotels, and stores sprang up almost daily, only to be destroyed by frequent fires and then quickly rebuilt. It was a wild and reckless time; rampant lawlessness was common, so much so that in 1851 concerned citizens banded together into vigilante groups and rounded up the worst violators, eventually restoring order to the town.

Gold Boom Goes Bust; Industry, Shipping Thrive

The gold boom declined by the mid-1850s, but the town continued to grow with increases in industry and shipping. The 1859 silver boom in Nevada and the completion of the transcontinental railroad in 1869 also contributed their share to the city's prosperity. The downtown area grew full of large stone buildings and warehouses along the docks, and the surrounding hills were filled with impressive residential homes. By the turn of the century, San Francisco was home to a population of more than a third of a million people and was the ninth largest city in the country.

April 18, 1906, brought disaster to the city in the form of a major earthquake and fire that killed more than 500 people, devastated 3,000 acres in the heart of the city, and left almost 1,000 residents homeless. Among the heroes of the day were the U.S. Navy, who stretched a mile-long fire hose from Fisherman's Wharf over Telegraph Hill and down to Jackson Square, saving historic buildings. Before the ashes were cold, the townspeople set out to rebuild the city, and by 1915, when San Francisco hosted the Panama-Pacific International Exposition in honor of the opening of the Panama Canal, no traces of the fire and earthquake were visible.

Rise of Finance, Commerce, Culture

During the mid-twentieth century, San Francisco secured its position as the financial, commercial, and cultural center of northern California. The completion of the Golden Gate Bridge in 1937, after four years of exhausting work, was the major event of the period and a symbol of the city's new-found prominence. Designer Joseph Strauss tried for more than a decade to convince disbelievers that the plans for the construction of the bridge were feasible, and many people still doubted that it could stand for long even after its completion. The structure is more than three-quarters of a mile in length, supported by two 746-foot towers. It was one of the outstanding engineering achievements of all time and continues to draw hundreds of thousands of tourists each year.

World War II boosted the already strong economy of the city, which became a major supply and troop shipping port for the Pacific fronts and an important area for defense industries. It was also during this time that large numbers of the area's Asian citizens were interred in work camps in the region. After the war, the city pointed the way to peace when delegates representing almost all of the world's countries gathered in San Francisco to draw up the charter of the United Nations.

The post-war era brought continued growth and prosperity. San Francisco's downtown area began to develop a skyline of high-rise buildings while carefully preserving many of the historical structures and green spaces. A large stretch of high-technology industries eventually built up in the nearby area known as Silicon Valley. The city fought problems of urban blight encountered in the 1960s and 1970s with an extensive urban-renewal program, developing the downtown section and introducing a major Rapid Transit System in 1974 to provide access to the center city. The assassinations of Mayor George Moscone and City Supervisor Harvey Milk in November 1978 were a blow to the city's progressive image. The city elected its first woman mayor, Diane Feinstein, in 1979.

Another major earthquake occurred on October 17, 1989, ending decades of tranquility in the San Francisco Bay Area. But the region recovered strongly, showing a spirit of cooperation and determination. San Francisco was home to many dot-com operations in the 1990s. When the dot-com bubble began to burst in 2000, the city was quickly left with many vacant office spaces. The recession of the early 2000s brought more unemployment to the city.

In 2004 Gavin Newsom took office as city mayor and began to undertake a number of ambitious, and sometimes controversial, programs. In February 2004 Newsom directed the city clerk to allow for the issuance of marriage licenses to same-sex couples, a direct violation of California state law which prohibits same sex marriages. Within one month, thousands of same-sex couples from across the country came to San Francisco to be married. In March 2004 the Supreme Court of California, based in San Francisco, issued the order for the county to stop issuing the licenses pending future legal review. These events set off a national controversy and brought the issue of same-sex marriages more firmly into the realm of the national court systems, where debate has persisted.

With somewhat less controversy, within the first three years in office Newsom initiated measures that decreased unemployment by about 26 percent and welcomed over 50 new companies into the city. Newsom also initiated a Climate Action Plan to reduce local greenhouse gas emission by more than 2.5 million tons by 2012. In 2005 Newsom began work on a program of universal health care for all city residents. The first version of the plan, Healthy San Francisco, was launched in September 2007. Under the plan, uninsured residents (an estimated 82,000 adults in 2007) who enroll in the plan are offered free health care through 14 community-based clinics and the San Francisco General Hospital. The plan was initiated primarily through government funding; however, the plan includes a future requirement for contributions by businesses with over 50 employees.

Historical Information: California Historical Society, 678 Mission Street, San Francisco, CA 94105; telephone (415)357-1848; www.califrorniahistoricalsociety. com. Chinese Historical Society of America, 965 Clay Street, San Francisco, CA 94108; telephone (415)391-1188; www.chsa.org. San Francisco African American Historical and Cultural Society, Fort Mason Center, Bldg. C, Room 165, San Francisco, CA 94123; telephone (415)441-0640; www.sfblackhistory.org

■ Population Profile

Metropolitan Area Residents

1980: 1,489,000
1990: 1,603,678
2000: 1,731,183
2006 estimate: 4,180,027
Percent change, 1990–2000: 7.8%

U.S. rank in 1980: 5th (CMSA)
U.S. rank in 1990: 4th (CMSA)
U.S. rank in 2000: 5th (CMSA)

City Residents

1980: 678,974
1990: 723,959
2000: 776,733
2006 estimate: 744,041
Percent change, 1990–2000: 3.0%
U.S. rank in 1980: 13th
U.S. rank in 1990: 14th
U.S. rank in 2000: 18th

Density: 16,634.4 people per square mile (2000)

Racial and ethnic characteristics (2005)

White: 382,220
Black: 46,779
American Indian and Alaska Native: 2,098
Asian: 238,133
Native Hawaiian and Pacific Islander: 2,726
Hispanic or Latino (may be of any race): 98,891
Other: 27,558

Percent of residents born in state: 51.2% (2000)

Age characteristics (2005)

Population under 5 years old: 39,718
Population 5 to 9 years old: 23,755
Population 10 to 14 years old: 29,156
Population 15 to 19 years old: 25,756
Population 20 to 24 years old: 38,924
Population 25 to 34 years old: 133,331
Population 35 to 44 years old: 140,775
Population 45 to 54 years old: 105,896
Population 55 to 59 years old: 43,051
Population 60 to 64 years old: 33,539
Population 65 to 74 years old: 50,928
Population 75 to 84 years old: 38,735
Population 85 years and older: 15,513
Median age: 39.4 years

Births (2006, MSA)

Total number: 56,369

Deaths (2006, MSA)

Total number: 28,874

Money income (2005)

Per capita income: $39,554
Median household income: $57,496
Total households: 322,399

Number of households with income of . . .

less than $10,000: 33,435

$10,000 to $14,999: 19,306
$15,000 to $24,999: 29,867
$25,000 to $34,999: 23,579
$35,000 to $49,999: 35,635
$50,000 to $74,999: 53,420
$75,000 to $99,999: 37,626
$100,000 to $149,999: 46,496
$150,000 to $199,999: 19,639
$200,000 or more: 23,396

Percent of families below poverty level: 9.9% (2005)

2005 FBI Crime Index Property: 34,269

2005 FBI Crime Index Violent: 5,985

■ Municipal Government

The governments of the city and county of San Francisco are consolidated into one unit. San Francisco adopted a mayor-council form of government in 1932. The council, however, is known as the Board of Supervisors. There are eleven supervisors, who represent specific districts, elected to four-year terms. The mayor is directly elected to a four-year term. A city administrator is appointed by the mayor, with approval of the board, to serve a five-year term.

Head Official: Mayor Gavin Newsom (D) (since 2004; term expires 2008)

Total Number of City Employees: 30,000 (2007)

City Information: City Hall, Mayor's Office, 1. Dr. Carlton B. Goodlett Place, San Francisco, CA 94102; telephone (415)554-6141; www.sfgov.org

■ Economy

Major Industries and Commercial Activity

Since the days of the Gold Rush, San Francisco has been an important financial center. Located halfway between London and Tokyo as well as between Seattle and San Diego, San Francisco is at the center of global business. Because of its natural, landlocked harbor, San Francisco has thrived on trade and shipping since its early days. Today, through its main port in Oakland, eight smaller ports, and three key airports, the Bay area handles some 30 percent of West Coast trade. The port system is augmented by San Francisco International Airport, the country's fourteenth and the world's twenty-first largest airport.

San Francisco's economic activity attracts and supports a range of industries. As the base for some of the country's largest banks and scores of international financial institutions, San Francisco is a center for world

Image copyright CAN BALCIOGLU, 2007. Used under license from Shutterstock.com.

commerce. Most recently San Francisco is being considered the birthplace of new media; its South Park neighborhood houses some of the most innovative new technology companies in the world. San Francisco's Mission Bay neighborhood is a model for collaborative innovation between the biotechnology industry and academic researchers.

World War II started a local boom in defense industries, resulting in subsequent high-technology development that hasn't ceased. Nearby Silicon Valley, along with Stanford University, are considered to be among the places where the worldwide technology boom began, and they remain on the leading edge today. More than 4,100 Bay Area companies produce computers, semiconductors and related components, scientific instruments, and various other electronic systems and equipment. The IT industry employs more than 214,000 people in San Francisco. With 78.8 percent of households wired to the Internet, San Francisco is one of the top 10 cities for high-speed connection. San Francisco has become a center for digital entertainment companies with more than 50 companies in the city, including LucasArts, Pixar, Sony, Electronic Arts, Dolby, Sega of America, Konami Digital Entertainment America, and PDI DreamWorks SKG. Aerospace industries such as the National Aeronautic and Space Administration (NASA) and Lockheed Martin also maintain major research facilities in the area.

Another important high-technology industry in the area is medical science; several hundred companies in the Bay Area are setting the pace in research and development of pharmaceutical products, medical electronics, and genetic engineering. Almost one third of the total worldwide biotechnology workforce is employed in San Francisco and the surrounding region—250,000 strong. Over 820 biotech companies are based in the San Francisco Bay Area, including Genentech, Chiron, Amgen, Gilead Sciences, Bayer, Berlex, Applied Biosystems, Exelixis, and Genecor.

The San Francisco/Silicon Valley Area also boasts the largest concentration of environmental technology investors in the United States. Other prominent industries are tourism, which is the largest industry in the region; fashion apparel, with the Bay Area home to the world's largest apparel maker, Levi Strauss & Co.; health care; education; and restaurants. Regarding the tourism industry, the number of visitors to San Francisco in 2006 was 15.8 million, up 0.40 percent over 2005. In 2006, visitors spent $7.76 billion, an increase of 5.3 percent over 2005 and an all-time high.

In 2007 the non-profit Wikimedia Foundation announced plans to relocate its headquarters from St. Petersburg, Florida, to San Francisco.

Items and goods produced: paper boxes, confectionery, paints, chemicals, glass, leather, lumber, textiles, steel, clothing, bags, furniture, auto parts, electric machinery, matches, clay, rubber products, tools, beverages

Incentive Programs—New and Existing Companies

Local programs: Businesses that create new permanent jobs in San Francisco receive a two-year credit against their city payroll tax liability for the new employees as part of the New Jobs Tax Credit. San Francisco's enterprise zone offers a variety of city and state economic benefits for businesses that locate within it. With the Mayor's Office of Community Development Loan Fund, companies that create jobs in the city and meet certain federal criteria are eligible for loans ranging from $1,000 to $250,000. SFWorks is a program that assists employers in hiring low-income individuals who are transitioning to work or trying to advance their careers. Many businesses that participate may qualify for a number of federal and state hiring tax credits, ranging from $2,400 to $8,500. The city also offers a Payroll Tax Exclusion for up to 7.5 years for biotech and clean energy tech companies in the city. There are several local business associations assisting entrepreneurs, including the San Francisco Black Chamber of Commerce and the Bayview Merchants Association.

State programs: The San Francisco Enterprise Zone, which covers about 11 square miles around Bayview Hunters Point, is one of the state's designated Enterprise Zones. Business incentives and tax credits are provided to those businesses that operate or invest within a designated Enterprise Zone. Benefits of operating in the Enterprise Zone include sales and use tax credits; hiring tax credits; net operating loss carryover and net interest deduction for lenders programs. San Francisco is also a state-designated Recycling Market Development Zone, enabling businesses involved in recycling to utilize low-interest loans, technical assistance, siting and permitting assistance, and reduced permit application fees. A Research & Development Tax Credit is available of up to 15% against bank and corporate tax liability for certain in-house research. An additional 24 percent credit is available for basic research payments to outside organizations. This is one of the highest research and development tax credits in the nation. A Child Care Tax Credit is available for companies establishing on-site child care facilities. A Net Operating Loss Carryover and New Market Tax Credits are also available. A Work Opportunity Tax Credit is offered for employers who hire individuals from certain target groups.

Job training programs: The San Francisco Private Industry Council (PIC), the organization responsible for administering the federal Workforce Investment Act (WIA) programs, offers significant benefits to employers who hire PIC trainees. Under the on-the-job training program, the PIC will reimburse employers 50 percent of wages paid to participants for as long as the first six months of employment. The California Employment Training Panel assists businesses through performance-based customized training contracts for new or existing employees. Reimbursement of costs for developing, implementing, and completing training programs may range from $1,500 to $2,000 per employee.

Development Projects

Pacific Bell Park, the home of the San Francisco Giants, was completed in April 2000 (its current name is AT&T Park). The $306 million project took more than 2,000 construction workers and more than 650,000 bricks to build the 42,000-seat stadium. San Francisco's premier convention facility, Moscone Center, added an additional 300,000 square feet of function space in 2003. With the completion of Moscone West, which opened in 2003, today's Moscone Center is a collection of facilities covering more than 20 acres on three adjacent blocks. It anchors the 87-acre Yerba Buena Center redevelopment district in a neighborhood of hotels, theaters, restaurants, museums, galleries, housing, parks, and urban recreation centers. The Sony Metreon retail and entertainment complex and Children's Center are also located in the Yerba Buena Center. The Children's Center includes facilities for childcare, ice skating, and bowling, as well as an arts and technology center.

San Francisco continues to invest in improvements that fuel its world-class reputation. Located midway between London and Tokyo, America's closest major city to the Pacific Rim, it sits at the center of the global community. A multiyear, $2.4 billion program to bring San Francisco International Airport into the twenty-first century includes new parking garages, a consolidated rental car center, and other amenities. In 2003, a $1.5 billion Bay Area Rapid Transit (BART) station began connecting trains to the heart of San Francisco and the East Bay; an intra-airport rail system links airport terminals and facilities together. Revitalization of San Francisco's scenic waterfront, which runs 7.5 miles along its northern and southern perimeters, is an ongoing project to reconnect the city to this historic area and enliven the area for both residents and visitors; the project will include the addition of an expanded ferry terminal and new office space.

Economic Development Information: San Francisco Partnership, 465 California Street, 9th Floor, San Francisco, CA 94104; telephone (415)352-8801; fax (415) 956-3844; email info@sfp.org

Commercial Shipping

Cargo service at San Francisco International Airport is available from 57 airlines, including 17 cargo-only airlines. The airport supports 11 cargo facilities with a total of about 989,000 square feet of warehouse and office space. At Oakland International Airport there are 16 airlines providing cargo service. The Port of San Francisco has five berths, on-dock rail, and over 550,000 square feet of covered storage for weather-sensitive cargo. There are six shipping service companies serving the port. The port is part of Foreign Trade Zone No. 3.

Labor Force and Employment Outlook

San Francisco has the highest concentration of new immigrants in the nation, providing a continuous supply of workers at all levels of expertise. The city also boasts some of the most well-trained professionals in the United States, with nearly 70 percent of San Franciscans having educational training beyond high school. In 2006, of U.S. cities with populations of more than 250,000, San Francisco was tied for second place with Raleigh, N.C., behind Seattle as the most well-educated city in the nation; 50.1 percent of residents 25 years of age and older held a bachelor's degree, double the percentage for the state. As well, more than 16 percent of San Franciscan residents hold a graduate or professional degree, compared to some 10 percent for the state.

The city's workforce is a magnet for business and employment. According to the U.S. Department of Labor, San Francisco's diverse and educated population results in one of the most productive workforces in the country and the world. Growth is expected to continue in the areas where San Francisco is already strong: high-technology industries, medical science and health-related fields, and finance. As the sixth largest metropolitan market in the United States, San Francisco offers future opportunities in areas such as retail trade, service industries, and restaurants.

Small businesses thrive in San Francisco; according to the city there are a multitude of small and medium sized businesses in the city, and 95 percent of all of the city's businesses employ 50 workers or less.

The following is a summary of data regarding the San Francisco-Oakland-Fremont metropolitan area labor force, 2006 annual averages.

Size of nonagricultural labor force: 2,007,300

Number of workers employed in . . .

  construction and mining: 117,700
  manufacturing: 140,400
  trade, transportation and utilities: 358,500
  information: 68,600
  financial activities: 158,000
  professional and business services: 346,500
  educational and health services: 225,600
  leisure and hospitality: 205,800
  other services: 73,300
  government: 313,000

Average hourly earnings of production workers employed in manufacturing: $17.98

Unemployment rate: 4.4% (June 2007)

Largest employers (2007)	*Number of employees*
United States Postal Service	704,716
State of California	227,531
Wells Fargo & Co.	153,000
Kaiser Permanente	152,368
Gap Inc.	128,917
City and County of San Francisco	28,000
PG&E Corp.	19,800
University of California, San Francisco	18,000
California Pacific Medical Center	5,569
San Francisco Unified School District	5,557

Cost of Living

San Francisco's cost of living is one of the highest in the country, due in part to the tight labor market and the high cost of housing, food, and other consumer goods. It is reported that Bay Area residents possess the third-highest discretionary income in the United States. This is because the workforce is highly educated and jobs are concentrated in high-paying industries. Its housing market has experienced record-breaking appreciation, with the median home price increasing by nearly 96 percent since the early 1990s. Although the residential property tax is low, because property values are high, the absolute payment is relatively high.

The following is a summary of data regarding several key cost of living factors for the San Francisco area.

2007 (1st quarter) ACCRA Average House Price: $874,795

2007 (1st quarter) ACCRA Cost of Living Index: 171.1

State income tax rate: 1.0% to 9.3%

State sales tax rate: 6.25%

Local income tax rate: None

Local sales tax rate: 2.25% (county)

Property tax rate: Not available

Economic Information: San Francisco Partnership, 465 California Street, 9th Floor, San Francisco, CA 94104; telephone (415)352-8801; fax (415)956-3844; email info@sfp.org

■ Education and Research

Elementary and Secondary Schools

Founded in 1851, the San Francisco Unified School District (SFUSD) was the first public school district established in California. The SFUSD is a multicultural, multilingual, major urban public school system in which ethnic and racial diversity are considered to be strengths. English is the second language of nearly one-third of SFUSD students. With this in mind, the district offers Language Immersion Programs at 17 schools. These include programs in Spanish, Mandarin, Cantonese and Korean. In 2007 *Newsweek* named seven SFUSD schools as "America's Best High Schools." Gifted and Talented Education (GATE) Programs and special education programs are offered for all grade levels. In 2007 there were nine charter schools in the district. Special programming for high school students is available at schools such as the International Studies Academy and the School of the Arts. Advanced Placement and honors classes are also available.

The SFUSD encompasses all of San Francisco County, making it one of the largest in the state of California. The school board consists of seven partisan members who appoint the superintendent. The San Francisco school system provides a rigorous curriculum that develops student curiosity and creativity while preparing them for success at college and in careers.

The following is a summary of data regarding the San Francisco Unified School District as of the 2005–2006 school year.

Total enrollment: 55,000

Number of facilities

 elementary schools: 67
 junior high/middle schools: 15
 senior high schools: 21
 other: 0

Student/teacher ratio: 20.2:1

Teacher salaries (2005–06)

 elementary median: $54,580
 junior high/middle median: $57,630
 secondary median: $58,070

Funding per pupil: $8,044

A number of private and parochial schools provide alternative forms of education in the San Francisco area.

Public Schools Information: San Francisco Unified School District, 555 Franklin Street, San Francisco, CA 94102; telephone (415)241-6000; www.portal.sfusd.edu

Colleges and Universities

The eight academic colleges of San Francisco State University offer bachelor's degree programs in 111 fields, along with 95 master's programs and two doctoral degrees (in education). Total enrollment in 2006 was over 29,620. The University of California, San Francisco (UCSF) is the only University of California campus dedicated exclusively to health sciences. The UCSF campus serves about 2,860 students, offering graduate degrees in dentistry, medicine, nursing, and pharmacy. The campus supports the UCSF Medical Center, the UCSF Children's Hospital, and Langley Porter Psychiatric Institute. UCSF also hosts over 60 specialized research centers and institutes.

Golden Gate University offers certificate programs and undergraduate and graduate degree programs in accounting, business, law, taxation, information technology and related professions such as psychology and public administration. While San Francisco is the main campus site, there are six other campuses on the West Coast. Total enrollment is over 5,300 students.

The University of San Francisco is a private, Jesuit Catholic university with an annual enrollment of about 8,568. The school offers graduate and undergraduate degrees in six schools: Arts and Sciences, Business and Management, Education, Law, Nursing, and Professional Studies. Advanced study options are available through 19 specialized centers and institutes, including the Center for Latino Studies in the Americas, the Ricci Institute for Chinese-Western Cultural History, and the Center for Law and Global Justice.

City College of San Francisco offers associate's degrees and certificate programs in a wide variety of fields through seven schools: Science and Math, Business, Applied Science and Technology, Behavioral and Social Sciences, Health and Physical Education, Liberal Arts, and International Education and ESL. The ESL Department is the largest department of the college, with over 700 course offerings.

The University of California Hastings College of the Law, in downtown San Francisco, has a total enrollment of about 1,276. The school offers undergraduate programs in 18 fields and 20 advanced degrees. The Academy of Art University offers undergraduate and graduate programs in a wide spectrum of art-related fields, such as architecture, fashion, industrial design, motion pictures and television, digital arts, and advertising. The San Francisco campus of the California College of the Arts houses the school's graduate program and hosts the CAA

Watts Institute for Contemporary Arts, established in 1998 as a forum for the presentation and discussion of international contemporary art and curatorial practices. The undergraduate programs of the school are located at the Oakland campus.

Nearby Stanford University and the University of California, Berkeley, two schools with international reputations, provide still more opportunities for educational pursuits.

Libraries and Research Centers

The San Francisco Public Library consists of the main library and 27 branches throughout the city, providing a total of more than 2.4 million volumes, as well as films, videotapes, CDs, and other recordings. There are also three bookmobiles. The main library houses several special collections and centers, including special collections on calligraphy, the history of printing, Panama Canal manuscripts, science fiction and fantasy, San Francisco history, gay and lesbian history, and a document department featuring United Nations, federal, state, and local documents. The library is one of five in the state to be designated as a U.S. Patent and Trademark Depository Library. The Deaf Services Center and the Library for the Blind and Print Disabled are also at the main branch.

The J. Paul Leonard Library at SFSU holds over 4 million items and serves as a federal depository library of the 12th congressional district. Special collections include the Marguerite Archer Collection of Historic Children's Materials, the San Francisco State College Strike Collection, and San Francisco Bay Area Television Archives. The Labor Archives and Research Center collection includes historic documents and materials from several surrounding counties. Many unions have made the Labor Archives the official repository for their historical records. This center also contains personal memorabilia, photographs, and oral histories that document the lives and stories of working men and women from the region.

The city's proximity to Silicon Valley produces a large amount of research activity. The University of California, San Francisco hosts over 60 specialized research centers and institutes. These include California Institute for Quantitative Biosciences, Center for Aging in Diverse Communities, the Center for BioEntrepreneurship, the Center for Consumer Self Care, the Center for Pharmacogenomics, the Institute of Regeneration Medicine, and the Gladstone Institute of Virology and Immunology. There are five centers conducting research in AIDS/HIV and at least three specializing in cancer research.

The Public Research Institute (PRI) at San Francisco State University offers a wide variety of research services to government agencies, non-profit organizations, community groups, and academic researchers.

Public Library Information: San Francisco Public Library, 100 Larkin Street, San Francisco, CA 94102; telephone (415)557-4400; sfpl.lib.ca.us

■ Health Care

The major hospitals in San Francisco are affiliated with the University of California, San Francisco. The UCSF Medical Center, part of the UCSF campus at Parnassus, features a 600-bed main hospital occupying two buildings. Along with a full spectrum of medical care and services, the hospital has special departments for cancer care, fertility treatments, nanosurgery, cardiac care, ophthalmology, and orthopedics. There is also a transplant department for liver, kidney, pancreas, heart, and heart-lung transplants. Within the Medical Center is the UCSF Children's Hospital, a 180-bed center with a specialized pediatric surgical suite, pediatric and neonatal intensive care units, and a Birth Center. Outpatient clinics of the UCSF Medical Center are part of the Ambulatory Care Center by the hospital. Specialized clinics include an AIDS treatment center, a cochlear implant center, epilepsy care, occupational medicine, and dermatology center, among others. The UCSF Medical Center at Mount Zion, only a few miles away from Parnassus, features specialized clinics and surgery services as well as a center for comprehensive cancer care. Mount Zion has eight operating rooms and a 50-bed inpatient unit.

The San Francisco General Hospital is a public general acute care hospital that serves as a regional teaching hospital through partnership with UCSF. The 24-acre hospital complex contains an internationally-recognized emergency and Level I Trauma Center (the only one in the city), psychiatric services, the nation's first AIDS unit, the Alternative Birth Center, and the innovative Women's Health Center. In 2003 the Avon Comprehensive Breast Center was opened, which planned to increase the number of underserved women who receive mammograms by 5,000 annually. The Psychiatric Care and Psychiatric Emergency Services department is a 24-hour, 7-day a week specialized emergency assessment, stabilization, and hospital placement program. Primary care services are also available through the San Francisco General Medical Center complex.

■ Recreation

Sightseeing

San Francisco contains so many interesting attractions in such a small area that visitors find something unique on almost any street. Most points of interest are within walking distance or a short ride away. The ride itself can be an attraction when taken on one of the city's famous cable cars, the nation's only moving historical landmarks, now restored and servicing a 10-mile route in the heart of the city.

Historic and scenic beauty is evident all over the city. The original mission and the Presidio, both built in 1776 out of simple adobe brick, can still be toured. Jackson Square, the former Barbary Coast, and Portsmouth Square, the original center of the early town, are both in renovated areas that highlight different periods of the city's history. Many of the residential sections that surround the downtown district were spared destruction in the earthquake and fire of 1906, and they offer examples of Victorian architecture. Displayed in hillside vistas, the colorful houses give the city a Mediterranean look. The downtown area also contains a number of striking modern structures like the pyramidal Transamerica Building, and the impressive Civic Center complex, including the domed City Hall.

Perhaps the most unique features of San Francisco are its clusters of distinct ethnic neighborhoods. The most famous is Chinatown, the largest Chinese district outside of Asia, a 24-block area of authentic bazaars, temples, restaurants, and distinctive Oriental architecture. Recent additions to the area include a two-level gateway to the district, ornately carved by Taiwanese craftsmen, and the Chinese Cultural Center. Next to Chinatown is the North Beach area, once home to the "beatnik" culture. Filled with Italian influences—cafes, gelato parlors, delicatessens, cappuccino houses, and restaurants—the area also contains a number of jazz clubs, art galleries, and theaters. The Mission District, a business and residential area of colorful Victorian buildings, is home to a predominantly Spanish-speaking population and the original Levi Strauss clothing factory, still in operation. A five-tiered pagoda welcomes visitors to Nihonmachi, a section of sushi bars, theaters, shops, restaurants, and hotels that reflect the Japanese culture.

Golden Gate Park, just west of the downtown area, is more than 1,000 acres of landscaped greenery that was once a barren area of windswept sand dunes. The park was created in 1846 and houses flowered meadows, an arboretum and botanical garden containing more than 6,000 plant species, and a 5-acre Japanese tea garden. Also located in the park are the Conservatory of Flowers, a children's playground with an antique carousel, and a small herd of bison, a tradition since 1890.

The city's waterfront offers a variety of entertainments. Several islands in the bay provide scenic picnic areas. Alcatraz Island, home of "The Rock," the former escape-proof federal prison, is now open for tours; advance reservations are suggested. Ocean Beach, on the Pacific side of the peninsula, provides a view of Seal Rocks, a small island occupied by a colony of sea lions. At the northern end of Ocean Beach is the San Francisco Zoo, one of the top ten in the nation. More than 1,000 animals inhabit the exhibits, including snow leopards, a rare white tiger, and a colony of koala bears. The zoo also features the computer-designed Primate Discovery Center, Gorilla World, the world's largest natural gorilla habitat, and a children's zoo.

Golden Gate National Recreation Area, one of the largest urban parks in the world and host to more than 16 million visitors each year, is located on both sides of the Golden Gate, the entrance to San Francisco Bay. Its 75,398 acres contain stunning cliff-top views of the bay and the ocean, a network of hiking trails, valleys, and beaches, and the Fort Point National Historic Site, a brick fort built in 1861. The Golden Gate Bridge, with its pedestrian walkway, connects the two sides of the park.

The Randall Museum is a special hands-on facility for families sponsored by the San Francisco Recreation and Parks Department. Situated on a 16-acre hill overlooking San Francisco and the Bay, the museum features a live animal exhibit, a greenhouse and garden, an earthquake exhibit with a working seismograph, and a replica of a 1906 Earthquake Refugee Shack. The Randall Museum Theatre hosts concerts, movies, plays and lectures year-round. A hiking trail leads to the top of Corona Heights with stunning views of San Francisco and the Bay.

Arts and Culture

San Francisco enjoys a cultural scene as varied as its population. Theater, music, and dance can be found in a multitude of outlets. The heart of the city's cultural life is located in the area around the Civic Center Plaza, where the San Francisco War Memorial and Performing Arts Center blends in with the neighboring civic buildings. The Center's Louise M. Davies Symphony Hall is home of the San Francisco Symphony, a world-class orchestra that is one of the oldest in the United States. The War Memorial Opera House is home to the internationally acclaimed San Francisco Opera and the equally renowned San Francisco Ballet.

Visitors and residents enjoy Broadway shows, improvisational comedy, musical revues, and dramatic theater throughout the city. Situated on San Francisco's Union Square is TIX Bay Area, a half-price ticket booth that has day-of tickets to performances at many of the large and smaller houses. Within walking distance are American Conservatory Theater, Cable Car Theater, Curran Theater, Mason Street Theater, and Theater on the Square.

Museums in San Francisco are varied and plentiful. Located on the waterfront is the National Maritime Museum, a collection of ship models, relics, photographs, and paintings, as well as several restored vessels docked at the adjacent pier. The American Carousel Museum features a collection of hand-carved antique carousel figures. Other area museums include the San Francisco African American Historical and Cultural Society, the Museum of the California Historical Society, and the Wells Fargo History Museum.

The California Academy of Sciences, formerly in Golden Gate Park, is now located downtown and consists of an aquarium, a planetarium, and a natural history museum. The Steinhart Aquarium houses more than 14,000 aquatic specimens including penguins, dolphins, seals, crocodiles, and rare Australian lungfish. The Natural History Museum houses many exhibits of natural science including the Earth and Space Hall with its simulated earthquake and the Gem and Mineral Hall.

The Exploratorium: The Museum of Science, Art and Human Perception, in the Palace of Fine Arts, was founded by the renowned physicist and educator Dr. Frank Oppenheimer in 1969. The museum offers hands-on exhibits on what might be considered an eclectic range of topics, including weather, the human body, space and astronomy, earth science, cooking, languages, the science of wine, and sports science.

The M. H. de Young Museum in Golden Gate Park houses a diverse collection, including galleries tracing the history of art, as well as displays of American art, pre-Columbian gold work, and works by masters such as El Greco and Rembrandt. The nearby Asian Art Museum houses the Avery Brundage Collection, which contains more than 500 examples of Chinese art in addition to art of the Middle East, the Indian subcontinent, and Southeast Asia.

At the heart of San Francisco's Yerba Buena Gardens, situated south of Market Street near the Financial District, is a bustling center for arts and culture that includes the San Francisco Museum of Modern Art, which is the first museum on the West Coast devoted solely to twentieth-century art. The Jewish Museum and Mexican Museum are two of the many organizations in the process of building their new facilities nearby. Other area art museums include the San Francisco Crafts and Folk Art Museum, the Chinese Culture Center Museum, the Galeria de la Raza, the Ansel Adams Center for Photography, the Cartoon Art Museum, and the Museo Italo Americano.

The Mint Plaza, opened in 2007, is one of the latest public space developments in the heart of downtown. It consists of an 18,000-square-foot portion of Jessie Street (between Fifth and Mint) that has been closed to vehicle traffic. The area is lined with cafes and art, with open spaces available for events including theater, live music, and street fairs.

Festivals and Holidays

San Francisco is known for its celebratory spirit, which is reflected in the calendar of festivals and special events. One of the biggest celebrations occurs in February with the week-long Chinese New Year festival, an exotic blend of parades, outdoor festivals, and other cultural programs in America's largest Chinese community. March brings the seven-day St. Patrick's Day Celebration. The attention shifts to the Japanese district for the annual Cherry Blossom Festival in April, consisting of cultural programs, exhibitions, and a parade of dancers and costumed performers.

For almost a century, thousands of runners have flocked to San Francisco in May for the annual Bay to Breakers, which is part fundraiser for a variety of charities and part celebration of the city's diversity. June brings the two-day San Francisco Lesbian, Gay, Bisexual and Transgender Parade, the world's largest gay pride event. The San Francisco Waterfront Festival is an Independence Day party that unfailingly delivers brilliant fireworks over the Bay. Also in July is the North Beach Jazz Festival, which underscores the rich history of the San Francisco jazz scene. This five-day celebration of the Soul of San Francisco begins on Wednesday when more than 40 bars and clubs along Grant Street host local and national jazz talent. In September, people can sample the sinful fruits of chocolatiers at the Ghirardelli Square Chocolate Festival. The San Francisco World Music Festival had its eighth annual celebration in October 2007 with the theme of "The Lutes of the Deserts and the Mountains: An Exploration of the Ancient Roots of Music." October is also the month for the Hardly Strictly Bluegrass Festival at Golden Gate Park. The Holiday Festival of Lights in December takes place at Fisherman's Wharf and launches the Bay Area holiday season in style.

Sports for the Spectator

The Bay Area is home to two Major League Baseball franchises, the American League Oakland A's and the National League San Francisco Giants, as well as to the National Basketball Association's Golden State Warriors (Oakland), the National Hockey League's San Jose Sharks, and the pro-soccer league's San Jose Clash. The National Football Leagues' San Francisco 49ers was the first professional sports franchise on the West Coast; they have made several trips to the Super Bowl. Thoroughbred racing can be enjoyed at Golden Gate Fields or Bay Meadows, two of America's premier horse racing facilities. The Laguna Seca Raceway and the Infineon Raceway provide a variety of motor sports nearby. The city annually sponsors one of the largest marathons in the country, the San Francisco Marathon, as well as several other running events throughout the year. Area colleges and universities also field teams in most sports and maintain extensive spectator facilities.

Sports for the Participant

San Francisco offers a wide array of choices for those who are sports minded. Aquatic sports are especially popular because of the city's proximity to water. Yachting, boating, swimming, water skiing, boardsailing, surfing, fishing, and hang gliding from cliffs are among the favorite activities. The 75,398-acre Golden Gate Recreation Area is filled with hiking and bicycling trails, campgrounds, and wildlife preserves. The San Francisco Recreation and

Parks Department administers and maintains more than 200 parks, playgrounds, and open spaces throughout the city, including two outside the city limits: Sharp Park in Pacifica and Camp Mather in the High Sierras. The system also includes 15 large, full-complex recreation centers; 9 swimming pools; 6 golf courses; and 132 tennis courts, indoor and outdoor soccer facilities, ball diamonds, athletic fields, and basketball courts. The department is also responsible for the Marina Yacht Harbor, Candlestick Park, the San Francisco Zoo, and the Lake Merced Complex, which is operated for recreational purposes under the San Francisco Water Department.

Shopping and Dining

San Francisco offers some of the best shopping in the world, so it is no wonder that tourists and serious shopaholics alike want to spend some time and money in San Francisco's varied shopping centers, districts and malls. Union Square, Hayes Valley, upper Fillmore, the Mission, Sacramento Street, Chinatown and downtown's San Francisco Shopping Center offer a unique style with one-of-a-kind shops; each mall and neighborhood offers a distinctive feel suited to any shopper's mood. Other major shopping districts include Ghirardelli Square, which is a group of stores built around the Ghirardelli chocolate factory, and the Cannery, a lavishly remodeled former produce processing plant. Other popular shopping destinations are the Anchorage at Fisherman's Wharf and downtown's Embarcadero Center. In addition, each ethnic neighborhood supports its own distinctive section of shops, open-air markets, and restaurants.

San Francisco has been called "the weight watcher's Waterloo" because of its tempting restaurants, many holding international reputations. Nearly 4,000 restaurants in the city are geographically concentrated at the rate of about 95 per square mile. The Dining Room, offering French cuisine, is a five-star rated restaurant (*Mobil Travel Guide*). Four-star dining establishments include Campton Place Restaurant (American), Aqua (seafood), La Folie (French), Fleur de Lys (French), and Gary Danko (American). Dining styles and venues include supper clubs, American grills, California-Asian hybrids, haute vegetarian, modest bistros, and fine-dining destinations.

Seafood fresh off the boat can be obtained at restaurants along Fisherman's Wharf; farmland, vineyards, and cattle ranches in the surrounding area provide an abundance of other fresh ingredients. Sourdough bread is a San Francisco specialty. Many international restaurants, serving dishes from around the world and prepared with exact authenticity, are scattered throughout the city's numerous ethnic neighborhoods.

Visitor Information: San Francisco Convention and Visitors Bureau, Convention Plaza, 201 Third Street, Suite 900, San Francisco, CA 94103; telephone (415) 974-6900; www.onlyinsanfrancisco.com

■ Convention Facilities

The city of San Francisco hosts more than a million meeting, convention, and trade show delegates annually. Convention planners come to San Francisco not only because of the attractions in the Bay Area, but also for the excellent facilities. The city's Civic Center, called "the grandest Civic Center in the country" by architectural critics, houses extensive meeting facilities. The Bill Graham Civic Auditorium seats 7,000 people, with two adjoining halls that seat another 900 people. Underneath the auditorium is the Brooks Exhibit Hall, a 90,000-square-foot open exhibition area. The Moscone Center offers 600,000 square feet; a 300,000-square-foot expansion was completed in 2003. The Concourse Exhibition Center offers a 2,500-seat theater and a total of about 125,000 square feet of meeting and exhibit space. Monster Park at McLaren Lodge has a total of 170,000 square feet of exhibit and meeting space.

The city has nearly 32,719 hotel rooms available. All the rooms are within easy traveling distance of the main convention sites. Most of the major hotels in the area provide ample meeting space, ballrooms, registration lobbies, and exhibit areas. Several local theaters, galleries, and museums also offer rental spaces for meetings, banquets, and other special events.

Convention Information: San Francisco Convention and Visitors Bureau, Convention Plaza, 201 Third Street, Suite 900, San Francisco, CA 94103; telephone (415) 974-6900; www.onlyinsanfrancisco.com

■ Transportation

Approaching the City

The San Francisco International Airport is one of the busiest in the nation, handling over 20 million passengers every year on over 40 domestic and international airlines. An efficient customs clearance, modern facilities, and computerized ground transportation information make the airport easy to use. A 24-hour AirTrain people-mover system helps passengers navigate the airport grounds. SamTrans provide 24-hour service from the airport to parts of San Francisco, Palo Alto, and San Mateo County. Many of the downtown hotels offer free transportation to and from the airport. Travelers may choose to fly in at Oakland International Airport, which is served by 13 domestic and international airlines.

The city is at the intersection of several major highways. U.S. 101 and S.R. 1, the Pacific Coastal Highway, converge on San Francisco from the north and south. From the east, Interstate 80 and U.S. 50 serve the city. Interstate Loops 580 and 680 provide access to Interstate 5, the major north-south route from Canada to Mexico.

Amtrak rail service is available, as is CalTrain, a commuter service that operates from San Francisco to Gilroy. Bus service is offered via Greyhound Bus Lines.

Traveling in the City

Because of the city's compact size, walking is a favored means of transportation, but when the distance is too great, several public transportation options are available. The famous cable cars are not only a tourist attraction, but also a convenient way for commuters to travel in the downtown area. The city's Municipal Railway System (Muni) light-rail vehicles, descendants of the cable cars, travel underground in the inner city and above ground in the outlying areas. A Muni Visitor Passport allows unlimited access to Muni's entire fleet of buses, trolleys, light-rail vehicles, and cable cars. Passports are available for one, three, or seven days. There are about 80 Muni routes in the city. The Bay Area Rapid Transit (BART) is an ultra-modern train system linking the city with 43 stations in the East Bay Area. Five ferry services also connect the city with Oakland and Berkeley across the bay.

■ Communications

Newspapers and Magazines

San Francisco is prominent in the publishing industry on both the regional and national levels. The city is served by two major daily newspapers, the morning *San Francisco Chronicle* and, in the evening, *The Examiner. The San Francisco Chronicle* is one of the top twenty largest newspapers in the country; daily circulation in 2007 was estimated at about 398,246. The city's diversity is reflected in the wide array of special interest and ethnic publications. The *Sun-Reporter* (Thursdays), *Metro Reporter* (Tuesdays), and *California Voice* (Sundays) are weeklies serving the African American community; all three are published by Sun-Reporter Publishing Company, one of the oldest black presses in the nation. The *San Francisco Bay Guardian* and *SF Weekly* are alternative press publications. The *Bay Area Reporter* is a weekly serving the gay and lesbian community. Spanish weeklies include *El Bohemio News* and *El Latino*. The Japanese *Hokubei Manichi* and *Nichibei Times* are distributed twice a week. *Vestkusten*, in both English and Swedish, comes out twice a month. The *Jewish News Weekly of Northern California* is distributed on Fridays.

Several nationally distributed magazines are based in the city, as are many trade, industry, and technical journals. Among the many local and national publications are *San Francisco, Mother Jones,*and *MacWorld*. A variety of scholarly, medical, and professional journals are published in San Francisco.

Television and Radio

About fifteen television stations provide viewing choices from the commercial networks, public television, and foreign-language stations. Additional channels are available through cable service. Thirty-one AM and FM radio stations broadcast in San Francisco, offering a range of music, news, and informational programming.

Media Information: *San Francisco Chronicle*, 901 Mission Street, San Francisco, CA 94103-2988; telephone (415)777-1111; www.sfgate.com/chronicle. *The Examiner,* 110 Fifth Street, San Francisco, CA 94103; telephone (415)777-5700; www.examiner.com/san_francisco

San Francisco Online

California Historical Society. Available www .californiahistoricalsociety.org

City of San Francisco Home Page. Available www .sfgov.org

San Francisco Chamber of Commerce. Available www.sfchamber.com

San Francisco Chronicle. Available www.sfgate .com/chronicle

San Francisco Convention & Visitors Bureau. Available www.onlyinsanfrancisco.com

San Francisco Examiner. Available www.examiner .com/san_francisco

San Francisco Public Library. Available sfpl.lib.ca.us

San Francisco Unified School District. Available www.sfusd.k12.ca.us

BIBLIOGRAPHY

Caen, Herb, *Baghdad by the Bay* (Garden City, NY: Doubleday, 1949)

Gold, Herbert, *Bohemia: Where Art, Angst, Love, and Strong Coffee Meet* (New York: Simon & Schuster, 1993)

Lewis, Oscar, *San Francisco: Mission to Metropolis* (San Diego, CA: Howell-North Books, 1980)

Richards, Rand, *Historic San Francisco: A Concise History and Guide* (San Francisco, CA: Heritage House Publishers, 2007)

Twain, Mark, *Mark Twain's San Francisco* (New York: McGraw-Hill, 1963)

Twain, Mark, *Roughing it in California* (Kentfield, CA: L-D Allen Press, 1953)

Twain, Mark, *The Washoe Giant in San Francisco* (San Francisco, CA: G. Fields, 1938)

Wheeler, Richard S., *Aftershocks* (New York: Forge, 1999)

San Jose

■ The City in Brief

Founded: 1777 (incorporated 1850)

Head Official: City Manager Debra Figone (since 2007)

City Population
- 1980: 629,442
- 1990: 782,224
- 2000: 894,943
- 2006 estimate: 929,936
- Percent change, 1990–2000: 13.6%
- U.S. rank in 1980: 17th
- U.S. rank in 1990: 11th
- U.S. rank in 2000: 11th

Metropolitan Area Population
- 1980: Not available
- 1990: 6,253,311
- 2000: 7,039,361
- 2006 estimate: 1,787,123
- Percent change, 1990–2000: 12.6%
- U.S. rank in 1980: 4th
- U.S. rank in 1990: 4th
- U.S. rank in 2000: 5th

Area: 175 square miles (2000)

Elevation: 67 feet above sea level

Average Annual Temperature: 57.1° F

Average Annual Precipitation: 18.5 inches

Major Economic Sectors: services, wholesale and retail trade, government

Unemployment Rate: 4.8% (June 2007)

Per Capita Income: $30,769 (2005)

2005 FBI Crime Index Property: 22,930

2005 FBI Crime Index Violent: 3,492

Major Colleges and Universities: San Jose State University, San Jose/Evergreen Community College District

Daily Newspaper: *San Jose Mercury News*

■ Introduction

Once a quiet, medium-sized city at the center of a thriving agricultural area, San Jose was transformed in less than 30 years into a huge metropolis and a phenomenon in U.S. economic history. As the result of the computer revolution, San Jose became the capital of the "Silicon Valley," a vast complex of electronics industries that stretches throughout California's Santa Clara County. From 1950 to 1980, a period of tremendous growth and prosperity, the population of San Jose increased fourfold. Like other major urban areas, however, the city has been forced to confront the problems that come with unbridled development: traffic congestion, air pollution, housing shortages, and a strained infrastructure. A 1985 recession in the Silicon Valley produced a stagnant economy, from which the city recovered by the twenty-first century. San Jose consistently ranks high in polls that rate cities for business climate, livability, and fun.

■ Geography and Climate

San Jose is located in the Santa Clara Valley at the southern tip of San Francisco Bay, 48 miles south of San Francisco and 40 miles south of Oakland. The area is known as the Southern Peninsula. San Jose is the seat of Santa Clara County and the center of a large and expanding metropolitan area bordered by the Santa Cruz Mountains on the west and the Diablo Mountain range on the east. The Coyote and Guadalupe rivers run through the city. San Jose's climate is mild and semi-arid, with humidity varying from 67 percent in January to 51 percent in July. The city boasts of having about 300 sunny days per year.

The city of San Jose lies on the boundary zone between two of the major tectonic plates: the Pacific and North American plates. The city also lies between three active fault lines, including the San Andreas to the west. As such, the city is highly susceptible to earthquakes, which are sometimes quite damaging.

Area: 175 square miles (2000)

Elevation: 67 feet above sea level

Average Temperature: 57.1° F

Average Annual Precipitation: 18.5 inches

■ History

San Jose Begins as Agricultural Center for State

San Jose was California's first civic settlement, founded in 1777 by Mexican colonists and named El Pueblo de San Jose de Guadalupe for St. Joseph and the Guadalupe River near the town site. The town was established in order to bring agricultural development to the Alta California territory; each settler was issued animals, farm implements, seeds, and a $10 monthly stipend. These farmers joined Spanish missionaries who were already in the area. The Native American inhabitants of the region were the Olhone. The disruption of their culture by the missionaries and farmers and the spread of diseases eventually led to their virtual extermination.

As a supply station for prospectors during the gold rush, San Jose underwent a population explosion; upon incorporation in 1850 the city's inhabitants numbered 5,000 people. San Jose was the state capital from 1849 to 1851, and then became an important stage and boat link on the route to San Francisco until the advent of the railroad in 1864. Growth continued through the 1880s, reaching a culmination with the real estate boom and bust of 1887 when land sales totaled $2 million per day before the market collapsed. By the turn of the century San Jose was a major center for the cultivation of apricots, prunes, and grapes; with rail connections to other cities, it was also an important regional shipping hub.

High-Technology Revolution

Prior to World War II, San Jose, with its 18 canneries and 13 packing houses, was the world's largest canning and dried-fruit packing center. The city also pioneered the manufacture of specialized mechanical farm equipment in California; among the other products introduced by local inventors were the spray pump and the steam-powered stemmer-crusher for wine making. In the 1950s,

however, San Jose was transformed from a farming community to a high-technology capital by another of its natural resources: silicon. This element is used in making semiconductors, a basic component in high-technology industries. Thus San Jose and Santa Clara County came to be known as "Silicon Valley." Originating at Stanford University in nearby Palo Alto, a vast military-industrial complex, which includes the Ames Research Facility of the National Aeronautics and Space Administration (NASA) at Moffett Field, ultimately spread throughout the Southern Peninsula.

San Jose's largest population boom was triggered by this high-technology revolution. This growth continued unabated from the 1950s through the early 1980s. It was in 1971 that a journalist first referred to the area as the "Silicon Valley," and the name has since stuck. Buoyed by the success of computer companies, a steady flow of venture capital poured into San Jose and Santa Clara County to finance new firms that sprang up almost overnight. Companies that got their start in the Silicon Valley area include Hewlett-Packard, Apple, Intel, Adobe, eBay, and Sun Microsystems. Expansion began to moderate only with the 1985 recession in the computer industry, followed by a new swell in the economy developed with the growth of the dot-com industry in the 1990s. Unfortunately, when that bubble burst, so did many local businesses. While the strength of other, more established businesses seemed to help the city from a major recession—more than 20 percent of the semiconductors and related devices made in the United States continue to be produced in the Silicon Valley—the city nevertheless has been faced with problems resulting from uncontrolled development. The city government faced budget shortfalls from 2002 through 2007. In 2007 government officials projected that the shortfalls could continue through 2012. Since the city charter requires a balanced budget, the shortfalls resulted in the reduction of services that further resulted in a backlog of necessary repairs and renovation on city properties, such as roads and a wastewater treatment plant. The city has taken several measures to cut costs and reduce spending. Development plans to encourage the growth of retail establishments may prove beneficial for the increase of general funds through sales tax revenues.

Historical Information: History San Jose, 1650 Senter Road, San Jose, CA 95112; telephone (408)287-2290; www.historysanjose.org

■ Population Profile

Metropolitan Area Residents

1980: Not available
1990: 6,253,311
2000: 7,039,361
2006 estimate: 1,787,123

Image copyright Albert Cheng, 2008. Used under license from Shutterstock.com.

Percent change, 1990–2000: 12.6%
U.S. rank in 1980: 4th
U.S. rank in 1990: 4th
U.S. rank in 2000: 5th

City Residents

1980: 629,442
1990: 782,224
2000: 894,943
2006 estimate: 929,936
Percent change, 1990–2000: 13.6%
U.S. rank in 1980: 17th
U.S. rank in 1990: 11th
U.S. rank in 2000: 11th

Density: 5,117.9 people per square mile (2000)

Racial and ethnic characteristics (2005)

White: 447,079
Black: 29,295
American Indian and Alaska Native: 3,530
Asian: 271,900
Native Hawaiian and Pacific Islander: 3,099
Hispanic or Latino (may be of any race): 279,420
Other: 107,507

Percent of residents born in state: 44.8%
(2000)

Age characteristics (2005)

Population under 5 years old: 73,444
Population 5 to 9 years old: 62,908
Population 10 to 14 years old: 67,324
Population 15 to 19 years old: 57,524
Population 20 to 24 years old: 54,342
Population 25 to 34 years old: 133,144
Population 35 to 44 years old: 155,311
Population 45 to 54 years old: 122,112
Population 55 to 59 years old: 49,223
Population 60 to 64 years old: 33,562
Population 65 to 74 years old: 45,370
Population 75 to 84 years old: 23,408
Population 85 years and older: 9,658
Median age: 34.7 years

Births (2006, MSA)

Total number: 27,639

Deaths (2006, MSA)

Total number: 8,953

Money income (2005)

Per capita income: $30,769
Median household income: $70,921
Total households: 288,339

Number of households with income of...

less than $10,000: 15,367
$10,000 to $14,999: 11,094
$15,000 to $24,999: 22,929
$25,000 to $34,999: 18,782
$35,000 to $49,999: 33,646
$50,000 to $74,999: 50,666
$75,000 to $99,999: 38,175
$100,000 to $149,999: 56,018
$150,000 to $199,999: 22,275
$200,000 or more: 19,387

Percent of families below poverty level: 8.4% (2005)

2005 FBI Crime Index Property: 22,930

2005 FBI Crime Index Violent: 3,492

■ Municipal Government

San Jose operates under a council–manager form of government. The council consists of ten council members elected by districts and the mayor, who is elected at-large. All council members serve four-year terms. The city manager is appointed by the mayor and the council to an open-ended term. San Jose is the seat of Santa Clara County.

Head Official: City Manager Debra Figone (since 2007)

Total Number of City Employees: 6,672 (2007)

City Information: City of San Jose, 200 East Santa Clara St., San Jose, CA 95113; telephone (408)535-3500; www.sanjoseca.gov

■ Economy

Major Industries and Commercial Activity

The rapid expansion of high-technology industries triggered uninterrupted growth in the Silicon Valley—San Jose and Santa Clara County—from the 1950s through the early 1980s. The 1985 recession, however, left a stagnant economy, pointing to a need to diversify the economic base of the area. Studies indicated that high-technology companies had to move toward decreased reliance on the defense industry. By the early 1990s businesses in San Jose and Santa Clara County showed less than 20 percent of their budgets devoted to government contracts. The city was encouraged by a 1992 study that reported the nation's beleaguered

semiconductor industry claimed 43.8 percent of the world market, up from a low of 36.9 percent in 1988.

By 1997 the nation was riding the wave of a booming New Economy—involving the creation of new companies that put the Internet to use to change the way business was done. High technology had become a major factor in the economic growth of U.S. cities, and San Jose was at the center of it all. By 2000 San Jose was a mecca for hot startup companies and venture capital dollars. San Jose, and in particular the Silicon Valley region, is a hotbed of technology and technological innovation. The area has received more patents than any other technology region in the United States. Technology businesses centered here continue to grow and expand in the twenty-first century, as does the growth of service and support businesses to the industry. The San Jose Metropolitan Area in 2007 was home to over 4,500 high technology companies employing more than 182,300 people. Companies in the Silicon Valley area include Hewlett-Packard, Apple, Intel, Intuit, Oracle, Yahoo!, Google, Adobe, eBay, and Sun Microsystems.

Items and goods produced: missiles; rocket boosters; computers; atomic electrical equipment; fruit, vegetable, and fish cans; dairy products; chemicals; aluminum; paint; fiberglass; matches; medical equipment

Incentive Programs—New and Existing Companies

Local programs: The city of San Jose adopted a Local Preference Policy in May 2004. The policy works to encourage local companies to work with other local companies and the city to promote further job growth for residents and to keep local spending within the regional economy. The Local Preference Policy goes hand in hand with the Small Business Opportunity Program, which works to smooth the process for small businesses of selling their products and services to the city.

A variety of loans, bonds, and special funds are available to local businesses in San Jose. Among them are the Development Enhancement Special Fund, which helps businesses secure loan funds for expansion, working capital, inventory, or other qualified business expenses; Industrial Development Bonds, which offer financing options for manufacturing firms that are job-generating; the Lenders for Community Development program, which provides access to small business loans and lines of credit; and the Revolving Loan Fund, which makes funds available to small businesses for a variety of uses.

The San Jose Silicon Valley Chamber of Commerce works to develop and maintain the metropolitan area economy. Their particular focus is on aiding small and medium-sized companies involved in international business. The chamber's international trade program includes seminars, networking events, and exhibitions. The San Jose Downtown Association also works to stimulate and improve business conditions. The SBA/CiscoSystems/San Jose Entrepreneur Center provides services to entrepreneurs and small businesses.

State programs: An 18-square mile state-designated Enterprise Zone offers businesses operating in the zone significant tax savings and other financial benefits. The zone consists of San Jose's downtown area and benefits retail, commercial, and high-tech businesses located there. Benefits of operating in the Enterprise Zone include sales and use tax credits; hiring tax credits; net operating loss carryover and net interest deduction for lenders programs. A Research & Development Tax Credit is available of up to 15 percent against bank and corporate tax liability for certain in-house research. An additional 24 percent credit is available for basic research payments to outside organizations. This is one of the highest research and development tax credits in the nation. A Child Care Tax Credit is available for companies establishing on-site child care facilities. A Net Operating Loss Carryover and New Market Tax Credits are also available. A Work Opportunity Tax Credit is offered for employers who hire individuals from certain target groups. San Jose is part of a state-designated Recycling Market Development Zone, enabling businesses involved in recycling to utilize low-interest loans, technical assistance, siting and permitting assistance, and reduced permit application fees. San Jose is also a designated Foreign Trade Zone, which allows companies to reduce, delay, or eliminate customs fees on imported goods. The Silicon Valley Export Assistance Center offers state and government programs that assist companies who wish to export goods.

Job training programs: The Silicon Valley Workforce Investment Network works with local businesses and residents. The network's one-stop system offers resources for job seekers, as well as services to businesses that include pre-employment screening, access to qualified applicants, training programs, and assistance with employee transitions. Work2future offers training and workforce assistance for local businesses and job-seekers. The California Employment Training Panel assists businesses through performance-based customized training contracts for new or existing employees. Reimbursement of costs for developing, implementing, and completing training programs may range from $1,500 to $2,000 per employee.

Development Projects

In 2003 and 2004, more than 240,000 square feet of retail space was added in downtown San Jose. The Neighborhood Business Districts (NBD) program was established as part of an effort to boost retail business in San Jose's older neighborhoods; its efforts resulted in 40 new restaurants and retail stores opening among the districts by early 2005. CIM Group's Central Place was approved in early 2005; construction on the downtown mixed-use highrise housing project began in 2006 and was scheduled to be complete in 2009.

A massive plan for the redevelopment of North San Jose, or the Innovation Triangle, was adopted by the city council in June 2005. The North San Jose 2030 plan calls for a redevelopment of the approximately 42 million square feet of industrial space in the Innovation Triangle, which is currently home to more than 1,200 multinational companies employing more than 55,000 people. The plan cites that the space is currently "functionally obsolete," and calls for renovations as well as an additional 26.7 million square feet of new research and development space and office space, 32,000 new housing units, and 1.4 million square feet of retail space. As of 2007, it was estimated that up to 83,000 new jobs would be brought to San Jose as a result of the North San Jose redevelopment.

A $2.8 billion expansion of the San Jose International Airport was underway in 2007, with phased completion dates and expansions and improvements ranging from new concourses and parking garages, terminal and roadway improvements, and an Automated People Mover. When completed in 2010, the airport will have the capacity to serve approximately 17.6 million passengers annually, up from the 11.5 million it currently serves.

San Jose has one of the fastest growing life science clusters in the U.S.; San Jose had invested some $6.5 million in contemporary bioscience laboratory facilities by 2007. The recently developed Edenvale Technology Park is home to over 300 companies located on 2,312 acres with 12 million square feet of research and development, office, and manufacturing space. The Edenvale Technology Park is also home to the San Jose BioCenter, a world-class life sciences research facility and business incubator sponsored by the Redevelopment Agency.

Economic Development Information: San Jose Silicon Valley Chamber of Commerce, 310 South First Street, San Jose, CA 95113; telephone (408)291-5250; fax (408)286-5019; email info@sjchamber.com

Commercial Shipping

Nearly half of the traffic at Mineta San Jose International Airport is business related, which makes the facility an important factor in the Silicon Valley economy. Revenues from freight shipments average more than $10 million annually. There are 12 cargo and freight airline services with facilities at the airport. Two major rail freight lines and a number of motor freight carriers also operate in the metropolitan area. The city is part of Foreign Trade Zone 18 and the U.S. Customs services are available at the airport.

Labor Force and Employment Outlook

According to San Jose's Office of Economic Development, more than 85 percent of the region's new jobs come from companies that are less than 10 years old. As of 2007, small businesses created eight out of ten new jobs in the Silicon Valley. A well-educated and abundant work force coupled with the great quantity of high-level jobs created annually combine to create a shortage of qualified employees in the region. One out of every five workers in Santa Clara County is employed in manufacturing (169,600 workers out of a total employment of 799,600). San Jose has ranked first among large metropolitan areas as a world class manufacturing community based on manufacturing strength and the high productivity of its workers. The San Jose region continues to have the highest productivity level of any region in the U.S. The workforce is highly educated: 67 percent of the workforce has some college education and 40 percent of workers have earned a college degree.

The following is a summary of data regarding the San Jose-Sunnyvale-Santa Clara metropolitan area labor force, 2006 annual averages.

Size of nonagricultural labor force: 892,400

Number of workers employed in . . .

    construction and mining: 47,300
    manufacturing: 171,000
    trade, transportation and utilities: 135,800
    information: 38,500
    financial activities: 37,100
    professional and business services: 164,700
    educational and health services: 101,300
    leisure and hospitality: 75,500
    other services: 25,000
    government: 96,400

Average hourly earnings of production workers employed in manufacturing: $22.60

Unemployment rate: 4.8% (June 2007)

Largest employers (2007)	Number of employees
Cisco Systems	17,200
County of Santa Clara	15,360
City of San Jose	6,840
IBM	6,650
San Jose State University	3,030
eBay	3,010
Hitachi	2,800
San Jose Unified School District	2,670
Xilinx	2,440
Kaiser Permanente	2,120

Cost of Living

San Jose suffers from a severe shortage of affordable housing and is among the most expensive cities in which to live; conversely, San Jose residents also have the highest disposable income in the nation.

The following is a summary of data regarding key cost of living factors for the San Jose area.

2007 (1st quarter) ACCRA Average House Price: $827,270

2007 (1st quarter) ACCRA Cost of Living Index: 155.1

State income tax rate: 1.0% to 9.3%

State sales tax rate: 6.25%

Local income tax rate: None

Local sales tax rate: 2.0% (county)

Property tax rate: Average 1.1% of full cash value

Economic Information: San Jose Silicon Valley Chamber of Commerce, 310 South First St., San Jose, CA 95113; telephone (408)291-5250; fax (408)286-5019; email info@sjchamber.com. State of California, Employment Development Department, 800 Capitol Mall, MIC 83, Sacramento, CA 95814

■ Education and Research

Elementary and Secondary Schools

The city of San Jose is served by 19 school districts, but not every district serves all ages of students. For instance, the Evergreen Elementary School District serves elementary and middle school students while the East Side Union High School District serves only high school students. Charter schools are available in some districts. The largest district in the city is the San Jose Unified School District, which serves children of all ages with a variety of curriculums, including programs for advanced students as well as those for at-risk or special education students.

The following is a summary of data regarding the San Jose Unified School District as of the 2005–2006 school year.

Total enrollment: 31,658

Number of facilities

    elementary schools: 31
    junior high/middle schools: 7
    senior high schools: 7
    other: 0

Student/teacher ratio: 21:1

Teacher salaries (2005–06)

elementary median: $54,720
junior high/middle median: $56,350
secondary median: $60,120

Funding per pupil: $8,123

More than 60 private and parochial schools serve San Jose.

Public Schools Information: San Jose Unified School District, 855 Lenzen Avenue, San Jose, CA 95126; telephone (408)535-6000; www.sjusd.org

Colleges and Universities

San Jose State University is the oldest public institution of higher learning on the West Coast, as well as one of the largest universities in the 23-campus California State University system. San Jose State University educates nearly 30,000 students and offers 134 bachelor's and master's degrees in 110 concentrations; the university prides itself on being the top supplier of engineering, computer science, and business graduates to the Silicon Valley high-tech workforce.

The San Jose/Evergreen Community College District is comprised of San Jose City College and Evergreen Valley College; both award associate's of arts and science degrees and offer occupational and technical training to more than 30,000 students.

The National Hispanic University is a four-year institution offering associate's and bachelor's degrees in business administration, computer information systems, and liberal studies. Associate's degrees are also available in early childhood education and mathematics and science. The school offers special programs for middle and high school students to encourage their educational goals. The Lincoln Law School of San Jose offers part-time evening study programs for students seeking a legal education leading to the Bar Examination. Most students complete their course of studies in about four years.

The University of Phoenix-North California campuses have a facility in San Jose, which awards bachelor's and master's degrees. Also located in the San Jose area are technical and vocational schools, adult learning centers, and extension facilities. Several colleges and universities—some of them considered among the best in the nation—are within driving distance of San Jose. They include Stanford University, Santa Clara University, and the University of California campuses at Berkeley and Santa Cruz.

Libraries and Research Centers

The San Jose Public Library system operates the Dr. Martin Luther King, Jr. Main Library, 17 branches, and a bookmobile. Library holdings consist of more than two million items. The Dr. Martin Luther King, Jr. Main Library opened in 2003 as a joint development effort between the city, San Jose State University, and the San Jose Redevelopment Agency. It is the first library of its kind in that the combined services and collections of the city system and the university library are made available to all. With eight floors and more than 475,000 square feet, the library is among the largest in the country and serves more than one million visitors annually. The Main Library also houses a special collection in the California Room, featuring state and local history from 1849 to the present; the Cultural Heritage Center; and the Ira F. Brilliant Center for Beethoven Studies. The Steinbeck Research Center contains the writings and memorabilia of novelist John Steinbeck, a San Jose area native, as well as the world's largest collection of the writer's first edition books.

San Jose State University has partnerships with over 45 research institutes and facilities serving a wide variety of fields. These include the Bay Area Earth Science Institute, the Carl W. Sharsmith Herbarium, the Center for Development of Recycling, the Center for Educational Research on Dyslexia, the Silicon Valley Ergonomics Institute, and the Institute of Nursing Research. Other fields of interest include gerontology, the environment, and telecommunications. IBM's Almaden Research Center conducts industrial research in computer science, software, computer storage technology, and physical and materials science and technology.

Public Library Information: Dr. Martin Luther King, Jr. Main Library, 150 E. San Fernando Street, San Jose, CA 95112; telephone (408)808-2000; www.sjlibrary.org

■ Health Care

HCA Healthcare Corp. owns two major hospitals in San Jose. The Regional Medical Center of San Jose has 204 licensed beds and serves about 45,000 patients annually in its emergency/trauma department, which is one of six Centers of Excellence at the hospital. The other five are cardiovascular, women's and children's health, neuroscience, cancer care, and medical/surgical services. The trauma department is a level II facility. Good Samaritan Hospital is a general acute-care hospital with a licensed bed capacity of 422. Good Samaritan is accredited as a primary stroke center and offers one of the few behavioral health centers in the area. Other specialized departments include mother and baby care, the Cardiac and Vascular Institute, and the Arthritis and Joint Replacement Center.

Santa Clara Valley Medical Center, one of California's most high-tech public hospitals, is a 524-bed acute-care facility that houses a burn unit, a rehabilitation center for patients with spinal and head injuries, a level 1 trauma center, a high-risk maternity program, and a neonatal intensive-care unit. The 358-bed O'Connor Hospital, sponsored by the Daughters of Charity of

St. Vincent de Paul, offers heart and cancer care, sports medicine, and a Wound Care Center. O'Connor Hospital also supports a satellite pediatric facility and a family health center. Stanford Hospital in nearby Palo Alto is highly regarded for its work in a wide variety of specialties, notably cardiovascular treatment, and is the teaching facility for the Stanford University medical school. Only 20 minutes from San Jose, the hospital's 613 beds and more than 1,800 medical staff personnel serve more than 400,000 area residents annually. Stanford Clinics offer treatment in more than 100 specialties and subspecialties.

■ Recreation

Sightseeing

Most of the attractions in San Jose are related to the natural beauty of the area or to its historical past. Kelley Park is a popular site, offering a variety of diversions, including Happy Hollow Park and Zoo, where visitors can enjoy family-oriented amusements and view wildlife in a 12-acre natural setting. The 16-acre San Jose Historical Museum on the park grounds features a recreated turn-of-the-century town with such exhibits as a working blacksmith shop, a Victorian home, and a doctor's office. Also located in Kelley Park is the Japanese Friendship Garden, featuring flowering trees and shrubs, waterfalls, and koi fish. Other botanical gardens in San Jose are Overfelt Botanical Gardens and the Municipal Rose Garden.

Alum Rock Park is a wildlife refuge containing mineral springs, trails, and picnic facilities; the Youth Science Institute based in the park offers educational programs and special events to acquaint children with nature. Ardenwood Historic Farm in neighboring Fremont is a working farm that demonstrates agrarian life from 1880 through the 1920s; among the exhibits are soap and candle making and the planting and harvesting of crops with horse-drawn equipment.

Especially popular with tourists is the Winchester Mystery House; according to legend, this "haunted" Victorian mansion, containing 160 rooms, was built by the wealthy but eccentric widow of the maker of the Winchester rifle to appease the spirits of the rifle's victims.

Families with children will not want to miss a trip to several of the special areas in Guadalupe River Park and Gardens. The park's Discovery Meadow is home to the Children's Discovery Museum, featuring 150 interactive exhibits, and Monopoly in the Park, the world's largest Monopoly game board at 930 square feet. McEnery Park includes a playground and 12 sculptures that represent the wildlife of the river. Arena Green has a carousel. The Guadalupe Gardens are a relaxing place for a stroll or a guided tour, for a small fee.

Nationally known for its table wines, the San Jose area boasts dozens of wineries; many offer wine-tasting and tours of their facilities. Several theme parks operate in Santa Clara County, including Paramount's Raging Waters in San Jose's Lake Cunningham Regional Park and Paramount's Great America in nearby Santa Clara.

Arts and Culture

San Jose is becoming a regional center for the arts as local performing groups and organizations consistently draw larger audiences from throughout the Bay Area. The American Musical Theatre of San Jose at the San Jose Center for the Performing Arts entertains capacity crowds with three to four annual Broadway musicals. The San Jose Repertory Theatre produces classic and contemporary drama. Plays for children are staged by the San Jose Children's Musical Theater. The California Theatre is home to the San Jose Wind Symphony, Symphony Silicon Valley, and Opera San Jose. The Ballet San Jose Silicon Valley is considered one of the country's most innovative ballet companies, with a repertoire of more than 120 modern and traditional classical ballets. The San Jose Stage Company produces plays by contemporary playwrights. HP Pavilion at San Jose hosts varied performers such as U2 and the Mormon Tabernacle Choir.

San Jose's museums and galleries specialize in a variety of fields. Attractions include the Children's Discovery Museum, offering hands-on exhibits, and The Tech Museum of Innovation, offering an IMAX theater and interactive experiences in new technologies. The Rosicrucian Egyptian Museum features the city's only planetarium as well as astronomical and scientific displays, a full-scale Egyptian tomb exhibit, and a collection of Egyptian artifacts.

The San Jose Museum of Art holds over 2,000 objects in a variety of media with a focus on twentieth- and twenty-first century artwork, particularly of artists from the West Coast. The San Jose Museum of Quilts and Textiles, one of the few museums of its kind in the country, provides a showcase for the history of quilts and textiles. The work of local and Bay Area artists is shown at the Institute of Contemporary Art and at the Works Gallery. The Works Gallery is a mixed-use space for contemporary art, music, and other performances. Movimiento de Arte y Cultura Latino Americana (MACLA) offers a place for the contemporary art and performances of Latino artists.

Arts and Culture Information: San Jose Convention and Visitors Bureau, 408 Almaden Blvd., San Jose, CA 95110; telephone (408)295-9600; toll-free (800) SAN-JOSE/726-5673; www.sanjose.org

Festivals and Holidays

Special events and celebrations take place in the San Jose area throughout the year, many of them focusing on the cultural heritages of the region's diverse population. Winter events include January's San Jose International Auto Show; in February, the Vietnamese Spring Festival and Parade offers food, entertainment, games, and other fun events highlighting Vietnamese culture in the city. Spring offerings include the San Jose Art Festival, a juried art show; and the Golden Circle Theatre Party, an annual black-tie benefit, both in March. March is also the month for the annual Cinequest Film Festival. April's annual Iris Show is a favorite of gardeners and iris aficionados; May brings cultural celebrations including the Nikkei Matsuri, Cinco de Mayo Parade and Festival, and the Zee Heritage India Festival. June events include the Juneteenth Festival and the San Jose Gay Pride Festival and Parade. In July, visitors and residents can enjoy the San Jose America Festival (multicultural), the International Mariachi Festival, the Tahiti fete of San Jose, and the Chinese Summer Festival. August ushers in the Comcast Jazz Festival and the Santa Clara County Fair. Fall offers Halloween at Bonfante Gardens. San Jose's year winds down with a Holiday River Parade and Lighting Ceremony and the Nuestra Navidad, a celebration of Christmas in the Mexican tradition.

Sports for the Spectator

San Jose is in an advantageous location for fans of professional sports. The National Hockey League's San Jose Sharks play at the HP Pavilion. The HP Pavilion also hosts the San Jose Stealth of the National Lacrosse League and Arena Football League's SaberCats, as well as figure skating, boxing, and other sporting events. Major League Soccer's San Jose Earthquakes play at San Jose State University's Spartan Stadium. The San Jose Giants, the farm club for the San Francisco Giants National League baseball team, play their home games at Municipal Stadium in San Jose. Horse racing is on view at Bay Meadows Racecourse in San Mateo and at the Santa Clara County Fairgrounds.

Several professional teams compete within driving distance of San Jose; among them are baseball's San Francisco Giants and Oakland Athletics, and Oakland's Golden State Warriors of the National Basketball Association.

Sports for the Participant

A variety of neighborhood and regional parks in the San Jose area provide facilities for a variety of activities such as water sports, baseball, tennis, golf, hiking, horseback riding, and wildlife study. San Jose's 152 large and small neighborhood parks and gardens, and another 9 regional parks, are maintained by the city; especially popular are Almaden Quicksilver Park, Alum Rock Park, and Lake Cunningham Regional Park. Numerous reservoirs and lakes are located throughout the region for sailing, waterskiing, and windsurfing. Over 15 local and championship golf courses exist in the area, including two Jack Nicklaus-designed golf courses and the Los Lagos Golf Course spanning Coyote Creek. Runners have two major fall events to choose from: the Metro Silicon Valley Marathon and the Rock 'n' Roll Half Marathon San Jose.

Shopping and Dining

With several major and outlet malls, regional shopping centers, and myriad neighborhood stores and specialty shops, San Jose can meet the needs of most consumers. San Jose's largest shopping center is Valley Fair Westfield Shoppingtown, boasting of over 360 stores and 20 dining establishments. Santana Row, directly across the street from the mall, includes 70 shops, 5 spas, 18 restaurants, and a full-service hotel in a complex set up like European streets. The Oakridge Mall (the city's other Westfield mall) has about 100 shops as well as cafes and restaurants. The San Jose Flea Market is one of the nation's largest flea markets and attracts more than 2,000 sellers and more than 80,000 shoppers per week to its 8 miles of corridors and alleys. Shoppers will find anything from antiques and collectibles to freshly-made foods. The "Produce Row" section of the market is touted as California's largest farmer's market. San Jose Market Center downtown features about 50 retail and dining establishments.

Restaurants are plentiful in San Jose, offering American cuisine and ethnic specialties ranging from German and French to Mexican, Persian, Moroccan, and Thai dishes. Several authentic Japanese restaurants are clustered in historic Japantown. Santana Row offers ethnic restaurants such as Amber India, The Left Bank, and Maggiano's. Local favorites include Paolo's, an Italian restaurant with a 5,000-bottle wine collection; Emiles, hosted by the Swiss Chef Emile; and Original Joe's, featuring Italian-American family-style dining. Santa Clara Valley wineries combine brunches, luncheons, and picnics with wine tastings; the area is noted for its Chardonnay, Zinfandel, and Johannisburg Riesling wines.

Visitor Information: San Jose Convention and Visitors Bureau, 408 Almaden Blvd., San Jose, CA 95110; telephone (408)295-9600; toll-free (800)SAN-JOSE/ 726-5673; www.sanjose.org

■ Convention Facilities

The principal convention and meeting place is the San Jose McEnery Convention Center. It offers a total of 432,000 square feet of event space with 30 meeting rooms and a 22,000-square-foot ballroom. South Hall, adjacent to the convention center, has 80,000 square feet of column-free exhibit space. Directly across the street from the convention center is the Civic Auditorium, a Spanish Mission style dual-level auditorium seating 3,060. The 523-seat Montgomery Theater is in the same building as the Civic Auditorium. Next door is Parkside Hall, featuring 30,000 square feet of unobstructed exhibit space. This space can be divided into two smaller sections. The 1,100-seat California Theatre downtown has conference and meeting rooms available.

There are more than 4,000 hotel and motel rooms in San Jose's downtown and another 4,400 citywide. Hotels and motels in the San Jose metropolitan area, many of them new or recently renovated, provide accommodations for a variety of group functions. Among the unique meeting facilities are the Bay Meadows Racecourse, and the many museums and wineries in the area.

Convention Information: San Jose Convention and Visitors Bureau, 408 Almaden Blvd., San Jose, CA 95110; telephone (408)295-9600; toll-free (800)SAN-JOSE/726-5673; www.sanjose.org

■ Transportation

Approaching the City

The Norman Y. Mineta San Jose International Airport, located 10 minutes from downtown, is rated among the busiest airports in the world, handling more than 10.9 million passengers annually; it is served by 13 airlines with more than 384 daily flights. In 2007 major construction was underway at the airport, with projects including new terminals, a people mover, more parking, runway extensions, and advanced security systems, all slated for completion in phases by 2015. Corporate and private aircraft are accommodated at the San Jose Jet Center and the Reid-Hillview Airport.

Three interstate highways serve San Jose: I-680 (north-south), which becomes I-280 (east-west), and I-880 (north-south). U.S. Route 101 runs northeast-southwest. State routes 87 and 17 also lead into the city.

Amtrak serves the San Jose Diridon station; rail commuter service to San Francisco is provided by Cal-Train. Other intercity rail connections are made via the county bus system that links with BART (Bay Area Rapid Transit), an ultra-modern train system based in San Francisco; a $1 billion transit plan approved in 2000 will fund an eventual BART extension to San Jose. In late 2007, engineering plans were completed but construction had not yet begun.

Traveling in the City

The Santa Clara Valley Transportation Authority (VTA) operates a 30-mile-long light rail system out of the downtown Transit Mall, which also provides antique trolleys and county transit buses in and around the city and connecting the city with Bay Area Rapid Transit (BART) to East Bay and San Francisco. The light rail system runs from Mountain View through downtown San Jose and ends in south San Jose residential and shopping areas. DASH Shuttles provide service around downtown and connect the VTA Light Rail to the Diridon CalTrain Station, the convention center, and San Jose State University. The Altamont Commuter Express train runs six times a day between Stockton and San Jose.

■ Communications

Newspapers and Magazines

San Jose's daily newspaper is the *San Jose Mercury News.* Weekly community papers include the *Almaden Resident, Rose Garden Resident,* and *Willow Glen Resident,* all published by Silicon Valley Community Newspapers. The metropolitan area is also served by such publications as the weekly *Silicon Valley/San Jose Business Journal* and the *San Jose Post-Record,* a daily legal newspaper. *El Observador* and *Alianza Metropolitan News* are published weekly in Spanish and English. *Viet Mercury* is a Vietnamese weekly paper.

Television and Radio

Because of the proximity of communities in the Bay Area, San Jose shares a number of television and radio stations with other cities. Based in San Jose are 3 television stations—1 public and 2 commercial—and 11 AM and FM radio stations.

Media Information: *San Jose Mercury News,* 750 Ridder Park Drive, San Jose, CA 95190; telephone (408) 920-5000; www.mercurynews.com

San Jose Online

City of San Jose home page. Available www.sanjoseca.gov

History San Jose. Available www.historysanjose.org

San Jose Convention & Visitors Bureau. Available www.sanjose.org

San Jose Mercury News. Available www.mercurynews.com

San Jose Public Library. Available www.sjlibrary.org

San Jose Silicon Valley Chamber of Commerce. Available www.sjchamber.com

San Jose Unified School District. Available www.sjusd.org

BIBLIOGRAPHY

Beers, David, *Blue Sky Dream: A Memoir of America's Fall From Grace* (New York: Doubleday, 1996)

Branson, Po, *The First $20 Million is Always the Hardest: A Silicon Valley Novel* (New York: Random House, 1997)

Farrell, Harry, *Swift Justice: Murder and Vengeance in a California Town* (New York: St. Martin's Press, 1992)

Lecuyer, Christopher, *Making Silicon Valley: Innovation and the Growth of High Tech, 1930-1970* (Cambridge, MA: MIT Press, 2006)

Santa Ana

■ The City in Brief

Founded: 1869 (incorporated 1886)

Head Official: Mayor Miguel A. Pulido (since 1986)

City Population

    1980: 203,713
    1990: 293,827
    2000: 337,977
    2006 estimate: 340,024
    Percent change, 1990–2000: 14.8%
    U.S. rank in 1980: 69th
    U.S. rank in 1990: 52nd
    U.S. rank in 2000: 51st

Metropolitan Area Population

    1980: 1,933,000
    1990: 2,410,668
    2000: 2,846,289
    2006 estimate: Not reported
    Percent change, 1990–2000: 12.9%
    U.S. rank in 1980: 2nd (CMSA)
    U.S. rank in 1990: 2nd (CMSA)
    U.S. rank in 2000: 2nd (CMSA)

Area: 27.2 square miles (2000)

Elevation: 110 feet above sea level

Average Annual Temperature: 65.0° F

Average Annual Precipitation: 13.17 inches

Major Economic Sectors: services, wholesale and retail trade, government

Unemployment Rate: 4.7% (June 2007)

Per Capita Income: $14,110 (2005)

2005 FBI Crime Index Property: 10,292

2005 FBI Crime Index Violent: 1,845

Major Colleges and Universities: Rancho Santiago Community College, Santa Ana College

Daily Newspaper: *The Orange County Register; Los Angeles Times–Orange County*

■ Introduction

Santa Ana is the seat and largest city of California's Orange County. Surrounded by the rich farmland of the Santa Ana Valley, the city is part of a megalopolis that includes several incorporated cities; among them are Anaheim, Buena Park, and Fullerton. It is close to both the Los Angeles metropolitan area to the northwest and the San Diego metropolitan area to the southeast along the Pacific Coast. About 76 percent of its residents are of Hispanic origin; thus, Santa Ana has retained its rich cultural heritage. Founded as a farming town, the city is now the financial and governmental center for Orange County.

■ Geography and Climate

Santa Ana is located in the Santa Ana Valley in southwestern California. The seat and largest city of Orange County, it is located about 30 miles southeast of Los Angeles and 90 miles north of San Diego. Situated on the Santa Ana River, it is near the Santa Ana Mountains and about 12 miles from the coast of the Pacific Ocean. For statistical purposes, the city is sometimes linked in a metropolitan division with Anaheim and Irvine and sometimes listed as part of a Metropolitan Statistical Area (MSA) encompassing Los Angeles and Long Beach. The weather is typically warm and sunny, as in most of Southern California. The sun shines approximately 300 days out of the year. Year-round humidity at noon is usually around 53 percent. The Santana Winds (or Santa

Ana Winds) that typically occur from late summer to spring bring warm and dry air down from the high deserts to the San Bernardino Mountains and through the Los Angeles–Orange County Basin. These winds are sometimes accompanied by brush and wildfires. The region of Southern California, with several fault lines, is susceptible to earthquakes, though most are of a relatively low magnitude.

Area: 27.2 square miles (2000)

Elevation: 110 feet above sea level

Average Temperature: 65.0° F

Average Annual Precipitation: 13.17 inches

■ History

Franciscans Settle Santa Ana Valley

The valley in which Santa Ana is located was discovered in July 1769, during a Franciscan expedition led by Don Gaspar Portola. The explorers christened the valley Santa Ana in honor of Saint Anne, also giving the name Santa Ana to the river flowing through the valley. One of the members of the Portola party, Father Junipero Serra, later founded a chain of Franciscan missions that still can be seen today. The El Camino Real, the King's Highway, which linked the missions, passes through the Santa Ana Valley.

Another member of the Portola group, a soldier named Antonio Yorba, and his nephew, Juan Peralta, received a Spanish grant for land extending from the foothills of the Santa Ana Canyon to the ocean. They used the land for grazing cattle and later developed irrigation systems fed by water from the Santa Ana River. The land was thus quite fertile, and the area soon became an agricultural center, with several ranches established in the valley.

City of Santa Ana Prospers

The 1849 California Gold Rush brought the region a population boom, which was followed by another major expansion during the Civil War. The valley's large ranches were subdivided and sold to the newcomers, many of whom later founded the cities of Santa Ana, Orange, and Tustin. Santa Ana's modern history began in 1869 when William H. Spurgeon purchased 70 acres from the Yorba heirs and drew up a town plan. Since the land had been part of the Santiago de Santa Ana ranch and since it was also near the Santa Ana River, the town was called Santa Ana.

Soon the new town became prosperous, boasting mail delivery twice a week and a number of stores and residences within its boundaries. Farms also were established throughout the valley; the rich soil and favorable climate permitted the cultivation of several crops. Santa Ana became a commercial center; because of its central location in the valley, it was a natural marketplace for crops produced in the surrounding region that is now Orange County. When rail transport arrived in the area in 1877, the town developed and population increased; in 1886 Santa Ana was incorporated. Three years later Orange County was separated from Los Angeles County and Santa Ana was named the county seat.

World War II brought further development as industry moved into the area. The population of Santa Ana increased from around 49,000 people in 1900 to nearly 210,000 residents in 1950. A city charter, providing for a council-manager form of government, was adopted in 1952. Since World War II Santa Ana has become a financial and governmental center of Orange County.

Efforts began in the 1980s to restore and revitalize the city of Santa Ana, especially its downtown. As a result the city became known for its historic downtown and MainPlace shopping center, which created thousands of jobs in the heart of the city. In 1993 the city gained a designation as an Enterprise Zone by the State of California and in 1999 was recognized as a Federal Empowerment Zone. The tax credits allowed by these designations encouraged development of new and existing business. The development of Artists Village in the downtown area contributed significantly to the city's pride in its arts and culture and the development of neighborhood associations (55 by 1999) also helped bring city residents together. In the mid-1990s city officials took on the challenge of reducing crime in the city, a goal which has been fairly successfully accomplished. In 2007 crime was down by an estimated 64 percent and Santa Ana was considered to be one of the safest among the 50 most populated cities in the nation.

Historical Information: Santa Ana Public Library, History Room, 26 Civic Center Plaza, Santa Ana, CA 92701; telephone (714)647-5267. Santa Ana Mountain Historical Society, 28192 Silverado Canyon Road (PO Box 301), Silverado, CA 92676; telephone (714)649-2216

■ Population Profile

Metropolitan Area Residents

1980: 1,933,000
1990: 2,410,668
2000: 2,846,289
2006 estimate: Not reported
Percent change, 1990–2000: 12.9%
U.S. rank in 1980: 2nd (CMSA)
U.S. rank in 1990: 2nd (CMSA)
U.S. rank in 2000: 2nd (CMSA)

aerialphotoshop.com/David Price 2008

City Residents

1980: 203,713
1990: 293,827
2000: 337,977
2006 estimate: 340,024
Percent change, 1990–2000: 14.8%
U.S. rank in 1980: 69th
U.S. rank in 1990: 52nd
U.S. rank in 2000: 51st

Density: 12,451 people per square mile (2000)

Racial and ethnic characteristics (2005)

White: 155,335
Black: 2,905
American Indian and Alaska Native: 945
Asian: 25,370
Native Hawaiian and Pacific Islander: 546
Hispanic or Latino (may be of any race): 238,773
Other: 112,617

Percent of residents born in state: 38.6% (2000)

Age characteristics (2005)

Population under 5 years old: 31,572
Population 5 to 9 years old: 29,846
Population 10 to 14 years old: 30,114
Population 15 to 19 years old: 23,019
Population 20 to 24 years old: 24,996
Population 25 to 34 years old: 49,187
Population 35 to 44 years old: 44,954
Population 45 to 54 years old: 32,269
Population 55 to 59 years old: 11,294
Population 60 to 64 years old: 6,325
Population 65 to 74 years old: 10,370
Population 75 to 84 years old: 6,657
Population 85 years and older: 1,699
Median age: 27 years

Births (2006, Metropolitan Division)

Total number: 46,345

Deaths (2006, Metropolitan Division)

Total number: 16,689

Money income (2005)

Per capita income: $14,110
Median household income: $47,438
Total households: 68,790

Number of households with income of...

less than $10,000: 3,269
$10,000 to $14,999: 3,999
$15,000 to $24,999: 6,593
$25,000 to $34,999: 10,443
$35,000 to $49,999: 11,537
$50,000 to $74,999: 14,744
$75,000 to $99,999: 8,205
$100,000 to $149,999: 7,870
$150,000 to $199,999: 1,406
$200,000 or more: 724

Percent of families below poverty level: 8.8% (2005)

2005 FBI Crime Index Property: 10,292

2005 FBI Crime Index Violent: 1,845

■ Municipal Government

In accordance with a charter adopted in 1952, Santa Ana operates under a council-manager form of government. The city is governed by a council consisting of six council members and an elected mayor. Council members are nominated from wards but are elected by voters from the entire city. Council members are elected to four-year terms and are limited to two consecutive terms. The mayor is elected every two years. The council hires a city manager.

Head Official: Mayor Miguel A. Pulido (since 1986; term expires November 2008)

Total Number of City Employees: 1,753 full-time (2007)

City Information: Santa Ana City Council, 20 Civic Center Plaza, PO Box 1998 M31, Santa Ana, CA 92701; telephone (714)647-6900; www.ci.santa-ana.ca.us

■ Economy

Major Industries and Commercial Activity

Santa Ana in 2006 boasted of having more than 13,000 businesses; major industries include a mix of retail trade, services, and manufacturing firms.

Government is a major employer in Santa Ana; as the county seat, the city has offices at the county, state, and federal levels. Santa Ana is also a financial center. The aerospace and electronics industries, among the area's largest employers, figure significantly in the city's economy. Santa Ana's major employers in 2006 were First American Title, Orange County Register, Western Medical Center, Ingram Micro, and Diversified Maintenance Service.

Santa Ana was the recipient of California's largest commercial loan program, which contributed to redevelopment of the downtown district. Part of the project were 10 new banking and financial buildings and the Civic Center, which houses city, county, state, and federal government buildings. Several *Fortune* 500 companies, including Textron's Cherry Division, ITT Cannon, and Xerox, are located in Santa Ana.

Tourism is a major industry in Santa Ana and Orange County. Within a radius of 10 miles of the city are several of California's most popular tourist attractions, such as Disneyland, Knott's Berry Farm, and southern California beaches. Forty-five million people visit the Orange County area each year, spending more than $8 billion.

Items and goods produced: sugar; glass products; plumbing material; foam rubber products; dehydrating, electronic, and sporting equipment; concentrates; extracts; agricultural machinery; perfumes; feed; cement pipes; soft drinks; rivets; fasteners; canned and dried fruits and vegetables; packaged walnuts and oranges; poultry

Incentive Programs—New and Existing Companies

Local programs: The Orange County Business Council (OCBC) concentrates on attracting and retaining high-quality, high-paying and low-polluting jobs to Orange County. For business development, the OCBC is the single business point-of-contact for economic development and related business information in Orange County. As well, the OCBC leads the county in ensuring a quality workforce and advocating legislation to benefit businesses.

State programs: A variety of programs administered by state and federal sources are available to Santa Ana businesses. Parts of Santa Ana are designated as a Federal Empowerment Zone. Santa Ana is currently the only town west of the Rockies to receive such a designation. As a Federal Urban Empowerment Zone, the city of Santa Ana receives up to $100 million in performance grants to be used in the designated area. Up to $10 milllion will be paid out each year through 2008. Part of the city also has a designation as an Enterprise Zone. Enterprise Zone Credits include a Sales and Use Tax Credit and Hiring Tax Credits. Research & Development Tax

Credit is available of up to 15 percent against bank and corporate tax liability for certain in-house research. An additional 24 percent credit is available for basic research payments to outside organizations. This is one of the highest research and development tax credits in the nation. A Child Care Tax Credit is available for companies establishing on-site child care facilities. A Net Operating Loss Carryover and New Market Tax Credits are also available. A Work Opportunity Tax Credit is offered for employers who hire individuals from certain target groups.

Job training programs: The Santa Ana Work/ Opportunities/Resources/Knowledge (W/O/R/K/) Center is a non-profit organization comprised of a partnership between several agencies: The Santa Ana Workforce Investment Board, State Employment Development Department, Santa Ana College, and Orange County Social Services. The W/O/R/K Center is designed to meet the job training and placement needs of the community. The center was awarded the largest grant ($867,000) given by the State of California for such programs in 2000. The Marketplace Education Center in downtown Santa Ana offers free non-credit courses to those seeking occupational training and basic skills. The Workforce Development and Career Center, sponsored in part by Santa Ana College, serves as a resource for continuing education and for specialized training programs for local business and industry. The Workplace Learning Resource Center, available in Santa Ana through the Rancho Santiago Community College District, is part of a statewide network that offers assessments and low cost customized on-site training for some businesses. The California Employment Training Panel assists businesses through performance-based customized training contracts for new or existing employees. Reimbursement of costs for developing, implementing, and completing training programs may range from $1,500 to $2,000 per employee.

Development Projects

Major recent commercial developments in Santa Ana include the MainPlace regional shopping center, MacArthur Place mixed use area, and the Santa Ana Auto Mall. More than 5,000 acres of the city are within six focused redevelopment areas that include a variety of governmental, infrastructure, retail and residential projects.

As of 2007, Santa Ana was pursuing a development plan for a centralized area encompassing over 350 acres including the train depot, downtown, the Civic Center, the Santa Ana Boulevard Corridor, and the Logan and Lacy neighborhoods. The purpose of the Renaissance Specific Plan is to create a land use plan that builds upon the urban environment, while at the same time ensuring that future development continues to enhance the area's strengths.

City Place, an 18-acre mixed-use project located across the street from the MainPlace Mall, will soon include 242 live/work townhomes and 60,000 square feet of restaurants and retail space. There are also plans for a 33-story residential tower, which includes a proposal for 350 units for sale. Other residential and mixed-use projects in the works in 2007 included Santiago Street Lofts, Olson Lofts, the SKYLINE at MacArthur Place, Promenade Pointe, and Cordoba Courtyards. Also, One Broadway Plaza, an office tower, once constructed will be Orange County's tallest building at 37 stories.

Economic Development Information: Orange County Business Council, 2 Park Plaza, Suite 100, Irvine, CA 92614-5904; telephone (949)476-2242; fax (949) 476-9240.

Commercial Shipping

The John Wayne Airport has two all-cargo airlines. Rail freight service is provided by the Southern Pacific and Union Pacific railroads. The Los Angeles International Airport (LAX), about 37 miles northwest of the city, has 1,000 cargo flights each day. Handling facilities include the 98-acre Century Cargo Complex, the 57.4-acre Imperial Complex, the Imperial Cargo Center, and several terminals on the south side of the airport. More than 100 motor freight carriers link Santa Ana with markets throughout the country; overnight delivery service is available to several West Coast cities as well as to Tucson, Phoenix, Las Vegas, and Reno.

Labor Force and Employment Outlook

Santa Ana has a young, well-trained work force that comprises over 10 percent of Orange County's labor pool. The workforce numbered nearly 160,000 in 2006. Employment forecasts in the Orange County area are positive, with growth of 15 percent expected between 2001 and 2008. Unionization is prevalent in manufacturing, trucking, retailing, the hotel industry, warehousing, and some grocery and drugstore chains. The top three business activities are retail trade; services, hotels, personal, and business; and manufacturing.

The following is a summary of data regarding the Santa Ana-Anaheim-Irvine Metropolitan Division metropolitan area labor force, 2006 annual averages.

Size of nonagricultural labor force: 1,520,100

Number of workers employed in . . .

construction and mining: 107,600
manufacturing: 183,400
trade, transportation and utilities: 270,700
information: 31,700
financial activities: 139,000

professional and business services: 274,800
educational and health services: 138,900
leisure and hospitality: 169,500
other services: 47,900
government: 156,500

Average hourly earnings of production workers employed in manufacturing: $14.59

Unemployment rate: 4.7% (June 2007)

Largest private employers
(2007)   *Number of employees*

New Century Mortgage	Not available
First American Title	Not available
Orange County Register	Not available
Western Medical Center	Not available
Power Wave Technologies	Not available
ITT	Not available
Cannon	Not available
Open Source	Not available
United Building Services	Not available
Diversified Maintenance	Not available
Ingram Micro, Inc.	Not available

Cost of Living

The following is a summary of data regarding key cost of living factors for the Santa Ana area.

2007 (1st quarter) ACCRA Average House Price: $855,232

2007 (1st quarter) ACCRA Cost of Living Index: 154.7

State income tax rate: 1.0% to 9.3%

State sales tax rate: 7.25%

Local income tax rate: None

Local sales tax rate: 1.25% county and city, plus any district taxes imposed by the county (0.50% to 1.0%); comes into effect through general election

Property tax rate: limited to 1% of assessed value by state law. The local taxing body can add bonds approved by popular vote.

Economic Information: Santa Ana Chamber of Commerce, 2020 N. Broadway, 2nd Floor, Santa Ana, CA 92702; telephone (714)541-5353; fax (714)541-2238

■ Education and Research

Elementary and Secondary Schools

The Santa Ana Unified School District (SAUSD), the largest in Orange County and the fifth largest in the state (in 2007), is administered by a five-member, nonpartisan board of education that appoints a superintendent.

The district boasts of past distinctions such as two Nationally Distinguished Schools, several State Distinguished Schools, and numerous first or second place "Golden Bell" awards from the California School Boards Association for excellence in innovative programs. McFadden Intermediate received a GEARINGUp federal grant in 2004 to create the McFadden Mathematics Institute; the Institute offers advanced instruction and technology-based materials for seventh and eighth grade students with proven math skills. Several schools offer year-round programs. As of 2007, about 92 percent of the student body was Hispanic. The school system offers some bilingual education programs.

The Achievement Reinforcement Center opened in December 2006 as an alternative school environment for at-risk students. A number of pre-K/early childhood programs are available. The system also has a Gifted and Talented Education (GATE) program. Occupational programs are available for high school students. There were eight charter schools in the district in 2007.

The following is a summary of data regarding the Santa Ana Unified School as of the 2005–2006 school year.

Total enrollment: 58,832

Number of facilities

elementary schools: 36
junior high/middle schools: 9
senior high schools: 8
other: 10

Student/teacher ratio: 22.3:1

Teacher salaries (2005–06)

elementary median: $61,360
junior high/middle median: $62,040
secondary median: $63,410

Funding per pupil: $7,519

A variety of private schools also operate in the city.

Public Schools Information: Santa Ana Unified School District, 1601 East Chestnut Avenue, Santa Ana, CA 92701; telephone (714)558-5501; www.sausd.us

Colleges and Universities

Santa Ana College, the fourth oldest junior college in the state, offers numerous programs leading to an associate's degree in science or arts or a vocational certificate of competency. Enrollment in 2006 was about 25,231 students. The college also offers a number of local off-site programs. The Centennial Education Center offers non-credit continuing education that includes English-as-a-Second-Language courses, citizenship preparation, high school completion, parent education, and vocational training. The Marketplace Education Center offers free non-credit courses to those seeking occupational training, basic skills, English language development and related instruction for independent living. A Regional Fire Training Center offers classes for students enrolled in the Fire Academy program as well as for fire professionals seeking continuing education credits. Santa Ana College is part of the Rancho Santiago Community College District, which also sponsors Santiago Canyon College in Orange.

The Santa Ana campus of Newbridge College offers diploma programs for surgical technology, medical laboratory technicians, medial assistants, ultrasound technicians, and medical office administration. The Technological Institute of Southern California offers career based programs in a variety of fields, including data entry processing, electronic fuel injection, fashion design, floral design, medical office administration, and professional child care.

Located within commuting distance of Santa Ana, other Orange County colleges include the University of California at Irvine, California State University at Fullerton, and Chapman College in Orange.

Libraries and Research Centers

The Santa Ana Public Library system operates a main library at Civic Center Plaza and the Newhope Library Learning Center. The main library houses the Santa Ana History Room, a computer lab, and a Passport Application Acceptance Center. The Newhope Library Learning Center also contains a computer lab. A bookmobile is available for service to shut-ins. Holdings consist of more than 335,000 volumes and more than 400 periodicals, plus CDs, tapes, videos, and maps. Special collections include California and Santa Ana history, foreign language books and cassettes, and federal and state documents.

The Orange County Public Library, based in Santa Ana and operating 32 branches, holds more than 2.5 million volumes and 5,000 periodicals and maintains a special collection of the Orange County Law Library documents. Other libraries and research centers are affiliated with government agencies, colleges, hospitals, and private corporations.

Research activities in botany are conducted at the Ranch Santa Ana Botanical Garden. The Apex Research Institute in Santa Ana conducts clinical trials for several major pharmaceutical companies.

Public Library Information: Santa Ana Public Library, 26 Civic Center Plaza, Santa Ana, CA 92701; telephone (714)647-5250; www.ci.santa-ana.ca.us/

library. Orange County Public Library, 1501 East St. Andrew Place, Santa Ana, CA 92705; telephone (714) 551-7159; www.ocpl.org

■ Health Care

Three general hospitals are located in Santa Ana. They offer a range of specialties such as cardiac rehabilitation and hospice care. The largest medical facility is Western Medical Center with 283 beds, a Level II Trauma Center, and 800 primary care physicians. Western also hosts the Grossman Burn Center, a seven-bed specialized care unit; a 16-bed Neonatal Intensive Care Unit; and a kidney transplant unit. Coastal Communities Hospital is a 178-bed acute care hospital offering community health programs as well as basic health care services, an emergency room, and outpatient surgical units. Kindred Hospital–Santa Ana is a long-term, acute care facility. Also located in Santa Ana is Bienstar Medical Center, which specializes in care for women, particularly prenatal and family planning services.

Nearby is the teaching hospital of the medical school at the University of California at Irvine; other medical schools in the area are the University of California at Los Angeles, the University of Southern California, and Loma Linda University.

■ Recreation

Sightseeing

A major tourist attraction in Orange County is the historical district in downtown Santa Ana. Placed on the National Register of Historic Places in 1984, the 21-block area is among the largest such districts in the state of California. It contains 100 buildings constructed between 1877 and 1934; among them are the Old County Courthouse (now a museum featuring changing exhibits related to local and regional history), the Fox West Coast Theatre, and Old City Hall. The district also features homes of prominent Santa Ana citizens. Tours of the Dr. Willella Howe-Waffle House, a restored Queen Anne Style home built in the 1880s, are available the first Saturday of each month.

Fairhaven Memorial Park is situated on 73 acres and features an arboretum harboring nearly 1,000 trees and numerous plants from around the world. The park's historic mausoleum was built in 1916 of European marble and granite, with handcrafted stained-glass windows.

The Santa Ana Zoo is home to 260 animals and 84 species; among the rare and endangered species living at the zoo are the ring-tailed lemur, the margay cat, the white-handed gibbon, and the golden lion tamarin; the zoo welcomes 270,000 visitors each year. There are several other points of interest in Orange County, including world-famous Disneyland amusement park in Anaheim, and Knott's Berry Farm and the Movieland Wax Museum in Buena Park.

Within driving distance of Santa Ana are the Universal Studios tour, Magic Mountain, Raging Waters amusement park, Sea World, and the San Diego Zoo.

Arts and Culture

More than 1,000 cultural organizations are active in Orange County; among them are symphony orchestras, ballet companies, theater groups, and modern and folk dance troupes. Santa Ana is the headquarters for the Pacific Symphony Orchestra, which presents its summer season at Irvine Meadows Amphitheater and performs its regular season concerts at Segerstrom Hall in the Orange County Performing Arts Center at Costa Mesa. The center is one of three theater facilities in the nation to house four performing arts—musical theater, symphony, opera, and ballet.

Among the other orchestras in the metropolitan area are the Orange County Youth Symphony and the American Youth Symphony. Theater groups include the South Coast Repertory Theatre; dance companies are the Gloria Newman Dance Theatre and the Penrod-Plastino Movement Theatre. The Santa Ana Performing Arts and Event Center is home to Tibbies Great American Cabaret dinner theater. A variety of special events and banquets are held there throughout the year.

Artists Village is a thriving area of art galleries and studios. It includes the Santora Arts Complex, renowned for its flamboyant churrigueresque architecture, which offers the works of more than 38 artists in five galleries, including the Santa Ana College gallery; the Empire Market Building, which contains several galleries, artists' studios and a small theater; and the Cal State Fullerton Grand Central Art Center, which houses a student gallery and studios and the Alternative Repertory Theatre. The Orange County Center for Contemporary Art is also located in the village.

One of Orange County's most prominent museums is located in Santa Ana. The famous Bowers Museum of Cultural Art, a Spanish mission style building, houses collections pertinent to Orange County and California history; Native American, Pacific Rim, and African cultures; and natural history. It also features a hands-on Kidseum, a five-star restaurant, and shops. The Discovery Science Center houses hands-on exhibits in themed areas that include Discovery Stadium, Quake Zone, Dynamic Earth, Air and Space Exploration, and Kidstation.

The Centennial Heritage Museum (formerly known as the Discovery Museum of Orange County) has exhibits that chronicle the history of Orange County back to the nineteenth century. Special demonstrations and hands-on activities draw visitors to imagine what life was like in that earlier time in history. The Natural History Museum in nearby Newport Beach displays fossils unique to Orange County and marine life such as whales and walrus. Art museums in the area include the Laguna Beach Art Museum Annex, the Muckenthaler Cultural Center, and the Newport Harbor Art Museum.

Festivals and Holidays

The Black History Parade and Festival takes place in February. Santa Ana College serves as the site for the annual Memorial Day Festival. The annual Imagination Celebration (usually in April and May) features art and cultural programs at a variety of venues throughout Orange County, including some within Santa Ana. The annual Fiestas Patrias Santa Ana celebrates the independence day of Mexico (September 16). The Santa Ana Zoo hosts an annual Boo at the Zoo event for families in October. The same month, the Santa Ana Historic Preservation Society sponsors a Cemetery Tour.

Sports for the Spectator

While there are no professional sports teams in Santa Ana, residents are within an easy drive of sporting events in Anaheim. The Major League Los Angeles Angels of Anaheim baseball team, World Series Champion in 2002 and American League West Champions in 2007, plays its home games at Angel Stadium of Anaheim. The National Hockey League Anaheim Ducks and the National Lacrosse League's Anaheim Storm play at Honda Center.

The Santa Ana College Dons play in the Orange Empire Conference. Sports include football, soccer, water polo, volleyball, cross country, basketball, baseball, badminton, golf, tennis, track and field, and wrestling. The Fullerton State Titans and the Anteaters of the University of California at Irvine field National Collegiate Athletic Association (NCAA) Division I teams. Los Alamitos Race Course features parimutuel thoroughbred and harness racing.

Sports for the Participant

Santa Ana's mild climate invites year-round athletic enjoyment. Some of Southern California's finest beaches are minutes away, and the city is located only 12 miles from the Pacific Ocean. The city maintains a system of 41 parks and 11 bicycle trails. There are also 17 city recreation centers and 5 municipal swimming pools. Mountain ski resorts are within easy driving distance.

Shopping and Dining

With 25 incorporated cities in Orange County, each with its own central shopping district and community shopping centers, the shopper has endless opportunities. More than 20 major regional shopping malls feature national department stores, specialty shops, and boutiques. Santa Ana is also within easy driving distance of Beverly Hills' famous Rodeo Drive, which is lined with luxury and designer shops.

In the city itself, prime shopping locations include the South Coast Plaza Village, which is a European-style marketplace, and MainPlace, a Westfield shopping mall.

Santa Ana has dozens of restaurants that offer a variety of cuisine, including traditional American, Continental, Italian, Asian, and Mexican dishes.

Visitor Information: Anaheim/Orange County Visitor and Convention Bureau, 800 West Katella Avenue, Anaheim, CA 92802; telephone (714)765-8888; fax (714)991-8963; www.anaheimoc.org. The California Welcome Center–Santa Ana, Westfield MainPlace, 2800 N. Main St., Suite 112, Santa Ana, CA 92705; telephone (714)667-0400; www.visitcwc.com

■ Convention Facilities

The largest convention facilities are located in nearby Anaheim. These include the Anaheim Convention Center, which houses 815,000 square feet of exhibit space, making it the largest exhibit facility on the West Coast. The Marriott Anaheim offers 35,000 square feet of exhibit space, three flexible ballrooms and eleven meeting rooms. The Disneyland Hotel at Disneyland Resort offers dozens of meeting spaces, the largest one being the 50,000-square-foot Disneyland Exhibit Hall in Magic Tower. There is a banquet hall to accommodate up to 2,000 people and three restaurants.

A number of Santa Ana's hotels and motels provide conference and convention facilities. Among the major hotels with meeting rooms are Saddleback Inn, Compri, the Grand Plaza Hotel, and Quality Inn Suites. The Doubletree Hotel Santa Ana offers 253 hotel rooms, two board rooms, a 7,000-square-foot ballroom, reception space for more than 1,000 participants, and private dining.

Convention Information: Anaheim/Orange County Visitor and Convention Bureau, 800 West Katella Avenue, Anaheim, CA 92802; telephone (714)765-8888; fax (714)991-8963; www.anaheimoc.org.

■ Transportation

Approaching the City

Several airports are located in the Santa Ana metropolitan area. The John Wayne Airport in Santa Ana, owned and operated by Orange County, is about 5 miles from downtown. It is served by 11 commercial airlines and 3 commuter lines, all providing transportation for 9.6 million passengers each year. Los Angeles International Airport (LAX), located about 37 miles northwest of the city, is one of the top ten largest airports in the world in terms of passengers handled. The airport is served by over 50 airlines with thousands of flights each year. Long Beach Airport is served by four airlines and LA/Ontario

International Airport supports 12 airlines. The Fullerton Municipal Airport is a general aviation airport accommodating about 600 planes.

Four major highways lead into Santa Ana: Interstate-5 (the Santa Ana Freeway), State Route 55 (Costa Mesa Freeway), State Route 57 (Orange Freeway), and State Route 22 (Garden Grove Freeway). Amtrak and Greyhound have stops at the Santa Ana Transit Terminal (also known as the Santa Ana Regional Transportation Center).

Traveling in the City

The Orange County Transportation Authority operates buses daily with about 80 routes throughout Orange County. OCTA Metrolink, a regional commuter rail system, links travelers to activity centers in Orange and surrounding counties. The Metrolink stops at the Santa Ana Transit Terminal. Special services are available for the handicapped and the hearing impaired. The Regional Transportation Center is a hub for Amtrak, intercity buses, urban transit, a future rapid transit system, taxi cabs, an airport shuttle, and other transportation services.

■ Communications

Newspapers and Magazines

The Orange County Register is the morning daily published in Santa Ana with a circulation of about 300,000. Readers also find some local news in the *Los Angeles Times–Orange County*, published in Costa Mesa. *OC Weekly,* an alternative press, and *Excélsior,* a Spanish-language newspaper, are both published in Santa Ana. *Azteca News* is another weekly Spanish community newspaper. *SqueezeOC* is a weekly arts and entertainment paper.

Television and Radio

The city sponsors its own local access television station (Channel 3). While there are no major television stations in the city, there are about thirteen television stations serving the city from the surrounding area; cable is also available. Only one radio station, KWIZ (in Spanish), broadcasts directly from Santa Ana. However, the city receives broadcasts from about 69 AM and FM radio stations in the area.

Media Information: *Orange County Register,* 625 N. Grand Ave., PO Box 11626, Santa Ana, CA 92702; telephone (714)796-7000; www.ocregister.com

Santa Ana Online

City of Santa Ana Arts and Culture Information home page. Available www.aplaceforart.org

City of Santa Ana home page. Available www.ci.santa-ana.ca.us

Orange County Business Council home page.
Available www.ocbc.org

Orange County Department of Education home
page. Available www.ocde.k12.ca.us

Orange County Register home page. Available www
.ocregister.com

Santa Ana Chamber of Commerce home page.
Available www.santaanacc.com

Santa Ana History home page (Historical
Preservation Society). Available www
.SantaAnaHistory.com

Santa Ana Public Library home page. Available
www.ci.santa-ana.ca.us/library

Santa Ana Unified School District home page.
Available www.sausd.k12.ca.us

BIBLIOGRAPHY

Haas, Lisbeth, *Conquests and Historical Identities in California, 1769–1936* (Berkeley, CA: University of California Press, 1995)

Colorado

The State in Brief

Nickname: Centennial State

Motto: Nil sine numine (Nothing without providence)

Flower: Rocky Mountain columbine

Bird: Lark bunting

Area: 104,093 square miles (2000; U.S. rank 8th)

Elevation: Ranges from 3,350 feet to 14,433 feet above sea level

Climate: Dry and sunny, with a wide daily and seasonal variation in temperature and with alpine conditions in the high mountains

Admitted to Union: August 1, 1876

Capital: Denver

Head Official: Governor Bill Ritter (D) (until 2010)

Population

  1980: 2,890,000
  1990: 3,377,000
  2000: 4,302,015
  2006 estimate: 4,753,377
  Percent change, 1990–2000: 30.6%
  U.S. rank in 2006: 22nd
  Percent of residents born in state: 42.08% (2006)
  Density: 45.0 people per square mile (2006)
  2006 FBI Crime Index Total: 182,670

Racial and Ethnic Characteristics (2006)

  White: 3,934,971
  Black or African American: 177,902
  American Indian and Alaska Native: 41,161
  Asian: 133,079
  Native Hawaiian and Pacific Islander: 3,745
  Hispanic or Latino (may be of any race): 934,410
  Other: 337,442

Age Characteristics (2006)

  Population under 5 years old: 338,995
  Population 5 to 19 years old: 958,152
  Percent of population 65 years and over: 10.0%
  Median age: 35.4

Vital Statistics

  Total number of births (2006): 68,957
  Total number of deaths (2006): 30,419
  AIDS cases reported through 2005: 8,480

Economy

  Major industries: Services, manufacturing, communications, transportation, agriculture
  Unemployment rate (2006): 5.5%
  Per capita income (2006): $27,750
  Median household income (2006): $52,015
  Percentage of persons below poverty level (2006): 12.0%
  Income tax rate: 4.63%
  Sales tax rate: 2.9%

Aurora

■ The City in Brief

Founded: 1891 (incorporated 1903)

Head Official: City Manager Ronald S. Miller (appointed 1997)

City Population

1980: 159,000
1990: 222,103
2000: 276,393
2006 estimate: 303,582
Percent change, 1990–2000: 24.6%
U.S. rank in 1980: Not available
U.S. rank in 1990: Not available
U.S. rank in 2000: 61st

Metropolitan Area Population

1980: Not available
1990: Not available
2000: Not available
2006 estimate: Not available
Percent change, 1990–2000: Not available
U.S. rank in 1980: Not available
U.S. rank in 1990: Not available
U.S. rank in 2000: Not available

Area: 142.7 square miles

Elevation: 5,435 feet above sea level

Average Annual Temperature: 64° F

Average Annual Precipitation: 17.69 inches

Major Economic Sectors: services, wholesale and retail trade, government

Unemployment Rate: 3.9% (June 2007)

Per Capita Income: $23,060 (2005)

2005 FBI Crime Index Property: 14,718

2005 FBI Crime Index Violent: 1,836

Major Colleges and Universities: The Community College of Aurora, University of Denver Daniels School of Business, University of Colorado at Denver, Metropolitan State College of Denver, Community College of Denver, Colorado School of Mines

Daily Newspaper: *Aurora Sentinel*

■ Introduction

Aurora began as a small farmer's and rancher's town on the frontier. For much of the twentieth century, Aurora was seen as a suburb of its larger neighbor Denver, but its strong growth and easy livability soon distinguished Aurora as a city in its own right. Today, set on 144 square miles beneath the towering Rocky Mountains, Aurora is Colorado's third-largest city. It is known for its beautiful weather, proximity to a plethora of outdoor activities and cultural opportunities, and pro-business climate.

■ Geography and Climate

Aurora is located just east of Denver on high plains at the foot of the Rocky Mountains. These mountains, reaching higher than 14,000 feet, are the dominant feature of the area. Much of the area's precipitation tends to fall as snow on the Rockies rather than as storms on the plains, sparing Aurora itself, and the city thus enjoys abundant sunshine.

Aurora has four seasons and an annual average high temperature of 64 degrees. The region's climate is semi-arid and relatively mild. The city has the lowest average relative humidity of 25 major cities surveyed on a list that includes Los Angeles, San Francisco, Dallas, and Minneapolis.

Area: 142.7 square miles

Elevation: 5,435 feet above sea level

Average Temperature: 64° F

Average Annual Precipitation: 17.69 inches

■ History

The City of Aurora got its start under a different name, in 1891, when westward-moving Chicagoan Donald Fletcher staked out a town named Fletcher on the high plains beneath the Rocky Mountains. In 1907 residents decided to rename their town Aurora, after the Latin word for dawn. The town remained a sleepy one until 1921, when the United States government selected Aurora to build a new army hospital, Fitzsimons Army Hospital. The new facility treated the wounded—especially those affected by mustard gas and tuberculosis—during World War I and provided an impetus to growth in the small town just outside of Denver. By 1929, the town had reached 2,000 residents and was finally recognized by the state of Colorado. Sewers, roads and fire stations were built. During the Great Depression, Fitzsimons was considered for cost-cutting closure by the Army, but the congressional delegation from Aurora managed to save the facility from that fate; in fact, when President Roosevelt visited the facility, shortly afterwards, he decided instead to allocate more funds for its improvement.

The Second World War proved to be another boon for Aurora's infrastructure. In 1942 the Army Air Corps built Buckley Field (later renamed the Naval Air Station, then Buckley Air National Guard Base), followed by Lowry Field, further increasing the military presence in the city. By 1960, Aurora had accumulated 60,000 residents. Growth continued through the 1970s, helped along in part by the construction of a new highway system through the Denver area that connected Aurora to more of its Western neighbors. Though Aurora's economy was based strongly on the U.S. military presence, it remained closely tied in with that of nearby Denver. In the 1980s Denver, along with most of Colorado and its close neighbor Aurora, experienced serious economic setbacks as energy prices fell and plans for oil shale development were curtailed. The 1990s represented an economic comeback of sorts for Aurora, as population grew to 292,393 residents by the end of the decade. The decade also saw the expansion of the aerospace engineering sector in Aurora, as well as the beginning of biotechnology as a major local industry. However, the city experienced a major setback in the mid-90s when first Lowry Air Force Base and then Fitzsimons were targeted for closure. In 1995 officials from the City of Aurora, University of Colorado Health Sciences Center, and the

University of Colorado Hospital presented the U.S. Department of Defense with a plan to transform the decommissioned base as a world-class medical campus. The government agreed, and work continued for over a decade on Fitzsimons. By 2004, a number of facilities within the base had been completed, including the University of Colorado Hospital and Health Sciences Center, Rocky Mountain Lions Eye Institute, the Nighthorse Campbell Native Health Building, Research Complex I and Colorado Bioscience Park Aurora. By the early part of the twenty-first century, Aurora had established itself as a thriving city in its own right and was no longer considered merely a large suburb of Denver.

Historical Information: Boulder Public Library, Carnegie Branch Library for Local History, 1125 Pine St., Boulder, CO 80302; telephone (303)441-3110

■ Population Profile

Metropolitan Area Residents

  1980: Not available
  1990: Not available
  2000: Not available
  2006 estimate: Not available
  Percent change, 1990–2000: Not available
  U.S. rank in 1980: Not available
  U.S. rank in 1990: Not available
  U.S. rank in 2000: Not available

City Residents

  1980: 159,000
  1990: 222,103
  2000: 276,393
  2006 estimate: 303,582
  Percent change, 1990–2000: 24.6%
  U.S. rank in 1980: Not available
  U.S. rank in 1990: Not available
  U.S. rank in 2000: 61st

Density: Not available

Racial and ethnic characteristics (2005)

  White: 202,340
  Black: 44,235
  American Indian and Alaska Native: 3,162
  Asian: 12,459
  Native Hawaiian and Pacific Islander: 252
  Hispanic or Latino (may be of any race): 79,494
  Other: 20,471

Percent of residents born in state: 33.9% (2006)

Age characteristics (2005)

  Population under 5 years old: 25,274

Airphoto - Jim Wark

Population 5 to 9 years old: 20,443
Population 10 to 14 years old: 23,236
Population 15 to 19 years old: 20,427
Population 20 to 24 years old: 20,724
Population 25 to 34 years old: 49,670
Population 35 to 44 years old: 44,887
Population 45 to 54 years old: 37,918
Population 55 to 59 years old: 16,934
Population 60 to 64 years old: 8,173
Population 65 to 74 years old: 13,253
Population 75 to 84 years old: 8,532
Population 85 years and older: 1,846
Median age: 32.1 years

Births (2006, MSA)

Total number: 37,672

Deaths (2006, MSA)

Total number: 14,824

Money income (2005)

Per capita income: $23,060
Median household income: $48,309
Total households: 111,072

Number of households with income of...

less than $10,000: 6,663
$10,000 to $14,999: 5,438
$15,000 to $24,999: 11,665
$25,000 to $34,999: 15,706
$35,000 to $49,999: 17,815
$50,000 to $74,999: 26,117
$75,000 to $99,999: 14,110
$100,000 to $149,999: 9,348
$150,000 to $199,999: 2,350
$200,000 or more: 1,860

Percent of families below poverty level: 9.9% (2005)

2005 FBI Crime Index Property: 14,718

2005 FBI Crime Index Violent: 1,836

■ Municipal Government

Aurora operates under a council-manager form of government. Councilmembers are elected and the city manager is appointed. The city manager is in charge of hiring city officials and preparing a recommended budget for the council, while city council sets long- and short-term goals and engages in strategic planning. There are also three deputy city managers and an assistant city manager.

Head Official: City Manager Ronald S. Miller (since 1997)

Total Number of City Employees: 3,826 (2007)

City Information: City of Aurora, 15151 E. Alameda Parkway, First Floor, Aurora, CO 80011; telephone (303)739-7000; email access@auroragov.org

■ Economy

Major Industries and Commercial Activity

The aerospace and bioscience industries are the two most significant industries in Aurora. The city is home to major aerospace suppliers that include the Boeing Company, Lockheed Martin, Northrop Grumman and Raytheon Company, which employ a combined 4,600 workers. Bioscience research is conducted at the University of Colorado at Denver Health Sciences Center, The Children's Hospital, and Colorado Bioscience Park Aurora.

In recent years the city has also become a hub for the transportation and logistics industries; between 1995 and 2007, the warehouse and distribution real estate inventory in Aurora's I-70 corridor more than doubled to about 16 million square feet. Major corporations with warehouses in Aurora include General Motors, L'Oreal, Kroger, Whole Foods, and Simmons. The area is also home to several third-party warehousing companies, such as Advanced Logistics, Usco, and Acme Distribution.

Merrick & Company, an internationally known engineering and architectural firm, is also headquartered in Aurora.

Items and goods produced: mattresses, biotechnology, airplane parts, defense technology

Incentive Programs—New and Existing Companies

Local programs: Aurora's low tax rates are a draw for businesses looking to relocate to the city. City council also has the power, on a case-by-case basis, to offer new, expanding, and existing businesses financial incentives, usually in the form of Aurora local sales and use tax rebates. Additionally, portions of Aurora have been designated by the state as enterprise zones to encourage investment and job creation.

State programs: The Colorado Office of Economic Development & International Trade offers several types of incentives to attract and retain businesses. Its Infrastructure Assistance Program is designed to create new jobs, mainly in the low- and moderate-income ranges, in certain cities and counties within the state. Other business incentives include enterprise zone tax credits, local property tax incentives, and manufacturing revenue bonds.

Job training programs: The Colorado Community College System has joined with the Colorado Office of Economic Development & International Trade to administer Colorado FIRST/Existing Industry Customized Training Programs. These programs, which received $2.7 million in funding in 2005-2006, are designed to fund employee training for transferable job skills to benefit a company's competitive strength as well as an employee's long-term employment opportunities.

Development Projects

In 2005 the Medical Center of Aurora began work on a new $10-million office building with three stories and 68,000 square feet of space; its anchor tenant is a cardiac care center. As of 2007 a completion date had not been announced.

In 2007 the 578-acre former Fitzsimons Army Medical Center was nearing the end of a $4.3-billion transformation into a major biomedical research center. The plan called for up to 15 million square feet of new construction dedicated to patient care, education, and research. The project was expected to result in the creation of approximately 32,000 jobs. Fitzsimons will be accompanied by an urban village center including a student center and library, 400 to 600 multifamily housing units, plus retail and recreation facilities.

Economic Development Information: Aurora Economic Development Council, 562 Sable Boulevard, Ste. 240, Aurora, CO 80011; telephone (303)340-2101; fax (303)340-2111

Commercial Shipping

Aurora's extensive warehouse industry means that it is also a shipping hub. There are twelve major long-haul trucking companies in Aurora, including Roadway, GP Xpress and Yellow Transportation. Nearby Denver International Airport Denver handled 622 million pounds of cargo in 2006. The Metro Denver area, which includes Aurora and is located strategically between Canada and Mexico, is an ever-expanding center for international trade; Colorado exports of manufactured goods, minerals and agriculture products reached almost $8 billion in 2006, a boost of 17.3 percent over 2005.

Labor Force and Employment Outlook

Colorado has the nation's third most educated workforce. The Aurora workforce is spread fairly evenly thoughout a variety of industries. Thirty-two percent of workers are employed in sales and office occupations; 31 percent in management, professional, and related occupations; 13 percent in the service industry; 11 percent in production, transportation, and material moving; and 10 percent in construction, extraction, and maintenance.

In August 2007 the unemployment rate for the Denver-Aurora metropolitan area was 3.8 percent, back to the level of the late 1990s boom and reflecting a steady drop since a ten-year high of seven percent occurred in 2003. The unemployment rate in Aurora has been below the national average since 2005. In 2007 analysts expected the medical and bioscience industries to continue their growth, thanks in part to the ongoing expansion of the Fitzsimons complex. The warehousing and aerospace industries also appeared to be well-primed to continue expansion. However, the one major foreseeable bump on the region's economic outlook was the real estate industry; in 2006 foreclosures were up in the greater Denver area to record levels, and house sales were down nearly 3 percent from the previous year. That trend was expected to continue and perhaps even escalate in 2007, thanks to the national mortgage crisis in August of that year.

The following is a summary of data regarding the Denver-Aurora metropolitan area labor force, 2006 annual averages.

Size of nonagricultural labor force: 1,214,700

Number of workers employed in...

   construction and mining: 94,100
   manufacturing: 72,200
   trade, transportation and utilities: 239,100
   information: 47,700
   financial activities: 100,700
   professional and business services: 199,800
   educational and health services: 122,900
   leisure and hospitality: 125,200
   other services: 46,400
   government: 166,700

Average hourly earnings of production workers employed in manufacturing: $17.64

Unemployment rate: 3.9% (June 2007)

Largest employers (2007)	*Number of employees*
Raytheon Company	2,600
ADT Security Systems	1,585
Kaiser Permanente	1,493
The Medical Center of Aurora	1,380
Northrop Grumman	1,100
Lockheed Martin Astronautics	800
Wagner Equipment Co.	596
Dex Media	550
Nelnet Group	550
Advantage Security, Inc.	500

Cost of Living

The following is a summary of data regarding several key cost of living factors for the Aurora area.

2007 (1st quarter) ACCRA Average House Price: $356,705

2007 (1st quarter) ACCRA Cost of Living Index: 102.7

State income tax rate: 4.63% of Federal Taxable Income

State sales tax rate: 2.9%

Local income tax rate: 8.0%

Local sales tax rate: 3.75%

Property tax rate: Not available

Economic Information: Aurora Chamber of Commerce, 562 Sable Blvd., Ste. 200 Aurora, CO 80011; telephone (303)344-1500; fax (303)344-1564; email info@aurorachamber.org

■ Education and Research

Elementary and Secondary Schools

The Aurora Public Schools District is the sixth largest in the state of Colorado. The district had an operating budget of $377 million in 2006-2007 and operates 49 schools serving 32,495 students. Nearly 40 percent of the students in the district speak two languages, with the majority of these being native Spanish-speakers. The school district's VISTA 2010 plan is an effort to get every graduating senior to the level of academic acheivement needed to be admitted to college without remediation; nearly 88 percent of the district's students graduate. In 2007 the district was taking the first steps toward creating a "Pilot Schools" program, wherein individual schools would have a greater level of control over budget and curriculum, in order to foster a culture of high expectations. The District operates five charter schools and several alternative and vocational high schools.

Part of the city of Aurora is also served by the Cherry Creek Public Schools District, known for consistently exceeding state and national acheivement standards.

The following is a summary of data regarding the Aurora Public Schools as of the 2005–2006 school year.

Total enrollment: 32,495

Number of facilities

   elementary schools: 31
   junior high/middle schools: 7
   senior high schools: 4
   other: 7

Student/teacher ratio: 18.1:1

Teacher salaries (2005–06)
elementary median: $46,070
junior high/middle median: $47,040
secondary median: $47,990

Funding per pupil: $6,361

There are over 20 private and parochial schools located within the city of Aurora.

Public Schools Information: Aurora Public Schools, 1085 Peoria St., Aurora, CO 80011; telephone (303) 344-8060; email webmaster@aps.k12.co.us

Colleges and Universities

In the Aurora-Denver metropolitan area, there are 21 institutions offering baccalaureate degrees or higher and six colleges that grant associate degrees. The Community College of Aurora offers 32 associate degree programs and 40 certificates in vocational education and technical fields. The school has two campuses, located at Lowry and CentreTech Parkway, and offers classes at seven outreach locations throughout Aurora.

Nearby Denver offers a number of opportunities in higher education, including the University of Denver, which is ranked second in the nation among doctoral and research universities for the percentage of undergraduate students studying abroad. The University of Denver Daniels School of Business has been ranked 7th in the *Wall Street Journal* for producing graduates with high ethical standards. Other area private colleges are Johnson & Wales University, Regis University, and Teikyo Loretto Heights University. Public schools include University of Colorado at Denver, Metropolitan State College of Denver, Community College of Denver, and the Colorado School of Mines. Non-traditional education is well represented by such institutions as the Colorado Free University, which has an open admissions policy and is known for its adult and continuing education programs.

Libraries and Research Centers

There are 103 total libraries within 15 miles of Aurora, seven of which are branches of the Aurora Public Library. The library also operates a Business Resource Center and The Book Outlet, which sells former library books at deeply discounted prices. The Learning Resource Center at the Community College of Aurora features a lending library, career resources, and computer access to online resources.

The greater Denver area, which includes Aurora, boasts a number of other public, special interest, and research libraries. Among them are the Colorado Talking Book Library, the Denver Medical Library, the University of Colorado Law Library, and many high-technology and university-related libraries. The University of Denver's Penrose Library features rare book and manuscript collections, the Beck Archives of Rocky Mountain Jewish Historical Society, and the Carson-Brierly Dance Library.

Research activities in such fields as environmental sciences, allergy and immunology, biochemical genetics, health services, mass spectrometry, biochemical parasitology, alcohol, taste and smell, sports sciences, applied mechanics, public management, social science, mineral law, mass communications, family studies, the Holocaust, Islamic-Judaic studies, and international relations are conducted at centers in the Denver area.

The former Fitzsimons Medical Center, now home to the Anschutz Medical Center, among other facilities, is a major research site for biotechnology firms.

Public Library Information: Aurora Public Library Administrative Offices, 14949 E. Alameda Parkway, Aurora, CO 80012; telephone (303)739-6600; email library@auroragov.org

■ Health Care

The Medical Center of Colorado is Aurora's only full-service hospital and employs a total of 1,500 staff and 450 active physicians at its facilities. The Medical Center has a total of 346 licensed beds and 240 staff beds at its North Campus, South Campus, and Centennial Medical Plaza. The Center offers services in cardiac care, breast cancer care, and emergency response, in addition to a number of educational services and programs. In 2006 the Medical Center of Aurora was named in the top five percent of hospitals for clinical excellence in HealthGrades' Hospital Quality and Clinical Excellence study. The University of Colorado Hospital recently moved to a new campus in Aurora, the Anschutz Medical Campus, which includes a cancer pavilion and eye institute.

Aurora is also close to the University of Colorado at Denver and Health Sciences Center and The Children's Hospital of Colorado.

■ Recreation

Sightseeing

There are a number of interesting historical, natural, and cultural sites for tourists to see, both within Aurora proper or just a day trip away. Nearby Manitou & Pikes Peak Cog Railway is the highest cog railroad in the world and offers tours to the summit of Pikes Peak at 14,110 feet. Near the peak of the mountain lies Garden of the Gods, the famous red rock sandstone formation that is a popular destination for hikers and walkers. Free tours are available. The Cave of the Winds, which also offers free guided tours, features 20 beautiful caverns. The Flying W ranch, in nearby Colorado Springs, is a recreated Old West town from the late 1800s. Visitors love to experience its authentic chuck wagon supper and famous Flying W Wranglers stage show. Also in Colorado Springs is the U.S. Olympic Training Center, where 12,000 athletes train annually.

The Royal Gorge is the world's highest suspension bridge and spans the Arkansas River at a height of 1,050 feet. At the base of the Royal Gorge is offered a 24-mile scenic train ride around the gorge that has been called "the most arresting scenic site in all of American railroading"; another option includes an aerial tram ride though the gorge itself. Tours are available at the Stanley House, an historic hotel dating from 1909, that inspired Stephen King to write *The Shining*. Within driving distance of Aurora are over 30 casinos in Central City and Blackhawk, with over 10,000 slot machines, blackjack tables and poker tables. Central City, an historic old mining town featuring Victorian homes and storefronts, is itself a tourist destination and was once called the "Richest Square Mile on Earth." The Gilpin County Historical Society features artifacts from Colorado's mining days, in addition to featuring the Teller House Museum, where President Grant once stayed. The Leanin' Tree Museum of Western Art displays over 200 paintings and 85 bronze statues. Tours are available at the nearby Anheuser-Busch Brewery for the beer afficianado. The Aurora History Museum features exhibits on the city's past, in addition to the environment, diversity, and contemporary life in Aurora.

Arts and Culture

Although Aurora's Arts District is small, in the early twenty-first century, city leaders placed strong emphasis on maintaining and growing a cultural presence in the city's downtown area. The Original Arts District on East Colfax Avenue is home to the Aurora Fox Theater, which holds a capacity crowd of 245 and is home to the Aurora Fox Theatre Company and the Aurora Fox Children's Theatre Company. The theater also co-sponsors with the Colorado Cultural Connections, *Aurora Sentinel*, *La Voz*, and Colorado Folk Arts Council an annual multi-cultural performance series that highlights Aurora's various ethnic groups. In addition to staging several productions annually, the Children's Theatre Company hosts theater classes, workshops, and summer camps. The Aurora Dance Arts Office, established in 1973, offers 100 classes weekly in various dance disciplines. The Bicentennial Arts Center, originally a satellite building operated as part of the Lowry Air Force Base, is now a pottery center that also organizes music and fine arts programs throughout the city. The nearby Central City Opera House opened in 1878 and is home to an ensemble repertory each summer that performs opera classics in English.

Festivals and Holidays

Art Walks are held by the City of Aurora each June and November and lead participants through local studios, galleries, and shops in Aurora's East End Arts District.

Banks in Harmony is a free concert series held on Thursday nights each summer at various parks throughout Aurora, featuring jazz, big band, Motown, and country performers. Another ongoing summer festival is Flicks on the 'FAX, held on seven summer Saturday nights in Fletcher Plaza, where popular, family-friendly films are shown on the big screen. JavaFest, held in May, is Colorado's only coffee-dedicated festival. The Aurora Asian Film Festival celebrated its 10th anniversary in June 2007. Fiesta Aurora, held each year in June, celebrates the heritage of the city's Latino residents. July brings KidsFest in Bicentennial Park, which is Colorado's largest children's festival. The Fourth of July Spectacular is the largest fireworks display in the metro region. In October, the city hosts Jack-O-Launch at PumpkinFest, which features hay rides, scarecrow making, a pumpkin patch, and music.

Sports for the Spectator

Although Aurora has no professional sports teams of its own, fans can root for the Buffalos at nearby University of Colorado Boulder, who compete in football, men's and women's basketball, cross country, golf, skiing, tennis, track and field, and women's soccer and volleyball. They can also cheer for any of Denver's pro teams, which include the Nuggets in the National Basketball Association, the Major League Baseball Rockies, the National Hockey League's Colorado Avalanche, and the National Football League's Broncos.

Sports for the Participant

In 2004 Aurora was selected as the *Sports Illustrated* Colorado "Sportstown" for its 50th anniversary issue. The city was chosen for its involvement in facilitating and enhancing the athletic experiences of its residents. The same year, the metro region was chosen as the fourth most fit area in the nation by *Men's Fitness Magazine*. The city of Aurora maintains 1,800 acres of developed parkland in 108 sites, which include a variety of athletic fields, playgrounds, picnic shelters, tennis courts, a skateboard bowl, basketball courts, a disc golf course, and a water sprayground. Major trail corridors for biking or walking include Cherry Creek Spillwood Trail, High Line Canal Trail, and Sand Creek Regional Greenway Trail. Popular parks in the region include Horsetooth Reservoir, a state park featuring a mountain lake, and Rocky Mountain National Park, with numerous opportunities for wildlife viewing and hiking. Aurora boasts 14 golf courses and there are a total of 83 within 30 miles of the city. The 212-acre Aurora Sports Park, opened in 2003, is home to 22 multi-use field game areas, one championship soccer field, and 12 youth baseball and softball fields.

Shopping and Dining

Aurora is a mecca for mall shopping. Local complexes include Southlands Shopping Center, Buckingham Square Shopping Center, Gateway Square, Tamarac Square Shopping Center, Simon Malls Town Center at Aurora, and the Aurora Mall. Shoppers can also drive to nearby Denver, Boulder, or Littleton for even more mall selection.

Aurora boasts a variety of restaurants—4,683 within a 15-mile radius. The city has both national chains and local favorites, such as Helga's German Restaurant & Deli or Lupita's Restaurant. Cuisines include Italian, American, German, Mexican, Hawaiian, and more.

Visitor Information: Visitor Information Department, Aurora Chamber of Commerce, 562 Sable Blvd., Ste. 200, Aurora, CO 80011; telephone (303)344-1500; fax (303)344-1564; email info@aurorachamber.org

■ Convention Facilities

The Summit Conference and Events Center in Aurora has 9,000 square feet of meeting space and can accommodate groups of up to 500 people. Nearby Denver offers a plethora of convention and meeting options; the Colorado Convention Center in downtown Denver is within walking distance of more than 7,000 hotel rooms and 300 restaurants. The convention center, located along the river in the heart of downtown, contains more than 600,000 square feet of exhibit space, 100,000 square feet of meeting rooms, two ballrooms (including a 35,000-square-foot ballroom and a 50,000-square-foot ballroom), theater-style seating for 7,000 people, 1,000 covered parking spaces, and state-of-the-art multimedia facilities. The center underwent a massive $268 million expansion that nearly doubled its space, completed in 2003.

The National Western Complex, located at the northern end of the downtown area near I-70, contains a 6,600-seat stadium arena, a 40,000-square-foot exhibit hall, a multi-use events center, and the 120,000-square-foot Hall of Education.

Other meeting and exhibition facilities include the Denver Coliseum, Red Rocks Amphitheater, the Denver Merchandise Mart and Exposition Center, and the Adams County Regional Park Complex.

Convention Information: Denver Metro Convention and Visitors Bureau, 1555 California, Suite 300, Denver, CO 80202; telephone (800)480-2010

■ Transportation

Approaching the City

Aurora is served by the Denver International Airport, which is the fifth busiest airport in the United States and 10th busiest in the world. In 2006 it served a total of 47.3 million passengers, an increase of 9.1 percent over 2005 rates. Aurora is easily accessible through the Interstate 70, Interstate 225, and E-470 thoroughfares.

Traveling in the City

Aurora is served by Denver's Regional Transportation District, which offers 170 bus routes, 14 miles of light rail and SkyRide transportation to and from Denver International Airport. The RTD was named the top transit agency in the United States in 2003. FasTracks, an ambitious expansion of Denver's public transportation system, was scheduled to be completed by 2016.

■ Communications

Newspapers and Magazines

The only paid newspaper published in Aurora is the *Aurora Sentinel,* a weekly with a subscription of around 7,000. The company also distributes the *Aurora Sentinel Free Daily* four days a week. Residents can get their daily news from *The Denver Post* and the *Rocky Mountain News,* both published in nearby Denver. *Minority Golf Magazine* is published in Aurora, and other area magazines include *Colorado Country Life, Colorado Outdoors,* and *The Bloomsbury Review.*

Television and Radio

The only television station broadcasting from Aurora is a public access station that broadcasts municipal events. Aurora is largely served by nearby Denver's broadcast media. Six major television stations in the Denver area represent commercial networks, public television, independent stations, and special interest channels; a number of channels are offered by area cable systems as well. More than 45 AM and FM radio stations provide listeners with a variety of musical and special programming.

Media Information: Aurora Sentinel, 10730 E. Bethany Drive Ste. 304, Aurora, CO 80014; telephone (303)750-7555; fax (303)750-7699

Aurora Online

Aurora Economic Development Council. Available www.auroraedc.com

Aurora Public Library. Available www.auroralibrary.org

Aurora Public Schools. Available www.aps.k12.co.us

The Aurora Sentinel. Available www.aurorasentinel.com

Chamber of Commerce. Available www.aurorachamber.org

City of Aurora Home Page. Available www.auroragov.org

The Medical Center of Aurora. Available www .auroramed.com

BIBLIOGRAPHY

Pettem, Silvia, *Behind the Badge: 125 Years of the Boulder, Colorado, Police Department* (Boulder, CO: The Book Lode LLC, 2003)

Pettem, Silvia, and Liston Leyendecker, *Boulder: Evolution of a City* (Niwot, CO: University Press of Colorado, 1994)

Whitney, Gleaves, *Colorado Front Range: A Landscape Divided* (Boulder, CO: Johnson Books, 1983)

Boulder

■ The City in Brief

Founded: 1859 (incorporated 1871)

Head Official: Mayor Shaun McGrath (since 2007)

City Population

    1980: 76,685
    1990: 85,127
    2000: 94,673
    2006 estimate: 91,481
    Percent change, 1990–2000: 11.2%
    U.S. rank in 1980: 250th
    U.S. rank in 1990: 257th
    U.S. rank in 2000: 283th (State rank: 9th)

Metropolitan Area Population

    1980: 189,625
    1990: 225,339
    2000: 291,288
    2006 estimate: 282,304
    Percent change, 1990–2000: 29.3%
    U.S. rank in 1980: 21st (CMSA)
    U.S. rank in 1990: 22nd (CMSA)
    U.S. rank in 2000: 19th (CMSA)

Area: 25.37 square miles (2002)

Elevation: 5,340 feet above sea level

Average Annual Temperature: 51.8° F

Average Annual Precipitation: 102.13 inches total; 83.1 inches of snow

Major Economic Sectors: services, wholesale and retail trade, government

Unemployment Rate: 3.3% (June 2007)

Per Capita Income: $32,326 (2005)

2005 FBI Crime Index Property: 3,624

2005 FBI Crime Index Violent: 216

Major Colleges and Universities: University of Colorado at Boulder, Naropa University, Front Range Community College

Daily Newspaper: *Daily Camera, Colorado Daily*

■ Introduction

Boulder is sometimes called the "Athens of the West" in tribute to its dedication to education and the arts. The University of Colorado at Boulder and a host of private industries make the city one of America's leading science and research towns. Boulder also maintains a commitment to the arts, presenting a number of renowned music, theater, and arts festivals each year. The city's attractive setting near the Rocky Mountains and its abundant cultural and entertainment offerings make it a popular stop for business or recreation.

■ Geography and Climate

Boulder lies in a wide basin beneath Flagstaff Mountain just a few miles east of the continental divide and about 30 miles west of Denver. The large Arapahoe glacier provides water for a number of mountain streams that pass through Boulder, including Boulder Creek, which flows through the center of the city. The climate in Boulder is typically mild with dry, moderate summers and relatively comfortable winters. The city boasts around 300 sunny days each year. Nearby mountains shield Boulder from the most severe winter storms. Most precipitation occurs during the winter and spring months, with snowfall averaging about 83 inches.

Area: 25.37 square miles (2002)

Elevation: 5,340 feet above sea level

Average Temperature: 51.8° F

Average Annual Precipitation: 102.13 inches total; 83.1 inches of snow

■ History

A City Born of a Newspaper

For centuries before the coming of European explorers, the area surrounding what is now Boulder was a favorite winter campsite for a number of Native American groups, including the Arapaho, Ute, Kiowa, Comanche, Cheyenne, and Sioux. The area was rich in buffalo, elk, and antelope.

Economic depression in the East brought many pioneers and gold seekers to Colorado in the 1850s, and the first settlement in Boulder County was established at Red Rocks in 1858. An early settler, A. A. Brookfield, organized the Boulder City Town Company in 1859. The company laid out more than 4,000 lots, each with a price of $1,000. Few people could afford such a price, and by 1860 the population numbered only 364 residents.

Boulder City grew slowly through the 1860s, competing for prominence in the county with nearby Valmont, where the only newspaper in the area was printed. A group of Boulder citizens stole the printing press, and soon Boulder City was named the county seat, selected because it published the only newspaper in the area. In November 1871, Boulder was incorporated as a Colorado town, and "City" was dropped from the name.

A site for the University of Colorado was chosen in Boulder in 1872, and the Colorado state legislature appropriated funds for the institution in 1874, the same year that Boulder's first bank opened its doors. The city grew steadily through the turn of the century. In 1880 the population totaled 3,000 people, but modern conveniences like the installation of electricity in 1887 and a new railway depot in 1890 boosted the population to more than 6,000 people by 1900.

The twentieth century brought moderate growth for Boulder. In the late 1950s and early 1960s the development of high-technology industries had a great impact in the area. Companies like IBM and Rockwell and governmental agencies like the National Oceanic and Atmospheric Administration and the National Bureau of Standards moved into the area, resulting in an economic surge due to the creation of many new jobs. The development of the Boulder-Denver Turnpike further bolstered the area, driving Boulder's population from 20,000 in 1950 to 72,000 in 1972.

A Rocky Period for a Rocky Mountain Town

The convergence of the university environment with research centers and science and technology companies fueled continued growth in the 1990s. By the turn of the century, however, the economic scene had begun to change. A national and international recession contributed to a migration of residences and businesses from Boulder to neighboring communities, where real estate was often cheaper. Lower facility costs fostered a wide variety of businesses, and stores located outside the city began winning in competition for the retail spending of Boulder residents. Sales tax revenue in Boulder dropped by 20 percent between 2000 and 2003. Local businesses began to struggle, as did their employees, many of whom were forced to move from the city to less expensive locales.

Despite media attention in the 1990s and a rocky economical start to the new century, Boulder is an evolving and forward-looking city. Today, Boulder consistently ranks high in polls by magazines and organizations that rate cities based on livability, fitness, and "greenness."

Historical Information: Boulder Public Library, Carnegie Branch Library for Local History, 1125 Pine St., Boulder, CO 80302; telephone (303)441-3110

■ Population Profile

Metropolitan Area Residents

1980: 189,625
1990: 225,339
2000: 291,288
2006 estimate: 282,304
Percent change, 1990–2000: 29.3%
U.S. rank in 1980: 21st (CMSA)
U.S. rank in 1990: 22nd (CMSA)
U.S. rank in 2000: 19th (CMSA)

City Residents

1980: 76,685
1990: 85,127
2000: 94,673
2006 estimate: 91,481
Percent change, 1990–2000: 11.2%
U.S. rank in 1980: 250th
U.S. rank in 1990: 257th
U.S. rank in 2000: 283th (State rank: 9th)

Density: 3,884.1 people per square mile (2000)

Racial and ethnic characteristics (2000)

White: 83,627
Black: 1,154
American Indian and Alaska Native: 450

©James Frank/Alamy

Asian: 3,806
Native Hawaiian and Pacific Islander: 48
Hispanic or Latino (may be of any race): 7,801
Other: 3,318

Percent of residents born in state: 24.2% (2000)

Age characteristics (2005)

Population under 5 years old: 3,748
Population 5 to 9 years old: 4,078
Population 10 to 14 years old: 2,976
Population 15 to 19 years old: 5,154
Population 20 to 24 years old: 14,038
Population 25 to 34 years old: 15,919
Population 35 to 44 years old: 11,368
Population 45 to 54 years old: 10,968
Population 55 to 59 years old: 4,876
Population 60 to 64 years old: 3,258
Population 65 to 74 years old: 3,909
Population 75 to 84 years old: 2,451
Population 85 years and older: 689
Median age: 31.5 years

Births (2006, County)

Total number: 3,533

Deaths (2006, County)

Total number: 1,419

Money income (2005)

Per capita income: $32,326
Median household income: $46,002
Total households: 38,898

Number of households with income of . . .

less than $10,000: 5,222
$10,000 to $14,999: 2,499
$15,000 to $24,999: 3,662
$25,000 to $34,999: 4,093
$35,000 to $49,999: 4,696
$50,000 to $74,999: 6,170
$75,000 to $99,999: 3,977
$100,000 to $149,999: 4,040
$150,000 to $199,999: 2,725
$200,000 or more: 1,814

Percent of families below poverty level: 11.8% (2005)

2005 FBI Crime Index Property: 3,624

2005 FBI Crime Index Violent: 216

■ Municipal Government

Boulder has a council-manager form of government with a nine-member council elected to two- or four-year terms. The council elects the mayor from among its number for a two-year term and elects a deputy manager to a four-year term.

Head Official: Mayor Shaun McGrath (since 2007; current term expires 2009)

Total Number of City Employees: 1,212 (2005)

City Information: City of Boulder, 1777 Broadway, Boulder, CO 80302; telephone (303)441-3388

■ Economy

Major Industries and Commercial Activity

The predominant industries in the Boulder are science and technology related. Helped out by the research activity at the University of Colorado at Boulder, a large high-technology, electronic, and aerospace industry has developed in and around the city. The phenomenal growth of these industries attracted the establishment of defense contractors, applied and pure research centers, and satellite and communications companies, which bring millions of dollars into the local economy each year.

The technology boom has filtered down into other Boulder industries, increasing the city's manufacturing and retail base. Other key industries include the manufacture of natural and organic products, and outdoor/sporting goods. Tourism, education, health care, and government are also important sectors of the Boulder economy.

The arts and culture sectors have also become important to Boulder's economy in recent years, to the tune of $27.58 million in revenue in 2006, in addition to supporting 812 full-time equivalent jobs and creating $1.83 million in local and state government revenue.

Items and goods produced: electronic devices, space hardware, recreational equipment, natural and organic food products

Incentive Programs—New and Existing Companies

Local programs: In an effort to reverse a downward economic trend early in the twenty-first century, the City of Boulder established an Economic Vitality Program in 2003. Guided by the Economic Vitality Advisory Board, the program's primary purpose is to attract new businesses and retain and expand existing businesses. Among the challenges it faces are Boulder's high facility costs, limited space for expansion, and poor condition of many older buildings. As a remedy, the program applies industry-cluster initiatives—partnerships between businesses, government agencies, and research institutions involved in similar industries—to foster innovation and efficiency. The city's current clusters include software, bioscience, creative services, natural and organic food, and sustainable technologies.

In 2005 the Business Innovation Center was opened and provides research and support for small companies, particularly technology start-ups.

In 2006 City Council approved a new pilot program spearheaded by the Economic Vitality Program, which allocated $850,000 to create a flexible rebate program, employee training assistance, an owner-occupied loan pool, and a parks and recreation employee discount program. The pilot program was to be evaluated at the close of 2007.

Additionally, Boulder's Small Business Development Center provides valuable assistance to new and established small businesses. It offers three types of support: counseling, short- and long-term training, and access to such resources as market data, financing, and competitive information.

State programs: The Colorado Office of Economic Development & International Trade offers several types of incentives to attract and retain businesses. Its Infrastructure Assistance Program is designed to create new jobs, mainly in the low- and moderate-income ranges, in certain cities and counties within the state. Other business incentives include enterprise zone tax credits, local property tax incentives, and manufacturing revenue bonds.

Job training programs: The Small Business Development Center of Boulder provides both short- and long-term employee training to businesses seeking to expand or relocate to the area. Front Range Community College, through its Center for Workforce Development, offers a variety of training programs for both employer and employee. The Colorado Community College System has joined with the Colorado Office of Economic Development & International Trade to administer Colorado FIRST/Existing Industry Customized Training Programs. These programs, which received $2.7 million in funding in 2005-2006, are designed to fund employee training for transferable job skills to benefit the company's competitive strength as well as the employee's long-term employment opportunities.

Development Projects

The Economic Vitality Program has several specific initiatives, in various stages of development. Among them is the development of the Boulder Transit Village, an 11.2-acre site that will combine transit service, including commuter rail, with residential and commercial space. The first phase of the project began in 2007, and rail service was expected within 10 years. A second major project, completed in 2006, is Twenty Ninth Street, an

850,000-square-foot shopping complex built on the site of the former Crossroads Mall. It is an open-air shopping and entertainment venue anchored by Foley's, a 16-screen cinema, and The Home Depot.

The Leeds School of Business at the University of Colorado Boulder broke ground in spring 2006 on a $38 million renovation and expansion of the Koelbel business building. It was scheduled to be complete by the end of 2007. Construction was expected to begin in 2009 on a new multi-use path on 28th Street adjacent to the CU Boulder campus.

Economic Development Information: Boulder Chamber of Commerce, 2440 Pearl St., Boulder, CO 80302; telephone (303)442-1044; fax (303)938-8837; email info@boulderchamber.com. Economic Vitality Program, City of Boulder, PO Box 791, Boulder, CO 80306; telephone (303)441-3090

Commercial Shipping

Commercial air shipping is available from a number of carriers at Denver International Airport (DIA). Approximately 400,000 tons of U.S. cargo pass through the airport each year. Commercial cargo carriers include FedEx, UPS, DHL, and Airborne, though nearly half of DIA's air cargo is handled by passenger carriers. In 2004 the airport's cargo facilities completed an expansion, adding 288,000 square feet of space. WorldPort at DIA, adjacent to the freight operations site, provides an additional 100,000 feet of office space. The airport is the site of Foreign Trade Zone #123, as well as areas for U.S. Customs and Department of Agriculture clearance. Approximately 50 freight forwarders and customs brokers also serve in the area. More than one dozen motor freight carriers maintain facilities in Boulder.

Labor Force and Employment Outlook

Boulder business managers and owners cite a high quality of life and a talented work base among the advantages of doing business in Boulder. The workforce is educated well above the national average, as 66.9 percent of Boulder residents had received a bachelor's degree or higher degree in 2000, compared with 24.4 percent in the U.S. as a whole. The university and the many technology- and research-oriented companies draw a large number of college graduates and professionals into the labor market.

A 2006 report comissioned by the Boulder's economic outlook described Boulder's economy as "slowing but growing" in the years ahead. However, national economic slowdowns in late 2006 and 2007 were expected to curb Boulder's growth somewhat, and fewer jobs were expected to be created. In July 2007 the unemployment rate in Boulder stood at 3.4 percent, the 44th lowest in the nation, while the labor force rose to over 175,000. This represented a drastic improvement over unemployment rates topping 6 percent five years

earlier, and is indicative of the generally positive recent trend in the Boulder economy. The growth is driven by the business services sector, in particular technology startups, in addition to the expanding retail base.

The following is a summary of data regarding the Boulder metropolitan area labor force, 2006 annual averages.

Size of nonagricultural labor force: 163,100

Number of workers employed in . . .

construction and mining: 6,300
manufacturing: 18,700
trade, transportation and utilities: 23,300
information: 8,800
financial activities: 7,300
professional and business services: 29,400
educational and health services: 18,200
leisure and hospitality: 16,600
other services: 5,000
government: 29,500

Average hourly earnings of production workers employed in manufacturing: Not available

Unemployment rate: 3.3% (June 2007)

Largest county employers (2006)	*Number of employees*
IBM Corp.	4,200
Sun Microsystems Inc.	3,800
Ball Corp.	3,000
Boulder Community Hospital	2,350
Level 3 Communications Inc.	2,000
Seagate Technology LLC	1,300
Valleylab	1,300
Safeway Inc.	1,245
Longmont United Hospital	1,237
Exempla Good Samaritan	1,142

Cost of Living

Boulder's cost of living is higher than in neighboring communities.

The following is a summary of data regarding key cost of living factors for the Boulder area.

2007 (1st quarter) ACCRA Average House Price: $356,705 (Denver metro)

2007 (1st quarter) ACCRA Cost of Living Index: 102.7 (Denver metro)

State income tax rate: 4.63% of Federal Taxable Income

State sales tax rate: 2.9%

Local income tax rate: None

Local sales tax rate: 3.41%

Property tax rate: $10.005 per $1,000 of assessed value (2004)

Economic Information: Boulder Chamber of Commerce, 2440 Pearl St., Boulder, CO 80302; telephone (303)442-1044; fax (303)938-8837; email info@boulderchamber.com

■ Education and Research

Elementary and Secondary Schools

The Boulder Valley School District regulates the public schools in Boulder as well as the neighboring communities of Broomfield, Lafayette, Louisville, Mountain, Nederland, and Superior. The district's open enrollment policy enables students to enroll in a variety of schools, including focus or alternative schools. The board, comprised of seven members elected at-large to four-year terms, employs the superintendent.

The District boasts the distinction of consistently ranking among the top two districts in Colorado as measured by the Colorado Student Assessment Program; 26 of the district's 58 schools received an evaluation of "Excellent," with 21 achieving a "High" ranking.

The following is a summary of data regarding the Boulder Valley School District as of the 2005–2006 school year.

Total enrollment: 28,196

Number of facilities

    elementary schools: 29
    junior high/middle schools: 10
    senior high schools: 10
    other: 6

Student/teacher ratio: 17.2:1

Teacher salaries (2005–06)

    elementary median: $53,210
    junior high/middle median: $52,940
    secondary median: $53,630

Funding per pupil: $7,713

A number of private and parochial schools also serve the Boulder area—5 high schools and 20 elementary/middle schools.

Public Schools Information: Boulder Valley School District, 6500 Arapahoe, Boulder, CO 80303; telephone (303)447-1010

Colleges and Universities

Boulder is the main campus of the University of Colorado (CU) university system. Other campuses in the system include the University of Colorado at Colorado Springs, and the Denver and Health Sciences Center. The Boulder campus is a major research and educational institution, with an enrollment of more than 29,000 students in 2007. It offers 2,500 courses in 150 areas of study in nine colleges and schools, both graduate and undergraduate. CU has strong ties to the astronautics and astrophysics disciplines. The university is a primary research center in space sciences, and 17 of its alumni have become astronauts in the National Aeronautics and Space Administration (NASA) program. It boasts of being the only research institution in the world to have designed and built space instruments for NASA that have been launched to every planet in the solar system. Additionally, it is the top ranked public university in federally financed research in environmental sciences. CU had an operating budget of $1.9 billion in 2006.

Front Range Community College promotes academic and career advancement through associate degree and certificate programs in business, health, mathematics, advanced sciences, arts and humanities, world languages, computer information sciences, communication, and social sciences. The Naropa University is a Buddhist-inspired institution offering four-year degrees in an academic program that blends intellectual, artistic, and meditative disciplines. Accredited by the North Central Association of Colleges and Schools, Naropa enrolls more than 450 students; the school also features internship programs and a study-abroad program in Prague, Czech Republic, and is home to the Jack Kerouac School of Disembodied Poetics, founded by Allen Ginsberg and Anne Waldman. The Boulder College of Massage Therapy offers a 1,000-hour certificate program in a variety of massage styles, as well as an Associate Degree of Occupational Studies in Massage Therapy.

Libraries and Research Centers

The Boulder Public Library consists of a main building and three branches. The library maintains special collections of children's literature, a Colorado Artists Registry, and municipal government. The Carnegie Branch Library for Local History contains a manuscript collection of more than 700,000 items, including some from before the area received the name Colorado, as well as historic photographs, newspapers, and oral histories. The University of Colorado library system consists of the central Norlin Library, which hosts the humanities and social science collections, and six discipline-specific branch libraries. The total system contains more than 11 million books, periodicals, and microforms, as well as special collections in juvenile literature, the history of silver, mountaineering, and Western history. The National Indian Law Library, which houses 4,000 items, is the only law library specializing in practice materials relating to federal and tribal Indian law. The Allen Ginsberg Library of the Naropa University houses books, journals, audio/visual media, and artwork, as well as special collections in university recordings, Tibetan volumes, and small press and chapbooks. A number of private and special interest libraries are also located in the city.

In 2005 the University of Colorado at Boulder (CU) received more than $640 million in sponsored research monies, and was ranked sixth among all public universities in the U.S. in federal research. Its nearly 100 research centers and institutes are involved in everything from music entrepreneurship to high energy physics. Some of the largest facilities are the Institute of Arctic and Alpine Research, the Institute for Behavioral Genetics, the Institute of Cognitive Science, the Colorado Center for Information Storage, the Joint Institute for Laboratory Astrophysics, and the Laboratory of Atmospheric and Space Physics. A $70 million instrument designed by researchers at the Center for Astrophysics and Space Astronomy was scheduled to be installed on the Hubble Space Telescope during a servicing mission in May 2008. Three CU professors are recipients of a Nobel Prize, the most recent bestowed to John Hall for physics in 2005, for the development of laser-based precision spectroscopy.

Boulder is home to several research institutions of the federal government. The Cooperative Institute for Research in Environmental Sciences is a joint venture of CU and the National Office of Oceanic and Atmospheric Research. The National Weather Service maintains a weather forecast office in the city, which provides weather forecasts and data for a large chunk of Colorado. The National Center for Atmospheric Research offers free, guided tours of such exhibits as lightning, a tornado, a solar eclipse telescope, and aircraft models. Visitors can view the atomic clock and other science displays at the National Institute of Standards and Technology Boulder Laboratories, which attracts 100 visiting researchers each year in addition to its 350 resident scientists, engineers, and other personnel.

Public Library Information: Boulder Public Library, 1000 Canyon Blvd., Boulder, CO 80302; telephone (303)441-3100

Health Care

Boulder Community Hospital is the largest health-care institution in the Boulder area, with 265 beds and a $250 million operating budget. It is a full-service hospital with a 24-hour emergency room, an intensive care unit, a cardiac care unit, and a network of facilities that includes the Boulder Center for Sports Medicine, Boulder Community Foothills Hospital, Community Medical Center (an urgent care facility), the Sleep Disorder Lab, and the Miriam R. Hart Regional Radiation Therapy Center.

Other hospitals within driving distance of Boulder include Centennial Peaks Hospital, Avista Adventist Hospital, Longmont United Hospital, Centennial Peaks Hospital, Devereux Cleo Wallace, Lutheran Medical Center, Mediplex Specialty Hospital, and Saint Joseph Hospital.

Recreation

Sightseeing

A highlight of downtown Boulder is the 16-mile-long Boulder Creek Path, which runs along the creek through the center of the city. The banks of the creek have been restored to their natural state, parks and picnic areas have been formed—including the attractive Boulder Sculpture Park—and many small waterfalls along the way are perfect for kayaking and tubing. The Open Space & Mountain Parks division of the City of Boulder encompasses 43,000 square feet and a number of free public nature hikes of varying difficulty, each offering some of the most scenic views in the region. Among them is Sawhill Ponds, featuring 18 ponds; Flagstaff Mountain, a 6,850-foot peak that is home to the Flagstaff Nature Center; Royal Arch, a sandstone arch through which the city of Boulder can be viewed from above; and Boulder Falls, a five-acre site known as the "Yosemite of Boulder Canyon."

Boulder also caters to those who prefer less strenuous sightseeing excursions. Free tours are offered by the Celestial Seasonings Tea Co., including a tea sampling bar and a walk through the Mint Room, and by the Redstone Meadery, brewer of a honey wine known as mead. Gateway Park Fun Center features go-karts, batting cages, and miniature golf.

Arts and Culture

The Boulder Philharmonic Orchestra has been performing since 1958, and holds the majority of its performances at the Macky Auditorium Concert Hall on the campus of the University of Colorado at Boulder. Also performing at the Macky is Boulder Ballet, the major dance company of Boulder County. The Boulder Concert Band, comprised of 70 community members, offers a concert series and summer concerts in the area parks. Other musical institutions include the Boulder Chorale, the Boulder Youth Choir and Youth Symphony, and the Boulder Chamber Orchestra, which was founded in 2004. The Nomad Theatre is Boulder's only professional resident theater. Upstart Crow is an ensemble acting company whose season runs from early fall to mid-summer and offers four major works. Boulder's Dinner Theatre entertains 80,000 attendees each year with food, drink, and major Broadway musicals.

The University of Colorado at Boulder (CU) Museum of Natural History houses nearly four million specimens of biology, anthropology, and geology, including fossils, local animals, and Southwestern cultural artifacts.

The CU Heritage Center contains exhibits that chronicle the university's past, such as the baseball bat and glove used by alumnus Robert Redford in *The Natural,* as well as space suits worn by former graduates who became astronauts. CU is also the site of the Sommers-Bausch Observatory and the Fiske Planetarium, which features the largest projection dome between Chicago and Los Angeles.

The city's many museums are not limited to the CU campus. The Boulder History Museum houses nearly 35,000 objects from Boulder's past, dating back to the 1800s. The Carnegie Branch Library for Local History, located in Boulder's original library building, contains thousands of books, diaries, photographs, oral history audiotapes, and genealogical papers. The Leanin' Tree Museum of Western Art houses one of the largest collections of contemporary Western art in America.

Boulder offers a variety of art galleries, as well as several art museums. In 2005 the city was mamed 18th among the "Top 25 Art Cities" by *American Style Magazine*. The Boulder Museum of Contemporary Art features regional, national, and international exhibitions and performances. The University of Colorado at Boulder Art Galleries contain the works of regional artists and students as well as major national and international artists, and house the Colorado Collection, a state-owned collection of 5,000 pieces. The Charles A. Haertling Sculpture Park displays the work of such artists as Jerry Wingren, Dennis Yoshikawa Wright, Tom Miller, and Beth Juliar-Skodge.

Festivals and Holidays

Boulder's most famous festival is the Colorado Shakespeare Festival, regarded as one of the best in the nation. The festival is held each summer at the University of Colorado at Boulder's outdoor Mary Rippon Theatre and the indoor University Theatre. January brings the Boulder Bach Festival, a three-day event featuring an orchestra, chorus, and soloists performing the works of Johann Sebastian Bach. For more than a month during the summer, the Colorado Music Festival presents classical music performed by musicians from around the world. The Pearl Street Art Fair is held each July, and the Aerial Dance Festival, featuring demonstrations of dancing through the air, takes place the following month. Film festivals include the Boulder International Film Festival, held for four days in February, and the Moondance International Film Festival, a competition that takes place each May. A variety of aspects of adventure is presented at the Boulder Adventure Film Festival each April.

The city hosts a number of unique festivals and events. The annual Polar Bear Plunge attracts participants intrepid enough to jump into the Boulder Reservoir on New Year's Day. The International Mead Festival, held in February, features more than 80 meads from seven countries and is the world's largest competition for mead, a beverage made of wine fermented with honey. Another record-setting event is held the following month, as the world's shortest parade—Boulder's St. Patrick's Day Parade—takes place over a course covering less than one city block. The Kinetics Sculpture Challenge, preceded a week earlier by the Kinetics Parade, invites teams to race kinetically designed sculptures over both land and water. The Boulder Creek Festival, which draws approximately 130,000 people over Memorial Day Weekend, features a rubber duck race, a children's fishing derby, and dog-agility demonstrations along with typical festival activities and fare. The Boulder Shoot-Out, marking its fourth year in October 2007, is a filmmaking festival. Several holiday events take place in November and December, including Switch on the Holidays, the Holiday Festival, and the Lights of December Parade.

Sports for the Spectator

The University of Colorado at Boulder provides the major sporting attractions in the city. The university's football team, the *Buffaloes,* is a member of the Big 12 Conference. The university also offers men's and women's basketball, cross country, golf, skiing, tennis, and track and field, and women's soccer and volleyball.

Professional sports fans can turn to any of nearby Denver's clubs: The Nuggets in the National Basketball Association, the Major League Baseball Rockies, the National Hockey League's Colorado Avalanche and the National Football League's Broncos.

Sports for the Participant

Boulder was voted the "Nation's Reigning Bike Friendly Community" by the League of American Bicyclists in 2004. A 2006 article in the *Washington Post* named it one of "10 other great bike cities" in the United States. Residents love to bicycle, and Boulder boasts 150-plus miles of bike paths and 192 miles of bike lanes. On occasion, the city will even plow snow off important bike paths before plowing certain roads. Each year Boulder turns national Bike to Work Day in June into Bike to Work Week and offers free tune-ups, and safety clinics.

Boulder offers a variety of outdoor activities the year round. Natural areas like the seven-mile-long Boulder Creek Path and the city's large mountain park feature hiking, camping, and boating. The city operates more than 60 parks—800 acres of maintained park land and an additional 200 acres of natural land—offering recreational facilities of all kinds. There are 48 tennis courts, 22 ballfields, and 15 soccer fields, and as well as the public Flatirons Golf Course. Boulder is also a short distance away from several popular ski resorts and dozens of state and national parks.

Boulder, named seventh on the list of "America's Best Running Cities" by *Runner's World* magazine in 2005, hosts several athletic competitions. The Bolder

Boulder 10K race brings 50,000 runners from around the world to the city on Memorial Day. Three weeks later is the 5430 Sprint Triathlon, the first of three races making up the Boulder Triathlon Series. The second race is the Boulder Peak Triathlon, held in July, followed in August by the 5430 Long Course Triathlon. Colorado's largest running event is the Nike ACG Boulder Backroads Marathon & Half Marathon, which takes place each September at the Boulder Reservoir.

Shopping and Dining

A major attraction in the downtown area is the historic Pearl Street Mall district. Set up for pedestrian traffic, the mall is lined with shops, galleries, and restaurants. Along the way, street performers, gardens, and sculptures make the stroll enjoyable. Several large suburban malls add to countless smaller shops and specialty stores scattered throughout the area. Just completed in the autumn of 2006 is Twenty Ninth Street, an 850,000-square-foot shopping center with an open-air environment that is anchored by Foley's and a 16-theater cinema. More than 300 restaurants in Boulder offer a wide variety of foods, from traditional Western fare to exotic ethnic foods. Patrons won't find a smoking section in any of these establishments, as the city has adopted a no-smoking policy in its restaurants and taverns.

Visitor Information: Boulder Convention & Visitors Bureau, 2440 Pearl St., Boulder, CO 80302; telephone (303)442-2911; toll-free (800)444-0447; fax (303)938-2098; email visitor@bouldercvb.com

■ Convention Facilities

Although lacking a full-fledged convention center, Boulder has 14 facilities offering meeting space. In 2006 the city was named the ninth "Best City for Green Meetings" by *Meetings and Conventions*. The Millennium Harvest House can accommodate small functions as well as up to 500 people on its outdoor pavilion and up to 600 in its Grand Ballroom. The historic Hotel Boulderado, a national registered landmark accommodates meetings for up to 200 people and receptions up to 300. Several other hotels provide meeting space, as do facilities at the University of Colorado at Boulder, namely the 2,047-seat Macky Auditorium Concert Hall and the University Memorial Center, whose 9,418-square-foot Glenn Miller Ballroom can accommodate 700 attendants. The Boulder Theater can seat up to 860 conference delegates.

Convention Information: Boulder Convention & Visitors Bureau, 2440 Pearl St., Boulder, CO 80302; telephone (303)442-2911; toll-free (800)444-0447; fax (303)938-2098; email visitor@bouldercvb.com

■ Transportation

Approaching the City

The majority of air traffic comes through Denver International Airport, located 42 miles from Boulder and served by 23 passenger airlines. The recently built Northwest Parkway toll road, which had a planned extension approved in summer 2007, connects the airport with Boulder. Hourly shuttle service and limousine service from the airport to Boulder is also available. Rocky Mountain Metropolian Airport is located 11 miles from Boulder, and provides commuter air service in addition to corporate air facilites. Boulder Municipal Airport, located three miles northeast of the central business district, also provides commuter air service.

Interstate 25, Colorado's major north-south highway, runs just to the east of Boulder. The Boulder-Denver Turnpike connects the two cities, and I-70 at Denver provides links east and west. Other major highways include U.S. Highways 36, 52, 93, and 287.

Traveling in the City

Major thoroughfares in the city include Broadway and Twenty-Eighth Street, running north and south, and Iris Avenue, Pearl Street, Canyon Boulevard, Arapahoe Road, and Baseline Road, all running east and west. The Regional Transportation District (RTD) operates a fleet of buses serving the metropolitan area. The HOP line makes 40 stops in a loop throughout central Boulder, while the SKIP lines runs north and south along Broadway; other RTD bus lines in Boulder are the JUMP, DASH, BOUND, and STAMPEDE. In 2006 Boulder began to cut back RTD services—particularly the frequency of service—because of ongoing funding problems and underuse.

Bicycling is extremely important to travel in Boulder, as 10 percent of its residents ride bikes on a regular basis. Bicycle paths parallel all major traffic arteries, and total more than 200 miles. A fleet of 150 bright green bicycles, part of the Spokes for Folks "Green Bikes Program," are provided free to residents as loaner vehicles to be shared by all residents of the city. The Annual Walk and Bike Week encourages commuters to get out of their cars and either pedal or walk to and from work. Local businesses, such as restaurants and bicycle mechanics, offer free incentives to participants.

■ Communications

Newspapers and Magazines

Boulder is served by two daily newspapers, the morning *Daily Camera* and the morning *Colorado Daily*. *Boulder Weekly* is a free, alternative newspaper, and the *Boulder County Business Report* focuses on economic, industrial, and business news every other week. The *Campus Press,* written by and for students of the University of Colorado at Boulder, is distributed each Thursday. Boulder's love of outdoor sports is reflected in some of the nationally distributed magazines published in the city, including *Inside Triathlon, Ski, Skiing,* and the competitive bicycling magazine *VeloNews.* Other publications include *Delicious Living* and *Soldier of Fortune,* as well as a number of several scholarly journals and trade publications.

Television and Radio

Five television stations broadcast to Boulder audiences, three representing the major commercial networks and two independent stations; cable service is available. Two AM and two FM radio stations broadcast alternative/new music, public radio, and University of Colorado programming.

Media Information: *Daily Camera,* 1048 Pearl St., Boulder, CO 80302; telephone (303)442-1202

Boulder Online

Boulder Chamber of Commerce. Available www .boulderchamber.com

Boulder Community Hospital. Available www.bch .org

Boulder Convention & Visitors Bureau. Available www.bouldercoloradousa.com

Boulder Public Library System. Available www .boulder.lib.co.us

Boulder Valley School District. Available www.bvsd .org

City of Boulder Home Page. Available www.ci .boulder.co.us

Daily Camera. Available www.thedailycamera.com

Economic Vitality Program. Available www.ci .boulder.co.us/economic_vitality

University of Colorado at Boulder. Available www .colorado.edu

BIBLIOGRAPHY

Pettem, Silvia, *Behind the Badge: 125 Years of the Boulder, Colorado, Police Department* (Boulder, CO: The Book Lode LLC, 2003)

Pettem, Silvia, and Liston Leyendecker, *Boulder: Evolution of a City* (Niwot, CO: University Press of Colorado, 1994)

Whitney, Gleaves, *Colorado Front Range: A Landscape Divided* (Boulder, CO: Johnson Books, 1983)

Colorado Springs

■ The City in Brief

Founded: 1871 (incorporated 1872)

Head Official: Mayor Lionel Rivera (since 2003)

City Population

    1980: 215,150
    1990: 283,112
    2000: 360,890
    2006 estimate: 372,437
    Percent change, 1990–2000: 27.5%
    U.S. rank in 1980: 66th
    U.S. rank in 1990: 54th
    U.S. rank in 2000: 48th (State rank: 2nd)

Metropolitan Area Population

    1980: 309,000
    1990: 397,014
    2000: 516,929
    2006 estimate: 599,127
    Percent change, 1990–2000: 31.3%
    U.S. rank in 1980: 105th
    U.S. rank in 1990: 90th
    U.S. rank in 2000: 80th

Area: 186 square miles (2000)

Elevation: 6,035 feet above sea level

Average Annual Temperatures: January, 28.1° F; July, 69.6° F; annual average, 47.8° F

Average Annual Precipitation: 17.40 inches of rain; 42.4 inches of snow

Major Economic Sectors: services, wholesale and retail trade, government

Unemployment Rate: 4.3% (June 2007)

Per Capita Income: $26,001 (2005)

2005 FBI Crime Index Property: 19,619

2005 FBI Crime Index Violent: 1,792

Major Colleges and Universities: University of Colorado at Colorado Springs, United States Air Force Academy, Colorado Technical College, Colorado College

Daily Newspaper: *The Gazette*

■ Introduction

At the foot of Pikes Peak, the highest peak of the Rocky Mountains, Colorado Springs is a city surrounded by natural beauty that draws millions of visitors a year. Its municipal parks include the breathtaking Garden of the Gods, once sacred Native American tribal grounds. Upon ascending Pikes Peak in 1893, Katharine Lee Bates wrote the words to "America the Beautiful;" the lyrics "purple mountains' majesty" refer to the vistas around Colorado Springs. Now an important center of military installations, Colorado Springs is home to the United States Air Force Academy, the North American Aerospace Defense Command (NORAD), U.S. Air Force and U.S. Space Commands, Consolidated Space Operations Center, and Fort Carson.

■ Geography and Climate

Colorado Springs is located on a high, flat plain at the foot of the Rocky Mountains in eastern central Colorado. To the east of the city are rolling prairie lands and to the north is Monument Divide. The climate of Colorado Springs is relatively mild and dry, since the city is protected from harsh weather by the Rocky Mountains in the west. In the winter, Colorado Springs is warmed by the Chinook, a wind whose name means "snow eater."

Area: 186 square miles (2000)

Elevation: 6,035 feet above sea level

Average Temperatures: January, 28.1° F; July, 69.6° F; annual average, 47.8° F

Average Annual Precipitation: 17.40 inches of rain; 42.4 inches of snow

■ History

Rowdiness and Refinement Coexist in City's Early Days

The history of Colorado Springs is the history of two very different communities, one wild and rowdy, the other a model of controlled growth. The area was first discovered by settlers of European descent in 1806 when Zebulon Montgomery Pike came upon a mountain he named Pikes Peak and attempted to climb it. Later, several tribes of Native Americans, namely the Ute, Arapaho, and Cheyenne, lived and battled in the region. They declared what is now called the Garden of the Gods to be sacred ground where the tribes could meet in peace and bathe in the mineral springs.

Mountains rich in silver and gold brought miners into the area. A settlement developed and was called El Dorado City, because of its proximity to the gold mines. This became Colorado City, a rough town full of saloons where frequent brawls and gun fights raged. In 1871, the Denver & Rio Grande Western Railroad, the first narrow-gauge line in Colorado, came to the region. The railroad was directed by General William Jackson Palmer, who began to plan a community near Colorado City. Palmer envisioned the town as a playground for the rich, rivaling the elegant resorts on the East Coast. First called the Fountain Colony, the town was incorporated as Colorado Springs in 1872. According to what was called "The Palmer Pattern of Responsibility," Colorado Springs was planned with schools, libraries, churches, parks, and a college. Citizens of "good moral character and strict temperance habits" were purposely sought; intemperance and industry were relegated to Colorado City across the railroad tracks.

City Becomes Tourist and Military Center

Tourists from throughout the country flocked to Colorado Springs and to the spa at nearby Manitou Springs. By the turn of the century Colorado Springs was the wealthiest city per capita in the United States. At this time it earned the nickname Little London, reflecting the number of Tudor-style houses constructed in the area. During this age of the elegant hotel, the rich and the titled were drawn to the Rocky Mountains—especially Colorado Springs—to play polo and hunt foxes. Colorado City, after suffering great economic vicissitudes tied

to the mining industry, was absorbed by Colorado Springs in 1971.

Since World War II, Colorado Springs has become an important focal point of the U.S. military. Fort Carson Army Base was established in the early 1940s; the United States Air Force Academy was completed in 1958. In 1966 the North American Air Defense Command (NORAD) was installed inside Cheyenne Mountain as the first warning system for North America against a nuclear missile strike. The United States Olympic Committee created an Olympic Training Grounds in Colorado Springs in 1978. Athletes come from throughout the world to train there, surrounded by the beauty of the Rocky Mountains. With a young, educated work force, beautiful weather, and an expanding military and high tech economy, Colorado Springs' future as a growth center in the West will continue for some time to come. In fact, *Money Magazine* rated the city the "Best Big City" in the nation to live and work in its August 2006 issue.

Historical Information: Colorado College, Charles Leaming Tutt Library, 1021 North Cascade Avenue, Colorado Springs, CO 80903; telephone (719) 389-6184

■ Population Profile

Metropolitan Area Residents

    1980: 309,000
    1990: 397,014
    2000: 516,929
    2006 estimate: 599,127
    Percent change, 1990–2000: 31.3%
    U.S. rank in 1980: 105th
    U.S. rank in 1990: 90th
    U.S. rank in 2000: 80th

City Residents

    1980: 215,150
    1990: 283,112
    2000: 360,890
    2006 estimate: 372,437
    Percent change, 1990–2000: 27.5%
    U.S. rank in 1980: 66th
    U.S. rank in 1990: 54th
    U.S. rank in 2000: 48th (State rank: 2nd)

Density: 1,942.9 people per square mile (2000)

Racial and ethnic characteristics (2005)

    White: 302,784
    Black: 23,831
    American Indian and Alaska Native: 3,322
    Asian: 9,856

Colorado Springs Convention & Visitors Bureau. Reproduced by permission.

Native Hawaiian and Pacific Islander: 935
Hispanic or Latino (may be of any race): 51,755
Other: 22,192

Percent of residents born in state: 29.6%
(2000)

Age characteristics (2005)

Population under 5 years old: 27,564
Population 5 to 9 years old: 25,254
Population 10 to 14 years old: 27,887
Population 15 to 19 years old: 25,532
Population 20 to 24 years old: 28,026
Population 25 to 34 years old: 60,253
Population 35 to 44 years old: 57,947
Population 45 to 54 years old: 53,178
Population 55 to 59 years old: 20,620
Population 60 to 64 years old: 15,012
Population 65 to 74 years old: 19,926
Population 75 to 84 years old: 11,823
Population 85 years and older: 3,963
Median age: 34 years

Births (2006, MSA)

Total number: 8,567

Deaths (2006, MSA)

Total number: 3,430

Money income (2005)

Per capita income: $26,001
Median household income: $47,854
Total households: 155,980

Number of households with income of...

less than $10,000: 11,510
$10,000 to $14,999: 8,764
$15,000 to $24,999: 19,720
$25,000 to $34,999: 17,532
$35,000 to $49,999: 23,707
$50,000 to $74,999: 31,299
$75,000 to $99,999: 18,462
$100,000 to $149,999: 16,347
$150,000 to $199,999: 5,112
$200,000 or more: 3,527

Percent of families below poverty level: 10.7% (2005)

2005 FBI Crime Index Property: 19,619

2005 FBI Crime Index Violent: 1,792

■ Municipal Government

Colorado Springs operates under a council-mayor form of government. Elections are held every four years for mayor, four council members-at-large, and four council members from the districts where they reside. Colorado Springs is the seat of El Paso County.

Head Official: Mayor Lionel Rivera (since 2003; current term expires 2011)

Total Number of City Employees: 2,500 (2004)

City Information: City Hall, PO Box 1575, Colorado Springs, CO 80901; telephone (719)385-CITY

■ Economy

Major Industries and Commercial Activity

The economy of Colorado Springs is based primarily on the military installations in the area as well as on the aerospace and electronics industries and tourism. Fort Carson, a U.S. Army base, has more than 15,000 people on its payroll. The U.S. Air Force Academy, Fort Peterson Air Force Base (AFB), and the North American Aerospace Defense Command (NORAD) are also major employers.

Colorado Springs is a center for space research. The city is the site of the Combined Services Space Center and the Space Defense Operations Center, which are involved in the Strategic Defense Initiative and handle military missions of the Space Shuttle. The U.S. Space Foundation (USSF) and the Space Commands at Peterson AFB also provide a conducive environment for developing future space-related projects. As a result of growth in the aerospace industry, several high-technology firms have been attracted to Colorado Springs, and the Colorado Springs Technology Incubator provides support for firms seeking to launch in the area. Two Colorado Springs based tech firms were among the 2006 Deloitte Technology Fast 500 listing for fastest growing technology companies: Intelligent Software Solutions Inc. and Ramtron International Corportation.

Since the turn of the century, when the city's grand hotels made it famous, Colorado Springs has been a major tourism center. Pikes Peak and the natural beauty of the surrounding area daws an average of over six million visitors per year. The city's average gross income from tourism is near $1 billion, providing a substantial boost to the construction industry and creating 16,000 tourism-sepcific jobs in the city.

Items and goods produced: advertising film, granite, concrete, dairy products, brooms, novelties, chemicals, pottery, bricks, airplane engine mounts, machine tools, shell fuses, electric motors, castings, electronics, plastics, steel culverts, printed and published works

Incentive Programs—New and Existing Companies

Local programs: At the local level, El Paso County contains an Urban Enterprise Zone offering state and local credits for new jobs, investment, and research and development expenditures. The Greater Colorado Springs Economic Development Council will package private and public incentives for relocating or expanding companies that are tailored to the specific needs of the company. The Council also sponsors the Business Expansion & Retention Visitation (BREV) Program, which seeks to nurture local investment and job retention with a pro-business attitude. The private sector and government in Colorado Springs cooperate to encourage new business and industry through such incentives as low corporate tax rates, a Foreign Trade Zone, and training programs. The Colorado Office of Business Development and International Trade offers services in bringing national and foreign investment to the state.

State programs: The Colorado Office of Economic Development & International Trade offers several types of incentives to attract and retain businesses. Its Infrastructure Assistance Program is designed to create new jobs, mainly in the low- and moderate-income ranges, in certain cities and counties within the state. Other business incentives include enterprise zone tax credits, local property tax incentives, and manufacturing revenue bonds. There are numerous venture capital firms throughout the state, including the Colorado Quality Investment Capital Program.

Job training programs: The Pikes Peak Workforce Center helps with placement, job matching, and training workers. The Colorado Office of Business Development and International Trade offers Colorado First grants for new businesses and Existing Industry grants for training and staff retention purposes.

Economic Development Information: The Greater Colorado Springs Economic Development Corporation, 90 S. Cascade Ave. Suite 1050 Colorado Springs, CO 80907; telephone (719)471-8183; fax (719)471-9733; email csedc@csedc.org

Development Projects

Development in the downtown area is booming due to the Colorado Springs Downtown Partnership. The Depot Arts District is undergoing a long-term revitalization, planned to offer affordable housing, studio, and retail space.The Art Mill, its central development and the product of a partnership among four local galleries, opened its doors in 2006. Projects underway in the downtown area in 2007 included the Colorado College

Cornerstone Arts Center, the Palmer Village residential development, Stratton Pointe office buildings, and a parking garage at Colorado and Nevada Avenues. The Gold Hill Mesa Urban Renewal Plan, begun by the city of Colorado Springs in 2005, is a long-term effort intended to rebuild and rezone a portion of the downtown area to attract more businesses in Colorado Springs. The Lowell Project, underway in 2007, is intended for the restoration and rehabilitation of Lowell Elementary School, built in 1891, in addition to the redevelopment of the surrounding property to include residential lofts, apartments and housing, as well as supporting retail, office and commercial space.

St. Francis Medical Center, a $200-million full-service hospital, was scheduled to open in August 2008 in Northeast Colorado Springs. Services will include a birth center, emergency service, Level III neonatal intensive care unit, inpatient-outpatient surgery and pediatric unit. In 2006 construction began on a new 54,000-square-foot recreation center at University of Colorado Colorado Springs, scheduled to be complete by the end of 2007.

Commercial Shipping

Established as a Foreign Trade Zone, Colorado Springs is a link in the country's import-export shipping network. Air cargo carriers operating from Colorado Springs Municipal Airport include Airborne Express, America West Freight, Cargo City, Sprint Colorado Air Cargo, Inc., Continental Air Cargo, Delta Airlines Cargo, Emery Worldwide, Federal Express Corp., Northwest Airlines, Trans World Airlines, Inc., and United Parcel Service. The metropolitan area is served by two major rail freight lines. About 20 motor freight carriers ship goods through terminals in the city.

Labor Force and Employment Outlook

Colorado Springs boasts a youthful, well educated labor force. Sources of labor include former military personnel, military dependents, retirees, college students, and commuters from other Colorado cities. Labor/management relations are described as excellent; there is a low level of unionization throughout Colorado. Between 1997 and 2007 the labor force grew rapidly in Colorado Springs, from about 260,000 workers to nearly 320,000 workers. The labor force was predicted to continue its growth as Colorado Springs becomes an increasingly popular spot for relocations; in 2007 the city was ranked the 4th best city to live by Cities Ranked & Rated, 2nd Edition.

Analysts believe the high-tech sector will continue to be an area of growth for Colorado Springs. The city ranked 11th in the nation in high-tech exports. From 2006 to 2007, Colorado's high-tech exports grew by 16 percent, for a total of $592 million. In July 2007 the unemployment rate stood at 4.3 percent, down from its high of over 7 percent in 2002.

The following is a summary of data regarding the Colorado Springs metropolitan area labor force, 2006 annual averages.

Size of nonagricultural labor force: 258,500

Number of workers employed in...

construction and mining: 18,000
manufacturing: 18,000
trade, transportation and utilities: 40,700
information: 8,000
financial activities: 18,200
professional and business services: 39,700
educational and health services: 25,600
leisure and hospitality: 31,100
other services: 14,800
government: 44,300

Average hourly earnings of production workers employed in manufacturing: Not available

Unemployment rate: 4.3% (June 2007)

Largest employers (2007)	*Number of employees*
Memorial Health Services	Not available
Penrose-St. Francis	Not available
Hewlett Packard	Not available
Lockheed Martin Corporation	Not available
Atmel Corporation	Not available
Broadmoor Hotel	Not available
Progressive Insurance Company Finance	Not available
Verizon Business	Not available
ITT Industries Inc	Not available
Focus on the Family	Not available

Cost of Living

The following is a summary of data regarding key cost of living factors in the Colorado Springs area.

2007 (1st quarter) ACCRA Average House Price: $267,028

2007 (1st quarter) ACCRA Cost of Living Index: 94.8

State income tax rate: 4.63% of Federal Taxable Income

State sales tax rate: 2.9%

Local income tax rate: None

Local sales tax rate: 2.5% city and 1.0% county

Property tax rate: Ranges between 59 mills and 90 mills depending on school district and other special taxing districts; the average in 2003 was 67 mills. The 2003

residential assessment rate for taxes due in 2004 was 7.96 percent of market value

Economic Information: The Greater Colorado Springs Chamber of Commerce, 2 North Cascade Avenue, Suite 110, Colorado Springs, CO 80903; telephone (719)635-1551; fax (719)635-1571

■ Education and Research

Elementary and Secondary Schools

In Colorado, school district boundaries are independent of city or other political boundaries. A 1993 state law allows parents to send their children to any public school, as long as there is room in the facility. There are 15 public school districts within El Paso County; six districts of varying size serve urban areas of Colorado Springs. Colorado Springs School District Eleven, the fourth largest system in the state and largest in the city, is administered by a seven-member, nonpartisan board of education that appoints a superintendent to a two-year contract. Composite SAT scores are consistently above the national average. There are seven charter schools in District 11, in addition to six alternative education programs. Pine Creek High School, a $16 million technology magnet school in District 20, prepares students for college or employment in regional business and provides them with a sense of community.

The following is a summary of data regarding the Colorado Springs School District 11 as of the 2005–2006 school year.

Total enrollment: 30,000

Number of facilities

    elementary schools: 41
    junior high/middle schools: 9
    senior high schools: 5
    other: 13

Student/teacher ratio: 16.4:1

Teacher salaries (2005–06)

    elementary median: $41,070
    junior high/middle median: $39,860
    secondary median: $40,170

Funding per pupil: $8,094

About 7,300 students attend 39 parochial and private schools in Colorado Springs, Pre-K through 12th grade.

Public Schools Information: Colorado Springs School District Eleven, 1115 North El Paso Street, Colorado Springs, CO 80903; telephone (719)520-2000; fax (719)577-4546

Colleges and Universities

The Colorado Springs area is home to a number of colleges and universities, including the United States Air Force Academy, the University of Colorado at Colorado Springs, and Colorado College. The University of Colorado is a state school offering both undergraduate and master's degrees in interdisciplinary programs such as geography, earth sciences, and environmental studies. The 2008 *U.S. News & World Report* "Best Colleges" list ranks the UCCS undergraduate engineering program ninth in the nation among public engineering schools offering bachelor's or master's degrees. Colorado College, opened in 1874, has grown with the city, and offers an unusual learning environment: the Block Plan has students take only one intensive course at a time. The Air Force Academy, which trains officers, is among the most selective insitutions in the country.

Other schools include Nazarene Bible College, DeVry College, Blair College and the Colorado School for the Blind and Deaf. Thirty technical, professional, and business schools, including Colorado Technical College, are also located in Colorado Springs. The city was ranked among the "Top 25 Cities to Live To Go To School" in 2007 by RelocateAmerica.com.

Libraries and Research Centers

The Pikes Peak Library District (PPLD) serves the residents of El Paso County except Manitou Springs and Widefield School District #3. Residents in those two areas can check out PPLD materials through the Colorado Library Card program. Library facilities include two main facilities—Penrose Public Library and the East Library and Information Center—as well as nine branches and two bookmobiles for the city and county. A new building for the Fountain Branch was completed, and the Carnegie Garden, an outdoor reading area, was opened in 2007. The library district maintains several diverse and specialized collections. The circulating collection includes books, vertical file materials, audio and video cassettes, record albums, CDs, and DVDs. The library subscribes to hundreds of periodicals and newspapers. The Local History and Genealogy collections, housed in the 1905 Carnegie Library, include books, photographs, manuscripts, maps, blueprints, newspapers, city directories, oral histories, and other items spanning more than 125 years of local and regional history. A number of other libraries and research centers are housed in the city; most are affiliated with educational institutions, government agencies, hospitals, and churches. The United States Air Force Academy Library, with more than 480,000 volumes, maintains a collection on aeronautics history before 1910; special interests also include falconry and military history. The Charles Leaming Tutt Library at Colorado College houses periodicals, a government documents repository, the college's Special Collections & Archives, and the

Crown Tapper Teaching & Learning Center devoted to exploring ways to improve teaching in the electronic age.

Public Library Information: Pikes Peak Library District, 5550 North Union Boulevard, PO Box 1579, Colorado Springs, CO 80918; telephone (719)531-6333

■ Health Care

The Colorado Springs metropolitan area is served by several major hospitals. Memorial Hospital is ranked among the top 10 percent of hospitals nationwide for heart surgeries. It is also a regional center for high-risk pregnancies, with a Level III Neonatal Intensive Care Unit. Its new North Hospital facility, opened in 2007, has nearly 500 beds. Memorial Hospital also was awarded 11 "Best Of" awards by *Colorado Springs Business Journal*, including Best Hospital, Best Place to Work, and Best Large Company With Most Promising Future.

Penrose-St. Francis Health Services runs Penrose Hospital, Penrose Community Hospital, and St. Francis Health Center. In 2006 and 2007 Penrose-St. Francis was ranked among the *U.S. News and World Report* top hospitals, in addition to receiving HealthGrades 2007 awards in Gastrointestinal Care Excellence, Critical Care Excellence and Pulmonary Care Excellence. Penrose Hospital completed a $52 million expansion in 2005 with the opening of "E Tower," containing critical care and cardiac units, a wellness center, a chapel, and a new main lobby. In addition, the Emergency Department on the Penrose Hospital campus was expanded in 2007.

There are a variety of rehabilitation centers, nursing homes and behavioral health centers in the city and surrounding county. In addition, there are a number of alternative centers of healing and medicine, including Inner Connection, Inc. and Health Quarters Ministries, Inc.

■ Recreation

Sightseeing

Colorado Springs is one of the premier vacation spots in the United States, the majestic natural beauty of Pikes Peak being a principal attraction. Visitors can venture up High Drive, a one-way road without guardrails, to see the spectacular vistas. North Cheyenne Canyon contains unusual rock formations and waterfalls that cascade down the mountains. In the Garden of the Gods, northwest of the city, visitors can hike or horseback ride through huge red sandstone rock formations; the Garden of the Gods is particularly lovely to visit at sunrise or sunset, when the sun's rays set off the natural splendor of the rocks. At High Point a camera obscura is provided for viewing the landscape that surrounds the point.

Cheyenne Mountain Zoo displays more than 600 wild animals from around the world in the U.S.'s only mountain zoo. The African Rift Valley area opened in 2003 and features Colobus monkeys, giraffes, other African animals and birds, and an interactive African Play Village for kids. The price of admission includes a visit to the Will Rogers Shrine of the Sun, which exhibits mementos of this famous American humorist and an 80-foot high observation tower. The May Natural History Museum of the Tropics houses more than 7,000 exotic insects from jungles around the globe.

The U.S. Air Force Academy is one of Colorado Springs's most popular tourist attractions. Visitors can tour the unusual multi-spired chapel, Honor Court and visitor's center. The Pikes Peak Cog Railway takes visitors on a 3-hour round trip tour to the summit of the mountain, at 12,110 feet above sea level. At the U.S. ProRodeo Hall of Fame, rodeo memorabilia is on display.

Arts and Culture

The Colorado Springs Philharmonic presents classical, pops and jazz performances October through May at the Pikes Peak Center. The Chamber Orchestra of the Springs performs five programs a year of pieces meant for small orchestras. The DaVinci Quartet plays concerts in various venues in Colorado Springs and Denver and offers community outreach to local schools. The Colorado Springs Choral Society has been performing classical and modern pieces since 1956. Students from Colorado College perform during the school year and during the Summer Music Festival, Vocal Arts and New Music Symposia, and during Extraordinary Dance Festival. The famous Broadmoor Hotel resort complex features international performers and hosts concerts.

The Star Bar Players presents four plays per season in the Lon Chaney Theater at the Civic Auditorium. Theatreworks at the University of Colorado presents Shakespeare and contemporary and classic plays. The Fine Arts Theatre Company presents musicals at the Fine Arts Center of Colorado Springs. Drama and dance students at Colorado College perform regular seasons at the college. Colorado Springs Dance Theatre sponsors national and international companies to perform at the Pikes Peak Center.

Colorado Springs is home to 20 major museums and galleries, including the Museum of the American Numismatic Association, which houses one of the largest collections of coins and medals in the world. The Fine Arts Center of Colorado Springs is a regional center for all the arts, containing the Taylor Museum of Art, the Bemis School of Art, and a performing arts department, presenting plays, dance, music, and films. Also located in Colorado Springs are the World Figure Skating Hall of Fame and Museum and the Pioneer's Museum, which exhibits displays pertaining to the history of the region. Featuring demonstrations of gold-panning techniques, the Western Museum of Mining and Industry showcases machinery used in early gold and silver mining operations. The Peterson Air and Space Museum displays historic aircraft and a moon rock. The Taylor Collection, which includes collections of Native American and Hispanic Art, is maintained at the Fine Arts Center. The Rock Ledge Ranch Historic Site celebrates the history of Colorado Springs by recreating the settlements of Native Americans and the lives of the settlers of the frontier in the 1800s, with costumed interpreters and special programs.

Festivals and Holidays

Among the annual events in Colorado Springs is the impressive Easter Sunrise Service, celebrated at Gateway Rocks in the Garden of the Gods. Territory Days on Memorial Day weekend brings 100,000 visitors to Colorado Avenue for free entertainment, food, and crafts. In early July is the Fire Fighter Chili Cook-off, featuring a beer garden and car displays. At the end of July the Annual Broadmoor Ice Revue at the Broadmoor World Arena features Olympic skaters. The Pikes Peak or Bust Rodeo in Penrose Stadium, one of the top 10 outdoor rodeos in the country, takes place in July as well. The celebration includes a parade through downtown Colorado Springs and a street breakfast. August also brings the national Little Britches Rodeo in which children from ages 8 to 18 compete for titles at the Penrose Stadium. Labor Day weekend features the Hot Air Balloon Classic, with the ascension of scores of colorful hot air balloons. December brings the Festival of Lights Christmas Parade and Gallery of Trees at the Fine Arts Center.

Sports for the Spectator

A number of sports events are available for viewing in Colorado Springs. The Sky Sox play professional Triple A baseball at Sky Sox Stadium as an affiliate of the Colorado Rockies in the Pacific Coast League. Football fans enjoy watching the U.S. Air Force Academy team compete against top college teams. Basketball, hockey and other college sports are played at University of Colorado and Colorado College. The Pikes Peak Auto Hill Climb and rodeo events also interest spectators in the Colorado Springs area. Greyhounds race at Rocky Mountain Greyhound Park from late August to late November. The U.S. Olympic Complex periodically hosts Olympic Sports Festivals. Pikes Peak International Raceway hosts NASCAR and Indy car races

Sports for the Participant

Outdoor activities abound in Colorado Springs, including climbing, white-water rafting, fishing, hiking, horseback riding, cave exploring, and gliding. The city maintains over 12,000 acres with 15 community and regional parks (including Garden of Gods and North Cheyenne Canon Parks), biking and hiking trails, 6 sports complexes, and 123 neighborhood parks. The El Pomar Youth Sports Complex includes 12 baseball fields of various sizes, 8 soccer/lacrosse fields, 6 volleyball courts, and a playground. The Broadmoor Hotel resort complex offers skeet and trap shooting as well as skiing and ice skating in the winter and golfing on three challenging courses during the warmer months. Echo Canyon River Adventures offers half- and multi-day rafting adventures on the Arkansas River. Summit Expeditions and Pikes Peak Alpine School offers instruction for all levels in rock and ice climbing, mountaineering, and back country skiing.

Shopping and Dining

Colorado Springs is served by three major malls: The Citadel, The Outlets at Castle Rock, and The Promenade Shops at Briargate. Stores specializing in Western gear and Native American art can be found in many areas. In addition, the Old Colorado City Historic District contains many small shops, and the Garden of the Gods Trading Post stocks fine Indian jewelry and Colorado giftware.

Because Colorado Springs is at the center of a popular resort area, it enjoys cuisine from around the world, as well as local Western-style establishments offering barbecue and chuck-wagon fare and Mexican foods. Rocky Mountain trout is a local delicacy. The Broadmoor Hotel maintains nine dining rooms with a range of prices and cuisines. Gourmet food is served at the historic Briarhurst Manor Inn. The Flying W Chuckwagon Supper and Western Show combines fine dining for the family with cowboy music.

Visitor Information: Colorado Springs Convention and Visitors Bureau, 515 South Cascade, Colorado Springs, CO 80903; telephone (719)635-7506; toll-free (877)745-3773; fax (719)635-4968

■ Convention Facilities

Since the turn of the century, Colorado Springs has drawn a steady flow of tourists; since the 1970s the city has made itself equally amenable to conventions and conferences, providing a number of meeting facilities. The Colorado Springs World Arena accommodates 8,000 people for general sessions and the exhibit floor offers 19,500 square feet of space or 180 booths. The Phil Long Expo Center has over 100,000 square feet of exhibition space and can accommodate up to 455 booths. There are many hotels that offer convention and meeting facilities. The luxurious 700-room Broadmoor has 114,000 square feet of meeting space and the 316-room Cheyenne Conference Mountain Resort offers 40,000 square feet. There is also the Marriott Colorado Springs Hotel and the DoubleTree Hotel Colorado Springs World Arena with 299 rooms and 21,135 square feet of meeting space. There are more than 13,500 hotel rooms in the city.

Convention Information: Colorado Springs Convention and Visitors Bureau, 515 South Cascade, Colorado Springs, CO 80903; telephone (719)635-7506; toll-free (800)888-4748; fax (719)635-4968

■ Transportation

Approaching the City

The Colorado Springs Airport, located east of the city, is served by eight major airlines, providing 110 daily flights to 13 cities. More than two million people travel through the airport each year. The airport sits on more than 7,200 acres with two parallel runways and one crosswind runway. It has one of the lowest rates of delays of major airports in the country, and also boasts valet parking service and free wireless Internet access.

Four major highways lead into Colorado Springs: I-25 (north-south), U.S. 85/87 (north-south), I-70 (east-west), and U.S. 50 (north-south). Commercial bus transportation into the city is available through interstate bus lines, including Greyhound.

Traveling in the City

The main north-south thoroughfare in Colorado Springs is I-25, called Monument Valley Freeway within the city. Midland Expressway (U.S. 24) runs east and west, becoming Platte Avenue after it crosses I-25. Other important arteries are Garden of the Gods Road, Uintah Street, and Fillmore Street, all running east and west. Some of the mountain roads are not furnished with guardrails and are not accessible to such vehicles as recreational vans.

Mountain Metropolitan Transit is the city's mass transportation system, which began running express routes in the spring of 2007.

■ Communications

Newspapers and Magazines

The major daily newspaper in Colorado Springs is the morning *The Gazette*. Weekly publications include *The Colorado Springs Independent* and the *Colorado Springs Business Journal*. The *Hispania News* and *Colorado Catholic Herald* are also published in Colorado Springs. Local concerns publish sports and hobby oriented magazines of interest to fans of hockey, whitewater kayaking, rafting, canoeing, cycling, hang gliding, rodeo, skating, coin collecting, and table tennis.

Television and Radio

Three commercial television stations broadcast in Colorado Springs; one cable provider is based in the city. The city also receives broadcasts from television stations located in nearby Grand Junction and Pueblo. Seven AM and 16 FM radio stations in Colorado Springs schedule a range of music, news, and information programming.

Media Information: The *Gazette*, 30 South Prospect, Colorado Springs, CO 80903; telephone (716)632-5511.

Colorado Springs Online

City of Colorado Springs Home Page. Available www.springsgov.com

Colorado Springs Convention & Visitors Bureau. Available www.experiencecoloradosprings.com

Colorado Springs Gazette Available www.gazette.com

Colorado Springs School District Eleven. Available www.cssd11.k12.co.us

Greater Colorado Springs Chamber of Commerce. Available www.coloradospringschamber.org

Greater Colorado Springs Economic Development Corporation. Available www.coloradosprings.org

Pikes Peak Library District. Available library.ppld.org

BIBLIOGRAPHY

Finley, Judith Reid, *On the Wings of Modernism: The United States Air Force Academy* (Urbana, IL: University of Illinois Press, 2004)

Nauman, Robert Allen, *Time Capsule 1900: Colorado Springs A Century Ago* (Colorado Springs, CO: Pastword Publications, 1998)

Denver

■ The City in Brief

Founded: 1858 (incorporated 1861)

Head Official: Mayor John W. Hickenlooper (D) (since 2003)

City Population

1980: 493,000
1990: 467,610
2000: 554,636
2006 estimate: 566,974
Percent change, 1990–2000: 18.6%
U.S. rank in 1980: 24th
U.S. rank in 1990: 26th
U.S. rank in 2000: 31st

Metropolitan Area Population

1980: 1,429,000
1990: 1,622,980
2000: 2,109,282
2006 estimate: Not reported
Percent change, 1990–2000: 29.9%
U.S. rank in 1980: 21st
U.S. rank in 1990: 22nd
U.S. rank in 2000: 19th

Area: 153 square miles (2000)

Elevation: 5,332 feet above sea level

Average Annual Temperatures: January, 29.2° F; July, 73.4° F; annual average, 50.1° F

Average Annual Precipitation: 15.81 inches of rain; 60.3 inches of snow

Major Economic Sectors: services, wholesale and retail trade, government

Unemployment Rate: 3.9% (June 2007)

Per Capita Income: $27,715 (2005)

2005 FBI Crime Index Property: 33,902

2005 FBI Crime Index Violent: 4,492

Major Colleges and Universities: University of Denver, Metropolitan State University, University of Colorado at Denver

Daily Newspaper: *The Denver Post, Rocky Mountain News*

■ Introduction

Denver, dubbed the Mile High City, is the commercial, financial, and transportation capital of the Rocky Mountain region. A concentration of federal government offices makes it the administrative center of this area as well. Denver's history has included frequent boom periods, but redirection and economic diversification became necessary during the late 1960s through the early 1980s. The city is undergoing a renaissance, with downtown development paving the way for Denver's projected ascendance in high-technology industries as the nation's population shifts southwestward. Set in a verdant plain at the foot of the Rocky Mountains, Denver is noted for its quality of life and the blending of modern innovation and Western tradition.

■ Geography and Climate

Denver is situated in the high plains at the eastern edge of the Rocky Mountains, which protect the city from severe winter weather. These mountains, reaching higher than 14,000 feet, are the dominant feature of the area. The South Platte River bisects the city, and many creeks, small lakes, and reservoirs grace the metropolitan area. Denver's climate is semiarid and relatively mild, with more sunny days than either Miami, Florida or San Diego, California. Although visitors must make some adjustment to the high altitude, they find that the area's low humidity makes even the highest and lowest temperatures seem less extreme.

Area: 153 square miles (2000)

Elevation: 5,332 feet above sea level

Average Temperatures: January, 29.2° F; July, 73.4° F; annual average, 50.1° F

Average Annual Precipitation: 15.81 inches of rain; 60.3 inches of snow

■ History

Discovery of Gold Brings Settlers to Denver Area

For centuries, the mountains and plains of Colorado were used as hunting grounds by Native Americans, and eventually the more sophisticated, agricultural tribes like the Anasazi established villages. In the sixteenth century, the Spanish explored the region where Denver is now located, but no Europeans established permanent settlements until the mid-1800s, when gold was discovered at Pikes Peak. In 1858, a supply center for the mining towns was established on the site of a tribal village at the junction of the South Platte River and Cherry Creek. The town was called St. Charles; later it was renamed Denver City after James W. Denver, governor of the Kansas Territory, and was incorporated in 1861.

The gold boom soon ended, but some of the fortune hunters stayed on to settle in the new town. During the 1860s, much of the town was destroyed by fire; a ravaging flash flood killed 20 people; and the citizens repelled frequent attacks from the Plains tribes and even an assault by a Confederate Army. With the arrival of rail transportation in 1870 a steady influx of settlers insured the future of the thriving town, and when Colorado attained statehood in 1876, Denver was named the state capital. By 1879 it boasted a population of 35,000 people and the first telephone service in the West.

Silver Boom and Bust; Economy Diversifies

A silver boom in the 1880s ushered in another period of rapid growth, filling Denver with the Victorian mansions of silver barons and making it the most elegant city in the West. The collapse of the silver market in the panic of 1893 staggered the city's economy, so the city began to diversify. By the early 1900s, Denver had become the commercial and industrial center of the Rocky Mountain region, as well as a leader in livestock sales, agriculture, and tourism.

Denver sustained a period of relatively slow development until the 1930s. Prior to World War II, when such federal government agencies as the Geological Survey, the U.S. Mint, Lowry Air Force Base, the Bureau of Land Management, and the Air Force Accounting Center were established in the area, Denver experienced another population surge that continued through the 1950s. During the 1960s Denver lost population as residents moved to the suburbs to escape inner city deterioration. Growth slowed again in the mid-1970s as a result of the oil industry crisis. The effects of this downturn, however, were ultimately positive. As a result of efforts to diversify the economy, Denver became known as "the energy capital of the west," with a focus on alternative energy sources such as solar and wind power. In fact, by 1980 approximately 1,200 energy companies were located in Denver.

Growth slowed again in the mid-1980s when plans for oil shale development were curtailed; construction of high-rise office buildings downtown nevertheless continued unabated. A sleek, modern landscape has emerged in Denver where a Western frontier town once stood. As Denver entered the twenty-first century, it reflected the economic downturn due to the high-tech industry but has since stabilized and strengthened to remain the principal commercial, financial, and industrial hub of the Rocky Mountain region.

Historical Information: Colorado Historical Society, Stephen H. Hart Library, 1300 Broadway, Denver, CO 80203; telephone (303)866-2305; email research@chs.state.co.us

■ Population Profile

Metropolitan Area Residents

1980: 1,429,000
1990: 1,622,980
2000: 2,109,282
2006 estimate: Not reported
Percent change, 1990–2000: 29.9%
U.S. rank in 1980: 21st
U.S. rank in 1990: 22nd
U.S. rank in 2000: 19th

City Residents

1980: 493,000
1990: 467,610
2000: 554,636
2006 estimate: 566,974
Percent change, 1990–2000: 18.6%
U.S. rank in 1980: 24th
U.S. rank in 1990: 26th
U.S. rank in 2000: 31st

Density: 3,616.7 people per square mile (2000)

Image copyright Evan Meyer, 2007. Used under license from Shutterstock.com.

Racial and ethnic characteristics (2005)

White: 392,164
Black: 54,693
American Indian and Alaska Native: 6,627
Asian: 15,905
Native Hawaiian and Pacific Islander: 108
Hispanic or Latino (may be of any race): 191,510
Other: 61,464

Percent of residents born in state: 40.1%
(2006)

Age characteristics (2005)

Population under 5 years old: 51,160
Population 5 to 9 years old: 36,066
Population 10 to 14 years old: 30,985
Population 15 to 19 years old: 26,907
Population 20 to 24 years old: 33,829
Population 25 to 34 years old: 102,202
Population 35 to 44 years old: 87,998
Population 45 to 54 years old: 69,598
Population 55 to 59 years old: 29,456
Population 60 to 64 years old: 18,385
Population 65 to 74 years old: 28,264
Population 75 to 84 years old: 23,129
Population 85 years and older: 7,219
Median age: 34.3 years

Births (2006, MSA)

Total number: 37,672

Deaths (2006, MSA)

Total number: 14,824

Money income (2005)

Per capita income: $27,715
Median household income: $42,370
Total households: 241,579

Number of households with income of...

less than $10,000: 22,618
$10,000 to $14,999: 15,739
$15,000 to $24,999: 32,678
$25,000 to $34,999: 29,748
$35,000 to $49,999: 37,182
$50,000 to $74,999: 41,801
$75,000 to $99,999: 23,659
$100,000 to $149,999: 22,166
$150,000 to $199,999: 8,111
$200,000 or more: 7,877

Percent of families below poverty level: 9.9% (2005)

2005 FBI Crime Index Property: 33,902

2005 FBI Crime Index Violent: 4,492

■ Municipal Government

The city and county of Denver share the same boundaries and operate under a government that performs both municipal and county functions. Denver's mayor-council form of government invests its mayor, who is elected to a four-year term, with strong executive powers. The 13 council members also serve for four years.

Head Official: Mayor John W. Hickenlooper (D) (since 2003; current term expires 2011)

Total Number of City Employees: 12,485 (2005)

City Information: City of Denver, 945 S. Huron St., Denver, CO 80223; telephone (303)698-4900

■ Economy

Major Industries and Commercial Activity

Following record economic and population growth in the 1950s, Denver weathered reversals tied to the fluctuating petroleum market in the 1970s and 1980s. By the late 1980s the city had taken measures toward establishing a diversified economic base. Major companies in the Denver metropolitan area employ workers in a range of fields such as air transportation, telecommunications, aerospace, and manufacturing, along with a growing high-tech sector. The city is also a major energy research center and a regional headquarters for government agencies. As of 2007 Denver had made *Fortune* magazine's list of "Best Cities for Business" for each of the past five years and Dun and Bradstreet's "Top 10 Cities for Small Business" for the previous six years.

The financial and commercial capital of the Rocky Mountain region, Denver's downtown banking district—dubbed the "Wall Street of the Rockies"—consists of major national and international institutions. The city is the transportation hub for a large portion of the western United States; consumer and industrial goods are transported by air, rail, and truck through Denver to more than 30 million people annually. Denver is a Foreign Trade Zone, providing advantages to companies involved in international trade.

Denver's central location—it is 346 miles west of the exact geographic center of the country—places it in an advantageous position for future economic development and growth. Analysts predict that the U.S. population is shifting south and west, with future concentration expected in the area from California to Utah and to the Gulf Coast in Texas. Denver is at the center of this region; projections indicate that the city will become a high-technology research, development, and manufacturing hub for the entire Southwest. In 2006 the city witnessed strong growth in the natural resources; mining and construction; transportation; warehousing and utilities; and professional and business services sectors.

Items and goods produced: computer storage and peripherals, beverages, mining and farming machinery, rubber goods, fabricated metals, chemicals and allied stone and clay products, western clothing, transportation equipment, scientific instruments, feed, flour, luggage

Incentive Programs—New and Existing Companies

Local programs: The Mayor's Office of Economic Development & International Trade (MOED/IT) works to retain and create quality jobs, assists organizations in expansion or relocation, and provides a multitude of business development services. It promotes the city as a business location particularly for foreign companies and promotes Denver companies entering international markets. MOED/IT assists with financing, economic incentives, regulatory requirement assistance, and other services as needed. MOED/IT also administers the Denver Urban Enterprise Zone, which assists business with state tax credits for job creation. Additionally, the WIRED grant program, administered by the Metro Denver EDC and the Denver Office of Economic Development, is intended to coordinate workforce development, economic development and education on a regional level for the aerospace, bioscience, energy, and information technology sectors.

State programs: A variety of state and federal programs are available to assist businesses in relocating and expanding in Denver. Enterprise Zone Tax Credits and Manufacturing Revenue Bonds are among them. The State of Colorado's Business Retention and Expansion program helps smooth the path for area businesses by removing local or statewide barriers.

Job training programs: The Mayor's Office of Workforce Development offers the Colorado FIRST program which connects employment, job readiness, education, and training services into a network of resources at the local and state level. This system links Colorado's employers to a variety of qualified applicants and provides job-seekers with access to employment and training opportunities at workforce training centers throughout the city as well as additional resources across the country. The menu of core services includes: career counseling and assessment, employer and job-seeker access to automated job postings, information on job trends, assistance in filing unemployment insurance claims, and help in finding federal, state, and city dollars to cover some or all of the costs of training opportunities. Metro Denver also has 17 Colorado Workforce training centers.

Development Projects

In 2006—a full two years ahead of schedule—the $1.67 billion T-REX project reached completion. It widened Interstates 25 and I-225 and added 19 miles of light rail connecting Metro Denver's two largest employment centers: The Central Business District and the Denver Tech Center. FasTracks, a 12-year project begun in 2004, planned to bring 119 miles of new light rail and commuter rail, 18 miles of bus rapid transit service, and 21,000 new parking spaces to Denver.

The health care industry is also a fertile source of development in metropolitan Denver. HealthONE announced plans in November 2005 for $255 million in expansions for three Metro Denver hospitals, all expected to be completed by 2008. The $111 million expansion at Presbyterian/St. Luke's Medical Center includes the new 100,000-square-foot HealthONE Children's Hospital at P/SL and a 120,000-square-foot medical office building. The Swedish Medical Center will receive an $84 million improvement for its surgical services, intensive care unit, and Emergency Department/Level I Trauma Center, while Medical Center of Aurora will recieve a $60 million, 140,000-square-foot tower for a new cardiovscular center.

Economic Development Information: Denver Office of Economic Development; 201 W. Colfax Ave., 2nd Floor, Dept. 1005, Denver, CO 80202; telepone (720) 913-1999; fax (720)913-1802; email econdev@Denver-Gov.org

Commercial Shipping

Denver is the commercial transportation center for an eight-state area, providing a hub for two major rail freight companies, more than 160 motor freight carriers, and a number of air cargo services. With negotiated motor freight rates and the city's designation as a Free Trade Zone, Denver has created a competitive marketplace for the import and export of goods. Denver International Airport handled 622 million pounds of cargo in 2006. The city, located strategically between Canada and Mexico, is an ever-expanding center for international trade; Colorado exports of manufactured goods, minerals and agriculture products reached almost $8 billion in 2006, a boost of 17.3 percent over 2005.

Labor Force and Employment Outlook

Employers in Denver choose from a highly educated labor pool. The city boasts the nation's third-most educated city. Thirty-eight percent of residents are college graduates and 89.1 percent have graduated from high school. Colorado has the nation's third most educated workforce. The workforce is also young, with a median age of 34.5 in the metro region. Local analysts predict a healthy economy, based on Denver's quality labor force, affordable cost of living, high quality of life, and low commercial lease rates. With a diverse employment base across many sectors, Denver is in a prime position for growth well into the twenty-first century. Growing industries include the aerospace, bioscience, energy, financial services, and information technology/software sectors.

Since 2005 employment growth in metro Denver has been greater than that of the nation as a whole. With the exception of information services, all industry sectors added jobs in 2006, and retail experienced perhaps the most stunning growth rate, at 8.8 percent. Also in 2006 population increased 1.6 percent, the largest annual percentage increase since 2002. Employment has kept pace with population growth, however; about 22,300 jobs were expected to be added in 2007 for a 1.6 percent increase in total employment. The one major bump on the Denver economic outlook is the real estate industry; foreclosures were up in 2006 to record levels and house sales were down nearly 3 percent from the previous year. 2007 was expected to see that trend continue and perhaps even increase, thanks to the national mortgage crisis in August of that year. In 2008 analysts expected the real estate market to perhaps slow, but not stop, Denver's overall growth and anticipated that further industry diversification, an expanding employment base, continued wage growth, and only modest inflation would keep Denver above national employment levels.

The following is a summary of data regarding the Denver-Aurora metropolitan area labor force, 2006 annual averages.

Size of nonagricultural labor force: 1,214,700

Number of workers employed in ...

> construction and mining: 94,100
> manufacturing: 72,200
> trade, transportation and utilities: 239,100
> information: 47,700
> financial activities: 100,700
> professional and business services: 199,800
> educational and health services: 122,900
> leisure and hospitality: 125,200
> other services: 46,400
> government: 166,700

Average hourly earnings of production workers employed in manufacturing: $17.64

Unemployment rate: 3.9% (June 2007)

Largest private employers (2005)	*Number of employees*
Wal-Mart Stores Inc.	23,730
King Soopers Inc./Division of Dillon Co. Inc.	17,134
Centura Health	12,000

Largest private employers (2005)

	Number of employees
Safeway Inc.	11,621
Qwest Communications International Inc.	10,400
HCA-HealthOne LLC	8,800
Exempla Healthcare	6,850
Target Stores	6,296
IBM	6,100
University of Denver	5,650

Cost of Living

The costs for housing and health care in Denver are somewhat above the national average, while the cost of utilities is substantially below the national average.

The following is a summary of data regarding key cost of living factors for the Denver area.

2007 (1st quarter) ACCRA Average House Price: $356,705

2007 (1st quarter) ACCRA Cost of Living Index: 102.7

State income tax rate: 4.63% of Federal Taxable Income

State sales tax rate: 2.9%

Local income tax rate: $5.75 per month per employee for all workers who receive income greater than $500 a month (occupational tax)

Local sales tax rate: 3.5%

Property tax rate: In Colorado, the tax assessor first determines the actual value of a property, then applies the residential rate to get the assessed value. In 2004 the residential rate was 7.96%.

Economic Information: Metro Denver Chamber of Commerce, 1445 Market Street, Denver, CO 80202; telephone (303)620-8092; fax (303)534-3200

■ Education and Research

Elementary and Secondary Schools

The Denver Public School system is directed by a seven-member board of education that administers policy and establishes direction. The Denver public schools provide programs for slow and gifted learners, college preparation, and career training. It also features a Junior level ROTC program. The four goals of the system are literacy, school readiness, school-to-career, and neighborhood centers. The district's recently-established Professional Compensation System is a groundbreaking teacher pay plan that links compensation to job performance.

The metropolitan area is served by 19 other public school districts, and Denver features an open enrollment policy and the opportunity for charter school formation. As of 2007 there were 19 charter schools operating at all grade levels.

The following is a summary of data regarding the Denver Public Schools as of the 2005–2006 school year.

Total enrollment: 73,399

Number of facilities

elementary schools: 88
junior high/middle schools: 17
senior high schools: 14
other: 32

Student/teacher ratio: 18.1:1

Teacher salaries (2005–06)

elementary median: $46,070
junior high/middle median: $47,040
secondary median: $47,990

Funding per pupil: $7,852

There are numerous private and parochial institutions, including the Colorado Academy and St. Mary's Academy for Girls. In 2004 just under 10 percent of the metro Denver population attended private schools.

Public Schools Information: Denver Public Schools, 900 Grant Street, Denver, CO 80203; telephone (720) 423-3411; email communications@dpsk12.org

Colleges and Universities

The metropolitan Denver area supports 12 four-year public and private colleges and universities with enrollments totaling over 140,300. A wide variety of undergraduate degrees and numerous graduate and professional degrees are offered along with the opportunity to study at several excellent research institutions. The University of Denver is ranked second in the nation among doctoral and research universities for the percentage of undergraduate students studying abroad. The University of Denver Daniels School of Business has been ranked 7th in the *Wall Street Journal* for producing graduates with high ethical standards. Other area private colleges are Johnson & Wales University, Regis University, and Teikyo Loretto Heights University. Public schools include University of Colorado at Denver, Metropolitan State College of Denver, Community College of Denver, and the Colorado School of Mines. Non-traditional education is well represented by such institutions as the Colorado Free University, which has an open admissions policy and is known for its adult and continuing education programs. More than 60 vocational and technical schools serve the region.

Libraries and Research Centers

Denver's Central Library underwent expansion in the mid-1990s to its current square footage of 540,000. The addition houses the Children's Library, the Burnham Hoyt Room popular adult library, and Marietta Baron Teen Space. The Denver Public Library maintains 22 branches, including an African-American research library and a bookmobile. It holds more than 2.5 million books, periodicals, subscriptions, microforms, and audiovisual materials, plus 2.2 million government publications.

The Denver area boasts a number of other public, special interest, and research libraries. Among them are the Colorado Talking Book Library, the Denver Medical Library, the University of Colorado Law Library, and many high-technology and university-related libraries. The University of Denver's Penrose library features rare book and manuscript collections, the Beck Archives of Rocky Mountain Jewish Historical Society and the Carson-Brierly Dance Library.

Research activities in such fields as environmental sciences, allergy and immunology, biochemical genetics, health services, mass spectrometry, biochemical parasitology, alcohol, taste and smell, sports sciences, applied mechanics, public management, social science, mineral law, mass communications, family studies, the Holocaust, Islamic-Judaic studies, and international relations are conducted at centers in the Denver area.

Public Library Information: Denver Public Library, 10 West Fourteenth Avenue Parkway, Denver, CO 80204-2731; telephone (720)865-1111

■ Health Care

For years Denver has attracted those seeking to enjoy the respiratory benefits of the area's climate and mountain air. Today, Denver is the medical center of the Rocky Mountains, operating more than 25 major hospitals, many of which have earned national and international reputations as leading medical research and treatment facilities. The city has a large number of physicians practicing in every specialty. Additionally, since Colorado has the lowest obesity rate in the nation, annual health insurance rates in the Denver area are about $400 cheaper than the national average.

Among the city's most prominent hospitals are Children's Hospital, a state-of-the-art children's hospital serving a 10-state area. It was ranked seventh nationally in pediatric care by *U.S. News and World Report* in 2006; the University of Colorado Hospital ranked in the top 50 in 9 of 16 specialties. The National Jewish Medical and Research Center is a teaching and research center for respiratory, allergic, and immunological diseases; the center also houses the Environmental Lung Center. In 2006 it was named the best hospital in the country for the treatment of respiratory diseases by *U.S. News and World*

Report for the ninth year in a row. The Rose Medical Center offers a wide range of services and specializes in diabetes treatment, obstetrics, and videoscopic surgery and is the health care provider for several of the area's professional sports teams.

Other major hospitals in the city include the AMC Cancer Research Center, Denver General Hospital, the Swedish Medical Center, the Colorado Psychiatric Hospital, the St. Anthony Central Hospital, and Fitzsimmons Army Medical Center.

■ Recreation

Sightseeing

Denver offers attractions ranging from historic Western landmarks to modern amusement parks. Downtown, the Colorado State Capitol features a 24-carat gold-plated dome; the 13th step of its stairway is set at the altitude of exactly one mile above sea level. A few blocks away is the United States Mint, where nearly a third of the nation's gold supply is stored. Larimer Square, Denver's first main street and a restored Victorian historical district, is an especially popular tourist site. Also downtown is Elitch Gardens, a year-round amusement park offering thrill rides, formal gardens, restaurants, and shops. Across the river, the recently renovated Downtown Aquarium combines the qualities of aquariums and sea life parks in an exciting interactive experience that is both fun and educational. The 80-acre Denver Zoo is a modern facility, housing more than 4,000 animals in natural environments; the zoo is also in the beginning stages of a long-term plan to transform itself into a major conservation center.

The Denver area is filled with historic buildings, homes, and mansions that are open to the public. Many neighborhoods retain a large part of their historical and architectural integrity, offering excellent examples of Victorian, Georgian, and Italianate styles. Popular tour sites in the area include the Coors Brewery in nearby Golden; the Denver Botanic Gardens; and Washington Park, a replica of President Washington's gardens at Mount Vernon. Another area landmark, located in City Ditch, is a statue of "Wynken, Blynken, and Nod," dedicated to Denver poet Eugene Field, author of the popular children's rhyme "Dutch Lullaby." Several bus and guided walking tours of Denver are also available.

Arts and Culture

The arts are well supported in Denver, both in recently constructed facilities and elegant historically preserved buildings. The Denver Performing Arts Complex (PLEX), covering a four-block area and 12 acres, is an $80 million, architecturally stunning complex which offers almost every facet of the cultural world from Shakespearean drama to popular music. It regularly hosts

Colorado Ballet, the Colorado Symphony Orchestra, the Denver Center Theatre Company and the National Theatre Conservatory. Many small theaters, galleries, and open-air exhibits can also be found throughout the city.

Denver enjoys a thriving performance community comprised of a number of theater and dance companies, as well as music and opera groups. Germinal Stage Denver, a non-profit avant-garde theater, stages five or six productions a year, and each summer the University of Colorado at Boulder sponsors a Shakespeare Festival. Dance in all its forms, from folk to ballet to modern, is performed frequently throughout the area. The Boettcher Concert Hall, considered one of the great music halls in the country, was the first symphony hall in the round in the United States, and is the home of the renowned Colorado Symphony Orchestra. Opera is presented by Opera Colorado in the Ellie Caulkins Opera House, where it has performed since 2005.

The Colorado History Museum displays exhibitions highlighting the history of Colorado and the West with changing and permanent exhibits on Native Americans, miners, and other settlers. The Museum of Outdoor Arts is a unique museum without walls that showcases a blend of architecture, fine art, and landscaping. Offering a versatile collection of activities for children of all ages, the Children's Museum of Denver includes live theater, playscapes for children of all ages, a market, assembly plant, and a fire station.

The Denver Art Museum is an impressive seven-story structure containing more than 30,000 art objects; a highlight is the world's leading collection of Native American art. The Colorado Railroad Museum, housed in a replica of an 1880s depot, is considered to be one of the best privately supported rail museums in the United States. Also of interest is a Museum of Miniatures, Dolls and Toys and the Denver Firefighters Museum.

Festivals and Holidays

Denver schedules an abundance of festivals and special events throughout the year. The National Western Stock Show, Rodeo and Horse Show, which has been called the "Super Bowl of cattle shows," occurs each January. It features nearly a month of western music performances, prize-winning livestock exhibitions, and rodeo events with the country's top rodeo stars. The show culminates with the award for Livestock's Man of the Year. From May through September, outdoor shows and musical events are held at Red Rocks and Coors amphitheaters and in the LoDo district.

Another special event in Denver is the nation's largest St. Patrick's Day parade west of the Mississippi in March. The Colorado Renaissance Festival, a recreation of medieval England, takes place each weekend during June and July. The Colorado Indian Market, featuring the art, dances, food, and culture of native Americans, is

held in January. Larimer Square is the site of the annual Oktoberfest.

Sports for the Spectator

Denver fields a professional team in almost every major sport. The Denver Broncos of the National Football League won back-to-back Super Bowls in 1998 and 1999. The team moved to Invesco Field at Mile High Stadium in 2001. The National Basketball Association's Nuggets have had several playoff successes. The Colorado Rockies National League Baseball team play home games at Coors Field. The Colorado Avalanche, Denver's National Hockey League team won the Stanley Cup in 2001. Denver area colleges and universities compete in a variety of sporting events.

Auto racing takes place at the Colorado National Speedway, and for those who enjoy parimutuel betting, the greyhound races at the Mile High Kennel Club in Commerce City provide plenty of excitement. Denver is also a major stop on the National Rodeo Circuit.

Sports for the Participant

The nearby Rocky Mountains provide abundant opportunities for sports-minded individuals year round. In the winter, skiers from the world over come to try their luck on the famous slopes. Rock and mountain climbing, fly fishing in the clear mountain streams, white-water canoeing and rafting, and hiking through the splendid mountain vistas are among the most popular recreations in spring, summer, and fall.

A $45 million, 24-year project to clean up the stretch of the South Platte River that runs through Denver has resulted in bike paths and a series of 11 beautiful parks; man-made boat chutes provide kayaking and rafting opportunities, and the banks of the river are lined with picnic areas and wetlands. Denver County maintains 250 urban parks, 14,000 acres of mountain park land and an extensive urban trail system in addition to 29 recreation centers, 19 swimming pools, numerous baseball fields, basketball courts, and other sports venues. In fact, Denver has the largest public parks system of any U.S. city. There are more than 75 public and private golf courses in the metropolitan area and several area lakes offering water skiing, sailing, swimming, and fishing.

Shopping and Dining

Denver's newest shopping venue, Colorado Mills, opened in 2004 and offers 200 stores. In downtown, Denver Pavilions retail and entertainment center covers two square blocks in the heart of downtown Denver. Flatiron Crossing offers indoor/outdoor shopping in 200 stores and a 14-theater movie complex. A variety of other shopping experiences can be found in Denver, ranging from small, specialized shops to large national outlet malls. The Sixteenth Street Mall, a sculptured pedestrian walkway stretching for over a mile in the downtown district, is lined with shops and restaurants. The recently revitalized Cherry Creek Shopping Center features upscale department stores and more than 160 specialty shops in an enclosed mall. The adjacent Cherry Creek Shopping District is known for its aesthetically appealing shops and galleries. With the success of Larimer Square, a renovated historical area of specialty stores, the entire lower downtown area is rapidly attracting unique shops, galleries, and restaurants. Denver's Tattered Cover Book Store has been hailed by *The New York Times* as "one of the truly great independent book stores in America."

Other interesting areas include Sakura Square, a group of Asian markets and art galleries; and Tivoli, a converted brewery that houses many shops, movie theaters, and some of Denver's finest restaurants. Park Meadows is a 1.5-million-square foot shopping center located 12 miles south of the city; it is designed to resemble a mountain ski resort.

Denver is well known for its fine beefsteak and traditional Western fare, but a much wider range of dining experiences is also available, from fast food to haute cuisine. Area specialties include spicy Mexican dishes, local fish and game delicacies such as buffalo, elk, venison, and Rocky Mountain trout, and native Southwestern food. A large number of international and ethnic restaurants complete the dining choices. A favorite nighttime gathering spot is LoDo, or Lower Downtown, which has been transformed since the opening of nearby Coors Field from an industrial warehouse district into a thriving area of elegant restaurants and sports bars that attracts Denver's young population.

Visitor Information: Denver Metro Convention and Visitors Bureau, 1555 California, Suite 300, Denver, CO 80202; telephone (303)892-1112

■ Convention Facilities

The Colorado Convention Center in downtown Denver is within walking distance of more than 7,000 hotel rooms and 300 restaurants. The convention center, located along the river in the heart of downtown, contains more than 600,000 square feet of exhibit space, 100,000 square feet of meeting rooms, two ballrooms (including a 35,000-square-foot ballroom and a 50,000-square-foot ballroom), theater-style seating for 7,000 people, 1,000 covered parking spaces and state of the art multimedia facilities. The center underwent a massive $268 million expansion that nearly doubled its space, completed in 2003.

The National Western Complex, located at the northern end of the downtown area near I-70, contains a 6,600-seat stadium arena, a 40,000-square-foot exhibit hall, a multi-use events center, and the 120,000-square-foot Hall of Education.

Other meeting and exhibition facilities include the Denver Coliseum, Red Rocks Amphitheater, the Denver Merchandise Mart and Exposition Center, and the Adams County Regional Park Complex. Most of the major hotels in the city offer extensive meeting, banquet, and ballroom facilities, as do many of the larger mountain resorts.

Convention Information: Denver Metro Convention and Visitors Bureau, 1555 California, Suite 300, Denver, CO 80202; telephone (800)480-2010

■ Transportation

Approaching the City

Denver International Airport is the fifth busiest airport in the United States and 10th busiest in the world. In 2006 it served a total of 47.3 million passengers, an increase of 9.1 percent over 2005. Amtrak provides passenger rail service with westbound passengers treated to a scenic route through the Rocky Mountains.

Denver is at the crossroads of three major interstate highways. A new beltway highway system that encircles the metro area and provides easy access to the airport was nearly complete in 2007, including C-470, E-470, and the Northwest Parkway.

Traveling in the City

Orienting oneself in Denver is made considerably easier by the natural landmark of the Rocky Mountains, readily visible to the west. Denver's street numbers are divided north and south by Ellsworth Avenue and east and west by Broadway. In general, east-west roads are called "avenues" and north-south designated as "streets." Above Ellsworth, the streets bear numbers; below Ellsworth the streets are named.

The Regional Transportation District (RTD) offers 170 bus routes, 14 miles of light rail and SkyRide transportation to and from Denver International Airport. The RTD was named the top transit agency in the United States in 2003. FasTracks, an ambitious expansion of Denver's public transportation system, was scheduled to be completed by 2016.

■ Communications

Newspapers and Magazines

Denver readers are served by two major daily morning newspapers, *The Denver Post* and the *Rocky Mountain News,* as well as by many smaller neighborhood weeklies and a business weekly—*The Denver Business Journal.* Local magazines include *Colorado Country Life, Colorado Outdoors,* and *The Bloomsbury Review.* Many trade and collegiate publications are based in the city as well.

Television and Radio

The six major television stations in the Denver area represent commercial networks, public television, independent stations, and special interest channels; a number of channels are offered by area cable systems as well. More than 45 AM and FM radio stations provide listeners with a variety of musical and special programming.

Media Information: *The Denver Post,* 101 W. Colfax Ave, Denver, CO, 80202; telephone (303)832-3232; toll-free (800)832-4609. *Rocky Mountain News,* 101 West Colfax Avenue, Denver, CO 80204; telephone (303)954-5000

Denver Online

City of Denver. Available www.denvergov.org

Colorado Historical Society. Available www
.coloradohistory.org

Denver Metro Convention & Visitors Bureau.
Available www.denver.org

Denver Post. Available www.denverpost.com

Denver Public Library. Available www.denverlibrary
.org

Denver Public Schools. Available www.denver
.k12.co.us

Mayor's Office of Employment and Training.
Available www.moet.org

Metro Denver Chamber of Commerce. Available
www.denverchamber.org

Rocky Mountain News. Available www
.rockymountainnews.com

BIBLIOGRAPHY

Everett, Derek R., *The Colorado State Capitol: History, Politics, and Preservation* (Boulder, CO: University Press of Colorado, 2005)

Noel, Thomas J.,*The City and the Saloon: Denver, 1858– 1916* (Lincoln, NE: University of Nebraska Press, 1982)

Fort Collins

■ The City in Brief

Founded: 1862 (incorporated 1869)

Head Official: Mayor Doug Hutchinson (R) (since 2005)

City Population

    1980: 64,092
    1990: 87,491
    2000: 118,652
    2006 estimate: 129,467
    Percent change, 1990–2000: 33.5%
    U.S. rank in 1980: Not reported
    U.S. rank in 1990: 230th (State rank: 7th)
    U.S. rank in 2000: 206th (State rank: 5th)

Metropolitan Area Population

    1980: 149,184
    1990: 186,136
    2000: 251,494
    2006 estimate: 276,253
    Percent change, 1990–2000: 35.1%
    U.S. rank in 1980: Not reported
    U.S. rank in 1990: 166th
    U.S. rank in 2000: 142nd

Area: 47 square miles (2000)

Elevation: 5,003 feet above sea level

Average Annual Temperature: 47.9° F

Average Annual Precipitation: 15 inches of rain; 55 inches of snow

Major Economic Sectors: services, wholesale and retail trade, government

Unemployment Rate: 3.3% (June 2007)

Per Capita Income: $25,408 (2005)

2005 FBI Crime Index Property: 4,434

2005 FBI Crime Index Violent: 442

Major Colleges and Universities: Colorado State University, Front Range Community College

Daily Newspaper: *Fort Collins Coloradoan*

■ Introduction

Fort Collins is located on the Cache la Poudre River at the foot of the Rocky Mountains. The city's clean water and clean air make for a healthy environment. Fort Collins boasts a very active cultural scene, which is enhanced by events offered at Colorado State University. The surrounding countryside has breathtaking cliffs, clear skies, and beautiful lakes and waterfalls—nature at its best. The city consistently appears on lists of the best places to live in the United States, and in 2006 it was chosen as America's best small city in which to live by *Money* magazine.

■ Geography and Climate

Located at the western base of the "Front Range" of the Rocky Mountains, Fort Collins is about 65 miles north of Denver and 45 miles south of Cheyenne, Wyoming. The city lies along the banks of the Cache La Poudre River, and the Great Plains lie to the east.

Fort Collins lies in a semi-arid region and experiences four seasons. The city has 300 days per year with sunshine, and the average summer high temperature is 85 degrees. Annual snowfall averages 55 inches, and the snow generally melts within a few days.

Area: 47 square miles (2000)

Elevation: 5,003 feet above sea level

Average Temperature: 47.9° F

Average Annual Precipitation: 15 inches of rain; 55 inches of snow

■ History

Travelers crossing the country on the Overland Trail often stopped at Camp Collins, which was established on the Cache La Poudre River in 1862. The camp was named for Colonel W. O. Collins, a commander of the eleventh Ohio Cavalry at Fort Laramie, Wyoming. The fort was built to protect the important trading post from attacks by native Americans. In 1864 a community grew around the fort and became a center of trading, shipping, and manufacturing. Fort Collins was incorporated in 1869.

As farmers settled in the outlying areas, other settlers began moving to the new town, where they opened stores, livery stables, and other businesses. The first buildings of the state agricultural college, located in Fort Collins by vote of the state legislature, were erected in the 1870s. By that time the town boasted a post office, a general store, a rooming house, a mill, and its first school house.

During the first half of the 1870s the town population began to dwindle due to the failure of the town's first bank, a grasshopper infiltration, and business problems. The economy was given a boost by the arrival of the Colorado Central Railroad later in the decade. Soon after, the development of irrigation canals brought water to the area, greatly expanding farming options. Barley, wheat, and oat growing were especially successful, as were the cultivation of sugar beets and alfalfa.

The 1880s saw the construction of a number of elegant homes and commercial buildings. Beet tops proved to be excellent and abundant food for local sheep, and by the early 1900s the area was being referred to as "Lamb feeding capital of the world." In 1903 the Great Western sugar processing plant was built in the city.

Fort Collins gained a reputation as a very conservative city in the twentieth century, with prohibition of alcoholic beverages being retained from the late 1890s until 1969. Although the city was affected by the Great Depression, it nevertheless experienced slow and steady growth throughout the early part of the twentieth century. During the middle of the century the population of the city doubled, and an era of economic prosperity occurred. Old buildings were razed to make way for new, modern structures. By the 1960s, though, citizens had formed a group to preserve and restore the older buildings that add such beauty and character to the city. The Fort Collins Historical Society was formed in 1974 to encourage the preservation of historic buildings and documents, and to provide educational opportunities for people to learn about the city's past.

Today's Fort Collins offers a rich mix of history with the cultural interest of a university town and an attractiveness to new, higher-tech businesses; add to that the plethora of outdoor activities and beauty offered in and around the city. Fort Collins is known above all for its small town familiarity, outdoor activities, cultural amenities, and active lifestyle.

Historical Information: Fort Collins Public Library, Local History Collection, 201 Peterson Street, Fort Collins, CO 80524; telephone (970) 221-6740

■ Population Profile

Metropolitan Area Residents
    1980: 149,184
    1990: 186,136
    2000: 251,494
    2006 estimate: 276,253
    Percent change, 1990–2000: 35.1%
    U.S. rank in 1980: Not reported
    U.S. rank in 1990: 166th
    U.S. rank in 2000: 142nd

City Residents
    1980: 64,092
    1990: 87,491
    2000: 118,652
    2006 estimate: 129,467
    Percent change, 1990–2000: 33.5%
    U.S. rank in 1980: Not reported
    U.S. rank in 1990: 230th (State rank: 7th)
    U.S. rank in 2000: 206th (State rank: 5th)

Density: 2,549.3 people per square mile (2000)

Racial and ethnic characteristics (2005)
    White: 110,626
    Black: 1,314
    American Indian and Alaska Native: 855
    Asian: 3,193
    Native Hawaiian and Pacific Islander: 201
    Hispanic or Latino (may be of any race): 13,792
    Other: 3,035

Percent of residents born in state: 36.2% (2000)

Age characteristics (2005)
    Population under 5 years old: 7,558
    Population 5 to 9 years old: 6,200
    Population 10 to 14 years old: 7,784
    Population 15 to 19 years old: 7,691
    Population 20 to 24 years old: 20,583
    Population 25 to 34 years old: 23,926
    Population 35 to 44 years old: 15,794

Landscape Imagery.

Population 45 to 54 years old: 14,493
Population 55 to 59 years old: 5,576
Population 60 to 64 years old: 3,239
Population 65 to 74 years old: 3,730
Population 75 to 84 years old: 4,070
Population 85 years and older: 1,653
Median age: 28.5 years

Births (2006, MSA)

Total number: 3,226

Deaths (2006, MSA)

Total number: 1,581

Money income (2005)

Per capita income: $25,408
Median household income: $44,261
Total households: 52,144

Number of households with income of...

less than $10,000: 6,199
$10,000 to $14,999: 3,410
$15,000 to $24,999: 7,005
$25,000 to $34,999: 4,740
$35,000 to $49,999: 8,100

$50,000 to $74,999: 8,913
$75,000 to $99,999: 5,603
$100,000 to $149,999: 5,863
$150,000 to $199,999: 1,242
$200,000 or more: 1,069

Percent of families below poverty level: 11.9% (2005)

2005 FBI Crime Index Property: 4,434

2005 FBI Crime Index Violent: 442

■ Municipal Government

The City of Fort Collins operates within a council-manager form of government. The City Manager is the chief executive officer of the city and is responsible for the overall management of city operations. The City Council is composed of six district council members who are elected for a term of four years, and a Mayor who is elected at-large for a two-year term. The Mayor Pro Tem is chosen from among the entire council and serves a term of two years.

Head Official: Mayor Doug Hutchinson (R) (since 2005)

Total Number of City Employees: 1,800 (2007)

City Information: City of Fort Collins, 300 LaPorte Avenue, PO Box 580, Fort Collins, CO 80522-0580; telephone (970) 221-6878

■ Economy

Major Industries and Commercial Activity

Fort Collins' economy has been described as well-balanced, with a good mix of manufacturing and service-related businesses. Local business leaders claim that the city's economy is insulated from some of the ups and downs in the regional and the national economies by the "highly sophisticated and rapidly advancing technological progress" of the city's industries. Fort Collins has a strong manufacturing base and is home to such firms as Hewlett Packard, WaterPik, Woodward, In-Situ, and Anheuser-Busch; however, in the early 2000s growth in the manufacturing segment slowed dramatically due in part to the nationwide trend of outsourcing. However, during the same time period, high-tech firms, including major information technology companies like HP, Intel, Advanced Microdevices, and LSI Logic, became an integral part of the Northern Colorado economy. Many of these high-tech companies have relocated to Fort Collins because of the resources of Colorado State University and its research facilities. Clean energy is also an emerging field in the Fort Collins area, with local businesses focusing on aspects such as distributed power generation, biofuels, energy efficiency, power management and intelligent grid technologies. In 2006 Fort Collins was rated 16th among the "Best Cities for Business and Career" by *Forbes* magazine, thanks in part to its numerous business incentives and programs intended to attract high-tech firms to the area.

Items and goods produced: pharmaceuticals, electronic components and accessories, aircraft and parts, scientific instruments, measuring and controlling instruments, radio and TV equipment, industrial chemicals, engines, turbines, communications equipment

Incentive Programs—New and Existing Companies

Local programs: The city of Fort Collins has established an economic development policy that allows the rebate of use taxes paid by qualifying firms on qualifying equipment. On a case-by-case basis, the county will consider negotiating financial incentives, giving up to a 50 percent credit towards a company's personal property tax liability for up to four years. Additionally, the Northern Colorado Economic Development Corporation will work with individual firms to locate resources or assist in the development of a financial package. In 2004, the community created the Fort Collins Technology Incubator, acquiring 6,500 square feet of office space and transforming the seven-year-old Fort Collins' "Virtual Incubator" into an incubator with walls. The technology incubator is a cluster of programs designed to nurture startup businesses. Incubator companies receive discounted business services from top-notch community resources, advisory groups, Colorado State University resources, and strategic planning counseling as well as idea sharing amongst other entrepreneurs.

The Northern Colorado Economic Development Corporation supports existing employers and recruits new employers to the region. It assists local companies to grow and expand and, in partnership with Colorado State University, encourages technology transfer to nurture local start-up companies. Fort Collins can negotiate with new business facilities an incentive payment equal to not more than the amount of the increase in property tax liability over pre-enterprise zone levels; and a refund of local sales taxes on purchases of equipment, machinery, machine tools, or supplies used in the taxpayer's business in the Enterprise Zone.

State programs: Colorado's Enterprise Zone tax benefits offer incentives for private enterprise to expand and for new businesses to locate in economically distressed areas of the state. They include a three percent investment tax credit for equipment investment, a $500 job tax credit for hiring new employees in an enterprise zone, double job tax credits for agricultural processing, a $200 job tax credit for employer health insurance, research and development tax credits, credits for the rehabilitation of vacant buildings, and exemptions from state sales and use tax on the purchase of manufacturing and mining equipment.

Job training programs: The Colorado FIRST customized job training program assists employers in training new or current workers in permanent, non-seasonal jobs and job-specific training programs, including the Existing Industry Customized Job Training program. FIRST provides financial assistance to eligible businesses for direct training costs including instructor wages, travel, and per diem allowances; development of curriculum and instruction materials; cost of essential training supplies, equipment and space; and training at the employer's location or at local community college or vocational schools. Front Range Community College and Colorado State University provide excellent employee training resources. Larimer County offers comprehensive, coordinated employment and training services at its WorkForce Center.

Development Projects

Development of the downtown Fort Collins area is largely spurred by the Downtown Development Authority, which uses tax increment financing to stimulate redevelopment in the central business district. In 2006 the old Sears Trostel Building was completely rebuilt, making extensive use of green construction techniques and with the help of the Authority. The Downtown Development Authority was behind the creation of the "Beet Street" initiative which was launched in 2007 and was intended to be an entirely self-supporting arts and culture community by 2011, with plans for an outdoor civic center intended to be explored in 2008. The development features cultural, musical, and seasonal festivals and performances, in addition to academic lectures. It was also intended to spur increased activity in Old Town restaurants and shops. Another major unteraking was the revitalization of the River District, which was a joint effort of the City and Development Authority, and was completed in summer 2007. It sought to improve the streetscape, traffic circulation, parking, and overall attractiveness of the area, in addition to creating a better link to the downtown area. In 2007 plans were underway to bring a light rail or trolley service to the area.

In 2006 a private developer announced plans to transform 50 city blocks on the north side of town into a $1 billion research campus and a mixed-use village with housing for 12,000, tentatively dubbed Airpark Village. The development was projected to generate an estimated $16 million in annual revenues and nearly $2 million in property taxes for the city; initial plans called for tenants to conduct research in fields including transport, robotics, conservation, renewable energy, water recycling and automation in order to lesson the nation's dependence on foreign oil.

Soapstone Natural Area was acquired by the city of Fort Collins in 2004. Covering more than 16,000 square miles, the area is known as an important archaeological site and is admired for its varied terrain. Improvements on Soapstone were begun in 2007 and it was expected to open to the public in 2009.

Economic Development Information: Northern Colorado Economic Development Corporation, 2725 Rocky Mountain Avenue #410, Loveland, CO 80538; telephone (970)667-0905; fax (970)669-4680

Commercial Shipping

Parcel service for Fort Collins is provided by companies that include Federal Express, Airport Express, Airborne, Burlington Air Express, Emery, United Parcel Service, Pony Express, and Purolator. Fort Collins has two-day rail freight access to the west coast or the east coast and has a number of motor freight carriers. Many local industrial sites have rail freight spur service. The city is served by the Union Pacific and Burlington Northern Santa Fe railroads.

Labor Force and Employment Outlook

Fort Collins' labor force has been described as young, well-educated, and energetic. Studies have indicated that many of the graduates of Colorado State University stay in the city. The state of Colorado boasts the fifth most educated workforce in the nation, with 33.7 percent of its residents having a bachelor's degree; Northern Colorado has the second largest workforce in the state, with an especially high concentration of high tech workers. In 2005 *Expansion Management* magazine ranked Fort Collins/Loveland one of the "Top 15 Best Educated Workforces" in the nation, in addition to being one of the "Top Ten Metros for Scientists & Engineers Per Capita."

In 2007 the Fort Collins labor force was over 170,000 strong, an increase of around 40,000 in a period of ten years, according to the Bureau of Labor Statistics. In August of the same year the unemployment rate stood at 3.2 percent, down from 4.6 percent in 1997 and below the national average.

According to the 2007 Colorado Business Economic Outlook the Northern Colorado economy continued to outpace the state in growth, thanks to increases in hospitality and food services, finance and insurance, healthcare and social assistance. Those sectors, along with retail and construction accounted for 85 percent of new jobs. The manufacturing industry, though, continued to slide in 2006, and was expected to continue to do so into 2008 and beyond. The high tech sector, with the added help of the Fort Collins Business Incubator, was expected to become increasingly important to Fort Collins. The Larimer County Bioscience Initiative, a group of organizations and individuals that include CSU, Fort Collins Technology Incubator, Colorado Bioscience Association, NCEDC and several bioscience firms created a strategic plan in 2006 that they hoped would augment the growth of a bioscience cluster in Larimer County and bring new jobs to the area.

The following is a summary of data regarding the Fort Collins-Loveland metropolitan area labor force, 2006 annual averages.

Size of nonagricultural labor force: 133,400

Number of workers employed in . . .

    construction and mining: 10,800
    manufacturing: 12,000
    trade, transportation and utilities: 22,700
    information: 2,500
    financial activities: 5,900
    professional and business services: 17,400
    educational and health services: 14,100
    leisure and hospitality: 16,000
    other services: 4,700
    government: 27,500

Average hourly earnings of production workers employed in manufacturing: Not available

Unemployment rate: 3.3% (June 2007)

Largest county employers	Number of employees
Colorado State University	6,948
Poudre School District	3,732
Hewlett Packard	3,000
Poudre Valley Health System	2,814
Agilent Technologies	2,800
Thompson School District	2,000
City of Fort Collins	1,400
Larimer County	1,394
McKee Medical Center	950
Advanced Energy	800

Cost of Living

The following is a summary of data regarding several key cost of living factors for the Fort Collins metropolitan area.

2007 (1st quarter) ACCRA Average House Price: $240,980

2007 (1st quarter) ACCRA Cost of Living Index: 103.1

State income tax rate: 4.63% of Federal Taxable Income

State sales tax rate: 2.9%

Local income tax rate: None

Local sales tax rate: 3.0%

Property tax rate: 7.96% of actual value based on market values as of June 30, 2006

Economic Information: Northern Colorado Economic Development Corporation, 2725 Rocky Mountain Avenue #410, Loveland, CO 80538; telephone (970)667-0905; fax (970)669-4680; email mfoley@ncedc.com.

■ Education and Research

Elementary and Secondary Schools

The Poudre School District is led by a seven-member Board of Education committed to actively recruiting administrators and teachers displaying high standards of excellence. The school district is the second largest employer in Fort Collins. Special programs within the district include specialized non-neighborhood elementary schools that offer bilingual immersion and a multi-age, non-graded program; two charter schools; and multiple alternative secondary schools. The metro area is also served by the Loveland-based Thompson School District. The combined graduation rate for both of the area

districts is consistently above 80 percent, and both districts boast test scores above the state average.

The following is a summary of data regarding the Poudre School District as of the 2005–2006 school year.

Total enrollment: 24,629

Number of facilities

elementary schools: 31
junior high/middle schools: 10
senior high schools: 5
other: 4

Student/teacher ratio: 17.2:1

Teacher salaries (2005–06)

elementary median: $30,030–$70,839 (all levels)
junior high/middle median: Not available
secondary median: Not available

Funding per pupil: $11,689

Public Schools Information: Support Services, Poudre School District, 2407 La Porte Avenue, Fort Collins, CO 80521; telephone (970)482-7420; fax (970) 490-3403

Colleges and Universities

Three doctoral-level universities and two community colleges in the greater Fort Collins area turn out approximately 14,600 newly minted graduates each year. Colorado State University (CSU), with 25,000 students, is a land-grant institution that consists of 8 colleges and more than 150 programs of study. Founded in 1870, its campuses cover 5,612 acres in Larimer County, including the main campus, a foothills campus, an agricultural campus, and the Pingree Park mountain campus, which is the summer campus for natural resources education. CSU offers eight major degree programs including agricultural sciences, applied human sciences, liberal arts, business, engineering, natural resources, veterinary medicine and biomedical sciences, and natural sciences. CSU also offers a unique major called equine science, in which prospective veterinarians or those pursuing a career in equine production learn about the behavior, nutrition, management, reproductive management, disease management, and the training of horses. The school was ranked 124th of 248 national universities in the 2007 *U.S. News and World Report's* rankings of "America's Best Colleges and Universities." The University of Northern Colorado, located in nearby Greeley, offers more than 100 undergraduate programs and 100 graduate programs, with a total enrollment of about 13,000 students in 2006.

Front Range Community College (FRCC), the largest community college in Colorado, grants associate's degrees in arts, science, general studies, and applied science at its four campuses. The college offers 12 high school vocational programs, and more than 100 degree and certificate programs, in addition to a growing online learning program. The Larimer Campus of FRCC offers partnerships with Colorado State University, Poudre Valley Hospital, McKee Medical Center, Columbine Health Systems, Village Homes' Observatory Village, Microsoft, and Oracle.

Libraries and Research Centers

The Fort Collins Public Library was established in 1900. The library maintains the Gates Computer Learning Lab and, in partnership with Front Range Community College, the Harmony Library branch and Harmony Library Electronic Learning Center. The library also hosts a number of monthly programs and panels. The library holds around 400,000 items and has a special local history archive, now partly digitized.

Wildlife is the focus of the special library at the Colorado Division of Wildlife, which has over 24,000 items in its collection. Special collections of the Colorado State University Library include agriculture, agricultural economics, biomedical science, engineering, hydrology, and natural resources. The university has over 2 million books in its total library holdings.

Fort Collins has a great range of research institutes covering a myriad of subjects. Facilities are maintained by the Centers for Disease Control Division of Vector-Borne Infectious Diseases, the Colorado Cooperative Fish & Wildlife Research Unit, the Colorado Water Resource Research Institute, and the Cooper Institute for Research in the Atmosphere. The Rocky Mountain Research Station conducts research on experimental forests, ranges, and watersheds, and oversees research on more than 200 natural areas.

Colorado State University has a variety of research groups focusing on subjects such as animal reproduction, biotechnology, engineering, environmental toxicology, irrigation management, microscopy, nutrition, hydraulics, manufacturing, marrow transplantation, vehicle emissions, and solar energy. The University spends over $210 million annually on research, with about 65 percent of that sum coming from the federal government.

Public Library Information: Fort Collins Public Library, 201 Peterson St., Fort Collins, CO 80524-2990; telephone (970)221-6740; fax (970)221-6398 (circulation)

■ Health Care

By virtue of the broad scope of medical services available, Fort Collins has become a regional health center. Poudre Valley Hospital System, a not-for-profit organization, has 417 beds, 35 operating rooms, and 55 critical care patient rooms; it is home to a regional heart center, a regional neurosciences center that cares for victims of head and back injury, stroke, spinal cord and nervous system diseases, and a regional orthopedic program. The hospital also offers a surgery center, oncology unit, regional wound care center, a 24-hour emergency department, adult and adolescent psychiatric programs, and a breast diagnostic center. The hospital has a birthing center and Level II nursery, and offers an off-site comprehensive homecare program, home infusion therapy, and comprehensive rehabilitation programs. It was named a "Top 100 Hospital" in 2007, for the fourth year in a row, by Solucient, a national health care consulting firm.

McKee Medical Center, owned by Banner Health System, is based in Loveland and has 132 beds. It offers heart, cancer, trauma and intensive care units, rehabilitation programs, home-health services, inpatient and outpatient surgical facilities and a birthing center. Banner Health System also operates Northern Colorado Medical Center in Greeley.

■ Recreation

Sightseeing

More than 40 historic sites can be visited in the Fort Collins Area, with over half of them listed in or eligible for the National Register of Historic Places. Tours of Avery House, a restored Victorian residence built by one of the city's prominent citizens, are offered year round. Visitors may also tour the two-story Strauss Cabin, which was built in 1864 by George Strauss and modeled after structures found in South Carolina. The Old Federal Building is a 1912 structure that housed the post office on its main floor for 60 years. The 1881 Spruce Hall on the campus of Colorado State University is the oldest complete building still standing on the campus. Ammons Hall, also on the campus, is a 1922 Italian Renaissance building that is still being used a women's physical education facility. Many other sites worth observing are on the Historic Buildings map available through the Fort Collins Convention and Visitors Bureau.

Fort Collins boasts of being the "Napa Valley of Beer." Beer enthusiasts and those merely curious will enjoy touring the Anheuser-Busch Brewery, which includes a visit with the famous Clydesdale horses and a trip to the sampling room. Several micro-breweries in town invite visitors to enjoy their variety of offerings. A metal menagerie of mythical and real creatures are on view at farmer/sculptor Bill Swets' dairy farm, known as the Swetsville Zoo. The zoo also has a miniature live steam railroad train and a display of antique farming equipment. Young and old enjoy hopping a ride aboard the Fort Collins Municipal Railway streetcar, which runs May to September, weather permitting.

Arts and Culture

The premier facility for the performing arts in Fort Collins is Lincoln Center, with its 1,180-seat performance hall, two theaters, and four exhibit galleries. The center hosts over 1,500 events each year, among them an annual season of Broadway shows, dance, and musical events. OpenStage Theater Company, a regional professional theater group, stages its seasons in the Lincoln Center's 220-seat Mini-Theater. Based on the tradition of eighteenth-century salons, the 48-seat Bas Bleu Theater provides an intimate setting for poetry, plays, and musical performances. Good food and theater can be combined at the Carousel Dinner Theater, which presents dramas, comedies, and popular musicals. Colorado State University presents several plays each year at the school's Johnson Hall. Other theater groups in the city include the Debut Theater Company, Fort Collins Children's Theater, and the Front Range Chamber Players. A variety of dance performances is offered by the Canyon Concert Ballet. Several performing halls are located at Colorado State University.

Musical experiences in the city come in many forms, featuring such groups as the Larimer Chorale, Opera Fort Collins, and the Fort Collins Symphony. The primary visual arts center of the city is the Fort Collins Museum of Contemporary Art, located in a renovated power plant. The Fort Collins Museum highlights the area's past, including a display of pre-Columbian Folsom points discovered at a major archaeological site in northern Larimer County. Other displays range from those of the Plains Indians to Fort Collins' beginnings as a trade and agricultural center. Experiences with hands-on science are available to youngsters at the Discovery Center Museum, with its opportunities for experimenting and testing scientific theories. Visitors can visit pioneer cabins and a one-room school house.

Festivals and Holidays

Fort Collins' festival season begins with its annual St. Patrick's Day Celebration downtown. The city's Hispanic community is honored at the Cinco De Mayo celebration, which features dancing, entertainment, and food. Patrons are invited to tap kegs of beer at June's Colorado Brewers' Festival downtown. Fireworks light the sky at City Park's annual Fourth of July Celebration. On Skookum Day, also in July, Fort Collins' history is re-enacted with demonstrations of blacksmithing, milking, quilting, branding, and weaving. August is enlivened by the Larimer County Fair & Rodeo, and by the New West Fest, featuring more than 300 booths, events, performances, evening concerts, and children's activities.

The city celebrates the harvest during Oktoberfest, and the holiday season is launched with Lincoln Center's Great Christmas Hall, with its juried art exhibit, homemade crafts, and decorated trees. In December, festivities include carolers and Christmas celebrations in Old Town, and the New Year is welcomed in with a community-wide celebration for the whole family called First Night.

Sports for the Spectator

Colorado State University students engage in a variety of sports competitions throughout the year. The CSU Rams are represented by both male and female teams in a variety of sports, including football, basketball, cross country, golf, softball, swimming and diving, tennis, track and field, volleball, and water polo.

Sports for the Participant

Fort Collins is home to a variety of walking, running, and bicycling events and tournaments. In 2005 the city was named one of the "Top 25 Running Cities in America" by *Runner's World* magazine. The Cache La Poudre River provides some of the finest fishing in the state. The city has more than 280 miles of designated bikeways through many natural areas in the city, in addition to 800 acres of dedicated parkland at over 44 sites. It also boasts several recently revamped or built park areas: Oak Street Plaza Park in the downtown area, Stewart Case Neighborhood Park, Washington Park, and Lincoln Park. Additionally, Lory State Park offers 2,400 acres for horseback riding, boating, hiking, and picnicking. Duffers may choose from three public golf courses in Fort Collins, in addition to several area private courses. The Edora Pool and Ice Center and Mulberry Pool feature swimming and exercise programs, as well as youth and adult hockey and public ice skating. The young or young at heart will enjoy skateboarding at Northside Azatlan Community Center, Edora Skateboard Park, and Fossil Creek Skateboard. In winter, Lory State Park's trails and rolling hills attract cross country skiers; tubing and sledding are also popular. Several renowned Colorado mountain ski resorts are within a few hours of Fort Collins. Rocky Mountain National Park offers scenic drives and hikes and is only one hour's drive away.

Shopping and Dining

Shopping in Fort Collins can involve browsing antique stores and flea markets or seeing the latest fashions at one of its major malls, such as Foothills Mall or University Mall. At Historic Old Town, restored buildings filled with specialty shops, galleries, boutiques, and outdoor cafes beckon the visitor. Fort Collins boasts over 300 restaurants, with American and ethnic cuisines.

Visitor Information: Fort Collins Convention and Visitors Bureau, 19 Old Town Square, Suite 137, Ft. Collins, CO 80524; telephone (970)232-3840; fax (970) 232-3841; email information@ftcollins.com

■ Convention Facilities

Fort Collins has nearly 2,000 hotel rooms, ranging from budget rooms to luxury suites. Colorado State University, in the heart of Fort Collins, has 50,000 square feet of convention facilities at its Lory Students Center. Other convention facilities include 10 auditoriums with accommodations for up to 400 in the Clark Building, a total of 4,400 beds in the residence halls, dining facilities in each residence hall, and an arena that seats 6,000. Lory's main ballroom has 12,728 square feet of space. The Pingree Park Conference Center, 53 miles west of Fort Collins and affiliated with Colorado State University, offers seven meeting rooms, two dorms and seven cabins on its 1,200 acre campus. Campus lodging is available late May through mid-August. There are several facilities around the city that can handle small group meetings.

Convention Information: Fort Collins Convention and Visitors Bureau, 19 Old Town Square, Suite 137, Ft. Collins, CO 80524; telephone (970)232-3840; fax (970) 232-3841; email information@ftcollins.com

■ Transportation

Approaching the City

Fort Collins/Loveland Airport is a small, general aviation facility with limited commercial flights and corporate service. Denver International Airport, which is 25 miles to the south, is the closest commercial/commuter airport. Fort Collins can be approached from Denver by car via Interstate 25. Greyhound offers bus service into the city.

Traveling in the City

Fort Collins' downtown streets form a grid with Interstate 25 running north and south on the east side of the city. U.S. Highway 287 runs east and west in the northwest sector of the city. Transfort, Fort Collins' local bus transportation system, operates daily. Alternative transportation is encouraged in the city; bicycle commuters benefit from city incentives and excellent bike paths through town. Maps for a walking tour of the historic downtown district can be obtained from the Downtown Business Association.

■ Communications

Newspapers and Magazines

The *Fort Collins Coloradoan,* which appears Monday through Sunday mornings, is the city's daily paper.

The *Fort Collins Weekly* serves Larimer and Weld Counties. The bimonthly *Northern Colorado Business Report,* reports on the growing business market in Northern Colorado with an increasing emphasis on high-tech and e-business. Other publications include *Fort Collins Now, Rocky Mountain Chronicle, Scene Magazine,* and *Fort Collins Forum.*

Television and Radio

There are six television stations in the greater Fort Collins area, in addition to available cable television. Ten local AM and FM stations serve the city with a variety of programming including public radio, news/talk, adult contemporary, and alternative music formats.

Media Information: The *Fort Collins Coloradoan,*PO Box 1577, Fort Collins, CO 80524; telephone (970) 493-6397

Fort Collins Online

City of Fort Collins Home Page. Available fcgov .com

Colorado Department of Labor & Employment, Labor Market Information. Available www .coworkforce.com

Coloradoan. Available www.coloradoan.com

Fort Collins Convention & Visitors Bureau. Available www.ftcollins.com

Fort Collins Public Library. Available fcgov.com

Larimer County. Available www.co.larimer.co.us

Northern Colorado Economic Development Corporation. Available www.ncedc.com

BIBLIOGRAPHY

Fleming, Barbara Allbrandt, *Fort Collins, A Pictorial History* (Virginia Beach, VA: Donning, 1992)

Fort Collins Friends of the Library, comp. *Talking About Fort Collins: Selections from Oral Histories* (Fort Collins, CO: City of Fort Collins, 1992)

Horan, Bob, *Colorado Front Range Bouldering: Fort Collins* (Evergreen, CO: Chockstone Press, 1995)

Swanson, Evadine Burris, *Fort Collins Yesterdays* (Fort Collins, CO: G & H Morgan, 1993)

Hawaii

The State in Brief

Nickname: Aloha State

Motto: Ua mau ke ea o ka aina i ka pono (The life of the land is perpetuated in righteousness)

Flower: Hibiscus

Bird: Hawaiian goose

Area: 10,930 square miles (2000; U.S. rank 43rd)

Elevation: Ranges from sea level to 13,796 feet above sea level

Climate: Mild, tropical

Admitted to Union: August 21, 1959

Capital: Honolulu

Head Official: Governor Linda Lingle (R) (until 2010)

Population

    1980: 965,000
    1990: 1,135,000
    2000: 1,211,537
    2006 estimate: 1,285,498
    Percent change, 1990–2000: 9.3%
    U.S. rank in 2006: 42nd
    Percent of residents born in state: 55.16% (2006)
    Density: 198.5 people per square mile (2006)
    2006 FBI Crime Index Total: 57,997

Racial and Ethnic Characteristics (2006)

    White: 337,507
    Black or African American: 28,062
    American Indian and Alaska Native: 4,153
    Asian: 512,995
    Native Hawaiian and Pacific Islander: 111,488
    Hispanic or Latino (may be of any race): 99,664
    Other: 14,513

Age Characteristics (2006)

    Population under 5 years old: 87,179
    Population 5 to 19 years old: 243,230
    Percent of population 65 years and over: 13.9%
    Median age: 37.2

Vital Statistics

    Total number of births (2006): 17,782
    Total number of deaths (2006): 9,189
    AIDS cases reported through 2005: 2,857

Economy

    Major industries: Government; services; finance, insurance, and real estate; agriculture; tourism
    Unemployment rate (2006): 4.4%
    Per capita income (2006): $27,251
    Median household income (2006): $61,160
    Percentage of persons below poverty level (2006): 9.3%
    Income tax rate: 1.4% to 8.25%
    Sales tax rate: 4.0%

Hilo

■ The City in Brief

Founded: 1822 (incorporated 1911)

Head Official: Mayor Harry Kim (since 2000)

City Population

    1980: 35,269
    1990: 37,808
    2000: 40,759
    2006 estimate: Not available
    Percent change, 1990–2000: 7.8%
    U.S. rank in 1980: Not reported
    U.S. rank in 1990: Not reported
    U.S. rank in 2000: Not reported

Metropolitan Area Population

    1980: Not available
    1990: 120,317
    2000: 148,667
    2006 estimate: 171,191
    Percent change, 1990–2000: 23.6%
    U.S. rank in 1980: Not reported
    U.S. rank in 1990: Not reported
    U.S. rank in 2000: Not reported

Area: 54 square miles (2000)

Elevation: 38 feet above sea level

Average Annual Temperatures: January, 71.4° F; July, 75.9° F; annual average, 73.9° F

Average Annual Precipitation: 126.27 inches of rain

Major Economic Sectors: services, wholesale and retail trade, government

Unemployment Rate: 3.0% (June 2007)

Per Capita Income: $18,220 (Hilo CDP) (1999)

2005 FBI Crime Index Property: Not available

2005 FBI Crime Index Violent: Not available

Major Colleges and Universities: University of Hawaii at Hilo, Hawaii Community College

Daily Newspaper: *Hawaii Tribune-Herald*

■ Introduction

The city of Hilo is the main port of the island of Hawaii, the largest island in the chain. It is the business and government center of the island, as well as the shipping and service center of the various industries in the vicinity. With more than 100 inches of rain annually, the city is the rainiest in the United States. The rainfall encourages the city's major industries—raising tropical flowers and fruit. Tourism is growing rapidly, spurred in part by the Hawaii Volcanoes National Park, which is 30 miles away. Hilo curves around a crescent bay where the lower foothills of Mauna Loa and Mauna Kea emerge. In recent years the city has attracted retirees and escapees from the faster-paced life on other islands. The city boasts a modern, convenient airport and a deep water harbor, and serves as the transportation hub for the island. The city, whose name means "new moon," is slowly transforming itself from a plantation town whose economy centered on sugar cane to a university town that is attracting a slew of new construction and research dollars. With the addition of the Imiloa Astronomy Center of Hawaii (formerly the Mauna Kea Astronomy Education Center) in November 2005 and the Hilo Art Museum in 2007, the city is well on its way to creating an even more enriching environment.

■ Geography and Climate

Hilo is located on Hilo Bay on the eastern side of the island of Hawaii, 216 miles southeast of Honolulu (on the island of Oahu). The area's topography is mostly sloping, from the tops of the scenic Mauna Kea and Mauna Loa mountains to the sea. Hilo is located less than 30 miles from Kilauea, one of the most active volcanoes on earth, which has been emitting lava since 1983. Lava flows have been responsible for the destruction of nearly 200 homes since then, and they continue to menace the island. Much of the lava has reached the ocean, enlarging the island of Hawaii by about 500 acres.

The Hilo region has a warm semitropical climate and experiences abundant rainfall without the droughts and shortages that trouble other parts of the island. The rain, which generally falls during the night, keeps the area fresh and green. It also results in many waterfalls. Hilo's rich soil is conducive to the growth of a variety of diversified agricultural products. At the summit of Mauna Kea the temperature ranges from about 31 to 43 degrees. In winter there is frost above the 4,000-foot level and snow above the 10,000-foot level.

Area: 54 square miles (2000)

Elevation: 38 feet above sea level

Average Temperatures: January, 71.4° F; July, 75.9° F; annual average, 73.9° F

Average Annual Precipitation: 126.27 inches of rain

■ History

Popular Trading Post Attracts Missionaries, Scientists

The city of Hilo has been a trading place from the time Hawaiian tribes came up the Wailuku River, which separated Hilo from Hamakua, and shouted out what goods they had to offer. In the 1800s, although Honolulu reigned supreme as the principal whaling base of the Pacific, Hilo came in third behind Koloa as alternative anchorages. Foreign ships found anchorages between the coral heads of Hilo's wide bay, and thereafter the dredging of a channel permitted steamships to enter the area.

Missionaries settled Hilo in 1822. The region was first studied scientifically by Lord Byron and his men of the ship *Blonde* in 1825. Titus Cona, a missionary at Hilo, was the foremost volcanologist of his time and made frequent visits to the volcano.

The beginnings of Hilo's tourist industry date back to the 1870s when Hilo was one of a number of sites on a standard sightseeing route. Particularly popular were visits to the volcano of Kilauea east of Mauna Loa.

By the early 1900s, Hilo's sugar industry was booming and the city became the commercial center of the island. A railroad connected Hilo with other parts of the island. Hilo became the seat of Hawaii County in 1905 and was incorporated as a city in 1911.

Hilo Beset by Volcanic Eruptions and Tidal Waves

In March 1868, a volcanic eruption resulted in formidable destruction. The city experienced close calls from the eruptions of Mauna Loa in 1942 and in 1984. Two tsunamis have also caused major damage. In 1946 a tidal wave swept half the town inland and then dragged the remains out to sea. Hilo rebuilt and constructed a stone breakwater across the bay to protect the harbor. Another tidal wave destroyed a major part of the waterfront business district and the city's beachfront in 1960, sweeping 61 Hiloites out to sea. Civic leaders, vowing that such destruction would never recur, drained the lowland crescent and raised a new hill 26 feet above sea level and mounted a new government and commercial center. Today, however, the beach is still gone.

Hilo's cultural diversity adds to the city's charm. Japanese, Polynesian, Filipino, Chinese, Puerto Rican, Portuguese, and Russian residents make up the city's mixed-race culture of today. Since their arrival, Japanese people have had an important influence on the city, from serving on the city council to starting businesses. Business people of all races join the Japanese Chamber of Commerce and Industry, and the Japanese newspaper, the *Hilo Times,* is published in the city. The city still strives to preserve its presence as one of the few surviving examples of a Hawaiian plantation town, and the Hilo Downtown Improvement Association serves to provide leadership in developing a safe and attractive community.

■ Population Profile

Metropolitan Area Residents

    1980: Not available
    1990: 120,317
    2000: 148,667
    2006 estimate: 171,191
    Percent change, 1990–2000: 23.6%
    U.S. rank in 1980: Not reported
    U.S. rank in 1990: Not reported
    U.S. rank in 2000: Not reported

City Residents

    1980: 35,269
    1990: 37,808
    2000: 40,759
    2006 estimate: Not available
    Percent change, 1990–2000: 7.8%
    U.S. rank in 1980: Not reported
    U.S. rank in 1990: Not reported
    U.S. rank in 2000: Not reported

Density: 750.8 per square mile (2000)

©Douglas Peebles/drr.net

Racial and ethnic characteristics (2000)

White: 15,764

Black: 471

American Indian and Alaska Native: 1,078

Asian: 25,172

Native Hawaiian and Pacific Islander: 13,922

Hispanic or Latino (may be of any race): 3,579

Other: 385

Percent of residents born in state: 78.7% (2000)

Age characteristics (2000)

Population under 5 years old: 2,301

Population 5 to 9 years old: 2,859

Population 10 to 14 years old: 2,965

Population 15 to 19 years old: 3,319

Population 20 to 24 years old: 2,806

Population 25 to 34 years old: 4,352

Population 35 to 44 years old: 5,576

Population 45 to 54 years old: 5,842

Population 55 to 59 years old: 2,215

Population 60 to 64 years old: 1,701

Population 65 to 74 years old: 3,473

Population 75 to 84 years old: 2,471

Population 85 years and older: 879

Median age: 38.6 years

Births (2006, Micropolitan Statistical Area)

Total number: 2,164

Deaths (2006, Micropolitan Statistical Area)

Total number: 1,254

Money income (1999)

Per capita income: $18,220 (Hilo CDP)

Median household income: $39,139

Total households: 14,577

Number of households with income of...

less than $10,000: 1,876

$10,000 to $14,999: 919
$15,000 to $24,999: 1,977
$25,000 to $34,999: 1,824
$35,000 to $49,999: 2,253
$50,000 to $74,999: 2,655
$75,000 to $99,999: 1,650
$100,000 to $149,999: 1,061
$150,000 to $199,999: 196
$200,000 or more: 182

Percent of families below poverty level: 13.2% (1999)

2005 FBI Crime Index Property: Not available

2005 FBI Crime Index Violent: Not available

■ Municipal Government

The Island of Hawaii has one governmental unit, the County of Hawaii. There is no formal government at the city or municipal level, although Hilo serves as the headquarters for all government activities on the Island. The city is governed by the county of Hawaii, which has a mayor elected for up to two four-year terms and nine council members representing each of the county's nine districts during two-year terms. Mayor Harry Kim, first elected to office in 2000, is the first mayor of Korean descent in the United States.

Head Official: Mayor Harry Kim, County of Hawaii (since 2000; current term expires 2008)

Total Number of County Employees: 2,300 (2007)

County Information: Hawaii County, 25 Aupuni Street, Hilo, HI 96720; telephone (808)961-8521

■ Economy

Major Industries and Commercial Activity

Hilo has a diversified economy that includes agriculture, tourism, aquaculture, livestock, trade, education, and government.

The Big Island was a world center for the production of raw sugar from 1876 to 1994, when the last plantation closed. Today, the tremendous rainfall produces a genuine paradise of flowers, from exotic anthuriums and orchids to tropical blooms of all sorts. The city, which is the center for the world's largest tropical flower industry, exports fresh cut flowers, sprays, and potted plants from various farmer cooperatives and flower farms. About 1 million acres of the island's total 2.4 million acres are devoted to agriculture, an over $500 million per-year industry.

Livestock is an economic mainstay, with sales of beef, hogs, dairy and poultry products, and honey totaling more than $25 million annually. Cattle ranches, including Parker Ranch, one of the largest in the country (150,000 acres), produce the majority of the state's beef supply About 440 cattle farms are run on the Big Island with a value of about $27 million; most are shipped to the U.S. mainland and Canada for processing. The Big Island is Hawaii's largest producer of honey, with its honey and queen bee industries producing more than nearly 930,000 pounds in 2006.

Aquaculture, another important industry on the island, has been a mainstay of economic life since the first Polynesian settlers came to the Big Island. Abalone, carp, catfish, clams, flounder, milkfish, moi, mullet, ornamental fish, oyster, prawns, sea cucumber, seaweed, shrimp, snails, sturgeon, tilapia, and rainbow trout are among the fish and seafood harvested. Several types of microalgae are also cultivated for pharmaceutical and nutritional products. In 2005 there were 31 aquaculture industries on the Big Island that produced over $19 million of aquaproducts.

Despite serious agricultural problems ranging from drought to harmful bacteria, the Big Island produces almost the whole of the state's production of fruit (other than pineapples), including bananas, guavas, oranges, tangerines, and avocados; the bulk of the state's macadamia nuts and papaya; the vast majority of its coffee; crops such as ginger, Chinese cabbage, leaf lettuce, greenhouse tomatoes, and cucumbers; and orchids, anthuriums, and other nursery products for domestic and foreign markets. A recent problem for Hilo's agricultural industry has been the infestation of the coqui frog. The increasing population of this amphibian has threatened the island's ecosystem. It is a community effort to control and prevent further coqui infestations; coqui control classes are held in partnership with the State of Hawaii Department of Agriculture.

Until recently, the tourism industry had all but bypassed the town of Hilo due to its lack of a decent beach and the annual surplus of rainfall. Since Hilo had never been a tourist destination, the town retained its historic character and has not suffered from the infrastructure problems associated with high-rises and big-city development. However, it just may be that historic character that is attracting new visitors to the city. Leisure and hospitality services comprised the largest of the major industrial sectors in the area in 2003. The total number of visitors to Hilo, both domestic and international, had reached some 668,900 by 2006. In an effort to bolster tourism even more so, the Hawaii Tourism Authority (HTA) planned in their "Hawaii Strategic Plan 2005–2015" to put aside funds for each county. Rather than looking at tourism just from a state level, HTA planned to assist individual counties in creating a strategic plan tailored to specific tourism goals in that area.

Hilo's Foreign Trade Zone (FTZ) is ideally situated adjacent to Hilo Harbor and the Hilo International Airport, less than a mile from downtown Hilo. This 31-acre site is the first such zone designated by the State of Hawaii to attract manufacturers to Hawaii. The FTZ allows companies locating there to import parts for assembly and export the finished product without paying import duties. It was given a boost when NIC Americas, Inc., became its first tenant. NIC Americas manufactures a device that uses electrical arcing to destroy used needles from health care facilities. The company represented Hilo's first significant new manufacturing facility in recent times; if successful it could lead to other FTZ tenants. Hilo's FTZ's performance increased significantly in 2006; 337 firms used the zone that year, which was a 30 percent increase. Future goals included promoting the FTZ program on a statewide level as well as educating international firms about the advantages of doing business in Hawaii through the program.

Television, film and commercial production also contributes to Hilo's economy. The County of Hawaii hosted 129 film productions from ten countries in 2003-2004, an increase from the prior year. With television series such as ABC's *Lost* and Fox's *North Shore* filming on location, the state reached a record in production expenditures in 2004, totaling $164 million.

Items and goods produced: flowers, fruit, cattle, fish, macadamia nuts, coffee

Incentive Programs—New and Existing Companies

Local programs: Hawaii's economy relies heavily on small business entrepreneurs, as they account for over 96 percent of all businesses in the state. Hawaii's Small Business Development Center Network is a partnership of the University of Hawaii at Hilo and the U.S. Small Business Administration. With the aim of helping small business become established or expand, the Network offers one-on-one counseling, seminars, workshops and conferences.

State programs: Most business incentives are offered at the state level. These include direct financial incentives such as Industrial Development Bonds, a Capital Loan Program, customized industrial training, and investment of public funds in return for equity or ownership positions in private businesses. Tax incentives are also offered along with the Hawaii Urban Enterprise Zones Program. Other tax incentives for businesses on the Big Island include no personal property taxes; no taxes on inventory, equipment, furniture and machinery; no tax on goods manufactured for export; no unincorporated business tax; and only one business tax for banks and financial institutions. High technology businesses can also take advantage of unparalleled tax breaks through legislative initiatives

(ACT 221, SLH 2001) and the State Foreign Trade Zone program and Enterprise Zone Partnership.

Job training programs: The Workforce Development Division of Hawaii's Department of Labor and Industrial Relations oversees One-Stop Workforce Assistance Centers, a job placement and training system to help people find work and employers find suitable workers, and the Employment & Training Fund (ETF), a job skills upgrade program for current workers. Employers can receive customized training grants for their workplace or they can nominate a current worker for an established training course. HireNet Hawaii was created as a "virtual one-stop employment center." The site allows individuals to post resumes online, search for available jobs in the state, and view current labor market data, among other features. Training providers can also use HireNet Hawaii as a tool to post program information.

Job Training Information: Workforce Development Division, Hawaii Department of Labor and Industrial Relations, Princess Ruth Keelikolani Building, 830 Punchbowl Street, Honolulu, HI 96813; telephone (808)586-8842; fax (808)586-9099

Development Projects

Since the fall of the Big Island's sugar plantations in the mid-1990s, "Hilo has transformed itself from a plantation town to a university town," according to Richard West, executive director of the Hawaii Island Economic Development Board, in a 2004 article in *Hawaii Business Magazine*. Hilo has seen the addition of several new science and technology developments in the early 2000s. One of the largest projects was the Imiloa Astronomy Center of Hawaii (formerly the Mauna Kea Astronomy Education Center), a $28 million facility that showcases exhibits that focus on the connection between Hawaiian culture and astronomy. The center opened in November 2005 and is located in the University of Hawaii at Hilo's University Park of Science and Technology. The U.S. Department of Agriculture's Agricultural Research Service broke ground on a $60 million research lab in fall 2004. In 5 stages, the Pacific Basin Agricultural Research Center (PBARC) will eventually encompass 120,000 square feet of laboratories, an administration building, greenhouse facilities, and insect rearing facilities. Additional research dollars will come to Hilo with the opening of the U.S. Forest Service Institute of Pacific Islands Forestry, a $12 million forest research laboratory. The laboratory is one of few that studies invasive plants in native ecosystems—important to the region, as invasive exotic species of plants are a major threat to Pacific Island forests.

Economic Development Information: County of Hawaii Department of Research and Development, 25 Aupuni Street, Hilo, HI 96720; telephone (808)961-

8366. Hawaii Department of Labor and Industrial Relations; telephone (808)586-8842. Hilo Hamakua Community Development Corporation, County of Hawaii, 25 Aupuni Street, Hilo, HI 96720.

Commercial Shipping

Hilo Harbor has an entrance depth of 35 feet, and the harbor basin has a length of 2,300 feet and a width of 1,400 feet. There are 2,787 linear feet of piers, and storage area totals 122,000 square feet of shedded and 492,000 square feet of open space. Plans on the drawing board for the harbor include the separation of the commercial shipping and cruise ship activities to accommodate the increasing demand of cruise lines that would like to dock there. An expansion plan scheduled to continue through 2020 recommends more passenger terminals at Hilo Harbor to accommodate the growing number of cruise passengers.

Labor Force and Employment Outlook

Hilo's job outlook has been improving steadily. The city's economic recovery has mirrored the state's reviving economy. The County of Hawaii's unemployment rate has improved from 9.6 percent in 1995 to an estimated 2.8 percent in 2006. This is compared to an estimated 2.4 percent for the entire state—one of the lowest in the nation. According to the FDIC, every major industry in the State of Hawaii posted employment gains as of the second quarter in 2007 except for manufacturing. Solid job gains were seen in the production of non-manufactured goods and private service sectors. The Department of Business, Economic Development & Tourism reported that forecasts for solid growth in employment and income continued through 2008.

The following is a summary of data regarding the Hilo CDP metropolitan area labor force, 2000 annual averages.

Size of nonagricultural labor force: 16,766

Number of workers employed in...

   construction and mining: 1,104
   manufacturing: 377
   trade, transportation and utilities: 2,681
   information: 374
   financial activities: 768
   professional and business services: 1,254
   educational and health services: 4,306
   leisure and hospitality: 1,782
   other services: 797
   government: 4,904

Average hourly earnings of production workers employed in manufacturing: $13.13

Unemployment rate: 3.0% (June 2007)

Largest non-government employers, Hawaii County (2005)

	Number of employees
Hilton Waikoloa Village	1,128
Hilo Medical Center	929
The Fairmount Orchid	800
Four Seasons Resort	676
Meuna Luni Bay Hotel and Bungalows	630
Kona Community Hospital	471
North Hawaii Community Hospital	469
Sheraton Keauhou Bay Resort and Spa	450

Cost of Living

Median single family home resale price in Hawaii County in 2002 was $194,500. The following is a summary of data regarding key cost of living factors for the Hilo area.

2007 (1st quarter) ACCRA Average House Price: Not reported

2007 (1st quarter) ACCRA Cost of Living Index: Not reported

State income tax rate: 1.4% to 8.25%

State sales tax rate: 4.0%

Local income tax rate: None

Local sales tax rate: None

Property tax rate: $9.10 per $1,000 assessed valuation for improved land and buildings; $5.55 per $1,000 valuation for owner-occupied residences

Economic Information: County of Hawaii, Department of Economic Development and Tourism, 25 Aupuni Street Room 219, Hilo, HI 96720; telephone (808)961-8366; fax (808)935-1205. Hawaii Island Chamber of Commerce, 106 Kamehameha Ave, Hilo, HI 96720; telephone (808)935-7178; fax (808)961-4435; email hicc@interpac.net

■ Education and Research

Elementary and Secondary Schools

Hawaii is the only state with a single, unified statewide school system, comprised of seven districts, one of which is the Hawaii District, which covers the island of Hawaii. An elected board of education formulates educational policy and supervises the public school system. Ten members are elected from Oahu and a total of three from all other islands. One non-voting student member from grades 7–12 is appointed.

The following is a summary of data regarding the Hawaii District as of the 2005–2006 school year.

Total enrollment: 26,108

Number of facilities

elementary schools: 8
junior high/middle schools: 2
senior high schools: 2
other: 0

Student/teacher ratio: 16.8:1 (statewide average)

Teacher salaries (2005–06)

elementary median: $29,000–58,000 (all levels)
junior high/middle median: Not available
secondary median: Not available

Funding per pupil: $7,455

There are six private schools in Hilo. They are Emakaala School; Haili Christian School; Hale Aloha Nazarene School; Kamehamaha Schools; Mauna Loa School; and St. Joseph School of Hilo.

Colleges and Universities

The city of Hilo is the home to the University of Hawaii at Hilo. The school offers two- and four-year programs in areas such as agriculture, arts and sciences, and vocational and technical training. It also currently offers five master's degrees and will offer two doctoral programs in the mid-2000s. Hawaii Community College has career, technical and academic programs. Akamai University is an alternative online graduate school designed for mid-career adult students.

Libraries and Research Centers

The Hilo Public Library, part of the Hawaii State Public Library System, contains books, periodicals, videotapes, sound recordings, and provides internet access to its patrons. It is the largest public library on the island and the second busiest in circulation statewide. Other libraries in the city include the Hilo Hospital Medical Library, which features consumer health materials; the State Supreme Court Third Circuit Court Law Library; and the University of Hawaii at Hilo Libraries, whose system holds more than 250,000 volumes, 1,650 periodical subscriptions, and 225,000 microfiche titles. Several floors of the UH Hilo's Edwin H. Mookini Library were closed temporarily starting in 2006 for extensive renovations; construction was expected to be completed by 2008.

University Park of Science and Technology on the campus of the University of Hawaii at Hilo (UH-Hilo) is home to several U.S. and international observing facilities. They include the British-Canada-Netherlands Joint Astronomy Centre, Gemini North Telescope, Caltech Submillimeter Observatory, Subaru National Astronomical Observatory of Japan, University of Hawaii Institute for Astronomy, and Smithsonian Submillimeter Array. The Imiloa Astronomy Center of Hawaii (formerly the Mauna Kea Astronomy Education Center) is a state-of-the-art interpretive research center and planetarium, located in University Park. The U.S. Geological Survey's Hawaiian Volcano Observatory is located at the rim of Kilauea, 30 miles from Hilo; Kilauea is said to be the most studied volcano in the world.

Public Library Information: Hilo Public Library, 300 Waianuenue Avenue, PO Box 647, Hilo, HI 96720; telephone (808)933-4650

■ Health Care

Hilo Medical Center is the city's primary hospital with 264 beds offering general medical, surgical and obstetric care, as well as emergency services. Other east Hawaii medical facilities include the Hale Hoola Hamakua long-term care facility in Honokaa and the Kau Hospital in Pahala. The North Hawaii Community Hospital in Kameula serves the 30,000 residents in the northern region of the Big Island. These facilities have led to growth in the island's medical profession and to an expectation that the region will become the health and medical center of the Pacific Rim; this in turn could make the island attractive as a retirement center. Federal funding of $18.4 million was approved in December 2003 to build Hawaii's first state veterans' home in Hilo. The hospital will be a 95-bed long-term care and adult day-care center and was expected to open in late 2007.

■ Recreation

Sightseeing

Hilo's quaint downtown contains wooden clapboard and stucco buildings with corrugated tin overhangs covering the sidewalks. A walk through town reveals flower and fruit stalls, fish markets, butcher shops, soda fountains, seed shops, and luncheonettes. Hilo has many magnificent gardens and parks.

At Hawaii Volcanoes National Park, a powerful active volcano can be glimpsed firsthand by car or helicopter at the fire pit crater of Kilauea. Rangers can provide maps and directions for optimum viewing of the volcano, if it is active, and for walks or hikes along 150 miles of trail. Educational programs and seminars are available to the public and include talks on topics such as endangered and unique local animal species and technology used to monitor volcanoes.

The center of the historic downtown is Kalakaua Park, a grassy square with a large banyan tree, a statue of the king, and a reflecting pool. On one side of the square is the 1919 Federal building, which combines Neo-Classical and Spanish Mission characteristics. Opposite the Federal Building is the East Hawaii Cultural Center. Other buildings of interest are the Zen Buddhist Temple, Taishoji Soto Mission, and the Haili Church, built in 1857 by missionaries from New England.

The Naha Stone, a gigantic stone sitting in front of the Hilo Public Library, is said to have been upended by King Kamehameha with his bare hands. Legend has it that only a chief of royal blood can budge it at all and anyone who can turn it over is a potential island king.

The Panaewa Rainforest Zoo is the only natural tropical rainforest zoos in the United States. Admission is free and animals on display include pygmy hippopotamuses, rainforest monkeys, a tapir, jungle parrots, rainforest tigers, and endangered species of Hawaiian birds.

A drive down Banyan Drive offers views of tree-lined lanes with 50-year-old banyan trees planted by President Franklin D. Roosevelt and other celebrities of the times. Old Mamalahoa Highway Scenic Drive, five miles north of the city, follows the Hamakua Coast through beautiful rainforest jungles with scenic views of the coast.

Rainbow Falls provides a view of cascading water surrounded by beautiful flowers. Nearby the Boiling Pots are turbulent rapids with deep, swirling pools and falls. Coconut Island, just offshore from Liliuokalani Park, contains picnic tables and shelters and is often used for local cultural events. Leleiwi Beach Park provides another ideal picnic spot and a good place for swimming, snorkeling, surfing, and netfishing since its seawall offers easy access to the ocean. The park's Richardson Ocean Center is a free marine life interpretive center.

The Suisan Fish Market Auction is a multilingual auction, held Monday through Saturday, of tuna and other tropical fish and seafood delicacies. On Wednesdays and Saturdays the Hilo Farmers' Market features breadfruit, papaya, avocados, stalks of ginger and other tropical flowers, as well as craft and gift items from more than 100 area farmers and crafters.

The Hawaii Tropical Botanical Garden, just a little over eight miles north of Hilo, provides views of hundreds of waterfalls and numerous varieties of flowers and native animals. The Nani Mau Gardens feature 20 acres of flowers, fruit trees, walking paths, pools and waterfalls.

Arts and Culture

The East Hawaii Cultural Center features changing art exhibits and dance and musical performances. The University of Hawaii-Hilo Performing Arts Center is the primary center for performing arts in the area. The theater seats 600 and each season hosts over 150 performances including dance, mime, lectures, and children's programs.

The Lyman Mission House and Museum, built in 1839, is the oldest wooden structure in Hilo. The restored house is furnished with period antiques that reflect the time when early Christian missionaries lived on the island. An attached museum features exhibits of Stone Age implements, feather leis, a large house made of grass, and various artifacts from Japan, Portugal, Korea, and the Philippines. The museum's Earth Heritage Gallery showcases the island's natural history including specimens of volcanic minerals and Hawaiian land shells, and the Island Heritage Gallery showcases native history and culture.

The Pacific Tsunami Museum in Downtown Hilo provides educational exhibits about tsunamis, which have caused more damage in Hilo than anywhere on all the Hawaiian Islands.

The Hilo Art Museum was a new addition in 2007. Founded in April of that year by resident Ted Coombs, the museum opened with a small permanent collection featuring original pieces by Picasso, Salvador Dali, and several local artists. With an in-house youth educational facility planned and a growing collection of artwork, the museum was expected to become a highlight not only in the Hilo community but for the state as well.

Festivals and Holidays

Hilo welcomes the Chinese New Year in February with a festival in Kalakaua Park featuring food, crafts, art, exhibitions, demonstrations, fireworks, and traditional dancers. The Kona Brewers Festival in March showcases 60 types of beer and chefs from 25 local restaurants preparing tropical culinary creations. Bluegrass, Hawaiian, and rock music, a "trash fashion show," hula and fire dancers are also part of the festivities. The Merrie Monarch Festival, held for a week each spring, is the state's biggest hula festival and draws the most publicity. Started in 1971, the festival offers parades and other attractions in addition to the three-night hula competition, which is the festival's claim to fame. The Annual Parker Ranch Horseraces & Rodeo is a Fourth of July celebration. Festivities at the rodeo include children's activities, food, and paniolo (Hawaiian cowboys) competing in traditional rodeo events.

Sports for the Spectator

The University of Hawaii at Hilo Vulcans offer intercollegiate basketball, volleyball, baseball, and softball competitions. The Hawaii Winter Baseball League (HWB) held a few games in 2007 at the Francis Wong Stadium, the former home of the Hilo Stars. Teams that year included the Waikiki Beach Boys, West Oahu Canefires, North Shore Honu, and Honolulu Sharks.

Sports for the Participant

Water sports reign supreme in Hilo and include fishing, skin diving, and sailing. Also popular are hunting, horseback riding, mountain biking, and other outdoor activities. The Big Island offers black, white, and green sand beaches; among them are Leleiwi Beach Park, a black sand beach that offers swimming, snorkeling and fishing, and Onekahakaha Beach Park, the city's only white sand beach with a safe inlet for swimming. The best surfing is found off Leleiwi and Richardson beaches. One of the oldest surf contests on the Big Island is the Quiksilver-Kamaaina Nissan Big Island Pro AM Surfing Trials. Held on the bayfront in downtown Hilo, amateur surf athletes use this open tournament as a platform toward a professional surfing career.

Two golf courses are located in the town of Hilo— the Hilo Municipal Golf Course and the Naniloa Golf Club. Several more public and semi-private courses are a short drive away. Skiing is occasionally possible atop Mauna Kea.

Shopping and Dining

Hilo offers a variety of shopping opportunities, ranging from national chain stores to bookstalls and specialty shops that carry such items as Hawaiian handicrafts, wooden bowls, jewelry, and native furniture. The major shopping centers in the city include the multimillion-dollar Prince Kuhio Plaza shopping center, Hilo Shopping Center, and Puainako Town Center, as well as the revitalized "Main Street" of downtown Hilo. Hilo's Bayfront area along Kamehameha Avenue is home to shops in historic buildings featuring native Hawaiian art and authentic Hawaiian wear. The East Hawaii Cultural Center is a good spot to find authentic, locally made Hawaiian gifts and souvenirs such as books, cards, jewelry, sculptures, and wood objects.

Hilo's residents and visitors enjoy a variety of dining spots that feature Cajun, Mexican, Italian, Japanese, Thai, Filipino, Chinese, Hawaiian, and traditional American fare. The fresh catch of the day is forever popular with visitors, especially the Aholehole, or Hawaiian flagtail, a reef fish raised in island ponds. Ahi (tuna), Mahi-Mahi and Opakapaka (pink snapper) are also served in area restaurants. Suman, a Filipino sticky-rice sweet wrapped in a banana leaf and cooked in coconut milk, is a favorite dish sold by street vendors in Hilo. Café Pesto is a popular local restaurant that features fresh local Hawaiian Regional foods. Other unique dining spots include an espresso bar featuring pure Kona coffee and various places with evening luaus.

Visitor Information: Big Island Visitors Bureau, 250 Keawe Street, Hilo, HI 96720; telephone (808)961-5797; fax (808)961-2126. Destination Hilo, 106 Kamehameha Ave, Hilo, HI 96720; telephone (808) 969-4999; fax (808)969-4999

■ Convention Facilities

The county of Hawaii's Hoolulu Park Complex provides the Afook-Chinen Civic Auditorium, with 11,342 square feet that can accommodate 3,550 people theater-style, 1,000 people classroom-style, and 500 people banquet-style. The Conference Center at the University of Hawaii at Hilo can host groups as small as 25 and as large as 600, with reception facilities for 1,000 people. The Edith Kanakaole Multipurpose Pavilion, with 18,720 square feet of space, can seat 4,500 people theater-style, 2,000 people for a reception, and 750 people banquet-style. The Seven Seas Luau House's 5,000 square feet can seat 700 people theater- or classroom-style, and 500 people for banquets. The Hilo Hawaiian Hotel offers a 5,040-square-foot banquet room that can accommodate small and large groups. The Hawaii Naniloa Resort offers seating for up to 400 people.

Convention Information: Big Island Visitors Bureau, 250 Keawe Street, Hilo, HI 96720; telephone (808)961-5797; fax (808)961-2126

■ Transportation

Approaching the City

The county of Hawaii's airports are Hilo International and Kona International. There are frequent inter-island flights by Aloha Airlines, Island Air, Pacific Wings and Hawaiian Airlines, as well as flights to major U.S. cities; daily direct flights from Tokyo are available. Four hotels are located within a five mile radius of the Hilo airport. A major highway system encircles the island of Hawaii, and driving time from the Kona International Airport to Hilo is about two hours and 15 minutes. State Highway 19 approaches Hilo from the north and State Highway 11 approaches from the south. State Highway 200 runs west into the interior of the island.

Traveling in the City

The island of Hawaii has more than 1,450 miles of highways. Since the area surrounding the city of Hilo is large, a rental car may be preferable to depending on taxi service. Major streets in Hilo include Kinoole St. and Kilauea Avenue, which run northwest to southeast, and Waianuenue Avenue, which runs east and west. Bayfront Highway follows the coastline and scenic Banyan Drive curves around the major resort area. County bus service is provided by "Hele-On." The Hawaii County Mass Transit Agency offers a Shared Ride Taxi program, which provides inexpensive door to door transportation in the cities of Hilo and Kona.

■ Communications

Newspapers and Magazines

The *Hawaii Tribune-Herald* is Hilo's daily morning paper.

Television and Radio

No network television stations broadcast from Hilo, but all major networks are available for viewing from Hilo via programming from neighboring Oahu. Hawaiian Cablevision system offers a wide selection of programming. The county is served by 5 AM and 14 FM radio stations.

Media Information: *Hawaii Tribune-Herald,* 355 Kinoole Street, Box 767, Hilo, HI 96720; telephone (808)935-6621; fax (808)969-9100

Hilo Online

Destination Hilo. Available www.destinationhilo.org

Downtown Improvement Association. Available www.downtownhilo.com

Hawaii County Home Page. Available www.hawaii-county.com

Hawaii Department of Education. Available doe .k12.hi.us

Hawaii Department of Labor and Industrial Relations. Available www.hawaii.gov/labor

Hawaii Island Chamber of Commerce. Available www.hicc.biz

Hawaii Tribune-Herald. Available www .hawaiitribune-herald.com

Hawaii Visitors and Convention Bureau. Available www.gohawaii.com/big_island

Hilo Public Library. Available www.librarieshawaii .org/locations/hawaii/hilo.htm

State of Hawaii. Available www.ehawaii.gov/dakine

BIBLIOGRAPHY

Ball, Pamela, *Lava: A Novel* (New York: Henry Holt, 1998)

Honolulu

■ The City in Brief

Founded: 1100 (by Hawaiians); 1795 (incorporated 1907)

Head Official: Mayor Mufi Hannemann (since 2005)

City Population

    1980: 365,048
    1990: 377,059
    2000: 371,657
    2006 estimate: 377,357
    Percent change, 1990–2000: −1.4%
    U.S. rank in 1980: 36th
    U.S. rank in 1990: 44th
    U.S. rank in 2000: 55th

Metropolitan Area Population

    1980: 763,000
    1990: 836,231
    2000: 876,156
    2006 estimate: 909,863
    Percent change, 1990–2000: 4.8%
    U.S. rank in 1980: 47th
    U.S. rank in 1990: 51st (State rank: 1st)
    U.S. rank in 2000: 55th

Area: 86 square miles (2000)

Elevation: 15 feet above sea level

Average Annual Temperatures: January, 73.0° F; July, 80.8° F; annual average, 77.5° F

Average Annual Precipitation: 18.29 inches of rain

Major Economic Sectors: services, wholesale and retail trade, government

Unemployment rate: 2.9% (June 2007)

Per Capita Income: $27,661 (2005)

2005 FBI Crime Index Property: 42,383

2005 FBI Crime Index Violent: 2,570

Major Colleges and Universities: University of Hawaii at Manoa, Chaminade University of Honolulu, Hawaii Pacific University, Brigham Young University-Hawaii

Daily Newspaper: *The Honolulu Advertiser; Honolulu Star-Bulletin*

■ Introduction

Honolulu, the capital of Hawaii and the seat of Honolulu County, is a cosmopolitan city. Its name means "protected harbor," and it serves as the crossroads of the Pacific Ocean with ship and air connections to the U.S. mainland, Asia, Australia, and New Zealand. The city is the principal port for the Hawaiian Islands and an important center for military defense with several bases, including Pearl Harbor Naval Base, located in the area. Millions of visitors are drawn annually to Honolulu's mild, semitropical climate and to the beautiful beaches of Waikiki.

■ Geography and Climate

Honolulu as a city is defined by the U.S. Census Bureau as the area from Makapuu south of the Koolau Mountain range summit to the western edge of Halawa Valley. Located along the southern coast of Oahu, Honolulu is the third largest of the Hawaiian Islands, just south of the Tropic of Cancer in the Pacific Ocean. The city is situated on a narrow plain between the ocean and the Koolau mountain range; it climbs the Punchbowl, an extinct volcano. Although the climate is semitropical, the trade winds usually keep the city comfortable, until the "kona" or southerly winds blow for a few weeks in the summer. Honolulu's weather exhibits the least seasonal change of any city in the United States, with only a few degrees difference between winter and summer.

Area: 86 square miles (2000)

Elevation: 15 feet above sea level

Average Temperatures: January, 73.0° F; July, 80.8° F; annual average, 77.5° F

Average Annual Precipitation: 18.29 inches of rain

■ History

Native Hawaiians Meet Westerners, Begin Trading Goods

Historians estimate that the first settlers, Polynesians, came to the Hawaiian Islands fifteen hundred years ago, with the last migration occurring around 750 A.D. By the time Westerners came to the islands, the Hawaiian people had developed a highly structured society composed of chiefs, who claimed the right of divine rule, and commoners, who worked the land and the sea.

British Captain James Cook first sighted Oahu in 1778, when he named the islands the Sandwich Islands after the Earl of Sandwich. William Brown was the first to enter Honolulu's harbor, in 1794. In 1795, King Kamehameha I unified the Hawaiian Islands, conquering the king of Oahu. Kamehameha settled at Waikiki, turning the harbor at Honolulu into a center of trade with the West for such goods as fur, sandalwood, and whale products. While bringing the islands into the modern world, such trade also threatened the native Hawaiian culture.

Rise of Sugar Industry Erodes Traditional Way of Life

Honolulu was such a convenient center of trade between the Orient and the West that it became the seat of a series of European occupations: Russia in 1816, England in 1843, and France in 1849. New England missionaries began arriving in 1820; some of their buildings, preserved by the Mission Houses Museum, can be seen today. The missionaries established schools and also functioned as government advisors to the royal Hawaiians. During the mid-nineteenth century the whaling industry began to decline and the sugar industry grew. The cultivation of sugar cane brought in a great influx of immigrant labor from throughout the Pacific basin; the descendants of these peoples are partially responsible for modern Honolulu's cosmopolitanism. A 1876 treaty that admitted sugar duty-free into the United States strengthened the power of this industry.

King Kamehameha III proclaimed Honolulu as the capitol city in 1850. The territorial legislature created county level governments in 1905. Incorporated that year, the County of Oahu included that island plus all the small islands beyond Niihau to, but not including, Midway Island 2,000 miles away. In 1907 the county was renamed the City and County of Honolulu.

At the time Honolulu was named the capitol city, traditional Hawaiian life was breaking down. The islands were basically ruled by the sugar interests consisting of an oligarchy of plantation owners. Native customs were declining both through the breakdown of taboos and the introduction of guns and liquor. Furthermore, the Hawaiian people were not immune to diseases brought to them by the Westerners; within a hundred years of the islands' discovery by the West, 80 percent of the native population was dead. The language and history of the Hawaiians is nevertheless preserved, partly through native dance and folklore.

In 1893 Queen Liliuokalani, the last Hawaiian monarch, was deposed by a group of American businessmen and U.S. Marines, and in 1898 the islands were annexed by the United States. In 1907 Honolulu was incorporated as a city and county. Through the efforts of Prince Jonah Kuhio Kalanianaole, a member of Congress from 1902 to 1922, Pearl Harbor was dredged, extending the sea power of the United States. On December 7, 1941, Pearl Harbor was bombed by the Japanese, but it survived to become the most important staging area for the United States in the Pacific during World War II. The area around Honolulu is still an important constellation of military bases.

Hawaii achieved statehood in 1959 and joined the Union as the 50th state with Honolulu as its capital. Today Honolulu is the Aloha state's center of business, culture, and politics. In recent years, Hawaiian sovereignty has become a contested political issue. In 1993 President Clinton signed an official apology acknowledging the U.S. role in the overthrow of the Hawaiian kingdom. A 2003 U.S. Supreme Court decision addressed the issue of sovereignty and the elections of government officials in Hawaii. In 2005, the Native Hawaiian Government Reorganization Act was reintroduced in the House and Senate. The legislation calls for the U.S. government to recognize Native Hawaiians as it does American Indians and Native Alaskans. The legislation would also provide a process by which the U.S. recognizes the Native Hawaiian governing entity.

As Honolulu continued to be a prime destination for travelers and developers alike, in the 21st century officials turned their focus toward preservation of the lush land. Taking initiative towards maintaining a balance between the natural setting of Hawaii and the ongoing development as a center for business and tourism, Mayor Mufi Hannemann presented the "21st Century Ahupuaa" campaign in April 2007. The campaign pushed the promotion of public

Image copyright Bryan Busovicki, 2007. Used under license from Shutterstock.com.

awareness and initiative in areas concerning conservation, alternative energy use, and economic development.

Historical Information: Bernice P. Bishop Museum Library, 1525 Bernice Street, Honolulu, HI 96817; telephone (808)847-3511; fax (808)841-8968

■ Population Profile

Metropolitan Area Residents

1980: 763,000
1990: 836,231
2000: 876,156
2006 estimate: 909,863
Percent change, 1990–2000: 4.8%
U.S. rank in 1980: 47th
U.S. rank in 1990: 51st (State rank: 1st)
U.S. rank in 2000: 55th

City Residents

1980: 365,048
1990: 377,059
2000: 371,657

2006 estimate: 377,357
Percent change, 1990–2000: −1.4%
U.S. rank in 1980: 36th
U.S. rank in 1990: 44th
U.S. rank in 2000: 55th

Density: 4,336.6 people per square mile (2000)

Racial and ethnic characteristics (2005)

White: 66,702
Black: 6,787
American Indian and Alaska Native: 456
Asian: 212,346
Native Hawaiian and Pacific Islander: 22,804
Hispanic or Latino (may be of any race): 13,268
Other: 2,912

Percent of residents born in state: 52.5% (2000)

Age characteristics (2005)

Population under 5 years old: 22,325
Population 5 to 9 years old: 15,724
Population 10 to 14 years old: 16,639
Population 15 to 19 years old: 19,818

Population 20 to 24 years old: 23,613
Population 25 to 34 years old: 45,233
Population 35 to 44 years old: 51,280
Population 45 to 54 years old: 55,438
Population 55 to 59 years old: 27,971
Population 60 to 64 years old: 20,198
Population 65 to 74 years old: 25,901
Population 75 to 84 years old: 27,950
Population 85 years and older: 10,162
Median age: 42.7 years

Births (2006, MSA)

Total number: 12,901

Deaths (2006, MSA)

Total number: 6,515

Money income (2005)

Per capita income: $27,661
Median household income: $50,793
Total households: 146,070

Number of households with income of . . .

less than $10,000: 14,457
$10,000 to $14,999: 7,540
$15,000 to $24,999: 14,545
$25,000 to $34,999: 13,875
$35,000 to $49,999: 21,635
$50,000 to $74,999: 27,170
$75,000 to $99,999: 16,513
$100,000 to $149,999: 18,332
$150,000 to $199,999: 7,370
$200,000 or more: 4,633

Percent of families below poverty level: 9.4% (2005)

2005 FBI Crime Index Property: 42,383

2005 FBI Crime Index Violent: 2,570

■ Municipal Government

The city of Honolulu and the county of Honolulu are administered jointly by a mayor-council form of government. The mayor and nine council members serve four-year terms.

Head Official: Mayor Mufi Hannemann (since 2005; current term expires 2009)

Total Number of City Employees: 8,000 (2006)

City Information: Mayor's Office, 530 South King Street, Honolulu, HI 96813; telephone (808)523-4141; fax (808)527-5552

■ Economy

Major Industries and Commercial Activity

Honolulu began its economic life in the mid-nineteenth century as a port for whalers; it was also a trade center for nations bordering the Pacific, dealing in such goods as sandalwood, whale oil, and fur. While markets for sandalwood and whale oil decreased, sugar and pineapple markets increased dramatically. In fact, the powerful sugar industry, owned mainly by Americans, engineered the downfall of Hawaii's last monarch and the islands' annexation by the United States. One-fifth of the land in Honolulu County is zoned for agriculture, but fields are now giving way to new homes and commercial development. With the closure of sugar plantations, challenges arise to find the most productive use for these lands. Diversified agriculture has been on a steady upward trend. Aquaculture, which includes cultivated species of shellfish, finfish and algae, has grown in recent years. As reported in 2006, at latest count Honolulu County had 46 aquaculture operations, which produced approximately $5.2 million in sales.

In addition to serving as the business and trading hub of the Hawaiian Islands, Honolulu is the transportation crossroads of the Pacific, connecting East with West. The city's recently expanded harbor facilities handle cargo for several international steamship companies, and a Foreign Trade Zone is based there. Other important elements of Honolulu's economic base include tourism, military defense, research and development, and manufacturing. With millions of visitors coming each year to enjoy Honolulu's climate and beaches, tourism contributes significantly to the local economy—in 2006 alone, the island of Oahu attracted more than 4.6 million visitors. Pearl Harbor Naval Shipyard, Marine Corps Base Hawaii in Kaneohe, and Schofield Barracks Army base provide revenues that are unaffected by the normal business cycle. As the home of the University of Hawaii at Manoa, Honolulu is a center for research and development, especially in the areas of oceanography, astrophysics, geophysics, and biomedicine. The city and county of Honolulu also contains many commercial, industrial and retail properties.

Items and goods produced: jewelry, clothing, food and beverages, rubber products, construction materials, and electronics and computer equipment

Incentive Programs—New and Existing Companies

Local programs: Honolulu's Office of Economic Development provides assistance to entrepreneurs; supports programs that stimulate business development; advocates for the removal of impediments to business;

sponsors conferences and events to attract investments; underwrites marketing outreach; provides extensive international networking; provides advice and guidance to businesses; and reinforces Honolulu's position as an important player in the global economy. Enterprise Honolulu, a non-profit economic development organization, works to retain existing businesses and assist in their expansion; encourage growth and diversification amongst existing businesses; attract and recruit new businesses; and help entrepreneurs in their business development initiatives.

State programs: State programs available include direct financial incentives such as Industrial Development Bonds, a Capital Loan Program, the Urban Honolulu Enterprise Zone Program, customized industrial training, and investment of public funds in return for equity or ownership positions in private businesses. Also at the state level, tax incentives for technology-related companies are available through 2010 with the extension of Hawaii's Act 215 relating to capital investment.

Job training programs: The Workforce Development Division of Hawaii's Department of Labor and Industrial Relations oversees One-Stop Workforce Assistance Centers, a job placement and training system to help people find work and employers find suitable workers, and the Employment & Training Fund (ETF), a job skills upgrade program for current workers. Employers can receive customized training grants for their workplace or they can nominate a current worker for an established training course. HireNet Hawaii was created as a "virtual one-stop employment center." The site allows individuals to post resumes online, search for available jobs in the state, and view current labor market data, among other features. Training providers can also use HireNet Hawaii as a tool to post program information.

Development Projects

With available research centers at the University of Hawaii as well as the area's defense contracting industry, Honolulu is looking to diversify its economy in the following areas: alternate energies, astronomy and space sciences, defense-dual use technologies, diversified agriculture, information and communication technologies, life science-biotech, and marine sciences. Mayor Mufi Hannemann presented the "21st Century Ahupuaa" campaign in April 2007, promoting public awareness and initiatives in areas concerning conservation, alternative energy use, and economic development. The film and digital media industry is growing and is supported by the City and County Honolulu Film Office.

A private and local government-supported "Second City," Kapolei, is constructed in an area 20 miles from downtown Honolulu. The Kapolei region is one of the

fastest growing areas in the state with 24,860 jobs in 2005 and a projected total reaching 46,000 by 2015. New amenities to the area included shopping centers, golf courses, parks, and the Hawaiian Waters Adventures Park. Public infrastructure was targeted in 2007 with a $172 million agreement aimed at improving roads, drainage, water services, and sewer systems as well as constructing a transit facility.

The $535 million Waikiki Beach Walk redevelopment project rejuvenated walkways, hotels, retail complexes and entertainment areas along one of the most visited beaches in Honolulu. Opening its doors in January 2007, the complex included 5 hotels and 47 restaurant and retail tenants. Over $75 million was released by Governor Linda Lingle for continued renovations planned at Honolulu International Airport. Construction projects at the airport were expected to be completed by 2010.

Economic Development Information: The Office of Economic Development, 530 South King Street, Suite 305, Honolulu, HI 96813; telephone (808)527-5761; fax (808)523-4242

Commercial Shipping

Honolulu's location in the mid-Pacific makes it a major stopover for trans-Pacific sea and air shipments. Honolulu Harbor has a highly successful Foreign Trade Zone and several major shipping companies serving the port. The harbor also has terminals for commercial fishing, cruise ships, and ferries. In the "Oahu Commercial Harbors 2020 Master Plan," the development of a commercial fishing "village" was introduced. The finished "village" was expected to consolidate services scattered across the waterfront, producing more efficiency in the fishing market.

Labor Force and Employment Outlook

Honolulu County's four major industry sectors are government; trade, transportation, and utilities; leisure and hospitality; and professional and business services. These four industries account for the majority of the total employment in Honolulu County. Services and trade are considered the two largest growth industries for the County. *Inc.* magazine ranked Honolulu eighth in employment growth for the areas of information and transportation in 2007. Proving growth overall in employment, Honolulu was recognized as a "large-size city" in the magazine that same year, qualifying with at least 450,000 jobs. The previous year the city had been in the "midsize" category.

The following is a summary of data regarding the Honolulu metropolitan area labor force, 2006 annual averages.

Size of nonagricultural labor force: 453,100

Number of workers employed in . . .

construction and mining: 24,700
manufacturing: 11,700
trade, transportation and utilities: 86,300
information: 9,100
financial activities: 22,900
professional and business services: 63,500
educational and health services: 56,000
leisure and hospitality: 62,500
other services: 20,500
government: 96,000

Average hourly earnings of production workers employed in manufacturing: $16.14

Unemployment rate: 2.9% (June 2007)

Largest non-government employers (2007)	*Number of employees*
Marriot International Inc.	6,710
Starwood Hotels and Resorts	5,357
Hawaii Pacific Health	5,313
Wal-Mart	4,594
Hawaiian Airlines Inc.	4,200
Kaiser Foundation Health Plan and Hospitals	4,004
The Queen's Health Systems	3,812
Hawaii Health Systems Corp.	3,723
Hawaiian Electric Industries Inc.	3,569
Alpha Airlines Inc.	3,375

Cost of Living

Because land is scarce and tourist development has driven up the cost of living, Hawaii is one of the top ranking states in housing costs. About 65 percent of housing in Honolulu is condominiums. The median single family home resale price in 2002 was $335,000. Housing rentals, fuel, and food costs are among the highest in the country. These conditions force many Hawaiians to work two or three jobs to survive, ranking it second in the nation for multiple part-time employment.

The following is a summary of data regarding key cost of living factors for the Honolulu area.

2007 (1st quarter) ACCRA Average House Price: $785,680

2007 (1st quarter) ACCRA Cost of Living Index: 162.6

State income tax rate: 1.4% to 8.25%

State sales tax rate: 4.0%

Local income tax rate: None

Local sales tax rate: None

Property tax rate: $3.75–$5.72 per $1,000 valuation (residential)

Economic Information: Chamber of Commerce of Hawaii, 1132 Bishop St. Suite 402, Honolulu, HI 96813; telephone (808)545-4300; fax (808)545-4369

■ Education and Research

Elementary and Secondary Schools

Hawaii is the only state with a single, unified statewide school system, comprised of seven districts, four on the island of Oahu and three on the neighbor islands. The four districts on Oahu are in the city and county of Honolulu; metropolitan Honolulu falls in the Honolulu District. An elected board of education formulates educational policy and supervises the public school system. Seven members are elected according to geographic region and six are elected at-large. One non-voting student member is appointed.

The following is a summary of data regarding the Honolulu District as of the 2005–2006 school year.

Total enrollment: 31,274

Number of facilities

elementary schools: 40
junior high/middle schools: 9
senior high schools: 6
other: 3

Student/teacher ratio: 16.6:1

Teacher salaries (2005–06)

elementary median: $37,710
junior high/middle median: $46,050
secondary median: $53,250

Funding per pupil: $7,455

A variety of private and special education schools are licensed by the state and serve the school-age population. There are six private schools in the Downtown Honolulu area. They are Hawaii Pacific University (post-secondary), Hongwanji Mission School, Kawaiahao School, Pacific Buddhist Academy, St. Andrew's Priory School, and Word of Life Academy.

Public and Private Schools Information: Department of Education, 1390 Miller St., PO Box 2360, Honolulu, HI 96804; telephone (808)586-3230; fax (808)586-3234

Colleges and Universities

The University of Hawaii at Manoa, with an enrollment of more than 20,000 in 2006, offers both undergraduate and graduate programs. It is especially known for its programs in the marine sciences, tropical agriculture, geophysics, astronomy, and Asian and Pacific cultures. On the campus of the University of Hawaii at Manoa is the East-West Center, which is an institution of technical and cultural exchange with Asian and Pacific countries.

Chaminade University of Honolulu is a small, private institution affiliated with the Society of Mary of the Roman Catholic Church. Also located in Honolulu is Hawaii Pacific University (HPU), Hawaii's largest private university. HPU was named "Best in the West" according to *The Princeton Review*'s "Best Colleges: Region by Region" list and was ranked in the 2008 edition of *U.S. News & World Report* as one of "America's Best Colleges." There are four community colleges.

Libraries and Research Centers

The Hawaii State Public Library System is based in Honolulu and operates 50 libraries throughout the state. Holdings consist of more than two million volumes (more than 1.5 million housed on Oahu) as well as newspapers, magazines, tapes, films, and special collections, including Hawaiian history and state and federal documents. The system also maintains the Library for the Blind and Physically Handicapped, located in Honolulu.

Specialized libraries are affiliated with local colleges and universities, government agencies, hospitals, and corporations. Research activities in such fields as agriculture, livestock, the environment, freshwater and marine ecology, marine biology, marine mammalogy, water resources, cancer, biomedicine, astronomy, geophysics, labor, and industrial relations are conducted primarily by the University of Hawaii and federal government agencies. A new $150 million biomedical research and education center was built in Kakaako in partnership with the University of Hawaii at Manoa.

Public Library Information: Hawaii State Public Library System, 478 South King Street, Honolulu, HI 96813; telephone (808)586-3500

■ Health Care

The city and county of Honolulu is served by 13 hospitals. The Queen's Medical Center in downtown Honolulu is the largest private hospital in the state, with 505 acute care beds and 28 sub-acute care beds. Cardiac rehabilitation centers are maintained at Kuakini Medical Center and Tripler Army Medical Center. Gamma Knife technology became available at the St. Francis Medical Center at the Gamma Knife Center of the Pacific. In 2006 more than 44,000 people were employed by the health care and social assistance services in the Honolulu area.

■ Recreation

Sightseeing

The beauty of Honolulu's natural surroundings, its fascinating mix of cultures, and its unique layering of history offer much for the visitor to see and do. Honolulu abounds in the exotic flora and fauna of a semitropical island. The Honolulu Zoo houses an excellent collection of tropical birds as well as animals from around the world. A highlight of the zoo is the Kubuni Reserve. In this 12-acre African savanna, animals roam free within 30 different habitats. The Waikiki Aquarium has exhibits that educate visitors and promote conservation of marine life, including coral reef environments and endangered species such as the monk seal. In 2000, the Waikiki Aquarium was designated as a Coastal Ecosystem Learning Center. At Sea Life Park, visitors can watch dolphins, penguins, and sea lions perform as well as swim with stingrays and dolphins.

The University of Hawaii at Manoa maintains the 200 acre Lyon Arboretum, which offers paths and trails throughout its beautifully landscaped gardens. The Foster Botanical Garden was established in 1855 by Queen Kalama, wife of King Kamehameha III, and features a prehistoric glen planted with grasses, ferns, and palms. Other botanical gardens include Ho'omaluhia, Koko Crater, Liliuokalani, and Wahiawa. Exotic flowers can also be seen at the Queen Kapiolani Hibiscus Garden.

A number of historic buildings are located in Honolulu. The stately Iolani Palace is the only royal palace in the United States, although it was inhabited by Hawaiian royalty for only 11 years. Completed by King David Kalahaua in 1862, it served as a prison for Queen Liliuokalani. Honolulu's first church, the Kawaiahao Church, was built in 1841 from blocks of coral and was the place of worship for Hawaiian rulers. The State Capitol, resembling a volcano, is designed to reflect various facets of the state of Hawaii.

The exhibits at the Hawaii Maritime Center focus on Hawaii's whaling days, the history of the Honolulu Harbor and the *Falls of Clyde*, a four-masted sailing ship built in 1878, which carried passengers and cargo between Honolulu and San Francisco. An underwater park is located at Hanauma Bay Beach Park, where novices at snorkeling and SCUBA diving can view a coral reef. Other historical sites include Diamond Head State Monument, the U.S.S. Arizona Memorial, the Battleship Missouri Memorial, and the National Cemetery of the Pacific.

Arts and Culture

With a symphony, opera, theater groups, and numerous museums, Honolulu is the cultural center of the state of Hawaii. The Honolulu Symphony presents a classical concert series as well as a pop series at the Blaisdell Center Concert Hall. Also housed at Blaisdell Center is the

Hawaii Opera Theater, which provides a season of grand opera and operettas. The Waikiki Shell is also a part of the Blaisdell Center and is an open-air amphitheater that hosts a variety of concerts and events. Broadway performances and dramatic classics are presented at Diamond Head Theatre and Manoa Valley Theatre, while the Kennedy Theatre at the University of Hawaii at Manoa is the site of student productions. Adjacent to the Waikiki Shell is a Hula Show Area where performances take place several times a week.

Honolulu's museums offer a range of experiences. The Bishop Museum is known for its collection of Polynesian artifacts, considered to be among the best in the world. The museum also presents hands-on exhibits and a planetarium where the constellations may be viewed as they appear from the island of Hawaii. The Bishop Museum opened a new $17 million Science Adventure Center in 2005. The center consists of 16,500 square feet of interactive displays and exhibits that feature volcanology, oceanography, and biodiversity. The Honolulu Academy of Arts houses permanent exhibits of oriental and occidental art, including the Kress collection of Italian Renaissance paintings and the Asian collection, featuring art and artifacts from throughout the Orient. In 2001, the museum opened its $28 million Luce Pavilion Complex which added two 4,000-square-foot galleries. The Mission Houses Museum is comprised of the three oldest American buildings in Hawaii; the Frame house, the oldest, was built in 1821 and is furnished with period pieces that help show how the missionaries lived.

Festivals and Holidays

A number of holidays and festivals celebrating Honolulu's unique mix of cultures are held throughout the year. The Narcissus Festival, in January or early February, marks the Chinese New Year with lion dances and pageants. The Cherry Blossom Festival runs from January to March and is the largest running ethnic celebration in the state. A highlight of the event is the selection of a Cherry Blossom Queen and Court. Prince Kuhio Day on March 26, a state holiday, is held in honor of the prince who served in the U.S. Congress for 20 years. The Honolulu Festival takes place in March and celebrates ethnic harmony. The Hawaii Invitational International Music Festival occurs in April with high school, junior high, and college band participants. Lei Day on May 1st is one of Honolulu's most popular unofficial holidays; festivities include hula dances, contests for the best lei, and the crowning of the Lei Queen. The Hawaii State Fair occurs on weekends from mid-May through mid-June at the Aloha Stadium. The Pan Pacific-Matsuri Festival held in June promotes cultural exchange between Hawaiian and Japanese cultures. In addition to dance, art, and music, the Festival includes a golf open and a half marathon run.

The King Kamehameha Celebration, a state holiday observed on June 11, honors the king who united the Hawaiian Islands. The Hawaii International Jazz Festival held in late July celebrates jazz with international artists. The Ukulele Festival held annually in July presents a variety of ukulele players during free concerts. The Prince Lot Hula Festival in July showcases ancient and modern versions of the dance at Queen Kapiolani Bandstand. The Aloha Festival celebrates *Makahiki*, the traditional harvest time when taxes were paid, with pageants and street parties known as *Ho'olaule'a*. The Annual Orchid Show in late October shows thousands of varieties of plants and flowers, especially the exotic orchids that grow in the area. The Hawaii International Film Festival in late November and early December brings together award-winning film directors from the nations that border the Pacific Ocean.

Sports for the Spectator

Honolulu sports fans enjoy a variety of college sports, which include baseball, softball, basketball, soccer, golf, tennis, and track and field. The NFL Pro Bowl is held in February each year at the Aloha Stadium. The American Basketball Association welcomed the new Hawaii Hurricanes; the team began play in the 2007-08 season. Honolulu is also home to the Hawaii Winter Baseball League's Honolulu Sharks and Waikiki Beach Boys. Spectators can enjoy car racing at Hawaii Raceway Park.

Sports for the Participant

Honolulu's Waikiki beach draws more visitors than any other beach on the island, offering a host of water sports such as swimming, sailing, snorkeling, surfing, scuba diving, kayaking, or outrigger canoeing. Scuba equipment, surfboard and windsurf boards can be rented; lessons are also available. Charter boats for deep-sea fishing can be rented; during spring and summer there are particularly rich runs of game fish such as marlin and tuna.

Honolulu is also popular for hang gliding and parasailing. Visitors can take helicopter tours or go whale watching. Other activities include hiking, jogging, biking, horseback riding, tennis, and golf. Thousands of runners convene in Honolulu in December for the 26.2 mile Honolulu Marathon. The Honolulu Triathlon takes place every year in April.

Shopping and Dining

Shopping is a pleasurable pastime in Honolulu. Located in the city is Ala Moana, one of the largest open-air shopping centers in the world. After completion of a multi-million dollar expansion in 2008, Ala Moana will offer 290 stores, including 70 restaurants. Hotels along the beach in Waikiki are full of shops, and downtown Fort Street has been converted into a pedestrian mall. Also located within the city are the Royal Hawaiian and the

Kahala Mall Shopping Centers. The Cultural Plaza in Chinatown Historic District features a variety of ethnic shops and stores. Temari, a center for Asian and Pacific arts that is not actually a store, offers two- to three-hour workshops to visitors. The former Dole Pineapple Cannery now houses retail shops oriented toward tourists. The newly developed Aloha Tower Marketplace next to the Hawaii Maritime Center offers many shops and restaurants catering to tourists.

Honolulu cuisine is truly international. Hawaiian specialties include *mahimahi* (dolphin fish), *poi* (rounded taro root), and *puaa kalua* (a whole pig slow-roasted in a pit). One restaurant in particular that boasts authentic Hawaiian cuisine is Alan Wong's Restaurant in Honolulu. The restaurant was ranked eighth on *Gourmet* magazine's "America's Top 50 Restaurants" in 2006 and in 2007 won "Best Restaurant of the Year" in *Honolulu Magazine*'s Hale Aina Awards—its eighth time receiving this award. Local restaurants offer a range of Oriental foods—Chinese, Japanese, Thai, and Korean—as well as European fare such as French, German, and Italian. Restaurants also serve popular Cajun and Creole dishes.

Visitor Information: Hawaii Visitors & Convention Bureau, 2270 Kalakaua Avenue, Suite 801, Honolulu, HI 96815; telephone (808)923-1811; toll-free (800)GO HAWAII (464-2924); fax (808)923-0290.

■ Convention Facilities

Honolulu's principal meeting facility is the beautiful four-story Hawaii Convention Center, which offers a 200,000-square-foot ground floor exhibition hall; a second floor exclusively for parking; a third floor with meeting room space totaling 149,768 square feet; and a 35,000-square-foot grand ballroom and rooftop garden on the fourth floor. Inside, a $2 million Hawaiian art collection with paintings of volcanoes, mountains, ocean, waterfalls, taro, and fishponds are displayed alongside images of Hawaiian royalty, gods, and myths; above, soaring rooftop canopies recall images of Polynesian sailing canoes. The building is open to the outdoors and sits on landscaped grounds featuring terraces, lanais, and courtyards that occupy more than six acres of the 10-acre site.

Convention Information: Hawaii Visitors & Convention Bureau, 2270 Kalakaua Avenue, Suite 801, Honolulu, HI 96815; telephone (808)923-1811; fax (808)923-0290

■ Transportation

Approaching the City

Isolated from the mainland, Honolulu is reached primarily by plane. Honolulu International Airport, a major center for Pacific air travel, is served by over 20 domestic and foreign airlines as well as inter-island carriers. Hawaii's Department of Transportation arranged for the airport to undergo a terminal modernization project; all construction projects at the airport are expected to be completed by 2010. Honolulu may also be reached by ship; cruise lines sail regularly between Honolulu and cities in California.

Traveling in the City

Because of the irregular shape of the city, Honolulu residents define directions according to landmarks such as the mountains and the sea rather than standard compass orientations.

TheBus, owned by the City and County of Honolulu but operated separately, provides public transportation to the entire island on a fleet of over 525 buses. Oahu Transit Service also provides a service called HandiVan that transports people with disabilities. The Waikiki Trolley Service, with a fleet of over 50 trolleys, provides transportation to shopping centers, museums, and other points of interest.

■ Communications

Newspapers and Magazines

Honolulu's daily newspapers are *The Honolulu Advertiser* and the *Honolulu Star-Bulletin*. There are also several non-English papers serving Honolulu. *Honolulu Magazine* features topics and events of local interest. Among the periodicals published in Honolulu are *Bamboo Ridge, The Hawaii Writers' Quarterly,* a literary magazine; *Biography,* a journal acting as a forum for learned articles dealing with life-writing; *Building Management Hawaii*; and *China Review International.* Business publications include *Hawaii Business* and *Pacific Business News.*

Television and Radio

Nine television stations broadcast from Honolulu; cable service is also available. Over 35 FM and AM radio stations broadcast in Honolulu; several offer multilingual programming.

Media Information: *The Honolulu Advertiser;* telephone (808)525-8090; fax (808)525-8037. *Honolulu Star-Bulletin,* telephone (808)529-4747; fax (808)529-4750

Honolulu Online

Chamber of Commerce of Hawaii. Available www .cochawaii.com

City and County of Honolulu. Available www.co .honolulu.hi.us

Hawaii Department of Education. Available www .doe.k12.hi.us

Hawaii Department of Labor and Industrial Relations. Available www.hawaii.gov/labor

Hawaii Visitors and Convention Bureau. Available www.gohawaii.com

Honolulu Advertiser. Available www.honoluluadvertiser.com

Honolulu Star-Bulletin. Available www.starbulletin.com

Oahu Visitors Bureau. Available www.visit-oahu.com

Social and economic trends. Available www.Hawaii.gov/dbedt

State of Hawaii. Available www.ehawaii.gov/dakine

BIBLIOGRAPHY

Cowing, Sue, ed., *Fire in the Sea: An Anthology of Poetry and Art* (Honolulu, HI: University of Hawaii Press in association with the Honolulu Academy of Arts, 1996)

Penisten, John, *Honolulu* (Minneapolis, MN: Dillon Press, 1989)

Twain, Mark, *Letters from Honolulu* (Honolulu, HI: T. Nickerson, 1939)

Tyau, Kathleen, *A Little Too Much Is Enough* (New York: Norton, 1995)

Idaho

The State in Brief

Nickname: Gem State

Motto: Esto perpetua (Let it be perpetual)

Flower: Syringa

Bird: Mountain bluebird

Area: 83,570 square miles (2000; U.S. rank 14th)

Elevation: Ranges from 710 feet to 12,662 feet above sea level

Climate: Tempered by Pacific westerly winds, varying by altitude; hot summers in the arid south and cold, snowy winters in the central and northern mountains

Admitted to Union: July 3, 1890

Capital: Boise

Head Official: Governor C.L. "Butch" Otter (R) (until 2010)

Population

1980: 944,000
1990: 1,006,749
2000: 1,293,953
2006 estimate: 1,466,465
Percent change, 1990–2000: 28.5%
U.S. rank in 2006: 39th
Percent of residents born in state: 45.12% (2006)
Density: 17.3 people per square mile (2006)
2006 FBI Crime Index Total: 39,096

Racial and Ethnic Characteristics (2006)

White: 1,357,129
Black or African American: 6,842
American Indian and Alaska Native: 16,250
Asian: 15,335
Native Hawaiian and Pacific Islander: 2,021
Hispanic or Latino (may be of any race): 138,871
Other: 37,435

Age Characteristics (2006)

Population under 5 years old: 112,366
Population 5 to 19 years old: 326,943
Percent of population 65 years and over: 11.6%
Median age: 34.3

Vital Statistics

Total number of births (2006): 22,888
Total number of deaths (2006): 10,894
AIDS cases reported through 2005: 578

Economy

Major industries: Mining, lumbering, agriculture, high technology, tourism
Unemployment rate (2006): 5.3%
Per capita income (2006): $21,000
Median household income (2006): $42,865
Percentage of persons below poverty level (2006): 12.6%
Income tax rate: 1.6% to 7.8%
Sales tax rate: 6.0%

Boise

■ The City in Brief

Founded: 1834 (incorporated 1864)

Head Official: Mayor David H. Bieter (D) (since 2004)

City Population
> 1980: 102,451
> 1990: 125,685
> 2000: 185,787
> 2006 estimate: 198,638
> Percent change, 1990–2000: 37.5%
> U.S. rank in 1980: 162nd
> U.S. rank in 1990: 145th
> U.S. rank in 2000: 105th

Metropolitan Area Population
> 1980: 256,881
> 1990: 295,851
> 2000: 464,840
> 2006 estimate: 567,640
> Percent change, 1990–2000: 45.4%
> U.S. rank in 1980: Not reported
> U.S. rank in 1990: Not reported
> U.S. rank in 2000: 97th

Area: 63.8 square miles (2000)

Elevation: 2,842 feet above sea level

Average Annual Temperatures: January, 30.2° F; July, 74.7° F; annual average, 51.9° F

Average Annual Precipitation: 12.19 inches of rain; 20.7 inches of snow

Major Economic Sectors: services, wholesale and retail trade, government

Unemployment Rate: 2.1% (June 2007)

Per Capita Income: $24,657 (2005)

2005 FBI Crime Index Property: 7,484

2005 FBI Crime Index Violent: 748

Major Colleges and Universities: Boise State University, University of Idaho-Boise Center

Daily Newspaper: *The Idaho Statesman*

■ Introduction

Boise, the capital of Idaho and the largest city in the state, is the commercial, financial, and cultural center of the northern Rockies region. Known as the "City of Trees," Boise is among the fastest-growing metropolitan areas in the nation; according to the U.S. Census Bureau it grew by 4.1 percent between 2005 and 2006. At the same time, the city has maintained a high quality of life through cooperation between business, government, and citizens. An easy blending of historic structures and modern buildings in the downtown district attests to the fact that Boise remains close to its Western heritage while moving with the times. Noted for its mild climate, clean environment, and friendly people, Boise is set in a fertile agricultural area called "Treasure Valley."

■ Geography and Climate

Boise is situated in a wide river valley at the foot of the Rocky Mountains. The Boise River runs out of a canyon to the south and through the center of the city, joining the Snake River about 40 miles to the north. The climate is tempered year-round by air from the Pacific Ocean. Summers are dry with hot periods that rarely last more than a few days; autumn weather is usually ideal. Winter storms produce much of the yearly precipitation; cold spells are common, but warm Chinook winds (moist air from the Pacific) bring periods of mild weather. Low humidity is raised slightly by agricultural irrigation.

Area: 63.8 square miles (2000)

Elevation: 2,842 feet above sea level

Average Temperatures: January, 30.2° F; July, 74.7° F; annual average, 51.9° F

Average Annual Precipitation: 12.19 inches of rain; 20.7 inches of snow

■ History

Gold Brings Prospectors, Settlers

In 1834 the Hudson's Bay Company founded a trading post for wagon trains along the Oregon Trail on the Snake River northwest of Boise's present site. The region that is now Boise was originally a small forested area along the Boise River, an oasis in the arid northwestern mountains. The spot was called "Les Bois," which means "wooded" in French, and thousands of emigrants passed through on their way to settle in Oregon. Gold was discovered in the area in 1862, bringing a number of prospectors, and the site became a convenient supply point for the mining camps in the mountains.

The U.S. Army constructed Fort Boise in 1863, and the town became the territorial capital in 1864, when it was also incorporated as a city. Several more gold strikes occurred in the next few years, and by1868 the town had more than four hundred permanent structures, more than half of which were residential. The Idaho Penitentiary was built in the town in 1870 and at one time or another housed many legendary western desperadoes.

Gold Dries Up; Irrigation Systems Bring Farms

After the gold boom ended, the population declined, and Boise faced an uphill battle for survival. The town was in an isolated location, far off the major lines of transportation, and the climate was too dry to support farming. A determined core of citizens set out to make the area livable by developing irrigation systems, planting crops, and mapping out a town with shady streets running along the river.

Boise approached the twentieth century as a remote place, reachable only by the difficult wagon trails. The city became the state capital when Idaho entered the Union, and the Capitol building was erected in 1920. A long struggle to obtain railway service finally succeeded when the elegant Union Pacific Depot (now the Boise Depot) was built in 1925. A number of dams and reservoirs were constructed in the years before World War II to improve the agricultural outlook and provide a water supply and hydroelectric power for the growing city.

During World War II the military became a strong presence in the Boise area when a flying and training base was established at Gowen Field. In the 1960s, a new city charter was drawn up, allowing the city to annex many of the suburban areas and doubling the population. The 21st century brought continued population growth due to Boise's urban renewal, job opportunities, quality of life, and favorable climate. Lending to some these positive qualities, the city was named the eighth "Best Place to Live" in the "small cities" category by *Money* magazine in 2006.

Historical Information: Idaho State Historical Society, Public Archives and Research Library, 2205 Old Penitentiary Road, Boise, ID 83712; telephone (208) 334-3356; fax (208)334-3198

■ Population Profile

Metropolitan Area Residents

1980: 256,881
1990: 295,851
2000: 464,840
2006 estimate: 567,640
Percent change, 1990–2000: 45.4%
U.S. rank in 1980: Not reported
U.S. rank in 1990: Not reported
U.S. rank in 2000: 97th

City Residents

1980: 102,451
1990: 125,685
2000: 185,787
2006 estimate: 198,638
Percent change, 1990–2000: 37.5%
U.S. rank in 1980: 162nd
U.S. rank in 1990: 145th
U.S. rank in 2000: 105th

Density: 2,913.1 people per square mile (2000)

Racial and ethnic characteristics (2005)

White: 177,851
Black: 1,995
American Indian and Alaska Native: 1,050
Asian: 3,801
Native Hawaiian and Pacific Islander: 43
Hispanic or Latino (may be of any race): 11,295
Other: 2,101

Percent of residents born in state: 43.2% (2000)

Age characteristics (2005)

Population under 5 years old: 12,713
Population 5 to 9 years old: 11,723
Population 10 to 14 years old: 12,614
Population 15 to 19 years old: 11,985
Population 20 to 24 years old: 16,057
Population 25 to 34 years old: 30,182
Population 35 to 44 years old: 26,842

The Idaho State Capitol building in Boise. *Image copyright Randy Allphin, 2007. Used under license from Shutterstock.com.*

Population 45 to 54 years old: 30,903
Population 55 to 59 years old: 11,937
Population 60 to 64 years old: 7,036
Population 65 to 74 years old: 10,366
Population 75 to 84 years old: 6,453
Population 85 years and older: 2,856
Median age: 35.2 years

Births (2006, MSA)

Total number: 9,036

Deaths (2006, MSA)

Total number: 3,649

Money income (2005)

Per capita income: $24,657
Median household income: $46,342
Total households: 82,587

Number of households with income of . . .

less than $10,000: 6,006
$10,000 to $14,999: 4,450
$15,000 to $24,999: 9,375
$25,000 to $34,999: 9,912
$35,000 to $49,999: 14,508
$50,000 to $74,999: 18,168
$75,000 to $99,999: 9,479
$100,000 to $149,999: 7,370
$150,000 to $199,999: 1,992
$200,000 or more: 1,327

Percent of families below poverty level: 11.9% (2005)

2005 FBI Crime Index Property: 7,484

2005 FBI Crime Index Violent: 748

■ Municipal Government

Boise has been led by a mayor-council form of government since the adoption of a new city charter in 1961. The council is comprised of six part-time members, elected to four-year terms. A full-time mayor is elected every four years.

Head Official: Mayor David H. Bieter (D) (since 2004; current term expires 2008)

Total Number of City Employees: 1,539 (2007)

City Information: City of Boise Mayor's Office, PO Box 500, Boise, ID 83701; telephone (208)384-4422; fax (208)384-4420; email mayor@council@cityofboise .org

■ Economy

Major Industries and Commercial Activity

Boise began as a supply and service center for the mining camps in the nearby mountains. It continues today as an important commercial hub for smaller towns and agricultural establishments in the northern Rockies. In addition to mining, farming and timber have played important roles in the development of the Boise economy.

The economy continued to grow in 2006 and 2007 with major growth in nonfarm employment, construction, trade, and professional services. Professional and business services, leisure and hospitality, and education and health services were expected to be the next main growth drivers. State government is one of the city's main employers, since Boise is the capital of Idaho. Boise is home to over a dozen corporate headquarters; corporate headquarters in the city include Albertsons, a supermarket chain; Boise Cascade wood and paper products; Washington Group International, an engineering and construction firm; the J.R. Simplot Company with frozen foods, phosphates, and cattle; Micron Technology, which manufactures semiconductors; and TJ International, with specialty building products. Over 18,000 other businesses have major facilities in the area. Tourism is another large source of revenue for the Boise area. High technology industries were becoming an increasingly important sector, and the Army National Guard's Gowen Field also has an economic impact.

Incentive Programs—New and Existing Companies

Local programs: Boise State University provides various services for the business community through its Idaho Business and Economic Development Center's TECenter, Boise Future Foundation, Center for Professional Development, Simplot/Micron Instructional Technology Center, Small Business Development Center, and the College of Technology.

State programs: Idaho is an aggressive pro-business state. The Idaho Department of Commerce and Labor provides services to business owners to assist them in starting, relocating, running, and closing a business. The state offers several incentives to business owners, including a three percent income tax credit to qualifying new investments. A five percent research and development tax credit is offered for qualified research performed in Idaho. The state also offers 100 percent tax exemptions on property tax, and 100 percent sales tax exemption on goods in transit, pollution control equipment, industrial fuels and raw materials, and production equipment and materials used to produce goods. Reimbursements and credits are available for employee training and the creation of new jobs. Smaller businesses can qualify for a 3.75 percent investment tax credit as well as new job credits of up to $3,000 per job.

Job training programs: IdahoWorks is a combination of state and local workforce development groups. IdahoWorks provides career centers with over 17 programs geared toward those seeking employment or education. Programs include workshops on application and interview skills, resume and cover letter writing, and job fairs. The Boise State University Selland College of Applied Technology provides apprenticeship and job training programs to students who are enrolled in the college's Apprenticeship Programs offered by the Center for Workforce Training. Students receive on-the-job training while working as full-time, paid employees. Students also receive classroom training related to their chosen profession. The Center for Workforce Training offers career training programs for adults as well as programs to help businesses increase their productivity. In addition to training in the classroom, the Center offers online training programs and courses.

Development Projects

Boise is working on three major ongoing urban renewal projects. The oldest project, called the Central renewal project, focuses on downtown Boise's core and has resulted in the vibrant downtown Boise visitors and residents see today. Ongoing funding of the Central project was planned for use in additional infrastructure, beautification and public arts projects. The River Myrtle-Old Boise renewal project, also underway, is located south of downtown Boise. With a focus on attracting high-tech tenants, this urban renewal project is developing a technical infrastructure. The Westside renewal project encompasses 47 acres of downtown Boise. Renewal plans encompass a 25-year span with completion of all projects in 2025. The Westside project is expected to bring multi-use development to downtown, including office, residential, retail, restaurants, entertainment venues, and hotels. Both the Boise Airport and Boise Public Library were undergoing expansion as of 2006 and 2007. The Boise Airport secured an agreement to build a new control tower and the library moved towards adding four new branches.

Economic Development Information: Boise Valley Economic Partnership, 250 S. 5th St., Suite 300, Boise, ID 83702; telephone (208)472-5230, email sboyce@ boisechamber.org

Commercial Shipping

A Grant Thornton *General Manufacturing Climates* study ranked Idaho the best state in the nation for transportation because of its infrastructure and strategic location in the Pacific Northwest. Rail freight carriers serve the Boise metropolitan area via the Union Pacific Railroad. A variety of motor freight lines, air freight, package express companies, and air courier services are also part of Boise's commercial transportation industry.

Labor Force and Employment Outlook

Boise's skilled work force is educated above the national average and it remains diverse because of a high percentage of immigration. Thirty-four percent of residents have a bachelor's degree or higher; the Boise metro area was ranked the fourth best place to do business in the nation by *Forbes* magazine in 2006. Employment overall continued to grow; according to the March 2006 "Idaho Employment" report the Boise Metro area increased employment by 4.4 percent from the previous year. The unemployment rate decreased to 2.8 percent. Although employment rates were on the rise, the city was experiencing difficulty finding qualified trade and skilled workers.

The following is a summary of data regarding the Boise City-Nampa metropolitan area labor force, 2006 annual averages.

Size of nonagricultural labor force: 270,500

Number of workers employed in . . .

    construction and mining: 24,600
    manufacturing: 31,500
    trade, transportation and utilities: 51,800
    information: 4,600
    financial activities: 14,900
    professional and business services: 39,700
    educational and health services: 31,700
    leisure and hospitality: 23,400
    other services: 7,600
    government: 40,600

Average hourly earnings of production workers employed in manufacturing: Not available

Unemployment rate: 2.1% (June 2007)

Largest private employers (2004)	Number of employees
Micron Technology, Inc.	9,500
Saint Luke's Regional Medical Center	4,250
Hewlett-Packard Company	4,000
J.R. Simplot Co.	3,800
Albertsons	3,800
Saint Alphonsus Regional Medical Center	3,373
Boise State University	2,895
DirecTV	1,400
Wal-Mart	1,200
Fred Meyer	1,200

Cost of Living

Boise boasts rates for residential, commercial, and industrial electricity and natural gas that are among the lowest in the country.

The following is a summary of data regarding key cost of living factors for the Boise area.

2007 (1st quarter) ACCRA Average House Price: Not reported

2007 (1st quarter) ACCRA Cost of Living Index: 97.5

State income tax rate: 1.6% to 7.8%

State sales tax rate: 5.0%

Local income tax rate: None

Local sales tax rate: None

Property tax rate: average 1.7% in 2004; ranges from 1 to 2.7%

Economic Information: Idaho Department of Commerce, 700 West State Street, PO Box 83720, Boise, ID 83720-0093; telephone (208)334-2470; toll-free (800)842-5858; fax (208)334-2631. Boise Metro Chamber of Commerce, 250 South 5th Street, PO Box 2368, Boise, ID 83702; telephone (208)472-5200; fax (208)472-5201; email info@boisechamber.org

■ Education and Research

Elementary and Secondary Schools

The Independent School District of Boise City #1 is the city's public elementary and secondary school system. The largest district in the state, it is administered by a seven-member, nonpartisan board of trustees that appoints a superintendent. In 2004 the Boise School District received the Gold Medal Award presented by *Expansion Management* magazine. Factors weighed included graduation rates and college board scores; the community's financial commitment to its children's education; student-teacher ratios, per-pupil expenditures and teachers salaries; and level of affluence and adult education in the district. The ranking placed the Boise School District in the upper 16 percent of all districts nationwide; Boise was the only district with this award in the state of Idaho. Adding to the school system's accolades, both Boise High School and Timberline High School were ranked on *Newsweek*'s 2007 "Top High Schools" list.

The following is a summary of data regarding the Boise School District as of the 2005–2006 school year.

Total enrollment: 25,000

Number of facilities

elementary schools: 9
junior high/middle schools: 9
senior high schools: 22
other: 1

Student/teacher ratio: 18.7:1

Teacher salaries (2005–06)

elementary median: $31,000–64,442 (all levels)
junior high/middle median: Not available
secondary median: Not available

Funding per pupil: $7,144

There are 22 private and parochial schools, with a total enrollment of nearly about 3,100 students in the Boise area.

Public Schools Information: Boise School District Services Center, 8169 W. Victory Rd., Boise ID 83709; telephone (208)854-4000; fax (208)854-4003

Colleges and Universities

Boise State University is the largest institution of higher learning in the state with an enrollment of 19,540 students in 2007, setting an all-time record for Idaho higher education schools. The university offers more than 180 degree programs, including 95 baccalaureate, 73 master's, 4 doctorate, and 12 graduate certificate programs. The Simplot/Micron Technology Center, located on the university campus, has formed a partnership with the public and private sectors designed to develop and present effective training programs. The facility contains state-of-the-art computer systems and video and audio production studios. Students in Boise may earn bachelor's, master's, and doctoral degrees in civil, electrical, and mechanical engineering from the University of Idaho while attending classes on the Boise State campus, where the College of Technology has been in operation since 1990. Boise State University and the Boise community began planning for a community college in 2004 and the Idaho State Board of Education approved a petition for the plan in March 2007; the community college district will include 11 public school districts within its proposed parameters. The metropolitan area is also served by three private colleges: Albertson College of Idaho in Caldwell, Northwest Nazarene University in Nampa, and Boise Bible College.

Libraries and Research Centers

The Boise Public Library serves the greater Boise area and circulated more than 1.4 million materials in 2006 including books, videos, CDs, cassette tapes, Kidpacks, books on tape, and computer software. A branch is located at Boise Towne Square Mall and a bookmobile and personal delivery of materials to the homebound are available. The Boise City Council approved funding in 2007 for a plan to construct four new full-service branches throughout the city. The Idaho State Library officially changed its name to the Idaho Commission for Libraries in July 2006. The name change was said to "reflect the mission to assist libraries to build the capacity to better serve their clientele." The Idaho Commission for Libraries heads LiLI (Libraries Linking Idaho), an alliance of libraries throughout the state. LiLI creates an extensive network through services such as databases and LiLI Express, a program that allows members to borrow from collections across the state, waiving borrowing fees and waiting period for interlibrary loans. Boise State University's library holds more than 560,000 books and more than 29,000 total periodicals, newspapers, and serial subscriptions. A number of smaller private, corporate, and special interest libraries are also located in the Boise metropolitan area. Research activities in such fields as technology, audio and video production, computers, and data processing are conducted at centers in the Boise area. Boise State University is home to the Raptor Research Center for research in biology and the conservation of natural resources. The university has focused on creating a stronger research core and received a record-breaking $26.8 million for sponsored projects in 2007.

Public Library Information: Boise Public Library, 715 South Capitol Boulevard, Boise, ID 83702-7115; telephone (208)384-4076

■ Health Care

The Boise medical community has two major regional medical facilities: Saint Alphonsus Regional Medical Center, an acute-care facility featuring a regional trauma center; and St. Luke's Regional Medical Center. St Luke's was the 2006 Microsoft "Hospital of the Year," awarded for use of technology in health care; the hospital provides general treatment, specialty care, and surgical services, as well as neonatal and pediatric intensive care. Both hospitals are among the city's largest employers with some 2,500 employees at St. Luke's and 1,800 at Saint Alphonsus. The Idaho Elks Rehabilitation Hospital specializes in rehabilitation services in the areas of audiology, brain injury, cardio-pulmonary, orthopedics, pediatrics and stroke/neurology. To better accommodate the growing community the hospital opened a new state of the art facility in 2001. The Veterans Administration Medical Center, a teaching hospital affiliated with the

University of Washington School of Medicine, offers general care and outpatient, mental health, and substance abuse clinics. Also located in Boise are Treasure Valley Hospital for patients needing surgery, Mountain States Tumor Institute, and several nursing homes.

■ Recreation

Sightseeing

The best way to see Boise is on the popular Tour Train, a replica of an 1890s steam-powered locomotive that originates in Julia Davis Park and takes an hour-long trip through the city's historic neighborhoods and the central business district. Other attractions in the park include Zoo Boise, the Julia Davis Park Rose Garden, and an outdoor band shell where summer concerts are performed.

The downtown area contains several historic points of interest. The Idaho State Capitol, erected in 1920, is a smaller version of the Capitol building in Washington, D.C., and is the only statehouse in America heated by natural geothermal energy. The Capitol building underwent extensive exterior renovation, completed in 2006, and funding was put in place that same year for future interior renovations. At the other end of Capitol Boulevard is the Boise Depot, constructed in 1925 and modeled after a Spanish mission. The station is surrounded by the beautiful Platt Gardens. Other historic sites in Boise include the Old Boise district and the Eighth Street Marketplace, two restored neighborhoods. The O'Farrell Cabin, the first structure built in Boise, is located in Military Reserve Park. The area surrounding Boise offers many attractions, including restored wild west towns like Idaho City and the Snake River Birds of Prey area. Other pleasurable activities are scenic mountain and canyon drives and tours of the local vineyards in Idaho's wine country.

Arts and Culture

The Morrison Center for the Performing Arts, a 2,030-seat facility located on the Boise State University campus, is the site of much of the city's cultural activity. The center hosts performances by the Boise Philharmonic Orchestra, Ballet Idaho, and Opera Idaho as well as special events that range from rock concerts to touring Broadway productions. The city holds an annual Shakespearean festival, and several area theatrical groups perform throughout the year. Among them are the Boise Little Theater, the Idaho Theater for Youth, and the Stage Coach Theater.

The city is home to a number of museums and art galleries. The Idaho Historical Museum, located in Julia Davis Park, is a unique open-air museum that features an Old West saloon, a blacksmith's shop, and western and Native American artifacts. The restored Idaho State Penitentiary (called the "Old Pen") now houses several museums, including the Idaho Transportation Museum and the Electricity Museum. The Idaho Black History Museum relocated from the former penitentiary to St. Paul Baptist Church in Julia Davis Park; exhibits relate the importance of the African American culture to the heritage of Idaho and the nation. The Boise Art Museum, also in Julia Davis Park, contains a permanent collection of regional and national art; it also hosts a number of traveling exhibits each year. The Idaho Botanical Garden, featuring a variety of themed gardens, is adjacent to the Old Pen. Other art galleries in the city include the Art Attack Gallery, Brown's Galleries, Gallery 601, and the Art Source Gallery.

Festivals and Holidays

A number of special events are scheduled in the Boise area throughout the year. Spring is celebrated with the Apple Blossom Festival; seven days of festivities include a rodeo, parade, carnival, festival, and crowning of the Apple Blossom Queen. The National Old Time Fiddlers' Contest takes place for seven days each June in nearby Weiser, Idaho, one hour northwest of Boise. Summer also brings the Spirit of Boise Balloon Classic in late June; the Idaho Shakespeare Festival, featuring Shakespeare under the Stars; and the Western Idaho Fair, an old fashioned country fair that lasts for 10 days in August. Boise's Basque population, the largest concentration in North America, presents three days of cultural activities every July, including performances by the famous Oinkari Basque Dancers. Oktoberfest at the Idaho Botanical Garden includes music, dance, food and beverage.

Sports for the Spectator

The Boise Hawks, members of the Northwest League and affiliated with the Chicago Cubs, play baseball from mid-June through early September at Memorial Stadium. The Hawks won their sixth Northwest League Championship in 2004 and eleventh division title in 2006. The Qwest Arena (formerly the Bank of America Center) hosts hockey action from the Idaho Steelheads of the East Coast Hockey League and satisfies basketball fans by also hosting the Idaho Stampede of the Continental Basketball Association.

A complete program of collegiate sports is offered at Boise State University, featuring a championship football team and a nationally recognized basketball team. Thoroughbred and harness racing, along with parimutuel wagering, are featured at Les Bois Race Track. Championship drag racing is held at Firebird Raceway. Fans of rodeo enjoy the famous Snake River Stampede in Nampa and the Caldwell Night Rodeo in Caldwell. Meridian Speedway offers drag racing and stock car racing. In women's sports action, there is the annual St. Luke's Women's Fitness Celebration, a run/walk event that ranks among the largest of its kind in the nation. The

Albertsons Boise Open golf tournament is part of the PGA Tour.

Sports for the Participant

Boise offers an abundance of outdoor activities. The area's 107 park sites feature facilities for boating, tennis, golf, swimming, jogging, cycling, and other recreational activities. The Boise River, which runs through downtown Boise, is a popular spot for tubing, canoeing, and fishing; 16 acres on both sides of the river form the Boise River Greenbelt offering 25 miles of paved and graveled paths. Many area reservoirs offer a full range of water activities. Both day and night skiing can be enjoyed at Bogus Basin, a 45-minute drive from downtown Boise; five other ski areas are within a three-hour drive. The nearby mountains are favorite hiking, fishing, and camping locations, while the nearby Payette and Salmon rivers are known worldwide by kayakers and rafters for their exciting white water.

Shopping and Dining

Old Boise and the Eighth Street Marketplace, two distinctive historical districts in Boise, have been converted into unique shopping areas. The Hyde Park district features a number of antique shops, and State Street marketplace is a group of specialty shops in a modern complex. Several shopping malls are open in the area, including Boise Towne Square, which offers more than 175 stores, and the Boise Factory Outlet Mall.

Dining opportunities in Boise are diverse and usually inexpensive. Cuisines range from simple yet filling Western fare to exotic international specialties such as Basque, Mexican, Chinese, Indian, Egyptian, and Vietnamese. Several elegant dining places feature French, Continental, and New American dishes.

Visitor Information: Boise Convention and Visitors Bureau, PO Box 2106, Boise, ID 83701; telephone (208)344-7777; toll-free (800)635-5240; fax (208)344-6236; email info@boisechamber.org

■ Convention Facilities

The Boise Center on the Grove offers over 80,000 square feet of meeting space and features a glass-fronted lobby, a 7,600-square-foot auditorium that will seat 350 people, and an almost 25,000-square-foot central meeting space. Other facilities include Boise State University's Taco Bell Arena, which seats up to 13,000 spectators and has 17,472 square feet of open floor space. The Morrison Center for the Performing Arts, also on the Boise State campus, has a 2,000 seat main hall and two teaching/studying halls. The Nampa Civic Center in nearby Nampa offers banquet seating for up to 1,000 people, and a 648-seat auditorium. There are more than 4,600 hotel rooms in Boise; most of the major hotels provide meeting, banquet, and ballroom facilities.

Convention Information: Boise Convention and Visitors Bureau, PO Box 2106, Boise, ID 83701; telephone (208)344-7777; toll-free (800)635-5240; fax (208)344-6236; email info@boisechamber.org

■ Transportation

Approaching the City

The Boise Airport, located a few miles south of downtown, is served by eleven major national and regional airlines and seven charter airlines carrying over three million passengers in 2006.

Two major highways lead into Boise. I-84 runs east and west, connecting the metropolitan area with the West Coast and the midwestern states. U.S. 20/26 runs diagonally west to southeast through the center of the city.

Traveling in the City

Streets south of the Boise River tend to form a grid pattern; north of the river, streets follow the contours of the foothills of the Rocky Mountains and the streams that flow through town.

ValleyRide provides bus service on fixed routes as well as access services for people with disabilities.

■ Communications

Newspapers and Magazines

Boise is served by one daily newspaper, *The Idaho Statesman,* and two weekly papers. Locally-published magazines focus on religion, families, wildlife, farming, and sheep and cattle growing.

Television and Radio

Four television stations broadcast from Boise. Approximately 15 AM and FM radio stations serve the Boise area with a diverse blend of music, news, and information.

Media Information: *The Idaho Statesman,* PO Box 40, Boise, ID 83707; telephone (208)377-6200; toll-free (800)635-8934

Boise Online

Boise Convention & Visitors Bureau home page. Available www.boise.org

Boise Metro Chamber of Commerce home page. Available www.boisechamber.org

Boise Public Library home page. Available www.boisepubliclibrary.org

Boise School District home page. Available www.boiseschools.org

City of Boise home page. Available www.cityofboise
.org

Idaho Commerce & Labor home page. Available
www.cl.idaho.gov

Idaho Commission for Libraries home page.
Available www.libraries.idaho.gov

*The Idaho Statesman home page.*Available www
.idahostatesman.com

BIBLIOGRAPHY

Harris, Richard, *Hidden Idaho: Including Boise, Sun
Valley and Yellowtone National Park* (Berkeley, CA:
Ulysses, 2004)

MacGregor, Carol Lynn, *Boise, Idaho, 1882–1910:
Prosperity in Isolation* (Missoula, MT: Mountain
Press Pub., 2006)

Nampa

■ The City in Brief

Founded: 1891

Head Official: Mayor Tom Dale (since 2002)

City Population

    1980: Not available
    1990: 28,365
    2000: 51,876
    2006 estimate: 76,587
    Percent change, 1990–2000: 73.5%
    U.S. rank in 1980: Not reported
    U.S. rank in 1990: Not reported
    U.S. rank in 2000: 688th (State rank: 2nd)

Metropolitan Area Population

    1980: Not available
    1990: 295,851
    2000: 432,345
    2006 estimate: 567,640
    Percent change, 1990–2000: 46.1%
    U.S. rank in 1980: Not available
    U.S. rank in 1990: Not available
    U.S. rank in 2000: 96th

Area: 20 square miles (2000)

Elevation: Average 2,492 feet above sea level

Average Annual Temperature: 64.4° F

Average Annual Precipitation: 11.7 inches of rain; 21.4 inches of snow

Major Economic Sectors: services, wholesale and retail trade, government

Unemployment Rate: 2.1% (June 2007)

Per Capita Income: $14,491 (1999)

2005 FBI Crime Index Property: Not available

2005 FBI Crime Index Violent: Not available

Major Colleges and Universities: Northwest Nazarene University, Boise State University, Albertson College of Idaho

Daily Newspaper: *Idaho Press-Tribune*

■ Introduction

Nampa, the second-largest city in Idaho, was established in the late 1800s as a result of the completion of the Oregon Short Line railroad. Although the origins of the name Nampa are unknown, it is believed to be a Shoshoni Indian word meaning "moccasin," or "footprint." Once highly dependent on agricultural production, the city's economy has become more diverse and now also relies on manufacturing. Nampa boasts a mild climate, excellent parks and recreation, and proximity to Idaho's state capital, Boise. Northwest Nazarene University is located in Nampa, and the Snake River Stampede, one of the nation's top 10 rodeos, is held every year in July. Nampa continued to thrive as the second largest city in terms of population, contributing to the over 50 percent population growth between 1996 and 2006 for Canyon County. As the population grows and diversifies, the city also benefits from a growing labor force and new economic developments.

■ Geography and Climate

Located in the heart of Idaho's Treasure Valley, or "Banana Belt," Nampa enjoys a mild climate year-round. Its high desert location is bordered to the north by the Front Range of the Rocky Mountains and to the south by the Owyhee Mountains. Nampa enjoys warm summers with an average temperature of 92° F, but the low humidity makes for a pleasant environment. Winter lows average 20.2° F. Nampa's winters are mild, with minimal snowfall. Blizzards are rare, and snow that does fall rarely stays on the ground for more than a few days. Nampa's climate is ideal for the production of agricultural goods, which make up a substantial part of the region's economy. Nampa is located just 16 miles from Boise, Idaho's state capital.

Area: 20 square miles (2000)

Elevation: Average 2,492 feet above sea level

Average Temperature: 64.4° F

Average Annual Precipitation: 11.7 inches of rain; 21.4 inches of snow

■ History

Nampa's Early Years

Although Native American tribes had settled in Idaho for hundreds of years, little human settlement occurred in the area that is now Nampa until the late 1800s. Settlement in Nampa began in 1883, a direct result of the completion of the Oregon Short Line Railroad. At that time, Caldwell resident James A. McGee and businessman Alexander Duffes decided to invest in the development of this new town. Duffes filed a claim under the Idaho Homestead Act, and in 1886 McGee and Duffes formed the Nampa Land and Improvement Company and filed the town's articles of incorporation. Initially, the Short Line bypassed Nampa, but due to increased traffic it soon became necessary to provide a connecting line between the Oregon Short Line and Boise. The Idaho Central Railway was built to make that connection, and Nampa was a stop along the way.

Nampa was incorporated in 1891. Population and business development continued to grow into the 1890s, mainly a result of irrigation made possible by the Phyllis Canal, but in 1894 Duffes mortgaged Nampa's unsold lots in an attempt to boost the slowing economy. The loan source defaulted and the town spiraled into debt. In 1896, Colonel W.H. Dewey paid the debt and received 2,000 deeds to town lots. He was crucial to the continued development of Nampa, as he began a survey of a route for the Boise, Nampa, Owyhee Railway that eventually linked Boise with the mining towns of the Owyhee Valley.

A Modern City Emerges

As the 20th century began, the Western Idaho Sugar Company and the Crescent Brewing Company were both established in Nampa. These companies utilized local farmers and created jobs at their processing plants. But a business decline was followed by a fire in 1909, which caused the destruction of more than 60 stores in downtown Nampa. By the 1920s, however, Nampa had once

again established itself as a stable community. The Northwest Nazarene School, now Northwest Nazarene University, was established in 1913 by Eugene Emerson. During World War I, Nampa's farming community benefited from high crop prices. However, when the bottom of the market fell out after the war was over, many farmers were bankrupted. The economy was revived in 1942, when the Amalgamated Sugar Company opened a sugar beet plant in Nampa, which spurred farm productivity.

In 1949, the Nampa Industrial Corporation (NIC) was formed to encourage other economic development beyond farming. By the 1970s the NIC's investment in land and facility improvements had resulted in a more diverse economy, having encouraged new businesses and industries to locate in Nampa.

Nampa has grown to become Idaho's second-largest city, boasting a thriving economy and excellent quality of life. Building a strong and progressive community, Nampa was ranked as one of the "100 Best Communities for Young People" by America's Promise Alliance in 2007. The city also won a community achievement award from the City Achievement Program for its innovative training program designed to teach all citizens how to help keep drugs and other criminal activity off of their property.

Historical Information: Canyon County Historical Museum, 1200 Front Street, Nampa, ID 83651; telephone (208)467-7611

■ Population Profile

Metropolitan Area Residents

1980: Not available
1990: 295,851
2000: 432,345
2006 estimate: 567,640
Percent change, 1990–2000: 46.1%
U.S. rank in 1980: Not available
U.S. rank in 1990: Not available
U.S. rank in 2000: 96th

City Residents

1980: Not available
1990: 28,365
2000: 51,876
2006 estimate: 76,587
Percent change, 1990–2000: 73.5%
U.S. rank in 1980: Not reported
U.S. rank in 1990: Not reported
U.S. rank in 2000: 688th (State rank: 2nd)

Density: 2,612 people per square mile (2000)

©IdahoAirships/Leo Geis

Racial and ethnic characteristics (2000)

    White: 43,281

    Black: 206

    American Indian and Alaska Native: 490

    Asian: 484

    Native Hawaiian and Pacific Islander: 92

    Hispanic or Latino (may be of any race): 9,282

    Other: 5,833

Percent of residents born in state: 46.1% (2000)

Age characteristics (2000)

    Population under 5 years old: 5,465

    Population 5 to 9 years old: 4,651

    Population 10 to 14 years old: 3,800

    Population 15 to 19 years old: 3,849

    Population 20 to 24 years old: 4,797

    Population 25 to 34 years old: 9,112

    Population 35 to 44 years old: 6,606

    Population 45 to 54 years old: 4,747

    Population 55 to 59 years old: 1,723

    Population 60 to 64 years old: 1,324

    Population 65 to 74 years old: 2,574

    Population 75 to 84 years old: 12,282

Population 85 years and older: 937

Median age: 28.5 years

Births (2006, MSA)

    Total number: 9,036

Deaths (2006, MSA)

    Total number: 3,649

Money income (1999)

    Per capita income: $14,491

    Median household income: $34,758

    Total households: 18,270

Number of households with income of . . .

    less than $10,000: 1,713

    $10,000 to $14,999: 1,327

    $15,000 to $24,999: 3,015

    $25,000 to $34,999: 3,141

    $35,000 to $49,999: 4,022

    $50,000 to $74,999: 3,333

    $75,000 to $99,999: 1,123

    $100,000 to $149,999: 435

    $150,000 to $199,999: 86

    $200,000 or more: 75

Percent of families below poverty level: 11.9% (1999)

2005 FBI Crime Index Property: Not available

2005 FBI Crime Index Violent: Not available

■ Municipal Government

Nampa operates under a mayor-council form of government. The mayor is elected at large every four years; the four council members serve staggered four-year terms.

Head Official: Mayor Tom Dale (since 2002; current term expires 2010)

Total Number of City Employees: 700 (2007)

City Information: City Hall, 411 3rd Street South, Nampa, ID 83651; telephone (208)465-2200

■ Economy

Major Industries and Commercial Activity

Historically, Nampa has been known as a strong agricultural base. Canyon County produces more than 90 percent of the world's sweet corn seed, and is also a leader in the production of livestock, dairy, and alfalfa. Located in the heart of Idaho's wine country, Nampa also produces its share of grapes. Vineyards in Nampa and surrounding areas grow Cabernet Sauvignon, Cabernet Franc, Roussanne, Pinot Gris, Merlot, and Syrah varietals. The climate, geography, and location along the Snake River make for ideal growing conditions. Nampa also has a strong manufacturing base with over 9,300 employees in Canyon County as of 2006, with goods produced such as furniture, boxes, wood products, and computer chips. Nampa has benefited from the technology boom: computer equipment manufacturer Plexus is headquartered in Nampa. It is among the city's top employers. Education continues to be a major source of employment in Nampa, with Nampa School District 131 and higher education institutes Northwest Nazarene University and Boise State University's Canyon County Center providing jobs. Other major employers include Woodgrain Millwork Inc, J.R. Simplot, and Mercy Medical Center.

Items and goods produced: sweet corn, livestock, alfalfa, dairy products, grapes, computer equipment, cardboard boxes, and furniture

Incentive Programs—New and Existing Companies

Local programs: Between 1995 and 2006, Nampa experienced rapid economic growth and development. Several companies make their headquarters in Nampa, and many national retailers have opened outlets in Nampa, attracted by Nampa's explosive population growth and pro-business environment. Several entities have been established to encourage business growth and development. The Nampa Industrial Corporation was formed in 1949 to create business opportunities in Nampa through the investment in and development of industrial property. The NIC also assists with community initiatives. The Chamber of Commerce supports local businesses by providing services such as monthly luncheons, small business consultations, networking opportunities, marketing ideas, and sponsorship opportunities for its members. The Boise Valley Economic Partnership (BVEP) serves the Boise-Nampa area with the goals of creating long-term jobs and encouraging economic development in the community. The BVEP provides free, customized services to businesses relocating, expanding, or establishing themselves in the Boise Valley Area.

State programs: Idaho is an aggressive pro-business state. The Idaho Department of Commerce and Labor provides services to business owners to assist them in starting, relocating, running, and closing a business. The state offers several incentives to business owners, including a three percent income tax credit to qualifying new investments. A five percent research and development tax credit is offered for qualified research performed in Idaho. The state also offers 100 percent tax exemptions on property tax, and 100 percent sales tax exemption on goods in transit, pollution control equipment, industrial fuels and raw materials, and production equipment and materials used to produce goods. Reimbursements and credits are available for employee training and the creation of new jobs. Smaller businesses can qualify for a 3.75 percent investment tax credit as well as new job credits of up to $3,000 per job.

Job training programs: The Boise State University Selland College of Applied Technology provides apprenticeship and job training programs to students who are enrolled in the college's Apprenticeship Programs offered by the Center for Workforce Training. Students receive on-the-job training while working as full-time, paid employees. Students also receive classroom training related to their chosen profession. The Center for Workforce Training offers career training programs for adults as well as programs to help businesses increase their productivity. In addition to training in the classroom, the Center offers online training programs and courses. IdahoWorks is a combination of state and local workforce development groups. IdahoWorks provides career centers with over 17 programs geared towards those seeking employment or education. Programs include workshops on application and interview skills, resume and cover letter writing, and job fairs.

Development Projects

As Idaho's second-largest city, Nampa continues to attract new business development. In 2004 home improvement retailer Home Depot opened a 102,000-square-foot store in Nampa. In early 2004 Costco announced plans to build a retail center adjacent to the new Karcher Interchange off of Interstate 84. A Costco opened in 2006 as one of two anchors of the new, 700,000-square-foot Treasure Valley Marketplace, which was the only retail center on the I-84 interchange to date.

In early 2005 the Nampa Industrial Corporation gave a $1,132,000 gift to Boise State University to help construct a Center for Construction and Transportation Technology on the BSU West campus in Nampa. The technical building will train students for careers and spur workforce development in fields such as automotive repair, welding, plumbing, and automotive and diesel technology. As of 2007 additional funding was still needed to begin the project.

Nampa city officials launched a downtown redevelopment project fronted by the construction of a new urban park, public library, and City Hall building. Construction of the new 80,000-square-foot library, 60,000-square-foot Public Safety Building, and 90,000-square-foot urban park was anticipated to begin in 2008. RxElite Holdings, Inc., a generic prescription drug manufacturer, chose Nampa as its new headquarters, distribution, and future production site in 2007. The construction of the first new 76,000 foot building began in August 2007. City and state officials pledged funds towards the relocation, looking forward to new job and economic growth. That same year, the Nampa Civic Center began an expansion project that would add new stage space for larger shows, several new restroom areas, and a scene construction shop. Hosting over 700 events annually, the center is one of the busiest event locations in the entire state; the additions were planned to help accommodate the growing number of shows and patrons. Construction was expected to be complete by October 2008.

Economic Development Information: Idaho Department of Commerce, 700 West State Street, Boise, ID 83720; telephone (208)334-2470. Idaho Department of Labor, 317 West Main Street, Boise, ID 83735; telephone (208)332-3570; fax (208)334-6300. Center for Workforce Training, Selland College of Applied Technology, Boise State University, 1464 University Drive, Technical Services Building, Boise, ID 83725; toll-free (800)632-6586; fax (208)426-4487

Commercial Shipping

Nampa is served by the Union Pacific Railroad and several commercial truck lines that transport goods produced in Nampa throughout the country. Air freight is handled at Nampa Municipal Airport.

Labor Force and Employment Outlook

Nampa's economy has become less dependent on agriculture as it has become a center for business and manufacturing. Canyon County boasted a 44.1 percent increase in labor force between 1996 and 2006 and a record unemployment rate of 3.6 percent in 2006. Almost all industries saw job increases that year; the most significant increases were in manufacturing and construction, gaining 1,000 and 1,207 new jobs respectively. Professional and business services also grew somewhat significantly with new jobs totaling 845. The county expected employment numbers to continue to increase as the development of several new retail stores in Nampa late in 2006 would impact future growth.

The following is a summary of data regarding the Boise City-Nampa metropolitan area labor force, 2006 annual averages.

Size of nonagricultural labor force: 270,500

Number of workers employed in . . .

    construction and mining: 24,600
    manufacturing: 31,500
    trade, transportation and utilities: 51,800
    information: 4,600
    financial activities: 14,900
    professional and business services: 39,700
    educational and health services: 31,700
    leisure and hospitality: 23,400
    other services: 7,600
    government: 40,600

Average hourly earnings of production workers employed in manufacturing: Not available

Unemployment rate: 2.1% (June 2007)

Largest employers (2007)	Number of employees
Nampa School District No. 131	1,300
MPC	1,000
Mercy Medical Center	650
Armour Foods	550
Amalgamated Sugar Company	500
Plexus (MCMS)	460
Nestle Brands	350
Woodgrain Millwork, Inc.	350

Cost of Living

Nampa's cost of living, as well as its housing prices, are slightly below the national average.

The following is a summary of data regarding several key cost of living factors for the Nampa area.

2007 (1st quarter) ACCRA Average House Price: Not reported

2007 (1st quarter) ACCRA Cost of Living Index: 97.5

State income tax rate: 1.6% to 7.8%

State sales tax rate: 5.0%

Local income tax rate: 1.0% (occupational)

Local sales tax rate: None

Property tax rate: 2.209% (2004)

Economic Information: Nampa Chamber of Commerce, 312 13th Avenue, Nampa, ID 83651; telephone (208)466-4641. Boise Valley Economic Partnership, 250 South 5th Street, Boise, ID 83702; telephone (208)472-5230.

■ Education and Research

Elementary and Secondary Schools

Nampa School District 131 (NSD) is the third largest school district in the state of Idaho. More than 13,000 students attend the district's elementary, middle, and high schools, as well as alternative programs. A growing district, NSD opened two new schools in 2007: Endeavor Elementary and Ridgeline High School. The new Lone Star Middle School is expected to open fall 2008. Nampa School District offers special education and gifted programs to help meet the needs of its student population.

The following is a summary of data regarding the Nampa Public Schools as of the 2005–2006 school year.

Total enrollment: 14,000

Number of facilities

elementary schools: 13
junior high/middle schools: 3
senior high schools: 3
other: 3

Student/teacher ratio: 18.7:1

Teacher salaries (2005–06)

elementary median: $36,057
junior high/middle median: Not available
secondary median: $38,759

Funding per pupil: $5,134

Nampa Christian Schools and St. Paul's Catholic School are private schools that offer religious-based educations.

Public Schools Information: Nampa School District 131, 619 S. Canyon, Nampa, ID 83686; telephone (208) 468-4600; fax (208)468-4638

Colleges and Universities

Four institutions of higher learning serve the Nampa area, including Northwest Nazarene College and Boise State University Selland College of Applied Technology, both located in Nampa. Boise State University is located in Boise, and Albertson College is in nearby Caldwell. Northwest Nazarene University is a four-year, private Christian liberal arts university offering undergraduate and graduate degrees in such fields as arts, humanities, science, theology, and education. Boise State University is a public university that offers undergraduate, graduate, and technical programs. Courses are offered in eight colleges: applied technology, arts and sciences, business and economics, education, engineering, graduate studies, health sciences, and social sciences and public affairs. In 2006 the University conferred 3,129 degrees. On-campus residential colleges, based on the Oxford system, is the University's housing program; residential students are assigned to residence halls and dormitories based on common interests or fields of study. The Boise State University Selland College of Applied Technology, one of Boise State University's eight colleges, operates a campus at the Canyon County Center in Nampa. The college offers degree and certificate programs; it is the only public technical college in southwest Idaho. Boise State University and the Boise community began planning for a community college in 2004 and the Idaho State Board of Education approved a petition for the plan in March 2007; the community college district will include 11 public school districts within its proposed parameters with a proposed Nampa campus. Albertson College, in Caldwell, is the state's oldest four-year institution of higher education. The school is a private liberal arts college offering a total of 27 majors.

Libraries and Research Centers

The Nampa Public Library serves the Nampa community; non-residents may obtain a library card and utilize the library's resources for an annual fee. Nampa Public Library card holders are allowed to borrow materials from six other area consortium libraries, including the Boise Public Library. The consortium has a collection of more than 500,000 books, videos, sound recordings, and other materials. In addition to a wide selection of current books, magazines, and media materials, the library has computer terminals with Internet access available for patron use. Patrons may also access the library's database via its Internet website. The Northwest Nazarene University Riley Library is open to students and faculty, as well as members of the Nampa community. Materials at Albertsons Library at Boise State University are available to students, faculty, and staff, as well as "special borrowers" who meet certain criteria. As part of a downtown redevelopment project launched by Nampa officials, plans to start construction of a new $30.8 million, 80,000-square-foot library were set for 2008.

A variety of research centers, including one at the Technology and Entrepreneurial Center at Boise State University West, exist in Nampa and conduct research in the fields of biology and agriculture, among others.

Public Library Information: Nampa Public Library, 101 Eleventh Avenue South, Nampa, ID 83651; telephone (208)468-5800

■ Health Care

Mercy Medical Center, the only hospital within Nampa city limits, is a private hospital affiliated with the Catholic Church. Founded in 1917 by the Sisters of Mercy, the hospital has grown to include two medical campuses in Nampa. The hospital provides 152 beds, emergency services as well as outpatient and hospice services; cancer care, maternity care, surgery, and interventional cardiology services are among the hospital's specialties. Mercy Medical has invested in state of the art technology and equipment, including the Galileo computerized system for orthopedic surgery. In order to better serve the growing demand in emergency care, Mercy Medical celebrated a groundbreaking ceremony in August 2007 in honor of an emergency department expansion.

■ Recreation

Sightseeing

Visitors to Nampa enjoy a wealth of activities and recreational opportunities. Museums that celebrate Nampa's heritage, year-round outdoor activities, and a variety of shopping and dining experiences help make Nampa a great place to work and live.

Nampa museums celebrate the history of Nampa, Canyon County, and the United States. The Warhawk Air Museum is a 20,000-square-foot facility dedicated to preserving the country's World War II history from the home front to the war front, as well as to trace the history of flight from the advent of aviation through the space age. Its collection includes two of the few remaining Curtiss P-40 World War II fighter airplanes and a rare World War II P-510 razorback Mustang fighter plane. The museum also hosts traveling NASA space exhibits, and often hosts special events and ceremonies to honor veterans and commemorate World War II events.

The Canyon County Historical Museum, located in Canyon County's original train depot, displays both Canyon County and Union Pacific Railroad memorabilia. An authentic 1940s era caboose and model railroad are among the exhibits in the building that has been called "Idaho's finest example of Baroque architecture." A farmer's market is held outside the museum on Saturdays during the months of May through October.

The Van Slyke Agricultural Museum, located in Caldwell Memorial Park, is an open-air museum that features log cabin replicas and antique farm equipment. Visitors to the Deer Flat National Wildlife Refuge at Lake Lowell enjoy swimming, fishing, hunting, boating, and bird watching on more than 11,000 acres of land.

Arts and Culture

With several state of the art exhibit and performance facilities, Nampa is becoming known for its arts scene. The Brandt Center at Northwest Nazarene University is a performing arts center that attracts musical and dramatic performances attended by both students and the community at large. Its Samuel Swayne theatre can accommodate up to 1,500 people, and two guest suites accommodate up to 15 guests each for private viewings and receptions. The Brandt Center's Friesen Art Galleries provide gallery space for Northwest Nazarene University's art students to exhibit their work.

The Caldwell and Nampa Alliance of Community Theatre (CAN-ACT) was started in 1991 and is housed at the Caldwell Center for the Arts. The not-for-profit troupe performs comedies, dramas, and musicals in the CAN-ACT Theater located in the Karcher Mall. Auditions for CAN-ACT's four yearly plays are open to community members.

In 2003 the Majestic Entertainment Foundation, Inc. was formed to refurbish downtown Nampa's historic Pix Theater, which was closed in 2002. Shortly after purchasing the already deteriorating building, the theater lost its roof in a severe storm. The owners and foundation received funding support from the community and as of 2006 the reconstruction of the roof was near completion. There was no projected completion date for the entire restoration project as it relies heavily on outside donations and grants. Once finished, the facility will be used for the viewing of films as well as lectures, religious services, educational programs, and community events.

Festivals and Holidays

Parade America, Idaho's largest patriotic parade, is held in May. Each July, the Snake River Dayz Festival is held in conjunction with the Snake River Stampede rodeo. The week-long festival features concerts, a parade, a pageant and golf tournament, a fun zone for children, and a "movie under the stars" to cap off the pre-rodeo festivities. Nampa Community Fun Night is held in late August or early September and includes games for children, music, and food. The Nampa Festival of the Arts is held annually in August. The festival features live music performances ranging from jazz to Celtic, over 200 artists, and a variety of food vendors.

Sports for the Spectator

Although Nampa has no professional sports teams, Boise State University's indoor track team competes at Nampa's Idaho Center. The state-of-the-art track facility has also been used for other prestigious events such as the USA Masters Indoor Track and Field Championships and the Western Athletic Conference Indoor Championships. Sports fans can also take in collegiate-level sports played by Northwest Nazarene University's teams, including baseball and softball, basketball, cross country, track and field, men's golf, and women's volleyball.

The Snake River Stampede, held annually in July, is ranked among the country's top 10 professional rodeos. The arena at the Idaho Center seats up to 10,000 people who take in bull riding, barrel racing, mutton busting (for children), bareback riding, steer wrestling, and roping events.

Sports for the Participant

Nampa residents enjoy a wealth of outdoor activities year-round. Nineteen city parks cover more than 200 acres. Available facilities include play areas, covered picnic shelters, baseball and softball fields, tennis courts, archery ranges, Little League fields, swimming pools, basketball courts, and a BMX track. A 140,000-square-foot recreation center provides residents with a climbing wall, basketball courts, an indoor track, six swimming pools, activity rooms, and a senior center.

Nampa has two public golf courses and one private golf course. Ridgecrest Golf Course has received a four-star rating from *Golf Digest* magazine. Runners can participate in a 5K fun run during July's Snake River Dayz festivities.

Shopping and Dining

Nampa retailers range from national chains to locally owned specialty stores, ensuring something for everyone. Karcher Mall's tenants include Macy's, Radio Shack, Sam Goody, and Big 5 Sporting Goods. As Karcher Mall was scheduled to undergo massive exterior remodeling, new stores such as Burlington Coat Factory and Starbucks were expected to open. Mass retailers such as Ross, Old Navy, and Bed, Bath, & Beyond can be found in the Meridian Crossroads development. Downtown Nampa is home to many unique retailers, including antique, book, jewelry, and flower stores. The Boise Factory Outlet is just a short drive away, and includes outlet stores for companies such as Reebok and Eddie Bauer. In early 2004 Costco announced plans to build a retail center adjacent to the new Karcher Interchange off of Interstate 84. A Costco opened in 2006 as one of two anchors of the new, 700,000-square-foot Treasure Valley Marketplace, which was the only retail center on the I-84 interchange to date. Other major stores at the Marketplace include Target, Kohls, and Office Max.

Nampa diners enjoy a variety of restaurants, from national chains to local establishments. The family-owned Generations restaurant offers steak and seafood, with their French dip sandwich among the more popular menu items. Copper Canyon is an upscale eatery known for its elegant presentation and extensive wine list. Asian restaurant House of Kim, located in downtown Nampa, serves Chinese, Thai, and Malaysian cuisine. The Dutch Inn, known for its salad bar, also serves breakfast, lunch, and dinner entrees. The Mona Lisa is a fondue restaurant that has found its niche as a special occasion restaurant. Cheese fondue appetizers and chocolate dessert fondues are part of a meal package that allows diners to cook their own main courses at pots on their table. Other area eateries include chains such as Applebee's, Denny's, Sizzler, and various fast food establishments.

Visitor Information: Nampa Chamber of Commerce, 312 13th Ave. So., Nampa, ID 83651; telephone (208)466-4641; fax (208)466-4677.

■ Convention Facilities

The Nampa Civic Center is Idaho's second largest full-service convention and performing arts center. With 42,500 square feet of space, the Civic Center hosts more than 750 events each year. Meetings, conventions, banquets, receptions, trade shows, and performing arts programs are among the events hosted there. Up to 14 separate meeting spaces can accommodate groups of up to 1,000. In addition to the 30,000 square feet of meeting space, the Civic Center boasts a 12,200 square foot exhibit area and a 640 seat theatre.

The Idaho Center Complex is comprised of four venues: an amphitheatre, an arena, the Idaho Horse Park, and the Idaho Sports Center. The arena can accommodate over 12,000 people, and the amphitheatre seats 10,500 people. Events such as concerts, basketball games, and ice shows, as well as trade shows and conventions, are held at the Idaho Center. The Idaho Horse Park, opened in 2002, consists of indoor and outdoor arenas, an English riding facility, warm-up pens, stalls, and stock pens. The Idaho Sports Center Complex is the newest addition to the Idaho Center. The 100,000 square foot multi-purpose building is the indoor track facility for Boise State University and is home to the only Mondo 200-meter banked track west of Nebraska.

Convention Information: Nampa Civic Center, 311 Third Street South, Nampa, ID 83651; telephone (208) 468-5500. Idaho Center, 16114 Idaho Center Blvd., Nampa, ID 83687; telephone (208)468-1000.

■ Transportation

Approaching the City

The nearby Boise Airport is served by eleven major national and regional airlines and seven charter airlines carrying over three million passengers in 2006. The Nampa

Municipal Airport handles only charter flights. By car, Nampa is accessible via Interstate 84. Greyhound provides bus service to Nampa.

Traveling in the City

Nampa is accessible from Interstate 84 via three interchanges and is relatively easy to navigate. Highway 45 extends through downtown Nampa toward the Snake River and Owyhee County. Roads in downtown Nampa are numbered, with avenues running north-south and streets running east-west. ValleyRide provides public transportation services for the Treasure Valley. Although ValleyRide provides transit service throughout Boise, it also provides fixed-line and door-to-door bus service in Nampa and Caldwell. The Ada County Highway District offers a commuter bus from Caldwell to Boise that stops in Nampa. The Treasure Valley Metro provides commuter service between Nampa, Meridian, and Boise during peak commute times.

■ Communications

Newspapers and Magazines

The *Idaho Press-Tribune* is published in Nampa and serves the Canyon County market. Published daily in the morning, the paper also maintains an Internet presence on its website.

Television and Radio

Nampa has one television station and four radio stations broadcasting within city limits; the city also receives programming from nearby Boise.

Media Information: *Idaho Press-Tribune*, PO Box 9399, Nampa, ID 83652; telephone (208)467-9251

Nampa Online

Boise State University Canyon County Center. Available www.boisestate.edu/bsuwest/ canyoncounty/studentservices.shtml

Boise Valley Economic Partnership. Available www .bvep.org

City of Nampa Home Page. Available www.ci .nampa.id.us

Idaho Center. Available www.idahocenter.com

Idaho Department of Commerce. Available www .commerce.idaho.gov

Idaho Department of Labor. Available www.labor .idaho.gov

Idaho Press-Tribune. Available www.idahopress.com

Nampa Chamber of Commerce. Available www .nampa.com

Nampa Public Library. Available www.nampalibrary .org

Nampa Public Schools. Available www.sd131.k12 .id.us

Northwest Nazarene University. Available www .nnu.edu

BIBLIOGRAPHY

Harris, Richard, *Hidden Idaho: Including Boise, Sun Valley and Yellowtone National Park* (Berkeley, CA: Ulysses, 2004)

Montana

The State in Brief

Nickname: Treasure State

Motto: Oro y plata (Gold and silver)

Flower: Bitterroot

Bird: Western meadowlark

Area: 147,042 square miles (2000; U.S. rank 4th)

Elevation: Ranges from 1,800 feet to 12,799 feet above sea level

Climate: Continental; heavy snows in the west and hot, dry summers in the east

Admitted to Union: November 8, 1889

Capital: Helena

Head Official: Governor Brian Schweitzer (D) (until 2008)

Population

1980: 786,690
1990: 799,065
2000: 902,195
2006 estimate: 944,632
Percent change, 1990–2000: 12.9%
U.S. rank in 2006: 44th
Percent of residents born in state: 53.49% (2006)
Density: 6.4 people per square mile (2006)
2006 FBI Crime Index Total: 27,784

Racial and Ethnic Characteristics (2006)

White: 847,192
Black or African American: 4,470
American Indian and Alaska Native: 59,500
Asian: 5,525
Native Hawaiian and Pacific Islander: 866
Hispanic or Latino (may be of any race): 20,513
Other: 8,195

Age Characteristics (2006)

Population under 5 years old: 57,577
Population 5 to 19 years old: 188,682
Percent of population 65 years and over: 13.9%
Median age: 39.5

Vital Statistics

Total number of births (2006): 11,558
Total number of deaths (2006): 8,778
AIDS cases reported through 2005: 372

Economy

Major industries: Services, trade, government, agriculture
Unemployment rate (2006): 4.8%
Per capita income (2006): $21,067
Median household income (2006): $40,627
Percentage of persons below poverty level (2006): 13.6%
Income tax rate: 1.0% to 6.9%
Sales tax rate: None

Billings

■ The City in Brief

Founded: 1882 (incorporated 1885)

Head Official: Mayor Ron Tussing (D) (since 2006)

City Population

 1980: 66,798
 1990: 81,125
 2000: 89,847
 2006 estimate: 100,148
 Percent change, 1990–2000: 10.7%
 U.S. rank in 1980: 294th
 U.S. rank in 1990: 263rd
 U.S. rank in 2000: 307th

Metropolitan Area Population

 1980: 108,035
 1990: 113,419
 2000: 129,352
 2006 estimate: 148,116
 Percent change, 1990–2000: 14.0%
 U.S. rank in 1980: Not available
 U.S. rank in 1990: Not available
 U.S. rank in 2000: 221st

Area: 33.82 square miles (2000)

Elevation: 3,126 feet above sea level

Average Annual Temperatures: January, 24.0° F; July, 72.0° F; annual average, 47.4° F

Average Annual Precipitation: 14.77 inches of rain; 56.7 inches of snow

Major Economic Sectors: services, wholesale and retail trade, government

Unemployment Rate: 2.1% (June 2007)

Per Capita Income: $23,884 (2005)

2005 FBI Crime Index Property: 5,520

2005 FBI Crime Index Violent: 201

Major Colleges and Universities: Montana State University-Billings, Rocky Mountain College

Daily Newspaper: *The Billings Gazette*

■ Introduction

Billings is the largest city in Montana and the commercial, cultural, and industrial center of a large region of the northern Rocky Mountains. Known as the "Magic City," Billings has grown phenomenally since its founding in 1882, until 1970 doubling in size every 30 years. The city is also the processing and distribution hub for a rich agricultural area that encompasses more than 125,000 miles. There are excellent road, rail, and air transportation networks. Many scenic attractions such as Yellowstone National Park are nearby, and the wide variety of available recreation activities make the Billings area a popular vacation spot. Such "pluses" are reasons why *U.S. News & World Report* listed Billings as one of the best places to retire in 2007.

■ Geography and Climate

Billings is located in southern Montana in the fertile Yellowstone River valley, with mountains on three sides. The Yellowstone River flows along the eastern boundary of the city. The mountains shelter the city from the most severe winter weather, but blizzard conditions are not uncommon in the spring and fall. Moist air from the Pacific Ocean, called "Chinook winds," often brings surprisingly warm weather in the winter and cooler temperatures in the summer. Spring features the most unpredictable weather, and summers are typically dry with cool nights.

Area: 33.82 square miles (2000)

Elevation: 3,126 feet above sea level

Average Temperatures: January, 24.0° F; July, 72.0° F; annual average, 47.4° F

Average Annual Precipitation: 14.77 inches of rain; 56.7 inches of snow

■ History

Native Americans Resist Settlement

For thousands of years before the coming of European settlers, the site of present-day Billings was hunted by migratory peoples. Traces of their camps and elaborate cave drawings have been discovered and preserved at many sites in the region. By the time of America's westward expansion, the predominant tribes in the area included the Crow, Sioux, and Cheyenne.

The Lewis and Clark Expedition of 1806 passed through the present site of Billings, and just 30 miles away William Clark climbed Pompey's Pillar, a 200-foot-high natural rock formation, which he named after the son of his female Indian guide. Although many Europeans explored the area, fierce resistance from the natives prevented any settlement. This led to the so-called "Sioux War," one of the more intense struggles between the U.S. Army and the native people. The infamous Battle of the Little Bighorn, where a large group of Sioux and Cheyenne warriors killed General George Custer and his entire 7th cavalry, took place 65 miles to the southeast of the future site of Billings.

Railroad Brings Ranchers, Farmers

Billings was founded in 1882 by the Northern Pacific Railroad as a rail head for the company's western line and named for the president of the railroad, Frederick Billings. Over the next six months more than 2,000 people settled in the town, which was incorporated as a city in 1885. The wide-open prairie lands were ideal for cattle grazing, and a number of large ranches grew up around the town. During the early twentieth century, families of settlers known as "homesteaders" arrived in the area, taking advantage of the offer of free land. Typically, a family and all its possessions would arrive in one freight car and receive a 40-acre plot of land. Conditions were difficult, but many families struggled through their first years and eventually developed successful farms.

Irrigation had been introduced in the Yellowstone Valley in 1879. Sugar beet growing was thus made possible, and a sugar refinery was built in 1906. Immigrant laborers came to work the fields—first Japanese, then Russo-Germans, and finally Mexicans. The Russo-German workers were unusually industrious; soon they bought their own land at the Huntley Irrigation project outside Billings, where they constituted a third of the population by 1940.

Abundant Natural Resources Contribute to Growth

Billings grew steadily during the 1900s, spurred on by the development of vast natural resources such as minerals, coal, natural gas, and oil. At one time Billings was the largest inland wool shipping point in the United States. In 1933 pulp-drying equipment was installed at the sugar refinery; a thriving livestock industry developed around animals fed on beet pulp. By 1938 more than 600,000 acres of land around Billings was irrigated.

A true hub city and gateway to the West, Billings has become the commercial, health care, and cultural capital of the "Midland Empire," a vast area of agricultural, mountainous, wilderness, and sometimes forbidding terrain that includes eastern Montana, the western Dakotas, and northern Wyoming. It is also an important refining and shipping center for agricultural and energy products. On its way to the 2010s, Billings remains "Star of the Big Sky Country."

Historical Information: Montana State University-Billings Library, 1500 University Dr., Billings, MT 59101; telephone (406)657–2262

■ Population Profile

Metropolitan Area Residents
   1980: 108,035
   1990: 113,419
   2000: 129,352
   2006 estimate: 148,116
   Percent change, 1990–2000: 14.0%
   U.S. rank in 1980: Not available
   U.S. rank in 1990: Not available
   U.S. rank in 2000: 221st

City Residents
   1980: 66,798
   1990: 81,125
   2000: 89,847
   2006 estimate: 100,148
   Percent change, 1990–2000: 10.7%
   U.S. rank in 1980: 294th
   U.S. rank in 1990: 263rd
   U.S. rank in 2000: 307th

Density: 2,656 people per square mile (2000)

Racial and ethnic characteristics (2000)
   White: 82,539
   Black: 495
   American Indian and Alaska Native: 3,088

Photograph by Phil Bell. Reproduced by permission.

Asian: 533
Native Hawaiian and Pacific Islander: 38
Hispanic or Latino (may be of any race): 3,758
Other: 1,300

Percent of residents born in state: 57.2% (2000)

Age characteristics (2005)

Population under 5 years old: 5,725
Population 5 to 9 years old: 5,028
Population 10 to 14 years old: 5,481
Population 15 to 19 years old: 5,505
Population 20 to 24 years old: 7,901
Population 25 to 34 years old: 11,645
Population 35 to 44 years old: 12,145
Population 45 to 54 years old: 14,392
Population 55 to 59 years old: 5,707
Population 60 to 64 years old: 5,519
Population 65 to 74 years old: 7,073
Population 75 to 84 years old: 5,636
Population 85 years and older: 1,087
Median age: 40.2 years

Births (2006, MSA)

Total number: 1,994

Deaths (2006, MSA)

Total number: 1,402

Money income (2005)

Per capita income: $23,884
Median household income: $38,711
Total households: 40,526

Number of households with income of...

less than $10,000: 5,042
$10,000 to $14,999: 2,201
$15,000 to $24,999: 6,685
$25,000 to $34,999: 4,949
$35,000 to $49,999: 6,548
$50,000 to $74,999: 7,752
$75,000 to $99,999: 3,068
$100,000 to $149,999: 3,113
$150,000 to $199,999: 705
$200,000 or more: 463

Percent of families below poverty level: 13.6% (2005)

2005 FBI Crime Index Property: 5,520

2005 FBI Crime Index Violent: 201

■ Municipal Government

Billings has a mayor-council form of government with ten council members elected to four-year terms. Until the 1995 election the mayor was elected to a two-year term; the mayor now serves a four-year term. The mayor and city council are the city's only policy-making bodies. A city administrator is hired by the mayor and city council and may be removed by a simple majority vote of the mayor and council. Billings is the seat of Yellowstone County.

Head Official: Mayor Ron Tussing (D) (since 2006; current term expires 2010)

Total Number of City Employees: 850 (2007)

City Information: City of Billings, 210 North 27th Street, Billings, MT 59101; telephone (406)657-8200; email tussingr@ci.billings.mt.us

■ Economy

Major Industries and Commercial Activity

Agriculture has been one of the leading economic forces in Billings since its founding, and it continues to play a major role today. Because of extensive irrigation, the Yellowstone Valley and the northern Great Plains are some of the nation's most fertile agricultural regions. The city is the transportation, processing, and packaging center for this large, productive area. The main agricultural products include sugar beets, grain, and livestock such as cattle and sheep.

The energy industry (oil, natural gas, and coal) is also an important part of the economic picture in Billings. The mountains around the city and throughout eastern Montana are a rich source of coal, oil, and natural gas. A number of refineries and purification plants are located in the Billings area to process the raw materials into usable energy resources.

Billings is the retail and wholesale trade center for a vast area of land in the northern Rocky Mountain states and a primary and secondary market population of almost half a million people, reaching from Denver, Colorado to Calgary, Alberta, and from Minneapolis, Minnesota to Seattle, Washington. Billings is also the medical and educational capital of the region. The city's medical community, including two major hospitals and more than 40 clinics, provides the most advanced health care in the four-state area. Two major colleges and a highly-rated public school system provide jobs and a well-trained workforce. It is also difficult to underestimate the impact of tourism and recreational diversity on the area's economy. The proximity of nearby Yellowstone National Park, as well as a wide array of other wilderness territories, mountain trails, rivers, and streams in the area bring much-needed tourist dollars and act as a magnet to companies and workers looking to relocate.

Items and goods produced: raw and refined energy products, sugar, flour, farm machinery, electric signs, furniture, paint, metal ornaments, cereal, creamery and meat products, canned vegetables, concrete, sugar beets, wheat, beans, livestock

Incentive Programs—New and Existing Companies

Local programs: The Billings Small Business Development Center (SBDC) is part of a statewide network of resource and technical service providers that assist start-up and existing businesses. The SBDC staff provides confidential business counseling, training and information to small business leaders and entrepreneurs. Services are provided at no charge and are funded by the Small Business Administration, Montana Department of Commerce, Yellowstone County, and local organizations. Areas of assistance include technical assistance in writing business plans for new and existing businesses, financial analysis, planning and state and private capital sources; assistance with marketing research, analysis and strategy as well as advertising, packaging and promotion; business plan review and critique; pre-business workshops; and one-on-one counseling for existing and start-up business management. Additionally, the Business Development Council of the Chamber of Commerce maintains a comprehensive inventory of local and state programs. It also helps identify location alternatives, provides technical assistance, and maintains current information on Billings and its trade area.

State programs: State of Montana tax incentives include property tax reduction; no inventory, use, or sales tax; new industry income tax credits; small business investment tax credit; and tax reduction on pollution control equipment. In 2003 the Montana legislature created the Certified Regional Development Corporations (CRDC) program in the Montana Department of Commerce. The CRDC program is designed to encourage a regional approach to economic development. State law also provides for the creation of a tax increment financing (TIF) industrial district for industrial development projects. A local government can issue bonds for a wide variety of development purposes such as: financing land acquisition, industrial infrastructure, rail spurs, buildings, and personal property related to the public improvements.

Job training programs: The Primary Sector Workforce Training Grant (WTG) program is a state-funded program; $3.9 million is available annually for this program. The WTG program is targeted to businesses that are creating at least one net, new job that pays at least the lower of the current county average wage or the state current average wage.

Development Projects

In 2004 renovations were completed on the historic Acme Hotel on North Broadway. Built in 1911 and rich with local history, the hotel was converted to residential homes, lofts, and commercial space in an area that included several more loft developments from refurbished buildings such as the Securities Building, Montana Avenue Lofts, and a proposed development at One South Broadway. Recent additions to the city's cultural and commercial growth include the $6 million Skyfest Amphitheatre, which presents outdoor concerts alongside the Yellowstone River, a $6.2 Yellowstone Art Museum expansion, and the conversion of several former hotels that were once stops on the Northern Pacific Railroad into coffee shops, antique stores, and restaurants.

As of 2007, the TransTech Center was in its fourth year of development. It is a high-tech business park specifically designed to support the communication, power, and workforce needs of technology-based businesses and e-commerce. A data center and Tech Plaza at the TransTech Center are two projects planned for future implementation.

Also in 2007, a new urban design neighborhood, Josephine Crossing, was being developed. The Southern Lights housing project was near completion at the end of 2007; the project was developed by the same company that developed the Acme hotel.

In the mid-1990s, an urban renewal plan for a Tax Increment Finance (TIF) District downtown was conceived. As of 2007, the East Billings Urban Renewal District was being developed into a vibrant and flourishing place of business and living opportunities.

Economic Development Information: Billings Area Chamber of Commerce, 815 South 27th Street, PO Box 31177, Billings, MT 59107-1177; telephone (406)245-4111; toll-free (800)711-2630; fax (406)245-7333; email info@billingschamber.com. Big Sky Economic Development Corporation, 222 North 32nd St., Suite 200, Billings, MT 59101; telephone (406)256-6871; fax (406)256-6877

Commercial Shipping

A number of carriers provide air freight and express mail service to the city via Billings Logan International Airport. Burlington Northern Railroad and Montana Rail Link operate rail lines from the Billings area. Burlington Northern also operates an intermodal (surface, sea, and air transportation) hub in Billings.

Labor Force and Employment Outlook

The Billings-area work force is educated above the national average, and a recent study found that one in four workers was overqualified for the jobs they were performing, creating an excellent climate for technical and higher-wage businesses looking to relocate to the area.

The Billings area economy is service-based, which includes specialized manufacturing, processing, and professional services to support the region's rural agricultural and energy economies. Billings serves as the regional hub for medical services, higher education, professional business services, retail and distribution, and travel and lodging.

The following is a summary of data regarding the Billings metropolitan area labor force, 2006 annual averages.

Size of nonagricultural labor force: 77,500

Number of workers employed in . . .

> construction and mining: Not available
> manufacturing: Not available
> trade, transportation and utilities: 19,500
> information: Not available
> financial activities: Not available
> professional and business services: 9,500
> educational and health services: 11,800
> leisure and hospitality: 9,800
> other services: Not available
> government: 9,200

Average hourly earnings of production workers employed in manufacturing: Not available

Unemployment rate: 2.1% (June 2007)

Largest county employers (2007)	*Number of employees*
Billings Clinic	2,919
School District No. 2	2,200
St. Vincent Healthcare	2,020
Stillwater Mining Co.	1,575
Montana State University – Billings	1,000
City of Billings	810
Wells Fargo Bank	615
Albertsons Food and Drug	600
First Interstate Bancsystems, Inc	595
US Postal Service	531

Cost of Living

The following is a summary of data regarding key cost of living factors for the Billings area.

2007 (1st quarter) ACCRA Average House Price: Not available

2007 (1st quarter) ACCRA Cost of Living Index: Not available

State income tax rate: 1.0% to 6.9%

State sales tax rate: None

Local income tax rate: None

Local sales tax rate: None

Property tax rate: 3.22% per $150,000 of assessed value

Economic Information: Billings Area Chamber of Commerce, 815 South 27th Street, PO Box 31177, Billings, MT 59107-1177; telephone (406)245-4111; toll-free (800)711-2630; fax (406)245-7333. Office of Research & Analysis, Montana Department of Labor & Industry, PO Box 1728, Helena, MT 59624; telephone (406)444-2430; fax (406)444-2638 or (800)633-0229 (within Montana) or (800)541-3904 (outside Montana)

■ Education and Research

Elementary and Secondary Schools

The Billings Public Schools District is governed by a nine-member School Board, which appoints a superintendent. With more than 15,000 students, it is the largest district in Montana. In addition to elementary, middle, and high schools, the district runs an alternative high school, a Career Center, and an Adult Education program that offers GED accreditation, basic math, English, science, and other pre-collegiate coursework. Special education, enrichment programs, education for disadvantaged children, adult education, and extracurricular activities are offered by the district. Billings Public Schools employs about 1,748 full-time equivalent positions. The 2007 budget was approximately $110 million dollars.

The following is a summary of data regarding the Billings Public Schools as of the 2005–2006 school year.

Total enrollment: 15,321

Number of facilities

 elementary schools: 21
 junior high/middle schools: 4
 senior high schools: 3
 other: 0

Student/teacher ratio: 15.3:1

Teacher salaries (2005–06)

 elementary median: $39,910
 junior high/middle median: $31,060
 secondary median: $42,660

Funding per pupil: $7,660

A number of private and parochial schools also serve the metropolitan area.

Public Schools Information: Billings Public Schools, 415 North 30th St., Billings, MT 59101-1298; telephone (406)247-3777; fax (406)247-3882

Colleges and Universities

There are two four-year institutions of higher education in Billings. Montana State University-Billings is a public, state-supported school with a 2007 enrollment of 4,912 students. A satellite campus of Montana State University-Bozeman, the college offers two-year associate's and four-year bachelor's degrees in more than 100 programs of study on a 112 acre-campus in Montana's largest city. The University is strongest in areas of Arts and Sciences, Allied Health, Education, Business, and Technology (including nursing); students can earn master's degrees in education and business administration. Rocky Mountain College is affiliated with the United Church of Christ, the United Methodist Church, and the United Presbyterian Church. It offers undergraduate degrees in more than 40 liberal arts and professionally-oriented majors and has an enrollment of about 1,000 students on a 60-acre Billings campus.

Libraries and Research Centers

The Parmly Billings Library contains more than 300,000 items, including 250,000 books (of these, more than 9,000 are large-print editions). There are also 190 magazine subscriptions, 7,000 music CDs, approximately 8,000 books on tape or CD, 11,000 videos, and 1,400 interactive CDs (games and other software). There are also five word processing centers and 18 Internet stations. Key collections include a full-text database research center, an Auto Repair Reference Center, Heritage Quest Online Genealogy Resources, and the NoveList Fiction Guide. There is an Outreach program and Infomobile for senior citizens. Other major libraries in the community are those of Montana State University-Billings and Rocky Mountain College.

Public Library Information: Parmly Billings Library, 510 North Broadway, Billings, MT 59101; telephone (406)657-8258; email refdesk@billings.lib.mt.us

■ Health Care

Billings provides the main medical services for a four-state area, with state-of-the-art equipment and highly skilled personnel. The community is served by nearly 500 physicians and dentists. Most of the health care facilities are concentrated in a 114-acre medical corridor that encompasses both of the city's major hospitals and 20 other health-related facilities.

Billings Clinic is a 272-bed Level II trauma center with general care and specialized services that include a cardiac care center, cancer services, an intensive care unit, the Kidney Center, a psychiatric center, pulmonary services, Women's Resource Center, occupational health and wellness, orthopedics and sports medicine, and a Research Institute. In 2004 ground was broken on a $27 million expansion to the hospital's Regional Emergency and Trauma Center. Off of the main campus are branch clinics which include Billings Clinic Heights and Billings Clinic West. In addition, the Aspen Meadows Retirement Community is part of Billings Clinic.

A 314-bed Level II trauma center, St. Vincent Healthcare is operated by the Sisters of Charity of Leavenworth and provides comprehensive inpatient and outpatient services, special services for women and seniors, and expertise in cardiology, orthopedics, general internal medicine, pediatrics, emergency and trauma, neurosciences, rehabilitation, neonatology, and oncology. St. Vincent Healthcare serves the medical needs of more than 400,000 people.

Other medical facilities in Billings are the Northern Rockies Radiation Oncology Center; Rimrock Foundation, which provides treatment for addictive disorders such as chemical dependency, co-dependency, compulsive gambling, and eating disorders; and several mental health facilities.

■ Recreation

Sightseeing

Downtown Billings contains the Billings Historical District, a renovated area that consists of most of the original business district. The Castle Corner is a replica of the Potter Palmer Mansion in Chicago, an interesting structure modeled after English castles. The railroad brought prosperity to Billings, and prosperity brought Preston B. Moss. In 1901, architect H.J. Hardenbergh (designer of the Waldorf-Astoria and Plaza Hotels in New York City) created the elegant Moss estate. The three-story Moss Mansion remains authentically furnished and is open year-round at 914 Division Street. The Black Otter Trail, beginning at the edge of the city, is a winding highway that follows the "rimrocks," natural sandstone cliffs that border the city on the north and east. Boothill Cemetery, burial ground for residents of the frontier town of Colson, and the Range Rider of Yellowstone, a life-sized bronze statue by artist Charles Christadora, are both located along the Black Otter Trail, as are Sacrifice Cliff and Yellowstone Kelly's gravesite. Pictograph Cave State Park, southeast of Billings, has cave paintings made by Indians who lived and hunted for wooly mammoth in the region some 4,500 years ago.

A number of national monuments, parks, and recreation areas are located near Billings, most within a two-hour drive. Little Bighorn Battlefield National Monument, site of Custer's Last Stand, is 65 miles southeast of the city, and Pompey's Pillar, a spectacular natural rock formation, is 28 miles east of Billings.

The Little Bighorn Battlefield National Monument lets visitors relive the clash between General George Custer's 7th Cavalry and more than 3,000 warriors led by Crazy Horse. Yellowstone National Park is the world's

first such; President Theodore Roosevelt proclaimed it so during his presidential tenure, and visitors today can see its famous geysers, painted canyons, and wildlife much as the way Roosevelt saw it. On the way from Billings to Yellowstone, Montana's highest peak is on view from Highway 212 over the Beartooth Mountain Pass.

Arts and Culture

The main performing arts center in the region, the Alberta Bair Theater for the Performing Arts is the site of most of the cultural activity in Billings. The Fox Committee for the Performing Arts and the Billings Community Concert Association are both responsible for bringing a wide range of cultural events to the city each year, including jazz, opera, ballet, and popular music concerts. The Billings Symphony Orchestra and Chorale performs approximately ten concerts each season, including an annual free concert in the park.

The Billings Studio Theatre (BST), established in 1953, mounts a five-show Mainstage Season along with a major fall production at the Alberta Bair Theater, special events, and experimental plays in its Dark Night Series. BST also showcases two Rocky Mountain College productions annually and hosts many community events. In addition, BST operates a children's theatre, the Growing Stage. Montana Shakespeare in the Parks is the only professional theatre program in the state producing Shakespearean plays; it offers its performances free to the public. Since its inception in 1973, Montana Shakespeare in the Parks has traveled over 400,000 miles and presented over 1,500 performances to a cumulative audience of more than a half million people. It began as an amateur 12-city tour but has become a nationally known, professional company which presents an eight-week tour of 70 performances in 50 communities every summer throughout Montana, northern Wyoming, and eastern Idaho.

The Western Heritage Center features changing exhibits pertaining to the region's history, and the Yellowstone County Museum contains historical relics and dioramas depicting scenes from Billings's past. The Yellowstone Art Museum holds one of the region's best collections of contemporary and historic art, including an impressive collection of Western art particularly strong in the works of Montana artists Russell Chatham and Deborah Butterfield; it also sponsors lectures and concerts.

MetraPark fairground holds concerts, rodeos, and the annual MontanaFair. Canyon Creek and a nature trail wind through ZooMontana's 70 acres of exotic animal exhibits.

Festivals and Holidays

Annual events in and around Billings include ArtWalk and the MSU-Billings Wine and Food Festival in May, the Moss Mansion County Fair and Strawberry Festival in

June, and July's Crazy Days downtown and the Skyfest Parade and Balloon Rally. In August the Magic City Blues Festival graces downtown, and the MontanaFair is held at the MetraPark fairgrounds. On the fourth weekend in September the traditional German harvest festival, Herbstfest, is held in nearby Laurel. German foods, dancing, and music are featured. Downtown Billings is the site of Harvest Fest each October. Late November has the Holiday Parade, and Christmas Stroll occurs each December downtown.

Sports for the Spectator

Billings supports three professional sports teams. The Billings Mustangs, a baseball farm team of the Cincinnati Reds, play at Cobb Field; the Billings Outlaws of the United Indoor Football League play at the 8,700-seat MetraPark Arena; and the Billings Bulls play junior hockey at the Centennial Ice Arena. The city features several rodeo events each year, including the Northern Rodeo Association finals, which have been held in Billings for 30 years. Auto racing takes place at Billings Motorsports Park.

Sports for the Participant

The mountains near Billings offer a complete range of year-round outdoor activity in some of America's most spectacular terrain: skiing (at nearby Red Lodge Mountain, and farther away Big Sky and the new Moonlight Basin resort); hiking; hunting; fishing (some of the world's legendary trout streams are nearby, such as Rock Creek and the Stillwater, Boulder, Musselshell, Big Horn, and Yellowstone rivers); camping; and a wide variety of water recreation. At a number of lakes and reservoirs, swimming, boating, sailing, and water skiing can be enjoyed. The city of Billings operates more than 40 parks that feature swimming pools, tennis courts, athletic fields, jogging and biking paths, and other recreational facilities. There are several public and private golf courses in the city.

Shopping and Dining

Rimrock Mall downtown is the largest shopping area, with more than 85 shops, including Dillard's, JCPenney, Eddie Bauer, Gap, and Bath and Body Works. West Park Plaza is another large enclosed shopping center, with more than 30 stores. There are at least a dozen smaller shopping areas in Billings. Western boutiques to specialty shops serve up quality merchandise and great bargains, all with no sales tax, in the historic downtown shopping district or the Billings Heights area on Main Street.

Restaurants in Billings feature traditional Western fare as well as exotic ethnic cuisine in settings ranging from casual and inexpensive to elegant and intimate. Most restaurants are clustered around the main shopping and commercial areas of downtown on Montana Avenue and North Broadway.

Visitor Information: Billings Area Chamber of Commerce, 815 South 27th St., PO Box 31177, Billings, MT 59107-1177; telephone (406)245-4111; toll-free (800)735-2635

■ Convention Facilities

The primary meeting facility in Billings is MetraPark, a multipurpose major event center located on the Rimrocks overlooking downtown. MetraPark features a 30,000-square-foot arena in addition to an exhibition space totaling more than 200,000 square feet with 10 break-out rooms. Total seating capacity is about 12,000 people. The complex contains an art pavilion and a covered grandstand for outdoor events, a half-mile track used for both horse racing and auto racing, and is surrounded by nearly 90 acres of parking. The facility is diverse enough to hold large trade shows, professional sporting events for three local franchises, national touring shows and musical acts, and Gold Wing Road Riders Wing Ding gatherings.

The Holiday Inn Grand Montana Hotel & Convention Center is the largest facility in the four-state region to be built in conjunction with a hotel; recently renovated, it contains 50,000 square feet of meeting space in 17 rooms that accommodate groups from 10 to 3,200. Located downtown is the Alberta Bair Theater, which serves as the site of business meetings and conventions as well as performances, with a theater capacity of 1,400 people.

Conference and convention facilities for large and small groups are available in several hotels, motels, and bed-and-breakfast establishments throughout the Billings metropolitan area, including the Historic Northern Hotel, Sheraton Billings Hotel, and the Billings Hotel and Convention Center. Billings offers more than 3,400 hotel rooms and nearly 350 million square feet of meeting space. Alternatives to city hotel accommodations can be found outside Billings at the Double Spear Ranch in Pryor, Montana.

Convention Information: Billings Area Chamber of Commerce, 815 South 27th Street, PO Box 31177, Billings, MT 59107-1177; telephone (406)245-4111; toll-free (800)711-2630

■ Transportation

Approaching the City

Billings Logan International Airport is only two miles from the downtown district and serves most of eastern Montana and northern Wyoming with more than 50 flights daily from major airlines and regional carriers. Allegiant Air, Atlantic Southeast Airlines, Big Sky, Delta, Frontier, Horizon, Northwest, Skywest, and United all service Billings with planes as large as 757s.

Billings is at the junction of two interstate highways: I-90, connecting the city with the Pacific Northwest and the southern Rocky Mountain states; and I-94, providing a link with the midwestern states. U.S. 87, 310, and 212 also meet in Billings.

Billings is served by Greyhound and Rimrock Trailways bus services. The nearest Amtrak stop is on the Hi-Line, 200 miles north of Billings. As of 2007 there was talk of bringing regular passenger rail service through Billings as part of a route through southern Montana.

Traveling in the City

Billings Metropolitan Transit operates 18 routes within the city and serves approximately 5,000 customers. Auto traffic on major thoroughfares is light compared to most metropolitan areas. The downtown area is laid out in a grid pattern with numbered streets.

■ Communications

Newspapers and Magazines

Billings has one major daily newspaper, *The Billings Gazette* (morning). *Montana Land Magazine* is published quarterly.

Television and Radio

Bresnan Communications provides cable television and high-speed internet service in Billings; in 2007, Bresnan teamed up with Fujitsu Network Communications to offer free high-speed broadband Wi-Fi access for Bresnan's customers in Billings. All four major television networks (ABC, CBS, NBC, Fox) broadcast to the Billings area. Fifteen AM and FM radio stations broadcast from Billings.

Media Information: *The Billings Gazette,* 401 N. Broadway, Billings, MT 59101; telephone (406)657-1200; toll-free (800)543-2505; email sprosinski@billingsgazette.com

Billings Online

Big Sky Development Authority. Available www .bigskyedc.org

Billings Area Chamber of Commerce. Available www.billingschamber.com

Billings Convention and Visitors Bureau. Available billingscvb.visitmt.com

Billings Cultural Partners. Available www .downtownbillings.org

*The Billings Gazette.*Available www.billingsgazette .com

Billings Public Schools. Available www.billings .k12.mt.us

City of Billings home page. Available www.ci .billings.mt.us

Parmly Billings Library. Available www.billings.lib .mt.us

BIBLIOGRAPHY

Raban, Jonathan, *Bad Land: An American Romance* (New York: Pantheon, 1996)

Van West, Carroll, *Capitalism on the Frontier: Billings and the Yellowstone Valley in the Nineteenth Century* (Lincoln, NE: University of Nebraska Press, 1993)

Butte

■ The City in Brief

Founded: 1864 (incorporated 1879)

Head Official: Chief Executive Paul Babb (since 2005)

City Population

> 1980: 37,205
> 1990: 33,336
> 2000: 33,892
> 2006 estimate: 32,110
> Percent change, 1990–2000: 1.6%
> U.S. rank in 1980: 605th
> U.S. rank in 1990: 806th
> U.S. rank in 2000: 887th

Metropolitan Area Population

> 1980: 38,092
> 1990: 33,941
> 2000: 34,606
> 2006 estimate: 32,801
> Percent change, 1990–2000: 1.9%
> U.S. rank in 1980: Not available
> U.S. rank in 1990: Not available
> U.S. rank in 2000: 1,262

Area: 716.2 square miles (2000)

Elevation: Ranges from 5,484 to 6,463 feet above sea level

Average Annual Temperatures: 53.2° F (maximum), 27.1° F (minimum)

Average Annual Precipitation: 12.75 inches

Major Economic Sectors: services, wholesale and retail trade, government

Unemployment Rate: 6.0% (January 2005, Silver Bow County)

Per Capita Income: $17,068 (1999)

2005 FBI Crime Index Property: Not available

2005 FBI Crime Index Violent: Not available

Major Colleges and Universities: Montana Tech of the University of Montana

Daily Newspaper: *The Montana Standard*

■ Introduction

Once dependent almost solely on the mining industry—in the early 1900s it was called "the richest hill on earth" because of the valuable ores that lay beneath it—Butte, like many older American cities, is in the midst of a transition toward a more diversified economy. With easy access to western and midwestern markets, Butte is one of the west's major transportation hubs; the city is also moving into enterprises related to energy research and high-altitude sports training. Despite the changes underway, Butte retains its multiethnic heritage and its connection to the breathtaking natural beauty of the surrounding Rocky Mountains. For statistical and other purposes, Butte is traditionally linked with Silver Bow County.

■ Geography and Climate

Butte is located in Summit Valley in the heart of the Rocky Mountains on the west slope of the Continental Divide in southwestern Montana. Silver Bow Creek, part of the Columbia River system—and called Clark Fork outside the city—runs through Butte. The climate is semi-arid, with a growing season of about 80 days.

Area: 716.2 square miles (2000)

Elevation: Ranges from 5,484 to 6,463 feet above sea level

Average Temperatures: 53.2° F (maximum), 27.1° F (minimum)

Average Annual Precipitation: 12.75 inches

■ History

Discovery of Gold and Silver Brings Settlers to Region

The area surrounding Butte's present location remained uninhabited before gold was discovered in 1864 in Silver Bow Creek. Native Americans and explorers passed through the region, but found no attractions for permanent settlement until two prospectors detected placer deposits in the creek; they named the site the Missoula lode. Other prospectors came, and by 1867 the population of the mining settlement reached 500 people. Water was scarce, however, and the town began to decline; the 1870 census recorded only about 200 people.

One of the region's first prospectors, William Farlin, returned in 1874 to claim several outcrops of quartz that he had discovered previously. Before long a silver boom began, bringing a chaos of claim staking and claim jumping as prospectors overran the site. Investors William Clark and Andrew Davis constructed mills for extracting gold and silver, and by 1876, when a townsite patent was issued, the prosperous camp numbered 1,000 residents. Marcus Daly, representing Salt Lake City mining entrepreneurs, arrived that same year and bought the Alice Mine, naming it Walkerville for his employers. In 1879 Butte, which had been named for Big Butte, a volcanic cone to the northwest, was incorporated as a city.

Copper Discovered; Butte Thrives; Unions Formed

In 1880 Daly sold his interest in the Walker mining operations and bought the Anaconda Mine. As he was digging for silver, Daly struck copper, thus initiating the industry that eventually made him one of the country's wealthiest and most powerful men. Daly attracted investors from as far away as Boston and New York, and within a year the town had several mines and mining companies. In a lifelong rivalry with William Clark for control of Butte, Daly finally won out as the "boss" of a one-industry town. The arrival of the Union Pacific Railroad in 1881 ensured Butte's success as the leading producer of copper in the United States.

With a population of 14,000 people in 1885, Butte supported banks, schools, a hospital, a fire department, churches, and a water company. Copper production and the development of mining companies continued until the turn of the century, when Daly joined with the Rockefeller family to form the Amalgamated Copper Mining Company, one of the early twentieth-century trusts. By the first decade of the twentieth century Butte was a major rail hub, with four railroads connecting in the city. Amalgamated, having bought out other mining companies in Butte, changed its name back to the Anaconda Copper Mining Company in 1915.

The labor movement was important to Butte's history. The Butte Miner's Union was formed in 1878 to protect miners from the dangers of working underground. The Butte delegation was the largest at the 1906 founding convention of the International Workers of the World (IWW) in Chicago. During the early twentieth century the union's power began to decline when mining companies were consolidated and management became indifferent to worker demands. The dynamiting of the union hall in 1914 and the lynching of an IWW organizer in 1917 led to seven years of martial law in Butte. The worst hardrock mining disaster in American history, the Spectacular Mine Fire, also took place in 1917, killing 168 miners.

Present-day Butte neighborhoods such as Dublin Gulch, Finntown, Chinatown, and Corktown attest to the city's diverse ethnic roots. Since the community's earliest days immigrants from all over the world settled in Butte to work the mines. When the placer camp was started in 1864, Chinese miners were the first to arrive. Later came Cornish, Irish, and Welsh laborers, and for a time Irish workers formed the dominant group. Then Serbs, Croats, French Canadians, Finns, Scandinavians, Jews, Lebanese, Mexicans, Austrians, Germans, and African Americans added to the ranks of miners.

Mining Declines; Economy Diversifies

Throughout the first half of the twentieth century, the mining industry continued to dominate the Butte economy. Changes began to take place, however; underground mining gave way to pit mining in the 1950s when high-grade copper-ore deposits were exhausted and above-ground exploration for low-grade ore began. In 1976 Anaconda was bought by Atlantic Richfield Company; in 1983 the mines were completely closed. Unemployment rose to more than 17 percent and Butte's survival seemed threatened. That same year a task force composed of government and business leaders was formed to ensure a future for Butte through a concerted effort to diversify the city's economy. Since then, mines have reopened, a transportation hub was built at the Port of Montana, the U.S. High Altitude Sports Center was located in the city, and several high-technology firms have established facilities in the area. These efforts at economic stability, diversification, and growth have been recognized by the Montana Ambassadors, the Pacific Institute, the U.S. Corporation for Economic Development, and *Newsweek* magazine, which commented in an article about the area's steady decline and stagnant

©*Chuck Haney/DanitaDelimont.com/drr.net*

economy, that "in Montana, Butte has engineered the most dramatic turnaround." In 2002 Butte was named one of the National Trust for Historic Preservation's "Dozen Distinctive Destinations." In 2005 Butte gained international recognition as the location for the Hollywood film *Don't Come Knocking* directed by Wim Wenders and starring Sam Shepard and Jessica Lange. In 2007 *U.S. News & World Report* named Butte one of the best places to retire.

Historical Information: Butte Silver-Bow Public Archives, PO Box 81, 17 W. Court St., Butte, MT 59703; telephone (406)782-3280; email info@buttearchives.org

■ Population Profile

Metropolitan Area Residents

1980: 38,092
1990: 33,941
2000: 34,606
2006 estimate: 32,801
Percent change, 1990–2000: 1.9%
U.S. rank in 1980: Not available

U.S. rank in 1990: Not available
U.S. rank in 2000: 1,262

City Residents

1980: 37,205
1990: 33,336
2000: 33,892
2006 estimate: 32,110
Percent change, 1990–2000: 1.6%
U.S. rank in 1980: 605th
U.S. rank in 1990: 806th
U.S. rank in 2000: 887th

Density: 47.3 people per square mile (2000)

Racial and ethnic characteristics (2000)

White: 32,325
Black: 53
American Indian and Alaska Native: 675
Asian: 147
Native Hawaiian and Pacific Islander: 21
Hispanic or Latino (may be of any race): 927
Other: 200

Percent of residents born in state: 73.3% (2000)

Age characteristics (2000)

Population under 5 years old: 1,947
Population 5 to 9 years old: 2,250
Population 10 to 14 years old: 2,407
Population 15 to 19 years old: 2,451
Population 20 to 24 years old: 2,231
Population 25 to 34 years old: 3,796
Population 35 to 44 years old: 5,246
Population 45 to 54 years old: 4,801
Population 55 to 59 years old: 1,820
Population 60 to 64 years old: 1,491
Population 65 to 74 years old: 2,628
Population 75 to 84 years old: 2,057
Population 85 years and older: 767
Median age: 38.9 years

Births (2006, Micropolitan Statistical Area)

Total number: 369

Deaths (2006, Micropolitan Statistical Area)

Total number: 449

Money income (1999)

Per capita income: $17,068
Median household income: $30,516
Total households: 14,176

Number of households with income of…

less than $10,000: 1,720
$10,000 to $14,999: 1,558
$15,000 to $24,999: 2,577
$25,000 to $34,999: 2,175
$35,000 to $49,999: 2,251
$50,000 to $74,999: 2,427
$75,000 to $99,999: 758
$100,000 to $149,999: 463
$150,000 to $199,999: 108
$200,000 or more: 139

Percent of families below poverty level: 10.7% (2000)

2005 FBI Crime Index Property: Not available

2005 FBI Crime Index Violent: Not available

■ Municipal Government

The governments of the city of Butte and Silver Bow County are combined and are administered by a Chief Executive and council. The twelve council members and the Chief Executive all serve four-year terms.

Head Official: Chief Executive Paul Babb (since 2005; current term expires 2009)

Total Number of City Employees: 470 (2007)

City Information: Butte/Silver Bow Government Courthouse, 155 West Granite St., Butte, MT 59701; telephone (406)497-6200; fax (406)497-6328

■ Economy

Major Industries and Commercial Activity

Since Butte's founding during a gold boom, its principal industry has been mining. From the mid-1880s to the 1980s, Butte produced an estimated $22 billion in minerals mined. More than 8 percent of the nation's copper continues to be produced in Butte, joining other important minerals such as lead, zinc, and magnesium. In the 1970s, when underground mines were closed, the copper industry began to decline; it reached its lowest point in 1983 when mining operations in the Butte area completely ceased for a time.

This recession began to ease in 1986 when copper mines were reopened, creating more than 300 jobs. This upsurge brought development in other areas such as transportation, tourism and recreation, small businesses, technology, energy research, medicine, and communications. Accolades have poured in during recent years, lauding Butte's economic resurgence, even earning the town a four-minute spot on the Paul Harvey radio program. Lou Tice of the Pacific Institute in Seattle hailed Butte as a "city on the move." Citing the economic rebirth of Butte, Tice attributed the successes to "its people—their tenacity, their hard work and the remarkable goals they set."

As of 2007 Montana's economy as a whole was growing, due in part to demands in Asia for precious metals. Butte's economy is tied to this performance. The reopening of Montana Resources, the stabilization of existing businesses, and the addition of new companies helped increase employment in Butte by 800 workers, or 5.4 percent from 2003-2006. Montana Resources was selected as the 2005 Business of the Year for Butte/Silver Bow. In 2005, unemployment fell to a 30-year low of 4.7 percent in Butte. The economy has become much more diversified. Major employers such as ASiMi and St. James Healthcare have reported plans for steady employment in the short-term and increases in the long-term.

Items and goods produced: motors, dairy and food products, compressed and liquefied gases, beverages, optical goods, chemicals, steel fabrications, phosphate products

Incentive Programs—New and Existing Companies

Local programs: The Butte/Silver Bow Tax Increment Financing Industrial District (Butte has two, comprising 1,300 acres) directs new tax dollars accrued from new development within the district to assist further development within the boundaries of the district. There are four other tax incentive programs available to local businesses that qualify. The Butte Local Development Corporation (BLDC), a principal catalyst in the region's economic turnaround, is considered one of the best economic development organizations for its size in the country. Its mission is to create jobs through industrial development. BLDC accomplishes these goals through capital acquisition, land and infrastructure development, development and maintenance of informational tools, economic analysis and planning, and numerous other activities. The BLDC also administers five loan programs. In addition, property used by certain new or expanding industries is eligible for a reduced taxable valuation (up to 50 percent of its taxable valuation for the first five years) during the first nine years after construction or expansion.

State programs: State of Montana tax incentives include property tax reduction; no inventory, use, or sales tax; new industry income tax credits; small business investment tax credit; and tax reduction on pollution control equipment. In 2003 the Montana legislature created the Certified Regional Development Corporations (CRDC) program in the Montana Department of Commerce. The CRDC program is designed to encourage a regional approach to economic development. State law also provides for the creation of a tax increment financing (TIF) industrial district for industrial development projects. A local government can issue bonds for a wide variety of development purposes such as: financing land acquisition, industrial infrastructure, rail spurs, buildings, and personal property related to the public improvements.

Job training programs: The Primary Sector Workforce Training Grant (WTG) program is a state-funded program; $3.9 million is available annually for this program. The WTG program is targeted to businesses that are creating at least one net, new job that pays at least the lower of the current county average wage or the state current average wage.

Development Projects

Government and industry leaders have organized to encourage expansion of Butte's economic base by capitalizing on the area's natural resources: agriculture, forest products, and mining. Steps have been made to reopen mines or help existing mines stay in business. The Montana Copper mine was reopened in 2003, creating 330 jobs and $11 million in annual payroll for local workers. The BDLC in 2004 announced renewed efforts to keep the Golden Sunlight and Luzenac America mines in operation, as well as provide assistance to the Northwestern Energy Corporation as it went through bankruptcy proceedings. The recently completed Port of Montana Hub, intended to facilitate the loading and transporting of minerals and forest products by rail and motor freight carriers, is expected to contribute significantly to the area's economic development. Other steps toward economic stabilization include the opening of a small business incubator, the establishment of Butte's Cyber Village and Silicon Mountain Technology Park where several science and technology firms have started up or relocated, and the development of the U.S. High Altitude Sports Center. Other recent development projects have included the development of an East Side Urban Renewal Area, a music and entertainment district downtown, a new community ice center and jail, and improvements to the Civic Center.

Once called an "environmental wasteland" because of the damage done to it by mining and smelting, Butte is gradually recovering. The Atlantic Richfield Corporation (ARCO) spent more than $400 million on reclamation work to repair damage in the area by capping mine tailings with clean dirt, landscaping, and re-vegetating damaged land. In 2004 ARCO agreed to contribute an additional $50 million to the Montana Superfund in efforts to clean up the Clark Fork Basin.

Economic Development Information: Butte Local Development Corporation, 480 East Park St. Butte, MT 59701; telephone (406)723-4349; fax (406)723-1539

Commercial Shipping

Butte is a major inland port from which imported cargo is shipped via rail and motor carrier to points throughout the Midwest. Butte is located at the only rail interline in the state of the Union Pacific and Burlington Northern railroads. Piggyback service is provided, and trains run up to twelve times weekly from Butte. Several motor freight carriers regularly transport goods through facilities in Butte, with overnight and second-day delivery to major cities in the West and Midwest; in addition, well over 1,000 motor freight carriers serving the state have access to Butte. Some of the trucking firms serving the county are Western Transport Line, Yellow Freight, Molerway Freight Lines, Consolidated Freightways, Transystems, Roadway Express, ANA Transport, Biggers Transport, Irving Trucking, Americana Expressways, Highland, S&J Trucking, Prince, Kenyon-Noble, Rob Clark, RB&C Trucking, Solberg, and Ward Trucking.

Labor Force and Employment Outlook

When the Butte Job Service surveyed 10 major employers in the Butte area, they reported rates of absenteeism from 1 to 2 percent, and turnover rates that average 3 percent. Butte's labor force in 2007 included many potential employees and other well-trained workers with skills and experience beyond their present employment. Silver Bow County has experienced ups and downs in employment levels as it has made the difficult transition to a more diversified economy. Growth in the 1990s was driven in a large part by construction of the American Silicon Minerals corporate headquarters in Butte. Following the loss of construction jobs in 1999, employment losses were once again experienced with the shutdown of Montana Resources in mid-2000. However, in August 2003 Montana Resources' copper and molybdenum mine reopened; Montana Resources currently employs approximately 350 people residing in Butte and Anaconda and neighboring communities. By 2007 Butte and Montana's economy were growing steadily—predictions were for 4 percent growth a year until 2009. A particular bright spot has been the city's success in luring international firms to the Silicon Mountain Technology Park and Cyber Village.

The following is a summary of data regarding the Butte-Silver Bow (balance) metropolitan area labor force, 2000 annual averages.

Size of nonagricultural labor force: 15,439

Number of workers employed in ...

    construction and mining: 823
    manufacturing: 616
    trade, transportation and utilities: 4,186
    information: 445
    financial activities: 606
    professional and business services: 1,091
    educational and health services: 3,696
    leisure and hospitality: 1,764
    other services: 784
    government: 2,529

Average hourly earnings of production workers employed in manufacturing: Not available

Unemployment rate: 6.0% (January 2005, Silver Bow County)

Largest employers (2004)	Number of employees
St. James Health Care	548
NorthWestern Energy	502
Wal-Mart	465
Town Pump	386
Montana Resources	335
Community Counseling and Correctional	308
Advanced Silicon Materials	307
MSE/MERDI	177
Kids Behavioral Health	174
Butte Convelescent Center	130

Cost of Living

The following is a summary of data regarding key cost of living factors for the Butte area.

2007 (1st quarter) ACCRA Average House Price: Not available

2007 (1st quarter) ACCRA Cost of Living Index: Not available

State income tax rate: 1.0% to 6.9%

State sales tax rate: None

Local income tax rate: None

Local sales tax rate: None

Property tax rate: $669.24 per $1,000 of taxable value; assessed at 1.82% to 1.54% of the actual market value (2005)

Economic Information: Butte/Silver Bow Chamber of Commerce, 1000 George St., Butte MT 59701; telephone (406)723-3177; toll-free (800)735-6814; fax (406)723-1215; email chamber@buttechamber.org. Montana Department of Labor & Industry, PO Box 1728, Helena, MT 59624; telephone (406)444-2840

■ Education and Research

Elementary and Secondary Schools

The public elementary and secondary school system in Butte is Butte School District #1. The district is overseen by an eight-member elected school board and is administered by a superintendent appointed by the board. The district considers itself one of the most technologically advanced in Montana, with 100 percent Internet access for all students. The district offers a full range of after-school latchkey and enrichment programs, adult education, homebound services, special education, and a unique Retired Seniors Volunteer Program (R.S.V.P.) that brings local retirees together with students to form tutoring and mentoring relationships. The 21st Century Community Learning Centers (R.O.C.K.I.E.S.) program offers elementary students and their parents such services as after-school childcare; enrichment activities; reading and math instruction; and recreational activities.

The following is a summary of data regarding the Butte School District #1 as of the 2005–2006 school year.

Total enrollment: 4,604

Number of facilities

    elementary schools: 6
    junior high/middle schools: 1
    senior high schools: 1
    other: 1

Student/teacher ratio: 15.6:1

Teacher salaries (2005–06)

elementary median: $35,058 (all levels)
junior high/middle median: Not available
secondary median: Not available

Funding per pupil: $6,305

Several religious and secular parochial elementary and high schools provide alternatives to public education in the Butte metropolitan area.

Public Schools Information: Butte School District #1, 111 North Montana, Butte, MT 59701; telephone (406)496-2000

Colleges and Universities

Montana Tech of the University of Montana, originally chartered as the Montana State School of Mines, comprises the College of Humanities, Social Sciences, and Information Technology; the College of Mathematics and Sciences; the School of Mines and Engineering; the College of Technology; and the Graduate School. Montana Tech offers 6 certificate, 9 associate's, 19 bachelor's, and 11 master's programs. With a 2006 enrollment of 2,232 students, the school conducts basic and applied research and provides graduates with degrees in such fields as geophysical engineering, mineral processing, and petroleum engineering. A $20 million dollar construction and renovation project was recently completed, which modernized laboratory, classroom, and office facilities for the biology and chemistry programs. Both Montana State University-Bozeman and the University of Montana in Missoula are within a two-hour drive of Butte.

Libraries and Research Centers

The Butte-Silver Bow Library is located in Butte. Holdings consist of 75,000 volumes and nearly 200 periodical subscriptions, with special collections relating to Montana architecture, historic preservation, and fishing. The library is the headquarters for the Montana Public Library Film Service. The Butte-Silver Bow Public Archives holds information on local families and history, plus more than 30 labor history and 70 personal collections. The Historic Hearst Free Library in Anaconda offers more than 43,000 volumes, 66 periodicals, 16 newspapers, and a repository of historic memorabilia.

The Montana Tech Library houses nearly 50,000 volumes, 80,000 maps, and 425,000 documents including paper, microform, and electronic media. The library is a depository for federal and state government documents. In addition, Montana Tech conducts research activities in such fields as water resources, earthquakes, mines, and geology. Butte is home to the National Center for Appropriate Technology Research Library. Most of the other libraries and research centers in the city also specialize in energy and technology.

Public Library Information: Butte-Silver Bow Library, 226 West Broadway Street, Butte, MT 59701; telephone (406)723-3361

■ Health Care

The chief medical provider for the Butte-Silver Bow area is the St. James Healthcare system, part of the Montana region of the Sisters of Charity of Leavenworth Health System, which also has operations in Billings and Miles City. The Butte facility employs more than 450 people, including 64 doctors, and has more than 100 beds. St. James provides medical services in the fields of cardiology, neurosciences, oncology, orthopedics, women's and children's services, emergency services, MRI, pain management, renal dialysis, and others. A number of other institutions provide mental health services, dental care, hospice care, chiropractic care, chemical dependency rehabilitation, and more.

■ Recreation

Sightseeing

A popular Trolley Tour takes visitors to all the key sights—Old No. 1, a replica of the city's original electric trolley car system, operates four times daily from the first of June through Labor Day. Both St. Lawrence Church and the Serbian Orthodox Church have stunning frescoes that are open to public viewing. Butte's historic district also showcases several homes built during the days of the mining barons. The Copper King Mansion, built in 1888, was the Elizabethan-Victorian-style home of William S. Clark, whose battle with Marcus Daly for control in Butte has become a local legend; the mansion is now a bed and breakfast inn. Another impressive structure is the Charles Clark Mansion, also called the W.A. Clark Chateau, home of William A. Clark's son and a replica of a French chateau; completely restored and housing an arts center and gallery, it has been designated as a National Historic Structure. On the west side of the city are other fashionable, late-nineteenth-century homes.

Overlooking Butte from Montana Tech Hill is a statue of Marcus Daly by Augustus Saint-Gaudens. North of the downtown district stands the "gallows frame" of the Original Mine, which was used to raise and lower miners and ores from the underground mine. To the east of the city is the Berkeley Pit, started in 1955, and once the largest truck-operated open pit copper mine in the United States; it is an example of the process that replaced underground vein mining. The Granite Mountain Memorial commemorates the 168 miners who died during a 1917 fire at the Granite Mountain and Speculator mines. Also east of Butte, atop the Continental Divide, is Our Lady of the Rockies, a statue of the Christian religion's Virgin Mary. Standing 90 feet high and floodlighted at night, the statue is a nondenominational monument to motherhood that was built with donated materials and labor and completed in 1985.

Among the points of interest within driving distance of Butte are ghost towns such as Alder Gulch, Cable, Granite, and Philipsburg, where legends were formed and fortunes made during the gold and silver booms.

Arts and Culture

A culturally active city, Butte supports a symphony, a community arts center, and a theater company. The Mother Lode, completed in 1923 as a Masonic Temple but never occupied by Masons, has been rehabilitated and serves as southwest Montana's premier performing arts center. The Butte Symphony Orchestra programs a four-concert season featuring a choral group and soloists. Theater is presented by Orphan Girl Theater and the Mother Lode Theater. Opera productions and appearances by national touring groups and speakers are also scheduled in the city.

Butte's principal museums are related to the mining industry. The World Museum of Mining and Hell Roarin' Gulch, a popular attraction in the area, features indoor and outdoor exhibits that replicate an early mining environment. Among the indoor displays are models of mines, minerals, fire fighting equipment, a Stanley steam engine, and an electric hoist. Outdoor exhibits include a reconstructed 1900 mining camp, with a print shop, Chinese laundry, bank, drug store, millinery shop, and other authentic structures. Also featured at the museum is a tour on the Neversweat and Washoe Railroad aboard a train drawn by an M-10 locomotive; the tour starts at the museum, traveling past mines and head frames, to nearby Kelly mine. Commentary on mine history is presented. The Dumas Brothel was the longest-running establishment of its kind in America; Butte once had as many as 2,400 ladies of the evening working in town. The Mineral Museum at Montana Tech exhibits 1,300 items from its collection of more than 15,000 mineral specimens gathered from throughout the world; a highlight is a display of fluorescent minerals. The Mai Wah preserves the history of Butte's Chinese miners.

The Piccadilly Museum of Transportation houses a fascinating array of exhibits about transportation in America, from antique cars to gas pumps to road signs. The Mother Bottego House honors Celestine Mary Bottego, who spent 15 years in Butte and has been nominated for beatification. The Butte-Silver Bow W.A. Clark Chateau, a professional art gallery, mounts changing exhibits of works by local and national artists. Several private art galleries are also located in the city.

Festivals and Holidays

The W.A. Clark Chateau holds a Wine Tasting Festival in February. The Winternational Sports Festival, a multi-sport event, begins in February and continues into March, when St. Patrick's Day festivities such as a parade and the Friendly Sons of St. Patrick Banquet also take place. On March 16 the Finnish-American community gives thanks to St. Urho for chasing the grasshoppers out of Finland. Ghost Walks takes place in April at the Mining Museum. July is an event-filled month; included among the activities are the National Folk Festival, Evel Knievel Days, and the Freedom Festival parade and community picnic. An Ri Ra—the Montana Gaelic Cultural Festival—takes place each August. Mining Heritage Day happens in September. The year ends with the annual Christmas Stroll, Ice-Sculpting Contest, and Festival of Trees.

Sports for the Spectator

Butte's U.S. High Altitude Sports Center has three times been chosen as the site of the World Cup Speedskating competition. Other sporting events include state wrestling tournaments and rodeos.

Sports for the Participant

Butte has some 30 parks ranging from mini parks on lots to major parks such as Stodden and the recently built Copper Mountain Sports and Recreation Complex north of Timber Butte. Municipal parks located in Butte provide such facilities as a swimming pool, basketball courts, baseball and football fields, tennis courts, golf courses, an Olympic-sized skating rink, and running/walking tracks. Recreational areas outside the city include the Blacktail Creek and Alice Pit Walking Trails, the Red Mountain Highlands (a 10,000 foot peak), Humburg Spires rock climbing site, kayaking on Big Hole and Madison rivers, downhill skiing at Maverick Mountain and Discovery Basin, and a number of golf layouts that offer spectacular scenery in the Butte foothills. Golfers may particularly wish to visit town of Anaconda, 26 miles from Butte, where an $11 million, 200-acre golf course designed by Jack Nicklaus has been built atop the ruins of a smelting plant. Butte is surrounded by lakes, streams, and reservoirs where trout fishing, boating, and waterskiing are popular pastimes.

Shopping and Dining

Historic Uptown has several unique stores that deal in antiques, toys, and tools, and art galleries that specialize in Western art. In addition to the Butte Plaza Mall, Butte's Harrison Avenue has small shops and stores with specialties ranging from locally made crafts and gifts to sporting equipment.

More than 80 restaurants in Butte provide a variety of choices that include fast food and family dining, as well as the more formal atmosphere of supper clubs. Among the cuisines offered are Chinese, Greek, Italian, and traditional American. Local favorites include The Acoma on Broadway, Gamer's Café on Park, the Gold Rush Casino and Restaurant on Galena, and Pork Chop John's (three locations). A local specialty is pasties, which are meat pies that were originally brought to Butte by Cornish miners in the 1870s.

Visitor Information: Butte Convention and Visitors Bureau, 1000 George St., Butte MT 59701; telephone (406)723-3177; toll-free (800)735-6814; fax (406)723-1215; email chamber@buttecvb.com

■ Convention Facilities

The Butte Civic Center, accessible to about 1,300 hotel and motel rooms and bed and breakfast inns in the metropolitan area, is a prime meeting facility both in the city and in the Northwest. Located in close proximity to major population centers, the complex offers a range of facilities for large and small group functions and sporting and recreational events. Total seating capacity is approximately 7,500 people, with parking for up to 1,500 vehicles on site. Total exhibit space is 26,923 square feet.

Meeting and convention accommodations are also available at the city's two major hotels. The Copper King Park Hotel features ten multipurpose meeting rooms, including a recreation area with approximately 8,000 square feet of space; a convention center providing more than 5,000 square feet; smaller rooms with seating for small groups; and a ballroom accommodating up to 1,200 participants. The Best Western features large and small meeting rooms, indoor pool, spa, and fitness center, and the Hops Bar and Casino. The Fairmont Chalets and Fairmont Hot Springs Resort offer a more relaxed, country setting outside of Butte.

Convention Information: Butte Convention and Visitors Bureau, 1000 George St., Butte MT 59701; telephone (406)723-3177; toll-free (800)735-6814; fax (406)723-1215; email chamber@buttecvb.com

■ Transportation

Approaching the City

The Bert Mooney Airport is served by Alaska Airlines, Horizon Air, Sky West, and Delta Airlines. Most flights connect in Salt Lake City or through Bozeman/Seattle. Greyhound and Intermountain lines provide bus transportation.

The principal highways into Butte are Interstate-15, running north and south, and Interstate-90, approaching from the northwest, which intersect in the city. Two state highways also serve Butte.

Traveling in the City

Butte is laid out on a grid pattern, although some streets run diagonally to follow railroad or freeway routes. Harrison Avenue is the main north-south thoroughfare. Butte Transit System provides bus service.

■ Communications

Newspapers

Butte's daily morning newspaper is *The Montana Standard*. Students at Montana Tech publish the *Technocrat*. *Butte Weekly* is a free weekly paper.

Television and Radio

In 2003 Bresnan Communications bought the rights to Butte cable television and invested several million dollars to upgrade the number of channels available and to bring high-speed Internet to Butte citizens. Viewers have access to ABC, CBS, and NBC television broadcasts. 91.3 FM is the city's Public Radio outlet. Six other AM and FM radio stations originate their signals from Butte. A number of other radio stations can be picked up from neighboring communities.

Media Information: *The Montana Standard*, 25 W. Granite St., Butte, MT 59701; telephone (406)496-5500; toll-free (800)877-1074

Butte Online

Butte Local Development Corporation. Available www.buttemontana.org

Butte Public School District #1. Available www.butte.k12.mt.us

Butte-Silver Bow Chamber of Commerce. Available www.butteinfo.org

Butte-Silver Bow Local Government. Available www.co.silverbow.mt.us

The Montana Standard. Available www.mtstandard.com

Only in Butte. History stories about Butte's past. Available www.butteamerica.com/hist.htm

BIBLIOGRAPHY

Hammett, Dashiell, *Red Harvest* (South Yarmouth, MA: J. Curley, 1983)

Morris, Patrick F., *Anaconda Montana: Copper Smelting Boomtown on the Western Frontier* (Bethesda, MD: Swann Pub., 1997)

Helena

■ The City in Brief

Founded: 1864 (chartered 1881)

Head Official: Mayor James E. Smith (I) (since 2001)

City Population

    1980: 23,938
    1990: 24,699
    2000: 25,780
    2006 estimate: 27,885
    Percent change, 1990–2000: 2.8%
    U.S. rank in 1980: Not available
    U.S. rank in 1990: Not available
    U.S. rank in 2000: Not available

Metropolitan Area Population

    1980: 43,039
    1990: 47,495
    2000: 55,716
    2006 estimate: 70,558
    Percent change, 1990–2000: 17.3%
    U.S. rank in 1980: Not available
    U.S. rank in 1990: Not available
    U.S. rank in 2000: 847th (for counties; state rank 6th)

Area: 14 square miles (2000)

Elevation: 4,090 feet above sea level

Average Annual Temperatures: January, 20.2° F; July, 67.8° F; annual average, 44.0° F

Average Annual Precipitation: 11.32 inches of rain; 46.9 inches of snow

Major Economic Sectors: services, wholesale and retail trade, government

Unemployment Rate: 5.5% (January 2005)

Per Capita Income: $20,020 (2000)

2005 FBI Crime Index Property: 1,046

2005 FBI Crime Index Violent: 99

Major Colleges and Universities: Carroll College, Helena College of Technology

Daily Newspaper: *Helena Independent Record*

■ Introduction

Helena, known as the "City of Gold," lies at the heart of the Rocky Mountains in a fertile region with rolling hills. On the outskirts of the city lies the giant Helena National Forest, which provides spectacular scenery and many opportunities for outdoor activities. Once a mining boom town, Helena is now a major social and governmental center of the American west, offering amenities not usually found in a city of its size.

■ Geography and Climate

Helena is located in west-central Montana in the foothills of the Big Belt Mountains on the eastern slope of the Continental Divide, 48 miles north-northeast of Butte, Montana. Helena is located midway between Glacier and Yellowstone national parks and fertile valleys lie to the north and east. The Missouri River flows northward nearly 10 miles east of the city.

Helena has a modified continental climate with warm, dry summers and moderately cold winters. Mountains located to the north and east of the city sometimes deflect shallow masses of arctic air to the east, but at times cold air can be trapped in the valley for days. During the coldest period, from November through February, temperatures sometimes drop to 0° F or below. Summer temperatures are usually under 90° F and the mountains account for marked changes in temperature from day to night. April through July is the rainy season, while late summer, fall, and winter are quite dry.

Area: 14 square miles (2000)

Elevation: 4,090 feet above sea level

Average Temperatures: January, 20.2° F; July, 67.8° F; annual average, 44.0° F

Average Annual Precipitation: 11.32 inches of rain; 46.9 inches of snow

■ History

Land of the Prickly Pear

Archaeological evidence shows that native Americans inhabited the valley in which greater Helena is situated more than 12,000 years ago. Although never serving as the permanent home of any particular tribe, the valley was a crossover area for Salish, Crow, Bannock, and Blackfeet tribal members.

In 1805, members of the Lewis and Clark expedition were the first white men to visit the valley. While investigating the area on foot, William Clark stepped on and had to remove 17 cactus spines from his feet. This caused him to name the nearby creek and valley Prickly Pear. In the early nineteenth century trappers came to the area, later to be pushed aside by groups of white settlers.

In 1862 a group of immigrants in a wagon train decided to build houses for the winter in Prickly Pear Valley, but this settlement proved temporary. In 1864, four ex-Confederate soldiers from Georgia discovered placer gold in Last Chance Gulch, the heart of Helena's present-day downtown. The gold strike attracted hundreds of miners eager to find riches. Over the next 20 years, 3.5 billion dollars worth of gold was discovered in the gulch. By 1888 Helena was home to more millionaires per capita than anywhere else in the world.

Early settlers considered naming their new boom town "Pumpkinville" or "Squashtown," but instead settled on the suggestion of John Somerville, who named the place after his hometown of Helena in Minnesota. The inhabitants chose to pronounce it HELL-uh-nuh, with the accent on the first syllable. Its original residents were mainly of English, Scottish, Irish, and German descent.

Becomes Territorial, Then State Capital

By 1870, Helena, with a population of 3,106 people, had become the most important town in the Montana Territory. Other nearby settlements turned into ghost towns after gold supplies were exhausted. But Helena's geographical location helped it become a business hub for other mining communities, such as Marysville to the west

and Rimini to the southwest. It became a vital bank, trade and farming town.

In the late 1870s the discovery of rich silver and lead deposits in nearby Wickes, Corbin, and Elkhorn further stimulated development in the area and helped Helena grow and prosper. The fact that Helena was on an important stagecoach route also spurred its growth as a hub city.

In 1875 Helena was made the capital of the Montana Territory. When Montana became a state in 1889, citizens disputed whether the capital should be Helena or Anaconda, another popular mining town. Copper rivals Marcus Daly, who supported Anaconda, and William A. Clark, who supported Helena, spent more than $3 million as each fought to have his city chosen for the honor. Helena finally won the vote in 1894. The city soon saw a tremendous amount of new construction. In time, Helena became the center of Montana political, social, and economic life. Between 1880 and 1890, the population grew from 3,624 to 13,834 people.

City Experiences Booms and Busts

By the late 1880s, wealthy Helena citizens had erected pretentious mansions and constructed a streetcar to transport them to the outskirts of town where they lived. They also drove about town, first in coaches driven by top-hatted drivers, and later in electric cars that stalled on the hills. Their Italianate, Romanesque, baroque, and Gothic-style houses featured cupolas, turrets, and hand-carved trim. The inhabitants of the mansions were served by a small army of maids and butlers.

The good times for many of the city's more than 13,000 residents continued until 1893, when the price of silver fell and many of the nouveau riche moved away. The spacious mansions were then taken over by members of the middle class who sometimes had problems paying to heat them. Many of the Mansion District homes can still be viewed today.

Like other Montana towns, Helena experienced boom-or-bust cycles. Prosperity returned once again between 1900 and 1910 when gold mining activity geared up at nearby Marysville and with the construction of the Canyon Ferry, Hauser, and Holter dams on the Missouri River, which employed a number of Helena residents. Then came a slump that lasted until the war years of 1914-1918, when once again the mines worked to meet the demand for metals during World War I. But another slump followed.

Helena in the Twentieth Century and Beyond

In the first part of the twentieth century, Helena's population showed modest growth, rising from 12,515 people in 1910 to 15,056 by 1940. This growth occurred despite several major fires and a 1935 earthquake that caused four deaths and $4 million in damages. Shocks of lesser intensity occurred in 1936 and 1937 but did no further harm.

During the mid-1930s, at the time of the Great Depression, the federal government employed hundreds of Helena citizens to repair the State Capitol and the county courthouse and to landscape a city park. New federal monetary policies increased the price of gold and silver and stimulated mining, which once again regained its importance in the life of the city.

The city's population stood at 17,581 people in 1950. During the 1960s, urban renewal changed the face of downtown Helena, and a pedestrian mall was built to attract tourists. Preservation fervor and urban renewal programs in the 1970s resulted in further downtown development. In recent decades, Montana residents have begun to truly appreciate and make efforts to preserve the beautiful terrain of their state. In 1992, the Montana House of Representatives voted to protect 1.5 million acres of Montana from development, including some local Helena area sites. In 2005, the National Trust for Historic Preservation named Helena one of America's Dozen Distinctive Destinations, recognizing the city as "unique and lovingly preserved."

Today, Helena is an attractive place that retains vintage residential and commercial structures while providing modern shops, distinctive restaurants, and entertainment centers for residents and visitors alike.

Historical Information: Montana Historical Society, PO Box 201201, 225 N. Roberts, Helena, MT, 59620-1201; telephone (406)444-2694; email mhslibrary@mt.gov

■ Population Profile

Metropolitan Area Residents

1980: 43,039
1990: 47,495
2000: 55,716
2006 estimate: 70,558
Percent change, 1990–2000: 17.3%
U.S. rank in 1980: Not available
U.S. rank in 1990: Not available
U.S. rank in 2000: 847th (for counties; state rank 6th)

City Residents

1980: 23,938
1990: 24,699
2000: 25,780
2006 estimate: 27,885
Percent change, 1990–2000: 2.8%
U.S. rank in 1980: Not available
U.S. rank in 1990: Not available
U.S. rank in 2000: Not available

Density: 1,840.7 people per square mile (2000)

Racial and ethnic characteristics (2000)

White: 24,434
Black: 59
American Indian and Alaska Native: 541
Asian: 201
Native Hawaiian and Pacific Islander: 18
Hispanic or Latino (may be of any race): 430
Other: 98

Percent of residents born in state: 55.5% (2000)

Age characteristics (2000)

Population under 5 years old: 1,501
Population 5 to 9 years old: 1,558
Population 10 to 14 years old: 1,628
Population 15 to 19 years old: 1,962
Population 20 to 24 years old: 1,999
Population 25 to 34 years old: 2,931
Population 35 to 44 years old: 3,919
Population 45 to 54 years old: 4,309
Population 55 to 59 years old: 1,414
Population 60 to 64 years old: 975
Population 65 to 74 years old: 1,640
Population 75 to 84 years old: 1,403
Population 85 years and older: 541
Median age: 38.8 years

Births (2006, Micropolitan Statistical Area)

Total number: 805

Deaths (2006, Micropolitan Statistical Area)

Total number: 597

Money income (2000)

Per capita income: $20,020
Median household income: $34,416
Total households: 11,476

Number of households with income of...

less than $10,000: 1,438
$10,000 to $14,999: 908
$15,000 to $24,999: 1,725
$25,000 to $34,999: 1,767
$35,000 to $49,999: 1,809
$50,000 to $74,999: 2,228
$75,000 to $99,999: 911
$100,000 to $149,999: 464
$150,000 to $199,999: 130
$200,000 or more: 96

Percent of families below poverty level: 12.1% (2000)

2005 FBI Crime Index Property: 1,046

2005 FBI Crime Index Violent: 99

The Montana State Capitol building in Helena. *Image copyright Alan Scheer, 2007. Used under license from Shutterstock.com.*

■ Municipal Government

Helena, the capital of Montana and the seat of Lewis and Clark County, has a city charter form of government. The mayor and four commissioners are elected to the city commission, each serving four-year terms. The daily affairs of the city are administered by a city manager, who is appointed by the commission.

Head Official: Mayor James E. Smith (since November 2001; current term expires 2009)

Total Number of City Employees: 275 (2005)

City Information: Mayor's Office, City of Helena, 316 N. Park Avenue, Helena, MT 59623; telephone (406)447-8410

■ Economy

Major Industries and Commercial Activity

For many years Helena has enjoyed a record of economic stability. It serves as a major governmental center for the county, state, and federal government. It is also a trading and transportation center for nearby livestock, mining, and farming enterprises. In an area rich in silver and lead deposits, Helena maintains an interest in mineral production and processing, and the nearby city of East Helena is the site of smelters, quartz crushers, and zinc reduction works. The Helena area is also a telephone communications center, and industries such as sand, gravel, and ranching remain important. Statewide, Montana's fastest-growing industries include education and instruction, waste management, and construction. Specific occupations showing significant growth include textile machinery operation, septic and sewer maintenance, and computer software engineering.

Government positions account for 31 percent of Helena's workforce, while private sector jobs comprise 62 percent. Many of the private businesses rely on the government and its employees as their customers.

Items and goods produced: refined and smelted metals, paints, ceramics, concrete, machine parts, baking products, sheet metal, prefabricated houses, bottled beverages

Incentive Programs—New and Existing Companies

Local programs: The Montana Business Information Center (BIC) in Helena is a one-stop center that provides a multitude of planning tools as well as free onsite counseling provided by the Service Corps of Retired Executives (SCORE), Small Business Development Center (SBDC), and other Small Business Administration resources. The Montana BIC's resources include a reference library, a video center, and a computer lab designed specifically for small business research. The Small Business Administration offers a variety of financing options for small businesses, including long-term loans for machinery and equipment, general working capital loans, revolving lines of credit, and microloans. Similarly, Gateway Economic Development Corp. offers loans and tax rebates to new or expanding businesses in Lewis and Clark County and the surrounding area. The Downtown Helena Business Improvement District offers grants up to $2,000 for retailers opening or expanding in the downtown area.

State programs: The state of Montana offers general incentives including net operating loss carry backs and carry forwards, depreciation, and dependent care assistance. New and expanding incentives include license tax credit for new or expanded jobs and reduced property assessments for research and development. Various tax exemptions are available for qualified businesses in research and development, domestic international sales corporations, free port merchandise, and business inventories.

Job training programs: The Small Business Development Center provides training, counseling, research, and other specialized assistance through its Helena office. NxLevel Entrepreneurial Training Programs, available through the Montana Department of Commerce, are in-depth training courses for entrepreneurs and business owners. NxLevel for Entrepreneurs is a 12-session course designed to help existing business owners improve growth and profits. NxLevel for Agricultural Entrepreneurs and NxLevel for Microentrepreneurs are similar programs aimed at new ventures and the self-employed.

Development Projects

Projects currently planned for Helena focus on business development, transportation, and branding. An ongoing downtown revitalization planning process has resulted in suggestions for an outdoor market, building restoration, and increased residential space. The City Commission voted to construct a new traffic lane on the Downtown Walking Mall, and to rename the road leading from the I-90 to downtown Last Chance Gulch (currently the name of the main downtown street only) to improve accessibility for tourists. Other plans call for new or upgraded freeway interchanges and improvements in water quality and availability.

Recently completed projects include the full restoration of the State Capitol building and construction of the Great Northern Town Center, a main street business and shopping district.

Economic Development Information: Small Business Administration-Montana District Office, 10 West 15th Street, Suite 1100, Helena, Montana, 59626; telephone (406)441-1081; fax (406)441-1090. Montana Finance Information Center, 301 S. Park, Helena, MT 59601; telephone (406)841-2732; fax (406)841-2771. Downtown Helena, Inc., 225 Cruse Ave., Suite B, Helena, MT 59601; telephone (406)447-1535. Montana Department of Commerce, PO Box 200501, Helena, MT 59620-0501; telephone (406)841-2700; fax (406)841-2701

Commercial Shipping

Air freight service is provided by FedEx, Airborne Express, and UPS. Freight service is also provided by Montana Rail Link, which provides national coverage in connection with Burlington Northern & Santa Fe Railway.

Labor Force and Employment Outlook

The Helena area labor force includes a high percentage of young, educated workers. The percentage of adults in the community who have received high school and college diplomas is considerably higher than the state and national averages. Helena's stable economy is based primarily on a range of government agencies and small businesses. Skills in demand include textile machinery operation, septic and sewer maintenance, and computer software engineering. In recent years, growth has been observed in the fields of education and instruction, waste management, and construction.

The following is a summary of data regarding the Helena city metropolitan area labor force, 2000 annual averages.

Size of nonagricultural labor force: 13,291

Number of workers employed in...

    construction and mining: 692
    manufacturing: 349
    trade, transportation and utilities: 1,875
    information: 583
    financial activities: 902
    professional and business services: 1,290
    educational and health services: 2,840
    leisure and hospitality: 1,282
    other services: 679
    government: 4,127

Average hourly earnings of production workers employed in manufacturing: Not available

Unemployment rate: 5.5% (January 2005)

Largest private employers	Number of employees
St. Peter's Community Hospital	565

Largest private employers	Number of employees
Blue Cross/Blue Shield	470
Veterans Administration Hospital	375
Shodair Children's Hospital	220
Qwest	210
Dick Anderson Construction	198
Carroll College	189

Cost of Living

The cost of living for Helena residents is comparable to the national average. According to the Helena Chamber of Commerce, housing, utilities, and goods and services all have lower than average cost. The cost of health care in Helena is slightly higher than the national rate.

The following is a summary of data regarding several key cost of living factors for the Helena area.

2007 (1st quarter) ACCRA Average House Price: Not available

2007 (1st quarter) ACCRA Cost of Living Index: Not available

State income tax rate: 1.0% to 6.9%

State sales tax rate: None

Local income tax rate: None

Local sales tax rate: None

Property tax rate: 647.74 mills minimum; applies to taxable value as set by the state of Montana

Economic Information: Montana Department of Commerce, Census and Economic Information Center, 301 S. Park Ave., PO Box 200505, Helena, MT 59620-0505; telephone (406)841-2740

■ Education and Research

Elementary and Secondary Schools

Helena Public Schools states that its mission is to challenge and empower each student to become a competent, productive, responsible, caring citizen. Nearly half of the teachers have a master's degree or beyond, while 42 percent have one to three years of education beyond a bachelor's degree. Students consistently score above average in national standardized testing in all academic areas.

The Helena school district enjoys one of the lowest teacher-to-pupil ratios in the state. The curriculum includes many accelerated and advanced placement courses. Nearly 60 percent of the district's graduating

seniors attend four-year colleges or universities, earning over $3 million annually in scholarships. Another 25 percent of high school graduates move on to trade school, two-year colleges or the military.

The following is a summary of data regarding the Helena Public Schools as of the 2005–2006 school year.

Total enrollment: 7,983

Number of facilities

elementary schools: 11
junior high/middle schools: 2
senior high schools: 3
other: 3

Student/teacher ratio: 15.7:1

Teacher salaries (2005–06)

elementary median: $45,789 (all levels)
junior high/middle median: Not available
secondary median: Not available

Funding per pupil: Not available

Public Schools Information: Helena Public Schools, 55 South Rodney, Helena, MT 59601; telephone (406) 324-2000; fax (406)324-2022

Colleges and Universities

Helena's Carroll College, established in 1909, is a Catholic liberal arts college with an enrollment of about 1,500. Students enjoy small classes and easy access to faculty members, and half of the students go on to graduate school. In 2005 *U.S. News & World Report* ranked Carroll among the Western region's best colleges for the 11th year in a row. Carroll College offers bachelor of arts degrees in a variety of fields, as well as eight pre-professional programs and a variety of research and internship opportunities in the capital city.

Helena College of Technology is a two-year college that is part of the University of Montana. More than 700 students receive technical education in accounting, computer science, aviation, construction, nursing, machine tooling, and other fields. The college also offers associate of science and arts degrees in general studies. Montana University also provides graduate programs and continuing education classes in Helena.

Libraries and Research Centers

The Lewis & Clark County Library's main facility is in downtown Helena and the system has three branches in nearby towns. The library contains 115,000 items, including books, periodicals, vertical files, and audio-visual tapes. Built in 1976, the library serves 50,000 patrons annually.

The Research Center of the Montana Historical Society, also in Helena, contains more than 40,000 books and pamphlets relating to Montana, 2,000 bound volumes of Montana newspapers, and more than 8,000 maps, as well as initial township plots, topographical maps, music scores, and other items. Its special collections focus on the Lewis & Clark expedition, fur trading, and General Custer and the Battle of the Little Big Horn. It also has an extensive photograph collection featuring approximately 400,000 images.

The Montana State Library is the primary facility for state government as well as for the blind, physically handicapped, and learning disabled. Its focus is on Montana's natural resources. Every Montanan is entitled to borrow from the State Library, although local libraries often borrow titles on behalf of their patrons.

Other local libraries include the college libraries of Carroll College and the Helena College of Technology, and those of St. Peter's Community and Shodair hospitals, the Montana state legislature, the Montana Department of Commerce, the Montana Natural Heritage Program, the Montana Department of Special Resources, the State Law Library, and the U.S. Geological Survey Water Resources Division Library.

Research institutions include the Montana Science Institute, which explores natural history and ecology of the Missouri River and conservation of native species, and the Nature Conservancy-Montana Chapter, which identifies rare plants and animals and works to protect rare species.

Public Library Information: Lewis & Clark County Library, 120 S. Last Chance Gulch, Helena, MT 59601; telephone (406)447-1690; fax (406)447-1687

■ Health Care

Helena citizens have the service of two local hospitals. St. Peter's Community Hospital offers comprehensive inpatient, outpatient, and home care service. The facility, founded in 1883, provides obstetrics, surgery, emergency care, a cancer treatment center, and a full range of diagnostic services. In 2004 St. Peter's began an expansion project to meet the anticipated needs of Helena's growing population. Shodair Children's Hospital provides inpatient and outpatient psychiatric services, and treatment of genetic disorders. Located just outside Helena is Fort Harrison Veterans Hospital.

Health Care Information: St. Peter's Community Hospital, 2475 Broadway, Helena, MT 59601; telephone (406)442-2480. Shodair Hospital, 2755 Colonial Drive, PO Box 5539, Helena, MT 59604; telephone (406)444-7500

■ Recreation

Sightseeing

The focal point of sightseeing in Helena is the 17-block Historic Downtown District. This part of town offers a mix of retail stores, galleries, lodging, restaurants, historic buildings, and entertainment centers. The imposing State Capital Building is constructed of Montana granite and boasts a classic dome made of radiant copper. It now serves as the symbol of Montana. The interior is decorated with murals by artists E.S. Paxon, Charles M. Russell, and others. The meeting of Lewis and Clark with a group of native Americans is depicted in a large mural by Russell.

Tours are offered of several impressive local structures. The original governor's mansion, which was built in 1888 in the Queen Anne style, contains furnishings popular during the early twentieth century. Helena Civic Center, built in 1921, is a Moorish-style edifice with a 175-foot minaret, an onion dome, and intricate exterior brickwork. Just outside Helena to the north is another impressive facility, Fort Harrison, which was once an army garrison and is now a veterans' hospital.

The Montana Historical Society Museum features the C.M. Russell painting collections, as well as temporary exhibits of western art. The Montana Homeland Exhibit portrays Montana history throughout the eras.

The imposing St. Helena Cathedral, with its white marble altar, stained-glass windows, and 230-foot spires, is modeled after famous churches in Austria and Germany. Gold nuggets, gold wire, gold coins, and gold dust are on display at the Gold collection at downtown's Norwest Bank and the Federal Reserve Bank on Neill Avenue. The Guardian of the Gulch is a landmark fire tower built in 1876 and one of just five similar towers remaining in the United States.

Dotting the hillsides on Helena's west side are dozens of stately private homes, built by rich merchants and miners a century ago. The Last Chance Tour Train provides hour-long tours of the city. A guided Missouri riverboat tour follows the path taken by Lewis and Clark nearly two centuries ago. Northeast of Helena, Canyon Ferry Dam offers information and interactive displays of the region's wildlife as well as the Lewis and Clark expedition.

Arts and Culture

A major cultural facility in Helena is the Myrna Loy Center, named after the beloved Montana-born actress. It is housed in the city's 1880s-era former jailhouse and features performing arts activities, literary events, films, and art shows. The Carroll College Theatre presents live performances throughout the year. The Toadstone Theatre Company offers professional and community childrens' theater and Grandsteet Theatre offers live performances of Broadway shows using community-based volunteers. The

Montana Shakespeare Company presents Shakespeare's classics in Performance Park Square, an outdoor venue.

Helena's Holster Museum of Art displays various works of art from historical to contemporary times. It also offers workshops, readings, and discussions. The Archie Bray Foundation for Ceramic Arts, which offers beautiful display pieces for sale, has attained a national reputation for training potters. The Ghost Art Gallery in Helena's old mining district features architecture and themes from nearby ghost towns, as well as western and wildlife art by fine local artists.

Music lovers attend performances of the Helena Symphony; in addition to a regular season of performances by its own chorale of 150 members, it offers community concerts. Four-part harmony is the focus of the Sweet Adelines Performing Chorus.

Festivals and Holidays

Downtown Helena is the site of many special events, including festivals, street dances, theater productions, sled dog races, car rallies, art exhibits, and street fairs. The annual Western Rendezvous of Art takes place in August, featuring art shows, seminars, an auction and a fixed price sale, and a gala awards banquet. Music fills the air in September during the Last Chance Bluegrass Festival, while October is enlivened by Bullfest and Oktoberfest celebrations. November brings the Bald Eagle Migration and Downtown Helena Fall Art Walk, while December hails the holidays with the Festival of Trees and Winter Fair.

The excitement of the Race to the Sky Sled Dog Race warms hearts in February, and children of all ages enjoy April's Railroad Fair and Kite Festival. The Governor's Cup Marathon and the Sleeping Giant Swing 'n Jazz Jubilee draw crowds in June, while July brings the excitement of the Last Chance Stampede & Rodeo and the Mt. Helena Music Festival.

Sports for the Spectator

Helena is the home of the Helena Brewers minor league baseball team of the Pioneer League; the Helena Bighorns hockey club, which plays NAHL hockey at the Helena Ice Arena; the Carroll College Fighting Saints; and high school teams that compete in tennis, baseball, football, soccer, hockey, golf, rugby, and basketball.

Sports for the Participant

Within easy access to Helena residents and visitors are millions of acres of public lands, top rated fisheries, and many lakes, rivers, and reservoirs that are used for boating, sailing, wind surfing, and other water sports. Also available are hunting, backpacking, biking, skiing, and snowmobiling. There are more than 25 area parks. Mount Helena City Park and Helena National Forest each have miles of hiking and biking trails. The local recreation department offers facilities for running, racquetball, weight training, and horseback riding.

Centennial Waterslide Park is a family-focused indoor facility with slides and swimming pools. Helena Skate Park offers ledges, quarter pipes, and banks with free access for skateboarders and in-line skaters. There are two public golf courses and one private golf course, numerous tennis courts, and several health clubs. Hikers on the Blackfoot Meadows or the Continental Divide trails may spot such wildlife as elk, moose, mountain goats, bighorn sheep, black bears, otters, beavers, and mink.

Shopping and Dining

Helena's largest shopping center is Capital Hill Mall, which is located near the Capital complex and contains 40 specialty shops and two major department stores. What was once the Last Chance Gulch mine is now Helena's main street and a pedestrian mall. Downtown Helena is dotted with specialty shops and galleries, especially throughout the Walking Mall and Reeders' Alley, a complex of red brick buildings from the 1870s that once served as miners' shanties. Principal shopping centers include Northgate Plaza and Lundy Center. Discount shopping can be found at WalMart, Shopko, Target, Big-K and Gibson's.

For a small city, Helena has a varied selection of ethnic dining spots that feature Mexican, Thai, Chinese, Mediterranean, French, German, Italian, and classic American cuisines. Beer lovers can sample local micro brews from the Sleeping Giant Brewery, Kessler Brewery, or Blackfoot River Brewing Company.

Visitor Information: Helena Convention & Visitor Bureau, 225 Cruse Ave., Helena, MT 59601; telephone (406)447-1530 or (800)743-5362

■ Convention Facilities

Most conferences in Helena are held at one of three facilities. The Best Western Helena Great Northern Hotel offers sleeping accommodations in 101 rooms and a convention capacity of 600 people. The Holiday Inn Helena Downtown has 71 sleeping rooms and can host up to 200 people in its newly remodeled meeting and banquet facilities. Jorgenson's Inn and Suites has 115 sleeping rooms and can accommodate up to 250 people for banquets or conventions.

Convention Information: Helena Convention & Visitors Bureau, 225 Cruse Ave., Suite A, Helena, MT 59601; telephone (406)447-1530 or (800)743-5362

■ Transportation

Approaching the City

Interstate 15 runs along the east side of Helena, northward toward Great Falls and southward toward Butte. It intersects with U.S. Highways 12/287 that run east and west and extend toward East Helena. Helena Airport is located 2.5 miles from the center of the city. SkyWest, Comair, Horizon, Northwest, and Big Sky Airlines provide 14 daily flights to the city. Bus service is provided by Rimrock Trailways, which connects with Greyhound.

Traveling in the City

The major north-south routes are U.S. 12, which is known as Montana Avenue, and North Last Chance Gulch, also known as Main Street. Neill Avenue, 6th, 9th and Lyndale are major east-west streets. Transportation is provided by door-to-door bus service and a city taxi service.

■ Communications

Newspapers and Magazines

Helena's local newspapers include the *Helena Independent Record,* a daily, and the *Adit,* a shopping weekly. Magazines published locally include *Montana Magazine,* a regional interest magazine, *The Montana Catholic,* and the *Montana* historical magazine, as well as the *Montana Stockgrower,* the *Montana Food Distributor, Trial Trends* and *U.S. Toy Collector Magazine.*

Television and Radio

One private television station broadcasts from Helena, and there is one local cable company. The city has four local FM radio stations and three AM stations. They feature adult contemporary, easy listening, country, classic rock, and news and talk formats.

Media Information: *Independent-Record,* PO Box 4249, Helena, MT 59604; telephone (406)447-4000

Helena Online

City of Helena. Available www.ci.helena.mt.us

Helena Chamber of Commerce. Available www .helenachamber.com/index.html

Helena Convention & Visitors Bureau. Available helenacvb.visitmt.com

Helena Public Schools. Available www.helena .k12.mt.us

Independent-Record. Available www.helenair.com

Lewis & Clark County Library. Available www .lewisandclarklibrary.org

Montana Business Information Center. Available www.sbaonline.sba.gov/regions/states/mt/ mtbics.html

BIBLIOGRAPHY

Evans, Nicholas, *The Horse Whisperer* (New York: Delacourte Press, 1995

Petrick, Paula Evans, *No Step Backward: Women and Family on the Rocky Mountain Mining Frontier, Helena, MT: 1865-1900* (Helena, MT: Helena Montana Historical Society Press, 1987)

Rodgers, Joni, *Crazy for Trying* (Denver, CO: Mac-Murray & Beck, 1999)

Missoula

■ The City in Brief

Founded: 1860 (incorporated 1883)

Head Official: Mayor John Engen (since 2006)

City Population

1980: Not available
1990: 42,918
2000: 57,053
2006 estimate: 64,081
Percent change, 1990–2000: 17.8%
U.S. rank in 1980: Not available
U.S. rank in 1990: Not available
U.S. rank in 2000: Not available

Metropolitan Area Population

1980: Not available
1990: Not available
2000: Not available
2006 estimate: 101,417
Percent change, 1990–2000: Not available
U.S. rank in 1980: Not available
U.S. rank in 1990: Not available
U.S. rank in 2000: 263rd (MSA)

Area: 24 square miles (2000)

Elevation: 3,210 feet above sea level

Average Annual Temperatures: January, 23.5° F; July, 66.9° F; annual average, 44.8° F

Average Annual Precipitation: 13.82 inches of rain; 46.3 inches of snow

Major Economic Sectors: services, wholesale and retail trade, government

Unemployment Rate: 5.2% (June 2007)

Per Capita Income: $17,166 (1999)

2005 FBI Crime Index Property: 3,629

2005 FBI Crime Index Violent: 254

Major Colleges and Universities: University of Montana

Daily Newspaper: *Missoulian*

■ Introduction

The birthplace of Jeannette Rankin, the first woman elected to the U.S. House of Representatives (1916), Missoula has many claims to fame. Known as the "Garden City" for its dense trees and lush green landscape, Missoula is a vibrant and friendly town. Perfect for outdoorsmen, Missoula offers much to those who cherish nature and wildlife. Indeed, the International Wildlife Film Festival, the largest animal-themed film festival in the world, is held annually at Missoula's historic Wilma Theatre. The main campus for the University of Montana, Missoula is a center of higher education. In 2006 Missoula was awarded a *Preserve America* designation based on its long-standing program in historic preservation and the broad base of community efforts dedicated to the preservation and conservation of Missoula's place in the history of Montana. Also in 2006 Missoula was named "Tree City USA" and one of the nation's "100 Best Communities for Young People."

■ Geography and Climate

Missoula is situated in a deep valley surrounded by the Bitterroot and Sapphire Mountains in western Montana. It is traversed by three rivers: the Clark Fork River, the Bitterroot River, and the Blackfoot River. The city is the namesake and center of the Glacial Lake Missoula, which caused tremendous flooding across the northwest between 15,000 and 13,000 years ago.

From December to February, temperatures average in the 20 degree range, with highs in the 30s and lows in the 10s. From June to September average monthly temperatures fall to the 50s and 60s, with highs in the 70s and 80s.

Because Missoula is located in a valley, there is a significant amount of smoke, soot, and fog during the winter months. Emissions restrictions have been placed on certain industries, and on the burning of wood in wood stoves. In recent years, the pollution problem has improved.

Area: 24 square miles (2000)

Elevation: 3,210 feet above sea level

Average Temperatures: January, 23.5° F; July, 66.9° F; annual average, 44.8° F

Average Annual Precipitation: 13.82 inches of rain; 46.3 inches of snow

■ History

"Nemissoolatakoo"
Native Americans from the Salish tribe originally inhabited the Missoula area. They called the area "Nemissoolatakoo," meaning "near the cold, chilling waters." In 1805 the Lewis and Clark expedition passed through the Missoula Valley, and 400 members of the Salish tribe met the whites south of what is now Darby, Montana. The Indians treated Lewis and Clark and their companions well, as they did later white settlers.

An Important Trading Center
In 1860 the Washington Territorial Legislature created Missoula County. C.P. Higgins and Francis Worden opened a trading post called the Hellgate Village on the Blackfoot River near the eastern edge of the Missoula Valley; this was the first white settlement in the area. Later a sawmill and a flourmill were built, which the settlers called the "Missoula Mills." The city began to grow and develop quickly when the Mullan Road connecting Fort Benton, Montana, with Walla Walla, Washington, was completed; the road passed through the Missoula Valley. The U.S. Army established Fort Missoula in 1877. In 1883 the Northern Pacific Railroad came through Missoula. These developments led to Missoula becoming an important trading center; produce and grain grown in the Bitterroot Valley could be easily transported. Businessmen A.B. Hammond, E.L. Bonner, and R.A. Eddy established the Missoula Mercantile Company in the early 1880s. On March 8, 1883, Missoula became an officially incorporated town under the territory of Montana. Missoula reincorporated when Montana became a state in 1889.

Twentieth Century Developments
In September 1893 the University of Montana opened to serve as the center of public higher education for western Montana. In 1908 Missoula became a regional headquarters for the Forest Service. That year, Missoula experienced its worst natural disaster, a flood that washed away the Higgins Avenue Bridge, which had first been built in 1873.

Missoula is the birthplace of Jeannette Rankin, the first woman elected (in 1916) to the U.S. House of Representatives. Rankin was the only member of Congress to vote against U.S. entry into World War II and only one of 50 to vote against U.S. entry into World War I. A lifelong pacifist, she later led resistance to the Vietnam War.

In 1954, President Dwight D. Eisenhower dedicated the Aerial Fire Depot. Big industry came to Missoula in 1956, with the groundbreaking for the first pulp mill. Logging became a major industry, with log yards throughout the city. Many ran teepee burners to dispose of waste material, creating the smoky haze that sometimes covered the city. However, by the early 1990s changes in the economic fortunes in the city had shut down all the Missoula log yards.

In 1996, Missoula adopted a charter form of government; the charter went into effect in 1997. Missoula has a thriving tourism industry based on outdoor activities, such as hunting, fishing, and skiing. Missoula is located within the so-called fly-fishing "Golden Triangle" and is a popular area for hunting mule deer, elk, bear, moose, and other game animals.

Historical Information: Historical Museum of Fort Missoula, Building 322, Fort Missoula, Missoula, MT 59804; telephone (406)728-3476; fax (406)543-6277; e-mail ftmslamuseum@montana.com

■ Population Profile

Metropolitan Area Residents

1980: Not available
1990: Not available
2000: Not available
2006 estimate: 101,417
Percent change, 1990–2000: Not available
U.S. rank in 1980: Not available
U.S. rank in 1990: Not available
U.S. rank in 2000: 263rd (MSA)

City Residents

1980: Not available
1990: 42,918
2000: 57,053
2006 estimate: 64,081
Percent change, 1990–2000: 17.8%

Dariusz Janczewski/BigStockPhoto.com

U.S. rank in 1980: Not available
U.S. rank in 1990: Not available
U.S. rank in 2000: Not available

Density: 2,397 people per square mile (2000)

Racial and ethnic characteristics (2000)

White: 53,387
Black: 207
American Indian and Alaska Native: 1,341
Asian: 703
Native Hawaiian and Pacific Islander: 57
Hispanic or Latino (may be of any race): 1,004
Other: 290

Percent of residents born in state: 48.9% (2006)

Age characteristics (2000)

Population under 5 years old: 3,043
Population 5 to 9 years old: 3,049
Population 10 to 14 years old: 3,162
Population 15 to 19 years old: 4,994
Population 20 to 24 years old: 8,833
Population 25 to 34 years old: 8,947
Population 35 to 44 years old: 7,832

Population 45 to 54 years old: 7,494
Population 55 to 59 years old: 2,213
Population 60 to 64 years old: 1,564
Population 65 to 74 years old: 2,703
Population 75 to 84 years old: 2,334
Population 85 years and older: 885
Median age: 30.3 years

Births (2006, Missoula County)

Total number: 1,216

Deaths (2006, Missoula County)

Total number: 658

Money income (1999)

Per capita income: $17,166
Median household income: $30,366
Total households: 24,014

Number of households with income of . . .

less than $10,000: 3,492
$10,000 to $14,999: 2,338
$15,000 to $24,999: 4,353
$25,000 to $34,999: 3,518

$35,000 to $49,999: 3,512
$50,000 to $74,999: 3,833
$75,000 to $99,999: 1,569
$100,000 to $149,999: 976
$150,000 to $199,999: 197
$200,000 or more: 226

Percent of families below poverty level: 11.7% (1999)

2005 FBI Crime Index Property: 3,629

2005 FBI Crime Index Violent: 254

■ Municipal Government

Missoula's mayor and city council are elected on a nonpartisan basis. There are 12 city council members. Each council member is elected in odd-numbered years for staggered four-year terms. The mayor serves a term of four years.

Head Official: Mayor John Engen (since 2006; current term expires 2010)

Total Number of City Employees: approximately 500 (2007)

City Information: City Hall, 435 Ryman, Missoula, MT 59802; telephone (406)552-6000

■ Economy

Major Industries and Commercial Activity

Industries that support Missoula include: wood products, government, medical, education, small business, and tourism. Missoula has long relied upon its lumber industry for its economic well-being. However, lumber mills in Missoula have had to implement curtailments and closures in the 21st century. Plywood plants in particular have had to close operations in response to burgeoning competition from a product called oriented strand board, or OSB. As a result of the decline in the nation's housing market in the mid-2000s, housing starts fell 12 percent through 2006 and were expected to fall an additional 15 percent by the end of 2007, to about 1.5 million units. That caused a substantial decline in lumber and plywood prices—15 to 25 percent depending on the grade or species of lumber.

Tourism, the arts, and education are important industries for Missoula. Seasonal tourism in the summer months increases revenue. In 2007 it was reported that Missoula's nonprofit arts and culture industry generated $34 million in economic activity annually, including 1,174 full-time equivalent jobs. Missoula benefits from the growth of the University of Montana, both economically and culturally. Nearly 70 percent of all of the university's graduates find jobs in Montana. The

University of Montana alone accounts for 11 percent of Missoula County's economy.

Missoula encourages sustainable development. Individuals, businesses, and organizations in the Missoula area aware of their relationship to the environment are utilizing sustainable business practices.

The largest employers in Missoula in 2007 were the Community Medical Center, Plum Creek Timber, St. Patrick's Hospital, the University of Montana, Montana Rail Link, Nightingale Nursing, and Southgate Mall.

Items and goods produced: lumber, plywood, wood panels, food

Incentive Programs—New and Existing Companies

Local programs: The Missoula Area Economic Development Corporation (MAEDC) provides three loan fund programs for job creation and business retention. Loans can range from $20,000 to $400,000. MAEDC works on business recruitment and relocation, and can provide demographic and statistical area information. Other financing options are a Community Reinvestment Fund and a Community Development Block Grant.

State programs: State of Montana tax incentives include property tax reduction; no inventory, use, or sales tax; new industry income tax credits; small business investment tax credits; and tax reduction on pollution control equipment. In 2003 the Montana legislature created the Certified Regional Development Corporations (CRDC) program in the Montana Department of Commerce. The CRDC program is designed to encourage a regional approach to economic development. State law also provides for the creation of a tax increment financing (TIF) industrial district for industrial development projects. A local government can issue bonds for a wide variety of development purposes, such as financing land acquisition, industrial infrastructure, rail spurs, buildings, and personal property related to the public improvements.

Job training programs: The Missoula Workforce Center provides assistance to job seekers, from resume reviews to mock interviews and other resources. The Workforce Center also has recruitment and selection services, comprehensive applicant testing capabilities, and interviewing facilities to offer employers the tools they need to attract and retain a superior workforce. Business consultants offer services that enable employers to stay abreast of changing regulatory issues, in order to avoid potential employer-related liability, and assist with management and employee training needs. Montana's JobLINC is the statewide coordination and collaboration of employment and training organizations, workforce development organizations, and other community service providers. Some of the organizations involved with JobLINC are workforce services divisions, local job service workforce centers, Chambers of Commerce, educational entities, economic development corporations, offices of public assistance, rural employment opportunities, human resource development councils, vocational rehabilitation, and other community-based organizations.

Development Projects

In 2007 improvements were being made to the Technology District of the Missoula Development Park. The Missoula Development Park is located on 446 acres between Interstate 90 and the airport. It has a Special Zoning District, which accommodates hotel/conference centers, restaurants, convenience and specialty stores, gas stations, banks, cultural centers, research and development technical training facilities and business and technology parks, warehouses, manufacturing, parks, and trails. The Missoula Development Park is located within two Tax Increment Financing districts, one industrial and one for technology.

In 2007 the Missoula Area Chamber of Commerce was undertaking a study of the potential economic impact of the proposed Bitterroot Resort, which would be a ski area and four-season resort including Lolo Peak and the 2,900-acre Maclay & Son Ranch.

Economic Development Information: Missoula Area Chamber of Commerce, 825 E. Front St., Missoula, MT 59802; telephone (406)543-6623; fax (406)543-6625

Commercial Shipping

Common carriers use Interstate 90, U.S. Highway 10/93, and Montana State Highway 200 to access Missoula. Missoula International Airport (Johnson-Bell Field) provides service for cargo operations.

Labor Force and Employment Outlook

Missoula is a university town and it provides employers with a high-quality workforce. The civilian labor force in Missoula in September 2007 was 61,400. Approximately 1,300 workers were unemployed, for an unemployment rate of 2.1 percent, well below the national average of 4.7 percent. Missoula has seen a steady increase in wages since 1999, with an increase of more than 4 percent each year from 2002–2005. The major industry subsectors are retail trade, health care and social assistance; local, state, and federal government; and educational services. Other major subsectors include transportation and construction. The fastest growing subsectors of the economy in recent years have included mining, utilities, finance and insurance, and real estate rental and leasing.

The following is a summary of data regarding the Missoula metropolitan area labor force, 2006 annual averages.

Size of nonagricultural labor force: 57,000

Number of workers employed in . . .

  construction and mining: Not available

  manufacturing: Not available

  trade, transportation and utilities: 12,700

  information: Not available

  financial activities: Not available

  professional and business services: 5,100

  educational and health services: 8,400

  leisure and hospitality: 7,300

  other services: Not available

  government: 10,700

Average hourly earnings of production workers employed in manufacturing: Not available

Unemployment rate: 5.2% (June 2007)

Largest employers (2007)	*Number of employees*
Community Medical Center	1,000+
Missoula County Public Schools	1,000+
Plum Creek Timber	1,000+
St. Patrick Hospital	1,000+
University of Montana	1,000+
Montana Rail Link	750-1,000
Nightingale Nursing	750-1,000
Southgate Mall	750-1,000

Cost of Living

The following is a summary of data regarding several key cost of living factors in the Missoula area.

2007 (1st quarter) ACCRA Average House Price: $309,018

2007 (1st quarter) ACCRA Cost of Living Index: 102.5

State income tax rate: 1.0% to 6.9%

State sales tax rate: None

Local income tax rate: None

Local sales tax rate: None

Property tax rate: 1.3%

Economic Information: Office of Research & Analysis, Montana Department of Labor & Industry, PO Box 1728, Helena, MT 59624; telephone (406)444-2430; toll-free (800)541-3904; fax (406)444-2638

■ Education and Research

Elementary and Secondary Schools

Missoula County Public Schools (MCPS) serves 8,600 students in 17 schools in Missoula. The district also provides preschool programs and adult and continuing education. MCPS offers an innovative, multi-disciplinary curriculum that is research-based and reflects the needs of all students. MCPS provides challenging programs to assist students with special needs and talents. These include agriculture education, bilingual education programs, a deaf education program, fine arts programs, gifted education programs, Indian education programs, special education programs, and Title I programs.

The following is a summary of data regarding the Missoula County Public Schools as of the 2005–2006 school year.

Total enrollment: 8,600

Number of facilities

    elementary schools: 9
    junior high/middle schools: 3
    senior high schools: 5
    other: 0

Student/teacher ratio: 16.2:1

Teacher salaries (2005–06)

    elementary median: $27,240
    junior high/middle median: $33,780
    secondary median: $41,160

Funding per pupil: $6,844

There are two private schools in Missoula: Valley Christian School and Loyola Sacred Heart High School.

Public Schools Information: Missoula County Public Schools, 215 South Sixth West, Missoula, MT 59801; telephone (406)728-2400

Colleges and Universities

Missoula is home to the University of Montana, which was founded in 1893. Since then students have been provided with a high-quality, well-rounded education and training for professional careers in the University's three colleges—arts and sciences, forestry and conservation, and technology—and six schools—journalism, law, business, education, pharmacy, and the fine arts. The 200-acre campus is one of the most beautiful in the nation and is home to 12,000 students.

Libraries and Research Centers

Since 1894, the Missoula Public Library has been working to provide programs, materials, and services to meet the informational, cultural, recreational, and educational needs of its patrons. As of 2007 the Missoula Public Library was in the process of expanding Internet access and electronic resources, including building a dedicated Internet Access room on the lower level. The main library and its two branches cooperate with other libraries, educational institutions, and agencies to gain information resources for residents within its

service area. The library's collection numbers 230,000 items.

Public Library Information: Missoula Public Library, 301 E. Main St, Missoula, MT 59802; telephone (406)721-2665; email mslaplib@missoula.lib.mt.us

■ Health Care

Missoula offers a wide range of medical services as the major medical hub between Minneapolis and Seattle. The city has over 5,200 people working in the health services industry. There are two major medical centers in Missoula: the 146-bed Community Medical Center and the 195-bed St. Patrick Hospital & Health Sciences Center.

■ Recreation

Sightseeing

The Missoula County Courthouse, designed by A.J. Gibson, Missoula's premier architect, was constructed between 1908 and 1910 and occupies an entire city block. The neoclassical sandstone block building has an integral iron-clad dome that is crowned externally by a clock tower, with clocks on all four sides. Within the tower is a two-ton bell that rings on the half hour and the hour. The courthouse is listed on the National Register of Historic Places. The Historical Museum at Fort Missoula was established by community effort in 1975 to save what remained of the original Fort Missoula and to interpret the area's history. The museum's collection includes 24,000 objects. Also for the history enthusiast, located downtown is the Higgins Block, one of Missoula's uniquely designed and preserved buildings.

One of Missoula's most cherished attractions is A Carousel for Missoula; it is one of the first fully hand-carved carousels to be built in the United States since the Great Depression. The carousel has 38 horses and two chariots. The carousel's band organ is the largest band organ in continuous use in the nation. Its 400 square wooden pipes make the music of 23 instruments and 45 musicians. In 2001 over 4,000 volunteers gathered to build a play area next to the carousel, called Dragon Hollow. The playground is complete with a three-headed dragon, numerous slides (one over 25 feet tall), musical instruments, an obstacle course, and a variety of child-created artwork. Also for young ones, the Children's Museum offers fun, interactive learning opportunities that allow children to explore their interests and abilities through play. The museum provides hands-on exhibits and weekly programs for infants through 10-year-old children.

The Forest Service Smokejumper Visitor Center gives tours that look at the methods used to train smokejumpers, highly skilled firefighters who parachute into forested areas to stop the spread of wildfires. The Montana Natural History Center has great displays on the local and regional geology, flora and fauna and provides guided tours of the Philip L. Wright Zoological Museum on the University of Montana campus. The Museum of Mountain Flying seeks to interpret and preserve the history of mountain flying in Montana and the northern Rockies. There are aircraft displays as well as interactive history displays. The Rocky Mountain Elk Foundation Elk Country Visitor Center is one of the best conservation education facilities in the Northwest. The Elk Country Visitor Center features hands-on conservation and hunting heritage exhibits for all ages. The center also includes a Lewis and Clark display, a collection of world record elk mounts, a western wildlife diorama, and a conservation theater.

Arts and Culture

The MCT Center for the Performing Arts opened in 1998. It is home to the internationally renowned Missoula Children's Theatre, which takes original musical theater productions on the road to nearly 1,100 communities around the world each year. The Wilma Theatre is a historical landmark theater built in 1921 by William Simons, who produced an early Wild West show. He named it after his wife, Edna Wilma Simons, a renowned light-opera star who performed on the Pantages vaudeville circuit. The building has as a centerpiece a 1,067-seat theater, which shows first-run films and presents live events. It also has two smaller theaters of 125 seats each, which show second-run movies.

The Missoula Art Museum (MAM) is dedicated to contemporary art. The MAM has grown from a summer arts festival to a thriving institution serving the Northwest. MAM develops and hosts approximately 25 exhibitions annually in six galleries located in its Carnegie building. MAM's exhibition programs encompass diverse media from local and international contemporary artists.

The Montana Museum of Art & Culture serves the University of Montana community and the Missoula public at large. The permanent collection, begun in 1894, now includes more than 10,000 original works. It is among the largest and oldest collections in Montana and the Rocky Mountain Northwest.

Art galleries in Missoula include the Dana Gallery, Gallery Saintonge, and Monte Dolack Gallery.

In the summer playgoers can enjoy Montana Shakespeare in the Parks, which is the only professional theater program in the state producing Shakespearean plays and the only company that offers its performances free to the public. Since its inception in 1973, Montana Shakespeare in the Parks has traveled over 400,000 miles and presented over 1,500 performances to a cumulative audience of more than half a million people. What began as an amateur 12-city tour has become a nationally known, professional company that presents an eight-week tour of 70 performances in 50 communities to approximately 30,000 people every summer throughout Montana, northern Wyoming, and eastern Idaho.

The Missoula Symphony Orchestra and Chorale was organized in 1954. Today, the orchestra puts on a five-concert season. In addition to the regular concert season, the orchestra performs a free outdoor summer concert in August in downtown Missoula, performs two youth concerts each year for 2,000 fourth grade students, performs an annual family concert, and provides educational performances in Missoula schools and in outlying communities.

Festivals and Holidays

In April the University of Montana holds its annual Buddy DeFranco Jazz Festival, which is a celebration of jazz performance and education. In May the International Wildlife Film Festival is held; it is the largest animal-themed film festival in the world.

Summertime brims with activities in Missoula. At the Missoula Saturday Market each summer, the city of Missoula closes a downtown street for a Saturday craft and food market run by local artisans. From June through August at lunchtime, Out to Lunch is a weekly performing arts festival at Caras Park on the Clark Fork river, featuring musicians and over 20 varied food vendors. Downtown Tonight takes place Thursday evenings June through August, featuring live music, food vendors, and a beverage garden. The International Choral Festival is held in July.

In September Germanfest is held. It is an annual ethnic heritage celebration that highlights Missoula's Sister City relationship with Neckargemund, one of the oldest communities in Germany. In November the annual Renaissance Arts and Crafts Fair is held. This juried arts and crafts show features some of the Northwest's best artists and craftspeople. Jewelry, photography, sculpture, weaving, wooden toys, handmade furniture, stained glass, glass beads, and pottery are displayed.

First Night Missoula is an all-day, alcohol-free celebration of the arts taking place on New Years Eve. More than 100 music, theater, dance, children's programs, and visual arts performances and activities in more than 30 venues throughout downtown Missoula, the University of Montana campus, and Southgate Mall are held from noon until midnight.

Sports for the Spectator

The Missoula Osprey is a minor league baseball team affiliated with the Arizona Diamondbacks. They play at Ogren Park at Allegiance Field. The Montana Grizzlies are the sports teams of the University of Montana. Men's teams include basketball, football, cross country, track and field, and tennis. Women's teams include basketball, tennis, soccer, volleyball, golf, cross country, and track and field.

Sports for the Participant

Recreational opportunities abound in the Missoula area; there are 50 parks, 21 health clubs, 11 golf courses, three rivers, four ski areas, and miles of hiking and biking. In addition to hiking, biking, and skiing, outdoor activities include snowmobiling and ice skating, fishing, hunting, mountain climbing, river rafting, and wildlife viewing. The millions of acres of wilderness surrounding Missoula are home to a rich variety of trees, plants, flowers, and wildlife for the nature enthusiast.

Mount Sentinel, embellished by a huge concrete letter "M," offers a great view of the area, especially the rugged Hellgate River Canyon. Trails explore the Rattlesnake Wilderness, which, nonetheless, is free of snakes. The most developed of the city's ski areas is Montana Snowbowl, 12 miles northwest, which has a good range of slopes for all abilities and boasts a summer chairlift. Marshall Mountain, seven miles east of Missoula, is geared toward the novice.

Shopping and Dining

Missoula is home to western Montana's largest indoor shopping mall, national discount and department stores, and dozens of interesting and unique downtown stores and boutiques. The downtown area is Missoula's newest and fastest growing shopping district, and is also an excellent place to dine in a number of ethnic and traditional restaurants.

Visitor Information: Missoula Convention & Visitors Bureau, 1121 E. Broadway, Number 103, Missoula, MT 59802; telephone (406)532-3250; fax (406)532-3252; toll-free (800)526-3465

■ Convention Facilities

The University of Montana's Adams Center offers 42,846 square feet of conference space and can seat 7,290 in theater- and classroom-capacity. The University Center has 37,000 square feet and 17 conference rooms; the University Center can seat 1,000 in theater-capacity and 400 in classroom-capacity.

The Doubletree Hotel Missoula Edgewater, the Hilton Garden Inn Missoula, the Holiday Inn Parkside, Ruby's Inn and Convention Center, and the Wingate Inn are some of the larger hotels and inns with both conference facilities and lodging.

Convention Information: Missoula Convention & Visitors Bureau, 1121 E. Broadway, Number 103, Missoula, MT 59802; telephone (406)532-3250; fax (406) 532-3252; toll-free (800)526-3465

■ Transportation

Approaching the City

Interstate 90, U.S. Highway 10/93, and Montana State Highway 200 intersect in Missoula.

Missoula International Airport (Johnson-Bell Field) is a primary commercial service airport with scheduled airline and air taxi service, military operations, U.S. Forest Service operations, cargo operations, and recreational flying services. Delta Airlines, Horizon, Northwest Airlines, United Express, Big Sky Airlines, and Allegiant Airlines serve the Missoula International Airport.

Buses serving Missoula are Greyhound and Rimrock Trailways.

Traveling in the City

Missoula Urban Transportation District does business as Mountain Line. Mountain Line operates regular route bus transit services within the Missoula urban area. In addition to a number of established bus stops around Missoula, a wave of the hand at any safe intersection along the bus routes will allow you to board.

■ Communications

Newspapers and Magazines

Missoulian is the city's daily newspaper. The *Missoula Independent* is western Montana's weekly alternative newspaper featuring political and arts coverage. The *Montana Kaimin* is the student daily of the University of Montana at Missoula. *Western Montana InBusiness Monthly* focuses on business news around the region.

Television and Radio

Affiliates of ABC, CBS, NBC, and PBS television broadcast in Missoula. Eleven AM and FM radio stations broadcast everything from National Public Radio, talk radio, and sports, to country, classic rock, Christian, oldies, adult contemporary, and alternative music.

Media Information: *Missoulian*, 500 S. Higgins, Missoula, MT 59807; telephone (406)523-5200; toll-free (800)366-7102; fax (406)523-5221

Missoula Online

City of Missoula home page. Available www.ci .missoula.mt.us

Missoula Area Chamber of Commerce. Available www.missoulachamber.com

Missoula Convention and Visitors Bureau. Available www.missoulacvb.org

Missoula County Public Schools. Available www .mcps.k12.mt.us/portal

Missoula Public Library. Available www
.missoulapubliclibrary.org

Missoula.com Magazine. Available www.missoula
.com

Missoulian. Available www.missoulian.com

Montana Community Development Corporation.
Available www.mtcdc.org

BIBLIOGRAPHY

Koelbel, Lenora, *Missoula the Way It Was: A Portrait of an Early Town* (Helena, MT: Gateway Print and Litho, 1972)

Wetzle, Betty, *Missoula, the Town and the People* (Helena, MT: Farcourt Press, 1987)

Nevada

The State in Brief

Nickname: Silver State

Motto: All for our country

Flower: Sagebrush

Bird: Mountain bluebird

Area: 110,560 square miles (2000; U.S. rank 7th)

Elevation: 479 feet to 13,140 feet above sea level

Climate: Semi-arid, with temperatures that vary with altitude as well as season; extremely cold winters in the north and west, ovenlike summer heat in parts of the south

Admitted to Union: October 31, 1864

Capital: Carson City

Head Official: Governor Jim Gibbons (R) (until 2010)

Population

    1980: 800,493
    1990: 1,201,833
    2000: 1,998,257
    2006 estimate: 2,495,529
    Percent change, 1990–2000: 66.3%
    U.S. rank in 2006: 35th
    Percent of residents born in state: 23.06% (2006)
    Density: 22.0 people per square mile (2006)
    2006 FBI Crime Index Total: 120,544

Racial and Ethnic Characteristics (2006)

    White: 1,837,860
    Black or African American: 183,064
    American Indian and Alaska Native: 30,413
    Asian: 147,363
    Native Hawaiian and Pacific Islander: 11,169
    Hispanic or Latino (may be of any race): 610,051
    Other: 206,079

Age Characteristics (2006)

    Population under 5 years old: 183,437
    Population 5 to 19 years old: 509,972
    Percent of population 65 years and over: 11.0%
    Median age: 35.6

Vital Statistics

    Total number of births (2006): 37,290
    Total number of deaths (2006): 18,974
    AIDS cases reported through 2005: 5,481

Economy

    Major industries: Services; finance, insurance, and real estate; trade; government
    Unemployment rate (2006): 5.2%
    Per capita income (2006): $26,340
    Median household income (2006): $52,998
    Percentage of persons below poverty level (2006): 10.3%
    Income tax rate: None
    Sales tax rate: 6.5%

Carson City

■ The City in Brief

Founded: 1858 (incorporated 1875)

Head Official: Mayor Marv Teixeira (R) (since 2005)

City Population

    1980: 32,022
    1990: 40,443
    2000: 42,457
    2006 estimate: 55,289
    Percent change, 1990–2000: 29.7%
    U.S. rank in 1980: Not available
    U.S. rank in 1990: Not available
    U.S. rank in 2000: 680th (State rank: 9th)

Metropolitan Area Population

    1980: 32,022
    1990: 40,443
    2000: 52,457
    2006 estimate: 55,289
    Percent change, 1990–2000: 29.7%
    U.S. rank in 1980: Not available
    U.S. rank in 1990: Not available
    U.S. rank in 2000: 680th (State rank: 9th)

Area: 155.66 square miles (2000)

Elevation: 4,600 feet above sea level

Average Annual Temperatures: January, 33.6° F; July, 69.9° F

Average Annual Precipitation: 11.8 inches of rain, 22 inches of snow

Major Economic Sectors: services, wholesale and retail trade, government

Unemployment Rate: 5.0% (June 2007)

Per Capita Income: $20,943 (1999)

2005 FBI Crime Index Property: Not available

2005 FBI Crime Index Violent: Not available

Major Colleges and Universities: Western Nevada Community College

Daily Newspaper: *The Nevada Appeal–Carson City Edition*

■ Introduction

Carson City, Nevada's state capital, is also a year-round vacation destination offering a wide variety of recreational activities. Long called the "hub of the Sierras," the city's distinct character was molded by the industries that dominated the area in the late 1800s—logging, mining, and the railroad. Carson City is now mainly a center of government, but entertainment, shopping, skiing, golf, and fishing keep the thriving capital alive with a sense of its own unique culture, charm, and Wild West adventure. In recent times, the city has seen a migration of people seeking an improved quality of life, many of them from California. Today, the city boasts a beautiful historic district amid an actively growing business environment that provides ample opportunities for companies and workers alike. Lively casinos continue to flourish and complement the small-town feel of the community.

■ Geography and Climate

Carson City is located in northwestern Nevada in the foothills of the Sierra Nevada range. It lies 30 miles south of Reno, Nevada in the Carson River Valley near Lake Tahoe, which is 14 miles to the west. Carson City includes an area that stretches across the Carson Range of the Sierra Mountains to Eagle Valley and the Pine Nut Mountains. It is bordered on the north by Washoe and

Storey counties, and on the west by the state of California.

Carson City has a pleasant, semi-desert climate, and boasts an average of over 260 sunny days annually. Summers are warm and dry with peak temperatures reaching into the 90° F range, while temperatures can drop into the 50° F range during the evenings. Winters are cold and dry with snow, but not in the amounts of nearby areas that are at a much higher elevation. The temperatures range from the high teens to the 40° F range. Annual snowfall in the city averages about 22 inches.

Area: 155.66 square miles (2000)

Elevation: 4,600 feet above sea level

Average Temperatures: January, 33.6° F; July, 69.9° F

Average Annual Precipitation: 11.8 inches of rain, 22 inches of snow

■ History

Gold Leads the Way

For nearly 4,000 years before the coming of white settlers, the Washoe Indians occupied the land along the Sierra Nevada Mountain Range that borders Nevada and California. In 1851 a group of prospectors decided to look for gold in the area that is now Carson City. Unsuccessful in that attempt, they opened up a trading post called Eagle Station on the Overland Stagecoach route. It was used by wagon trains of people moving westward. The surrounding area came to be called Eagle Ranch, and the surrounding meadows as Eagle Valley. In time, a number of scattered settlements grew up in the area and the Eagle Ranch became its social center.

As a growing number of white settlers came to the area and began to develop the valleys and mountains of the Sierra Nevada, the Washoe people who for so long had occupied the area were overwhelmed. Although lands were allotted to individual Indians by the federal government starting in the 1880s, they did not offer sufficient water. As a result, the Washoe tended to set up camp at the edges of white settlements and ranches in order to work for food. It would not be until the twentieth century that parcels of reservation land were established for them.

Many of the earliest settlers in the Carson City area were Mormons led to Eagle Valley by Colonel John Reese. When the Mormons were summoned to Salt Lake City, Utah, by their leader, Brigham Young, many sold their land for a small amount to area resident John Mankin, who later laid claim to the entire Eagle Valley. In time he subdivided the land and sold tracts of it.

Birth of Carson City

In 1858, an ambitious New Yorker named Abraham Curry, along with three partners, bought most of Eagle Valley, including the ranch and trading post. Curry was correct in his prophecy that the western part of Utah Territory was soon to become a state, and he had the present-day site of Carson City surveyed. He promoted Eagle Valley, a fertile though rather deserted place, as the site of the future state capital.

Soon Major William M. Ormsby also became an enthusiastic promoter of a town that did not yet exist. He named it in honor of legendary mountain man Kit Carson, whose name was also borne by a nearby river. The town was laid out with wide streets and had a four-square city area that he named Capitol Square, but that later came to be called the Plaza.

In 1859 the rich Comstock Lode (chiefly silver) was discovered mere miles from the site of Carson City, setting off a rush to the area. Curry sold his claim to the Comstock for a few thousand dollars, but those who bought it became millionaires. Still, Curry is remembered in the name of the mine, the Gould and Curry.

By 1860 the town's population stood at 500 people. Soon Abe Curry took steps to have Carson City named territorial capital. He argued that it was close to the main lines of travel in the region. On November 25, 1861, Carson City was named the permanent capital of Nevada Territory and the Ormsby County seat. A plaza was established at the site for future public buildings.

Carson Named Capital of New State

Just one year later, the population of the town had nearly doubled. The year 1862 saw Carson become a station on the Pony Express and the eastern end of a telegraph line from San Francisco. Soon the town became a freighting and supply point for many mining and ranching communities in the central and southern part of Nevada.

About this time, both Carson and the entire surrounding area were having problems with cattle rustlers, claim jumpers, and other outlaws. As a result, the legislature passed laws designed to establish order. When the new legislature could not find a site large enough to accommodate its numbers, Abe Curry offered it the use of his Warm Springs Hotel, a rather primitive building located near the Carson River. In the early days a canvas curtain was used to divide the Nevada senate from the state assembly.

In October 1864, Nevada became a state, and Carson City was chosen to serve as the state capital. By then, Curry owned a sandstone quarry, a brickyard, a saloon, and the Great Basin Hotel. When a courthouse was needed, Curry again came to the rescue. He sold his Great Basin Hotel to the State of Nevada and it was used as a courthouse and legislature building into the 1870s. Because it was two miles out of town, Curry transported the legislators in Carson's first horse-drawn streetcar.

The Early Years of a Capital City

A few years later the Warm Springs building was converted into a territorial prison and Curry became its first warden. Prison labor used local sandstone to construct many of Carson City's early buildings. In 1870, a branch of the U.S. Mint was built in Carson and Curry was appointed its first superintendent. The mint processed the rich ore found in nearby mines. In rapid succession, Curry resigned that position, lost a bid to become Nevada's lieutenant governor, and built the huge stone roundhouse and shops for the Virginia & Truckee Railroad. This became America's richest short-line railroad, connecting the Comstock mines with mills on the Carson River. In 1873 Curry died of a stroke.

During those early years, Nevada's legislative business was punctuated by fistfights, vote-buying, and other acts of political corruption. In 1872, a State Capitol building, a large square stone structure with rafters made of hewn logs, was completed. That same year saw the completion of a 52-mile railroad linking Carson City to Virginia City, and other lines were to follow. In 1880, the population stood at about 8,000 people.

As a New Century Dawned

During the last decades of the nineteenth century, Carson City experienced boom and bust cycles common to the area. With the decline of the nearby mines, the population too began to decline. Railroad traffic through Carson City came to a halt when the Southern Pacific Railroad built a branch rail line that bypassed the city. That, and the departure of the rootless, restless miners, resulted in Carson City's settling down into a quiet community. In the late 1800s Carson City became home to the Stewart Indian School, which educated thousands of native American children between 1890 and 1980, teaching them English and the ways of the white people.

In 1897, Carson City became the focus of worldwide attention when it became the site of a world heavyweight championship fight in which Britain Bob Fitzsimmons won over "Gentleman Jim" Corbett. A motion picture of the fight, the first of its kind, thrilled audiences, despite its bluish tint and flickering images. But soon after, between 1890 and 1900, the population of Carson City dropped from nearly 4,000 to just over 2,000 people.

Carson City in the Twentieth Century

Carson City's fortunes gradually declined through World War I and with the coming of the worldwide economic downturn known as the Great Depression. By 1930, the population had declined to only about 1,500 citizens, a quarter of what it had been 50 years earlier. Then in 1931 state legislation was enacted that permitted gambling in the area and provided for speedy divorce and simple marriage procedures. These moves brought more tourists into the area.

Soon the population began to grow again, reaching 2,478 in 1940, doubling to 5,163 by 1960, then tripling that figure by 1970, when the population stood at 15,468 people. In 1969, Ormsby County was merged with Carson City, and government services were consolidated. The population doubled again in 1980 to 32,022, then jumped by 20,000 more in 2000.

Today, as the site of a state prison, the Nevada Gaming Commission, and a variety of state department headquarters and federal agencies, the small city is economically thriving and serves as the power center of Nevada. The business climate is diverse, expansive and driven by a highly educated workforce and prime open land for future development. Pleasant weather conditions throughout the year draw visitors to outdoor activities in addition to the wide array of entertainment options, and Carson City has been rated among the most pleasant small metropolitan areas in which to live.

Historical Information: Nevada State Library and Archives, 716 N. Carson Street, Suite B, Carson City, NV 89701; telephone (775)687-8393; fax (775)684-5446; email nslref@clan.lib.nv.us. State of Nevada, Department of Cultural Affairs, Division of Museums and History Office, 716 N. Carson Street, Suite B, Carson City, NV 89701; telephone (775)687-8393; fax (775)684-5446; email lmlibby@clan.lib.nv.us

■ Population Profile

Metropolitan Area Residents

1980: 32,022
1990: 40,443
2000: 52,457
2006 estimate: 55,289
Percent change, 1990–2000: 29.7%
U.S. rank in 1980: Not available
U.S. rank in 1990: Not available
U.S. rank in 2000: 680th (State rank: 9th)

City Residents

1980: 32,022
1990: 40,443
2000: 42,457
2006 estimate: 55,289
Percent change, 1990–2000: 29.7%
U.S. rank in 1980: Not available
U.S. rank in 1990: Not available
U.S. rank in 2000: 680th (State rank: 9th)

Density: 365.9 people per square mile (2000)

Racial and ethnic characteristics (2000)
White: 44,744

AP Images

Black: 946
American Indian and Alaska Native: 1,259
Asian: 930
Native Hawaiian and Pacific Islander: 76
Hispanic or Latino (may be of any race): 7,466
Other: 3,391

Percent of residents born in state: 23.8% (2000)

Age characteristics (2000)

Population under 5 years old: 3,289
Population 5 to 9 years old: 3,495
Population 10 to 14 years old: 3,473
Population 15 to 19 years old: 3,196
Population 20 to 24 years old: 2,946
Population 25 to 34 years old: 6,766
Population 35 to 44 years old: 8,370
Population 45 to 54 years old: 7,724
Population 55 to 59 years old: 2,949
Population 60 to 64 years old: 2,412
Population 65 to 74 years old: 4,096
Population 75 to 84 years old: 2,950
Population 85 years and older: 791
Median age: 38.8 years

Births (2006, County)

Total number: 751

Deaths (2006, County)

Total number: 710

Money income (1999)

Per capita income: $20,943
Median household income: $41,809
Total households: 20,237

Number of households with income of...

less than $10,000: 554
$10,000 to $14,999: 499
$15,000 to $24,999: 1,473
$25,000 to $34,999: 1,689
$35,000 to $49,999: 2,560
$50,000 to $74,999: 3,299
$75,000 to $99,999: 1,728
$100,000 to $149,999: 1,129
$150,000 to $199,999: 257
$200,000 or more: 245

Percent of families below poverty level: 6.9% (1999)

2005 FBI Crime Index Property: Not available

2005 FBI Crime Index Violent: Not available

■ Municipal Government

The city and county of Carson, Nevada, have been co-extensive since 1969, when the city merged with what was formerly Ormsby County to form a consolidated municipality. The city is governed by a council-manager form of government. Carson City has a mayor and a four-member board of supervisors, all elected to serve over-lapping four-year terms. An appointed city manager performs administrative functions for the city's board of supervisors and oversees city staff and departments.

Head Official: Mayor Marv Teixeira (R) (since 2005; current term expires 2008)

Total Number of City Employees: 830 (2007)

City Information: City Hall, Carson City, 201 N. Carson St., Suite 1, Carson City, NV 89701; telephone (775)887-2100; fax (775)887-2286

■ Economy

Major Industries and Commercial Activity

Carson City has a growing and diverse economy, with a population that increased by 64 percent between 1980 and 2000. It is the regional retail and commercial center for northwestern Nevada, which is devoted to irrigated farming, livestock raising, and mining of silver and other minerals. It draws from a trade area of about a quarter of a million people, with 15 percent of the city's employees working in the manufacturing industry, compared to the state average of just 4 percent.

Since gambling was legalized in 1931, tourism has also been important to the Carson City economy, and the resort city is drawing increasingly more visitors to its casinos and hot springs. The service industry is by far the largest in the city, representing 30 percent of the local workforce, which includes hotel, gaming, and tourism workers. In an effort to bolster the arts sector alongside tourism, the Carson City Arts and Culture Coalition (CCACC) provides advocacy for arts with the explicit goal of becoming the region's cultural hub.

As the seat of state government, which meets in the city for two months every two years, and a center for federal government, the government sector accounts for 53 percent of the contributory earnings of Carson City's economy. The state of Nevada is the area's largest employer, the Carson City School District the second, and the City of Carson City is the fourth-largest.

The cost of doing business in Carson City is about 10 percent less than in Nevada's larger metropolitan areas, and land and labor costs are also lower. Carson City serves as one of the health care hubs for the region, providing hospitals and multispecialty clinics.

Items and goods produced: calculators and computers, refurbished aircraft turbines, retail display furniture, plastic moldings, plumbing supplies, fiberglass light poles, aerospace components, and welding accessories

Incentive Programs—New and Existing Companies

Local programs: Carson City is able to save employers time and money through the major project review process, and a local one-stop shop that issues building permits. Additionally, new and expanding businesses can defer sales and use taxes interest free for up to five years on certain capital goods purchased. Both Nevada and Carson City rely largely on having very few taxes to make its cities very competitive in business. In addition, accessible government, a thriving business climate, and sensible regulations also draw business.

State programs: The State of Nevada administers Small Business Administration loans. The Nevada Development Capital Corporation (NDCC) provides more than $3 million from Nevada banks, utilities, and mining companies and other firms to help finance growth opportunities for new and existing businesses. It provides flexible financing to small Nevada businesses that do not qualify for more conventional financing. The state has no personal state income tax, no unitary tax, no corporate income tax, no inventory tax, no estate and/or gift tax, no franchise tax, no inheritance tax, and no special intangible tax.

The Nevada Revolving Loan Fund (NRLF) offers loans of up to $100,000 to for-profit businesses in need of gap financing to complete business projects. The Nevada Industrial Development Revenue Bond Program makes loans available to qualified manufacturers who are buying land, building new facilities, and purchasing new equipment. It creates an estimated 4,000 new jobs annually statewide.The Micro Enterprise Loan Fund works with the Community Business Resource Center (CBRC) to help provide economic self-sufficiency for entrepreneurs through training, technical assistance, and access to credit.

Job training programs: Western Nevada Community College works closely with area businesses in providing specialized training courses for employees. Nevada's "Train Employees Now" (TEN) program has customized industrial training programs to assist new and expanding businesses in training new or potential employees. Eligible businesses contribute 25 percent of the total training costs. Working to ensure that companies have an adequate workforce is Job Opportunities in Nevada (JOIN), which offers training and educational opportunities for job seekers; Nevadaworks assists employers in developing employees' skills. Manufacturers Assistance Partnership (MAP) is an industrial outreach program affiliated with local community colleges and is dedicated to training employees to meet the hiring goals of specific companies.

Development Projects

In 2003 the city held a groundbreaking for the new Carson City Freeway that was intended to provide another north-south option for local travelers. It was estimated that the challenging and long-discussed project would cost over $70 million by its full completion in late 2010; the 4.8-mile northern half opened in 2006.

In 2005 work began on the restoration and expansion of the historic Virginia and Truckee Railroad Line, and the Nevada Department of Transportation awarded a $3.8 million contract to extend the railroad south from Gold Hill. Work on the $30 million first leg of the project was expected to be complete by 2009, with long-term plans calling for 20 years of work on the railroad. It was hoped that the completed railway would be a tourist attraction drawing 140,000 visitors per year and bringing 885 new jobs to the area.

Also in 2005 the Carson City Board of Supervisors approved a "Master Plan" for the city, which called for a new focus on better utilization of land through vertical development of properties and mixed-use developments, and also included plans to create a historic retail zoning district. Plans extending into the 2010s called for an overhaul of a new Parks, Recreation and Trails project. In 2005 the Casino Fandango announced plans for a $60 million expansion that could include a hotel with up to 200 rooms, but completion dates for the project were not finalized.

Economic Development Information: Carson City Economic Development, 201 North Carson Street, Carson City, NV 89701; phone (775)887-2101; fax (775) 887-2286; email information@carsoncityecondev.com

Commercial Shipping

With a strategic location on three major highway corridors, including Interstate 80, more than 60 local, regional, and national carriers provide trucking services in nearby Reno. Shipments from Carson City are able to reach nine western states on a next-day basis. The Union Pacific Railroad provides regional freight service through Reno.

Labor Force and Employment Outlook

Nevada and Carson City's abundant availability of skilled workers and the area's moderate salaries have made the area attractive to new businesses. A 2007 projection showed that the Carson City population was expected to grow to 63,515, or an influx of around 100 new workers per month, by the year 2010. Despite the rapid growth of the region, the cost of living was expected to remain fairly reasonable. Nineteen percent of the local residents hold college degrees, and 82 percent have earned high school diplomas.

In August 2007 the unemployment rate in Carson City stood at 5.1 percent, reflecting a drastic decrease since the 1997 rate of over 9 percent but remaining in line with the general unemployment trend of the region since 2002. Despite the strong manufacturing base in Carson City, analysts in 2007 did not expect to see growth in that sector, in keeping with the national trend of slowed maufacturing. Growth in Carson City was expected to come from the tourism and government sectors, with low Nevada taxes continuing to attract new businesses and spur continued population increases. In particular, the announced expansion of Casino Fandango was interpreted as a strong indicator for the continued growth of the gambling and tourism industries.

The following is a summary of data regarding the Carson City metropolitan area labor force, 2006 annual averages.

Size of nonagricultural labor force: 32,800

Number of workers employed in . . .

construction and mining: Not available
manufacturing: 3,200
trade, transportation and utilities: 4,700
information: Not available
financial activities: Not available
professional and business services: 2,400
educational and health services: Not available
leisure and hospitality: 4,000
other services: Not available
government: 11,200

Average hourly earnings of production workers employed in manufacturing: Not available

Unemployment rate: 5.0% (June 2007)

Largest employers (2006)	*Number of employees*
State of Nevada	5,000–5,499
Carson City School District	1,000–1,499
Carson-Tahoe Hospital	800–899
City of Carson City	700–799
Nevada Department of Transportation	700–799
Western Nevada Community College	500–599
Carson City Nugget	500–599
Casino Fandango	400–499

Chromalloy Nevada	300–399
Legislative Counsel	
Bureau	300–399

Cost of Living

The following is a summary of data regarding several key cost of living factors for the Carson City area.

2007 (1st quarter) ACCRA Average House Price: Not available

2007 (1st quarter) ACCRA Cost of Living Index: Not available

State income tax rate: None

State sales tax rate: 6.5%

Local income tax rate: None

Local sales tax rate: None

Property tax rate: $2.63 per $100 assessed value

Economic Information: Carson City Area Chamber of Commerce, 1900 S. Carson St., Carson City, NV 89701; telephone (775)882-1565; fax (775)882-4179; email ccchamber@carsoncitychamber.com. Nevada Department of Business & Industry, Office of the Labor Commissioner, 675 Fairview Dr., Ste. 226, Carson City, NV 89701; telephone (775)687-4850; fax (775)687-6409

■ Education and Research

Elementary and Secondary Schools

Carson High School is one of the top-rated schools in Nevada. Since 1999 it has shared a $5 million joint-use project—the Jim Randolph High-tech Center—with Western Nevada Community College. It assists students in preparing for careers in electronics, automated technology, drafting, business, and allied health.

The following is a summary of data regarding the Carson City School District as of the 2005–2006 school year.

Total enrollment: 9,613

Number of facilities

    elementary schools: 6
    junior high/middle schools: 2
    senior high schools: 3
    other: 1

Student/teacher ratio: 18.6:1

Teacher salaries (2005–06)

    elementary median: $26,220–$51,242 (all levels)

    junior high/middle median: Not available
    secondary median: Not available

Funding per pupil: $6,953

Five schools provide private, religion-based education in the city.

Public Schools Information: Carson City Schools, 1402 W. King St., Carson City, NV 89703; telephone (775)283-2110; fax (775)283-2092

Colleges and Universities

Western Nevada Community College is a two-year public institution that offers about 50 associate degree programs, as well as basic education and job development skills programs. It enrolls more than 6,000 students at its campuses in Carson City and in Fallon and Douglas counties, totaling an 18,000-square-foot service area. The college offers diverse degree and certificate programs, schedules evening and weekend as well as daytime classes, and provides small class sizes and one-on-one counseling opportunities for students.

The University of Nevada, Reno, is located 30 miles north of Carson City and enrolls over 16,000 students per semester. It is ranked among the top 150 national research univsersities, according to the Carnegie Foundation's listing of colleges and universities, and receives more than $130 million in external grants and contracts annually.

Other area schools include Truckee Meadows Community College and Sierra Nevada College, which was named among the top 50 regional colleges and universities for entrepreneurial study in the May 2004 issue of *Entrepreneur* magazine.

Libraries and Research Centers

Carson City Library, built in 1966, offers over 116,000 volumes, 200 periodical subscriptions, and 3,200 audio tapes. The library has a collection on Nevada history and a large print section.

Western Nevada Community College opened the 34,000-square-foot Library & Student Center on its Carson City campus in January 2004. The university's total holdings number 46,000 books, 185 magazines, 12 newspaper subscriptions, over 1,000 maps, and other materials. The University of Nebraska, Reno, is a major reseach center, with strong programs in Great Basin Studies, Basque Studies, and Genomics and Proteomics. Its library holdings include the Basque Library, the Keck Earth Sciences and Mining Research Information Center, and the Nevada Inventors Database.

Other libraries in the city include the Nevada State Library & Archives, the library of the Nevada State Museum, and the Nevada Supreme Court Library.

Public Library Information: Carson City Library, 900 N. Roop St., Carson City, NV 89701; telephone (775)887-2244

■ Health Care

The Carson-Tahoe Hospital is the city's not-for-profit community hospital and largest area hospital, which employs over 200 physicians spread throughout 6 total facilties. The hospital system includes a Life Stress Center featuring in- and out-patient psychiatric and addiction services, a 24-hour emergency room that is northern Nevada's designated trauma center, state-of-the-art diagnostic facilities, nutritional counseling, wellness programs, and a cardiac care center along with a separate rehabilitation and physical therapy facility. In December 2005 the hospital opened the new Carson-Tahoe Regional Medical Center with 352,000 square feet, over double the capacity of the previous building.

Other nearby hospitals include St. Mary's Reno, Renown Health, which operates a series of hospitals throughout Northern Nevada, and Nevada Health Centers, Inc., which operates a community clinic in Carson City.

Health Care Information: Carson City Government, Health and Human Services, 900 East Long Street, Carson City, NV 89706; telephone (775)887-2190; fax (775)887-2248

■ Recreation

Sightseeing

The Carson City Chamber of Commerce provides an illustrated map with details about various local historic sites. Tours in a horse-drawn surrey are available. The Governor's Mansion, a 1909 example of classic southern Colonial design, is on the 2.5-mile Kit Carson Trail, a blue line painted on the sidewalk that takes visitors past a variety of historic sites. The route passes 60 historical homes, churches, and buildings featuring Victorian architecture. Also along the route are several museums. Visitors to the State Library and Archives Building can peruse its rich collection on Nevada history and view the original Nevada Constitution.

Historical homes that highlight the tour include the Bliss Mansion, an 1879 15-room mansion with seven marble fireplaces; the 1859 Roberts House, a Gothic revival structure that was moved to the city from its first site in Washoe City; and the 1876 Chartz House.

The silver-domed State Capitol, rebuilt during the 1970s, features portraits of Nevada governors, Nevada artifacts, and old Nevada Supreme Court and legislative chambers that are open to the public when not in use. The Federal Building, once the federal courthouse, a post office, and a state library, and now the Paul Laxalt State Office Building in honor of a popular Nevada politician, houses the state Tourism Commission.

The Nevada State Museum, inside the old Carson City U.S. mint, has displays on the history of the area, an exhibit that illustrates the process of making coins, a realistic mock underground mine, and an exhibit showing bears, bobcats, and other animals native to the area. The Fire Museum displays a century's worth of fire-related memorabilia, including goggles, helmets, hose carts, and Currier & Ives prints of New York fires. The Children's Museum of Northern Nevada offers displays and activities for the younger set, such as 25 hands-on exhibits and a walk-in kaleidoscope.

The Stewart Indian School Museum houses the Cassinelli arrowhead collection, traditional basketry, grinding rocks, Great Basin artifacts, and the Indian School collection, as well as a gift shop. The Dat-So-La-Lee House features memorabilia of the famed Nevada basket weaver of the same name. Her original baskets, worth up to $250,000 each, remain on display at the Nevada State Museum and in other museums throughout the country.

Focusing on Nevada's rich railroad heritage, the Nevada State Railroad Museum's collection contains more than 60 pieces of rolling stock, including 6 steam locomotives, and more than 50 passenger and freight cars, many of which once operated on the famous Virginia and Truckee line. The museum also contains an assortment of exhibits relating to railroading in Nevada.

A short drive from Carson City is Virginia City, site of the legendary Virginia City mining operation, which produced both gold and silver. Virginia City provides a glimpse into the days of the Old West. The booming mines there spurred the construction of quartz reduction mills along the Carson River and helped Carson City become a thriving commercial center beginning in the 1860s. Today's shops, saloons, museums, and rides on the Virginia & Truckee Railroad are fun for visitors old or young. Major sites in Virginia City include the Comstock State Fire Museum, with memorabilia from the Comstock Era; the mining and silver artifacts displayed at the MacKay Mansion; and the Territorial Enterprise, a newspaper office that gave famous writer Mark Twain his start in journalism.

Carson City draws visitors with its major gambling casinos, including Best Western Carson Station Hotel-Casino, Best Western Pinon Plaza Hotel Resort, Cactus Jack's, Carson City Nugget, the Carson Horseshoe Club, Casino Fandango, Comstock Casino, Ormsby House Hotel & Casino, Silver Dollar Casino, Slotworld, and Slotworld's Cabaret.

Arts and Culture

The King Street Gallery, a showcase of the Nevada Artists Association, displays the works of over 75 local artists. Western Nevada Community College Art Gallery features works by local and regional artists. The Great Basin Gallery features fine contemporary art from Nevada and the region.

The Proscenium Players, Nevada's second-oldest year-round theater company, present dramas and comedies at the Brewery Arts Center, which also features other performing groups. Affiliated with Western Nevada Community College, the Western Nevada Musical Theatre Company stages plays and musicals on campus.

The Carson City Symphony presents five annual classical concerts. Residents also enjoy the music of the Carson Chamber Singers, who perform occasional concerts.

Festivals and Holidays

September calls for a trip to nearby Virginia City for the annual International Camel Races. Begun as a hoax, the event is now one of the most popular in the state. Since 1997 September has also been the time for the three-day *Salsa y Salsas* family celebration with food, entertainment, and dancing. October's special events in Carson City include the Nevada Day Parade and four-day celebration, the La Ka Le'l Be Pow Wow, filled with arts, crafts, dancing, the Chili Cook-Off, and the Ghost Walk tour of homes decorated for Halloween. The December holidays are ushered in by the Silver & Snowflake Holiday Tree Lighting ceremony, which includes caroling, and the Victorian Christmas Tour of houses on the Kit Carson Trail.

March is the month for the Mother Earth Pow Wow and the Cowboy Jubilee & Poetry Evening, which features cowboy poets and barbecues. March also features a traditional St. Patrick's Day parade. April brings the Eagle Valley Muzzle Loaders Spring Rendezvous. June's big events are the Downtown A-Fair, and the Stewart Indian Museum Pow Wow, as well as A Taste of Downtown, which features a food tasting from the city's restaurants along with live music and dancing. The Kit Carson Rendezvous and Wagon Train event, also in June, features a mountain man encampment, trader's row, an Indian pow wow, and mock gunfights, all in celebration of Nevada's history. Independence Day in July is hailed by a four-day celebration with the traditional fireworks and the Silver Dollar Car Classic, a street dance, and music concerts.

Sports for the Spectator

While no professional sports teams play in Carson City, nearby Reno offers viewing opportunities of several athletic programs. Reno is making a name for itself as the mountain golf capital of the world. Since 1999 the PGA Tour's Reno-Tahoe Open has taken place at Montreux Golf and Country Club in August, where some of the world's best professional golfers compete. A celebrity-packed golfing event, the American Century Celebrity Championship, is also held annually at Edgewood-Tahoe in July. Two of the country's largest bowling organizations, the American Bowling Congress (ABC) and the Women's International Bowling Congress (WIBC), hold tournaments at the National Bowling Stadium. Dubbed "Pin Palace" by *USA Today*, it draws thousands of bowlers to its high-technology facility on a regular basis.

The University of Nevada, Reno, offers spectators the chance to cheer on teams playing football, basketball, softball, volleyball, and other popular sports. The collegiate sports program, dubbed "Wolf Pack Athletics," was declared "best in the nation" in terms of sports opportunities offered to female students in a 2005 study orchestrated by a Penn State University-York professor.

Sports for the Participant

Included within about 600 acres of city parks is Mills Park, which offers tennis courts, indoor and outdoor pools, a mini-golf course, and a children's one-mile train ride. The park is also the home of the Carson City Skateboard Park, which provides a skateboard area with platforms, ramps, and spectator seating. Centennial Park has several soccer and softball fields, tennis courts, a public golf course, and shady picnic sites. Residents and visitors can make use of the "Divine Nine" golf courses within the city limits. Horseback riding is also popular in the area, especially on the Mount Rose Wilderness trails. At the edge of town is an old hot springs where bathers can soak in a 100° F spring water pool, and make use of hot tubs, massage facilities, and an adjoining restaurant and motel.

Sports enthusiasts enjoy hunting for birds and big game such as elk, deer, antelope, and bighorn sheep. In addition, the city is only 45 minutes from several prime skiing areas at nearby Lake Tahoe.

Shopping and Dining

The once shabby block that houses the landmark St. Charles Hotel has been transformed into a delightful collection of shops and restaurants. Other major shopping areas include various downtown blocks, as well as Eagle Station Shopping Center, Carson Valley Plaza shopping center, and Silver City.

Diners in Carson City can choose from among over 40 restaurants with American and ethnic cuisines, including Basque, Asian, Southwestern, and Italian. The Carlson House is a popular modern restaurant set in the wonderfully restored 1876 Rinckel Mansion, the city's second-oldest residence, with service offered in the garden during the summer months. Adele's French restaurant is set in a lovely Victorian house near the town center, while nearby Silvana's features Italian dishes. Breakfast lovers enjoy the hearty omelets at the Cracker Box or Heidi's Dutch Mill Restaurant.

Visitor Information: Carson City Convention & Visitors Bureau, 1900 S. Carson St., Ste. 100, Carson City, NV 89701; telephone (775)687-7410 or (800) NEVADA-1; fax (775)687-7416

Convention Facilities

Carson City has a variety of meeting and convention facilities. The 31,020-square-foot Pony Express Pavilion can accommodate up to 3,000 people and offers table, theater, or bleacher-style seating. The Carson City Community Center can seat 803 people theater-style, and the Carson City Nugget has facilities for about 500 people on 8,600 square feet. The Best Western Pinon Plaza Resort can handle groups of 30 to 250 people in its 3,000-square-foot facilities. The meeting room at the Plaza Hotel offers an outstanding panoramic view of the city. Historic Brewery Arts Center offers its art gallery for smaller groups while its restored meeting room has space for up to 300 guests.

Convention Information: Carson City Convention & Visitors Bureau, 1900 S. Carson St., Ste. 100, Carson City, NV 89701; telephone (775)687-7410; toll-free (800)NEVADA-1; fax (775)687-7416

Transportation

Approaching the City

The Carson City Airport does not provide commercial services, but Reno-Cannon International Airport, just 30 miles to the north of Carson City, is served by many major airlines and offers over 170 flights daily. Carson City is located at the intersection of U.S. Highway 395, which links cities from Canada to Mexico, and U.S. Highway 50, a direct route from west to east. Amtrak provides rail service to the Reno/Sparks area, 30 miles north of Carson City. The RTC Intercity provides express weekday intercity bus service among Carson City, Reno, North Douglas County, and the Reno/Tahoe International Airport. Greyhound bus lines offer daily service to Los Angeles, Sacramento, Las Vegas, Reno, and other destinations.

Traveling in the City

Because the city has no freeway off-ramps, U.S. 395 and U.S. 50 serve as the main north-south and east-west highways, as well as the main streets in the city. However, the 9.7-mile Carson City Freeway project that began in 2003 is expected to be fully complete in 2010 and provide an alternate north-south route. The city began its bus service, Jump Around Carson (JAC) in 2004, and a dial-a-ride service is available to residents.

Communications

Newspapers and Magazines

The *Nevada Appeal*–Carson City Edition is the daily newspaper. *Nevada Magazine*, a bimonthly that carries feature stories on events and people in the state, is also published in Carson City. Other locally published magazines include *The Wine Trader* and *Range Magazine*, a consumer magazine covering cowboys and people who work the land in the western United States.

Television and Radio

Carson City receives its television coverage from nearby Reno's network and public stations but has its own cable company. The city has several AM and FM radio stations broadcasting religious, county, and oldies formats.

Media Information: *Nevada Appeal* PO Box 2288, Carson City, NV 89702; telephone (775)882-2111 or (800)221-8013

Carson City Online

Carson City Area Chamber of Commerce. Available www.carsoncitychamber.com

Carson City Convention & Visitors Bureau. Available www.carson-city.org

Carson City Economic Development. Available www.carsoncitycondev.com

Carson City Library. Available www.carson-city .nv.us/library

Carson City School District. Available www .carsoncityschools.com

City of Carson City home page. Available www .carson-city.nv.us

Nevada State Library and Archives. Available dmla .clan.lib.nv.us

State of Nevada, Department of Cultural Affairs, Division of Museums and History. Available dmla.clan.lib.nv.us

BIBLIOGRAPHY

McLaughlin, Mark, *Sierra Stories: True Tales of Tahoe* (Carnelian Bay, CA: Mic Mac Publishers, 1997)

Twain, Mark, *Roughing It* (Berkeley, CA: University of California Press, 1996)

Henderson

■ The City in Brief

Founded: 1941 (incorporated 1953)

Head Official: Mayor Jim Gibson (D) (since 1997)

City Population

1980: 24,363
1990: 62,942
2000: 175,381
2006 estimate: 240,614
Percent change, 1990–2000: 169.4%
U.S. rank in 1980: Not available
U.S. rank in 1990: Not available
U.S. rank in 2000: 118th (State rank: 2nd)

Metropolitan Area Population

1980: 528,000
1990: 852,737
2000: 1,563,282
2006 estimate: Not available
Percent change, 1990–2000: 83.3%
U.S. rank in 1980: 72nd
U.S. rank in 1990: 53rd
U.S. rank in 2000: 32nd

Area: 80 square miles (2000)

Elevation: 1,940 feet above sea level

Average Annual Temperature: 68.0° F

Average Annual Precipitation: 4.5 inches of rain

Major Economic Sectors: services, wholesale and retail trade, government

Unemployment Rate: 5% (August 2007)

Per Capita Income: $32,335 (2005)

2005 FBI Crime Index Property: 6,654

2005 FBI Crime Index Violent: 432

Major Colleges and Universities: Nevada State College; University of Nevada, Las Vegas; Community College of Southern Nevada

Daily Newspaper: *Las Vegas Review-Journal*

■ Introduction

Henderson, Nevada was pronounced a "city of destiny" by then-president John F. Kennedy while on a visit to Southern Nevada during his brief time in office. Incorporated during World War II, Henderson had become known only 10 years prior when it sprung up from the desert floor as the home of the Basic Magnesium Plant, which supplied the U.S. forces with magnesium for munitions and airplane parts during the war. Post-war, Henderson quieted as the plant closed and out-of-work residents sought greener pastures. Quick thinking and creativity by city leaders and developers brought money and new residents back to Henderson, saving it from "ghost town" status. Now a bustling metropolis making its own name in the shadow of a glittering Las Vegas, Henderson is the second largest city in Nevada.

■ Geography and Climate

Henderson sits at the southern rim of the Las Vegas Valley. At an elevation of 1,940 feet above sea level, the city is only 7 miles southeast of Las Vegas and about midway between Las Vegas and Boulder City (home of the Hoover Dam). Residents and visitors enjoy warm weather, with an average temperature of just under 70 degrees most months of the year, low humidity, and very little rain. Winter snows are visible in the mountains, but snow is rare in the city.

Area: 80 square miles (2000)

Elevation: 1,940 feet above sea level

Average Temperature: 68.0° F

Average Annual Precipitation: 4.5 inches of rain

■ History

Spanish Move Through Area

Spanish explorers moved through Southern Nevada in the early 1800s, discovering and naming Las Vegas as a stop on their way to California. Mormon missionaries established a settlement and built a fort in 1855 in Las Vegas but didn't stay long. In the latter half of the century, Las Vegas, and with it the area that is now Henderson, was detached from Arizona territory to become part of Nevada. Small farming communities developed, but things were quiet in the area until construction on the Boulder Dam was begun in 1931, bringing thousands to the area for work.

A City Born Overnight

Southern Nevada had but a handful of residents in the early decades of the twentieth century. Henderson, quite literally, was created almost overnight in 1941, as building began on a plant that was, at the time, a massive undertaking in the middle of desert land. Magnesium and its importance in munitions and to the brewing war were the key to the city's beginning.

In 1941 a Cleveland, Ohio manufacturer named Howard Eells and his newly formed Basic Magnesium Inc. (BMI) company signed a contract with the U.S. Defense Plant Corp. to build the Basic Magnesium Plant. Only days after signing, the government asked Eells to expand the planned site to 10 times its original size, making it 1.75 miles long and .75 miles wide, the largest such magnesium plant in the world. More than 13,000 workers—which was 10 percent of the entire state's population at the time—lived in ramshackle housing or "tent cities" until construction began on a company town in 1942. Under scrutiny for attempting to profit from the war, Eells sold BMI to Anaconda Copper Mining Co. that year. Anaconda was charged with finishing the plant, and the burgeoning city was named not after Eells, but for former senator Charles P. Henderson for his role in helping to get the plant financed and built.

For the next few years, BMI exceeded its planned production rates and employees numbered 14,000 at peak production. However, by 1947 magnesium was no longer needed for defense, the plant closed, and more than half of the employees left. Almost as quickly as the city was built, it all but disappeared. Henderson stood in danger of becoming a ghost town, and in 1947 the U.S. War Asset Administration offered the entire city for sale as war surplus property. In a brochure created to help sell the city, a description was provided that outlined the housing, streets, alleys, sanitary systems, schools, general buildings, shops, churches, and other city amenities.

Last Ditch Effort Saves City

In an effort to save Henderson, the Chamber of Commerce convinced the Las Vegas Chamber of Commerce to issue an invitation to the entire Nevada Legislature to come visit Boulder Dam (now Hoover Dam). They were asked to evaluate the Basic Magnesium site and explore the possibility of construction of a power generator at the dam, which would bring new workers and provide work for those Henderson residents that remained. The plan worked—a bill was unanimously approved, giving the Colorado River Commission of Nevada authority to purchase the plant. By 1953 signs of improvement were well underway and the city was officially incorporated, with a population of 7,410 residents.

Modern Henderson Emerges

Throughout the 1960s and 1970s, Henderson remained a relatively small factory town. In the early 1980s, the first master planned community, Green Valley, was plotted. Henderson's population in 1980 was 24,363; by 1990 it had more than doubled, and by the end of the twentieth century Henderson had reached 175,381. By 1999 Henderson overtook Reno as Nevada's second largest city, and by 2007 estimates showed that Henderson had grown over 195 percent since 1990, with an average of 1,000 new residents moving into the city per month since 1997.

The city celebrated its 50 year birthday in 2003. Henderson's unparalleled growth in the past two decades shows little signs of slowing. As Nevada's second largest city, with a thriving economy, master-planned communities, world-class recreation, and proximity to several of the country's national and man-made treasures, it's no wonder that Henderson remains one of the fastest-growing cities in the nation.

Historical Information: City of Henderson, City Hall, 240 Water Street, Henderson, NV 89009. Nevada State Museum & Historical Society, 700 Twin Lakes Drive, Las Vegas, NV 89107; telephone (702)486-5205

■ Population Profile

Metropolitan Area Residents

    1980: 528,000
    1990: 852,737
    2000: 1,563,282
    2006 estimate: Not available
    Percent change, 1990–2000: 83.3%
    U.S. rank in 1980: 72nd

Ethan Miller/Getty Images

U.S. rank in 1990: 53rd
U.S. rank in 2000: 32nd

City Residents

1980: 24,363
1990: 62,942
2000: 175,381
2006 estimate: 240,614
Percent change, 1990–2000: 169.4%
U.S. rank in 1980: Not available
U.S. rank in 1990: Not available
U.S. rank in 2000: 118th (State rank: 2nd)

Density: 2,200.8 people per square mile (2000)

Racial and ethnic characteristics (2005)

White: 181,638
Black: 11,017
American Indian and Alaska Native: 1,850
Asian: 9,476
Native Hawaiian and Pacific Islander: 2,560
Hispanic or Latino (may be of any race): 26,071
Other: 10,042

Percent of residents born in state: 18.7% (2000)

Age characteristics (2005)

Population under 5 years old: 12,603
Population 5 to 9 years old: 15,325
Population 10 to 14 years old: 15,166
Population 15 to 19 years old: 15,928
Population 20 to 24 years old: 14,201
Population 25 to 34 years old: 28,949
Population 35 to 44 years old: 34,692
Population 45 to 54 years old: 33,603
Population 55 to 59 years old: 14,063
Population 60 to 64 years old: 13,684
Population 65 to 74 years old: 16,832
Population 75 to 84 years old: 7,336
Population 85 years and older: 1,394
Median age: 37.3 years

Births (2002, Clark County)

Total number: 23,756

Deaths (2003, Clark County)

Total number: 12,751

Money income (2005)

Per capita income: $32,335

Median household income: $61,483
Total households: 86,924

Number of households with income of ...

less than $10,000: 4,071
$10,000 to $14,999: 2,545
$15,000 to $24,999: 5,710
$25,000 to $34,999: 8,151
$35,000 to $49,999: 14,013
$50,000 to $74,999: 16,910
$75,000 to $99,999: 13,560
$100,000 to $149,999: 15,149
$150,000 to $199,999: 3,322
$200,000 or more: 3,493

Percent of families below poverty level: 3.9% (2000)

2005 FBI Crime Index Property: 6,654

2005 FBI Crime Index Violent: 432

■ Municipal Government

The city of Henderson received its charter only relatively recently, in 1965. The mayor and city council have legislative power of the city through the charter; the city manager is charged with executive duties and general administration of the city. The mayor and four city councilmen are elected at large on a nonpartisan basis, and councilmen must be from different wards of the city's four wards. Majority vote by the mayor and city council decides all issues, including land use, business licensing, city ordinances, and city fund expenditures.

Head Official: Mayor Jim Gibson (D) (since 1997; current term expires 2009)

Total Number of City Employees: 3,000 (2007)

City Information: City Hall, 240 Water St., Henderson, NV 89009; telephone (mayor and council) (702) 267-2085

■ Economy

Major Industries and Commercial Activity

For most of Henderson's short history, the city has been a manufacturing center. Though its beginnings were fast and furious as a magnesium producer for World War II efforts, Henderson's economy today has diversified. The city is still a manufacturing center and a producer of metals and industrial chemicals, but its diversification includes a competitive marketplace for communications technology.

In the past two decades, city leaders, businesses, and the community have been working together to diversify the city's economy with aggressive programs to attract modern industries. The top industries showing growth in Henderson are education services, medical and biomedical technology, the supplier industry, and computer and electronic transfer. In addition, businesses that service senior citizens are sprouting up in the area as more seniors relocate there.

A modern "boom town," Henderson's growth shows no signs of slowing. Major corporations with large offices or headquarters in Henderson include Levi Strauss & Company, Ocean Spray Cranberries, Ford Credit, and Good Humor-Breyers. Henderson's growing community and highly favorable business climate continues to attract businesses to the area. The ever-growing population provides a built-in customer base for Las Vegas' World Market Center, opened in 2005, which is the largest new home and hospitality contract furnishings showroom complex in the Western United States. Real estate continues to be an important part of Henderson's expanding economy as well.

Due only in part to Henderson's proximity to Las Vegas, it goes without saying that a large portion of economic gain stems from the tourism and services industry. The military also maintains a presence near Henderson; Nellis Air Force base, located about twenty miles northeast of the city of Henderson, has an average of 9,500 civilian and military personnel at any given time.

Items and goods produced: baked goods, clothing, food products, metal and chemical products

Incentive Programs—New and Existing Companies

Several city and state programs are available to assist new, current, or expanding businesses in the City of Henderson.

Local programs: The City of Henderson can offer partial exemption from public utilities license or franchise fees for gas or electricity; businesses must meet stringent requirements to take advantage of this program. The city's department of economic development staff, along with community resource partners, work together to provide relocating or expanding businesses with needed resources. The city's Redevelopment Agency, as part of the Downtown Investment Strategy plan, offers development incentives via grants, low-interest loans, and other financing to businesses for building improvements, equipment, start-up capital, and other expenses; one of the most successful programs is the Facade Improvement Program.

State programs: The State of Nevada administers Small Business Administration loans, in addition to the Modified Business Tax Abatement Program, which provides a partial abatement of taxes to qualified new businesses and local businesses that are expanding. The Nevada Development Capital Corporation (NDCC) provides more than $3 million from Nevada banks, utilities, and mining companies and other firms to help finance growth opportunities for new and existing businesses. It provides flexible financing to small Nevada businesses that do not qualify for more conventional financing. The state has no personal state income tax, no unitary tax, no corporate income tax, no inventory tax, no estate and/or gift tax, no franchise tax, no inheritance tax, and no special intangible tax.

Job training programs: The Nevada Department of Employment, Training, and Rehabilitation offers a variety of job training services to both employers and job seekers, including applicant recruitment and screening, tax credit benefits, training programs and career enhancement programs, and labor market information. The Train Employees Now (TEN) program, administered by the State of Nevada Commission on Economic Development, helps new and expanding firms by providing intensive skills-based training programs tailored to the company's needs. The TEN program utilizes training providers such as local businesses and community colleges. The Family Support Center at Nellis Air Force Base offers job information and employer connections to spouses and family members of base personnel. A variety of programs exist through the area's educational institutions, including the College of Southern Nevada, which makes job training an explicitly stated part of its educational goals.

Development Projects

The Henderson Redevelopment Agency was created in 1995 and utilizes tax increment financing funds for projects in three designated areas of Henderson: downtown, Tuscany, and Cornerstone. In 2005 a variety of projects began construction in the Water Street District, totaling more than 230,000 square feet of residential, retail, and office space, alongside sidewalk expansions and beautification of pedestrian areas. Many of the projects were designed to fit into the emerging "Art Deco" theme city planners selected for the downtown area.There was no comprehensive completion date reported in 2007.

In 2006 the Eastside Redevelopment Area was officially adopted, encompassing over 4,500 square acres, including Pittman, the Sunset Industrial Corridor, Valley View and Landwell. The city of Henderson pledged to provide financial support for homes and businesses requiring substantive imrovements; the goal of the project was to attract more building projects in the area.

As one of the fastest-growing cities in the U.S., Henderson is also home to a number of new private, residential developments.

Economic Development Information: City of Henderson Economic Development, 240 Water Street, Henderson, NV 89009; telephone (702)267-1650.

Commercial Shipping

Southern Clark County is the hub of an extensive transportation network serviced by three highway corridors: Interstate 15, U.S. Highway 95, and U.S. Highway 93. More than 50 motor freight carriers serve the area. In addition, a variety of warehousing and support services are available in Clark County, including foreign trade zone accommodations, packaging support, and U.S. customs service. McCarran International Airport handles in excess of 600,000 pounds of arriving and departing cargo, and has an annual economic impact of more than $29.8 billion in Clark County. Additionally, the McCarran International Air Cargo Center offers cargo storage and handling and operates in a designated Foreign Trade Zone (FTZ). Union Pacific Railroad runs northeast/southwest through Clark County, linking the area to markets in most states.

Labor Force and Employment Outlook

Henderson's rapid population expansion in the last several decades especially means that local businesses experience no shortages of labor supply. Area businesses draw from a southern Nevada workforce of more than 800,000 people. Additionally, the array of vocational and technical trade schools, higher education institutions, and opportunities for customized training programs enhance both business and employment prospects.

The Las Vegas-Henderson rate of unemployment stood at five percent in August 2007, remaining fairly consistent with its 10-year trend. Analysts expected that rate to remain fairly steady. Henderson's population boom showed no signs of slowing in 2007, and it was expected that the economy would keep pace. The only question mark was whether new residential building would continue at the same rate in the wake of the summer 2007 mortgage crisis; in early 2007 home prices already showed a drop over the previous year's highs.

The following is a summary of data regarding the Henderson city metropolitan area labor force, 2005 annual averages.

Size of nonagricultural labor force: 118,448

Number of workers employed in ...

    construction and mining: 9,861
    manufacturing: 5,364
    trade, transportation and utilities: 23,946
    information: 2,155
    financial activities: 9,116
    professional and business services: 12,208
    educational and health services: 16,645
    leisure and hospitality: 28,753
    other services: 3,979
    government: 15,292

Average hourly earnings of production workers employed in manufacturing: Not available

Unemployment rate: 5% (August 2007)

Largest county employers	Number of employees
Clark County School District	20,000+
Clark County	9,000-9,999
Bellagio Hotel & Casino	8,000-8,999
MGM Grand Hotel & Casino	7,000-7,999
Mandalay Bay Resort & Casino	7,000-7,999
Mirage Hotel & Casino	5,000-5,999
State of Nevada	5,000-5,999
Caesars Palace Hotel & Casino	4,000-4,999
Las Vegas Metropolitan Police	4,000-4,999
University of Nevada, Las Vegas	4,000-4,999

Cost of Living

Henderson's cost of living, as well as its housing prices, are somewhat above the national average.

The following is a summary of data regarding several key cost of living factors for the Henderson area.

2007 (1st quarter) ACCRA Average House Price: Not available

2007 (1st quarter) ACCRA Cost of Living Index: Not available

State income tax rate: None

State sales tax rate: 6.5%

Local income tax rate: None

Local sales tax rate: 7.5%

Property tax rate: 2.9027-2.9468 (depending on tax district) per $100 assessed value (2005)

Economic Information: Sierra Pacific Power Company Economic Development; Grant Sims, Economic Development Manager; phone (775)834-3716; fax (775)834-3384; email gsims@sppc.com. City of Henderson Economic Development, 240 Water Street, Henderson, NV 89009; telephone (702)267-1650

■ Education and Research

Elementary and Secondary Schools

The Clark County School District serves about 306,000 students in all of Clark County—a 7,910 square mile section of Nevada—which includes the city of Henderson, and serves nearly three quarters of all students in the state. The large system, which celebrated its 50th anniversary in 2006, is divided into five regions; the population of Henderson is served by the Southeast Region. A variety of magnet schools exist throughout the district, in addition to English as a second language programs, vocational training, language immersion, and fine arts specialties. The school district is constantly expanding along with the reigion; in 2002 the district reported a "typical year" as including 14,000 new students, 12-14 new schools, and 1,300 new employees. There were 317 schools operating in the system in 2007, with several in the planning stages. In 2007 the school district was the region's largest employer, with more than 26,000 people on its payroll. Nearly $100 million dollars in college scholarships were awarded to members of the district's class of 2006; that same year the district reported significant gains in students taking Advanced Placement classes, schools with high rankings on the Nevada state proficiency tests, and percentage of students enrolling in college.

The following is a summary of data regarding the Clark County School District (Southeast Region) as of the 2006–2007 school year.

Total enrollment: 59,221

Number of facilities

elementary schools: 41
junior high/middle schools: 13
senior high schools: 8
other: 0

Student/teacher ratio: 18:1 elementary; 30:1 secondary

Teacher salaries (2005–06)

elementary median: $30,299–63,544
junior high/middle median: Not available
secondary median: Not available

Funding per pupil: $5,501

Public Schools Information: Clark County School District, 2832 East Flamingo Road, Las Vegas, NV 89121; telephone (702)799-5011

Colleges and Universities

Henderson offers residents several major institutions of higher learning. The College of Southern Nevada (CSN) system, with a campus in Henderson, educates more than 70,000 students as the fourth-largest community college in the nation. It operates in over 50 locations and offers 100 fields of study and more than 200 degrees and certificates. CSN's top disciplines include dental hygiene, culinary arts, computing and information technologies, resorts and gaming, nursing and other health professions, automotive technology, air conditioning, and criminal justice. The Nevada State College at Henderson was founded in 2002, and places a particular focus on training in the nursing and healthcare industries.

The University of Nevada, Las Vegas (UNLV) in nearby Las Vegas enrolls more than 28,000 students and confers 220 undergrad, graduate, and doctoral degrees, with a total staff of more than 3,300. In 2006 UNLV received more than $94 million in funding from outside sources, with $68 million of that going to support research. UNLV also has a School of Dental Medicine and a School of Medicine; both educate students as well as provide low-cost health care to residents. Also in Las Vegas, the International Academy of Design & Technology offers two- and four-year programs in Fashion Design, Interior Design, and Visual Communications.

Libraries and Research Centers

The Henderson District Public Libraries operate four branches throughout the city and served nearly 700,000 visitors in 2004, with holdings of about 289,000 items in all branches. The newest of the branches, the Paseo Verde Library, was constructed in 2002 and houses a Genealogy Collection, a Government Documents Collection, library administrative offices, and a Friends of Henderson Libraries Bookstore and Coffee Shop. Friends of the Henderson Libraries actively advocates for increased private donations, since growth in the area is far outpacing the growth of the library system; in 2007 the state legislature allocated $1.2 million dollars for the Nevada Public Libraries Collection Development fund, or just over a dollar per person.

The Las Vegas-Clark County Library District serves all of Clark County with 24 branches and a comprehensive resource of informational materials. The district's Green Valley branch resides in Henderson. Its holdings include special collections on African-American history, Asian history, health and medicine, international language, gaming/local history, grants, government Documents, and patents. The Community College of Southern Nevada library system, as well as the University of Nevada Las Vegas libraries, are available for public use as well.

The Desert Research Institute's (DRI) main research campus in Las Vegas carries out about 300 scientific research projects at any given time. It is a stand-alone institution that falls under the umbrella of the Nevada System of Higher Education (NSHE), thanks to generous outside research funding. In 2007 the institute had grown 85 percent since 1999 while using only 1 percent of NSHE's annual budget. Environmental research programs focus on three core divisions of atmospheric sciences, earth and ecosystems sciences, and hydrologic sciences. DRI maintains a library that is available to researchers and scholars. A variety of other specialized libraries and research centers are located in the area.

Public Library Information: Henderson District Public Libraries, 280 S. Green Valley, Henderson, NV 89012; telephone (702)492-7252

■ Health Care

St. Rose Dominican Hospitals operates three medical campuses, with the Rose de Lima Campus and the Siena Campus both in Henderson. The third facility, the San Martín Campus in Warm Springs, opened in November 2006. It has 111 private rooms, with space for an additional 90 in the future. Rose de Lima, with 138 beds, offers emergency and surgical services, rehabilitation, obstetrical services, community outreach, and kidney stone treatment services, among others. Siena opened in 2000 and is a 214-bed acute care facility with pediatrics services, neurosurgery, an open-heart surgery center, emergency department, obstetrics and surgical services, diagnostic imaging, and others. The hospital system also operates two Womens Care centers, one in Las Vegas and one in Henderson, which offer treatment and guidance on health and wellness to area women. A variety of hospitals and clinics exist in nearby Las Vegas.

■ Recreation

Sightseeing

Less than 20 miles southeast of Henderson is the Hoover Dam. A National Historic Landmark, and recognized as one of America's Seven Modern Civil Engineering Wonders by the American Society of Civil Engineers, the dam entertains more than a million visitors and tourgoers annually. Lake Mead National Recreation Area in nearby Boulder City offers opportunities for a leisurely afternoon outdoors or multi-day, multi-activity trips, and dinner or dinner-and-dance cruises are available on a Mississippi-style paddlewheeler.

Ghost towns of the Old West are popular tourist destinations; several exist within an hour's drive of the city. Ethel M. Chocolates, a mainstay in Henderson though originating in Tacoma, Washington, offers tours of the chocolate factory (samples included) and the botanical cactus gardens on its grounds.

Arts and Culture

Henderson's Veterans Memorial Wall on Water Street honors not only those who have fought for their country, but those who played a part in Henderson's heritage. The wall was dedicated in 2004 and is inscribed with more than 1,500 names.

The Clark County Museum tells the story of southern Nevada in a variety of exhibits, including prehistoric dioramas, Native American collections, a walk-in mine, and a pueblo. Heritage Street, an outdoor exhibit of the museum, offers a look at the structures and homes of the early 1900s, including a replicated newspaper print shop, historic homes, and the 1932 Boulder City Depot. The Howard W. Cannon Aviation Museum at the airport tells of the history of aviation in the region.

The Arts Council of Henderson, a nonprofit group, works to bring arts programming to Henderson residents. One of the Council's ventures is the annual Nevada Shakespeare in the Park, presented in cooperation with the city of Henderson, American Nevada Corporation, and the Clark County School District. Shakespeare in the Park, which celebrated its twentieth anniversary in 2006, presents one play per season over one October weekend, with a performance each day. An Elizabethan Festival precedes each daily performance. Theatre in the Valley presents community theater in a season of four to five shows per year.

Festivals and Holidays

The St. Patrick's Day Parade and Block Party, which celebrated 40 years in 2006, takes place each March in downtown Henderson. For nearly a week in late March or early April the FLW Outdoors EverStart Series offers fishing competition action at Lake Mead. In early May at the Lake Las Vegas Resort, crews compete in the Dragon Boat Race and Festival. ArtFest happens over Mother's Day weekend in May in downtown Henderson's Water Street district, featuring more than 200 artists, music, food, and fun kids' events. Also in May, *Bon Appetit* magazine spends the weekend at several area hotels and resorts, offering culinary demonstrations, wine tastings, brunches, and dinners during the Annual Bon Appetit Wine & Spirits Focus. Fourth of July events and fireworks happen citywide. September features the Super Run Car Show, with car cruises and drag racing, concerts, and food at Water Street and various locations throughout the city. The Nevada Silverman, an iron-distance triathlon event in November, offers spectators and participants views of the Lake Mead National Recreation Area.

Sports for the Spectator

While no sports teams reside in the city of Henderson, nearby Las Vegas offers enthusiasts many opportunities to cheer for their favorite sports. The Las Vegas 51s, triple A affiliate of the Los Angeles Dodgers, play minor league baseball at Cashman Field in Las Vegas. The AFL's Las Vegas Gladiators play professional indoor football at the Orleans Arena. The Las Vegas Wranglers, members of the ECHL Division, also play at the Orleans Arena. The Las Vegas Strikers of the National Premier Soccer League play at the Bettye Wilson Soccer Complex, but the team announced a hiatus for the 2007-2008 season. The University of Las Vegas Rebels' most popular sports include baseball, soccer, football, and basketball. The Las Vegas Moter Speedway offers NASCAR and other motor sports events. High-profile boxing matches are often scheduled in Las Vegas.

Sports for the Participant

Henderson and nearby areas are an outdoor lover's paradise. In 2007 Henderson was named one of the top 10 walking cities in America by *Prevention Magazine's*

annual "Best Walking Cities" list. The city of Henderson offers visitors more than 1,200 acres of outdoor opportunities in 44 developed parks—Henderson's parks and recreation system is nationally recognized. Among Henderson's outdoor amenities in the park system and beyond are 65 athletic fields, 42 tennis courts, nine pools, six recreation centers, more than 57 miles of trails, and 12 golf courses. The city of Henderson's bird viewing preserve is a 147-acre migratory bird and wetland area featuring basins, ponds, and lagoons; signs, kiosks and nature trails guide visitors.

The Lake Mead National Recreation Area consists of a man-made lake in a massive crater created during the building of the Hoover Dam, offering opportunities for boating, swimming, kayaking, hiking, horseback riding, and fishing. Bootleg Canyon, in nearby Boulder City, is heralded as one of the best mountain biking spots in the U.S. and offers more than 20 miles of challenging terrain. Red Rock Canyon, a 197,000-acre National Conservation Area, presents a variety of outdoor opportunities, including hiking and biking trails, rock climbing, a visitor's center with interpretive programs, and Spring Mountain State Park.

Shopping and Dining

The Galleria at Sunset mall, which was the first enclosed mall in the city, is anchored by Dillard's, Robinsons May, JCPenney, and Mervyn's, and has two levels with fountains, skylights, and desert flowers in its indoor landscaping. The District at Green Valley Ranch, part residential development and part stylish shopping mecca, offers a "main street" shopping experience for its loft residents and visitors alike, with over 40 upscale shops and restaurants on the development's street level. Shoppers looking for bargains can head to the Las Vegas Outlet Center, featuring 130 outlet shops. Shoppers in Henderson's Water Street District area will find a variety of unique shops, boutiques, galleries, and restaurants. The Country Fresh Farmers Market operates throughout the spring and summer on Fridays in the Water Street District. Henderson's variety of restaurants satisfy urges for area favorites like steak and Mexican food; other tastes tempted include French, Chinese, Italian, Japanese, Greek, and Thai.

Visitor Information: Henderson Convention and Visitors Bureau, 200 Water Street, Henderson, NV 89009; telephone (702)267-2171; toll-free (877)775-5252; fax (702)267-2177; email info@visithenderson.com

■ Convention Facilities

The Henderson Convention Center offers over 10,000 feet of meeting space, and can accommodate wedding receptions, corporate and civic functions, class and family reunions, dances, and charity events. The Ritz-Carlton

Lake Las Vegas opened in 2003 in the new resort development area of Lake Las Vegas in Henderson, offering 32,000 square feet of flexible indoor meeting space, in addition to its outdoor space. Other hotels with convention facilities in Henderson include The Fiesta-Henderson Hotel Casino, Green Valley Ranch Resort, Hyatt Regency Lake Las Vegas Resort, and Sunset Station Hotel Casino. By the end of 2007, there were expected to be over 5,000 hotel rooms available in the city of Henderson, alongside a grand total of 253,000 square feet of meeting space.

Convention Information: Henderson Convention and Visitors Bureau, 200 Water Street, Henderson, NV 89009; telephone (702)267-2171; toll-free (877)775-5252; fax (702)267-2177; email info@visithenderson.com

■ Transportation

Approaching the City

McCarran International Airport serves Henderson, Las Vegas, and all of Clark County and southern Nevada. In April 2005 the airport debuted its $125 million expansion, consisting of a new gate wing that allows the airport to handle an additional estimated 3.1 million passengers annually. The fifth busiest airport in the nation, McCarran has 95 total gates, and averaged 121,280 passengers per day in 2005. The Henderson Executive Airport accommodates private and general aviation aircraft.

Four major highways bring travelers into and out of Henderson: I-15, US 93/95, Highway 146, and the Southern Nevada Beltway (I-215). North-south I-15 links travelers west to California and east to the East Coast via I-80, I-70, and I-40.

Traveling in the City

Amtrak Thruway provides bus service between Los Angeles, California, and Las Vegas. Greyhound provides bus service to and from nearby Las Vegas with connections throughout the west; in 2005, an additional stop was added in Henderson itself. The Citizens Area Transit (CAT) provides local bus service throughout Clark County; in 2005 the system had over 55 million riders, with 51 routes served by 365 vehicles.

■ Communications

Newspapers and Magazines

Henderson residents are served by the daily *Las Vegas Review-Journal*, the alternative weekly the *Las Vegas Weekly*, the *Showbiz Weekly* covering local entertainment in Las Vegas, and a variety of other publications coming from Las Vegas.

Television and Radio

Henderson's one commercial television station is a Fox network; the area is served by Las Vegas' nine total television stations. No radio stations broadcast from Henderson proper, although residents enjoy programming from Las Vegas' numerous AM and FM channels.

Media Information: *Las Vegas Review-Journal*, PO Box 70, Las Vegas, NV 89125; telephone (702)383-0211

Henderson Online

Center for Business and Economic Research at the University of Nevada, Las Vegas. Available www.unlv.edu/Research_Centers/cber

City of Henderson. Available www.cityofhenderson.com

Clark County School District. Available ccsd.net

Henderson Chamber of Commerce. Available www.hendersonchamber.com

Las Vegas-Clark County Library District. Available www.lvccld.org

Las Vegas Review-Journal. Available www.reviewjournal.com

Las Vegas Sun. Available www.lasvegassun.com

Nevada State Museum and Historical Society. Available dmla.clan.lib.nv.us

This Was Nevada (internet column on Nevada History from the State of Nevada Department of Culture, originally printed in the Henderson Home News). Available dmla.clan.lib.nv.us

BIBLIOGRAPHY

Armstrong-Ingram, Jackson R., *Henderson, Nevada: Images of America* (Mount Pleasant, SC: Arcadia Publishing, 2002)

Bowers, Michael W., *The Sagebrush State: Nevada's History, Government, and Politics* (Reno, NV: University of Nevada Press, 2002)

City of Henderson, ed., *An American Journey: Henderson, 50 Years* (Henderson, NV: City of Henderson, 2004)

Hulse, James W., *The Silver State: Nevada's Heritage Reinterpreted* (Reno, NV: University of Nevada Press, 2004)

Toll, David W., *The Complete Nevada Traveler: The Affectionate and Intimately Detailed Guidebook to the Most Interesting State in America* (Virginia City, NV: Gold Hill Pub., 2002)

Las Vegas

■ The City in Brief

Founded: 1905 (incorporated 1911)

Head Official: Mayor Oscar B. Goodman (D) (since 1999)

City Population

1980: 164,674
1990: 258,877
2000: 478,434
2006 estimate: 552,539
Percent change, 1990–2000: 84.1%
U.S. rank in 1980: 89th
U.S. rank in 1990: 63rd
U.S. rank in 2000: 39th (State rank: 1st)

Metropolitan Area Population

1980: 528,000
1990: 852,737
2000: 1,563,282
2006 estimate: 1,777,539
Percent change, 1990–2000: 83.3%
U.S. rank in 1980: 72nd
U.S. rank in 1990: 53rd
U.S. rank in 2000: 32nd

Area: 113 square miles (2000)

Elevation: 2,180 feet above sea level

Average Annual Temperatures: January, 47.0° F; July, 91.2° F; annual average, 68.1° F

Average Annual Precipitation: 4.49 inches of rain; 1.2 inches of snow

Major Economic Sectors: services, wholesale and retail trade, government

Unemployment rate: 4.7% (June 2007)

Per Capita Income: $24,887 (2005)

2005 FBI Crime Index Property: 62,013

2005 FBI Crime Index Violent: 9,530

Major Colleges and Universities: Nevada State College, University of Nevada at Las Vegas, Community College of Southern Nevada

Daily Newspaper: *Las Vegas Review-Journal*

■ Introduction

Las Vegas is unique among U.S. cities. Famous for luxury casinos and show palaces offering non-stop recreation on the "Strip" and in downtown Casino Center, the city has over the years become synonymous with glitter and glamour. Las Vegas since the late 1980s has acquired another identity as a center for business, finance, transportation, and services; still the "Entertainment Capital of the World," it has actively and successfully cultivated a diversified economy. The Las Vegas resident can enjoy legalized gaming, yet may more often take advantage of the diverse range of cultural and recreational opportunities offered in the city and in the surrounding area.

■ Geography and Climate

Las Vegas is located in the center of Vegas Valley, a desert region of about 600 square miles, which is surrounded by the Sierra Nevada Mountains and the Spring Mountains. The seasons are hot, windy, and dry, with desert conditions and maximum temperatures of 100° F during the summer; because of the mountains, however, summer nights are cool. Winters are mild. The mountains around Las Vegas reach elevations of over 10,000 feet, acting as barriers to moisture from the Pacific Ocean. Rainfall is minimal and there are approximately 215 clear days during the year. Snowfall is rare.

Area: 113 square miles (2000)

Elevation: 2,180 feet above sea level

Average Temperatures: January, 47.0° F; July, 91.2° F; annual average, 68.1° F

Average Annual Precipitation: 4.49 inches of rain; 1.2 inches of snow

■ History

Forts Built; Farmers Settle; Hoover Dam Built

Las Vegas was discovered by Spanish explorers, who gave the site its name—meaning "meadows"—because of the verdant grassland fed by natural aquifers. Las Vegas served as a watering place on the Spanish trail to California. In 1855 Mormon missionaries established a settlement, cultivating the land and building a fort to provide protection to travelers on the Salt Lake—Los Angeles Trail. They abandoned the place two years later when the enterprise became unprofitable, but their fort is still standing and is the oldest historical site in Las Vegas. In 1864 Fort Baker, a U.S. Army post, was built nearby; in 1867 Las Vegas was detached from the Arizona territory and became part of the Nevada territory.

Around that time Las Vegas began to expand as a series of farmers cultivated the land. The area encompassed 1,800 acres when it was sold to William Clark, a Montana senator. In 1905 Clark auctioned off parcels of land for the building of the Union Pacific Railroad link between Salt Lake City and Los Angeles. The town was incorporated in 1911. Construction on the Hoover Dam—originally the Boulder Dam—on the Colorado River was begun in 1931, bringing to the area thousands of men seeking employment. The 70-story dam, which is regarded as one of the wonders of the modern world, still supplies affordable power to parts of California, Arizona, and Nevada.

Gaming, Lenient Laws, Climate Attract Visitors, Settlers

Another significant event occurred in 1931: the legalization of casino gambling in Nevada. The gaming and entertainment industries boomed in Las Vegas after World War II. A street lined with large, glittering casino hotels came to be known as the "Strip"; downtown, in Casino Center, lavish palaces featured the country's top entertainers. By the 1950s Las Vegas, dubbed the "Entertainment Capital of the World," had become synonymous with the unique form of recreation it had created. Because of lenient state laws, Las Vegas also became popular as a wedding site; eventually wedding chapels were operating around the clock, and each year thousands of couples were coming to the city to be married.

Since the 1930s Las Vegas's population has steadily increased, jumping from slightly under 8,500 people in 1940 to nearly 25,000 people in 1950. By 1960 almost 65,000 people lived in Las Vegas, and in 1980 the census figure was 164,674 people. Between 1980 and 1990 there was a more than 60 percent increase, or a total of 278,000 people. Newcomers, primarily from California, are attracted by the favorable climate, the high standard of living, low tax rate, and jobs produced by a boom in business and the entertainment and gaming industries. In the 1990s an average of 6,000 to 7,000 people moved into Clark County each month; in the mid 2000's, a quick rate of growth appeared to be a permanent fixture.

On May 15, 2005, Las Vegas celebrated its centennial birthday with citywide parties and events on the day and throughout the year—one such celebration included a 130,000-pound cake registered with the Guinness Book of World Records.

Historical Information: Nevada State Museum & Historical Society, 700 Twin Lakes Drive, Las Vegas, NV 89107; telephone (702)486-5205

■ Population Profile

Metropolitan Area Residents

  1980: 528,000
  1990: 852,737
  2000: 1,563,282
  2006 estimate: 1,777,539
  Percent change, 1990–2000: 83.3%
  U.S. rank in 1980: 72nd
  U.S. rank in 1990: 53rd
  U.S. rank in 2000: 32nd

City Residents

  1980: 164,674
  1990: 258,877
  2000: 478,434
  2006 estimate: 552,539
  Percent change, 1990–2000: 84.1%
  U.S. rank in 1980: 89th
  U.S. rank in 1990: 63rd
  U.S. rank in 2000: 39th (State rank: 1st)

Density: 4,222.5 people per square mile (2000)

Racial and ethnic characteristics (2005)

  White: 400,007
  Black: 60,602
  American Indian and Alaska Native: 3,845
  Asian: 25,779

©Joseph Sohm/drr.net

Native Hawaiian and Pacific Islander: 2,206
Hispanic or Latino (may be of any race): 153,813
Other: 29,916

Percent of residents born in state: 19.7% (2000)

Age characteristics (2005)

Population under 5 years old: 42,540
Population 5 to 9 years old: 41,537
Population 10 to 14 years old: 39,976
Population 15 to 19 years old: 33,569
Population 20 to 24 years old: 29,733
Population 25 to 34 years old: 84,418
Population 35 to 44 years old: 85,401
Population 45 to 54 years old: 64,654
Population 55 to 59 years old: 28,432
Population 60 to 64 years old: 26,244
Population 65 to 74 years old: 36,901
Population 75 to 84 years old: 19,704
Population 85 years and older: 5,544
Median age: 34.8 years

Births (2006, Las Vegas-Paradise MSA)

Total number: 27,916

Deaths (2006, Las Vegas-Paradise MSA)

Total number: 12,789

Money income (2005)

Per capita income: $24,887
Median household income: $47,863
Total households: 204,688

Number of households with income of . . .

less than $10,000: 15,360
$10,000 to $14,999: 10,134
$15,000 to $24,999: 23,930
$25,000 to $34,999: 22,984
$35,000 to $49,999: 33,431
$50,000 to $74,999: 39,176
$75,000 to $99,999: 25,358
$100,000 to $149,999: 24,169
$150,000 to $199,999: 5,224
$200,000 or more: 4,922

Percent of families below poverty level: 11.2% (2005)

2005 FBI Crime Index Property: 62,013

2005 FBI Crime Index Violent: 9,530

■ Municipal Government

Las Vegas has a council-manager form of government. The five council members and the mayor are elected to four-year terms. The city's foremost spending priority is public safety.

Head Official: Mayor Oscar B. Goodman (D) (since 1999; current term expires 2011)

Total Number of City Employees: 3,000 (2007)

City Information: City of Las Vegas, 400 East Stewart Avenue, Las Vegas, NV 89101; telephone (702) 229-6241; fax (702)385-7960

■ Economy

Major Industries and Commercial Activity

Tourism drives the economy in Las Vegas, with 38.9 million people visiting the city each year. According to the Las Vegas Convention and Visitors Authority, Research Department, the figure for visitor spending in 2006 was a staggering $39.4 billion, up over $2 billion from the previous year. Around 20 percent of all jobs are gaming-related, and the gambling industry accounts for $8.2 billion in annual revenues.

Though many miles away, the terrorist attacks of September 11, 2001, had a devastating effect on the Las Vegas economy, costing thousands who worked in the entertainment and service industries their jobs in the weeks following. By 2007 revenues had risen steadily, thanks in part to the focus of the city's economic development department on the downtown area (including the promotion of the Freemont Street Experience entertainment area and mall) in addition to a nationwide marketing campaign. In fact, since 2005 large building projects on the Strip have increased dramatically.

Constant population growth means that the housing construction industry is vitally important. In 2005 more than one third of Las Vegas homes were only five years old or less.

While the entertainment and service industries are, collectively, the largest employers in Las Vegas, the major single employer is the Clark County School District.

Incentive Programs—New and Existing Companies

Local programs: To encourage industrial development, the Las Vegas business community works in cooperation with the state of Nevada to provide various incentives through minimal taxation, vocational training programs, no-cost site location services, special loan plans, and limited liability protection. The city is a foreign trade zone, making it an attractive foreign business destination.

State programs: The State of Nevada administers Small Business Administration loans, in addition to the Modified Business Tax Abatement Program, which provides a partial abatement of taxes to qualified new businesses and local businesses that are expanding. The Nevada Development Capital Corporation (NDCC) provides more than $3 million from Nevada banks, utilities, and mining companies and other firms to help finance growth opportunities for new and existing businesses. It provides flexible financing to small Nevada businesses that do not qualify for more conventional financing. The state has no personal state income tax, no unitary tax, no corporate income tax, no inventory tax, no estate and/or gift tax, no franchise tax, no inheritance tax, and no special intangible tax.

Job training programs: The Nevada Department of Employment, Training, and Rehabilitation offers a variety of job training services to both employers and job seekers, including applicant recruitment and screening, tax credit benefits, training programs and career enhancement programs, and labor market information. The Train Employees Now (TEN) program, administered by the State of Nevada Commission on Economic Development, helps new and expanding firms by providing intensive skills-based training programs tailored to the company's needs. The TEN program utilizes training providers such as local businesses and community colleges. The Family Support Center at Nellis Air Force Base offers job information and employer connections to spouses and family members of base personnel. A variety of programs exist through the area's educational institutions, including the College of Southern Nevada, which makes job training an explicitly stated part of its educational goals.

Development Projects

The 1990s saw major developments in the casino/resort area, with 18 new venues alone built in the last two years of the century, many themed after famous cities throughout the world. The race to build the most outrageous casino/resort in Las Vegas may be never-ending, but the area's more established resorts are quick to follow suit with expansions to match. The 2000-2005 expansion at Caesars Palace included a 949-room, 26-story tower that brought the resort's number of hotel rooms to more than 3,300. In 2006 even more expansion projects were announced by Ceasar's Palace: three new pools; the Octavius Tower, a 350-foot, 23-story tower; and a 263,000-square-foot ballroom added to the Convention Center, all to be completed by 2009. The Cosmopolitan Resort and Casino on the Strip, expected to be complete by 2010, is a $3 billion undertaking featuring 3,000 condo-hotel and hotel rooms managed by Grand Hyatt.

Also slated for completion by 2010 is the $4.8 billion Echelon on the Strip, with 4,713 rooms to be divided among five towers.

Wynn Las Vegas opened in spring 2005, topping out as the world's most expensive casino resort with a price tag of $2.7 billion. On 217 acres and with 2,716 rooms—each at a minimum of 630 square feet and built at a price tag of $1 million per room—the hotel is extravagantly appointed. Wynn Las Vegas features an 18-hole golf course; its own Ferrari-Maserati dealership; an art gallery featuring the likes of Picasso, Vermeer, Cezanne, Gauguin, and Rembrandt; and 18 restaurants.

In 2007 work began on MGM Mirage's CityCenter Las Vegas, a $7.4 billion, 68 acre project on the Las Vegas Strip between Bellagio and Monte Carlo. It represents the largest building project in U.S. history. The first phase of the project was tentatively scheduled to be completed by 2009.

At any given time in Las Vegas, planned community developments are in various construction phases. In fact, in 2007, over 110 high-rise, condo, hotel, mixed-use and other major projects in the Las Vegas area were in various stages of development. Summerlin, one such community along the western rim of the Las Vegas Valley, is the fastest growing master planned community in the country. At 22,500 acres and with 16 separate villages, each with its own major park, golf course, and schools, Summerlin had growth planned until approximately 2020.

In 2007 work began on the Downtown Connector rapid transit project, which was intended to connect Downtown Las Vegas with the Sahara Monorail Station, the Las Vegas Strip and McCarran International Airport.

Economic Development Information: Office of Business Development, City of Las Vegas, 400 Las Vegas Boulevard South, Las Vegas, NV 89101; telephone (702) 229-6551; fax (702)385-3128. City of Las Vegas Economic Development Division; telephone (702)229-6551. Las Vegas Chamber of Commerce, 3720 Howard Hughes Pkwy., Las Vegas, NV, 89109-0320; telephone (702)735-1616; fax (702) 735-2011; email info@lvchamber.com

Commercial Shipping

Southern Clark County is the hub of an extensive transportation network serviced by three highway corridors: Interstate 15, U.S. Highway 95, and U.S. Highway 93. More than 50 motor freight carriers serve the area. In addition, a variety of warehousing and support services are available in Clark County, including foreign trade zone accommodations, packaging support, and U.S. customs service. McCarran International Airport handles in excess of 600,000 pounds of arriving and departing cargo, and has an annual economic impact of more than $29.8 billion in Clark County. Additionally, the McCarran International Air Cargo Center offers cargo storage and handling and operates in a designated

Foreign Trade Zone (FTZ). Union Pacific Railroad runs northeast/southwest through Clark County, linking the area to markets in most states.

Labor Force and Employment Outlook

The labor force in Las Vegas continues to expand as people move into the region in record numbers (estimated at as many as 6,000 each month). Las Vegas boasts one of the highest rates of new job growth in the country. The gaming and hospitality industries in Las Vegas are expected to continue to improve. The Las Vegas-Henderson rate of unemployment stood at five percent in August 2007, remaining fairly consistent with its 10-year trend.

Though the forecast was generally rosy for Las Vegas' economic future, in 2007 analysts were concerned with the trend in the Las Vegas housing construction industry. The prices of new and existing homes had fallen by over 13 percent in Las Vegas from mid-2006 to mid-2007, and were expected to continue to fall into 2008 and possibly beyond, slowing the previously steady expansion of the region. Some forecasters predicted that home prices could drop as much as 15 to 20 percent from their 2007 values by 2010.

The following is a summary of data regarding the Las Vegas-Paradise metropolitan area labor force, 2006 annual averages.

Size of nonagricultural labor force: 918,800

Number of workers employed in . . .

   construction and mining: 400
   manufacturing: 27,100
   trade, transportation and utilities: 156,200
   information: 11,100
   financial activities: 50,400
   professional and business services: 115,300
   educational and health services: 60,000
   leisure and hospitality: 271,900
   other services: 25,200
   government: 92,000

Average hourly earnings of production workers employed in manufacturing: $15.02

Unemployment rate: 4.7% (June 2007)

Largest county employers (2006)	*Number of employees*
Clark County School District	26,700
Bellagio Hotel	8,300
Clark County Government	8,200
MGM Grand Hotel	7,200
Mirage Hotel	5,800
Mandalay Bay	5,000

Largest county employers

(2006)	*Number of employees*
State of Nevada	4,900
UNLV	4,800
Caesars Palace Hotel	4,400
Las Vegas Metro Police	4,300

Cost of Living

Nevada's low taxes make everything else cheaper: wages, rent, and energy costs.

The following is a summary of data regarding several key cost of living factors for the Las Vegas area.

2007 (1st quarter) ACCRA Average House Price: $421,667

2007 (1st quarter) ACCRA Cost of Living Index: 108.8

State income tax rate: None

State sales tax rate: 6.5%

Local income tax rate: None

Local sales tax rate: 1.25%

Property tax rate: 3.0815% of assessed value

Economic Information: Las Vegas Chamber of Commerce, 3720 Howard Hughes Pkwy., Las Vegas, NV 89109-0320; telephone (702) 735-1616; fax (702) 735-2011; email info@lvchamber.com. Nevada Department of Employment, Training and Rehabilitation, Information Development and Processing, Research and Analysis Bureau, 500 E. Third St., Carson City, NV 89713-0001; telephone (775)684-0450; email lmi@govmail.state.nv.us.

■ Education and Research

Elementary and Secondary Schools

The Clark County School District serves about 306,000 students in all of Clark County—a 7,910 square mile section of Nevada—which includes the city of Las Vegas, and serves nearly three quarters of all students in the state. The large system, which celebrated its 50th anniversary in 2006, is divided into five regions; the population of Las Vegas is served by the Southeast Region. A variety of magnet schools exist throughout the district, in addition to English as a second language programs, vocational training, language immersion, and fine arts specialties. The school district is constantly expanding along with the region; in 2002 the district reported a "typical year" as including 14,000 new students, 12-14 new schools, and 1,300 new employees. There were 317 schools operating in the system in 2007, with several in the planning stages.

In 2007 the school district was the region's largest employer, with more than 26,000 people on its payroll. Nearly $100 million dollars in college scholarships were awarded to members of the district's class of 2006; that same year the district reported significant gains in students taking Advanced Placement classes, schools with high rankings on the Nevada state proficiency tests, and percentage of students enrolling in college.

The following is a summary of data regarding the Clark County School District (Southeast Region) as of the 2006–2007 school year.

Total enrollment: 59,221

Number of facilities

elementary schools: 41
junior high/middle schools: 13
senior high schools: 8
other: 0

Student/teacher ratio: 13.4:1

Teacher salaries (2005–06)

elementary median: $33,570
junior high/middle median: $40,890
secondary median: $41,260

Funding per pupil: $6,108

More than thirty private and parochial elementary and secondary schools serve the Las Vegas metropolitan area. There are also more than 90 preschools and day care centers.

Public Schools Information: Clark County School District, 2832 East Flamingo Road, Las Vegas, NV 89121; telephone (702)799-5011

Colleges and Universities

Officially opened in 1957 and occupying 337 acres in the metropolitan area, the University of Nevada at Las Vegas (UNLV) enrolls more than 28,000 students and confers 220 undergrad, graduate, and doctoral degrees, with a total staff of more than 3,300. In 2006 UNLV received more than $94 million in funding from outside sources, with $68 million of that going to support research. UNLV also has a School of Dental Medicine and a School of Medicine; both educate students as well as provide low-cost health care to residents. Also in Las Vegas, the International Academy of Design & Technology offers two- and four-year programs in Fashion Design, Interior Design, and Visual Communications.

Located in the Las Vegas area are three campuses of the College of Southern Nevada (CSN) system, which educates more than 70,000 students as the fourth-largest community college in the nation. It operates in over 50 locations and offers 100 fields of study and more than 200 degrees and certificates. CSN's top disciplines include dental hygiene, culinary arts, computing and information technologies, resorts and gaming, nursing and other health professions, automotive technology, air conditioning, and criminal justice. The Nevada State College at nearby Henderson was founded in 2002, and places a particular focus on training in the nursing and healthcare industries.

Libraries and Research Centers

The Las Vegas-Clark County Library District serves all of Clark County with 24 branches and a comprehensive resource of informational materials. Its holdings include special collections on African-American history, Asian history, health and medicine, international language, gaming/local history, grants, government documents, and patents. The Community Colleges of Southern Nevada library system, as well as the University of Nevada Las Vegas libraries, are available for public use as well.

The Desert Research Institute's (DRI) main research campus in Las Vegas carries out about 300 scientific research projects at any given time. It is a stand-alone institution that falls under the umbrella of the Nevada System of Higher Education, thanks to generous outside research funding. In 2007 the institute had grown 85 percent since 1999 while using only one percent of NSHE's annual budget. Environmental research programs focus on three core divisions of atmospheric sciences, earth and ecosystems sciences, and hydrologic sciences. DRI maintains a library that is available to researchers and scholars. The Church of Jesus Christ of Latter-Day Saints maintains a branch of its genealogical library in Las Vegas. A variety of other specialized libraries and research centers are located in the area.

Public Library Information: Las Vegas-Clark County Library District, 833 Las Vegas Boulevard North, Las Vegas, NV 89101; telephone (702)382-3493

■ Health Care

Among the 11 major hospitals serving the area is the Sunrise Hospital and Medical Center. With over 700 beds and 1,500 physicians, it also maintains centers for renal transplants, breast cancer, sleep disorders, and epilepsy. Affiliated with the University of Nevada School of Medicine, the University Medical Center (UMC) was named in 2005-2006 as being among the top 10 percent of hospitals nationwide in women's health, cardiology, spine surgery, and pulmonary services by HealthGrades. It also is home to Nevada's only children's hospital. UMC's Lions Burn Care Center, the only such facility in Nevada, has gained national recognition; the center also maintains a free-standing trauma center and the state's first pediatric emergency department. Mountain View Hospital features 1,100 physicians and a popular weight loss center, while the Desert Springs Hospital Medical

Center has 286 beds and is the only diabetes treatment center in the area accredited by the American Diabetes Association. In addition to its approximately 400 beds and more than 2,800 staff members, Valley Hospital Medical Center also operates "Flight for Life," an emergency helicopter service for a wide area surrounding Las Vegas. It is one of only 47 hospitals in the nation to be designated as an "Accredited Chest Pain Center with PCI" by the Society of Chest Pain Centers. The University of Nevada School of Medicine's Genetics Program, based in Las Vegas, offers counseling to prospective parents about inherited diseases and provides clinical care to children with birth defects.

■ Recreation

Sightseeing

Most people visit Las Vegas to see shows featuring world-famous entertainers and to try their luck at the gaming tables. But the city offers much more to see and do. The streets of Las Vegas, with neon and glittering lights, are themselves a popular attraction. Also within the city limits is the Old Mormon Fort; built in 1855, it is the oldest structure in the area and tours are offered daily.

East of the city, Lake Mead National Recreation area boasts 500 miles of scenic shoreline created when the Hoover Dam was constructed. Located 30 miles southeast of the city is Hoover Dam, the tallest concrete dam in the Western Hemisphere. The popular site draws about one million visitors annually to its tourist center while millions more drive over it. Only 15 miles west of Las Vegas is Red Rock Canyon, where a 13-mile scenic route winds through a natural landscape inhabited by wild burros and bighorn sheep; hikers and bicyclists can also enjoy 30 miles of trails in the 197,000-acre National Conservation Area. Some 50 miles north, the Valley of Fire State Park contains beautiful desert land, rock formations, and rock drawings surviving from ancient civilizations. Tour buses travel from Las Vegas to Grand Canyon National Park in northern Arizona, where visitors can choose from hiking, camping, biking, fishing, and boating. Several ghost towns are within an hour's drive of Las Vegas; Bonnie Springs Old Nevada, southwest of the city, is a recreated town that evokes the lawless days of the Old West.

Arts and Culture

World famous for entertainment, Las Vegas is a city where nightlife lasts 24 hours a day and spectacular casino resorts and venues feature international stars. There is also an active and acclaimed arts community in Las Vegas; theater, dance, and concert performances as well as lectures are staged at the Reed Whipple Cultural Arts Center. The center is home to the Las Vegas Youth Orchestra and the Rainbow Company Youth Theatre.

The Charleston Heights Arts Center presents theater and musical performances as well as exhibits by local and regional artists. The College of Southern Nevada offers dance, theater, and musical performances.

The University of Nevada at Las Vegas, with three performing arts venues, is the heart of the cultural community. The university hosts performances by Nevada Ballet Theatre, Nevada Symphony Orchestra, Chamber Music Southwest, and the Charles Vanda Master Series.

The Las Vegas Clark County Library District kicked off a partnership with the Nevada Chamber Symphony in the 2004-2005 season, with concerts scheduled in the main theater of the Clark County Library on Flamingo Road. The Library District also hosts theatrical, dance, and other musical performances.

Several museums are located in the city. The Liberace Museum exhibits a collection of rare pianos, including pianos owned by Frederic Chopin and George Gershwin. The Nevada State Museum and Historical Society specializes in the natural history of Southern Nevada, while the Las Vegas Natural History Museum focuses on the region's wildlife and natural environment, both past and present. The Lied Discovery Children's Museum offers hands-on exhibits that let children explore science, arts, and humanities in a fun and educational way.

The Bellagio Gallery of Fine Art in the Bellagio Resort features two to three exhibitions annually, with works from top art museums and private collections. The Las Vegas Art Museum, situated on 30,000 square feet, offers works from a variety of mediums, with a focus on contemporary art. The University of Nevada at Las Vegas maintains an art gallery in the Ham Fine Arts Building on campus, featuring the work of faculty members, touring artists, and students. Las Vegas area commercial galleries show the work of local and nationally known artists.

Festivals and Holidays

Las Vegas hosts the Antiquarian and Used Book Fair in January. The entire month of May is designated Jazz Month, showcasing local and national artists. Helldorado Days in May celebrate the Old West era with rodeos and parades. The Greek Festival in September features authentic food and dancing. National Finals Rodeo is held in December at the Thomas & Mack Center.

Sports for the Spectator

Las Vegas offers enthusiasts many opportunities to cheer for their favorite sports. The Las Vegas 51s, triple A affiliate of the Los Angeles Dodgers, play minor league baseball at Cashman Field in Las Vegas. The AFL's Las Vegas Gladiators play professional indoor football at the Orleans Arena. The Las Vegas Wranglers, members of the ECHL Division, also play at the Orleans Arena. The Las Vegas Strikers of the National Premier Soccer League play at the Bettye Wilson Soccer Complex, but the team announced a hiatus for the 2007-8 season. The University of Las Vegas Rebels' most popular sports include baseball, soccer, football, and basketball. The Las Vegas Moter Speedway offers NASCAR and other motor sports events. High-profile boxing matches are often scheduled in Las Vegas.

Sports for the Participant

Although Las Vegas is in the desert, there are facilities for a number of water sports, including fishing, boating, waterskiing, and canoeing at nearby Lake Mead and on the Colorado River. Nearby Henderson is nationally renowned for its recreational facilities. Las Vegas City parks and Clark County parks continue to be developed to meet the needs of an expanding population; both provide a variety of athletic programming, tennis courts and ballfields, swimming pools, golf courses, community centers, activities, classes, and workshops. The Clark County Wetlands Nature Preserve, which includes two miles of walking trails, is a habitat for numerous species of wildlife and seeks to create a cleaner natural water system in Southern Nevada. More than 30 golf courses exist in the area as well.

Shopping and Dining

Shopping center construction is constantly taking place in the city. A major attraction is the $100 million Forum Shops at Caesars Palace, which opened in 1992 and expanded to 675,000 square feet (an increase of 175,000 square feet) in 2004. Described as combining the opulence of Rodeo Drive with the glitter of the Las Vegas Strip, the Roman-inspired complex houses about 160 upscale shops, art galleries, and a $5 million animated fountain. The Galleria at Sunset Mall in nearby Henderson features one million square feet of enclosed mall space. Boulevard Mall has about 140 shops and eateries. The Fashion Show has seven anchor department stores: Saks Fifth Avenue, Dillard's, Neiman Marcus, Macy's, Nevada's only Nordstrom, and Bloomingdale's Home. It also features "The Cloud," a canopy that is suspended 20 stories over the mall and serves the dual purpose of sunshade during the day and movie projection screen at night. An unusual shopping experience can be found at the Rue de la Paix center, featuring all that is French.

More than 750 restaurants with choices ranging from haute cuisine to inexpensive fare are located in Las Vegas. One such place is Spago, run by internationally-known chef Wolfgang Puck, who uses French cooking techniques to create an eclectic menu. Puck also features a more casual bar and grill within the city bearing his name. In 2004 Bobby Flay, successful chef and star of a popular television show on the Food Network, opened the Mesa Grill at Caesars Palace. Major resort hotels all feature gourmet menus; most hotels on "the Strip" and downtown offer buffet dining. Some examples of the culinary variety available include: AJ's Steakhouse, located in the Hard Rock Hotel; Hard Rock Cafe, residing just outside of the hotel; Planet Hollywood, at Caesars Palace; and the Eiffel Tower Restaurant, inside the Paris Las Vegas Hotel that is shaped to resemble the famous French structure.

Visitor Information: Las Vegas Visitor Information Center, 3150 Paradise Rd., Las Vegas, NV 89109-9096; telephone (702)892-7575; toll-free (877)VISITLV

■ Convention Facilities

Las Vegas is among the nation's foremost meeting destinations, with convention trade being one of the city's major industries. Las Vegas hosted more than 23,825 conventions in 2006, bringing in 6,307,961 convention delegates who have a non-gaming economic impact of $8.2 billion. Along with entertainment and recreation, well-appointed meeting facilities and luxury hotels and resorts are the attractions that consistently draw large and small groups to the city. There are about 133,000 hotel rooms in Las Vegas alone and a total of 9.5 million square feet of meeting and exhibit space citywide.

The Las Vegas Convention Center, after expansions in the late 1990s and then further expansion in the early 2000s, encompasses 3.2 million square feet. Nearly 2 million square feet are available for exhibit space in 16 exhibit halls, while 144 meeting rooms (more than 241,000 square feet) handle seating capacities ranging from 20 to 5,500 people. A grand lobby and concourse area of 225,000 square feet, catering services, state-of-the-art technological service, and ample parking round out the offerings.

Cashman Center in downtown Las Vegas contains 98,100 square feet of exhibit space, 12 meeting rooms, a 1,922 seat state-of-the-art theatre, over 2,500 spaces for parking, and a 10,000 seat baseball stadium. Many of the hotels and motels in the city provide facilities for large and small group functions.

Convention Information: LVCVA Meetings Division, 3150 Paradise Road, Las Vegas, NV 89109; telephone (702)892-0711; fax (702)892-2824 (ask for the Meetings Division)

■ Transportation

Approaching the City

Seemingly isolated in the middle of the desert, Las Vegas is, in fact, easily accessible. McCarran International Airport, located five miles south of the business district, serves Henderson, Las Vegas, and all of Clark County and southern Nevada. In April 2005 the airport debuted its $125 million expansion, consisting of a new-gate wing that allows the airport to handle an additional estimated 3.1 million passengers annually. The 5th busiest airport in the nation, McCarran has 95 total gates and averaged 121,280 passengers per day in 2005.

The city is served by three major highways. I-15 connects Las Vegas with Los Angeles and Salt Lake City. U.S. 95 leads into the city from the northwest and U.S. 93/95 enters from the southeast.

Amtrak Thruway provides bus service between Los Angeles, California, and Las Vegas. Greyhound provides bus service to and from nearby Las Vegas with connections throughout the west.

Traveling in the City

The streets of Las Vegas are laid out in a grid system. The primary north-south routes are Main Street and Las Vegas Boulevard—locally known as the "Strip"—which runs parallel to I-15. Main east-west thoroughfares are Flamingo Road, Tropicana Avenue, and Sahara Avenue. Within the city U.S. 95 is known as the Las Vegas Expressway.

Citizens Area Transit (CAT) operates routes to points throughout the city and metropolitan area, with buses and trolleys serving the Strip every 15 minutes. CAT services extend throughout Clark County; in 2005 the system had over 55 million riders, with 51 routes served by 365 vehicles. The MAX project, or Metropolitan Area Express, is the first transportation system in the United States to operate the Civis vehicle to provide an environmentally-friendly transit alternative to rail service. The Las Vegas Monorail, the only privately owned public transportation system, runs along a four mile route along the Strip, linking major resorts, hotels, attractions, and the convention center along its seven stops.

■ Communications

Newspapers and Magazines

The major daily newspaper is the *Las Vegas Review-Journal,* a morning paper. *Las Vegas Sentinel-Voice* is a weekly African American community newspaper, and the *Sun* is a general weekly community newspaper. *Nevada Senior World* is a monthly newspaper focusing on active seniors. Several small, special interest journals and magazines are also published in the city; among them are *Nevada Business Journal,* which focuses on the Nevada business climate, and *What's On In Las Vegas Magazine,* published every other week. Other publications include scholarly journals, Jewish publications, and those focused on art, foodservice, and business.

Television and Radio

There are nine total television stations broadcasting from the greater Las Vegas region. Cable television service is available by subscription.

Sixteen AM and FM radio stations broadcast from Las Vegas, featuring diverse programming, including news, information, and music ranging from jazz to classical. Additional stations are received from surrounding communities.

Media Information: *Las Vegas Review-Journal,* PO Box 70, Las Vegas, NV 89125; telephone (702)383-0211

Las Vegas Online

Center for Business and Economic Research at the University of Nevada, Las Vegas. Available www.unlv.edu/Research_Centers/cber

City of Las Vegas home page. Available www.lasvegasnevada.gov

Clark County home page. Available www.co.clark.nv.us

Clark County School District. Available ccsd.net

Las Vegas Chamber of Commerce. Available www.lvchamber.com

Las Vegas-Clark County Library District. Available www.lvccld.lib.nv.us

Las Vegas Convention and Visitors Authority. Available www.visitlasvegas.com

Las Vegas Review-Journal. Available www.reviewjournal.com

*Las Vegas Sun.*Available www.lasvegassun.com

Nevada State Museum and Historical Society. Available dmla.clan.lib.nv.us

"One City One Site." Available www.lasvegas.com

Vegas.com (entertainment, dining, attractions, book a room, travel tips). Available www.vegas.com

BIBLIOGRAPHY

Hopkins, A.D., and K.J. Evans, eds., *The First 100: Portraits of the Men and Women Who Shaped Las Vegas* (Las Vegas, NV: Huntington Press, 2000)

Kranes, David, *Low Tide in the Desert: Nevada Stories* (Las Vegas, NV: University of Nevada, 1996)

Vinson, Barney, *Las Vegas Behind the Tables* (Grand Rapids, MI: Gollehon, 1986)

Reno

■ The City in Brief

Founded: 1868 (incorporated 1903)

Head Official: Mayor Robert Cashell (R) (since 2002)

City Population
- 1980: 100,756
- 1990: 133,850
- 2000: 180,480
- 2006 estimate: 210,255
- Percent change, 1990–2000: 34.5%
- U.S. rank in 1980: 169th
- U.S. rank in 1990: 132nd
- U.S. rank in 2000: 130th

Metropolitan Area Population
- 1980: 193,623
- 1990: 254,667
- 2000: 339,486
- 2006 estimate: 400,560
- Percent change, 1990–2000: 33.3%
- U.S. rank in 1980: Not available
- U.S. rank in 1990: 132nd
- U.S. rank in 2000: 119th

Area: 69.34 square miles (2000)

Elevation: 4,400 feet above sea level

Average Annual Temperatures: January, 33.6° F; July, 71.3° F; annual average, 51.3° F

Average Annual Precipitation: 7.48 inches of rain; 24.3 inches of snow

Major Economic Sectors: services, wholesale and retail trade, government

Unemployment rate: 4.4% (June 2007)

Per Capita Income: $24,801 (2005)

2005 FBI Crime Index Property: 10,989

2005 FBI Crime Index Violent: 1,518

Major Colleges and Universities: University of Nevada, Reno, Truckee Meadows Community College, Morrison University, Sierra Nevada College

Daily Newspaper: *Reno Gazette-Journal*

■ Introduction

Reno is known as "The Biggest Little City in the World" because of its outstanding western hospitality, fine dining, entertaining stage shows, top-name performers, history, culture, and 24-hour gaming excitement. The region also offers a wide variety of outdoor recreation including golf and skiing. Golfers can choose from courses in lake, high desert, and mountain settings. Lake Tahoe, located less than an hour's drive from downtown Reno, boasts the largest concentration of ski resorts in North America. Nevada's liberal tax structures, along with Reno's free port status and central location in the West, also make the area an important regional warehouse and distribution center.

■ Geography and Climate

Reno is located at the western border of Nevada—in a valley known as the Truckee Meadows—about 20 miles east of the Sierra Nevada mountains and Lake Tahoe, the second largest alpine lake in the world. The Truckee River passes between Reno and its sister city, Sparks. Temperatures in the region are mild, but can fluctuate as much as 45 degrees between day and night. The temperature at night during the summer rarely rises above 60 degrees. More than half the annual precipitation falls from December to March, in the form of mixed snow and rain, with snow accumulation seldom lasting longer than three or four days. Low humidity and sunny skies are prevalent throughout the year.

Area: 69.34 square miles (2000)

Elevation: 4,400 feet above sea level

Average Temperatures: January, 33.6° F; July, 71.3° F; annual average, 51.3° F

Average Annual Precipitation: 7.48 inches of rain; 24.3 inches of snow

■ History

Reno's Beginnings

Reno's history began when Charles William Fuller arrived in the Truckee Meadows in 1859 and occupied a piece of land on the south bank of the Truckee River. By early 1860, he had constructed a bridge and small hotel, and the place was known as Fuller's Crossing. In the following year, Fuller sold his bridge and hotel to Myron C. Lake, who renamed the spot Lake's Crossing and soon was charging a toll on the bridge. The Crossing became an important station on one of the main routes between northern California and the silver mines of Virginia City and the Comstock Lode.

Lake was the crossing's only property owner until the Central Pacific Railroad (later renamed Union Railroad) crossed the Sierra Nevada in 1868 and pushed its tracks into the Truckee Meadows. Under terms of an agreement between Myron Lake and Central Pacific, a new town was laid out at the crossing; ownership was divided between Lake and the railroad. Almost overnight, buildings began to appear on the town site and the new settlement was named Reno in honor of General Jesse Lee Reno (1823–1862), a Union army officer who was killed during the Civil War.

In 1871, the Nevada State Legislature moved the Washoe County seat to Reno, where one year later the Virginia & Truckee Railroad extended its line. The town soon became an important commercial center on the transcontinental railroad and a transfer point for the immense wealth coming out of the Comstock Lode. The University of Nevada was moved from Elko to Reno in 1885.

Gaming Gains Prominence; Modern Times

At the beginning of the twentieth century, Reno gained national notoriety after a number of famous people obtained divorces in the city under Nevada's lenient laws. Newspapers sensationalized the incidents, dubbing Reno the "divorce capital." Reno's sister city, Sparks, was established in 1904 as a division point on the Southern Pacific Railroad. After the legalization of casino gambling by the state legislature in 1931, Reno filled with gambling

establishments–marking the start of a tourist industry that flourishes today.

In the shadow of the casinos, Reno has quietly grown into an important transportation hub for the western United States and has developed a diverse economic base. The city leaders have recognized this and responded by creating aggressive expansion plans including a railroad system that will eventually bolster travel in the area along with the boom the construction brings. Modern Reno boasts a thriving cultural scene, a refurbished downtown area, and an expanding tourist industry fueled not only by the casinos, but by the many year-round resorts in the nearby mountains. The area's mix of recreational opportunities—from outdoor activities to gambling to plush accommodations—coupled with a warm climate that features more than 300 sunny days every year, has been the backbone to the success of the city. The effects are evident in its population and business growth, so much so that *Inc. Magazine* named Reno the "No. 1 Place for Doing Business in America 2005."

Historical Information: Nevada Historical Society-Research Library, 1650 N. Virginia St., Reno, NV 89503; telephone (775)688-1190; fax (775)688-2917

■ Population Profile

Metropolitan Area Residents

  1980: 193,623
  1990: 254,667
  2000: 339,486
  2006 estimate: 400,560
  Percent change, 1990–2000: 33.3%
  U.S. rank in 1980: Not available
  U.S. rank in 1990: 132nd
  U.S. rank in 2000: 119th

City Residents

  1980: 100,756
  1990: 133,850
  2000: 180,480
  2006 estimate: 210,255
  Percent change, 1990–2000: 34.5%
  U.S. rank in 1980: 169th
  U.S. rank in 1990: 132nd
  U.S. rank in 2000: 130th

Density: 2,611.4 people per square mile (2000)

Racial and ethnic characteristics (2005)

  White: 155,991
  Black: 6,025
  American Indian and Alaska Native: 2,997
  Asian: 12,067

Courtesy of the Reno Sparks Convention & Visitors Authority. Reproduced by permission.

Native Hawaiian and Pacific Islander: 1,783
Hispanic or Latino (may be of any race): 45,665
Other: 20,696

Percent of residents born in state: 24.1%
(2006)

Age characteristics (2005)

Population under 5 years old: 15,131
Population 5 to 9 years old: 12,190
Population 10 to 14 years old: 12,737
Population 15 to 19 years old: 12,968
Population 20 to 24 years old: 20,270
Population 25 to 34 years old: 31,894
Population 35 to 44 years old: 28,745
Population 45 to 54 years old: 27,373
Population 55 to 59 years old: 11,192
Population 60 to 64 years old: 9,348
Population 65 to 74 years old: 12,523
Population 75 to 84 years old: 7,692
Population 85 years and older: 2,415
Median age: 34.3 years

Births (2006, MSA)

Total number: 5,721

Deaths (2006, MSA)

Total number: 3,076

Money income (2005)

Per capita income: $24,801
Median household income: $42,214
Total households: 88,118

Number of households with income of . . .

less than $10,000: 7,716
$10,000 to $14,999: 6,294
$15,000 to $24,999: 12,379
$25,000 to $34,999: 10,604
$35,000 to $49,999: 13,916
$50,000 to $74,999: 15,453
$75,000 to $99,999: 9,956
$100,000 to $149,999: 7,728
$150,000 to $199,999: 2,290
$200,000 or more: 1,782

Percent of families below poverty level: 10.3% (2005)

2005 FBI Crime Index Property: 10,989

2005 FBI Crime Index Violent: 1,518

■ Municipal Government

Reno operates under a mayor-city council-city manager form of government. The seven council members and the mayor, who appoint a city manager, all serve four-year terms.

Head Official: Mayor Robert Cashell (R) (since 2002; current term expires 2010)

Total Number of City Employees: 1,500 full-time (2007)

City Information: City of Reno, PO Box 1900, Reno, NV 89505; telephone (702)334-INFO; fax (702) 334-3110; email renodirect@cityofreno.com

■ Economy

Major Industries and Commercial Activity

Tourism is the major industry in the Reno area. The hotel and casino industry attracts more than five million visitors annually and adds over $4 billion to the local economy each year. The business climate also has a strong presence in manufacturing and logistics in industries such as computers, electronics, financial services, and communications. Thirty-five *Fortune* 500 companies and nine Top 20 *Fortune* "America's Most Admired Companies" have major offices in the Reno area. This diversity supports the thriving local economy and includes a wide range of restaurants and retail options. The nearby mountains draw many tourists to the highest concentration of ski resorts in America, and contribute to the unlimited year-round recreational opportunities.

Items and goods produced: cement, labeling devices, suntan lotion, valves, dairy and food products, pet food, microwaves, electronic equipment, livestock, agricultural produce

Incentive Programs—New and Existing Companies

Local programs: To encourage industrial development, Reno offers tax deferral, exemption, and abatement programs, further reducing the already-low tax rates in the state. Reno is part of northern Nevada's foreign trade zone, which, at nearly 7,500 acres, is one of the largest in the nation.

State programs: The State of Nevada administers Small Business Administration loans, in addition to the Modified Business Tax Abatement Program, which provides a partial abatement of taxes to qualified new businesses and local businesses that are expanding. The Nevada Development Capital Corporation (NDCC) provides more than $3 million from Nevada banks, utilities, and mining companies and other firms to help finance growth opportunities for new and existing businesses. It provides flexible financing to small Nevada businesses that do not qualify for more conventional financing. Because a majority of tax revenues in Nevada are generated from the tourism and gaming industries, Nevada's tax burden is one of the lightest in the nation. The state has no personal state income tax, no unitary tax, no corporate income tax, no inventory tax, no estate and/or gift tax, no franchise tax, no inheritance tax, and no special intangible tax.

Job training programs: The Nevada Department of Employment, Training, and Rehabilitation offers job training services to both employers and job seekers, including applicant recruitment and screening, tax credit benefits, training programs and career enhancement programs, and labor market information. The Train Employees Now (TEN) program, administered by the State of Nevada Commission on Economic Development, helps new and expanding firms by providing intensive skills-based training programs tailored to the company's needs. The TEN program utilizes training providers such as local businesses and community colleges. Job Opportunities in Nevada (JOIN) works to ensure that companies have an adequate workforce while offering training and educational opportunities for job seekers; Nevadaworks assists employers in developing employees' skills. The public school district's Glenn Hare Occupational Center provides training in areas identified by local employers. Training, recruiting, and continuing education resources in Reno also include Truckee Meadows Community College and the University of Nevada, Reno. Several other educational programs are geared toward meeting the needs of employers such as the Nevada Prepaid Tuition Program and the Millennium Scholarship Plan.

Development Projects

The city of Reno is bustling with economic development in the downtown area, and the local government actively creates plans to ensure progress continues. Over thirty million dollars of city and one billion dollars in private/ other public investment has been made to modernize downtown Reno in recent years. Also critical to the success of the area has been the fulfillment of a long-anticipated $282 million plan to build depressed railroad tracks, named ReTRAC, to facilitate travel. Discussed for many decades, the construction, completed in 2006, was estimated to have an overall $360 million economic impact and won an "Aon Build America" award for its design in 2007.

In 2007 more than 2,000 luxury condominiums were under construction, in addition to a 127-room Hyatt Hotel underway at the Reno-Tahoe International Airport. Expected to be complete by early 2008 was a 28,000-square-foot ballroom built by the City of Reno to host meetings and conventions, located across from the National Bowling Museum. Station Casinos, a Las Vegas-based company, announced plans to complete four casino/hotels in the Reno area by 2010-2011. In 2007 the Reno City Council approved plans to bring a Triple A ballpark to the area, as well as funding for a "Ballpark District," featuring shopping, dining, and entertainment; no completion date was yet finalized but start-up costs were estimated at $81 million.

Economic Development Information: Economic Development Authority of Western Nevada (EDAWN), 5190 Neil Rd., Ste. 111, Reno, NV 89502; telephone (702)829-3700; fax (702)829-3710; email info@edawn.org

Commercial Shipping

Reno/Sparks is situated at the hub of an extensive transportation network. Nevada borders five western states and provides overnight ground service to ten of the eleven West Coast major markets.

The area is also located on two major highway corridors: Interstate 80 and US 395. Over 60 local, regional and national carriers provide trucking service in the Reno/Sparks area including the United Parcel Service (UPS) regional package-sorting hub in Sparks. Rail freight service is provided by Burlington Northern Santa Fe and Union Pacific Railroads.

The Reno/Tahoe International Airport is the nation's 45th busiest airport, with 170 daily departures/arrivals. Air Cargo in the Reno/Sparks area handled 55,551 metric tons of cargo in 2006.

The Reno/Sparks foreign trade zones are popular to business, as they provide economically favorable conditions and operational flexibility. Reno/Sparks has eight sites with more than 7,500 acres of building space.

Labor Force and Employment Outlook

The availability of skilled workers and competitive compensation levels makes the Reno/Sparks area especially attractive to new businesses. More than 20,000 students attend the five colleges in the area, many of whom remain in the region following graduation. State-supported training programs and pro-business policies have helped make Nevada the fastest growing state in the nation. As a right-to-work state, Nevada's law states that no person shall be denied the opportunity to obtain or retain employment because of non-membership in a labor organization.

In August 2007 the unemployment rate stood at 4.4 percent, down from 5.8 in 1997, but fairly consistent with the overall 10-year trend. There was an annual job growth rate of around 1.7 percent. Approximately 65 percent of workers in the Reno area are employed in the trade and services sectors (including casino and hospitality jobs), while 25 percent are employed in

construction, manufacturing, transportation, communications, public utilities, and finance related services.

The following is a summary of data regarding the Reno-Sparks metropolitan area labor force, 2006 annual averages.

Size of nonagricultural labor force: 223,500

Number of workers employed in . . .

    construction and mining: 24,100
    manufacturing: 14,500
    trade, transportation and utilities: 47,200
    information: 2,800
    financial activities: 10,700
    professional and business services: 28,800
    educational and health services: 19,900
    leisure and hospitality: 39,500
    other services: 7,300
    government: 28,600

Average hourly earnings of production workers employed in manufacturing: Not available

Unemployment rate: 4.4% (June 2007)

Largest county employers (2007)	*Number of employees*
University of Nevada	4,000–4,499
International Game Technology	2,500–2,999
Washoe Medical Center	2,000–2,499
Silver Legacy	2,000–2,499
Peppermill Hotel Casino	1,500–1,999
City of Reno	1,500–1,999
Reno Hilton	1,500–1,999
Atlantis Casino Resort	1,500–1,999
Eldorado Hotel & Casino	1,500–1,999
Sparks Nugget, Inc.	1,500–1,999
Circus Circus Casinos, Inc.	1,500–1,999
St. Mary's	1,500–1,999
Harrah's Reno	1,000–1,499
Hire Dynamics LLC	1,000–1,499
United Parcel Service	1,000–1,499

Cost of Living

The following is a summary of data regarding key cost of living factors for the Reno area.

2007 (1st quarter) ACCRA Average House Price: $359,100

2007 (1st quarter) ACCRA Cost of Living Index: 108.5

State income tax rate: None

State sales tax rate: 6.5%

Local income tax rate: None

Local sales tax rate: 0.875%

Property tax rate: $3.64 per $100 assessed value

Economic Information: Economic Development Authority of Western Nevada (EDAWN), 5190 Neil Rd., Ste. 111, Reno, NV 89502; telephone (702)829-3700; fax (702)829-3710; email info@edawn.org. Nevada Department of Employment, Training & Rehabilitation, Information Development and Processing, Research and Analysis Bureau, 500 E. Third St., Carson City, NV 89713; telephone (775) 684-0450; email detradmn@nvdetr.org

■ Education and Research

Elementary and Secondary Schools

Reno is part of the Washoe County School District, the second-largest district in the state. The district is governed by a board of trustees that consists of seven nonpartisan members. The superintendent is appointed by the board. Total district enrollment is more than 63,000.

Reno public school students consistently score above state and national averages on standardized tests, including the Iowa Test of Basic Skills/Iowa Test of Educational Development (ITBS/ITED) and, for high school students, the ACT and SAT college entrance exams. Five Reno public high schools have been named by *Newsweek* as among the best in the country. Of 16 Nevada public schools recognized as "exemplary" in 2006, twelve were in Washoe County. Special programs include the Parent/School Partnership training, co-sponsored by the Mexican American Legal Defense and Educational Fund, as well as charter and magnet schools at the primary and secondary levels.

The following is a summary of data regarding the Washoe County School District as of the 2005–2006 school year.

Total enrollment: 64,696

Number of facilities

    elementary schools: 64
    junior high/middle schools: 15
    senior high schools: 12
    other: 3

Student/teacher ratio: 21:1

Teacher salaries (2005–06)

    elementary median: $27,907–57,292

    junior high/middle median: Not available
    secondary median: Not available

Funding per pupil: $6,430

Public Schools Information: Washoe County School District, 425 E. Ninth St., PO Box 30425, Reno, NV 89520-3425; telephone (775)348-0200

Colleges and Universities

The University of Nevada, Reno, founded in 1864, enrolled 16,336 degree-seeking students in fall 2005 at both the undergraduate and postgraduate levels. It has a total budget of $500 million, and offers 75 bachelor's degree programs in addition to 100 at the master's and doctorate level. The university includes schools of medicine, journalism, and education; a college for training judges (National Judicial College); and the only program in Basque studies in the country (many Nevadans trace their ancestry to Basque sheepherders from Spain). The Truckee Meadows Community College offers two-year associate's degrees as well as adult education programs in more than 50 different fields of study. A number of business, vocational, and professional schools are also located in the Reno area. Morrison University focuses on business degrees while the Sierra Nevada College in Lake Tahoe takes advantage of its location by presenting many science and environmental programs, in addition to hosting nationally recognized speakers on various topics—from poetry to politics—from time to time.

Libraries and Research Centers

The Washoe County Library System consists of 14 library branches strategically placed around the county with the newest branch, Spanish Springs, which opened in early 2005. In addition, there is a Mobile Branch and an "Internet Branch." Six of the branches are "Partnership Libraries," which are housed in public school libraries but serve the entire public in their neighborhoods. The library has nearly 950,000 items including books, videos, audios, and materials in microformat, CD-ROMs, database access, and several hundred periodical subscriptions. Special collections focus on gambling, Nevada history, and U.S. and Nevada documents.

The University of Nevada, Reno Libraries offer resources in paper and electronic formats, including over one million texts and journals available in-house, as well as electronic access to the full-text articles of over 8,000 journals. Films, audio and video tapes, maps, and government documents are also available. Special collections include Basque materials (50,000 volumes and 1,500 journals), Nevada and the Great Basin collection (which includes over 200,000 photographs), rare books and prints, and a collection of contemporary arts books.

The Desert Research Institute (DRI) maintains facilities in Reno (the 470-acre Dandini Research Park) and oversees about 300 separate projects throughout the state, conducting studies in areas such as air quality and climactic changes in the western United States over the last two million years. The University of Nevada is a hotbed for research activities and spent over $80 million on research in 2006.

Public Library Information: Washoe County Library, 301 S. Center St., Reno, NV 89501; telephone (775) 327-8300; fax (775)327-8393; email internet@washoe.lib.nv.us

■ Health Care

Twelve hospitals and clinics serve Reno, including Renown Health, known as Washoe Medical Center until 2006. The system, which serves a 17-county area, features institutes for cancer, cardiac health, and neurosciences. Its hospitals provide 24-hour emergency room facilities and various specialized treatment programs. The medical community consists of about 800 physicians and approximately 3,000 registered and licensed practical nurses. Renown Health planned to open Tahoe Towers in late fall 2007, which was billed as "the most advanced health care facility in the region," with 190 private rooms. Other health-related facilities include West Hills Hospital, Tahoe Pacific Hospital, St. Mary's At Galena Urgent, and the Surgical Arts Surgery Center. The University of Nevada School of Medicine, with a campus in Reno, is the state's only public medical school.

■ Recreation

Sightseeing

Downtown Reno glitters with brightly-lit casinos and 24-hour entertainment. In the middle of it all stands the city's best-known symbol, the Reno Arch. The arch welcomes visitors with its slogan, "The Biggest Little City In The World." There have been four arches since the original was erected in 1929; the current disco ball version has been there since 1987. The arch that welcomed visitors from 1934 to 1963 can now be seen on Lake Street, in front of the National Automobile Museum.

One of the country's finest and most extensive collections of antique cars is on display at the National Automobile Museum (The Harrah Collection). Opened in 1989, more than 220 vehicles are featured, including horseless carriages, cars owned by celebrities, and experimental cars of the future.

Described by the *Los Angeles Times* as the "Taj Mahal of Tenpins," the National Bowling Stadium is the only facility of its kind in the world. The stadium features 78-championship lanes, Paul Revere's Kick's Diner & Dance Club, and an IWERKS theater where giant screen movies

are shown daily. In 2005 the facility began a $1.3 million renovation, which involved the installation of a massive, state of the art scoring system.

The Wilbur D. May Center features a museum, an indoor arboretum, and a botanical garden surrounded by a beautiful park. During summer months, the center's Great Basin Adventure provides children with a full day of activities including pony rides, a "hands-on" discovery room, a log flume ride, a petting zoo, and a playground complete with dinosaurs.

Daytrip excursions also provide visitors with a number of sightseeing options. Reno serves as a base camp to some of the most unique attractions on the West Coast. Pyramid Lake, just east of Reno, is shrouded in the mysteries of Indian legend and prehistoric past; Virginia City, still the liveliest ghost town in the West, is only a 35-mile drive from Reno; Carson City, Nevada's State Capital, is only 30 miles from Reno; and nearby Lake Tahoe was described by Mark Twain as "surely the fairest picture the whole earth affords."

Arts and Culture

Reno offers a flourishing and diverse community of artistic talent. The 1,500-seat Pioneer Center for the Performing Arts is the home of the Reno Philharmonic Orchestra, the Sierra Nevada Master Chorale, and the Reno Dance Company. A chamber orchestra, opera company, and two ballet troupes round out the Reno experience. The University of Nevada, Reno, presents a variety of art galleries, music, and performing arts.

The Nevada Museum of Art, originally called the Nevada Art Gallery in 1931, debuted its new four-level, 55,000 square foot location in May 2003 and features a permanent collection along with video and experimental exhibitions. A library, cafe, sculpture garden, and store are among the other modern amenities offered.

Reno's own summer arts festival, Uptown Downtown ARTown, was named one of the top 100 Events in North America by the American Bus Association. The festival takes place every July, when more than 150 events at three dozen locations are featured throughout the month.

Festivals and Holidays

Special events are plentiful and varied in Reno. The Reno Rodeo, the "wildest, richest rodeo in the west," takes place over nine days in June and infuses nearly $35 million into the local economy. In August, the Reno area celebrates America's love affair with cars and rock 'n' roll during the five-day Hot August Nights. The celebration features more than 5,000 classic cars, vintage music, parades, and drag racing. September is full of celebrations, which include the Great Reno Balloon Race, the National Championship Air Races and Air Show, and Street Vibrations (which attracts more than 30,000 motorcycle enthusiasts annually). October brings the Eldorado's Great Italian Festival and the Celtic Festival.

Sports for the Spectator

Reno is making a name for itself as the mountain golf capital of the world. Since 1999 the PGA Tour's Reno-Tahoe Open has taken place at Montreux Golf and Country Club in August, where some of the world's best professional golfers compete. A celebrity-packed golfing event, the American Century Celebrity Championship, is also held annually at Edgewood-Tahoe in July.

Two of the country's largest bowling organizations, the American Bowling Congress (ABC) and the Women's International Bowling Congress (WIBC), hold tournaments at the National Bowling Stadium. Dubbed "Pin Palace" by *USA Today*, it draws thousands of bowlers to it's high-technology facility on a regular basis.

Sports for the Participant

Reno offers a seemingly limitless variety of indoor and outdoor activities. Snow-packed mountains, less than an hour from Reno, feature the largest concentration of world-class ski/snowboard resorts in North America. In the summer months, the same mountains, as well as the valley below, offer hiking and mountain biking. Since 1994 the three-day annual Mighty Tour De Nez Classic has featured different levels of regional bicyclers. Lake Tahoe, "the Jewel of the Sierra," is the perfect place for a day of canoeing, water skiing, swimming, and more.

High desert, rolling hills and mountainous alpine terrain make for some of the greatest golf courses found anywhere. The Reno-Tahoe area boasts more than 40 courses, 4,000 feet above sea level so golfers can watch their balls fly further through the thin air. The Reno area also offers great fishing in a variety of streams, rivers, and lakes. Non-resident fishing licenses are available at most sporting goods stores.

Shopping and Dining

More than 90 area shopping centers sell items ranging from the usual designer apparel to Native American handicrafts and Western art and clothing. Popular centers in Reno include Arlington Gardens Mall, Franktown Corners, Southwest Pavilion, Meadowood Mall, Park Lane Mall, and Indian Colony Corners. Sparks is home to Victorian Square Plaza.

Restaurants in Reno range from simple to extravagant. A local specialty is family-style Basque dinners.

Visitor Information: Reno-Sparks Convention & Visitors Authority, PO Box 837, Reno, NV 89504-0837; general information number telephone (800)FOR-RENO; email info@visitrenotahoe.com

■ Convention Facilities

In the heart of downtown is the two-floor Reno Events Center, which has a capacity of 7,000 and hosts everything from business conventions to rock concerts. In July 2002 the Reno-Sparks Convention Center completed an extensive expansion costing more than $100 million that provides convention and meeting planners with a modern, high-tech facility. The convention center's space increased to nearly 500,000 square feet and includes 53 meeting rooms and exhibit space totaling 381,000 square feet.

Meeting attendees can visit the National Bowling Stadium in Reno, where customized tournaments on its 78 championship lanes can be arranged for groups of anywhere between 50 and 2,000 people in the four-story facility that boasts a 172-seat theater.

The Motel 6 Reno Livestock Events Center provides space for livestock and equestrian events, as well as meetings. It includes 35,000 square feet of exhibit space, a climate-controlled indoor arena seating 6,200 and a lighted, 9,000-seat outdoor arena.

Theater-style seating for more than 1,500 people is available at the Pioneer Center for the Performing Arts in downtown Reno. The Lawlor Events Center, a large multipurpose arena on the campus of the University of Nevada, Reno is also available for conventions and can seat around 1,200.

Reno has more than 20,000 first-class guestrooms all within minutes of the Reno-Sparks Convention Center and Reno-Tahoe International Airport. Eighteen local properties also offer facilities for meetings and conventions.

Convention Information: Reno-Sparks Convention & Visitors Authority, PO Box 837, Reno, NV 89405-0837; telephone (800)FOR-RENO; email info@visitrenotahoe.com

■ Transportation

Approaching the City

The Reno/Tahoe International Airport (RTIA) is located three miles south of downtown Reno. The airport handles about 14,000 arriving and departing passengers on about 170 flights per day, and is an international Port of Entry. In 2006 five million passengers travelled through RTIA. Reno Stead Airport is a small general aviation airport located north of Reno, with two runways located on 5,000 acres. Passenger rail service is available from Amtrak via the "California Zephyr," described as the most scenic train ride in the United States, with daily service from San Francisco and Chicago. The city is also served by commercial bus lines.

Interstate highway 80 runs through Reno's downtown region, west to San Francisco, and east to Salt Lake city. The US 395 freeway passes just to the east of the city, connecting Reno with Portland and Seattle to the north and Los Angeles to the south.

Traveling in the City

Washoe County's Regional Transportation Commission (RTC) runs the Reno Citifare, which provides continuous travel throughout the metropolitan area; most of its buses have wheelchair accessibility. RTC's CitiLift offers bus service to those with special transportation needs. The Sierra Spirit bus line gives free rides to passengers in the downtown area. Citifare also offers commuter bus service, PRIDE, between Reno and Carson City. Major thoroughfares in the city include Virginia Street, Plumb Lane, Kietzke Lane, and Mill Street.

■ Communications

Newspapers and Magazines

The *Reno Gazette-Journal* is the city's daily and Sunday newspaper, published in the morning. The *Daily Sparks Tribune* is a daily newspaper published in neighboring Sparks since 1910. *Ahora Spanish News* is a semi-monthly Hispanic community newspaper. Also published in Reno are *Sagebrush* (a collegiate newspaper), *Reno News and Review*, and *Showtime Magazine*.

Television and Radio

Five commercial television stations are based in the greater Reno area; a variety of channels are available from the local cable system. Over 20 radio stations broadcast from the Reno/Tahoe area.

Media Information: *Reno Gazette Journal,* PO Box 22000, Reno, NV 89520; telephone (775)788-6200

Reno Online

City of Reno. Available www.cityofreno.com

Economic Development Authority of Western Nevada. Available www.edawn.org

Nevada Department of Employment, Training & Rehabilitation. Available detr.state.nv.us

Reno Gazette Journal. Available www.rgj.com

Reno-Sparks Chamber of Commerce. Available www.reno-sparkschamber.org

Reno-Sparks Convention & Visitors Authority. Available www.visitrenotahoe.com

Reno Visitor's Center. Available www .visitrenotahoe.com

Truckee Meadows Community College. Available www.tmcc.edu

Washoe County Library. Available www.washoe.lib .nv.us

Washoe County School District. Available www .washoe.k12.nv.us

BIBLIOGRAPHY

Betts, Doris, *The Sharp Teeth of Love: A Novel* (New York: Scribner, 1998)

Land, Barbara and Myrick Land, *A Short History of Reno* (Reno, NV: University of Nevada Press, 1995)

Twain, Mark, *Mark Twain of the Enterprise; Newspaper Articles and Other Documents, 1862–1864* (Berkeley, CA: U. of California Press, 1957)

New Mexico

The State in Brief

Nickname: Land of Enchantment

Motto: Crescit eundo (It grows as it goes)

Flower: Yucca

Bird: Roadrunner

Area: 121,589 square miles (2000; U.S. rank 5th)

Elevation: Ranges from 2,842 feet to 13,161 feet above sea level

Climate: Semi-arid and sunny, with temperatures varying according to elevation

Admitted to Union: January 6, 1912

Capital: Santa Fe

Head Official: Governor Bill Richardson (D) (until 2010)

Population
1980: 1,302,894
1990: 1,515,069
2000: 1,819,046
2006 estimate: 1,954,599
Percent change, 1990–2000: 20.1%
U.S. rank in 2006: 36th
Percent of residents born in state: 50.86% (2006)
Density: 15.9 people per square mile (2006)
2006 FBI Crime Index Total: 89,528

Racial and Ethnic Characteristics (2006)
White: 1,325,762
Black or African American: 39,654
American Indian and Alaska Native: 189,152
Asian: 25,983
Native Hawaiian and Pacific Islander: 1,396
Hispanic or Latino (may be of any race): 860,687
Other: 309,772

Age Characteristics (2006)
Population under 5 years old: 141,732
Population 5 to 19 years old: 427,441
Percent of population 65 years and over: 12.3%
Median age: 35.2

Vital Statistics
Total number of births (2006): 28,946
Total number of deaths (2006): 14,655
AIDS cases reported through 2005: 2,526

Economy
Major industries: Government; manufacturing; services; finance, insurance, and real estate; trade
Unemployment rate (2006): 6.4%
Per capita income (2006): $20,913
Median household income (2006): $40,629
Percentage of persons below poverty level (2006): 18.5%
Income tax rate: 1.7% to 5.3%
Sales tax rate: 5.0%

Albuquerque

■ The City in Brief

Founded: 1706 (incorporated 1891)

Head Official: Mayor Martin Chavez (since 2001)

City Population

> 1980: 332,920
> 1990: 384,915
> 2000: 448,607
> 2006 estimate: 504,949
> Percent change, 1990–2000: 15.9%
> U.S. rank in 1980: 44th
> U.S. rank in 1990: 38th (State rank: 1st)
> U.S. rank in 2000: 42nd (State rank: 1st)

Metropolitan Area Population

> 1980: 485,430
> 1990: 589,131
> 2000: 712,738
> 2006 estimate: 816,811
> Percent change, 1990–2000: 21.0%
> U.S. rank in 1980: 80th
> U.S. rank in 1990: 77th
> U.S. rank in 2000: 62nd

Area: 180.64 square miles (2000)

Elevation: 5,311 feet above sea level

Average Annual Temperatures: January, 35.7° F; July, 78.5° F; annual average, 56.8° F

Average Annual Precipitation: 9.47 inches of rain; 11.0 inches of snow

Major Economic Sectors: services, wholesale and retail trade, government

Unemployment Rate: 3.7% (June 2007)

Per Capita Income: $24,576 (2005)

2005 FBI Crime Index Property: 30,243

2005 FBI Crime Index Violent: 4,670

Major Colleges and Universities: University of New Mexico, University of Phoenix, Central New Mexico Community College, College of Santa Fe at Albuquerque

Daily Newspaper: *Albuquerque Journal; The Albuquerque Tribune*

■ Introduction

Surrounded by natural beauty, Albuquerque is at the center of Native American pueblo country in New Mexico, the "Land of Enchantment." The state's largest city, Albuquerque retains deep roots in the past and simultaneously stands on the cutting edge of the future. The original Spanish town was built on the site of the oldest farming civilization in North America; modern Albuquerque is the focal point of the "Rio Grande Research Corridor," one of the nation's primary space-research complexes. The city's residents have maintained ethnic traditions and preserved a high quality of life while at the same time fostering modern growth and economic development. Boasting a balance between natural settings and a thriving economy, Albuquerque was named as one of the "Top 50 Best Places to Live and Play" by *National Geographic Adventure* magazine in 2007.

■ Geography and Climate

Albuquerque is situated in the middle of the Rio Grande valley. To the east of the city are the Sandia and Manzano mountains; to the west are five volcanic cones that mark the beginning of high plateau country. The climate in

Albuquerque, termed "arid-continental," is sunny and dry with very low humidity. Half of the annual precipitation falls between July and September in heavy afternoon thundershowers. During the winter one can ski on Sandia Peak and play a round of golf on the same day.

Area: 180.64 square miles (2000)

Elevation: 5,311 feet above sea level

Average Temperatures: January, 35.7° F; July, 78.5° F; annual average, 56.8° F

Average Annual Precipitation: 9.47 inches of rain; 11.0 inches of snow

■ History

Early Native American and Spanish Influences

The region surrounding present-day Albuquerque was home to several groups of Native American peoples, including "Sandia Man," who lived there and hunted mastodon during the ice age 25,000 years ago. Albuquerque was later inhabited by the ancient Anasazi Indians. Their huge apartment-like buildings, constructed 3,000 years ago of stone and adobe, are still standing. The city continues to be a center of Native American culture; most of New Mexico's 19 pueblos—including the thousand-year-old, still-inhabited Acoma Pueblo—are within an hour's drive. To the north is Sandia Pueblo Indian Reservation. Albuquerque's modern architecture, particularly buildings on the University of New Mexico campus, combines modern design elements with Native American and Hispanic motifs.

Albuquerque was founded as a villa in 1706 by Spanish colonists, who were attracted to the banks of the Rio Grande by the green pastures they needed to graze their sheep. The city is named for a Spanish Duke, the tenth Duke of Alburquerque (over time the first "r" in his name was dropped). The first structure built in Albuquerque was a church named for the city's patron saint, San Felipe de Neri. The original adobe walls remain standing in the part of the city known as Old Town.

City Becomes Distribution Center

Although the topography of the land—the mountains to the east and the Rio Grande to the west—afforded the settlement natural protection, Albuquerque was regularly threatened during the nineteenth century by hostile attacks, particularly from the Navajo and Apache. In the meantime, the town assumed a role as purveyor of goods to the West and served as a link in trade with Mexico. Situated on the Old Chihuahua trail, an extension of the Santa Fe Trail, Albuquerque's stores and warehouses were perfectly positioned to supply forts that were established in the Southwest to protect westward-moving settlers. Albuquerque became a U.S. Army post in 1846 and was occupied by the Confederacy for two months during the Civil War.

In 1880 rail travel arrived in Albuquerque. The town's strength as a transportation and trade center grew as manufactured goods were shipped in from the East and raw materials and livestock were transported from the West. A bustling new town quickly sprang up around the railroad, then grew to take in historic Old Town. In 1883 Albuquerque became the seat of Bernalillo County, and in 1891 it was incorporated as a city. Already an established oasis of civilization, Albuquerque, unlike other southwestern towns, never suffered from the boisterousness of the Old West.

Development of Atomic Bomb Brings High Technology

Until World War II, Albuquerque remained a small, quiet city. Then the development of the atomic bomb at nearby Los Alamos brought the town into the nuclear age. Now an important part of the Rio Grande Research Corridor, Albuquerque has undergone record population growth. It is a center of large high-technology industries that have evolved around the research and development of atomic energy and space exploration, drawing as well hundreds of smaller research firms. The city celebrated its tricentennial in 2006 with events and exhibits honoring Albuquerque's art, history, and culture. With the passing of the tricentennial, city officials focused on continued success in economic development, particularly in the technology industry. In 2007 significant advances were made in aviation, with the beginning of an aviation campus at Eclipse Aviation; and film, as Sony Pictures Imageworks announced the opening of a new branch in Albuquerque.

■ Population Profile

Metropolitan Area Residents

   1980: 485,430
   1990: 589,131
   2000: 712,738
   2006 estimate: 816,811
   Percent change, 1990–2000: 21.0%
   U.S. rank in 1980: 80th
   U.S. rank in 1990: 77th
   U.S. rank in 2000: 62nd

City Residents

   1980: 332,920
   1990: 384,915
   2000: 448,607
   2006 estimate: 504,949
   Percent change, 1990–2000: 15.9%

©James Blank.

U.S. rank in 1980: 44th
U.S. rank in 1990: 38th (State rank: 1st)
U.S. rank in 2000: 42nd (State rank: 1st)

Density: 2,483.4 people per square mile (2000)

Racial and ethnic characteristics (2005)

White: 352,257
Black: 15,368
American Indian and Alaska Native: 21,327
Asian: 10,976
Native Hawaiian and Pacific Islander: 873
Hispanic or Latino (may be of any race): 213,289
Other: 70,604

Percent of residents born in state: 46.7% (2000)

Age characteristics (2005)

Population under 5 years old: 35,037
Population 5 to 9 years old: 30,866
Population 10 to 14 years old: 31,241
Population 15 to 19 years old: 33,544
Population 20 to 24 years old: 38,867
Population 25 to 34 years old: 66,925
Population 35 to 44 years old: 71,011

Population 45 to 54 years old: 71,746
Population 55 to 59 years old: 31,333
Population 60 to 64 years old: 19,424
Population 65 to 74 years old: 31,070
Population 75 to 84 years old: 20,455
Population 85 years and older: 6,614
Median age: 35.8 years

Births (2006, MSA)

Total number: 11,732

Deaths (2006, MSA)

Total number: 5,912

Money income (2005)

Per capita income: $24,576
Median household income: $41,820
Total households: 208,824

Number of households with income of ...

less than $10,000: 18,489
$10,000 to $14,999: 14,713
$15,000 to $24,999: 30,102
$25,000 to $34,999: 22,551
$35,000 to $49,999: 32,594

$50,000 to $74,999: 39,611
$75,000 to $99,999: 20,536
$100,000 to $149,999: 20,246
$150,000 to $199,999: 5,124
$200,000 or more: 4,858

Percent of families below poverty level: 14.5% (2005)

2005 FBI Crime Index Property: 30,243

2005 FBI Crime Index Violent: 4,670

■ Municipal Government

Albuquerque operates under a mayor-council form of government, with a full-time mayor, nine council members—all of whom serve staggered four-year terms—and a chief administrative officer, who is appointed by the mayor. The city is the seat of Bernalillo County.

Head Official: Mayor Martin Chavez (since 2001; current term expires 2009)

Total Number of City Employees: more than 7,000 (2007)

City Information: City of Albuquerque, PO Box 1293, Albuquerque, NM 87103; telephone (505)768-3000

■ Economy

Major Industries and Commercial Activity

The largest city in New Mexico, Albuquerque is also its economic center; it accounts for nearly half of the state's economic activity. Part of its success can be attributed to a diverse economic base consisting of government, services, trade, agriculture, tourism, manufacturing, and technology research and development. In 2006 *Forbes* magazine ranked Albuquerque the best city in the nation for business and careers.

The Rio Grande River valley contains rich farm and pasture lands that support a sizable food industry, based mainly on fruit and produce, in the Albuquerque area. Since its early years as a stop on the Santa Fe Trail, the city has been a transportation and service center. Albuquerque is also home to hundreds of manufacturing firms—many of them located in well-planned industrial parks—that produce such goods as trailers, food products, electronic components, neon and electric signs, hardware, and machine tools. Among the major manufacturing firms that call Albuquerque home are Intel, GE, and General Mills.

The Rio Grande Research Corridor, a constellation of high-technology industries, sprang up in the wake of the development of nuclear research during and after World War II. Each year, more than $4 billion is spent on research and development in the region. The area's major employers are part of this complex. Sandia National Laboratories, a government research and development lab, is involved in laser technology and solar energy, and employs about 8,500 workers. Kirtland U.S. Air Force Base, the area's largest employer with some 25,500 employees and the sixth-largest military base in the world, is a weapons research center. In 2006 the value of the base's economic impact to the local area was $8.2 billion and over 51,000 jobs. The technology field continued to grow in the city with business clusters in areas such as aerospace and aviation, alternative energy, biotechnology and biomedicine, film and multimedia, and information technology and software. With technology on the rise in Albuquerque, it reflected on a state level; according to the American Electronic Association, New Mexico had the sixth highest concentration of technology workers in the nation as of 2006.

For nearly a century people have valued Albuquerque for its dry air, which is especially beneficial to those with respiratory problems. Today the city's medical services and facilities are a vital part of the local economy. The biotechnology and biomedicine industry has more than 100 companies located in the area. Major medical based companies in Albuquerque include Johnson & Johnson's Ethicon Endosurgery (medical instruments) and Cardinal Health (pharmaceuticals). The year-round sunny weather attracts pleasure seekers as well; almost three million tourists visit Albuquerque each year spending more than $2 billion in Bernalillo County and supporting more than 30,000 local jobs.

Items and goods produced: machine tools, fabricated structural steel, furniture, hardware, textiles, paints, varnishes, fertilizers, scientific instruments, electronic equipment, neon and electric signs, Native American jewelry and curios

Incentive Programs—New and Existing Companies

Among the factors that draw businesses to Albuquerque are the city's affordable cost of living (based on cost of labor, energy, taxes, and office space) and its highly-educated workforce.

Local programs: Albuquerque Economic Development, Inc. (AED), is a private, nonprofit organization that recruits companies to the Albuquerque area. AED provides site-selection assistance, labor market analysis, business incentive analysis, workforce recruitment and job-training assistance, and coordination of state and local assistance, among other services. Many high technology activities are carried out in Albuquerque; Technology Ventures Corporation, a non-profit organization, serves as a bridge between the public and private sectors for the commercialization of technologies developed at the national labs and research universities, and assists in the expansion of existing businesses. The city of Albuquerque also issues industrial revenue bonds (IRBs) to companies looking to fund construction and renovation of manufacturing plants, research and development facilities, and corporate headquarters. Projects using IRBs may be exempt for up to 20 years from property taxes on land, buildings, and equipment.

State programs: New Mexico offers a variety of incentives to all new and expanding businesses. Its Build to Suit program facilitates building construction, and ePort New Mexico is a one-stop information source offering permitting and licensing. The state's financial incentives include: no inventory taxes; tax credits for high-wage jobs, technology jobs, and childcare; a tax deduction for research and development services; a job training incentive program (allowing New Mexico to pay half the salary for new hires for up to half a year, and 100 percent of classroom training costs and on-the-job training by state institutes); exemptions for qualified businesses from property taxes on land, buildings, and equipment, and from personal property tax on equipment; and laboratory partnerships with small businesses. The Angel Investment Tax Credit is available to those invested in New Mexico companies pursuing high-technology research or manufacturing. Qualified investors can receive a tax credit of up to $25,000 each year on up to two qualified investments. Further incentives are available for manufacturers, customer support centers, aerospace and aircraft industries, producers of agriculture or energy, and filmmakers. In addition, the state enacted a major personal income tax reduction in 2003, and New Mexico's property taxes are among the lowest in the nation.

Job training programs: In July 2007 the Governor's Office of Workforce Training & Development merged with the New Mexico Department of Labor to create a new branch called the New Mexico Department of Workforce Solutions. The new department focuses on preparing job seekers to meet current standards in the labor market as well as effectively matching citizens with businesses in need of help. Services available include job fairs, local workforce development centers, online job searches, and online registration for employment services. Through the Job Training Incentive Program (JTIP) companies can utilize features that include training customized to individual companies' needs and the freedom to select training candidates. JTIP is not limited to economically disadvantaged people.

Economic Development Information: Albuquerque Economic Development, University Center Research Park, 851 University Boulevard SE, Suite 203, Albuquerque, NM 87106; telephone (505)246-6200; toll-free (800)451-2933; fax (505)246-6219

Development Projects

Among the many businesses that have located or expanded in Albuquerque in the early 2000s are: Gap, Inc., which opened a corporate shared services center in 2001; Victoria's Secret Catalog, which expanded its support center in 2001, adding 380 jobs; Blue Cross/ Blue Shield, which expanded in 2002, adding 500 jobs; ClientLogic, a customer service and technical support center for high-technology companies, which expanded in 2002-2003, adding 500 jobs; and Tempur-Pedic Mattress, which broke ground on a $56 million manufacturing plant in 2004. Verizon Wireless began business in a new customer service and wireless data technical support center in November 2006. The support center began with 800 employees and by August 2007 that number had grown to 1,100 with company officials looking to hire 300 more. Eclipse Aviation, a personal jet manufacturer, opened a Customer Training Center in 2007 approximating 100 workers when in full operation. The new training center was the company's first step towards creating an Eclipse Aviation campus and boasts flight training devices as well as full motion simulators. Boosting the city's film industry, in 2007 Sony Pictures Imageworks announced plans to open a new branch in Albuquerque. The company planned to employ up to 300 people. The $73 million Alvarado Transportation Center Project was partially completed and operational as of 2005; in 2006 the center was successful in linking commercial and city/state bus and rail services. New routes included services between Rio Rancho and Albuquerque.

Commercial Shipping

Since the days of the Santa Fe Trail, Albuquerque has been an important center for the transportation of goods. The city's economy benefits from the Burlington Northern Santa Fe Railroad. The railroad carries 90 percent of freight originating in the state, linking Albuquerque with major markets throughout the country.

New Mexico is a Freeport State, meaning that business inventories for resale, raw materials, and interstate commerce products stored there temporarily are not subject to state or local property taxes. Albuquerque offers an international airport, Albuquerque International Sunport, with a port of entry from Mexico; the airport moved approximately 32,879 tons of freight cargo in 2006. Foreign trade zones operate in Albuquerque and nearby Rio Rancho.

Labor Force and Employment Outlook

Non-agricultural employment growth in Albuquerque as of July 2007 was 1.8 percent compared to the national growth of 1.3 percent. That same year the unemployment rate was at 3.3 percent and Albuquerque's employment made up 40 percent of the state's total employment. The city's labor force is relatively young, skilled, and educated; Albuquerque is notable for its high percentage of advanced degree holders thanks to the large student population affiliated with the University of New Mexico, Central New Mexico Community College, and the Albuquerque Public School District. Albuquerque's work force is routinely cited for its productivity. Analyzing employment trends across the nation, *Washington Business Journal* (*Bizjournals*) named Albuquerque 25th among America's "Hottest Job Markets" in 2007.

The following is a summary of data regarding the Albuquerque metropolitan area labor force, 2006 annual averages.

Size of nonagricultural labor force: 391,700

Number of workers employed in . . .

> construction and mining: 31,200
> manufacturing: 24,000
> trade, transportation and utilities: 67,600
> information: 9,400
> financial activities: 19,300
> professional and business services: 63,200
> educational and health services: 47,900
> leisure and hospitality: 38,400
> other services: 78,600
> government: 12,200

Average hourly earnings of production workers employed in manufacturing: $15.30

Unemployment rate: 3.7% (June 2007)

Largest employers (2007)	Number of employees
Kirtland Air Force Base	16,360
Albuquerque Public Schools	14,480
University of New Mexico	14,300
City of Albuquerque	6,680
Presbyterian Health Services	6,670
State of New Mexico	5,490
Lovelace	5,200
Kirtland Air Force Base (Military Active Duty)	5,100
Intel Corporation	4,700
UNM Hospital	4,600

Cost of Living

The following is a summary of data regarding key cost of living factors for the Albuquerque area.

2007 (1st quarter) ACCRA Average House Price: $325,310

2007 (1st quarter) ACCRA Cost of Living Index: 101.6

State income tax rate: 1.7% to 5.3%

State sales tax rate: 5.0%

Local income tax rate: None

Local sales tax rate: 0.5625% (city); 1.1875% (county)

Property tax rate: 27.027 to 43.860 mills (residential); 32.857 to 51.724 mills (non-residential)(2004)

Economic Information: Greater Albuquerque Chamber of Commerce, PO Box 25100, Albuquerque, NM 87125; telephone (505)764-3700; fax (505)764-3714.

■ Education and Research

Elementary and Secondary Schools

The Albuquerque Public Schools (APS) system, one of the largest in the nation, is administered by a nonpartisan, seven-member school board and a superintendency team.

The following is a summary of data regarding the Albuquerque Public Schools as of the 2005–2006 school year.

Total enrollment: 87,000

Number of facilities

> elementary schools: 84
> junior high/middle schools: 26
> senior high schools: 11
> other: 10

Student/teacher ratio: 15.5:1

Teacher salaries (2005–06)

> elementary median: $40,960
> junior high/middle median: $42,260
> secondary median: $44,340

Funding per pupil: $6,814

The Albuquerque area has more than 70 private or parochial schools. Among these schools, Albuquerque Academy is regarded as one of the top private schools in the nation.

Public Schools Information: Albuquerque Public Schools, PO Box 25704, Albuquerque, NM 87125; telephone (505)880-3700

Colleges and Universities

The University of New Mexico (UNM), the state's largest institution of higher learning and part of the Rio Grande Research Corridor complex, is based in Albuquerque, with branch campuses in Gallup, Los Alamos, Taos, Los Lunas, and west Albuquerque. The main campus had an enrollment of more than 25,000 students in fall 2007; the enrollment of all campuses totaled more than 32,000 students. UNM is particularly strong in Latin American studies, flamenco dance, anthropology, and medicine—its rural medicine and family medicine programs rank second and sixth in the nation respectively according to *U.S. News & World Report*. Other four-year institutions in Albuquerque include the New Mexico campus of the University of Phoenix, offering bachelor's and advanced degrees in business and nursing; a campus of ITT Technical Institute, which offers degrees in information technology, electronics technology, drafting and design, business, and criminal justice; and National American University, which offers degrees in accounting, business administration and management, and computer and information sciences. The city is also home to Central New Mexico Community College (CNM) (formerly Albuquerque Technical-Vocational Institute), the largest community college in New Mexico. The community college offers associate's degrees in occupational fields as well as liberal arts. Central New Mexico Community College and the University of New Mexico passed a joint agreement in 2007 to collaborate together, giving students access to several services at both schools. Plans for this new collaboration included dual enrollment, easier transition for CNM students to finish a four-year degree at UNM, and allowing CNM students to access UNM dorms and recreational services.

Libraries and Research Centers

The Rio Grande Valley Library System, the largest public library system in New Mexico, is a Consortium of the City of Albuquerque, Bernalillo County and the City of Rio Rancho. Public library service is available through a large Main Library and 16 branches throughout the Albuquerque area (including a Special Collections Library specializing in genealogy and regional history and the Erne Pyle Branch, former home of the famed World War II correspondent, displaying a collection of his memorabilia), and the nearby Rio Rancho Public Library. The library system has a collection of more than 1.4 million items, including periodicals and audio-visual materials.

The University of New Mexico has six branches and maintains more than 2.2 million volumes. The branches include the Health Sciences Library and Informatics, the Law School Library, Centennial Science and Engineering Library, Fine Arts Library, Parish Business and Economics Library, and the Zimmerman Library. Collection strengths include Latin American history, regional photography, music and architecture, American Indian affairs, and maps. The Health Sciences Library serves the Medical School and the health professions statewide. The Law School Library is the primary legal library in the state and has special collections in American Indian and Latin American Law.

Research activities in such fields as water resources, Southwestern biology, power systems, alternative energy, artificial intelligence, robotics, anthropology, satellite data analysis, business and economics, Native American law, aging and health policy issues, Latin America, and Hispanic and Chicano studies are conducted at centers in the Albuquerque area. The University of New Mexico (UNM) is the state's primary research university. Among its research units are the Center for Advanced Studies (quantum optics, laser physics, etc.), the Center of Biomedical Engineering, the New Mexico Engineering Research Institute, the Center for High Technology Materials, the High Performance Computing Educational Research Center, the Center for Micro-Engineered Materials, and the Latin American Institute. Many of UNM's research centers work in alliance with industry partners such as 3M Corporation, Toyota Motor Company, Intel, and Sandia National Laboratories. The school's Health Sciences Center for treatment, research, and education is the state's largest organization of its kind. Other research centers based in Albuquerque include the Behavioral Health Research Center of the Southwest, which conducts research on substance abuse and other behavioral health issues, and the Air Force Research Lab at Kirtland Air Force Base, where space- and missile-related research is performed. Sandia National Laboratories, based in nearby Sandia, performs national security research.

Public Library Information: Main Library, 501 Copper NW, Albuquerque, NM 87102; telephone (505) 768-5141

■ Health Care

In the 1920s Albuquerque, like many other cities in the Southwest, became a mecca for people suffering from respiratory diseases and allergies who seek relief in the warm, dry climate. Today, advanced medical care is available at the University of New Mexico Health Sciences Center, which encompasses the following patient facilities: UNM Hospital, New Mexico's only Level 1 Trauma Center; Carrie Tingley Hospital for pediatric rehabilitation and orthopedics; UNM Cancer Research & Treatment Center, New Mexico's only academic center for cancer treatment; UNM Psychiatric Center; and UNM Children's Psychiatric Hospital. The UNM Hospital began constructing the new UNM Children's Hospital and Critical Care Pavilion in 2004. The $233.8 million, 476,555-square-foot expansion opened its doors in June 2007, but final completion of the project was not expected until November of that year.

Albuquerque's other major hospitals are the 453-bed Presbyterian Hospital, New Mexico's largest acute care hospital and the 254-bed Lovelace Medical Center, which specializes in orthopedics, ophthalmology, neurology and neurosurgery, oncology, and cardiology. In 1959 the first Americans in space underwent a newly developed test series at the Lovelace Clinic in preparation for their mission.

■ Recreation

Sightseeing

Albuquerque's unique mixture of Native American, Hispanic, and Anglo heritages provides visitors with a variety of activities. Albuquerque's spiritual heart is Old Town, dating to the city's founding in 1706, where an arts community flourishes. Old Town is an atmospheric area of quaint adobe-style buildings with flat roofs and rounded edges, with windows frequently decorated with strings of dried chili peppers for good luck, and winding cobblestone or brick walkways leading to tucked-away patios and gardens. Old Town's Plaza features an outdoor Native American market offering traditional arts and crafts such as textiles, jewelry, and pottery. Also located in Old Town is San Felipe de Neri church, the city's oldest building, enclosing the adobe walls of the original presidio (fort).

The landscape surrounding the city is particularly scenic and provides some of the area's principal attractions. To the west are a high mesa and five extinct volcanos; to the east are the magnificent Sandia and Manzano mountains. Sandia Crest in the Cibola National Forest, 30 miles from Albuquerque, offers a breathtaking view that encompasses 11,000 square miles. A skylift operates there throughout the year, carrying skiers and hikers up the mountain. The Aerial Tramway, 2.7 miles in length and the longest tramway in the world, runs to the top of 10,378-foot Sandia Peak.

Evidence of Albuquerque's Native American roots can be found in the numerous pueblos around the city, many of them at least a thousand years old and some still inhabited. Active pueblos within an hour's drive of Albuquerque include Acoma, Cochiti, Isleta, Jemez, Laguna, Sandia, San Felipe, Santa Ana, Santo Domingo, and Zia. Acoma is perhaps the most spectacular; a walled adobe village atop a sheer rock mesa, the community dates to the 11th century or earlier and is thought to be the longest continuously-occupied community in the country. Reminders of the ancient native civilization also exist in dozens of ruins and archaeological sites, among them Petroglyph State Monument, where some 17,000 petroglyphs (images carved in rock) dating back as far as 1300, can be found.

The Rio Grande Nature Center State Park, located a few miles north of Old Town, already offers several miles of nature trails through the Southwest *bosque* (the grove of cottonwood growing along the Rio Grande) but in 2004 a statewide plan was set in place to extend the Rio Grande Trail by almost 40 miles. The Albuquerque Biological Park consists of four separate facilities: Rio Grande Zoo, Albuquerque Aquarium, Rio Grande Botanic Garden, and Tingley Beach. The zoo sits on 64 acres and is an oasis for both exotic and native species, such as seals and sea lions, gorillas, orangutans, elephants, polar bears, giraffes, camels, tamarins, koalas, Mexican wolves, mountain lions, monkeys, jaguars, zebras, and rhinoceros; one of the missions of the zoo is the breeding of endangered species. The zoo's Africa wing, opened in 2004, has 17 separate exhibits and 23 species of mammals and birds, including chimpanzees, warthogs, red river hogs, cheetahs, hippopotamus, DeBrazza's monkeys, spotted hyenas, African wild dogs, Marabou storks, Cape griffon vultures, lappet-faced vultures, wattled cranes, white-faced whistling ducks, Lady Ross's turacos, and golden-breasted starlings. At the Albuquerque Aquarium visitors can follow the story of a drop of water as it enters the upper Rio Grande high in the San Juan Mountains of Colorado and flows past canyons, deserts, and valleys in New Mexico, Texas, and Mexico, before reaching the Gulf of Mexico. The aquarium features exhibits of Gulf of Mexico saltwater species. A highlight is the 285,000-gallon tank housing brown, sandtiger, blacktip, and nurse sharks; brightly-colored reef fish; eels; and sea turtles. The Botanic Garden is 36 acres of developed land that includes a 10,000-square-foot conservatory divided into a Desert Pavilion and a Mediterranean Pavilion. New at the botanic garden in 2004 was the Rio Grande Heritage Farm, a 1930s-style farm with an adobe farmhouse, barn, farm animals, orchard, grape vineyard, flowers, and vegetable crops; a new Japanese garden was added in 2007 reflecting Japanese traditions that are similar to the Southwest. The Heritage Farm won an award for excellence in programming by the American Public Gardens Association in 2007 and received a chance to place an exhibit at the U.S. Botanic Garden in Washington, D.C.

Glancing skyward in Albuquerque, spectators frequently see the colorful spectacle of hang-gliders and hot-air balloons drifting slowly past. A combination of sunshine and topography produces steady geothermal winds, making the area ideal for wind sports and earning for the city the nickname of "Hot Air Balloon Capital of the World."

Albuquerque's Central Avenue, which runs east-west through the city, is considered one of the best-preserved sections of historic Route 66 in the state. Along the avenue are more than 100 classic structures, including diners, motor courts, and theaters, in architectural styles ranging from Streamline Moderne to Pueblo Deco.

Arts and Culture

Albuquerque actively promotes its rich cultural community. In 1979 City Council created an ordinance that assigns 1 percent of monies generated by revenue bonds and general obligation bonds to public construction and public art. Consequently, Albuquerque abounds with sculptures and murals attesting to the city's artistic

428

energies. Along Central Avenue, from historic Old Town on the east through downtown and the university area to Nob Hill on the west, is Albuquerque's "cultural corridor." In the numerous theaters, museums, galleries, and cafes, and at other sites along this route, the stimulating and diverse cultural life of Albuquerque is on view.

Albuquerque has more than 30 performing arts centers and groups. The KiMo Theater, an ornate 1927 Pueblo Deco-style landmark downtown, is on the National Register of Historic Places; it serves as a performing arts theater, hosting a number of groups, with seating for 700. The Albuquerque Little Theatre presents comedies, mysteries, and light classics in its own playhouse near Old Town. La Compañía de Teatro de Albuquerque—one of the few major Hispanic companies in the United States and Puerto Rico—stages a series of bilingual productions including comedies, dramas, and musicals. Vortex Theatre offers off-Broadway original and classic plays. A new African American Performing Arts Center opened in fall 2007. The new 23,000-square-foot facility planned to host several permanent and traveling art exhibits, music, theater, and dance performances, as well as educational programs about the history, culture, and arts of people of African descent.

Albuquerque is home to the New Mexico Ballet Company, founded in 1972, which performs classic dances in the KiMo Theatre and in Popejoy Hall on the University of New Mexico campus. Dance performances by visiting artists and groups can also be seen at KiMo Theatre. Popejoy Hall, the primary facility in the city for the performance of orchestral music and opera, is home to the Ovation Series—which offers a variety of events including drama and comedy, and ballet and modern dance—and the New Mexico Symphony. Based in the city and one of the southwest's most prestigious orchestras, the symphony presents classical, baroque, and pops, as well as Symphony Under the Stars and other special concerts. Musical Theatre Southwest, formerly the Civic Light Opera, performs classical and new musicals and is one of the largest producers of community theater in the country. Chamber Music Albuquerque, established in 1942, brings chamber ensembles from around the world to Albuquerque.

Many of Albuquerque's museums concentrate on area history and culture. The New Mexico Museum of Natural History and Science features exhibits exploring the geological and anthropological history of New Mexico, through Paleozoic-era fossils, full-scale dinosaur models, a walk-through volcano, and a replica of an ice-age cave. The Indian Pueblo Cultural Center specializes in the authentic history and culture of the Pueblo peoples. The center includes exhibits tracing the history, artifacts, and contemporary art of New Mexico's 19 pueblos; the Pueblo House Children's Museum; a restaurant serving Native American foods; and an outdoor arena where Native American dancers perform on weekends. The National Hispanic Cultural Center, opened in 2000, explores Hispanic history and literature as well as visual, performing, media, and culinary arts. Located on the University of New Mexico campus, the Maxwell Museum of Anthropology displays ethnic, anthropological, and archaeological artifacts. Some date back 10,000 years, with especially strong collections from Southwestern cultures. The National Atomic Museum exhibits the history of atomic energy, including the Manhattan Project that produced the first atomic bomb, as well as non-military applications of nuclear energy. The museum is set for relocation to a new 30,000-square-foot building in 2009. The new museum, to be renamed the National Museum of Nuclear Science and History, also plans to have an outdoor park for aircrafts and large artifacts.

The Albuquerque Museum of Art and History displays southwest art and explores 400 years of Albuquerque history. The museum features works by New Mexican artists from the early 20th century to the present, and numerous artifacts from the area's Spanish-American period, such as swords, helmets, and horse armor. A 40,000-square-foot expansion, completed in 2005, allowed the museum to display more of its permanent collection. With an emphasis on the early modernist period, the University of New Mexico Art Museum houses a collection of nineteenth- and twentieth-century American and European art, including one of the largest university-owned photography collections in the nation. The Jonson Gallery, located on the University of New Mexico campus, is the home of the late New Mexico modernist painter Raymond Jonson and exhibits more than 2,000 of his works. The National Hispanic Cultural Center's 11,000-square-foot gallery space displays contemporary and traditional Hispanic art. The KiMo Gallery at KiMo Theatre presents the work of local artists. The South Broadway Cultural Center Gallery mounts exhibitions by local and regional artists; workshops are available for emerging artists of all ages.

Festivals and Holidays

In 2006 Albuquerque turned 300 years old. The city celebrated its tricentennial for 18 months, from April 2005 to October 2006, with events and exhibits honoring Albuquerque's art, history, and culture. Many of Albuquerque's yearly events celebrate the city's ethnic heritage. At the National Fiery Foods and Barbeque Show, held in early March, attendees can sample spicy sauces, salsas, candies, and more. The Rio Grande Arts and Crafts Festival, held in mid-March, features some 200 artists and crafters from across the country. Native American dancing and feast-day observances take place at numerous pueblos located within an hour's drive of the city. In April, the Gathering of Nations Pow Wow, held on the University of New Mexico campus, features more than 3,000 Native American dancers and singers representing some 500 tribes; more than 800 artists, crafters, and traders at its Indian Traders Market; and a Miss Indian World pageant. The New Mexico Arts and Crafts Fair, in June, showcases the works of some 200 New Mexican artisans. Each Saturday during the summer, Summerfest at Civic Plaza celebrates the food and culture of the city's various ethnic groups, and presents live music and entertainment. In September, the New Mexico Wine Festival in nearby Bernillo offers wine tastings, an art show, and entertainment. Also in September, the 17-day New Mexico State Fair, regarded as one of the top fairs in the United States, presents a professional rodeo, concerts, livestock shows, and other events. The annual Albuquerque International Balloon Fiesta is one of the most-photographed events in the world. A 9-day festival in October, it features the mass ascension of some 700 hot air balloons; at night, balloons filled with luminous gas light the sky. The Weems Artfest, in November, is billed as New Mexico's number one arts and crafts festival; a three-day event, the Artfest shows the works of approximately 260 artisans from around the world. Albuquerque is known as the "City of Little Lights" during the annual Luminaria festival in December. Luminaria bus tours are available as well as maps of noted luminarias neighborhoods for self walking tours.

Sports for the Spectator

The Albuquerque Isotopes, part of the Pacific Coast League, bring minor league baseball to Albuquerque at the new Isotopes Park (a $25 million renovation of Albuquerque Sports Stadium), which has seating for 11,124. The city is famous for the University of New Mexico Lobos, especially the football and basketball teams; the football team plays a September to November season at the 37,370 seat University Stadium, and the basketball team plays from November to March at "The Pit," the university's Arena. The New Mexico Scorpions, part of the Western Professional Hockey League, play at Tingley Coliseum. Rodeos and horse racing are other popular spectator sports in Albuquerque.

Sports for the Participant

With 360 park sites, 12 public swimming pools, over 130 tennis courts, 5 public golf courses, 24 community centers, and 85 miles of urban and soft trails, Albuquerque has much to offer the outdoor enthusiast. Los Altos Park, the city's largest park, offers baseball and softball diamonds, an enclosed heated pool, tennis courts, a lighted golf course, and a children's recreational area. The Los Altos Skate Park is designed for BMX bikers, skateboarders, and in-line skaters. The city opened a covered BMX track in 2007 as part of the new Albuquerque VeloPort. The VeloPort will be an indoor center for cycling training and competition; construction of the next phase, building a 250-meter velodrome, was expected to begin by 2008. Biking trails can be found at Sandia Peak

and the Rio Grande Nature Center. Fishing is available in irrigation and drainage ditches, stocked with trout by the state, and in nearby mountain streams. Among other favorite outdoor adventures are hiking the trails in Cibola National Forest, camping, horseback riding, and downhill and cross-country skiing at Sandia Peak Ski area. Albuquerque's calm, steady winds also provide perfect conditions for hang gliding and hot-air ballooning.

Shopping and Dining

Albuquerque is a shopper's paradise. Numerous shops and galleries in Old Town specialize in art items and crafts produced by local artisans, such as textiles and the turquoise and silver jewelry for which the region is famous. Authentic pre-historic, historic, and contemporary Native American pottery, paintings, photography, and furniture are also for sale in Albuquerque. Sandia Pueblo, just north of Albuquerque, runs its own crafts market, Bien Mur Indian Market Center.

Other shopping needs can be met at Coronado Center and Cottonwood Mall, two of New Mexico's largest shopping centers; the historic Nob Hill district, offering some 130 shops, galleries, and restaurants; the underground First Plaza Galleria in the historic downtown district; and the flea market held every weekend at the New Mexico State Fairgrounds. The Winrock Center was slated for major redevelopment as of 2006; plans for the redevelopment included tearing down the old center to create an outdoor shopping center and building 66 multifamily housing units, 174 hotel rooms, and a new movie theater and office space.

For dining pleasure Albuquerque offers a diverse range of restaurants, from family to fancy. Many feature regional specialties, including authentic Native American food, Hispanic and Mexican cuisine, and western barbecue. The core ingredients of what is known as Northern New Mexican Cuisine—a blending of Hispanic and Pueblo cuisines—are beans, corn, and chili. Several restaurants in Old Town are housed in picturesque adobe buildings.

Visitor Information: Albuquerque Convention and Visitors Bureau, 20 First Plaza NW, Suite 601, Albuquerque, NM 87102; telephone (505)842-9918; toll-free (800)284-2282

■ Convention Facilities

As the economic and industrial heart of New Mexico, and as a city known for its commitment to the past and to the future, Albuquerque is an ideal meeting place for conferences and conventions. Albuquerque's unique ethnic heritage and spectacular setting, plus its generous meeting facilities and hotel guest rooms, promote the mixing of business with pleasure.

The city's primary meeting place is the Albuquerque Convention Center, located in the heart of downtown. The 600,000-square-foot complex offers over 167,562 square feet of exhibition space, a 31,000-square-foot ballroom, and a 2,350-seat auditorium. It can accommodate more than 9,000 attendees and has banquet space for up to 6,000 people. The convention center is within walking distance of more than 900 guest rooms, as well as restaurants and clubs offering a variety of entertainment. Facilities for large groups are also available at Expo New Mexico at the State Fairgrounds, which offers flexible indoor and outdoor space, with an indoor capacity of 12,000 and outdoor capacity of 20,000 people.

Convention Information: Albuquerque Convention and Visitors Bureau, 20 First Plaza NW, Suite 601, Albuquerque, NM 87102; telephone (505)842-9918; toll-free (800)284-2282

■ Transportation

Approaching the City

Albuquerque is a designated Port of Entry into the United States. When arriving in Albuquerque by plane, visitors are greeted by the Albuquerque International Sunport terminal, which introduces them to local art and pueblo architecture. Located within the city limits, the airport is served by 8 major commercial airlines and 4 commuter airlines. The airport offers nonstop service to 39 cities across the country, plus nonstop service to in-state cities. The airport served over 6.4 million passengers on 192,520 flights in 2006.

Albuquerque is at the crossroads of two major highway routes: Interstate 25, running from Canada to Mexico, and Interstate 40 (formerly Route 66), intersecting the city from east to west.

Passenger bus transportation into Albuquerque is available through commercial bus companies. Train service is provided by Amtrak; Albuquerque is a stop along its Southwest Chief route, a daily line between Los Angeles and Chicago.

Traveling in the City

The landscape surrounding Albuquerque—the Sandia Mountains to the east and mesas to the west—provides convenient landmarks for finding direction in the city. Dividing Albuquerque into quadrants are Interstate 40, which runs east to west, and Interstate 25, known as the Pan American Freeway, which runs north to south. The streets form a grid accommodating this intersection.

Albuquerque's mass transit service is provided by ABQ Ride. During the major festivals held in the city—such as the International Balloon Fiesta, the State Fair, and Luminaria—ABQ Ride supplies special service to and from the event venues. A trolley serves shoppers and tourists, running between Old Town, the zoo, and downtown. The New Mexico Rail Runner Express, a commuter rail system, started operation in 2006 with stations in Sandoval, Los Ranchos, and Downtown Albuquerque. Service extending to Santa Fe was expected to be completed by 2008.

The city also maintains a number of well-lit and well-paved paths for bicycle travel, including 70 miles of on-street bike lanes.

■ Communications

Newspapers and Magazines

Albuquerque is served by two daily newspapers, the morning *Albuquerque Journal* and the evening *Albuquerque Tribune*, and by the weekly newspapers *New Mexico Business Weekly*, which covers business media, and *El Hispano News*, a Spanish-language newspaper. Magazines published there include *albuquerqueARTS*, *New Mexico Business Journal*, and *New Mexico Woman*.

Television and Radio

Ten television stations, including affiliates for the major commercial networks and public television, serve metropolitan Albuquerque. Cable television is available by subscription. Approximately 55 AM and FM radio stations broadcast to Albuquerque-area listeners, offering a wide variety of programming, including Spanish- and Navajo-language features. Albuquerque Public Schools operates an instructional radio station that features educational programming as well as jazz and Latin music.

Media Information: *Albuquerque Journal,* 7777 Jefferson Street NE, Albuquerque, NM, 87109; telephone (505)823-3800. *The Albuquerque Tribune,* PO Drawer T, Albuquerque, NM, 87103; telephone (505) 823-3653

Albuquerque Online

Albuquerque Convention & Visitors Bureau. Available www.itsatrip.org

Albuquerque Journal. Available www.abqjournal.com

Albuquerque Public Schools. Available www.

Albuquerque Tribune. Available www.abqtrib.com

Bernalillo County home page. Available www.bernco.gov

City of Albuquerque home page. Available www.cabq.gov

Greater Albuquerque Chamber of Commerce. Available www.abqchamber.com

New Mexico Department of Workforce Solutions. Available www.dws.state.nm.us

Rio Grande Valley Library System. Available www
.cabq.gov/library

BIBLIOGRAPHY

Anaya, Rudolfo A., *Alburquerque* (Albuquerque, NM:
U. of New Mexico Press, 1992)

Chilton, Lance, et al., *A New Guide to the Colorful State*
(University of New Mexico Press, 1984)

Simmons, Mark, *Albuquerque: A Narrative History*
(University of New Mexico Press, 1982)

Las Cruces

■ The City in Brief

Founded: 1848 (incorporated 1907)

Head Official: Mayor Ken Miyagishima (D) (since 2007)

City Population

1980: 45,086
1990: 62,648
2000: 74,267
2006 estimate: 86,268
Percent change, 1990–2000: 19.5%
U.S. rank in 1980: 475th
U.S. rank in 1990: 396th (State rank: 2nd)
U.S. rank in 2000: 408th (State rank: 2nd)

Metropolitan Area Population

1980: 96,340
1990: 135,510
2000: 174,682
2006 estimate: 193,888
Percent change, 1990–2000: 28.9%
U.S. rank in 1980: Not available
U.S. rank in 1990: 208th
U.S. rank in 2000: 181st

Area: 52.22 square miles

Elevation: 3,909 feet above sea level

Average Annual Temperature: 64.0° F

Average Annual Precipitation: 8.5 inches of rain, 3.2 inches of snow

Major Economic Sectors: services, wholesale and retail trade, government

Unemployment Rate: 4.2% (June 2007)

Per Capita Income: $17,059 (2005)

2005 FBI Crime Index Property: 3,949

2005 FBI Crime Index Violent: 465

Major Colleges and Universities: New Mexico State University, Dona Ana Community College

Daily Newspaper: *Las Cruces Sun-News*

■ Introduction

Las Cruces, Spanish for "city of crosses," is located in the Mesilla Valley, a wonderfully varied area of forests, river valley, and vast desert. The seat of Dona Ana County, the city is near White Sands Missile Range, where the first atomic bomb was tested. The city's spectacular setting boasts the Organ Mountains to the east and the surrounding Chihuahua Desert, with the Rio Grande running through the middle. Since the end of the nineteenth century, the city has been the political, social, and business hub for southern New Mexico. *Forbes* ranked Las Cruces second in 2006 for "Best Small Places for Business and Careers," and in 2005 *Money* magazine dubbed it one of the top eight places to retire, based on factors such as weather, crime, and economy.

■ Geography and Climate

Las Cruces is located 45 miles from the Mexican border and 40 miles northwest of El Paso, Texas. Bordered by the Organ Mountains in the east and the legendary Rio Grande on the west, Las Cruces is located in the heart of the fertile Mesilla Valley.

Las Cruces enjoys 350 days of sunshine annually, with less than 9 inches of average annual rainfall, which happens mostly at night, and only 3.2 inches of snowfall. Because it is situated over a natural underground aquifer, it does not suffer the water problems of a number of southwestern cities. Also, unlike many desert cities, Las

Cruces experiences four mildly distinct seasons, with the harder part of the winter occurring during December and January, when the average daytime temperature is 57 degrees. Light snow does fall in the winter but seldom lasts longer than one day. June is generally the hottest month, with an average temperature of 94 degrees. The monsoon season, when heavy thunderstorms can occur daily, takes place in July and August.

Area: 52.22 square miles

Elevation: 3,909 feet above sea level

Average Temperature: 64.0° F

Average Annual Precipitation: 8.5 inches of rain, 3.2 inches of snow

■ History

Long Before Humans

Before the first human inhabitants, the area around Las Cruces was populated by a teeming variety of reptiles and amphibians, who left many fossils when the great inland sea that once covered southern New Mexico retreated 600 million years ago. The Smithsonian has stated that the area holds "the world's best-fossilized footprints from the Permian Period."

Early Paleolithic Indians traversed the area about 20,000 years ago, and Anasazi tribes built cliff dwellings over most of New Mexico 10,000 years ago. The Mogollon tribe thrived in the Las Cruces region until they mysteriously disappeared around 1450 A.D. They left many petroglyphs, or rock drawings, scattered around the vicinity for scientists to gain a glimpse into their way of life.

Blazing a Trail

The first European visitors came to the Las Cruces area in 1535 when Spanish explorers, led by Cabeza de Vaca, passed through. In 1589, the first colonists arrived, led by Don Juan Onate, motivated by legends of seven ancient cities of gold. The group's livestock were driven in front of them, blazing a trail called El Camino Real, which led from Chihuahua, Mexico to Santa Fe. Another trail blazed by this same group was dubbed Jornado del Meurto, or Journey of Death. As they attempted to forge a path more direct than the one which followed the meandering Rio Grande, the brutal desert conditions claimed the lives of many men and the Apaches claimed more.

Control of the region changed hands often from the 1600s to about 1850. The Pueblo Indians rebelled against their Spanish conquerors in the late seventeenth century and enjoyed self-rule for a time. In 1821 the Mexican Revolution overthrew the Spanish and created the Republic of Mexico. Soon after that, U.S. westward expansion caused friction and an eventual war with Mexico. This was resolved with the 1848 Treaty of Guadalupe Hidalgo, followed by the 1854 Gadsden Purchase, which claimed much of northern Mexico's land as U.S. territory. The region was even briefly under Confederate rule when Texas troops marched on it in 1862. They were later defeated by Union soldiers near Santa Fe.

After the Civil War ended, the Army installed Fort Selden to help guard travelers against attacks by the Apache. The Buffalo Soldiers of the 125th Infantry, African Americans, were among the first to man the fort. With the coming of the railroad and more and more new immigrants, the Apache threat abated and the fort officially closed in 1891.

The small town of Mesilla is intertwined with the history of Las Cruces. Mesilla was founded by residents who were not happy with the Treaty of Guadalupe Hidalgo and wished to remain Mexican citizens, hence moving across the Rio Grande. Ironically, the Gadsden Purchase a few years later placed them back under U.S. rule.

A Glimpse of Modern Las Cruces

In 1849 the first blocks of the city were laid out with rawhide ropes and stakes. Plots were quickly claimed by settlers and gold miners hoping to find their fortune in the Organ Mountains. The coming of the railroad increased growth of the town quickly. The Santa Fe Railroad had planned to lay track through Mesilla, which had been a depot of the Butterfield Stage Coach, but someone in Las Cruces offered them free land. From then on, Las Cruces grew rapidly while Mesilla remained a sleepy little border town.

Las Cruces continued to grow quickly yet rather quietly into the 1900s as New Mexico became the 47th state in 1912. The quiet was suddenly disturbed when the first atomic bomb was tested north of Las Cruces on July 16, 1945. The area used for the test site, fittingly, was the Jornado del Muerto area. The following year World War II ended and Las Cruces was officially incorporated as a city.

Las Cruces celebrated its 150th birthday in 1998 with festivities that carried on into the millennium. Today, Las Cruces remains one of the fastest growing metro areas in the nation, and the second largest city in New Mexico. In addition to thriving business in trade, government, and agriculture, the unique and stunning scenery of the region has made it an attractive place to film movies and music videos. Attractive to industry development, Las Cruces was labeled a "boomtown" by *Inc.* magazine and ranked ninth on the "Top 20 Small Cities for Doing Business" list in 2007. It remains a true crossroads, not only of highways but of cultures and

Airphoto-Jim Wark

customs, which blend together amiably to become a very pleasant place to live.

Historical Information: Rio Grande Historical Collections, New Mexico State University Library, PO Box 30006 Las Cruces, NM 88003-3006; telephone (505)646-3839; fax (505)646-7477; email archives@lib. nmsu.edu

■ Population Profile

Metropolitan Area Residents

1980: 96,340
1990: 135,510
2000: 174,682
2006 estimate: 193,888
Percent change, 1990–2000: 28.9%
U.S. rank in 1980: Not available
U.S. rank in 1990: 208th
U.S. rank in 2000: 181st

City Residents

1980: 45,086
1990: 62,648
2000: 74,267

2006 estimate: 86,268
Percent change, 1990–2000: 19.5%
U.S. rank in 1980: 475th
U.S. rank in 1990: 396th (State rank: 2nd)
U.S. rank in 2000: 408th (State rank: 2nd)

Density: 1,425.7 people per square mile

Racial and ethnic characteristics (2005)

White: 70,412
Black: 1,555
American Indian and Alaska Native: 1,240
Asian: 1,413
Native Hawaiian and Pacific Islander: 0
Hispanic or Latino (may be of any race): 48,333
Other: 7,843

Percent of residents born in state: 46.7% (2000)

Age characteristics (2005)

Population under 5 years old: 6,556
Population 5 to 9 years old: 4,747
Population 10 to 14 years old: 6,191
Population 15 to 19 years old: 6,687
Population 20 to 24 years old: 11,755
Population 25 to 34 years old: 11,827

Population 35 to 44 years old: 10,638
Population 45 to 54 years old: 8,471
Population 55 to 59 years old: 3,281
Population 60 to 64 years old: 3,176
Population 65 to 74 years old: 5,457
Population 75 to 84 years old: 4,212
Population 85 years and older: 1,031
Median age: 30.1 years

Births (2006, MSA)

Total number: 3,560

Deaths (2006, MSA)

Total number: 1,243

Money income (2005)

Per capita income: $17,059
Median household income: $29,363
Total households: 34,005

Number of households with income of...

less than $10,000: 5,246
$10,000 to $14,999: 3,921
$15,000 to $24,999: 5,291
$25,000 to $34,999: 5,707
$35,000 to $49,999: 5,216
$50,000 to $74,999: 3,365
$75,000 to $99,999: 2,325
$100,000 to $149,999: 2,166
$150,000 to $199,999: 425
$200,000 or more: 343

Percent of families below poverty level: 27.4%
(2005)

2005 FBI Crime Index Property: 3,949

2005 FBI Crime Index Violent: 465

■ Municipal Government

Las Cruces has a council-manager form of government with six council members, elected by district, serving staggered terms. Both the mayor and the council members serve four-year terms.

Head Official: Mayor Ken Miyagishima (D) (since 2007; current term expires 2011)

Total Number of City Employees: approximately 1,236 (2007)

City Information: City of Las Cruces; PO Box 20000, Las Cruces, NM 88004; telephone (505)541-2000

■ Economy

Major Industries and Commercial Activity

Like many other sunbelt communities, Las Cruces' economy is booming. The city is the fastest-growing metro area in New Mexico and was ranked ninth by *Inc.* magazine on the "Top 20 Small Cities for Doing Business" list in 2007. Private and public sectors continue to fuel the economy, whereas the conditions in other parts of the country, such as climate, cost of living, and quality of life, are less attractive to people and companies looking to relocate.

Mainstays of the local economy are agriculture, construction, government, retail trade, tourism, and services. Since World War II, federal, state, and local government have become the main source of jobs in the area, due to the proximity of New Mexico State University (NMSU) and White Sands Missile Range. NMSU is one of the city's largest employers with over 4,400 people on faculty and staff in 2006. The university also provides training and education for research facilities at White Sands. White Sands Missile Range is the Army's largest installation and the largest military installation in the Western Hemisphere, covering more than 2.2 million acres, and is used by the Navy, Air Force, and NASA. Other government agencies, universities, private industries, and even foreign militaries conduct research there as well. About 56 percent of White Sands' employees live in the Las Cruces area.

Although Las Cruces was never primarily an industrial town, manufacturing and commerce has been growing in importance. The North American Free Trade Agreement, or NAFTA, passed in 1994, has influenced this trend, as has the opening in 1991 of the border crossing at Santa Teresa, just 40 miles south of Las Cruces. Many companies are finding it advantageous to relocate in the Mesilla Valley area in order to do business with maquilladoras (factories) in Mexico. NAFTA and the Mexican government's maquilladora program enacted in the 1960s encourage this type of trade by lowering or completely eliminating tariffs. For example, a U.S. company may send automobile parts to be assembled in Mexico; when the assembled car is shipped back, duties are paid only on the value added in Mexico. As of 2006 the manufacturing sector was still seen as a small part of the overall economic development, but had grown to employ about five percent of the city's labor force.

On the U.S. side of the border, there are an abundance of established industrial and research parks in Dona Ana County. Parks in the county include the Arrowhead Research Park on the New Mexico State University campus, the 1,820-acre West Mesa Industrial Park, Santa Teresa Logistics Park, and the 230-acre Bi-National Park. As of 2007 existing and planned industrial research facilities occupied over three million square feet.

Las Cruces is definitely a land of peppers. Chile, cayenne, jalapeno, and bell peppers in every color imaginable are all raised locally. The pungent aroma of roasting peppers and the sight of strings of red peppers drying on rooftops enliven the local scene. Stahmann Farms on Highway 28, which originally focused on cotton and tomatoes, is now one of the world's largest producers of pecans. Dona Ana County led the state in pecan production in 2005 with $82 million of the state's total production of $110 million. Other agricultural products include cotton, onions and various other vegetables, and dairy products. Research into preserving species of chiles and developing new strains takes place at New Mexico State University at the Chile Pepper Institute Center for Chile Education.

Despite the lack of adequate convention space, the convention sales industry still saw growth in 2005-06, as did the tour sector of the tourism industry with an economic impact of over $73,500. That year future tours were booked with an estimated economic impact of over $79,400. Although tourism slowed in mid-2006 due to record high gas prices, by fall Las Cruces as well as other cities contributed to a rebound in the industry. By November 2006, New Mexico had drawn over one million visitors that year compared to just over 994,000 reported in November 2005.

Items and goods produced: peppers, pecans, cotton and other agricultural products, electronics parts and molded plastics, repair parts for machines, packaging materials, and chemicals.

Incentive Programs—New and Existing Companies

Local programs: The County may issue Industrial Development Bonds (IDBs) for new businesses and industries, and will work with private bond counsel of the company and the State Investment Council to have the bonds purchased by the State Investment Pool or through a private placement. These IDBs can be used for construction, site costs, equipment, and training. A less expensive alternative to IDBs is the Community Development Incentive Act that allows new businesses to be exempt from property taxes for up to 20 years. The Community Development Department assists in expediting all permit applications. Las Cruces' foreign trade zone exists in three sub-areas adjacent to the Las Cruces airport and West Mesa Industrial Park.

State programs: The city of Las Cruces participates in all of New Mexico's incentives for new and expanding businesses. Its Build to Suit program facilitates building construction, and ePort New Mexico is a one-stop information source offering permitting and licensing. The state's financial incentives include: no inventory taxes; tax credits for high-wage jobs, technology jobs, and

childcare; a tax deduction for research and development services; a job training incentive program (the cornerstone of the state's incentives, allowing New Mexico to pay half the salary for new hires for up to half a year and 100 percent of classroom training costs and on the job training by state institutes); exemptions for qualified businesses from property taxes on land, buildings, and equipment, and from personal property tax on equipment; and laboratory partnerships with small businesses. The Angel Investment Tax Credit is available to those invested in New Mexico companies pursuing high-technology research or manufacturing. Qualified investors can receive a tax credit of up to $25,000 each year on up to two qualified investments that must be in two different businesses. Further incentives are available for manufacturers, customer support centers, aerospace and aircraft industries, producers of agriculture or energy, and filmmakers. In addition, the state enacted a major personal income tax reduction in 2003, and New Mexico's property taxes are among the lowest in the nation.

Job training programs: In July 2007 the Governor's Office of Workforce Training & Development merged with the New Mexico Department of Labor to create a new branch called the New Mexico Department of Workforce Solutions. The new department focuses on preparing job seekers to meet current standards in the labor market, as well as, effectively matching citizens with businesses in need of help. Services available include job fairs, local workforce development centers, online job searches, and online registration for employment services. Through the Job Training Incentive Program (JTIP) (formerly the Industrial Development Training Program) companies can utilize features that include training customized to individual companies' needs and the freedom to select training candidates. It is not limited to economically disadvantaged people.

Development Projects

Housing needs are on the minds of developers and planners in Las Cruces and any fast growing city. Las Cruces issued over 4,073 permits in 2006 for construction of all types of commercial and residential buildings. The Community Development Department has cooperated with some 16 agencies to obtain over $1.1 billion for services for low income families, including helping 36 families through its Home Rehabilitation Program between 2003 and 2005. As the productivity of the program began to decrease, helping only 5 families in 2005, plans to revise and analyze its structure were expected to be completed between 2006 and 2010. This city department has also helped rewrite zoning codes according to citizen's requests and has designed the Mesquite Neighborhood Plan, approved in July 2007. The Mesquite Neighborhood Plan focuses on expanding and revitalizing the oldest district in Las Cruces. Design goals for the plan included preserving the Mesquite

St. Original Townsite Historic District, encouraging re-location of small and new businesses with expanded street parking, creating and maintaining affordable housing, and implementing urban design concepts to create a physically safe environment. Priority projects are expected to completed or at least started by 2012.

The importance of water and wastewater management to the region was not overlooked. A two million gallon capacity Telshor water tank was restored and nearly $1 million was spent for various upkeep projects on Las Cruces's more than 390 miles of water lines and 50 wells. With over 50 new and expanding industries in the city and sur-rounding area, economic development in Las Cruces continued to grow at an accelerated rate in 2007. One of the newest and largest additions that year was Spaceport America, the first purpose-built commercial spaceport in the nation. Located about 45 miles north of the city and controlled by White Sands Missile Range, Spaceport America completed its first successful commercial launch in April 2007. Continued construction of the facility includes a 100,000-square-foot hangar was scheduled to begin in 2008. The economic impact of this state-of-the-art spaceport was projected to reach over $1 billion in total revenues by 2020 and create more than 5,000 new jobs.

Economic Development Information: Mesilla Valley Economic Development Alliance, 505 S. Main, Suite 134, PO Box 1299, Las Cruces, NM 88004; telephone (505)525-2852; fax (505)523-5707.

Commercial Shipping

Overnight shipping is available to most major western cities, including Dallas, Houston, San Antonio, Phoenix, San Diego, Los Angeles, and Denver. Two railroads pro-vide direct rail services: Burlington Northern-Santa Fe and Union Pacific-Southern Pacific, and the newer border crossing at Santa Teresa's Intermodal Park is set to be a future site where truck, rail, and air modes can converge on the United States-Mexico border. Air freight service is provided by all major companies. Several major commer-cial trucking firms offer freight service for the area.

Labor Force and Employment Outlook

The city is within close proximity to 11 post-secondary institutions that create an abundant, strong, and techni-cally-skilled workforce. In 2006 the Las Cruces metro area employed over 82,000, with an employment rate of 4.7 percent. By March 2007 the unemployment rate had al-ready decreased slightly to 4.3 percent. Another source for skilled workers is the Technical Bridge Apprenticeship Program. This program prepares students for challenging careers in the technical industry and also provides low-wage workers with additional education to help them move up in their field. Degrees that workers can earn include a Manufacturing Technology Associate Degree and Engi-neering Technology Bachelor's Degree. Citing the city's

positive job growth, affordable cost of living, and low cost of doing business, *Forbes* ranked Las Cruces second on the "Best Small Metros for Business and Careers" list in 2006.

The following is a summary of data regarding the Las Cruces metropolitan area labor force, 2006 annual averages.

Size of nonagricultural labor force: 67,000

Number of workers employed in . . .

  construction and mining: 5,000
  manufacturing: 3,400
  trade, transportation and utilities: 10,200
  information: 1,200
  financial activities: 2,400
  professional and business services: 5,600
  educational and health services: 10,100
  leisure and hospitality: 6,900
  other services: 1,500
  government: 20,800

Average hourly earnings of production workers employed in manufacturing: Not available

Unemployment rate: 4.2% (June 2007)

Largest county employers	Number of employees
New Mexico State University	6,980
White Sands Missile Range	4,357
Las Cruces Public Schools	3,316
NASA	1,500
City of Las Cruces	1,251
Memorial Medical Center	1,198
Wal-Mart	700
Allied Signal Aerospace	667
Excel Agent Services	300

Cost of Living

The following is a summary of data regarding several key cost of living factors for the Las Cruces metropolitan area.

2007 (1st quarter) ACCRA Average House Price: $324,380

2007 (1st quarter) ACCRA Cost of Living Index: 100.3

State income tax rate: 1.7% to 5.3%

State sales tax rate: 5.0%

Local income tax rate: None

Local sales tax rate: 7.0%

Property tax rate: $27.53 per $1,000 of 33.3% of assessed value

Economic Information: Greater Las Cruces Chamber of Commerce, 760 W. Picacho, Las Cruces, NM 88005; telephone (505)524-1968. Mesilla Valley Economic Development Alliance, 505 S. Main, Suite 134, PO Box 1299, Las Cruces, NM 88004; telephone (505) 525-2852.

■ Education and Research

Elementary and Secondary Schools

Las Cruces Public Schools is the state's second largest school district and the third-largest employer in Dona Ana County. Specialized programs include a Bilingual Education Program geared towards English proficiency in academics and ultimately career success. There is also a preschool program for toddlers younger than kindergarten age, an in-school program for pregnant teens, and a drug abuse prevention program. A new "Drop Back In" mentorship program matches at-risk students with adult mentors. There are also special vocational/technical programs featuring nontraditional, nonacademic training for fields such as construction. Programs for special education students and for the gifted or talented are strong.

The following is a summary of data regarding the Las Cruces Public School District as of the 2005–2006 school year.

Total enrollment: 24,000

Number of facilities

elementary schools: 24
junior high/middle schools: 7
senior high schools: 4
other: 1

Student/teacher ratio: 15.2:1

Teacher salaries (2005–06)

elementary median: $35,310
junior high/middle median: $36,050
secondary median: $37,860

Funding per pupil: $6,907

Public Schools Information: Las Cruces Public Schools, 505 S. Main, Suite 249, Las Cruces, NM 88001; telephone (505)527-5800

Colleges and Universities

New Mexico State University (NMSU), with 16,415 students in fall 2006 is home to six colleges: Agriculture and Home Economics, Business Administration, Education, Engineering, Arts and Sciences, and Health and Social Service. NMSU offers 77 baccalaureate, 50 masters, and 22 doctoral programs, plus a specialist in education in two study areas. The university employs over 1,000 faculty members and approximately 3,300 staff members. NMSU offers Ph.D. degrees in agriculture, education, engineering, and the sciences. With 13 statewide research facilities, NMSU is regarded among the top 110 national institutions in federal research expenditures. Funding of $1.5 million was given to the College of Engineering in October 2007 for the development of a new water quality laboratory. When completed, the Freeport-McMoRan Copper & Gold Water Quality Laboratory will house cutting-edge research technology and will be the first of its kind within the state. A groundbreaking ceremony was also held that year for a Native American Cultural Center (NACC). The center includes new offices, classrooms, computer rooms, and multipurpose spaces in an effort "to recruit, retain, and educate American Indian students."

Dona Ana Branch Community College (DABCC), actually a branch of New Mexico State University and located on NMSU's campus, was instituted in 1973 to meet the needs of students who wish to achieve one year certificates and two year associate's degrees in medical, technical, and business fields. The college's Adult Basic Education Outreach Program and Community Education Program have been noted by the U.S. Department of Education for promoting literacy and preparing individuals for high school equivalency exams. DABCC also has programs for high school students in Dona Ana County. Enrollment is at nearly 7,000, with 37 academic and degree programs offered.

Libraries and Research Centers

The Las Cruces public library, called Thomas Branigan Memorial Library, has more than 200,000 items which include audio, video, and microform media as well as print items. The library provides free internet access seven days a week, a Bookmobile, a Spanish Language Collection, and a genealogy collection. The Thomas Branigan Memorial Library received $550,000 from the New Mexico State Legislature in 2007 to begin an expansion project. Finding solutions to acquire additional funding was the main goal that year; it was estimated that the expansion would take $15 million to complete. The New Mexico State University Library holds over a million volumes housed in two buildings on the Las Cruces main campus. The Branson Library houses items pertaining to engineering, agriculture, business, government publications, and special collections, while the Zuhl Library houses the arts, humanities, and sciences collections.

Major research centers at New Mexico State University include the Engineering Research Center, which coordinates research functions in many engineering disciplines; the Physical Science Laboratory, which performs research, development, testing, and evaluation for NASA; The Rio Grande Corridor, which includes the NMSU High Performance Computing Center, focusing on artificial intelligence and genetic engineering; and Arrowhead Research Park and Genesis Center, specializing in research and development and providing affordable incubator space for small technology based start-up companies. The Rocket Racing League, an aerospace sports and entertainment organization, opened development operations in 2006 at Arrowhead Research Park. The new addition sparked focus on attracting more aerospace industries in an effort to make Arrowhead a premiere hub for space-related research. The Carnegie Foundation ranked New Mexico State as a Level One research facility; it receives more than $150 million in total research contracts. Waste Management Education and Research Consortium helps develop environmental management resources; New Mexico Water Resource Research Institute explores water issues; New Mexico Border Research Institute plays an integral role in promoting international trade and cultural exchange; and the Advanced Manufacturing Center has a mission to enhance education, research, and business in the manufacturing industry. The College of Engineering received $1.5 million in October 2007 for the development of a new water quality laboratory. The Freeport-McMoRan Copper & Gold Water Quality Laboratory will house cutting-edge research technology and will be the first of its kind within the state. There are also the Arts and Sciences Research Center and an agricultural experiment station, and the university interacts with outside military and industrial research facilities in the area.

Public Library Information: Thomas Branigan Memorial Library, 200 E. Picacho, Las Cruces, NM 88001; telephone (575)528-4000

■ Health Care

Las Cruces has three main medical facilities serving its health care needs. Memorial Medical Center (MMC) signed a 40-year, $150 million agreement with Province Healthcare, which will enable it to add 99 private rooms to its 286-bed acute care facility. MMC offers emergency and urgent care, comprehensive cancer care at Ikard Cancer Treatment Center, imaging services, maternal/infant care, lab services, Memorial Heart Center for Heart and Vascular Care, outpatient surgery, Women's Health and Wellness, pediatrics, a neonatal care center, behavioral services, and various rehabilitation services among others. Additional services are offered at its freestanding annex, Memorial HealthPlex, an outpatient surgery center with diagnostic imaging, lab services, and endoscopy. The Mesilla Valley Hospital, with 86 beds, offers adult and child psychiatric care, and chemical dependency treatment. One of the newest

choices in health care in Las Cruces is the 172-bed MountainView Regional Medical Center, which opened in 2002. It boasts a state-of-the art, full service emergency room and all private inpatient rooms. Among other key services at MountainView are the Comprehensive Women's Center, cardiology services, surgery services, diagnostic imaging, inpatient rehabilitation, a pain management center, and an ADA certified diabetes program. The MountainView Surgical Center allows patients to have gastrointestinal, orthopedic, and pediatric surgeries in a relaxed out-patient setting. The Southern New Mexico Cancer Center also opened in 2002, providing patients with services including radiation therapy, medical oncology, and diagnostic radiology.

■ Recreation

Sightseeing

A popular attraction is the monument and white crosses that mark the graves of the travelers from Taos who were ambushed and killed by Apaches in 1830, and for which the city is purported to be named. White Sands Missile Range displays missiles and weapons at its visitor's center. Its museum traces the origins of space and nuclear research. Separate and distinct from the missile range is White Sands National Monument, an area of over 275 square miles of pure gypsum. Nature tours, including tours of Lake Lucero, are given. Visitors can explore the world's largest pecan farms at Stahmann Farms, about 7 miles south of the city. History buffs of the Old West will enjoy San Albino Church in old Mesilla, one of the oldest missions in the region; the Fort Selden State Monument on the site of the former cavalry fort; and the Historical Museum of Lawmen, located at the Dona Ana County Sheriff's Department, which displays law enforcement memorabilia. The only federally funded monument to the Bataan Death March heroes can be found in Veterans Park in Las Cruces along Roadrunner Parkway. It was sculpted by local artist Kelly Hester and dedicated in 2001.

Arts and Culture

Founded by Tony-award-winning playwright Mark Medoff, The American Southwest Theatre Company performs five or six regular season productions a year plus a children's show at New Mexico State University. Professional actors are hired each season through the Guest Artist Program and work alongside the resident company and New Mexico State University actors. The Las Cruces Community Theatre group produces five shows annually and holds a one-act festival of experimental plays in the winter. Opportunities for Creative Theater Students offers student performances at the NMSU Attic Theater.

Las Cruces boasts a number of interesting museums. Four are run by the city itself: the Branigan Cultural Center, the Museum of Natural History, The Museum of Art, and The Railroad Museum. The Bicentennial Log Cabin was a cabin originally in the Black Mountain range in Grafton, New Mexico in Sierra County until the mining industry ended and Grafton became a ghost town. The log cabin was given as a gift to Las Cruces in 1976 for its bicentennial celebration. It was then transported and completely rebuilt by Las Cruces Association of Home Builders, and featured original furnishings and artifacts from the 1880s. It was used as a museum and educational venue for many years, but public interest decreased and city revitalization plans included moving the cabin and expanding a highway intersection on the cabin's site. After a formal request by the Sierra County Board of County Commissioners, Las Cruces transferred the cabin back to its home county in 2006. The Branigan Cultural Center displays both historical and fine arts items in a building that was constructed as the city's main library during the Great Depression. The Museum of Art was completed in spring of 1999. The Las Cruces Railroad and Transportation Museum holds artifacts from New Mexico's railroading past. The museum was closed throughout most of 2007 for building renovations, but was expected to reopen in late fall 2007 with expanded hours and new exhibits. The museum of Natural History displays plants and animals from the Chihuahuan Desert region and has programs running the gamut from dinosaurs to astronomy. The New Mexico Farm and Ranch Heritage Museum is the largest of its kind in the world and educates the public on everything in the 3,000-year history of agriculture in New Mexico. New Mexico State University has its own University Museum in Kent Hall on the main campus, which holds mostly anthropological artifacts including historic and prehistoric art objects. Space Murals, Inc. is a combination giant water tower mural and museum honoring space exploration and astronauts. Visitors to the Gadsden Museum get a taste of the life and times of the Albert Jennings Fountain family, who played a crucial role in Las Cruces history. The museum exhibits Indian artifacts and objects from the Civil War, paintings and china, and outlines the history of the Gadsden Purchase.

Festivals and Holidays

Las Cruces hosts holidays and fiestas year round, many of them celebrating the city's Hispanic culture. Starting in mid-January is the Mesilla Valley Balloon Rally, when 70 or more colorful hot air balloons fill the sky. April offers four happenings: the La Vina Blues and Jazz Thing features cool music sponsored by New Mexico's oldest winery; the Trinity Site Tour in White Sands Missile Range, where the first atomic explosion was set off; the Border Book Festival, featuring renowned visiting authors, food, fun, and live acts; and the annual Frontier

Days at Fort Selden. Cinco de Mayo festivities take place in May, with Mexican food, dancing, and music in old Mesilla. Also in May, the Fiesta de San Ysidro celebrates agriculture and Hispanic traditions, and ends with a Blessing of the Fields and the hot GLASS Fly-In, showcasing the latest in flight technology. The Southern New Mexico Wine Festival is held at the end of May.

Fourth of July is celebrated with the Electric Light Parade and fireworks. In September and October, kids and grown ups alike enjoy the Mesilla Valley Maze, which includes hay rides to a pumpkin patch and finding one's way through twists and turns cut into a corn field. In early September is the Hatch Chile Festival, honoring the Mesilla Valley as the chile capital of the world with food, crafts, an auction, and more. An hour north of Las Cruces, Hillsboro holds its apple festival the first week of September. Diez y Seis de Septiembre commemorates Mexican Independence day with folk dances, mariachi music, and traditional Mexican foods. The world's largest enchilada is constructed each year at the Whole Enchilada Fiesta, with an accompanying parade and other festivities. The end of September and the beginning of October bring the Southern New Mexico State Fair, with food, music, an auction, livestock shows, and a rodeo. La Vina, New Mexico's oldest winery, holds its namesake festival in October. The Annual Mesilla Jazz Happening holds court in two places—the old Historic Plaza and the Mercado Plaza—with horse drawn shuttles giving free rides between the two plazas.

While the Anglo world celebrates Halloween, in Las Cruces there is Dia de los Muertos, or Day of the Dead, with candlelit processions, homemade altars in the streets, and a giant piñata. November brings the Annual Renaissance ArtsFaire where artisans present their works in a juried art show and exhibition. In mid-November the International Mariachi Conference and Concert arrives to New Mexico State University and Young Park. Finally, in December, Christmas Carols and Luminarias set historic old Mesilla aglow.

Sports for the Spectator

New Mexico State University offers Division I NCAA college sports with six men's and nine women's teams. Many games are held at Aggie Memorial Football Stadium with a capacity of more than 30,000 people. The city is home to over 25 sport facilities that host a variety of games. Las Cruces also hosts sporting events such as the American Bicycle Association National BMX Tournament, the American Junior Golf Association Nike All Stars Tournament, and a number of NCAA Collegiate games.

Sports for the Participant

Las Cruces is home to more than 60 parks, many of which have playgrounds, picnic tables, and special events throughout the year. The city's six recreation centers have weight rooms and racquetball and basketball courts. Therapeutic recreation is offered at Mesilla Park Recreation Center. Summer programs include swimming, tennis, track and field, and computer camp. Other city recreation department offerings are soccer, football, softball, basketball, BMX, track and field, swimming lessons, volleyball, and boxing.

Shopping and Dining

Shopping in Las Cruces can be a delightfully varied experience. Mesilla Valley Mall houses 115 stores, including both national chain stores and small boutiques. Rated one of the top 10 open-air markets in the country, the Las Cruces Farmers & Crafts Market presents more than 200 local artisans and farmers twice a week, year round. Visitors to Las Cruces are drawn to Old Mesilla, a picturesque village of galleries, unique stores and restaurants built around the town plaza, with buildings dating back to the 1850s. Mesilla is only five minutes from downtown Las Cruces.

Besides the wonderful Southwestern cuisine featuring dishes of local peppers and other produce, Las Cruces has more than 70 restaurants running the gamut from fast food and deli fare to Chinese, Japanese, continental, Italian, and, of course, Mexican fare.

Visitor Information: Las Cruces Convention and Visitors Bureau, 211 N. Water St., Las Cruces, NM 88001; telephone (575)541-2444; fax (575)541-2164.

■ Convention Facilities

The city of Las Cruces has more than 2,200 hotel rooms, 98,000 square feet of meeting space, and can accommodate groups from 10 to 1,000. The Las Cruces Hilton has 203 rooms and nearly 6,500 square feet of convention and meeting facilities, including a 5,000-square-foot Grand Ballroom and smaller executive conference rooms. The Best Western Mesilla Valley Inn is the second largest hotel with 160 rooms and 8,500 square feet of meeting space that can accommodate from 10 to 600 people.

Convention Information: Las Cruces Convention and Visitors Bureau, 211 N. Water St., Las Cruces, NM 88001; telephone (575)541-2444; fax (575)541-2142.

■ Transportation

Approaching the City

Interstate 10, which is a direct route to Phoenix, Los Angeles, Houston, and Dallas; and Interstate 25, which is the direct route to Albuquerque and Denver, traverse the city's south end. U.S. Highway 70 presents a direct route to Interstate Highway 40 at Amarillo. The Las Cruces

International Airport, eight miles west of the city, no longer offers commercial services; the last commercial flight was in July 2005. Air travel takes place at the El Paso International Airport in Texas, about 52 miles to the south of Las Cruces. American, Continental, Delta, United, Frontier, U.S., ExpressJet, and Southwest airlines fly to over 70 cities from El Paso.

Bus and shuttle service is offered by Greyhound-Trailways, Enchanted Lands Enterprise Tours, and the Las Cruces Shuttle Service.

Traveling in the City

Local bus service is offered by Roadrunner Transit and taxis are available from the Checker/Yellow Cab Company.

■ Communications

Newspapers and Magazines

The city is served by the *Las Cruces Sun-News,* which is published every morning, and *The Las Cruces Bulletin,* a community newspaper that comes out each Thursday. Locally published magazines include *New Mexico Farm and Ranch,* a monthly covering equipment, techniques, and laws affecting the farming industry in New Mexico. The scholarly journal *Tamara* covers organization science and is published out of New Mexico State University's Department of Management.

Television and Radio

Las Cruces has approximately 32 AM and FM radio stations that broadcast within close listening range. The stations have a variety of formats including country, Hispanic news/talk, adult contemporary, and public radio programming. The city has one public television station and one cable station.

Media Information: *Las Cruces Sun-News* 256 West Las Cruces Avenue, Las Cruces, NM 88005; telephone (505)541-5400; fax (505)541-5498. *The Las Cruces Bulletin,* 840 N. Telshor Boulevard Suite E, Las Cruces, NM 88011; telephone (505)524-8061; fax (505)526-4621.

Las Cruces Online

City of Las Cruces home page. Available www .las-cruces.org

Greater Las Cruces Chamber of Commerce. Available www.lascruces.org

Las Cruces Convention and Visitors Bureau. Available www.lascrucescvb.org

Las Cruces Sun-News. Available www.lcsun-news .com

Mesilla Valley Economic Development Alliance. Available www.mveda.com

New Mexico Department of Workforce Solutions. Available www.dws.state.nm.us

New Mexico Magazine. Available www .nmmagazine.com

New Mexico State University Library. Available lib .nmsu.edu

BIBLIOGRAPHY

Harris, Linda G., *Las Cruces: An Illustrated History* (Las Cruces, NM: Arroyo Press, 1993

Santa Fe

■ The City in Brief

Founded: 1607 (incorporated 1846)

Head Official: Mayor David Coss (since 2006)

City Population
> 1980: 48,953
> 1990: 56,537
> 2000: 62,203
> 2006 estimate: 72,056
> Percent change, 1990–2000: 8.0%
> U.S. rank in 1980: 431st
> U.S. rank in 1990: 428th
> U.S. rank in 2000: 508th (State rank: 3rd)

Metropolitan Area Population
> 1980: 93,118
> 1990: 117,043
> 2000: 147,635
> 2006 estimate: 142,407
> Percent change, 1990–2000: 26.1%
> U.S. rank in 1980: Not available
> U.S. rank in 1990: Not available
> U.S. rank in 2000: 205th (MSA)

Area: 37.33 square miles (2000)

Elevation: 7,000 feet above sea level

Average Annual Temperature: 49.3° F

Average Annual Precipitation: 14 inches of rain, 32 inches of snow

Major Economic Sectors: services, wholesale and retail trade, government

Unemployment Rate: 3.1% (June 2007)

Per Capita Income: $34,095 (2005)

2005 FBI Crime Index Property: 4,022

2005 FBI Crime Index Violent: 379

Major Colleges and Universities: The College of Santa Fe, St. John's College, Santa Fe Community College

Daily Newspaper: *The Santa Fe New Mexican*

■ Introduction

Founded before Massachusetts's Plymouth Colony and the second oldest city in the United States, Santa Fe is a cultural center for the Southwest. The Santa Fe Opera is known throughout the world, and the city is a gathering place for writers and artists. The capital of the state of New Mexico, Santa Fe is a blend of Native American, Spanish, New Mexican, and Anglo (English) cultures. The architectural integrity of the city's high-walled adobe structures and narrow, winding streets has been preserved through careful planning, attracting travelers world-wide and gaining recognition as the fifth "Top City in the U.S. and Canada" by *Travel + Leisure* magazine in 2006. At the same time Santa Fe is a center for commerce, light industry, and science, making advances in environmental conservation, digital technology, and medical services.

■ Geography and Climate

Santa Fe is located in the northern Rio Grande Valley at the southern end of the Rocky Mountains. Situated in the foothills of the Sangre de Cristo mountain range, the city has a nearby pine forest. Because of the mountain setting, Santa Fe enjoys a semi-arid continental climate, with moderate summers and winters. Humidity is low and the sun shines approximately 300 days per year. Snowfall averages 32 inches annually in the city; deep snow does remain at higher altitudes during the winter.

Area: 37.33 square miles (2000)

Elevation: 7,000 feet above sea level

Average Temperature: 49.3° F

Average Annual Precipitation: 14 inches of rain, 32 inches of snow

■ History

Native American and Spanish Influences

During prehistoric times a village built by the Tano tribe stood on the site now occupied by Santa Fe. Evidence from the Tano culture, uncovered in the few ruins left by Spanish settlers, indicates that civilization existed on the site as far back as 1050 to 1150 A.D. The settlement was abandoned around 200 years before the arrival of the Spanish. The spot was called Kuapoga—"place of the shell beads near the water"—by the Pueblos. Santa Fe was founded in either 1607 or 1609 (there is some confusion about the year) by Don Pedre de Peralta, the third governor of the Province of New Mexico, who built the Palace of Governors and the Plaza and planned a walled city. The palace was occupied by a succession of sixty Spanish governors for more than 200 years, and Santa Fe has been a seat of government since its founding.

Throughout Spanish rule of the territory Santa Fe was a center for exploration and mission work. Franciscan friars built eleven churches and by 1617 had converted more than 14,000 Native Americans to their form of Christianity. Conflict arose, however, when the Native Americans continued to practice their own religion. In 1680 a number of the Spanish settlers were killed in a conflict with natives; the survivors fled to El Paso del Norte, abandoning the town. The Native Americans established their own community in Santa Fe; occupying the palace and appointing a governor, they held the town for twelve years until the arrival of De Vargas, Spanish governor of the province. He made peace and returned the following year with a statue of the Christian New Testament's Virgin Mary. Making his entry on the site of present day Rosario Chapel, he vowed to pay yearly homage to "Our Lady of Victory." Since that time, in fulfillment of this vow the De Vargas Procession has been held in Santa Fe.

Mexico and United States Claim Santa Fe

When Mexico won independence from Spain in 1821, Santa Fe came under the control of Mexico. Trade was then opened between Santa Fe and the United States over a route that came to be known as the Santa Fe Trail. In 1846 the United States claimed Santa Fe; the city has been under U.S. jurisdiction ever since, except for two weeks during the Civil War when the Confederates seized control after the Battle of Valverde. The Santa Fe Trail eventually fell into disuse when rail travel advanced to the region. Santa Fe flourished, however, benefiting from the new trade connections that were made possible by the railroad.

City Becomes Art Colony, Capital of State

Around the turn of the century, artists, attracted by the climate and the beauty of the area, moved to Santa Fe, and the city soon became popular as an art colony. When New Mexico attained statehood in 1912, Santa Fe, as the capital, entered a period of prosperity; government workers arrived to live in the city and federal and state buildings were constructed around the Plaza. By 1920 the population had grown from 5,000 to more than 7,000 people, and by the 1940s it was over 20,000 people.

In 1957 the city established zoning codes designed to maintain a uniform architectural style. Two types of architecture are permitted: Pueblo, characterized by rounded parapets and rough-hewn woodwork, and Territorial, featuring brick coping and milled, often decorative woodworking.

Santa Fe's populace reflects the city's Native American, Spanish, and Anglo heritage, and the cultural traditions of these groups have been retained. However, after an influx of new residents in the 1980s, the 1990 census reported that for the first time since the city's founding, Hispanic residents were a minority. During the 1990s the city experienced some tensions between locals—many of them poor—and newcomers, who are driving up the cost of housing and otherwise altering the landscape. Economic frustrations continue into the early 2000s, as wages linger at almost 20 percent below the national average, while the cost of living remained well above the national average. The city has taken steps to remedy the issue; a "living wage" city ordinance was passed in 2003 to raise minimum wages and as of January 2007 the minimum wage had increased to $9.50 per hour for employers with 25 or more employees.

Historical Information: Fra Angelico Chavez Memorial History Library and Photographic Archive, 110 Washington Ave., Santa Fe, NM 87504; telephone (508) 476-5090. Special Collections, Santa Fe Community College Library; telephone (505)428-1341

■ Population Profile

Metropolitan Area Residents

1980: 93,118
1990: 117,043
2000: 147,635
2006 estimate: 142,407
Percent change, 1990–2000: 26.1%
U.S. rank in 1980: Not available

©Luc Novovitch/offiwent.com/drr.net

U.S. rank in 1990: Not available

U.S. rank in 2000: 205th (MSA)

City Residents

1980: 48,953

1990: 56,537

2000: 62,203

2006 estimate: 72,056

Percent change, 1990–2000: 8.0%

U.S. rank in 1980: 431st

U.S. rank in 1990: 428th

U.S. rank in 2000: 508th (State rank: 3rd)

Density: 1,666.1 people per square mile (2000)

Racial and ethnic characteristics (2000)

White: 47,459

Black: 409

American Indian and Alaska Native: 1,373

Asian: 791

Native Hawaiian and Pacific Islander: 49

Hispanic or Latino (may be of any race): 29,744

Other: 12,122

Percent of residents born in state: 44.8% (2000)

Age characteristics (2005)

Population under 5 years old: 2,944

Population 5 to 9 years old: 3,243

Population 10 to 14 years old: 3,583

Population 15 to 19 years old: 4,027

Population 20 to 24 years old: 5,053

Population 25 to 34 years old: 8,077

Population 35 to 44 years old: 9,484

Population 45 to 54 years old: 10,052

Population 55 to 59 years old: 6,055

Population 60 to 64 years old: 4,374

Population 65 to 74 years old: 5,007

Population 75 to 84 years old: 3,658

Population 85 years and older: 896

Median age: 41 years

Births (2006, County)

Total number: 1,588

Deaths (2006, County)

Total number: 828

Money income (2005)

Per capita income: $34,095

Median household income: $45,177
Total households: 27,481

Number of households with income of...

less than $10,000: 2,433
$10,000 to $14,999: 1,798
$15,000 to $24,999: 3,521
$25,000 to $34,999: 3,803
$35,000 to $49,999: 3,332
$50,000 to $74,999: 4,283
$75,000 to $99,999: 2,834
$100,000 to $149,999: 3,032
$150,000 to $199,999: 979
$200,000 or more: 1,466

Percent of families below poverty level: 13.1% (2005)

2005 FBI Crime Index Property: 4,022

2005 FBI Crime Index Violent: 379

■ Municipal Government

Santa Fe operates under a council-mayor, city-manager form of government, administered by an eight-member council and a mayor who are elected to four-year terms. Santa Fe is the seat of Santa Fe County and, as the state capital, the site of meetings of the State Legislature.

Head Official: Mayor David Coss (since 2006; current term expires 2010)

Total Number of City Employees: 1,489 (2007)

City Information: City of Santa Fe, PO Box 909, 200 Lincoln Avenue, Santa Fe, NM 87504-0909; telephone (505)955-6590

■ Economy

Major Industries and Commercial Activity

Santa Fe's economy has been based largely on government and tourism. As capital of New Mexico, the government is the largest employer in the area employing some 18,600 people in 2007 (29 percent of the total workforce). Santa Fe receives an average of more than one million visitors annually; *Outside Magazine* named Santa Fe as one of the "Best Towns" in 2007, noting that it is "fit, fun, and packed with adventure." Tourism boosts the city's retail industry, which employed approximately 9,800 people that year.

Because of the city's proximity to Los Alamos National Laboratory (LANL), 45 miles away, scientific research has also become a factor. Operated by the University of California for the U.S. Department of Energy, LANL is one of the largest research laboratories in

the nation. It is an important center for work on defense-related projects, conducting research on technology associated with nuclear weapons and deterrence, as well as energy production and health, safety, and environmental concerns, among other areas. Several LANL employees live in Santa Fe, and several new research-related firms and high-technology spinoff companies have located in Santa Fe.

Health care and light manufacturing are other significant economic sectors. Santa Fe has emerged as a regional medical center; St. Vincent Regional Medical Center is one of the city's largest employers and serves a 19,000-square-mile area in seven counties. Products manufactured by local companies include electronic instruments and textiles.

Santa Fe has become a leading city in the Art, Design, and Cultural Industry. The United Nations Educational Scientific and Cultural Organization (UNESCO) designated Santa Fe as a "Creative City" in 2005 as part of the "Creative Cities Network." It was the first U.S. city to receive the honor and was appointed a "City of Crafts and Folk Art." UNESCO bestows this title to global cities that demonstrate superior development in the creative industries. The title has seven subcategories including literature, cinema, music, craft and folk art, design, media arts, and gastronomy.

Items and goods produced: art, pumice products, weavings, Native American arts and crafts, textiles, electronic instruments, aluminum ware

Incentive Programs—New and Existing Companies

Local programs: The Santa Fe Business Incubator, considered one of the best of its kind in the nation, assists new businesses with all aspects of start-up. The Small Business Development Center provides one-on-one business advising, encourages and instructs entrepreneurs, and is a strong advocate for local business growth and development. SCORE (Service Corps of Retired Executives) provides business counseling and support. Santa Fe Economic Development, Inc. (SFEDI) supports entrepreneurs and works with businesses interested in relocating to the area.

State programs: New Mexico offers a variety of incentives to all new and expanding businesses. Its Build to Suit program facilitates building construction, and ePort New Mexico is a "one-stop" information source offering permitting and licensing. The state's financial incentives include: no inventory taxes; tax credits for high-wage jobs, technology jobs, and childcare; a tax deduction for research and development services; a job training incentive program (New Mexico can pay half the salary for new hires for up to half a year); exemptions for qualified businesses from property taxes on land, buildings, and equipment and from personal property tax on equipment; and laboratory partnerships with small businesses. The Angel Investment Tax Credit is available to those invested in New Mexico companies pursuing high-technology research or manufacturing. Qualified investors can receive a tax credit of up to $25,000 each year on up to two qualified investments. Further incentives are available for manufacturers, customer support centers, aerospace and aircraft industries, producers of agriculture or energy, and filmmakers. In addition, the state enacted a major personal income tax reduction in 2003, and New Mexico's property taxes are among the lowest in the nation.

Job training programs: In July 2007 the Governor's Office of Workforce Training & Development merged with the New Mexico Department of Labor to create a new branch called the New Mexico Department of Workforce Solutions. The new department focuses on preparing job seekers to meet current standards in the labor market, as well as effectively matching citizens with businesses in need of help. Services available include job fairs, local workforce development centers, online job searches, and online registration for employment services. Through the Job Training Incentive Program (JTIP) (formerly the Industrial Development Training Program) companies can utilize features that include training customized to individual companies' needs and the freedom to select training candidates. It is not limited to economically disadvantaged people.

Development Projects

To attract businesses that rely on high-speed technology, Santa Fe is constructing a "Santa Fe Light Trail" system of digital microwave and fiber facilities; it will be a hybrid network available to the business community as well as educational facilities and local and state government agencies. Construction and implementation were still underway as of 2007. Construction began in November 2006 on the Santa Fe Convention Center. The new 72,500-square-foot venue will replace the Sweeney Convention Center with more than 40,000 square feet of exhibit space; the center is scheduled to open in October 2008. The U.S. Department of the Interior's Bureau of Land Management released a Final Environmental Impact Statement (FEIS) in 2007 for the future Buckman Water Diversion Project. The project seeks a solution to the continuation of water shortages in the city and county of Santa Fe. If authorized, a water diversion would be implemented in the Buckman area pulling additional water supply from the Rio Grande.

Commercial Shipping

Santa Fe is linked with major western and midwestern markets via rail freight service provided by the Santa Fe Southern Railroad, which maintains a main line through nearby Lamy. Several rail sidings are conveniently located in the city's industrial areas. Several interstate motor freight carriers connect Santa Fe with markets on both the East and West Coasts; major parcel express lines also serve the city. Air cargo service is available at Santa Fe Municipal Airport.

Labor Force and Employment Outlook

Santa Fe's economy is lead by government and tourism, and as of 2006, 29 percent of people were employed by the government, 15 percent by the retail/wholesale sector, and 13 percent by accommodation and food services. Corporations of substantial size are absent from the economy with over 60 percent of all local businesses having fewer than five employees. In response, recruitment efforts encourage entrepreneurship and small business development. Unemployment dropped in 2006 to 3.5 percent, a whole percentage point decrease compared to 2005. A "living wage" ordinance, passed in 2003, attempts to raise minimum wages to remedy the imbalance of low wages with a high cost of living index. As of January 2007 the minimum wage in the City of Santa Fe had increased to $9.50 per hour for employers with 25 or more employees.

The following is a summary of data regarding the Santa Fe metropolitan area labor force, 2006 annual averages.

Size of nonagricultural labor force: 62,800

Number of workers employed in . . .

   construction and mining: 4,900
   manufacturing: 1,100
   trade, transportation and utilities: 10,600
   information: 1,100
   financial activities: 3,100
   professional and business services: 5,100
   educational and health services: 8,400
   leisure and hospitality: 9,100
   other services: 3,000
   government: 16,400

Average hourly earnings of production workers employed in manufacturing: Not available

Unemployment rate: 3.1% (June 2007)

Largest employers (2007)	*Number of employees*
State Government	18,600
Los Alamos National Laboratory	10,364
Santa Fe School District	1,850
U.S. Government	1,750
City of Santa Fe	1,719
St. Vincent Regional Medical Center	1,600
County of Santa Fe	808

Largest employers (2007)	Number of employees
Santa Fe Community College	717
Santa Fe Opera	640
College of Santa Fe	564
Albertson's Food Centers	510

Cost of Living

The following is a summary of data regarding key cost of living factors for the Santa Fe area.

2007 (1st quarter) ACCRA Average House Price: Not available

2007 (1st quarter) ACCRA Cost of Living Index: Not available

State income tax rate: 1.7% to 5.3%

State sales tax rate: 5.0%

Local income tax rate: None

Local sales tax rate: 1.0625% (city); 1.25% (county)

Property tax rate: 0.017494 multiplied by one-third of full market value (2004)

Economic Information: Santa Fe County Chamber of Commerce, 8380 Cerrillos Rd #302, Santa Fe, NM 87507; telephone (505)988-3279; fax (505)984-2205; email trish@santafechamber.com. University of New Mexico, Bureau of Business and Economic Research, 1 University of New Mexico, Albuquerque, NM 87131; telephone (505)277-6626; fax (505)277-2773

■ Education and Research

Elementary and Secondary Schools

The Santa Fe Public Schools system is one of the largest districts in the state of New Mexico. It is administered by a five-member, executive team that includes a superintendent, deputy superintendent, two associate superintendents, and a chief financial officer. The executive team establishes educational policies and appoints a superintendent.

The following is a summary of data regarding the Santa Fe Public Schools as of the 2005–2006 school year.

Total enrollment: 13,336

Number of facilities

elementary schools: 14
junior high/middle schools: 3
senior high schools: 1
other: 0

Student/teacher ratio: 14.9:1

Teacher salaries (2005–06)

elementary median: $34,356 (all levels)
junior high/middle median: Not available
secondary median: Not available

Funding per pupil: $6,512

Additionally, Santa Fe has a large network of private schools, consisting of over 30 schools ranging from pre-Kindergarten through 12th grade, one of which—the Santa Fe Indian School—is a federally funded boarding school for Native Americans, run by the All Indian Pueblo Council.

Public Schools Information: Santa Fe Public Schools, 610 Alta Vista Street, Santa Fe, NM 87501; telephone (505)467-2003; fax (505)995-3300

Colleges and Universities

Santa Fe has several institutes of higher learning, all of which have an enrollment of less than 2,000. The College of Santa Fe is a private college offering associate and baccalaureate degrees; it is particularly known for its programs in the performing, visual, moving image, and creative writing arts, and also has strong programs in the humanities, education, business, conservation science, and social science. Students have the ability to design their own majors by working with faculty and advisors if they choose. The College of Santa Fe was ranked by *U.S. News & World Report* as one of the top schools in the West for Master's programs in 2008. St. John's College, which has a campus in Annapolis, Maryland as well as in Santa Fe, offers baccalaureate and advanced degrees. St. John's is distinctive for its "great books" curriculum; learning is based upon the study of important books of the Western tradition, and no textbooks are used. There are no majors or departments; all students follow the same path of study including four years of language, four years of math, four years of interdisciplinary study, three years of laboratory science, and one year of music. The Institute of American Indian Arts, a fine arts college, offers associate and baccalaureate degrees in creative writing, studio arts, new media arts, and museum studies. Southwestern College, devoted to the study of mental health, offers master's degrees in counseling; counseling with a concentration in grief, loss, and trauma; and art therapy. Southwest Acupuncture College offers a Master of Science in Oriental Medicine. Santa Fe Community College serves area residents with two-year college preparatory and technical and vocational curricula.

Libraries and Research Centers

The Santa Fe Public Library operates two branches in addition to its main facility downtown. Holdings include over 198,000 titles and 337,797 separate items that include videos, DVDs, tapes, and CDs. The New Mexico State Library, with over two million items, is a federal and state documents depository. Research libraries located in Santa Fe house special collections pertaining to such diverse topics as Southwestern culture, comparative religion, and Sherlock Holmes; other libraries are affiliated with local colleges and government agencies. The Santa Fe Institute conducts research activities in the physical, biological, computational, and social sciences, in areas such as cognitive neuroscience, computation in physical and biological systems, economic and social interactions, evolutionary dynamics, network dynamics, and robustness. The National Center for Genome Resources examines the influence of genetic variability on infectious disease progression. The Georgia O'Keefe Museum Research Center, in downtown Santa Fe, provides a research library and archived materials supporting research in American Modernism. The Indian Arts Research Center (IARC) holds one of the most prominent collections of authentic Southwest Indian arts and artifacts in the world; most research focuses on the existing collection.

Public Library Information: Santa Fe Public Library, 145 Washington Avenue, Santa Fe, NM 87501; telephone (505)955-6780; fax (505)955-6676

■ Health Care

Santa Fe's St. Vincent Regional Medical Center is the largest medical center in Northern New Mexico, and has the region's only Level III Trauma Center. It is the major regional medical center for a 19,000-square-mile area covering seven counties. St. Vincent has 268 licensed beds, and employs some 300 physicians representing 22 medical specialties. Non-profit and non-affiliated, it was established in 1865 and is the oldest hospital in the state. The medical center is known for its heart and vascular center, which has the first rural EKG network in the nation; it allows rural EMS personnel to transmit an electrocardiogram directly to the medical center. The Cancer Institute of New Mexico, the combination of the New Mexico Cancer Care Associates and Radiation Oncology Associates, opened in 2003 in Santa Fe. Cancer patients are able to access doctors specializing in medical oncology, radiation oncology, diagnostic imaging, clinical research, and administrative support all in one facility.

■ Recreation

Sightseeing

Santa Fe's historic downtown plaza, once the terminus of the Santa Fe Trail, has been a center of activity in Santa Fe since the city's founding. The plaza area is full of restaurants, shops, art galleries, and museums. Also here is St. Francis Cathedral, a grand structure built in the French Romanesque style, unusual in this city of Spanish-Pueblo architecture. Santa Fe's first Roman

Catholic archbishop, Jean Baptiste Lamy, started the cathedral; both the bishop and the building were the inspiration for Willa Cather's novel, *Death Comes to the Archbishop.* A wooden icon in the cathedral's north chapel is the oldest representation of the Madonna in the United States.

Other historical buildings include Santuario de Guadalupe, the nation's oldest shrine dedicated to Our Lady of Guadalupe; built in the late 1700s, its adobe walls are three feet thick. Our Lady of Light Chapel, also known as Loretto Chapel, was built between 1873 and 1878 and is the oldest stone masonry building in the city; it is known for its spiral wooden Miraculous Staircase, apparently made without nails or a support beam. San Miguel Mission, one of the oldest mission churches in the nation, was built in 1610 by the Tlaxcala natives, who were servants of Spanish soldiers and missionaries; on display is a bell that was cast in Spain in 1356 and brought to Santa Fe in the early 19th century. The New Mexico State Capitol building, the only round capitol building in the United States, was built in the shape of a Southwestern Indian *zia*, which represents the circle of life. The Palace of the Governors has been home to 60 Spanish, Mexican, and American governors, among them Lew Wallace, who wrote the novel *Ben Hur* there during his 1877-1881 tenure. Built in 1610, it became a history museum in 1909.

Canyon Road, just north of the capitol building, was once a Native American trail and defines one of the oldest districts in the city. Just west of Canyon Road is Barrio de Analco, now called East de Vargas Street, among the oldest continuously inhabited streets in the nation; many historic homes are located here. The Cross of the Martyrs, overlooking the city, is a large white cross built in 1920 to commemorate the Franciscans killed by native Pueblos in 1680. The Commemorative Walkway leading to the monument has been the route for various religious processions, particularly in September during Fiesta, the celebration of the return of the Spanish to Santa Fe in 1692.

Santa Fe is surrounded by twelve Pueblo villages, each of which retains its own distinct culture and holds special events relating to its unique traditions; all are located within an hour's drive of the city.

Arts and Culture

Home of more than 20 music groups, theater companies, and dance groups, Santa Fe supports one of the best and most active arts communities in the country. The famous Santa Fe Opera, which attracts audiences from throughout the world, presents its performances in a partially open-air amphitheater located on a wooded hill north of the city. It is known for its performances of the classics, obscure works by classical composers, and American premiers of modern works. Its eight-week season runs from June to August. The Santa Fe Symphony Orchestra and Chorus performs classical and popular works at the Lensic Performing Arts Center; the center's lavish Lensic Theater, built in 1931 as a film and vaudeville house, received an $8.2 million restoration, which was completed in 2001. The Desert Chorale choral group performs at venues throughout the city and is known for blending Renaissance melodies and avant-garde compositions. The Desert Chorale also has a children's chorus. Children ages 8 to 14 can participate and take part in several public performances each season.

Students at the College of Santa Fe stage their productions in the Greer Garson Theatre. Their season, which runs from October to May, consists of several presentations of four plays. Santa Fe Playhouse, established in the 1920s, performs dramas, avant-garde works, and musical comedy in a historic adobe theater.

The María Benitez Teatro Flamenco performs flamenco music and dance in a summer season at the María Benitez Theatre at the Radisson Hotel. The company is comprised of Benitez, who has been named the best flamenco dancer of her generation by *Dance* magazine, and flamenco dancers and musicians from throughout the United States and Spain.

Santa Fe is home to several museums specializing in a variety of fields. The Museum of New Mexico, described as the most important modern cultural institution in the state, houses the Palace of Governors, Museum of Indian Arts and Culture/Laboratory of Anthropology, New Mexico Museum of Art, and Museum of International Folk Art. The Palace of the Governors, the nation's oldest continually used building, houses exhibits relating to Native American, Spanish, Mexican, and American frontier history. Its governor offices have been restored and preserved. The Museum of Indian Arts and Culture showcases exhibits pertaining to the history and contemporary culture of the Pueblo, Navajo, and Apache peoples, including pottery, basketry, woven fabrics, jewelry, and contemporary crafts. Opened in 1987, its massive collection has been built over the course of nearly 80 years of research and acquisition by the Laboratory of Anthropology. The New Mexico Museum of Art, built in 1917, is the oldest art museum in the state; it was built in the style of the mission church at nearby Acoma Pueblo. The museum maintains a collection of more than 23,000 works, with a specialty in regional art from throughout the 20th century to the present. The Museum of International Folk Art, the largest of its kind in the world, has more than 135,000 items of folk art from around the world, including dolls and puppets, masks, textiles, ceramics, furniture, clothing, and Spanish colonial artworks.

The Georgia O'Keeffe Museum houses the largest collection of the artist's work in the world. The museum features revolving exhibits of O'Keeffe's paintings, watercolors, pastels, charcoals, and sculptures, and also hosts exhibitions of works by some of O'Keeffe's

contemporaries. In July 2001 the Georgia O'Keeffe Research Center opened as the only museum-related, American Modernism-dedicated research facility in the world. The Wheelwright Museum of the American Indian, housed in a building shaped like a Navajo hogan, features rotating single-subject displays of jewelry, tapestry, pottery, baskets, and paintings crafted by Native Americans throughout the Southwest. The Institute of American Indian Arts Museum focuses on works by students and faculty members; with more than 7,000 works, it is one of the largest collections of contemporary American Indian art in the world. The Santa Fe Children's Museum was developed to offer hands-on exhibits for the whole family. One of Santa Fe's newest museums is the Museum of Spanish Colonial Art, which presents a variety of Hispanic media—including santos (painted and sculpted images of saints), textiles, tinwork, silverwork, goldwork, ironwork, straw appliqué, ceramics, furniture, and books—dating from the Middle Ages through the present.

Festivals and Holidays

Many of Santa Fe's events reflect the cultural diversity of the city. During the Chimayo Pilgrimage, on Good Friday, thousands walk on foot to the Santuario de Chimayo, a small church believed to aid in miracles. The Rodeo de Santa Fe, a popular regional competition, is held in June; the four-night rodeo features entrants from several states competing in such events as bareback bronco riding, calf roping, steer wrestling, and barrel racing. The annual Traditional Spanish Market is held in July; it is the oldest and largest market in the country for Spanish Colonial artists. More than 300 Hispanic artisans offer traditional artforms including santos, textiles, tinwork, furniture, straw appliqué, and metalwork. The market also presents live music, art demonstrations, and regional foods. The Santa Fe Indian Market, held in August, is the country's largest and most prestigious Native American art show. More than 1,000 artisans offer basketry, blankets, jewelry, pottery, woodcarvings, rugs, sandpaintings, and sculptures. Tribal dancing and craft demonstrations are also presented. Santa Fe Fiesta in September, which dates to 1712, is the oldest community celebration in the country. Highlights include Spanish dancing, mariachi music, food and craft booths, and parades and ceremonies including a pet parade, a historical/hysterical parade, and a fiesta mass of thanksgiving held at St. Francis Cathedral, followed by a candle-lit procession from the cathedral to the Cross of the Martyrs. The Santa Fe Wine and Chile Fiesta, a five-day event, is also held in September. The Winter Spanish Market, in December, is a smaller version of July's market; more than 100 artisans offer their wares.

Drawing on the traditions of three cultures—Native American, Spanish, and Anglo—Christmas celebrations in Santa Fe take on a special flair. As part of the festivities, *farolitos*—luminaries made of paper bags, sand, and candles—set the town aglow on Christmas Eve. The city also celebrates Las Posadas, the traditional Spanish play depicting the Christmas Eve plight of Mary and Joseph. Indian pueblos schedule winter dances, bonfires, and processions in late December and January.

Sports for the Spectator

Polo teams sponsored by local merchants compete in Sunday games from June through Labor Day at the Santa Fe Polo Club. For those interested in college sports, the College of Santa Fe plans to reintroduce an intercollegiate athletics program in fall 2008. Competition sports at the college were set to include women's and men's soccer, golf, tennis, women's softball, and men's baseball.

Sports for the Participant

Outdoor activities can be pursued throughout most of the year in Santa Fe. Outdoor enthusiasts can mountain-bike through the area's high-desert terrain, hike in the area's 1,002 miles of national forest trails, golf at one of Santa Fe's six golf courses, or play tennis at one of several tennis courts. Within the Santa Fe National Forest are wilderness areas—Pecos, Dome, and San Pedro parks, and the Chama River Canyon—that are ideal for hiking, camping, fishing, and hunting. Resorts at Ojo Caliente and Jemez Springs furnish bath houses for the enjoyment of the natural hot springs for which northern New Mexico is famous. Skiing is a flourishing sport in Santa Fe. Seven ski areas within a two-hour drive provide facilities for every level of skiing expertise. Ski Santa Fe, a 30-minute drive through the Sangre De Cristo Mountains from Santa Fe, is an especially popular spot. Cross-country skiing areas are also nearby.

Shopping and Dining

Santa Fe has been described as a shopper's "Shangri-La." With hundreds of stores in the downtown area alone, the city offers boutiques and specialty shops, art galleries, and several large shopping centers. Locally designed and crafted items such as clothing, jewelry, pottery, and furniture are featured.

Prime shopping areas include the historic Canyon Road area, home to a large, eclectic mix of small shops and galleries; the plaza area, which features the greatest concentration of Native American crafts; and the Santa Fe Arcade, a three-story shopping center that opened in 2004. The Guadalupe district, a redeveloped area close to the railyard, features numerous specialty stores and cafes. Located in this area is the Sanbusco Market Center, a remodeled warehouse occupied by unique shops and restaurants. Other Santa Fe shopping highlights include the local treats at the Santa Fe Farmer's Market and the variety of wares at the Tesuque Flea Market.

A specialty of Santa Fe is northern New Mexico cuisine, which is a mixture of Pueblo Indian, Spanish Colonial, and Anglo frontier cooking. It differs from "Tex-Mex" food in that northern New Mexican cooks use heavy meats for such dishes as *carne adovada,* or marinated pork. Green chiles, pinto beans, and blue corn tortillas are also used in local dishes. *Sopaipillas,* deep-fried puff pastries drizzled with honey, are especially popular. Among other dining options are Western-style steak and barbeque, vegetarian cuisine, and Italian, Chinese, Sushi, Thai, Indian, Korean, Mediterranean, French, and Native American restaurants. Trattoria Nostrani, located in downtown Santa Fe, was listed in *Gourmet* magazine as one of "America's Top 50 Restaurants" in 2006.

Visitor Information: Santa Fe Convention and Visitors Bureau, 201 West Marcy, PO Box 909, Santa Fe, NM 87504; telephone (505)955-6200; toll-free (800) 777-CITY

■ Convention Facilities

The principal meeting facility in Santa Fe is Sweeney Convention Center, located downtown within easy access of the historical district, cultural attractions, shopping, restaurants, and more than 1,500 hotel and motel rooms. Sweeney Convention Center has 22,000 square feet of space for exhibitions, banquets, and meetings. The center features flexible seating and exhibition arrangements in its 10,000-square-foot main floor area; up to 80 booths, banquets for 700 people, and theater-style seating for 1,200 people can be accommodated in this space. Six additional meeting rooms each provide 1,300 square feet with a seating capacity of approximately 150 people. Construction began in November 2006 on the Santa Fe Convention Center. The new 72,500-square-foot venue will replace the Sweeney Convention Center with more than 40,000 square feet of exhibit space; the new convention center is scheduled to open in October 2008.

Convention Information: Santa Fe Convention and Visitors Bureau, 201 West Marcy, PO Box 909, Santa Fe, NM 87504; telephone (505)955-6200; toll-free (800) 777-CITY

■ Transportation

Approaching the City

The major airport closest to Santa Fe is Albuquerque International Sunport, 65 minutes away. Shuttle companies offer transportation between the airport and Santa Fe. Santa Fe Municipal Airport, located nine miles southwest of the city's central business district, accommodates commuter flights and private aircraft. The

Roadrunner Shuttle meets every flight to transport travelers to any Santa Fe location.

The principal highway routes into Santa Fe are I-25, running east and west along the southern perimeter of the city, and I-84/285, which bisects the city from north to south.

Amtrak's Southwest Chief, a line running between Chicago and Los Angeles, schedules twice-daily arrivals and departures at Lamy, about 20 miles south of Santa Fe; regular shuttle service is provided from the village to Santa Fe.

Intercity commercial bus transportation is available through two bus lines.

Traveling in the City

Santa Fe Trails Bus System provides affordable public transportation on nine routes throughout the city. The New Mexico Rail Runner Express, a commuter rail system, started operation in 2006 with stations in Sandoval, Los Ranchos, and Downtown Albuquerque. Service extending to Santa Fe is expected to be completed by 2008. The closest Rail Runner Express entrance for Santa Fe as of late 2007 was the Sandoval County/US 550 Station, about 45 minutes away.

■ Communications

Newspapers and Magazines

Santa Fe's major daily newspaper is *The Santa Fe New Mexican*, the oldest newspaper in the West. The weekly *Santa Fe Reporter* is published on Wednesdays. Magazines published in Santa Fe include the *Santa Fean*, featuring articles on New Mexico history and travel, restaurants, events, and attractions; and *New Mexico Magazine*, founded in 1923, which covers such topics as the state's multicultural heritage, arts, climate, environment and diverse people.

Television and Radio

Two television stations broadcast from Santa Fe; several others, including network affiliates, are broadcast from nearby Albuquerque. Cable service is available by subscription. Eight FM and three AM radio stations broadcast in Santa Fe, one of which plays Spanish music. Santa Fe also receives programming from Albuquerque and other nearby cities.

Media Information: *The Santa Fe New Mexican*, 202 E Marcy Street, Santa Fe, NM 87501; telephone (505)983-3303; email info@sfnewmexican.com

Santa Fe Online

Bureau of Business and Economic Research, University of New Mexico. Available www.unm.edu/~bber

City of Santa Fe home page. Available www.santafenm.gov

New Mexico Department of Workforce Solutions. Available www.dws.state.nm.us

Santa Fe Economic Development, Inc. Available www.sfedi.org

The Santa Fe New Mexican. Available www.santafenewmexican.com

Santa Fe Public Library. Available www.santafelibrary.org

Santa Fe Public Schools. Available www.sfps.k12.nm.us

BIBLIOGRAPHY

Dennis, Lisl, and Landt Dennis, *Behind Adobe Walls: The Hidden Homes and Gardens of Santa Fe and Taos* (San Francisco, CA: Chronicle Books, 1997)

Oregon

The State in Brief

Nickname: Beaver State

Motto: Alis Volat Propriis (She flies with her own wings)

Flower: Oregon grape

Bird: Western meadowlark

Area: 98,380 square miles (2000; U.S. rank 9th)

Elevation: Ranges from sea level to 11,239 feet above sea level

Climate: Mild and humid with frequent rainfall in western third; dry with extremes of temperature in the interior two-thirds

Admitted to Union: February 14, 1859

Capital: Salem

Head Official: Governor Ted Kulongoski (D) (until 2010)

Population

1980: 2,633,105
1990: 2,842,321
2000: 3,421,399
2006 estimate: 3,700,758
Percent change, 1990–2000: 20.4%
U.S. rank in 2006: 27th
Percent of residents born in state: 45.03% (2006)
Density: 37.9 people per square mile (2006)
2006 FBI Crime Index Total: 146,268

Racial and Ethnic Characteristics (2006)

White: 3,186,177
Black or African American: 63,631
American Indian and Alaska Native: 67,269
Asian: 135,746
Native Hawaiian and Pacific Islander: 8,250
Hispanic or Latino (may be of any race): 379,034
Other: 128,670

Age Characteristics (2006)

Population under 5 years old: 229,956
Population 5 to 19 years old: 723,174
Percent of population 65 years and over: 12.9%
Median age: 37.6

Vital Statistics

Total number of births (2006): 45,287
Total number of deaths (2006): 31,349
AIDS cases reported through 2005: 5,740

Economy

Major industries: Manufacturing; finance, insurance, and real estate; trade
Unemployment rate (2006): 6.3%
Per capita income (2006): $24,418
Median household income (2006): $46,230
Percentage of persons below poverty level (2006): 13.3%
Income tax rate: 5.0% to 9.0%
Sales tax rate: None

Eugene

■ The City in Brief

Founded: 1846 (incorporated 1862)

Head Official: Mayor Kitty Piercy (D) (since 2005)

City Population

    1980: 105,624
    1990: 112,733
    2000: 137,893
    2006 estimate: 146,356
    Percent change, 1990–2000: 21.1%
    U.S. rank in 1980: 151st
    U.S. rank in 1990: 159th (2nd in State)
    U.S. rank in 2000: 160th (2nd in State)

Metropolitan Area Population

    1980: 275,000
    1990: 282,912
    2000: 322,959
    2006 estimate: 337,870
    Percent change, 1990–2000: 14.2%
    U.S. rank in 1980: 115th
    U.S. rank in 1990: 119th
    U.S. rank in 2000: 123rd

Area: 41.0 square miles (2000)

Elevation: 369 feet above sea level

Average Annual Temperatures: January, 39.8° F; July, 66.2° F; annual average, 52.1° F

Average Annual Precipitation: 50.9 inches of rain; 6.4 inches of snow

Major Economic Sectors: services, wholesale and retail trade, government

Unemployment Rate: 5.1% (June 2007)

Per Capita Income: $21,685 (2005)

2005 FBI Crime Index Property: 9,902

2005 FBI Crime Index Violent: 328

Major Colleges and Universities: University of Oregon, Lane Community College, Northwest Christian College, Gutenberg College, Eugene Bible College

Daily Newspaper: *The Register-Guard*

■ Introduction

Eugene is Oregon's second largest city and the seat of Lane County. Together with Springfield it is also the second largest metropolitan area in the state. It is the commercial and cultural center for a large agricultural and timber region, as well as an important retail trade and transportation hub in the state of Oregon. Situated halfway between the ocean and the mountains, Eugene offers many recreational possibilities year round.

■ Geography and Climate

Eugene is located in the center of western Oregon, about 100 miles south of Portland and halfway between the Pacific Ocean and the Cascade Mountains in the broad Willamette River valley. Temperatures are usually moderate throughout the year, with most rainfall occurring from October to May. Winters are warmed by prevailing winds from the southwest, and summers are kept mild and dry by cooling northwestern winds.

Area: 41.0 square miles (2000)

Elevation: 369 feet above sea level

Average Temperatures: January, 39.8° F; July, 66.2° F; annual average, 52.1° F

Average Annual Precipitation: 50.9 inches of rain; 6.4 inches of snow

■ History

A site near present-day Eugene was settled in 1846 by Eugene F. Skinner at the base of a mountain peak called Ya-po-ah by the Calapooya tribe. The settlement was named Skinner's, and in 1852 a townsite was laid out by Skinner and Judge D. M. Risdon, who erected the first house within the corporate limits. Attempts to establish the town were foiled by heavy rains, however, and it was given the nickname "Skinner's Mudhole." The settlers moved to higher ground, construction succeeded, and in 1853 the town, taking its founder's given name, was chosen as the seat of newly created Lane County. The first post office in the region was built there the same year; Eugene was incorporated in 1862. The University of Oregon was established in Eugene in 1876.

Agriculture, milling, and transportation were the principal industries during Eugene's early years. A steady steamship trade was conducted between the town and Portland from the late 1850s until 1871, when construction of the Oregon & California Railroad brought an end to water transportation. By the end of the Civil War, Eugene's population had reached 1,200 residents and the city was becoming highly industrialized. With lumbering as a principal industry, the city was the site of sawmills, shingle mills, planing mills, and box factories. Cottonwood and balm trees indigenous to the area were used to produce excelsior. Mining was also an important part of the economy. Agriculture continued to expand; wheat had been the major crop, and many farmers soon turned to fruit growing and dairy farming as well. Creameries, canneries, and flour mills were built for the processing of agricultural products. A major influence on the city as a cultural and education center began in 1872, when the University of Oregon was founded.

Along with industrial development, however, Eugene maintained a livable environment for its residents. By the 1940s the city was noted for its parklike appearance: comfortable, well-kept homes were set in landscaped lawns and shade trees lined the streets. Business districts occupied impressive brick and concrete buildings. With a major university, the city had also become the cultural center for the region. Eugene's population expanded steadily throughout the first half of the twentieth century, reaching nearly 51,000 people in 1967. By 1980, the population had nearly doubled. A slowdown in the timber industry during the early 1980s halted expansion.

Eugene is thriving in the mid 2000s. The city continues to be a lumber and wood-products center, where a high percentage of the nation's plywood is produced. It is also an increasingly important hub for Oregon high tech businesses and industries. With retail, industrial, educational, and professional institutions and enterprises serving a metropolitan population of nearly 338,000 people, Eugene remains one of the largest markets in the Pacific Northwest.

Historical Information: Lane County Museum Library Archives, P.O. Box 5407, Eugene, OR 97405-3819; telephone (541)687-4239

■ Population Profile

Metropolitan Area Residents

1980: 275,000
1990: 282,912
2000: 322,959
2006 estimate: 337,870
Percent change, 1990–2000: 14.2%
U.S. rank in 1980: 115th
U.S. rank in 1990: 119th
U.S. rank in 2000: 123rd

City Residents

1980: 105,624
1990: 112,733
2000: 137,893
2006 estimate: 146,356
Percent change, 1990–2000: 21.1%
U.S. rank in 1980: 151st
U.S. rank in 1990: 159th (2nd in State)
U.S. rank in 2000: 160th (2nd in State)

Density: 3,403.2 people per square mile (2000)

Racial and ethnic characteristics (2005)

White: 122,042
Black: 1,376
American Indian and Alaska Native: 1,345
Asian: 8,472
Native Hawaiian and Pacific Islander: 178
Hispanic or Latino (may be of any race): 9,025
Other: 5,445

Percent of residents born in state: 40.8% (2000)

Age characteristics (2005)

Population under 5 years old: 7,797
Population 5 to 9 years old: 7,084
Population 10 to 14 years old: 9,336
Population 15 to 19 years old: 7,830
Population 20 to 24 years old: 19,584
Population 25 to 34 years old: 22,782
Population 35 to 44 years old: 19,542
Population 45 to 54 years old: 18,750
Population 55 to 59 years old: 8,186
Population 60 to 64 years old: 5,125

Photograph by Len Stolfo/Upshotz.com. Reproduced by permission.

Population 65 to 74 years old: 6,589
Population 75 to 84 years old: 6,693
Population 85 years and older: 3,418
Median age: 33.5 years

Births (2006, MSA)

Total number: 3,416

Deaths (2006, MSA)

Total number: 2,986

Money income (2005)

Per capita income: $21,685
Median household income: $33,070
Total households: 63,312

Number of households with income of . . .

less than $10,000: 8,618
$10,000 to $14,999: 6,248
$15,000 to $24,999: 10,663
$25,000 to $34,999: 7,160
$35,000 to $49,999: 9,156
$50,000 to $74,999: 10,373
$75,000 to $99,999: 5,012
$100,000 to $149,999: 4,128

$150,000 to $199,999: 900
$200,000 or more: 1,054

Percent of families below poverty level: 16.1% (2005)

2005 FBI Crime Index Property: 9,902

2005 FBI Crime Index Violent: 328

■ Municipal Government

Eugene operates under a council-manager form of government with a mayor and eight council members elected in non-partisan elections for four-year terms. Half the council is elected every two years. The council hires the city manager.

Head Official: Mayor Kitty Piercy (D) (since 2005; current term expires January 2009)

Total Number of City Employees: 1,550 (2007)

City Information: Eugene City Hall, 777 Pearl Street, Eugene, OR 97401; telephone (541)682-5010; email webweaver@ci.eugene.or.us

■ Economy

Major Industries and Commercial Activity

Lumber is the largest industry in the Eugene area, where a number of manufacturing concerns produce lumber and wood products. The region is the nation's largest producer of softwood lumber and plywood products, although weak prices in the early 2000s, coupled with higher fuel costs, have hurt the industry somewhat. Since 2000 the high-tech industry has been increasingly important to the economic well-being of the area. Agriculture ranks second to the wood industry in the local economy, with a wide variety of crops grown. A sizable food processing industry has grown up around the agricultural activity, and the area is also known for its RV coach production. The top manufacturers in Lane County include Monaco Coach Corporation, Country Coach, Symantec Corporation, and Hynix Semiconductor America. Combined, government and education account for more than 20,000 jobs, while the health care industry adds another 5,000 jobs. Small business form the core of the Lane County economy.

Eugene serves central and southern Oregon as a retail and wholesale trade center. Services, government, and tourism are also contributors to the overall economy.

Items and goods produced: lumber, recreational vehicles, canned fruits and vegetables, dairy and meat products, chickens and chicken fryers, sheep, grass seed, metals, machinery, compact discs, computer software, plastics, electronic instruments, computer memory disks, sport and pleasure boats.

Incentive Programs—New and Existing Companies

Local programs: In recent years the emphasis in the Willamette Valley has switched from business recruitment to business retention and expansion programs designed to help resident companies "stay put and stay healthy." Among the many incentives available to businesses in Eugene are financial programs offered at the local level, such as the Eugene Business Development Funds. Cascades West Microloan Program provides new or existing businesses in Lane County with up to $25,000 for any purpose with a twenty percent match from owner equity, while the Cascades West Revolving Loans finance land and buildings, equipment and machinery, and working capital. Other incentives include enterprise zones, new construction exemptions, and tax credits. Workforce incentive programs include employee recruiting, screening, and evaluating; customized training at Lane Community College; on-the-job training reimbursement; and certification services.

State programs: The state of Oregon offers a number of incentive programs to attract new and expanding businesses to the state. State funding programs include the Oregon Research & Technology Development Accounts, the Brownfield Redevelopment Fund, the Business Development Fund, the Capital Access Program, the Entrepreneurial Development Loan Fund, and several others. Oregon's Department of Energy administers a Small Scale Energy Loan, which offers low-interest loans to businesses that save energy or produce energy from renewable resources.

Job training programs: The state of Oregon's education program includes a statewide apprenticeship program and has students choose between job training or a college preparatory program after the tenth grade. The program was to be installed in stages in schools through the year 2010. The Employer Workforce Training Fund is an Oregon grant program for employers wanting to upgrade the skills of their employees in the trade or healthcare sectors. The Lane Workforce Partnership oversees programs based on those grants, while the state runs the JOBS For Oregon's Future program. WorkSource Oregon centers not only help match employees and their skills with employers, but also help bring workers to training programs, such as those at Lane Community College.

Development Projects

Aggressive efforts to diversify the local economy have resulted in several industrial expansions in the area; software development, RV manufacturing, and environmental technology-related fields are especially high-growth businesses. Construction began in 2006 on the new research center for the Oregon Nanoscience and Microtechnologies Institute by the University of Oregon campus. Peace Health Medical Systems intended to open two new branches in the greater Eugene area; the first, a comprehensive regional medical center and Level II trauma center at RiverBend, was slated to open by 2008, while the second facility is scheduled to open at Springfield in 2010.

The Eugene Downtown Plan was adopted in 2004, and outlines as its broad goal the revitilization of the downtown area and eliminating blight by expanding housing, cultural and recreational opportunities within the boundaries of an appointed 70 acres of central Eugene.

Economic Development Information: Eugene Area Chamber of Commerce, 1401 Willamette Street, Eugene, OR 97401; telephone (541)484-1314; fax (541)484-4942. Lane Metro Partnership, PO Box 10398, Eugene, OR 97440; telephone (541)686-2741; fax (541)686-2325; email business@lanemetro.com. Oregon Employment Department, 875 Union Street N.E., Salem, OR 97301; telephone (800)237-3710; fax (503)947-1472; email info@emp.state.or.us

Commercial Shipping

A number of air-freight services operate out of Eugene Airport, notably Alaska/Horizon. A new air cargo facility at the airport was expected to be complete by late 2007 or early 2008. More than 50 interstate truck carriers serve metropolitan Eugene and the West Coast via Interstate 5. Eugene is close to three deep-water ports, including the Port of Portland and the International Port of Coos Bay, for shipping to Asia. The Union Pacific and Burlington Northern railroads run through the area for shipping goods throughout North America.

Labor Force and Employment Outlook

Eugene boasts a skilled labor force with a good work ethic and low turnover rates. Over 35 percent of Eugene residents have completed four or more years of college. The city is the hub of one of the country's top 100 industrial areas. Continued growth is forecast in non-lumber manufacturing sectors, such as electronic and biotech technologies. By 2010 the Eugene population was projected to hit 377,341, or an increase of around 10,000 people per year. In August 2007 the unemployment rate in the Eugene-Springfield region stood at 5.3 percent, down dramatically from ten year highs in 2003 that topped out at nearly nine percent.

The following is a summary of data regarding the Eugene-Springfield metropolitan area labor force, 2006 annual averages.

Size of nonagricultural labor force: 153,400

Number of workers employed in . . .

> construction and mining: 8,900
> manufacturing: 20,300
> trade, transportation and utilities: 28,900
> information: 3,700
> financial activities: 8,300
> professional and business services: 16,100
> educational and health services: 19,600
> leisure and hospitality: 14,200
> other services: 5,100
> government: 28,400

Average hourly earnings of production workers employed in manufacturing: $14.64

Unemployment rate: 5.1% (June 2007)

Largest county employers (2007)	*Number of employees*
PeaceHealth Oregon	4,300
University of Oregon	3,676
Lane Community College	2,531
Eugene School District	2,025
U.S. Government	1,800
Lane County	1,786
City of Eugene	1,452
Springfield School District	1,162
State of Oregon	1,100
McKenzie-Willamette Medical Center	750

Cost of Living

The Chamber of Commerce describes Eugene housing as "plentiful, varied and built to last." Eugene is the center of many environmentally friendly housing construction projects and developments.

The following is a summary of data regarding key cost of living factors for the Eugene area.

2007 (1st quarter) ACCRA Average House Price: $458,000

2007 (1st quarter) ACCRA Cost of Living Index: 108.4

State income tax rate: 5.0% to 9.0%

State sales tax rate: None

Local income tax rate: None

Local sales tax rate: None

Property tax rate: Real property tax rate for the city of Eugene is $5 to $10 per $1,000 assessed valuation (2005)

Economic Information: Eugene Area Chamber of Commerce, 1401 Willamette Street, Eugene, OR 97401; telephone (541)484-1314; fax (541)484-4942. Lane Metro Partnership, PO Box 10398, Eugene, OR 97440; telephone (541) 686-2741; fax 686-2325; email business@lanemetro.com. Oregon Employment Department, 875 Union Street N.E., Salem, OR 97301; telephone (503)378-4824 or (800) 237-3710; email info@emp.state.or.us

■ Education and Research

Elementary and Secondary Schools

Eugene is home to three school districts, with the largest being Eugene School District 4J, the fourth largest in Oregon. A seven-member board, elected at large, governs the district. The board employs the superintendent. Parents residing within the Eugene District may choose any 4J school for their child, provided that space is available.

Alternative public schools include International High School, three foreign language immersion schools (French, Spanish and Japanese), and an arts magnet school. Eugene's public school students consistently score higher on standardized tests than the state and national averages. Oregon state standards were projected to be the highest in the world by 2010.

The following is a summary of data regarding the Eugene School District 4J as of the 2005–2006 school year.

Total enrollment: 17,279

Number of facilities

elementary schools: 27
junior high/middle schools: 13
senior high schools: 9
other: 0

Student/teacher ratio: 19.8:1

Teacher salaries (2005–06)

elementary median: $45,670
junior high/middle median: $45,510
secondary median: $43,930

Funding per pupil: $6,969

Eugene is also served by three private high schools and 15 other private schools from Pre-K to grade 8, including religious and special education centers, as well as schools for the gifted and the physically and mentally challenged.

Public Schools Information: School District 4J, Eugene Public Schools, 200 North Monroe, Eugene, OR 97402; telephone (541)687-3123; fax (541)687-3691

Colleges and Universities

The University of Oregon, a major research and educational institution with an enrollment of about 20,000 students, is located in Eugene. The university has schools in the arts and sciences, in addition to professional schools in architecture, arts, business, education, journalism, law, music and dance. It generates an estimated $653 million worth of economic activity in the area, and faculty annually obtain more than $90 million annually in research funding. Lane Community College offers two-year associate and vocational degrees, serving more than 36,000 students in both credit and non-credit course study. It has the third-largest enrollment of Oregon's community colleges. Gutenberg College, with an enrollment of around fifty total students each year, offers liberal arts education from a Protestant Christian base and follows a "great books" program. Other educational institutions in Eugene are Northwest Christian College, Eugene Bible College, Oregon Business College, and the National Academy of Artistic Gymnastics.

Libraries and Research Centers

The Eugene Public Library consists of three locations: the Downtown Library, the Bethel Branch, and the Sheldon Branch. The system contains more than 375,000 items including books, CDs, DVDs, audio and video tapes, and art reproductions, in addition to 600 magazine and 55 newspaper subscriptions. The library's special collections include fine children's literature and a state documents department. The University of Oregon's Knight Library holds 2.5 million volumes, nearly 17,000 periodical subscriptions, and special collections on the American West, American missions and missionaries, Esperanto, Oriental literature and art, politics, and zeppelins. It is the largest library facility in Oregon. Other libraries at the university specialize in law, architecture, science, and mathematics. Northwest Christian College's Kellenberger library holds 74,000 volumes and Lane Community College holds 62,000 books.

Research activities in such fields as the environment, botany of the Pacific Northwest, molecular biology, marine biology, cellular biology, neuroscience, materials science, solar energy, chemical physics, applied materials, forest industries, labor, industrial relations, work organizations, ocean and coastal law, women and gender roles, human development, communication, recreation, mental retardation, and mass communications are conducted at centers in the Eugene area primarily through the University of Oregon. Technicians at Eugene's Riverfront Research Park engage in industrial research and development, data processing, and computer software development.

Public Library Information: Eugene Public Library, 100 West 10th Avenue, Eugene, OR 97401; telephone (541)682-5450

■ Health Care

Two major hospitals serve Eugene. The largest is Sacred Heart General Hospital, with 432 beds and a 32 bed intensive care neonatal unit. The largest hospital between Portland and San Francisco, it is a general-care facility that features a cancer care unit, a state-of-the-art heart center, and orthopedics and rehabilitation services. Sacred Heart intended to open another branch, a comprehensive regional medical center and Level II trauma center at RiverBend, by the end of 2008, and yet another branch at nearby Springfield by 2010, this one featuring 104 inpatient beds and costing over $97 million. All three branches fall under the umbrella of the PeaceHealth Medical Group, which has a total of 120 physicians and more than 600 staff members with clinic locations in Eugene-Springfield and Junction City.

The McKenzie-Willamette Medical Center is a full-care hospital and Level III Trauma Center containing 114 beds and 13 mother/newborn units; it offers short-stay surgery and home care services with nearly 200 physicians on staff. Traditional and alternative physical and mental health care services are offered at area clinics. The area boasts nearly 800 area physicians and surgeons covering 46 different fields and 12 surgical specialties.

Health Care Information: Sacred Heart Medical Center, 1255 Hilyard St., Eugene, OR 97401-3718; telephone (541) 686-7300. McKenzie-Willamette Medical Center, 1460 G Street, Springfield, OR 97477; telephone (541) 726-4400

■ Recreation

Sightseeing

Eugene's Willamette River banks are lined with miles of paths and a number of picnic areas and scenic parks, including the 5-acre Owen Memorial Rose Garden. The Hendricks Park Rhododendron Garden features more than 6,000 rhododendrons and azaleas. Culminating at Spencer Butte, the city's highest point, the South Hills Ridgeline Trail showcases a variety of plants and wildlife. The Mount Pisgah Arboretum has trails throughout its 209 acres and multiple habitats. Tours of many historic homes and buildings, such as the Shelton McMurphey Johnson House from 1888, are also available in Eugene.

The surrounding area offers a number of attractions, such as scenic drives, a national park, wildlife and natural areas, mine and winery tours, and historic sites.

Arts and Culture

Eugene has a large and varied arts community. Companies that perform music include the Eugene Symphony, the Eugene Opera Company, the Oregon Mozart Players, and the Eugene Youth Symphony/Arts Umbrella; all these groups call the Hult Center for the Performing Arts home. The Shedd Institute is home to the Oregon Festival of American Music, which runs year round and features an eclectic variety of performers. Summer music concerts are held at the Cuthbert Amphitheatre in Alton Baker Park. The McDonald Theater, a historic restored movie house, presents touring and local musicians and performers.

The Eugene Ballet performs several times during the year at the Hult Center. The Actor's Cabaret of Eugene has been presenting plays and musicals since 1979. The Very Little Theatre is a volunteer community theater group that dates back to 1929. The Lord Leebrick Theatre Company presents five plays a year. The Hult Center is also home to the Willamette Repertory Theatre.

The University of Oregon Natural History Museum contains exhibits in archeology, paleontology, and zoology. The Science Factory Children's Museum and Planetarium, formerly the Willamette Science and Technology Center, re-opened in 2002 with interactive exhibits and planetarium shows. Relics and memorabilia pertaining to the history of the Eugene area can be viewed at the Lane County Historical Museum. The Maude Kerns Art Center displays a number of works by local artists as well as traveling exhibits. The University of Oregon's Jordan Schnitzer Museum of Art reopened in 2005 with a new

addition that doubled the size of the museum. It houses a famous collection of Asian art and hosts numerous special exhibits each year.

Festivals and Holidays

The Oregon Bach Festival is an annual highlight of Eugene's special events calendar. Held for two weeks in late June and early July, the festival is hosted on the University of Oregon campus and at the Hult Center. It features performances by internationally acclaimed soloists and orchestral, choral, and chamber music groups interpreting the compositions of eighteenth-century German composer Johann Sebastian Bach. Eugene also celebrates with the Willamette Valley Folk Festival in May, a Country Fair in July, and Eugene Celebration, taking place for three days beginning in late September.

Sports for the Spectator

Professional baseball is represented in Eugene by the minor league Eugene Emeralds, a Class A farm club for the San Diego Padres that plays at Civic Stadium. The University of Oregon fields teams in every major sport, competing at the National Collegiate Athletic Association (NCAA) Division I level; games are played at the 10,000-seat MacArthur Court and at the 54,000-seat Autzen Stadium, while track and field events take place at Hayward Field. Eugene is also a major center of track and field events, hosting the National Track and Field Championships on a regular basis.

Sports for the Participant

A wide range of outdoor recreation activities are available in and around Eugene, located only 60 miles away from either the mountains or the ocean. The Cascade Mountains offer opportunities for winter skiing and summer hiking, camping, and rafting. The glacier-fed McKenzie and Willamette rivers offer water sports such as fishing, boating, and kayaking. The city maintains more than 3,000 acres of park land, with jogging trails, bike paths, pools, athletic fields, tennis courts, bowling alleys, a roller rink, an outdoor skateboard facility, and a major lighted softball complex. Emerald KIDSPORTS provides approximately 24,000 young people with organized sports programs such as soccer, baseball, softball, football, basketball, and volleyball. In 2006 Eugene was named one of the top 21 cities for bicycling by "Bicycling Magazine."

Shopping and Dining

Valley River Center is an enclosed mall with 130 retail, food, and specialty businesses. The Fifth Street Public Market is a collection of specialty and craft shops and restaurants, and hosts musicians, artists, and special events. Boutiques can be found in downtown Eugene. Saturday Market, an open-air market featuring fresh produce, handcrafted goods, and ethnic foods, is open from April to Christmas. Gateway Mall, in nearby

Springfield, has 80 stores and a 29-screen movie complex. Hundreds of area restaurants present fresh Oregon salmon, lamb, wines, apples, pears, and berries among their offerings. Coffee shops and cafes abound.

Visitor Information: Convention and Visitors Association of Lane County Oregon, 754 Olive St., Eugene OR 97401; telephone (541)484-5307; toll-free (800) 547- 5445; fax (541)343-6335; email info@cvalco.org

■ Convention Facilities

The Lane County Events Center/Fairgrounds in Eugene offers a convention center, an equestrian and livestock pavilion, a state-of-the-art ice arena, 2,500 parking spaces, and full catering service. Other Eugene venues include the Hult Center for the Performing Arts, the Florence Events Center in Florence, Oregon, the Valley River Inn and Convention Center, and the McKenzie River Conference Center. In addition, there are numerous hotels, motels, resorts, lodges, and conference facilities throughout Lane County, including the Hilton Eugene & Conference Center, one of the largest convention centers between San Francisco and Portland. It offers 30,000 square feet of meeting and exhibit space ranging from intimate boardrooms to convention halls and ballrooms.

Convention Information: Convention and Visitors Association of Lane County Oregon, 754 Olive St., Eugene OR 97401; telephone (541)484-5307; toll-free (800)547- 5445; fax (541)343-6335; email info@ cvalco.org

■ Transportation

Approaching the City

Eugene Airport is located 9 miles north of Eugene by Interstate 5, and is served by 5 major air carriers. It is the second busiest airport in the state and fifth largest in the Pacific Northwest. Amtrak provides passenger rail service north to Vancouver on the Amtrak Cascades Line, and south to Los Angeles on the Coast Starlight.

The major north-south route from Canada to Mexico along the West Coast, I-5, runs through Eugene. U.S. 126 connects the city with the Pacific coast and eastern Oregon.

Traveling in the City

Public transportation is provided by Lane Transit District buses to all parts of the city and to some rural areas. The system provides convenient stops at schools and downtown, and is 100 percent wheelchair accessible. The city maintains nearly 130 total miles of off-street bike paths and on-street bike lanes.

■ Communications

Newspaper and Magazines

Eugene is served by one daily morning newspaper, *The Register-Guard* (Oregon's second-largest daily), *Eugene Weekly,* a Thursday paper presenting arts and entertainment information along with news, and by several smaller neighborhood and special-interest weekly newspapers. The University of Oregon publishes the *Oregon Daily Emerald.* Magazines published in Eugene include *Skipping Stones,* an international, multicultural magazine for children; *Alternatives,* an environmental and political quarterly; *Oregon Voice,* a general interest magazine by students from the University of Oregon; and several scholarly journals.

Television and Radio

Television stations broadcasting from Eugene include ABC, NBC and CBS, as well as commercial/religious programming. Five AM and eight FM radio stations broadcast music, information, Christian and sports programs from Eugene, and many other stations are received from other communities in the metropolitan area.

Media Information: *The Register-Guard,* 3500 Chad Drive, PO Box 10188, Eugene, OR 97440-2188; telephone (541)485-1234

Eugene Online

City of Eugene home page. Available www.eugene-or.gov

Convention & Visitors Association of Lane County Oregon. Available www.cvalco.org

Eugene Area Chamber of Commerce. Available www.eugenechamber.com

Eugene School District 4J. Available www.4j.lane .edu

Lane Metro Partnership. Available www.lanemetro .com

Oregon Economic Development Department. Available www.econ.oregon.gov

*The Register-Guard.*Available www.registerguard .com

BIBLIOGRAPHY

Eugene 1945–2000: Decisions that Made a Community (Eugene, OR: The City Club of Eugene, 2000)

Moore, Lucia W., *The Story of Eugene* (Eugene, OR: Lane County Historical Society, 1995)

Portland

■ The City in Brief

Founded: 1845 (incorporated 1851)

Head Official: Mayor Tom Potter (D) (since 2005)

City Population
>
> 1980: 366,383
> 1990: 485,975
> 2000: 529,121
> 2006 estimate: 537,081
> Percent change, 1990–2000: 8.9%
> U.S. rank in 1980: 35th
> U.S. rank in 1990: 30th
> U.S. rank in 2000: 35th

Metropolitan Area Population
>
> 1980: 1,106,000
> 1990: 1,515,452
> 2000: 1,874,449
> 2006 estimate: 2,137,565
> Percent change, 1990–2000: 23.7%
> U.S. rank in 1980: 26th (CMSA)
> U.S. rank in 1990: 27th (CMSA)
> U.S. rank in 2000: 23rd (CMSA)

Area: 130 square miles

Elevation: Averages 173 feet above sea level

Average Annual Temperatures: January, 39.9° F; July, 68.1° F; annual average, 53.5° F

Average Annual Precipitation: 37.07 inches of rain; 6.5 inches of snow

Major Economic Sectors: services, wholesale and retail trade, government

Unemployment rate: 4.8% (June 2007)

Per Capita Income: $26,677 (2005)

2005 FBI Crime Index Property: 37,645

2005 FBI Crime Index Violent: 3,858

Major Colleges and Universities: Portland State University, Oregon Health & Science University, Reed College, Lewis & Clark College, University of Portland, Marylhurst University

Daily Newspaper: *The Oregonian*

■ Introduction

Portland, known as the "City of Roses," is the result of both chance and planning. Having obtained its name by the flip of a coin, the city is today the model of a metropolitan area that has been effectively integrated with its environment through controlled growth and development. Set in the natural beauty of northwest Oregon and lacking such big-city problems as traffic congestion, pollution, and litter, Portland is laced with parks, gardens, and fountains. A deep-water port, international airport, and a diverse economy make Portland a thriving commercial center, but the primary commitment is to preserving the city's individuality, its healthful environment, and its friendly atmosphere.

■ Geography and Climate

Located 110 miles from the Pacific Ocean, Portland lies between two mountain ranges, the Cascade Range to the east and the lower Coast Range to the west, in the Willamette River valley, one of the world's most fertile river valleys. The city is divided by the Willamette River, which flows into the Columbia River just to the north. Winters are rainy in Portland, with 55 percent of the annual rainfall occurring between the months of November and February, but the marine air keeps temperatures moderate, and the summers are mild, with temperatures rarely over 90 degrees.

Area: 130 square miles

Elevation: Averages 173 feet above sea level

Average Temperatures: January, 39.9° F; July, 68.1° F; annual average, 53.5° F

Average Annual Precipitation: 37.07 inches of rain; 6.5 inches of snow

■ History

The area surrounding present-day Portland was originally inhabited by the Multnomah and Clackamas tribes, who had established several villages by the 1830s. Most of these people died from smallpox epidemics and other diseases. Meriwether Lewis and William Clark were the first settlers of European descent to travel through the Portland area during their 1806 expedition. Clark named the Willamette River after the Multnomah village he found on Sauvie Island.

The future site of Portland was originally a clearing in the woods, appropriately known as "The Clearing," where Native Americans and traders stopped to rest on trips between Oregon City and Fort Vancouver. The land underwent a series of ownerships until Amos Lovejoy and Francis Pettygrove bought it and mapped out a town called "Stumptown" in 1845. Four years later the two men, Lovejoy from Boston and Pettygrove from Portland, Maine, decided to flip a coin to determine the town's new name. Pettygrove won and the town became Portland.

Portland grew steadily through the California gold rush, reporting a population of 821 residents, a post office, and a newspaper—the *Weekly Oregonian*—in the 1850 census. Portland was incorporated in 1851 and became the seat of newly created Washington County (later renamed Multnomah County) in 1854. That same year the town advanced toward becoming a major trade center when its harbor was selected as the West Coast terminal for *The Petonia*, the U.S. mail steamer. Prior to the Civil War the salmon industry began to grow, enhancing Portland's economic status. The city experienced catastrophe when, in 1872 and 1873, the downtown area was heavily damaged by fire; civic leaders subsequently decided to rebuild only with cast iron, brick, and stone. The construction of the first transcontinental railroad in 1883, linking Portland with the East Coast, brought renewed prosperity. By the turn of the century the population had grown to 90,000 people.

Portland continued to expand steadily through the early decades of the twentieth century; the Alaska gold rush, the 1905 Lewis and Clark Centennial Exposition, and the construction of the Bonneville Dam in the 1930s were important factors in its growth. During World War II the city was a ship-building and manufacturing center.

In the 1960s and 1970s Portland's city leaders were able to avoid problems experienced by other large metropolitan areas through economic diversification, controlled growth, and environmental planning. A precedent had already been set by early planners who had integrated parks and green spaces into the city's lay-out; later, city planners instituted an ordinance to protect scenic views. Local government continues to work on the Region 2040 growth plan to manage all aspects of growth in the metropolitan area to the year 2040. The city has been nationally recognized for its unique character and attention to the quality of life of its residents; in 2005 *Reader's Digest* honored Portland as "America's Cleanest City" and in 2007 it was named one of America's "Greenest Cities" by MSN City Guide. In the 2007 CNN survey of "Favorite American Cities," Portland rated among the top three in the quality of its flea markets, farmer's markets, access to the outdoors, cleanliness, and public parks.

Historical Information: Oregon Historical Society Regional Research Library, 1200 SW Park Avenue, Portland, OR 97204; telephone (503)222-1741

■ Population Profile

Metropolitan Area Residents

1980: 1,106,000
1990: 1,515,452
2000: 1,874,449
2006 estimate: 2,137,565
Percent change, 1990–2000: 23.7%
U.S. rank in 1980: 26th (CMSA)
U.S. rank in 1990: 27th (CMSA)
U.S. rank in 2000: 23rd (CMSA)

City Residents

1980: 366,383
1990: 485,975
2000: 529,121
2006 estimate: 537,081
Percent change, 1990–2000: 8.9%
U.S. rank in 1980: 35th
U.S. rank in 1990: 30th
U.S. rank in 2000: 35th

Density: 3,932.2 people per square mile (in 2000)

Racial and ethnic characteristics (2005)

White: 408,462
Black: 32,009
American Indian and Alaska Native: 4,342

©James Blank.

Asian: 36,536
Native Hawaiian and Pacific Islander: 1,890
Hispanic or Latino (may be of any race): 43,324
Other: 9,806

Percent of residents born in state: 44.0% (2000)

Age characteristics (2005)

Population under 5 years old: 33,946
Population 5 to 9 years old: 33,139
Population 10 to 14 years old: 27,739
Population 15 to 19 years old: 27,128
Population 20 to 24 years old: 30,424
Population 25 to 34 years old: 90,023
Population 35 to 44 years old: 84,148
Population 45 to 54 years old: 80,007
Population 55 to 59 years old: 33,827
Population 60 to 64 years old: 19,714
Population 65 to 74 years old: 25,784
Population 75 to 84 years old: 19,276
Population 85 years and older: 8,472
Median age: 36.4 years

Births (2006, MSA)

Total number: 27,916

Deaths (2006, MSA)

Total number: 15,394

Money income (2005)

Per capita income: $26,677
Median household income: $42,287
Total households: 228,167

Number of households with income of . . .

less than $10,000: 24,329
$10,000 to $14,999: 15,025
$15,000 to $24,999: 28,551
$25,000 to $34,999: 27,235
$35,000 to $49,999: 35,141
$50,000 to $74,999: 40,231
$75,000 to $99,999: 22,977
$100,000 to $149,999: 21,432
$150,000 to $199,999: 7,295
$200,000 or more: 5,951

Percent of families below poverty level: 12.8% (2005)

2005 FBI Crime Index Property: 37,645

2005 FBI Crime Index Violent: 3,858

■ Municipal Government

Portland is the last large city in the United States to operate under a commission form of government, with four commissioners, an auditor, and the mayor elected to staggered four-year terms. Each member casts an equal vote in council and each undertakes administrative responsibilities for a group of city bureaus. The mayor receives the authority to make budget assignments and traditionally proposes the annual budget for council approval; otherwise, governing power is invested in the council as a whole.

Portland is also home to the nation's only directly elected regional government. The body, known as Metro, controls growth by wielding authority over land use, transportation, and environment.

Head Official: Mayor Tom Potter (D) (since 2005; current term expires 2009)

Total Number of City Employees: 7,659 (2005)

City Information: Portland City Hall, 1221 SW 4th Avenue, Portland, OR 97204; telephone (503)823-3588; email cityinfo@ci.portland.or.us

■ Economy

Major Industries and Commercial Activity

Early in its history, Portland's economy was based on the Columbia and Willamette rivers and their access to the Pacific Ocean. The town was a supply hub for area farming communities and a regional shipping center. The deep, fresh-water port helped the city grow into an important part of the lumber industry, and a number of manufacturing concerns settled there because of the ease of transportation.

Today, Portland is the fifth largest export tonnage port on the West Coast and the 17th largest container port in the nation. Easy access to the north-south and east-west interstate freeway system, international air service, and both west coast intercontinental railroads make Portland an important distribution center.

Portland enjoys a long history of association with high-technology industries, beginning with Tektronix in 1946. There are now more than 1,200 technology companies currently operating in Portland. However, since its peak in 2005, high-tech investment in the Portland area has been down slightly, with real estate replacing it as the fastest-growing sector. Although maufacturing is down in recent years, the service, retail, and health care industries have grown. Portland has also become a center of intellectual property, with Intel filing more patents originating in its Oregon office than from anywhere else. Local analysts trumpet the diverse nature of Portland's economy, with plenty of small businesses, as contributing to its overall health.

Items and goods produced: electronics, machinery, food products, transportation equipment

Incentive Programs—New and Existing Companies

Local programs: World Trade Center Portland assists businesses involved in international trade. Business in Portland allows area businesses to access valuable information to help them succeed, including site location assistance, storefront improvement grants, contract opportunities, and economic and demographic data. The Port of Portland, working with other local and state departments, offers a variety of businesses development and incentive programs, including a Small Business Development Program, a Disadvantaged Business Enterprise Program, and a Mentor Program. The Portland Development Commission administers a variety of programs to assist new, existing, and expanding businesses, such as the Economic Opportunity Fund and the Enterprise Zone, E-Commerce Zone, Storefront Improvement Program, Quality Jobs Program, and other assistance programs.

State programs: Among the incentives available to businesses in Portland are several financial programs offered at the state level, together with tax incentives, new construction exemptions, and tax credits. These include the Brownfield Redevelopment Fund, Business Development Fund, Capital Access Program, Entrepreneurial Development Loan Fund, and several others. The State's Department of Energy administers a Small Scale Energy Loan, which offers low-interest loans to businesses that save energy or produce energy from renewable resources.

Job training programs: The state of Oregon administers an educational program, the first such in the nation, that establishes a statewide apprenticeship program and allows students to choose between job training or a college preparatory program after the tenth grade. The state's JOBS Plus program allows employers who hire a JOBS Plus-eligible worker to receive benefits that include reimbursements, the opportunity to train and evaluate the worker during the contract period, and the opportunity to treat the employee as a temporary employee.

Worksystems, Inc., funds providers of career placement and training services. The WorkSource Portland Metro network offers job-seekers assistance with their career planning and job search activities. Due to an increase in the non-native English speaking population, services are also provided in Spanish, Russian, Vietnamese, and Chinese.

Development Projects

In 1999 the North Macadam Urban Renewal Plan was adopted by the City Council. The plan seeks to develop vacant and underdeveloped land in the North Macadam area. Technical, environmental, and transportation difficulties had prevented previous efforts to develop the land. Redevelopment efforts have focused on providing transportation connections, space for housing and businesses, and greenway and open space connections. The city has since designated a number of other neighborhoods as Urban Renewal Areas, which are targeted for improvement projects by the Portland Development Commission. The URAs include Airport Way, Central Eastside, Downtown Waterfront, Gateway Regional Center, Interstate Corridor, Lents Town Center, Inner Northeast, River District, South Park Blocks, and Willamette Industrial. In 2007 development efforts were ongoing at all sites, and the stated goal is to stimulate further private investment.

In 2005 construction began to make improvements on NW Third and Fourth avenues between Burnside and Glisan streets, which encompass the Old Town/Chinatown area. The project is a partnership between the Portland Development Commission and the Portland Office of Transportation. The $5.35 million project includes improvements to streets and sidewalks, installation of trees and streetlights, and public art.

A new MAX light rail project, expected to open in 2009, runs the length of the Portland Mall and connects Union Station and Portland State University. Along with the construction of the tracks, the project was expected to bring refurbished streets and sidewalks, new transit shelters, better lighting and unique public art installations.

In 2005 phase one of construction was begun on the Oregon Entertainment Center, built on the site of what was formerly the Multnomah Kennel Club. The facility is to include a 1,500-seat live theater, restaurants, spa, bowling alley, retail shops, driving range, resort-style hotel and gaming center. In 2007 no completion date had been announced and the Center's gambling license was still pending approval; projections estimated that the casinos would generate over $100 million annually to be earmarked for the Oregon Public Schools.

Economic Development Information: Portland Business Alliance, 520 SW Yamhill Street, Portland, OR 97204; telephone (503)224-8684; fax (503)323-9186; email info@portlandalliance.com

Commercial Shipping

Portland's comprehensive transportation system comprises ocean shipping, transcontinental railways and highways, river barging, and a major international airport. The shipping industry is keyed to a lifeline of ship, rail, air, and truck services. Both West Coast transcontinental railroads and 110 trucking lines provide shippers with options for moving cargo. At the Port of Portland's five marine terminals, container ships, grain ships, bulk and breakbulk carriers, and auto carriers work around the clock. The Port of Portland leads the nation in wheat exports and is ranked fourth in the nation for auto imports. In addition, barges ply the Columbia/Snake river system, the second largest waterway in the nation, feeding the Port's Terminal 6 from as far upriver as Lewiston, Idaho, more than 300 river miles away. Foreign Trade Zone #45, administered by the Port of Portland, provides an additional incentive for international trade activity. Portland International Airport handles more than a quarter million tons of cargo a year.

Labor Force and Employment Outlook

The work force in Portland is well-educated and very stable; in recent years the city has been among the top in the nation at attracting college-educated 24-35 year olds. The job turnover rate is low and productivity is high, compared with other metropolitan areas. The unemployment rate has remained below the national average for several years. In August 2007 the unemployment rate stood at 5.0 percent, a sharp drop from its ten year high of over nine percent in 2003, despite an ever-growing workforce and population in the metropolitan area. In 2007 economic forecasters were concerned about the impact a negatively growing real estate market might have on Portland's economic growth, since in recent years real estate has become an increasingly important part of the city's broader economy.

The following is a summary of data regarding the Portland-Vancouver-Beaverton metropolitan area labor force, 2006 annual averages.

Size of nonagricultural labor force: 1,015,00

Number of workers employed in . . .

    construction and mining: 65,100
    manufacturing: 126,900
    trade, transportation and utilities: 203,100
    information: 23,800
    financial activities: 70,300
    professional and business services: 134,100
    educational and health services: 123,600
    leisure and hospitality: 93,700
    other services: 35,600
    government: 139,100

Average hourly earnings of production workers employed in manufacturing: $16.24

Unemployment rate: 4.8% (June 2007)

Largest metropolitan area employers (2007)	*Number of employees*
PeaceHealth Oregon	4,300
University of Oregon	3,676

Largest metropolitan area employers (2007)	*Number of employees*
Lane Community College	2,531
Eugene School District	2,025
U.S. Government	1,800
Lane County	1,786
City of Eugene	1,452
Springfield School District	1,162
State of Oregon	1,100
McKenzie-Willamette Medical Center	750

Cost of Living

The following is a summary of data regarding key cost of living factors for the Portland area.

2007 (1st quarter) ACCRA Average House Price: Not available

2007 (1st quarter) ACCRA Cost of Living Index: 98.5

State income tax rate: 5.0% to 9.0%

State sales tax rate: None

Local income tax rate: None

Local sales tax rate: None

Property tax rate: ranges from $14.00 to $20.30 per $1,000 of assessed value (Multnomah County, 2004–2005)

Economic Information: Portland Business Alliance, 200 S.W. Market Street, Suite 1770, Portland, OR 97201; telephone (503)224-8684; fax (503)323-9186. Oregon Employment Department, 875 Union Street NE, Salem, OR 97301; telephone (800)237-3710; email info@emp.state.or.us

■ Education and Research

Elementary and Secondary Schools

The Portland Public School District, the largest in the state of Oregon, is governed by a nonpartisan, seven-member board that appoints a superintendent. Special programs offered by the district include a gifted and talented program, summer school remedial and enrichment classes, special education, and career education. In fall 2007 nearly 47,000 students were enrolled in the district at 85 school buildings. Magnet schools in the district offer dual language immersion programs in Spanish, Japanese, and Chinese; a living history curriculum; schools for the performing arts; and early intervention programs.

Students can also apply to attend any school in the district outside of their geographically-assigned one, including the alternative schools listed previously.

The following is a summary of data regarding the Portland Public Schools as of the 2005–2006 school year.

Total enrollment: 47,000

Number of facilities

elementary schools: 27
junior high/middle schools: 16
senior high schools: 15
other: 30 (K-8; in transition)

Student/teacher ratio: 20.4:1

Teacher salaries (2005–06)

elementary median: $46,430
junior high/middle median: $46,790
secondary median: $48,380

Funding per pupil: $8,573

A variety of private education options exist in the Portland metro area, including the well-known Oregon Episcopal School and The Catlin Gabel School. Three Catholic high schools, several Montessori and Waldorf schools, and arts-centered schools serve the area's students.

Public Schools Information: Portland Public Schools, 501 North Dixon, Portland, OR 97227; telephone (503) 916-2000; email pubinfo@pps.k12.or.us

Colleges and Universities

Portland is home to several accredited institutions of higher education. Concordia College is a private four-year college affiliated with the Lutheran Church-Missouri Synod offering bachelor's degrees in business administration, education, health and social sciences, liberal arts, theological studies, and environmental remediation. It has a total enrollement of 1,600 students. Lewis & Clark College, founded by Presbyterian pioneers and set on 137 wooded acres, offers 26 majors and 23 minor programs. It was ranked among the 100 best liberal arts colleges in America in the 2008 listing by *U.S. News & World Report.* Marylhurst University is a private Catholic institution offering coursework leading to master's and bachelor's degrees to students of all ages. Oregon Health & Science University houses schools of medicine, nursing, and dentistry, and is Oregon's only academic health center.

Portland State University offers strong liberal arts and sciences programs to augment its concentration on engineering, computer science, international trade, and business. The schools also boasts Oregon's most diverse college campus. Reed College is an independent liberal arts and sciences college, and was ranked 54th among the

100 best liberal arts colleges in America in the 2008 listing by *U.S. News & World Report.* The college enrolls around 1,400 students and boasts 22 departmental majors and 12 interdisciplinary majors. The University of Portland, a Catholic university, offers 60 majors and 11 graduate degrees in its College of Arts and Sciences and four professional schools (Business, Education, Engineering, and Nursing). Based in the Portland metropolitan area is the Oregon Graduate Institute of Science and Technology.

Libraries and Research Centers

The Multnomah County Library, the oldest public library west of the Mississippi, maintains a Central Library and 16 other branches throughout the metropolitan area. Total holdings include more than 2 million items including books, periodicals, videos, audio cassettes, compact discs, films, records, and maps. The County Library and its branches together host more than 480 computer work stations. The Multnomah County Library is Oregon's largest public library system, and serves nearly a fifth of the total state population.

Area universities also offer extensive library services, and there are a number of special interest and research libraries in the area, serving science, industry, and business interests. Oregon Health & Science University is where both the artificial heart valve and cardiac angioplasty were developed; research there continues to be the catalyst for clinical and educational advancements in heart treatment. Cancer research in the areas of cancer biology, hematologic malignancies, solid tumors, and cancer prevention and control is also performed at Oregon Health & Science University. The Vollum Institute for Advanced Biomedical Research studies brain function at the molecular level, in addition to sponsoring a new center for the study of weight loss. At Oregon Medical Laser Center, researchers study the use of lasers in medicine. Other areas of medical research include cancer research at the Robert W. Franz Cancer Research Center and multidisciplinary research at the Earl A. Chiles Research Institute. Research activities in such fields as public health, computing and information systems, nuclear science, urban studies, population and census, sociology, psychology, aging, human services, and the Middle East are conducted at other centers in the Portland area.

Public Library Information: Multnomah County Library, 801 SW Tenth Avenue, Portland, OR 97205; telephone (503)988-5123

■ Health Care

Portland is the center for health care in the state of Oregon, with major hospitals collaborating to offer quality care at a moderate cost. Playing a prominent role is the Oregon Health & Science University (OHSU), which includes the University Hospital and Doernbecher Children's Hospital as well as the Casey Eye Institute, the Child Development and Rehabilitation Center, 9 primary care clinics, and numerous specialty and dental clinics. Its hospitals offer 560 beds and saw a total of nearly 700,000 visits in 2006. OHSU also operates four interdisciplinary centers that focus on aging, women's health, cancer, and interventional therapy. OHSU shares technology, personnel, and training with the Portland Veterans Affairs Medical Center to help keep health care costs down. Residents who seek nontraditional medical treatment have access to licensed acupuncturists and to practitioners trained at a local naturopathic college. Senior services are coordinated by the Multnomah County Aging Services Division to help senior citizens remain active in the community. Providence Health Services operates seven hospitals and medical centers in the Portland metro area. In 2005 Providence St. Vincent Medical Center was named among the top 100 hospitals in the nation by research company Solucient, a distinction it has received eight times. The facility has 523 licensed beds. One of the Portland area's top employers, Providence hospitals specialize in cancer care, rehabilitation, cardiac care, children's emergency care, surgical services, sports medicine, and maternity care.

■ Recreation

Sightseeing

Portland offers sightseeing attractions both in the city itself and in the surrounding area. A walking tour of downtown encompasses two separate national historical districts, including the largest preserved example of nineteenth-century cast iron architecture in the West, and a number of other nineteenth-century landmarks intermixed with distinctive modern buildings. The controversial Portland Building was the first major post-modern architectural structure in the country. The award-winning Pioneer Courthouse Square, which hosts over 300 events a year, bustles with activity from outdoor art exhibits, concerts, and sidewalk vendors.

Portland is proud of its outdoor public art and fountains, including Portlandia, a 35-foot tall hammered copper sculpture of a kneeling woman, and Ira's Fountain, a cascading water sculpture dotted with islands and terraces across from the Civic Auditorium. Other attractions include The Grotto, a 60-acre shrine; the Japanese Garden, the most authentic example of Japanese gardens outside of Japan; the International Rose Test Garden; and the Classical Chinese Garden in the Old Town/Chinatown district.

Many other attractions can be found just outside of the city. Vineyards in the Willamette Valley are open to the public for tours and wine tastings. Some of the nation's most beautiful natural scenery can be found around nearby Mount Hood and the Columbia Gorge. Portland is 110 miles away from the Pacific Ocean.

Arts and Culture

The Portland Center for the Performing Arts is the center of art activity in the city, presenting more than 900 annual events and featuring the Arlene Schnitzer Concert Hall, Newmark Theatre, Dolores Winningstad Theatre, and Keller Auditorium. Portland's performing arts groups include Oregon Symphony, Portland Opera, Oregon Ballet Theatre, Portland Center Stage, Portland Youth Philharmonic, Portland Gay Men's Chorus, and Chamber Music Northwest.

The Oregon Historical Society's History Center houses exhibits tracing the history of the Pacific Northwest from prehistoric times to the present. The Oregon Maritime Center and Museum features ship models, navigational instruments, hardware, and historical exhibits. The Oregon Museum of Science and Industry (OMSI), one of the nation's largest, offers hands-on displays pertaining to science, including a walk-in replica of a space station, a planetarium, and a computer center.

Displaying exhibits of commercial memorabilia, the American Advertising Museum specializes in the history of American marketing since 1683. The World Forestry Center has recreational and educational exhibits relating to the forestry industry; a special attraction is a 70-foot talking tree.

The Portland Art Museum houses collections of 35 centuries of world art, including European works from the Renaissance to the present, nineteenth- and twentieth-century American art, and Native American, Asian, and West African art. In 2000 the museum unveiled three new centers in its Millennium Project expansion: the Center for Native American Art, Center for Northwest Art, and the outdoor public sculpture gardens. A 2005 renovation of the Mark Building left it with a new Center for Modern and Contemporary Art, two ballrooms, a 33,000-volume Art Study Center and Library, and headquarters for the Northwest Film and Video Center, which features traditional, historical, and experimental exhibits in the media of film and video. One of the oldest nonprofit art galleries in the nation, the Contemporary Crafts Gallery displays artworks in clay, fiber, glass, wood, and metal.

Washington Park is home to many children's attractions, including the Portland Children's Museum. It features hands-on exhibits for children through 10 years of age. The Oregon Zoo, which opened in 1887, houses animals from around the world. Also of interest to children and book-lovers alike is the Beverly Cleary Sculpture Garden in Grant Park, which showcases bronze statues of Ramona Quimby and Henry Huggins and his dog Ribsy—characters made famous in the Portland author's classic children's books.

Festivals and Holidays

The centerpiece of Portland's special events schedule is the annual Portland Rose Festival, which lasts for 25 days each June and celebrated its 100th anniversary in 2007. The festival features more than 70 events, including the Grand Floral Parade (second largest all-floral parade in the nation), a waterfront carnival, a juried fine arts festival, and an Indycar race.

Spring and summer bring several area jazz festivals, including the Mt. Hood Jazz Festival in August, which brings renowned jazz musicians from all over the country to the Portland area. In August, "The Bite: A Taste of Portland" presents a three-day extravaganza of music while Portland's finest restaurants and cafes demonstrate their specialties. The Oregon Brewers Festival is held in July. The Christmas holidays are highlighted by the spectacular Holiday Parade of Christmas Ships. A variety of festivals and events throughout the year celebrate the region's microbreweries and wineries.

Sports for the Spectator

Professional sports in Portland are led by the National Basketball Association's Portland Trail Blazers, a frequent playoff contender, who play at the Rose Garden arena. Professional minor league baseball is represented by the Portland Beavers, a Triple-A affiliate of the San Diego Padres. The Portland Timbers are Portland's professional soccer franchise and members of the First Division of United Soccer Leagues. Both the Beavers and the Timbers play their home games at Portland's PGE Park. Hockey action is brought to fans by the Portland Winter Hawks of the Western Hockey League, which is a major source of talent for the National Hockey League. A wide range of other sports activities can be viewed at several of the area's universities.

Portland Meadows features quarterhorse and thoroughbred racing from October through April. Stock and Indycar racing take place at the Portland International Raceway.

Sports for the Participant

Portland offers a variety of ways to satisfy the sporting urge. The mountains provide opportunities for outdoor sports such as rock climbing and hiking. Timberline Lodge, a National Historic Landmark, serves one of Mt. Hood's five ski areas and offers the only lift-serviced summer skiing in the country. Local rivers feature all water sports; the Portland area is a fishing paradise, offering everything from fly fishing for trout in mountain streams and salmon-fishing in the rivers to all-day deep-sea excursions on charter boats. Hood River, Oregon, is a windsurfing mecca on the Columbia Gorge. The Portland Marathon, held in early October, has been ranked as one of the premier marathon events in the country; its 26.2-mile course is open to walkers as well as runners.

The Portland Parks & Recreation department maintains 10,000 acres at more than 250 locations throughout the city. Parks range in size from the 4,700-acre Forest Park to Mill Ends Park, the world's smallest park at 36 inches by 36 inches in diameter. Facilities include two amphitheaters; a skateboard park; tennis courts; sports fields; playgrounds; arts, music, and dance centers; and sports, fitness, and arts programming. There are over 220 miles of regional trails.

Shopping and Dining

Lloyd Center, Portland's first and largest shopping center, is located in the downtown core in the city's northeast section. Here, more than 200 stores surround an indoor ice rink. Washington Square, Jantzen Beach Super Center, and Clackamas Town Center are all located within a 20-minute drive of downtown. The Galleria includes several floors of unique urban shopping and dining. Pioneer Place in the heart of downtown features four city blocks of dining, shopping, entertainment, and the first-ever Sundance Film Center for Independent Film. Powell's City of Books, the world's largest new and used independent bookstore, is located in downtown Portland and stocks more than a million books.

The Skidmore/Old Town National Historic District at the north end of downtown offers many shopping possibilities. The New Market Theatre, renovated in 2002, also houses shops and restaurants. Saturday Market, which attracts an estimated 750,000 visitors to the area each year, is open Saturday and Sunday, March through December, and features more than 300 vendors. The Water Tower at John's Landing is the home of a unique blend of shops and restaurants. The Sellwood and Hawthorne Boulevard Districts in southeast Portland and the Multnomah District in southwest Portland are favorites of antique hunters.

Portland features a number of restaurants specializing in fresh, grown-in-Oregon foods, as well as spots to sample famous Pacific seafood. The Chinatown district offers regional Chinese cuisine; a large number of other restaurants specialize in many ethnic foods. More than a dozen nationally ranked restaurants emphasize elegance and formal dining, and there are many informal bistros and other places to mix dining with nightlife. In 2007 Portland was featured in the *New York Times* for its up-and-coming fine dining scene.

Visitor Information: Portland Oregon Visitors Association, 1000 SW Broadway, Suite 2300, Portland, OR 97205; telephone (503)275-9750; toll-free (800)962-3700; email info@pova.com

■ Convention Facilities

The Oregon Convention Center, located in the center of downtown along the Willamette River, contains a total of nearly one million square feet of enclosed space, with 250,000 square feet of exhibit space, 50 meeting rooms, two grand ballrooms, and an 800-space parking garage. The facility can accommodate groups of up to 10,000. In 2003, the Oregon Convention Center completed a major expansion that doubled the center's size. Offering greater flexibility and more options than ever before, the Oregon Convention Center is the largest meeting facility in the Pacific Northwest.

The Portland Memorial Coliseum Complex, in the Rose Quarter, features 108,000 square feet of exhibit space. In 2007 the City of Portland outlined a number of improvements to the coliseum, including new large-screen televisions and beer gardens.

Portland offers several convention complexes that are all within a few minutes of more than 11,000 hotel rooms. Montgomery Park is a unique trade center located five minutes northwest of downtown Portland. It contains 19,000 square feet of exhibition and meeting space complemented by a 135-foot-high glass atrium.

The Portland Center for the Performing Arts's Brunish Hall offers space for 200 people for meetings, conferences, or other events. Other meeting and exhibition facilities include the Portland Metropolitan Expo Center and the Washington County FairPlex. Most major hotels in the city offer extensive meeting, banquet, and ballroom facilities.

Convention Information: Portland Oregon Visitors Association, 1000 SW Broadway, Suite 2300, Portland, OR 97205; telephone (503)275-9750 or (800)962-3700; fax (503)275-9284

■ Transportation

Approaching the City

Portland's airport, Portland International Airport (PDX), is one of the fastest-growing major airports on the West Coast, with 16 commercial carriers offering daily nonstop flights from Portland to various destinations; there were over half a million flights into and out of the airport in 2006. Serving 13 million passengers annually, PDX offers more than 500 passenger flights daily. The airport is 9 miles east of the central city, a 15-minute car ride. The Portland International Airport is owned and operated by the Port of Portland.

Two major interstate highways intersect in Portland: I-5, running north-south from southern California into Canada, and I-84, running east-west. U.S. highways 26 and 30 are other east-west routes. Portland is bypassed by I-405, on the western edge of the downtown area, and I-205, running through the eastern suburbs.

Amtrak serves the Portland area with daily train service; commercial bus service is also available.

Traveling in the City

Portland is divided into five areas—southwest, southeast, north, northeast and northwest—with the Willamette River bisecting the city. Street addresses match the location of these areas. A total of eleven bridges cross the river. The major streets are Grand Avenue, Martin Luther

King Jr. Blvd., Sandy Boulevard, and SE Eighty-second Street. Downtown, streets are mostly one way, with adjacent streets flowing in opposite directions.

TriMet, Portland's mass transit system, is ultramodern and efficient, highlighted by MAX, a 44-mile light-rail system that connects the downtown area with three counties. Westside MAX serves commuters in suburbs west of town as far west as Hillsboro. This line boasts the deepest subterranean transit station in North America, and public artwork decorates all Westside MAX stations. A 330-block area in the heart of downtown has been designated as the Fareless Square, where trips beginning and ending within the area are free. TriMet also has over 90 bus lines that serve Multnomah, Clackamas, and Washington counties, in addition to the Portland Street Car, which connects the Cultural District, the Pearl District and the Nob Hill/Northwest Neighborhood.

■ Communications

Newspapers and Magazines

Portland's major daily newspaper, *The Oregonian*, has been in publication since the 1850s. The paper's affiliated website provides news and local coverage online as well as archives to past stories. *Willamette Week* and many smaller neighborhood weeklies, as well as *The Skanner* and *Portland Observer*, both serving the African American community, are among the other Portland area newspapers. *The Portland Business Journal* provides news pertaining to the Portland business community. Local magazines include *Oregon Business Magazine* and a quarterly publication of the Oregon Historical Society.

Television and Radio

Six television stations in the area represent the commercial networks and public television; other channels are available on cable and from neighboring communities.

Over 20 AM and FM radio stations serve the Portland area with a variety of musical and other programming.

Media Information: *The Oregonian,* 1320 SW Broadway, Portland, OR 97201; telephone (503)221-8327

Portland Online

City of Portland home page. Available www
.portlandonline.com

Multnomah County Library. Available www
.multcolib.org

Oregon Economic Development Department.
Available www.econ.oregon.gov

The Oregonian. Available www.oregonlive.com

Portland Art Museum. Available www
.portlandartmuseum.org

Portland Business Alliance. Available www
.portlandalliance.com

Portland Oregon Visitors Association. Available
www.travelportland.com

Portland Public Schools. Available www.pps.k12
.or.us

BIBLIOGRAPHY

Hawkins, William John, and William F. Willingham, *Classic Houses of Portland, Oregon: 1850–1950* (Portland, OR: Timber Press, 1999)

Will, Robin, *Beauty of Portland* (Portland, OR: LTA Publishing, 1989)

Salem

■ The City in Brief

Founded: 1848 (incorporated 1860)

Head Official: Mayor Janet Taylor (since 2003)

City Population

1980: 89,091
1990: 107,793
2000: 136,924
2006 estimate: 152,239
Percent change, 1990–2000: 25.8%
U.S. rank in 1980: 195th
U.S. rank in 1990: 178th
U.S. rank in 2000: 162nd

Metropolitan Area Population

1980: 250,000
1990: 278,024
2000: 347,214
2006 estimate: 384,600
Percent change, 1990–2000: 24.9%
U.S. rank in 1980: 126th
U.S. rank in 1990: 122nd
U.S. rank in 2000: 129th (CMSA)

Area: 46.37 square miles (2000)

Elevation: 171 feet above sea level at State Capitol

Average Annual Temperatures: January, 40.3° F; July, 66.8° F; annual average, 52.6° F

Average Annual Precipitation: 40 inches of rain; 6.6 inches of snow

Major Economic Sectors: services, wholesale and retail trade, government

Unemployment Rate: 5.2% (June 2007)

Per Capita Income: $21,671 (2005)

2005 FBI Crime Index Property: 9,004

2005 FBI Crime Index Violent: 706

Major Colleges and Universities: Willamette University, Chemeketa Community College, Corban College, Tokyo International University (branch)

Daily Newspaper: *Statesman Journal*

■ Introduction

Salem is the capital of Oregon and the third largest city in the state. Situated in the middle of a large, fertile agricultural region and known as the "Cherry City," Salem is the processing and transportation center for the surrounding area. A clean environment, the natural scenic beauty of its location, and the recreational activities afforded by the nearby mountains contribute to the high quality of life for which Salem is noted. In addition, careful planning and intelligent zoning have made the city attractive to new business and industry.

■ Geography and Climate

Salem is located about 60 miles inland from the Pacific Ocean in the Willamette Valley and about halfway between Portland and Eugene. The Willamette River flows on the western edge of the central city. The city is bounded by the Coast Range of mountains on the west and the Cascade Range on the east. Moist Pacific air is the dominant weather feature, moderating temperatures year round. The city and especially the nearby mountains receive a large amount of rainfall; more than 70 percent occurs between November and March and only about 6 percent during the summer. Severe storms and extreme temperatures are uncommon.

Area: 46.37 square miles (2000)

Elevation: 171 feet above sea level at State Capitol

Average Temperatures: January, 40.3° F; July, 66.8° F; annual average, 52.6° F

Average Annual Precipitation: 40 inches of rain; 6.6 inches of snow

■ History

The site of present-day Salem was called "Chemeketa" by the Calapooya tribe. The word means "meeting" or "resting place," and the tribe used the region for many years in that capacity. In 1840, Jason Lee, a Methodist-Episcopal missionary, moved his mission to the area and called it "Chemeketa," but most settlers referred to it as "The Mill," because of its proximity to Mill Creek. Two years later, the mission established the Oregon Institute, a training school for the local Native Americans that eventually became Willamette University.

The mission was closed in 1844, but in 1848, a town was laid out on the site and called Salem. Some controversy remains over who actually named the town Salem, but historians agree that it was either David Leslie or W. H. Wilson. A fierce battle over where to locate the capital of the Oregon Territory began when the capital was moved from Oregon City to Salem in 1851. In 1853 the Oregon State Legislature began debate on whether to change the town's name to Thurston, Valena, or Corvallis, but a vote in 1855 retained the town's original name. The capital was moved again in 1855, but it returned to Salem later that same year. A suspicious fire that destroyed the Capitol building in late 1855 added to the controversy. When Oregon became a state in 1859, Salem was named the tentative capital, but it was not until 1864 that the city was officially chosen as the capital by election. Salem was incorporated as a city in 1860, and the present Capitol building was built in 1938, after the previous building was destroyed by fire in 1935. Beginning as a wool processing center, Salem has grown to be an important center for the processing of agricultural products and lumber, as well as a hothouse for technology and information companies. The city's historic buildings, surrounding natural beauty, and modern amenities make it a draw for new residents and businesses alike.

Historical Information: Marion County Historical Society Museum, 260 Twelfth St., SE, Salem, Oregon 97301-4101; telephone (503)364-2128; Fax (503)391-5356; email mchs@open.org

■ Population Profile

Metropolitan Area Residents

1980: 250,000
1990: 278,024
2000: 347,214
2006 estimate: 384,600
Percent change, 1990–2000: 24.9%
U.S. rank in 1980: 126th
U.S. rank in 1990: 122nd
U.S. rank in 2000: 129th (CMSA)

City Residents

1980: 89,091
1990: 107,793
2000: 136,924
2006 estimate: 152,239
Percent change, 1990–2000: 25.8%
U.S. rank in 1980: 195th
U.S. rank in 1990: 178th
U.S. rank in 2000: 162nd

Density: 2,994.0 people per square mile (2000)

Racial and ethnic characteristics (2005)

White: 113,956
Black: 1,397
American Indian and Alaska Native: 2,310
Asian: 4,892
Native Hawaiian and Pacific Islander: 0
Hispanic or Latino (may be of any race): 30,734
Other: 15,694

Percent of residents born in state: 45.0% (2000)

Age characteristics (2005)

Population under 5 years old: 10,702
Population 5 to 9 years old: 10,935
Population 10 to 14 years old: 11,069
Population 15 to 19 years old: 7,939
Population 20 to 24 years old: 10,761
Population 25 to 34 years old: 22,656
Population 35 to 44 years old: 21,464
Population 45 to 54 years old: 17,664
Population 55 to 59 years old: 8,256
Population 60 to 64 years old: 5,079
Population 65 to 74 years old: 7,479
Population 75 to 84 years old: 5,786
Population 85 years and older: 2,216
Median age: 33.7 years

Births (2006, MSA)

Total number: 5,410

The State Capitol building in Salem. *Jim Corwin/Stone/Getty Images*

Deaths (2006, MSA)

Total number: 3,047

Money income (2005)

Per capita income: $21,671
Median household income: $39,259
Total households: 55,425

Number of households with income of...

less than $10,000: 4,644
$10,000 to $14,999: 3,615
$15,000 to $24,999: 7,772
$25,000 to $34,999: 8,614
$35,000 to $49,999: 9,371
$50,000 to $74,999: 10,594
$75,000 to $99,999: 5,391
$100,000 to $149,999: 3,382
$150,000 to $199,999: 1,029
$200,000 or more: 1,013

Percent of families below poverty level: 16.1% (2005)

2005 FBI Crime Index Property: 9,004

2005 FBI Crime Index Violent: 706

■ Municipal Government

Salem operates under a council-manager form of government with eight council members elected to four-year terms by wards; the mayor serves for two years and is elected at-large. The council hires the city manager. Salem is the seat of Marion County.

Head Officials: Mayor Janet Taylor (since 2003; current term expires 2008); City Manager Robert Wells

Total Number of City Employees: 1,200+ (2007)

City Information: City of Salem, 555 Liberty Street SE, Salem, OR 97301; telephone (503)588-6255; email Manager@open.org

■ Economy

Major Industries and Commercial Activity

Salem was named to the *Forbes* 2006 top 10 "Best Places for Business and Careers" list in the "Cost of Doing Business" category. The major industry in Salem, as the state's capital and county seat of Marion County, is government, where state, local, and federal governments employ 28 percent of Salem's workers. The service industry makes up 26 percent, and trade comprises 21 percent.

Agriculture and livestock, which is a highly diversified industry in the Salem area, has a total estimated economic impact of $1.2 billion dollars annually. Over 150 different cash crops are produced in the area. Vegetables and fruits, nursery and greenhouse crops, grass seed, and dairy products account for more than 50 percent of the total agricultural value.

Manufacturing in the Salem area has become increasingly diverse. The food product industry is the largest single manufacturing sector, employing 3,500 people on average each year and up to 10,000 during the peak of the processing season. Major manufacturing employers also include those that produce fabricated metal products and high-tech equipment such as cell phones, snow boards, and area newspapers. Most employment pertaining to lumber and wood products is actually in the manufactured building industry making pre-fabricated structures.

Items and goods produced: high-tech components, vegetable and fruit products, wood and paper products, grass seed, ornamental plants, dairy products, manufactured homes, and metal products

Incentive Programs—New and Existing Companies

Local programs: In recent years the emphasis in the Willamette Valley has switched from business recruitment to business retention and expansion programs designed to help resident companies "stay put and stay healthy." Most incentive programs are state loan, worker-training, and tax credit packages provided by the Oregon Economic Development Department and arranged through the Mid-Willamette Valley Council of Governments or the Salem Economic Development Corp. (SEDCOR). One such incentive program is the "Toolbox" loan and grant program, created to address vacancy in downtown Salem by providing grant and loan funds for rehabilitation and restoration of buildings The Salem area has three enterprise zones for qualified manufacturing and wholesale distribution firms that allow a three- to five-year property tax exemption on improvements.

State programs: Among the incentives available to businesses in Portland are several financial programs offered at the state level, together with tax incentives, new construction exemptions, and tax credits. These include the Brownfield Redevelopment Fund, Business Development Fund, Capital Access Program, Entrepreneurial Development Loan Fund, and several others. The state's Department of Energy administers a Small Scale Energy Loan, which offers low-interest loans to businesses that save energy or produce energy from renewable resources.

Job training programs: The state of Oregon has approved an education program, the first such in the nation, that establishes a statewide apprenticeship program and has students choose between job training or a college preparatory program after the tenth grade. The program is to be installed in stages in schools through the year 2010. The state's JOBS Plus program allows employers who hire a JOBS Plus-eligible worker to receive benefits that include reimbursements, the opportunity to train and evaluate the worker during the contract period, and the opportunity to treat the employee as a temporary employee. Chemeketa Community College's Training & Economic Development Center in downtown Salem has a variety of programs to help small businesses develop and to assist existing businesses to expand. SEDCOR has partnered with Chemeketa and the Oregon Manufacturers Extension Partnership (OMEP) to run the Oregon Gateway Project for Business and Education, a program for training businesses and workers in state-of-the-art manufacturing processes at the Advanced Manufacturing and Technology Institute (AMTI) at the college.

Development Projects

In 2005 the new Salem Conference Center and attached Phoenix Grand Hotel opened in the heart of downtown Salem, just a few blocks from the state capitol building. The Meridian, a 130,000-square-foot mixed-use development of luxury condominiums and medical offices, began construction in 2005 near Salem Hospital. The largest development project to be started in the mid-2000s was the development of the Mill Creek area labeled as "Salem Regional Employment Center." This 646-acre parcel began development in 2005 as an industrial area with business and industry parks, with 100 acres set aside as open space and wildlife habitat. Phased development of the area is expected to continue for 20 years, and it is hoped that the center will create 5,000 new jobs.

Salem Hospital's new seven-story patient tower is expected to be complete by 2009. Plans called for 30 patient rooms on each of the building's top three floors, in addition to operating rooms, a cardiac cath lab, surgery recovery, satellite pharmacy, and frozen-section lab.

Economic Development Information: SEDCOR, 350 Commercial St. NE, Salem, OR 97301; telephone (503)588-6225; fax (503)588-6240; email sedcor@sedcor.org. Salem Area Chamber of Commerce, 1110 Commerical Street NE, Salem, OR 97301; telephone (503)581-1466; fax (503)581-0972; email info@salemchamber.org.

Commercial Shipping

Salem is located on the main lines of the Union Pacific and Burlington Northern Santa Fe railroads. Located in Salem are 28 long haul truck lines with seven terminals.

Interstate 5, the primary north-south highway of the West Coast, passes through the east side of Salem, and Interstate 84 connects to states in the east. Nearby Portland has marine terminals and deep water ports, and is one of the busiest ports on the West Coast in cargo shipped. The Salem Municipal Airport at McNary Field is a 750-acre facility with a 5,800-foot ILS, precision runway that has full facilities for corporate and general aviation aircraft.

Labor Force and Employment Outlook

The Salem area labor force is diversified, with skilled and semi-skilled components including metal workers, assemblers, electrical/electronic technicians, machine operators, computer operators, and programmers. In August 2007 the unemployment rate stood at 5.2 percent, down from its ten-year high of nearly eight percent in 2004.

The Salem area economy in the mid-2000s was very healthy. Salem's workforce has expanded in recent years, and has grown by about 3,000 residents each year since the 2000 U.S. Census. The state Employment Department's industry and occupational projections for 2004-2014 show the greater Salem area growing at the same rate as the state, about 15 percent, over the ten year period. The high percentage of government workers has shown to have a stabilizing effect on the area's economy. There are projections that population growth will slow, but as baby boomers retire, more job openings should become available.

The following is a summary of data regarding the Salem metropolitan area labor force, 2006 annual averages.

Size of nonagricultural labor force: 149,400

Number of workers employed in . . .

    construction and mining: 10,700
    manufacturing: 15,400
    trade, transportation and utilities: 25,500
    information: 1,500
    financial activities: 7,500
    professional and business services: 12,300
    educational and health services: 19,100
    leisure and hospitality: 12,200
    other services: 5,200
    government: 40,100

Average hourly earnings of production workers employed in manufacturing: $11.92

Unemployment rate: 5.2% (June 2007)

Largest private employers (2007)	*Number of employees*
Salem Hospital	2,700
Spirit Mountain Casino	1,500
T-Mobile	1,100
Norpac Foods	1,000
Roth's-Your Family Market	1,000
Wal-Mart	1,000
Fred Meyer	700
Wachovia	690
Willamette University	627
Rainsweet	600

Cost of Living

The following is a summary of data regarding several key cost of living factors for the Salem area.

2007 (1st quarter) ACCRA Average House Price: Not available

2007 (1st quarter) ACCRA Cost of Living Index: Not available

State income tax rate: 5.0% to 9.0%

State sales tax rate: None

Local income tax rate: None

Local sales tax rate: None

Property tax rate: $19.32 per $1,000 assessed valuation

Economic Information: SEDCOR, 745 Commercial St. NE, Salem, OR 97301; telephone (503)588-6225; fax (503)588-6240. Oregon Employment Department, 875 Union Street, Salem, OR 97311; telephone (800) 237-3710

■ Education and Research

Elementary and Secondary Schools

Salem-Keizer Public Schools comprises the second largest school district in the state. It is governed by a seven-member, nonpartisan school board that appoints the superintendent. In 2006-2007 district-wide enrollment stood at 39,740, and the system was one of the largest employers in the metropolitan area, employing nearly 4,000 full-time staff. The district includes four charter schools and two alternative high schools.

The following is a summary of data regarding the Salem-Keizer Public Schools as of the 2005–2006 school year.

Total enrollment: 39,000

Number of facilities

    elementary schools: 45
    junior high/middle schools: 10
    senior high schools: 6
    other: 5

Student/teacher ratio: 18.9:1

Teacher salaries (2005–06)

elementary median: $45,760
junior high/middle median: $45,620
secondary median: $44,030

Funding per pupil: $6,979

Salem is also served by over twenty parochial and private schools spanning pre-K to 12th grade.

Public Schools Information: Salem-Keizer Public Schools, 2450 Lancaster Dr. NE, Salem, OR 97305; telephone (503)399-3000

Colleges and Universities

Salem is home to Willamette University, a private school affiliated with the Methodist Church that traces its roots back to 1842 and calls itself the first university in the West. With an enrollment of more than 1,800, the university offers a wide range of undergraduate degrees in many fields and a number of postgraduate programs, including law (the first program in the Pacific Northwest), teaching, and management. Recent additions to the campus include the F.W. Olin Science Center, the Hallie Ford Museum of Art, and the Mary Stuart Rogers Music Center, and the $14 million Kaneko Commons residence hall. Chemeketa Community College enrolled more than 64,000 students in 2006-2007, and offers one- and two-year associates degrees. The school also boasts nearly 500 staff members. A branch of Tokyo International University opened in Salem in 1989 to meet Japanese corporations' increased demand for a culturally adapted workforce. The branch is located directly across from Willamette University. Other area colleges and universities are Corban College (formerly Western Baptist College), George Fox University, and Western Oregon State College in Monmouth.

Libraries and Research Centers

The Oregon State Library provides quality information service to Oregon state government, provides reading materials to blind and print-disabled Oregonians, and provides leadership, grants, and other assistance to improve local library service for all Oregonians. Among its more than one million items are in-depth collections in business, history, political and social sciences, federal and state government publications, genealogy, and a comprehensive collection of materials about Oregon. In addition, its Library for the Blind and Physically Handicapped collection consists of more than 60,000 cassette, large print, Braille, and talking book titles.

The Salem Public Library maintains a main library, one branch, and a bookmobile with a total of more than 350,000 items, including more than 800 periodical titles. The library features a special photographic history collection. Around 1.2 million items circulate annually from the library. At Willamette University the Mark O. Hatfield Library houses more than 400,000 volumes and about 5,000 periodical subscriptions; the J.W. Long Law Library houses collections of Oregonian, national, and international law titles.

Public Library Information: Salem Public Library, 585 Liberty Street SE, Salem, OR 97301; telephone (503)588-6315

■ Health Care

Salem Hospital, with 464 physicians and 454 acute-care beds, is the major health-care facility in the city, providing a wide range of services in several locations. Salem Hospital's service area includes Marion, Polk, and portions of Yamhill counties. Salem Hospital is one of the largest of Oregon's 63 acute care hospitals, and is home to the state's busiest Emergency Room. The hospital's Center for Outpatient Medicine, just east of the hospital, houses outpatient programs, outpatient surgery, imaging, a Sleep Disorders Center, a SHAPES clinic, and other programs. In 2003, a $50 million Family Birth Center facility was added, and a brand-new patient tower is slated to open in 2009. The Salem Hospital Regional Rehabilitation Center, at 2561 Center Street NE, provides comprehensive inpatient and outpatient rehabilitation services as well as home care. Other Salem Hospital facilities include a Psychiatric Medicine Center, an Outpatient Mammography and MRI Center, and an Urgent Care Center.

Additional community health care providers are the Willamette Valley Hospice, Northbank Surgical Center, skilled nursing and adult foster care providers, and a number of physician clinics also furnishing care to Salem residents. Kaiser Permanente runs two medical office buildings in the city, and the company's Northwest Division was ranked fifth of Oregon's "100 Best Companies to Work For" by *Oregon Business*.

Health Care Information: Salem Hospital, Community Relations Office, 665 Winter St. SE, Salem, OR 97301-3919; telephone (503)370-5269; toll-free (800) 876-1718

■ Recreation

Sightseeing

The State Capitol building in downtown Salem is constructed of white marble and features a 22-foot bronze and gold leaf statue, "The Oregon Pioneer." Willson Park, next to the Capitol, contains the Waite Fountain, a replica of the Liberty Bell, and a gazebo for open-air concerts. Bush's Pasture Park is a large park near the

Willamette River and downtown Salem that features the Bush House, a Victorian mansion; historic Deepwood House and Gardens, a 5.5-acre estate built in the Queen Anne style; Bush Barn Art Center; and Bush Conservatory. The Salem Municipal Rose Garden is also located in the park. Riverfront Park on the Willamette River has an amphitheatre, a playground and picnic areas, and is home to Salem's Riverfront Carousel, featuring hand-carved horses. The A.C. Gilbert Discovery Village, a children's museum, is also in Riverfront Park. Salem Saturday Market brings local farmers and artisans to the corner of Marion and Summers streets May through October. The Reed Opera House, built in 1869, has been renovated and now contains a number of shops and restaurants.

Attractions at Enchanted Forest, a family-run amusement park, include Storybook Lane in a woodland setting, a Western mining town, summer comedy theater, a haunted house, the Ice Mountain roller coaster, and bobsled and log flume rides. The Salem area features more than 20 wineries within an hour's drive.

Arts and Culture

Theatrical performances are held year-round by the Pentacle Theatre, a community theater group. The Elsinore Theatre presents international and national tours of musicians and theatrical performances, hosts a children's play series, and presents films on Wednesdays. The Willamette Playhouse is where theatre majors from the Willamette University perform, along with the university's Distinguished Artists Series that brings speakers, concerts, and plays to the venue. Musical performances by local groups include classical and pops concerts backed by the Oregon Symphony Association of Salem. The Willamette Falls Symphony presents three concerts a year. Salem is also home to concert and jazz bands, a chamber music group, and men's and women's barbershop choirs. The Hallie Ford Museum of Art, the state's largest art museum, opened in 1998. It houses Willamette University's collection of Indian baskets, Northwest paintings, prints, photographs, sculptures, and European, Asian, and American art. The A.C. Gilbert Discovery Village is the largest children's museum in the Northwest and includes the National Toy Hall of Fame. Half of the museum is housed in a Victorian home once occupied by Gilbert's uncle and the other half is in a Victorian building separated from the first by a charming outdoor activity center.

Mission Mill Museum is a 5-acre site that is home to the Thomas Kay Woolen Mill, the historic buildings of the Jason Lee House, the Parsonage, the John D. Boon House, and Pleasant Grove Church. The modern PGE Waterpower Interpretive Center showcases the importance of waterpower to Salem's textile industry.

Arts and Culture Information: Mid-Valley Arts Council, 401 Center Street, Suite 1156, Salem, OR 97301; telephone 503-364-7474

Festivals and Holidays

The Oregon Wine and Food Festival, billed as "The first taste of the wine season," is held at the Oregon State Fairgrounds in January. In April, the Oregon Agricultural Fest at the State Fairgrounds brings over 20,000 visitors a year to enjoy the Trade, Garden and Craft Show, live entertainment, food, and petting zoo. In June, Riverfront Park hosts the Salem World Beat Festival, with music, dance, crafts, and food from around the world. The Salem Art Fair and Festival occurs annually in the third weekend in July and exhibits the works of artists from throughout the Northwest. Also in July is Salem Hoopla, an all-ages 3-on-3 basketball tournament held right on Court Street, and the Marion County Fair takes place at the State Fairgrounds. The Oregon State Fair is a 12-day celebration each August that features floral and art exhibits, agricultural displays, a midway, and live entertainment. The nearby Bavarian-style community of Mt. Angel holds a popular Oktoberfest each fall. The Festival of Lights Parade in December features floats and marching bands on a route through downtown at night.

Sports for the Participant

More than 1,874 acres within 101 park and open space areas and 29.53 miles of trails in Salem offer a variety of outdoor recreational activities. Water sports include fishing, swimming, and boating. Nearly thirty parks maintain ball fields, and there are also over twenty public tennis courts and 7 public golf courses; some provide accommodations for the handicapped. Minto Brown Island Park, the largest park at 900 acres, is located along the river about a mile from Salem's center city and contains picnic grounds, jogging and bike paths, and a wildlife refuge. Within 50 miles of Salem are coastal beaches and state and federal recreational areas and parks.

Shopping and Dining

The downtown Salem Center Mall, Lancaster Mall, and Woodburn Company Stores Outlet Mall are the three main shopping areas in Salem. A system of skywalks connects the four major department stores downtown. A number of other specialty stores and smaller shops, such as Mission Mill Village, featuring antiques and crafts in a historic village setting, are scattered throughout the area.

Salem restaurants specialize in fresh, grown-in-Oregon foods and famous Pacific seafood along with cuisine from around the world. The Willamette Valley's vineyards produce a variety of fine wines that area restaurants proudly feature.

Visitor Information: Salem Convention and Visitors Association, 1313 Mill Street SE, Salem, OR 97301; telephone (503)581-4325; toll-free (800)874-7012; fax (503)581-4540

■ Convention Facilities

There are numerous options when pondering where to meet and stay in Oregon's capital city. The Salem Convention Center, which opened in 2005, has 29,400 square feet of meeting and exhibition space in 14 rooms, and is attached to the all-suite, 193-room Phoenix Grand Hotel. The Pavilion at the Oregon State Fair & Exhibition Center offers more than 110,000 square feet of meeting and exhibit space for groups of 30 to 4,000 persons. There are eight other buildings available at the Fairgrounds, including a horse barn, a livestock building, and an amphitheater, all available for events or meetings. The historic Reed Opera House in downtown Salem has two ballrooms with catering facilities for elegant receptions for up to 300 people, and the Elsinore Theatre can be rented for events. In total, the city offers over 450,000 square feet of meeting and exhibit space and can accommodate groups of up to 7,000.

Convention Information: Salem Convention and Visitors Association, 1313 Mill Street SE, Salem, OR 97301; telephone (503)581-4325; toll-free (800)874-7012; fax (503)581-4540

■ Transportation

Approaching the City

Airport shuttles make round trips from Portland International Airport, 61 miles from Salem. Salem Municipal Airport, also known as McNalty Field, is located two miles outside the city. It is a general aviation facility, largely serving private flights and the Oregon Army National Guard. Interstate 5, the major West Coast interstate highway, and Interstate 84, for destinations to the east, run through Salem. Passenger rail service is available from Amtrak with two trains daily. The city is also served by Greyhound bus line.

Traveling in the City

The downtown area and much of the rest of Salem is laid out in a grid pattern. Major thoroughfares include State Street, Center Street, Commercial Street, and River Road. Salem-Keizer Transit, also known as Cherriots, operates a fleet of more than 50 buses throughout the metropolitan area, in addition to a Rideshares program. By 2008 Cherriot planned to begin replacing older and pollution-heavy diesel buses with a new fleet of "Clean Diesel Buses," 10 at a time.

■ Communications

Newspaper and Magazines

Salem readers support one major daily morning newspaper, the *Statesman Journal,* and a number of weekly papers that provide business, agricultural, government, and general news, including Willamette University's *Collegian.* Among the magazines published in Salem are *Dialogue,* a magazine for the visually impaired, and *The Capital Press,* a farming newspaper for the Pacific Northwest.

Television and Radio

Two television stations broadcast from Salem: PAX and CW affiliates. Salem is also served by a number of stations broadcasting from Portland, Oregon, as well as cable television. Seven FM and AM radio stations are located in Salem, and along with broadcasters from the surrounding communities, serve the area with an assortment of music, news, and informational programming.

Media Information: *Statesman Journal,* 280 Church St. NE, Salem, OR 97309; telephone (503)399-6611; toll-free (800)874-7012

Salem Online

City of Salem home page. Available www .cityofsalem.net

Oregon Economic Development Department. Available www.econ.oregon.gov

Salem Area Chamber of Commerce. Available www .salemchamber.org

Salem Convention & Visitors Association. Available www.travelsalem.com

Salem Economic Development Corporation. Available www.sedcor.org

Salem-Keizer Public Schools. Available www.salkeiz .k12.or.us

Salem Public Library. Available www.salemlibrary .org

*Statesman Journal.*Available www.statesmanjournal .com

BIBLIOGRAPHY

Price, Lorna, ed., *Oregon Biennial* (Portland, OR: Portland Art Museum, 2006)

Utah

The State in Brief

Nickname: Beehive State

Motto: Industry

Flower: Sego lily

Bird: California gull

Area: 84,898 square miles (2000; U.S. rank 13th)

Elevation: Ranges from 2,000 feet to 13,528 feet above sea level

Climate: Generally arid with abundant sunshine; higher temperatures in the southwestern desert, cooler weather and lower temperatures in high plateaus and mountains

Admitted to Union: January 4, 1896

Capital: Salt Lake City

Head Official: Governor Jon Huntsman Jr. (R) (until 2008)

Population

1980: 1,461,000
1990: 1,722,850
2000: 2,233,169
2006 estimate: 2,550,063
Percent change, 1990–2000: 29.6%
U.S. rank in 2006: 34th
Percent of residents born in state: 63.02% (2006)
Density: 30.1 people per square mile (2006)
2006 FBI Crime Index Total: 95,393

Racial and Ethnic Characteristics (2006)

White: 2,271,604
Black or African American: 22,742
American Indian and Alaska Native: 28,901
Asian: 49,079
Native Hawaiian and Pacific Islander: 18,958
Hispanic or Latino (may be of any race): 286,113
Other: 113,961

Age Characteristics (2006)

Population under 5 years old: 247,167
Population 5 to 19 years old: 628,967
Percent of population 65 years and over: 8.8%
Median age: 28.4

Vital Statistics

Total number of births (2006): 48,953
Total number of deaths (2006): 13,693
AIDS cases reported through 2005: 2,261

Economy

Major industries: Manufacturing; trade; government; finance, insurance, and real estate; services; mining; agriculture; tourism
Unemployment rate (2006): 4.4%
Per capita income (2006): $21,016
Median household income (2006): $51,309
Percentage of persons below poverty level (2006): 10.6%
Income tax rate: 2.30% to 6.98%
Sales tax rate: 4.75%

Provo

■ The City in Brief

Founded: 1849 (incorporated 1851)

Head Official: Mayor Lewis K. Billings (R) (since 1998)

City Population

1980: 74,111
1990: 86,835
2000: 105,166
2006 estimate: 113,984
Percent change, 1990–2000: 20.7%
U.S. rank in 1980: Not available
U.S. rank in 1990: 239th
U.S. rank in 2000: 244th (State rank: 3rd)

Metropolitan Area Population

1980: 218,000
1990: 263,590
2000: 368,536
2006 estimate: 474,180
Percent change, 1990–2000: 39.8%
U.S. rank in 1980: Not available
U.S. rank in 1990: 129th
U.S. rank in 2000: 111th

Area: 41.79 square miles (2000)

Elevation: 4,540 feet above sea level

Average Annual Temperature: 53.3° F

Average Annual Precipitation: 20.13 inches of rain; 60.40 inches of snow

Major Economic Sectors: services, wholesale and retail trade, government

Unemployment Rate: 2.8% (June 2007)

Per Capita Income: $15,072 (2005)

2005 FBI Crime Index Property: 3,298

2005 FBI Crime Index Violent: 182

Major Colleges and Universities: Brigham Young University, Utah Valley State College

Daily Newspaper: *The Daily Herald*

■ Introduction

Provo is the commercial center and county seat of Utah County, and one of the fastest growing areas in the nation. A high-technology mecca, the Provo area is home to one of the largest concentrations of computer software in the nation after California's Silicon Valley. The city is one of the top iron and steel producers in the West, as well as an agricultural center producing berries and orchard fruit. Many ski areas, campgrounds, state parks, lakes, and rivers are located within Utah County. Fishing, camping, hiking, and hunting facilities are nearby. Brigham Young University is the center for many local activities in the city, which is the headquarters of the Uinta National Forest with its many scenic drives through the Wasatch Mountains and Provo Canyon. The city has a very well-educated population—more than 90 percent of its residents have graduated from high school. Housing is affordable and the crime rate is two to three times lower than in most comparable cities. In 2007 Provo was ranked second in the "Best Places for Business and Careers" survey by *Forbes* magazine, which considered job and income growth, cost of doing business, and workforce qualification in its rankings.

■ Geography and Climate

Provo is located in Utah Valley, 38 miles south of Salt Lake City, 263 miles northeast of St. George, and 80 miles south of Ogden. It is situated on the Provo River between Utah Lake to the west and the Wasatch Mountain Range to the east. It sits on a shelf along the famous shoreline of prehistoric Lake Bonneville and is nurtured by the Provo River.

The area experiences four seasons with low humidity that makes the air cool rapidly after sunset, resulting in comfortably cool evenings. The temperature dips below zero on only three days per year on average. Generally 57 days of the year are above 90 degrees and 15 days are below freezing. The wettest month of the year is usually May while June is the driest month.

Area: 41.79 square miles (2000)

Elevation: 4,540 feet above sea level

Average Temperature: 53.3° F

Average Annual Precipitation: 20.13 inches of rain; 60.40 inches of snow

■ History

Two Franciscan friars, Francisco Dominguez and Silvestre de Escalante, were the first Spaniards to visit the area that makes up present-day Utah County. They arrived in the area from Santa Fe, New Mexico, in search of a direct route to Monterey, California. Arriving in 1776, Father Escalente described the Provo/Orem Valley as having comfortable weather both day and night. "This place is the most pleasant, beautiful, and fertile land in all New Spain," he wrote. The two priests instructed the native Americans in Christian teachings, and though they promised to return, no further record of them remains.

Etienne Provost, a French Canadian trapper, was the next recorded European visitor. He arrived in the area in 1825 with a band of men in search of fur-bearing animals. The trappers were visited by 20 or 30 natives, whose leader told them that they could not smoke peace pipes together because there was iron in the vicinity. Provost and his men moved their knives and guns further away, and subsequently the natives attacked them with hidden knives and tomahawks, killing 17 of the 22 men. Provost and four other men escaped and made their way to the mountains.

The Mormon pioneers, fleeing religious persecution in Illinois, were the next European visitors to the area. Brigham Young led his followers to Salt Lake Valley in 1847, where they immediately began planting crops and constructing houses. In 1849 a permanent settlement in Provo was established by Mormon pioneers.

Provo was founded in 1849 as Fort Utah, named after the Ute tribe that inhabited the region. Later, the name was changed to Fort Provo in honor of Provost, the French trapper.

A war between the settlers and the native tribes took place in 1850, and the Walker War followed in 1853. The Mormons built a fort that they called Fort Utah as a

protection against their native enemies. Shortly after, settlers began building houses around the fort. By 1852 hotels and businesses had been established.

By 1861 all of the Utah Valley was being settled. Even though lack of water remained a problem, many of the earlier settlers from nearby valleys began living on the lands that now comprise the city of Orem. When railroad connections were built from Salt Lake City (1873) and Scofield (1878), Provo became a shipping point for the region's mines. Provo is the seat of Brigham Young University (founded in 1875) and Utah Valley State College. Nearby are the Uinta National Forest, with headquarters in Provo; a state fish hatchery; a wild bird refuge; and Provo Peak.

Today, Provo is one of the fastest growing metropolitan areas in the nation, with population gains of nearly 40 percent in the 1990s and into the new millennium. The area boasts a high quality of life due in part to its proximity to an abundance of recreational and leisure options in the nearby Wasatch Mountains and Utah Lake. Provo is a family-friendly city, too; in 2007, *Kiplinger's Personal Finance* magazine ranked the city fifth on its list of "Best Cities for Families."

Historical Information: Department of History, Brigham Young University, 2130 JFSB, Provo, UT 84602; telephone (801)422-4335

■ Population Profile

Metropolitan Area Residents
    1980: 218,000
    1990: 263,590
    2000: 368,536
    2006 estimate: 474,180
    Percent change, 1990–2000: 39.8%
    U.S. rank in 1980: Not available
    U.S. rank in 1990: 129th
    U.S. rank in 2000: 111th

City Residents
    1980: 74,111
    1990: 86,835
    2000: 105,166
    2006 estimate: 113,984
    Percent change, 1990–2000: 20.7%
    U.S. rank in 1980: Not available
    U.S. rank in 1990: 239th
    U.S. rank in 2000: 244th (State rank: 3rd)

Density: 2,653.2 people per square mile (2000)

Racial and ethnic characteristics (2000)
    White: 93,094
    Black: 486
    American Indian and Alaska Native: 846

Photograph by Ron H. MacDonald. Provo City Corporation, Economic Development Office. Reproduced by permission.

Asian: 1,924
Native Hawaiian and Pacific Islander: 882
Hispanic or Latino (may be of any race): 11,013
Other: 5,368

Percent of residents born in state: 46.3% (2000)

Age characteristics (2005)

Population under 5 years old: 10,535
Population 5 to 9 years old: 5,386
Population 10 to 14 years old: 3,357
Population 15 to 19 years old: 7,244
Population 20 to 24 years old: 27,404
Population 25 to 34 years old: 24,513
Population 35 to 44 years old: 6,291
Population 45 to 54 years old: 5,564
Population 55 to 59 years old: 2,951
Population 60 to 64 years old: 2,497
Population 65 to 74 years old: 2,342
Population 75 to 84 years old: 2,187
Population 85 years and older: 893
Median age: 24.5 years

Births (2006, MSA)

Total number: 10,674

Deaths (2006, MSA)

Total number: 1,765

Money income (2005)

Per capita income: $15,072
Median household income: $31,603
Total households: 31,795

Number of households with income of ...

less than $10,000: 2,546
$10,000 to $14,999: 3,633
$15,000 to $24,999: 6,629
$25,000 to $34,999: 4,366
$35,000 to $49,999: 5,010
$50,000 to $74,999: 5,225
$75,000 to $99,999: 1,891
$100,000 to $149,999: 1,721
$150,000 to $199,999: 549
$200,000 or more: 225

Percent of families below poverty level: 12.1% (2005)

2005 FBI Crime Index Property: 3,298

2005 FBI Crime Index Violent: 182

■ Municipal Government

Provo has a council-mayor form of government with a mandatory chief administrative officer. Seven members make up the Provo Municipal Council—five representing municipal districts and two city-wide representatives.

Head Official: Mayor Lewis K. Billings (R) (since 1998; current term expires 2010)

Total Number of City Employees: 740 (2004)

City Information: Provo City Mayor's Office, 351 West Center St., Provo, UT 84603; telephone (801) 852- 6100

■ Economy

Major Industries and Commercial Activity

According to a 2005 article in *Inc.* magazine, "Utah has become the epicenter of the *Inc.* 500 Fastest-Growing Private Companies in recent years, specifically Provo." The Provo-Orem area has a diverse economy with every employment sector well represented. The area is home to one of the largest concentrations of high-tech and software technologies companies in the United States. There is also a large concentration of biotech companies located in the area.

Some of the world's major software companies are located in the area, including Novell, Inc., Symantec and Corel, creating opportunities for more than 400 small to mid-range high-technology companies. Provo is also home to such giants as Nestle Frozen Foods and Nu Skin Enterprises Inc. High-technology companies in the Provo/Orem area include Micron Technology, Ameritech Library Services, Convergys, Folio Corporation, Viewsoft, and Nimbus Manufacturing, among others.

The notable work ethic of local employees and the appeal of a serene mountain community have made Provo ideal for a wide variety of manufacturers, communications firms, and marketing and retail organizations, including Banta Press, Nature's Sunshine, PowerQuest Corp., and Powder River Manufacturing. Many industrial parks offer a variety of settings for light to heavy industry with abundant, low-cost utilities.

Tourism is also an important industry, especially as the Sundance Film Festival's international profile has become more prominent in recent years. As other sectors of the economy have prospered in recent years, retailers have seen dramatic increases as well. Provo is a magnet for many of the surrounding counties and the major shopping areas are easily accessible from I-15 and other main routes.

Items and goods produced: iron, steel, software, fruit, electronics, apparel

Incentive Programs—New and Existing Companies

Local programs: Most incentive programs are at the state level. Provo City's Redevelopment Agency provides support for starting a new business by offering assistance in preparing a business plan and demographic information necessary for decision making. The city's Revolving Loan Fund offers new or existing businesses loans of up to $100,000 dollars. Provo also offers a city-wide broadband high speed internet capacity fiber network in an effort to entice new businesses.

State programs: Utah's Centers of Excellence Program funds viable research at the college and university level, bridging the gap between technological innovation and marketplace success. Since its creation in 1986 the program has resulted in thousands of new high-tech jobs and significant growth for many of the state's tech companies. In 2006 there were 2,000 tech jobs that had resulted from the CEP program. The Economic Development Corporation of Utah plays a dual role in the state's commercial success, promoting expansion of local companies as well as relocation for out-of-state firms. EDCUTAH offers a considerable network of public- and private-sector contacts, as well as support for site selection, media relations, and industry research. The Utah Small Business Development Center (USBDC) helps established and start-up companies prepare business plans, set sales goals, identify customers and the competition, analyze the market, and research financing sources. The USBDC operates in partnership with the U.S. Small Business Administration, the Utah Department of Community and Economic Development, and Salt Lake Community College. It offers training and resources in the areas of entrepreneurship, business development, the law, international business, financial management, e-commerce, and computer technology. The Salt Lake Chamber of Commerce represents businesses across the state, lobbying the government and providing networking opportunities to benefit its member companies.

Job training programs: The Small Business Development Center in Orem/Provo provides free personal consulting services and low-cost skill-based training to owners and managers of small businesses and to prospective entrepreneurs. State funding is also provided for Short Term Intensive Training programs across Utah. Training is offered at the state college level at a 66 percent discount to potential employers or employees. The program is customized to match full-time job seekers with the needs of specific companies.

Development Projects

One of the largest redevelopment projects Provo City has undertaken has been the Ironton Redevelopment Project. Plans for the 338-acre former Ironton Steel mill, abandoned since 1962, include the 200,000-square-foot Mountain Vista Business Park, the largest undeveloped tract of land in the area, owned by the city and available for rent. Environmental clean-up to remove contaminants from the coke and iron-making operations were underway in 2007 and the city had completed part of the construction of South Mountain Vista Parkway at Ironton.

In 2007 plans were announced for three new buildings downtown, to be located near the Wells Fargo Tower and tentatively occupied by an unnamed Fortune 100 company. The project, called University Towers, is slated to include both commercial and residential space. Highlights of the plan include a 10-story high-rise, new parking garage, and sky bridge between buildings.

Economic Development Information: Provo City Economic Development, 425 West Center St., Provo, UT 84603; telephone (801)852-6160

Commercial Shipping

Provo is served by the Union Pacific railroad, which offers second-morning service to the majority of the Western markets. The Provo area is served by approximately 40 major trucking lines. The expanding Provo Municipal Airport can serve and handle most aircraft and is equipped with an instrument-landing system and a weather-reporting capability. The nearby Salt Lake International Airport handled more than $148 million pounds of cargo in 2006.

Labor Force and Employment Outlook

The Provo-Orem area boasts low unemployment; favorable taxes; a young, educated, "internationally skilled" work force; and a growing population. Utah's labor market is made up of a large percentage of young people. The Provo work force not only has a high education level. Among its other qualities are foreign language ability, foreign service experience, and a strong work ethic; over 45 percent of Provo's work force is between 20 and 34 years old, while 35 percent of the population over 25 has a bachelor's degree or higher. Utah Valley remains one of the hottest high-tech areas in the nation, which continues to bring in entrepreneurs, big business, and new and higher-paying jobs.

In August 2007 the unemployment rate in Provo stood at 2.6 percent, well below the national average, and down from ten-year highs in 2002 that topped six percent. Between 1997 and 2007 the workforce in the Provo MSA grew from approximately 160,000 to over 220,000 workers. This steady influx of new workers, coupled with consistently low unemployment and the city's investment in the high-tech sector, indicated that Provo was on pace to continue its steady growth into the 2010s.

The following is a summary of data regarding the Provo-Orem metropolitan area labor force, 2006 annual averages.

Size of nonagricultural labor force: 180,300

Number of workers employed in...

construction and mining: 16,400
manufacturing: 18,700
trade, transportation and utilities: 29,200
information: 8,100
financial activities: 6,400
professional and business services: 22,100
educational and health services: 37,200
leisure and hospitality: 13,500
other services: 4,100
government: 24,600

Average hourly earnings of production workers employed in manufacturing: $12.85

Unemployment rate: 2.8% (June 2007)

Largest employers, Utah County (2002)	*Number of employees*
Brigham Young University	14,500
Alpine School District	6,213
IHC Health Care Services	3,650
Utah Valley State College	3,165
Nebo School District	2,371
Convergys	2,000
Provo School District	1,900
Nestle USA Food Group Inc.	1,899
Novell, Inc.	1,800
Modus Media International	1,200

Cost of Living

Overall cost of living in the Salt Lake City area, which includes Provo, ranks close to the national average.

The following is a summary of data regarding key cost of living factors for the Provo area.

2007 (1st quarter) ACCRA Average House Price: $310,631 (Salt Lake City metro)

2007 (1st quarter) ACCRA Cost of Living Index: 99.9 (Salt Lake City metro)

State income tax rate: 2.3% to 7.0%

State sales tax rate: 4.75%

Local income tax rate: None

Local sales tax rate: 6.25%

Property tax rate: Property tax assessment rate: .002787 applied to 55% of assessed value for residential property and 100% of assessed value for commercial property (2005)

Economic Information: The Provo Orem Chamber of Commerce, 51 South University Avenue, Suite 215, Provo, UT 84601; telephone (801)851-2555

■ Education and Research

Elementary and Secondary Schools

In addition to educating students from kindergarten to grade twelve, the Provo School District assists students in preschool and latch-key programs, as well as through programs for the physically challenged. In addition to the traditional schools, Provo has one school for children with physical and emotional challenges too severe for mainstreaming. For 18 percent of Provo students, English is their second language; Provo students speak 43 different languages, and the district offers a strong English for Speakers of Other Lanuages (ESOL) program. Scores on college entrance exams are above state and national averages. The system is home to several charter schools; one, the Walden School of Liberal Arts, was ranked the third-best high school in the state in 2007 by utahschools.org.

The following is a summary of data regarding the Provo City School District as of the 2005–2006 school year.

Total enrollment: 13,039

Number of facilities

elementary schools: 13
junior high/middle schools: 2
senior high schools: 3
other: 1

Student/teacher ratio: 20.9:1

Teacher salaries (2005–06)

elementary median: $37,870
junior high/middle median: Not available
secondary median: $44,730

Funding per pupil: $5,776

Because public education in the Utah Valley is highly regarded, there are few private schools. Among the private schools are Challenger School, a K-12 school based on a structured learning environment; Provo Canyon School, an alternative school; and several Montessori Schools.

Public Schools Information: Provo City School District, 280 West 940 North, Provo, UT 84604-3394; telephone (801)374-4800. Utah State Office of Edu-

cation, 250 East 500 South, Salt Lake City, UT 84111-4200; telephone (801)538-7500

Colleges and Universities

Brigham Young University (BYU) is located in the city at the base of the Wasatch Mountains. Founded in 1875 by Brigham Young, BYU is the largest private university in the United States. Owned by the Mormon Church, the university enrolled over 26,000 full-time day students in 2006. The vast majority of its students are members of the Church of the Latter Day Saints. Particularly notable are its business administration programs, broadcast journalism program, and law and engineering schools. The 2007 *U.S News and World Report* "America's Best Colleges" issue singled BYU out for several honors, including 70th in the category of "Best National Universities," 19th in the "Great Schools, Great Prices" category, and 12th for least student-incurred debt.

Utah Valley State College enrolled more than 23,000 students in fall 2006 and awards bachelor's degrees in accounting, behavioral science, biology, business management, business/marketing education, chemistry, computer science, early childhood and elementary education, environmental tech, criminal justice, integrated and paralegal studies, fire science, history, hospitality management, mathematics, nursing, information technology, and technology management. Other Provo institutions of higher learning include Provo College (with Schools of Healthcare, Business, Health & Wellness, Justice, and Design & Technology) and Stevens Henager College of Business, which train students in special and entry-level skills.

Libraries and Research Centers

The Provo City Library at Academy Square, opened in 2001, holds 176,496 volumes, 350 periodicals, and more than 10,000 records and audio tapes, video tapes, and compact discs. Its special collections center on Utah and Utah County history. Other libraries in the city include the Utah State Hospital's Patient Library and Brigham Young University's Harold B. Lee Library, which houses more than 3.5 million volumes and features special collections on linguistics, poetry, children's literature, Victorian literature, and oral history. The rapidly growing library serves well over three million patrons per year.

Provo has many research centers affiliated with Brigham Young University. They encompass such areas as engineering, computers, cancer, sociology, literature, thermodynamics, Western studies, communications, international studies, earth science, agriculture, psychology, religion, life science, anthropology, business, religion, and women's studies. BYU maintains an Office of Research and Creative Activities that apportions grants annually. The U.S. Forest Service has a Shrub Sciences Laboratory maintained in cooperation with Brigham Young University. Utah State University supports 16 undergraduate research projects each term, in addition to its faculty research. The University houses the Ross A. Smart Veterinary Diagnostic Laboratory, engaging in animal disease diagnosis.

Public Library Information: Provo City Library at Academy Square, 550 North University Ave., Provo, UT 84601; telephone (801)852-6650

■ Health Care

The Provo/Orem area is served by three major hospitals—Utah Valley Regional Medical Center (UVRMC) in Provo, Orem Community Hospital in Orem, and Timpanogos Regional Hospital in Orem. UVRMC is a 330-bed tertiary and acute care facility. Special features at UVRMC include magnetic resonance imaging and computerized tomographic scanning capabilities, laser technology, intensive care and coronary care units, the Newborn ICU and Cancer Services, Emergency and Trauma Services, Critical Care, Women's and Children's Services, and Behavioral Health. The majority of health care facilities in the area are run by Intermountain Health Care (IHC), the regional health care provider that operates UVRMC and Orem Community Hospital, in addition to nineteen other facilities. OCH specializes in same-day surgery and obstetrics. MountainStar Health Care operates Timpanogos Regional Hospital in Orem, built in 1999; services include open heart surgery, obstetrics, and a variety of health and wellness centers. Other IHC facilities in Provo are the Utah Valley Heart Center and the Utah Valley Rehabilitation Center. Surgical facilities in Provo include the Central Utah Surgical Center. Mental health care services are available at Utah State Hospital and Wasatch Mental Health Center.

■ Recreation

Sightseeing

The Provo/Orem area is one of the most scenic in the country. Visitors can view the breathtaking Bridal Veil Falls from the Provo Canyon floor. The falls can be seen from Highway 189, which curves alongside the Provo River up the beautiful Provo Canyon Scenic Byway. A turn onto the Alpine Loop Scenic Backway (Highway 92) goes past the Sundance Resort and the Timpanogos Cave National Monument. Located in American Fork Canyon, the cave is actually three highly decorated limestone caverns that can be observed on a 1.5-mile hike.

Built in 1972, Provo Latter Day Saints Temple is located on a hillside above the Brigham Young University campus. It is an architecturally striking building faced with white cast stone and topped with a segmented spire. The Provo Latter Day Saints Tabernacle is a historic structure built in 1898 that is still in active use, hosting many religious and cultural events.

The award-winning McCurdy Historical Doll Museum has more than 4,000 dolls, 47 miniature rooms, toys, and a toy shop. The Monte L. Bean Life Science Museum on the Brigham Young University campus contains a large collection of trophy animals and displays of animal habitats. The Brigham Young University Earth Science Museum features animals large and small from dinosaurs to ancient forms of sea life.

The Sundance Resort, 15 miles northeast of Provo, provides fine dining, a spa, plays, art workshops, and nature experiences throughout the summer in addition to excellent skiing in winter.

The Trafalga Family Fun Center in Orem contains a 400-foot waterslide, indoor and outdoor miniature golf courses, and a game room. Thanksgiving Point in nearby Lehi is a 700-acre oasis featuring restaurants, a visitor center and giftshop, a professional golf course, academy driving range, clubhouse, tennis ranch, animal farm, equestrian center, shopping village, North American Museum of Ancient Life, and acres and acres of awe-inspiring gardens. Recent additions to Thanksgiving Point are a dinner theater seating more than 1,000 and Electric Park for parties, reunions, and fairs.

Arts and Culture

Hundreds of cultural events are sponsored annually in Provo, including concerts, symposiums, plays, lectures, classes, art exhibits, and museum displays. The Museum of Art at Brigham Young University (BYU) is one of the largest of its kind in the intermountain West and houses an impressive permanent collection of fine art. The B. F. Larson Gallery at BYU exhibits works by contemporary artists. Fine art is on display at the Brownstone Gallery. The Springville Museum of Art in nearby Springville houses an extensive collection of the works of Utah artists, highlighted by the month-long National Art Exhibit in April.

The Sundance Institute, an arts community near Provo, fosters creativity in film and visual and performing arts, and presents arts events throughout the year, including children's theater.

The historic Latter Day Saints Tabernacle hosts a roster of internationally known performers as well as the Utah Valley Symphony, an 80-member community orchestra. Brigham Young University is a major source of music, dance, and drama events at its Harris Fine Arts Center. Utah Regional Ballet is the resident ballet company at Utah Valley State College in Orem. The Center Street Musical Theater presents dinner theater in downtown Provo. The Provo Theatre Company stages five to six musical, comedy, and dramatic productions from September through July.

Festivals and Holidays

Provo kicks off the New Year with its First Night community celebration of the arts in an alcohol-free setting. Utah Pioneer Days in May features the Miss Orem

Pageant. America's Freedom Festival in Provo on July 4 is the largest Independence Day celebration in the country. This grand three-week event begins with balloon festivals; gala balls; clogging competitions; 10K, 5K, and one mile runs; and explodes with an enormous parade and a "Stadium of Fire" concert and fireworks display. More than 700 folkdancers from many countries gather at the Springville World Folkfest in July for the largest event of its kind in the country. From May through September, many cities in Utah County hold individual city festivals. WinterFest in downtown Provo during the month of December celebrates the holiday season with concerts, a parade, living nativity, decorated storefronts and a "Lights On" celebration.

Sports for the Spectator

Brigham Young University's (BYU) basketball team plays its games throughout the winter at the 23,000-seat Marriott Center arena. The BYU Cougars hold home football games at their 65,000-seat stadium on campus. The Utah Valley State Wolverines play basketball at the McKay Events Center in Orem. Some of the other sports presented at BYU and Utah Valley State College are basketball, baseball, track, volleyball, gymnastics, rugby, wrestling, and swimming.

Sports for the Participant

The city of Provo has ten golf courses, 37 public tennis courts, 32 public parks, five softball complexes, and two ice rinks. The city maintains a rifle and pistol shooting range year-round for public use. Within an hour's drive from Provo are 7 downhill ski resorts, including Park City and Snowbird. Sundance Resort, which offers mountain biking trails as well as skiing, is 20 minutes from the city of Provo Canyon. Nearby Utah Lake State Park and Deer Creek Reservoir in Heber Valley provide water skiing, fishing, boating, camping, canoeing, and other water sports, in addition to being popular spots for hiking. Fly-fishing in the Provo River is popular, and hunting of elk, deer, moose, and bighorn sheep is also possible. Maps and trail guides to the area can be obtained at the U.S. Forest Service's main office in Provo. Climbers have access to both indoor and outdoor ropes courses at the CLAS (Challenging Leadership Adventure Systems, Inc.) Ropes Course facility. The High Uintas Mountain Range is a challenge for climbers and home to the highest Boy Scout Camp in the country.

Seven Peaks Resort, located at the foot of Maple Mountain in Provo, is a waterpark with a variety of water amusements including the world's tallest water slides, a wave pool, and children's activity areas. The park's acres of lush lawns and pavilions make it a favorite site for picnics and parties. Thanksgiving Point in nearby Lehi is a 700-acre oasis featuring a variety of outdoor activities.

Shopping and Dining

Provo boasts two newer malls: the modern Provo Towne Center and The Shops at Riverwoods. Provo Town Center Mall is anchored by Dillard's, JCPenney, and Sears department stores. The Shops at Riverwoods features modern, upscale shops in a nostalgic Main Street USA setting. Provo Town Square is a specialty theme mall in the heart of the city. All the buildings are restored historic structures housing restaurants, shops, and entertainment facilities. Provo University Parkway has recently developed into a major shopping area with large department stores and small specialty shops. University Mall in the University Parkway corridor in Orem contains 185 stores and restaurants.

The city of Provo has more than 200 eating places. The Provo/Orem area hosts a variety of ethnic restaurants including American, Chinese, Japanese, Indian, Italian, and Mexican establishments. Vegetarian fare, bars/nightclubs, and fast foods of all kinds are also popular. Allie's American Grill at the Provo Marriott, Los Hermanos, and Magelby's are local favorites for dining. At Sundance Resort, The Tree Room offers elegant dining by candlelight; the Foundry Grill Room features lighter, bistro-style dining; and the Owl Bar offers spirits, local brews, and a bistro-style menu for the benefit of private club members (temporary memberships are available); all rooms are known for their exceptional fare.

Visitor Information: The Utah County Convention & Visitors Bureau, 111 S. University Ave., Provo, UT 84601; telephone (801)851-2100

■ Convention Facilities

The cities of Provo and Orem have two major conference facilities and one special events center. The Provo Marriott Hotel and Conference Center has 21 meeting rooms for a total of more than 28,000 square feet, and 330 sleeping rooms, including more than 100 suites. The Brigham Young University Conference Center is a full-service facility featuring 34 conference rooms. It can be scheduled for programs that are consistent with BYU's educational mission and is a smoke- and alcohol-free facility.

Provo hotels with conference facilities are: Best Western CottonTree Inn, Courtyard by Marriott, Hampton Inn, and Holiday Inn. Other nearby hotel conference facilities are located in Orem, American Fork, and Payson.

In addition to the conference centers, the Provo area offers many options for hosting large groups, including the Provo City Library at Academy Square, Historic County Courthouse, Springville Museum of Art, Thanksgiving Point, Alpine Art Center, and Scera Theater in Orem, among others.

The David O. McKay Events Center at Utah Valley State College features an 8,500-seat arena, four multi-purpose athletic courts of 5,000 square feet each, two 2,500-square-foot meeting spaces, four concession stands, six locker rooms, in-house catering, full equipment rental, and ticketing services. Sundance Resort's facilities include more than 11,000 square feet of meeting space and 102 sleeping units in a rustic, alpine atmosphere. The fairground facilities at Spanish Fork include a 7,000-seat main arena, plus two additional arenas totaling more than 60,000 square feet.

Convention Information: The Utah County Convention & Visitors Bureau, 111 S. University Ave., Provo, UT 84601; telephone (801)851-2100

■ Transportation

Approaching the City

Provo/Orem is intersected by U.S. Highways 50, 89, 91, and 189, as well as by Interstate 15. Provo is located within an hour's drive of Salt Lake International Airport, which offers over 900 daily flights on 15 airlines. In 2006 the airport served 21.5 million customers as the 22nd busiest airport in the United States. Bus service to the city is also available.

Traveling in the City

The Utah Transit Authority provides daily mass transit service to both the Provo/Orem and Salt Lake City metropolitan areas. It offers complete routes serving all of the major business areas in Provo. The metropolitan area is served by one taxi company.

■ Communications

Newspapers and Magazines

The Daily Herald is Provo's daily newspaper. The *Daily Universe* newspaper is published by the students at Brigham Young University. Magazines published in Provo include *BYU Studies, BYU Magazine, Al-Arabiyya* (a scholarly journal for Arabic language teachers), *The Western North American Naturalist,* and *Scandinavian Studies.*

Television and Radio

Provo has five AM and FM radio stations that encompass religion, music, talk, and public broadcasting, and three television stations, including one that broadcasts from the campus of Brigham Young University.

Media Information: The Daily Herald, 1555 North Freedom Blvd., PO Box 717, Provo, UT 84603; telephone (801)375-5050; toll-free (800)880-8075.

Provo Online

City of Provo home page. Available www.provo.org

The Daily Herald. Available www.harktheherald .com

Provo City Economic Development. Available www .provo.org/econdev.econdev_main.html

Provo City Library. Available www.provo.lib.ut.us

Provo City School District. Available www.provo .edu

Provo Orem Chamber of Commerce. Available www.thechamber.org

Utah County Convention & Visitors Bureau. Available www.utahvalley.org/p_home.asp

Utah State Office of Education. Available www.usoe .k12.ut.us

BIBLIOGRAPHY

Smoot, L. Douglas, *The Miracle at Academy Square* (Provo, UT: Brigham Young University Press, 2003)

Salt Lake City

■ The City in Brief

Founded: 1847 (incorporated 1851)

Head Official: Mayor Ralph Becker (D) (since 2007)

City Population
> 1980: 163,033
> 1990: 159,928
> 2000: 181,743
> 2006 estimate: 178,858
> Percent change, 1990–2000: 13.6%
> U.S. rank in 1980: 90th
> U.S. rank in 1990: 108th
> U.S. rank in 2000: 129th

Metropolitan Area Population
> 1980: 910,000
> 1990: 1,072,227
> 2000: 1,333,914
> 2006 estimate: 1,067,722
> Percent change, 1990–2000: 24.4%
> U.S. rank in 1980: 41st
> U.S. rank in 1990: 38th
> U.S. rank in 2000: 35th

Area: 109 square miles (2000)

Elevation: 4,330 feet above sea level

Average Annual Temperatures: January, 29.2° F; July, 77.0° F; annual average, 52.0° F

Average Annual Precipitation: 16.50 inches of rain; 58.5 inches of snow

Major Economic Sectors: services, wholesale and retail trade, government

Unemployment Rate: 2.8% (June 2007)

Per Capita Income: $23,286 (2005)

2005 FBI Crime Index Property: 15,859

2005 FBI Crime Index Violent: 1,283

Major Colleges and Universities: University of Utah, Westminster College, Salt Lake Community College-South City Campus, LDS Business College

Daily Newspaper: *The Salt Lake Tribune; Deseret News*

■ Introduction

Salt Lake City is the state capital and largest city in Utah. Founded in 1847 by religious leader Brigham Young, the city is the world headquarters of the Church of Jesus Christ of Latter-day Saints (Mormons). From its early days as a mining and railroad town, Salt Lake City has emerged as the commercial and cultural hub for a large area of the western mountain region. The city played host to the 2002 Winter Olympics, which proved to be an economic boon to the area and raised the international profile of the city. The nearby mountains, historical and religious landmarks, and the uniqueness of the Great Salt Lake also make the city a prominent tourist attraction.

■ Geography and Climate

Salt Lake City is bounded on three sides by mountain ranges and on the northwest by the Great Salt Lake. The Jordan River flows just to the west of the downtown district. Mountains shield the city from much of the severe winter weather common to the area, and the lake also serves to moderate the temperatures. Summer days are typically hot and dry, with cool nights and little precipitation. The winters are cold but not severe, with snow remaining on the ground through most of the season.

Spring, especially in March, is the season of heavy rain and high winds from Pacific storms.

Area: 109 square miles (2000)

Elevation: 4,330 feet above sea level

Average Temperatures: January, 29.2° F; July, 77.0° F; annual average, 52.0° F

Average Annual Precipitation: 16.50 inches of rain; 58.5 inches of snow

■ History

European Explorers Replace Native Americans

For thousands of years, the inhabitants of the northern Utah region were hunter-gatherers. Artifacts dating as far back as 12,000 years have been found in caves near the Great Salt Lake. About 500 B.C. the Fremont tribe, a less nomadic, agricultural society, settled in the area, building impressive cliff dwellings and drawing elaborate rock paintings, many of which can still be viewed today. Changing environmental conditions eventually made primitive farming impossible, and by the twelfth century, the area was populated mainly by the Ute, Paiute, and Shoshone tribes of nomadic hunters.

The first Europeans to travel through the area were the Spanish, coming from New Mexico in search of a direct route to Monterey, California, in 1776. In the early 1800s, fur trappers and "mountain men" explored the region, discovering the Great Salt Lake and mapping the mountain passes. A number of government expeditions explored the area, and a steady stream of settlers bound for California began to pass through.

Mormons Settle, Lay Out Town; Religious Beliefs Questioned

A group of Mormon pioneers led by Brigham Young settled in the Salt Lake Valley in 1847, laying out a town they called Great Salt Lake City. From the beginning the city was well planned, with a grid of ten-acre plots separated by streets 132 feet wide. The industrious settlers began planting crops and developing intricate irrigation systems, eventually forming more than 500 settlements in the Utah area. Disaster was averted in 1848 when, as drought and plagues of insects threatened the crops, flocks of seagulls arrived to consume the insects, thereby saving the harvest.

In 1848 the settlers organized the State of Deseret and applied for statehood with a government headed by the Mormon Church. Congress denied the petition and instead created Utah Territory in 1850. Salt Lake City was incorporated in 1851, and in 1856 it replaced Fillmore as the territorial capital. Misunderstandings about Mormon religious beliefs and political outrage at the Mormon practice of polygamy led to the so-called "Utah War" in 1857 between the Mormon settlers and the U.S. government. Although the dispute was settled peacefully in 1858, relations between the church and the territorial government were strained for many years.

City Becomes State Capital; Regional Mines, Industry Thrive

The two ends of the transcontinental railroad met just 40 miles north of Salt Lake City in 1869, tying Utah with the outside world. Over the next 20 years, hundreds of copper, silver, and lead mines were developed in the region, bringing a large number of non-Mormon settlers. Under continued pressure, the practice of polygamy was officially stopped by the church in 1890. This paved the way for women's suffrage in Utah, which had been a political lever in the national polygamy debate. The majestic Mormon Temple, begun in 1853, was completed in 1892, and Utah entered the Union in 1896 as the third suffrage state, with Salt Lake City as the capital.

During the early twentieth century Salt Lake City assumed the look of a modern city. The State Capitol building and a number of other impressive structures were built, electric trolley cars began service on the city's streets, and large residential sections developed around the city. Like most cities, Salt Lake City suffered during the Great Depression, but prosperity returned during World War II amidst a construction boom and increased demand for metals. Industrial expansion continued postwar with downtown development and beautification projects becoming a focus in the 1970s and 1980s.

In 2002 Salt Lake City hosted the "best attended" Olympic Winter Games in history, with 1.6 billion tickets sold and another 4 billion television viewers. The city continues to reap the benefits of improved infrastructure and a significant increase in tourism, and in 2007 was experiencing a post-Olympic downtown building boom.

In recent years Salt Lake City has been consistently recognized for its prosperity and quality of life. In 2006 *Fortune* magazine ranked the state fourth-best in America for business, and it is recognized annually on lists of the healthiest cities.

Historical Information: Utah State Historical Society Library, 300 South Rio Grande Street, Salt Lake City, UT 84101; telephone (801)533-3500; fax (801)533-3503

■ Population Profile

Metropolitan Area Residents

    1980: 910,000
    1990: 1,072,227
    2000: 1,333,914
    2006 estimate: 1,067,722

©Joseph Sohm; ChromoSohm Inc./Corbis.

Percent change, 1990–2000: 24.4%
U.S. rank in 1980: 41st
U.S. rank in 1990: 38th
U.S. rank in 2000: 35th

City Residents

1980: 163,033
1990: 159,928
2000: 181,743
2006 estimate: 178,858
Percent change, 1990–2000: 13.6%
U.S. rank in 1980: 90th
U.S. rank in 1990: 108th
U.S. rank in 2000: 129th

Density: 1,666.1 people per square mile (2000)

Racial and ethnic characteristics (2005)

White: 142,877
Black: 5,413
American Indian and Alaska Native: 2,636
Asian: 7,235
Native Hawaiian and Pacific Islander: 1,388
Hispanic or Latino (may be of any race): 41,745
Other: 20,245

Percent of residents born in state: 49.1%
(2000)

Age characteristics (2005)

Population under 5 years old: 16,278
Population 5 to 9 years old: 11,097
Population 10 to 14 years old: 9,206
Population 15 to 19 years old: 8,842
Population 20 to 24 years old: 18,932
Population 25 to 34 years old: 41,400
Population 35 to 44 years old: 23,557
Population 45 to 54 years old: 18,880
Population 55 to 59 years old: 9,986
Population 60 to 64 years old: 5,472
Population 65 to 74 years old: 9,237
Population 75 to 84 years old: 7,090
Population 85 years and older: 2,693
Median age: 30.8 years

Births (2006, MSA)

Total number: 19,213

Deaths (2006, MSA)

Total number: 5,866

Money income (2005)

Per capita income: $23,286
Median household income: $37,287
Total households: 75,028

Number of households with income of...

less than $10,000: 7,907
$10,000 to $14,999: 5,283
$15,000 to $24,999: 11,379
$25,000 to $34,999: 10,550
$35,000 to $49,999: 13,193
$50,000 to $74,999: 13,002
$75,000 to $99,999: 4,241
$100,000 to $149,999: 5,892
$150,000 to $199,999: 1,969
$200,000 or more: 1,612

Percent of families below poverty level: 9.4% (2005)

2005 FBI Crime Index Property: 15,859

2005 FBI Crime Index Violent: 1,283

■ Municipal Government

Salt Lake City has a council-mayor form of government with the mayor elected at large. The mayor and seven council members serve four-year terms. The city is also the seat of Salt Lake County and the capital of Utah.

Head Official: Mayor Ralph Becker (D) (since 2007; current term expires 2011)

Total Number of City Employees: 3,000 (2007)

City Information: Salt Lake City Corporation, 451 South State Street, Salt Lake City, UT 84111; telephone (801)535-6333

■ Economy

Major Industries and Commercial Activity

Salt Lake City was originally a farming community; it also depended on mining until the early 1980s when foreign competition began to erode profits from that industry. Today it has grown into a diverse economic region. As the state capital, county seat of Salt Lake County, and the largest city in the four-county Wasatch Front metropolitan area, the city is a government, commercial, and industrial center for Utah and much of the Intermountain West.

The service sector produces the most jobs in the city, especially computer and health care services. Government employment is considerable, with the State of Utah, University of Utah, and Salt Lake County among the city's top employers. A number of national financial institutions have established branch offices in Salt Lake City, making it the center of banking and finance for the region; there are 56 financial organizations in the county, employing over 20,000 workers. The city boasts a lower-than-the-national average cost of doing business. Manufacturing is the third-largest industry in the area, with over 51,000 workers. Salt Lake City is the largest retail and wholesale market in Utah. The construction industry remains significant, and bioscience is a growing sector, with over 300 firms in the Salt Lake City area. The city supports a thriving tourism industry, especially in the wake of the 2002 Olympics, which brought in over $2 billion dollars of directly related spending; the industry continues to benefit from the city's increased international profile. Salt Lake City is the international headquarters of the Church of Jesus Christ of Latter-day Saints.

Items and goods produced: petroleum products, electronics, missiles, pharmaceuticals, medical products

Incentive Programs—New and Existing Companies

Local programs: The Salt Lake County Office of Business Economic Development offers incentives to new and existing companies in the form of loans, grants, and on-the-job training. Most incentives are targeted toward the unincorporated areas of the county. It also provides no-cost monthly workshops. The Salt Lake City Department of Economic Development offers similar incentives as well as assistance with site selection, financial planning, and permit applications.

State programs: Utah's Centers of Excellence Program funds viable research at the college and university level, bridging the gap between technological innovation and marketplace success. Since its creation in 1986 the program has resulted in thousands of new high-tech jobs and significant growth for many of the state's tech companies. In 2006 there were 2,000 tech jobs that had resulted from the CEP program. The Economic Development Corporation of Utah plays a dual role in the state's commercial success, promoting expansion of local companies as well as relocation for out-of-state firms. EDCUTAH offers a considerable network of public- and private-sector contacts, as well as support for site selection, media relations, and industry research. The Utah Small Business Development Center (USBDC) helps established and start-up companies prepare business plans, set sales goals, identify customers and the competition, analyze the market, and research financing sources. The USBDC operates in partnership with the U.S. Small Business Administration, the Utah Department of Community and Economic Development, and Salt Lake Community College. It offers training and resources in the areas of entrepreneurship, business development, the law, international business, financial management, e-commerce, and computer technology. The Salt Lake Chamber of Commerce represents businesses across the state, lobbying the government and providing networking opportunities to benefit its member companies.

Job training programs: Custom Fit is an employee training program offered through the Utah College of Applied Technology, state colleges, and the local business community. It provides training in specific technologies, computer skills, safety certification, leadership, management and team-building. The Utah State Legislature allocates annual funding to Custom Fit, covering a substantial portion of the cost to employers.

State funding is also provided for Short Term Intensive Training programs across Utah. Training is offered at the state college level at a 66 percent discount to potential employers or employees. The program is customized to match full-time job seekers with the needs of specific companies.

Development Projects

In 2007 it was estimated that total investment in downtown Salt Lake City would exceed $1.5 billion by 2012, representing the most concentrated period of investment in Salt Lake City's history, according to the city's Downtown Alliance.

Among the new constructions expected to be complete by the end of 2007 was Intermountain Health Care's $362 million, 468-bed flagship hospital in the Salt Lake Valley. A commuter railway from Weber County to downtown Salt Lake City, run by the Utah Transit Authority, was expected to open in 2008. The Salt Palace Convention Center completed its latest expansion in 2006. City Creek Center, a major office and residential development on twenty acres in downtown Salt Lake City, was expected to be finished by 2012. The new Frank E. Moss Courthouse, covering 367,188 square feet, was expected to open in 2011. A new light rail line stemming from the Intermodal Hub began construction in 2006 and was slated to begin service by fall 2008.

Other projects in the planning phase or under construction include the Marmalade, a $47 million commercial and residential development; Gateway Olympic Plaza, a $10 million dollar commercial and retail center; and The Leonardo, an arts, culture, and science center co-sponsored by Global Artways, the Center for Documentary Arts, and the Utah Science Center.

Economic Development Information: Economic Development Corporation of Utah, 201 South Main Street, Suite 2010, Salt Lake City, UT 84111; telephone (801)328-8824; fax (801)531-1460. Salt Lake Chamber and Downtown Alliance, 175 East 400 South, Suite 600, Salt Lake City, Utah 84111; telephone (801) 328-5073; fax (801)328-5093; email downtownrising@saltlakechamber.org

Commercial Shipping

Utah's free port law makes it an ideal location for the import and export of goods. Salt Lake City is a full-service customs port city with a foreign trade zone. The Salt Lake International Airport handled more than $148 million pounds of cargo in 2006.

Southern Pacific and Union Pacific railways offer freight service throughout Utah. The state's railroad lines all converge in the Salt Lake-Ogden area, making it a convenient interline switching route for destinations across the country. About 2,000 interstate and intrastate motor freight carriers operate in Utah.

Major distribution operations in Salt Lake County include RC Willey Furnishings, Nicholas & Company, Inc., Costco Western Distribution Center, and Schiff Nutrition International, Inc.

Labor Force and Employment Outlook

The services sector is Salt Lake City's largest employment division, with over a thousand new jobs added on average each year. Health care and computer technology are two dominant subsections. Construction remains important to the local economy, especially in the midst of the downtown building boom. Trade employment also remains high.

In 2007 the unemployment rate in Salt Lake City stood at 2.8 percent, well below the national average and down dramatically from its 10-year high in 2002 of over six percent unemployment. Between 1997 and 2007 the labor force grew by nearly 100,000 workers. Analysts expected steady growth and employment to continue, thanks to an influx of capital investment in downtown Salt Lake City and a diversified economy.

The following is a summary of data regarding the Salt Lake City metropolitan area labor force, 2006 annual averages.

Size of nonagricultural labor force: 614,700

Number of workers employed in...

construction and mining: 44,900
manufacturing: 55,300
trade, transportation and utilities: 126,500
information: 18,900
financial activities: 48,900
professional and business services: 98,100
educational and health services: 56,600
leisure and hospitality: 54,700
other services: 19,100
government: 91,700

Average hourly earnings of production workers employed in manufacturing: $16.13

Unemployment rate: 2.8% (June 2007)

Largest employers (2006)	*Number of employees*
University of Utah	15,000-19,999
State of Utah	10,000-14,999
Intermountain Health Care	10,000-14,999
Granite School District	7,000-9,999
Jordan School District	7,000-9,999
Salt Lake County	5,000-6,999
Wal-Mart	3,000-3,999
Discover Financial Services Inc.	3,000-3,999
Delta Airlines	3,000-3,999
U.S. Post Office	3,000-3,999

Cost of Living

Overall cost of living in the Salt Lake City area ranks close to the national average.

The following is a summary of data regarding several key cost of living factors for the Salt Lake City area.

2007 (1st quarter) ACCRA Average House Price: $310,631

2007 (1st quarter) ACCRA Cost of Living Index: 99.9

State income tax rate: 2.3% to 7.0%

State sales tax rate: 4.75%

Local income tax rate: None

Local sales tax rate: 6.6%

Property tax rate: Levied at the state and local level, based on assessed valuation; rate in 2005, .015288%

Economic Information: Economic Development Corporation of Utah, 201 South Main Street, Suite 2010, Salt Lake City, UT 84111; telephone (801)328-8824; fax (801)531-1460. Governor's Office of Planning and Budget, Demographic and Economic Analysis, 116 State Capitol, Salt Lake City, UT 84114; telephone (801)538-1036; fax (801)538-1547. Utah Department of Workforce Services, PO Box 45249, Salt Lake City, UT 84145-0249; telephone (801)526-9675; fax (801)526-9211; email dwscontactus@utah.gov. Bureau of Economic and Business Research, University of Utah, David Eccles School of Business, 1645 E Campus Center Dr., Rm 401, Salt Lake City, UT 84112-9302; telephone (801)581-6333; fax (801)581-3354; email bureau@business.utah.edu

■ Education and Research

Elementary and Secondary Schools

The Salt Lake City School District is sixth-largest in Utah, serving approximately 24,000 total students from diverse socioeconomic backgrounds. Its stated mission is to advocate for all students, provide education of the highest quality, and prepare students for opportunities in the future. In 2004 the Board of Education instituted a five-year "Student Achievement Plan," which was to be evaluated in 2009; a key component of the program is school choice. The district operates several charter, magnet, and alternative schools. New options for the 2006-7 school year included Salt Lake School for the Performing Arts, the Health Professions Academy, and Open Classroom Expansion.

The following is a summary of data regarding the Salt Lake City School District as of the 2005–2006 school year.

Total enrollment: 23,595

Number of facilities

elementary schools: 27
junior high/middle schools: 5
senior high schools: 4
other: 4

Student/teacher ratio: 20.8:1

Teacher salaries (2005–06)

elementary median: $42,620
junior high/middle median: $48,730
secondary median: $47,970

Funding per pupil: $5,822

Public Schools Information: Salt Lake City School District, 440 East 100 South, Salt Lake City, Utah 84111-1891; telephone (801)578-8599; fax (801)578-8248. Utah State Office of Education, 250 East 500 South, PO Box 144200, Salt Lake City, UT 84114-4200; telephone (801)538-7500

Colleges and Universities

Salt Lake City is home to the University of Utah, the oldest university in the West. Founded in 1850, the university covers more than 1,000 acres and includes the Red Butte Garden and Arboretum. One of the country's top 30 public research universities, the University of Utah is known for its technology transfer program to move research into practical applications in the business world; it also has a medical school. In fall 2006 the University's enrollment stood at 24,558, and there are over 2,000 graduate degrees awarded each year. The College of Social and Behavioral Sciences has the largest total enrollment of the University's 16 different academic divisions, and Economics, Political Science, Mass Communication, Psychology and Sociology are the most popular concentrations.

Salt Lake City is also home to prestigious Westminster College, a private non-denominational institution founded in 1875, offering 24 undergraduate majors and a range of post-graduate degree and certificate programs. It enrolls approximately 2,000 students each year in its four colleges: the School of Arts and Sciences, Bill and Vieve Gore School of Business, School of Education, and the School of Nursing and Health Sciences. Other local colleges include the Salt Lake Community College and LDS Business College. Adult education is available through the Salt Lake City campus of the University of Phoenix.

Libraries and Research Centers

The Salt Lake City Public Library System consists of a main library and 5 branch locations, with a total of more than 750,000 volumes and 600 periodical subscriptions, as well as films, audio tapes, maps, and art reproductions. The library also contains special collections of old and rare material from the region's past. A new Main Library was unveiled in 2003, featuring a six-story curving, climbable wall, spiraling fireplaces, a multi-level reading area and a rooftop garden. The 240,000-square-foot space is double the size of the previous library, and houses over 500,000 volumes. Several other branches were also remodeled or expanded in 2003.

The Salt Lake County Library System consists of a main library and 18 branches offering a variety of exhibits, events and collections. Salt Lake City is also home to the Utah State Library Program for the Blind and Disabled, which serves visually impaired, physically disabled, and reading disabled patrons across the western states with Braille books, books on cassette, and large-print books. The University of Utah maintains a large library system. A number of private, research, and special interest libraries also serve the city.

The Church of Jesus Christ of Latter-Day Saints Library houses a genealogical library, considered to be the largest of its kind in the world. Open to the public free of charge, the collection contains family history, local history, and vital records. The library is visited by approximately 1,900 patrons each day.

Centers in the Salt Lake City area conduct research activities in such fields as the environment, entomology, engineering design, biomedical engineering, toxicology, lasers, radiobiology, occupational and environmental health, astrophysics, astronomy, communications, nuclear engineering, physical electronics, remote sensing and cartography, mineral technology, isotope geology, seismology, mining, business and economics, finance, public affairs, politics, energy law, gerontology, the American West, the Middle East, and archaeology.

Public Library Information: Salt Lake City Public Library, 210 East 400 South, Salt Lake City, UT 84111; telephone (801)524-8200. Salt Lake County Library System, 2197 Fort Union Blvd, Salt Lake City, UT 84121-3139; telephone (801)943-4636; fax (801)942-6323

■ Health Care

Utah boasts some of the healthiest people in the country. In 2006 the state was ranked sixth-healthiest in the U.S. by the United Health Foundation. Utah has the lowest smoking rate in the nation (the only state with a smoking rate under 10 percent), and also records some of the lowest cancer, heart disease, and infant mortality rates.

A major focus for health care in Salt Lake City is the University Health Services Center, the teaching and research hospital for the University of Utah Medical School. The system consists of 850 physicians and health-care professionals, inpatient and outpatient services, same-day surgery, a 90-bed psychiatric hospital, and 24-hour assessment and referral services. In 2006 University Health Services Center was named to the *U.S. News & World Report* list of "America's Best Hospitals" for the thirteenth time. In 2005 the hospital was named to Solucient's list of the "One Hundred Most Improved Hospitals." Intermountain Health Care is a non-profit organization based in Salt Lake City. It includes 21 hospitals and has a mandate to provide quality care regardless of a patients' abilities to pay. In 2006 *Information Week* ranked Intermountain Healthcare as one of the nation's top 50 innovative users of information technology; in that same year, *Verispan* and *Modern Healthcare* ranked Intermountain Healthcare second in the nation in a study of more than 550 integrated health systems. It has been cited as an example of a well-run hospital system on ABC News and in *Newsweek*. The Intermountain Shriners Hospital for Children provides no-cost care and services for children with disorders of the bones, muscles and joints.

■ Recreation

Sightseeing

Downtown Salt Lake City boasts a number of popular attractions. The State Capitol with its spectacular copper-clad dome is located on Capitol Hill, which offers a view of the city and surrounding area. At Temple Square, the headquarters of the Mormon Church, the Salt Lake Temple displays six spires, 15-foot-thick granite walls, and a golden statue of the Angel Moroni. Also on the square are the famous Mormon Tabernacle, built in 1867 with no interior supports, and the Seagull Monument, honoring the birds that saved the settlers' first crops.

Other sights in the city include Beehive House, the restored residence of Brigham Young, who gave it the name because he wanted his followers to be as industrious as bees. Fort Douglas, a 9,000-acre historical fort, is filled with interesting military architecture dating from 1862. Utah's Hogle Zoo contains a collection of exotic birds and animals in a natural setting, including an elephant habitat and an Asian Highlands exhibit. This Is The Place Heritage Park contains an operational pioneer community as it was in 1847, as well as the "This Is The Place" Monument, marking the spot where Brigham Young chose the area as a home for the Mormons.

The Great Salt Lake, over 90 miles long and 48 miles wide, is the second most salty body of water in the world. The high salinity makes it a unique swimming experience: it is almost impossible for a person to sink in the water. A different type of aquatic entertainment is found at Raging Waters, a family-oriented theme park with more than 30 different water rides and a picnic area. Clark Planetarium presents daily star shows and images from the Hubble Telescope. Olympic Cauldron Park is a stunning addition to the city, featuring the 72-foot Olympic Cauldron, which housed the Olympic Flame; the Hoberman Arch, where athletes stood to receive their medals; a visitor center; and a theatre dedicated to the memory of the 2002 Olympic Winter Games.

Arts and Culture

Salt Lake City is home to a number of acclaimed cultural organizations. The world-famous Mormon Tabernacle Choir, an American institution for many years, is based in Salt Lake City. The Utah Symphony performs over 260 concerts nationally and internationally each year; the orchestra performs locally in Maurice Abravanel Hall, a world-class acoustic space. The historic Capitol Theatre is home to the Utah Opera and Ballet West, one of the nation's leading companies. The Rose Wagner Performing Arts Center includes an art gallery and several performance spaces for new and established artists.

Theatrical performances are scheduled at Desert Star Playhouse, featuring live musical comedy melodrama, honky-tonk piano, and audience participation; Hale Center Theater, offering comedies and musicals for the whole family to enjoy; Off Broadway Theatre, staging comedy and improvisation; Promised Valley Playhouse, presenting theater in a restored turn-of-the-century showplace; and Salt Lake Community College Grand Theatre, featuring Broadway musicals.

Several interesting museums are located in Salt Lake City. The Daughters of the Utah Pioneers Museum houses a collection of dolls, textiles, and frontier furniture in a replica of the famous Salt Palace. Located in a restored nineteenth century railroad station, the Utah Historical Society features exhibits on the history of Utah's various ethnic groups. The Fort Douglas Military Museum inside the restored fort displays items relating to the military history of the state. Hill Air Force Base Aerospace Museum maintains a collection of military aircraft, missiles, vehicles and uniforms. The Utah Museum of Natural History contains a large collection of dinosaur skeletons excavated from many local sites, as well as exhibits on animals and minerals of the region.

The Salt Lake Art Center houses traveling art exhibits from around the world as well as a permanent collection and a sculpture garden. On the campus of the University of Utah, the Utah Museum of Fine Arts contains paintings by artists such as Rubens, antique tapestries, and Louis XIV furniture. The Museum of Church History and Art chronicles the early development of the Church of Jesus Christ of Latter-day Saints. The Chase Home Museum of Utah Folk Arts is dedicated to the work of Utah's ethnic, native, and rural artists.

Festivals and Holidays

The Utah Arts Festival, the nation's first statewide arts festival, takes place in June and provides exciting performances and visual art, crafts, and ethnic foods. June is also the time for the prestigious Gina Bachauer International Piano Foundation Festival and Competition. In 2006, the American West Heritage Center inaugurated the reformatted Festivals of the American West, a change from the previous format of a single, large festival held each year in August to several smaller festivals held throughout the year. These include Baby Animal Days, Spirit of '47 Pioneer Jubilee, Tellabration!, and Frontier Christmas. Pioneer Harvest Days happens every September in Pioneer Trail State Park, featuring authentic examples of historic craftwork, including butter making, weaving, blacksmithing, adobe brick making, and pioneer games. September is a busy month in Salt Lake City, with the Salt Lake City Jazz Festival and the Utah State Fair, which features midway rides, livestock and art exhibits, and special entertainment nightly. The Christmas season begins the day after Thanksgiving, when more than 300,000 lights are turned on in Temple Square. The Sundance Film Festival takes place in the Salt Lake area every January. The Madeleine Festival takes place at the Cathedral of the Madeleine each spring, offering free cultural performances to the community. The annual Great Salt Lake Bird Festival takes place in May, as well as Living Traditions, a three-day festival honoring folk artists of the Salt Lake Valley.

Sports for the Spectator

Salt Lake City is home to one professional basketball team: the NBA's Utah Jazz, which plays in the $90 million, state-of-the-art EnergySolutions Arena. Hockey is represented by the Utah Grizzlies, who are an affiliate of the New York Islanders. The Salt Lake Bees, a Triple A affiliate of the Anaheim Angels, play baseball at Franklin Covey Field from April through mid-September. The University of Utah fields competitive teams in most major collegiate sports. Salt Lake City is also host to Major League Soccer's Real Salt Lake, the Utah Blaze arena football team, and a number of rodeo events on the national rodeo circuit. The nearby Bonneville Salt Flats is the site of numerous auto races and frequent attempts to set the land speed record.

Sports for the Participant

The Salt Lake City area offers an abundance of outdoor activities. The nearby mountains provide year-round recreation: hiking, fishing, camping, and winter skiing. Some of the nation's most popular ski resorts such as Snowbird, Park City, Deer Valley, Sundance, Alta, and Solitude are within a 40-minute drive of the city. Non-traditional sports such as ski-jumping and luge are offered at new facilities constructed for the 2002 Olympic Winter Games. The area's rivers offer white-water rafting, canoeing, and innertubing. Many area lakes are ideal spots for all forms of water activity—boating, sailing, water skiing, and swimming.

Gallivan Utah Center Plaza, a four-acre public plaza in downtown Salt Lake, has a skating rink. Salt Lake City operates a number of parks that feature swimming pools, jogging trails, playing fields, tennis courts, and other recreational facilities. Several championship-grade golf courses are located in the city as well.

Shopping and Dining

America's first department store, the Zions Cooperative Mercantile Institution, opened in Salt Lake City in 1868 and continues to operate today in ZCMI Center Mall. A number of major shopping centers are located in the city, including Crossroads Plaza and Trolley Square, a theme mall located in a group of restored trolley barns. The Gateway, Salt Lake's only open-air entertainment, dining, and shopping venue, was completed in 2001. Set on thirty acres, it features 90 shops and restaurants, a restored 1908 Union Pacific Depot and the Olympic Legacy Plaza. Many small shops and boutiques are scattered throughout the metropolitan area.

Because of its diverse ethnic population, Salt Lake City features a variety of international restaurants; many are prominent nationally. Everything from inexpensive fast food to elegant, intimate dining can be found in the more than 300 restaurants located in the valley.

Visitor Information: Salt Lake City Convention & Visitors Bureau, 90 South West Temple, Salt Lake City, Utah 84101; telephone (801)521-2822; fax (801)534-4927

■ Convention Facilities

The Salt Palace Convention Center, located in the center of the downtown district, is the city's major convention facility. After an extensive renovation completed in 2006, the Palace features over half a million square feet of continuous exhibition space, catering services, and a business center.

There are more than 4,200 hotel rooms and 90 restaurants within walking distance of the Salt Palace Convention Center and another 7,000 hotel rooms in the city. Several of the major hotels also contain extensive meeting, banquet, and ballroom accommodations. The EnergySolutions Arena offers meeting rooms ranging in size from 400 to 10,000 square feet.

Convention Information: Salt Lake City Convention & Visitors Bureau, 90 South West Temple, Salt Lake City, Utah 84101; telephone (801)521-2822; fax (801) 534-4927

■ Transportation

Approaching the City

The Salt Lake International Airport offers over 900 daily flights on 15 airlines, and is located just minutes from downtown Salt Lake City. In 2006 the airport served 21.5 million customers as the 22nd busiest airport in the United States. The Utah Transit Authority provides transportation to and from the airport; taxis are available, and many area hotels provide complimentary shuttle service.

Salt Lake City is at the junction of two major interstate highways, Interstate 15 running north-south and Interstate 80 running east-west. Interstate 215 forms a commuter loop and by-pass around the inner city.

Amtrak provides national passenger rail service from Salt Lake City's Gateway area. The TRAX light rail system serves Salt Lake County.

Traveling in the City

Walking is perhaps the best way to see the city's sights. Salt Lake City was laid out in a grid pattern with exceptionally wide streets by the early Mormon pioneers, which makes automobile travel easy and pleasurable compared to most larger metropolitan areas. Streets are named according to their distance and relationship to Temple Square. Salt Lake City recently implemented an intelligent CommuterLink system to decrease traffic congestion.

The Utah Transit Authority (UTA) operates 69 light rail vehicles, 30 commuter rail cars and more than 600 buses. Free fare zones operate downtown. UTA also provides service to ski resorts in winter and door-to-door transportation for the disabled.

■ Communications

Newspapers and Magazines

Salt Lake City is served by two major daily newspapers, *The Salt Lake Tribune* and *Deseret News*. The Latter-Day Saints publish three titles: *Church News,* a weekly newspaper; *The Friend,* a magazine for children aged three to eleven; and *New Era,* a magazine for teens. Other magazines published in the city include *Salt Lake*

Magazine and several scholarly, medical, and industry magazines.

Television and Radio

Salt Lake City's 10 television stations represent the commercial networks and independent and instructional channels. The city is also served by a variety of cable channels. Nearly two dozen AM and FM radio stations broadcast from Salt Lake City, providing a wide range of music, news, and informational programming.

Media Information: *The Salt Lake Tribune,* 143 S. Main Street, Salt Lake City, UT 84111; telephone (801) 257-8742. *Deseret News,* 30 E 100 South, PO Box 1257, Salt Lake City, UT 84110; telephone (801)237-2100

Salt Lake City Online

City of Salt Lake City home page. Available www.ci .slc.ut.us

Deseret News. Available www.deseretnews.com/dn

Discover Southern Utah! Available www.infowest .com/Utah

Salt Lake City Public Library. Available www.slcpl .lib.ut.us

Salt Lake City Public Schools. Available www.slc .k12.ut.us

Salt Lake Convention and Visitors Bureau. Available www.saltlake.org

The Salt Lake Tribune. Available www.sltrib.com

Utah State Office of Education. Available www.usoe .k12.ut.us

BIBLIOGRAPHY

Ayres, Becky, *Salt Lake City* (Minneapolis, MN: Dillon Press, 1990)

Miller, Marjorie, *Salt Lake City: Jewel of the Wasatch* (Yellow Cat Flats, UT: Yellow Cat Publishing, 2000)

Naifeh, Steven W., *The Mormon Murders: A True Story of Greed, Deceit, and Death* (New York: Weidenfeld and Nicolson, 1988)

Washington

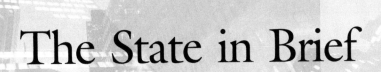

The State in Brief

Nickname: Evergreen State

Motto: Al-Ki (By and by)

Flower: Coast rhododendron

Bird: Willow goldfinch

Area: 71,299 square miles (2000; U.S. rank 18th)

Elevation: Ranges from sea level to 14,410 feet above sea level

Climate: Generally mild and humid in the western region dominated by the Pacific Ocean; semi-arid in the eastern region; heavy snows in higher elevations

Admitted to Union: November 11, 1889

Capital: Olympia

Head Official: Governor Chris Gregoire (D) (until 2008)

Population

1980: 4,132,000
1990: 4,866,692
2000: 5,894,121
2006 estimate: 6,395,798
Percent change, 1990–2000: 21.1%
U.S. rank in 2006: 14th
Percent of residents born in state: 47.21% (2006)
Density: 94.5 people per square mile (2006)
2006 FBI Crime Index Total: 308,653

Racial and Ethnic Characteristics (2006)

White: 5,148,130
Black or African American: 217,868
American Indian and Alaska Native: 92,791
Asian: 423,976
Native Hawaiian and Pacific Islander: 27,186
Hispanic or Latino (may be of any race): 580,027
Other: 276,396

Age Characteristics (2006)

Population under 5 years old: 406,816
Population 5 to 19 years old: 1,301,428
Percent of population 65 years and over: 11.5%
Median age: 36.7

Vital Statistics

Total number of births (2006): 80,334
Total number of deaths (2006): 46,377
AIDS cases reported through 2005: 11,438

Economy

Major industries: Trade; manufacturing; finance, insurance, and real estate; government; services; agriculture
Unemployment rate (2006): 6.4%
Per capita income (2006): $27,346
Median household income (2006): $52,583
Percentage of persons below poverty level (2006): 11.8%
Income tax rate: None
Sales tax rate: 6.5%

Bellingham

■ The City in Brief

Founded: as Whatcom, 1852; renamed Bellingham, 1903

Head Official: Mayor Dan Pike (NP) (since 2007)

City Population

    1980: 45,794
    1990: 52,179
    2000: 67,171
    2006 estimate: 75,150
    Percent change, 1990–2000: 28.7%
    U.S. rank in 1980: 466th
    U.S. rank in 1990: 477th (State rank: 9th)
    U.S. rank in 2000: 461st (State rank: 10th)

Metropolitan Area Population

    1980: 107,000
    1990: 127,780
    2000: 166,814
    2006 estimate: 185,953
    Percent change, 1990–2000: 30.5%
    U.S. rank in 1980: Not available
    U.S. rank in 1990: Not available
    U.S. rank in 2000: 185th

Area: 31.74 square miles (2000)

Elevation: 68 feet above sea level

Average Annual Temperature: 51.5° F

Average Annual Precipitation: 58 inches

Major Economic Sectors: services, wholesale and retail trade, government

Unemployment Rate: 4.0% (June 2007)

Per Capita Income: $22,801 (2005)

2005 FBI Crime Index Property: 5,573

2005 FBI Crime Index Violent: 174

Major Colleges and Universities: Western Washington University, Whatcom Community College, Northwest Indian College

Daily Newspaper: *The Bellingham Herald*

■ Introduction

Bellingham, a coastal city built around the deep water harbor of Bellingham Bay, is set against the backdrop of the Cascade Mountains. Bellingham is the last major city before the coast of Washington state meets the border of Canada. It was named in honor of Sir William Bellingham, who was director of stores for the British Admiralty. The renovated old, historic buildings, views of the water and the mountains, and gorgeous sunsets make for a picture-postcard setting. In 2006 Bellingham made the American Lung Association's list of top twenty cities for clean air for the sixth year in a row.

■ Geography and Climate

Bellingham is the seat of Whatcom County, the most northwestern county in the United States. The city is located 90 miles north of Seattle, 50 miles south of Vancouver, British Columbia, and 20 miles from the Canadian border at Baline. Bellingham, situated at the foot of 10,788-foot Mount Baker, is set on several hills overlooking the 172 San Juan Islands.

    Bellingham has a mild, maritime climate with temperatures ranging from 45 to 60 degrees in spring and fall, 30 to 50 degrees in winter, and 60 to 80 degrees in summer. Most days have at least partial sunshine and snow; sleet and hail occur only about 15 days per year.

Area: 31.74 square miles (2000)

Elevation: 68 feet above sea level

Average Temperature: 51.5° F

Average Annual Precipitation: 58 inches

■ History

European Contact with Natives Minimal at First

Long before the coming of Europeans, ancestors of local Bellingham tribes—the Lummi, the Nooksack, and the Semiahmoo—established camps along the bay as part of the great migration over the land bridge that once extended from Asia to North America. Salmon from the surrounding waters was their dietary mainstay, supplemented by roots, berries, and shellfish. The tribes engaged in both warfare and trade at various times. Some historians contend that Spanish explorers were the first white men to visit the area; if so, little evidence of them remains. The Lummi and Semiahmoo still live in the area and salmon remains their chief source of sustenance.

British Captain George Vancouver weighed anchor in nearby Birch Bay during his explorations of the Puget Sound in 1792, and Lt. Joseph Widbey charted Vancouver Bay. Widbey and his men may have seen a community of more than 3,000 natives living near the bay. Vancouver is said to have named the site of present-day Bellingham after the British admiralty controller who outfitted his ships.

As a result of reports carried back to Europe about the bounty of the region, traders began to arrive and a fur industry burgeoned in the early 1800s. From 1825 to 1846 the Hudson's Bay Company held domain over the region, but in the latter year the United States and Great Britain established a boundary at the 49th Parallel, and the Hudson's Bay Company relocated to Vancouver.

Industries Emerge; A Rush for Gold

In 1852, assisted by Lummi tribesmen, Henry Roeder built a sawmill on what is now Whatcom Creek. This initiated a period of coal mining and milling that continued for many decades. Whatcom County was established in 1854. Although the area of Bellingham remained untouched during the Indian War of 1855–1856, an infantry group was sent to Bellingham Bay in 1856 to establish Fort Bellingham.

More than 10,000 people were drawn to Bellingham during the Fraser River Gold Rush of 1858. A tent city mushroomed, until would-be prospectors were advised by Canadian officials that before starting digging they had to report to Victoria, British Columbia.

Eventually, fire and fatalities brought difficult times to the mining industry, and Roeder's mill site was sold to a company from Kansas City. Soon after, a boom was initiated by the building of a railroad that connected Bellingham to the trans-Canada railroad line. Other major segments of the economy at that time were farming, fishing, and canning. In the late 1880s the town of Fairhaven, now part of Bellingham, was promoted as the "next Chicago" by entrepreneur Nelson Bennett, and hundreds of workers were hired to build hotels, homes, and office buildings. People began arriving at the rate of 300 per month, among them gamblers and prostitutes. A vigilante group tried to keep the peace until a police force was finally formed in 1890. In 1902 a brewery was founded in Bellingham that at its height produced more than 100,000 barrels of beer annually. However, the Bellingham Bay Brewery disappeared forever with the beginning of prohibition in 1917.

Bellingham was formed in 1903 with the consolidation of four towns—Whatcom, New Whatcom, Fairhaven, and Bellingham—into one town with the name Bellingham. During the late 1800s tall ships could be seen loading coal, salmon, and timber for transport to cities around the globe. Prosperous businessmen began building impressive homes in the Sehome Hill section of the city, many of which are now used for student housing. The Whatcom Normal School opened in 1899, later to become Western Washington College of Education in 1937, Western Washington Sate College in 1961, and finally Western Washington University within the following decade.

Bellingham in the New Millennium

In June 1999 a fuel pipeline exploded along Whatcom Creek, killing three people along with thousands of fish and other wildlife. The tragedy resulted in major changes to federal pipeline laws and the creation of a Washington State Office of Pipeline Safety. After a rocky economical start to the twenty-first century, today's Bellingham is a growing and vibrant community set to the scenic backdrop of majestic Mt. Baker.

Plans to develop Bellingham's waterfront were underway in 2007. The waterfront is home to the 137-acre site of Georgia Pacific's former pulp and chemical plant and tissue mill, the latter scheduled to stop operating in December 2007. Efforts to redevelop the site are controversial, particularly regarding the issue of the disposal of mercury-contaminated sediments and soils.

As of 2007 the city had made the protection of Lake Whatcom a high priority. The Lake Whatcom Reservoir is the source of drinking water for about 95,000 people in Whatcom County, including the 82,000 served in Bellingham. The health of the reservoir is declining, as algae growth is requiring more expensive treatment to keep the water safe. Steps to be taken to

©*Tore Ofteness 2008*

protect the lake include protecting more undeveloped land in the watershed, improving stormwater treatment, and helping watershed residents become better stewards of the lake.

Historical Information: Center for Pacific Northwest Studies, Goltz-Murray Archives Building, Western Washington University, Bellingham, WA 98225-9123; telephone (360)650-7747; fax (360)650-3323; email cpnws@wwu.edu

■ Population Profile

Metropolitan Area Residents

 1980: 107,000
 1990: 127,780
 2000: 166,814
 2006 estimate: 185,953
 Percent change, 1990–2000: 30.5%
 U.S. rank in 1980: Not available
 U.S. rank in 1990: Not available
 U.S. rank in 2000: 185th

City Residents

 1980: 45,794

 1990: 52,179
 2000: 67,171
 2006 estimate: 75,150
 Percent change, 1990–2000: 28.7%
 U.S. rank in 1980: 466th
 U.S. rank in 1990: 477th (State rank: 9th)
 U.S. rank in 2000: 461st (State rank: 10th)

Density: 2,619.3 people per square mile (2000)

Racial and ethnic characteristics (2005)

 White: 60,149
 Black: 526
 American Indian and Alaska Native: 802
 Asian: 2,280
 Native Hawaiian and Pacific Islander: 492
 Hispanic or Latino (may be of any race): 3,646
 Other: 2,586

Percent of residents born in state: 49.4% (2000)

Age characteristics (2005)

 Population under 5 years old: 3,165
 Population 5 to 9 years old: 3,398
 Population 10 to 14 years old: 2,361
 Population 15 to 19 years old: 4,066

Population 20 to 24 years old: 14,303
Population 25 to 34 years old: 11,552
Population 35 to 44 years old: 6,691
Population 45 to 54 years old: 8,993
Population 55 to 59 years old: 4,580
Population 60 to 64 years old: 2,086
Population 65 to 74 years old: 3,387
Population 75 to 84 years old: 3,796
Population 85 years and older: 679
Median age: 30.1 years

Births (2006, MSA)

Total number: 2,009

Deaths (2006, MSA)

Total number: 1,380

Money income (2005)

Per capita income: $22,801
Median household income: $35,612
Total households: 32,385

Number of households with income of...

less than $10,000: 3,944
$10,000 to $14,999: 3,016
$15,000 to $24,999: 5,071
$25,000 to $34,999: 3,901
$35,000 to $49,999: 5,253
$50,000 to $74,999: 5,406
$75,000 to $99,999: 2,910
$100,000 to $149,999: 1,936
$150,000 to $199,999: 609
$200,000 or more: 339

Percent of families below poverty level: 13.7% (2005)

2005 FBI Crime Index Property: 5,573

2005 FBI Crime Index Violent: 174

■ Municipal Government

Bellingham has a mayor-council form of government. Six council members serve four-year terms and a seventh council member serves a two-year term as a council person-at-large. The mayor serves a four-year term.

Head Official: Mayor Dan Pike (NP) (since 2007; current term expires 2011)

Total Number of City Employees: 841 (2007)

City Information: City of Bellingham, Bellingham City Hall, 210 Lottie St., Bellingham, WA 98225; telephone (360)676-6900; email info@cob.org

■ Economy

Major Industries and Commercial activity

The year 2001 delivered a number of blows to Bellingham's economy. Georgia-Pacific Corp. closed its pulp and paper mill, resulting in the loss of 420 high-paying jobs and nearly $1 million to the local economy each year since. Alcoa's Intalco Works aluminum plant also shut down part of its Bellingham operations, further trimming the local workforce. Heightened border security after the September 11th terrorist strikes significantly reduced the number of visitors from Canada that spent their retail and entertainment dollars in Whatcom County.

Local officials realized that the area's dependence on resource-based industries made it particularly susceptible to such events, and that diversification was necessary to ensure future stability and growth. The downfall of diversification is that tourism- and other service-related jobs tend to pay far less than manufacturing jobs. While hospitality jobs paid an average of $26,000 per employee per year in Whatcom County, the jobs lost at Georgia-Pacific paid about $52,000 a year.

Still, jobs in service industries are increasingly important, not just to Bellingham's economy but to that of the nation as a whole. This is due in large part to the emergence of technology-driven sectors in the 1990s. Whatcom County employment in services increased from 18.9 percent in 1981 to 25.6 percent in 2000, while manufacturing employment shrunk from 20.8 percent to 14.3 percent over the same period.

Bellingham's economy had been traditionally based on agriculture, fishing, and timber. Today, these segments are still vital components of the local economy, though of less importance than they once had been. The bulk of Whatcom County's agricultural activity involves berry and dairy farming. Although the number and size of farms has been steadily declining, production has been climbing. In 2001 the county's 201 dairy farms produced milk valued at $185 million, compared to the 480 farms and $130 million in production in 1985. During 2000, workers in Whatcom County's berry farms produced more blueberries and raspberries than any other county in the state, and ranked second in strawberries. Seed potatoes and apples are also important crops.

Commercial fishing, one of the area's oldest industries, has taken a drastic downturn due to overfishing, shortened seasons, and falling prices. Once home to one of the largest commercial fishing fleets, Whatcom County had 740 commercial vessels in 1985; by 2002 the Port of Bellingham reported only 177 such vessels. The forestry industry tends to be more stable, as loggers in Whatcom County rely more on private lands than on public timberlands, making them more impervious to federal environmental restrictions on public resources.

Despite the losses in paper and aluminum segments, manufacturing remains an important industry in Whatcom County. Manufacturing of wood products and transportation equipment has seen gains in recent years. Boatbuilding is a crucial segment of the transportation equipment sector, as its focus has shifted from fishing vessels to the production of luxury yachts and military boats. Whatcom County in 2007 was home to over 245 manufacturing companies.

Healthcare is becoming increasingly vital to the local economy. Comprised of such areas as hospitals, nursing and residential care, ambulatory clinics, and social assistance, the healthcare field employs some 7,600 residents of Whatcom County.

The top ten employers in Whatcom County in 2007 were: St. Joseph Hospital; Haggen Inc.; BP Cherry Point Refinery; Brown and Cole; Sodexho; T Mobile; Fred Meyer; Alcoa Intalco Works; Madrona Medical Group; and Silver Reef Casino.

Items and goods produced: boats, lumber and wood products, tissue paper, refined oil and petroleum products, blueberries, strawberries, raspberries, seed potatoes, apples, processed frozen foods, baked goods

Incentive Programs—New and Existing Companies

Local programs: The Bellingham Whatcom Economic Development Council promotes local businesses, products, and services, and helps firms in interfacing with regional, national, and international markets. It assists businesses by providing information on expansion and investment decisions, and by providing liaison with government officials and community leaders. It also offers a revolving loan program and a public infrastructure program. Additionally, the Port of Bellingham, a municipal corporation, offers an industrial revenue bond program and a foreign trade zone program to benefit local businesses.

State programs: The state of Washington offers a number of incentive programs to attract new and expanding businesses to the state. Among them are B & O tax credits; sales/use tax deferrals for technology and manufacturing companies as well as for firms relocating or expanding in distressed areas; and loan programs that apply to rural areas and the redevelopment of brownfields.

Job training programs: Job training programs are offered by the state of Washington, and the Bellingham Whatcom Economic Development Council facilitates the implementation of workforce development programs. Training programs for a variety of industries, including healthcare and manufacturing, are offered by such institutions of higher learning as Bellingham Technical College, Northwest Indian College, Western Washington University, and Whatcom Community College. The WorkSource Partnership also provides start-up services to recruit, screen, test, and refer potential employees. Federal tax credits are available for targeted new jobs.

Development Projects

Funding for the Depot Market Square was secured in 2004, and the new square was dedicated on July 6, 2006. The development serves as the permanent home of the Bellingham Farmers Market, which attracted approximately 10,000 visitors a day in 2007. Depot Market Square also serves as a community gathering place for public and private events. Elsewhere in Bellingham, Bellwether on the Bay is a mixed-use complex occupying 15 acres of waterfront property. As of 2007, Phase I was complete: there were two office buildings, the four-star Hotel Bellwether, a fitness center and spa, and a variety of restaurants and shops. Planning for Phase II was underway that year, and is expected to include two or three additional mixed use buildings with residential areas on upper floors.

Aside from commercial developments, Bellingham has devoted considerable resources to improving culture, recreation, and the general quality of life. The Taylor Avenue Dock and Boardwalk was completed in 2004; this $2.9 million project restored and improved the historic dock and includes a new boardwalk connecting the dock to Boulevard Park. September 2004 hailed the grand opening of the Studio Theatre, a 3,000-square-foot room within the historic Mt. Baker Theatre built to host small-scale musical and theatrical productions. Also in 2004, a clean-up and restoration project was initiated at the Holly Street Landfill. Reconstruction of portions of the Civic Field Complex, including its grandstands, football field and track, stadium, and skate park, was completed by 2007 at a cost of $9.9 million.

Plans to develop Bellingham's waterfront were underway in 2007. The waterfront is home to the 137-acre site of Georgia Pacific's former pulp and chemical plant and tissue mill. The disposal of mercury-contaminated sediments and soils will have to be addressed as development begins.

Economic Development Information: Bellingham/ Whatcom Chamber of Commerce & Industry, 1201 Cornwall Ave., Ste. 100, Bellingham, WA 98225; telephone (360)734-1330; fax (360)734-1332; email chamber@bellingham.com. Bellingham Whatcom Economic Development Council, 105 E Holly St., PO Box 2803, Bellingham, WA 98227; telephone (360)676-4255; toll-free (800)810-4255; fax (360)647-9413; email info@bwedc.org

Commercial Shipping

Whatcom County has four major locations for U.S.-Canada border crossings: two in Blaine, one in Lynden, and one in Sumas. Freight rail service is offered in Bellingham by the Burlington Northern Santa Fe, Canadian Rail, and Canadian Pacific railroads. Among its motor freight companies are Puget Sound Truck Lines, Roadway Express, Yellow Transportation, LTI Inc., Machine Transport, Inc., AES Transportation, JIT Transport, Oak Harbor Freight Lines, and Peninsula Truck Lines. The area is also home to 11 local freight brokers. Bellingham International Airport (BIA) serves as a base for charter airlines and is a port of entry for general aviation aircraft. The airport is home to Foreign Trade Zone #129, an area where foreign goods bound for international destinations can be temporarily stored without incurring an import duty. BIA also offers customs brokerage and air cargo services, and houses a U.S. Customs office.

The Port of Bellingham, a municipal corporation dedicated to fulfilling the essential transportation needs of the region, operates a cargo terminal with three ship berths, backed up by two warehouses. Among its exports are wood pulp and aluminum ingots from local factories; its primary import is cottonseed pulp for cattle feed. The port administers five federally designated foreign trade zones to promote manufacturing, warehousing, and trade in the region.

Labor Force and Employment Outlook

As of 2006, Whatcom County had more than 68,000 private wage and salaried workers, 15,700 government workers, and 6,580 self-employed workers. Bellingham's workforce is highly educated. Approximately 90.8 percent of Whatcom County's population over 25 years of age had graduated from high school, and 32.2 percent of 25-year-olds and above had earned a bachelor's degree or higher; both figures are above state averages. Washington is a "right to work" state. Unions are primarily active in the public sector, health care, and construction trades. Whatcom County employers are mostly small business operations and experience little union activity. Most Whatcom County businesses are non-union shops.

The following is a summary of data regarding the Bellingham metropolitan area labor force, 2006 annual averages.

Size of nonagricultural labor force: 82,100

Number of workers employed in ...

    construction and mining: 8,100
    manufacturing: 8,800
    trade, transportation and utilities: 15,600
    information: Not available
    financial activities: 3,100
    professional and business services: 6,800
    educational and health services: Not available
    leisure and hospitality: 9,600
    other services: Not available
    government: 15,700

Average hourly earnings of production workers employed in manufacturing: Not available

Unemployment rate: 4.0% (June 2007)

Largest employers (2007)	*Number of employees*
Bellingham School District	Not available
Bellis Fair Mall	Not available
BP Cherry Point Refinery	Not available
Brown & Cole	Not available
City of Bellingham	Not available
County of Whatcom	Not available
Fred Meyer	Not available
Georgia Pacific	Not available
Haggens, Inc.	Not available
St. Joseph Hospital	Not available
Western Washington University	Not available
Whatcom Community College	Not available

Cost of Living

The following is a summary of data regarding several key cost of living factors for the Bellingham metropolitan area.

2007 (1st quarter) ACCRA Average House Price: $435,000

2007 (1st quarter) ACCRA Cost of Living Index: 109.3

State income tax rate: None

State sales tax rate: 6.5%

Local income tax rate: None

Local sales tax rate: 1.7%

Property tax rate: $11.40 per $1,000 of assessed value (2005)

Economic Information: Bellingham/Whatcom Chamber of Commerce & Industry, 1201 Cornwall Ave., Ste. 100, Bellingham, WA 98225; telephone (360)734-1330; fax (360)734-1332; email chamber@bellingham.com

■ Education and Research

Elementary and Secondary Schools

The Bellingham School District offers special programs for disabled students, those with learning disabilities, and exceptionally capable students. The schools have computers and related technology in every classroom. An early childhood preschool program and Head Start classes are offered. In 2000 the Bellingham School District was one of only 10 districts in the state to be recognized as a "model of achievement" and receive a five-year, $4.49 million Bill & Melinda Gates Foundation Grant. In October 2007 Bellingham's Columbia Elementary and Sunnyland Elementary received School of Distinction awards from the state Office of Superintendent of Public Instruction. Only 86 schools, or the top 5 percent of Washington's 2,500 schools, earned this honor for learning improvement in reading and math over the previous six years.

The following is a summary of data regarding the Bellingham Public School District as of the 2005–2006 school year.

Total enrollment: 9,000

Number of facilities

> elementary schools: 13
> junior high/middle schools: 4
> senior high schools: 5
> other: 0

Student/teacher ratio: 19:1

Teacher salaries (2005–06)

> elementary median: $46,690
> junior high/middle median: $47,300
> secondary median: $45,610

Funding per pupil: $7,175

Bellingham has 12 private schools, including two Montessori schools, five religious schools, three alternative schools, a day-care center, and the Whatcom Day Academy.

Public Schools Information: Bellingham Public Schools, 1306 Dupont St., Bellingham, WA 98225-3198; telephone (360)676-6400; fax (360)676-2793; email mgude@bham.wednet.edu

Colleges and Universities

Western Washington University, with nearly 12,500 students, overlooks the city on Sehome Hill. Founded in 1893, the school became a regional university in 1977. College programs include business and economics, fine and performing arts, humanities and social sciences, science and technology, the Huxley College of the Environment, the Woodring College of Education, and Fairhaven College, an interdisciplinary liberal arts college. Western Washington University's graduate school offers master's degrees in art, business administration, accounting, education, music, science, and teaching.

More than 7,000 students are enrolled in Whatcom Community College, which offers a variety of two-year programs in such areas as accounting, computer

information sciences, education, English, graphic design, library and information science, massage, paralegal studies, and visual and performing arts; a program in nursing was added in the fall of 2005. Northwest Indian College, one of the fastest-growing Native American colleges in the country, offers its more than 1,200 students associate degrees in Native American Studies, Oksale Native Education, Chemical Dependency Studies, and Life Sciences, as well as a certificate program in Native American Studies; additional programs in a variety of areas of professional development and vocational training are offered through the Training Institute. Degree and certificate programs in more than 50 fields, from culinary arts to radiologic technology, are offered at Bellingham Technical College. Washington State University, based in Pullman, has a Whatcom County Extension that offers non-credit education and degree programs in the fields of gardening and agriculture, family living, and environment and natural resources.

Libraries and Research Centers

The Bellingham Public Library's main building was built in 1949 and was remodeled and expanded in 1985. Its Fairhaven branch, which celebrated its centennial in December 2004, occupies an original 1912 Carnegie building on the south side of the city. The library system has a collection of more than 400,000 items that range from original manuscripts to the latest CDs, videos, and books on tape. The library maintains current subscriptions to more than 50 newspapers. The library offers free Internet access to patrons, quality programs for children, reference services for adults, and an online local newspaper index and catalogue, as well as a complete database of community resources. The library has a special collection on local history and is a U.S. and state documents depository. In 2006, nearly 750,000 people used the library's resources, and checked out more than 1.2 million items, record-breaking figures that put Bellingham's library among the top circulating libraries in the nation for communities of Bellingham's size. On an annual basis, 16.4 items per person are checked out in Bellingham's library, compared to the state of Washington's average of 10.9 items, and the nation's average of 7.1 items.

Bellingham's colleges and universities maintain a number of libraries, many of which are open to the public. Western Washington University has a number of research institutes and libraries, including those focusing on such areas as Canadian-American studies, Pacific Northwest studies, demographics, watershed studies, economic education and research, environmental toxicology, and vehicle research. Its special collections include the Ford Fly Fishing Collection, Northwest Collection, Rare Books Collection, and the Western Collection. The Whatcom County Law Library houses more than 15,000 books and CDs covering Washington laws and practice guides, federal laws, U.S. Supreme

Court reports, and regional case law, as well as legal reference materials. Bellingham Technical College maintains an Information Technology Resource Center.

Public Library Information: Bellingham Public Library, 210 Central Ave., Bellingham, WA 98225; telephone (360)676-6860

■ Health Care

The people of Bellingham are served by St. Joseph's Hospital, which has 253 beds across two campuses. The hospital has a staff of 270 physicians, a medical surgical intensive care unit, a trauma center, and emergency, obstetrics, and oncology departments. Services offered include open heart surgery, outpatient surgery, psychiatric and addiction care for children and adults, and geriatric services. St. Joseph's Cardiovascular Center has a brand-new facility. The Cardiovascular Center is award-winning and nationally recognized. The city is also home to more than 80 dentists, some 15 naturopathic physicians, and 80 chiropractors.

■ Recreation

Sightseeing

Bellingham's museums are devoted to an array of topics. The Whatcom Museum of History & Art, located in downtown Bellingham, is comprised of four buildings, each with its own theme: the 1892 Old City Hall, Whatcom Children's Museum, Syre Education Center, and Arco Exhibits Building. The American Museum of Radio and Electricity is the only one of its kind in North America. This museum, which completed an expansion in 2001, houses artifacts and interactive exhibits spanning from the onset of the scientific exploration of electricity in the 17th century to the evolution of broadcast radio and its impact on American culture. The Bellingham Railway Museum chronicles the heritage and operation of railroads in Whatcom and Skagit counties. Mindport Exhibits is a collection of interactive and fine arts exhibits designed to encourage exploration, discovery, and thought. Nearby, the Lynden Pioneer Museum focuses on the heritage of Whatcom County prior to World War II, with exhibits covering Front Street, agriculture, rural Victorian lifestyles, transportation, natural resources, veterans, and the military.

The International Peace Arch, located about 20 miles north of Bellingham, is one of the world's few landmarks to be listed on the national historic registries of two countries. The 67-foot-tall arch has one foot in Canada and the other in the United States, and represents the longest undefended boundary—3,000 miles—in the world. It commemorates the signing of the Treaty of the Ghent, which ended the war between Britain and the United States. A number of celebrations take place there each year. From May to September a sculpture exhibition of both Canadian and American artists includes festivities each weekend. The Peace Arch Celebration, also known as Hands Across the Border, is held in June. September brings the annual Peace Arch Dedication Days, or "Sam Hill Days," that reenact the anniversary of the arch.

Arts and Culture

The Mt. Baker Theatre has been offering theatrical entertainment since 1927. The Moorish-Spanish style former vaudeville movie palace, which is on the National Historic Register, seats 1,500 people. The theater boasts a 100-foot Moorish tower, open-beamed lobby, 80-foot interior dome, an original 215-pipe organ, state-of-the-art staging capabilities, and, some speculate, a resident ghost. The theater hosts more than 100 live events annually, including touring Broadway shows. The Studio Theatre, a 2004 addition to the Mt. Baker Theatre, stages performances in an intimate setting. Mt. Baker Theatre is also the site for performances by the Whatcom Symphony Orchestra, Mt. Baker Youth Symphony, and Mt. Baker Organ Society.

The oldest community theater company in the Northwest, the Bellingham Theatre Guild, presents a year-round venue of comedies, dramas, and musicals. Western Washington University offers a wide range of performances, including its summer stock season, a theatre arts series of dramas and comedies, and a performing arts series featuring world-renowned musicians and dance companies. Other theaters include the iDiOM Theater and the Upfront Theatre.

The Art of Jazz Series takes place on the last Sunday of each month from January through November (11 shows), featuring trio and quartet performances by Northwest Regional players from Vancouver, Seattle, Portland, and beyond.

Arts and Culture Information: Bellingham/Whatcom County Convention & Visitors Bureau, 904 Potter St., Bellingham, WA 98229; telephone (360)671-3990; fax (360)647-7873; email tourism@bellingham.org

Festivals and Holidays

The highlight of Memorial Day weekend is Bellingham's annual Sea to Ski Race, an athletic contest dating from the 1800s that is accompanied by parades, carnivals, art and garden shows, house tours, and street fairs. The Bellingham Scottish Highland Games take place in early June. Later that month in nearby Fairhaven is the annual Bowler Hat Bocce Ball Tournament, in which teams are encouraged to dress in 1890s period attire. Aerial acrobatics and fireworks turn the eyes toward the skies above the Port of Bellingham in June for AirFest. The Fourth of July is celebrated with the Viewing of the Blast Over Bellingham Bay. Later that month brings the Raspberry

Festival at the Bellingham Farmers Market, and cowboys turn out for the International Bull-A-Rama. The Mount Baker Blues Festival in July has been voted the Best Blues Event in the state. The Bellingham Festival of Music, held in July, features classical, chamber, jazz, and world music. Families flock to downtown's Chalk Art Festival in August.

For hundreds if not thousands of years, Native Americans in the Pacific Northwest have held ceremonies in honor of the salmon. This tradition is carried on at the Salmon and Corn Festival/Oktoberfest. Also in autumn is the Eldridge Area Historical Home Tour. Mount Baker is the site for the Mount Baker Country Christmas and the Western Washington University Department of Music's *Messiah* production. In December the Lights of Love is celebrated at Bellingham Public Library. Also in December the Holiday Port Festival and Holiday Festival of the Arts are held.

Sports for the Spectator

The Bellingham Bells, with a season that runs from June through August, is a part of the West Coast Collegiate Baseball League. The Western Washington University Vikings compete in cross country, football, softball, track and field, volleyball, rowing, golf, soccer and men's and women's basketball. Students of Whatcom Community College participate in men's and women's basketball and soccer, and women's volleyball.

Sports for the Participant

In 2001 *Outside* magazine named Bellingham one of its top 10 "Dream Towns" for outdoor recreation. The city has an extensive network of hiking and biking trails, swimming pools and beaches, picnic grounds, fishing sites, softball and soccer fields, and beautiful gardens. At 10,788 feet, Mt. Baker is the highest peak in the North Cascade mountain range. It not only offers some spectacular views, it has the longest ski season in the state, with runs that curve below Mt. Shuksan. Bellingham ranked number seven of the "Best Golf Cities" by *Golf Digest* in 2002, and with 14 courses, Whatcom County boasts the largest concentration of public golf courses in the Pacific Northwest. Water sports abound, with sailing, kayaking, rafting, and whale watching among the favorites. Charter trips are available to the San Juan Islands or Victoria, B.C.

More than 110,000 athletes from around the world participate in the annual Sea to Ski Race, an 82.5-mile relay for teams of eight. The race begins with cross-country skiing at Mount Baker, followed by downhill skiing, running, road cycling, canoeing, mountain biking, and kayaking to the finish at Bellingham Bay. The Human Race, held each June, is a 5K/10K walk-run event in which participants raise money for their favorite charities. The course of the Baker's Healthy Start Foundation Triathlon, held each August, begins from the banks of Lake Whatcom and ends at Bloedel Donovan Park. September brings the Bellingham Traverse, a team event involving running, mountain and road biking, and canoeing/kayaking around downtown Bellingham, as well as the Discover Bellingham VolksFest, a three-day event comprised of a variety of walks.

Shopping and Dining

Shopping opportunities in Bellingham encompass both large regional malls and charming boutiques. Downtown Bellingham boasts two million square feet of businesses and shops. The Victorian buildings in the city's Fairhaven District hold a variety of specialty shops and eateries. Bellis Fair, the regional shopping mall, has Macy's, Mervyn's, Target, JCPenney, Sears, and 140 specialty stores plus a six-screen cinema. Outlet centers just a few miles from the town center draw bargain hunters. The Sunset Square Shopping Center houses more than 40 stores and restaurants, as well as a movie theater. Unique shops can be found at the new Bellwether on the Bay development on Squalicum Harbor.

Beer-lovers enjoy the fare at the Boundary Bay Brewery Company, where hand-crafted ales and lagers are served in a historic warehouse. Local eateries range from casual cafes and burger joints to restaurants offering Italian, Mexican, and Chinese cuisine, to an upscale steak house with scenic views. The Silver Reef Casino, located in Ferndale, offers food and drink, live entertainment, and gaming, as does the Skagit Valley Casino Resort.

Visitor Information: Bellingham/Whatcom County Tourism, 904 Potter St., Bellingham, WA 98229; telephone (360)671-3990; fax (360)647-7873; email tourism@bellingham.org

■ Convention Facilities

The Bellingham/Mt. Baker region offers more than 2,200 guest rooms and 175,000 square feet of meeting space. Northwest Washington Fairgrounds, located in nearby Lynden, offers more than 70,000 square feet of meeting space in eight rooms, the largest of which can seat 5,000 people. Within the city of Bellingham, the Mt. Baker Theatre offers three meetings rooms that can accommodate 120-1,500 people. The Bellingham unit of the Boys & Girls Clubs of Whatcom County provides more than 13,000 square feet of meeting space, and Western Washington University offers 24 separate rooms that can each seat up to 750 attendees.

A number of area facilities provide both meeting space and lodging. Semiahmoo Resort offers 7,200 square feet in the largest of its 17 meeting rooms. The Best Western Lakeway Inn & Conference Center has 12 meeting rooms that can seat from 504 to 700 people. The Homestead Farms Golf Resort & Convention Center, located 20 miles north of Bellingham in Lynden, has 6 meeting rooms, the largest of which is 2,400 square feet in size.

Convention Information: Bellingham/Whatcom County Tourism, 904 Potter St., Bellingham, WA 98229; telephone (360)671-3990; fax (360)647-7873; email tourism@bellingham.org

■ Transportation

Approaching the City

Bellingham is located along western America's Interstate-5 corridor, nearly equidistant from Seattle and Vancouver, British Columbia. State routes 11, 539, 542, and 544 form a highway grid that covers most of the interior of western Whatcom County, linking with I-5 near Bellingham. Bellingham International Airport provides service to more than 250,000 passengers annually. Delta Air Lines offers two flights daily from Bellingham to Salt Lake City. Horizon Airlines flies passengers to the Seattle-Tacoma International Airport. Allegiant Air provides direct service to Las Vegas and Reno, NV, and to Phoenix and Mesa, AZ; it is also slated to provide service to Palm Springs, CA. San Juan Airlines runs daily to Friday Harbor and San Juan Island. Skybus Airlines offers daily non-stop flights to Columbus, OH. The Airporter Shuttle delivers passengers to local points. At the Port of Bellingham, the Bellingham Cruise Terminal and Fairhaven Station launch cruises by ferry to Alaska, the San Juan Islands, and Victoria, British Columbia. Amtrak provides passenger rail service to Seattle and Vancouver, B.C., and Canadian Pacific and Rail Canada travel east through Canada. Regional bus service is offered by Greyhound Bus Lines.

Traveling in the City

Interstate 5 runs north and south through the center of Bellingham. State Highway 11 runs north and south down the coast of Bellingham Bay at the south end of town. The Whatcom Transportation Authority (WTA) provides local bus service around Bellingham and to Blaine, Ferndale, and Lynden. In 2007 WTA was remodeling its downtown Bellingham Station; passengers at that time were being served by a temporary station. The remodeled station was scheduled to reopen in fall 2007 to provide a more spacious passenger lobby, enlarged restrooms, and improved facilities for riders' customer service needs.

■ Communications

Newspapers and Magazines

Bellingham's daily paper is *The Bellingham Herald,* which appears every morning. *The Western Front* is published twice-weekly from fall to spring by students of Western Washington University. The *Bellingham Business Journal* and the *Northwest Business Monthly* focus on local business news and features each month. Other papers published in Bellingham include *Cascadia Weekly, Whatcom Watch,* and the *Whatcom Independent.*

Television and Radio

One independent television station broadcasts out of Bellingham, which has two cable TV stations. Bellingham has three AM and five FM radio stations, covering classical music, jazz, rock, news, talk, and public radio.

Media Information: *The Bellingham Herald,* 1155 N. State St., Bellingham, WA 98225; telephone (360) 676-2600

Bellingham Online

The Bellingham Herald. Available www .bellinghamherald.com

Bellingham Public Library. Available www .bellinghampubliclibrary.org

Bellingham Public Schools. Available www.bham .wednet.edu

Bellingham/Whatcom Chamber of Commerce and Industry. Available www.bellingham.com

Bellingham/Whatcom County Tourism. Available www.bellingham.org

Bellingham Whatcom Economic Development Council. Available www.bwedc.org

City of Bellingham home page. Available www .cob.org

BIBLIOGRAPHY

Dillard, Annie, *The Living* (New York: HarperCollins Publishers, 1992)

Gilliland, Miki, *Entering Bellingham* (Bellingham, WA: Bayside Press, 1989)

Manning, Harvey, *Walking the Beach to Bellingham* (Corvallis, OR: Oregon State University Press, Reprint Edition, 2002)

Roth, Lottie Roeder, *The History of Whatcom County* (Seattle, WA: Pioneer Historical Publishing Co., 1926)

Olympia

■ The City in Brief

Founded: 1846 (incorporated 1859)

Head Official: Mayor Mark Foutch (NP) (since 2004)

City Population

1980: 27,447
1990: 33,729
2000: 42,514
2006 estimate: 44,645
Percent change, 1990–2000: 26.0%
U.S. rank in 1980: Not available
U.S. rank in 1990: Not available
U.S. rank in 2000: Not available (State rank: 17th)

Metropolitan Area Population

1980: 124,264
1990: 161,238
2000: 207,355
2006 estimate: 234,670
Percent change, 1990–2000: 28.6%
U.S. rank in 1980: Not available
U.S. rank in 1990: 12th (CMSA)
U.S. rank in 2000: 13th (CMSA)

Area: 18.52 square miles (2000)

Elevation: 221 feet above sea level

Average Annual Temperatures: January, 38.1° F; July, 62.8° F; annual average, 49.6° F

Average Annual Precipitation: 50.79 inches of rain; 16.7 inches of snow

Major Economic Sectors: services, wholesale and retail trade, government

Unemployment Rate: 4.2% (June 2007)

Per Capita Income: $22,590 (1999)

2005 FBI Crime Index Property: 2,549

2005 FBI Crime Index Violent: 115

Major Colleges and Universities: The Evergreen State College, South Puget Sound Community College, Saint Martin's University

Daily Newspaper: *The Olympian*

■ Introduction

Olympia, Washington's capital, is a city rich in history and natural beauty. Known for its spectacular view of the Olympic Mountains, the city serves as the gateway to Olympic National Park and headquarters for the Olympic National Forest. Local residents enjoy quiet neighborhoods with lovely tree-lined streets, an abundance of parks, good schools, and a high overall quality of life.

■ Geography and Climate

Olympia sits on a low flat at the southern end of Puget Sound on the shores of Budd Inlet's two bays, between Seattle and the Olympic Mountains to the north, Mt. Rainier to the northeast, and Mt. Saint Helens to the south. The city is further divided by Capitol Lake.

The city and the surrounding area experience fair-weather summers and the gray, wet overcast winters of the Pacific Northwest. Tempered by the Japanese trade current, the mild northwest climate favors lushly forested landscapes replete with ferns and mosses. Rainfall tends to be spread out over a large number of days. With about 52 clear days out of every 365, Thurston County residents live under some form of cloud cover 86 percent of the year, with more than a trace of rain falling on almost half of the days of the year.

Area: 18.52 square miles (2000)

Elevation: 221 feet above sea level

Average Temperatures: January, 38.1° F; July, 62.8° F; annual average, 49.6° F

Average Annual Precipitation: 50.79 inches of rain; 16.7 inches of snow

■ History

Territorial Days

Before British Captain George Vancouver sailed into Puget Sound Bay in 1791 and made the first known European contact with the native tribes, the Nisqually, Duwamish, Suquamish, and Puyallup Indians hunted, gathered, and fished in the region where Olympia now stands. The United States and Great Britain jointly controlled the region until the boundary between U.S. territory and Canada was established in 1846. The Pacific Northwest Region was then called Oregon Territory.

White settlement of what later became Olympia began in 1846 with a joint claim filed under a homestead law by partners Edmund Sylvester, a Maine fisherman, and Levi Lathrop Smith, an easterner who wanted to be a minister but was prevented by epilepsy from pursuing that career. Smith called his portion of the claim Smithfield. For two years, Smith and Sylvester were the only white residents in Smithfield (then Oregon Territory); the area was covered with virgin forest. When Smith drowned in Puget Sound in 1848, Sylvester took over his partner's claim. By the end of 1848, a trail had been cleared between Smithfield and New Market to the south (now Tumwater), and four families, about fifteen single men, and Father Pascal Ricard and his small band of Oblate missionaries had settled in Smithfield. In 1850 a city was laid out and Smithfield was renamed Olympia after the Olympic Mountains that can be seen in the distance. In 1853 Washington Territory became separate from Oregon Territory. Olympia (population 150), the largest settlement in Washington Territory, was named its capital and Isaac Stevens arrived to serve as Washington's first territorial governor.

Governor Stevens predicted a golden future for Washington Territory. He moved quickly to open up the area to white settlement, promising to survey a route for a transcontinental railway and to convince the natives to cede their land and move to reservations. By 1854 most of the tribes had done so, but intermittent outbreaks of hostility throughout the 1850s deterred extensive settlement. Delays in constructing a transcontinental railroad and the 1849 discovery of gold in California drew prospective settlers from the Northwest. The outbreak of the Civil War in 1861 nearly halted the westward migration of settlers.

City's Desire for Prominence Thwarted

Blessed with abundant natural resources, Olympia remained small but prospered. The year 1852 marked many firsts for the town. Coal was discovered, saw mills were built, a fledgling trade industry was started with California, road and school districts were established, and Washington's first newspaper, the weekly *Columbian,* published its first issue. In 1853 a Methodist minister took up residence and began to build a church, classes began at the Olympia Public School, and the city's first theatrical performance was held. Olympia's population grew from fewer than 1,000 people in 1860 to 1,203 residents in 1870. By 1872 Olympia seemed on its way to becoming Washington's great city; that year, however, a severe earthquake shook Olympia, as did the decision by the Northern Pacific railroad not to end the line at Olympia. Instead, the railway went to Tacoma, taking with it much of Olympia's trade and industry.

Meanwhile, people began moving to Seattle instead of Olympia. Still, with its strategic location near virgin forestland and the waterfalls at Tumwater, Olympia flourished as a sawmill town. Furniture, shingles, timber, pilings, and coal were loaded aboard ships bound from Olympia Harbor to California. Olympia served as a social center for isolated settlers throughout Washington, who traveled by steamboat to attend picnics and fairs there. By 1890 Olympia's population stood at 4,698 inhabitants. A year earlier, in 1889, Washington had become a state; Olympia fought bids by several other cities for the right to remain state capital and won in a statewide vote. At the time, state government was housed in a single frame building.

The decade of the 1890s was marked by progress and disappointments. The Olympia Brewing Company, which would become one of Olympia's greatest claims to fame, was founded in 1896 in Tumwater. Telephone lines and electric light poles were erected, dredging began for a modern port, a street railway system was built, and the elegant Olympia Hotel was completed (but destroyed by fire in 1904); however, an economic depression left citizens complaining that their diet consisted of nothing but clams, and Olympia's population fell to 3,863 residents by 1900. By this time, Seattle and Tacoma had surpassed Olympia as the big cities of the Puget Sound area.

Twentieth-Century Advances

In 1901 the state bought Olympia's Thurston County Court House to serve as the Capitol building, but Olympians could not rest easy with their title of state capital until the present Capitol complex was finally completed in 1935, after delays due to the 1890 and 1930 depressions.

Olympia had escaped the worst of the Indian wars of the 1850s, and in the twentieth century managed to escape the labor troubles and various upheavals that beset other Washington cities. The city benefited when World

War I brought a huge demand for Olympic peninsula spruce to make airplanes. Waterborne trade lost by 1920 to other Puget Sound ports picked up after a 1925 revitalization of the Port of Olympia, and ships once again began loading lumber bound for the Orient.

Olympia suffered a severe earthquake in 1949. A year later the city celebrated its centennial, 100 years from the date Olympia was laid out. By then Olympia ranked twelfth among Washington's cities in population and boasted one high school, one radio station, a "video" station, and two newspapers. With a population in 1953 of 16,800 people, Olympia was a typical small town where the sidewalks were "rolled up" each evening. One by one, state government offices were moving from Olympia to Seattle, and the city feared it would lose its capital status. Finally, four local businessmen filed a lawsuit against the state to stop the exodus; the eighteen state agencies were ordered back to Olympia in a decision that opined: "it was not the intention of the framers of the constitution that the state capital should be composed of empty buildings to collect cobwebs and stand in disuse."

Then began a flurry of construction of government buildings on what had once been residential streets. Despite decades of effort, Olympia was less successful in luring industry, thus managing to escape the attendant smog and pollution. In the 1960s and 1970s Olympia lost many of its downtown retail businesses to shopping malls in the then-rural towns of Lacey and Tumwater.

Efforts to preserve the downtown emphasized people-friendly projects while discouraging skyscrapers. Olympia served as a west coast port of entry and exit from which agricultural products and oysters were shipped. However, government had become the leading source of local employment and has a strong influence on most aspects of life in the city.

Challenges in the New Century

The turn of the century brought several challenges to Olympia. Some, like a national recession and the terrorist attacks of 2001, affected the entire United States and beyond. Others were more specific to the region. On February 28, 2001, the 6.8-magnitude Nisqually Earthquake occurred, with an epicenter only 10 miles from Olympia. A gradual yet significant loss of manufacturing jobs spurred the goal of diversification, particularly into technology—a segment in which Olympia was lagging behind the state's other regions. The question of the new resident of Olympia's Executive Mansion hung in the balance for two months. The gubernatorial race between Democrat Christine O. Gregoire and Republican Dino Rossi was finally settled, after several recounts, in Gregoire's favor in January 2005.

Olympia was listed in tenth place on *Forbes* magazine's 2007 list of Best Places for Business and Careers; number 16 on *Sperling's* 2007 ranking of Best

U.S. cities; number 10 on the *Men's Journal* 2005 list of Top 50 Best Places to Live; number 27 on *Kiplinger's* 2006 list of 50 Smart Places to Live; featured in the 2006 edition of *50 Fabulous Places to Raise Your Family!*; and ranked number 36 on the 2007 *Country Home Magazine* list of Best Green Cities in America.

Olympia's Evergreen State College is the alma mater of two of the nation's top television icons: Matt Groening, creator of "The Simpsons"; and Michael Richards, who played Kramer on "Seinfeld."

Historical Information: Washington State Capital Museum, 211 W. 21st Ave., Olympia, WA 98501; telephone (360)753-2580

■ Population Profile

Metropolitan Area Residents

  1980: 124,264
  1990: 161,238
  2000: 207,355
  2006 estimate: 234,670
  Percent change, 1990–2000: 28.6%
  U.S. rank in 1980: Not available
  U.S. rank in 1990: 12th (CMSA)
  U.S. rank in 2000: 13th (CMSA)

City Residents

  1980: 27,447
  1990: 33,729
  2000: 42,514
  2006 estimate: 44,645
  Percent change, 1990–2000: 26.0%
  U.S. rank in 1980: Not available
  U.S. rank in 1990: Not available
  U.S. rank in 2000: Not available (State rank: 17th)

Density: 2,544.4 people per square mile (2000)

Racial and ethnic characteristics (2000)

  White: 36,246
  Black: 805
  American Indian and Alaska Native: 553
  Asian: 2,473
  Native Hawaiian and Pacific Islander: 125
  Hispanic or Latino (may be of any race): 1,863
  Other: 713

Percent of residents born in state: 45.3% (2000)

Age characteristics (2000)

  Population under 5 years old: 2,307
  Population 5 to 9 years old: 2,449
  Population 10 to 14 years old: 2,664
  Population 15 to 19 years old: 2,859

The State Capitol building in Olympia. *©James Blank.*

Population 20 to 24 years old: 3,914
Population 25 to 34 years old: 6,471
Population 35 to 44 years old: 6,436
Population 45 to 54 years old: 6,434
Population 55 to 59 years old: 2,029
Population 60 to 64 years old: 1,279
Population 65 to 74 years old: 2,449
Population 75 to 84 years old: 2,261
Population 85 years and older: 962
Median age: 36.0 years

Births (2006, MSA)

Total number: 2,548

Deaths (2006, MSA)

Total number: 1,698

Money income (1999)

Per capita income: $22,590
Median household income: $40,846
Total households: 18,673

Number of households with income of . . .

less than $10,000: 1,923
$10,000 to $14,999: 1,340

$15,000 to $24,999: 2,511
$25,000 to $34,999: 2,519
$35,000 to $49,999: 2,931
$50,000 to $74,999: 3,826
$75,000 to $99,999: 1,835
$100,000 to $149,999: 1,370
$150,000 to $199,999: 226
$200,000 or more: 192

Percent of families below poverty level: 11% (1999)

2005 FBI Crime Index Property: 2,549

2005 FBI Crime Index Violent: 115

■ Municipal Government

Olympia has a council-manager form of government. Power lies with the council, which sets policy and makes budgetary decisions. Seven elected, non-partisan council members representing the community at-large, not individual districts, serve staggered four-year terms, with Position 1 designated as the Mayor's position. A city manager is hired by the council to advise and administer all city affairs.

Head Officials: Mayor Mark Foutch (NP) (since 2004; current term expires 2008); City Manager Steve Hall (since 2003)

Total Number of City Employees: approximately 600 (2007)

City Information: City of Olympia, 900 Plum St. SE, PO Box 1967, Olympia, WA 98507-1967; telephone (360)753-8447; email cityhall@ci.olympia.wa.us

■ Economy

Major Industries and Commercial Activity

The city's early development was based on its port facilities and lumber-based industries, and later oyster farming and dairying. Following World War II, Olympia served as a major service center for lumber communities west of Thurston County, while the Port of Olympia remained a major transportation center for shipping logs and finished lumber. But during the mid-twentieth century, the decline of the local timber industry resulted in the loss of many of the local associated milling and secondary operations.

During the 1970s, Olympia expanded as a center of offices and homes for state employees, military personnel, and their respective families. This further diminished Thurston County's already modest farm sector as housing development pushed into the remaining fertile prairies. Dairy and truck (mostly berry) farming continued in the south county, interspersed with small hobby farms.

In the late 1960s and early 1970s, the state legislature approved and financed construction of the Evergreen State College. The four-year public institution became an economic and cultural fixture in Thurston County with faculty, staff, and students contributing to the local housing and retail sectors. On a smaller scale, South Puget Sound Community College and Saint Martin's University in nearby Lacey also drove the housing demand. In the late 1980s the Olympia waterfront and downtown were revitalized, and an effort began to draw new businesses to the area.

Manufacturing continued to be a major economical segment in the early 2000s, though a setback was experienced with the closure of the famous Olympia Brewing Company (then owned by Miller) in June 2003. The company had been in business since 1896. Wood and food processing segments were stagnating, while plastics, industrial supplies, and machinery were experiencing growth. Area companies in these growth segments include Dart Containers, Inc.; Albany International Corp.; Big Toys, Inc.; and Amtech Corp. Overall, though, the number of manufacturing jobs was projected to decrease slightly until the late 2000s, when it is expected to regain the employment level it had in 1990.

Agriculture, another industry traditional to Olympia, also waned, although production is still higher than in nearby counties. Although the size of farms continues to decrease, the number of farms has actually increased. As with agriculture, the timber industry is dominated by smaller, family-owned operations.

As the capital of the state of Washington, Olympia relies on the state government to be a stabilizing factor for the local economy. In addition to the jobs it supports directly, state government also supports the economy by attracting tourists, as does the region's gambling industry. The annual sessions of the state legislature in the winter and spring mark the first tourist season of the year, with summertime recreation and attractions, including tours of state buildings, following.

Compared to other regions in the state, Olympia and Thurston County are home to a relatively small number of technology companies. To attract them, economic development officials promoted the area's telecommunication infrastructure, low property price, and educated workforce. In 2004 Univera Inc., a biotechnology firm, relocated to Thurston County from Colorado. Other recent additions to the area are Reach One, an Internet service provider, and Fast Transact, a processor of credit card transactions.

Among Thurston County's largest employers in 2006 were St. Peter's Hospital, Safeway Stores, Group Health Cooperative, Red Wind Casino, Capital Medical Center, and Panorama Corp.

Items and goods produced: wood products, processed foods, metal and paper containers

Incentive Programs—New and Existing Companies

Local programs: Olympia has no corporate or personal income tax, and no inventory tax. Thurston County offers exemptions on sales and use tax for manufacturing equipment, repair and replacement parts, and labor; for manufacturing machinery and equipment used for research and development; and for warehouse/distribution facilities and equipment. A tax credit of up to $2 million is available for research and development in the high technology industry. Tax exempt revenue bonds for manufacturing, ranging from $1 million to $10 million, are also available.

State programs: The state of Washington offers a number of incentive programs to attract new and expanding businesses to the state. Among them are B & O tax credits; sales/use tax deferrals for technology and manufacturing companies as well as for firms relocating or expanding in distressed areas; and loan programs that apply to rural areas and the redevelopment of brownfields.

Job training programs: South Puget Sound Community College provides specialized job training for public and private employees, contracts with businesses to provide specialized job training, and operates a comprehensive Cooperative Work Experience program. The Washington state Job Skills Training Program offers employers a 50 percent match for training costs. The federal Workforce Investment Act (WIA), formerly Job Training Partnership Act (JTPA), may match up to 50 percent of wages for on-the-job training of dislocated workers.

Development Projects

Faced with a higher cost of living, residents of such large cities as Seattle were migrating to Thurston County by the beginning of the twenty-first century. According to the Thurston Regional Planning Council, 77 percent of the county's increase in population between 1990 and 2000 was attributed to in-migration. This influx, combined with relatively low interest rates, drove development projects. In 2004 the Red Wind Casino completed a $31 million expansion, and the area's other tribal casinos completed similar upgrades. The Westfield Shoppingtown Capital mall expanded and renovated, and a 16-screen movie complex was added. Elsewhere in Thurston County, construction of new office buildings for the state government has been in progress, including the 160,000-square-foot, $35-million Cherry Street Plaza in Tumwater, which was dedicated in 2006.

In February 2007 the Olympia City Council identified a site at the corner of State Avenue and Jefferson Street (East Bay site) in downtown Olympia as the preferred location for a new City Hall/Police Station. The City Hall project will cost approximately $35 million. The site satisfies one of the Council's four primary goals, which is to invest in downtown. The city will collaborate with the Hands on Children's Museum (HOCM), LOTT Alliance, and Port of Olympia to clean up and redevelop this prime piece of downtown Olympia waterfront. The LOTT and HOCM have each announced their plans to build projects adjacent to the new City Hall site. The Port is planning for additional future mixed-use redevelopment of the 14 acres on the west side of Marine Drive at East Bay.

Economic Development Information: Economic Development Council of Thurston County, 665 Woodland Square Loop SE, Ste. 201, Lacey, WA 98503; telephone (360)754-6320; fax (360)407-3980; email busdev@thurstonedc.com. Thurston Regional Planning Council, 2404 Heritage Ct. SW, Ste. B, Olympia, WA 98502; telephone (360)786-5480; fax (360)754-4413; email info@trpc.org

Commercial Shipping

After years of struggling with an identity as a failing bastion of log exporting, the Port of Olympia reported its first profitable year in nearly a decade with a surplus of $400,000

in 2004. The turnaround was primarily due to diversification into such bulk commodities as metals and limestone, and the controversial move into military shipments to support the war in Iraq. The 60-acre, deepwater port offers three berths, a U.S. Customs bonded warehouse, and a cargo yard for breakbulk, bulk, rolling stock, and containerized cargoes. The Port of Olympia is also the site of Foreign Trade Zone #216, an area where foreign goods bound for international destinations can be temporarily stored without incurring an import duty. As of 2007 the Port of Olympia generated some 2,600 jobs in Thurston County and indirectly more than 5,000 in the state of Washington.

The Port of Olympia owns and operates Olympia Regional Airport, a general aviation-transport facility for corporate, commercial, and recreational users. The airport is 20 minutes by air to the Seattle-Tacoma International Airport and 50 minutes away from Vancouver, B.C. Nearly 90 miles of active rail lines lie in Thurston County. Burlington Northern Santa Fe, Union Pacific, and the Puget Sound & Pacific Railroad serve the area, with the Tri-City & Olympia Railroad also serving the Port of Olympia.

Labor Force and Employment Outlook

Olympia's workforce surpasses much of the nation in educational attainment. Of adults aged 25 years or older in 2000, 91.6 percent of Olympians had obtained a high school diploma, compared to the national average of 80.4 percent. That discrepancy is even greater in terms of college education, with 40.3 percent of Olympia's residents earning a bachelor's degree or higher, while only 24.4 percent did so across the United States as a whole. In September 2007 the civilian labor force in Olympia numbered 127,300. Approximately 5,400 workers were unemployed, leading to a 4.2 percent unemployment rate, which was below the national average of 4.7 percent for that month.

The following is a summary of data regarding the Olympia metropolitan area labor force, 2006 annual averages.

Size of nonagricultural labor force: 98,600

Number of workers employed in ...

    construction and mining: 6,000
    manufacturing: 3,200
    trade, transportation and utilities: 15,900
    information: Not available
    financial activities: 4,000
    professional and business services: 7,600
    educational and health services: Not available
    leisure and hospitality: 8,300
    other services: Not available
    government: 36,600

Average hourly earnings of production workers employed in manufacturing: Not available

Unemployment rate: 4.2% (June 2007)

Largest Thurston County employers (2006)	*Number of employees*
St. Peter's Hospital	2,300
North Thurston Public Schools	1,600
Olympia School District	1,336
Safeway Stores	825
Tumwater School District	815
South Puget Sound Community College	725
Group Health Cooperative	700
Red Wind Casino	610
Lucky Eagle Casino	534
Capital Medical Center	450
Panorama Corporation	360

Cost of Living

Rising real estate prices in the area are driven by people migrating from more crowded and costly counties to the north.

The following is a summary of data regarding several key cost of living factors for the Olympia area.

2007 (1st quarter) ACCRA Average House Price: $300,991

2007 (1st quarter) ACCRA Cost of Living Index: 104.0

State income tax rate: None

State sales tax rate: 6.5%

Local income tax rate: None

Local sales tax rate: 1.9%

Property tax rate: 13.119 per $1,000 of assessed value (2005)

Economic Information: Thurston County Chamber, 809 Legion Way SE, Olympia, WA 98501; telephone (360)357-3362; fax (360)357-3376; email info@thurstonchamber.com

■ Education and Research

Elementary and Secondary Schools

One of the oldest districts in the state of Washington, the Olympia School District was founded in 1852, nearly 40 years before Washington statehood. The district offers five alternative programs for students in elementary,

middle, or high school grades. It also offers an Early Childhood Program for children under five years with developmental disabilities and the Program for Academically Talented Students, which serves students in grades two through five. The district has strong programs in Advanced Placement, the International Baccalaureate, fine arts, technology, and athletics.

Olympia High School, one of the oldest public secondary schools in Washington, was built in 1906. The building was completely renovated in the late 1990s, and rededicated in October 2000. Taxpayers in February 2004 approved additional funds to renovate and update the district's other facilities.

Beginning with the graduating class of 2008, all students enrolled in the Olympia School District must meet new graduation requirements that include the earning of 22 credits, completion of the "High School and Beyond" plan, the attainment of a Certificate of Academic Achievement, and the completion of a culminating project.

The following is a summary of data regarding the Olympia School District as of the 2005–2006 school year.

Total enrollment: 40,019

Number of facilities
elementary schools: 11
junior high/middle schools: 4
senior high schools: 3
other: 0

Student/teacher ratio: 20.3:1

Teacher salaries (2005–06)
elementary median: $51,200
junior high/middle median: $49,460
secondary median: $50,180

Funding per pupil: $7,115

Olympia is home to a number of private and religious schools.

Public Schools Information: Olympia School District, 1113 Legion Way SE, Olympia, WA 98501; telephone (360)596-6100; fax (360)596-6111

Colleges and Universities

The Evergreen State College, a public liberal arts and sciences institution founded in 1969, enrolled approximately 4,500 students in 2007. The Olympia campus accounted for 93 percent of enrollment, with Grays Harbor, Tacoma, and Tribal Reservations sharing the remainder. Emphasizing interdisciplinary studies rather than traditional majors, Evergreen offers a Bachelor's of Arts and a Bachelor's of Science in Liberal Arts and Sciences, with the opportunity to concentrate in biology, communications, computer science, energy systems, environmental studies, health and human services, humanities, language, management and business, marine studies, mathematics, Native American studies, performing arts, physical science, politics and economics, pre-law, pre-medicine, and visual arts. Master's degree programs are offered in environmental studies, public administration, and teaching. In 2005 the *Princeton Review* listed Evergreen as "Best in the West" and a "Best-Value College."

South Puget Sound Community College is a two-year, public institution that serves all adults regardless of their previous education. More than 6,300 students each semester pursue associate's degrees in arts, general studies, technical arts, and nursing. The college also offers non-credit community education classes, adult literacy, and high school completion programs.

U.S. News & World Report ranked Saint Martin's University 44th among the best Western universities for Master's programs in its "America's Best Colleges 2005." St. Martin's, located in nearby Lacey, is a four-year, co-educational college with a strong liberal arts foundation that also encompasses business, education, and engineering. Known as Saint Martin's College until changing its name in August 2005, the school offers 21 undergraduate programs, six graduate programs, and numerous pre-professional and certification programs. St. Martin's, one of 18 U.S. Benedictine Catholic colleges, has more than 1,250 full- and part-time students enrolled at its main campus and 650 at its five extension campuses at the Fort Lewis Army Post, McChord Air Force Base, Centralia Community College, Tacoma Community College, and Olympic College at Bremerton.

Libraries and Research Centers

The Timberland Regional Library system has 27 community libraries, including the Olympia branch, and five cooperative library centers across the counties of Grays Harbor, Lewis, Mason, Pacific, and Thurston. The system encompasses some 1.6 million items, including books, electronic books, magazines, online reference databases, and numerous videos, CDs/records/cassettes, audio books, pamphlets, CD-ROMs, and DVDs. The Olympia Timberland Library was founded in 1909 with a collection of 900 books. In 2003 the Timberland Regional Library system became the state's first public library system to join with the Library of Congress as a partner in the national Veterans History Project.

Other local libraries include the college libraries at the Evergreen State College, whose special collections include a Rare Books room and the Chicano/Latino Archive, South Puget Sound Community College, Providence St. Peter Hospital, and the Washington State Capital Museum. The college's Daniel J. Evans Library re-opened after a renovation in Fall 2006, with improved study spaces, integrated technology, and world-class stained glass art by Evergreen alumnus Cappy Thompson.

The Washington State Library has more than half a million volumes and periodicals, with special collections on Washington newspapers, Washington authors, and Washington state documents. It is a U.S. government and Washington State depository library.

State of Washington governmental libraries include those of the Attorney General's Office, the Department of Information Services, the Department of Natural Resources, the Office of the Secretary of State, the State Superintendent of Public Instruction, and the Washington State Law Library.

Local research institutes include the Cascadia Research Collective, the Evergreen Freedom Foundation, The Evergreen State College Labor Education and Research Center, the Washington State Institute for Public Policy, and the Washington Department of Fish and Wildlife Fish Program.

Public Library Information: Olympia Timberland Library, 313 8th Ave. SE, Olympia, WA 98501; telephone (360)352-0595. Washington State Library, PO Box 42460, Olympia, WA 98504-2460; telephone (360)704-5200

■ Health Care

Olympia has two hospitals and functions as the regional medical center for five surrounding counties. The Providence Health System operates the 390-bed Providence St. Peter Hospital and the 191-bed Providence Centralia Hospital, each of which have served the community's health care needs for a century. Providence St. Peter is the largest hospital in the region, offering a full spectrum of acute care, specialty and outpatient services, including cardiac surgery, obstetrics, medical rehabilitation, emergency care, and outpatient surgery. Providence St. Peter has been named one of the 100 Top Hospitals in the nation for cardiology, orthopedics, and stroke care.

Capital Medical Center, established in 1985, has 119 beds and 238 physicians. The full-service hospital includes emergency care, private birthing suites, a same-day private-room surgery center, pain management services, a lymphedema program, senior programs, and a sleep disorder center.

Health Care Information: Providence St. Peter Hospital, 413 Lilly Rd NE, Olympia, WA 98506; telephone (360)491-9480; toll-free (888)492-9480. Capital Medical Center, 3900 Capital Mall Dr. SW, Olympia, WA 98502; telephone (360)754-5858; fax (360)956-2574

■ Recreation

Sightseeing

Located on the Olympic Peninsula, nearby Olympic National Park encompasses the Olympic Mountains and Pacific Ocean beaches. Beautiful Olympic National

Forest, which surrounds the park, is the site of three rain forests.

Capitol Lake Park provides a spectacular view of the state capitol buildings, the lake, and surrounding wooded bluffs. The Capitol grounds feature the Executive Mansion, the campus gardens, war memorials, and a conservatory. The Capitol group of buildings, completed in 1935, consists of six white sandstone structures located on a hill in the city's southern section. The marble interior Legislative Building at the center of the cluster has a 287-foot high dome, similar to that of the U.S. Capitol, and one of the highest of its kind in the world.

Heritage Fountain invites children and adults to don a swimsuit and splash among its 47 waterspouts. The fountain is part of the Heritage Park, a scenic pedestrian district stretching from the Capitol Grounds to Percival Landing. Percival Landing, on the city's waterfront, has a 1.5-mile boardwalk featuring works of art and interpretive displays outlining the history of the harbor. A walk along the Port Plaza provides mountain views from the working waterfront and a visit to the nationally recognized Batdorf and Bronson Coffee roasters shop.

Yashiro Japanese Garden, a traditional Asian garden designed in the ancient hill and pond style, honors Olympia's sister city of Yashiro, Japan. The walled garden features classic gates built without nails. The City of Yashiro presented two cutstone lanterns and a 13-tier pagoda as gifts to the garden.

Chief William Shelton's Story Pole, located on the Washington State Capitol Campus, was dedicated in 1940 to commemorate the relationship between Northwest Native tribal governments and the State of Washington. The American Revolution is remembered in downtown Sylvester Park with a monument to the End of the Oregon Trail, a leg of a pioneer trail that ran to the shores of Puget Sound.

The Nisqually Wildlife Refuge has 3,000 acres of land and waters to provide refuge and nesting places for migratory waterfowl, songbirds, raptors, and wading birds. The Woodard Bay Natural Resource Conservation Area is a wildlife sanctuary for bald eagles, seals, otters, and bats, and is one of the most important heron rookeries in Washington.

Four tribal casinos operate in Thurston County. Located in Olympia, the Red Wind Casino features slot machines, table games, dining, and live entertainment. The area's other casinos are Hawk's Prairie, Little Creek, and Lucky Eagle.

Arts and Culture

Olympia residents enjoy a variety of arts and cultural facilities and events. Each year, the Capitol Campus draws more than half a million visitors who tour the Legislature as well as the stately buildings, grounds, gardens, and artwork. The State Capital Museum, adjacent to the Capitol Campus, houses exhibits that document the story and political and cultural life of the city and state. Built in the 1850s, the Bigelow House Museum, one of the oldest homes in the Pacific Northwest, offers tours of the house's original furnishings. The exhibits at the Hands-On Children's Museum, across from the Capitol Campus, allow children to enjoy a first-hand experience of science and art. At the east side of the Olympia Airport, the Olympic Flight Museum features historic aircraft from around the world.

The Washington Center for the Performing Arts presents a full season of performances by resident and touring groups, offering music, dance, theater, and family entertainment. Groups in residence at the center include Ballet Northwest, Youth Symphonies, the Olympia Chamber Orchestra, the Olympia Symphony Orchestra, and Opera Pacifica. The Masterworks Choral Ensemble is a southwest Washington chorus based in Olympia. The Capital Playhouse, a semi-professional theater company, presents five musical performances in its season. The State Theater is the venue for Harlequin Productions, whose eclectic performances include both new works and innovative treatments of classics. The Olympia Film Society shows independent, international, and classic film year-round at the Capital Theater, offers special live performances, and annually produces a nationally recognized film festival.

The city's popular Music in the Park program takes place at noon each Friday from mid-July through August; its sister program, Music in the Dark, offers evening concerts on Wednesdays. The largest Art Walk in the state occurs in Olympia in April and October, with businesses featuring visual arts, performances, and poetry of local artists.

Olympia's downtown art galleries include the Childhood's End Gallery, Side Door Studio, Studio-FOUR18, Van Tuinen Art, and State of the Arts Gallery. The Evergreen Galleries on that college's campus feature changing exhibits.

Olympia is known as a center for independent rock and punk music produced and performed locally. Cover charges are generally low or non-existent, venues are often no-frills, and shows are frequently all-ages events. Folk, jazz, and bluegrass are traditionally strong draws as well. The Capitol Theater Backstage offers all-ages shows.

Festivals and Holidays

Olympia's first celebration of the year is April's Procession of the Species, a celebration of arts and the natural world that culminates in a procession of residents in masks and costumes. Percival Landing is the site of May's annual Wooden Boat Fair, which features wooden boats, international foods, and craft booths. Also in May is the annual Swantown Boatswap & Chowder Challenge, a day dedicated to boats, marine equipment, and clam chowder. Nearby that same month are the annual Harbor Shorebird Festival at the Grays Harbor National Wildlife

Refuge, and the Lacey Grand Prix Electric Car Race & Alternative Fuel Fair.

Summer begins with Duck Dash & Bite of Olympia, a June event featuring entertainment, children's activities, and a rubber duck race. Evergreen State College sponsors Super Saturday, a free festival for all ages, that same month. Also in June is the annual Olympic Air Show, held at the Olympic Flight Museum. July brings the Dixieland Jazz Festival, a four-day event, and Capital Lakefair, one of the largest community festivals in the state. The Thurston County Fair is held over the first weekend of August. For more than 60 years, the Pet Parade has invited the children of the city to parade the downtown streets with their favorite pets or toys, costumes, or creations of their own. Sand in the City, Washington's largest sand sculpting competition, takes place at the Olympia Waterfront Port Plaza each August.

Olympia Harbor Days is held over Labor Day weekend, and features the Tugboat Races & Festival. In September the Percival Play Day features activities and attractions for families. Octoberfest at the Farmers Market highlights the month, which also includes the Arts-Walk and the Children's Halloween Party at Olympia Center. In December, the spotlight is on the Parade of Lighted Boats at the city's waterfront.

Sports for the Spectator

The Geoducks, the sports teams of Evergreen State College, compete in cross country, track and field, volleyball, and men's and women's basketball and soccer. St. Martin's University teams, nicknamed the Saints, participate in baseball and softball, cross country, track and field, volleyball, and men's and women's basketball and golf. Nearby Tacoma is home to the Tacoma Rainiers baseball team, a Triple-A affiliate of the Seattle Mariners.

Sports for the Participant

Olympia's location on the Puget Sound and nearby mountains make outdoor recreation very popular, especially hiking, kayaking, skiing, and sailboating. Thurston County boasts a number of golf courses, including Vicwood, one of Washington's newest championship-rated courses. An abundance of parks and forests nearby and in the city include the very popular Tolmie State Park and Millersylvania State Park. Burfoot Park, which covers 50 acres of property with 1,100 feet of saltwater beach frontage on Budd Inlet, offers nature trails and beach access that feature beautiful views of the State Capitol and the Olympic Mountains.

The Capital City Marathon winds through various parts of town each May. Nearby Rochester is the site for June's Swede Day 5K Fun Run/Walk. The following month the Washington State Senior Games take place throughout Thurston County, with a series of athletic competitions in 20 sports for men and women aged 50 and older.

Shopping and Dining

The Westfield Shoppingtown Capital mall encompasses more than 100 stores and restaurants, and is anchored by JCPenney and Macy's. Olympia's Farmers Market, the second largest in the state, offers the finest in handicrafts, baked goods, and fresh produce. It is located on Budd Inlet, the southernmost reach of the Puget Sound.

Naturally, the stars of Olympia's cuisine are the wonderful fish and seafood that have made the area famous. In addition to Northwest fare, diners may choose from ethnic cuisine, oven fired pizza, or family dining spots. Jean-Pierre's Garden Room in Tumwater is known for fine dining.

Visitor Information: State Capital Visitor Center, 14th Ave. and Capitol Way, Olympia, WA 98504; telephone (360)586-3460; fax (360)586-4636. Olympia-Thurston County Visitor & Convention Bureau, PO Box 7338, Olympia, WA 98507; telephone (360)704-7544; toll-free (877)704-7500; fax (360)704-7533; email info@visitolympia.com

■ Convention Facilities

Thurston County offers more than 2,500 hotel rooms and over 100,000 square feet of meeting space. The Thurston County Fairgrounds, located in Olympia, feature three buildings including the Thurston Expo Center. The Olympia Center and the Washington Center for the Performing Arts each offer facilities for a variety of meeting and exhibition events. The Washington State Capital Museum houses several venues for conferences, among them the Coach House and the Conference Room. The Norman Worthington Conference Center on the St. Martin's University campus in nearby Lacey has 4,752 square feet of open area that can be partitioned into four smaller rooms of approximately 1,100 square feet each. Other meeting venues include the Heritage Room at Capital Lake, the Jacob Smith House, Lucky Eagle Casino, Lacey Community Center, facilities at Evergreen State College, the Indian Summer Golf and Country Club, the Masonic Center and New Masonic Center, the Olympic Flight Museum, Squaxin Island Museum Library and Research Center, Stampfer Center, the State Theater, Tugboat Annie's, Mercato Ristorante, Olympia Tumwater Foundation Schmidt House, the Pavilion at American Heritage Campground, Ramblin' Jacks, and Tumwater Valley Lodge.

Convention Information: Olympia-Thurston County Visitor & Convention Bureau, PO Box 7338, Olympia, WA 98507; telephone (360)704-7544; toll-free (877)704-7500; fax (360)704-7533; email info@visitolympia.com

■ Transportation

Approaching the City

Olympia can be approached from the east by Interstate 5. In the center of the city, Interstate 5 turns southward. State highway 12 runs westward beginning at the center of the city. State highway 101 runs northward from the west side of Olympia.

Olympia is served by Seattle-Tacoma International Airport. Located 45 miles northwest of downtown Olympia, "Sea-Tac Airport" handled almost 30 million passengers in 2006. The Olympia Regional Airport, situated in Tumwater, is home to aircraft service operations, hangars, corporate offices, and a modern public terminal. The airport provides tower-controlled and full-instrument approach access for a variety of recreational, commercial, and corporate users.

Traveling in the City

Olympia's downtown streets are arranged in a grid to the east of Budd Inlet. Local bus transportation is available on the free Capitol Shuttle. The Intercity Transit has routes to nearby cities. Amtrak provides rail transportation, and bus service is provided by Greyhound.

■ Communications

Newspapers and Magazines

The Olympian is the city's daily newspaper. Three monthly newspapers published locally are *The Thurston-Mason Senior News; Washington State Grange News,* an agricultural paper; and *Works in Progress,* a community newspaper.

Television and Radio

Olympia has one cable television station, as well as two FM and two AM radio stations with nostalgia, country music, classical, soft rock, and eclectic programming.

Media Information: *The Olympian,* 111 Bethel St. NE, PO Box 407, Olympia, WA; 98507; telephone (360) 754-5400; fax (360)754-5408; email service@theolympian.com

Olympia Online

City of Olympia. Available www.ci.olympia.wa.us

Olympia-Thurston County Visitor & Convention Bureau. Available www.visitolympia.com

The Olympian. Available www.theolympian.com

Thurston County Chamber. Available www .thurstonchamber.com

Thurston County Economic Development Council. Available www.thurstonedc.com

Thurston Regional Planning Council. Available www.trpc.org

Timberland Regional Library. Available www .timberland.lib.wa.us

BIBLIOGRAPHY

Christie, Rebecca A., *Workingman's Hill: A History of an Olympia Neighborhood* (Olympia, WA: Bigelow House Preservation Association, 2001)

Newell, Gordon, *So Fair a Dwelling Place: A History of Olympia and Thurston County, Washington* (Olympia, WA: Gordon Newell and F. George Warren, 1984)

Seattle

■ The City in Brief

Founded: 1851 (incorporated 1869)

Head Official: Mayor Greg Nickels (D) (since 2001)

City Population

    1980: 493,846
    1990: 516,259
    2000: 563,374
    2006 estimate: 582,454
    Percent change, 1990–2000: 9.1%
    U.S. rank in 1980: 23rd
    U.S. rank in 1990: 21st
    U.S. rank in 2000: 30th

Metropolitan Area Population

    1980: 1,607,000
    1990: 2,033,108
    2000: 2,414,616
    2006 estimate: 3,263,497
    Percent change, 1990–2000: 18.76%
    U.S. rank in 1980: 18th (CMSA)
    U.S. rank in 1990: 14th (CMSA)
    U.S. rank in 2000: 13th (CMSA)

Area: 83.9 square miles (2000)

Elevation: Ranges from sea level to 450 feet above sea level

Average Annual Temperatures: January, 41.5° F; July, 65.5° F; annual average, 52.9° F

Average Annual Precipitation: 38.25 inches of rain; 7.3 inches of snow

Major Economic Sectors: services, wholesale and retail trade, government

Unemployment Rate: 4.2% (June 2007)

Per Capita Income: $36,392 (2005)

2005 FBI Crime Index Property: 43,471

2005 FBI Crime Index Violent: 4,109

Major Colleges and Universities: University of Washington, Seattle Pacific University, Seattle University

Daily Newspaper: *The Seattle Times; Seattle Post-Intelligencer*

■ Introduction

Little more than a century ago, Seattle—nicknamed "The Emerald City"—was a pioneer outpost and a quiet lumbering town. Transformed by the Yukon gold rush into a thriving metropolis, Seattle has become the transportation, manufacturing, commercial, and services hub for the Pacific Northwest as well as the largest urban area north of San Francisco, California. The city's arts community has gained an international reputation, annually drawing audiences from throughout the United States and abroad. Nestled between two magnificent mountain ranges, with a breathtaking view of a lake and bay, Seattle enjoys a climate one observer has likened to "an airborne ocean bath."

■ Geography and Climate

Seattle is situated on a series of hills in a lowland area on Puget Sound's eastern shore between the Olympic Mountains to the west and the Cascade Mountains to the east. Westerly air currents from the ocean and the shielding effects of the Cascade range produce a mild and moderately moist climate, with warm winters and cool summers. Extremes in temperature are rare and of short duration, and the daily fluctuation is slight. While Seattle is known for its pronounced rainy season and frequent cloudy weather, the average annual rainfall is actually less than that of many other cities in the United States, including New York and Atlanta.

Area: 83.9 square miles (2000)

Elevation: Ranges from sea level to 450 feet above sea level

Average Temperatures: January, 41.5° F; July, 65.5° F; annual average, 52.9° F

Average Annual Precipitation: 38.25 inches of rain; 7.3 inches of snow

■ History

Illinois Farmers Build Sawmills in Seattle

The original inhabitants of the region surrounding the site of present-day Seattle were the Suquamish tribe. Their chief, Sealth, befriended a group of Illinois farmers who settled in the area in 1851. These settlers, the first people of European descent to arrive north of the Columbia River, had established a town at Alki Point on Elliott Bay then moved to the location of present-day Pioneer Square. They named their new town Seattle in gratitude to Chief Sealth.

Finding an abundant lumber resource in the rich forests, the settlers set up sawmills for the preparation of logs for export to San Francisco, where the 1849 gold rush had generated a building boom. By 1853 the lumber industry was thriving in the area, and for several years it provided the sole economic base of Seattle, which was incorporated in 1869.

City Rebuilds After Fire; Becomes Commercial Center

In 1889 a great fire, ignited by a flaming glue pot in a print shop, destroyed the entire business district, consuming sixty blocks. Damaged wood-frame buildings were replaced by masonry structures on a higher elevation than the original storefronts, resulting in the creation of an underground city that is a popular tourist attraction in modern Seattle. The city recovered fairly quickly from the setback caused by the fire.

During the last decade of the nineteenth century Seattle became a rail and maritime commercial center when the Great Northern Railroad reached town and the city was selected by a major shipping line as the port of entry for trade with the Orient. The Alaska gold rush brought further growth and development, and Seattle, dubbed the "gateway to the Klondike," increased in population from 56,842 people in 1897 to 80,600 people in 1900. Prosperity continued and within the next decade the population grew to 240,000 residents.

Rise of Aerospace Industry; World's Fair Brings Tourists

Seattle's aerospace industry began when a small local firm that became the Boeing Company—now the world's foremost manufacturer of jet aircraft and spacecraft—started making two-seater biplanes in 1916. The shipping and aircraft industries continued to play an important role in the city's economy during both world wars and into the 1960s. Boeing moved its corporate headquarters from Seattle to Chicago in 2001.

The Seattle World's Fair in 1962 brought new economic dimensions to the region, establishing Seattle as a tourist and entertainment center. As a result of the reduction of federal support for aerospace projects in the 1970s, the city's reliance on the aircraft industry shifted to development of its position as a transportation hub in the international market. Since 1975 Seattle has undergone renewed economic expansion to become the financial, industrial, and trade center for the Pacific Northwest.

Seattle made international headlines in 1999 when the city played host to the World Trade Organization meeting. Forty thousand demonstrators gathered to protest globalization; city leaders had hoped that the summit would showcase Seattle as a world-class friend to free trade. The event highlighted the tension between those who liked the new high-tech, high-wealth Seattle and those who believed that Seattle is losing its small-town charm.

Today, Seattle is a hotbed of activity in the Pacific Northwest. Located just two hours south of Vancouver, Canada, the city of Seattle is an international port that boasts several professional sports teams, hundreds of restaurants, a myriad of cultural venues, and a lifestyle that is unique to the Pacific Northwest.

■ Population Profile

Metropolitan Area Residents

1980: 1,607,000
1990: 2,033,108
2000: 2,414,616
2006 estimate: 3,263,497
Percent change, 1990–2000: 18.76%
U.S. rank in 1980: 18th (CMSA)
U.S. rank in 1990: 14th (CMSA)
U.S. rank in 2000: 13th (CMSA)

City Residents

1980: 493,846
1990: 516,259
2000: 563,374
2006 estimate: 582,454
Percent change, 1990–2000: 9.1%

Image copyright Alex Stepanov, 2007. Used under license from Shutterstock.com.

U.S. rank in 1980: 23rd
U.S. rank in 1990: 21st
U.S. rank in 2000: 30th

Density: 6,717.0 people per square mile (2000)

Racial and ethnic characteristics (2005)

White: 369,689
Black: 43,914
American Indian and Alaska Native: 6,336
Asian: 77,363
Native Hawaiian and Pacific Islander: 1,666
Hispanic or Latino (may be of any race): 33,707
Other: 16,940

Percent of residents born in state: 38.8% (2000)

Age characteristics (2005)

Population under 5 years old: 31,852
Population 5 to 9 years old: 22,672
Population 10 to 14 years old: 21,424
Population 15 to 19 years old: 20,805
Population 20 to 24 years old: 41,462
Population 25 to 34 years old: 108,525
Population 35 to 44 years old: 95,502

Population 45 to 54 years old: 75,485
Population 55 to 59 years old: 35,744
Population 60 to 64 years old: 24,959
Population 65 to 74 years old: 25,309
Population 75 to 84 years old: 22,297
Population 85 years and older: 10,910
Median age: 36.8 years

Births (2006, MSA)

Total number: 40,948

Deaths (2006, MSA)

Total number: 21,253

Money income (2005)

Per capita income: $36,392
Median household income: $49,297
Total households: 261,433

Number of households with income of . . .

less than $10,000: 24,932
$10,000 to $14,999: 15,525
$15,000 to $24,999: 27,521
$25,000 to $34,999: 26,124
$35,000 to $49,999: 38,061

$50,000 to $74,999: 44,504
$75,000 to $99,999: 27,491
$100,000 to $149,999: 30,810
$150,000 to $199,999: 14,191
$200,000 or more: 12,274

Percent of families below poverty level: 9.6% (2005)

2005 FBI Crime Index Property: 43,471

2005 FBI Crime Index Violent: 4,109

■ Municipal Government

Seattle operates under a mayor-council form of government. The mayor is elected to a four-year term; the nine council members, elected at large, serve staggered four-year terms. Seattle is the seat of King County.

Head Official: Mayor Greg Nickels (D) (since 2001; current term expires December 31, 2009)

Total Number of City Employees: 14,297 (2006)

City Information: City Hall, 600 4th Avenue Floor 1, PO Box 94726, Seattle, WA 98124; telephone (206) 684-2489

■ Economy

Major Industries and Commercial Activity

While Seattle had in the past been largely dependent on the aerospace industry (until 2001 it was the corporate headquarters of the Boeing Company, the world's largest aerospace firm), the city's diverse economy is also based on the manufacture of transportation equipment and forest products as well as food processing and advanced technology in computer software, biotechnology, electronics, medical equipment, and environmental engineering. In 2003 Corbis, one of the world's leading providers of digital images, moved its headquarters to downtown Seattle. Nonmanufacturing activities, however, comprise more than 85 percent of the Seattle economy; international trade, for instance, is a leading industry, accounting for a large portion of jobs statewide.

The Port of Seattle, the second largest handler of container cargo in the country, provides a direct connection to the Orient and serves as a major link in trade with markets in Alaska, on the Gulf of Mexico, and on the Atlantic Coast. With its multifaceted transportation network of freeways, railroads, an airport, a ferry system, and port facilities, Seattle is the principal trade, distribution, financial, and services center for the Northwest. Tourism continues to be a vital part of the city's economy.

Five companies on the 2006 *Fortune* 500 list are headquartered in Seattle: financial services company Washington Mutual, Internet retailer Amazon.com, department store Nordstrom, coffee chain Starbucks, and insurance company Safeco Corporation. Although Boeing moved its headquarters to Chicago in 2001, Boeing remains the Seattle area's largest private employer. In 2006 *Expansion Magazine* ranked Seattle among the top 10 metropolitan areas in the nation for climates favorable to business expansion.

Items and goods produced: food products, textiles, aluminum, iron and steel products, lumber, flour, clothing, airplanes, canned fish and fruit

Incentive Programs—New and Existing Companies

Local programs: There are many incentives available to businesses in Seattle/King County. These include aerospace industry incentives, a manufacturing machinery sales and use tax exemption, tax deferrals, a research and development business and occupation credit, and international services tax credits.

State programs: The state of Washington offers a number of incentive programs to attract new and expanding businesses to the state. Among them are B & O tax credits; sales/use tax deferrals for technology and manufacturing companies as well as for firms relocating or expanding in distressed areas; and loan programs that apply to rural areas and the redevelopment of brownfields.

Job training programs: The Washington state Job Skills Training Program offers employers a 50 percent match for training costs. The federal Workforce Investment Act (WIA), formerly Job Training Partnership Act (JTPA), may match up to 50 percent of wages for on-the-job training of dislocated workers. Washington also offers a credit for Job Training Services, which is a credit of 20 percent of the cost spent on job training by firms eligible for an Empowerment Zone sales tax deferral/exemption. This may be taken as a business and occupation tax credit. The amount of credit for a particular firm is limited to $5,000 annually.

Development Projects

With Seattle mired in a recession in the aftermath of the September 11, 2001, terrorist attacks on the United States, Mayor Greg Nickels created the Economic Opportunity Task Force to revitalize distressed neighborhood business districts and work on policies that benefit the University of Washington. Also at the top of the mayor's economic development agenda were transportation issues, including replacement of the Alaskan Way

538

Viaduct, the expansion of the Seattle monorail, and the improvement of Sound Transit's light rail line.

Perhaps one of the area's most ambitious projects is the replacement of the Alaskan Way Viaduct with a tunnel. Because the adjacent seawall is deteriorating and the viaduct itself was severely damaged in the 2001 Nisqually earthquake, both structures need to be rebuilt in order to remove a threat to public safety and the economy. The viaduct is one of the state's most important transportation corridors, carrying 110,000 vehicles a day. Since 2001, millions of dollars have been spent to secure it. Construction on the viaduct's first Moving Forward project began in 2007. All of the Moving Forward projects are expected to be completed by 2012, when the viaduct along the central waterfront will be removed.

Numerous apartments, condominiums, hotels, and retail spaces are under construction or renovation in the downtown area. The 362,987-square-foot Downtown Central Library opened in May 2004. Construction to transform nine acres of waterfront property adjoining Myrtle Edwards Park into an open space began in June 2004. The park has a two-story pavilion, parking for 54 vehicles, and pedestrian walkways as well as a pedestrian overpass. The Olympic Sculpture Park is also included in the green space.

In addition to a massive, $300 million expansion of Terminal 18, the Port of Seattle has been carrying out other projects as a part of the Seattle Seaport Terminal Project. The plan consists of numerous smaller projects that are expected to improve the port's terminals for businesses, tourists, and passengers. In past decades, the Port has invested $2.1 billion in facilities improvements and plans to invest an additional $2.9 billion over the next decade. Dredging the east waterway of the Duwamish River is expected to cost $7.5 million and will help make several more of the Port's container berths deep enough to accommodate the next generation of container ships. This will also create jobs both on the waterfront and throughout the region. The first phase of a $12.7 million cruise terminal began in 2000; Norwegian cruise Line and Royal Caribbean International use the port for new cruise services. In 2007 the Port completed construction of a new concrete bridge between Terminals 25 and 30. With the bridge, the area can now be used as one contiguous 70-acre container terminal. The second of three project phases of Terminal 18 was completed in September 2007. When construction on Terminal 18 is complete, the facility will have four active container berths. Completion is scheduled for September 2008.

Economic Development Information: City of Seattle Office of Economic Development, 700 Fifth Avenue, Suite 5752, PO Box 94708, Seattle, WA 98124-4708; telephone (206)684-8090; fax (206)684-0379. Trade Development Alliance of Greater Seattle, 1301 Fifth Avenue, Suite 2500, Seattle, WA 98101; telephone (206) 389-7301; fax (206)624-5689

Commercial Shipping

Seattle's economy benefits from Seattle-Tacoma International Airport (Sea-Tac); total air cargo for 2006 was 341,952 metric tons. Sea-Tac is the nineteenth busiest U.S. cargo airport. The city's most important commercial asset is Elliott Bay, one of the finest deep-water ports in the world. The Port of Seattle can accommodate ships up to 1,400 feet in length and provides generous warehouse space. In 2006 the total tonnage of sea cargo handled was 20,769,134. Two transcontinental railroads and more than 170 motor freight carriers transport goods to and from Seattle.

Labor Force and Employment Outlook

Seattle offers an educated, skilled, productive, and stable work force, and workers are attracted to the area by the quality of life. Local analysts expect continued growth in the Seattle area, especially in manufacturing industries (mainly aircraft and biotechnology) and services. The total labor force of the Seattle metropolitan region in September 2007 was 1,823,711. That month 74,769 workers were unemployed, for an unemployment rate of 4.1 percent, below the national average of 4.7 percent.

The following is a summary of data regarding the Seattle-Tacoma-Bellevue metropolitan area labor force, 2006 annual averages.

Size of nonagricultural labor force: 1,688,700

Number of workers employed in . . .

    construction and mining: 115,800
    manufacturing: 181,100
    trade, transportation and utilities: 319,500
    information: 81,500
    financial activities: 105,300
    professional and business services: 226,900
    educational and health services: 186,300
    leisure and hospitality: 156,900
    other services: 62,400
    government: 253,100

Average hourly earnings of production workers employed in manufacturing: Not available

Unemployment rate: 4.2% (June 2007)

Largest employers (2007)	*Number of employees*
The Boeing Company	62,000
Port of Seattle	11,225
Alaska Air Group Inc.	11,150
Microsoft Corporation	11,000

Largest employers (2007)	Number of employees
University of Washington	10,000
Safeway Stores	9,293
VA Puget Sound Health Care System	8,500
Virginia Mason	7,957
Amazon.com Inc.	7,500
AT&T	7,328

Cost of Living

The cost of living in Seattle is not inexpensive, given the relatively high price of housing. According to the Northwest Multiple Listing Service, the median price of condominiums and houses in King County, which includes Seattle, was $365,000 in March 2006, a 12.3 percent jump from the same period in 2005.

The following is a summary of data regarding several key cost of living factors for the Seattle area.

2007 (1st quarter) ACCRA Average House Price: Not available

2007 (1st quarter) ACCRA Cost of Living Index: 115.9

State income tax rate: None

State sales tax rate: 6.5%

Local income tax rate: None

Local sales tax rate: 1.0%

Property tax rate: $10.21-12.18 per $1,000 assessed value (2004)

Economic Information: The Greater Seattle Datasheet, City of Seattle, Office of Intergovernmental Relations, 600 Fourth Ave., 5th Floor, Seattle, WA 98124; telephone (206)684-8055; fax (206)684-8267

■ Education and Research

Elementary and Secondary Schools

Seattle Public Schools is the largest district in the state and the 44th largest in the nation. The system is administered by a nonpartisan, seven-member school board that appoints a superintendent. Six Seattle schools were named "Washington State 2007 Schools of Distinction." The award is given to only 86 schools in the state, and is based on steady improvement in student achievement in reading and mathematics over a six-year period.

The following is a summary of data regarding the Seattle Public Schools as of the 2005–2006 school year.

Total enrollment: 45,800

Number of facilities

elementary schools: 59
junior high/middle schools: 10
senior high schools: 12
other: 16

Student/teacher ratio: 20.5:1

Teacher salaries (2005–06)

elementary median: $49,180
junior high/middle median: $49,000
secondary median: $51,150

Funding per pupil: $8,655

More than 300 private and parochial schools, preschools, and special schools also operate in the Seattle metropolitan area.

Public Schools Information: Seattle Public Schools, PO Box 34165, Seattle, WA 98124-1165; telephone (206)252-0000

Colleges and Universities

The University of Washington (which enrolls nearly 40,000 students), Seattle Pacific University (which enrolls 3,800), and Seattle University (which enrolls 4,100) are the major four-year accredited institutions of higher learning in Seattle. They offer baccalaureate degrees in a wide range of disciplines and graduate degrees in such fields as education, law, software engineering, and medicine. A number of community colleges, vocational schools, and adult-education centers serve Seattle residents.

Libraries and Research Centers

In addition to its main branch downtown, the Seattle Public Library system operates 26 branches throughout the city. Its collection consists of nearly 2.3 million items. Total patron visits in 2006 (including the Central Library, branches, website visits, and TeleCirc) was 10,889,752. Special collections focus on aeronautics, African Americans, and Northwest history. In 1998 Seattle voters approved a $196.4 million bond measure to upgrade the Seattle Public Library system with new facilities, technology, and books. The 362,987-square-foot facility, which opened in 2004, includes a 275-seat auditorium and parking for 143 vehicles.

The University of Washington's library, said to be the largest and most comprehensive in the Northwest, holds more than six million volumes. Special libraries there are affiliated with universities, government agencies, hospitals, and local corporations, concentrating on such fields as medicine, business, banking, law, and science.

The University of Washington is the heart of research study in Seattle, including the areas of microcomputer architecture, digital systems theory, speech and image processing, artificial intelligence, and metallurgical and ceramic engineering. Other major research facilities are the Fred Hutchinson Cancer Research Center and the Battelle Memorial Institute.

Public Library Information: Seattle Public Library, 1000 Fourth Avenue, Seattle, WA 98104-1109; telephone (206)386-4636

■ Health Care

With a national reputation for its diagnostic and treatment facilities, which include more free clinics than in any other West Coast city, Seattle-King County is the health care center for the Pacific Northwest. The metropolitan area offers more than 25 general acute-care and five special purpose centers providing thousands of beds and physicians. University of Washington Hospital is the teaching hospital for the University of Washington. Among Seattle's other leading health care institutions are Children's Hospital and Regional Medical Center, the Fred Hutchinson Cancer Research Center, Virginia Mason Medical Center, and Swedish Medical Center. Bailey-Boushay House, a residence where people with HIV can be treated less expensively than at traditional centers, has provided over a decade of life-changing care. The Seattle Cancer Treatment and Wellness Center is the only cancer center in the Pacific Northwest where medical oncologists work side by side with practitioners of alternative medicine.

■ Recreation

Sightseeing

Seattle is consistently ranked among the top U.S. tourist destinations. Many attractions are located in the pedestrian-scale downtown area or within easy access by bus and monorail. Tourists can choose from several diversions, including historical sites, internationally acclaimed cultural events, and outdoor activities in the spectacular mountains, forests, and waters surrounding the city.

A popular Seattle landmark is the Space Needle, focal point of the Seattle Center, the 74-acre park and building complex constructed for the 1962 World's Fair. The 605-foot Space Needle features an observation deck for viewing the city, Puget Sound, and adjacent Cascade and Olympic mountains. At its base is the $100 million Experience Music Project, a nonprofit interactive museum tracing the history of American music, which was funded entirely by Microsoft co-founder Paul Allen. The Seattle Center, linked to the central business district by free bus service and the high-speed Monorail, contains an amusement park and sponsors outdoor concerts as well as other events.

Pioneer Square, near the waterfront downtown, is the city's historic district. This area offers a trip back to late-1800s Seattle via cobblestone streets, the original Skid Road (an expression that later evolved into Skid Row), and restored brick and sandstone buildings, many of them housing shops and restaurants. A unique point of interest beneath Pioneer Square is the "underground city," five blocks of sidewalks and storefronts that were left standing after the 1889 fire, when the street levels were raised.

Seattle offers an abundance of attractions related to the maritime industry. Harbor traffic on Elliott Bay can be observed from Waterfront Park, located in the pier area just off Alaskan Way. South of the park at Pier 53, the Seattle Fire Department boats *Alki* and *Chief Seattle* are berthed; a favorite local event is practice day, when the fireboats shoot high water arcs into the bay. As of 2007 the *Chief Seattle* was being upgraded, and the *Alki* was due to be retired from service. Two new fireboats, *Engine One*, built in 2006, and the *Leschi*, built in 2007, are based at Elliott Bay. At Fishermen's Terminal, a working commercial fishing port, residents and visitors enjoy watching fishermen mend nets and tend their boats. Hiram M. Chittenden Locks (Ballard Locks), among the busiest locks in the world, furnish diversion for navigation enthusiasts as scores of large and small vessels are transferred daily between salt and fresh water. The Seattle Aquarium on the downtown waterfront links the waterfront to First Avenue, which lies just above. For those wanting to go out onto the water, ferries provide rides along the coast and across the sound; tour boats offer longer cruises and excursions to points of interest in the area.

Seattle is known for the Woodland Park Zoo, which contains about 1,000 animals in their natural habitats with minimal fencing and barriers; special features are 50 endangered species and the world's largest group of liontail macaques. Washington Park on the University of Washington campus is the setting for the Arboretum, 200 acres of public gardens, including a Japanese tea garden, with especially striking displays of blossoms and foliage during spring and fall.

Arts and Culture

Seattle is the cultural and entertainment hub of the Pacific Northwest as well as one of the nation's leading cities for theater and opera. Rivaled only by New York in the number of equity theaters based in the area and considered one of the leading U.S. cities for opera performances, Seattle is the only place in the Western Hemisphere where Richard Wagner's *Ring* cycle is performed annually. Attaining wide recognition has in fact become a Seattle tradition, yet cultural events also emphasize regional artists and performers.

The arts scene includes the Seattle Symphony, located in the world-class Benaroya Hall; Seattle Opera; the Pacific Northwest Ballet; numerous art galleries; the

Seattle Art Museum; the Seattle Asian Art Museum; the Seattle Repertory Theatre; Intiman Theatre; and the Experience Music Project rock and roll museum.

The city is rich in theater arts with 80 companies, 13 of which are professional. The Seattle Opera, recognized internationally for its compelling and accomplished performances, moved into its new state-of-the-art home, Marion Oliver McCaw Hall, in 2003. The Seattle Repertory Theatre Company, the city's principal and nationally acclaimed professional theater company, stages its annual productions at the Bagley Wright Theater at Seattle Center. Downtown's Paramount Theatre houses both the Fifth Avenue Theatre and visiting Broadway shows. Live theater is presented by area companies, including A Contemporary Theater (ACT), now housed at the renovated Eagle's Auditorium; Empty Space; and Intiman. Several small theaters are also active in the Seattle metropolitan area. Dramatic and musical performances are regularly scheduled at the University of Washington. Seattle hosts large-scale musical concerts and has gained international attention as the place of origin of many trend-setting rock and pop groups.

Seattle supports a number of museums and galleries specializing in a wide range of areas. The Seattle Art Museum displays a large collection of Oriental, Asian, African, and modern art; of special interest is a collection of paintings by the Northwest Mystics school. The Charles and Emma Frye Art Museum downtown features exhibits of eighteenth- and nineteenth-century and contemporary paintings. The Bellevue Art Museum in Bellevue Square specializes in works by regional artists. The Henry Art Gallery at the University of Washington is one of the oldest art museums in the state. Commercial galleries, most of them clustered around Pioneer Square, regularly schedule shows.

The Museum of Flight traces the history of flight from Leonardo da Vinci to the present with such exhibits as "Apollo," which chronicles manned space exploration and displays more than forty aircraft. The Suquamish Museum is devoted to the preservation of Puget Sound native culture; artifacts, photographs, and oral histories are featured. Daybreak Star Arts and Cultural Center in Discovery Park pays homage to Northwest Coast tribes through indoor and outdoor displays of paintings and carvings. The Burke Museum of Natural History and Culture displays artifacts and geological materials relating to Northwest Coast native and Pacific Rim cultures; dinosaur exhibits are a highlight. The Museum of History and Industry concentrates on the heritage of Seattle, King County, and the Pacific Northwest. The Pacific Science Center, located at Seattle Center, presents exhibits pertaining to science; laser shows and films are shown at the Eames/IMAX Theater. The Science Center also is home to the Boeing 3D IMAX Theatre. The Seattle Children's Museum, also at Seattle Center, offers such hands-on activities as a child-size neighborhood for both adults and children.

Festivals and Holidays

Seattle and its environs, a major attraction for the television and film industry, support an annual, world-famous international film festival. Other festival celebrations include the Seattle International Children's Festival and the Bite of Seattle food festival. The Northwest Folklife Festival is held at Seattle Center on Memorial Day weekend in May; this annual event features traditional folk music, folk dances, and the culture of the people of the Pacific Northwest. Held annually for 23 days from mid-July to early August, the Seattle Seafair includes boat races and exhibitions, parades, a queen coronation and pageant, fishing derbies, food, and entertainment. Also in July and August is the famous Pacific Northwest Wagner Festival, presenting performances of the composer's complete *Ring* cycle, staged at Marion Oliver McCaw Hall. Seattle Center is the site on Labor Day weekend of the Seattle Arts Festival, popularly known as "Bumbershoot"; rated as one of the five top festivals in the nation, it is a celebration of the city's arts community with more than 400 performances ranging from grunge bands to Russian tightrope walkers. The year closes with the Harvest Festival in November and the Christmas Cruise in December.

Sports for the Spectator

Seattle is the only city in the Northwest to support professional teams in all three major sports. The Seattle Seahawks of the American Football Conference play at Qwest Field, a 72,000-seat, open-air stadium. The Seattle Mariners play American League baseball at Safeco Field, which has a retractable roof. The SuperSonics, a National Basketball Association team, hold their games in the Key Arena in the Seattle Center, which is also the scene of hockey action from the Seattle Thunderbirds of the Western Hockey League. Soccer fans enjoy matches featuring the Seattle Sounders at Qwest Field. WNBA women's basketball is played by the Seattle Storm. Area colleges and universities field teams in all primary sports. There is also horse racing at Emerald Downs, minor league baseball with the Everett Aquasox and Tacoma Rainiers, the Professional Rodeo Cowboys Association (PRCA) Rodeo, and numerous other spectator and participatory sports.

Sports for the Participant

Considered one of the best recreational cities in the United States, Seattle offers a variety of outdoor activities. Especially popular are water sports such as fresh- and salt-water fishing, boating, swimming, scuba diving, and whitewater rafting on lakes and waterways within an hour of downtown. Hiking and horseback riding can be enjoyed on miles of forest trails maintained in area parks and mountains; skiing and mountain climbing, including guided climbs to the top of Mount Rainier, can be pursued at several locations in the mountains surrounding Seattle. Five golf courses, more than 150 tennis courts, 12 beaches, 10 swimming pools, and more than 30 play fields can be found in the area's nearly 400 parks and open spaces.

Shopping and Dining

Shopping can be a unique experience in Seattle, where high-fashion merchandise and recreational gear coexist on shop counters. Major department stores and designer boutiques are located downtown within walking distance of hotels and in suburban shopping centers throughout the area. Seattle is the nation's primary manufacturing and retail center for recreational and outdoor equipment. Northwest Native American handicrafts and art items are available at local artisan centers, specialty shops, and galleries and museums; goods imported from the Orient are featured at shops in Seattle's International District, where Chinatown is located. Historic Pike Place Market near Pioneer Square is one of the few remaining authentic farmer's markets in the nation. A terraced walkway leads from the market to Alaskan Way, a colorful waterfront streetcar route lined with piers, marine equipment shops, and seafood restaurants.

Seafood is a Seattle specialty, and seafood stands and restaurants featuring dishes prepared from daily catches abound. The city has also gained a national reputation as the center for "Northwest cuisine": Olympia oysters, geoduck clams, wild mushrooms, fresh produce, whole-grain breads, and local cheeses and wines. Many restaurants feature scenic locations that enhance dining pleasure, and opportunities for alfresco dining are plentiful. Asian food is found on many local menus, and citizens have gone wild for coffee—coffee shops and espresso carts can be found in the usual locations and even in gas stations and hardware stores.

Visitor Information: Seattle/King County Convention & Visitors Bureau, 701 Pike Street, Suite 800, Seattle, WA 98101; telephone (206)461-5800; fax (206) 461-5855; email admin@visitseattle.org

■ Convention Facilities

The Washington State Convention and Trade Center is the city's major meeting and conference facility. The facility currently offers up to 61 meeting rooms and ball-rooms totaling approximately 105,000 square feet of space, and exhibit space totaling 205,700 square feet. The Convention Center expansion, which was completed in 2001, includes a magnificent new arch spanning Pike Street, along with an office tower at the northeast corner of 7th and Pike. The center sits on top of Interstate 5, within walking distance of more than 9,000 hotel rooms. Just north of downtown, the 831,000-square-foot Seattle Center also hosts conventions and meetings. Lynnwood

Convention Center, Meydenbauer Center (which completed a $1.92 million renovation of its 36,000-square-foot Center Hall in April 2007), and Bell Harbor International Conference Center are among other locations used for trade shows and meetings. Hotels and motels throughout the metropolitan area provide a total of some 25,000 rooms as well as additional convention and meeting accommodations.

Convention Information: Seattle/King County Convention & Visitors Bureau, 701 Pike Street, Suite 800, Seattle, WA 98101; telephone (206)461-5800; fax (206)461-5855; email conventions@visitseattle.org

■ Transportation

Approaching the City

Air travelers to Seattle are served by the Seattle-Tacoma International Airport (Sea-Tac), the seventeenth busiest commercial airport in the United States. The airport is currently being upgraded with a new runway that will enable aircraft to land in any weather conditions. A new South Terminal and new Central Terminal and Pacific Marketplace were completed in 2004. Plans are also underway for a multi-year capital improvement project slated for completion by 2010 that will add needed capacity.

Two interstate highways serve Seattle: I-5 (north-south) and I-90 (east-west). Seattle is the southern terminus of the Alaska Marine Highway System; ferries transporting passengers and motor vehicles operate year round from points in southeast Alaska. Passenger rail service to major U.S. destinations is provided by Amtrak, and buses connect Seattle with U.S. and Canadian cities and with Tijuana, Mexico.

Traveling in the City

Avenues in Seattle run north and south and streets run east and west. The city center is perhaps best explored on foot. Seattle's bus- and trolley-based mass transit system, Metro Transit, operates routes throughout the Seattle-King County area, with service in downtown Seattle provided free of charge from 6 a.m. to 7 p.m. Metro Transit operates a fleet of about 1,300 vehicles that serves an annual ridership of 100 million within a 2,134 square mile area. Metro Transit operates the largest publicly owned vanpool program in the country, with more than 600 vans making more than 2.9 million trips per year.

■ Communications

Newspapers and Magazines

Seattle's major daily newspapers are the evening *The Seattle Times* and the morning *Seattle Post-Intelligencer*. Seattle is also the headquarters for several weekly, biweekly, or monthly publications appealing to ethnic groups, such as *Northwest Asian Weekly,* and *Korea Central Daily News. Slate,* an online publication developed by Microsoft, was started in Seattle.

Television and Radio

All major television networks have affiliates in Seattle, and cable service is available. More than 30 AM and FM radio stations are based in Seattle, providing music, news, and features; other stations broadcast from neighboring communities.

Media Information: *The Seattle Times,* 1120 John St., Seattle, WA 98109; telephone (206)464-2111. *Seattle Post-Intelligencer,* 101 Elliott Ave. W, Seattle, WA 98119; telephone (206)448-8000

Seattle Online

City of Seattle home page. Available www.pan.ci .seattle.wa.us

EnterpriseSeattle. Available www.enterpriseseattle .org

Greater Seattle Chamber of Commerce. Available www.seattlechamber.com

Seattle Daily Journal of Commerce. Available www .djc.com

Seattle-King County Convention & Visitors Bureau. Available hwww.visitseattle.org

Seattle Post-Intelligencer. Available www.seattlepi .nwsource.com

Seattle Public Library. Available www.spl.org

Seattle Public Schools. Available www.seattleschools .org

*The Seattle Times.*Available www.seattletimes .nwsource.com

Washington State Tourism home page. Available www.tourism.wa.gov

BIBLIOGRAPHY

Dillard, Annie, *The Living* (New York: HarperCollins, 1992)

Ochsner, Jeffrey Karl, *Shaping Seattle Architecture: A Historical Guide to the Architects* (Seattle, WA: University of Washington Press, 1994)

Rex-Johnson, Braiden, and Paul Souders, *Inside the Pike Place Market: Exploring America's Favorite Farmer's Market* (Seattle, WA: Sasquatch Books, 1999)

Spokane

■ The City in Brief

Founded: 1878 (incorporated 1881)

Head Official: Mayor Mary Verner (since 2007)

City Population

    1980: 171,300
    1990: 177,196
    2000: 195,629
    2006 estimate: 198,081
    Percent change, 1990–2000: 9.8%
    U.S. rank in 1980: Not available
    U.S. rank in 1990: 94th
    U.S. rank in 2000: 110th

Metropolitan Area Population

    1980: 341,835
    1990: 361,333
    2000: 417,939
    2006 estimate: 446,706
    Percent change, 1990–2000: 15.7%
    U.S. rank in 1980: 96th
    U.S. rank in 1990: 101st
    U.S. rank in 2000: 98th

Area: 58 square miles (2000)

Elevation: Ranges from 1,898 to 2,356 feet above sea level

Average Annual Temperatures: January, 27.3° F; July, 68.6° F; annual average, 47.3° F

Average Annual Precipitation: 16.67 inches of rain; 48.8 inches of snow

Major Economic Sectors: services, wholesale and retail trade, government

Unemployment Rate: 4.0% (December 2007)

Per Capita Income: $20,914 (2005)

2005 FBI Crime Index Property: 12,170

2005 FBI Crime Index Violent: 1,120

Major Colleges and Universities: Eastern Washington University, Gonzaga University, Whitworth College, Washington State University-Spokane, Community Colleges of Spokane, City University

Daily Newspaper: *The Spokesman-Review*

■ Introduction

Spokane is the commercial and cultural hub of a large area known as the "Inland Empire" or the "Inland Northwest," a rich agricultural region. The picturesque beauty of its surroundings makes the city an attractive vacation spot, and population and economic growth have brought many metropolitan amenities to the once quiet, out-of-the-way town. Although the city suffered from decay during the late 1980s and early 1990s, Spokane has undergone an impressive $1 billion urban renaissance and, through its many development projects, has ensured its status as a hub of economics, recreation, and culture in the Pacific Northwest.

■ Geography and Climate

Spokane is located near the eastern border of Washington, about 20 miles from Idaho and 110 miles south of the Canadian border. The city lies on the eastern edge of the Columbia Basin, a wide sloping plain that rises sharply to the east toward the Rocky Mountains. The Spokane River and its waterfalls bisect the city. Summers are typically dry and mild, and winters can bring periods of cold, wet weather. Snowfall rarely accumulates to depths greater than one foot.

Area: 58 square miles (2000)

Elevation: Ranges from 1,898 to 2,356 feet above sea level

Average Temperatures: January, 27.3° F; July, 68.6° F; annual average, 47.3° F

Average Annual Precipitation: 16.67 inches of rain; 48.8 inches of snow

■ History

Spokane Area Popular with Traders

For years before the coming of European explorers, the land around the present-day city was settled by the Spokane tribe. Explorers and trappers passed through the area, but no settlements were built until 1810, when Finan McDonald and Joco Finlay built a trading post called Spokane House at the junction of the Spokane and Little Spokane rivers. In 1812, John Clarke of the Pacific Fur Company built Fort Spokane not far from the trading post. The house and fort soon became a popular meeting place for traders, trappers, and Native Americans, and the buildings were sold to the North West Company in 1813.

The Hudson's Bay Company bought the North West Company in 1821 and dismantled Spokane House. The area was once again left to local tribes. Chief Garry, the leader of the Middle and Upper Spokane tribes, had been educated at the Red River Mission school and converted to Presbyterianism. He built a school for his people and taught them English and religion, as well as modern agricultural methods. At about the same time, the first missionaries arrived in the area, establishing a mission on Walker's Prairie, 25 miles north of Spokane Falls.

The great westward expansion of the 1840s attracted a number of settlers to the area, but a clash with local tribes, culminating in the Whitman Massacre, led to the closing of eastern Oregon (the Spokane area was then part of the Oregon Territory) to settlement in the 1850s. In 1871 J. J. Downing and his family located a claim on the banks of the Spokane River. Within a year, the small settlement included a sawmill, a post office, and a general store. In 1873, James N. Glover, who is called the "father of Spokane," rode through the area on horseback. He was, he wrote, "enchanted...overwhelmed...with the beauty and grandeur of everything." Glover bought the rights to Downing's land and sawmill and opened a store and stable. His early trade was with the Spokane and Coeur d'Alene Indians who lived in the region. The town was registered as Spokane Falls in 1878. By 1880, the town had a population of 75 people, a weekly newspaper, and several baseball teams. In 1881 it was incorporated.

Rapid Population Growth Builds Sophisticated City

Spokane Falls grew steadily throughout the ensuing decades, changing from a rough frontier community into a solid city, complete with all the trappings of Eastern culture: a college, a library, and a number of theaters. The transcontinental railroad reached Spokane Falls in 1883, ensuring the town's success. Fire destroyed much of the town in 1889, but residents quickly rebuilt. By 1890, the city had a population of 30,000 people and changed its name to Spokane when Oregon entered the Union. By 1910, the population had jumped to over 100,000 people.

In 1974 the city was host to the World's Fair, Expo '74, which focused the world's attention on Spokane. Development of Expo '74 buildings and other improvements at the fair site in downtown Spokane created a modern city center with an extensive system of enclosed skywalks. Expansion and development continued through the 1990s and into the new century. Faced with the possibility of losing important downtown retailers, Spokane embarked upon an ambitious and large-scale effort at renewing the city center. These efforts have been enormously successful, as Spokane has continued to attract new retailers and businesses as well as residents who are fleeing high prices in California and in Seattle. In 2004 Spokane was one of just ten cities nationwide to be named an "All-American City."

Historical Information: Eastern Washington State Historical Society/Northwest Museum of Arts and Culture, Research Library and Archives, 2316 W. First Avenue, Spokane, WA 99204; telephone (509)456-3931; fax (509)456-2770

■ Population Profile

Metropolitan Area Residents

    1980: 341,835
    1990: 361,333
    2000: 417,939
    2006 estimate: 446,706
    Percent change, 1990–2000: 15.7%
    U.S. rank in 1980: 96th
    U.S. rank in 1990: 101st
    U.S. rank in 2000: 98th

City Residents

    1980: 171,300
    1990: 177,196
    2000: 195,629
    2006 estimate: 198,081
    Percent change, 1990–2000: 9.8%
    U.S. rank in 1980: Not available
    U.S. rank in 1990: 94th
    U.S. rank in 2000: 110th

Density: 3,343.36 people per square mile (2000)

©David Smith 2008/drr.net

Racial and ethnic characteristics (2005)

> White: 171,312
> Black: 3,861
> American Indian and Alaska Native: 2,899
> Asian: 4,815
> Native Hawaiian and Pacific Islander: 367
> Hispanic or Latino (may be of any race): 6,732
> Other: 1,112

Percent of residents born in state: 52.7%
> (2000)

Age characteristics (2005)

> Population under 5 years old: 11,141
> Population 5 to 9 years old: 11,599
> Population 10 to 14 years old: 12,132
> Population 15 to 19 years old: 14,468
> Population 20 to 24 years old: 17,743
> Population 25 to 34 years old: 28,371
> Population 35 to 44 years old: 25,224
> Population 45 to 54 years old: 27,914
> Population 55 to 59 years old: 10,819
> Population 60 to 64 years old: 7,789
> Population 65 to 74 years old: 11,932
> Population 75 to 84 years old: 10,036

> Population 85 years and older: 3,609
> Median age: 35.4 years

Births (2006, County)
> Total number: 5,372

Deaths (2006, County)
> Total number: 3,834

Money income (2005)
> Per capita income: $20,914
> Median household income: $34,752
> Total households: 85,594

Number of households with income of . . .
> less than $10,000: 10,262
> $10,000 to $14,999: 6,490
> $15,000 to $24,999: 14,453
> $25,000 to $34,999: 11,932
> $35,000 to $49,999: 14,242
> $50,000 to $74,999: 15,044
> $75,000 to $99,999: 6,050
> $100,000 to $149,999: 4,408
> $150,000 to $199,999: 1,299
> $200,000 or more: 1,414

Percent of families below poverty level: 14.5% (2005)

2005 FBI Crime Index Property: 12,170

2005 FBI Crime Index Violent: 1,120

■ Municipal Government

Spokane's mayor-council form of government formerly elected a mayor and six other council members to four-year terms; the council employed a city manager for the day-to-day operation of the city. In 1999 Spokane voters adopted a strong-mayor form of government, eliminating the city manager position. The city council still has seven members; a council president now presides over meetings instead of the mayor, so there are eight elected city officials instead of seven.

Head Official: Mayor Mary Verner (since 2007; current term expires December 2011)

Total Number of City Employees: 1,943 (2007)

City Information: City Hall, West 808 Spokane Falls Boulevard, Spokane, WA 99201; telephone (509)625-6250; email jwest@spokanecity.org

■ Economy

Major Industries and Commercial Activity

Natural resources have traditionally provided much of the economic activity for the Spokane area, a major center for the timber, agriculture, and mining industries in the region. A number of manufacturing companies have located in Spokane, drawn by the easy access to raw materials. Finished wood products, metal refinery and fabrication, and food processing are among the leaders in manufacturing. The outlying areas are part of an abundant agricultural system, providing a large amount of the nation's apples, peas, hops, pears, asparagus, lentils, soft wheat, and sweet cherries. A number of wineries and breweries also operate in the area. These industries continue to be important elements in the local economy, but in recent years the economy has diversified to encompass high-technology and service companies. Health-related industries employ more people than any other industry in Spokane; health care accounts for over 13 percent of the local employment base. The city provides specialized care to many patients from the surrounding areas, as far north as the Canadian border. The city is also the wholesale and retail trade and service center of the 80,000-square-mile Inland Northwest region.

All branches of the U.S. armed forces are represented in Spokane County. The largest military facility is Fairchild Air Force Base, which employed 4,992 personnel in 2007. The military units and their personnel combine to have an economic impact on the regional economy of over $400 million annually. Tourism is one of the top industries in the state, and Spokane is a center for tourist activity. Spokane has also seen the recent development of economic activity in the lucrative high-tech and biotech sectors. The city is the site of a 100-block wireless network (the Spokane Hot Zone), among the largest of its kind in the country, which is seen as symbolic of its dedication to the development of technological opportunities and resources. The recently built Sirti Technology Center has been a hub for attracting high-tech companies; in 2007 there were 10 high-tech and nine life-sciences companies and organizations headquartered at Sirti.

In 2002 Kaiser Aluminum, a major employer with a 60-year presence in the region, filed for bankruptcy. Despite the loss of jobs and revenue, Spokane has rebounded by working to make the city attractive to retail and small businesses.

Items and goods produced: silver, lead, zinc, timber, poultry, dairy, vegetable, fruit, meat products, aluminum, magnesium, clay and cement products, machinery and metal products, flour, feed, cereal, petroleum products, paper, electrical fixtures

Incentive Programs—New and Existing Businesses

Local programs: The Spokane Area Economic Development Council works with businesses to locate and utilize local and state business incentives. The Spokane Neighborhood Economic Development Alliance offers two revolving loans to businesses and nonprofits expanding or creating new jobs in Spokane.

State programs: The state of Washington offers a number of incentive programs to attract new and expanding businesses to the state. Among them are B & O tax credits; sales/use tax deferrals for technology and manufacturing companies as well as for firms relocating or expanding in distressed areas; and loan programs that apply to rural areas and the redevelopment of brownfields.

Job training programs: Spokane businesses are assisted largely by working with the higher education community, including such organizations as Applied Technology Center, part of the Community Colleges of Spokane; ITT Technical Institute, which focuses on preparing graduates for careers in technology; and the Spokane Intercollegiate Research and Technology Institute, which uses the collective resources of local colleges to accelerate the development of technology companies. The Spokane Area Workforce Development Council administers employment and training programs for local economically disadvantaged youths and adults through the Spokane City-County Employment and Training Consortium. The Council also supports local economic growth by working to improve the workforce development system. The Washington state Job Skills Training Program offers employers a 50 percent match for training costs. The federal Workforce Investment Act (WIA), formerly Job Training Partnership Act (JTPA), may match up to 50 percent of wages for on-the-job training of dislocated workers. Washington also offers a credit for Job Training Services, which is a credit of 20 percent of the cost spent on job training by firms eligible for an Empowerment Zone sales tax deferral/exemption. This may be taken as a business and occupation tax credit. The amount of credit for a particular firm is limited to $5,000 annually.

Development Projects

In 2000, the Spokane Symphony purchased the 1931 Art Deco Fox Theater and conducted a $28.4 million renovation and restoration of the building. The new 1,600-seat home for the Spokane Symphony celebrated its grand opening in November 2007. Development was ongoing in 2007 in the Davenport Arts District, a 10-block area adjacent to the Davenport Hotel (which was reopened in 2002 after renovations). Renovations were underway on various small businesses, Steam Plant Square, and the Big Easy nightclub.

Also begun in 2003 and completed in 2007 was a major expansion of the Spokane Convention Center. Budgeted at $80 million total, the renovation and construction consisted of new amenities in the existing areas, and a new 100,000-square-foot exhibition hall. Developers were committed to employing environmentally-friendly building techniques throughout the project, including non-toxic materials and the utilization of efficient energy, natural light, and water conservation.

The city of Spokane set aside $117 million for street improvements over a 10-year period, work which began in 2005. The project was expected to repair about 110 miles of residential streets and arterials throughout Spokane. In 2007 renovations and modernizations were underway at John R. Rogers High School and Shadle Park High School. A new Sirti Technology Center was opened in 2006, which includes 30,000 square feet of space housing wet labs, offices and light manufacturing areas. Also in 2006, WSU-Spokane opened a new $33.85 million Academic Center on its Riverpoint Campus, and broke ground on a new nursing building at Riverpoint. The 80,000-foot nursing building was expected to open by 2008.

Economic Development Information: Economic Development Council, 801 West Riverside, Suite 302, Spokane, WA 99201; telephone (800)SPOKANE; email edc@EDC.Spokane.net.

Commercial Shipping

Four air cargo carriers fly out of Spokane International Airport: DHL Express 800, UPS Worldwide, Federal Express, and United Parcel Service. The Burlington Northern & Sante Fe and Union Pacific railroads also serve the city. Many motor freight concerns operate regularly scheduled trucks in and out of Spokane.

Labor Force and Employment Outlook

A large, experienced work force is available in Spokane; about 80 percent of workers are native Washingtonians. The health and service industries enjoy strong employment outlooks. Seasonal employment at harvest time is always available.

In September 2007 the unemployment rate in Spokane was 4.3 percent, representing a fairly steady decline in the rate since its 10-year peak above 8 percent in early 2003. Between 1997 and 2007 the greater Spokane work force grew by nearly 30,000 workers.

The following is a summary of data regarding the Spokane metropolitan area labor force, 2006 annual averages.

Size of nonagricultural labor force: 213,000

Number of workers employed in . . .

construction and mining: 13,400
manufacturing: 18,500
trade, transportation and utilities: 43,200
information: 3,200
financial activities: 13,500
professional and business services: 23,300
educational and health services: 34,300
leisure and hospitality: 20,100
other services: 9,200
government: 34,200

Average hourly earnings of production workers employed in manufacturing: Not available

Unemployment rate: 4.0% (December 2007)

Largest employers (2007)	*Number of employees*
Fairchild AFB	4,992
Spokane Public Schools	3,231
Sacred Heart Medical Center	3,040
State of Washington	3,020
U.S. Government	2,790
Spokane County	2,083
City of Spokane	1,943
Empire Health Services	1,700
Community Colleges of Spokane	1,368
Eastern Washington University	1,280

Cost of Living

The following is a summary of data regarding key cost of living factors for the Spokane area.

2007 (1st quarter) ACCRA Average House Price: $278,033

2007 (1st quarter) ACCRA Cost of Living Index: 97.7

State income tax rate: None

State sales tax rate: 6.55%

Local income tax rate: None

Local sales tax rate: 2.0%

Property tax rate: Averages $14.94 in city, $14.21 in county, per $1,000 of assessed value (2005)

Economic Information: Economic Development Council, 801 West Riverside, Suite 302, Spokane, WA 99201; telephone (800)SPOKANE; email edc@EDC. Spokane.net. Spokane Area Chamber of Commerce, 801 West Riverside Avenue, Spokane, WA 99201; telephone (509)624-1393; fax (509)747-0077; email info@chamber.spokane.net

■ Education and Research

Elementary and Secondary Schools

Spokane School District Number 81, representing all city schools, is the second largest in the state. Students' test scores are consistently above the national average, and over 70 percent of teachers hold master's degrees. The district boasts a number of alternative schools, including a homeless education program, school-parent partnerships, and a Montessori school. The district received a $16.4 million gift from the Bill and Melinda Gates Foundation, which was used to create a program encouraging professional develeopment and individualized learning programs, known as SHAPeS, or Spokane High Achieving and Performing Schools.

In 2007 renovations and modernizations were underway at John R. Rogers High School and Shadle Park High School.

The following is a summary of data regarding the Spokane Public Schools as of the 2005–2006 school year.

Total enrollment: 30,945

Number of facilities

elementary schools: 35
junior high/middle schools: 6
senior high schools: 8
other: 30

Student/teacher ratio: 19.6:1

Teacher salaries (2005–06)

elementary median: $51,340

junior high/middle median: $51,570
secondary median: $50,990

Funding per pupil: $7,771

A variety of state-approved private elementary and secondary schools augment the public school system, including parochial schools, special schools such as the Lilac Blind Foundation, Montessori programs, and the Spokane Guild's School and Neuromuscular Center. The Spokane Art School offers classes, workshops, and master classes.

Public Schools Information: Spokane Public Schools, 200 North Bernard, Spokane, WA 99201; telephone (509)354-5900

Colleges and Universities

Eastern Washington University (EWU), a state-operated school located 17 miles from Spokane in Cheney, Washington, offers four-year undergraduate degrees in more than 100 academic majors, 10 master's degrees, and 55 graduate programs of study. The university operates a branch in downtown Spokane and enrolls more than 10,000 students. The school boasts a student-teacher ratio of 20:1. Two-thirds of its alumni live and work in the state of Washington.

Gonzaga University, founded by the Jesuits in 1887, offers 92 undergraduate degree programs and 21 graduate programs. The school enrolls around 6,700 students. Washington State University at Spokane, a multi-campus research university, enrolls more than 23,000 students throughout the university system, 1,580 of whom study at the Spokane campus. There are 150 majors, 70 master's degree programs, and 44 doctoral programs. The school offers 100 study-abroad programs in more than 70 countries. These three institutions, together with Whitworth College and the Spokane Community Colleges, operate as a collaborative project the Spokane Intercollegiate Research and Technology Institute, which uses the collective resources of the institutions to improve the economic vitality of the region. Community Colleges of Spokane serves students in a six-county region, awarding more than 4,400 two-year degrees each year in 120 professional and technical programs. There are 6,710 enrolled at its downtown Spokane location.

Libraries and Research Centers

Founded in 1904, the Spokane Public Library system comprises a Downtown Library overlooking Spokane Falls and five branch libraries. Total holdings include approximately 600,000 volumes; more than 35,000 video, music, and audiotapes and CDs; and a periodicals collection numbering more than 700 titles. Special collections include Northwest history; history of the book; genealogy; oral history; an African American collection; and U.S., Washington state, and Spokane County government documents. The downtown library features a gallery, three works of permanent public art, a skywlk connection to downtown shopping and restaurants, and wireless Internet service. The library system also sponsors community programs for residents of all ages.

Special libraries in Spokane include the Crosby Library at Gonzaga University, which contains a collection of Bing Crosby records and other memorabilia. Research at the Spokane Intercollegiate Research and Technology Institute at Riverpoint focuses on technology transfer for commercial uses. Sirti, as it is called, is the headquarters for ten high-tech and nine life-sciences companies and organizations. A new Sirti Technology Center was opened in 2006, made possible by a $3 million grant from the U.S. Department of Commerce, as well as private funds. The Health Research and Education Center at Washington State University Spokane develops clinical and applied research in biomedical and social health areas. The Washington Institute for Mental Illness Research and Training recruits and retrains qualified professionals at state hospitals in the use of modern treatments.

Public Library Information: Spokane Public Library, 906 West Main Avenue, Spokane, WA 99201; telephone (509)444-5300

■ Health Care

Six major hospitals are located in Spokane, four of which are full service facilities. The city is the center of specialized care for the entire Inland Northwest area, offering an expert team of cardiac surgeons and more than 18,500 health care professionals, including more than 900 physicians. Sacred Heart Medical Center, a 623-bed facility, is a leader in heart, lung, and kidney transplant services. Sacred Heart, which is a non-profit Catholic institution, has 4,000 employees, 800 of whom are medical specialists. In 2003, the hospital opened the region's first full-service children's hospital; a Women's Health Center was added in 2004. In 2007 Sacred Heart was named a Bariatric Surgery Center of Excellence by the American Society for Bariatric Surgery, and in 2006-2007 it was selected by the National Foundation for Trauma Care as one of five "best preparedness practice trauma centers" in the nation. The Shriners Hospital for Children is also based in Spokane; in 2006, it approved 38,984 new patient applications. The Community Mental Health Center, which provides mental health services to children, adults, and the elderly, is nationally recognized and the largest and most comprehensive community mental health center in Washington.

■ Recreation

Sightseeing

Riverfront Park, the site of Expo '74, is a 100-acre urban park that has been developed into a collection of cultural and recreational attractions including an IMAX theater,

art gallery, a skating rink, an antique carousel composed of 54 hand-carved horses, a train, and an exciting gondola ride over Spokane Falls. Historic Fort George Wright, a 1,500-acre complex, was established in 1894 on a plateau overlooking the river. Other points of interest in the city include Manito Park, with its beautiful Rose Hill and Japanese garden, and Cliff Park, site of Review Rock, a large formation with steps cut into the sides that offers a beautiful view of the city.

The area around Spokane offers a number of attractions, including several ghost towns, the Spokane Plains Battlefield, and the Turnbull National Wildlife Refuge. A variety of historic homes, churches, and architecture are available for touring in the Spokane area. Spokane's local wineries have won prestigious awards and offer tours, tastings, and sales.

Arts and Culture

Spokane's 12,500-seat Veteran's Memorial Arena is a focal point for special events. In addition, the 2,700-seat Opera House and the more intimate The Met Performing Arts Center host national and international touring companies and entertainers. Music is provided by the Spokane Symphony, housed in the Opera House, which presents a full season of classical music, including special children's performances and Super Pops! by the Spokane Jazz Orchestra; and by Allegro-Baroque and Beyond, Connoisseur Concerts, the Spokane Chamber Music Association, and Uptown Opera. Theater is represented by the region's only resident professional company, Interplayer's Ensemble, whose seven-play season runs from September to June; by Spokane Civic Theatre; and by several amateur community theaters and smaller groups. The Big Easy Concert House, home to a concert hall and dance club, has opened in a renovated office block adjacent to the arts district. Area colleges and universities also contribute to the cultural scene.

The new Northwest Museum of Arts and Culture (formerly the Cheney Cowles Museum) reopened after a major $26 million expansion. The museum houses permanent collections of regional history and American Indian artifacts, as well as five art galleries and educational facilities. The historic Campbell House, a museum since 1925, is now a part of the Northwest Museum complex, with tours of the home available by reservation. Additionally, the Jundt Art Museum on the campus of Gonzaga University includes two large gallery spaces and an exhibition lounge.

Festivals and Holidays

Bloomsday, the country's largest timed road race, is held on the first Sunday in May. Later that month, the Spokane Lilac Festival runs for 10 days and features such activities as a flower show, parades, concerts, games, entertainment. Begun in 1938, the festival also showcases local foods and crowns a lilac queen. In June, Spokane plays host to Hoopfest, the world's largest three-on-three basketball tournament. The Spokane County Fair, a tradition since the late 1800s, happens in September. The Northwest Bach Festival celebrates the music of J.S. Bach in venues throughout the city for one week at the end of January or early February.

Sports for the Spectator

The remodeled Spokane Arena hosts the Spokane Chiefs of the Western Hockey Association. The Spokane Indians, a minor league farm team of professional baseball's Texas Rangers, play at Avista Stadium. The Gonzaga Bulldogs athletic teams, members of the National Collegiate Athletic Association (NCAA) Division I, engage in intercollegiate competition at Gonzaga University. Spokane Raceway Park offers stock car and drag racing, while Playfair offers thoroughbred horse races during the summer and fall.

Sports for the Participant

Seventy-six lakes and four major rivers within a 50-mile radius of Spokane offer a wide variety of water activity. For hikers and nature lovers, a 70-mile pathway called Centennial Trail begins near the old Spokane House fur trading post and winds through Riverside State Park, Riverfront Park in downtown Spokane, and eastward past Coeur d'Alene, Idaho. The Trail was expanded to include 37 paved miles on the Spokane River. The city and county maintain more than 75 parks, many of which feature athletic fields, tennis courts, swimming pools, skating rinks, recreational programming, and other facilities. In total, the city boasts 3,488 acres of protected green space. More than 30 public and private golf courses exist in the county. The nearby mountains offer year-round recreation: skiing in the winter and fishing, hunting, camping, canoeing, hiking, and other outdoor activities in the warmer months. In the summer months, floating excursions are available on the Spokane River, while several nearby rivers provide whitewater rafting opportunities. Rock climbing is available just outside of Spokane, and seven ski areas are within a two hour drive.

Shopping and Dining

Spokane shoppers are served by several major shopping centers in the city and a number of smaller plazas and specialty shopping districts. Retail establishments in downtown Spokane are connected by a 16-block system of enclosed skywalks. The shopping opportunities at River Park Square and in the retail district are unmatched in the Inland Northwest. Spokane's restaurants offer fine international and traditional American dishes. Specialties include fresh salmon and locally-produced wines. More than 500 dining establishments can be found in the Spokane area.

Visitor Information: Spokane Area Visitor Information Center, 201 W. Main, Spokane, WA 99201; telephone (509)747-3230; toll-free (888)SPOKANE

■ Convention Facilities

The Spokane Convention Center is located on the banks of the Spokane River in the downtown district. As of 2007 a renovation of the Convention Center was nearing completion; the plan called for 164,307 square feet of meeting space, with a 25,310-square-foot, fully finished ballroom. A roof deck holds up to 500 people, and the new addition also features Group Health Exhibit Hall. The adjoining 28,000-square-foot Washington State International Agricultural Trade Center, with a 300-seat theater, expands the capacity, offering space to more than 8,000 people. The Spokane Veterans Memorial Arena provides 173,100 square feet of exhibit space and festival seating for 12,500 people. The Joe A. Albi Stadium is a large outdoor arena that seats 28,500 people.

More than 2,000 hotel rooms are available within walking distance of the major convention sites in Spokane; nearly 7,000 hotel rooms total exist in the surrounding area. Most of the larger hotels maintain ample facilities for conventions, such as banquet space, conference rooms, and ballrooms.

Convention Information: Spokane Convention and Visitors Bureau, 801 W. Riverside, Spokane, WA 99201; telephone (509)624-1341

■ Transportation

Approaching the City

The Spokane International Airport is a multimillion-dollar complex located a few minutes from the downtown area and served by ten major airlines and four air cargo carriers. In the first six months of 2007 the airport served 1,643,855 passengers. The city is also served by three commercial bus lines and by Amtrak.

Interstate 90 passes through Spokane, connecting the city with Seattle to the west and with points east. U.S. Highway 2 also runs east and west through the city. U.S. 395 continues north out of Spokane into Canada, and U.S. 195 leads south from the city.

Traveling in the City

Generally in Spokane, the east-west roads are designated as avenues, and the north-south roads are referred to as streets. Major east-west thoroughfares in the city include Francis, Wellesley, Mission, Sprague, and 29th avenues. North-south arteries include Maple, Monroe, Division, Hamilton, Greene-Market, Argonne, and Sullivan streets.

■ Communications

Newspaper and Magazines

Spokane readers are served by one daily newspaper, *The Spokesman-Review*, which presents a special entertainment section on Friday. *Journal of Business* is among the biweekly business journals published in the city. *The Pacific Northwest Inlander*, a weekly newspaper, has an extensive arts and entertainment section. Other newspapers focus on senior living, the outdoors, and collegiate interests.

Television and Radio

Spokane has six television stations representing the major commercial networks and public television. The area is also served by a cable system that provides a wide variety of viewing options. Nearly thirty AM and FM radio stations broadcast in Spokane, which also receives programming from neighboring communities.

Media Information: *The Spokesman-Review,* West 999 Riverside Avenue, PO Box 2160, Spokane, WA 99210; telephone 509(459-5068); email danc@spokesman.com

Spokane Online

City of Spokane home page. Available www .spokanecity.org

Spokane Area Chamber of Commerce. Available www.spokanechamber.org

Spokane Area Convention & Visitors Bureau. Available www.visitspokane.com

Spokane Public Library. Available www .spokanelibrary.org/

Spokane Public Schools. Available www .spokaneschools.org

Spokane Veterans Memorial Arena. Available www .spokanearena.com

The Spokesman-Review. Available www.spokane.net

BIBLIOGRAPHY

Alexie, Sherman, *Reservation Blues* (New York: Warner Books, 1995)

Tacoma

■ The City in Brief

Founded: 1852 (incorporated 1884)

Head Official: Mayor Bill Baarsma (D) (since 2002)

City Population

> 1980: 158,501
> 1990: 176,664
> 2000: 193,556
> 2006 estimate: 196,532
> Percent change, 1990–2000: 9.1%
> U.S. rank in 1980: 97th
> U.S. rank in 1990: 95th
> U.S. rank in 2000: 114th

Metropolitan Area Population

> 1980: 486,000
> 1990: 586,203
> 2000: 700,820
> 2006 estimate: Not available
> Percent change, 1990–2000: 19.5%
> U.S. rank in 1980: 18th (CMSA; includes Seattle)
> U.S. rank in 1990: 14th (CMSA; includes Seattle)
> U.S. rank in 2000: 13th (CMSA; includes Seattle)

Area: 50 square miles (2000)

Elevation: 380 feet above sea level

Average Annual Temperature: 53.1° F

Average Annual Precipitation: 39.2 inches

Major Economic Sectors: services, wholesale and retail trade, government

Unemployment Rate: 4.0% (December 2007)

Per Capita Income: $22,854 (2005)

2005 FBI Crime Index Property: 16,802

2005 FBI Crime Index Violent: 2,014

Major Colleges and Universities: Pacific Lutheran University, University of Puget Sound, University of Washington Tacoma

Daily Newspaper: *The News Tribune*

■ Introduction

Tacoma's name is derived from the Native American word "Tahoma," meaning "Mother of the Waters," referring to Mt. Tacoma, which is now known as Mt. Rainier. Tacoma's beautiful natural setting affords views of the nearby Cascade Range and the more distant Olympic Mountains. Tacoma is home to a deep-water harbor that is among the busiest in the nation and has played an important role in the city's economic development. Nationally recognized for careful municipal planning, Tacoma has been nicknamed the "City of Destiny." In 2004 Partners for Livable Communities named the Tacoma and Pierce County area one of "America's Most Livable Communities."

■ Geography and Climate

Situated on Commencement Bay, an inlet of Puget Sound, Tacoma lies at the foot of Mt. Rainier in the Puyallup River valley, bordered by mountains. The Tacoma Narrows Bridge links the city to the Olympic Peninsula. Tacoma is about 36 miles south of Seattle. The climate is quite mild throughout the year. Although the area has the reputation of being rainy, Tacoma actually receives less rain than New York City. Most of the precipitation falls in the winter, when snow blankets the mountains. Tacoma is the seat of Pierce County. The city lies near active fault lines making the area susceptible to earthquakes; however, very few damaging quakes have occurred in the recent past.

Area: 50 square miles (2000)

Elevation: 380 feet above sea level

Average Temperature: 53.1° F

Average Annual Precipitation: 39.2 inches

■ History

Slow Rise of Lumber Industry; Arrival of Settlers

The first people to live in the Puyallup Valley on the shore of Commencement Bay were the Nisqually and Puyallup Native American tribes. Captain George Vancouver was the first person of European descent to explore the area when, in 1792, he sailed his ship up Puget Sound and named Mt. Rainier for Peter Rainier, an officer in the British Navy. Commencement Bay was charted and named in 1841 by a member of the Charles Wilkes Expedition. Permanent European settlement was achieved in the region in 1852 when a Swedish immigrant, Nicholas De Lin, built a sawmill at the junction of two creeks and soon conducted a thriving lumber business.

Settlers fled the area in 1855 after hearing rumors of native hostilities; they returned when the Commencement Bay tribe was relocated to a nearby reservation, leaving the area free for other settlers. General Morton Matthew McCarver, who named the settlement Tacoma, was responsible for promoting extensive development by buying tracts of land and bringing in other settlers.

When the Hanson & Ackerman Mill was built in 1869 by a group of San Francisco investors, Tacoma became established in the lumber industry. The mill started a boom, as laborers, artisans, and shopkeepers arrived with their families to settle in Tacoma; with a population of 200 people, the town soon boasted mail service, electric lights, and a telegraph. In 1873 Tacoma was selected as the terminus for the Northern Pacific Railroad; construction was stopped 20 miles short of Tacoma, however, when an economic crash forced the railroad's investors to pull out of the project. The government recalled the workers, who insisted upon being paid thousands of dollars in back wages before they completed the line.

Railroad Assists Industrial Development

The railroad increased Tacoma's industrial development. Coal mines were opened and Tacoma became the major coaling station on the Pacific Coast. The lumber industry expanded while new industries included a flour mill, a salmon cannery, and machine shops. The town continued to grow, and with a population of 4,400 residents, Tacoma was incorporated in 1884. During the following year a group of residents, who blamed Chinese workers for an employment recession that came with the com-

pletion of the railroad, formed the Law and Order League and forcibly deported the Chinese. The insurgents were tried in court but were later acquitted.

Transcontinental rail service to Tacoma was completed in 1887, bringing further development; the completion of the Stamford Pass Tunnel and the establishment of the Northern Pacific Railroad general offices in Tacoma gave an even greater boost to the lumber and coal industries. Record numbers of settlers arrived and the town flourished. Since Tacoma's economy was closely tied to the railroad industry, however, more than half of the city's banks closed when the Reading Railroad went bankrupt. The economy recovered to some degree with the creation of the Weyerhaeuser Timber Company in 1900. During World War I the shipping industry boomed, and the city profited from its proximity to Camp Lewis (later renamed Fort Lewis). Commencement Bay was declared an official U.S. Port of Entry in 1918.

Although the Great Depression of the 1930s brought hard times to Tacoma, World War II stimulated industrial growth and prosperity because of the city's location near Fort Lewis and McChord U.S. Air Force Base. During the 1950s Tacoma underwent extensive city planning. Voters adopted a progressive council-manager form of government, and massive renovation of the city's infrastructure was implemented.

While the presence of the military has long had a stabilizing effect on the city economy, economic diversification into the early 2000s has offered the promise of continued growth. In particular, the health care and financial services industries have gained importance to the local economy. Educational institutions have expanded in the area, most notably through the University of Washington Tacoma, which opened its campus in 1990 as a degree completion site and expanded to a four-year institution by 2006. The City of Tacoma, along with investors from the private sector, spent over $300 million on the city's telecommunications infrastructure through Click! Network. Becoming a "wired" city has helped attract new industries while balancing environmental and quality-of-life concerns. In 2004 the city was named one of "America's Most Livable Communities" by the national nonprofit organization Partners for Livable Communities. City and county development officials have been hard at work to continue on this success, particularly through major redevelopments in the downtown areas. From 2000 to 2007 over 74 new projects were completed or under construction in downtown Tacoma. These included expansion and development of the Foss Waterway, with many residential, retail, and business locations; construction of a new convention and trade center; and hundreds of new residential units.

Historical Information: Washington State History Museum, 1911 Pacific Avenue, Tacoma, WA 98402; telephone (253)272-3500; www.wshs.org

©Chuck Pefley 2007/drr.net

■ Population Profile

Metropolitan Area Residents

1980: 486,000
1990: 586,203
2000: 700,820
2006 estimate: Not available
Percent change, 1990–2000: 19.5%
U.S. rank in 1980: 18th (CMSA; includes Seattle)
U.S. rank in 1990: 14th (CMSA; includes Seattle)
U.S. rank in 2000: 13th (CMSA; includes Seattle)

City Residents

1980: 158,501
1990: 176,664
2000: 193,556
2006 estimate: 196,532
Percent change, 1990–2000: 9.1%
U.S. rank in 1980: 97th

U.S. rank in 1990: 95th
U.S. rank in 2000: 114th

Density: 3,864.9 people per square mile (2000)

Racial and ethnic characteristics (2005)

White: 125,620
Black: 22,920
American Indian and Alaska Native: 2,498
Asian: 19,936
Native Hawaiian and Pacific Islander: 2,904
Hispanic or Latino (may be of any race): 16,238
Other: 8,018

Percent of residents born in state: 48.6% (2000)

Age characteristics (2005)

Population under 5 years old: 13,474
Population 5 to 9 years old: 13,484
Population 10 to 14 years old: 15,826

Population 15 to 19 years old: 12,189
Population 20 to 24 years old: 14,251
Population 25 to 34 years old: 30,207
Population 35 to 44 years old: 31,720
Population 45 to 54 years old: 24,577
Population 55 to 59 years old: 8,981
Population 60 to 64 years old: 6,934
Population 65 to 74 years old: 9,301
Population 75 to 84 years old: 8,253
Population 85 years and older: 2,737
Median age: 33.7 years

Births (2006, Metropolitan Division)

Total number: 9,939

Deaths (2006, Metropolitan Division)

Total number: 5,326

Money income (2005)

Per capita income: $22,854
Median household income: $40,290
Total households: 78,806

Number of households with income of . . .

less than $10,000: 9,308
$10,000 to $14,999: 4,192
$15,000 to $24,999: 10,106
$25,000 to $34,999: 10,281
$35,000 to $49,999: 14,695
$50,000 to $74,999: 15,529
$75,000 to $99,999: 6,736
$100,000 to $149,999: 5,597
$150,000 to $199,999: 995
$200,000 or more: 1,367

Percent of families below poverty level: 11% (2005)

2005 FBI Crime Index Property: 16,802

2005 FBI Crime Index Violent: 2,014

■ Municipal Government

Tacoma's council-manager form of government provides for the election of nine city council members—a mayor, five members serving districts, and three at-large members. All serve four-year terms. The council hires a city manager.

Head Official: Mayor Bill Baarsma (D) (since 2002; current term expires 2009)

Total Number of City Employees: 2,044 (2006)

City Information: City Hall, 747 Market Street, Tacoma, WA 98402; telephone (253)591-5000; www.cityoftacoma.org

■ Economy

Major Industries and Commercial Activity

Tacoma has attracted companies of all sizes and is making every effort to build on past achievements in continuing to grow a diverse economy. Into the 2000s, the health-care industry has quickly gained ground in Tacoma. Franciscan Health System (with headquarters in Tacoma) and MultiCare Health System both operate hospitals and health clinics in the city and have become top employers for both the city and the county. InVivo Health Partners, offering support services to hospitals and physician groups, has also made Tacoma the site of regional headquarters. The financial sector has also seen growth in the new century. Columbia Bank and Rainier Pacific Bank opened headquarters in the city in 2001 and 2004 respectively. KeyBank (2001) and Union Bank of California (2005) opened major offices in downtown.

The Port of Tacoma continues to have a major impact on the local economy. It is home to the sixth largest container handling port in the United States. Top imports include machinery, toys, sports equipment, footwear, and furniture. Top exports include grains, machinery, automobiles, auto parts, meat, and plastics. A major gateway port for international trade, the Port of Tacoma covers more than 2,400 acres of land. Port activities generate more than 43,000 jobs in Pierce County. Port activities generate over $637 million in annual wages.

The military also holds a strong foothold in the local economy through the presence of McChord U.S. Air Force Base and Fort Lewis Army Post. There are nearly 35,000 military and civilian personnel on the bases with the total annual payroll at about $2 billion. On-base retail spending has been estimated at over $200 million annually. The U.S. Department of Defense has sponsored approximately $20 million in contracts in Pierce County.

Significant work in satellite imaging, automated fingerprint and radio frequency identification systems, and Internet and computer services continues because of multiple broadband telecommunications systems, including the city's fiber-optic Click! Network, launched in November 1998. Over the past several years, the City of Tacoma, along with investors from the private sector, has spent over $300 million on the city's telecommunications infrastructure through Click! Network, which continues expansion with new construction and additional services for customers.

Tacoma's economy is still heavily involved with timber. Regional enterprises produce more flower bulbs than the Netherlands, as well as crops, such as berries and rhubarb, which require heavy seasonal employment. Tourism is also important to Tacoma's economy. Visitors are attracted to the waters of Commencement Bay and the state and national parks surrounding Tacoma.

Items and goods produced: lumber products, pulp, paper, clothing, chemicals, furniture, flour, furnaces, railroad car wheels, candy, food products, meat and fish

Incentive Programs—New and Existing Companies

Local programs: The City of Tacoma offers a variety of business loan programs, tax credits for new job creation, industrial revenue bonds, sales and use tax exemption on machinery and equipment, a variety of housing-related programs, financial incentives for historic properties, and others.

State programs: Part of Tacoma is a designated state Empowerment Zone; employers located within this area who meet certain hiring requirements are eligible for tax credits, special financing, and contracting programs. The state of Washington offers a number of incentive programs to attract new and expanding businesses to the state. Among them are B & O tax credits; sales/use tax deferrals for technology and manufacturing companies as well as for firms relocating or expanding in distressed areas; and loan programs that apply to rural areas and the redevelopment of brownfields.

Job training programs: The Washington state Job Skills Training Program offers employers a 50 percent match for training costs. The federal Workforce Investment Act (WIA), formerly Job Training Partnership Act (JTPA), may match up to 50 percent of wages for on-the-job training of dislocated workers. Washington also offers a credit for Job Training Services, which is a credit of 20 percent of the cost spent on job training by firms eligible for an Empowerment Zone sales tax deferral/exemption. This may be taken as a business and occupation tax credit. The amount of credit for a particular firm is limited to $5,000 annually. The Local Employment and Apprenticeship Training Program (LEAP) provides Tacoma residents with opportunities to access training, enter apprenticeship programs, acquire skills, and perform work on city public works projects that provide living wages.

Development Projects

Development of the downtown waterfront has been on-going since about 2000 through the efforts of the Foss Waterway Development Authority. The Foss Waterway Marina was renovated in 2003. Foss Harbor, a mixed-use development nearby, includes plans for 350 condominiums and retail space to be developed in phases. Thea Foss Esplanade has been expanded and private development efforts have begun. The $63 million Museum of Glass at the waterfront has become a prime attraction. A new set of condominiums is under construction as Nineteen Thirty-Three at Dock Street, scheduled for completion in 2008.

The University of Washington Tacoma has grown considerably since it opened as a degree completion center in 1990. The school added its Science and Keystone buildings in 2001 and the Institute of Technology in 2002. Additional classrooms, offices, and retail space were added in 2003. In 2006 the school was able to welcome its first freshman class into a comprehensive, four-year institution. Court 17, an apartment complex for students was completed in 2006. However, the university is looking toward the private sector to develop additional student housing off-campus.

New residential units have been added to the downtown area through the redevelopment of the old city hall into Renaissance at Old City Hall (completed in 2007) and of the former Spring Air Mattress building (to be completed in 2008). Several other apartment, loft, and condo units have been added since 2000 and a number of projects were still in planning and construction phases as of 2007.

The $89.7 million Greater Tacoma Convention and Trade Center, anchored in the heart of downtown Tacoma, opened in 2004. Developments surrounding and supporting the Convention Center include Courtyard by Marriott, a 162-room hotel with additional meeting facilities, an upscale restaurant, and a day spa. Tollefson Plaza, one of the newest urban parks in the city, opened in 2006 with an investment of $3.5 million. The $11 million Tacoma Dome Best Western opened the same year.

In 2007 construction was completed on the Tacoma Narrows Bridge, a suspension bridge across Puget Sound. At a final cost of about $1 billion, the bridge deck is 5,400 feet long. The new bridge was built parallel to the existing bridge, the latter of which will be repaired and reconstructed with seismic improvements through 2008.

Economic Development Information: Tacoma-Pierce County Chamber, 950 Pacific Ave., Ste. 300, P.O. Box 1933, Tacoma, WA 98401-1933; telephone (253) 627-2175; www.tacomachamber.org. Community and Economic Development, City of Tacoma, 747 Market Street, 9th Floor, Tacoma, WA 98402; telephone (253) 591-5364; www.cityoftacoma.org

Commercial Shipping

The Port of Tacoma is the 6th largest container port in North America and the 25th largest worldwide. It serves as one of the country's primary gateways for trade with Japan, China, Taiwan, and Thailand. Tacoma is also strongly tied to Alaska's economy, with the port handling more than 75 percent of all waterborne commerce going from the lower 48 states to Alaska. A 171-acre mega-container terminal opened in January 2005, part of a $34.1 million plan to meet the needs of the Port's existing customers and to attract additional customers. The Port services over 15 steamship lines.

The city is also an important rail shipping hub and is served by two major transcontinental railroads: Burlington Northern–Santa Fe and Union Pacific. These two railroads link Tacoma to major markets in the Midwest and East Coast. Rail is also used to move a variety of export commodities through Tacoma—everything from Midwest corn to John Deere tractors. More than 200 trucking companies work to move goods through the city and major air freight carriers serve Seattle-Tacoma International Airport (Sea-Tac), which is located about 30 minutes from Tacoma. Sea-Tac is one of the top 20 busiest air cargo airports in the nation.

Labor Force and Employment Outlook

Tacoma draws from a stable work force of skilled and unskilled workers that has steadily attracted new business and industry. Local firms can rely on more than one million workers who live within an hour's commute of the city. Pierce County is expected to gain 143,400 new jobs between 2002 and 2012. The highest demand is expected in labor, freight and stock handling, maintenance, and skilled trades. Retail sales jobs are also expected to increase.

The following is a summary of data regarding the Seattle-Tacoma-Bellevue metropolitan area labor force, 2006 annual averages.

Size of nonagricultural labor force: 1,688,700

Number of workers employed in . . .

> construction and mining: 115,800
> manufacturing: 181,100
> trade, transportation and utilities: 319,500
> information: 81,500
> financial activities: 105,300
> professional and business services: 226,900
> educational and health services: 186,300
> leisure and hospitality: 156,900
> other services: 62,400
> government: 253,100

Average hourly earnings of production workers employed in manufacturing: Not available

Unemployment rate: 4.0% (December 2007)

Largest employers (2006)	*Number of employees*
U.S. Army, Fort Lewis	39,204
Public school districts	13,275
U.S. Air Force, McChord	10,772
Washington state	7,649
Franciscan Health System	3,896
MultiCare Health System	3,874

Madigan Hospital	3,231
Pierce County	3,160
State higher education	2,958
City of Tacoma	2,044

Cost of Living

The following is a summary of data regarding several key cost of living factors in the Tacoma area.

2007 (1st quarter) ACCRA Average House Price: $357,943

2007 (1st quarter) ACCRA Cost of Living Index: 108.0

State income tax rate: None

State sales tax rate: 6.5%

Local income tax rate: None

Local sales tax rate: 8.4 to 8.8%

Property tax rate: $3.23 per $1,000 assessed value (2004; assessed yearly)

Economic Information: Tacoma-Pierce County Chamber, 950 Pacific Ave., Ste. 300, P.O. Box 1933, Tacoma, WA 98401-1933; telephone (253)627-2175; www.tacomachamber.org. Washington State Workforce Explorer, P.O. Box 9046, Mail Stop: 46000, Olympia, WA; telephone (360)438-4800; www.workforce explorer.com

■ Education and Research

Elementary and Secondary Schools

Tacoma Public Schools offer a wide range of academic services for students of all ages. High school students may participate in dual credit programs through which they may gain up to two years of college credits while completing their graduation requirements. Foss High School offers an International Baccalaureate program. Through a program called Great Start, the school system has been attempting to reduce the class sizes in first grade classrooms to 17 or fewer students in order to ensure that all children begin their first year of classes with the one-on-one attention they may need to succeed. Magnet schools are also available. Oakland Alternative High School assists children with learning differences. The Tacoma School of the Arts offers a focus on arts education for eligible high school students. Special education programs for developmentally disabled students are also available.

The following is a summary of data regarding the Tacoma Public Schools as of the 2005–2006 school year.

Total enrollment: 29,785

Number of facilities

elementary schools: 37
junior high/middle schools: 12
senior high schools: 7
other: 0

Student/teacher ratio: 20.5:1

Teacher salaries (2005–06)

elementary median: $51,680
junior high/middle median: $49,860
secondary median: $53,810

Funding per pupil: $7,783

Many private and parochial schools in Tacoma offer alternative and religious curricula.

Public Schools Information: Tacoma Public Schools, Central Administration, PO Box 1357, Tacoma, WA 98401-1357; telephone (253)571-1000; www.tacoma.k12.wa.us

Colleges and Universities

The University of Washington Tacoma opened in 1990 to offer bachelor's and master's degree completion programs for students with two or four years of college. The school welcomed its first freshman class in 2006 with a total enrollment of about 2,292 students. Bachelor's and master's degrees are available through seven academic divisions: the Milgard School of Business, the Institute of Technology, Interdisciplinary Arts and Sciences, Nursing, Social Work, Urban Studies, and Education. The school also sponsors the KeyBank Professional Development Center, offering continuing and executive education programs.

The University of Puget Sound is a private liberal arts college with an enrollment of about 2,576. The school offers three bachelor's degrees. four master's degrees, and a doctorate in physical therapy. Pacific Lutheran University is affiliated with the Evangelical Lutheran Church in America. The school has an enrollment of about 3,500 students and offers bachelor's degrees in a wide variety of majors through eight academic divisions. The school sponsors five graduate programs.

Tacoma Community College, Bates Technical College, and Pierce College provide occupational training and college preparatory curricula, as well as two-year degree programs and certificates. The Tacoma Campus of Evergreen State College offers bachelor's degree completion programs with flexible class schedules. Evergreen has a bridge program with Tacoma Community College.

Libraries and Research Centers

Tacoma is served by two public library systems. The Tacoma Public Library, with a downtown Main Library housed in a renovated 1903 Carnegie Library building, plus nine branches, maintains holdings of nearly 1 million items including books, periodical subscriptions, records, slides, tapes, films, maps, and art reproductions. Special collections include city archives and World War I books and posters; the library is a depository for federal and state government documents. The Pierce County Library System operates 17 branches and two bookmobiles; holdings consist of more than 1.3 million items. Several specialized libraries in the city are affiliated with government agencies, universities, corporations, churches, and a local newspaper.

The UW Tacoma Library is part of the University of Washington Library System, which is ranked 15th largest by the Association of Research Libraries. Students and researchers with borrowing privileges through the library have access to over 6 million items available through 33 regional consortium libraries. The Collins Memorial Library at the University of Puget Sound has a stock of 538,488 books, 1,658 periodical subscriptions, and over 344,409 microfilms.

Research activities in such fields as invertebrate zoology, herpetology, and ornithology are conducted at the University of Puget Sound's James R. Slater Museum of Natural History in Tacoma. The Franciscan Health System Research Center at St. Joseph Medical Center conducts clinical trials.

Public Library Information: Tacoma Public Library, 1102 Tacoma Avenue South, Tacoma, WA 98402-2098; telephone (253)591-5666; www.tpl.lib.wa.us. Pierce County Library System, 3005 112th Street East, Tacoma, WA 98446; telephone (253)536-6500; www.piercecountylibrary.org

■ Health Care

Franciscan Health System (FHS) operates the 320-bed St. Joseph Medical Center in Tacoma. St. Joseph Medical Center offers a comprehensive range of medical and surgical services including a burn clinic, endoscopy center, the Franciscan Spine Center, the St. Joseph Heart and Vascular Center, a Wound Care Center, Hyperbaric Oxygen Center, and a cancer treatment center that is affiliated with the Fred Hutchinson Cancer Research Center in Seattle. An outpatient clinic and mental health services are available, as is a hospice program. Other FHS facilities in the city include the Day Surgery Center, the St. Joseph Medical Clinic, the St. Joseph Women's Clinic, the Port Clinic (for occupational therapy and health), the Orthopaedic Center, Tacoma South Medical Center, and Neurosurgery Northwest.

MultiCare Health System (MHS) is the largest provider of medical services in Pierce County. MultiCare sponsors the Mary Bridge Children's Hospital and Health Center, which is the only dedicated pediatric hospital in southwest Washington. The MHS Tacoma General Hospital is a 391-bed facility that features a Level II adult trauma center and a Level III neonatal intensive care unit. Tacoma General has a special Family Birth Center. Allenmore Hospital is a 130-bed facility that features the Kelley Eye Center, a regional cancer center, orthopedic services, and a pulmonary conditioning department. The Allenmore Medical Center, Frank S. Barker Center, Jackson Hall, Westgate MultiCare Clinic, and University Place Multi-Care Clinic all offer primary care services in Tacoma.

Governmental agencies provide a number of programs that assist in substance abuse care, mental health, preventive medicine, and family planning.

■ Recreation

Sightseeing

Tacoma offers the sightseer a variety of diversions. The city is bordered by miles of waterfront parks and beaches. One of several parks located in the city is the 702-acre Point Defiance Park, which includes miles of walking trails through the wilderness and along the waterfront. Its Point Defiance Zoo and Aquarium includes animals native to the Puget Sound area as well as such exotic animals as Sumatran tigers and polar bears. Other attractions within Point Defiance Park include the Fort Nisqually Living History Museum, a restored trading post, and Camp 6, a re-creation of a logging camp. The city's first off-leash dog park is located at Rogers Park. The Narrows Bridge, spanning the Sound between Tacoma and the Gig Harbor Peninsula, is the fifth longest suspension bridge in the United States.

Wright Park downtown offers lawn bowling and horseshoe pitching; it is also the site of the Seymour Botanical Conservatory, a 1908 Victorian-style conservatory that contains about 500 species of exotic tropical flowers and foliage. Other points of interest are Union Station and the Old City Hall, built in the style of the Italian Renaissance; both are National Historic Landmarks.

A little more than an hour from Tacoma is Mt. Rainier National Park, which provides a closer view of the mountain that dominates the city's landscape. More than 300 miles of trails in the park provide plenty of opportunity for hiking and exploring. Climbing courses and skiing instruction are available. Plans are currently underway at the park to prepare an Intelligent Transportation System to enhance visitors' experiences there, including web cameras showing traffic conditions, interactive websites, and toll-free numbers to obtain road, weather, and traffic conditions. Kopachuck State Park and Penrose Point State Park are also in the vicinity.

Arts and Culture

Tacoma has a vibrant arts community with excellent museums and professional theater and opera companies. Downtown Tacoma, which in recent years has been attempting to re-establish the theater district as the "heart of the city," has revitalized its Broadway Center for the Performing Arts. The Broadway Center, which includes the historic Pantages Theater, the Rialto Theater, and the Theatre on the Square, is home to many performances year-round. Often programs at the Broadway Center feature companion education activities for school children. In addition, the University of Puget Sound and Pacific Lutheran University offer ongoing performances from September through June.

In 2002 Tacoma became home to the new Museum of Glass, featuring works of glass artists from throughout the world. Recognized glass artist Dale Chihuly is a Tacoma native. His work can be viewed in the historic Union Station on Pacific Avenue. The Tacoma Art Museum has a rich collection of American, European, and Asian art and offers stimulating rotating exhibits on an ongoing schedule. Its new facility opened in May 2003 and is twice the size of its previous location. The Antoine Predock–designed building features a unique flexible exhibition area that wraps around an indoor, open-air stone garden.

The Washington State History Museum has the largest collection of Northwest artifacts in the state. Its interactive exhibits chronicle the natural, social, and industrial history of the Pacific Northwest. The Washington State Capitol Museum features exhibits that reflect regional Native American history. The Karpeles Manuscript Library Museum has a collection of original manuscripts from American authors of the nineteenth century.

Tacoma's anchor arts groups include the Northwest Sinfonietta, Tacoma Philharmonic, Tacoma Symphony Orchestra, Tacoma Actors Guild, Tacoma Art Museum, Tacoma Little Theatre, Children's Museum of Tacoma, and Tacoma Youth Symphony. Visitors to Tacoma can also enjoy a variety of public art. Highlights not to be missed include displayed public art projects on the Ruston Way waterfront and the literary, visual, and sound art forms at the walkway at Point Defiance. The University of Washington Tacoma campus is located in the middle of downtown Tacoma. A stroll through the campus takes the visitor past a variety of contemporary art created by some of Washington state's finest artists, including Buster Simpson, Dan Senn, and Dale Chihuly.

Festivals and Holidays

Tacoma's special events calendar is filled throughout the year. The Home and Garden Show, the Palmer/Wirfs Antique Show, and the Northwest Bridal Expo are held in January. The Wintergrass Bluegrass Festival takes place in February, followed by the Northwest Antique Show in March. The Annual Daffodil Festival and the Annual Spring Barrel Wine Tasting Tour are fun April events. The Sound to Narrows Race draws crowds annually in June. July in Tacoma is especially festive, with the Fourth of July Celebration in Old Town, the Tacoma Freedom Fair and Fireworks Display, and the Taste of Tacoma. Summer festivals continue with the Pierce County Fair, Downtown Farmers Market, and the Tall Ships Festival, which includes world-class sailing ships at the waterfront.

Fall brings the Western Washington Fair, Oktoberfest, the Puyallup Canine Fest, and the Holiday Food and Gift Festival. The year closes with the Victorian Country Christmas in December, followed by the Downtown Tacoma Tree Lighting Ceremony, and First Night Celebrations on New Year's Eve.

Sports for the Spectator

The Tacoma Rainiers, the Triple A farm team for professional baseball's American League Florida Mariners, play baseball at Cheney Stadium. Both Pacific Lutheran University and the University of Puget Sound field teams in major sports.

Sports for the Participant

In addition to the recreational opportunities provided by the Cascade Mountains and the 361 freshwater lakes in Pierce County, Tacoma operates four public golf courses and tennis courts are located in the public parks. MetroParks Tacoma maintains 57 parks, including the Point Defiance Park Zoo and Aquarium. The city has five municipal pools. There are five parks with wading pools and four parks with spraygrounds. The city also maintains a number of public beaches and piers for swimming and fishing. Three skateparks are available. Those looking for a more relaxing day may visit a number of spas in the city, including Avanti Spas, Body Evolution, and the Tacoma Women's Fitness and Day Spa.

Shopping and Dining

Boutiques and antique shops can be found at Tacoma's Old Town Historic District, the city's original business district. The downtown business district has shops, boutiques, and galleries. Freighthouse Square is a public market with restaurants, specialty shops, an antique mall, and special events. The Tacoma Mall, one of the largest in the Northwest, contains about 150 specialty stores, 5 department stores and a food court. The Pacific Northwest Shop in the historic Proctor district features "Gifts Made in Our Corner of America," including wine and specialty foods.

Tacoma is salmon country and the city is home to numerous seafood restaurants. Ruston Way, along the western side of the peninsula, is dotted with restaurants and is referred to as "Restaurant Row."

Visitor Information: Tacoma Regional Convention and Visitor Bureau, 1119 Pacific Avenue, 5th Floor, Tacoma, WA 98402; telephone (253)627-2836; toll-free (800)272-2662; www.traveltacoma.com

■ Convention Facilities

The Greater Tacoma Convention and Trade Center in the heart of downtown features a 51,000-square-foot Exhibition Hall, a 13,650-square-foot ballroom (which can be divided into 4 smaller rooms), and 15 meeting rooms. An 18,000-square-foot outdoor event space is also available. A light rail train connects the center to the Tacoma Dome.

Meeting facilities are available at the 6.1-acre Tacoma Dome Entertainment Complex. The Dome, located near Commencement Bay in downtown Tacoma, contains a 30,000-square-foot Convention Hall with a seating capacity for 2,000 participants. The hall can be divided into six soundproof rooms, providing seminar space. The dome's arena can provide additional seating space for 3,000 persons. The Shanaman Sports Museum, which aims to preserve the area's sports heritage, is also located inside the Dome. Along with the arena, the Convention Hall offers 150,000 square feet of space. Banquet and meeting space are available at Saint Helens Convention Center, a historic landmark. Several other hotels and motels providing additional meeting space are located in the Tacoma area.

Convention Information: Tacoma Regional Convention and Visitor Bureau, 1119 Pacific Avenue, 5th Floor, Tacoma, WA 98402; telephone (253)627-2836; toll-free (800)272-2662; www.traveltacoma.com

■ Transportation

Approaching the City

Seattle-Tacoma International Airport (Sea-Tac) is a modern facility serving over 29 million passengers each year with over 22 airlines. In 2007 it was the 17th busiest commercial service airport in the nation. Tacoma Narrows Airport is a municipally-owned field handling corporate commuter flights.

The primary north-south motor route to Tacoma is Interstate 5, which runs between Canada and Mexico. East-west access is provided by S.R. 16. Amtrak furnishes rail service into Tacoma with several trains each day. Greyhound also stops in the city.

Traveling in the City

Tacoma occupies an irregular peninsula with its street pattern conforming roughly to a grid within those constraints. The principle north-south arteries are Pacific Avenue, North Pearl, and Ruston Way. The major east-west thoroughfares are Sixth Avenue and S.R. 16, which enters Tacoma across the Narrows Bridge. Interstate 5 bisects the city on a southwest to northeast axis.

Sound Transit offers several ways of getting around. ST Express buses run from Tacoma, Gig Harbor, and Lakewood to downtown Seattle and back. ST Express buses also run from Lakewood and Tacoma to Seattle-Tacoma International Airport. Sounder commuter trains run some 80 miles on weekdays, connecting from Everett and Tacoma into Seattle and back. The Tacoma Link light rail trains began operating in August 2003 and have become a primary factor in the renaissance of downtown Tacoma. Construction is currently underway on a 14-mile Central Link light rail line, to begin carrying passengers in 2009. Future Sound Transit plans include adding more bus transit facilities and increasing the hours of operation for all services. Pierre Transit (PT) is another regional public transportation service serving Tacoma and Pierce County. PT offers daily commuter buses to Seattle and Olympia as well as dozens of fixed routes in and around the city.

Washington State Ferries offer service between Pt. Defiance Park and Vashon Island.

■ Communications

Newspaper and Magazines

The major daily newspaper in Tacoma is *The News Tribune*. *The Ranger* is a weekly paper for military personnel. The *Pierce County Business Examiner* is available in a print edition once a week; an email daily subscription is also available. The *Tacoma Reporter* is a weekly alternative press newspaper. The *Northwest Dispatch* is a weekly serving the African American community.

Television and Radio

Two television stations are based in Tacoma; because of the city's proximity to Seattle, broadcasts from Seattle television stations are also received in the metropolitan area. Ten AM and FM radio stations broadcast from Tacoma with music, news, and special interest programming.

Media Information: *The News Tribune,* 1950 South State Street, Tacoma, WA 98411; telephone (253)597-8742; www.thenewstribune.com

Tacoma Online

City of Tacoma home page. Available www.cityoftacoma.org

The News Tribune. Available www.thenewstribune.com

Pierce County Library System. Available www.piercecountylibrary.org

Tacoma-Pierce County Chamber of Commerce. Available www.tacomachamber.org

Tacoma Public Library. Available www.tpl.lib.wa.us

Tacoma Public Schools. Available www.tacoma.k12.wa.us

Tacoma Regional Convention and Visitor Bureau. Available www.traveltacoma.com

BIBLIOGRAPHY

Alexie, Sherman, *Reservation Blues* (New York: Warner Books, 1995)

Vancouver

■ The City in Brief

Founded: 1825 (incorporated 1857)

Head Official: Mayor Royce Pollard

City Population
- 1980: 43,000
- 1990: 46,380
- 2000: 143,560
- 2006 estimate: 158,855
- Percent change, 1990–2000: 209%
- U.S. rank in 1980: Not available
- U.S. rank in 1990: Not available
- U.S. rank in 2000: 145th

Metropolitan Area Population
- 1980: Not available
- 1990: 1,477,895
- 2000: 2,265,223
- 2006 estimate: Not available
- Percent change, 1990–2000: 53.2%
- U.S. rank in 1980: Not available
- U.S. rank in 1990: Not available
- U.S. rank in 2000: Not available

Area: 46.1 square miles (2000)

Elevation: Ranges from 150 to 290 feet above sea level

Average Annual Temperature: 51.8° F

Average Annual Precipitation: 41.92 inches

Major Economic Sectors: services, wholesale and retail trade, government

Unemployment Rate: 8.6% (2005)

Per Capita Income: $23,084 (2005)

2005 FBI Crime Index Property: 7,943

2005 FBI Crime Index Violent: 626

Major Colleges and Universities: Clark College, Washington State University–Vancouver

Daily Newspaper: *The Columbian*

■ Introduction

Washington's fourth largest city and the county seat of Clark County, Vancouver celebrated its 150th anniversary as an incorporated city in 2007. Vancouver is a historic and cultural gem of southwest Washington, replete with natural beauty. It offers the services of a large metropolitan city with the charm and hospitality of a small urban town. Residents and visitors can engage in a wide variety of outdoor recreational activities and be entertained by a symphony orchestra, different theater troupes, or popular musical and comedy acts. Vancouver's proximity to Portland, Oregon, also offers residents and visitors additional opportunities for business and pleasure. The economy is diversifying, with growth in high technology industries. Vancouver is undertaking a major plan to develop its downtown, including the city waterfront. The future looks promising for this Columbia River city.

■ Geography and Climate

Vancouver sits on the north bank of the Columbia River directly across from Portland, Oregon. The Pacific Coast is less than 90 miles to the west. The Cascade Mountain Range rises on the east. The city has a total area of 46.1 square miles. Vancouver has a climate similar to Portland—temperate and seasonal. The rainy season lasts from November through April, with 80 percent of the total annual rainfall occurring in those months. Winter low temperatures hover around 35 degrees and summer highs average around 80 degrees. Summers are usually very pleasant with abundant sunshine. However,

Vancouver's climate is different from Portland's in a few key ways. Being unsheltered by the Willamette Valley, high pressures east of the Cascade Range lead to cold east winds down the Columbia River Gorge. Vancouver can experience freezing rain. Until the building of dams, close proximity to the river was a concern for flooding, destroying features such as Celilo Falls. Two of the most destructive floods took place in June 1894 and May 1948. Offsetting the cold gorge winds is a subtropical jet stream that brings warm moist air from the southern Pacific Ocean.

Area: 46.1 square miles (2000)

Elevation: Ranges from 150 to 290 feet above sea level

Average Temperature: 51.8° F

Average Annual Precipitation: 41.92 inches

■ History

A Habitable Place

For thousands of years, the Vancouver area was home to native people, including the Chinook and Klickitat nations. In May 1792 American trader and sailor Robert Gray became the first non-native to enter the Columbia River. Later that year, British Lieutenant William Broughton, serving under Captain George Vancouver, explored 100 miles upriver. Broughton named a point of land along the shore in honor of Vancouver. In 1806 Meriwether Lewis and William Clark camped near the Vancouver waterfront on the return trip of their western expedition. Lewis called the area "the only desired situation for settlement west of the Rocky Mountains."

In 1825 Dr. John McLoughlin, the chief agent of the Hudson Bay Company's Columbia District, made a decision to move the company's northwest headquarters from Astoria (now Oregon) upriver. He named the site after Point Vancouver on Broughton's original map. This was the founding of Fort Vancouver.

From a Fur Trading Center to Military Headquarters

For many years, Fort Vancouver was the main location for fur trading in the Pacific Northwest. It was settled by both Americans and British under a "joint occupation" agreement. Fort Vancouver was a center of British control over the Oregon Territory. However, in 1846 American control was extended north to the 49th parallel with the Oregon Treaty. The northwest became part of the United States.

In 1849 American troops arrived to establish Columbia (later Vancouver) Barracks. It served as military headquarters for much of the Pacific Northwest. U.S. Army Captain Ulysses S. Grant was quartermaster at the Columbia Barracks for 15 months beginning in September 1852. The neighboring settlement was named the "City of Columbia." The city of Vancouver was incorporated on January 23, 1857. Through the rest of nineteenth century, Vancouver developed and grew. In 1908 the first rail line east through the Washington side of the Columbia River Gorge reached Vancouver. In 1910 a railroad bridge was opened south across the Columbia River. In 1917 the Interstate Bridge was completed, which replaced ferries.

Wartime Activities

During World War I, the site later named Pearson Field was the location of the world's largest spruce cut-up mill. The mill cut raw timber into the lumber used to build planes that fought in World War I. After the bombing of Pearl Harbor, Henry Kaiser opened a shipyard next to the U.S. Army reserve, which by 1944 employed as many as 36,000 people. Vancouver's Kaiser Shipyard built a variety of craft that were used in World War II. The large number of shipyard workers who came to work in Vancouver increased the population from 18,000 to over 80,000 in just a few months. This led to the creation of the Vancouver Housing Authority and six new residential developments that became neighborhoods.

Sesquicentennial Celebration

Vancouver celebrated its 150th anniversary as an incorporated city in 2007. Vancouver has gone through many transformations in its history, including growing from a population of about 250 people in 1857 to more than 158,000 today. Twice Vancouver has been honored with being an "All American City." As its motto says, Vancouver, with a colorful past, has a bright future.

Historical Information: Washington State History Museum, 1911 Pacific Avenue, Tacoma, WA 98402; telephone (253)272-3500; toll-free (888)BE-THERE; fax (253)272-9518

■ Population Profile

Metropolitan Area Residents

1980: Not available
1990: 1,477,895
2000: 2,265,223
2006 estimate: Not available
Percent change, 1990–2000: 53.2%
U.S. rank in 1980: Not available
U.S. rank in 1990: Not available
U.S. rank in 2000: Not available

City Residents

1980: 43,000
1990: 46,380

Airphoto-Jim Wark

2000: 143,560
2006 estimate: 158,855
Percent change, 1990–2000: 209%
U.S. rank in 1980: Not available
U.S. rank in 1990: Not available
U.S. rank in 2000: 145th

Density: 3,354,7 people per square mile (2000)

Racial and ethnic characteristics (2005)

White: 128,837
Black: 3,108
American Indian and Alaska Native: 2,953
Asian: 7,258
Native Hawaiian and Pacific Islander: 1,433
Hispanic or Latino (may be of any race): 12,957
Other: 4,648

Percent of residents born in state: 28.9% (2000)

Age characteristics (2005)

Population under 5 years old: 10,656
Population 5 to 9 years old: 10,238
Population 10 to 14 years old: 11,213
Population 15 to 19 years old: 7,951

Population 20 to 24 years old: 12,846
Population 25 to 34 years old: 25,789
Population 35 to 44 years old: 23,165
Population 45 to 54 years old: 21,288
Population 55 to 59 years old: 9,972
Population 60 to 64 years old: 6,229
Population 65 to 74 years old: 7,929
Population 75 to 84 years old: 6,211
Population 85 years and older: 2,001
Median age: 34.6 years

Births (2005)

Total number: 5,110

Deaths (2005)

Total number: 2,235

Money income (2005)

Per capita income: $23,084
Median household income: $40,743
Total households: 63,693

Number of households with income of...

less than $10,000: 6,782
$10,000 to $14,999: 3,337

$15,000 to $24,999: 8,207
$25,000 to $34,999: 9,071
$35,000 to $49,999: 11,161
$50,000 to $74,999: 12,230
$75,000 to $99,999: 6,130
$100,000 to $149,999: 5,083
$150,000 to $199,999: 788
$200,000 or more: 904

Percent of families below poverty level: 12.8% (2005)

2005 FBI Crime Index Property: 7,943

2005 FBI Crime Index Violent: 626

■ Municipal Government

The city has a council/manager form of government. Seven council members (including a mayor) are elected to staggered four-year terms.

Head Official: Mayor Royce Pollard (since 1996; current term expires 2009)

Total Number of City Employees: 1,050 (2007)

City Information: City Hall, 210 E. 13th St., Vancouver, WA 98668; telephone (360)696-8121; fax (360) 696-8049

■ Economy

Major Industries and Commercial Activity

Vancouver's economy has diversified over the past two decades, resulting in a healthy climate for business investment, as well as creating markets for a wide array of products and services. The expansion of the manufacturing base and growth in the high-tech and service sector has improved the economic outlook. Although traditional industries like agriculture, wood products, and natural resources and mining are no longer contributing materially to job growth, industries such as construction, professional and scientific services, software publishing, biotechnology, education, heath care, and retail trade have recently seen measurable gains. Many residents commute to Portland, Oregon. As of 2007, the largest employers in Clark County were government agencies (including school districts) and Kroger Corporation's Fred Meyer grocery stores. High-tech manufacturers such as Hewlett-Packard, WaferTech, and SEH America, and labor subcontractors such as Volt Services Group are also located in the city. Vancouver is home to the corporate headquarters of Nautilus, Inc., and The Holland (parent company of the Burgerville restaurant chain).

Items and goods produced: electronic goods, software, agricultural products, foodstuffs, wood products, fitness equipment

Incentive Programs—New and Existing Companies

Local programs: The Columbia River Economic Development Council (CREDC) helps companies find profitable locations in the Vancouver and Portland Metropolitan area. The council offers such services as site location and acquisition, business demographics, and permit and process facilitation. It helps businesses relocate, expand, and increase their competitiveness in a cost-effective manner. CREDC markets tax-exempt industrial revenue bonds on behalf of the Industrial Revenue Bonds Public Corporation of Clark County. IRBs can be used to finance real estate, machinery, and equipment for eligible manufacturing companies. The CREDC also has connections that can introduce businesses to private equity and government backed financing for projects. CREDC promotes funding programs that leverage research and development support for targeted industries.

State programs: The state of Washington offers a number of incentive programs to attract new and expanding businesses to the state. Among them are B & O tax credits; sales/use tax deferrals for high technology and manufacturing companies as well as for firms relocating or expanding in distressed areas; and loan programs that apply to rural areas and the redevelopment of brownfields.

Job training programs: The Southwest Washington Workforce Development Council (SWWDC) provides leadership and resources to increase economic development with a trained and productive workforce in Clark, Cowlitz, and Wahkiakum Counties. WorkSource and other partners offer resources and a variety of services to help youth, adults, and dislocated workers secure gainful employment. There is a WorkSource center in Vancouver, which offers job search assistance, access to current job openings, career development and assistance, and training and skill development.

Development Projects

In 1997 Vancouver dedicated the next 15 to 20 years to redeveloping and revitalizing a large section of downtown. The first projects started in the early 2000s with the construction of high-rise condominiums around Esther Short Park and in the Uptown Village neighborhood. A Hilton hotel was built directly across from the park. As of 2007 Vancouver was building a new shopping complex just outside of the downtown area. *The Columbian* newspaper was in the final stages of constructing a new seven-story building adjacent to the Hilton. As of 2007 a new development along C Street downtown that would include a new library, a Marriott hotel, and approximately 250 condominiums was in the planning stages. In 2006 the Boise Cascade site on the Columbia River waterfront was sold, which has the potential to transform the waterfront into an active living area for both residents and visitors.

In June 2007 the City Council adopted the Vancouver City Center Vision and Subarea Plan for future development. The boundary of the City Center Plan was expanded to approximately 130 city blocks including the city center waterfront. The Plan will encourage residential development; the creation and support of what the city calls "messy vitality"—a mix of residential, civic, retail, and entertainment places that will attract growth, jobs, and activity; focused waterfront redevelopment; protection of key historic buildings and established residential neighborhoods; and revitalization of the Main Street Corridor to establish downtown as a regional center for commerce, culture, and urban living.

Economic Development Information: City of Vancouver, Economic Development Services, City Hall, 210 E. 13th St., Vancouver, WA 98668; telephone (360)696-8121; fax (360)696-8049. Columbia River Economic Development Council, 805 Broadway, Suite 412, Vancouver, WA 98660-3237; telephone (360)694-5006; fax (360)694-9927; email info@credc.org

Commercial Shipping

The Port of Vancouver is a multi-purpose port authority located along the banks of the Columbia River. The Port has over 1,000 acres available for expansion and development of heavy and light industry, manufacturing, distribution warehousing, research and business-park uses. The Port also has versatile cargo handling facilities, a skilled labor force, personal customer service, and extensive transportation networks. The Port is a hub of marine, rail, highway, and air cargo transportation connections. The Port of Vancouver has handled a variety of bulk and break bulk cargoes since 1912.

Labor Force and Employment Outlook

Many Vancouverites work in Portland. Job opportunities are increasing in the high technology, education, healthcare, and other service sectors, while employment in traditional industries such as agriculture, wood products, and natural resources and mining is decreasing.

The following is a summary of data regarding the Portland-Vancouver-Beaverton OR-WA metropolitan area labor force, 2006 annual averages.

Size of nonagricultural labor force: 1,015,200

Number of workers employed in . . .

    construction and mining: 1,700
    manufacturing: 126,900

    trade, transportation and utilities: 203,100
    information: 23,800
    financial activities: 70,300
    professional and business services: 134,100
    educational and health services: 123,600
    leisure and hospitality: 93,700
    other services: 35,600
    government: 139,100

Average hourly earnings of production workers employed in manufacturing: $16.24

Unemployment rate: 8.6% (2005)

Largest employers (2006)	Number of employees
Vancouver School District	3,380
Southwest Washington Medical Center	3,229
Evergreen School District	3,052
Hewlett-Packard	1,800
Clark County	1,703
City of Vancouver	1,438
Clark College	1,297
Fred Meyer, Inc.	1,295
Safeway	1,205
Bonneville Power Administration	1,139

Cost of Living

The following is a summary of data regarding key cost of living factors for the Vancouver area.

2007 (1st quarter) ACCRA Average House Price: Not available

2007 (1st quarter) ACCRA Cost of Living Index: 98.5 (Portland-Vancouver-Beaverton metro)

State income tax rate: None

State sales tax rate: 6.5%

Local income tax rate: None

Local sales tax rate: 8.10%

Property tax rate: 1.0% per $100 of assessed valuation

Economic Information: Greater Vancouver Chamber of Commerce, 1101 Broadway, Suite 100, Vancouver, WA 98660; telephone (360)694-2588; fax (360)693-8279. Columbia River Economic Development Council, 805 Broadway, Suite 412, Vancouver, WA 98660-3237; telephone (360)694-5006; fax (360)694-9927; email info@credc.org

■ Education and Research

Elementary and Secondary Schools

The Vancouver School District employs 2,352 people full time, 1,345 of whom are certified. Teachers have an average 13.5 years of experience, and 958 teachers had an advanced degree as of 2007.

All schools in the district offer extended day activities. Approximately 2,000 students participate in summer programs. About 12 percent of students receive special education services. The graduation rate is 75 percent. Minority students make up 25 percent of total enrollment. Students in the Vancouver School District speak over 30 different languages. Approximately two percent are gifted students enrolled in the Challenge Program.

The following is a summary of data regarding the Vancouver School District as of the 2005–2006 school year.

Total enrollment: 326,673

Number of facilities

elementary schools: 22
junior high/middle schools: 7
senior high schools: 6
other: 1

Student/teacher ratio: 20.4:1

Teacher salaries (2005–06)

elementary median: $46,430
junior high/middle median: $46,790
secondary median: $48,380

Funding per pupil: $7,221

Private schools include the Cascadia Montessori School, the Clark County Christian School, the Columbia Adventist Academy, the Columbia Ridge Baptist Academy, the Cornerstone Christian School, the Firm Foundation Christian School, the Gardner School, Kings Way Christian School, Our Lady of Lourdes, Vancouver Christian High School, Vancouver Community Christian, and St. Joseph Catholic Grade School. The Washington School for the Deaf and the Washington State School for the Blind are also located in Vancouver.

Public Schools Information: Vancouver School District, 2901 Falk Road, Vancouver, WA 98661; telephone (360)313-1000

Colleges and Universities

Originally founded as a private two-year junior college in 1932, Clark College provides a variety of associate degrees, general adult education, and preparation for four-year university degrees. Clark College has well-regarded programs in nursing, dental hygiene, and industrial arts such as welding and auto maintenance.

Enrollment for fall quarter 2007 was 11,422 students (full- and part-time).

Washington State University (WSU), a major public research university with a main campus in Pullman, Washington, has a regional 350-acre campus in Vancouver. WSU-Vancouver is a non-residential research university with access to the resources of the WSU system. WSU-Vancouver offers 14 bachelor's degrees, 9 master's degrees, 1 doctorate degree, and more than 35 fields of study. Enrollment for fall 2007 was 2,555 students. WSU-Vancouver has more than 90 full-time Ph.D. faculty.

Libraries and Research Centers

Fort Vancouver Regional Library District serves southwest Washington state. With a library collection that includes more than 725,000 books, magazines, videotapes, DVDs, playaways, and audio book CDs and tapes, the library district serves all of Clark, Skamania, and Klickitat counties, and the city of Woodland and the independent Yale Valley Library District in Cowlitz county. The district has 13 libraries, 3 bookmobiles, a Vancouver operations center, and dial-up and Internet access to electronic services. Fort Vancouver Regional Library District provides information resources and services and community and cultural events for a population of more than 400,000 residents. Branch libraries are located in the communities of Battle Ground, Cascade Park, Goldendale, La Center, North Bonneville, Ridgefield, Stevenson, Three Creeks (Salmon Creek area), Vancouver (Main), Vancouver Mall, Washougal, White Salmon Valley, and Woodland.

Washington State University-Vancouver's library has more than 800 journals in hardcopy and over 9,000 full-text online journals and newspapers. It also has a core collection of more than 20,000 books and access to more than 100 major bibliographic databases. The library participates in several local and regional library consortia, including the Portland Area Library System and ORBIS/CASCADE (the Oregon and Washington Cooperative Library Project). It also houses the Environmental Information Cooperative Library.

Public Library Information: Fort Vancouver Regional Library District, 1007 E. Mill Plain Blvd., Vancouver, WA 98663; telephone (360)695-1561

■ Health Care

Southwest Washington Medical Center in Vancouver offers comprehensive hospital services, with special heart and vascular, cancer, brain and spine, bone and joint, and trauma centers. It is community owned and operated and has 360 licensed beds. An active medical staff of more than 600 physicians is supported by a staff of over 3,200 highly skilled professionals. Southwest

Washington Medical Center was established in 1858 as the first permanent hospital in the Northwest Territories, and is now the largest private employer in Clark County and one of the major employers in the Portland metropolitan region.

Legacy Salmon Creek Hospital is part of the Legacy Health System. The 220-bed, full-service community hospital celebrated its second anniversary in 2007.

Medical centers in Portland within a ten-mile radius of Vancouver include the Providence Portland Medical Center, Woodland Park Hospital, and Legacy Emanuel Hospital and Health Center.

■ Recreation

Sightseeing

A must-see for any visitor to the city is the Fort Vancouver National Historic Site. Headquarters for the British Hudson's Bay Company, the fort was once the center of political, cultural, and commercial activities in the Pacific Northwest. Interpreters in period clothing re-enact daily fort life in this reconstructed mid-19th century fur trading outpost. Officers Row is the location for 22 preserved Victorian homes on the National Historic Register. Built in the mid- to late-1800s, these beautifully restored homes were built to house U.S. Army officers and their families stationed at Vancouver Barracks. They include the Marshall House, the O.O. Howard House, and the Grant House (featuring the Restaurant at the Historic Reserve and Commanders Whiskey and Wine Bar). On Main Street, the Clark County Historical Museum showcases the history of Clark County housed in a former Carnegie Library that was built in 1909. Exhibits feature a Native American gallery, railroad exhibit, American military memorabilia, and other artifacts dating back to the 13th century.

Located at the oldest continually operating airfield in the nation, the Pearson Air Museum houses a collection of vintage airplanes, interpretive displays, an interactive children's center, theater presentations, a restoration shop, and gift shop. The Water Resources Education Center teaches people of all ages about water resources and includes hands-on activities in the Exhibit Hall, artwork in the Center's White Sturgeon Art Gallery, live sturgeon in a 350-gallon aquarium, and a panoramic view of the Columbia River. The Salmon Run Bell Tower and Glockenspiel is located in Esther Short Park. The bells were cast in the Netherlands, and there are four five-foot bronze jumping salmon on the tower and several jets that spray water down the column. A Chinook Indian story is inscribed in the basalt column around the base of the tower and a fully animated, three-scene glockenspiel depicts Chinook Indian legend. The Ilchee Monument features a seven-foot tall statue, overlooking the Columbia River, honoring the daughter of Comcomly, a

19th century Chinook chief. According to Native American lore, Ilchee had the power of a shaman, and she paddled her own canoe, the sign of a chief. The four-mile Waterfront Renaissance Trail connects downtown Vancouver with the retail shops and restaurants along the Columbia River waterfront.

The Ridgefield National Wildlife Refuge offers over 5,000 acres of vital migration and wintering habitat for spring and fall migrating birds. The mild winter climate and wetlands along the Columbia River create ideal resting and feeding areas for 180 species of birds such as Canada Geese, Sandhill Cranes, Great Blue Herons, swans, shore and song birds, and a variety of waterfowl.

The Cedar Creek Grist Mill in Woodland is the only grain-grinding mill in Washington that has maintained its original structural integrity, grinds with stones, and is water-powered. Built in 1876, the mill has been fully restored as a working museum and is registered as a National Historic Site. The covered bridge spanning Cedar Creek adjacent to the mill was rebuilt in 1994. Cathlapotle Plankhouse is a full-scale replica of a Chinookan-style cedar plankhouse located at the Ridgefield National Wildlife Refuge at the location of Cathlapotle, one of the largest Chinookan villages in the area. At Hulda Klager Lilac Gardens in Woodland, visitors can step back in time to discover an 1880s Victorian farmhouse and country garden with more than 150 varieties of lilacs and some rare and unusual plants and trees. The 1889 farmhouse contains many of the original furnishings as well as featured displays of handmade quilts, artwork, antiques, and collectibles.

In Yacolt visitors can experience 1920s farm life at the Pomeroy Living History Farm. Period-dressed interpreters help visitors participate in farm activities such as grinding grain, washing clothes, feeding livestock, and making rope. Also in Yacolt, the Chelatchie Prairie Railroad is pulled by an 1841 diesel locomotive, transporting passengers through scenic northern Clark County from Yacolt to Mouton Falls and Chelatchie Prairie and back. Special events include casino nights, murder mysteries, staged hold-ups, and barbeque trips.

Arts and Culture

The Main Street Theater offers an intimate theater in downtown Vancouver with multiple live performances for adult audiences each week. Next to Esther Short Park, the Old Slocum House Theater is Vancouver's oldest non-profit community theater. It is located in the historic Slocum House and can seat 60. The Clark College Theatre blends theatre, music, dance, and art into entertaining and award-winning productions. For the past two decades, the theatre has been recognized as a leader in Southwest Washington.

The Vancouver Symphony Orchestra, with critically acclaimed music director and conductor Salvador Brotons, puts on musical performances from October through May, plus a summer outdoor evening concert in Esther Short Park. The Bravo! Concert Series is one of the premiere choral groups in the Pacific Northwest. Singers perform a diverse repertoire, and are equally at home performing jazz and popular music. In Ridgefield the Amphitheater at Clark County is a 60,000-square-foot live music venue located next to the Clark County Event Center and Fairgrounds. The facility seats almost 8,000 in the covered pavilion and an additional 10,000 on the lawn. The Camas Performing Arts Series presents five musical concerts between September and May in the 720-seat Joyce Garver Theater in Camas. The 90-minute concerts feature national and international artists in a variety of musical genres.

Festivals and Holidays

True to its reputation as a great city for walking, Vancouver hosts the Discovery Walk Festival each April. The Discovery Walk Festival is sponsored by International Walk Fest and the city of Vancouver to foster international friendship. Walkers and military units come from a dozen different nations to participate.

The Sturgeon Festival is held at the Water Resources Education Center in June. The festival is a celebration of the sturgeon and its Columbia River ecosystem. Each Fourth of July, fireworks are set off on the grounds of Fort Vancouver National Historic Site. The display is the largest west of the Mississippi River.

In late August the Vancouver Wine and Jazz Festival is held in Esther Short Park, where attendees can sample excellent wine and food while listening to great music. Also in August, Founders Day is held to commemorate the anniversary of the founding of the National Park System. Admission to Fort Vancouver National Historic Site is free, and there are craft demonstrations by carpenters, blacksmiths, bakers, and cooks.

St. Joseph Catholic School hosts the Vancouver Sausage Fest in September; more than 100,000 people attend the festival over three days. October brings the Old Apple Tree Celebration, an annual celebration in honor of the Northwest's oldest living apple tree, originally planted at Fort Vancouver in 1826. The celebration features a Heritage Tree bike ride, children's activities, tree expert presentations, a fruit tree pruning workshop, and a chance to sample apples from the Old Apple Tree itself.

WinterFaire is held on the weekend before Thanksgiving at the Water Resources Education Center. The fair features some of the region's foremost artisans and craft artists who display treasures such as turned wooden vessels, precious stone jewelry, ceramics, garden art, photography, and paintings, with a focus on nature. In December visitors can experience the festive traditional sights, smells, and sounds of the holiday season at Fort Vancouver, just as the employees of Hudson's Bay Company may have been doing in preparation for the holidays.

Sports for the Spectator

When not rooting for other Washington teams, Vancouverites and visitors can take advantage of the city's close proximity to Portland, Oregon to watch spectator sports. Portland hosts NBA basketball, pre-NHL hockey, minor league baseball, and A-League soccer. The Rose Garden Arena is home to the NBA's Portland Trail Blazers and the Portland LumberJax professional indoor lacrosse team. The Portland Winter Hawks hockey team plays at the Memorial Coliseum, which is located next door to the arena. PGE Park is home to Triple-A baseball's Portland Beavers, an affiliate of the San Diego Padres. The A-League Portland Timbers' soccer games are also played there. The season at the Portland International Raceway is highlighted by G.I. Joe's Presents Champ Car Grand Prix of Portland, the largest auto racing event in the Pacific Northwest. Portland Meadows is a horse-racing track.

Washington State University-Vancouver belongs to the Pacific-10 Conference for football, basketball, baseball, and track and field.

Sports for the Participant

Vancouver offers recreation and sports programs for residents of all ages. There are nearly 7,000 acres of parkland, over 44 miles of trails, and facilities including pools, a tennis/racquetball center, and community centers. Opportunities for hiking, biking, camping, fishing, boating, swimming, kayaking, golf, windsurfing, skiing, and snowboarding abound. The rivers and lakes in southwest Washington offer some of the best fishing. There are many fine steelhead streams and one of the only wild Fall Chinook salmon runs in the state. The Columbia River also offers some of the best sturgeon fishing. The Columbia River Gorge has become known as one of the best locations worldwide for windsurfing—some even call it the windsurfing capital of the world. There are approximately 50 approved windsurfing sites along the east and west sides of the Gorge. Hikers can climb in Gifford Pinchot National Forest to the east. Trails range from easy nature trails to rugged terrain at varying difficulties. *Walking Magazine* awarded Clark County the Walkable Community Award for the more than 44 miles of urban walking trails in the Vancouver region. Mt. Hood in Oregon, about an hour's drive away from Vancouver, offers everything from the best powder skiing and snowboarding, to tubing, sleigh rides, and dog sled rides. Mt. Hood Skibowl also offers the nation's largest night ski area. For golf, the area offers 10 public courses and numerous driving ranges. For those who like to camp, the area also has two state parks with tent and RV sites, as well as a number of well-kept RV campgrounds.

Shopping and Dining

Vancouver offers a variety of shopping opportunities. The Vancouver Farmers Market operates year-round indoors in the Esther Short Commons next to Esther Short Park. It features an eclectic mixture of food, high-end crafts, farm-direct produce, and nursery stock. From April through October, the Market expands outdoors into the streets with more than 150 vendors offering local produce, plants, and arts and crafts. There are also food booths with local and international specialties, and entertainers provide live music.

If one is shopping for antiques, gifts, or in boutique shops, Uptown Village in the upper Main Street area is the place to go. In downtown Vancouver, there are many art galleries, clothing and shoe stores, and gift and specialty shops. Westfield Shoppingtown is Southwest Washington's largest mall. It features more than 140 specialty shops, 5 major anchor retailers, and a food court with 11 restaurants. Downtown Camas, just east of Vancouver, boasts a variety of shops where one can find antiques, ladies fashions, accessories, jewelry, and home décor.

There are many wonderful restaurants in the heart of Vancouver and surrounding areas. From seafood restaurants, steak houses, vegetarian restaurants, pubs, wine bars, delis, and coffee shops to such ethnic specialties as Italian, Greek, Mexican, Thai, Chinese, and Japanese, diners have a wide variety of choices from which to sate their palates.

Visitor Information: Southwest Washington Convention & Visitors Bureau, 101 East 8th Street, Suite 240, Vancouver, WA 98660-3294; toll-free (877)600-0800; telephone (360)750-1553; fax (360)750-1933; email admin@SouthwestWashington.com

■ Convention Facilities

Conveniently located only 15 minutes from Portland International Airport, Vancouver is an ideal setting for conventions. In the heart of downtown, the Hilton Vancouver Washington and Vancouver Convention Center provide 226 guest rooms and 30,000 square feet of flexible meeting space for conferences and events. The Exhibition Hall at the Clark County Event Center has 97,200 square feet of space with a maximum occupancy of 13,844 people and up to 551 booths. In total Clark County has 32 lodging properties offering over 2,400 guest rooms. Outdoor venues include Esther Short Park and Alderbrook Park, which can each accommodate 10,000 people. Facilities at Pearson Air Museum can accommodate 450, Clark Community College can accommodate 350, and the Marshall House can accommodate 225, in addition to other off-site venues.

Convention Information: Southwest Washington Convention & Visitors Bureau, 101 East 8th Street, Suite 240, Vancouver, WA 98660-3294; toll-free (877)600-0800; telephone (360)750-1553; fax (360)750-1933; email admin@SouthwestWashington.com

■ Transportation

Approaching the City

Portland International Airport (PDX) is just across the river from Southwest Washington and only 15 minutes from downtown Vancouver. The airport is served by more than 17 regional, national, and international airlines. Clark County has two airfields that accommodate private aircraft: Pearson Airfield, near downtown Vancouver, and Grove Field, near the Port of Camas/Washougal.

Interstate 5, the major north-south artery, goes directly through the Vancouver area. I-84, running along the Oregon side of the Columbia River, provides easy access from the West. A number of other state highways provide southwest Washington with access from the northwest and southwest.

Amtrak provides passenger rail service and Greyhound provides bus service to Vancouver.

Traveling in the City

C-Tran is Clark County's public bus service. C-Tran has 27 routes covering Clark County and connecting into Portland. C-Tran also offers curb-to-curb service for people who are unable to use regular service, as well as carpool and vanpool services. Three transit centers and five park-and-ride facilities serve the area.

■ Communications

Newspaper and Magazines

The Columbian is Vancouver's daily newspaper. The *Vancouver Business Journal* is also published in the city.

Television and Radio

Two television stations and four AM and FM radio stations broadcast from Vancouver, but the city also receives broadcasts from surrounding areas, especially Portland, Oregon.

Media Information: *The Columbian*, 701 W 8th St., Vancouver, WA 98666; telephone (360)694-3391; toll-free (800)743-3391

Vancouver Online

City of Vancouver home page. Available www .cityofvancouver.us

The Columbian. Available www.columbian.com

Fort Vancouver Regional Library District. Available www.fvrl.org

Greater Vancouver U.S.A. Chamber of Commerce. Available www.vancouverusa.com

Southwest Washington Convention and Visitors Bureau. Available www.southwestwashington. com

Vancouver School District. Available www.vansd .org

BIBLIOGRAPHY

Blumenthal, Richard W., ed., *With Vancouver in Inland Washington Waters: Journals of 12 Crewmen, April–June 1792* (Jefferson, NC: McFarland and Co., 2007)

Wyoming

The State in Brief

Nickname: Equality State; Cowboy State

Motto: Equal rights

Flower: Indian paintbrush

Bird: Meadowlark

Area: 97,813 square miles (2000; U.S. rank 10th)

Elevation: Ranges from 3,100 feet to 13,084 feet above sea level

Climate: Continental; semi-arid and cool, with mild summers and severe winters; temperature varies with elevation

Admitted to Union: July 10, 1890

Capital: Cheyenne

Head Official: Governor Dave Freudenthal (D) (until 2010)

Population

1980: 470,000
1990: 453,588
2000: 493,782
2006 estimate: 515,004
Percent change, 1990–2000: 8.9%
U.S. rank in 2006: 51st
Percent of residents born in state: 42.59% (2006)
Density: 5.2 people per square mile (2006)
2006 FBI Crime Index Total: 16,584

Racial and Ethnic Characteristics (2006)

White: 472,937
Black or African American: 3,686
American Indian and Alaska Native: 11,505
Asian: 4,656
Native Hawaiian and Pacific Islander: 350
Hispanic or Latino (may be of any race): 35,732
Other: 12,442

Age Characteristics (2006)

Population under 5 years old: 34,128
Population 5 to 19 years old: 101,604
Percent of population 65 years and over: 12.0%
Median age: 37.5

Vital Statistics

Total number of births (2006): 6,846
Total number of deaths (2006): 4,092
AIDS cases reported through 2005: 225

Economy

Major industries: Mining; finance, insurance, and real estate; government; construction
Unemployment rate (2006): 3.5%
Per capita income (2006): $24,544
Median household income (2006): $47,423
Percentage of persons below poverty level (2006): 9.4%
Income tax rate: None
Sales tax rate: 4.0%

Casper

■ The City in Brief

Founded: 1888 (incorporated 1889)

Head Official: Mayor Kate Sarosy (since 2007)

City Population

 1980: 51,016
 1990: 46,742
 2000: 49,644
 2006 estimate: 52,089
 Percent change, 1990–2000: 6.2%
 U.S. rank in 1980: Not available
 U.S. rank in 1990: 559th (2nd in state)
 U.S. rank in 2000: Not available

Metropolitan Area Population

 1980: 71,856
 1990: 61,226
 2000: 66,533
 2006 estimate: 70,401
 Percent change, 1990–2000: 8.6%
 U.S. rank in 1980: Not available
 U.S. rank in 1990: Not available
 U.S. rank in 2000: 275th

Area: 23.9 square miles (2000)

Elevation: 5,140 feet above sea level

Average Annual Temperatures: January, 22.3° F; July, 70.0° F; annual average, 44.9° F

Average Annual Precipitation: 13.03 inches rainfall; 77.9 inches snowfall

Major Economic Sectors: services, wholesale and retail trade, government

Unemployment Rate: 2.9% (June 2007)

Per Capita Income: $19,409 (1999)

2005 FBI Crime Index Property: 2,699

2005 FBI Crime Index Violent: 135

Major Colleges and Universities: Casper College, University of Wyoming–Casper College Center

Daily Newspaper: *Casper Star-Tribune*

■ Introduction

In the days of the Wild West and Manifest Destiny, all roads led to Casper. The city was sited at the nexus of a number of important trails of the time, including the Oregon Trail, the Pony Express route, the Mormon Trail, the Bozeman Trail, the California Trail, and the Bridger Trail. The city has kept much of its history while beginning to develop a more modern and diverse economy. While the economy of the surrounding area still includes the oil and petroleum exploration and thriving livestock ranches that built the town, new developments have been established to strengthen the city in fields such as health care and tourism. In 2007 *Forbes Magazine* ranked Casper in the "Top 100 Best Small Places for Business and Careers," a designation earned in part by a low cost of living, a low cost of doing business, and excellent potential in job growth.

■ Geography and Climate

At almost a mile above sea level, Casper rests at the foot of Casper Mountain and follows the contours of the North Platte River. With the Laramie Mountain Range of the Rocky Mountains to the west and the Wyoming plains to the east, Casper has been uniquely situated between natural resources for energy and outdoor adventure exploration on the one hand and agricultural endeavors on the other.

Casper sits within the area characterized by the National Weather Service as the "comfort zone," with year-round low humidity moderating the cold of winter and the heat of summer. Casper averages 275 days of sunshine every year and experiences an average wind speed of 12.9 miles per hour. The city's location and climate make it a jumping-off point for outdoor adventures. The city is the seat of Natrona County.

Area: 23.9 square miles (2000)

Elevation: 5,140 feet above sea level

Average Temperatures: January, 22.3° F; July, 70.0° F; annual average, 44.9° F

Average Annual Precipitation: 13.03 inches rainfall; 77.9 inches snowfall

■ History

Back to the Source

Before there were people, there was the river. The North Platte River begins its meandering journey in the mountains near Casper, running east across the Great Plains to merge with its sister river, the South Platte, to become simply the Platte River. Water, mountains, and plains were a lure from the beginning. Evidence of human occupation dates back more than 12,000 years with the Clovis peoples, followed by the Folsom and the Eden Valley peoples. A mix of hunting and gathering tribes occupied the area until approximately 500 A.D., eventually morphing into Native American tribes more familiar in today's world.

The original residents of Wyoming were nomadic Plains Indians, including tribes as disparate as the Arapaho, Sioux, Cheyenne, Crow, Lakota, Blackfeet, Kiowa, Nez Perce, and Shoshone. The tribes relied on the land and the roaming buffalo herds for sustenance. When European explorers and hunters began a wholesale slaughter of the buffalo that coincided with an interest in herding native peoples to a containment area in Oklahoma, armed conflicts escalated in the clash of cultures and interests. In 1812 fur trappers had followed beaver and buffalo populations to the northern Rockies. The Oregon Trail had been scouted out in 1823 and its ever-deepening ruts reflected the entrenched U.S. belief in its manifest destiny to expand westward.

The Western Civil War

By 1847 a network of travel routes converged at a spot just west of present-day Casper. Here the Emigrant Trail crossed from the south side to the north side of the North Platte River. When the first Mormon wagon train passed through this area on its way to what would become Utah, Brigham Young arranged for a ferry to be set up for the

use of future travelers. The Mormon Ferry soon faced competition as more emigrants passed that way and decided to cash in on a good idea. One entrepreneurial French Canadian trader named John Baptiste Richard decided to build a bridge across the North Platte and charge a toll for crossing it. The area was now not just a way-station but an encampment.

Local residents established a trading post along the Emigrant Trail in 1859, taking advantage of the growing stream of wagon trains. As the local population grew along with the number of emigrants, friction developed with local tribes of Lakota, Arapaho, and Cheyenne. As a result, the trading post was transformed into a fort by the military, and two pitched battles between the army and the native tribes took place in 1865. In the first conflict, Lieutenant Caspar Collins was killed while attempting to rescue another soldier. Lt. Collins' father already had a fort named after him in Colorado, so the military named the Wyoming fort "Casper" in his honor, inadvertently using a misspelling that had been transmitted by telegraph. The seeds of present-day Casper had been planted.

Black Gold, Texas Tea

Casper in 1888 was a true Wild West town. A railroad had been built through the town in an effort to ease travel to riches of gold in California and fertile land in Oregon. Isolation and lawlessness attracted a rough crowd of renegades and outlaws and the original township developed a main street lined with saloons on one side. By necessity, the first public building in Casper was a jail. Lynchings were not an uncommon occurrence.

Oil was struck in nearby Salt Creek Field in 1889, an event that has come to define Casper as the "oil capital of the Rockies." The city was flooded with an influx of claim jumpers looking to capitalize on the promised wealth. In 1895 the first oil refinery was constructed. Oil workers known as "roughnecks" followed, along with gamblers, prostitutes and corrupt businessmen. Cattlemen went to war against the sheepmen. The local law struggled to keep up with the shenanigans of the populace, passing laws to prevent women from walking on the saloon side of Main Street and to make illegal the discharge of firearms within city limits.

Local municipal leaders were set on Casper becoming the state capitol and a centerpiece of the West. As the economy continued to thrive, construction began on some of the tallest buildings in Wyoming during the early 20th century. But, a city that lives on oil can die on oil.

Nearly a Ghost Town

Few communities escaped the repercussions of the Great Depression and Casper was not an exception. In 1929 the city's population diminished by 50 percent. The struggle continued until World War II spurred renewed demand for oil and gas supplies. The city experienced a ten-year cycle of

Casper Area Convention and Visitors Bureau. www.casperwyoming.info. Reproduced by permission.

boom and bust beginning in the 1960s, riding the wave of oil and gas prices. Then in 1991 the Casper Refinery, operated by Amoco, closed down. The city began to consider redevelopment efforts that would diversify the economy in fields such as health care, social services, and tourism, in part through revitalization of its downtown areas. Beginning in 1998, city residents and officials teamed up with British Petroleum (the new owners of Amoco) and the state Wyoming Department of Environmental Quality to clean up and redevelop the old refinery site. In 2000 the city council established the West Central Corridor (from David Street to Poplar Street and from West 1st to Collins Drive) as an urban renewal zone, offering special funding incentives for development. The result by 2005 was a new development that included the Robert Trent Jones-designed Three Crowns Golf Course, the Casper White-water Park, and three commercial parks.

In 2006 the city created the Urban Renewal Division within the city government structure to implement redevelopment plans for these and future renewal districts. The city began focusing specifically on the possibilities of mixed-use developments, renovation of historic buildings through tax incentive programs, and the recruitment of commercial and residential businesses to the downtown area.

Historical Information: Fort Caspar Museum, 4001 Fort Caspar Road, Casper, WY 83604; telephone (307) 235-8462; www.fortcasparwyoming.com

■ Population Profile

Metropolitan Area Residents

1980: 71,856
1990: 61,226
2000: 66,533
2006 estimate: 70,401
Percent change, 1990–2000: 8.6%
U.S. rank in 1980: Not available
U.S. rank in 1990: Not available
U.S. rank in 2000: 275th

City Residents

1980: 51,016
1990: 46,742
2000: 49,644
2006 estimate: 52,089
Percent change, 1990–2000: 6.2%
U.S. rank in 1980: Not available

U.S. rank in 1990: 559th (2nd in state)

U.S. rank in 2000: Not available

Density: 2,073.2 people per square mile

Racial and ethnic characteristics (2000)

White: 46,680

Black: 428

American Indian and Alaska Native: 495

Asian: 425

Native Hawaiian and Pacific Islander: 10

Hispanic or Latino (may be of any race): 2,656

Other: 1,011

Percent of residents born in state: 46.4% (2000)

Age characteristics (2000)

Population under 5 years old: 3,264

Population 5 to 9 years old: 3,458

Population 10 to 14 years old: 3,758

Population 15 to 19 years old: 4,122

Population 20 to 24 years old: 3,455

Population 25 to 34 years old: 6,125

Population 35 to 44 years old: 7,649

Population 45 to 54 years old: 7,016

Population 55 to 59 years old: 2,211

Population 60 to 64 years old: 1,852

Population 65 to 74 years old: 3,606

Population 75 to 84 years old: 2,402

Population 85 years and older: 746

Median age: 36.1 years

Births (2006, MSA)

Total number: 933

Deaths (2006, MSA)

Total number: 608

Money income (1999)

Per capita income: $19,409

Median household income: $36,567

Total households: 20,343

Number of households with income of...

less than $10,000: 1,761

$10,000 to $14,999: 1,689

$15,000 to $24,999: 3,101

$25,000 to $34,999: 3,185

$35,000 to $49,999: 3,680

$50,000 to $74,999: 3,948

$75,000 to $99,999: 1,772

$100,000 to $149,999: 866

$150,000 to $199,999: 196

$200,000 or more: 238

Percent of families below poverty level: 9.4% (1999)

2005 FBI Crime Index Property: 2,699

2005 FBI Crime Index Violent: 135

■ Municipal Government

The City of Casper has a council-manager form of government with a nine-member city council. The city is divided into three wards. Three council members are elected for each ward with staggered four-year terms. The council appoints a mayor and vice president from among the members. The mayor and vice president each serve for one year. The council hires a city manager.

Head Official: Mayor Kate Sarosy (since 2007; term expires December 2008)

Total Number of City Employees: 520 full-time (2007)

City Information: City of Casper, 200 N. David, Casper, WY 82601; telephone (307)235-8400; www.casperwy.gov

■ Economy

Major Industries and Commercial Activity

In 2007 *Forbes Magazine* named Casper one of the nation's "Top 100 Best Small Places for Business and Careers" based on the comparatively low costs of operating in the Casper area. The city was ranked 14th in the nation for job growth in the same survey. The city's central location and proximity to a wealth of natural resources has attracted mining and petroleum exploration industries to the area.

Casper also grew up as a cattle and sheep ranching town, and remains as such today. Businesses related to the care and feeding of livestock have maintained a hold on the economy in Casper and the surrounding Natrona County area.

The medical industry is healthy, as Casper serves as the site for a Department of Veterans Affairs Clinic in addition to the Wyoming Medical Center. The tourism trade is growing as well, grounded in local Wild West history, rodeos, and proximity to natural wonders such as Grand Teton National Park and Yellowstone.

Items and goods produced: oil, natural gas, coal, gravel, fire equipment, agricultural products

Incentive Programs—New and Existing Companies

Local programs: The lack of a local income tax and a low municipal sales tax rate are the main business incentives employed by the City of Casper. General assistance to local business owners can be found through the Casper Area Chamber of Commerce, the Casper Area Economic Development Alliance, and the Downtown Development Authority.

State programs: Wyoming's primary business incentive is a non-existent corporate income tax rate, coupled with relatively minimal sales tax rates. The state also does not tax intangibles or inventory and has kept property taxes low. The Wyoming Business Council provides several financing programs for businesses, including the Business Ready Community Grant and Loan Program and the Wyoming Partnership Challenge Loan Program. The Community Development Block Grant and Industrial Development Revenue Bonds programs are also administered by the Wyoming Business Council. The Foreign Trade Zone at Natrona County International Airport provides further encouragement for importers to frequent Casper, as international goods can be warehoused at the airport without undergoing full U.S. Customs scrutiny.

Job training programs: The Casper Workforce Center (a branch of the Wyoming Department of Workforce Services–DWS) is part of a statewide network of workforce development resources, including services for businesses, job seekers and employment data researchers. Expanding and new businesses can tap into the Business Training Grant program through which employers may receive up to $2,000 per trainee per year for existing employees and $4,000 per employee per year for new hires. Large and small business owners can take advantage of the Wyoming Job Network to search online for prospective employees; the Workforce Center additionally operates an Alien Labor Certification program, which allows employers to utilize immigrant labor for positions that are difficult to fill with U.S. citizens. The state also sponsors a Pre-Hire Economic Development Grant program to offer training for new hires in particular businesses and industries.

Job seekers can avail themselves of several programs organized under the Workforce Investment Act passed in 1998. The intent of the act was to create a seamless continuum of employment, education, and training programs to support business with a skilled workforce. Programs supported by the act include Title II Adult Basic Education, Title IV Vocational Rehabilitation programs, dislocated worker programs, youth tutoring, alternative secondary school services, youth summer employment programs, youth internships, and job shadowing. The Workforce Center offers specialized programs for older workers and workers who identify themselves as having disabilities.

The McMurray Training Center at Casper College is a program of the Wyoming Contractor's Association designed to offer job training for those interested in certain heavy industry trades. Contractors and other businesses may seek help through the center for specialized employee training programs.

Development Projects

Development in Casper was moving at a fast pace in 2007, particularly in the areas of residential housing and business developments. The McMurry Business Park along the extension of 2nd Street in Casper is a $25 million investment property zoned for commercial use. Covering 500 acres, the project involves access road improvements and major utility installations.

The Natrona County International Airport Business Park has undergone a sizable expansion during the last few years, including up to 18,000-square-feet of available office space, approximately 135 buildings that can accommodate businesses that range from manufacturing to retail to aviation, and an adjacent acreage that has been designated for future development.

The Downtown Casper Reconstruction and Improvement Project is designed to revitalize an aged and deteriorating area in an effort to make it more inviting to tourists and businesses. A one-cent sales tax is providing the funding. The improvements include replacement light fixtures, serpentine sidewalks, parkway landscaping, pavers, and street furniture.

Commercial Shipping

The largest airport in Wyoming, the Natrona County International Airport, is located in Casper and encompasses Foreign Trade Zone No. 157, which allows imported goods to remain onsite without undergoing full U.S. Customs processing. Three regional carriers offer business class travel. Northwest Airlines, Action Cargo express, and Blue Streak Express offer cargo transportation services. The airport is additionally home to the air cargo facilities of UPS, FedEx and DHL package delivery services. A full-time U.S. Customs Agent is onsite.

Burlington Northern Santa Fe (BNSF) Railway passes through Casper, with routes to the West Coast, the Southwest, the Midwest, and other points west of the Mississippi River. Freight services are available for agricultural, mineral, industrial, and consumer goods. Freight forwarding and direct connections with dock spurs are available.

Casper's central location makes it a highway hub, with Interstate 25, U.S. Highways 20/26 and 87, and State Routes 220, 254 and 20 all meeting within its city limits. Casper is served by approximately 50 motor freight carriers and has access to package delivery services such as UPS, FedEx and DHL.

Labor Force and Employment Outlook

While it is expected that Wyoming will remain identified with production of natural gas and coal, a slight decline in total mining jobs is anticipated. Most employment growth is expected to occur in non-goods producing sectors, including service and retail trade. The State of Wyoming predicts that the aging of the baby boomer generation will result in possible labor shortages as that group retires. An aging population will also increase demand for health care and social services, creating a potential spike in those professions. In August 2007 the civilian labor force was 40,700, with 1,000 workers unemployed. The unemployment rate was 2.5 percent, well below the national average of 4.6 percent for that month.

The following is a summary of data regarding the Casper metropolitan area labor force, 2006 annual averages.

Size of nonagricultural labor force: 39,000

Number of workers employed in . . .

    construction and mining: 6,800
    manufacturing: 1,900
    trade, transportation and utilities: 8,700
    information: 600
    financial activities: 2,100
    professional and business services: 2,900
    educational and health services: 4,700
    leisure and hospitality: 3,700
    other services: 1,900
    government: 5,700

Average hourly earnings of production workers employed in manufacturing: Not available

Unemployment rate: 2.9% (June 2007)

Largest employers (2004)	*Number of employees*
Natrona County School District No. 1	1,427
Wyoming Medical Center	921
The Industrial Company	600
Key Energy	558
City of Casper	505
Casper College	343
OfficeMax	339
Wyoming Machinery Company	315
Natrona County Government	278
McMurry Ready Mix	225
True Companies	201

Cost of Living

In 2000 the median value of a home in Casper was $84,500 according to the U.S. Census Bureau.

The following is a summary of data regarding key cost of living factors for the Casper area.

2007 (1st quarter) ACCRA Average House Price: Not available

2007 (1st quarter) ACCRA Cost of Living Index: Not available

State income tax rate: None

State sales tax rate: 4.0%

Local income tax rate: None

Local sales tax rate: 1.0%

Property tax rate: assessed at 9.5% of market value

Economic information: Casper Area Economic Development Alliance, 300 South Wolcott Suite 300, Casper, WY 82601; telephone (307)577-7011; toll-free (800)634-5012

■ Education and Research

Elementary and Secondary Schools

The Natrona County School District serves students not just in Casper but also the communities of Midwest, Edgerton, Mills, Evansville, Bar Nunn, Alcova, Mountain View, and Powder River. The school district emphasizes site-based decision making in schools of choice, a system that allows parents to enroll students in any school without regard to location. Ideally, this encourages a cooperative approach between school administration, parents, and students in targeting an educational environment that best fits the needs of the individual.

The district operates a K-12 substance abuse program that has been recognized at the national level, along with specialized services for English language learners. Since 2001, the school district has offered an after-school program and community learning center at two elementary schools, with stated goals of retention, improved academic performance, life-long learning, and a safe drug-free environment. Outreach is also conducted for students who are homebound and those who are homeless.

The Natrona County School District created a planetarium in 1966, which over the years has brought the stars and planets to more than 500,000 students. The Casper Planetarium also presents programs for the public throughout the year, including the This Month's Sky series.

The following is a summary of data regarding the Natrona County School District #1 as of the 2005–2006 school year.

Total enrollment: 11,500

Number of facilities

    elementary schools: 27

junior high/middle schools: 7

senior high schools: 4

other: 0

Student/teacher ratio: 15.2:1

Teacher salaries (2005–06)

elementary median: $42,286 (average)

junior high/middle median: Not available

secondary median: Not available

Funding per pupil: $8,329

There are a few private schools in the city, primarily church-based.

Public Schools Information: Natrona County School District, 970 N. Glenn Rd., Casper, WY 82601; telephone (307)577-0200; www.natronaschools.org

Colleges and Universities

Perched in the foothills of Casper Mountain, higher education takes on a literal meaning at Casper College. One of the largest community colleges, Casper College offers students a choice of 50 academic majors and more than 30 technical and career programs. The college enrolls over 5,000 students in small, personal classes in business, education, communications, health sciences, trades and technology, and life sciences programs, among others. The college also provides free Adult Basic Education and General Educational Development (GED) assistance in the Werner Technical Center.

The University of Wyoming in nearby Laramie maintains an outreach school as the UW Casper College Center. Students typically complete their first two years of study as Casper College students and then enroll as students of the University of Wyoming. Coursework is completed onsite, via teleconferencing or through web-based instruction, with internships and educational travel experiences offered in various degree programs. About 14 baccalaureate degrees, 13 master's programs, and a variety of certification programs are available through the UW Casper College Center.

The McMurray Training Center, a program of the Wyoming Contractor's Association, offers training programs for heavy industry trades. At the Natrona County International Airport, the Aircraft Rescue Firefighting training program offers classroom and hands-on experience with firefighting techniques unique to aeronautical equipment. Small classes ensure individual attention as students learn to deal with hazardous materials, ventilation issues, fire behavior, and search and rescue procedures.

Libraries and Research Centers

The Natrona County Library's Main Library is located in the heart of Casper with branch libraries maintained in the communities of Edgerton and Mills and a bookmobile. The library offers access to over 204,922 books, 4,312 audio materials and 4,264 video materials, supplemented by 352 serial subscriptions and online research resources. Children's programs include a Reader's Advisory program that recommends books tailored to particular ages and interests; outreach programs to schools and community groups; educational games and reference programs; storytime; a summer reading program; and Dial-a-Story with a new story available by phone every week. The library also maintains a special multicultural literature collection for children.

The Goodstein Foundation Library at Casper College contains a collection of 118,000 volumes. The library subscribes to more than 500 periodicals, with access to more than 30,000 full-text periodicals available online. A statewide interlibrary loan service is available. The library is also home to a Western history collection, with materials focused on Casper and Natrona County.

Public Library Information: Natrona County Public Library (Main Library), 307 East Second Street, Casper, WY 82601; telephone (307)237-4935; www.natronacountylibrary.org

■ Health Care

The Wyoming Medical Center in Casper serves the Natrona County area and also draws patients from rural communities of greater distances. The state's largest medical facility is a full-service facility licensed for 206 beds. The facility houses an emergency and trauma department and two Centers of Excellence, the Heart Center of Wyoming and the Wyoming Neuroscience and Spine Center. In addition to those specialties, the Wyoming Medical Center provides a full range of specialized care services including such fields as epilepsy, sleep disorders, allergies, addiction medicine, infectious diseases, neurology, obstetrics, pulmonology, wound care, and more. The McMurray Medical Arts building houses offers outpatient services and the Casper Medical Imaging department. The Casper Surgical Center offers outpatient procedures. The hospital is served by Wyoming Life Flight, the only emergency air transportation service in the state.

The main campus of the Wyoming Behavioral Institute is located in Casper, with substance abuse and mental health services for adults, adolescents, and children. The facility offers initial assessment, intensive inpatient treatment, detoxification programs, and outpatient therapy. The Wyoming Orthopaedic Institute in Casper sponsors the Wyoming Orthopaedic and Sports Therapy Center and the Wyoming Surgical Center. These facilities offer a wide range of programs in orthopaedic injury diagnosis and care, rehabilitation, and sports medicine. There are five skilled nursing care facilities in the city.

The Department of Veterans Affairs Casper Clinic serves as an outreach center connecting military veterans to health care and counseling services, including making arrangements for bus travel to V.A. hospitals in Cheyenne or Sheridan.

■ Recreation

Sightseeing

A sightseeing tour of Casper would start where the town started—at the convergence of the multiple travel routes to the West. The National Historic Trails Interpretive Center accurately portrays the experiences of emigrants who traversed the Oregon, California, Mormon, Bridger, Bozeman, and Pony Express Trails. The museum has incorporated the history of Wyoming's native peoples in displays that include a simulated crossing of the North Platte River in a replica Conestoga wagon. An award-winning audiovisual feature recreates the days of early Casper in a way that brings pioneer existence alive for modern visitors.

The natural segue is to next visit the Fort Caspar Museum and Historical Site, located along the historical trail system. The buildings of the original fort have been reconstructed, with structures including the 1859 Guinard bridge and the 1847 Mormon ferry utilized in crossings of the North Platte. Exhibits range from prehistoric natural history items to recent regional development in central Wyoming.

While in the vicinity, visitors can enjoy a leisurely ramble along the Platte River Parkway, an 11-mile paved path that connects residential neighborhoods to natural areas. The Platte River Commons in downtown Casper continues along the riverbank; within the downtown area, the Art for the Streets program has sprinkled the historic area with 31 sculptures. "Painted Past" Living History Tours through the downtown area highlight myths, legends and true stories of Casper's checkered past.

The Mormon Handcart Visitors' Center commemorates the hardships and survival of members of the Church of Jesus Christ of Latter-day Saints traveling as part of the Martin and Willie Handcart Companies in 1856. As the group traveled westward, it encountered a raging blizzard that forced the company to hole up in a local cove for four days. During the ensuing wait for rescuers, many members of the group died from starvation or exposure. Visitors to the site today can pull a handcart to the cove or can participate in guided camping treks.

Arts and Culture

The Nicolaysen Art Museum and Discovery Center contains one large and six small galleries exhibiting art from or about the Rocky Mountain Region. Exhibitors at "the Nic" often include contemporary living artists from the area. The Discovery Center allows visitors to create their own art in a self-guided studio containing interactive exhibits, and the Wyoming Science Adventure Center generates interest in sciences through fun, interactive displays. Workshops and educational programs are offered throughout the year as well, with a special emphasis on quilting.

The West Wind Gallery is operated by the Casper Artists' Guild, the members of which show and sell their works under the gallery's roof. The gallery occasionally hosts artists from out of state and also offers classes.

The Tate Geological Museum is located on the grounds of Casper College and is home to a collection of more than 3,000 fossil and mineral specimens. The museum offers a Saturday Club experience for local youth in which they study local geology and animal fossils. Adults can take part in paleontology and geology fieldwork expeditions coordinated through the museum, with visits to Wind River Reservation, and the Morrison and Lance Formation sites. Casper College also houses the Werner Wildlife Museum featuring more than 285 birds and 100 other various species.

The formative history of Casper is further represented at the Salt Creek Museum in the city of Midwest, where books, memorabilia and reminiscences reflect on more than 100 years of oil field action in the area. The Wyoming Veteran's Memorial Museum at the airport is located in the building where bombing crews trained during World War II.

The Wyoming Symphony Orchestra performs "The Nutcracker" seasonally in conjunction with the Western Ballet Theater, which involves local dancers for that event. Five more performances per season round out the orchestra's schedule at the John F. Welsh Auditorium.

Young musicians from 4th graders to 21-year-olds participate in The Troopers Drum and Bugle Corps, regardless of musical experience. The Troopers travel around the U.S. throughout the summer, performing and competing in drum and bugle corps contests. Further musical offerings are provided through the Casper Chamber Music Society, the Casper Children's Chorale, Casper Civic Chorale, Casper Fiddle Club, Casper Municipal Band, Choral Arts Ensemble, Metropolitan Brass Quintet, Oil City Slickers, and ARTCORE.

Productions ranging from the classical to the contemporary are performed by the players of Stage III, an all-volunteer community theater located in historic downtown Casper. The theater department at Casper College presents similarly varied fare to audiences in the Gertrude Krampert Theatre. A musical and three plays are presented each academic year, while the summer season offerings are often musicals or comedies.

Arts and Culture Information: Wyoming Arts Council, 2320 Capitol Ave., Cheyenne, WY 82002; telephone (307)777-7742; http://wyoarts.state.wy.us. Casper Area Convention & Visitors Bureau, 992 N.

Poplar St., Casper, WY 82601; telephone (307)234-5362; toll-free (800)852-1889; www.casperwyoming.info

Festivals and Holidays

The year kicks off in January with the Windy City Quilt Festival. Casper residents fire up for the Cowboy State Games in February, an Olympic-style event composed of a mix of indoor and outdoor competitive sports. The Games run for five weekends during the month. Casper sees a local version of March Madness with the 1A and 2A State Basketball Tournament being held at the Casper Events Center early in the month. March is also time for the Super Flea Market at the Fairgrounds. The spring winds of April support the Central Wyoming Kite Flyers Fun Fly at the Soccer Complex, and Casper College hosts its rodeo. Temperate May weather ushers in a flock of activities such as the high school rodeo, the Kid's Fishing Derby, a dog show, and a car exhibition. The festivities continue in June with the Casper Antique Show early in the month and the Governor's Cup Sailboat Regatta at Alcova Lake a few weeks later.

The Fourth of July blasts off with a Fireworks Festival and a Cavalry baseball game, followed by the Rocky Mountain Regional Dance Festival, the Whitewater Kayak Rodeo, and the Beartrap Music Festival at the end of July. The Kiwanis Club hosts a golf tournament at the end of August, and cooler fall temperatures in September are perfect for the Platte River Fall Festival and Great Duck Derby. In mid-October, Casper hosts the local Special Olympics events. The holiday months of November and December respectively see the advent of the Meals on Wheels Craft Fair and the Tate Museum Holiday Open House.

Sports for the Spectator

Casper grew up around the livestock industry, so it's no surprise that rodeo is the major spectator sport. Casper hosts two large rodeo events: the College National Finals Rodeo and the Central Wyoming Fair and Rodeo. The College National Finals Rodeo takes place in mid-June each year and features the top rodeo event qualifiers from colleges and universities from across the United States. Events include barrel racing, calf roping, and bull riding. The Central Wyoming Fair and Rodeo is held in mid-July, with Pro Rodeo Cowboys Association competitions in roping, bareback riding, saddle bronc and bull riding events among others.

During the summer months, baseball fans can see tomorrow's stars playing for the Casper Rockies, the minor league affiliate of the Colorado Rockies. The team plays at Mike Lansing Field. In the spring, sports are still staying indoors with the Wyoming Cavalry football team, a member of the National Indoor Football League. Formed in 2001, the Cavalry finished the inaugural season second in the nation and have a rowdy,

faithful following. The Casper College Thunderbirds play volleyball and basketball at the Erickson Thunderbird Gymnasium.

Sports for the Participant

Aficionados of the Wild West will relish the opportunity to participate in historic wagon train trips arranged through local companies. A similar desire to experience pioneer Casper could spur a visit to a working cattle and guest ranch located about 65 miles southwest of the city.

For folks who prefer to provide their own locomotion, the Casper Marathon takes place in early June, with marathon, half-marathon, and marathon relay options. The course is described as flat with few hills, and runners are invited to "come run with the herd."

A slightly less strenuous workout can be found at the Casper Municipal Golf Course, an 18-hole course with a practice range, putting and chipping greens, and a 19th Hole Restaurant and Lounge. The course is open from April 1st to November 1st each year.

The North Platte River offers ample outdoor recreation opportunities, such as kayaking through the Platte River Parkway Whitewater Park. This man-made whitewater facility runs for half a mile over structures that create turbulent water for kayak maneuvers. Canoes and rafts can also navigate through the Whitewater Park or pursue a more relaxed pace on other stretches of the North Platte. Fly fishing along the river can yield large brown and rainbow trout. The Dirt Riders Motocross Club has a facility offering both adult and peewee ridging courses. Day passes are available for non-members.

Birding excursions at the Audubon Center, Edness Kimball Wilkins State Park, and Jackson Canyon may produce sightings of bald and golden eagles, hummingbirds, bluebirds, hawks, sandpipers, wild turkeys, and grosbeaks. Birding field trips are offered almost every weekend of the year through the Murie Audubon Society.

Casper Mountain is the scene of outdoor adventure year-round, with alpine skiing, Nordic skiing and snowshoeing in the winter and hiking during the spring, summer and fall seasons. Casper is within an easy day's drive of Yellowstone National Park, Grand Teton National Park, and Devil's Tower Monument, all of which offer a range of trails in addition to campsites. Serious rock climbers can head east a few hours to Vedauwoo in southeast Wyoming; this startling and impressive collection of rock formations has something for everyone, from the scrambler to the multi-pitch climber.

Shopping and Dining

Casper's historic downtown area contains a mix of antique shops and other retailers, including the largest western merchandise store in Wyoming. The Eastridge Mall is the site of a number of national franchise stores combined with shops owned locally. Fast food outlets, grocery stores, and home supply stores are located nearby. Based near the foothills of Casper Mountain, the Sunrise Shopping Center is anchored by a restaurant and a bowling alley at one end and a gym at the other. The Hilltop Shopping Center focuses on local businesses, while the Beverly Plaza Shopping Center is home to national franchises. Other shopping areas include Plaza East, Millview Center, and CY Avenue/Highway 220 Shopping Strip.

Traditional American cuisine rules in Casper, with at least 36 restaurants offering downhome and family-style cooking. Approximately eight Mexican eateries meet the needs of spice-craving palates, while another eight establishments serve up varieties of Asian fare. As might be expected in cattle country, steakhouses are popular as well. A handful of fine dining, Italian, seafood, and barbecue restaurants flesh out the dining options in Casper. Basic and gourmet coffees are available at the six java houses in town.

Visitor Information: Casper Area Convention & Visitors Bureau, 992 N. Poplar St., Casper, WY 82601; telephone (307)234-5362; toll-free (800)852-1889; www.casperwyoming.info

■ Convention Facilities

The Casper Events Center was constructed on a hill at the north end of the city and its massive maroon roof is visible from practically all points in Casper. The arena is shaped like a horseshoe, with a 28,200-square-foot main floor that can hold up to 154 exhibition booths. Concourse exhibit space encompasses 7,900 square feet, while meeting rooms add another 6,204 square feet of usable space. Sound and lighting systems can be configured for sporting events, concerts, trade shows and banquets. The Parkway Plaza Hotel and Convention Center has three large exhibit rooms and a grand ballroom that can be divided into three smaller sections.

The Central Wyoming Fairgrounds can accommodate trade shows, conferences, receptions, rodeos, and RV parking. A multi-purpose sports facility opened in 2000 and covers 76,875 square feet, while the Grandstand and Arena have seating capacity for 5,200.

Several local hotels offer meeting, convention, and conference space, including the Holiday Inn on the River and the Ramkota Hotel Casper.

Convention Information: Casper Area Convention & Visitors Bureau, 992 N. Poplar St., Casper, WY 82601; telephone (307)234-5362; toll-free (800)852-1889; www.casperwyoming.info

■ Transportation

Approaching the City

Natrona County International Airport (NCIA), about seven miles to the northwest of Casper, is Wyoming's largest airport and is located at the geographic center of the state. Three regional carriers provide service through NCIA, including Delta Airlines, United Airlines, and Northwest Airlines. There are about 12 daily departures with links to non-stop service.

Casper's central location makes it a highway hub, with Interstate 25, U.S. Highways 20/26 and 87, and State Routes 220, 254, and 20 all meeting within its city limits. Casper is served by the Greyhound, which maintains a station in the Parkway Plaza Hotel. Powder River Coach offers scheduled bus services between Casper and Denver, Colorado, with a stop in Cheyenne and from Casper to Lowell with stops in Greybull, Basin, Worland, and Thermopolis.

Traveling in the City

While Casper is fitted to the meandering contours of the North Platte River, the streets are laid out on a straightforward north-south, east-west grid pattern. Numbered streets run east and west, while name streets run north and south for the most part, making navigation simpler.

The Casper Area Transportation Coalition operates The Bus with 6 routes and over 60 stops. The Bus offers reduced fares and dial-a-ride services to elderly and disabled patrons. Children under five years old ride free.

The 11-mile Platte River Parkway provides a safe and fast route for bike commuters to ride into downtown Casper.

■ Communications

Newspapers and Magazines

Casper's daily paper is the *Casper Star-Tribune,* delivered mornings and providing comprehensive coverage of international, national, regional, and local news stories. A special insert on Saturdays conveys community events and special features. Billed as "Casper's community newspaper," the *Casper Journal* is a weekly focused on local news, sports, and community events. The *Wyoming Business Report* is an affiliate of two similar periodicals published along the Front Range in Colorado. The bimonthly paper is circulated to 10,000 readers, providing coverage of banking, technology, energy, investing, and agribusiness issues.

Television and Radio

Only one network television affiliate (ABC) is located in Casper, but the community has relays for transmissions of public television and other network stations. Casper's 19 AM and FM radio stations offer a variety of programming, including classic rock, country, top 40, talk radio, news, public radio. and Christian music.

Media Information: *Casper Star-Tribune,* 170 Star Lane, Casper, WY 82601; telephone (307)266-0500; http://casperstartribune.net

Casper Online

Casper Area Chamber of Commerce. Available www.casperwyoming.org

Casper Wyoming Convention & Visitors Bureau. Available www.casperwyoming.info

City of Casper. Available www.casperwy.gov

Natrona County School District. Available www .natronaschools.org

BIBLIOGRAPHY

Casper Chronicles (Casper, WY: Casper Zonta Club, 1964)

Cheyenne

The City in Brief

Founded: 1867 (incorporated 1867)

Head Official: Mayor Jack R. Spiker (since 2001)

City Population

1980: 47,283
1990: 50,008
2000: 53,011
2006 estimate: 55,314
Percent change, 1990–2000: 5.6%
U.S. rank in 1980: 451st
U.S. rank in 1990: 504th
U.S. rank in 2000: 520th

Metropolitan Area Population

1980: 68,600
1990: 73,142
2000: 81,607
2006 estimate: 85,384
Percent change, 1990–2000: 11.57%
U.S. rank in 1980: Not available
U.S. rank in 1990: Not available
U.S. rank in 2000: 637th

Area: 21.19 square miles (2000)

Elevation: 6,062 feet above sea level

Average Annual Temperatures: January, 25.9° F; July, 67.7° F; annual average, 44.9° F

Average Annual Precipitation: 15.45 inches of rain; 55.6 inches of snow

Major Economic Sectors: services, wholesale and retail trade, government

Unemployment Rate: 3.9% (June 2007)

Per Capita Income: $19,809 (1999)

2005 FBI Crime Index Property: 2,585

2005 FBI Crime Index Violent: 97

Major Colleges and Universities: Laramie County Community College, University of Wyoming-Laramie

Daily Newspaper: *Wyoming Tribune-Eagle*

Introduction

Cheyenne, the capital of Wyoming, began as a railroad town and, during the height of the colorful cattle days, became the wealthiest city in the world. Cheyenne has retained its Western frontier traditions while keeping pace with the twenty-first century. The seat of Laramie County, Cheyenne continues to be a railroad and transportation center. While the military (at the F.E. Warren Air Force Base) and government have been major employers in the past decade, the city has taken measures to diversify its economy primarily in the service and retail trade industries. In the 2000s, the city welcomed several high-tech businesses with plans to encourage and recruit many more in the future. Cheyenne continues to be known for its quality of life and for high clean air ratings.

Geography and Climate

Surrounded by rolling prairie, Cheyenne is located between the North and South Platte rivers. The Laramie Mountains 30 miles west of the city form a ridge that is part of the Rocky Mountain range and that significantly influences local temperature and weather. Winds passing over the ridge from the northwest through the west to southwest produce a Chinook effect, particularly during the winter. (Chinooks are warm, moist winds from the sea.) Because of the terrain and wind patterns, Cheyenne experiences wide daily temperature fluctuations of 30 degrees in the summer and about 23 degrees in the winter. Snow falls during late winter and early spring, with yearly snowfall averaging 55.6 inches. Cheyenne is the seat of Laramie County.

Area: 21.19 square miles (2000)

Elevation: 6,062 feet above sea level

Average Temperatures: January, 25.9° F; July, 67.7° F; annual average, 44.9° F

Average Annual Precipitation: 15.45 inches of rain; 55.6 inches of snow

■ History

Rough-and-Tumble Beginnings of Railroad Terminus

The region where present-day Cheyenne stands was originally occupied by a Native American Plains tribe in the Algonquian linguistic family. The townsite was initially a campsite for the U.S. Army's Major General Grenville M. Dodge and his troops, who were charged in 1865 with finding a railroad route over the Laramie Mountains. In 1867, when Dodge became chief engineer for the Union Pacific Railroad, he established a terminal town there; he named it Cheyenne for the local tribe. Dodge received some criticism in the local press for his mispronunciation of the word, which was actually "shai-en-na;" but his two-syllable version was accepted through usage.

Fort D. A. Russell was built in 1867 to protect railroad construction crews. Soon real estate speculators, merchants, gamblers, and tradesmen converged on Cheyenne in hopes of profiting from the construction project. Violent disputes arose over ownership of the land, since the railroad had already claimed it and citizens questioned the company's right to do so. Eventually troops from Fort Russell were called in; land jumpers were run out of town and could not return until they promised to acknowledge the railroad's claim.

A town charter was accepted by the Dakota Territorial Legislature in 1867 and Cheyenne was thereupon incorporated. By the end of that year the population had risen to 4,000 people, and lots were selling for $2,500. Makeshift buildings gave the town a raffish appearance, but even before railroad construction began, Cheyenne enjoyed the elements of a stable community; churches had been built and the first school, with 114 pupils, was opened in 1867. Within a year Cheyenne was thriving. More than 300 businesses were in operation, and the diverse citizenry included engineers, lawyers, artists, Native Americans, trappers, hunters, laborers, gamblers, and gunslingers. The town, however, was soon overrun by lawlessness.

The early Cheyenne closely resembled the Wild West towns depicted in novels and films. Dodge named it the gambling center of the world and some dubbed it "Hell on Wheels." Mayhem and violence were a way of life with the saloon and the cemetery being the most important places in town. In an attempt to impose order, the churches backed an ordinance that closed saloons for four hours on Sundays; another ruling required visitors to check their guns. But laws were virtually unenforceable, so the vigilante "committee" became a substitute for the courts. Although the city government had been given powers by the Dakota Legislature upon incorporation, civic leaders found the vigilante approach to be more effective. When the jail became full, for instance, prisoners were driven from town with a whip or a six-shooter; frequently the committee executed perpetrators of severe crimes.

Riches Flow from Cattle, Sheep, Gold

A degree of peacefulness returned when railroad construction moved on toward Sherman Pass and transients followed. But then the first Sioux War broke out north of the Platte River, and Fort Russell became the supply depot for the Rocky Mountain region. In 1868 Cheyenne was made the seat of Laramie County; the following year it was named the capital of the new Wyoming territory. By the 1870s Cheyenne was the center of a prosperous ranching area where cattle were bred for a European beef market. Visiting Englishmen, who spent summers in Cheyenne and winters in Europe, joined wealthy cattle owners to found the Cheyenne Club, where they dined in luxury and struck deals that affected the cattle industry throughout the West. Furnished in the English style and serving the finest liquors in the world, the club employed a foreign chef whose cuisine was known nationwide.

With the opening of the Black Hills gold fields in 1875, the town profited from a new industry as Cheyenne merchants supplied miners and prospectors with provisions and equipment. The Cheyenne and Black Hills Stage Company was formed to transport passengers and cargo between the railroad and the mines. When electric lights were installed in 1882, Cheyenne was the wealthiest city per capita in the world. Cheyenne was named the capital of the new state of Wyoming in 1890 and the Capitol building was erected in the city. By 1890 the population had reached 10,000 people.

Before the turn of the century many ranchers had begun raising sheep, which adapted well to the climate and the native grasses; sheep raising continues to be an important industry in the area. During the twentieth century Cheyenne became an industrial and manufacturing center. The Francis E. Warren U.S. Air Force Base was established at Fort Russell in 1947. While undergoing several realignment plans through the early 2000s, the base continued to remain active and was still

The Wyoming State Capitol building in Cheyenne. *Image copyright Jonathan Lenz, 2007. Used under license from Shutterstock.com.*

considered to be one of the largest employers in the city. State government also maintained a large number of employees.

In the late 1990s and early 2000s city officials began making plans to expand and encourage new business, primarily through the revitalization of the downtown areas with mixed-use developments. Through the efforts of Cheyenne LEADS, a local development organization, they city welcomed two new business parks and helped recruit new technology-based companies to the area, in efforts to further diversify the economy. In 1994 EchoStar Communications selected the Cheyenne Business Parkway as the site for its multimillion dollar satellite uplink center. In 2006 Nanomaterials Discovery Corporation agreed to build a specialized laboratory at Cheyenne Business Parkway. In January 2007 the National Center for Atmospheric Research announced that it would build a supercomputer in Cheyenne to study climate and weather. The city has made plans to continue this recruitment of new high-tech industries in conjunction with plans to bring other new retail and commercial establishments into the city.

Historical Information: Wyoming State Archives, 2301 Central Avenue, Cheyenne, WY 82002; telephone (307)777-7826; fax (307)777-7044; http://wyoarchives.state.wy.us

■ Population Profile

Metropolitan Area Residents

1980: 68,600
1990: 73,142
2000: 81,607
2006 estimate: 85,384
Percent change, 1990–2000: 11.57%
U.S. rank in 1980: Not available

U.S. rank in 1990: Not available
U.S. rank in 2000: 637th

City Residents

1980: 47,283
1990: 50,008
2000: 53,011
2006 estimate: 55,314
Percent change, 1990–2000: 5.6%
U.S. rank in 1980: 451st
U.S. rank in 1990: 504th
U.S. rank in 2000: 520th

Density: 2,511.4 people per square mile (2000)

Racial and ethnic characteristics (2000)

White: 46,707
Black: 1,472
American Indian and Alaska Native: 430
Asian: 561
Native Hawaiian and Pacific Islander: 59
Hispanic or Latino (may be of any race): 6,646
Other: 2,356

Percent of residents born in state: 36.9% (2000)

Age characteristics (2000)

Population under 5 years old: 3,422
Population 5 to 9 years old: 3,677
Population 10 to 14 years old: 3,755
Population 15 to 19 years old: 3,683
Population 20 to 24 years old: 3,337
Population 25 to 34 years old: 7,362
Population 35 to 44 years old: 8,387
Population 45 to 54 years old: 7,423
Population 55 to 59 years old: 2,562
Population 60 to 64 years old: 2,090
Population 65 to 74 years old: 3,723
Population 75 to 84 years old: 2,638
Population 85 years and older: 952
Median age: 36.6 years

Births (2006, MSA)

Total number: 1,246

Deaths (2006, MSA)

Total number: 687

Money income (1999)

Per capita income: $19,809
Median household income: $38,856
Total households: 22,346

Number of households with income of...

less than $10,000: 1,744
$10,000 to $14,999: 1,587
$15,000 to $24,999: 3,245
$25,000 to $34,999: 3,435
$35,000 to $49,999: 4,502
$50,000 to $74,999: 4,456
$75,000 to $99,999: 2,076
$100,000 to $149,999: 935
$150,000 to $199,999: 154
$200,000 or more: 933

Percent of families below poverty level: 9.5% (1999)

2005 FBI Crime Index Property: 2,585

2005 FBI Crime Index Violent: 97

■ Municipal Government

Cheyenne operates under a mayor-council form of government; the nine council members and the mayor serve four-year terms. Three council members are elected to represent each of the three city wards and serve staggered terms. A council president and vice-president elected from among the council members each serve one-year terms. The mayor and council members serve as Cheyenne's legislative body, which is responsible for regulating city growth and development, enacting ordinances, appropriating city funds, and establishing city rules and regulations.

Head Official: Mayor Jack R. Spiker (since 2001; term expires 2008)

Total Number of City Employees: 591 full-time (2007)

City Information: City of Cheyenne, 2101 O'Neil Avenue, Cheyenne, WY 82001; telephone (307)637-6200; www.cheyennecity.org

■ Economy

Major Industries and Commercial Activity

As of 2007 the largest industries in the Cheyenne area (by percentage of employment) were services, the military and government, and retail trade. Financial, insurance, and real estate; light manufacturing; construction; and transportation also held fairly important positions in the local economy. Farming only accounted for about 1.1 percent of employment.

F. E. Warren U.S. Air Force Base, site of a major installation of the Strategic Air Command, was the city's largest employer; federal, state, and county government offices are located in Cheyenne. Major private sector employers included Cheyenne Regional Medical Center, Lowe's Companies Inc., Union Pacific Railroad, Sierra Trading Post, WalMart Retail, Frontier Refining Inc.,

EchoStar Communications, Magic City Enterprises (rehabilitation facility), JELD WEN (window and door manufacturing), and Great Lakes Aviation.

Items and goods produced: oil refining, fertilizer, food service equipment, rail switching equipment, windows and doors

Incentive Programs—New and Existing Companies

Local programs: At the local level, Cheyenne LEADS, a private, not-for-profit economic development organization, assists non-retail businesses through such services as site location, employee training, and demographic and financial assistance. The Cheyenne Workforce Center, a regional office of the Wyoming Business Council, offers expansion assistance for current businesses, and relocation assistance for businesses looking to expand into the area. Most local business incentive packages are customized for the particular needs of the business.

State programs: Wyoming's primary business incentive is a non-existent corporate income tax rate, coupled with relatively minimal sales tax rates. The state also does not tax intangibles or inventory and has kept property taxes low. The Wyoming Business Council provides several financing programs for businesses, including the Business Ready Community Grant and Loan Program and the Wyoming Partnership Challenge Loan Program. The Community Development Block Grant and Industrial Development Revenue Bonds programs are also administered by the Wyoming Business Council.

Job training programs: Laramie County School District provides education programs at the secondary level in areas such as agricultural science, industrial technology, business and marketing education, health occupations, and core employability skills. Cheyenne colleges work with both businesses and the community to develop training programs for businesses and potential employees. Our Families Our Future in Cheyenne provides assistance to populations living below poverty through training programs and job search help. Our Families Our Future works with Wyoming agencies, community colleges, and employers; the organization began the CLIMB program in 2004 to train eligible single mothers in the field of medical transcription. The Cheyenne Workforce Center is part of a statewide network of workforce development resources, including services for businesses, job seekers and employment data researchers. Expanding and new businesses can tap into the Business Training Grant program through which employers may receive up to $2,000 per trainee per year for existing employees and $4,000 per employee per year for new hires. Customized workforce training programs can be designed through the Laramie County Community College Business Training and Development department.

Development Projects

In 2001, city leaders, the chamber of commerce, and other individuals and organizations got together to begin a development planning process known as Vision 2020 plan. That process lead to the adoption of a community-driven Cheyenne Area Master Plan commonly referred to as PlanCheyenne. PlanCheyenne will serve as a guiding principle for development in three key areas: community, transportation, and parks and recreation.

Cheyenne LEADS (Cheyenne-Laramie County Corporation for Economic Development) is a private, not-for-profit organization promoting economic development for both the city and the county. The organization is responsible for much of the most recent development activity, including the construction of Cheyenne Business Parkway and North Range Business Park and continual recruitment efforts to draw new or expansion businesses to these facilities. In 2006, the Nanomaterials Discovery Corporation announced plans to build a specialized laboratory and high-tech office spaces at the Cheyenne Business Parkway. In 2007 WalMart celebrated the grand opening of its new distribution center at North Ridge. The same year, the National Center for Atmospheric Research announced plans to build a new supercomputing facility at North Range and Allstate Insurance Company announced plans to establish a claim services call center in Cheyenne. VAE Nortrak North America Inc. purchased a property adjacent to their existing manufacturing facility on Pacific Avenue in order to expand production of pre-stressed concrete switch ties.

Economic Development Information: Cheyenne LEADS, 1 Depot Square, 121 W. 15th Street, Suite 304, Cheyenne, WY 82001; telephone (307)638-6000; toll-free (800)255-0742; www.cheyenneleads.org

Commercial Shipping

With access to two railroads, to interstate freeways, and to commercial air service, the city is a vital transportation center for the state of Wyoming. Great Lakes Airlines routes light cargo through Cheyenne Regional Airport. Union Pacific and Burlington Northern Santa Fe provide daily freight transportation and a variety of motor freight carriers move goods through facilities in Cheyenne and onto interstates 80 and 25.

Labor Force and Employment Outlook

Cheyenne's labor force is described as available, educated, and productive. The civilian labor force numbered 42,100 in August 2007; there were 1,400 workers unemployed, for an unemployment rate of 3.4 percent, compared with 4.6 percent nationwide for that month.

Although the local unemployment rate is low, a recent study conducted by PathFinders Resources found there are about 12,300 underemployed workers in Laramie and Goshen counties in Wyoming and portions of nearby Larimer and Weld counties in Colorado.

Wyoming residents gain from the state's lenient tax structure, including no personal income tax, capital gains tax, and corporate income taxes. The state does not levy estate tax beyond the federal pick-up level, nor does it levy an electric utilities tax. Low health insurance rates are also in effect.

The following is a summary of data regarding the Cheyenne metropolitan area labor force, 2006 annual averages.

Size of nonagricultural labor force: 42,800

Number of workers employed in . . .

> construction and mining: 3,300
> manufacturing: 1,600
> trade, transportation and utilities: 9,200
> information: 1,000
> financial activities: 2,000
> professional and business services: 3,300
> educational and health services: 3,400
> leisure and hospitality: 4,400
> other services: 1,700
> government: 12,800

Average hourly earnings of production workers employed in manufacturing: Not available

Unemployment rate: 3.9% (June 2007)

Largest employers (2005)	*Number of employees*
F.E. Warren U.S. Air Force Base	4,190
State of Wyoming	3,574
U.S. Government	1,811
Laramie County School District No. 1	1,794
Cheyenne Regional Medical Center (formerly United Medical Center)	992
Union Pacific Railroad	700

Cost of Living

The following is a summary of data regarding key cost of living factors for the Cheyenne area.

2007 (1st quarter) ACCRA Average House Price: $331,600

2007 (1st quarter) ACCRA Cost of Living Index: 101.9

State income tax rate: None

State sales tax rate: 4.0%

Local income tax rate: None

Local sales tax rate: 1.0%

Property tax rate: 77.31 mills on 9.5% of residential market value (2004)

Economic Information: Greater Cheyenne Chamber of Commerce, One Depot Square, 121 W. 15th Street, Suite 204, Cheyenne, WY 82001; telephone (307)638-3388; fax (307)778-1407. Laramie County Community College, Center for Economic and Business Data, 1400 E. College Drive, Cheyenne, WY 82007; telephone (307)778-5222

■ Education and Research

Elementary and Secondary Schools

Public elementary and secondary schools in Cheyenne are part of Laramie County School District #1 (LCSD1). The district, the largest in the state, is administered by a seven-member Board of Trustees and a superintendent. The Cheyenne Schools Foundation works "to engage community interest and support for enhanced academic, personal, and vocational opportunities for LCSD1 students beyond the capacity of the local school district budget." The Foundation also provides grants to benefit district and school-wide projects as well as teachers for classroom projects that address student needs.

Among the special programs offered by the school district is a magnet school for high-potential elementary students. Eighty percent of elementary and secondary students are involved in one or more extracurricular activities, which include music, sports, clubs, and after-school projects. The Community Based Occupational Education (CBOE) program at Triumph High School is an alternative education program that helps students meet the academic standards for the State of Wyoming and LCSD1 as well as gain employable business skills for the future.

The following is a summary of data regarding the Laramie County School District #1 as of the 2005–2006 school year.

Total enrollment: 13,954

Number of facilities

> elementary schools: 26
> junior high/middle schools: 3
> senior high schools: 4
> other: 0

Student/teacher ratio: 13.6:1

Teacher salaries (2005–06)

elementary median: $26,450–40,455 (all levels)

junior high/middle median: Not available

secondary median: Not available

Funding per pupil: $8,150

There are a few private schools located in Cheyenne, primarily affiliated with Christian churches.

Public Schools Information: Laramie County School District No. 1, 2810 House Avenue, Cheyenne, WY 82001; telephone (307)771-2100; www.laramie1.org

Colleges and Universities

Laramie County Community College (LCCC), which provides a two-year curriculum, is based in Cheyenne. The college offers associate's degrees in 72 academic programs and 15 certificate programs. Enrollment is about 3,500 full-time students per year. The Adult Career Education Center at LCCC offers basic adult education and English as a second language programs.

The University of Wyoming is the state's only public provider of baccalaureate and graduate education, research, and outreach services. The main campus at Laramie is less than 45 miles west of Cheyenne. Popular majors there are elementary and secondary education and social work. The UW Family Medicine Residency Program is based in Cheyenne at the Cheyenne Regional Medical Center.

The Cheyenne Campus of Embry-Riddle Aeronautical University is located at the F.E. Warren Air Force Base. Students there may achieve a bachelor's degree in professional aeronautics or technical management, a master's degree in aeronautical science and management, or a certificate in security and intelligence. Warren AFB is also the site for the Cheyenne Campus of Park University.

Libraries and Research Centers

The Laramie County Library System, established in 1886, is the oldest continually operating county library system in the country. In addition to its main library in Cheyenne, the Laramie County Library System operates two branches and a bookmobile serving the rural eastern portion of the county. Its holdings include over 275,000 volumes as well as periodical titles, microfiche, maps, CDs, videos, DVDs, and music CDs. The library also offers Internet connectivity, books-on-tape, video games, and art reproductions. Special collections are the Carpenter Collection of Western Americana and material on the elk of North America. The library's genealogy collection includes extensive materials that are part of a joint collection with the Family History Library of the Church of Jesus Christ of Latter Day Saints.

The Wyoming State Library is also located in Cheyenne. It contains more than 130,000 volumes and is a federal, state, and regional document depository. It is also the site of the Wyoming Patent and Trademark Depository Library. The Wyoming Center for the Book, established in 1995, operates as a program within the Wyoming State Library. A state affiliate of the Library of Congress Center for the Book, it "promotes the values of a literate and learned society through a variety of programs including a database of Wyoming writers and literary guide." The Ludden Library at Laramie County Community College has over 55,000 books and a continually growing collection of e-books.

The University of Wyoming-Laramie conducts research activities in dozens of disciplines, such as education; biological, physical, and social sciences; business and economics; mathematics; and politics and government in Wyoming. At the university's Archaeological Dig Site in Pine Bluffs, researchers extract relics and prehistoric artifacts dating back 8,000 years.

Public Library Information: Laramie County Library System, 2200 Pioneer Avenue, Cheyenne, WY 82001; telephone (307)634-3561; www.lclsonline.org

■ Health Care

The Cheyenne Regional Medical Center (CRMC) is a nonprofit county hospital system. The two main facilities, CRMC West and CRMC East, have a combined total of 218-beds. CRMC West contains a Level II Trauma Center, the Regional Cardiac Care Center, inpatient and outpatient surgery units, the Regional Cancer Treatment Center, a birthing center with a Level II neonatal intensive care unit, the Women's Imaging Center, physical therapy services, and a radiology department. CRMC East contains the Behavioral Health Services, a transitional care unit, home care and hospice services, the Rehabilitation Center, the Sleep Disorders Lab, and Home Away From Home, a nine-room facility to house out-of-town family guests. CRMC Health and Fitness Center offers physical and occupational therapy, sports medicine services, cardiac and pulmonary rehabilitation programs, as well as a full-service fitness center.

The Cheyenne Veteran's Administration Hospital provides medical care to military personnel and their families and to veterans. Facilities at the F.E. Warren U.S. Air Force Base provide medical and dental care for military personnel and their families.

■ Recreation

Sightseeing

Cheyenne features several sites that recall the city's past. The Tivoli Building, which houses the Chamber of Commerce, was completed in 1892. It is among the best examples of Victorian architecture in the Rocky Mountain region. The former Union Pacific Depot is an equally fine example of Romanesque architecture. Located on Capitol Avenue, the Wyoming State Capitol building contains historic photographs and a display of native wildlife; near the Capitol is a statue of Esther Hobart Morris, a pioneer in the women's suffrage movement. A guided walking tour of historic Cheyenne is available.

The French Merci Train was sent to the American people by French citizens in 1946 as a "thank-you" for the Friendship Train that carried food from America to France during World War II. The Big Boy steam engine—"Old Number 4004"—is the world's largest steam locomotive and was retired from the Union Pacific Railroad in 1956. F. E. Warren U.S. Air Force Base houses intercontinental ballistic missiles; free tours are conducted.

Recalling the days of cattle barons, the Wyoming Hereford Ranch east of Cheyenne was established in 1883; still in operation and producing Hereford cattle, it is the oldest continuous registered livestock operation in the county. The ranch hosts visitors and community events. Terry Bison Ranch is a working guest ranch that offers chuckwagon dinners, trout fishing, and horse-drawn wagon tours into a bison herd.

The Cheyenne Botanic Gardens in Lions Park, open 365 days a year, is a public botanical garden as well as a municipal nursery and community garden. Their conservatory is entirely solar heated; 50 percent of the garden's electricity is also solar-generated. Displays include rose, cacti, and herbs, and plants native to the area.

Other points of interest are historic Lakeview Cemetery and the Wyoming Game & Fish Visitors Center, featuring wildlife exhibits ranging from grizzly bears to big horn sheep.

Arts and Culture

Cheyenne supports an active cultural community. The Civic Center is the site of performances by Broadway touring companies, major symphony orchestras, and popular entertainers. Residents also enjoy concerts by the Cheyenne Symphony Orchestra at the Civic Center from September through May and occasionally in the summer. The Cheyenne Little Theatre stages plays with local directors and actors at its own playhouse; in the summer it stages melodramas at the historic Atlas Theatre. The Cheyenne All-City Children's Choir highlights the talents of children in grades four through eight, offering performances at the Laramie County School District Auditorium.

Several museums are located in Cheyenne. The Wyoming State Museum displays western memorabilia and chronicles the history of Wyoming. The Wyoming Arts Council Gallery displays the works of Wyoming artists. The Nelson Museum of the West houses cowboy and Indian collectibles and wildlife trophies from around the world. The Governors' Mansion, a state historic site and an example of colonial-revival architecture, was home

to the state's governors from 1905 to 1976; guided tours are available. At the Cheyenne Frontier Days Old West Museum, highlights include Oglala Sioux artifacts, a Union Pacific railroad exhibit, and a collection of horse-drawn vehicles.

For a unique tour of public art, maps are available to the Depot Visitor's Center to show the locations of the Cheyenne Big Boots. These eight-feet-tall cowboy boots have been decorated by local artists to reflect local and state history.

Local art galleries include the Painted Pony Gallery at Wyoming Home, the Wild Goose Gallery, and Manitou Galleries.

Arts and Culture Information: Wyoming Arts Council, 2320 Capitol Ave., Cheyenne, WY 82002; telephone (307)777-7742; http://wyoarts.state.wy.us

Festivals and Holidays

The foremost event in the Cheyenne area is Cheyenne Frontier Days. Taking place during the last full week in July, it is billed as the world's largest outdoor rodeo. Frontier Days features daily rodeos, concerts, parades, pancake breakfasts, Native American dances, shootouts, and a carnival. The festivities attract hundreds of thousands of people. Running concurrently is the annual Western Art Show at the Old West Museum in Frontier Park. In June and July Cheyenne Gunslinger Gunfights are enacted. In August Cheyenne hosts the Laramie County Fair. Oktoberfest is held in the fall. Highlights of the Christmas season are the Christmas parade, craft show, and concert, held at the end of November. An annual Festival of Trees event is sponsored as a fundraiser for the MentorAbility Program, a local group benefiting citizens with disabilities.

Sports for the Spectator

There are no major league professional sports teams in Wyoming. Cheyenne is home of the oldest rodeo event in the world, celebrated as part of the Cheyenne Frontier Days in July. Other rodeos are presented in the city throughout the year. The Wyoming State Open Golf Tournament is held at the Airport Golf Club, and Holiday Park in Cheyenne is host to the Wyoming Governor's Cup Tennis Tournament. The city is also the site of state youth baseball and softball tournaments.

Sports for the Participant

Cheyenne maintains 17 city parks which cover more than 600 acres, plus 15 miles of the Cheyenne Greenway Trail. Lion's Park features a special physical fitness course with activities at all levels of physical ability. The city maintains 23 baseball and softball fields, 13 soccer fields, 12 tennis courts, 2 golf courses, and 2 public swimming pools. A Spray Park is located at Lion's Park. Sloans Lake offers swimming, paddleboats, kayaks, and canoes. Curt Gowdy

State Park is located 25 miles outside of the city, while the Vedauwoo and Happy Jack recreational areas are approximately 30 miles away. Facilities for such sports as hunting, fishing, boating, camping, trap-shooting, snowmobiling, polo, tennis, and waterskiing are available.

Shopping and Dining

Shopping in downtown Cheyenne is enhanced by a sense of tradition; among the wide selection of stores, shops, and boutiques are several that have been in the city for many years. Nine shopping areas are located throughout the city. Frontier Mall features national retailers such as JCPenney, Bath and Body Works, American Eagle, and Dillard's, but also has local and regional stores such as Coral West Ranchwear and All Wild and Western. Visitors wanting to find a wide selection of Western clothing can visit Wrangler on Capitol Avenue. Cheyenne Farmer's Market, open half-days from August to October, sells fresh fruits, vegetables, and more.

Cheyenne offers a range of dining experience from traditional Southwestern specialties to Continental and ethnic cuisine such as Italian, Greek, Chinese, and Japanese. There are a large number of local Mexican restaurants. The Cheyenne Club frequently offers live country entertainment and the Outlaw Saloon has live country music seven nights a week. Numerous fast-food restaurants are also located in Cheyenne.

Visitor Information: Cheyenne Area Convention and Visitors Bureau, One Depot Square, 121 W. 15th Street, Suite 202, Cheyenne WY 82001; telephone (307) 778-3133; toll-free (800)426-5009; fax (307)778-3190; www.cheyenne.org. Wyoming Travel and Tourism, I-25 and College Drive, Cheyenne, WY 82002; toll-free (800) 225-5996; www.wyomingtourism.org

■ Convention Facilities

Little America Hotel and Resort offers a 10,360-square-foot meeting room at a facility that also includes 188 guest rooms and a nine-hole golf course. The Best Western Hitching Post Inn has 14,000 square feet of meeting space that can be divided into 10 smaller rooms. The Holiday Inn has 18,000 square feet of banquet and exhibition space. About 9,000 square feet of conference space is available at the Historic Plains Hotel. Other event and meeting venues include the Cheyenne Frontier Days Arena and Exhibit Hall, the City of Cheyenne–Kiwanis Community House, the Cheyenne Civic Center, Terry Bison Ranch, and Taco John's Event Center.

Convention Information: Cheyenne Area Convention and Visitors Bureau, One Depot Square, 121 W. 15th Street, Suite 202, Cheyenne WY 82001; telephone (307)778-3133; toll-free (800)426-5009; fax (307)778-3190; www.cheyenne.org

■ Transportation

Approaching the City

The major routes into Cheyenne are Interstate 25, which runs north and south; the east-west I-80; and U.S. 30, which bisects the city southwest to east. Highway 85 provides access from the northeast and southeast.

Great Lakes Airlines, operated out of Cheyenne Regional Airport, operates daily shuttle flights to Denver International Airport. From there travelers may connect to flights around the world. Shamrock Express offers shuttle service from the Denver Airport to Cheyenne. Casino Express operates monthly gambling excursion flights to Elko, Nevada. Greyhound bus service is available into the city. Thruway bus service is provided by Amtrak as well. Powder River Coach offers bus service from Cheyenne to Denver with stops at Fort Collins, Greeley, Longmont, and Boulder. Service from Cheyenne to Gillette includes stops at Douglas and Wheatland.

Traveling in the City

The Cheyenne Transit Program is Cheyenne's city-operated bus system. It serves Cheyenne and surrounding areas with six routes. The Cheyenne Street Railway Trolley takes visitors through the downtown and historic districts and to the air force base from mid-May through mid-September. Occasionally the governor will greet riders as they pass his residence.

■ Communications

Newspapers and Magazines

Cheyenne's daily newspaper is the *Wyoming Tribune-Eagle*, which has a circulation of about 16,500 daily and 18,500 on Sunday. With headquarters in Cheyenne, the paper is distributed throughout southeast Wyoming and into western Nebraska. *Warren Sentinel* is a weekly paper published by News Media Corporation for F.E. Warren Air Force Base. Also published in Cheyenne is *Wyoming Wildlife*, a Wyoming Fish and Game Department magazine on hunting, fishing, and environmental issues.

Television and Radio

One television station affiliated with a major network broadcasts from Cheyenne. The city also receives four stations from Denver and Casper; cable is available. The area is served by 13 AM and FM radio stations that feature news and information, music, and special programming.

Media Information: *Wyoming Tribune-Eagle*, 702 West Lincolnway, Cheyenne, WY 82001; telephone (307)634-3361; www.wyomingnews.com

Cheyenne Online

Cheyenne Area Convention and Visitors Bureau. Available www.cheyenne.org

City of Cheyenne. Available www.cheyennecity.org

Greater Cheyenne Chamber of Commerce. Available www.cheyennechamber.org

Laramie County School District. Available www .laramie1.org

Wyoming Tribune-Eagle. Available www .wyomingnews.com

BIBLIOGRAPHY

Dubois, William Robert, *We've Worked Hard to Get Here: The First 100 Years of the Greater Cheyenne Chamber of Commerce* (Cheyenne, WY: Greater Cheyenne Chamber of Commerce, 2007)

O'Neal, Bill, *Cheyenne: A Biography of the Magic City of the Old West* (Austin, TX: Eakin Press, 2006)

Cumulative Index

The 199 cities featured in *Cities of the United States,* Volume 1: *The South,* Volume 2: *The West,* Volume 3: *The Midwest,* and Volume 4: *The Northeast,* along with names of individuals, organizations, historical events, etc., are designated in this Cumulative Index by name of the appropriate regional volume, or volumes, followed by the page number(s) on which the term appears in that volume.

10/08

For Reference

Not to be taken from this room